Sybex's Quick Tour of Windows 98

THE DESKTOP

The Desktop is where your applications, folders, and shortcuts are located. You can choose between the classic Windows Desktop, which is familiar from previous versions of Windows, or you can use the new Active Desktop, which brings the Web directly to you.

My Computer lets you browse the contents of your computer, open folders, open documents, and run your favorite applications.

My Documents is a desktop folder you can use to store documents, graphics, and other files that you want to access quickly.

Internet Explorer starts up the Internet Explorer Web browser.

Network Neighborhood opens a viewer that presents system information about your computer's place in a network.

Recycle Bin makes it easy to delete and undelete files and folders.

The Microsoft Network opens a connection to Microsoft's online service.

My Briefcase lets you synchronize files between two computers.

Online Services allows you to access one of the popular commercial service providers, such as AOL.

Outlook Express opens the Outlook Express e-mail program.

The **Start button** pops up the Start menu, from which you can run almost all of your applications.

The **Quick Launch toolbar** provides an easy way to start frequently used applications.

The **Taskbar** displays a button for every program running on your computer.

The **Channel bar** lets you open your favorite Web site without first opening your Web browser.

Every **Window** has a **Minimize**, **Maximize** (alternating with **Restore**), and **Close** button.

The **Standard toolbar** provides fast access to common functions.

The **Address toolbar** shows the location of the page currently displayed in the main window; this may be an Internet address or a file or folder stored on your hard disk.

The **Links toolbar** lets you access different parts of Microsoft's Web site.

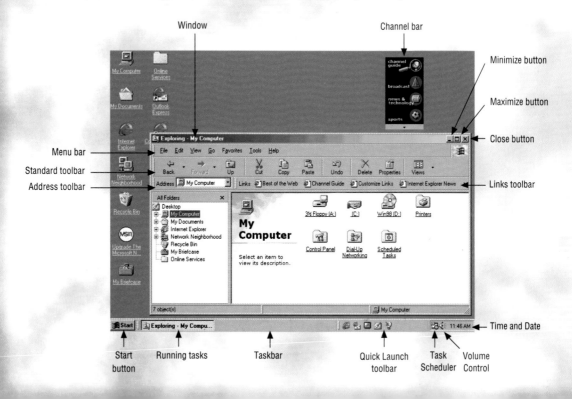

WINDOWS 98 AND THE INTERNET

Windows 98 and Internet Explorer bring the Internet right onto your Desktop. There are Internet access points available in every folder, and you can add Web content to your Desktop and folders to customize the way your system looks and feels.

CONFIGURING WITH THE CONNECTION WIZARD

Use the Connection Wizard to find an Internet Service Provider (ISP) and open a new account, or to configure an existing account. Plug your modem into the phone jack and choose Start ➤ Programs ➤ Internet Explorer ➤ Connection Wizard, then follow the instructions on the screen.

USING INTERNET EXPLORER

Once you have established an Internet account, click the Internet Explorer icon on the Desktop and start your explorations; you can also start Internet Explorer from the Quick Launch toolbar.

TUNING IN TO CHANNELS

The Channel bar on the Desktop lets you access the Channel Guide quickly and easily. You can use it to subscribe to the Web channels that you want to view or place on your Desktop. The channel content is updated by the content provider on a regular basis; all you have to do is sit back and watch.

BROWSING FROM EVERYWHERE

You will find Go and Favorites menus in all the windows, including Explorer, My Computer, My Briefcase, the Control Panel, the Printers folder; even the Recycle Bin has them.

You can also use the Address toolbar or the Links toolbar, available in all these windows and on the Taskbar, to access Web sites on the Internet. The Auto Complete

feature automatically completes a Web address that you have previously visited as you start to type the address into the Address toolbar.

 You can even access certain technical support Web sites from within the Windows 98 Help system.

WEB-RELATED APPLICATIONS

But it doesn't stop there; in addition to the Internet Explorer browser, Windows 98 also contains several other important Web-related applications, including:

Address Book Identifies the computers and individuals to which you may send and receive files and e-mail.

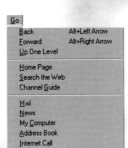

FrontPage Express A quick-and-easy Web-page editor you can use to create or customize your own Web pages.

NetMeeting A conferencing application which allows people working in different locations to collaborate simultaneously on the same project.

NetShow Player A viewer that displays streamed audio, video, and illustrated audio files downloaded from a Web site without waiting for long downloads.

Outlook Express An application used to send and receive e-mail and read and post messages to Internet news groups.

Personal Web Server Provides a Windows 98-based Web server you can use to set up a Web site on your local network or intranet, or to develop and test your Internet content before uploading it to your Internet Service Provider (ISP).

Web Publishing Wizard Manages the process of posting new Web content to a Web site.

Sybex, Inc.
1151 Marina Village Parkway
Alameda, CA 94501
Tel: 510.523.8233

Sybex's Quick Tour of Windows 98

Every application running on your computer and every open folder gets its own button on the Taskbar. The Taskbar may also show other icons from time to time, indicating that an e-mail message is waiting or that you are printing a document.

You can switch from one task to another by clicking its button on the Taskbar, but when you have a lot of applications running, the Taskbar can get pretty crowded. You can make it bigger by simply dragging the top edge of the Taskbar upward.

MOVING THE TASKBAR

You don't have to have the Taskbar at the bottom of the screen. If you'd prefer, you can have it at the top of the screen, on the left side, or on the right side. Just click a blank part of the Taskbar (not on one of the buttons), and drag the Taskbar to the new location.

TASK SWITCHING WITH ALT+TAB

Another quick way to switch from one running task to another is to hold down the Alt key on the keyboard and then press the Tab key once. A dialog box that contains an icon for each application running on your system will open. Each time you press the Tab key, a different icon is highlighted. This indicates the application that will run when you finally release the Alt key.

The name of each application or folder is displayed at the bottom of this dialog box.

ADDING A TOOLBAR

Windows 98 includes a default set of toolbars that you can add to your Taskbar.

Address Allows you to open an Internet address without first opening Internet Explorer.

Links Contains a set of Internet addresses, which users can add, remove, or re-arrange.

Desktop Adds a toolbar containing all your Desktop icons to the Taskbar. Because this toolbar is longer than the screen is wide, you can use the small arrows to see the other icons.

Quick Launch Adds buttons for commonly used applications.

To add one of these toolbars, right-click a blank part of the Taskbar, choose Toolbars from the pop-up menu, and then select a toolbar by name.

CREATING YOUR OWN TOOLBAR

To create a new toolbar, right-click an empty area on the Taskbar, and select Toolbars ➤ New Toolbar. Type the path to the folder (or the Internet address) that you want to appear as the toolbar and click OK.

Drag the new toolbar to the Desktop, and then position and size it accordingly.

USING THE QUICK LAUNCH TOOLBAR

The Quick Launch toolbar, located on the Taskbar, provides shortcuts to several often-used Windows features.

 Opens Internet Explorer.

 Opens Outlook Express.

 Opens the TV Viewer.

 Brings the Desktop back to the front.

 Views selected Web channels.

Click the Start button to do almost anything on your computer, from running an application to configuring your printer.

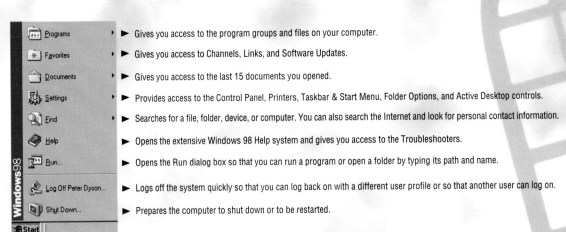

▶ Gives you access to the program groups and files on your computer.

▶ Gives you access to Channels, Links, and Software Updates.

▶ Gives you access to the last 15 documents you opened.

▶ Provides access to the Control Panel, Printers, Taskbar & Start Menu, Folder Options, and Active Desktop controls.

▶ Searches for a file, folder, device, or computer. You can also search the Internet and look for personal contact information.

▶ Opens the extensive Windows 98 Help system and gives you access to the Troubleshooters.

▶ Opens the Run dialog box so that you can run a program or open a folder by typing its path and name.

▶ Logs off the system quickly so that you can log back on with a different user profile or so that another user can log on.

▶ Prepares the computer to shut down or to be restarted.

RUNNING A PROGRAM

To start an application, click Start ➢ Programs, choose a program folder to open the next menu (if required), and then click the name of the program you want to run.

ADDING AN APPLICATION TO THE START MENU

The quickest way to add a program to the top of the Start menu is to open the folder that contains the program, and then drag the program's icon onto the Start button.

FINDING THINGS QUICKLY

Windows 98 adds several powerful items to the Find menu, which in

addition to finding files and folders, now includes options for finding a computer, information on the Internet, or information about people.

To locate a file, click Start ➢ Find ➢ Files or Folders. Type the name (or part of the name) into the Named field, enter any text you think the

file might contain into the Containing text field, and click Find Now. A window opens displaying the files that match as Windows finds them.

To locate a computer, click Start ➢ Find ➢ Computer, enter the name of the computer into the Named field, and click Find Now. To track down information on the Internet, use Start ➢ Find ➢ On the Internet. This option connects you to a single Web site giving you access to some of the most powerful and popular search engines on the Internet, including Infoseek, AOL NetFind, Lycos, Excite, and Yahoo. To find information such as a person's e-mail address, click

Start ➢ Find ➢ People. In the Look In list, select the name of the directory service you want to use, type in the information on the person you are looking for (usually just the first name followed by the last name), and click Find Now.

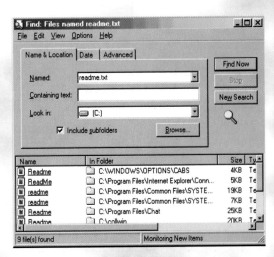

"I recommend this to all my customers because it's the most efficient way I have found to decrease my technical support calls."

ROBIN WARNER, Windows 9x and NT Systems Integrator and trainer

"As a photo-digital illustrator, I've been using Macs forever. Mastering Windows was indispensable in helping me make the transition to the PC platform."

KEN MILBURN, author of six computer books and over
250 computer magazine reviews

"I believe this book is one of the best I have read on the new and exciting operating system, Windows 95. It starts out very basic and jumps right into the core of the operating system. This book talks extensively about Windows 95 networking, Internet, the free applications that come with Win95, and the tips and tricks to optimize Windows 95 to fit your personal needs. The book also comes in handy for a quick off-the-shelf reference book. I found myself stuck many a time only to find the answer staring at me in this book. I highly recommend this book for anyone using or still considering the purchase of Windows 95."

HENRY TAYLOR, LAN administrator

"Finally, a book that has everything I've needed to know about Windows 95. From configuration to integration to optimization, this book is so readable that I wish I'd had like it for Windows years ago. The Internet communications and networking sections have proven particularly helpful."

GEOFF MARCY, Distinguished Professor of Physics and Astronomy,
San Francisco State University

"This is an excellent product for people already familiar with Windows 3.1 or Windows 95—there are detailed sections on using fonts effectively, working with multimedia files, and compressing your PC's hard drive. There also are lessons covering Windows 95 networking."

PC World, Nov 1997

Praise for Cowart's
Windows NT Server No Experience Required:

"I skimmed through your book during the flight to London. By the time I arrived, I knew more about NT Server than our consultant. Thanks."

TONY RINELLA, Information Systems Specialist (MIS chief) for Anshen & Allen,
a San Francisco-based architectural firm

WINDOWS 98

MASTERING™
WINDOWS® 98

Robert Cowart

SYBEX®

San Francisco • Paris • Düsseldorf • Soest

Associate Publisher: Gary Masters
Contracts and Licensing Manager: Kristine Plachy
Acquisitions & Developmental Editor: Peter Kuhns
Editor: Doug Robert
Technical Editors: Doug Langston, Doug Smith, Rima Regas
Book Designer: Patrick Dintino, Catalin Dulfu
Desktop Publishers: Franz Baumhackl, Kris Warrenburg
Production Coordinator: Charles Mathews
Production Assistant: Rebecca Rider
Indexer: Matthew Spence
Cover Designer: Design Site
Cover Illustrator: Design Site

Screen reproductions produced with Collage Complete.
Collage Complete is a trademark of Inner Media Inc.

SYBEX is a registered trademark of SYBEX Inc.
Mastering is a trademark of SYBEX Inc.

TRADEMARKS: SYBEX has attempted throughout this book to
distinguish proprietary trademarks from descriptive terms by
following the capitalization style used by the manufacturer.

The author and publisher have made their best efforts to prepare
this book, and the content is based upon final release software
whenever possible. Portions of the manuscript may be based upon
pre-release versions supplied by software manufacturer(s). The
author and the publisher make no representation or warranties of
any kind with regard to the completeness or accuracy of the contents herein and accept no liability of any kind including but not
limited to performance, merchantability, fitness for any particular
purpose, or any losses or damages of any kind caused or alleged
to be caused directly or indirectly from this book.

Photographs and illustrations used in this book have been downloaded from publicly accessible file archives and are used in this
book for news reportage purposes only to demonstrate the variety
of graphics resources available via electronic access. Text and
images available over the Internet may be subject to copyright and
other rights owned by third parties. Online availability of text and
images does not imply that they may be reused without the permission of rights holders, although the Copyright Act does permit
certain unauthorized reuse as fair use under 17 U.S.C. Section 107.

Library of Congress Card Number: 98-84008
ISBN: 0-7821-1961-1

Manufactured in the United States of America

10 9 8 7 6 5 4 3 2 1

Acknowledgments

I am indebted to all the talented people at Sybex for their invaluable assistance in the production of this book. Special thanks go to Doug Robert, who spent long hours recasting my often ambiguous statements and keeping track of all my changes.

A project as ambitious and time-pressured as this book required a team effort in the writing department, too. I am indebted to several people for their research, writing, and editorial contributions. For help in the networking section, thanks to Brian Knittel, Arthur Knowles, and Jim Blaney. For help with some aspects of Windows 98 communications, my appreciation goes to John Ross, Gene Weisskopf, and Pat Coleman. And special thanks to my multitalented friend and writing colleague Dr. Steve Cummings, whose assistance was responsible for portions of the Accessories section.

The world of the Internet is so quickly evolving that no one person can keep up with it. Janine Warner and many friends and acquaintances in the San Francisco Bay area, on the Web, and in newsgroups provided me with additional information essential to the Internet section of this book.

Finally, I want to thank Janine, my friends, and my family for their continued support during these seemingly endless writing projects.

Contents at a Glance

Introduction . . . . *xxvii*

PART I	UP AND RUNNING WITH WINDOWS 98	1
1	What Is Windows 98?	3
2	Getting Your Hardware and Software Ready for Windows 98	31
3	Getting to Know the Interface	57
4	Getting Down to Business: Running Your Applications	103
5	Organizing Your Programs and Documents	141
6	Sharing Data between Applications	193

PART II	EXPLORING WINDOWS 98	228
7	Basic Customizing with the Control Panel	231
8	Printers and Printing	293
9	Using Fonts Effectively	331
10	Windows Multimedia	367
11	Object Properties and the Right-Click	427
12	Working with the File System and Windows Explorer	437

PART III	COMMUNICATIONS AND USING THE INTERNET WITH WINDOWS 98	482
13	Introduction to Windows Communications	485
14	Communicating Using HyperTerminal	509
15	Connecting to the Internet	551
16	Browsing the World Wide Web with Internet Explorer 4	573
17	Communicating with Outlook Express News and Mail	627
18	Using the Active Desktop and Tuning In to Channels	695
19	Using NetMeeting	731

PART IV		USING THE SUPPLIED PROGRAMS	766
	20	Using WordPad for Simple Word Processing	769
	21	Using Paint and Kodak Imaging	821
	22	The Other Windows Accessories	869
	23	Maintaining Your System with the System Tools	911

PART V		NETWORKING WITH WINDOWS 98	988
	24	An Overview of Windows 98 Networking	991
	25	Planning Your Windows 98 Network	1013
	26	Setting Up a Peer-to-Peer Windows 98 Network	1031
	27	Internetworking Windows 98 Workstations with NT	1053
	28	Extending Your Reach with Dial-Up Networking	1065
	29	Troubleshooting Your Windows 98 Network	1093

APPENDIX

	A	Installing Windows 98 on Your Computer	1107
		Index	*1123*

Table of Contents

Introduction . . . . *.xxvii*

PART I • UP AND RUNNING WITH WINDOWS 98

1   What Is Windows 98?   **3**

So What Exactly *Are* Windows and Windows 98? 6
   Windows vs. Macintosh 7
Some Windows Background 8
   What Windows 95 Brought Us 10
Enter Windows 98 13
   Reliability and Performance Improvements 14
   Entertainment and Multimedia Enhancements 16
   Improved Ease of Use 17
   Seamless Internet Integration 19
   Increased Manageability and Other Business-Related Features 21
What Makes Windows Important 22
   Cost of Upgrade and Retraining 25
Is Windows 98 for You? 27
   What about NT? 28

2   Getting Your Hardware and Software Ready for Windows 98   **31**

What Software to Kiss Good-Bye and Why 34
   Applications vs. Utilities 34
   About APIs 35
   Protecting the System from Programs That Circumvent the API 37
   Device-Protection Capabilities Built Into Intel Chips 37
   So What Does This Mean to Me? 38
What Software to Keep and What to Upgrade 40
   Other Extinct and Unnecessary Utilities 41
   Faster 32-Bit Applications 47
   Flavors of 32-Bit Windows 48
What Hardware to Keep and What to Upgrade 49
   The Box 49
   RAM 50
   Hard Disk 51
   Monitor/Video-Card Support 52
   Plug-and-Play Items 53
   Other Items 55

3   Getting to Know the Interface   **57**

Windows 101 59
    Before Moving Ahead 61
Starting Windows 62
Parts of the Windows Screen 65
    The Desktop 65
    Icons 65
    Channel Bar 67
    Hey, What *Is* a Window, Anyway? 67
Types of Windows 68
    Application Windows 68
    Document Windows 69
Anatomy of a Window 70
    The Title Bar 70
    Minimize, Maximize, and Close 71
    The Control Box 77
    Scroll Bars, Scroll Buttons, and Scroll Boxes 78
All about Menus 80
    Selecting Menu Commands 82
    Special Indicators in Menus 82
All about Dialog Boxes 84
    Moving between Sections of a Dialog Box 85
    Entering Information in a Dialog Box 87
Using the New Web View 94
    Turning On Web View 96
Exiting Windows 100

4   Getting Down to Business: Running Your Applications   **103**

What Can and Can't Be Run 106
So, How Do I Run My Programs? 106
    Running a Program from the Start Button 107
Running a Program from My Computer 111
Running a Program from the Explorer or File Manager 114
    Running a Program from File Manager 117
Running a Program from Ye Olde Program Manager 119
Running Applications from the Find Command 120
Running a Program via One of Its Documents 123
    How Do File Types Become Registered? 124
Running an Application by Right-Clicking on the Desktop 124
Using the Start ➢ Documents List .126
Running DOS Programs 127
    So How Do I Run My DOS Programs? 128
    Options While Running a DOS Session 131
    Additional Property Settings for DOS Programs 133
What I Didn't Tell You—Shortcuts on the Desktop 136
Switching between Applications 137
    Switching with Alt-Tab 140

5   Organizing Your Programs and Documents   141

Putting Your Favorite Programs on the Start Button 143

Quick Launch and Other New Taskbar Features 146

Modifying the Start Button Menus 149

Removing an Item from a Menu 153

Advanced Options 154

Organizing Your Files and Folders 156

Making New Folders 156

Moving and Copying Items between Folders 158

Using Quick View to Examine a File 163

Deleting Items 165

Putting Items on the Desktop 166

Copying Files and Folders to and from Floppy Disks 171

Setting Options That Affect Viewing of Folders 176

Sorting and Tidying Up the Listing 177

Other Options on the View Menu 179

Using the Cut, Copy, and Paste Commands with Files and Folders 184

Checking and Chucking the Trash 187

Renaming Documents and Folders 191

6   Sharing Data between Applications   193

OLE Overview 195

Windows 98 and Data Exchange 196

The Clipboard 197

How It Works 197

Selecting, Copying, and Cutting in Windows Applications 198

Copying Text and Graphics from a DOS Box 200

Working with the Clipboard's Viewer 208

Viewing the Clipboard's Contents 209

Storing the Clipboard's Contents in a File 211

Retrieving the Contents of a Stored Clipboard File 212

Clearing the Clipboard 213

Object Linking and Embedding under Windows 98 213

Advantages of OLE 215

Basic OLE Concepts 217

Embedding Objects 220

Editing an Embedded Object 223

Linking Objects 224

Editing a Linked Object 226

PART II • EXPLORING WINDOWS 98

7   Basic Customizing with the Control Panel   231

Opening the Control Panel 234

Accessibility Options 238

Keyboard Accessibility Settings 239

Sound Accessibility Settings 240
Display Accessibility Settings 241
Mouse Accessibility Settings 243
Other Accessibility Settings 246
Adding New Hardware 247
Running the Install Hardware Wizard 248
When Your Hardware Isn't on the List 254
Adding and Removing Programs 255
Installing New Programs 255
Removing Existing Programs 257
Setting the Date and Time 258
Desktop Themes 260
Customizing Your Screen Display 261
Setting the Background and Wallpaper 262
Setting the Screen Saver 266
Adjusting the Appearance 269
Effects 275
Web 277
Driver Settings 277
Adjusting the Mouse 287
Switching the Buttons and Setting Double-Click Speed 287
Setting Your Pointers 288
Setting the Pointer Motion 289
General Mouse Settings 291

8   Printers and Printing   **293**

A Print-Manager Primer 297
Adding a New Printer 298
About Printer Installation 298
About Adding Printers 300
Running the Wizard to Add a New Printer 302
Altering the Details of a Printer's Setup—The Properties Box 311
Sharing a Printer for Network Use 312
Connecting to a Network Printer 314
How to Delete a Printer from Your Printers Folder 315
How to Print Out Documents from Your Programs 316
About the Default Printer 316
Printing from a Program 317
Printing by Dragging Files onto a Printer Icon or into Its Window 319
Printing by Right-Clicking on a Document 321
Working with the Print Queue 322
Refreshing the Network Queue Information 323
Deleting a File from the Queue 323
Canceling All Pending Print Jobs on a Given Printer 325
Pausing (and Resuming) the Printing Process .326
Rearranging the Queue Order 327
Printing to a Disk File instead of a Printer 328

9 Using Fonts Effectively **331**

Font Management in Windows 98 334
What Are Fonts and What Is TrueType? 334
   General Classes of Fonts 336
   About TrueType Fonts 337
   Comparing TrueType Fonts to Bit-Mapped and Vector Fonts 337
   How Does TrueType Work? 340
   Elements of TrueType Typography 341
   TrueType Font Embedding 345
Which Fonts Should I Use? 346
How Your Fonts Get Used by Windows 346
Building a Font Collection 347
   What about Other Scalable Type Alternatives? 349
   Choosing Specific Fonts 350
   Classes of Font Styles 350
Procuring Fonts 352
Adding and Removing Fonts Using Control Panel 353
   Adding Fonts 353
   TrueType Options 356
   Displaying and Printing Examples of Fonts with the Font Viewer ...357
   Removing Fonts 361
Some Basic Guidelines for Using Fonts 362
Deleting Font Files from Your Hard Disk 363
Font Utility Programs 363
   Managing Large Numbers of Fonts 363

10 Windows Multimedia **367**

Exactly What Is Multimedia? 371
What's New in Windows 98 Multimedia 373
Upgrading to Multimedia 374
The Supplied Multimedia Applications and Utilities 384
   Doing It All with DVD Player 386
   Assigning Sounds with the Control Panel's Sound Utility 392
   Playing Multimedia Files with Media Player 397
   Recording and Editing Sounds with Sound Recorder 399
   Playing Tunes with CD Player 403
   TV Viewer 411
   Using TV Viewer 413
   Tips for Using TV Viewer 416
Managing Multimedia Drivers and Settings 424

11 Object Properties and the Right-Click **427**

Right-Clicking around Windows 429
Property Sheets 431
   Who Will Use Property Sheets? 432
   Trying Out a Few Properties Boxes 432
   Making Property Settings from My Computer 435

12 Working with the File System and Windows Explorer **437**

A Review of DOS Directories 440
Exploring the Explorer 442
  Displaying the Contents of Your Computer 443
Working with Folders 445
  Selecting the Correct Drive and Choosing a Folder .446
  Creating a New Folder 449
  Deleting a Folder 450
  Moving Folders 451
Working with Files 453
  Refreshing the Directory 455
  Selecting Files 455
  Moving Files to Another Disk Drive 458
Working with Disks 459
  Formatting Disks and Making System Disks 459
  Copying Disks 461
Using Network Drives, Files, and Disks 463
  Mapping a Drive from a Windows 3.x File Dialog Box 465
  Mapping a Drive from Explorer—The Easy Way 466
  Disconnecting from a Network Drive or Folder 468
  Sharing Folders and Drives 468
  Changing a Share's Properties 471
Working with Other Objects in Explorer 472
Preview and Thumbnails View 474
  Enabling Thumbnail View 476
Customizing a Folder 478
Keep Experimenting with Windows Explorer 480

PART III • COMMUNICATIONS AND USING THE INTERNET WITH WINDOWS 98

13 Introduction to Windows Communications **485**

What's New in Windows 98 Communications? 488
The Windows Telephony Interface 491
Installing and Configuring a Modem 492
  Choosing a Modem 492
  Installing a Modem into Windows 98 494
  Changing Modem Properties 497

14 Communicating Using HyperTerminal **509**

Working with HyperTerminal 512
Setting Up Your Communications System 514
Setting Up a HyperTerminal Connection 515
  Starting HyperTerminal 516
  Entering a Phone Number 517
  Setting Dialing Properties 518
Choosing Communications Settings 519
  Choosing Basic Communications Settings 520

Choosing Terminal Settings 527
Setting Other HyperTerminal Preferences 531
Saving Your Settings 534
Making Connections 535
What Might Go Wrong 536
Disconnecting 537
Making a Different Connection 537
Connecting via Cable 538
Sending and Receiving Data 539
Communicating in Interactive Mode 539
Sending and Receiving Text Files 542
Sending and Receiving Documents and Other Files 544
Ending a Communications Session 548

15 Connecting to the Internet   551

What Kind of Connection? 554
Choosing a Service Provider 556
Using a National ISP 558
Using a Local ISP 559
Connecting through an Online Service 560
Getting Directly on the Internet—Finding a Local ISP 562
Setting Up Windows 98 Dial-Up Networking 564
Loading the Software 565
Creating a Connection Profile 566
Changing the Default Connection 568

16 Browsing the World Wide Web with Internet Explorer 4   573

Inside Internet Explorer 575
Starting Internet Explorer 575
The Components of Internet Explorer 577
Some Commands You'll Use Frequently 581
Using the Toolbars 582
Getting Help 584
Moving between Pages 585
Making the Jump with Hyperlinks 585
Other Ways to Move between Pages 586
Browsing Off-Line 588
Returning to Your Favorite Pages 591
The Structure of the Favorites Menu 591
Adding Items to the Favorites Menu 591
Organizing Your Favorites Menu 593
Subscribing to Your Favorite Websites 594
Using Subscriptions to Stay in Touch 595
Signing Up for a Subscription 595
Subscribing to a Site 596
Browsing Your Updated Subscriptions 597
Canceling a Subscription 599
Viewing Your Current Subscriptions 599

Defining Your Subscriptions 600
    Viewing Current Subscription Settings 601
    Choosing How You Want to Be Notified 602
    Choosing How Much Content Should Be Delivered 604
    Setting a Subscription Schedule 607
    Updating Your Subscriptions Manually 608
Viewing and Subscribing to Active Channels 609
    Viewing a Channel in Internet Explorer 610
    Viewing a Channel in the Channel Viewer 610
    Viewing a Channel from the Channel Bar 612
    Subscribing to an Active Channel 614
Some Tips on Web Searching 616
    Keywords 616
    Searching vs. Browsing 618
    Searching in the Explorer Bar 619
    Common Search Engines 623

17 Communicating with Outlook Express News and Mail   627

A Quick Tour of Outlook Express 629
    The Preview Pane 631
    The Outlook Bar 632
Getting Connected 633
    Establishing an Account with an ISP 633
    Setting Up an E-Mail Account 634
    Setting Up a News Account 636
Using Outlook Express Mail 637
Reading and Processing Messages 638
    Printing, Marking, and Moving Messages 638
    Saving Messages 639
    Replying to a Message 641
    Forwarding a Message 642
    Deleting a Message 643
Creating and Sending Messages 643
    Composing Your Message 643
    Sending Your Message 645
Retrieving Your Mail 646
Creating Designer E-Mail Messages 646
    Adding a Signature to Your Message 648
    Adding a Picture to Your Message 649
    Adding a Background Color to Your Message 651
Attaching Files to Your Messages 651
Setting Up and Using Your Address Book 653
    Accessing Address Book 654
    Creating a New Address Book from Scratch 654
    Setting Up a Group in Address Book 660
    Customizing Your Address Book Window 662
    Searching for Names in All the Right Places 662
    Printing from Your Address Book 664

Taking Control of Your Mail with Inbox Assistant 664
Using Outlook Express News 666
Newsgroups and the Internet 666
   A Little Background 668
   Using Outlook Express as Your News Reader 668
Starting Outlook Express News 669
Connecting to Newsgroups 669
   Finding a Newsgroup of Interest 670
   Reading a Newsgroup 671
Replying and Posting 672
Subscribing and Unsubscribing to Newsgroups 673
Filtering Out What You Don't Want to Read 674
Viewing, Marking, and Sorting Messages 676
   Interpreting the News Icons 677
   Marking Messages 678
   Sorting Messages 678
Reading the News Off-Line 679
Customizing Outlook Express 679
   Customizing the Toolbar 679
   Customizing Mail and News Options 680

18 Using the Active Desktop and Tuning In to Channels   **695**

Understanding the Active Desktop 697
   To Single-Click or Not to Single-Click 699
   The Active Desktop Work Area 700
   The Windows Taskbar 703
   The Windows Start Menu 704
   Program Windows 705
   Icons 705
   HTML Web Objects 705
Using the Active Desktop Toolbars 706
   Displaying Other Toolbars on the Desktop 707
   Manipulating Desktop Toolbars 707
Adding Content to Your Active Desktop 709
   Turning On or Off Desktop Components 710
   Adding an Item to the Desktop 711
   Using a Web Page as the Desktop Background 712
   Removing Desktop Components 713
Adding Content from the Active Desktop Gallery 713
   Installing the Investor Ticker 714
   Installing the Web Search Component 715
Using the Channel Screen Saver 716
   Running the Channel Screen Saver 716
   Setting Up the Channel Screen Saver 717
Browsing Resources with Windows Explorer 719
   The Personal Computer Merges with the Networked Terminal 719
   Browsing Your Computer 720
   Browsing the Internet 722

Browsing in Web View 723
Customizing a Folder 726
Rearranging Details View 729

19   Using NetMeeting — 731

New Stuff in NetMeeting Version 2.*x* 734
How You'll Use It 736
Installing NetMeeting 740
Running NetMeeting for the First Time 741
Using NetMeeting 744
Chat 756
Whiteboard 757
Sharing Documents and Applications 759
Sharing Your Clipboard 761
Doing File Transfers to Other Participants 762
Speed Dial, Viewing Dial History, and Sending E-Mail 764
For More Information about NetMeeting 765

PART IV • USING THE SUPPLIED PROGRAMS

20   Using WordPad for Simple Word Processing — 769

Creating a Document 773
Getting Help in WordPad 774
Working with the WordPad Window .774
Entering Text 776
Editing Your Text 778
Moving the Cursor 778
Scrolling in the Document 780
Making Selections in WordPad 781
Making Some Changes to the Text 785
Moving Selected Blocks 786
Inserting the Date or Time in a Document 790
Formatting Paragraphs 790
Using the Ruler as Your Guide 791
Adjusting Alignment 792
Setting Indents 793
Creating Bulleted Paragraphs 795
Formatting Characters 796
Formatting Existing Characters 797
Formatting Characters As You Type 799
Working with Tabs 800
Repositioning Existing Tab Stops 801
Clearing Custom Tab Stops 801
Reformatting the Whole Document 801
Using Undo to Reverse Mistakes 802
Searching for and Replacing Text 802
Finding a Specific Word or Text String 803
Replacing Specific Words 804

Copying between Two Documents 804
Hyphenating Text 806
Adding Graphics to Your WordPad Document 807
   Importing a Graphic from the Clipboard 808
   Positioning the Graphic 809
   Sizing the Graphic 809
   Inserting Graphics as Objects 810
Saving Your Work 810
Opening Other Documents 812
   A Shortcut for Opening Recent Documents 813
   Opening Documents Stored in Other Formats 813
   Converting ASCII Files 813
   Opening a New Document 814
Display Options 814
   Selecting Measurement Units and Controlling Word Selection 815
   Choosing Display Options for Each Type of Document 815
Printing Your Documents 816
   Seeing a Preview of Your Printed Document 817
   Printing 818
   Quick Printing with the Print Button 819

21 Using Paint and Kodak Imaging   **821**

Using Paint 824
Starting a New Document 824
   Understanding Computer Art 826
Opening an Existing Picture 828
Seeing More of the Picture 829
   Removing and Tearing Off the Tool and Color Boxes .829
   Displaying Only the Picture 830
Creating a New Picture 831
   Setting a Picture's Basic Characteristics 831
Basic Painting Techniques 834
   Setting the Foreground and Background Colors 835
   Using the Painting Tools 837
Manipulating Areas of a Picture 847
   Selecting an Area 847
   Moving a Selected Area 848
   Flipping and Rotating Selections 850
   Inverting Colors 851
   Stretching, Shrinking, and Slanting 852
Zooming In for Detail Work 853
Creating Custom Colors 854
Saving Your Work 855
Printing 856
Using Kodak Imaging 856
   Scanning Images 861
   Annotating Images 862
   Starting a New Document 866
   Saving Documents 867

22 The Other Windows Accessories 869

Jotting Down Notes with Notepad 872
So, What's a Text File? 872
Notepad's Limitations 873
Running Notepad 873
Opening Files 874
Entering and Editing Text 875
Entering the Time and Date in Your Text 877
Searching for Text 877
Setting Margins and Adding Headers and Footers 878
Printing a Notepad File 879
Performing Calculations with the Calculator 879
Getting Help with the Calculator 880
Calculating a Result 880
Using the Memory Keys 881
Copying Your Results to Other Documents 881
Copying Calculations from Other Documents to the Calculator 882
Computing Square Roots and Percentages 883
Using the Scientific Calculator 884
Entering Special Symbols with Character Map 888
Using Character Map 889
Entering Alternate Characters from the Keyboard 890
Character Sets: ANSI vs. IBM 891
Audio Control 893
Using the Phone Dialer 895
Starting Phone Dialer 895
Programming the Speed Dial List 896
Placing a Call 897
Finding People on the Internet 898
How to Get Registered in LDAP 902
Microsoft Chat (formerly Comic Chat) 903
Running Chat 903
Starting to Chat 906
Additional Chat Features 908

23 Maintaining Your System with the System Tools 911

Correcting Disk Errors with ScanDisk 913
Testing a Disk 917
Setting ScanDisk Options 918
Backing Up Your Files with Backup 924
Running Backup 925
Running Backup via the Wizard 926
Running Backup without the Wizard 930
Formatting, Erasing, and Other Operations for Backup Media 932
Restoring Files from Your Backups 933
Backup and Restore Option Settings 938
Increasing Disk Capacity with DriveSpace 3 939
How DriveSpace Works 939
When to Use DriveSpace 940

Compressing a Drive 942
Adjusting the Amount of Free Space 947
Uncompressing a Compressed Drive 948
Creating an Empty Compressed Drive from Free Space 949
Deleting a Compressed Drive 950
Mounting and Unmounting Compressed Drives 950
Changing the Estimated Compression Ratio 951
Advanced Settings: Compression Amounts and Auto Mounting 952
Compression Agent 953
Disk Defragmenter 956
When Should You Use Disk Defragmenter? 957
Running Disk Defragmenter 958
Disk Cleanup 961
Finding Even More Space 962
Drive Converter (FAT 32) 965
The Downside of FAT 32 966
Running the FAT 32 Converter (FAT 32) .970
System Monitor 973
Choosing Items to Display 975
Editing an Item's Display Properties 975
Choosing the Display Type 976
Removing Items from the Window 976
Other Display Options 976
Task Scheduler 977
Running a Task Immediately 980
NetWatcher 980
Checking Resources on Another Computer 982
Maintenance Wizard 982
Windows Update Wizard 985
The System Information Utility 987

PART V • NETWORKING WITH WINDOWS 98

24 An Overview of Windows 98 Networking   991

Networking Features of Windows 98 994
The OSI Reference Model 997
The Application Layer 999
The Presentation Layer 999
The Session Layer 1000
The Transport Layer 1000
The Network Layer 1001
The Data Link Layer 1001
The Physical Layer 1001
The Windows 98 Networking Model 1002
Network Drivers Interface Specification (NDIS) 1003
Open Datalink Interface (ODI) 1003
Which Protocol to Use? 1003
PPTP: Point-to-Point Tunneling 1011

25 Planning Your Windows 98 Network   **1013**

Ethernet Networks and Cabling Technologies 1016
    Which Type of Cable to Use? 1016
Which LAN Topology to Implement? 1020
    Thin Ethernet (10Base-2) 1021
    Twisted-Pair Ethernet (10Base-T) 1022
    Fast Ethernet (100Base-T) 1024
Choosing Your Cards 1026

26 Setting Up a Peer-to-Peer Windows 98 Network   **1031**

Getting Acquainted with Peer-to-Peer Networking 1033
Setting Up the Network 1035
    Buying Your Network Cards 1035
    Installing the Network Hardware 1036
Moving Into the Network Neighborhood 1044
    Sharing Resources on the Network 1045
    Security Features 1050

27 Internetworking Windows 98 Workstations with NT   **1053**

Some Networking Philosophy 1055
    Workgroups 1056
    Domains 1056
    NT Workstation vs. NT Server 1057
Adding Windows 98 Workstations to the Network 1059
    Adding Workstations to an NT Server 1059
    Using Shared Printers 1061
    Mapping Windows 98 and Windows NT Shared Drives 1061
Using Your NT/98 Network 1064

28 Extending Your Reach with Dial-Up Networking   **1065**

Remote Access—What Is It? 1068
    Remote Control vs. Remote Node 1069
Windows 98's Style of Dial-Up Networking 1069
    DUN and TAPI 1070
    Dial Helper 1070
    Connecting 1071
    Using Your Remote Connection 1072
    Setting Up Your Modem for Dial-Up Networking 1073
    Setting Up Dial-Up Networking on Your Computer 1075
    Using Dial-Up Networking 1076
    Advanced Configurations for Dial-Up Networking 1082
    Dial-Up Networking and Security 1085
Direct Cable Connect (DCC) Using a Serial or Parallel Port 1089

29 Troubleshooting Your Windows 98 Network   **1093**

Diagnosing Cable Problems 1097
Diagnosing Network Interface Card (NIC) and Driver Problems 1099
Restoring from a Downed Hard Drive 1102

What to Do If You Cannot Even Boot to a System Prompt 1105
Easiest Approach: A Full Upgrade from an Earlier Version of Windows 1110
Installing to a Fresh Disk or New Directory 1116
Finding and Fixing Hard-Disk Problems during Installation 1117
Reverting to the Previous Operating System 1118
Removing Uninstall Files to Free Up Disk Space 1119
Installing onto a Compressed Drive 1120
How to Install Windows 98 to a Machine Running Windows NT 1122

APPENDIX

A   **Installing Windows 98 on Your Computer**   **1107**

Index *1123*

INTRODUCTION

Thank you for purchasing (or considering the purchase of) this book! *Mastering Windows 98* is designed to help you get the most out of Microsoft's Windows 98 with the least amount of effort. You may be wondering if this is the right book for you. I've written this book with both the novice and the experienced PC user in mind. The intention was to produce a volume that would prove both accessible and highly instructive to all Windows users.

Based on my best-selling *Mastering Windows 95*, this new Windows 98 edition uses the same time-tested approach for teaching computer skills that has helped hundreds of thousands of beginners in many countries become Windows-literate. Windows 98 ushers in a whole new phase of Windows computing abilities that is very exciting. For example, numerous Internet-related tools are integrated directly into Windows now, so you can easily shift between tasks such as word processing, sending e-mail, and browsing the World Wide Web without having to buy separate products. Though you may have already used some of this technology if you're a veteran Windows 95 / Internet user, many of the features have not been available in any previous version of Windows.

Beginners and Power Users Alike Will Find This Book Valuable

What kind of background do I expect you to have to get the fullest use of this book? From the outset, this book doesn't require that you have a working knowledge of a previous version of Windows. All I assume is that you have a modicum of familiarity with a PC. So, no matter if on the one hand you are new to Windows and are a bit PC-literate, or on the other hand you already have a fair amount of experience with Windows computers but need to find out what makes this version and its newest features click, this book is a perfect choice. I think you'll find it easy to read and not over your head. There are everyday examples to explain the concepts, and all the accessory programs that come with Windows 98 are explained in detail so you can do it all with nothing more than this book, your computer, and Windows 98 itself.

For Beginning Users

I've written over 30 books at this point, spanning a range of computer topics over the past 15 years. A number of those books have been beginner books, so even though this book is thick, it doesn't mean it's impossible to read through, or that it's meant only for computer geeks. Nope—I know what beginners are looking for. After all, I haven't forgotten my friends who think you use a mouse like you use a TV remote control, and I know there are more of you out there! So in this book, I explain the basics and assume very little.

I have to admit that a lot of what's new in Windows 98 is of particular interest to experienced Windows users who have been looking for some of Win 98's latest features for years now. So as not to lose the experienced reader from the outset, I've used Chapter 1 to introduce the beginning user *and* the experienced user to what they'll find once they start working with Windows 98. If, as a beginner, you find that Chapter 1 gets over your head rather quickly, don't despair. The true step-by-step introduction to using Windows begins in Chapters 2 and 3; you can skip Chapter 1 until after you get your feet wet.

If you are new to computers, you should at least have some understanding of PC terminology. Though Windows 98 takes much of the effort out of using your computer, it's still a good idea for you to understand the difference between things such as RAM and hard-disk memory, for example. And although I'll be covering techniques for performing typical tasks in Windows—such as copying files, formatting disks, and moving stuff from one folder to another—I'm assuming that you already understand *why* you'd want to do these things in the first place. (Of particular importance is a basic understanding of the differences between data files and program files.) I'll be describing these types of things briefly within the book, but you may also want to take some time out to bone up on these topics if your knowledge is a little shaky.

What About Power Users?

If you're a power user, familiar with earlier versions of Windows and the intricacies of DOS, then the explanations and procedures here will quickly bring you up to speed with Windows 98 and how it differs from its predecessors. For example, the first chapter (which can be skipped by novices), is a thorough analysis of what's new in Windows 98 and how it compares to other members of the Windows family of operating systems. By quickly skimming the next several chapters, you'll learn how to use the new Web view, the folder system, property sheets, right-click menus, the Windows Explorer, how to share data between documents, and other necessary basics.

The advanced discussions in Parts II through V will be extremely useful whether you're an MIS professional, an executive, an instructor, or a home user. There's significant coverage of the increasingly important area of electronic communications from the Windows workstation, be it through the Internet, over a LAN, via services such as AOL, MSN, Prodigy, and CompuServe, or through an independent Internet service provider. You will learn how to get onto the Internet: that is, how to choose the correct transmission medium (whether it be analog modem, cable modem, ISDN, ADSL, or satellite dish); how to choose and install a typical modem; and how to choose and sign up (immediately) with an Internet service provider. Soon you'll be cruising the Web using Internet Explorer, reading newsgroups, sending e-mail with Outlook Express, and having live video chats with people around the world with NetMeeting.

A multimedia chapter explores the possibilities for adding high-performance audio, video, CD-ROM, MIDI, and DVD elements to your Windows setup. With the right hardware you'll be running 3-D games, watching DVD movies, and seeing streaming-video websites.

Local-area networking is an essential part of corporate computer use. Even many homes are networked with several computers these days. So, six chapters—something you're not likely to find in the other books of this type—tackle all the most salient aspects of Windows 98 networking, from the initial planning stages of choosing and routing cabling, through internetworking with Windows NT, Novell, TCP/IP, and using remote access services to dial in from the road. Of course, simple peer-to-peer networking—which, with the addition of a $5 cable, Windows 98 can do right out of the box— is covered, as is how to best manage and troubleshoot your network.

Customizing your computer by adding new hardware and software is something all users have to do from time to time. So extensive coverage of Control Panel, Plug-and-Play, dealing with "legacy" hardware, using the new Taskbar options, and how to add and manage typical items such as modems, new video boards, fonts, and Windows software modules (including the Accessibility options for folks who have bad eyesight or who are motor challenged) are all included in this tome. Technical tips and tricks are scattered liberally throughout.

Because Windows 9x (i.e., versions 95 and 98 considered together) has become such a complex system, maintaining a Windows computer and keeping it working has become a specialty unto itself. Windows 98 incorporates an extensive new set of maintenance and troubleshooting tools for system files, hard disks, and online communications. I'll show you when and how to use them in Chapter 23.

NOTE

Although for many users Windows 98 will be factory installed on the computer, this won't always be the case. If you're faced with installing Windows 98 on your own, turn to the appendix for installation procedures and considerations.

This is just a sample of the topics you'll find between the covers of this book. Please consult the table of contents (or the index, of course) for the exact topics covered.

Why This Book?

As you know, there is built-in online Help with Windows 98. So why do you need a book? Well, it's because the Help system doesn't tell you what you want to know. True, great efforts have been made on Microsoft's part to simplify Windows 98 and make it more intuitive and friendly in hopes that reference tomes like this one will no longer be necessary. The Help system has been revamped and is now a bit easier to use. But until a computer can rap with you in everyday language, like the one on the Starship Enterprise, you will still need a good book, especially when you're talking about a computer program or operating system that is as all-inclusive (read "complex") as Windows 98.

If you happen to find some technical manuals from the manufacturer, explanations are often written in computerese, assuming too much knowledge. Other times they only give you the bare rudiments of how to unpack the box and how to call their Customer Assistance number. This is often true of trade books as well; they're either too technical or they speak only to the novice user, with no recognition that the majority of interested users are intermediate or advanced users. The beginner books, in particular, don't give the novice anything to grow into.

Here I've done the legwork for you: I've boiled down the manuals, tested Windows 98 for almost a year before its release, had discussions with many Windows 98 testers, experimented on various machines from laptops to networked workstations, and finally wrote a book that was reviewed and revised by a whole group of critical editors, all with the goal of explaining Windows 98 in normal, everyday English.

The assistant authors of this book have a wide diversity of experience with both Windows 98 and other PC software and hardware. Pooling their knowledge and working with both Windows 95 and 98, I have come up with a thorough cross-section of useful information about this landmark operating system and condensed it into the book you see before you.

In researching this book, I have tried to focus not just on the How To's but also on the Whys and Wherefores. Too many computer books tell you only how to perform a simple task without explaining how to apply it to your own work. In this book, step-by-step sections explain how to perform specific procedures, and descriptive sections explain general considerations about what you've learned. As you read along and follow the examples, you will not only become adept at using Windows, but you will also learn the most efficient ways to accomplish your own work.

Conventions Used in This Book

There are a few conventions used throughout this book that you should know about before beginning. First, there are commands that you enter from the keyboard and messages you receive from Windows that appear on your screen. When you have to type something in, the text will be boldface. For example, "In the text field, type **a:setup**."

When referring to files and folders, the text may be on its own line like this:

`School Stuff\Sally's thesis on arthropods.doc`

or it might be included right in a line like this: "Now look for the folder named `Letters to the Editor`."

More often than not, responses from Windows will be shown in figures so you can see just what the screens look like. Sometimes, though, I'll skip the picture and just display the message in text.

Finally, there are many notes and tips in this book. They are generally positioned below the material to which they relate. Most are self-explanatory. The "Tech Tips" in particular, however, are directed at readers who may be interested in the behind-the-scenes workings of the program; you may safely skip them if you're not interested. Here's an example:

TECH TIP

Tech Tips are tips that are more technical in nature; they may be skipped by the non-technical reader.

Before You Begin . . .

Before you can begin working with Windows, make sure you have correctly installed Windows 98 on your computer's hard disk. A large percentage of what appear to be software problems are often the result of incorrect installation. If your copy of Windows is already installed and operating correctly, you have no need to worry about this and can move ahead to Chapter 1. However, if you haven't installed Windows, you should turn first to the appendix, which covers the Windows Setup program. If your copy of Windows is installed but appears to be operating significantly differently than what is discussed in this book, you might want to seek help from a computer professional or friend who can determine whether your Windows 98 system was installed correctly. For the purposes of this book I installed all the options in my machine, so my setup might look a little different from yours. The chapters about the Control Panel and Internet Explorer and the use of the new Web view explain how you can install options that may have been omitted when Windows 98 was initially installed on your computer.

Happy reading! I hope this book helps you on your way to success in whatever line of work (or play) you use your computer for.

PART I

Up and Running with Windows 98

CHAPTERS:

1. What Is Windows 98?

2. Getting Your Hardware and Software Ready for Windows 98

3. Getting to Know the Interface

4. Getting Down to Business: Running Your Applications

5. Organizing Your Programs and Documents

6. Sharing Data between Applications

Chapter

1

What Is Windows 98?

About Windows 98

Some Windows background

Features that Windows 95 introduced

New features in Windows 98

Windows 95 vs. the competition

What Is Windows 98?

A s of this writing, there were an estimated 60 million users of Windows 3.*x*
(3.*x* includes 3.0, 3.1, and 3.11), and
about 120 million users of Windows 95. And then there are hundreds of thousands of
Windows NT systems in place, with that number growing phenomenally. That's a lot
by any standards, certainly by the standards of PC software sales. Even if you've never
used Windows before, you are probably well aware of it as a household term, and that
it's one of those products that has made Bill Gates the richest man in the world. No
doubt Windows will be with us in some form for a good while.

NOTE

C|net (the web-based computer industry news service) reports that nearly 60 percent of
U.S. corporate PC users are still using Windows 3.1. If that number includes *you*, don't
worry—I've tailored many sections of this book for users considering making the switch
directly to Windows 98 from Windows 3.*x*.

It's likely you're upgrading to Windows 98 from one of its earlier incarnations, so this
book will discuss right up front just what's so new and great about Windows 98. Exactly
what Windows is in general, and what Windows 98 is in particular, are the topics of this

chapter. I'll discuss how Windows 98 differs from its predecessors, and what all its bells and whistles will give you in your day-to-day work with your computer.

Please bear in mind that some terms or concepts may not make sense to you just yet. Don't worry, you'll understand them later as you work through the various chapters in the book. With that said, let's dive into the world of the latest and greatest graphical operating system for IBM PCs.

So What Exactly *Are* Windows and Windows 98?

Windows 98 is Microsoft Corporation's latest upgrade to its phenomenally successful and ubiquitous software, which has been generically dubbed *Windows*.

Windows is a class of software called a GUI (graphical user interface). How you interact with your computer to do things like writing a letter, entering data into a mailing list, playing games, or doing simple housekeeping tasks such as backing up or organizing your important files, is determined by the *interface*. On most computers, the hardware part of the interface consists of your screen and the keyboard. But the software part of the interface determines what things look like on the screen, how you give commands such as "check the spelling" or "print this report" to the computer, how you flip between pages of text, and so forth.

In days of old, before Windows, these kinds of chores were all done with keyboard commands, and often very cryptic ones at that. With the advent of Windows, many everyday computer tasks—such as running programs, opening files, choosing commands, changing a word to italic, and so forth—can be done using a graphical approach that is much more intuitively obvious to people who are new to computers (Figure 1.1). Also, because all Windows programs (even ones from different software manufacturers) use essentially the same commands and graphical items on the screen, once you've mastered your first Windows program, learning others is much easier.

Windows has evolved into more than just a user interface over the last ten years, however. It is now a complete operating system— an environment hosting thousands of programs, recognizing and supporting a broad range of hardware, and interconnecting users of workstations on a global level. This is a far cry from the simple Windows 1.0 interface that Microsoft tacked on top of DOS back in the eighties. Today's Windows is a highly evolved product, tightly integrating the GUI, the operating and disk systems, and connections to the outside world.

FIGURE 1.1

Word for Windows displays text as it will print. Commands are found on menus and are fairly consistent between different Windows programs.

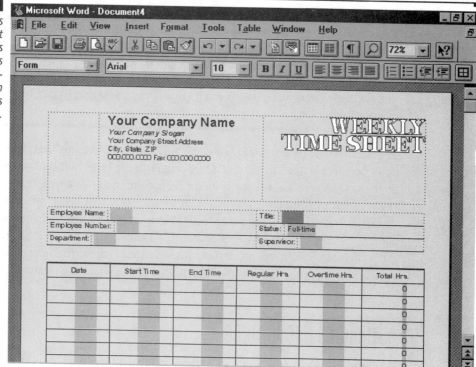

Windows vs. Macintosh

If you've used a Mac, you know all its programs work the same way and look much alike. They comply with a standard set of commands and comply with the Apple Human Interface (HI) Guidelines. Non–computer people gravitated to the Mac over the years primarily because it is easy to use and isn't intimidating. The problem is that up until recently the Mac's GUI could be used only on computers made by Apple Corporation; Apple didn't allow anyone to make Mac clones.

Windows changed everything about the PC market when it brought the essentials of the Macintosh interface (the mouse, the pointer arrow on the screen, the little icons on the screen, and so forth) to the IBM PC and the thousands of super-cheap IBM-compatible brands readily available in stores all over the world. The fact that Windows has always offered tremendous compatibility with affordable equipment, and that that equipment itself has proved to be eminently configurable to each user's desires, has made Windows today much more than just the PC's version of the Mac.

Apple loosened up its licensing agreements for a while between 1995 and 1997, but now has reverted once again to being strictly proprietary, much to the chagrin of many Apple enthusiasts. Still, for most of the early years of the PC era, if you wanted a computer that was easy for novices to master, you had to pay top dollar for an Apple computer.

Regardless of Apple's pricing or availability, the fact remains that the microcomputer business is software driven. More programs are being written for the Windows platform than all other microcomputer GUIs combined (for example, OpenSTEP, OS/2, variants of Unix, etc.). Windows is here to stay. This being the case, Windows detractors have slowly had to face facts: Windows is the only big game in town, and besides, it really isn't so bad after all. Most Windows applications look and feel identical to their Mac counterparts, and because most users are running programs just to get work done, not critiquing the finer points of the operating system, the issue of Mac vs. PC is technically almost moot at this point.

Some Windows Background

Targeting the needs and demands of home and small business users and hoping to keep Windows users from being wooed away by the competition (which included IBM's OS/2 and various Unix alternatives such as Linux and OpenSTEP), Microsoft spent several years developing a robust and feature-rich operating system intended to replace the somewhat glitchy Windows 3.1 and make us all (even Mac users) happy. That was Windows 95. And as we all know, it was a smashing success, despite legitimate complaints from detractors. People lined up outside of computer retail stores at midnight in cities around the globe just to get their copy the moment it went on sale. This is the level of hysteria we're used to seeing when Stones, Michael Jackson, or U2 tickets go on sale – not computer software.

Windows 95 was substantively very different from Windows 3.1 and considerably more user-friendly, and it introduced many modern features such as *Plug and Play*, eliminating some major headaches for PC users. Windows also now recognized and worked more efficiently with portable computers, since Microsoft thought it wise to address the needs of the burgeoning laptop-computer community. Upper management, sales personnel, and technical users who had shifted from desktop systems to portable computers by the mid-nineties had developed a new set of computing needs that Windows 95 addressed.

Despite the frenzied Windows 95 upgrade craze, powered to a great extent by the Microsoft's indefatigable advertising department, millions of PC users have resisted the temptation. For many of them, their resistance was due to the cost of hardware upgrades necessary to run Windows 95 (millions of PCs still have only 8MB of RAM and 286 or "slow" 386 CPUs). Or, when hardware wasn't the issue, the high cost of retraining and/or the fear of data loss on a new operating system dictated managers' decisions to stay with Windows 3.1.

Which brings me to my point. Many PC users, especially corporate types, have been waiting for "rev 2" of Windows 95 before upgrading. In essence, you can think of Windows 98 as that revision—not entirely different from Windows 95, but more like a Windows 95 with some niceties, some bug fixes, better hardware support, and integration with the Internet. It's a "modern" Windows 95, forming a bridge between Windows 95 and Windows NT (which is, incidentally, where Microsoft intends to take you next time around).

Since undoubtedly a large number of the 60 million users of Windows 3.x will be upgrading directly to Windows 98, there are references to Windows 3.x in this book, and some discussion in this chapter of the differences between Windows 98, Windows 95, and Windows 3.11. I've also decided not to pretend that Windows 95 isn't out there on 120 million machines. By referencing different versions, you'll get a bit of historical perspective, including what's new in Windows 98 relative to its several predecessors.

TIP

If you're an old hand with Windows 95, you may want to just skip to the "What's New in Windows 98" section. If you're a "new hand," and you don't want to know all this stuff about Windows 98's features, history, and other exciting but technical and geeky stuff, don't worry. Chapter 2 really does start out at the beginning, teaching you all you'll need to know to actually use Windows. Feel free to skip this chapter, or come back to it later.

For you computer history folks, here's a little background on Windows events that have shaped the developments in personal computing over the last decade (well almost a decade):

- May 1990. Windows 3.0 ships. Unlike versions 1 and 2, this one is actually usable.

- May 1992. Windows 3.1 ships, adding more stability and leaving first-generation and second-generation PCs (8086 and 80286) in the dust, since they can't run it.

- March 1993. Windows for Workgroups (also known as WFW, or Windows 3.11) ships—bringing effortless peer-to-peer networking and a bunch of faster 32-bit innards to Windows.

- July 1993. Windows NT (the first industrial-strength version of Windows) ships.

- August 1995. Windows 95 finally ships after 18 months of delays and hoopla.

- August 1996. Windows 95 version 2 (also known as 950B or OSR2) ships to computer makers, fixing some bugs and adding lots of little goodies. This is a non-publicity release, but buyers of new computers reap many benefits. Many of the additions are downloadable from the Microsoft web sites. Windows NT 4.0 also ships, gluing the Windows 95 interface onto Windows NT.

- Spring 1998. Windows 98 ships. If things go as planned at Microsoft, so will Windows NT 5.0.

What Windows 95 Brought Us

In technical terms, here are some of the features that Windows 95 introduced. (I'll explain many of these later in this chapter.) All of these features are also available in Windows 98. I'll describe in the next section what Windows 98 adds to the pie.

- A face-lift and reliability improvements over Windows 3.x.

- It ran DOS applications (aka software, programs, or "apps" as the trade press is calling them now—all names for the same thing), Windows 3.x applications, and some Windows NT 32-bit applications. This encouraged the development of the more-efficient 32-bit apps, which have proliferated in the last few years.

- Unlike Windows 3.x, Windows 95 wasn't planted on top of an old version of MS-DOS, but rather on a modern DOS (DOS 7) that was designed to work hand-in-hand with this new version of Windows. The new DOS/Windows 95 combination was finally a full-fledged graphical operating system in its own right, not a GUI tacked on top of a dinosaur. It was more stable as a result.

- *Multithreading* and *preemptive multitasking*. This means it could run multiple applications simultaneously more smoothly than did Windows 3.1, especially if those programs were of the new breed of 32-bit applications that were written for Windows 95 or Windows NT. In Windows 3.x, programs had to be written carefully to cooperate with one another, or one program might stall while waiting for another one to finish a task. This rarely happened in Windows 95 (and even less often in Windows NT).

- Major portions of Windows 95 were written in 32-bit code, taking better advantage of the Intel 80386, 80486, and Pentium processors. The memory manager, scheduler, and process manager are all 32-bit. Some sections of the operating system were still written in 16-bit code, however, to ensure compatibility with existing 16-bit applications.

- A more Mac-like interface, doing away with the confusing Program Manager/ File Manager design and incorporating a single integrated arrangement that allowed you to place document icons and folders right on the Windows desktop and work with them from there. A *Taskbar*, always easily accessible on screen, had buttons listing the currently running applications, letting you easily switch between them.

- Supported long file names rather than the severely limited eight-letter file names used by DOS. Finally, starting with Windows 95, files could have names up to 255 characters long.

- Consolidated the bulk of software and hardware settings in a central location called the *Registry*. These settings were previously stored in a number of different files such as autoexec.bat, config.sys, win.ini, and system.ini files. This arrangement allows for a more easily managed PC. These settings can be accessed from a remote PC on a network, allowing a network administrator to maintain a network of corporate PCs more easily than was possible with Windows 3.11.

NOTE

For backward compatibility with older device drivers and systems, the autoexec.bat and config.sys files are still used by Windows 95 and Windows 98, so the implementation of the Registry is not as complete as it is in Windows NT. However, reliance on the older files is greatly lessened, with Windows 95 and 98 doing more system housekeeping than before and using 32-bit device drivers when possible.

- Supported multiple users of the same computer, each with their own settings such as desktop icons, shared resources, user rights, and so forth.

- Had an installable 32-bit file system, allowing easier future expansion of Windows 95 to incorporate other file-system schemes. It also ensured faster disk performance than the 16-bit file system used by Windows 3.1 and DOS.

- Was more proficient at cleaning up after an application crash, often preventing Windows from crashing altogether (i.e., you'll see fewer General Protection Fault error messages). If a program crashed, you could often eliminate it from the task list without affecting other running applications. Memory and other resources the application was using were freed for use by the system.

- Automatically adapted more fully to the hardware it was running on and thus required less fine-tuning to take full advantage of your particular computer setup, available disk space, amount of RAM, and so forth.

- Windows 95 provided more DOS program *conventional memory* space by implementing device drivers such as SmartDrive, mouse drivers, share.exe, CD-ROM, and SCSI device drivers as 32-bit VxDs handled by Windows 95. There was now less chance of running out of memory space for your DOS applications.

- Like Windows for Workgroups, Windows 95 included built-in peer-to-peer networking, only with more efficient 32-bit network drivers as well as support for the increasingly popular TCP/IP protocol for accessing Unix-based systems such as the Internet. It supported NDIS 2.*x*, 3.*x*, and ODI drivers, and had 32-bit NetBEUI and IPX/SPX support. Redirectors for SMB and NCP-based networks were included. The upshot? You could hook up a Windows 95 PC really easily to most existing local-area and wide-area networks. That included the popular Novell NetWare, Banyan Vines, LANtastic, Windows NT, LAN Manager, and Windows for Workgroups. Also, users would see a fairly identical interface (dialog boxes) when interacting with any of these networks to share data, printers, and so on. With Windows 95, networking got easier.

- It incorporated Object Linking and Embedding (OLE) version 2.0. This meant users could easily create fancy documents combining information from several different application programs. This made it a cinch to incorporate graphs, charts, music, video, clip art, and so forth right into your word-processing documents.

- Windows 95 introduced the "document-centric" concept for managing your files. This means Windows let you organize your work on the computer in a way that's more similar to the way you work in the world. You organize your documents on the Windows desktop or in folders, then click on them to open them. You don't have to think about finding and running a specific program (such as Word or Excel), then finding and opening your document. You just organize your documents into folders that you can name as you wish, like My PhD Thesis, and click it. You can create a new document simply by clicking on the desktop and choosing New from a pop-up menu.

- Included some nifty administration and system management tools such as disk compression, networking monitoring, backup utilities, and a resource meter. Also available almost from the initial release of Windows 95 was the Plus! Pack, which included a bunch of goodies for adding neat sounds and wallpaper, color schemes, and font smoothing, and for automatically scheduling tasks such as defragmenting your hard disk at predetermined times. (Some of the Plus! Pack items cost extra with the original version.of Windows 95, but were thrown in for free later, in the second major version, which was known as OSR2.)

- Came bundled with Remote-Access Services, which allowed Windows 95 users on the road to call into a Windows 95 network, log on, and connect just as they do from their desktop machine, sharing data and resources supplied by network servers, printers, fax modems, and other workstations.

- Supported the new Plug and Play standard for hardware, developed by PC makers. Plug and Play lets you simply plug a new board (such as a video or network card) into your computer without having to set switches or make other settings. Windows 95 will figure out what you plugged in and make it work.

- Supported PCMCIA cards for laptop computers and the use of laptop docking stations. Without rebooting the operating system, it will acknowledge what you plugged in and automatically reconfigure the system accordingly.

- Included a new mail system called Microsoft Exchange for managing all the types of messages computer users typically have to deal with, such as e-mail, Internet communications, faxes, and documents. There was no need for separate communications programs (such as Microsoft Mail, WinCIM, or Eudora) or fax programs (such as WinFAX). Once it was set up, a single button click could get and send e-mail from CompuServe, the Internet, The Microsoft Network, or a network e-mail post office, and also send queued-up faxes. Although the program turned out to be unwieldy and buggy, it evolved into newer versions that were more reliable.

Enter Windows 98

All these bells and whistles didn't come cheaply. Not that Windows 95 itself was expensive (typically it was thrown in with a new computer; if sold separately it cost at most $150 or so). But there was the serious additional cost of upgrading machines to run Windows 95, not to mention the cost of training folks to use it (we'll talk about what you'll need for Windows 98 in the next chapter). And then there were bugs. As you may know, the press wasn't all positive about Windows 95, despite all the hoopla. Numerous Windows detractors busily published diatribes against it, and against Microsoft as well. Apple Computer sued Microsoft over parts of the interface, and some smaller software companies scurried for their piece of the litigation pie as well. Regardless, many of us accommodated Windows 95's quirks, and even learned to like them. A major migration to Windows 95 has occurred. Within a year, virtually all new PCs were loaded with it. It became the de facto standard.

With all that said, let's look at Windows 98. Is it really new? Why should you care? If you're already happy with Windows 95, should you upgrade? All good questions.

Analyzed bit by bit, Windows 98 is not a big deal, certainly not as big a deal as the upgrade from Windows 3.*x* to 95 was. But taken on the whole, it's certainly worth the hassle of upgrading. I've watched Windows 98 evolve through its couple of thousand "builds" while the programmers hammered away on it, and it wasn't long before I was hooked on some of its features. It sports a truckload of refinements, add-ons, conveniences, and some important networking and administrative enhancements. It integrates with the Internet really well (maybe *too* well, by some claims, such as one from the U.S. Justice System, but that's another story). Windows 98 is more reliable, lets you do "cool stuff" like watch TV on your computer (just what we needed more of), and talk with and see people in live conversations around the globe. You can see more of your work and documents at one time through use of multiple monitors, and have faster Internet connections by ganging up multiple modems. And then there's Internet Explorer 4.0 thrown into the package. (You could download that for free and use it with Windows 95, that's true. But it integrates more fully with Windows 98.) There's quite a collection of terrific new utility programs, such as improved backup, system file checkers, and such. That's it in a nutshell. Want to know the details? Read the rest of the chapter. (You'd rather get right into using it? Okay, skip to Chapter 2.)

Reliability and Performance Improvements

I'll break down Windows 98's improvements by category. Let's start with reliability and performance. Most important, especially to folks doing "mission critical" work (that's business speak for *really important* work), are the greater stability, improved system management tools, and better Help system that have been built into Windows 98. Microsoft had to respond to all the gripes and the overhead of running their tech support department, and I think they've made some intelligent improvements in this regard.

- **Windows 98 HelpDesk**: A built-in web page you use to handle Windows-related problems when you need help. The screen links you to various sources of information to resolve your technical problems, including the standard Help files and troubleshooting Wizards in your computer, but extending to the outside world via the Internet. Easy links to the Microsoft Knowledge Base, the Microsoft Technical Support for Windows Home Page, Windows Update Manager, and the Windows 98 Web-based Bug Reporting Tool are included.

- **Windows Tune-Up Wizard**: A new program in the System Tools group does its best to keep your operating system and hard disk in top condition by defragmenting the hard disk, culling unnecessary startup commands, deleting unnecessary temp, setup, and Internet files, and checking a hard disk for errors. Sort of like a self-cleaning oven. The result is faster program execution and more disk space.

- **Windows System Update**: A very nifty feature. This ensures you've got the latest system software such as drivers and system files that are available. This is a new Microsoft Web-based service you access over the Internet. True, the paranoid in us all could be concerned about what this feature does, since it's an ActiveX control that scans your system to check out what's in it (software and hardware), and then checks this against a database of the latest files at the Microsoft site—but what a godsend if your computer is suddenly freaking out after you've erased a file or installed some new program that futzed with your system files. Just run the update, and you're alerted if anything is out of date or missing. Also cool if you've just bought some new video card and want the latest driver without searching the entire web for it. And just in case the download causes trouble, such as a system lockup, you can use the "rollback" feature, which can remove a driver that was automatically installed via Windows System Update.

- **System File Checker Utility**: Along the same lines as the Windows System Update, which works on-line, this new utility works off-line to to verify if your Windows 98 system files (*.dll, *.com, *.vxd, *.drv, *.ocx, *.inf, *.hlp, and so on) are altered, dead, or missing. If it senses trouble, the program will tell you to load your Windows 98 CD so it can get the "real McCoy" files from it and reinstall them. This one is going to save Microsoft support folks a lot of time trying to solve system conflicts for users. It's included as part of the following utility package:

- **Microsoft System Information**: Spiffy new package of programs that collects a huge amount of information about your system, and displays it in a two-pane window, as Windows Explorer or Regedit does. Think of it as a combination of the Control Panel's *System* applet combined with the old MSD (Microsoft System Diagnostics)—but on steroids. Using this utility, a tech support person can easily walk a user through the necessary steps to find the data relating to a problem or conflict in the system.

- **Disk Defragmenter Optimization Wizard**: Uses the process of disk defragmentation to increase the speed with which your most frequently used applications run. To accomplish this the wizard creates a log file, which identifies your most commonly used programs. Once this log file has been created, it can be used by the disk defragmenter to store the files associated with those programs. By storing all of the files associated with a given application in the same location on your hard disk, this wizard optimizes the speed with which your application runs.

- **Enhanced Dr. Watson Utility:** This is a tool for capturing information about the system at the time of a program or system malfunction. Not often used by end users, but by programmers. Dr. Watson reports which program screwed up, records the relevant details, such as state of the system, and can display it and/or save it on disk for later perusal.

- **Automatic ScanDisk after Improper Shutdown:** This feature first appeared in Windows 95's OSR 2 update and carries over into Windows 98. After a system crash or after someone accidentally turns off the computer without exiting Windows properly, the ScanDisk program automatically runs, helping prevent hard drive errors, and assuring that disks are in proper working order, free of lost clusters, cross-linked files, etc.

- **New Backup Program:** The supplied backup program now supports SCSI tape devices, and has general enhancements so that backing up your data is simpler and quicker.

- **More Automated Setup:** Several enhancements speed up the process of installing and setting up Windows, as well as making setup more reliable. Among other things CD-ROM support is provided on the bootable Windows 98 CD. On many computers, you'll be able to boot right off the CD and install Windows easily without having to load special CD-ROM drivers.

- **New Tools for the Physically Challenged:** There are several new accessibility tools. Two of the more interesting are:
  - The Accessibility Configuration Wizard, which helps people adapt Windows' options to their needs and preferences.
  - A screen magnifier, which helps people with moderate vision impairments see the screen more clearly.

- **Faster Shutdown:** You won't have to wait as long for Windows 98 to shut down as you did for Windows 95. Microsoft heard that this was an annoyance.

Entertainment and Multimedia Enhancements

- **Support for New Generation of Hardware:** Since Windows 95 came out, lots of new types of hardware have shown up: Universal Serial Bus (USB), IEEE 1394, Accelerated Graphics Port (AGP), Advanced Configuration and Power Interface (ACPI), and Digital Video Disc (DVD), and some new video conferencing formats. Windows 98 supplies drivers, controls, and some software programs for these new hardware devices.

- **Support for Intel MMX Processors**: Provides support so that third parties can build software that exploits the Intel Pentium Multimedia Extensions (MMX) for fast audio and video support on the next generation of Intel Pentium processors.

- **Broadcast Architecture**: With a TV tuner board installed, Windows 98 allows a PC to receive and display television and other data distributed over the broadcast networks. Windows 98's Program Guide, which is updated continuously, lists television shows that are on now and in the future, and allows for instant tuning in to shows for viewing on the PC. Windows 98 can also receive Enhanced Television programs, which combine standard television with HTML information related to the programs, as they become available. Additionally, Windows 98 users will be able to receive Internet content or other data services via the broadcast networks, without tying up their existing phone lines.

- **ActiveMovie™**: ActiveMovie is a new media-streaming architecture for Windows that delivers high-quality video playback while exposing an extensible set of interfaces upon which multimedia applications and tools can be built. ActiveMovie enables playback of popular media types including MPEG audio, .WAV audio, MPEG video, AVI video, and Apple QuickTime video.

- **Display Setting Enhancements**: Now you can dynamically change your screen resolution and color depth without rebooting Windows. Adapter refresh rate can also be set with most newer display driver chipsets. Windows 98 also includes the display enhancements previously available in Microsoft Plus!. (Microsoft Plus! is an add-on pack for Windows 95 which provided several minor operating system enhancements.) The enhancements include: full window drag, font smoothing, wallpaper stretching, large icons, high-color icons, and complete desktop "themes" of designer-coordinated sounds, colors, backgrounds, and icons.

Improved Ease of Use

- **FAT32**: FAT32 is an improved version of the FAT file system that allows disks over two gigabytes to be formatted as a single drive. FAT32 also uses smaller clusters than FAT drives, resulting in a more efficient use of space on large disks.

- **FAT32 Conversion Utility**: For added flexibility, Windows 98 includes a graphical FAT32 conversion utility, which can quickly and safely convert a hard drive from the original version of FAT to FAT32. (However, it can't do the reverse.)

- **Power Management Improvements**: Windows 98 includes built-in support for Advanced Configuration and Power Interface (ACPI). ACPI is an open industry specification proposed by Intel, Microsoft, and Toshiba that defines hardware interfaces that allow for standard power management functionality throughout a PC system. In addition to ACPI support, Windows 98 Beta 2 includes support for the Advanced Power Management (APM) 1.2 extensions including: Disk spindown, PCMCIA modem power down, and resume on ring. Also supported are new power management "schemes".

- **Multiple Display Support**: Multiple Display Support allows you to use multiple monitors and/or multiple graphics adapters on a single PC. The ability to have your work environment displayed on several screens at once gives you extra room for viewing large documents, or having many document windows open at once. This can be beneficial for doing work such as: desktop publishing, Web development, video editing, and for playing computer games.

NOTE

Speaking of games, DOS-based games should run about 10 percent to 20 percent faster under Windows 98 because they'll be running on top of DOS32 rather than DOS 7.00. (DOS 32 is written in more-efficient 32-bit code, not 16-bit, so it executes on the 32-bit CPUs such as Pentiums much faster.) With Windows based games, the probability of incompatibility is about 5 to 15 percent higher than with Windows 95. However, if an existing game or program is compatible with both Windows 95 and Windows NT, it should be fully compatible with Windows 98. Some games that run flakily in Windows 95 may actually run better under Windows 98.

- **Remote Access Server**: Windows 98 includes all of the components necessary to enable your desktop to act as a dial-up server. This allows dial-up clients to remotely connect to a Windows 98 machine for local resource access or connecting to an IPX/SPX and/or NetBEUI network. However, compared to the dial-up server included with Windows 95, it has been reduced in capability. Apparently people were using the Windows 95 dial-up server to serve Web pages instead of using NT Server as Microsoft wished. The RAS server in Windows 98 severely restricts the number of simultaneous connections.

- **PCMCIA Enhancements**: There have been several enhancements to Windows 98 with respect to PCMCIA technology including:

  - Support for PC Card32 (Cardbus): Cardbus brings 32-bit performance to the small PC Card form factor. It enables notebooks to implement high-bandwidth applications like video capture and high-speed 100Mbps networking.

  - Support for PC Cards that operate at 3.3 Volts: This enables hardware manufacturers to lower the power consumption of their devices, giving you longer operational time when running your laptop computer on a battery.

- Support for Multifunction PC Cards: Allows two or more functions (such as LAN and Modem, or SCSI and sound) on a single physical PC Card. Supporting Multifunction Cards helps decrease the cost-per-function of PC Cards, and makes better use of the precious number of slots on most PCs, permitting more functions per PC.

- **Built-In Support for Infrared Data Association (IrDA) 3.0**: Windows 98 includes support for IrDA, the Infrared Data Association standard for wireless connectivity. IrDA support enables Windows 98 users to easily connect to peripheral devices or other PCs without using connecting cables. This driver set provides infrared-equipped laptop or desktop computers with the capability of networking, transferring files, and printing wirelessly with other IrDA-compatible infrared devices.

Seamless Internet Integration

- **Integrated Internet Shell**: Windows 98 has an optional "Web view" that you can turn on to change the way you interact with your computer. With Web view on, you interact with all the stuff in your computer (hard disk, files, folders, etc.) in a very similar way to how you use Web pages on the Net. Say goodbye to double-clicking, for example. Hard disk folders can have custom HTML files in them to present the contents to a viewer, such as by including instructions. JPG, GIF, HTML and other popular files display in "thumbnail" form in the Web view window simply by pointing to the file. A neat way to see what a file is, without opening it. The overall advantage is that new users will no longer have to learn to deal with the two disparate looks (single-clicking vs. double clicking, selecting objects, underlines for links, etc.) on and off the Internet. Microsoft is calling this the "Integrated Internet Shell" or "Web view." The result? You can now universally view local, network, intranet, and Internet data, so you can get to the information you need faster and easier. Web view is a feature that's actually built into Internet Explorer 4 (which also runs on Windows 95), so you could, if you'd rather, update a Windows 95 machine to do the same thing.

- **Dial-Up Networking Improvements**: It's now easier to set up new dial-up networking (DUN) connections. Also there are two major improvements to dial up networking:

  - Addition of dial-up scripting (which can automate the process of connecting to bulletin boards and online services);

  - Support for Multilink Channel Aggregation. Say what? That means you can connect multiple modems together (assuming you have multiple dial-up phone lines available) to get higher transfer speeds to the Internet, other dial-up services, or remote computers. For example, you can combine two or more ISDN lines to achieve speeds of up to 128K, or combine two or more standard modem lines. This can provide dramatic performance improvements when dialing into the Internet or corporate network.

- **Advanced Internet Browsing Functionality**: Internet Explorer isn't the only Web browser in town, as Microsoft has had to admit (they've had trouble from the Justice Department over requiring computer sellers to make IE the default browser on Windows machines). Still, IE is pretty darned good. With Windows 98 (via Internet Explorer 4) cruising the Web just got easier. It includes:

  - Advanced browsing capabilities such as AutoComplete, enhanced Web searching, improved Favorites list, navigation history on the Forward/Back buttons, and improved printing.

  - Support for all major Internet standards including HTML, Java, ActiveX, JavaScript, VisualBasic Scripting, and major security standards.

  - Improved performance with Dynamic HTML, a just-in-time Java compiler, and basic code "tuning."

- **Personalized Internet Information Delivery**: When folks were asked the biggest problem they have with the World Wide Web, the number one response was getting the information they need. IE 4 addresses this problem by providing a mechanism to automatically select and schedule downloads of the information you care about. This enables you to see what has changed on a Web site without physically visiting the site and even allows you to view the site when you are not connected to the Web.

- **Suite of Tools for Internet Communication**: Windows 98 also contains rich tools for online communication including:

  - Outlook™ Express, a full featured email and news reading client.

  - Microsoft NetMeeting™, a complete Internet conferencing solution providing standards-based audio, data, and video conferencing functionality.

  - Personal Web Server (and the Web Publishing Wizard), which provides an easy way to publish Web pages on intranets or the Internet.

- **Client Support for Point-to-Point Tunneling Protocol (PPTP)**: The Point-to-Point Tunneling Protocol (PPTP) provides a way to use public data networks, such as the Internet, to create virtual private networks connecting client PCs with servers. PPTP offers protocol encapsulation to support multiple protocols via TCP/IP connections and data encryption for privacy, making it safer to send information over non-secure networks. This technology extends the Dial-Up Networking capability by enabling remote access and securely extending private networks across the Internet without needing to change the client software.

- **Online Services Folder**: The Windows 98 desktop contains an Online Services Folder with links to America Online (AOL), AT&T WorldNet, CompuServe 3.0, and Prodigy clients. When you click the link to the client, a setup program starts that automatically registers you with that Internet Service Provider.

Increased Manageability and Other Business-Related Features

- **Win32 Driver Model (WDM)**: The Win32 Driver Model (WDM) is an all new, common driver model for Windows 95 and Windows NT. WDM will enable some common types of devices using USB and IEEE 1394 to have a single driver for both operating systems. The WDM has been implemented by adding selected NT Kernel services into Windows 98 via a special virtual device driver (NTKERN.VXD). This means that Windows 98 can use older "legacy" device drivers while also adding support for new WDM drivers.

- **Windows System Update**: Windows System Update, part of the "Zero Administration" initiative for Windows, helps a system administrator see to it that users have the latest drivers and file systems available. It is a new Web-based service (ActiveX control) that scans a user's system to determine what hardware and software they have installed, then compares that information to a back-end database to determine whether there are newer drivers or system files available. If there are newer drivers or system files, the service can automatically install the drivers. This process is completely configurable allowing the user to choose which updated drivers/system files to download, or it will simply download the drivers requiring no user interaction. There is even a "rollback" feature which can remove a driver which has been automatically installed via Windows System Update.

- **Windows Scripting Host**: Windows 98 supports direct script execution from the user interface or the command line (a script is simply a series of commands that can be automatically executed). This support is provided via the Windows Scripting Host (WSH) and allows administrators and/or users to save time by automating many user interface actions such as creating a shortcut, connecting to a network server, disconnecting from a network server, etc. The WSH is extremely flexible with built-in support for VisualBasic scripts, Java scripts, and a language independent architecture which will allow other software companies to build ActiveX™ scripting engines for languages such as Perl, TCL, REXX, and Python.

- **Distributed Component Object Model (DCOM)**: The Component Object Model (COM) allows software developers to create component applications.

PART

I

Up and Running

Now, Distributed COM (DCOM) in Windows 98 (and Windows NT 4.0) provides the infrastructure that allows DCOM applications (the technology formally known as Network OLE) to communicate across networks without needing to redevelop applications.

- **Client Support for NetWare Directory Services (NDS)**: Windows 98 includes Client Services for NetWare that support Novell NetWare Directory Services (NDS). This enables Windows 98 users to log on to Novell NetWare 4.*x* servers running NDS to access files and print resources. This service provides the key features that Novell users need, such as: NDS authentication, ability to browse NDS resources, ability to print to NDS print queues, and full support for processing NetWare login scripts, NDS property pages, and NDS passwords.

- **32-bit Data Link Control (DLC)**: The Data Link Control (DLC) protocol is used primarily to access IBM mainframe and IBM AS/400 computers. The 32-bit DLC protocol software built-in to Windows 98 enables a network administrator to add support for 32-bit and 16-bit DLC programs.

- **Dr. Watson and System Information Utility**: These two programs make it easier for product support staff to diagnose and correct problems.

- **Upgrade Wizard**: provides smooth migration paths from Windows 95 and Windows 3.*x*-based systems.

What Makes Windows Important

Even though the first iterations of Windows had shortcomings, the sheer number of software programs available for them ensured their success. If the demand were only for a serious operating system with most or even all of the features Windows provided, Windows never would have caught on as it has. Corporations heavily invested in PC-based information systems could have adopted Unix (or even the now pretty much defunct OS/2) en masse by now, but they didn't. These alternatives have been feature-rich, and each has had an advantage over Windows, but the success of an operating system, particularly in business settings, has more to do with application availability and compatibility than any other variable.

If the success of a computer operating system or GUI is dependent on application availability and timely and reliable upgrades, then it can also be said that application availability is tied to ease of writing for that platform. Microsoft is certainly well aware of this and is supplying programmers with Windows-related tool- and software-development kits.

Availability of applications isn't the only crucial variable when choosing an operating system. MIS professionals need to not only think about what software is available for the platform, but whether their current hardware, software, and training investments will be jeopardized or enhanced by a specific operating-system decision. There are many considerations in this decision-tree, but part of that formula includes usability. The more usable an operating system, the less likely it is that serious training costs will be involved in migrating to it.

Windows 98, like its immediate predecessor, makes single-user PCs and laptops simpler to learn and use than those running Windows 3.*x* or DOS. Significant expense, time, and scientific analysis were involved in the development of the Windows 9*x* interface (see sidebar below). The studies showed that the majority of PC users were confused by their computers and felt that they were not taking full advantage of the power they paid dearly for when purchasing their PC (as we all know). For example, it was shown that many Windows 3.1 users didn't know they could run multiple programs simultaneously, didn't know what happens to one program when another program's window overlaps it, or were afraid to use the File Manager. The Windows 9*x* (also incorporated into NT 4 and 5) interface was developed in response to these findings. Windows 98 takes these findings and extends the technology another step.

Usability Studies

In researching ways to improve the Windows user interface above Windows 3.*x*, Microsoft relied on several sources. In fact, it's quite likely that the interface of Windows 95/98 are the most thoroughly researched pieces of software ever developed. Several phases of study were conducted in a variety of settings:

- *Usability Lab test groups.* Users were watched from behind mirrors and taped with video cameras as they performed tasks such as launching programs, creating new files, and printing. Their interaction with the keyboard and mouse as well as their reactions were all recorded and later analyzed by experts in learning theory and cognition.

- *Long-Term Testing.* Longer-term testing, also know as *summative* testing, was conducted both at Microsoft and in the field at various customer locations.

- *Expert consultants.* Experts in user interfaces were hired to perform a professional critique of the Windows interface.

Reactions to the product design were then tabulated, digested, and fed back to the design, development, and programming staff.

What's the "another step" I referred to above? Windows 98 integrates emerging Internet technologies such as:

- displaying local resources as underlined "hot-links,"
- streaming video and audio,
- "push" technology, and
- "channels"

into the operating system interface itself. When using Windows 98, the experiential distinction between being on- and off-line becomes much more subtle. When using the optional Web View interface, for example, you interact with stuff inside your computers (such as hard disk directories, files, and printers), the same way you use and view links and data on web pages. The toolbar on a folder or Windows Explorer, for example, looks much like the Internet Explorer toolbar, with a Back button for returning to the last location you were viewing. (See Figure 1.2.)

Since the World Wide Web has become probably the single common denominator among computer users (regardless of whether they're using Macs, Unix, PCs, or whatever), it makes perfect sense for Microsoft to have revamped their GUI to mimic it and incorporate it. If you know how to interact with a Web page, you'll become conversant in the Windows GUI that much faster.

FIGURE 1.2

In Web View, file folders are displayed as links. Single-clicking will open the file, or folder, or launch the application. Many file types will be displayed as a "thumbnail" in the left side of the pane, simply by pointing to it. Sound files will play, and AVI or MPG video files will run in a little window. Notice the Back and Forward buttons, borrowed from Web browsers.

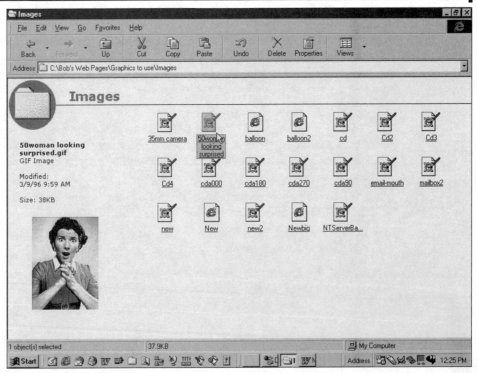

People always seem to be confused and intimidated by computers, regardless of usability advances. If you feel that way, you're not alone. This is why the demand for training materials (such as this book) remains high. So don't be misled. Especially if you choose to take advantage of the new bells and whistles (such as Web View), Windows 98 will take a little getting used to.

Cost of Upgrade and Retraining

What about the cost of upgrading and retraining? Whether you're using MS-DOS, Windows for Workgroups, Windows 3.*x*, or Windows 95, actual software migration to Windows 98 will be relatively painless. True, with the migration from 3.*x* to 95, there was a learning curve to climb. Despite Microsoft's hopes of making a computer interface more "discoverable" or immediately sensible, it's not really that obvious, and won't be until we can simply say "Open the pod bay door, Hal." And Hal doesn't then destroy all nearby life forms. But if you or your users are familiar with Windows 95 and a web browser such as Netscape or IE, retraining time should be negligible.

There are still plenty of things for newbies to learn, like using menus, saving files, cutting and pasting, and such, but major confusions such as when to single- vs. double-click are eliminated. Also eliminated, or at least minimized, is the hassle of learning *two* interfaces: the Windows GUI and a web browser. With e-mail, newsgroups, and Web access becoming so popular and important in business, Microsoft has seen to it that newly added tools can be relied upon to get the user connected to the internet. Whether you're setting up an initial account with an Internet Service Provider (ISP), or logging on to your ISP every time you ask for a web page or want to read your mail, it's all getting pretty seamless. The chore of tracking whether you're on or off the Net at any given time, or whether a particular resource requires Net access, can be left up to Windows. You no longer have to think "Gee, I want to do a Web search. First I'll call up my ISP and log on. Then I run my web browser … let's see, where is that program? Then I have to get to a search engine…" Nope. Instead you simply click Start, point to Find, and point to On the Internet:

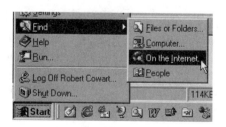

If you're not connected already (either via the company LAN or dial-up), Windows' Connection Manager senses this and can make the connection for you. Windows logs you into the Net, and loads a search engine web page where you're prompted to enter the search criteria.

The effect of the new Windows 98 Web View is a subtle one at first. But soon you find yourself performing a multitude of previously disparate tasks all from the same window. From either the Windows Explorer or Internet Explorer, you can now seamlessly switch between viewing local files and viewing Web pages, doing typical Web activities such as searching for people and information, or searching for local files. And while you're working away on one project, your system can be downloading pages of websites you've subscribed to, for viewing off line, when you are not paying for connect time, or tying up phone lines.

Another enticing feature for professionals is that Windows 9x makes the oft-confusing topic of local area networking surprising simple for average user folk. Workgroups that don't need serious data protection and/or security are no hassle to set up, configure, and maintain. Accessing LAN resources is as simple for the user as clicking on the Network Neighborhood icon on the desktop.

And setting up a simple peer-to-peer network with a bunch of Windows 98 machines—it's almost a no brainer, too. With Windows 98, networking is easy both to set up and to use. Windows 98 now offers even better remote management of the workstation than did Windows 95, so a manager can connect to and alter the security settings on a Windows 98 PC from anywhere on its network, even via remote access from home or another city.

Finally, Windows 98 implements some of the newest hardware technology available (such as Plug and Play, USB, and DVD), pushing PC manufacturers into finalizing design and development of those emerging technologies in hopes of maintaining a competitive edge against other lines of computers. All three of these strategies, of course, are geared towards making PCs friendlier and thus spurring on the sales of computers and software.

NOTE

Windows 3.*x* aficionados take heart. Actually a File Manager and Program Manager à la Windows 3.*x* are supplied with Windows 98 (as they were in 95), just to help veteran 3.*x* users get over the hump. However, the idea is that once you get used to the new interface, you won't find yourself using them much anymore. Instead, you'll use the Taskbar to launch and switch applications and the Desktop to manage your documents. To dig into the file system, you'll use the turbocharged File Manager replacement, Windows Explorer.

Is Windows 98 for You?

In my opinion, Windows 98 is currently the ideal solution for the bulk of Windows users. (For many, this will be a moot point anyway since new computers as of May 1998 will ship with it preinstalled.) Even stubborn OS/2 lovers will probably want to come back to the fold, because Windows 98 has everything that OS/2 does (except, of course, the ability to run OS/2-specific software). In my opinion, certainly everyone currently running Windows 3.1 and 95 should, assuming they have a 486DX-based PC or higher, with 16MB of RAM. Windows 98 runs much more smoothly and crashes less often than Windows 3.1, and recovers more gracefully from application crashes. Its refinements in both usage and system management far exceed Windows 95's. And once you get used to doing things a bit differently in Windows 98, your productivity will certainly increase.

 TIP

Not that Windows 3.*x* isn't perfect in certain situations. Sometimes it's just the ticket. Suppose you have a "legacy" machine (e.g. 286 or 386 or slow 486 with only 8M of RAM). Just stick with Windows 3.*x* on that baby until you're ready to trash it. Actually one of the best deals around these days, for simple tasks such as basic word processing, is to purchase a 386-based laptop for a hundred bucks or so and run Windows 3.1 on it. Then add an older version of Word for Windows, such as version 2.0, and you're in business.

Since close to half of the machines that will be purchased in the next year will be laptops, Microsoft has seen to it that Windows 98 is well-equipped for all us road warriors. (Personally, I'm very laptop-computer oriented and hate being tied to a desktop machine. Or even a desk.) It doesn't matter if you're using a desktop or a laptop machine. Windows 98 has been designed for—and will be bundled with—both types of machines.

As you're probably aware, the current crop of laptops is every bit as respectable as the desktop machines they aim to replace. Performance speed, usability, keyboards, and now even screens clearly rival the best desktop machines, have clearer displays, produce less radiation, and consume so much less space and electrical power.

Of course you pay a premium for this portability—an additional $500 to $1000 on average for a modest laptop. With decent desktop machines coming down to below $1000, and powerhouse laptops still tipping the scale at as high as $6000 or $7000 the range of price disparity is still pretty great at the extremes.

What about NT?

Because there are two Windows workstation operating systems (NT Workstation and Windows 95), which should you choose? And is Microsoft shooting itself in the foot by offering both?

Actually, Microsoft's strategy makes sense. There are two options because there are two markets for network workstations—high performance and low-to-medium performance.

Well, at least for the present time we'll have two workstation operating systems from Microsoft. But not for long. Actually Windows 98 will probably be the last non-NT version of Windows. After that, Microsoft will try to get us all to move into the NT camp. Why? Because NT is all 32-bit code, is more modular and easier for Microsoft to support, and is better in overall design. But it will mean saying goodbye to some of your legacy software and hardware. Since you'll have a couple of years before you have to seriously think about this, by then you may not care. During the interim, your new hardware and software will be designed with the NT migration in mind.

If your applications require the utmost in performance or if your application mix is highly network oriented, you are using large networks, and you need robust workstation and network management, you should be using a mix of NT Server and NT Workstation-based computers (or possibly Novell NetWare-based machines).

Windows NT provides US Government "C-2"-rated security features. For most intents and purposes, NT Server has essentially bulletproof security that can prevent an unauthorized user from entering the system or in other ways gaining access to files on the hard disk. Without a proper password, NT can effectively prevent sensitive files from being reached. Tools for assigning permission levels for various tasks are supplied, providing great flexibility in security arrangements.

If the application mix is heavy on the Windows side, I'd especially recommend NT (over NetWare) because NetWare tacked on top of DOS with Windows tacked on top of that can lead to some headaches. For one thing, it decreases the available conventional memory for DOS applications. NT removes at least one software level and has IPX/SPX drivers to connect with NetWare networks if you need to. Figure 1.3 demonstrates this. Connection to a NetWare network with Windows 3.1 and DOS requires three levels (four modules) of software. Connection with Windows 95 requires just one, with the inherent security and connectivity advantages of Windows 95. If you're running only DOS applications, stick with NetWare.

FIGURE 1.3

32-bit NetWare drivers are incorporated into both Windows 95 and Windows NT, improving performance and eliminating hassles caused by loading NetWare drivers into DOS.

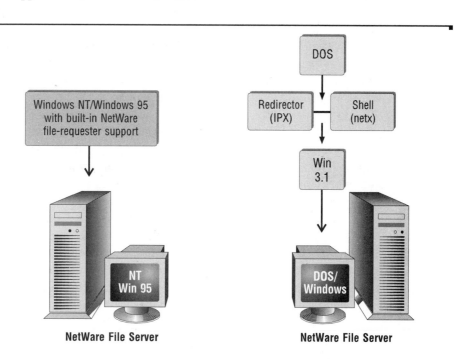

Unlike NT, which boasts the ability to escape crashed hard drives and power outages on huge networks with nary a hiccup, Windows 98 is no Houdini. It wasn't meant to be as robust as NT, which was designed for "mission critical" projects such as running an airline reservations system where downtime isn't acceptable. Still, Windows 98 has key features that redeem it. For example, the Windows 9*x* product was the first Microsoft operating system since Windows 3.0 to offer a significantly improved interface (one that has been incorporated into NT 4, and soon into NT 5). It was also designed to run fairly well without users having to do much of anything to their systems, particularly adding RAM or upgrading to a faster processor. Windows 98 should run fine on a 486 with 16M of RAM. (By contrast, Windows NT Workstation is more hungry, and should probably have 24 or 32M and a Pentium to run smoothly).

Consider that if you need to run Unix applications, NT may be able to run them because it can handle any Unix applications written to the POSIX specification.

Finally, if your machines are speedy 486s or Pentiums well-endowed with RAM (I'd say 32M for NT Workstation) and the applications you want are available for NT, my advice is to go for it. NT is where PCs are headed. But beware. Make sure that all your add-in boards and devices have NT device drivers available before you begin. Remember, NT can't use your old Windows 3.1 16-bit device drivers for your printers, video boards, mice, SCSI drives, CD-ROM drives, sound cards, and the like. It needs special 32-bit drivers written for NT. And some of the newer bells and whistles that Windows 98 touts will not be integrated with NT for some time. NT 5 will have some of them, but since Windows 98 is aimed at the consumer and home user, some of the entertainment niceties (such as fine tuning for games, TV viewing, DVD) will be offered for Windows 98 first.

Now for the Windows 98 argument. If the computers you are considering upgrading aren't top of the line, if having a full 32-bit operating system with high level system security is nothing more than academic to you, if you'd like to have the widest diversity of new technology available and supported, and enjoy the widest variety of software compatibility, Windows 98 is the clear winner.

If you own an expanding business and are in doubt about which workstation route to take, don't worry. You can start with all Windows 98 workstations connected to one another in a peer-to-peer fashion (see Part V on networking for more about peer-to-peer networks) and then add an NT Server station later if you want more network security and performance. And remember that if you have been using or are still using a NetWare network, 32-bit NetWare client support is built in. Getting a Windows workstation up and running on a NetWare network is finally a no-brainer.

Chapter

2

Getting Your Hardware and Software Ready for Windows 98

FEATURING

What Windows 3.1 software to kiss good-bye and why

What Windows 3.1 software to keep and what to upgrade

About 32-bit software

Hardware requirements and options for Windows 98

Getting Your Hardware and Software Ready for Windows 98

Assuming you made it through the last chapter unscathed, you should now have a pretty good idea of what Windows 98 is all about. Because this book is slated for publication roughly around the time Windows 98 is released, our mission here is not only to teach you how to use it, but also what it has to offer you, what benefit you will gain from it, and how to prepare yourself for it.

> If you are learning to use Windows for the first time and have recently purchased a computer with Windows 98 preinstalled, the information in this chapter will not be essential to your getting started, so you can move ahead to Chapter 3. But if you're migrating to Windows 98 from a previous incarnation of Windows (especially 3.1), or if you simply find this stuff interesting (is it my deathless prose?), you should read on.

What's the minimum base system you'll need to run Windows 98, really? And, beyond the minimum requirements, what can you do to upgrade your system to capitalize on Windows 98's coolest features, like its 32-bit operating-system underpinnings, advanced processing features, multimedia and Internet stuff, cool display options, gaming, and networking. Beyond Windows 98 itself, what new software will you have to (or want to) buy to really take advantage of what Windows 98 now makes available to you? (And what software will you have to jettison or pass on to Uncle George?) In this chapter I'll try to cover all these considerations, because knowing what you're getting into may help ease your transition to Windows 98.

NOTE

In that I don't know whether you're upgrading from Windows 3.1 or Windows 95, I'll cover both "upgrade paths" in this chapter.

What Software to Kiss Good-Bye and Why

In preparation for upgrading to Windows 98, assuming you *are* upgrading (versus simply purchasing a new computer that came with Windows 98 on it), you'll have to consider some things about your existing software. So, let's look at software compatibility first.

As I discussed in Chapter 1, Windows 98 was designed with backward compatibility in mind. Windows 98 should be compatible with most existing 16-bit DOS and Windows 3.*x* applications. Microsoft even claims that Windows 98 runs many old DOS applications better than Windows 3.*x* did. It's also compatible with 32-bit programs that were designed for Windows 95 and Windows NT. So, the good news is that compatibility with your existing PC software is likely to be high. Not only that, all your Windows 3.*x* software will benefit from having a face-lift—nicer borders, more options in the dialog boxes, an increased capability to work with larger files, and so forth.

But there is some bad news. There will be classes of programs that Windows 98 *won't* be able to run, at least not in their current incarnations. Also, there will be some programs that, even though they run okay, you should upgrade anyway.

Here's the skinny on all of that.

Applications vs. Utilities

As you probably know, there are two basic categories of PC applications for the mass market: *applications* and *utilities*. Applications are programs such as Microsoft Word, Microsoft Access, Adobe PhotoStyler, and Adobe PageMaker (to mention just a few of the thousands that are available). These programs, often called *productivity-enhancement software,* assist you in doing a certain class of work, such as generating textual documents, managing graphical images, or organizing huge amounts of data. By contrast, programs called utilities are for performing various types of computer housecleaning.

For example, the Norton Utilities can help you by undeleting files you accidentally erased, defragmenting your hard disk, combing through your hard disk to find files, or determining your system's speed by putting it through its paces.

NOTE

In common parlance, most people don't distinguish between utilities and applications, and simply use the word "application" (or just "program") to refer to any program other than Windows itself.

Applications work at the highest level of the operating system, a bit like a ship on the sea. They "ride" on top of the operating system and graphical user interface software and don't have to interfere with the lower *primitives* of the operating system to get things done. Let me explain.

About APIs

When an application needs the operating system to do something, such as display a dialog box on the screen, accept your keypress, or display letters you've typed, it does this by asking the operating system for help. This type of request is called an *API call*. (API stands for *applications programming interface*.) APIs are little tricks, if you will, that the operating system can do for the programmer. Sort of like you saying to your dog, "Spot, roll over," the application can say, "Display the Save As dialog box and ask for a filename." Then the application can say, "Okay, now store this file on the disk somewhere." The operating system then locates and utilizes unrecorded disk space to save the file for future use.

The operating system can do these things because it is directly in touch with the operating-system *primitives,* which include such operations as writing to the hard disk, reading the keyboard, putting graphics on the screen, reading data from the COM port, and so on. Because of APIs, applications don't have to handle the drudgery of system housekeeping on their own. The existence of an API makes writing Windows programs much easier, because the programmer doesn't have to write code to perform myriad common tasks that every program needs, such as having a window, having a menu bar, opening and closing files, and printing. The fact that Windows has a pretty good library of API calls has made life easier for Windows programmers, because a lot of their work is already done for them. (By comparison, writing 16-bit applications is a pain, and 16-bit DOS is itself a pain, which is why programmers like writing for Windows 9x and NT.)

There's another reason why operating-system primitives are handled by API calls—they help protect the operating-system software from failure. If every program running in the computer were allowed to have direct access to resources such as the screen, keyboard, hard disk, and ports, your computer could be in big trouble. For starters, your hard-disk file allocation table (FAT) could get trashed pretty quickly, and, in essence, you'd lose all your files. Or if you printed from two programs at the same time, both files would go to the printer at the same time (normally, in Windows, the print spooler sees to it that files are sent sequentially rather than simultaneously). The result would be a combination of, say, your 3rd Quarter Income and Expense Report with that Print Shop birthday card for Aunt Harriet. It wouldn't be pretty.

Here's another example. You may have used a disk defragmenting program, such as the one in Norton Utilities or PC-Tools. There's also one supplied with DOS called `defrag.exe`. Though useful, these programs can be dangerous to your data, because they fiddle directly with your hard disk. This is one reason you're not supposed to run them while other programs are also running on the same computer. Because they mess around with the hard disk's file allocation table, as well as moving your disk's files all over the place one block at a time, the whole process can be bollixed up if another program asks the operating system for disk access at the same time.

NOTE

What is defragmenting? When a file becomes too large for your computer to store in a single location on a disk, it becomes fragmented—the operating system splits it up and puts it into different sections of the hard disk. Fragmented files can still be used, but it takes the computer longer to find them because the hard-disk heads have to jump around on the disk, like the arm of a record player jumping from song to song. This slows down overall throughput in the computer. Defragmenting is the process of rearranging the files and free space on your computer in order to speed up disk access. After defragmenting, free space is consolidated in one contiguous block and files are stored contiguously on the rest of the disk.

When programs use the prescribed Windows API calls, everything is cool. Applications that obey the rules go sailing along minding their manners, receiving the proper help from Windows, and other programs that are running are happy too. Perhaps they will have to wait in line to gain access to the hard disk or printer, but that's okay. Spot knows how to roll over and does his job when asked.

When all the programs you're running are Windows programs, there usually isn't a problem. If a communications program needs access to a COM port, for example, it is supplied by Windows. If the particular COM port is already in use, Windows says, in effect, "Sorry, that port isn't available."

But things get tricky when you're running two DOS programs at once, or even a DOS program and a Windows program simultaneously. This is because DOS programs were written to think they are the only program running on the computer and they have the whole computer to themselves, including the hard disk, ports, screen, keyboard, printer, and any other resources. They don't know that other programs might be running at the same time. For this reason, Windows 9*x* enforces the rule that any requests for access to hardware *must* be made via the operating system calls (API), not executed directly by the program itself.

When programs try to bypass the API and directly access hardware that is normally controlled by the operating-system primitives, trouble can ensue. In Windows 3.*x*, such breaches of system security were often neither perceived nor prevented (especially if they originated with a DOS program), and this is one reason Windows 3.*x* wasn't a "secure" operating system. DOS-based viruses are a good case in point. Viruses make a hobby of fiddling with the innards of your operating system (typically by altering data on the hard disk), with insidious effects. Windows 3.*x* couldn't prevent such security breaches because it had no way of knowing they were occurring. Even Windows 98 can't prevent this, but it's a bit more secure.

Protecting the System from Programs That Circumvent the API

Although NT is really the flagship Microsoft product when security is the issue, Windows 98's designers hoped to make it at least more secure (*robust* is the popular adjective) than Windows 3.*x*. There are several means to this end, but the primary approach is to disallow any program direct access to the computer's hardware. Thus, any program that tries to perform an action that the operating system thinks would jeopardize its security will be stopped from doing so.

In the case of Windows 9*x*, the designers have achieved this kind of hardware isolation by "virtualizing" all the hardware. (This is the same approach used in Windows NT, incidentally.) Every physical piece of hardware in the computer is accessed only by *virtual device drivers* (called *VxD*s in Windows lingo). When an application wants the use of a device, it asks the operating system for it via the API call. Then the operating system validates the request and passes it along to the device driver, which in turn handles the actual communication with the device.

Device-Protection Capabilities Built Into Intel Chips

When you run a DOS program in Windows, all standard DOS calls (similar to Windows API calls, but invented for DOS applications way back before Windows was invented) are translated into Windows API calls and sent to the correct device. This works great until a DOS application tries to access hardware directly. Because of a nifty little feature called the *I/O permission bitmap* that is built into the Intel 386 and subsequent chips (486, Pentium and Pentium II), Windows 98 can detect any illegal attempt to directly access the computer's hardware.

Each time an application is run, Windows 98 knows whether it's a DOS or Windows application. If it's a DOS application, a *virtual DOS machine* (*VDM*) is created. A virtual DOS machine is a "software replica" of an IBM PC, providing all the services that a real PC running DOS would supply to a program. Such services would include means for hardware access to the screen, keyboard, memory, and disk drives, for example. Along with this VDM, Windows 98 creates an I/O permission bitmap for the application. The bitmap is essentially a table with entries for each of the computer's internal ports (there are many, used for different things, such as the system clock, network boards, and so on), and shows which, if any, of the ports allow direct access. If the DOS application tries any funny business, it will probably generate an error message indicating your program has done something naughty and Windows will terminate it. Not only that, instead of the program crashing Windows (as in Windows 3.*x*'s "General Protection Fault" error message and resultant system lockups), Windows 98 will terminate the errant program and remain operational.

Because the designers wanted to retain as much compatibility with older DOS programs as possible, they didn't want to go overboard on this protection thing, so some direct hardware calls are still allowed. For example, if a DOS communications program wants to access COM1, and COM1 isn't currently in use by another application, Windows 98 will allow it. However, some ports, such as the hard or floppy disk's, are off-limits.

So What Does This Mean to Me?

If all this sounds like a bunch of computer mumbo-jumbo, here's the bottom line. Any well-behaved Windows application or utility program is likely to run under Windows 98 without incident. However, some DOS programs, especially hard-disk utilities, may have trouble running. Windows 98's "DOS Mode" lets you run particularly demanding DOS programs by temporarily exiting Windows.

 WARNING

Just because you can run many of your older disk utilities by forcing the issue (i.e., temporarily exiting Windows) doesn't mean that it's advisable. Neither the standard VFAT disk directory structure that lets you store long filenames nor the new FAT32 file system will be recognized by your pre-Windows 95 utility programs. So if you're jumping to DOS just to run those utilities, keep in mind that those programs will probably stomp on any long filenames created by Windows 98. Even Microsoft-supplied DOS 6.*x* utilities such as DEFRAG don't know about long filenames, and will shorten them rather crudely. Running such programs is not recommended, and I suggest you relegate them to your personal computer museum.

Don't despair. There are scads of 32-bit utility programs written for Windows 9*x* that accomplish what your DOS or Windows 3.*x* did. There are also some workarounds that let you use picky DOS programs. The numerous DOS *properties settings* often provide workarounds to limitations imposed by Windows 98's DOS application defaults. But even these won't allow ambitious DOS programs access to your hard disk. Finally, realize that limitations imposed on DOS applications serve to protect your system and data against any errant programs, so in the long run it means happier computing.

The other good news is that Microsoft has built many tricks into Windows 98 to allow you to run far more DOS applications than you could under Windows 3.*x*, and still protect the system. So you should try each program first before concluding that it's history. As a rule, if an app ran under Windows 95, it will run under Windows 98.

Which programs can you run, and which ones can't you run? Well, providing an actual list here wouldn't be meaningful, because it changes every day, as more companies release Windows 98 versions of their software. When you go to purchase new software, just be sure to check the box for the Windows 98 logo, or ask the dealer. When you want to try out software you've already been using with your previous system, ask yourself first if it's designed to work directly with some aspect of the computer's hardware or peripherals. If it is, consider buying the updated version. If not, try it out; it may work fine.

Using Utility Programs under Windows 98

Do you have an MS-DOS utility that you just can't live without? Does it access hardware directly? Does it check to see if you are trying to run the program under Windows, and fail to run if it detects that? If so, don't despair: there may be hope for you. Just try the following steps:

1. Launch an MS-DOS session. (You can use the Start ➤ Programs ➤ MS-DOS Prompt or any other method that takes you there.)

2. Click on the system control box in the upper left corner of the MS-DOS Prompt window.

3. Select Properties.

4. Click on the Advanced button.

5. Enable (check) the *Prevent MS-DOS-based programs from detecting Windows* checkbox. Now the MS-DOS application will *think* it is running under MS-DOS rather than under Windows.

6. Click on the OK button of the Advanced Programs Settings dialog box.

Continued ▊▶

CONTINUED

7. Click on the OK button of the MS-DOS Prompt Properties Settings dialog box.

8. In the MS-DOS box, run the **lock** command by typing it and pressing Enter. This will give the MS-DOS session exclusive access and allow direct access to the hard disk.

9. In the MS-DOS box, run the utility program (again, by typing the proper command—usually the name of the program—and pressing Enter).

10. When you're finished with the utility program, run the **unlock** command. This will remove the ability to access the hard disk directly within the MS-DOS session and restore hard-disk access to other applications.

What Software to Keep and What to Upgrade

There will be at least three, possibly four, criteria on which to base your decision regarding whether to keep your software or upgrade it.

- Does it still run?
- Is it safe to use?
- Is it a Windows 3.x or Windows 95 program that does something that Windows 98 now has built in?
- Do I want a faster 32-bit version of the program?

The section above discussed why programs might not run. Consider now why you might not *want* to run a particular program. Consider programs such as Norton Desktop for Windows, WinTools, or another such "shell" replacement for Windows 3.x. These are programs that improve on what was a relatively useless, annoying, and confusing shell in Windows 3.x (the Program Manager / File Manager duo). They also tend to include a number of useful utility programs for organizing your hard disk, finding files, recovering files, and so on.

Because Windows 98 is backward-compatible with Windows 3.x applications, you'll still be able to run your favorite shell replacements, even various add-ons for Windows 95, such as Explorer+ (which is like the Windows Explorer but adds lots of useful goodies). For that matter, you'll be able to run Program Manager (`progman.exe`) and File Manager (`winfile.exe`) if you're a glutton for punishment. And if you've become so accustomed to organizing your work according to the Norton view of the world that going cold turkey would be a hardship, you can stick with it (but better yet, get the updated Norton Navigator for Windows 9x).

Of course, you might find that the Windows 98 Taskbar and toolbars, the new Active Desktop, and various other conveniences are enough like Norton Desktop / Norton Navigator for Windows that you can live with such add-ons. (At least Microsoft would like you to think so.) And because the Windows 95 Desktop gives you integrated drag-and-drop capabilities, property sheets, shortcuts, and other such niceties, I'll bet my two cents on people ditching their add-on shell programs. As usual, Microsoft has learned from the competition.

NOTE

A couple of years ago, after first starting to use Windows 95, it took me several months to get used to using the Desktop and the Taskbar. But soon I was a convert. Whereas my home base had been the 3.*x* Program Manager and File Manager, I quickly became addicted to dropping folders and documents right on the Desktop, dragging files to a floppy drive on the Desktop, and so forth. With Windows 98, a similar conversion has taken place. At first, using the Web View interface was weird, but in a week or so I became so hooked that I now use it exclusively.

Other Extinct and Unnecessary Utilities

Shells are only one class of popular Windows utilities. And we've already discussed disk managers that might be thwarted when attempting microsurgery on your hard disk. But there are scads of other utility programs for Windows, some of which you may rely on daily. For example, I have one called PowerScope that scans my hard disks and generates about five different views of where all my precious disk space went. I have others that test the speed of my Windows system, quit Windows really fast, speed up the floppy disk duplication, scour the disk for a particular file, and so on. Will you still be able to run utilities such as these, and will they work under Windows 98?

Well, unless the hard disk in your machine was set up for FAT32 right from the factory, or unless you convert to it at home, all Windows 95 utilities should still work under Windows 98. (After a FAT32 conversion, on the other hand, you'll need new disk utilities, or simply use the ones supplied with Windows 98). And because most Windows 3.*x* applications were written according to Microsoft's standard Windows 3.*x* API, execution of Windows 3.*x* utilities shouldn't be a problem, either. Theoretically, only a program that goes outside the API will bomb. However, I rely much less now on utilities such as Norton's FF (File Find) command, using instead the built-in services such as the Start button's Find option, which is worth its weight in gold. It gives you a box like that in Figure 2.1.

FIGURE 2.1

The built-in Find utility

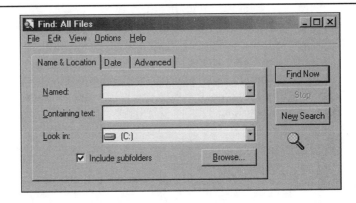

Find is not only always at your fingertips via the Start button, but once a file, folder, or computer is found, you can manipulate it in a manner consistent with other objects in the Windows 98 interface. That is, with a right click you could (depending on the type of item found) run it, view it, cut it, copy it, rename it, create a shortcut to place on the Desktop, or alter its properties (see Figure 2.2).

FIGURE 2.2

A found object with the right-click menu open. (You may notice that my right-click menu shows a few add-in programs such as PowerDesk and WinZip that are not supplied with Windows 98.)

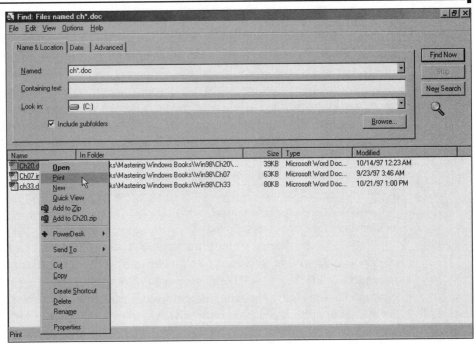

Find is a pretty comprehensive searching utility. It can scrutinize, for example, every file on your hard disk while prospecting for a particular string of text, or can list only files of a certain size, or those modified within the last week. If you're already familiar with it, you'll find that Windows 98's Find utility is not significantly improved over the one in Windows 95. It does have the "containing text" field moved to the first tab page, however, which serves to reduce the number of steps in the process if you're searching for all the files in your computer that contain, say, the word "aardvark."

What's even more useful is that the Find command from the Start button lists several new options:

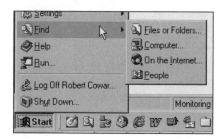

I guess the designers at Microsoft realized that folks spend half of their time on computers just trying to find stuff—people's e-mail or postal addresses, work files, other computers on the company network, or information on the Web. A single point for initiating searches is a welcome idea, and should replace several utility programs you might currently use.

Many other classes of Windows 3.x and Windows 95 utilities that are available from third parties, of course, will be operable under Windows 98. Not only that, but you might find you prefer to use third-party utilities, rather than their counterparts that are built into Windows 98, simply because you may already be familiar with those other programs. Until you play with the Windows 98 versions to get a feel for them, you might prefer to hold on to your favorite utilities of the following types:

- Advanced font management and font translation
- Screen panning and zooming
- Cursor shape alteration
- Macro recording and playback (but note that Windows 98 includes scripting)
- Mouse functionality enhancements
- More interesting screen savers (such as Berkeley Systems' *After Dark*)
- Floppy-backup and tape-backup programs
- Virus checkers (such as McAfee or Norton)
- Benchmarking programs

Then again, Microsoft has consistently added utility programs to the Windows package to the point that we're now dealing with a very rich collection. For example, the System accessories now include the items you see here:

Backup programs, automated hard-disk cleanup, disk compression, system-file validity checkers, you name it. As much as I support the idea of the free market and healthy competition in the software industry, I have to admit that I rarely need to go elsewhere for Windows utility products.

Just as with the upgrade to Windows 95 from Windows 3.11, it's difficult to prophesy just which older Windows utilities will and won't work, because Windows 98 compatibility will pivot on how strictly a program adheres to the Windows API. One class of utility that will *certainly* run into trouble on Windows 98 (if they don't bomb altogether) are Windows 3.*x* system optimization (tune-up) programs. Tune-up utilities (for example, WinSleuth and System Engineer, among others) are popular among power users who want to squeeze every last drop of performance from their Windows systems. By examining your computer's hardware and then thoroughly checking out its Windows configuration settings, these programs recommend changes, and some of them actually go ahead and make the changes. They churn through the `config.sys`, `autoexec.bat`, `win.ini`, and `system.ini` files, examining their contents, rearranging entries when necessary, deleting items as necessary, and so forth. They also typically optimize disk caching and virtual memory settings.

The problem with running these programs under Windows 98 is as follows: The configuration files that these programs fiddle with are either not actually used by Windows 98 or used very differently by Windows 98 than by DOS and Windows 3.*x*. Thus, many of the changes such a utility would make would not be appropriate or wouldn't make a difference in Windows 98's operation.

As mentioned in Chapter 1, Microsoft developed the Configuration Registry to provide a centralized, easily managed repository of system and applications settings. The Registry replaces (or augments, in certain cases) the following Windows 3.*x* files.

- `autoexec.bat`, which stores start-up information for the DOS operating system pertaining to some device drivers and TSR programs, declares the system search path, and executes any start-up programs

- `config.sys`, which also loads device drivers, memory managers, and sets up system variables

NOTE

For backward-compatibility reasons, `autoexec.bat` and `config.sys` files have not been completely replaced. That won't really happen until we all migrate to Windows NT in a couple of years. Windows 98 can boot up without them, using its own 32-bit Windows 98–supplied drivers for such things as disk-caching, CD-ROMs, and drive doubling, among others. However, these two files will likely still be in your start-up drive's root directory, and *will* be used by Windows 98 when booting if they are there. (When you run Setup to install Windows 98, however, the Setup program will do its best to pare down the `autoexec.bat` and `config.sys` files, removing or replacing older drivers and commands that are no longer valid or are not necessary, so even if the two files are in your start-up directory, Windows definitely relies on them less than it did in previous incarnations.)

- `win.ini`, which stores information about the appearance and configuration of the Windows environment

- `system.ini`, which stores software and hardware information that pertains directly to the operation of the operating system, its device drivers, and other system-specific information

- other `.ini` files, comprising various initialization files that store user preferences and start-up information about specific applications (for example, `winfile.ini` for File Manager, `clock.ini` for the `clock.exe` program, and `control.ini` for Control Panel)

There is still compatibility with 16-bit Windows 3.*x* applications that expect to find and modify the `win.ini` or `system.ini` files. Any applications that use the Windows 3.*x*

API for making ini settings will still be supported. However, that doesn't mean Windows 98 will actually use all those settings. Application-specific ini files will still be used by the source application (for example, when you run a 16-bit version of MS-Works, it'll read msworks.ini to load in user preferences), but win.ini settings and most system.ini settings won't have any effect on Windows 98. The only exception to this is the [enh 386] section of system.ini, which *will* be read. If there are any virtual device drivers in this section not already recorded in the Registry, they'll be noticed as Windows 98 boots and will be loaded.

Some Windows 3.*x* utility programs conceived to fine-tune Windows 3.*x* do so by futzing with the SmartDrive, virtual memory, drivers, and other base system settings. Windows 98 not only incorporates 32-bit drivers for disk caching and virtual memory management that would not be affected by these alterations, it dynamically and intelligently scales many resources to take the best advantage of the hardware and software mix on which it's running. Therefore, for example, a utility that adjusts the permanent swap file size will have no effect, because the swap file in Windows 98 is temporary and changeable in size.

The upshot of all this discussion is that if you are upgrading from Windows 3.*x* and you're attached to your system utilities, you should check to see if you can obtain a newer version of those utilities aimed at Windows 98, or at least at Windows 95.

For 3.*x* Upgraders

When you upgrade a Windows 3.*x* system to Windows 98, some application-specific win.ini settings *are* migrated into the Windows 98 Registry (for example, associations and OLE-related information). Any preexisting installed application packages—such as WordPerfect for Windows, Lotus 1-2-3, Microsoft Excel, and so on—are noted by the Windows 95 Setup program and incorporated into the Registry so you don't have to install them again. (If you opt to install Windows 98 into its own directory rather than on top of the old Windows 3.*x* so that you can run either Windows version, then you *will* have to install those applications again from within Windows 98.)

After this initial installation, 16-bit applications will still have their ini files and will use them to store their settings. 32-bit applications developers have been encouraged to use the Registry to stow application settings in hopes that one day a preponderance of system and applications settings for each workstation will live in a central repository that can be managed from anywhere on a network. As of this writing, though, the truth is that many programs still rely somewhat on their own ini files.

Faster 32-Bit Applications

As Windows 95 and NT have taken hold in the market, software developers have recompiled their applications into 32-bit versions. This has provided them a performance edge over their previous editions, satisfying the needs of users for faster, more reliable, and more efficient programs. Windows 98's compatibility with older 16-bit applications is really only a stopgap measure on Microsoft's part, allowing users to gracefully upgrade to Windows 95, Windows 98, and Windows NT while still using their existing applications.

Some of the decisions you'll make about what programs to keep or chuck (as discussed above) will become moot because the attraction to new features and faster performance of 32-bit applications will spur you to upgrade. Over the last few years, many software makers have offered various upgrade incentives, pushing their "Windows 95" versions. There's no reason to expect that they won't do the same for Windows 98.

**TIP**

Don't waste your hard-earned bucks. Before you replace your Windows 95 software packages with ones supposedly "made for Windows 98," check to see if they're actually something new! Windows 95 and Windows 98 both run 32-bit applications, so chances are good that if you already have a version that was designed for Windows 95, then maybe only the boxes and manuals have been changed for the Windows 98 version.

In the long run, though DOS and Windows 3.x applications support will probably be built into successive iterations of Windows for some time, the impetus really is toward the Windows 32-bit design model. Without 32-bit applications, many of the spiffy Windows 9x and NT features will not be exploited to any great degree. Until we're all running 32-bit, multithreaded, preemptive multitasking applications, supporting the latest in OLE (DCOMM) and slick connections to the Internet, and so forth, we're still kind of in the Dark Ages. In the coming year or two we're going to see a lot more video teleconferencing for the average user, more sophisticated multimedia CDs, interactive groupware and gaming on the Net, fancy computer-based video-editing systems for your home movies, CD-ROM and DVD ROM burners, and virtual-reality games. Software is a sort of virtual reality in and of itself, and developers' ideas seem limited only by the box with which they have to work.

The developments will affect not only the way we work (and play) but our buying decisions and purchasing patterns. The desire for more functionality in software will lead more software writers to market their software on DVD, because they can "bundle" video-based tutorials with the application. Already some CD-ROM–based programs such as Quicken Deluxe have short video and audio training lessons built in. My point is that there are many incentives for you to purchase the latest 32-bit software, just as there were reasons why you bagged your WordPerfect 5.1 in favor of a Windows word processor.

A little word of warning, though. Just because a program is "32-bit" doesn't guarantee it will be better than its 16-bit predecessor. For example, it might not run any faster. A program's speed of execution is dependent on the efficiency of the code the programmer writes. Some 16-bit programs run faster than their newer 32-bit cousins because the code was tighter and better thought out. However, whether the 16-bit version is faster or not, it's very likely you'll get more features in a newer 32-bit version of a program.

Flavors of 32-Bit Windows

A few years ago, there were numerous flavors of 32-bit Windows, with names like Daytona, Cairo, Chicago, Windows NT, Win32, Win32s, and Win32c. Which one of these you were using could affect which programs you could run. Microsoft has now consolidated their 32-bit API, so now average users needn't worry about such distinctions. There is only one 32-bit API. Think of the API as a list of ingredients. Depending on which subset of the ingredients from the API a program uses, it'll be able to run higher or lower on the Windows food chain. Thus, if a program uses all the ingredients, it can only run on NT. A slightly lesser use of the API will allow it to run on Windows 98. Even less, and it'll run in Windows 3.*x*.

NOTE

According to Microsoft, by following simple guidelines, third-party developers have been able to write 32-bit programs (not 16-bit, mind you) that will run on Windows 3.11, Windows 95, Windows 98, *and* Windows NT platforms with no modification. If this is so, these must be programs with the least amount of 32-bit goodies built in. (Unless they have conditional code, such as multithreading, that kicks in only once they sense they're running in Windows 9*x* or NT.) To keep the size of programs down, software makers are more likely to recompile their software into several versions, one for each platform. You'll be reading the labels on boxes much the way you read the ingredients on the back of a food jar in the grocery store. And you should! If you don't understand the label (or can't pronounce what's on it), start asking questions!

What the Terms Mean

Win32s: The Win32 Subset API, generally used as the base 32-bit API for Windows 3.*x*. This is the minimalist approach to writing 32-bit applications. A Win32s application will run on any 32-bit Microsoft platform (i.e., Windows 3.11, Windows 95, Windows 98, and Windows NT), but does not contain support for multiple threads, security APIs, or a few more APIs that are NT specific.

Win32c: Another Win32 Subset API. This approach includes support for multiple threads and will run on Windows NT, Windows 98, Windows 95, but not Windows 3.*x*. It also does not include support for security and a few other APIs that are NT specific.

Win32: The full-blown 32-bit API that is based on Windows NT. Some applications that use this API set will not run on Windows 3.11, Windows 95, or Windows 98 if those use APIs that are not supported by the other subset versions (Win32s/Win32c).

What Hardware to Keep and What to Upgrade

In the context of this chapter's discussion about "getting ready for Windows 98," next I'll provide an overview of the hardware requirements and considerations pertinent to running Windows 98 successfully.

The Box

Let's start with the basic box: the computer itself, if you will. Windows 98 is going to run its fastest, of course, on fast Pentium and Pentium II machines. Actual performance of Windows 98 is impossible to judge at this point because optimization of the Windows 98 code (called *performance tuning*) is the last stage of software development just before a product ships. However, Microsoft's advance documentation claims Windows 98 will run reasonably speedily on typical 386 DX machines.

TIP

If Windows 95 is successfully running on your current computer, you should have no trouble using the same machine for Windows 98. You should *not* require a hardware upgrade.

If you can lay your hands on a real Plug-and-Play machine (it needs a Plug-and-Play BIOS built in) that has ACPI (the new power management scheme) *and* a fast processor such as a Pentium 233, Pentium Pro, or Pentium II, this is the basis for a Windows 98 powerhouse that'll prove effortless to upgrade when it comes time to stuff in a new card or two.

If you're interested in running Windows 98 on an existing machine, here are some notes about what kind of performance you can expect. For sluggish to modest performance using productivity applications such as word processors (assuming you use a slim word processor, not something huge such as the entire Microsoft Office suite), even a 33-MHz 386 DX machines will likely prove adequate for Windows 98. For slightly slower—but still workable—performance, you may use an SX machine. For a middle-of the road workstation, you'll want to be using at least a 50Mhz 486 (even these are hard to find these days, but you may have them in your stockpile of working machines). For more demanding application mixes, such as graphics, computer-aided design, or heavy database use, use a quick 486 (for example DX4/100), a 100Mhz Pentium, or faster. The same goes for networked machines that will serve as printer and communication servers.

If you're planning to buy a new machine, it doesn't make sense to buy anything new short of a Pentium (or equivalent, such as a K6) or a Pentium II, running at 133Mhz or above, what with the price of systems dropping like lead balls off the Tower of Pisa. If you shop around, you should be able to get a Pentium 200 or 233, or a Pentium II 333, for only a tad more. Be sure, however, to purchase a system with a *local bus*. The VLB is now out of favor, so you should buy a machine based on the PCI bus. Even most laptops have internal PCI bus architecture.

NOTE

Suffice it to say that older 286-based machines are now out of the picture. They simply won't run the 32-bit code on which Windows 95 is built. If you want Windows or Windows networking compatibility on these machines, your only options are to run Windows 3.0 or Windows 3.1 in Standard mode or to run the DOS program *Workgroup Connection* (included with Windows for Workgroups) to connect to a Windows network.

RAM

Just as with Windows NT, Windows 98 scales automatically and intelligently to avail itself of any extra RAM you throw its way. I'm writing this on a Compaq 1680 that last week had 32 MB. I installed a fancy 64MB upgrade module this week and restarted the machine. Windows 98 knew immediately that the machine now had 96 MB of RAM and began to use it. The difference in performance would be seen as marginal for most users. Not necessarily worth the $390 I paid for the RAM. Two of the other machines I've been using to test the beta releases of Windows 98 have 16 MB and 64 MB respectively. The 16MB machine does a lot more disk swapping, which slows operations (as the operating system temporarily writes RAM data out to the hard disk or restores it from the disk back to RAM). However, this impact will probably be lessened once Windows 98 is fine-tuned before release by Microsoft. The 8MB machine works okay. If there is advice to be given, it's that 4 MB is the rock-bottom amount of RAM this OS will work on. I'd say aim at 16 MB as a minimum (and probably more like 32 MB if you're the kind of person who would rather dial 411 than look up a number in the phone book). If you have a choice between DRAM (Dynamic), EDO (Extended Data Out) RAM, and SDRAM (Synchronous Dynamic RAM), choose the latter. If not that, then buy a machine that supports EDO. The computer must be engineered for EDO or SDRAM, however, to use its faster data transfer ability.

System RAM is only one consideration, and only about half the story when it comes to deciding what kind of memory to get for your computer. A hotly discussed topic in the computer magazines is the amount and kind of "cache" RAM. Cache RAM is very fast RAM used by the CPU to temporarily store data as it is sent to and from system RAM, speeding up memory fetches. RAM caching has been shown to increase system speed considerably. When shopping for a notebook or desktop computer, go for 128K cache minimum, and preferably 256K. If your computer is very old, it might not have a built-in cache or even an option to add one.

Some CPUs have a cache built into them. The Pentium and Pentium Pro, for example, have 8K of internal cache. The Intel Pentium MMX and Pentium II have 16K. The Pentium Overdrive has 32K.

Hard Disk

You'll need approximately 120 MB of free hard disk space to install Windows 98. About 45 MB of this is temporary space used only during setup. You'll want a hard disk with plenty of space. For a full install (all options), I used up 251 MB on one of my computers! (Of course, this was before all the fine tuning that Microsoft does to the software, so it may be a bit less with final release software.) Add to this the advantage you'll get from having free disk space for the dynamically sized virtual-memory paging ("swap file"), and you can see why free disk space will be important when installation time comes rolling around. It remains to be seen how forgiving Windows 98's Setup program will be when upgrading from existing installations of Win95 and Windows 3.x (since files will be erased and/or replaced as part of the setup process). The good news is that drives are *cheap* now. You can buy a multi-gigabyte (GB) drive for about $300 these days if you know where to shop. Also, the Windows 98 support files (basically, everything you see in the directories) do not have to be on the boot drive. If you have a two-drive system, drive D can hold everything except the boot tracks. The Setup program sleuths around for a drive with enough space to handle the install process and suggests a drive and directory.

You'll want to use a fast hard disk. So what else is new, you ask. Well, not everyone knows that the hard disk and video card are the two most likely bottlenecks in a system. Your hard-disk system should preferably be a SCSI II system, but if not, it should at least be a SCSI or EIDE type using a local bus (typically PCI) controller. You'll want a drive with a fast access time, too: around 12 ms (milliseconds) average access time. ("Average access time" is a specification that will likely be advertised along with the drive's price.)

Monitor/Video-Card Support

Windows 98 is packaged with 32-bit driver support for many devices, including a wide variety of video cards. Even in the beta, support for all generic VGA cards and the more popular cards based on chip sets such as the Cirrus Logic, ATI Mach, NewMagic, Chips and Technologies, S3, ET-x000, Western Digital, various 2-D and 3-D accelerators, and Weitech were all on board. In fact, Setup will run around and look at your hardware, investigating the video card's identity and doing its best to load the appropriate drivers. In all four of my systems, this has worked reliably.

Because slowpoke video cards can bring even the zippiest of systems to a seeming crawl, and because Microsoft has gone video happy with Windows 98, if performance and high resolution with lots of colors is of interest to you, then get your hands on a fast video card before upgrading, if possible. The full-window drag option, for example, is so boss you'll definitely want to set this option *on*. But if your video card is slow (i.e., it's on the ISA bus and/or doesn't have a coprocessor), your windows will then leave trails as you move them around on screen. The only solution then is to turn off full-window drag, which only shows the outline of a window as you drag it.

Of course more and more programs and games are getting bit-blit intensive, meaning they rely on heavy-duty graphics and the ability to rapidly move images around the screen. Because some of the color schemes in such programs, and even in the Windows interface itself, call on a palette of 64 thousand colors, or even more (16 million), it'll serve you to shop for a video card with at least 1 MB of VRAM (Video RAM, not plain-old-vanilla DRAM), with a resolution equal to or above that of your monitor, and a refresh rate of at least 72 Hz, noninterlaced. For really great color, you'll want the card to display at least 64 thousand colors at your desired resolution. Nowadays, most folks are using a resolution of 800×600 (that's the number of dots across the screen, horizontally by vertically). If you have a larger screen, such as 17" or more, running in 1024×768 is a boon since you can see a lot more at once.

Better laptops these days come with 12" screens or larger, sporting either 800×600 or 1024×768 resolution. If you're interested in the latter, make sure you see a demonstration of the screen before buying, especially if the screen is a 13" model. Text can look pretty darn small on such a screen. I briefly had a portable with a 14" screen at 1024×768 and even that was a challenge. I prefer a 12" or 13" screen tuned for 800×600.

TIP

Laptop and other flat-panel screens look very good at only one resolution—the so-called "native resolution." Other resolutions may be displayable, but they'll look blocky.

Finally, if your computer has a "local" bus (such as PCI or VLB), get a video card that plugs into one of the edge connectors attached to this bus rather than into the normal, slower system-bus (ISA or EISA) slots. If your system doesn't have a local bus, don't lose any sleep over it. Windows 98 will still work fine with most types of popular applications such as word processing, spreadsheets, databases, and such. But with flashy graphics programs or games that do texture mapping, 2-D and 3-D animations will slow down. As far as operating Windows 98 itself goes, even the most prehistoric, simple VGA cards will run fine. I've been using a very old, generic VGA card on one of my systems. It's not flashy, but it works, and its speed is acceptable so long as I keep the resolution and color depth to something low (for example 640×480 at 16 or 256 colors). If I bump up the numbers of colors to, say, 64 thousand, then moving windows around the screen becomes a bit sluggish.

Plug-and-Play Items

Plug-and-Play (or *PnP*, as it is commonly abbreviated) is a technology that seems too good to be true. With PnP, you just plug in a board, reboot your computer, and you're off and running. All existing peripherals, sound boards, video boards, network cards, and so forth are automatically configured for you as the operating system boots up. No DIP switches to set, no IRQ conflicts, no hassles. Sounds impossible, right? Well, in the last few years since Windows 95 hit the streets, a plethora of PnP devices have shown up.

NOTE

You don't have to buy PnP devices for your Windows 98 machine. Non–Plug-and-Play cards will work fine in a PnP-enabled computer. You just give up the autoconfiguring features of the device. Also, in many cases Windows 98's hardware installation program is pretty intelligent about detecting and correctly installing non-PnP cards.

For PnP to work, three areas of technology must coordinate:

- the system BIOS,
- the operating system,
- and possibly some related hardware drivers.

That leaves out all "legacy" computers (which in this case would include any computer that doesn't have PnP specifically built into the BIOS). In regard to the first point, with the number of older computers around that do *not* have PnP-aware BIOS chips in them, such as traditional ISA and EISA machines, we've got major sticking point.

In regard to point number two in the preceding list, Windows 98 itself, of course, will be PnP-aware, so the operating-system angle is covered.

In regard to point number three, you should note that you can't expect to get PnP convenience with any existing 16-bit drivers from Windows 3.*x* or with the huge majority of older plug-in cards (with the exception of credit-card PCMCIA). But PnP drivers and applications have been making a strong appearance in the last few years.

So, in preparation for Windows 98 you should be considering buying PnP boards, PnP display monitors, PnP printers, PnP mice, PnP scanners, and PnP computers only. The majority of new systems are now PnP-ready. Ditto for add-in cards. Purchasing systems and boards now that comply with the PnP specification will save you precious time and Excedrin® headaches later.

NOTE

To be permitted to display the "Windows-95 compatible" or "Windows-98 compatible" logo, hardware and software must be PnP capable. Look for this logo when buying.

When you're shopping, be aware that new equipment must sport the full *Plug-and-Play* moniker (the whole term spelled out, with capital *P*s) to be truly compliant. Keep in mind also that, like other evolving industry standards (ADSL, SCSI, ACPI, PCMCIA, VLB, and PCI, just to name a few), the spec for PnP is likely to fluctuate as bugs or oversights become evident over time. We're all held hostage on that account. With

Windows 98 we're now into the second generation of PnP, so at least we can feel a little more confident that we're not shelling out good money for what a couple of years ago might have turned out to fit the description "Plug-and-Pray" more than it fit the term "Plug-and-Play."

Other Items

What else is there to consider when looking for sound cards, SCSI controllers, CD-ROM drives, DVD drives, USB ports, or network boards? Well, some of this is hard to predict, as the hardware is ever evolving. But here are a couple of tips.

For starters, if your existing hardware works with the version of Windows you're upgrading from (Windows 3.*x* or Windows 95), they'll operate correctly within Windows 98. If drivers for your cards aren't supplied initially by Windows 98, you can use your old ones. As mentioned in Chapter 1, eventually every hardware manufacturer will supply 32-bit NT-style (WDM) drivers for their hardware. In the meantime, either your old Windows 3.*x*-style 16-bit drivers or your Windows 95 drivers will do the job.

Second, get a machine that is *ACPI compliant*. As I mentioned in Chapter 1, ACPI is the new power conservation specification developed in 1997. Windows 98's *OnNow* capability and smartest battery management (for longer computing on batteries) requires ACPI. OnNow lets you power down your computer without closing all your apps, and then turn it on again, continuing right where you left off. It's a real time-saver. If you like this idea, check to see that any new computers you purchase meet the latest ACPI specification.

Chapter

3

Getting to Know the Interface

An overview of the Windows interface

Types of windows

Menus

Dialog boxes

Quitting Windows

Chapter 3

Getting to Know the Interface

In this chapter, I'll begin explaining Windows so you can start using your computer to get your work done. If you're an experienced Windows user, you can skim this chapter just to get the gist of the new features of Windows 98. If, on the other hand, you're new to Windows, you should read this chapter thoroughly because it will introduce you to essential Windows concepts and skills that you'll need to have no matter what your line of work is or what you intend to do with your computer. A solid grasp of these concepts will also help you understand and make best use of the rest of this book.

Windows 101

Windows owes its name to the fact that it runs each application or document in its own separate *window*. A window is a box or frame on the screen. Figure 3.1 shows several such windows.

You can have numerous windows on the screen at a time, each containing its own program and/or document. You can then easily switch between programs without having to close one down and open the next.

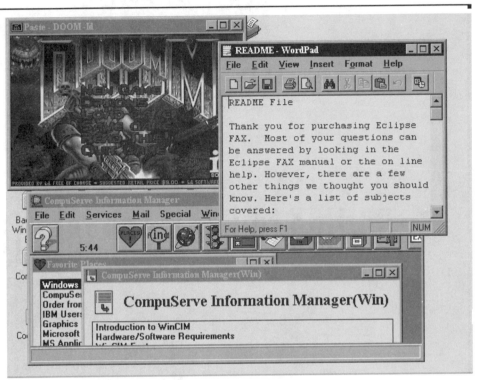

FIGURE 3.1

Windows are frames that hold informa-tion of some sort on the screen.

Another feature that Windows has is a facility—called the Clipboard—that lets you copy material between dissimilar document types, making it easy to *cut* and *paste* infor-mation from, say, a spreadsheet into a company report or a scanned photograph of a house into a real-estate brochure. In essence, Windows provides the means for seam-lessly joining the capabilities of very different application programs. Not only can you paste portions of one document into another, but by using an advanced document-link-ing feature—for example, OLE or DCOMM—those pasted elements remain *live*. That is, if the source document (such as some spreadsheet data) changes, the results will also be reflected in the secondary document (such as a word-processing document) containing the pasted data.

In addition to expediting the way you use your existing applications, Windows comes with quite a handful of its own little programs. For example, there's a word-processing program called WordPad, a drawing program called Paint, at least one e-mail program, Internet connectivity programs, several games, utilities for keeping your hard disk in good working order (or even doubling the amount of space on it), and a data-backup program—just to name a few.

Before Moving Ahead

Before going on in this book, make sure you've read the introduction and installed Windows correctly on your computer (installation is explained in the appendix). Then, while experimenting with Windows on your computer, you should feel free to experiment (if with some caution) as I explain things you can do, offer tips, and so forth. Experimentation is the best way to learn. I'll try to warn against things you shouldn't do, so don't worry. Experience really is the best teacher—especially with computers. Contrary to popular belief, they really won't blow up if you make a mistake!

If at any time while reading this chapter you have to quit Windows to do other work or simply because you want to turn off your computer, just jump to the end of this chapter and read the section called *Exiting Windows*. Also, if at any time you don't understand how to use a Windows command or perform some procedure, go to the newly improved Help facility available within any Windows application.

If you truly get stuck and don't know how to escape from some procedure you're in the middle of, the last resort is to reboot your computer and start up Windows again. Though this isn't a great idea, and you may lose part of any documents you're working on, it won't actually kill Windows or your computer. There are several ways to do this, but always try this one first:

- Click the Start button and choose Shut Down. Then choose Shut Down from the box of shut-down options.

If that doesn't work, try pressing the Ctrl, Alt, and Del keys simultaneously (in other words, press Ctrl and hold, press Alt and hold both, then tap Del. A box should appear, offering you a Shut Down button to click (no, Enter doesn't work). If your computer is really stuck, sometimes you might have to press Ctrl, Alt, and Del again (that is, twice in a row). This will likely restart Windows.

The most drastic but surefire way to reboot the computer is by pressing the reset switch on your computer or turning your computer off, waiting about five seconds, and then turning it on again. This will almost invariably get you out of what you were doing, and make the computer ready to use again.

 NOTE

All but the first method (the bulleted one) are last resorts to exiting Windows, and can result in losing some of your work! It's better to follow the instructions at the end of this chapter (in the section entitled "Exiting Windows").

Starting Windows

To start up Windows and get to work, follow these steps:

1. Remove any floppy disk from the computer's floppy disk drives.

2. Turn on your computer, monitor, and any other stuff you're likely to use (for example an external CD-ROM drive or external modem).

3. Wait. Unlike in the old days of Windows 3.1, the DOS prompt (C:>) will not appear. Instead, after a few seconds you'll see the Windows 98 start-up logo, which may seem to sit there a long time. You'll see some action on the screen, such as the blue bar moving across the bottom of the screen. This means Don't worry, your computer is still alive. Windows takes quite a while to load from your hard disk into RAM. You just have to wait.

TECH TIP

If you have 16-bit device drivers included in your `autoexec.bat` file, you may see a command prompt instead of the Windows 98 logo while Windows 98 loads. Also, if you press Esc while the Windows 98 logo is displayed, the logo will disappear and you'll see a listing of your `config.sys` lines as they load.

4. After about 15 seconds or so, the Windows sign-on dialog box appears and asks you to type in your user name and password.

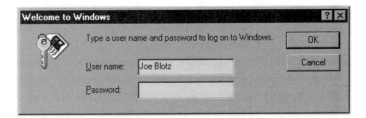

By pressing Esc or clicking on the Cancel button, you tell Windows that you will not be using a password. On subsequent startups, you will not be asked to enter a password. If you want a little more security, or will be using your computer on a network, enter name and a password at this point. If you upgraded from Windows 95 or Windows for Workgroups, your old user name and password should work just as it did before. Then click on OK (or press Enter).

NOTE

Clicking means positioning the mouse pointer on the item in question and then clicking the *left* button once (or, if you've custom configured your pointing device, whichever button you've assigned as the *primary* button). The middle and right (or secondary) mouse buttons won't cut it unless I mention them specifically—they are used for other things! *Double-clicking* means clicking on an item twice in quick succession.

5. If you are hooked up to a local area network (LAN) and Windows detected the network and installed itself for network activities, you may be prompted to enter your network password, like this:

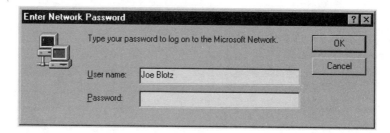

This might seem redundant, as you entered a password already. No, it's not Fort Knox. It's just that there are two possible password requirements—one that gets you into your own computer and into a workgroup, and another one for signing you onto a network domain. A typical peer-to-peer network of Windows 98 machines is considered a workgroup. If your workgroup machine is interconnected with a Windows NT Server, then the second password will be used by Windows 98 to authenticate you on the Microsoft Network domain. If you don't already have a network user name and password, invent one now. You'll be prompted to confirm it.

NOTE

The sequence of boxes that prompt you for your user name and password the first time you run Windows 98 will likely be different from subsequent sessions. You'll have fewer steps after signing in the first time because you won't be asked to confirm your password.

6. Click on OK (or press Enter).

Now the Windows 98 starting screen—the Desktop—appears, looking approximately like that in Figure 3.2. Take a look at your screen and compare it to the figure. Your screen may look a bit different, but the general landscape will be the same. You may see a Welcome to Windows 98 box and hear some jazzy music asking if you want to take a tour of Windows or get some help about Windows. Just click on the Close button (the X in the upper right-hand corner of the box) to close it. You can explore the Help system and the Windows Tour later. When you close the Welcome box, it will ask you if you want to see it every time you "log on" (start up) Windows. That's up to you. Click Yes or No. I find it a nuisance, and click No, but you might want to click Yes so it runs the next time you start up your computer. You can always turn it off later.

FIGURE 3.2

The initial Windows 98 screen. This starting screen is called the Desktop— the place where you can organize your work and interact with your computer a bit like the way you use your real desk.

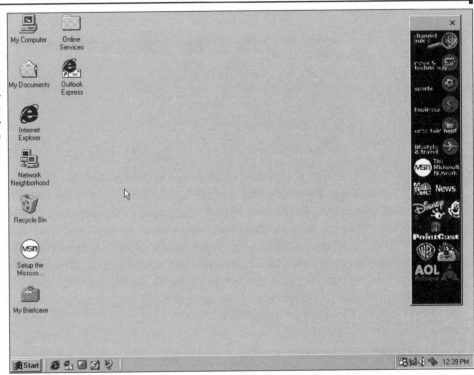

NOTE

If you or someone else has used your Windows 98 setup already, it's possible that some open windows will come up on the screen automatically when Windows boots (starts up). It's also possible that you'll see more icons on the Desktop than what's shown in Figure 3.2. That depends on what options you chose when Windows 98 was installed.

Parts of the Windows Screen

Now let's take a quick look at the basic parts of the Windows start-up screen: the Desktop, icons, Taskbar, and, optionally, the Channel bar. Once you understand these three essential building blocks (and one other—a *window*—which you'll see in a few minutes) you'll begin to get a feel for how Windows works.

The Desktop

The *Desktop* is your overall work area while in Windows. It's called the Desktop because Windows uses your whole screen in a way that's analogous to the way you'd use the surface of a desk. As you work in Windows, you move items around on the Desktop, retrieve and put away items (as if in a drawer), and perform your other day-to-day tasks. You do all of this using graphical representations of your work projects.

November Budget   Music School Logo   Letters

The analogy of the Desktop falls a bit short sometimes, but it's useful for understanding how the program helps you organize your activities.

You can put your favorite (e.g., most oft-used) items on the Desktop so getting to them requires less hunting around. Each time you run Windows, those items will be right there where you left them. This is a great feature of Windows 9*x*.

In Figure 3.2, which displays a "virgin" system where nobody has added anything new to the Desktop, there are several items ready to go. (Remember, you may have slightly different items, depending on options you chose when installing Windows.) We'll get to what those items are for, but you get the picture. When you add your own items, such as your thesis, your recipe list, or your latest version of Quake, they'll be represented by little graphics, also known as *icons*, in the same way that the items above are represented.

Icons

An icon is a graphical symbol that represents something in your computer. To get your work (and play) done, you interact with these little graphics. Notice the icons along the left side of your desktop. The icons have names under them. Windows 98 uses icons to represent folders, documents, and programs when they are not currently opened up and running. Below are a couple of icons.

My Computer

Research for Thesis

Icons that look like file folders are just that—folders. Folders (just like on the Mac), are used to keep related documents or programs together. You can even have folders within folders, a useful feature for really organizing your work from the top down.

NOTE

Folders were called *directories* in DOS and Windows 3.*x* terminology. As of Windows 95, the help system and manuals refer to directories (and program groups as well) as *folders*.

There's another kind of icon-ish sort of thing you'll need to know about. Technically, it's called a *minimized window*. When you want to get a window off the screen temporarily but within easy reach, you minimize it. This lets you do work with a document that's in another window without any extra clutter on the screen. When a window is *minimized* in this way, it's as if its program or document is shoved to the bottom of your desk for a moment and put in a little box on the Taskbar.

We'll cover this kind of icon later, when I discuss the Taskbar and running your programs.

There are several variations on these boxes, but the upshot is the same: the program or document's window will pop up again if you simply click or double-click on it (more about double-clicking later).

NOTE

Incidentally, while minimized, the program or document will actually be running. It's just that you can't interact with it while it's shrunken. This means a spread sheet could still be calculating, a database could be sorting, or a communications program could still be sending in your e-mail while it's minimized.

Channel Bar

If you have the Channel Bar on your desktop as shown in Figure 3.2, you're probably wondering what it is. As mentioned in Chapter 1, it's for taking advantage of one of the newer developments on the World Wide Web called "push" technology. Channels let you surf the Web in a way that's a little more like surfing your cable stations on TV. If you're connected to the Internet already, you can try clicking on one of the channel buttons in the Bar and see what happens. If you aren't Internet experienced, this would be getting a little ahead of yourself, though, and you should wait until the discussion of Internet connections and using Channels later in the book.

Hey, What *Is* a Window, Anyway?

Just in case this whole "windows" thing is eluding you, here's the scoop on what a window is and the various types of windows. Because there are different types, people can get somewhat confused when looking at a bunch of windows on the screen. You'll want to learn what they are and how they work, or the screen can be confusing.

It's actually simple. When you want to do some work, you open up a program or document with the mouse or keyboard, and a window containing it appears on the Desktop. This is similar to pulling a file folder or notebook off the shelf, placing it on the desk, and opening it up. In Windows, you do this for each task you want to work on.

Just as with a real desktop, you can have a number of project windows scattered about, all of which can be in progress. You can then easily switch between your projects, be they letters, address lists, spreadsheets, games, or whatever, as you see in Figure 3.3. This approach also allows you to copy material from one document to another more easily by cutting and pasting between them.

Another feature designed into Windows is that it can be instructed to remember certain aspects of your work setup each time you quit. For example, if you use a certain group of programs regularly, you can set up Windows to come up with those programs already running—or ready to run with just a click of the mouse. Programs you use less frequently will be stored away within easy reach without cluttering your Desktop.

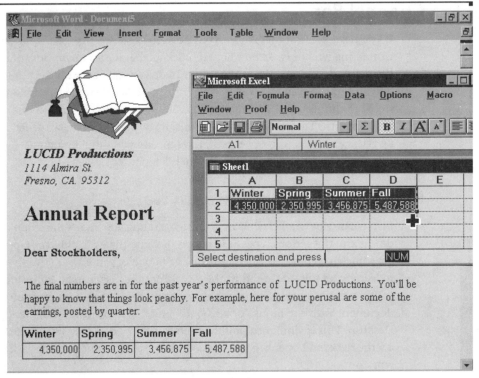

FIGURE 3.3

Windows let you see documents simultaneously.

Types of Windows

Now let's look a little more closely at the various parts of the Desktop. There are three types of windows that you'll encounter while working: *application windows, document windows,* and *folder windows.*

If you want to place a window on the screen that you can play with a bit as you read the next section about window sizing, double-click on the My Computer icon.

Application Windows

Application windows are those that contain a program that you are running and working with, such as Microsoft Word, Excel, PC Paintbrush, WordPerfect, and so on. Most of the work that you do will be in application windows. Figure 3.4 shows a typical application window, sometimes called a *parent window.*

FIGURE 3.4

An application window is a window that a program is running in.

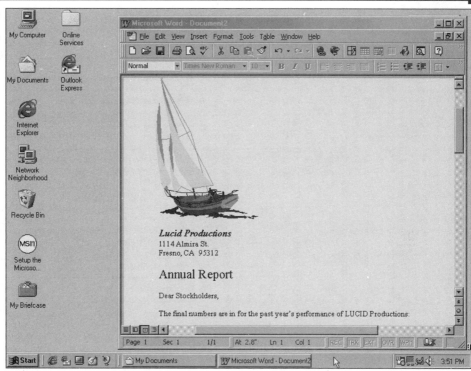

Document Windows

Some programs let you have more than one document open within them at a time. What does this mean? Well, take the spreadsheet program Microsoft Excel, for example. It allows you to have several spreadsheets open at once, each in its own document window. Instead of running Excel several times in separate application windows (which would use up too much precious RAM), it just runs once and opens several document windows within Excel's main window. Figure 3.5 shows Excel with two document windows open inside it.

NOTE

Incidentally, document windows are sometimes called *child windows*.

FIGURE 3.5

Two document (child) windows within an application (parent) window

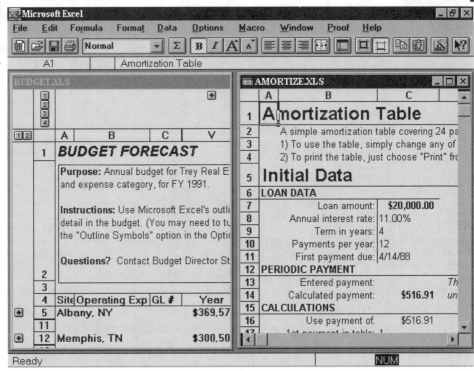

Anatomy of a Window

Now let's consider the parts of a typical window. All windows have the same elements in them, so once you understand the anatomy of one window, others will make sense to you. Of course, some programs have extra stuff like fancy toolbars built in, but you learn about those things as you experiment with the particular program. Here we're talking about the elements common to any kind of window.

The Title Bar

OK. Let's start from the top and work down. The name of the program or document appears at the top of its respective window, in what's called the *title bar*. In Figure 3.5, notice the title bars read Microsoft Excel, BUDGET.XLS, and AMORTIZE.XLS. If you were running another application, such as PageMaker or Paint, its name would be shown there instead.

Sometimes an application window's title bar also contains the name of the document being worked on. For example, here Notepad's title bar shows the name of the document being edited:

Notepad - NETWORKS.TXT

The title bar also serves another function: it indicates which window is *active*. Though you can have a lot of windows on the screen at once, there can be only one active window at any given time. The active window is the one you're currently working in. When a window is made active, it jumps to the front of other windows that might be obscuring it, and its title bar changes color. You make a window active by clicking anywhere within its border.

Minimize, Maximize, and Close

There are three small buttons at the right end of the title bar with small graphics in them—the Minimize button, Maximize or Restore button, and the Close buttons. These are little control buttons with which you can quickly change the size of a window, or close the window completely, as I'll explain in a moment.

Referring to Figure 3.6, the button with the skinny line in it is the *Minimize* button. The one to its right is the *Restore* button. (It changes to a *Maximize* button when the window is less than its full size—you can see the Maximize button in the preceding graphic.) The third button is called the *Close* button.

NOTE

3.*x* USERS: In Windows 3.*x* the Minimize, Maximize, and Close techniques varied too much between applications, and thus were confusing to users. Now you can close any application (including a DOS box) with a single click on the "X" button.

After a window has been maximized, the Maximize button changes to the *Restore* button. Restore buttons have two little boxes in them. (Restored size is neither full-screen nor minimized. It's whatever size it was when it was last *between* minimized and maximized.)

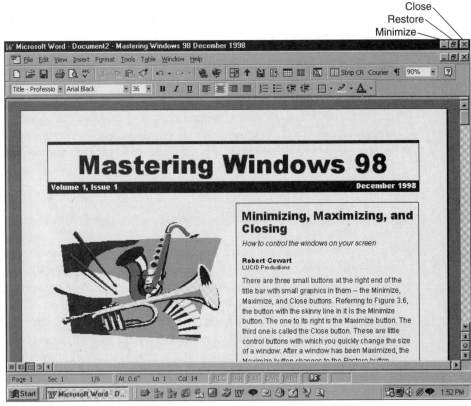

FIGURE 3.6

The buttons for resizing a window quickly

There are essentially three sizes that a window can have:

- Minimized: The window becomes an icon on the Taskbar (or on the application's window if it's a document or child window), where it's ready to be opened again but takes up a minimum of screen space.

- Normal: The window is open and takes up a portion of the Desktop, the amount of which is determined by how you manually size the window, as explained in the next section. This is also called the *restored* size.

- Maximized: The window takes up the whole Desktop. When you maximize a document window, it expands to take up the entire application window. This may or may not be the entire screen, depending on whether the application's window is maximized.

Here are the basic mouse techniques to quickly change the size of a window. To try these techniques, you'll first want to open a window on your screen. If you don't already have a window open, you can open one by double-clicking on the icon called My Computer. I'll explain this icon's purpose later. But just for discussion, try double-clicking on it. If nothing happens, you didn't click fast enough. Make sure you're clicking the left mouse button (on a standard right-handed mouse or trackball).

TIP

In Chapter 1 I talked about Web view, which replaced double-clicking with single clicking, and makes the whole interface act much like a web page. When you install Windows 98, Web view isn't the default setting; the so-called "Classic view" is. But you can turn on Web view if you want. I'll cover that later in this chapter.

To Minimize a Window

1. First, if you have a number of windows open, click inside the perimeter of one you want to work with. This will activate it.

2. Position the mouse pointer (the arrow that moves around on the screen when you move the mouse) on the Minimize button (the one with the short line in it) and click.

The window reduces to the size of an icon and "goes" down to the bottom of the screen in the Taskbar. The window's name is shown beside the icon so you know what it is. Notice here it says "My Computer." Sometimes this kind of icon is called a "button."

To Restore a Window from an Icon

OK. Now suppose you want to get the window back again. It's simple. The window is waiting for you, minimized down on the Taskbar.

1. Move the mouse to position the pointer just over the little My Computer button (icon) down at the bottom of your screen, in the Taskbar. (Unless for some reason your Taskbar has been moved to one of the other edges of the screen, in which case use that. Changing the Taskbar's location is covered in Chapter 4.)

2. Click on the button. The window is now restored to its previous size.

A new feature in Windows 98 is that you can alternately restore and minimize a window by clicking its button on the Taskbar. If a window is minimized, clicking on the button restores it to the screen. Click the button again, and the window is minimized.

To Maximize a Window

You maximize a window when you want it to be as large as possible. When maximized, a window will take up the whole screen. Unless you have a very large screen, or need to be able to see two application windows at the same time, this is the best way to work on typical documents. For example, in a word-processing program, you'll see the maximum amount of text at one time with the window maximized.

1. Activate the window by clicking within its perimeter.

2. Click on its Maximize button:

The window expands to fill the entire screen. If you're maximizing a child window (remember, that means a window within a window), the window can only be as big as its parent. So it might not be able to get as large as the screen; you'd have to maximize the parent window first. You have to look carefully to find the location of maximize and minimize buttons for child windows. Don't confuse them with the buttons for the parent application window. As an example, look at Figure 3.7.

After you maximize a window, its Maximize button changes to a Restore button.

Clicking on this button will restore the window to its "restored" size, which is neither full nor minimized; it's the intermediate size that you either manually adjusted it to (see below) or the size that it originally had when you opened the window.

FIGURE 3.7

Document windows have their own Minimize, Maximize, Close, and Restore buttons. Don't confuse them with the buttons for the parent application they're running in.

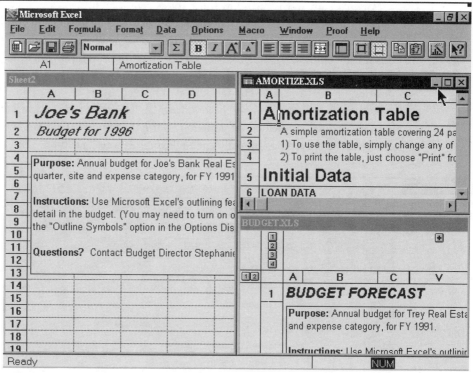

Up and Running

To Manually Adjust the Size of a Window

Sometimes you'll want to adjust the size of a window manually to a very specific size. You might want to arrange several windows side by side, for example, so you can easily see them both, copy and paste material between them, and so forth.

Clicking on and dragging a window's corner allows you to change both the width and height of the window at one time.

Dragging simply means keeping the mouse button depressed while moving the mouse.

You manually resize a window using these steps: Carefully position the cursor on any edge or corner of the window that you want to resize. The lower right corner is easiest on windows that have a little triangular tab there, designed just for resizing. (You'll only see this feature on newer programs, though not all of them. You can still resize a window if it's not there. Just click on any side or corner of a window.) When you are in the right position, the cursor shape changes to a two-headed arrow, as you can see in Figure 3.8. Press the left mouse button and hold it down. A "ghost" of the window's outline moves with the arrow to indicate that you are resizing the window. Drag the window edge or corner to the desired position and then release the mouse button.

FIGURE 3.8

Change a window's size by dragging its corner.

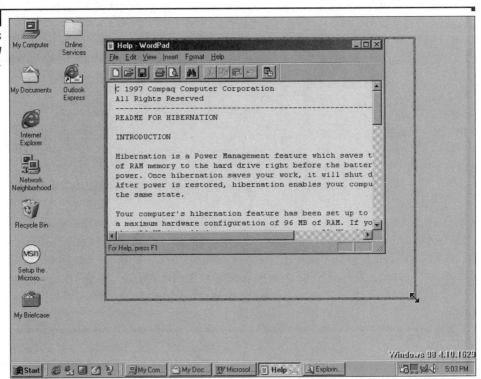

Instead of seeing a "ghost" line while resizing, you can set Windows to actually resize the contents as you drag the border. I'll cover this later in this chapter, but if you're impatient, right click on the desktop, choose properties, click on the Effects tab and turn on the "Show windows contents while dragging" option.

Moving a whole window: You can drag an entire window around the screen (to get it out of the way of another windows, for example) by dragging it from its title bar. Just click on the window's title bar, keep the mouse button, and drag it around. Then release when it's where you want it. (For this to work, the window can't be maximized, since that wouldn't leave any screen room for moving it.)

The Control Box

Every title bar has a little icon at its far left side. This is the Control box. It has two functions. First, it opens a menu, called the Control menu. Figure 3.9 shows a Control box with its Control menu open. This is the same menu you get when you single-click on an minimized window. This menu only comes up from the Control box when you single-click. Most of the commands on a Control menu let you control the size of the window, so you rarely have to use them. (Menus are covered in detail later in this chapter.) But some programs put special items on their control menus.

FIGURE 3.9

Single-clicking on the Control box brings up the Control menu.

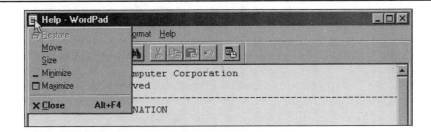

Second, the Control box for a program or document will close the window (terminate the program or close the document) when you double-click on it.

Pressing Alt-Hyphen opens the Control box of the active child window; Alt-spacebar opens the Control box of the active parent window.

Scroll Bars, Scroll Buttons, and Scroll Boxes

On the bottom and right edges of many windows, you'll find *scroll bars*, *scroll buttons*, and *scroll boxes*. These are used to "pan across" the information in a window: up, down, left, and right. This is necessary when there is too much information (text or graphics) to fit into the window at one time. For example, you might be writing a letter that is two pages long. Using the scroll bars lets you move around, or scroll, within your document to see the section you're interested in, as two full pages of text won't be displayed in a window at one time. Scrolling lets you look at a large amount of data through what amounts to a small window—your screen. Figure 3.10 illustrates this concept. Many Windows operations—such as listing files on your disks, reading Help screens, or displaying a lot of icons within a window—require the use of scroll bars and boxes.

FIGURE 3.10

Scrolling lets you work with more information than will fit on your screen at one time.

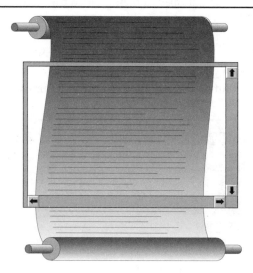

Scroll bars have a little box in them called the *scroll box*, sometimes called an *elevator*. Just as an elevator can take you from one floor of a building to the next, the scroll bar takes you from one section of a window or document to the next. The elevator moves within the scroll bar to indicate which portion of the window you are viewing at any given time. By moving the elevator with your mouse, you cause the document to scroll.

TIP

If you have a "scrolling" mouse, such as the Microsoft Intellimouse, you can scroll the window by simply turning the little roller on the mouse using your index finger.

Try these exercises to see how scroll bars and boxes work:

1. If you haven't already double-clicked on the My Computer icon, do so now. A window will open. (We'll discuss the purpose of the My Computer windows later. For now just use one as an example.) Using the technique explained above, size the window so that it shows only a few icons, as shown below. A horizontal or vertical scroll bar (or possibly both) appears on the bottom edge of the window. This indicates that there are more icons in the window than are visible because the window is now so small. What has happened is that several icons are now out of view.

2. Click on the elevator with the left mouse button, keep the button held down, and slide the elevator in its little shaft. Notice that as you do this, the elevator moves along with the pointer, and the window's contents are repositioned. (Incidentally, this mouse technique is called *dragging*.)

3. Now try another approach to scrolling. Click on the scroll buttons (the little arrows at the ends of the scroll bar). With each click, the elevator moves a bit in the direction of the button you're clicking on. If you click and hold, the elevator continues to move.

4. One more approach is to click within the scroll bar on either side of the elevator. Each click scrolls the window up or down a bit. With many programs, the screen will scroll one entire screenful with each click.

This example used only a short window with relatively little information in it. In this case, maximizing the window or resizing it just a bit would eliminate the need for scrolling and is probably a better solution. However, with large documents or windows containing many icons, scrolling becomes a necessity, as you'll see later.

All about Menus

The *menu bar* is a row of words that appears just below the title bar. (It appears only on application windows. Document windows do not have menu bars.) If you click on one of the words in the menu bar (called a menu *name*), a menu opens up, displaying a series of options that you can choose from. It is through menus that you tell all Windows programs what actions you want carried out.

Try this as an example:

1. With the My Computer window open and active, click on the word *File* in the menu bar. A menu opens, as you see in Figure 3.11, listing seven options. You can see why it's called a menu; it's a bit like a restaurant menu listing things you can order.

FIGURE 3.11

Open a menu by clicking on its name in the menu bar.

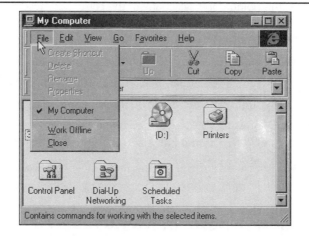

**TECH TIP**

You could also have pressed Alt-F to open the File menu. If there is an underlined letter in any menu's name, holding down the Alt key (either one, if your keyboard has two) and pressing that letter opens the menu.

2. Slide the mouse pointer to the right to open the other menus (Edit, View, or Help) and examine their choices.

As you might surmise, each menu contains choices somewhat relevant to the menu's name. The names on menus vary from program to program, but there are usually a few common ones, such as File, Edit, and Help. It may take a while for you to become familiar with the commands and which menus they're located on, but it will become more automatic with time. In any case, it's easy enough to look around through the menus to find the one you want.

Selecting Menu Commands

Once a menu is open, you can select any of the commands in the menu that aren't dimmed (dimmed choices are explained below).

NOTE

At this point, don't select any of the commands just yet. We'll begin using the commands in a bit.

When a menu is open, you can select a menu command in any of these ways:

- By typing the underlined letter in the command name
- By sliding the mouse down and clicking on a command's name
- By pressing the down-arrow or up-arrow keys on your keyboard to highlight the desired command name and then pressing Enter

You can cancel a menu (that is, make the menu disappear without selecting any commands) by simply pressing the Esc key or by clicking anywhere outside of the menu.

Special Indicators in Menus

Menus often have special symbols that tell you a little more about the menu commands. For example, examine the menus in Figure 3.12. Notice that many of these commands have additional words or symbols next to the command name. For example, the Options command has ellipses (three dots) after it. Other commands may have check marks, triangles, or key combinations listed beside them. The following paragraphs present the meanings of these words or symbols.

FIGURE 3.12

Typical menus

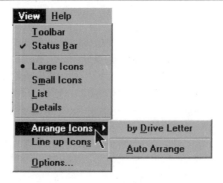

Up and Running

A Grayed (Dimmed) Command Name

When a command is shown as *grayed*, or *dimmed*, it means that this choice is not currently available to you. A command can be dimmed for a number of reasons. For example, a command for changing the typestyle of text will be grayed if you haven't selected any text. Other times, commands will be grayed because you are in the wrong program mode. For example, if a window is already maximized, the Maximize command on the Control menu will be dimmed because this choice doesn't make sense.

Ellipses (…)

Ellipses next to a command means that you will be asked for additional information before Windows or the Windows application executes the command. When you select such a command, a dialog box will appear on the screen, asking you to fill in the needed information. (I'll discuss dialog boxes in the next section of this chapter.)

A Check Mark (✔)

A check mark preceding a command means the command is a *toggle* that is activated (turned on). A toggle is a command that is alternately turned off and on each time you select it. It's like those old high-beam switches on the car floor that you step on to change between high beams and low beams. Each time you select one of these commands, it switches from *active* to *inactive*. If there is no check mark, then the command or setting is inactive. This is typically used to indicate things like whether selected text is underlined or not, which font is selected, what mode you are in within a program, and so on.

A Triangle (▶)

A triangle to the right of a menu command means that the command has additional subchoices for you to make. This is called a *cascading menu* (because the next menu starts to the right of the previous one and runs down from there, a bit like a waterfall of menus). You make selections from a cascaded menu the same way you would from a normal menu. The lower left example in Figure 3.12 shows a cascaded menu. The Taskbar also uses cascading menus, but we'll get to that in a moment.

A Dot

A dot to the left of the command means that the option is currently selected and is an exclusive option among several related options. For example, in Figure 3.12, the center section of one of the menus contains the options Large icons, Small icons, List, and Details. Only one of these options can be selected at a time. The dot indicates the current setting. By simply opening the menu again and clicking on one of the other options, you set that option on.

A Key Combination

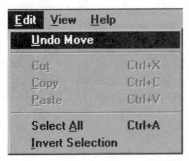

Some menu commands list keystrokes that can be used instead of opening the menu and choosing that command. For example, in the My Computer's Edit menu, shown below, notice that the Cut command could be executed by Ctrl-X, the Copy command could be executed by pressing Ctrl-C, and the Paste command with Ctrl-V. These alternative time-saving keystrokes are called *shortcut keys*. (Don't worry if you don't understand these commands yet. They will be explained later.)

NOTE

A keystroke abbreviation such as Ctrl-C means to hold down the Ctrl key (typically found in the lower left corner of your keyboard) while pressing the C key.

All about Dialog Boxes

As I said above, a dialog box will always appear when you select a command with an ellipsis (...) after it. Dialog boxes pop up on your screen when Windows or the Windows application program you're using needs more information before continuing. Some dialog boxes ask you to enter information (such as file names), while others simply require you to check off options or make choices from a list. The list may be in the form of additional sub-dialog boxes or submenus. In any case, after you enter the requested information, you click on OK, and Windows or the application program continues on its merry way, executing the command.

Though most dialog boxes ask you for information, other boxes are only informative, alerting you to a problem with your system or an error you've made. Such a box might also request confirmation on a command that could have dire consequences or explain why the command you've chosen can't be executed. These alert boxes sometimes have a big letter *i* (for "information") in them, or an exclamation mark (!). A few examples are shown in Figure 3.13.

More often than not, these boxes only ask you to read them and then click on OK (or cancel them if you decide not to proceed). Some boxes only have an OK button. Let's look at some typical dialog boxes and see how they work.

PART

I

FIGURE 3.13

Dialog boxes are used for a wide variety of purposes. Here are some examples of dialog boxes that are informative only and do not ask you to make settings or adjust options.

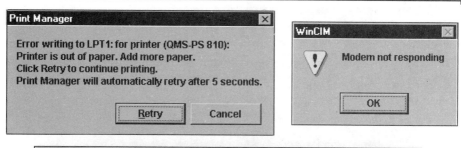

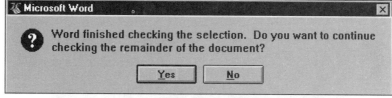

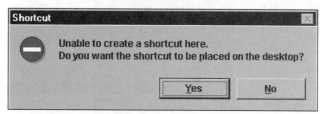

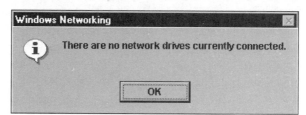

Moving between Sections of a Dialog Box

As you can see in Figure 3.14, dialog boxes often have several sections to them. You can move between the sections in three ways:

- The easiest way is by clicking on the section you want to alter.

- If you are using the keyboard, you can press the Tab key to move between sections and press the Spacebar to select them.

- You can also use the Alt key with the underlined letter of the section name you want to jump to or activate. Even when you are using a mouse, the Alt-key combinations are sometimes the fastest way to jump between sections or choose an option within a box.

FIGURE 3.14

Typical dialog boxes

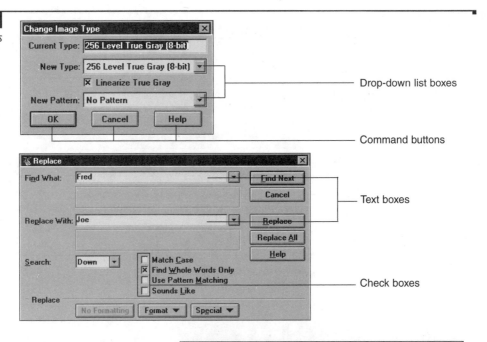

Drop-down list boxes

Command buttons

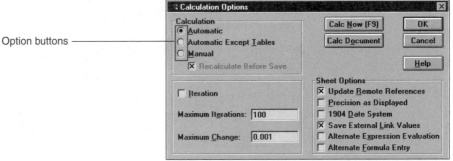

Text boxes

Check boxes

Option buttons

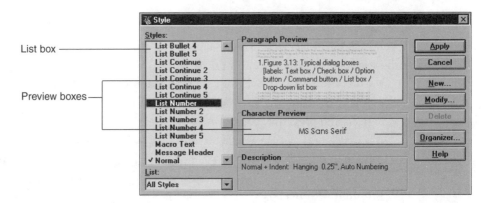

List box

Preview boxes

Notice that one of the dialog boxes here has a Preview section. This is a feature that more and more dialog boxes will be sporting as applications become more *user friendly*. Rather than having to choose a formatting change, for example, and then okaying the dialog box to see the effect on your document, a Preview section lets you see the effect in advance. This lets you "shop" for the effect you want before committing to it.

Many newer Windows programs have dialog boxes with *tab pages*, a new item introduced around the time of Windows 95. I discussed this feature somewhat in Chapter 1 but will mention it here in the context of dialog boxes. Tab pages keep a dialog box to a reasonable size while still letting you adjust a lot of settings from it. To get to the page of settings you want, just click on the tab with the correct name. Figure 3.15 illustrates this concept. I've clicked on the View menu of Word's Options dialog box.

FIGURE 3.15

Newer dialog boxes have multiple tabs that make the boxes easier to understand and appear less cluttered. Click on a tab, and a new set of options appears.

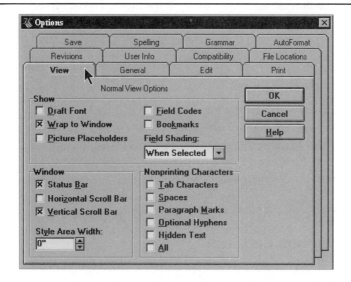

Entering Information in a Dialog Box

Now let's consider how you enter information into dialog boxes. There are seven basic types of sections in dialog boxes:

- text boxes
- check boxes
- option buttons
- command buttons
- list boxes
- drop-down list boxes
- file dialog boxes

Once you've jumped to the correct section, you'll need to know how to make choices from it. The next several sections explain how to use each kind. (Please refer to Figure 3.14 during the next discussions.)

Text Boxes

In this sort of section, you are asked to type in text from the keyboard. Sometimes there will be text already typed in for you. If you want to keep it as is, just leave it alone. To alter the text, simply type in new text. If the existing text is already highlighted, then the first key you press will delete the existing entry. If it is not highlighted, you can backspace over it to erase it. You can also edit existing text. Clicking once on highlighted text will *deselect* it and cause the *text cursor* (a vertical blinking bar) to appear when you put the pointer inside the text area. You can then move the text cursor around using the arrow keys or the mouse and insert text (by typing) or delete text (by pressing the Del key). Text is inserted at the position of the text cursor. Text boxes are most often used for specifying file names when you are saving or loading documents and applications or specifying text to search for in a word-processing document.

Check Boxes

Check boxes are the small square (or sometimes diamond-shaped) boxes. They are used to indicate nonexclusive options. For example, you might want some text to appear as bold *and* underlined. Or, as another example, consider the Calculation Options dialog box from Excel shown in Figure 3.14. In this box, you can have any of the settings in the Sheet Options section set on or off. These are toggle settings (as explained previously) that you activate or deactivate by clicking on the box. When the box is empty, the option is off; when you see an ×, the option is on.

Option Buttons

Unlike check boxes, which are nonexclusive, option buttons are exclusive settings. Sometimes called *radio buttons*, these are also round rather than square or diamond shaped, and only one option can be set on at a time. For example, using the same Calculation Options dialog box referred to above, you may select Automatic, Automatic Except Tables, *or* Manual in the Calculation section of the dialog box—not a combination of the three. Clicking on the desired button turns it on (the circle will be filled) and turns any previous selection off. From the keyboard, you first jump to the section, then use the arrow keys to select the option.

Command Buttons

Command buttons are like option buttons except that they are used to execute a command immediately. They are also rectangular rather than square or circular. An example of a command button is the OK button found on almost every dialog box. Once you've filled in a dialog box to your liking, click on the OK button, and Windows or the application executes the settings you've selected. If you change your mind and don't want the new commands on the dialog box executed, click on the Cancel button.

There is always a command button that has a thicker border; this is the command that will execute if you press Enter. Likewise, pressing the Esc key always has the same effect as clicking on the Cancel button (that's why there's no underlined letter on the Cancel button).

Some command buttons are followed by ellipses (...). As you might expect, these commands will open additional dialog boxes for adjusting more settings. Other command buttons include two >> symbols in them. Choosing this type of button causes the particular section of the dialog box to expand so you can make more selections.

List Boxes

List boxes are like menus. They show you a list of options or items from which you can choose. For example, when choosing fonts to display or print text in, WordPad shows you a list box. You make a selection from a list box the same way you do from a menu: by just clicking on it. From the keyboard, highlight the desired option with the arrow keys and then press Enter to choose it. Some list boxes are too small to show all the possible selections. In this case, there will be a scroll bar on the right side of the box. Use the scroll bar to see all the selections. Some list boxes let you make more than one selection, but most only allow one. To make more than one selection from the keyboard, press the Spacebar to select or deselect any item.

TECH TIP

You can quickly jump to an option in a list box by typing the first letter of its name. If there are two choices with the same first letter and you want the second one, press the letter again, or press the down-arrow key.

Drop-Down List Boxes

Drop-down list boxes are indicated by a small arrow in a box to the right of the option. The current setting is displayed to the left of the little arrow. Clicking on the arrow opens a list that works just like a normal list box and has scroll bars if there are a lot of options. Drop-down list boxes are used when a dialog box is too crowded to accommodate regular list boxes.

File Dialog Boxes

A dialog box like one of the three shown in Figure 3.16 often appears when you're working in Windows programs. This type of box is called a *file dialog box* or simply *file box*.

Though used in a variety of situations, you're most likely to run into file boxes when you want to open a file or when you save a document for the first time. For example, choosing File ➢ Open from almost any Windows program will bring up such a box asking which document file you want to open.

FIGURE 3.16

A file dialog box lets you scan through directories to load or save a document. Here you see three typical file dialog box types. The upper one is the newer Windows 95 style. The middle one is the Windows 3.x style, and the lowest one is the moldy, oldy 3.0 style.

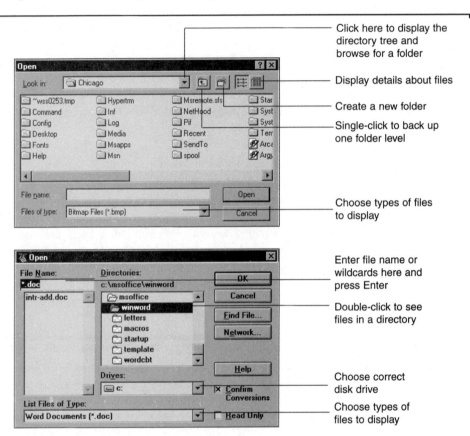

Click here to display the directory tree and browse for a folder

Display details about files

Create a new folder

Single-click to back up one folder level

Choose types of files to display

Enter file name or wildcards here and press Enter

Double-click to see files in a directory

Choose correct disk drive

Choose types of files to display

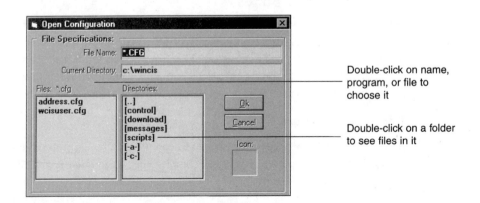

Double-click on name, program, or file to choose it

Double-click on a folder to see files in it

NOTE

If you're new to Windows, you may want to mark this section of the book with a paper clip and refer back to it when you have to save or open a file for the first time.

File dialog boxes vary somewhat from program to program, even though they perform the same job. Some boxes, as you will note in the figure, allow you to open a file as Read Only, for example, or help you search for a file with a Find button or a Network button (if you're connected to a network). The file box went through a major redesign by Microsoft after they finally figured out that novices were thoroughly confused by it. Now the new design is much more intuitively obvious and is very similar to the file boxes used on the Mac. Because the older two boxes and new type are pretty different from one another, I'll explain the steps for each separately, starting with the two older-style files boxes.

The two older-style boxes (which 16-bit Windows 3.*x* applications will use) are divided into two main sections, listing files on the left and directories on the right. In most applications, directories are represented by a folder. In really old programs you only see the directory's name enclosed in brackets, like this:

    [cserve]

Using Older-Style File Boxes   Here are the steps you can take to use these older boxes. If you know how to run a program (we'll cover that in the next chapter), you might try running a 16-bit program, opening its File menu, and choosing Open to experiment a bit.

NOTE

In this discussion, the words *directory* and *folder* are used interchangeably because in reality they are the same thing. In the older dialog boxes, *directory* refers to what are now called *folders* under Windows 95.

1. Make sure the correct disk drive is chosen down in the lower right side of the box. If it's not, open the drop-down *Drives* list box and select another drive if necessary. Normally, this setting will be set to drive C, which is your hard disk, and should be fine. On the oldest-style file box, you don't have a drop-down list for the drive. To change drives, you scroll to the bottom of the directory list and double-click on the name of the drive (e.g., [-a-], [-b-], [-c-]) to change drives.

2. Now select a directory on the right side by double-clicking on its little folder icon or name. Whatever files are stored in the directory you just chose will then show up in the list at the left. If you don't see the directory you're aiming for,

you may have to move down or back up the directory tree a level or two (see Chapter 12 for a review of DOS directory theory).

NOTE

Because these older programs were by definition written for Windows 3.*x*, their file boxes won't display long file or directory names. Long names will be converted to the "8.3" standard DOS file-name format for display in these boxes. Chapter 1 covered details of how the conversion process works.

In Windows 3.1-style boxes, you'd double-click on the folder just above the one that's currently open to back up a level or on the folder below the current one to move down a level. In Windows 3.0-style boxes, you'd have to double-click on the two dots (..) at the top of the directory list to back up one directory level. Each double click backs up one directory level. To move down a level, click on any directory name enclosed in brackets.

3. If you want to see only certain types of files, open the List Files of Type box (if there is one) to select the type of files you want to see (such as programs, or all files). If the options offered don't suit your needs, or if you're using the older-style box, you can type in DOS-like wildcards in the File Name area, then press Enter to modify the file list accordingly. For example, to show only Lotus 1-2-3 worksheet files, you'd enter ***.WK?** in the File Name area and press Enter.

4. Once the file you want is visible in the file box at the left, double-click on it or highlight it, and click on OK.

When saving a file for the first time, the file won't exist on the drive yet, so it won't show up in the file list box; you'll be giving it a name. To do this, select the drive and directory as outlined above, then move the cursor to the File Name area and type in the file name and extension. Make sure to delete any existing letters in the text area first, using the Backspace and/or Delete keys. (For more information about selecting, editing, and replacing text, see Chapter 19.)

The Newer-Style File Box The newer-style file box will show up in 32-bit programs written for Windows 95, 98 and NT. You'll also see it in portions of Windows 95 itself. Here's how to use this type of file box when you're opening or saving files.

NOTE

To see one of these new dialog boxes, you can run the Paint application found in the Accessories folder by clicking on the Start button, then choosing Start ➤ Programs ➤ Accessories ➤ Paint. Then choose File ➤ Open. (The ➤ symbol here indicates a chain of choices you make from the menus.)

1. First, notice the *Look in* section at the top of the box. This tells you what folder's contents is being displayed in the window below. You can click on this drop-down list to choose the drive or folder you want to look in. This will also list the folders you have on the Desktop so you can open or save files from/to the Desktop.

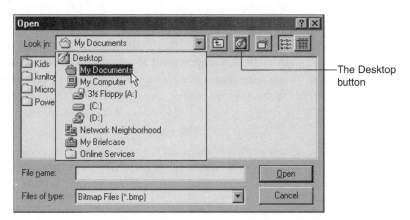

The Desktop button

2. If the file is on your desktop or in a folder on the desktop, click the Desktop button. That will instantly display the contents of the desktop.

3. You can create a new folder using the Create New Folder button in the dialog box's toolbar if you want to save something in a folder that doesn't already exist. This can help you organize your files. The new folder will be created as a subfolder to the folder shown in the Look in area. (After creating the new folder, you'll have to name it by typing in a new name just to the right of the folder.)

4. The object is to display the target folder in the window and then double-click on it. So, if the folder you want is somewhere on your hard disk (typically drive C), one way to display it is to choose *C:* from the Look in area. All the folders on your C drive appear in the window. *Don't forget about scrolling! You might have to scroll the contents of the window to display the folder you want if there are too many folders to fit in the window.*

5. In the large window, double-click on the folder you want to look in. If you don't see the folder you're aiming for, you may have to move down or back up the tree of folders a level or two (see Chapter 12 for a review of DOS directory theory). You back up a level by clicking on the Up One Level button. You move down a level by double-clicking on a folder and looking for its subfolders to then appear in the window. You can then double-click on a subfolder to open that, and so on.

6. Finally, click on the file you want to open. Or, if you're saving a file for the first time, you'll have to type in the name of the file. Of course, if you are saving a

PART

I

Up and Running

file for the first time, the file won't exist on the drive yet, so it won't show up in the list of files; you'll be giving it a name. To do this, select the drive and directory as outlined above, then click in the File Name area and type in the file name. Make sure to delete any existing letters in the text area first, using the Backspace and/or Delete keys. (For more information about selecting, editing, and replacing text, see Chapter 20.)

7. If you want to see only certain types of files, open the Files of Type box to select the type of files you want to see (such as a certain kind of document or all files). If the options offered don't suit your needs, you can type in DOS-like wildcards in the File Name area, then press Enter to modify the file list accordingly. For example, to show only Lotus 1-2-3 worksheet files, you'd enter ***.WK?** in the File Name area and press Enter.

8. Once the file you want is visible in the file box at the left, double-click on it or highlight it, and click on OK.

Here's a trick I use all the time. Instead of scrolling around to find a file or folder that I know I'm heading for, I can jump to it, or close to it, quickly. Just click once on a folder or file in the box (any one will do), then type the first letter of the item you're looking for. That will jump the highlight to the first item that starts with the letter, and probably bring your target into view. Successive keypresses will move through each item that starts with that letter.

Using the New Web View

As mentioned in Chapter 1, the use of the Internet and the World Wide Web (sometimes called "WWW," "W3" or simply the "Web") has escalated beyond anyone's wildest imaginations. You can't read a magazine, watch a TV commercial, or watch the evening news without seeing Web addresses. You can't even listen to the radio without hearing the words "dot com" in half of the commercials. Quite a few of my friends have their own Web sites, and so do I for that matter (*www.cowart.com*).

Since so many of us are using our computer to look at the Web, Microsoft decided to come up with an adjustment to the Windows interface to make for a more seamless meshing of stuff that's in your computer with stuff that's out there on the Internet. For instance, on Web pages, you click once on a link to go to a new Web page. In the new, optional, interface to Windows 98, you can also click once to go to files and launch programs.

The new look is called Web view, for obvious reasons. It's pretty nice, and I have to say I like it a lot. It cuts down on clicking (and resultant finger and carpal tunnel wear over the course of a day's work), and I don't have to remember if I'm on a Web page or looking at folders and files on my hard disk. Now everything works much more similarly.

Technically the Web view option is a feature of Internet Explorer, the Web browser from Microsoft. You might have heard of Netscape's Navigator or America OnLine's Web browser. They are the competition (well, they're the biggies; there are many others). But they don't have this feature. Even though lawsuits and Federal Trade Commission investigations are raging as of this writing, I'm going to assume that Internet Explorer 4 (IE4) is going to be shipped with Windows 98, and so you'll have Web view as an option in your copy of Windows 98. Even if IE does *not* ship with Windows 98, it will be free anyway, so I can safely assume that you'll probably have downloaded it off the Net or gotten it from a friend, and installed it. Despite the Microsoft bashing, IE is a terrific Web browser, and integrates with Windows 98 very nicely, as you'll see.

In the chapters on using the Internet, I'll cover the ins and outs of getting connected, browsing the Web, using search engines, e-mail, newsgroups and so forth. What's relevant to this overview chapter is how IE4 changes the look and feel of Windows. Here are the main points:

- Folder windows have new *Back* and *Forward* buttons. The Windows Explorer also has these buttons. These buttons let you easily review a sequence of folders you've recently been examining, without having to traverse the directory tree.

- The toolbars in Folder and Explorer windows are customizable, just like those in IE are. You can add an "address bar," for example—type in a Web address while you're exploring your hard drive's contents, hit Enter, and the window becomes a Web browser. It connects to the Internet and displays the page. (See Chapter 12 for more about Windows Explorer.) Type in a local hard disk name in the address bar (C: for example), and folders are displayed again.

- Files and Folders can act like "hot links" on a Web page: one click activates them.

- All folders can have a specialized Web page "look" that you can customize using a background, or custom HTML code. With a single menu choice, even non-programmers can choose a default Web view that has some useful features, including a display that shows thumbnail views (of pictures, local Web pages, text documents, etc.).

- Your desktop can be made "active," displaying data streaming in from the Internet (such as stocks, news, entertainment listings, etc.).

In this section, I'll cover only those effects that are related to the overall inter-face; I'll leave for later chapters any Web view effects that are directly related to IE or the Web.

Turning On Web View

Want to try Web view? Good. You just might like it. Of course, if you're in a business where you use lots of other people's computers and they aren't using Web view, you might confuse yourself a bit by mixing up your habits, but it's not really that mentally difficult to switch between them.

As the book progresses you'll see that a lot of the screen shots I made for the book use Web view, since that is what I use most of the time. So that you're not confused by the figures, you might want to try using Web view yourself as you read.

1. Open any folder. An easy one is My Computer, since you already know how to do that.

2. Choose View ➢ Folder Options. You'll see a dialog box.

3. Click on the Web Style radio button to turn on the option.

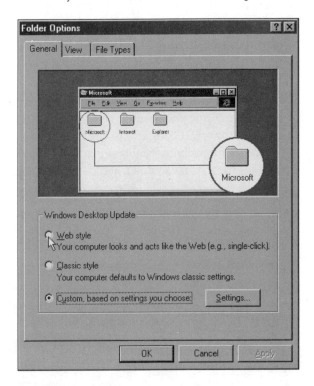

4. Click on OK. You'll be prompted to make sure this is what you want to do.

Now your Desktop should have changed its look, as you see in Figure 3.17.

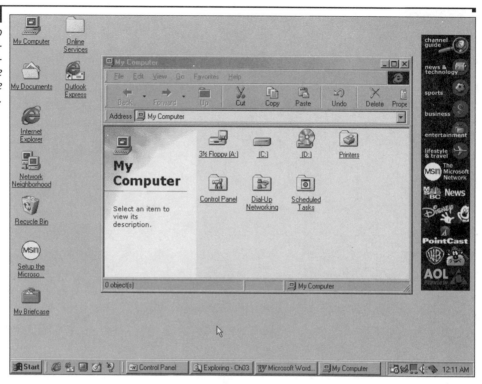

FIGURE 3.17

After turning Web view on, icons, folders, and other documents have a line under them like Web links.

Notice that the Channel bar has appeared over on the right side of my screen, since part of Web view is the "Active" desktop associated with IE. Also notice that the My Computer window now looks fancier and has a description. Most any folder window (including stuff like Printers or Control Panel, which you can reach now by single-clicking them in the My Computer window) will have a spiffed-up look, complete with descriptions.

An important skill with Web view is "pointing." See, in Classic view (the traditional view you're using when you're *not* using Web view) you select an object by clicking on it. But with Web view on, you select an object by just pointing to it. You don't click. Try out this example:

1. Adjust the My Computer window to a larger size, to give you some room to navigate.

2. Simply move the pointer to one of the icons such as Control Panel. Don't click, just keep the pointer still over the Control Panel icon. The window should change to look like Figure 3.18. Notice also that the pointer takes the shape of a pointing hand (though we couldn't capture that cursor for display here).

3. Try pointing to the C drive. You'll see a little pie chart indicating the amount of free space on the disk, and some other drive statistics. Pretty spiffy, eh?

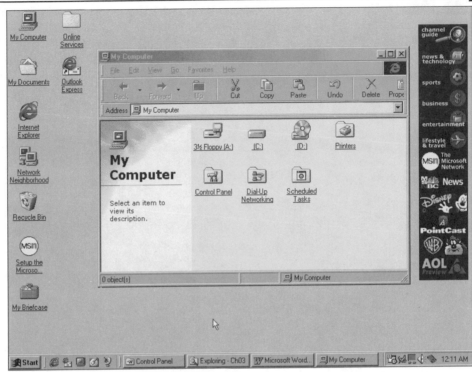

FIGURE 3.18

In Web view you simply point the cursor at an object to select it.

WARNING

This pointing technique has some important consequences which will become clearer in Chapters 4 and 5. But briefly, in Web view you have to be careful not to click on things unless you are ready to execute some action. That's because a single click is now the same as a double click in Classic view. Clicking a folder makes it open. Click a file and it opens. Click a program, it runs. And so forth. This also affects the selection of a *range* of objects, such as files or folders. Whereas in Classic view you click on the first item in the range, then hold down the Shift key and click on the last item, in Web view you point to the first item, wait a second for it to be selected, and then press Shift and—you guessed it—*point* to the last item in the range.

TECH TIP

Are you the nit-picky type? Want to control some of the details of Web view settings? You can do it. Click the Custom option from the View ➤ Folder Options dialog box, click on the Customize button, and change any settings that you would like to change. (Some of these are pretty technical though. If you don't understand a setting, don't touch it.) Personally, I think the standard Web style settings are right for most people. However, I do like the setting that eliminates the underline until you point to an object. See Chapter 5 for more details about custom settings.

Mess-O-Adjustments

There's a bushel of adjustments you can make to the user interface that I'm not going to go into here. Coverage of these is scattered throughout the book, in the appropriate places. But if you're brave or anxious to know, check them out by doing this:

1. Open up any folder in a window.

2. From that folder's menu bar, choose View ➢ Folder Options.

3. Click on the View tab. You'll see this list of options:

Study and remember these options. They could come in handy. Most germane to this discussion regarding the look of the interface are the last two options (you'll probably have to scroll down to see them):

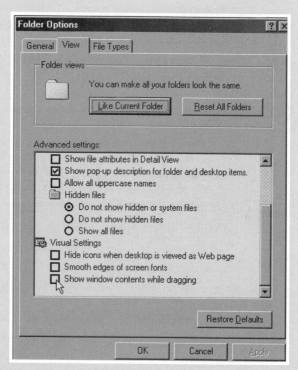

- **Smooth edges of screen fonts.** This smoothes out some smaller letters on screen that might otherwise look blocky, filling in the gaps with a sort of thin grayish blur. It's a nice feature, and easier on the eyes.

- **Show window contents while dragging.** I mentioned this earlier in this chapter. If this checkbox is on, you can make the innards of a window move around with your mouse as you resize it or drag it.

To activate one of these items, click in it so that a checkmark appears, then click Apply or OK.

If you later decide you've messed up the settings in this box, click the Restore Defaults button. Everything will be set back to the way it came from the factory.

Returning to Classic View

If you decide you don't like Web view, it's cool. You can easily return to regular old Windows 95-like operation:

1. Open the View ➤ Folder Options dialog as we did in the preceding examples.

2. Choose Classic Style.

3. Click on OK.

Exiting Windows

When you're finished with a Windows session, you should properly shut down Windows before turning off your computer. This ensures that Windows saves your work on disk correctly and that no data is lost. Even if you are running an application in Windows and you close that application, you *must* exit Windows, too, before turning off your computer.

WARNING

Exiting Windows properly is very important. You can lose your work or otherwise foul up Windows settings if you don't shut down Windows before turning off your computer. If you accidentally fail to do so, the computer probably won't die or anything, but the hard disk will be checked for errors the next time you turn it on.

Here are the steps for correctly exiting Windows:

1. Close any programs that you have running. (This can almost always be done from each program's File menu—choose Exit from the menu—or by clicking on the program's Close button.) If you forget to close programs before issuing the Shut Down command, Windows will attempt to close them for you. This is fine unless you were working on a document and didn't save your work. In that case you'll be prompted by a dialog box for each open document, asking you if you want to save your work. If you have DOS programs running, you'll have to close them manually before Windows will let you exit. You'll also be reminded if this is the case by a dialog box telling you that Windows can't terminate the program and you'll have to do it from the DOS program. Quit the DOS program and type **exit** at the DOS prompt, if necessary.

Save Energy! The Suspend Option for Laptops and Desktops with OnNow

If your computer has Advanced Power Manager (APM) or ACPI built in, you may have a Standby option in the Shutdown dialog box menu. This is like shutting down, only it lets you come right back to where you were working before you suspended. This means you don't have to exit all your applications before turning off your computer. You only have to choose Standby. It also means you can get right back to work where you left off without rebooting your computer, finding the document(s) you were working on, and finding your place in those documents. You can just press a key or button (depending on your computer) and in a few seconds you are up and running right where you left off.

An increasing number of laptop computers now support this Standby (sometimes called suspend) function. Note that there is a limit to the amount of time a laptop computer can stay in a suspended state. If the battery runs out, the computer will have to be rebooted when you turn it on, and your work may be lost. If you're going to standby on a laptop for very long, you should use the Hibernate function, if your laptop supports it (check the manual). Most new ones do. There is no time limit with Hibernate, though it takes a little longer to revive the machine (like about 15 seconds). Still, the effect is the same – you start working from where you left off.

My experience is that Toshiba computers hold the record in terms of how long they will stay in Suspend mode. I have had five Toshibas thus far, precisely for their well-engineered *Auto Resume* feature. A typical Toshiba laptop will stay suspended on a full battery charge for several days to a week or more. Most other brands won't stay suspended for more than a few hours. You'll want to check with the manufacturer of your computer about how long theirs will stay "alive" in a suspended state if you plan to use Windows 98's Standby option.

Due to the growing popularity of this idea on laptops, and the desire by the U.S. Department of Energy for us all to conserve power, the latest breed of desktop computers have OnNow technology built in. This means they, too, can be put in a suspended state, lowering power consumption considerably. That saves you lots on your electric bill (way too many offices leaves their PCs on all the time), and keeps the air cleaner (did you know that 80% of our power comes from burning fossil fuels and garbage?). If your desktop machine supports this feature, you'll have a Standby option in your Shutdown dialog box. Some machines, such as ones from Compaq, have a hardware button on the keyboard or computer box to engage Standby mode, too.)

WARNING: If you do have Standby capability on your computer, you should save your work before suspending. You don't necessarily have to close the applications you're using, but you should at least save any documents you're working on.

2. Next, click on the Start button and choose Shut Down. You'll now see a dialog box like that in Figure 3.19.

FIGURE 3.19

The Start ➢ Shut Down command offers a variety of ways to end your Windows session.

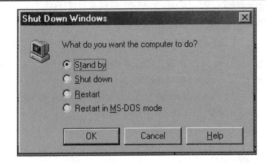

3. Choose Shut down or Standby, depending on which you want.

4. Click on Yes. Now take one of two actions:

- If you chose Standby, in a few seconds the computer will appear to shut off. There may be some indication that it's still semi-alive, such as a little light somewhere, indicator on an LCD panel or something (depends on the brand and model of your computer). If it's a laptop computer, you can now close the cover and pack it up if you need to take to the streets, etc.

- If you chose Shut Down, wait until Windows completely shuts down and tells you it's okay to turn off your computer. This can take up to about fifteen seconds. Just wait until the screen says "It's now safe to turn off your computer."

Then turn off the computer, printer, monitor, and other stuff you have attached. You're home free.

Chapter

4

Getting Down to Business: Running Your Applications

FEATURING

How to run your programs

Running programs from the Start button

Running programs from the My Computer icon

Using Find to locate programs, documents, and folders

Using Explorer or File Manager to run programs

Using the old Program Manager

Running DOS programs

Using and customizing the Taskbar

Using Alt-Tab to switch between applications

Getting Down to Business: Running Your Applications

I f you've just upgraded from Windows 3.1 or Windows 95, you already know a lot about how to use Windows and Windows applications. A few things will be different with Windows 98, but you'll probably pick those up quickly. If you're new to Windows, then getting used to the turf might take a little longer, though you'll have an advantage—you won't have to unlearn any bad habits that Windows 3.x veterans have ground into their craniums.

NOTE

Beginning with this chapter, I'm going to assume you're running Windows 98 in Web view rather than Classic view. (See Chapter 3 if you forget the difference or how to change views). We did have some debate at Sybex as far as which way to lean, especially since Classic view is the default setting until you change it. But I think that Web view is the wave of the future, and since it integrates so well with the Web, I've decided to go primarily with the Web view for illustrations and descriptions in this book. However, when something I'm talking about looks radically different in Classic view, I'll mention it in a note or an aside.

What Can and Can't Be Run

As I discussed in the opening chapters, Windows 98 was designed to be *backward-compatible* with previous versions of Windows and with DOS programs. And it's *forward-compatible* with most 32-bit programs designed for Windows NT. In a sense, Windows 98 is the best of all worlds when it comes to running your existing programs. You can pretty much bet that whatever is in your existing software arsenal won't be rendered obsolete by Windows 98.

Windows 98 will run your existing DOS programs quite nicely in scalable windows, offer them more conventional memory than previously possible, run many graphics programs in a window, and optionally give each DOS application its own custom DOS environment to run in. And as mentioned in Chapter 2, virtually all Windows programs will run just fine with smoother task switching and a more pleasant appearance than Windows 3.*x*, you'll have the Windows 9*x* Desktop to play with, the "single Explorer" approach regardless of whether you're looking at the Web or a local drive, and you get all the new Internet goodies. Finally, any and all programs can be run from the DOS command line, not just DOS programs.

So, How Do I Run My Programs?

As with many of the procedures you'll want to do while in Windows, starting up your programs can be done in myriad ways. Here's the complete list of ways to run programs. You can:

- Choose the desired application from the Start button's menus.
- Add the application to the "quick launch" bar and click it to run.
- Open My Computer, walk your way through the directories until you find the application's icon, and double-click on it.
- Run Explorer or File Manager, find the application's icon, and double-click on it.
- Run the old-style Windows 3.*x* Program Manager, open the group that contains the application's icon, and double-click on it.
- Find the application with the Find command and double-click on it.
- Locate a document that was created with the application in question and double-click on it. This will run the application and load the document into it.
- Right-click on the Desktop or in a folder and choose New. Then choose a document type from the resulting menu. This creates a new document of the type you desire, which, when double-clicked on, will run the application.
- Open the Documents list from the Start button and choose a recently edited document. This will open the document in the appropriate application.

- Enter command names from the MS-DOS prompt. In addition to the old-style DOS commands that run DOS programs and batch files, you can run Windows programs right from the DOS prompt.

For many users, the last three approaches will make the most sense because they deal with the document itself instead of the application that created it.

In deference to tradition, I'm going to cover the approaches to running applications in the order listed above. That is, application-centric first rather than document-centric. All the approaches are useful while using Windows, and you will probably want to become proficient in each of them.

Running a Program from the Start Button

Certainly the easiest way to run your applications is with the Start button. That's why it's called the Start button. On the next page, I describe how it works.

Running Applications from the Command Prompt

One of the nicest features of Windows 98 is that you can now run any application from the MS-DOS command prompt. If you're used to MS-DOS, you can open up a MS-DOS Prompt from the Start menu (Start ➢ Programs ➢ MS-DOS Prompt). If you use the command prompt frequently, you might want to create a shortcut on the Desktop to make access to the command prompt faster. To do this:

1. Click on the Desktop with the right mouse button.

2. Select New ➢ Shortcut.

3. In the Create Shortcut dialog box's Command line edit box enter **command.com**.

4. Click on Next.

5. As a Program-Information File already exists for this program, the *Select Title for the Program* dialog box's *Select name for the shortcut* edit box should already have *MS-DOS Prompt* listed, but if it doesn't, go ahead and enter it now. If you want another title to be displayed, you can enter that instead.

6. Click on Finish. A new shortcut should now be displayed on the Desktop.

7. At this point you can change the default start-up directory (the MS-DOS Prompt's default directory) by right-clicking on the program icon and selecting Properties. Choose the Program tab, then change the entry in the Working edit box to your desired directory. I often change this to C:\ instead of the default C:\Windows so I can browse around from the root directory.

Continued

Up and Running

CONTINUED

If you use a long-filename directory, remember to enclose the entire text string in quotes. For instance, if you want to start your command prompt in the Program Files directory, it should look like **"C:\Program Files"** in the Working edit box.

Once you have a command prompt, you can use your familiar MS-DOS commands like **CD** to change directories or **MD** to make a new directory, or you can run your programs (any `.bat`, `.pif`, `.com`, or `.exe` file). And you can run either MS-DOS or Windows programs. Just type in the program name, and it will start up. For instance, if you wanted to run the Windows 3.*x* version of File Manager, type **winfile** and press the Enter key. Or, for the Windows 98 Explorer, type **explorer** and press the Enter key.

When you install a new program, the program's name is almost always added to the Start button's Program menu system. Then you just find your way to the program's name, choose it, and the program runs. Suppose you want to run Notepad:

1. Click on the Start button.

2. Choose Programs because you want to start a program. Up comes a list of programs similar to what's shown in Figure 4.1. Your list may differ because this is the list of programs on *my* computer, not yours. Any selection that has an arrow pointer to the right of the name is not actually a program but a program *group*. If you've used Windows 3.*x*, you'll know that program groups are the collections of programs and related document files that were used to organize your programs in Windows 3.*x*'s Program Manager. Choosing one of these opens another menu listing the items in the group.

3. I happen to know that the Notepad program lies amongst the accessory programs that come with Windows 98. Slide the pointer up or over to highlight Accessories. Now a list of accessory programs appears. Slide the pointer down to Notepad and click, as shown in Figure 4.2.

You've successfully run Notepad. It's now sitting there with a blank document open, waiting for you to start typing. Chapter 22 covers the ins and outs of using Notepad, so I won't discuss that here. For now just click on the Close button, or open the File menu and choose Exit.

PART

I

Up and Running

FIGURE 4.1

The first step in running a program is to click on the Start button and choose Programs from the resulting list.

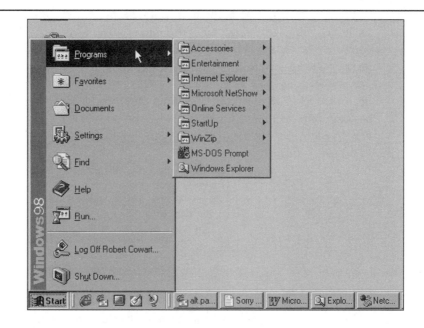

FIGURE 4.2

The second step in running a program from the Start button is to choose the program itself from the resulting Program list or to open a group such as Accessories and then choose the program.

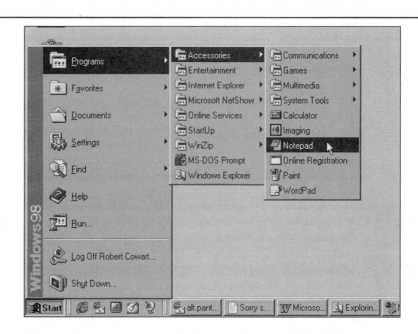

Because Windows 98 lets you nest groups of applications and documents into multiple levels, you might occasionally run into multiple levels of cascading menus when you're trying to launch (that's computerese for *run*) an application. For example, in the instance above, I had to open the Accessories group to find Notepad. If you open the Accessories group again you'll notice that there are a couple of groups within Accessories up at the top—Communications, Games, Multimedia, and System Tools. Sometimes because of the length of a list, the list might need to scroll off of the screen. In this case, you'll see arrows at the top or bottom of the list, like this:

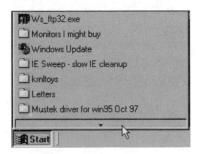

Just click on the arrow to scroll the list and release the mouse button when you see the one you want. Then click on it.

Sometimes spotting a program in a list is a visual hassle. Computers are smart about alphabetizing, so notice that the items in the lists are in order from A to Z. Folders appear first, in order, then programs after that. This ordering is something you'll see throughout Windows. To make things even simpler, you can press the first letter of the item you're looking for, and the highlight will jump to it. If there are multiple items starting with that letter, each key press will advance one in the list. This works fairly reliably unless the pointer is sitting on an item that has opened into a group.

Often you will accidentally open a list that you don't want to look at—say, Documents. Just move the pointer to the one you want, let's say it was Programs. The Document list will close and the Programs list will open. It takes a little getting used to, but you'll get the hang of it. Another way to close unwanted program lists is by pressing the Esc key. This has the effect of closing open lists one at a time. Each press of Esc closes one level of any open lists. To close down all open lists, just click anywhere else on the screen, such as on the Desktop or another window, and the all open Start button lists will go away.

Running a Program from My Computer

There are times when you might want to do a little sleuthing around on your hard disk using a more graphical approach as opposed to hunting for a name in the Start list. The My Computer icon lets you do this. My Computer is usually situated in the upper-left corner of your Desktop. Double-clicking on it reveals an interesting entry point to all the elements of your computer—hardware, software, printers, files, and folders.

NOTE

> Just a reminder: Remember that if you are using Classic view, a double-click is going to be necessary to open a folder, run a program, etc. I'm going to try to use consistent language throughout the book, based on Web view. Sometimes I'll just simplify matters by saying "open the folder," "run the program" or whatever, and you can decide how you're going to open it based on which view you're using.

The My Computer icon is the entry point for the file system and other parts of your computer including the Control Panel, Dial-up Networking, and Printers. It's a very Mac-like way of moving through the stuff in your computer. Getting to a program you want can be a little convoluted, but if you understand the DOS directory tree structure or you've used a Mac, you'll be able to grasp this fairly easily. Try it out.

1. Get to the Desktop by minimizing any windows that are on the screen. You can do this by clicking on each window's Minimize button, but the fastest way is by clicking on the Show Desktop icon to the right of the Start Button (this is a great little time saver, new to Windows 98).

TIP

> Yet another way to minimize all your windows and see the Desktop is to right-click on the clock in the Taskbar and choose Minimize All Windows.

2. Now open My Computer (you know, double-click on it, or single-click if in Web view). A window appears, looking something like this:

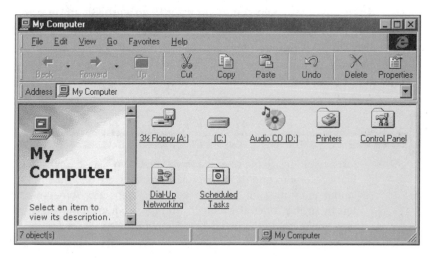

3. Typically, Drive C is where your programs will be located. Open the drive icon, and your hard drive's contents will appear (in the same window if you are in Web view, or in another window in Classic view) as shown in Figure 4.3.

FIGURE 4.3

Opening a drive icon displays its contents in a window. Here you see a portion of what I have on my C drive. Notice that folders (which used to be called directories in Windows 3.x) are listed first. Scrolling the listing would reveal files. Here we are in essence looking at the root directory of my C drive. Clicking a folder will reveal its contents.

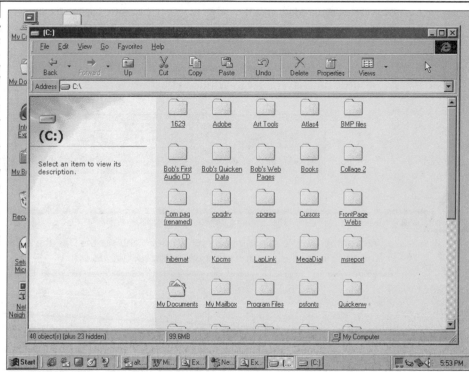

4. The object is to locate the folder containing the program you want and open it. (Some programs are so ferreted away that it's difficult to find them. You may have to search around a bit.) The standard setting shows folders and files as *large icons*. If you want to see more folders on the screen at once to help in your search, you have several options. The large icon view can be annoying because it doesn't let you see very many objects at once. Check out the View menu, and choose Small Icons, or better yet, click on the little arrow next to the View button in the tool bar a couple of times.

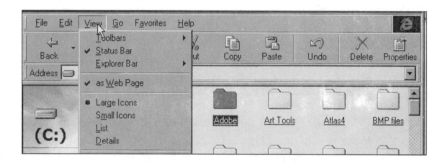

5. Choose Small Icons, List, or Details. *Details* will show the sizes of files and other information about the files and folders, such as the date they were created. This is useful when looking for applications because the Type column will indicate whether the file is an application program.

You can simply click repeatedly on the View button to cycle through the available views.

Pressing Backspace while in any folder window will move you back one level. While in the C drive window, for example, pressing Backspace takes you back to the My Computer window. Or, if you're looking at a directory, Backspace will take you up to the root level. The UP button on the toolbar works, too. And the Back and Forward buttons work just like they do in Help, as discussed in the last chapter. They'll move you forward and back through folders you've already visited.

6. When you see the program you want to run, click on it. For example, in Figure 4.4 I've found PhotoEnhancer.

FIGURE 4.4

*Run a program
by clicking its icon.
Regardless of
whether the view
is Large Icons,
Small Icons, List,
or Detailed view,
clicking (or double-
clicking in Classic
view) will run it.*

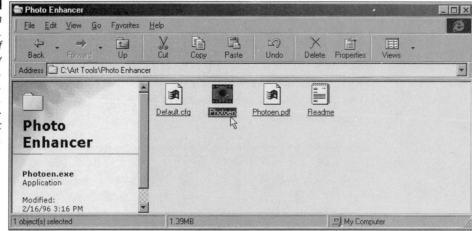

Note that many of the files you'll find in your folders are *not* programs. They are documents or other kinds of files that are used by programs. Programs tend to have specialized icons such as the one for PhotoEnhancer in Figure 4.4. Documents, as you will learn later, tend to look a bit different.

Normally, files with some specific extensions (the last three letters of a file's name) are hidden from display. Files with d11, sys, vxd, 386, drv, and cp1 extensions will not display. Nor will "hidden" system files and directories. This choice was made to prevent cluttering the display with files that perform duties for the operating system but not directly for users. It also prevents meddling with files that could affect how the system runs. If you want to see all the files and folders on your machine, do this: From a folder's window choose View ➢ Folder Options ➢ View and turn on Show all Files. In Chapter 5 I'll explain all the options you can use when displaying folder windows.

Running a Program from the Explorer or File Manager

On the Mac, all you get to work with to organize your documents and programs is folders—essentially the same arrangement the last section illustrated. This approach can be annoying when what you want is a grand overview of your hard disk's contents. Working your way through a lot of folder windows can get tedious and can clutter up the screen too much to be efficient. If you're running in Web view, when you open a folder the existing window is used to display the contents. (This is just like browsing the Web. When you click a link on a Web page, usually no new window appears. Only the window's content changes.) But in Classic view, you see a new window each time you double-click a folder. There are ways to reduce the resulting clutter when using this approach, as I'll explain in Chapter 5.

Regardless of view, if you're the kind of person who prefers the *tree* approach (a hierarchical display of your disk's contents) to your PC's hard disk, you might find the Windows Explorer a better means of running programs and finding documents. I'll be covering Explorer in depth in Chapter 12. But in the meantime, I'll explain how to run your programs using these two supplied applications.

The trick to using either of these two programs is that you need to know a little more about what's going on in your computer than many people care to. Principally, you'll need to know where your programs are located and what their names are. For example, Word for Windows is really called word.exe on the hard disk and is typically stored in the Program Files\Microsoft Office\Office directory, the C:\Winword directory, or Msoffice\Winword directory.

NOTE

Although not featured, the old-style Windows 3.*x* File Manager is actually supplied as part of Windows 98. It's not listed on the Start button menu, but it's most likely on your hard disk. Click Start ➤ Run, type **winfile** and press Enter.

Here's how to use Explorer to run your programs (I'll explain File Manager next):

1. Because Explorer is a program itself, you have to run it before you can use it to run other programs. So click on the Start button, choose Programs, and point to Windows Explorer as shown in Figure 4.5.

FIGURE 4.5

To run Windows Explorer, click on Start, then Programs, then Windows Explorer.

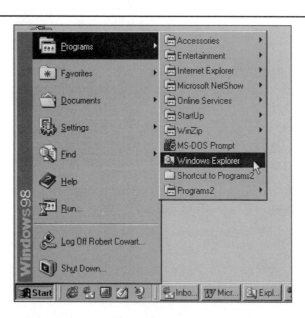

TIP

Another way to run Explorer is to right-click on My Computer or a drive's icon in the My Computer window and choose Explore.

2. When the Explorer window comes up, adjust the window size for your viewing pleasure. It should look something like Figure 4.6.

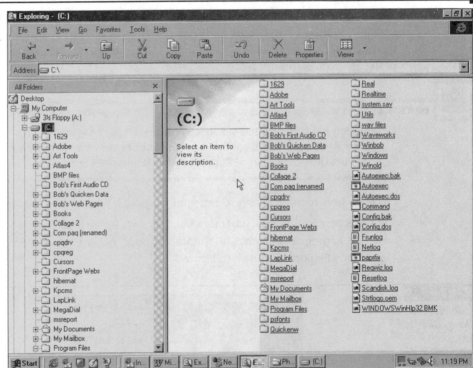

3. The items on the left side are folders. Scroll down to the folder that contains the program you're looking for (folders are listed in alphabetical order). If a folder has a + sign next to it, it has subfolders. Clicking on the + sign displays the names of any subfolders.

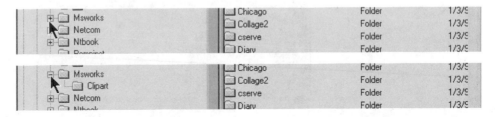

4. Single-click on the folder containing the program you want to run. Its contents will appear in the right-hand side (called the right *pane*) of the window.

5. Then click or double-click on the program. Here I'm about to run Microsoft Works.

Notice that the items in the right-hand pane are displayed as large icons. Just as when using folders, you can change the appearance of listed items by clicking the View button, using the little list next to the View button, or opening the View menu and choosing Large Icons, Small Icons, List, or Details. It's easier to see which file is a program when the display is set to Large Icons (because you can see the icon clearly) or Details (because the third column will say *application* if the file is a program).

Running a Program from File Manager

As I said above, the File Manager as we all knew it and love/hated it in Windows 3.*x* is alive and well in Windows 98. It's just sort of hidden. It's not on the Start button's menu, but you can run it with the Run command, which *is* on the Start button's menu.

File Manager is a useful tool for a number of tasks, including running programs. Although the Windows Explorer is more supercharged, File Manager is charming because of its simplicity. It doesn't confuse the issue by displaying everything in your computer including the kitchen sink. It works much the same way as Explorer, but the display is simpler. Unfortunately, File Manager doesn't display long file names, so long names will be shortened and have lots of tildes (~) in them.

To use File Manager to run a program:

1. Click on the Start button and choose Run.

2. In the resulting box, type **winfile** and click on OK.

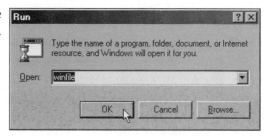

3. File Manager runs and appears in a window. Maximize the window, and File Manager will display as shown in Figure 4.7.

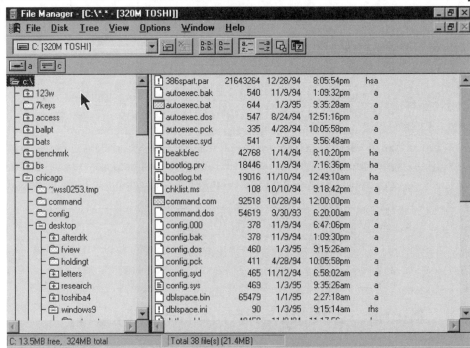

4. Select the folder you want by clicking on it. Normally, you won't see any indication of which folders have subfolders (subdirectories) under them. To see an indication of subfolders, you have to open the File Manager's Tree menu and choose Indicate Expandable Branches. After that, folders that have subfolders will be indicated by a + sign. Double-click on a + to display its subdirectories.

Even without the + sign showing, you can double-click on a folder to see any existing subfolders.

5. Scroll the display as necessary to show the name of the program you want to run. Programs have a special icon so you know which ones can be run. Here I'm about to run Works.

6. Double-click on the program file you want to run (regardless of whether you're using Web view or Classic view).

NOTE

As a general rule, four kinds of files can be run using this method: those with extensions of exe, com, bat, and pif. All other files will either not run when double-clicked or will run their *associated* programs and load into them. For example, files with the extension bmp are graphics. Double-clicking on such a file (e.g., arches.bmp) will run the Paint program and load the graphic into the Paint window for editing.

Up and Running

Running a Program from Ye Olde Program Manager

If you're a Windows 3.*x* veteran, you might be most at home running your programs from the good old Program Manager. That's the program organizer that was supplied with Windows 3.*x* and is now essentially replaced by the Start button's submenus. To get 3.*x* users over the hurdle of learning the new Win98 interface, Microsoft included Program Manager. Like File Manager, though, it's hidden away.

As I mentioned earlier, when you install a new program onto your computer (see Chapter 5), the new program usually creates what's called a *program group.* A program group is a window that contains items pertaining to the program, such as the program's icon (for running it), various Readme files, a Help file, and so forth. To run a program from Program Manager, you just open the desired window and double-click on the icon you want. It's the old version of Windows 98's Start menus, which are easier to get to.

When you install Windows 98 over an existing Windows 3.*x* setup, it pulls all your preexisting Program Manager groups and icons into the Start button's Program lists. So clicking Start ➤ Programs will list your Program Manager groups.

Enough theory. Try this to run Program Manager:

1. Click on the Start button.

TIP

You can press Ctrl-Esc to open the Start list from the keyboard at any time.

2. Choose Run. In the Run box enter **progman**.

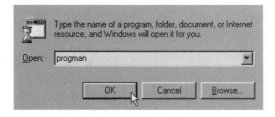

3. Click on OK, and you'll see your old familiar Program Manager. Figure 4.8 illustrates.

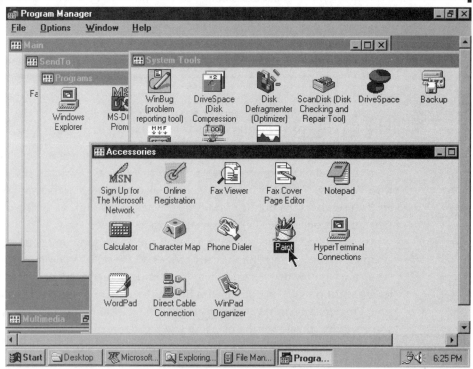

FIGURE 4.8

In Program Manager, double-clicking on a program's icon runs the program.

4. The trick with Program Manager is that you have to find and display a group's window before you can run a program in it. If the screen is cluttered, sometimes the easiest way to do this is simply by opening the Window menu and choosing from there. Of course, you could just click on the window if it's in view, but the Window menu approach is a no-brainer.

5. Once you've chosen the desired group, its window appears. Then double-click on the icon of the program you want to run. In Figure 4.8, for example, I'm about to run Paint from the Accessories group.

Running Applications from the Find Command

The Find command is covered in detail in Part V of this book, but I'll quickly mention how to use this indispensable little gadget. As with File Manager and Explorer, it helps if you know the file name of the program you're looking for, but at least Find cuts you some slack if you don't know the whole name. You can specify just part of it. Find will search a given disk or the whole computer (multiple disks) looking for something that looks like the program (or other file, such as a document) name you tell it. Once found, you can double-click on the program in the resulting list, and it will run. Pretty spiffy.

TIP

The Run box technique (described above) is easier than Find if you know the exact name of the program. But the catch is that Run requires the program to be in the DOS *search path.* If it's not, the program won't run and you'll just get an error message saying the program can't be found. Of course, if you know the drive and directory the program is in, you *can* enter its entire path name, in which case it will probably run.

Here's an example. I have the program called Dunmon somewhere on my computer. It's a program that doesn't have its own setup program so it never got added it my Start menus. I could do that manually, as you'll learn how to do later, but I'm too lazy to do that for all the programs I have. So I use the Find command. Why not the Run command? Well, the Run command won't run this program because Dunmon is stored in a folder that's not in my DOS search path. All I get when I try to find it is this message:

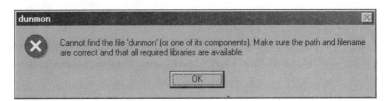

So I cancel the Run dialog box and try the Find command. Here's how:

NOTE

From here on out, I'm going to rely more heavily on the shorthand notation to describe making multiple menu choices. Instead of: "Click on the Start button, choose Programs, then choose Accessories, and then choose Paint," I'll say: "Choose Start ➢ Programs ➢ Accessories ➢ Paint."

1. Choose Start ➢ Find ➢ Folders and Files.

2. The Find dialog box appears, and I fill in the top part with at least a portion of the name of the file I'm looking for. (See Figure 4.9—I've enlarged the Find window to show you as much information as possible.) Note that I've set the *Look In* section to My Computer. As a default it will search your C drive, which is usually fine unless you have multiple hard disks on your computer and want Find to comb through them all.

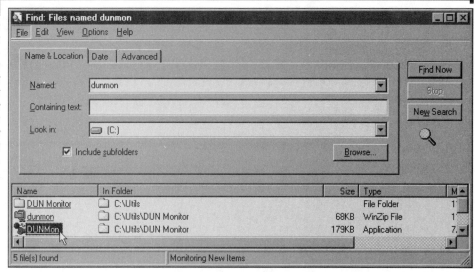

3. I click on Find Now. In a few seconds any files or folders matching the search request show up in the bottom pane, as the figure illustrates. Note that several Dunmon files were located, but that only one is an application (a program).

4. I click on the Dunmon application, and it runs.

   If you're running in Classic mode, be careful not to double-click on a file name slowly (click-one, second-click). If you do, this tells Windows that you want to change the object's name. You know this has happened when a little box appears around the name of the file like this:

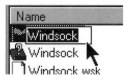

   Just press Esc to get out of editing mode. To be safe, it's better to click on any item's icon (the picture portion) when you want to run it, open it, move it around, and so forth.

Running a Program via One of Its Documents

As I mentioned above, some documents will open up when you click on their icons—if they are *registered*. Windows 98 has an internal registry (basically just a list) of file extensions that it knows about. Each registered file type is matched with a program that it works with. When you double-click on any document, Windows scans the list of registered file types to determine what it should do with the file. For example, clicking on a bmp file will run Paint and load the file.

The upshot of this is that you can run an application by clicking (or double-clicking in Classic view) on a document of a known registered type. For example, suppose I want to run Word. All I have to do is spot a Word document somewhere. It's easy to spot one, especially in Large Icon view, because all Word documents have Word's telltale identifying icon. Unregistered documents have no discernible icon. Check out Figure 4.10. There I'm about to double-click on a Word document I came across in a folder. Notice that the icon just above it is what an unregistered file icon looks like.

FIGURE 4.10

Double-clicking on a file of a registered type runs the program that created it.

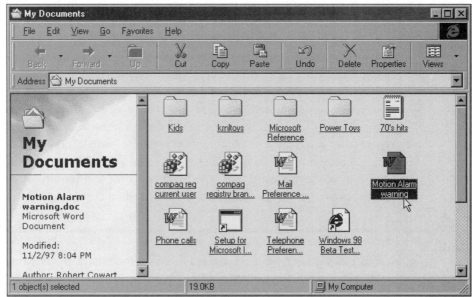

Once the program runs, you may decide you don't want to work with the actual document that you used as a trick to get the program going. That's OK because most programs will let you close the current document (try choosing File ➤ Close) and then let you open a new document (usually via File ➤ New) or an existing one with File ➤ Open.

TIP

Try clicking on the Start button and choosing Documents to see a list of the files you've recently edited. Depending on what's on the list, you may be able to run the program you're looking for.

TECH TIP

By default, file extensions of registered files are not displayed on screen. This cuts down on visual clutter, letting you see simple names that make sense, such as 1995 Report instead of 1995 Report.wk3. In later chapters I'll tell you how to turn off this option in case you always want to see and be able to change extensions at will.

How Do File Types Become Registered?

You may be wondering how documents with certain extensions become registered so they will run an application when double-clicked on. Some types are set up by Windows 98 when you install it. For example, hlp files (e.g., paint.hlp) are Help files and will open up in an appropriate window. Likewise, txt files will open in Notepad, pcx files in Paint, doc files in WordPad, ht files in HyperTerminal, and so on.

In addition to those extensions that are automatically established, some others might have been imported into your system from an earlier version of Windows. If you've upgraded to Windows 98 from Windows 3.*x*, then any previously registered types (called *associations* in Windows 3.*x*) are pulled into Windows 98.

Some programs register their file type when you install the program. So, for example, when you install Word, Windows 98 changes the registration list so that doc files will be opened by Word instead of by WordPad when clicked on.

TIP

You can register a file type yourself from any folder or Explorer window's View ➢ Options ➢ File Types command (see Chapter 5).

Running an Application by Right-Clicking on the Desktop

When you don't want to bother finding some favorite program just to create a new document, there's an easier way. How often have you simply wanted to create a To Do list, a shopping list, a brief memo, little spreadsheet, or what have you? All the time, right? Microsoft figured out that people often work in just this way—they don't think: "Gee, I'll root around for Excel, then I'll run it, and then I'll create a new spreadsheet file and save it and name it." That's counterintuitive. On the contrary, it's more likely they think: "I need to create a 'Sales for Spring Quarter' Excel spreadsheet."

Just create a new *empty* document of the correct type on the Desktop and name it. Then clicking on it will run the correct program. Windows 98 takes care of assigning the file the correct extension so that internally the whole setup works. Try an experiment to see what I'm talking about.

1. Clear off enough windows so you can see your Desktop area.

TIP

Remember, you can click on the Show Desktop button in the Taskbar to minimize all the open windows. You can reverse the effect and return all the windows to view by clicking on the button again.

2. Right-click anywhere on the Desktop. From the resulting menu choose New. You'll see a list of possible document types. The types in my computer are shown in Figure 4.11 as an example.

FIGURE 4.11

You can create a variety of new document types by right-clicking on the Desktop. This creates a blank document that you then name and run.

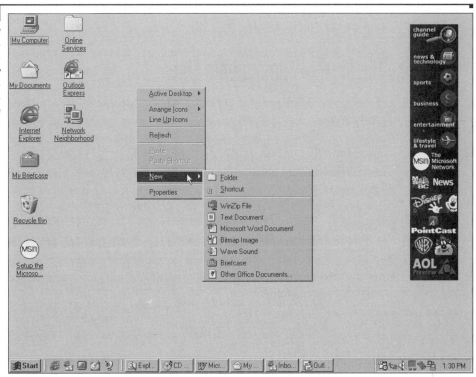

3. Choose a document type from the list by clicking on it. A new document icon appears on your Desktop such as this one that appeared when I chose *Text Document*:

4. The file's name is highlighted and has a box around it. This means you can edit the name. As long as the whole name is highlighted, whatever you type will replace the entire name. When you create a new document this way, you don't have to worry about entering the extension. For example, a text file normally has a txt extension, but you could just type in **Shopping List** for the name and press Enter (remember, you have to press Enter after typing in the name to finalize it). The actual file name will be Shopping List.txt because Windows 98 adds a hidden file extension for you.

5. Double-click on the icon and its associated program will run. In the case of the text file, the Notepad program will run, open the new file, and wait for me to start typing in my shopping list.

Using the Start ➤ Documents List

As I mentioned in a Tip above, choosing Start ➤ Documents lists the documents you've recently created or edited. It's an easy way to revisit projects you've been working on. This list is maintained by Windows 98 and is *persistent*, which means it'll be there in subsequent Windows sessions, even after you shut down and reboot. Only the last fifteen documents are remembered, though, and some of these won't be things you'd think of as documents. Some of them might actually be more like programs or folders. Check it out and see if it contains the right stuff for you. Figure 4.12 shows my list the day I wrote this section.

Notice the My Documents choice at the top of this list. This is a shortcut to the My Documents folder on the desktop. That's a folder that some programs use to store documents you've created. Office 97, for example, defaults to storing your documents in the My Documents folder.

FIGURE 4.12

The Document list from the Start button provides a no-brainer path to ongoing work projects, but only the last 15 documents you viewed or edited are shown.

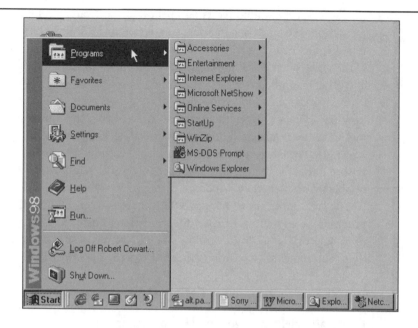

Many Windows programs have a similar feature that lists your most recently edited documents at the bottom of their File menus. Because many of my favorite programs sport this feature, I tend to rely on that more than on the Documents list.

You can clear off the items in the Documents list and start fresh if you want to. Click on the Start button, choose Settings ➢ Taskbar ➢ Start Menu Programs, and click on the Clear button.

Running DOS Programs

Though DOS applications are by no means the preponderant genre of PC programs being sold anymore, they certainly were for many years. Consequently, tens of thousands of useful and interesting programs exist for the IBM-PC DOS environment. Many of these programs are not easily replaced with popular Windows programs, because they were specialized programs custom designed for vertical market uses such as point of sale, transaction processing, inventory, scientific data gathering, and so on. It's safe to say that after a corporation invests significantly in software development, testing, implementation, and employee training, conversion to a Windows-based version just because it looks groovier isn't a very attractive proposition. As a result, much of the code that was written five to ten years ago and ran in DOS programs is still doing its job in companies and other institutions today.

If you're a gamer, you know that lots of games are actually written for DOS, even nowadays. Game programmers often want to control the computer like a miser controls money so their games will run as fast as possible, and so the hardware (game controllers, screen, etc.) will do exactly as they command without interference from Windows. The upshot is that plenty of games don't actually run *in* Windows, even though you might be able to run them *from* Windows.

The great thing about Windows 98 is that you can still run all those wonderful DOS programs, even multiple ones at the same time. And each can have its own DOS environment, tasking settings, window size and font, and so on, not to mention the ability to automate task execution and control with DOS *batch* files.

So How Do I Run My DOS Programs?

I'll explain briefly how you run DOS programs here.

First off, you can run DOS programs using most of the same techniques explained above, minus a few:

- clicking on the Start button, choosing Programs, and looking for the program on the resulting menus. It's not likely to be there unless you added it. (See Chapter 5)

- clicking on the program's name in a folder (pretty good method), File Manager or Windows Explorer

- entering the program's name at the Run command (acceptable method, but DOS path may be needed in command—cumbersome)

- running a "DOS session" and then typing in the program's name at the DOS prompt

- double-clicking on a document file with an extension that you've manually associated with the DOS program

I explained the first five of these techniques earlier when I told you how to run Windows programs. The only difference between running Windows programs and DOS programs using those techniques is that DOS programs don't normally have an identifying icon, such as a big "W" for Word. Instead, they tend to have a boring, generic icon that looks like:

Xtgold

Therefore, you have to rely on the icon's name alone. This one is for XTREE Gold, but because the actual program's name on disk is `xtgold.exe`, that's what you see. Well, actually, you don't see the `exe` part, because as I mentioned earlier, `exe` extensions are normally hidden from view.

Because the last two approaches in the above list differ from running Windows programs and haven't been covered, let's check those out. Then I'll tell you a bit about how DOS programs operate in Windows and what you can quickly do to modify their behavior.

First consider the option of running a DOS program from the good old DOS prompt.

NOTE

There isn't room in this book to discuss all the DOS commands and how DOS works. You should consult a book such as Sybex's *Mastering DOS 6.2* for more information about DOS commands. To get on-screen help with DOS, you can enter the command **help** at the DOS prompt and follow directions at that point.

To run a DOS session, do the following:

1. Click on the Start button.

2. Choose Programs, then MS-DOS Prompt, as shown in Figure 4.13.

FIGURE 4.13

Choose Start ➤ Programs ➤ MS-DOS Prompt to bring up a DOS command line.

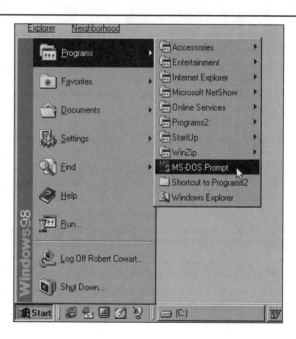

3. The result will be what's called a *DOS box*—a window that operates just like you're using a computer running DOS. Try typing in **DIR** and pressing Enter. You'll see a listing of files on the current drive, as shown in Figure 4.14. Note that short and long file names are both shown in this new version of DOS. Long file names are in the rightmost column, with corresponding short file names over on the left.

FIGURE 4.14

The DOS box lets you enter any standard DOS commands and see their output. Here you see the end of a DIR listing and the DOS prompt that follows it.

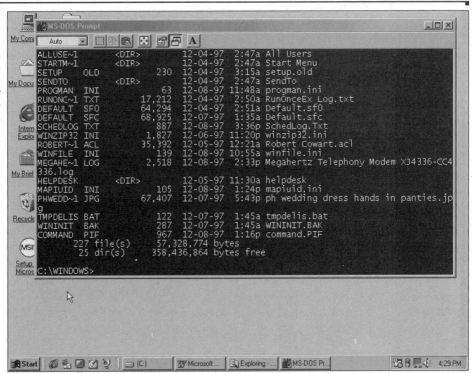

4. Enter the command **exit** when you are finished running DOS programs or executing DOS commands. This will close the DOS window and end the session.

NOTE

If no DOS program is actually running, clicking on the DOS window's Close button will also end the DOS session. If a DOS program is running, trying this results in a message prompting you to quit the DOS program first.

Options While Running a DOS Session

While running a DOS session, there are several easy adjustments you can make that are either cosmetic or actually affect the performance of the program. You can easily do any of the following:

- Toggle the DOS session between full screen and windowed.
- Turn the toolbar on or off.
- Adjust the font.
- Resize the DOS box.
- Allow the DOS session to work in the background.
- Cause the DOS session to take over the computer's resources when in the foreground.

Let me briefly discuss each of these options. Refer to Figure 4.14 for toolbar buttons.

First, if the DOS window is taking up the whole screen (all other elements of the Windows interface have disappeared) and you'd like to have the DOS program running in a window so you can see other programs, press Alt-Enter to switch it to a window. Once windowed, you can return it to full-screen mode either by clicking on the Full Screen button or pressing Alt-Enter again.

Next, you can turn on the toolbar if you want easy access to most of the nifty features. Then you won't have to use the menus. If you don't see the toolbar shown in Figure 4.14, click in the upper-left corner of the DOS window and choose Toolbar. (Choose the same command again, and the toolbar will turn off.)

Once the toolbar is showing, you can set several useful options. A nice feature in Windows 98 is the adjustable TrueType fonts you can use in a DOS box. The easiest way to change the font is to open the Font drop-down list (rather than clicking on the "A" button).

Fonts are listed there by the size of the character matrix (in pixels) that comprises each displayed character. The larger the matrix, the larger the resulting characters (and consequently the DOS box itself) will be. Setting the size to auto has the effect of scaling the font automatically if you resize the DOS box from its lower-left corner. When resizing, don't be surprised if the mouse pointer jumps around a bit wildly. The box is not infinitely adjustable as Windows programs are, so as you're adjusting, the outline of the window jumps to predetermined sizes.

NOTE

The *A* button on the toolbar lets you choose whether only bit-mapped fonts, TrueType fonts, or both will show in the Fonts listing on the left. By default, both types are available, giving you more size choices.

The Properties button we'll leave alone for the time being. Selections you make here are rather complicated and require some detailed discussion. So, moving right along, the other button of interest is the Background button which determines whether the DOS program will continue processing in the background when you switch to another program. By default, this setting is on. You can tell it's on because the button looks indented. You can turn it off if you want your DOS program to temporarily suspend when it isn't the active window (isn't the window in which you're currently working).

TECH TIP

The Exclusive button, seen on DOS boxes in Windows 95, has been removed for Windows 98. That button determined whether your DOS program, when in the foreground, would receive all of your CPU's attention, running as though there were no other programs running in the computer. Some programs—such as data-acquisition programs that expect total control of the computer, the screen, keyboard, ports, and so forth—may require this. If that's the case with your program, you'll have to run it in "MS-DOS mode" outside of Windows. The next section talks about more esoteric DOS-box settings such as this.

TIP

You can, of course, have multiple DOS sessions running at the same time in separate windows. This lets you easily switch between a number of DOS programs that can be running simultaneously.

NOTE

You can Copy and Paste data from and to DOS applications, using the Windows clipboard. See Chapter 6 for details.

Additional Property Settings for DOS Programs

DOS programs were designed to run one at a time and are usually memory hogs. They often need as much as 560K of free RAM, and some may require some additional expanded or extended memory to perform well. Since DOS programs think they don't have to coexist with other programs simultaneously, running a DOS program with several other programs (particularly other DOS programs) under Windows is conceptually like bringing a bunch of ill-mannered guests to a formal dinner.

The upshot is that Windows has a lot of housekeeping to do to keep DOS programs happy. When running from Windows, DOS programs don't really "know" that other programs are running, and they expect to have direct access to all the computer's resources: RAM, ports, screen, keyboard, disk drives, and so on.

In most cases, Windows 98 does pretty well at faking out DOS programs without your help, using various default settings and its own memory-management strategies. However, even Windows 98 isn't omniscient, and you may occasionally experience the ungracious locking up of a program or see messages about the "system integrity" having been corrupted.

TECH TIP

In reality, what Windows is doing when running DOS programs is giving each of them a simulated PC to work in, called a *VDM* (Virtual DOS Machine).

If a DOS program doesn't run properly under Windows 98 or you wish to optimize its performance, you must modify its PIF (Program Information File), declaring certain settings that affect the program within Windows. With Windows 3.*x*, making PIF settings for a program required using a program called the PIF Editor—a cumbersome program supplied with Windows. Things became simpler with Windows 95 and this carries over to Windows 98. Here's how it works: The first time you run a DOS program, a PIF is automatically created in the same directory as the DOS program. It has the same name as the program but looks like a shortcut icon. Examining the properties of the icon will reveal it has a .pif extension.

To adjust a program's PIF settings, simply open the Properties box for the DOS program and make the relevant settings. This can be done by running the DOS program in a window and clicking on the Properties button on the Toolbar or, without running the program, by right-clicking on its PIF icon and choosing Properties (but this requires finding the icon first, which is a hassle). When you close the Properties box, the new PIF settings are saved. From then on, those settings go into effect whenever you run the program from within Windows.

The PIF settings affect many aspects of the program's operation, such as, but not limited to:

- the file name and directory of the program
- font and window size
- the directory that becomes active once a program starts
- memory usage, including conventional, expanded, extended, and protected-mode memory usage
- multitasking priority levels
- video-adapter modes
- the use of keyboard shortcut keys
- foreground and background processing
- Toolbar display
- program-termination options

Some of these options were discussed above and are quickly adjustable from the DOS box Toolbar; others are not. To fine-tune the DOS environment for running a program:

- If the program will run without bombing:
  1. Run it as explained above.
  2. If it's not in a window, press Alt-Enter.
  3. Click on the Properties button if the Toolbar is showing or, if it isn't showing, click on the Control Box in the upper-left corner of the window and choose Properties.
- If the program won't run without bombing:
  1. Navigate with My Computer or Explorer to the folder containing the DOS program.
  2. Find the program's icon and click on it.
  3. Open the File menu and choose Create Shortcut. A new icon will appear in the folder, called "Shortcut to [*program*]."
  4. With the new shortcut highlighted, open the File menu and choose Properties.

Now you'll see the DOS program's Properties sheet, from which you can alter quite a healthy collection of settings (Figure 4.15). Unfortunately, there isn't room in this book for an explanation of all the settings available from this box. Remember, you can get some basic information about each setting via the ? button in the upper-right corner. Click on it, then on the exact button, line, or option in question.

FIGURE 4.15

*The Properties box
for the program
XTreePro Gold*

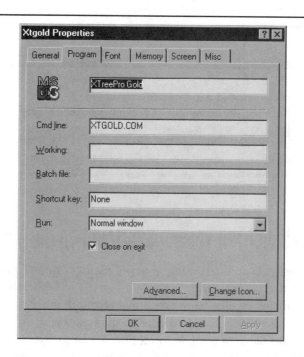

Simply make your settings as necessary. When you're happy with them, click on OK in the Properties box to save the settings. The next time you run the program by double-clicking on the shortcut or the program's icon, the settings will go into effect.

TECH TIP

When you run a DOS program by clicking on its icon or its PIF icon, the PIF settings go into effect and the program runs. However, if you run the program from the DOS command line (by typing in a command from a DOS box), the settings *don't* go into effect. *They simply aren't used.* Two other ways to ensure they are used are to use the Run command and enter the name of the PIF, such as ed.pif, and to use the Start command from the DOS prompt (e.g., **start ed.exe**). Also, aside from the active directory, only directories listed in the search path as set up by your autoexec.bat file are scanned for PIFs. If a PIF isn't found when a program is double-clicked on, it won't be loaded, and Window's default PIF settings will be used instead.

If you are having trouble getting a DOS program to even open, check that the memory settings for the PIF match those required by the program (check the program's user manual), and if the program can't run in a window, set the screen usage to Full Screen.

PIFs are one of two types of shortcut files. Shortcuts for Windows applications and documents are given the LNK extension. Only shortcuts for DOS applications actually are given the PIF extension. Even if you elect to display the MS-DOS extensions of all files (from the View ➤ Options menu in Explorer or a folder), you won't see the PIF extension in listings. Use the Find utility to look for PIFs by extension, if you need to.

What I Didn't Tell You—Shortcuts on the Desktop

When it comes to running your programs, Windows 98 has a spiffy feature called *shortcuts*. (If you haven't used Windows 95 or a Mac, this will be a new concept.) Shortcuts are alias icons (icons that represent other icons) that you can add almost anywhere, such as in folders or on the Desktop, or on the Task Bar's quick launch toolbar (later for that). The neat thing about shortcuts is that since they're really only a link or pointer to the real file or application it represents, you can have as many as you want, putting them wherever your heart desires, without duplicating your files and using up lots of hard disk space. So, for example, you can have shortcuts to all your favorite programs right on the Desktop. Then you can run them from there without having to click on the Start button, walk through the Program listings, and so forth as we've been doing.

In Chapter 5 I'll explain how you make, copy, and place shortcuts. I'll also cover how you can dump shortcuts of your favorite programs onto the Start button so they are right there on the first menu when you click on Start.

Automating Jobs with Batch Files

Because I am not a 200-word-per-minute typist, I like to create batch files to automate repetitive jobs or to create jobs to run at Windows start-up. For instance, if you want to automate the process of checking your hard disk for errors with ScanDisk every time you start Windows 98, try this:

1. Open up Notepad (Start ➤ Programs ➤ Notepad) or any other ASCII text editor.

2. To check just your C: drive, enter the following text:

```
SCANDISK C: /n
```

To check all of your local disk drives, enter the following text:

```
SCANDISK /a /n
```

3. Save the file with a .bat file extension. For instance, you might want to save it as Check Disk Drives for Errors.bat.

4. Then add this item to the Startup folder so that Windows 98 will run it every time you start it (see Chapter 5 for complete instructions on how to do this).

5. The check will now run automatically every time you start Windows 98. You can also run it anytime you desire by selecting it from the Start menu.

The really nice part about this process is that you can do this to automate any job. And you can make the process completely automatic by adding the batch file to the Startup group (as we did above), or you can choose to manually run it whenever you select it from the Start menu. For instance, I could have created a new folder under the Programs folder, called it Batch Jobs, and placed the Check Disk for Errors batch file there. Then anytime I wanted to run this process I would select Start ➤ Programs ➤ Batch Jobs ➤ Check Disk. You can use this same process to automate any job or start up multiple applications to create your daily working set. For instance, I could have created a batch file to launch Microsoft Mail, Schedule Plus, Word for Windows, and Excel all at once. This would save several mouse or keystroke commands because I would not have to return to the Start menu to launch them individually.

Switching between Applications

Remember, Windows lets you have more than one program open and running at a time. You can also have multiple folders open at any time, and you can leave them open to make getting to their contents easier. Any folders that are open when you shut down the computer will open again when you start up Windows again.

People often think they have to shut down one program before working on another one, but that's really not efficient nor true. When you run each new program or open a folder, the Taskbar gets another button on it. As you know from Chapter 3, simply clicking on a button switches you to that program or folder. For the first several programs, the buttons are long enough to read the names of the programs or folder. As you run more programs, the buttons automatically get shorter, so the names are truncated. For example:

You can resize the Taskbar to give it an extra line or two of buttons if you want to see the full names. On the upper edge of the Taskbar, position the cursor so that it turns into a double-headed arrow (this takes some careful aiming). Then drag it upwards a half inch or and inch and release. Here I've added an additional line for my current set of buttons:

Obviously as you increase the size of the Taskbar, you decrease the effective size of your work area. On a standard VGA screen, this means you'll be cutting onto your work area quite a bit if you go to two or three lines. On SVGA or SGA screens, the impact will be less.

Another nice feature is that you can set the Taskbar to disappear until you move the mouse pointer down to the bottom of the screen. This way, you sacrifice nothing in the way of screen real estate (see below).

TIP

If you prefer, you can also position the Taskbar on the right, left, or top of the screen. Just click on any part of the Taskbar other than a button and drag it to the edge of your choice.

Here's how to set the Taskbar options:

1. Choose Start ➢ Settings ➢ Taskbar.

2. You'll now see the dialog box shown in Figure 4.16. Click on *Auto hide* to turn that option on—this is the one that makes the Taskbar disappear until you move the pointer to the edge of the screen where you've placed the Taskbar.

FIGURE 4.16

You set the Taskbar options from this box. The most likely choice you'll make will be Auto Hide.

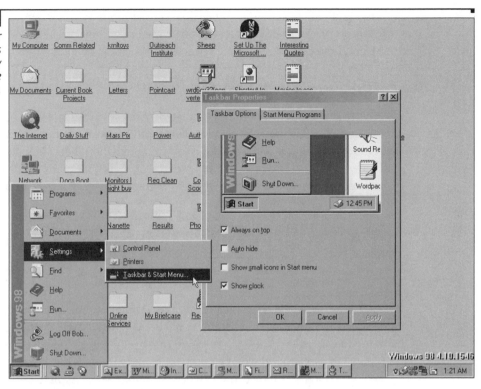

TIP

A quick way to get to the Taskbar's Property settings is to right-click on an empty area of the Taskbar and choose Properties.

3. If you'd like to see smaller icons in the first Start-up menu, set that option on, too.

4. OK the dialog box. Once you do so, the Taskbar will disappear. Try out the Auto Hide setting: Move the pointer down to the bottom and see how the Taskbar reappears.

TECH TIP

Even when set to Auto Hide, the Taskbar still uses one or two pixels (a very small area) at the edge of the screen to indicate where it is and to act as a trigger zone to pop up the Taskbar when the pointer touches it.

The Taskbar has become a very flexible animal in the Windows 98. Just like the toolbars on the Internet Explorer (if you've used that), you can add or remove various toolbars, and reposition them. I'll cover this in the next chapter.

Switching with Alt-Tab

Don't like the Taskbar? Are you a habituated Windows 3.*x* user? Okay. As you may know, there's another way to switch between programs and folders—the Alt-Tab trick. Press down the Alt key and hold it down. Now, press the Tab key (you know, that key just above the Caps Lock and to the left of the Q). You'll see a box in the center of your screen showing you an icon of each program or folder that's running, like this:

Each press of the Tab key will advance the outline box one notch to the right. The outline box indicates which program you'll be switched to when you release the Alt key. If you want to back up one program (move the box to the left), you can press Alt-Shift-Tab. Note that the name of the program or folder is displayed at the bottom of the box, which is especially useful when choosing folders, as all folders look the same.

Chapter

5

Organizing Your Programs and Documents

FEATURING

Setting up your Start button menus

Using the Quick Launch bar

Moving, copying, and deleting

Moving a file to a floppy disk

Creating shortcuts

Putting shortcuts on the Desktop

Customizing Folder views

Using the Recycle Bin

Organizing Your Programs and Documents

I n this chapter, we'll explore the best way to organize your own work within Windows 98 and just what steps to take to do so. I'll tell you how to use the Taskbar, the Windows 95 folder system, and the Explorer to arrange your programs and documents so you can get to them easily. With the techniques I'll show you in this chapter, you'll be ready to set up new folders and move your work files into them—just like setting up a new filing cabinet in your office. You'll also learn how to put your programs and projects on the Startup menus as well as on the Desktop so they are within easy reach.

Putting Your Favorite Programs on the Start Button

One thing every Windows user is bound to benefit from is knowing how to put their favorite programs and documents right on the Start button's menu. True, you can put your programs, folders, and documents on the Desktop and just click on them to use them. But it's sometimes a hassle to get back to the Desktop, because it can be obscured by whatever windows you might have open. Although there are ways around this (as in click on the Desktop icon near the Start button), dropping your favorite items on the Start button's first menu is easier. For example, Figure 5.1 shows you what my Start button's menu currently looks like.

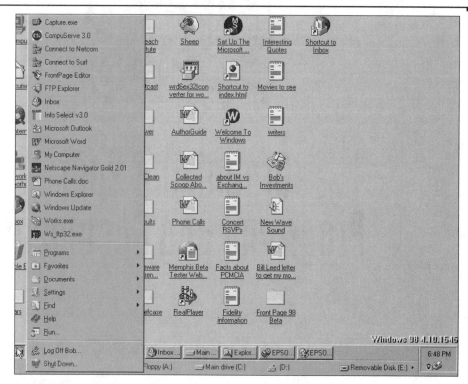

With a single click of the mouse, no matter what I'm doing in Windows with my other programs, I can quickly see the programs, folders, and documents I use most and open them.

As with most things in Windows, there are several ways to add items to the Start menu. I'll show you the two that are the most straightforward—dragging onto the Start button, and using the Start ➤ Settings ➤ Taskbar ➤ Start Menu Programs command. The first technique is simply to drag the application, folder, or document's icon onto the Start button. Windows will then create a *shortcut* and place the shortcut on the Start button's opening menu.

NOTE

As mentioned in Chapter 4, a shortcut is not the application, folder, or document's *real* icon, it's a pointer to that icon. The result is the same either way. Clicking on a shortcut has the same effect as clicking on the object's original icon. In the case of the Start button's menu, choosing the shortcut item from the menu will run the application, open the folder, or open the document.

1. First, you'll need to find an icon that represents the object you want to put on the menu. The icon can be a shortcut icon or the original icon, either in a folder, on the Desktop, in the Find box, in Windows Explorer, or displayed in any other window that supports drag-and-drop techniques. The Find box is probably the easiest: If you know the name of the file or document you're looking for just do a search using Start ➣ Find.

2. Once you've located the object you want to add, drag it over the Start button and then release the mouse button. Figure 5.2 shows an example of adding a program to the Start button. I'm dragging a program called Capture from the Collage 2 folder to the Start button.

FIGURE 5.2

Dragging from a folder to the Start button is simple. Just find the object you want to add, drag it over the Start button, and release.

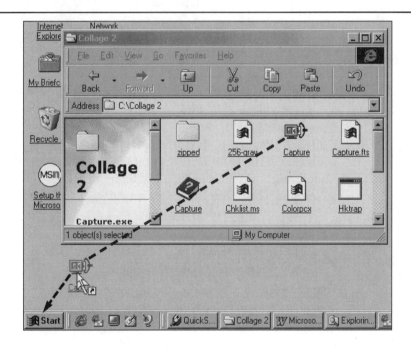

3. Now when you open the Start menu, you'll see the object has been added at the top of the list.

That's the easiest way to add new items to the Start button. You can also drag objects *off* the Start menu, but it follows a slightly different approach (see "Removing an Item from a Menu," later in the chapter).

Quick Launch and Other New Taskbar Features

As of Windows 98, the Taskbar has a few new features. For starters you can plop additional useful toolbars, icons, and folders on it. Do this by right-clicking on the clock area, and choose Toolbars. Then choose the toolbar you want to add to the Taskbar.

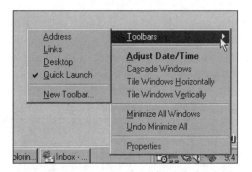

- **Address** adds an address area in which you can type in Web addresses or local resource addresses (for files, folders, or even network resources). This serves the same purpose as the Address bar in a folder window or a Windows Explorer / Internet Explorer window. An appropriate window will appear when you enter a resource name and press Enter. Typically you'll use this for Web page addresses, but you could enter **My Computer** to see your My Computer folder; **command.com** to get a DOS box; **printers** to see the printers folder; or **c:** to see the contents of your hard disk.

- **Links** adds a toolbar containing the same quick links that are currently set up in your Internet Explorer's Links bar. Clicking on a link brings up or switches you to IE, then connects to the predetermined website.

- **Desktop** adds a new row on the bar, containing replicas of all the icons you have on your desktop. If you have a cluttered desktop, this is sort of useless: If space is crammed on your Desktop, having all that stuff on your Taskbar will be worse!

- **Quick Launch** (which may already be checked) adds the Internet Explorer, Desktop, and Channels icons, typically to the immediate right of the Start Button. (We'll cover Explorer and Channels in the Internet section of the book.) Actually, you can add shortcuts to anything on your Quick Launch bar. This is an even faster way to run your favorite staple of programs, documents, folders, etc., than the Start menu is.

- **New Toolbar** gives you a Browse box to choose a folder or other item (such as a hard disk—its folders will appear, or Control Panel, or whatever). Note that if there are too many items to display at once, you'll have little scroll arrows on the toolbar row at least, so with a little work you can scroll through all the goodies on your Taskbar.

Of all the options, the Quick Launcher and Address are really the best. Also, I find adding the Control Panel (via the New Toolbar option) to be useful, since I do lots of system "tweaking" and access the Control Panel frequently.

As you turn on items, they are added to the Taskbar as sliders, looking like this:

You can grab any of the sliders and drag left or right to resize them and see the contents of the particular toolbar. With all the items I have added in the example, this would be an annoyance. Better to drag the top of the Taskbar up (as I showed you in Chapter 4) to give the toolbars more room to display their contents. If you work at it, you can construct a very unruly Taskbar like the one in Figure 5.3, which I provide only as an illustration of the possibilities (don't try to live with these settings!).

FIGURE 5.3

You can add new rows to the Taskbar. Here you see a barrage of new toolbars.

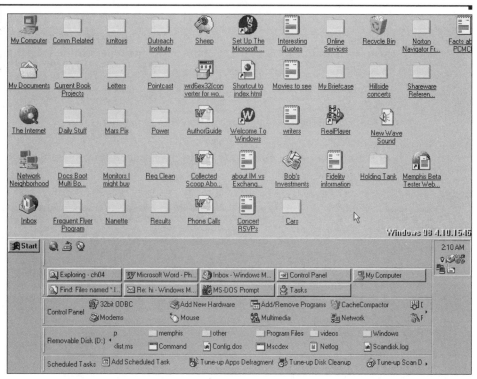

In addition to the sliders, the location of the toolbars is adjustable, in the same way as the toolbars at the top of Internet Explorer: you can move sections around by dragging them. For example, in Figure 5.3, I could exchange the position of the Control Panel row and the My Documents rows. Try sliding sections around, and with some luck, you'll be able to reposition them. It's a little tricky. You move a toolbar by dragging the slider (notice the pointer position in the graphic above the last paragraph) and drag the slider up or down. The toolbar will jump into the row above or below.

The Quick Launch toolbar is turned on by default when Windows 98 is installed, with a few items on it.

But you can add your own, and make it really easy to run your favorite programs:

Just drag items from folders, Windows Explorer, the Find box, the Desktop, even from the Control Panel (Control Panel is covered in Chapter 7), and drop them to the Quick Launch bar. Once on the bar, you can drag the icons left and right to rearrange them if you want to. Don't worry about accidentally relocating something important. These are only shortcuts you're creating on the Quick Launch bar. You can't damage anything. If you decide you want to remove an item from the bar, right-click on it and choose Delete.

To run an item on the Quick Launch bar, just click on it.

Remember you can add folders as well as programs, so if you have a favorite folder containing your work, for example, just drag its icon onto the bar. (Notice the folder example in the graphic above.)

TIP

Items on the Quick Launch bar don't have text names, so how do you remember what they do? Folders are especially confusing since they all look identical. Just let the mouse rest over the icon for a moment and its name will appear. Then click once if you're sure it's the one you want.

Modifying the Start Button Menus

When you want a little more control over what you're adding to the Start menu, there's a command for it. This command also lets you add to and remove items from submenu folders. Here's how it works.

1. Click on Start and choose Settings ➢ Taskbar & Start Menu.

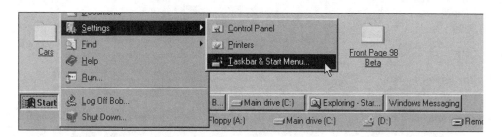

2. You now see a dialog box like the one shown in Figure 5.4. Click on the Start Menu Programs tab, then on OK.

FIGURE 5.4

The Start menu setup is reached from this tab.

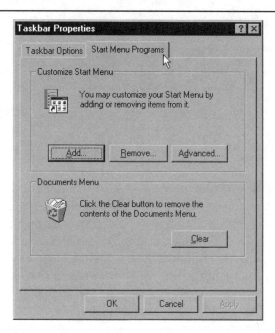

3. Now you see a box from which you can choose Add, Delete, or Advanced. Click on Add.

4. The result is a Wizard dialog box that guides you though choosing the program you want to add (Figure 5.5).

The Wizard walks you through adding an item to your Start button menu or submenus. Just fill in the name of the item or use the Browse button. Browse is probably easier.

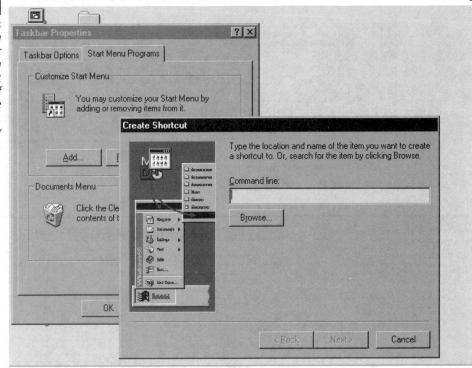

5. If you know the name of the item, just enter it into the box. The problem is that you need to know the full path name of the item or it must be in your DOS search path. Otherwise, when you click on Next, you'll be told the file can't be found. Any program in the DOS root directory, your Windows directory, or DOS directory will work even without a full path name entered. For example, entering **scandisk** will work fine without specifying its full path name, which is \Windows\Command\scandisk.exe. To make life easier on yourself and cut down on possible typing or naming mistakes, click on the Browse button and browse for the item graphically. You'll see a typical File box. Normally, the box only displays *programs*. But if you're trying to add a *document* to your Start button menu, open the *Files of type:* drop-down list and choose All Files. When you find the item you want, click on it, then click on Open.

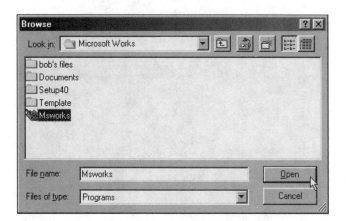

 **TECH TIP**

What if instead of adding a *program* or *document* to a Start menu you want to add a *folder?* Doing this can give you a shortcut to that folder as one of the options on your Start menu. The only catch is that you can't do it from the Browse box. You have to go back to Step 4. If the Browse box is open, close it by clicking on Cancel. Then enter the full path name of the folder.

6. Now you're back to the Create Shortcut dialog box. Your item's name is now typed in. Click on Next.

7. You'll see a large dialog box asking which folder you want the shortcut added to (Figure 5.6). Note that those listed in the box are the same folders and subfolders that are included on your Start ➢ Programs menu. As you can see, there's a lot of flexibility here. At this point you can choose to add the shortcut to any existing folder, to the Desktop, or to the Start menu. You can even create a new folder if you want to by clicking on New Folder. Just scroll the list and click on the folder you want to add the item to. If you're going to create a new folder, you have to decide where you want it to be added. For example, if I wanted to add a sub-folder under Berneze (see Figure 5.6), I'd first click on Berneze, then click on the New Folder button. A new folder is added there, waiting for me to edit its name.

FIGURE 5.6

Choose which group or other location the new shortcut will be added to. If you want the item on the Start menu, choose Start Menu. To put the folder on the Desktop, scroll up to the top of the list.

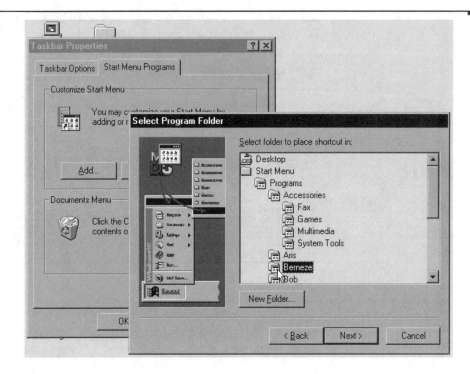

8. Click on Next.

9. Now you're asked to name your shortcut. This is thoughtful because it's more informative to have a menu item called *Word Perfect 5.1* than *WP51.EXE*. (When you just drop an icon on the Start button, incidentally, you're stuck with whatever name the icon has.) Enter the name you want, but don't make it incredibly long because that will widen the menu appreciably, possibly making it difficult to fit on the screen.

10. Click on Finish.

11. Back at the Taskbar Properties dialog box, click on Close. The new items should now appear in the location(s) you chose.

A few points to consider: If you chose to add the item to the Desktop, it would appear there, not on one of the menus. Also, note that you can add more than one item to your lists at a time. Rather than closing the Taskbar Properties box in step 11, just click on Add and do the whole megillah over again for your next item, starting from step 2.

Removing an Item from a Menu

There will no doubt be times when you'll want to remove an item from one of your Start button menus, such as when you no longer use a program often enough to warrant its existence on the menu. With Windows 98, you can now drag objects off the Start menu.

Note that moving an actual program or a document from one folder to another isn't reason enough to delete its choice on a Start menu. This is because shortcuts in Windows 98 are "self-healing." If an item that a menu item points to has been moved to another drive, directory, or computer, choosing the menu command results in a message similar to this:

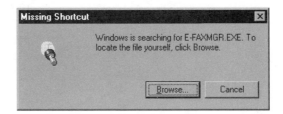

Windows will automatically scan your hard disk(s) looking for the item. In most cases, if you've moved rather than deleted the displaced item, Windows will find it, responding with a dialog box asking whether you want to repair the shortcut path.

Just click on Yes, and the shortcut on your Start menu will be repaired. Next time it will work flawlessly.

Here's how you remove an item:

1. Choose Start ➤ Settings ➤ Taskbar.

2. Click on the Start Menu Programs tab and click on Remove.

3. Wait a few seconds as Windows 98 updates your menus.

4. In the list that appears, scroll and otherwise maneuver the list until you get to the folder and item you want (see Figure 5.7). Note a couple of things here. All items with plus signs are folders that have sub-items. For example, on your computer you'll certainly have an Accessories folder. Clicking on the + sign to the left of Accessories will display all the program items on the Accessories submenu. Clicking on the minus (-) sign closes up the folder. Items that normally list on the first Start button menu are at the *bottom* of the list. You may have to scroll down to see them.

FIGURE 5.7

Remove any folder or item from the Start menus using this box. Click on the item you want to remove, then click on Remove.

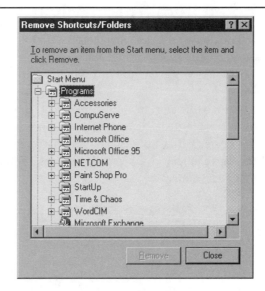

5. Click on the item you want to remove. It can be a folder name or an individual item in the folder. Note that removing a folder removes all the sub-items in the folder.

NOTE

Just as with Program Manager icons in Windows 3.*x*, removing a shortcut from the Start button menus does not remove the actual item from your hard disk. For example, if you remove a shortcut to Word for Windows, the program is still on your computer. It's just the shortcut to it that's been removed. You can always put the shortcut back on the menus again using the Add button.

Advanced Options

If you consider yourself a hotshot, you can wreak all kinds of havoc by clicking on the *Advanced* button from the Taskbar settings dialog box. What this really does is run the Explorer and let you copy, move, delete, and *rename* items on your menus. (This is *the* place to give any goofily named menu items a new name.) Clicking on it results in a display like that shown in Figure 5.8.

FIGURE 5.8

Exploring the Start button menus lets you easily modify them. You can use right mouse clicks for a variety of purposes. Here you see the right-click menu for a shortcut in the Internet Explorer group list. You can also drag-and-drop items if you want to move them between folders.

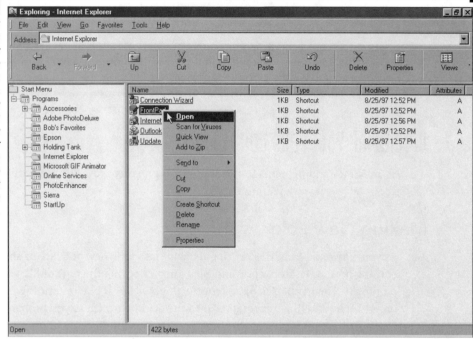

For details about using the Explorer, check out Part II of this book. For now, just note a few facts:

- Click on the topmost folder (Start Menu) to adjust the contents of the Start button's first-level menu.

- Change a name by clicking on the *name* once to highlight it, then once more. Alternatively, you can right-click on the name and choose Rename from the right-click menu.

- You can drag items in the right pane to destination menus in the left pane. Just drag-and-drop.

- You can create new submenus by clicking in the left pane on the menu you want to add to. Then right-click in the right pane and choose New ➤ Folder.

TECH TIP

I know it doesn't make sense to choose New and then choose Folder, because you want to create a menu, not a folder. But actually everything in Windows 98 is *folders* or *files*, and in reality this whole menu thing is based on directories. Check out the directory structure under your \Windows\Start Menu directory, and you'll find directories that correspond to each menu, with .lnk (link) files for each shortcut.

As a shortcut for modifying the contents of the Start button menus, right-click on the Start button. Then choose Open if you want to use the folder approach. Choose Explore if you like the Explorer approach.

Organizing Your Files and Folders

So much for adding items to the Start button menus. Now I'll show you a bit more about how you work with folders.

Making New Folders

As you may recall from the last chapter, you can create new documents simply by right-clicking on the Desktop, choosing New, then choosing the type of file you want and naming it. Then you click (or, of course, double-click if you're running in Classic view) on it to start entering information into the document. Or, as you probably know, you can create documents from within your programs and save them on disk using commands in the programs.

In either case you're likely to end up with a lot of documents scattered around your hard disk, or worse yet, a lot of documents lumped together in the same directory with no sense of organization. In interviewing users and teaching people about Windows over the years, I've found that most people haven't the foggiest idea where their work files are. They know they're on the hard disk, but that's about it.

To some extent, Windows 95 and 98 will exacerbate this problem because every document or folder that's on the Desktop is actually stored in the SystemRoot\Desktop directory on the disk. Typically this will be the C:\Windows\Desktop directory. Even though each folder the user has on the Desktop will be a subfolder of the desktop directory, it still means that wiping out the C:\Windows\Desktop directory or doing a clean install of Windows by wiping out everything in the \Windows directory and below would wipe out anything on the Desktop. This normally won't be a problem for most people, as this kind of willy-nilly removal of whole directories or directory trees is something only power users are likely to do. If you are the kind of computer user who is going to be poking around on the hard disk, handle your Windows\Desktop directory with due respect.

Saving all your files in one directory without sorting them into folders makes creating backups and clearing off defunct projects that much more confusing. It's difficult enough to remember which files are involved in a given project without having to sort them out from all of Word's program and support files, not to mention all the other writing projects stored in that directory.

TECH TIP

Unless your hard disk was formatted with FAT32, be cautious about storing a lot of files in the root directory of the disk. DOS and Windows limit the number of file or directories in the root to 512. This limit doesn't apply to subdirectories. Also, because long file names take up additional space in the directory, economizing on name length in the root directory can be a good idea if you're pushing the 512-entry limit.

Admittedly, organizing files was a bit difficult in Windows 3.*x*, but with Windows 98, there's no excuse for bad organizing. And there are plenty of reasons to organize your files: You'll know where things are, you'll be more likely to make backups, and you'll be less likely to accidentally erase your doctoral dissertation because it was in the WordPerfect directory that you deleted so you could install a new word-processing program.

Probably the most intuitive way for most people to organize their work is to do it right on the Desktop. You can create as many folders as you like right there on the Desktop, name them what you like, and voilà, you've done your homework.

If you want to get really tidy, you can pull all your subfolders into a single folder called something like My Work. To show you how to create folders and then move them around, I'm going to consolidate mine. First I'll create a new folder.

1. Right-click on the Desktop. Choose New from the resulting menu, then Folder.

2. A new folder appears, called New Folder. Its name is highlighted and ready for editing. Whatever you type will replace the current name. I'll enter the name *My Work*.

3. Now I'll open the folder by clicking on it (or double-clicking if in Classic view).

So much for creating a new folder on the Desktop.

Incidentally, you're not limited to creating new folders only on the Desktop. You can create new folders within other folders using the same technique. That is, open the destination folder's window. Then right-click on an empty area inside the folder's window and choose New ➢ Folder.

Moving and Copying Items between Folders

Now that I've got a new folder on the Desktop, I can start putting stuff into it. Let's say I want to pull several of my existing Desktop folders into it to reduce clutter. It's as simple as dragging and dropping.

1. Open the destination folder. (Actually you don't even have to open the destination folder, but what you're about to do is more graphically understandable if you do.)

2. Size and position the destination folder's window so you will be able to see the folder(s) you put in it.

3. Repeatedly drag folders from the Desktop inside the perimeter of the destination folder's window. Be careful not to drop items on top of one another. Doing that will put the dropped item *inside* the item under it.

That's it. Figure 5.9 illustrates the process.

NOTE

You can drag-and-drop most objects in Windows 95 using this same approach. Every effort has gone into designing a uniform approach for manipulating objects on screen. In general, if you want something placed somewhere else, you can drag it from the source to the destination.

WARNING

When dragging and dropping, aim carefully before you release the mouse button. If you drop an object too close to another object, it can be placed *inside* that object. For example, when moving folders around, or even repositioning them on the Desktop, watch that a neighboring folder doesn't become highlighted. If something other than the object you're moving becomes highlighted, that means it has become the target for the object. If you release at that time, your object will go inside the target. If you accidentally do this, just open the target and drag the object out again, or, if the incorrect destination was a folder, open any folder and choose Edit ➢ Undo Move or right-click on the Desktop and choose Undo Move from the pop-up menu. Also, if you press Esc before you drop an object, the process of dragging is canceled.

Now all I have to do is close the My Work folder, and there's that much less clutter on my desktop.

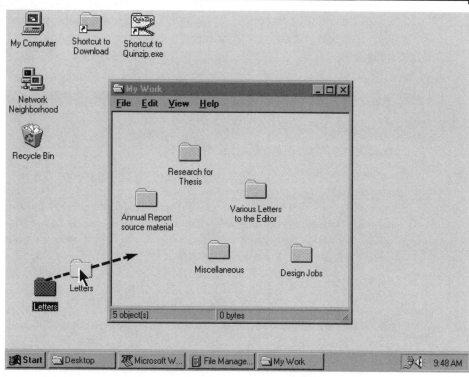

FIGURE 5.9

Working with folder windows and objects is as simple as dragging and dropping. Rearranging your work is as simple as organizing your desk drawer.

Moving vs. Copying

When you drag an item from one location to another, Windows does its best to figure out if you intend to copy it or move it. As you might surmise, copying means making a replica of the object. Moving means relocating the original.

In the procedure above, Windows assumed I wanted to move the folders from one location to another. This makes sense because it's not likely you'll want to make a copy of an entire folder. But you could.

The general rule about moving vs. copying is simple. When you *move* something by dragging, the mouse pointer keeps the shape of the moved object.

But when you *copy*, the cursor takes on a + sign.

To switch between copying and moving, press the Ctrl key as you drag. In general, holding down the Ctrl key causes a copy. The + sign will show up in the icon so you know you're making a copy. Pressing Shift as you drag ensures that the object is moved, not copied.

But Isn't There an Easier Way?

Here's a little technical tip you'll need to know regarding dragging. The easiest way to fully control what's going to happen when you drag an item around is to *right-click-drag*. Place the pointer on the object you want to move, copy, or make a shortcut for, then press the right mouse button (or left button if you're left-handed and have reversed the buttons) and drag the item to the destination. When you drop the object, you'll be asked what you want to do with it, like this:

Being able to create a shortcut this way is pretty nifty. Often, rather than dragging a document file (and certainly a program) out of its home folder just to put it on the Desktop for convenience, you'll want to make a shortcut out of it. There are important considerations when using shortcuts, however, so make sure you understand what they do.

Organizing Document Files

Once you've thought out how to name and organize your folders, you'll naturally want to start stashing your documents in their rightful folders.

As you might expect, moving and copying documents works just like moving and copying folders—you just drag-and-drop. When you want to copy files, you press the Ctrl key while dragging. If you want to create a shortcut, you right-click-drag and choose Shortcut from the resulting menu (see *But Isn't There an Easier Way?* above). Here's an example you might want to try.

1. Clear off the Desktop by clicking on the Desktop icon.

2. Create a new folder on the Desktop by right-clicking on the Desktop and choosing New ➤ Folder. Name it My Test Folder.

3. Now create a couple of new documents by right-clicking on the Desktop, choosing New, and then choosing a document type. Name the documents whatever you like.

Now let's say you want to put these three files into the new folder. You could just drag them in one by one. But here's a faster approach: You can select multiple objects at once. Selecting a number of objects can be useful when you want to move, copy, delete, or make shortcuts out of them in one fell swoop.

1. First, we're going to *snap a line* around the items we want to drag. Move the pointer to an empty area on the Desktop at the upper-left corner of the three documents and press the left mouse button. Now drag the mouse down and to the right. This draws a box on the screen, outlining the items you are selecting. You know which items you've selected because they become highlighted (see Figure 5.10).

FIGURE 5.10

You can select multiple objects by snapping a line around them.

Start here —

Release here —

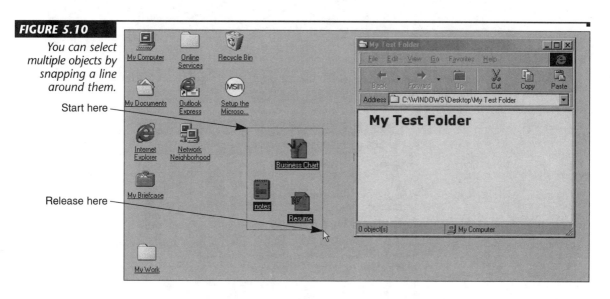

2. Once selected, you can perform a number of tasks on the group of items. For example, you could right-click on one and choose Open, which would open all three documents in their respective programs. In this case we want to move them. So while they are all selected, just drag one of them. The whole group will move (see Figure 5.11).

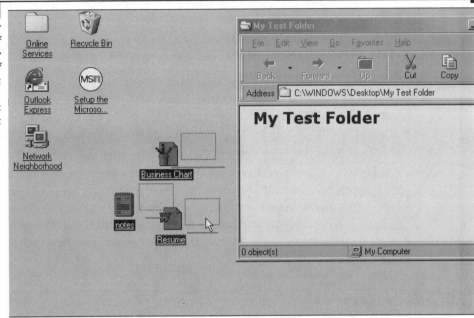

FIGURE 5.11

You can move or copy a group of selected items by dragging one of them. The others will come along. Notice the outlines of all three objects are moving.

3. Using this method, drag the items over the destination folder and release. They've all been moved into My Test Folder.

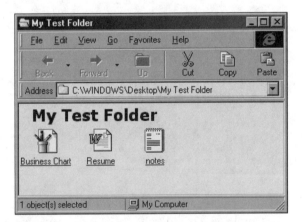

Not all the outlines of the items you're moving need to fit into the destination folder before you release the mouse button. If just a single document's outline falls within the boundary of the target, all the selected items will move to the target folder.

Using Quick View to Examine a File

In the process of organizing your documents, looking at e-mail attachments, or browsing the company network, you've certainly noticed that the name and/or last modification date alone are not always enough to go on when you're trying to guess a file's contents. Often you will need to open the file and look at it before you can determine if it's the one you want to take action on, such as moving, copying, editing, printing, e-mailing, or deleting. However, the process of opening a file isn't always a fast one, especially when it necessitates loading a large program such as Word or Photoshop from the hard disk into RAM, opening the file, and then displaying it. If all you want to do is view a file for basic identification purposes, there is a better and faster way—via the *Quick Viewers* in Windows 98.

The supplied Quick Viewers can display the most popular file formats quickly and easily from the file's right-click menu. You simply right-click on the file and choose Quick View. Assuming there is a Quick Viewer for the type of the file you're pointing to, the document will then open in a Quick View window (Figure 5.12).

FIGURE 5.12

Windows 98 includes Quick Viewers for many popular file types. This is a Quick View window for a Microsoft Works spreadsheet file.

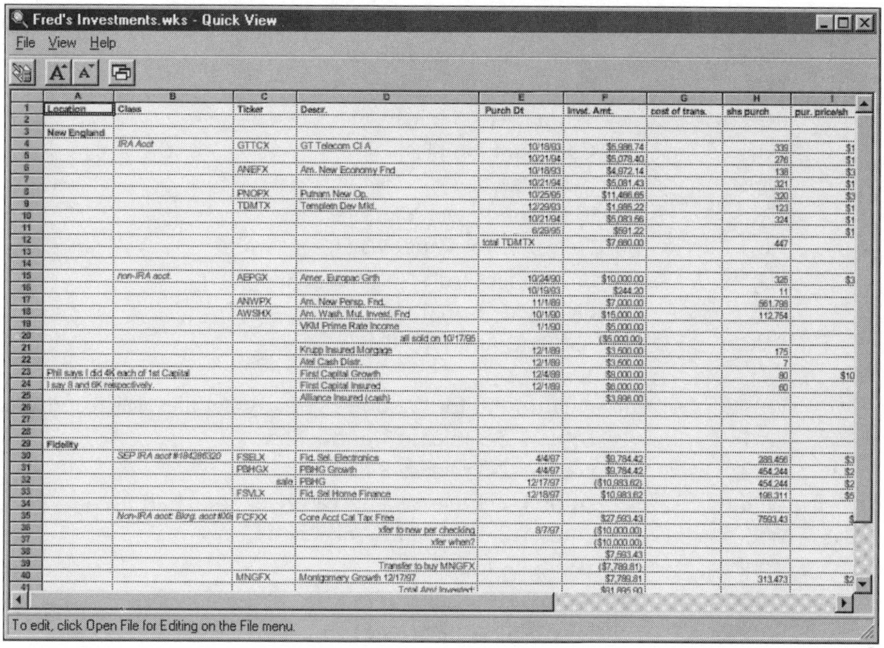

The formats that can be viewed with the Quick Viewers that are included on the Windows 98 CD are listed in Table 5.1.

Quick Viewers have different controls and menu choices, based on what you are viewing. Check the View menu: Page View shows an entire page at a time in the view window. If you're looking at a graphics or fax file, you can rotate the image for the best page orientation. For text files, check out the toolbar; you can click on the two "A" buttons in the toolbar to increase or decrease the font size for the text display.

Quick Viewer windows support drag-and-drop, so you can drag files from a folder or from Windows Explorer onto an open Quick View window to examine it if you want.

Quick viewing a program file (that is, a file that has the .EXE filename extension) will display information that would mainly be of interest to programmers.

TABLE 5.1: FILE FORMATS THAT ARE VIEWABLE WITH WINDOWS 98 QUICK VIEWERS

File Extension	Type of File
ASC	Plain ASCII files
BMP	Windows bitmapped graphics files (such as from Paint)
CDR	CorelDRAW files
DIB	Windows bitmapped graphics files
DLL	Dynamic Link libraries
DOC	Microsoft Word for DOS and Word for Windows; also WordPerfect
DRW	Micrografx Draw files
EXE	Executable files (programs)
INF	Setup files
INI	Configuration files
MOD	Multiplan files
PPT	Microsoft PowerPoint files
FRE	Freelance for Windows files
RLE	Bitmap files (run-lengthen coding)
RTF	Rich Text Format files
SAM	AMI and AMI PRO files
TXT	Text files
WB1	Quattro Pro for Windows spreadsheet files, Microsoft Works database files
WK1	Lotus 1-2-3 release 1 and 2 files
WK3	Lotus 1-2-3 release 3 files
WK4	Lotus 1-2-3 release A spreadsheet and chart files
WKS	Lotus 1-2-3 files and Works files
WMF	Windows Metafiles
WPD	WordPerfect demo files
WPS	Microsoft Works word processing files
WQ1	Quattro Pro for MS-DOS files
WQ2	Quattro Pro version 5 for MS-DOS files
WRI	Windows Write files
XLC	Excel 4 chart files
XLS	Excel spreadsheet and chart files

If you don't have the Quick View option on your right-click menus, even on common files such as .BMP (bit-mapped picture) files, you may have to install the viewers. See Chapter 7 ("Basic Customizing with the Control Panel") for a discussion of using the Add/Remove Programs applet for adding components of Windows 98. The component you'll want to add is *Viewers*, which is a subcomponent of *Accessories*.

The Quick Viewers were developed by Microsoft in collaboration with Systems Compatibility Corporation, which makes additional viewers available for purchase. Contact SCC or Microsoft for more information regarding additional viewers.

Deleting Items

Of course there will be times when you'll want to delete items, like that old report from last year. Regular file deletion is very important if you don't want to become like everyone else—strapped for disk space. The same techniques will apply to deleting other objects as well, such as printers and fax machines you have installed, because all objects in Windows 98 are treated much the same way regardless of their type or utility.

To Delete a File

So how do you delete a file? Let me count the ways. Because Windows 98 has a Recycle Bin, that's one of the easiest ways, assuming you can arrange things on your screen to find the Recycle Bin. But there are other ways that are even easier though less graphically pleasing than dragging an item over the Recycle Bin and letting go.

To delete a file,

1. Just select the file in its folder, on the Desktop, in the Find box, or wherever. (Remember, to select in Web view, just point to the item, don't click.)

2. Drag the item on top of the Recycle Bin, press the Del key on your keyboard, or right-click on the item and choose Delete from the resulting menu. Unless you drag to the Recycle Bin, you'll be asked to confirm the deletion.

3. Choose appropriately. If you choose Yes, the item goes into the Recycle Bin.

If you throw something away, you can still get it back, at least up until whenever you decide to empty the trash, as explained in the section "Checking and Chucking the Trash" later in this chapter.

To Delete a Folder

Deleting a folder works much the same way as deleting a file. The only difference is that deleting a folder deletes all of its contents. When you drag a file over to the Recycle Bin, or delete it with one of the other techniques explained above, you'll see a confirmation message warning you that all the contents—any shortcuts, files, and folders (including files in those folders) will be deleted. Take care when deleting folders, as they may contain many objects.

Before deleting a folder, you may want to look carefully at its contents. Open the folder and choose View ➢ Details or View ➢ List to examine what's in it, check on the dates the files were created, and so forth. Check the contents of any folders within the folder by opening them; you might be surprised by what you find.

Putting Items on the Desktop

The Desktop is a convenient place to store items you're working on regularly. Each time you boot up, the same files and folders you left there are waiting in easy reach. So how do you put things on the Desktop? You have probably figured out already that you simply drag them there from any convenient source such as a folder or the Find box.

You can also drag files and folders to the Desktop from the Windows Explorer and even from File Manager. See Chapter 12 for more details.

However, there are a few details to consider when using the Desktop that aren't immediately obvious. First, some objects can't actually be *moved* to the Desktop—only their shortcuts can. For example, if you open the Control Panel (Start ➢ Settings ➢ Control Panel) and try pulling one of the icons (called Control Panel *applets*) onto the Desktop, you'll see this dialog box:

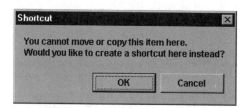

In the case of the Control Panel, setting up a shortcut is your only choice because Windows won't let you move it. As you drag an icon from the Control Panel onto the Desktop or into a folder, the icon turns into a shortcut icon (it has a little arrow in it). But in some other cases, you'll have the choice of moving, copying, or creating a shortcut. How do you choose? Here's a little primer about shortcuts.

Because a shortcut will work just as well as the real thing (the program or document file itself), in general shortcuts are a good idea. As I've said before, you can have as many shortcuts scattered about for a given item as you want. For example, suppose you like to use a particular set of programs. You can have shortcuts for them on the Start button menu, on the Quick Launch toolbar, on the Desktop, and in some folder such as, say, My Favorite Programs. You still have only one copy of the program, so you haven't used up a lot of disk space, but the programs are easily available from multiple locations.

Shortcuts do consume *some* disk space. Each shortcut file has the .LNK (for Link) extension and contains information about where the program, folder, or document it represents is stored. .LNK files will typically use up the smallest amount of space that the disk operating system (DOS) will allow. Most .LNK files consume 1K, though some you'll find to be 2K. If you convert to the FAT32 file system, the size will be even smaller.

The same holds true for other objects, such as folders or documents that you use a lot. You can have shortcuts to folders and shortcuts to documents. For example, try dragging a folder (the folder must be displayed as an icon) onto the Start button, and you'll see that a shortcut to the folder is created. A good way to create a shortcut to a document is, as I mentioned earlier, to right-click-drag it somewhere and choose Shortcut from the resulting menu.

I have to warn you of a few things when using shortcuts, however. Remember, shortcuts are *not* the real McCoy. They are *aliases* or pointers to an object only! Therefore, copying a document's shortcut to a floppy disk doesn't copy the document itself. A colleague will be disappointed if you copy only the shortcut of a document to a floppy and then give it to him or her, because there will be nothing in it. When you are in doubt about what is getting copied, look at the icon that results from the procedure. If it has a little arrow in it, it's a shortcut.

If no arrow, then it's the actual file.

And consider this: When you move the real McCoy around—whether a program, folder, or document—it may disable some shortcuts that point to it. For example, assume you've set up a bunch of shortcuts that expect your Annual Budget to be located in folder X. Then you move the budget document to folder Y. What happens? Nothing, until you try clicking on those shortcuts. Then you'll get an error message. Windows will try to find the missing object the shortcut is pointing to:

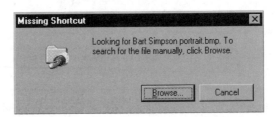

If the object is found, then the shortcut will be repaired and will work next time. If it's not found, Windows does its best to find something *like it*, but usually suggests something pretty bogus. You can click on the Browse button and use the resulting Browser box to poke around and find the file, fixing the link. If neither you nor Windows finds the target, the shortcut remains useless, and will do the same rigmarole next time you try it.

WARNING

Programs that are *installed* into Windows—these are typically big-time programs like those in Microsoft Office, Borland's or Lotus' office suites, database packages, communications packages, and so on—don't like to be moved around. Almost any program that you actually install with an "install" or "setup" program will register itself in Windows 98's internal *Registry*, informing Windows of the folder it is located in, what kinds of files it uses, and other details. Moving the program around after that (i.e., actually moving it rather than moving the shortcuts that point to it) will bollix up something somewhere unless the program actually comes with a utility program for relocating it as, say, WinCIM (a program for working with CompuServe Information Service) does. There are some third-party utility programs that will enable you to move programs around without having to reinstall them.

Saving Files on the Desktop from a Program

One of the features I like best about Windows 98 is the ability to use the Desktop as a sort of temporary holding tank. Here's one example. Suppose you want to copy some files from the floppy disk. It's as easy as opening the floppy disk window from My Computer, then dragging the desired file onto the Desktop. Voilà, it's on the hard disk! (Technically, it's in a Desktop subdirectory of your Windows 98 directory, but for all intents and purposes it's simply on "the Desktop.")

You can use the same kind of approach to move or copy items from one folder to another. Rather than having to open both folders and adjust your screen so you can see them both, you can just open the source folder and drag the items onto the Desktop temporarily. When you find or create the destination folder, you can later copy the items there.

But what about using the Desktop from your favorite programs? Although the Desktop is actually a subdirectory of your Windows directory, it's fairly easy to save a file to the Desktop. The newest programs use a File dialog box with a Desktop button that really makes this easy (Figure 5.13).

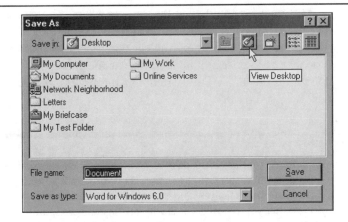

Some Windows 95 programs have a file box that doesn't have the button, but at least lets you open a list and choose Desktop, as in Figure 5.14.

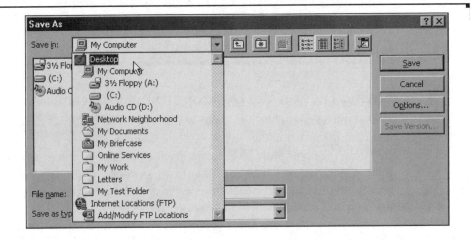

File boxes for Windows 3.*x* programs don't have this button on them. Sorry. It's because the Desktop didn't exist in that version of Windows. Anyway, as a result, saving a file to (or opening one from) the Desktop from a Windows 3.*x* program takes a little more doing. Still, you can do it. The next page shows you how.

NOTE

When your computer is set up for multiple users, there may be multiple Desktop directories, one for each user. They're located in subdirectories under `Windows\Profiles`. There will be one for each user who has an account. For example, for Joe, there will be a directory named `Windows\Profiles\Joe\Desktop`. These directories are *not* normally hidden and can be accessed from any program without modification.

1. Open the Save, or Save As, or Open dialog box from the File menu as usual.

2. In the dialog box, select the drive that contains Windows. This is probably your C drive.

3. Switch to the Windows directory. Then look for the Desktop subdirectory. Figure 5.15 shows an example.

FIGURE 5.15

Saving a file to the Desktop from Collage Complete, a 16-bit program.

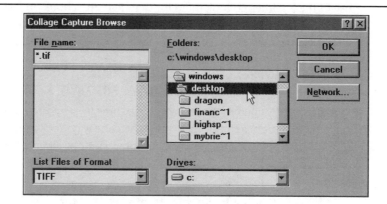

4. Enter or choose the file's name or open one of the subfolders on the Desktop. Remember that subfolders that have long names will show up in the 16-bit File boxes with shortened names. For example, in Figure 5.15, notice the folders on the Desktop that end with the ~ (tilde) character. For older programs, Windows removes any spaces that occur in the filename, shortens any names that are longer than eight characters (it shortens them to six characters), and for characters 7 and 8 inserts a ~ and a number. The number is helpful, because if the first six characters of two filenames are the same (for example, *Joe's resume* and *Joe's resume revised*), the number is incremented for each file. So those files would appear as joe'sr~1 and joe'sr~2. A later file named *joe's rock collection* would show up as joe'sr~3.

Copying Files and Folders to and from Floppy Disks

Whether you're sending a file to a colleague around the world, "sneaker-netting" some work down the hall, or simply making a backup of some important files, copying to and from floppy disks is one of those recurring computer-housekeeping chores.

As you might expect, there are multiple ways to copy files to and from floppies. You can use:

- My Computer
- the Send-To option

- drag-and-drop on a floppy-drive's shortcut
- Explorer
- File Manager
- the Command prompt

Here I'll briefly cover the basics of the first three items. In Chapter 12 I'll cover use of the Explorer, so look there for that. Refer to a book on DOS if you need help copying files by typing in copy commands at the DOS Command Prompt. Or open a MS-DOS window and type **copy /?** to read some help information about the Copy command.

Copying to and from a Floppy with My Computer

I've already explained in the sections above how to copy and move files between folders. Copying to or from a floppy disk works the same way. Your computer's floppy disk drives simply appear as icons in the My Computer window. Open a floppy drive icon and it brings up the contents of the floppy disk, displayed in the same format as a typical folder on your hard disk.

1. Clear off enough windows from your Desktop to see the My Computer icon.

2. Open My Computer.

3. In the My Computer window, open the appropriate floppy disk icon. Typically you'll only have one, but some computers have two or more floppy disk drives. In Figure 5.16, I'm about to open the $3^1/_2$-inch floppy A: drive in the illustration. (If you don't have a diskette in the drive, you'll see an error message.)

4. Once the floppy drive's window opens, you can easily work with it just as you do with other folders. Drag items from the window to other folders you might have opened on the Desktop, or vice versa.

TIP

When you replace one floppy diskette with another, the computer doesn't know about it automatically, as it does on the Mac. After you change the disk, the contents of an open floppy disk window will still be the same, even though the disk holds a completely different set of files. To update the contents of the floppy disk's window, press the F5 key. (This same technique is needed with File Manager and Explorer, incidentally, whenever you change a floppy.)

Up and Running

FIGURE 5.16

You can examine the contents of the floppy drive by opening My Computer and then opening the desired drive.

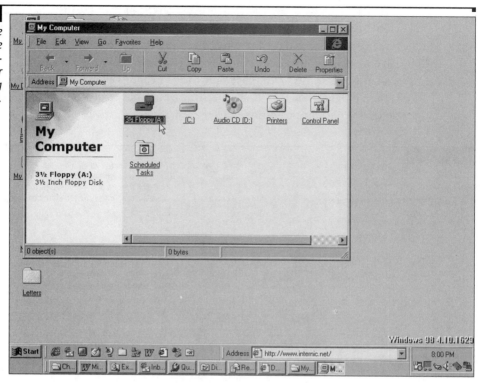

Remember, you're not limited to dragging between opened disk and folder *windows*. You can drop items on closed folders or disk icons, too. Here, I'm dragging Bart Simpson's portrait from the Desktop into My Test Folder.

Sometimes when using a floppy disk you'll see an error message alerting you that the disk has not yet been formatted, that the disk can't be read, or something else, such as the disk is *write protected*.

On 3½-inch diskettes, there's a little tab on the back of the disk that must be in the closed position for the disk to be written onto (new files put on it). On 5½-inch diskettes (rare these days, but older machines have them), if a stick-on write-protect tab covers the write-protect notch, writing will not be allowed. You should know that a disk must be *write-enabled* (have no write protection) even to open or read files with certain programs such as Word or any program that creates temporary or backup files on disk while you are editing. See Figure 5.17.

FIGURE 5.17

Location of write-protect slider and notch on 3½" and 5½" floppies

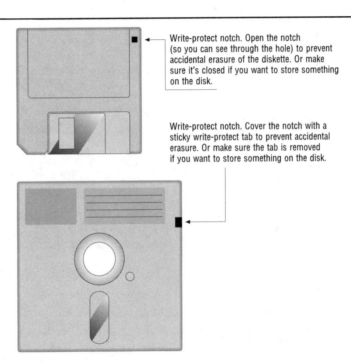

Write-protect notch. Open the notch (so you can see through the hole) to prevent accidental erasure of the diskette. Or make sure it's closed if you want to store something on the disk.

Write-protect notch. Cover the notch with a sticky write-protect tab to prevent accidental erasure. Or make sure the tab is removed if you want to store something on the disk.

If the disk isn't formatted—because you just bought it or it was formatted for use in another kind of computer or device, such as a Mac, and you want to use it on a PC—you simply can't write anything on it, regardless of the write-protect tab setting. You can format a floppy from:

- Explorer or My Computer by right-clicking on the floppy drive's icon and choosing Format
- any floppy-disk shortcut icon by right-clicking on it and choosing Format
- the DOS prompt's Format command
- the File Manager (using the Disk ➤ Format command)

I'll cover formatting more in Chapter 12 when I talk about the file system.

TIP

To see how much room is left on any disk drive, including a floppy, right-click on the drive in My Computer and choose Properties. You'll see a display of the disk's free and used space. Another approach is to open My Computer and set the view to Details. All drives' statistics will be reported. Disk properties are described more in Chapter 11, where I discuss right-clicking and property sheets.

Copying Files to a Floppy with Send To

Realizing that people wanted an easy way to copy a file or folder to a floppy disk, Microsoft has provided a cute little shortcut to the interface that copies to a floppy from almost anywhere.

1. Just right-click on any file or folder icon.

2. Then choose the Send To option.

Depending on your computer's setup, you'll have differing choices in the Send To list. You'll at least have one floppy-disk option.

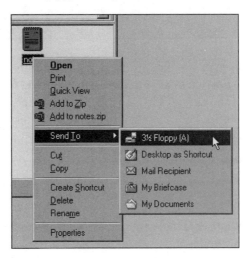

3. Insert a floppy disk that has some free space on it and choose the desired drive. The file will be copied to the drive you specify.

TIP

The Send To option is very handy. You can customize the Send To list for other purposes, such as sending a file to a viewer program, to the Desktop, a file-compression program, a network destination, and so on. Just add the destination shortcuts to the \windows\SendTo directory and they'll show up in the Send To list.

Copying Files to a Floppy's Shortcut

Because a shortcut works just fine as a drag-and-drop destination, one convenient setup for copying items to a floppy is this:

1. Place a shortcut of the floppy drive on the Desktop. You can do this by opening My Computer and dragging the desired floppy drive to the Desktop.

2. Now, whenever you want to copy items to the floppy drive, insert a diskette in the drive, adjust your windows as necessary so you can see the drive's shortcut, and simply drag-and-drop objects on it. They'll be instantly copied to the diskette.

And, of course, opening the shortcut icon will display the diskette's contents.

Setting Options That Affect Viewing of Folders

In the interest of consistency, Windows 98 puts the same menus and toolbar buttons on all Explorer windows:

The View menu in particular provides a number of other useful features you might want to know about as you work with your files, folders, floppy disks, and so forth. A couple of the settings I'll discuss here can be super useful, helping to keep your screen clear of clutter. From the View menu, you can control:

- Which toolbars appear on all Explorer windows

- Whether folders look like Web pages or not

- The custom look of a folder's display, including the use of custom HTML code

- The ordering of icons in the window

- Whether folders are displayed in Web view, Classic view, or a little of each (customized)

- Whether file extensions (the last three letters after the period) will be displayed

- Whether "system" and "hidden" files are displayed or are invisible

- Which programs are associated with given file extensions

Sorting and Tidying Up the Listing

As you drag icons around, they have a way of obscuring one another, falling behind the edge of the window, or otherwise creating an unsightly mess. Once a bunch of icons become jumbled up, it's often difficult to see or find the one you want. A few commands let you quickly clean up, arrange, and sort the display of files and folders in a window.

1. If you want to tidy up the Desktop or a folder's contents quickly, simply right-click on any free space on the Desktop or in the folder and choose Arrange Icons.

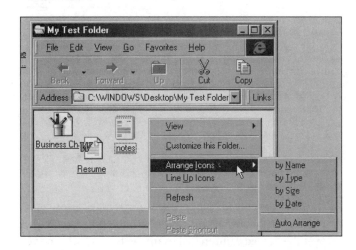

2. Then choose the appropriate command. The following list describes your options.

By Name	Sorts the display of objects alphabetically based on the name. Folders always appear first in the listing.
By Type	Sorts the display of objects according to type. (The type is only visible when you list the objects' details.) Folders always appear first in the listing.
By Size	Sorts the display of objects in increasing order of size. Folders always appear first in the listing.
By Date	Sorts the display of objects chronologically, based on the date the object was last modified.
Auto Arrange	Keeps the objects lined up nicely at all times. It doesn't ensure that they'll be in any particular order, however. This is a toggle: choose it once to turn it on and again to turn it off.

Right-clicking menus in certain specialized windows may give you additional Arrange options. For example, in the Recycle Bin window you'll see this:

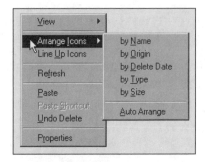

And in the My Computer folder you'll see this:

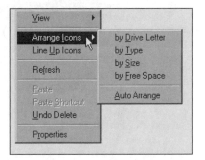

If you have the display set to show Details, a convenient feature lets you sort all the objects without using any of these commands. Simply click on the *column heading control* over the desired column. For example, to sort by Name you'd click on the Name heading:

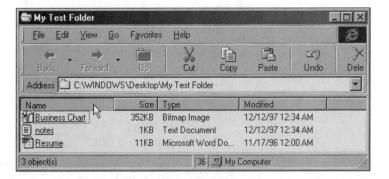

Clicking once on the heading sorts in ascending order (A to Z, 0 to 9). Clicking a second time sorts in descending order. This is particularly useful in the Size and Modified columns, letting you easily bring to the top of the list the files you've modified most recently *or* those you modified ages ago; or you can quickly find which files in a folder are very large and might be taking up significant space on your hard disk.

NOTE

Certain view settings you make in a folder pertain only to that folder. They don't affect other folders. The size, position, listing type and order, and auto-arrange settings are stored with the folder itself and will not affect other folders' settings. However, as discussed in Chapters 1 and 3, the view settings (Classic, Web, and Custom) *are* global, and will affect *all folder* windows, including the desktop. See the discussions in those chapters for a refresher on Web, Classic, and Custom views.

Other Options on the View Menu

As mentioned in Chapter 3 in the section covering Web view, there's quite a plethora of options that affect display of files and folders throughout your system. Let's take a look at some of them now.

Advanced Folder Settings

On any folder, or in the Windows Explorer, you can choose View ➤ Folder Options, and click on the View tab. You'll see the options displayed in Figure 5.18. These options can be tweaked if you wish. For most folks they are fine as set, but you may be the kind of user who really likes personalizing things. Some of these settings are new to Windows 98, and some options were available in Windows 95. This box is totally new, however, and is somewhat like some options boxes available in Internet Explorer that really let you get into the nitty-gritty of the Explorer's display settings.

FIGURE 5.18

This box, reachable from the View menu of any folder window, lets you set a number of options that affect display of files and folders.

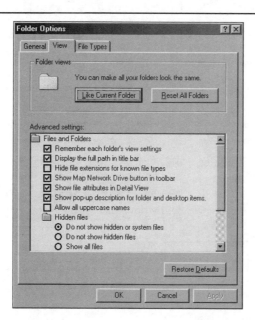

Table 5.2 describes what the various settings mean.

TABLE 5.2: THE FOLDER OPTIONS VIEW SETTINGS		
Setting	**Meaning**	**Effect**
Remember each folder's view settings	The Windows documentation states that when on, settings for each folder, such as location on the screen, window size, toolbar settings, whether in large icon, small icon, list, or details view will be remembered when you close the folder window. If off, these shouldn't be remembered. However, in my testing this didn't seem to work as expected. Window settings seem to be stored regardless.	Global
Display the full (MS-DOS) path in the Title bar	When set on, the entire path name of a open folder will be displayed in the Title bar of the folder's window. Normally, only the name of the folder itself is shown. For example, a full path name might be C:\joe's work\ budgets\1998, whereas the folder name alone would display as 1998.	Global
Hide MS-DOS file extensions for file types that are registered	When set on, files with recognized extensions won't have their last three letters (and the period) showing. Unrecognized (unregistered) file types will still show their extensions. Turn this off to see all extensions, even if they are registered in Windows 98. The reasoning behind hiding file extensions when possible is that it keeps extraneous information off the screen and makes life easier for normal mortals who don't want to be confused or hassled by file-name extensions. Once the extension is set and then hidden, you can rename a document file without fear of accidentally changing the extension and thus preventing the file from opening in the correct program when clicked on.	Global
Show Map Network Drive button in toolbar	When on, two new buttons appear in folder and Explorer windows, Map Network Drive and Disconnect Network Drive. (See networking chapters for explanation.)	Global
Show file attributes in Detail view	In Detail view, you'll be able to see normally hidden file "attributes" such as whether a file is marked Hidden, Archive, System, or Read Only. (These properties can be set by right-clicking a file and choosing Properties.)	Global

Continued ▶

TABLE 5.2: THE FOLDER OPTIONS VIEW SETTINGS (CONTINUED)		
Setting	**Meaning**	**Effect**
Show pop-up description for folder and desktop items	When not viewing a folder as a Web page (see View menu option), this enables a pop-up menu displaying the same info that's normally displayed in the left-hand pane of a folder when you highlight an icon in a folder or on the Desktop.	Global
Allow all upper-case names	Normally, a file with the name FRED will be displayed as Fred. With this setting on, folders, Explorer, and Find boxes will display FRED if that is how the file or folder was originally named.	Global
Do not show hidden or system files	When set on, files marked Hidden or System won't be displayed in folders, in the Explorer, in the Find box, etc. Also hidden are any files with extensions: .DLL, .SYS, .VXD, .386, or .DRV.	Global
Do not show hidden files	When set on, only files or folders marked as Hidden won't display.	Global
Show all files	When set on, any and all files and folders on your hard and floppy disks will display.	Global

Of all these settings, the only ones I really prefer to turn on are file extensions, and hidden files. Being an old DOS guy, I like to see all the files on the drive, and also see the file extensions.

WARNING

Beware, though, that turning on the display of all files can be a little dangerous because anyone using the computer could browse to your Windows directory and see all your system files, possibly deleting some of them accidentally. System files do not contain personal information, but they contain data and programming that are responsible for making Windows work correctly.

Once you get a folder looking the way you like, you can opt to have all other folders use the same display arrangement. Just click on the Like Current Folder button.

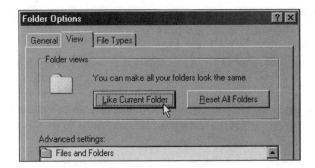

Click on the Restore Defaults button if you have doubts about what you've done or if, at a later date, you want to return the behavior of the system to its original state.

Turning Text Labels Off and On

You might have noticed a setting on the View ➤ Toolbars menu called Text Labels.

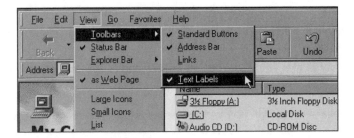

When this setting is on, you see descriptive names under each button in the toolbar. Choose the setting again, and the checkmark on the menu goes away, and so do the text labels, freeing up space for display of files and folders in a window. Once you know what the buttons do, you might want to turn off the labels.

Creating a Custom View

As mentioned in Chapter 3, the two primary choices for view in Windows 98 are Web and Classic. You can customize the view to something in between as well. Here's how:

1. Choose View ➤ Folder Options.

2. Click on Custom, then click Settings:

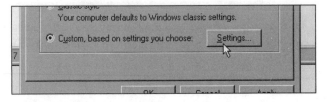

3. Make settings to the dialog box shown in Figure 5.19.

FIGURE 5.19

Making settings for a Custom display, somewhere between Web and Classic views.

The following paragraphs describe the settings found in this dialog.

Active Desktop

This section applies only to the Desktop itself, not other folders. Active Desktop is covered in Chapter 18, but for now just know that you can turn off the Active Desktop and display items on the Desktop in Classic mode irrespective of the settings for other folders.

Browse Folders as follows

- **Open each folder in the same window:** With this setting, if you open a folder from within another folder (as an example, open My Computer and then open the C drive), the window stays put. Only the content changes.

- **Open each folder in a new window:** With this setting, each time you open a folder from within an existing folder a new window appears. This can create clutter on your screen, but lets you drag-and-drop items between folder windows.

View Web Content in Folders

- **For all folders with HTML Content:** As mentioned earlier, each folder can have a customized look, using HTML programming code. Choosing View ➢ Customize, this folder walks you through the process of creating the HTML code.

The result is a file named `folder.htt` that determines the look of the folder when displayed in Windows Explorer or a folder window. Setting this option on causes all folders with predetermined Web content to display according to their `.HTT` files' stipulated format.

- **Only for folders where I select "as Web Page" (View menu):** Recall that the View menu (and View button in the toolbar) of a folder or Windows Explorer has an option called "as Web Page." Well, when this "Only for folders..." setting is on, then only the folders that have the Web page setting turned on will display their contents in Web page format.

Click Items as follows

- **Single-click to open an item:** The meaning is pretty obvious. When this is the setting, you open a folder, file, program, or other item such as a printer by pointing and clicking once. There are two options under this setting that you then have to think about that affect when an item is underlined (like a hyperlink in a browser). The default is the first one, and makes sense, since you'll typically want to have underlining appear consistent with what your Web browser is set to. As a default, underlines are on at all times. If you want the single-click behavior of Web view, but the on-screen look of Classic view without all the underlines, choose the second option ("...only when I point at them").

- **Double-click to open an item:** If you want the Classic view clicking arrangement, choose this setting.

Using the Cut, Copy, and Paste Commands with Files and Folders

You're probably well acquainted with the Cut, Copy, and Paste commands as they pertain to programs such as word processors. These commands let you remove, replicate, or move bits of data around while working on your documents.

NOTE

If you're *not* familiar with these concepts as applied to programs, don't worry. They'll be explained in Part IV, which covers the supplied accessory programs.

Just as in Windows 95, a Windows 98 feature is its inclusion of the Cut, Copy, and Paste commands when browsing folders, files, and other objects (such as printers, fax machines, fonts, and so forth). To Windows 3.*x* users, these commands might not make sense at first, because cutting and copying aren't commands that have been applied to files before. They're typically used within programs and apply to portions of documents. When I first saw this menu I wondered how *cutting* a file would differ from *deleting* it and why cutting it only made a file's icon grayed out rather than making it disappear. However, once you know how these commands work, you'll use them all the time.

As I mentioned earlier, the Desktop is a useful temporary storage medium when copying or moving objects between windows or folders. Having the Desktop available means you don't have to arrange *both* the source and destination windows on screen at once to make the transfer. Well, the Cut, Copy, and Paste commands do the same thing without the Desktop.

Here's how it works, using a real-life example. Today I downloaded a file from CompuServe called editschd.doc. My e-mail program dumped the file in my Download folder, but I want it in my Mastering Windows 98 folder instead. Well, I could open both folders, arrange them on screen, and drag the file from one to the other. Or I could drag the file first to the Desktop, then to the destination folder. But instead of either of these, I'll use the Cut and Paste commands to accomplish the same task more easily. Here are the steps I used:

1. First I opened the source folder—which in this case was the Download folder.

2. Next, I located the file in question, right-clicked on it, and chose Cut (not Delete, because that command actually trashes the file instead of preparing to put it somewhere else).

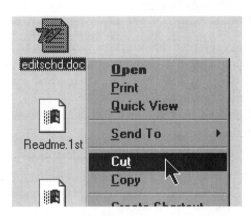

3. This turns the icon into a shadow of its former self, but it's still there in a ghostly form, which means it's waiting to be pasted into another location.

TIP

At this point, failing to paste the file into a destination or pressing Esc will abort the cutting and copying process. Nothing will be lost. The file will remain in its original location.

4. Next, I can close the current folder, browse around to my heart's content until I find the proper destination for my file, whether it be a floppy disk, the Desktop, or another folder. In this case, I opened the Mastering Windows 98 folder.

5. I now position the pointer on an empty space within the folder, right-click, and choose Paste. The file's icon appears in its new home. That's it.

NOTE

If, when you go to paste, the Paste command is grayed out, it means you didn't properly cut or copy the object. You must use the Cut or Copy commands on a file or other object *immediately* before using the Paste command, or it won't work. That is, if you go into a word processor and use the Cut or Copy commands in a *document*, then the Paste command for your *files* or other objects will be grayed out and won't work. (Chapter 6 discusses use of the Cut, Copy, and Paste commands within programs such as word processors.)

Now, a few points about cutting, copying, and pasting objects in this way. First, if you want to make a copy of the file rather than move the original, you'd choose Copy rather than Cut from the menu. Then, when you paste, a copy of the file appears in the destination location.

Second, you can cut or copy a bunch of items at once to save time. The normal rules of selection apply:

- Draw a box around them as I described in *Organizing Document Files*.
- Or press the Ctrl key and select each additional object you want to work with (remember, if in Web view, this just means pointing and waiting a second—no clicking).
- Or select the first of the items you want to select, hold down the Shift key, and click on the last of the items you want to select. This selects the entire *range* of objects between the starting and ending points.

Once a number of items is selected (they will be highlighted), right-clicking on any one of the objects will bring up the Cut, Copy, Paste menu. The option you choose will apply to *all* the selected items. Also, clicking anywhere outside of the selected items will deselect them all.

Take a look at the Edit menu in any folder window. There are two commands at the bottom of the menu—Select All and Invert Selection. These can also be useful when you want to select a group of files. Suppose you want to select all but two files; select the two you *don't* want, then choose Edit ➤ Invert Selection.

Finally, remember that you can cut, copy, and paste complete folders, too, just by choosing the folder's icon and then choosing the Cut or Copy command. When you paste the folder somewhere new, you get all of its contents, including any other folders within it.

What if you accidentally goof and realize that you didn't want to move an object or objects to the new location after all? After you perform the Paste, simply open the Edit menu in any folder and choose Undo. This is a great feature! Often I'll accidentally drag some folder somewhere due to a slip of the wrist or finger or something and not even know what I've done. Suddenly a folder is gone. Before doing anything else, I choose Undo, and the damage is undone.

Checking and Chucking the Trash

When right-clicking on an object, you may have noticed the Delete command in the menu.

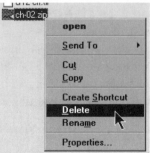

This command isn't the same as the Cut command. Delete sends the selected files, folders, or other objects to the Recycle Bin (essentially the trash can), while the Cut command puts the file on the Clipboard for pasting to another location.

When you delete a file, folder, or other item, it gets put into the Recycle Bin, which is actually a special folder on your hard disk. This folder or directory is called, as you might expect, Recycled, typically on your C drive.

Each logical drive (drive with a letter name) has a `Recycled` directory on it. So, if you have a C and D drive, you'll have two Recycle Bins. `Recycled` directories are "hidden" system files, so they don't normally show up in Explorer or folders. You'll just have a Recycle Bin on the Desktop. If you have access to the root directory of a networked drive, whether mapped to a logical drive on your machine or not, it too will have a `Recycled` directory. CD-ROM drives, even though given a logical drive letter, do not have `Recycled` directories for the obvious reason that you can't delete their files or folders.

The Recycle Bin temporarily holds things that you delete. Because items are not actually *erased* from your computer when you delete them with the Delete command, you can get them back in case you made a mistake! Even better than the Undo command discussed above, this is a terrific feature. How many times have you accidentally erased a file or directory and realized you goofed? For most people even a single accidental erasure was enough. Now with the Recycle Bin, all you have to do is open its folder, find the item you accidentally deleted, and choose the File ➤ Restore command to undelete it.

Well, actually there's a caveat here. The Recycle Bin will hang onto your deleted items only until you empty the bin. Once you empty the bin, anything in it is *gone*. At that point your only hope is one of the undelete programs like those from PC Tools, Norton, or the one supplied with DOS 5 or 6. (From the Start button, check your Programs menu for a Microsoft Tools option. You may have an undelete program on it.) If that fails, look in your DOS folder (`C:\DOS`) for `undelete.exe` and run that. Or, for an easier approach, simply click on the Start button, choose Run, and enter **undelete**. If you have the program in the DOS directory, it should run. Refer to a book on DOS or the DOS help system (type **Help Undelete** at an MS-DOS prompt) for more information about how to use Undelete.

When you're doing your hard-disk housecleaning, merrily wiping out directories and files in hopes of regaining some needed disk space, you should be aware of one thing: Because files aren't actually erased until you empty the Recycle Bin, you won't increase your available disk space until you do just that.

Restoring a File or Folder You Accidentally Trashed

If there's one single thing you'll want to know about using the Recycle Bin, it's how to get back something you accidentally put there. (This page alone may make this book worth your investment!)

1. Get to the Desktop one way or another.

You can also reach items in the Recycle Bin via any folder window, using the drop-down list in the Address bar. Just scroll down to it. The Windows Explorer is another way (see Chapter 12).

2. Open the Recycle Bin icon. The folder will list all the items you trashed since the last time the Recycle Bin was emptied. Figure 5.20 shows an example.

FIGURE 5.20

A typical Recycle Bin before emptying

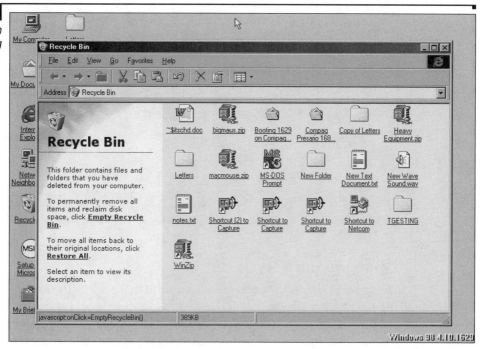

3. Hunt around for the thing(s) you accidentally trashed. When you find it, highlight it by clicking on it. (You can select multiple items using the techniques I described earlier in this chapter.) If you want to know more about an item, click on it and choose File ➢ Properties. A dialog box displays when the item was created and when deleted. (Or if you are in the Details view, a column appears displaying the deletion date of each item.)

You can also restore an item in the Recycle Bin or Windows Explorer by right-clicking on the item and choosing Restore.

4. Right-click on the item (or choose File ➢ Restore). This will move all selected item(s) back to their original locations. Figure 5.21 shows an example.

FIGURE 5.21

Undeleting (restoring) a file that was accidentally erased

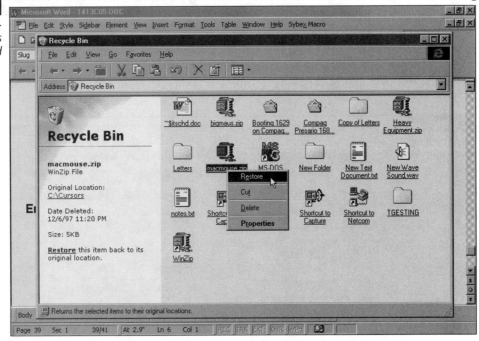

Emptying the Recycle Bin

You've probably already noticed the command that empties the Recycle Bin. It's on the File menu. When you want to free up some disk space and are sure that all the contents of the Recycle Bin can be dispensed with, go ahead and empty it. It's always a good idea to have plenty of free disk space for Windows 98 and your programs to work with, so regularly emptying the trash, just like at home, is a good practice.

Here's the easiest way to empty the Recycle Bin:

1. Get to the Desktop.

2. Double-click on the Recycle Bin.

3. Examine its contents to make sure you really want to jettison everything.

4. Choose File ➢ Empty Recycle Bin.

5. You'll be asked to confirm the process.

TIP

You can quickly empty the Recycle Bin by right-clicking on it right on the Desktop and choosing Empty Recycle Bin.

NOTE

We all love to accumulate junk on our hard disks. It doesn't matter whether the disk holds only 40 megabytes or a nine gigabytes. It will fill up. When your hard disk can gets too crammed, Windows 98 starts to strangle. At that point, a dialog box reporting the sorry state of your disk housekeeping will pop up on your screen. If there is stuff in the Recycle Bin, the box will have a button you can click to empty the trash for you, reclaiming some precious space. You'll also have the option of dumping Internet temp files that may have accumulated as you browsed the Web.

Renaming Documents and Folders

As you work with your files, folders, and other objects, you may occasionally need to rename them, either to more easily identify them later or because their purpose has changed and the current name is no longer valid. In any case, it's easy enough to change an object name. In fact, it's far easier than in Windows 3.x because you don't have to resort to the File Manager or DOS commands to do the renaming.

In general, renaming objects works similarly throughout Windows 98. The surest, though not necessarily the quickest, way is this:

1. Right-click on the object you want to rename and choose Rename from the resulting menu. (If you are using Web view, this is definitely the best way, short of using the File ➢ Rename command.)

2. At this point, the name will be highlighted and the text cursor (small vertical bar) will be blinking.

3. Here's the tricky part. Because the whole name is highlighted, whatever you type now will replace the whole name. More often than not, this isn't what you want to do. Typically you'll just want to add a word or two, fix a misspelling, or something. So, just press ← (the left arrow key). This will deselect the name and move the cursor one space to the left. Now use the normal editing procedures with Backspace, Del, arrow keys, and regular typing to modify the name.

Ap11base.bmp

4. Click outside the little text box encircling the name (or press ← once) when you're through; that will store the new name.

If you're in Classic view, a shortcut for editing a name is to do a *slow* double-click on the name. This puts the name into edit mode, with the cursor blinking away and the name highlighted. Be careful not to double-click quickly, or this will run the application or open the document. (Remember, this tip only works in Classic view!)

If, when renaming a file, you see an error message about how changing the extension of the file may make it unworkable, you'll typically want to choose No.

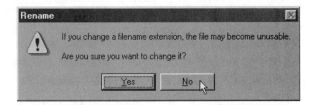

This message just means you forgot to give the file name an extension by typing in a period and the same three-letter extension it had before. So just rename it again, making sure to give it the same extension that it had before. So for example, let's say the file is named:

    Budget for Winter 1999.wks

and you change it to

    Budget for Spring 1999

You'll probably see an error message when you press the ← key. Renaming the file to

    Budget for Spring 1999.wks

would prevent the error message.

As I discussed earlier in this chapter, extensions for registered file types are normally hidden. So a Word for Windows file named Letter to Joe, for example, will simply appear as:

    Letter to Joe

not

    Letter to Joe.doc

which is the name that's actually stored on the disk. When you change the name of a file that doesn't have an extension showing, you don't have to even think about what the extension is or about accidentally typing in the wrong one.

Chapter

6

OLE 2.0 overview

Copying, cutting, and pasting

Using Clipboard Viewer

OLE overview

Using OLE to create complex documents

Sharing Data between Applications

As you now know, you can run several programs at one time and switch between them with a click of the mouse or a press of Alt-Tab. You may also know that you can cut, copy, and paste information between programs and documents, embedding bits and pieces of information, graphics, sound, and video from multiple sources into a single destination source to create complex documents. Previously disparate types of information are beginning to merge into a new synthesis, evidenced by products such as CD-ROM–based interactive encyclopedias, in-car electronic guidance (map) systems, and voice-controlled telephone systems. All these capabilities are outgrowths of the desire to mix and match heretofore unrelated kinds of data.

In this chapter, we'll look at data sharing on the Windows 98 platform, paying particular attention to the techniques you can use to create complex documents.

OLE Overview

As a result of the standardization of the Windows interface and API, users have become accustomed to being able to cut, copy, and paste not only within a given program but between Windows programs. Nowadays, thousands of applications can easily share data with one another through these commands that use the Windows Clipboard.

We still have the problem of proprietary file and data formats—the kind of thing that makes a WordPerfect file different from a Word for Windows file, or an Excel file different from a 1-2-3 file. These proprietary formats often seem to be promoted by software developers as a means of pushing their own programs by locking users into a particular file format. Unfortunately, the proprietary-file-formats marketing strategy has backfired, leaving users grumbling and feeling held hostage by a particular brand of program. The situation becomes even thornier when multimedia files are thrown in. We are now seeing competing formats for full-motion video, audio recording, MIDI files, and the like.

Software developers have finally figured this out, though, and have made working with "foreign" file formats much easier. With each new month, more applications have built-in file-format converters to allow applications to share files. For example, Word for Windows can read and write a whole gaggle of text and graphics file formats. Ditto for PageMaker, Ventura Publisher, Microsoft Access, and many others. Standards such as Rich Text Format (RTF), Windows Metafiles, HTML, and others are now emerging to facilitate data transfers between programs. Embedded TrueType fonts and utility programs such as Adobe's *Acrobat* even allow people to see and edit documents containing fonts not in their systems.

Windows 98 and Data Exchange

Actually, much more interesting than simply being able to use one program's document in another program is the ability to mix and match a great variety of document types, such as text, sound, graphics, spreadsheets, databases, and so forth. This lets you construct complex documents previously requiring physical cutting and pasting and possibly the aid of an art department.

Windows 98 offers three internal vehicles for exchanging data between programs: the Windows Clipboard, Object Linking and Embedding (OLE), and Dynamic Data Exchange (DDE). In this chapter, I'll explain each of them, and then describe some special considerations for data sharing across the network.

If you're new to Windows, you may only want to read the portion about the Clipboard. That's the part about the cut, copy, and paste commands. You'll use these commands much more often than the other stuff I talk about in this chapter. If you want to take full advantage of what Windows' OLE has to offer, read the entire chapter.

NOTE

Many of my examples in this chapter refer to Microsoft products. This isn't necessarily my endorsement of Microsoft products over other competing products! Competition in the software marketplace is a healthy force, ensuring the evolution of software technology, and I highly support it. But, because so many of you are bound to be familiar with the Microsoft product line, I use products such as Word, Excel, Graph, and Access in my examples in hopes of better illustrating the points I'm trying to make here.

The Clipboard

Though it's not capable of converting data files between various formats, such (such as xls to wk3 or rtf to doc) the Windows Clipboard is great for many everyday data-exchange tasks. Just about all Windows programs support the use of the ubiquitous cut, copy, and paste commands, and it's the Clipboard that provides this functionality for you.

Clipboard makes it possible to move any kind of material, whether text, data cells, graphics, video or audio clips, and OLE objects between documents—and since Windows 95, between folders, the desktop, the Explorer, and other portions of the interface. The actual form of the source data doesn't matter that much, because the Clipboard utility and Windows together take care of figuring out what's being copied and where it's being pasted, making adjustments when necessary—or at least providing a few manual options for you to adjust. The Clipboard can also work with non-Windows (DOS) programs, albeit with certain limitations that I'll explain later.

How It Works

How does the Clipboard work? It's simple. The Clipboard is built into Windows and uses a portion of the system's internal resources (RAM and virtual memory) as a temporary holding tank for material you're working with. For example, suppose you have cut some text from one part of a document in preparation for pasting it into another location. Windows stores the text on the Clipboard and waits for you to paste it into its new home.

The last item you copied or cut is stored in this no-man's-land somewhere in the computer until you cut or copy something else, exit Windows, or intentionally clear the Clipboard. As a result, you can paste the Clipboard's contents any number of times.

You can examine the Clipboard's contents using the Clipboard Viewer or Clipbook utility supplied with Windows. If you've used Windows for Workgroups or Windows NT, you'll be familiar with these applications. You can also use these applications to save the Clipboard's contents to disk for later use or to share specific bits of data for use by others on your network.

Selecting, Copying, and Cutting in Windows Applications

In Windows 98, the Windows 95 and 3.x standards and procedures for copying, cutting, and pasting apply. Even if you're mixing and matching 16- and 32-bit applications, the Clipboard will work just fine because in the internals of Windows 98, the 16-bit subsystem shares the same Clipboard as the 32-bit section.

You simply use each application's Edit menu (or Edit menu's shortcut keys) for copying, cutting, and pasting (Figure 6.1).

Here are the steps for cutting, copying, or pasting within a Windows program:

1. First, arrange the windows on screen so you can see the window containing the source information.

2. Now *select* the information you want to copy or cut, such as text, a graphic, spreadsheet cells, or whatever. In many programs, simply clicking on an object, such as a graphic, will select it. Other programs require you to drag the cursor over objects while pressing the left mouse button.

3. Once the desired area is selected, open the application's Edit menu and choose Copy or Cut depending on whether you want to copy the material or delete the original with the intention of pasting it into another location.

4. If you want to paste the selection somewhere, first position the cursor at the insertion point in the destination document (which may or may not be in the source document) you're working in. This might mean scrolling up or down the document, switching to another application using the Taskbar, or switching to another document within the *same* application via its Window menu.

5. Open the Edit menu and choose Paste. Whatever material was on the Clipboard will now be dropped into the new location. Normally, this means any preexisting material, such as text, is moved down to make room for the stuff you just pasted.

 TIP

There may be some shortcuts for cut, copy, and paste in specific programs, so you should read the manual or help screens supplied with the program. Generally, pressing Ctrl-X, Ctrl-C, and Ctrl-V are shortcuts for cutting, copying, and pasting, respectively.

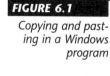

FIGURE 6.1

Copying and pasting in a Windows program

Select an item and choose Cut or Copy

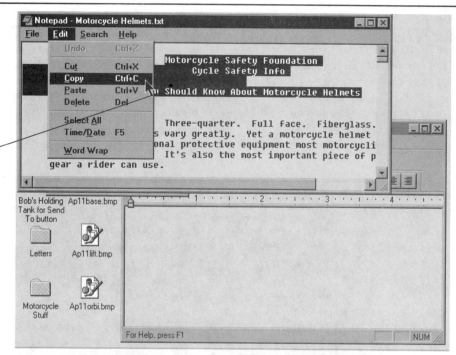

Move to a destination and choose Paste

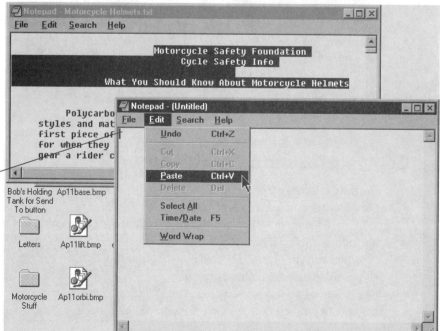

NOTE

When pasting in graphics, you'll typically have to reposition the graphic *after* pasting, rather than before. For example, Figure 6.2 shows a graphic (another copy of the Earth as taken from the moon on the Apollo 11 mission) just after pasting it into a Paintbrush window. It appears in the upper-left corner, waiting to be dragged to its new home.

FIGURE 6.2

Graphics applications typically accept pasted information into their upper-left corner, where they wait to be repositioned.

Copying Text and Graphics from a DOS Box

Copying selected graphics from DOS programs is also possible. This is a pretty nifty trick for lifting material out of your favorite DOS program and dropping it into a Windows document. There's only one caveat: the DOS program has to be running in a window, not full screen.

When you cut or copy selected material from the DOS box, it gets dumped into the Clipboard as text or graphics, depending on which mode Windows determines the DOS box (*box* means window) was emulating. Windows knows whether the application is running in character mode or graphics mode and processes the data on the Clipboard

PART

Up and Running

accordingly. If text mode is detected, the material is copied as characters that could be dropped into, say, a word-processing document. If the DOS application has set up a graphics mode in the DOS box (because of the application's video requests), you'll get a bit-mapped graphic in the destination document when you paste.

NOTE

As you may know, some fancy DOS programs may look as though they are displaying text when they're really running in graphics mode. For example, WordPerfect for DOS and Microsoft Word for DOS can both run in a graphics mode that displays text attributes such as underline, italics, and bold, rather than as boring block letters displayed in colors that indicate these attributes. When you copy text from such a program and then paste it into another document, you'll be surprised to find you've pasted a graphic, not text. This means you can't edit it like text because it's being treated like a bit-mapped graphic. The solution is to switch the DOS application back to Text mode and try again. Refer to your DOS program manual for help.

Because of the DOS box's toolbar, the procedure for copying is simple to learn. You can use the menus or the toolbar almost as if you were using another Windows program. Figure 6.3 illustrates the simple technique. Here are the steps:

1. First, switch to the DOS application and display the material you want to work with.

2. Make sure the application is running in a window, rather than running full-screen. If it's not, press Alt-Enter. (Each press of Alt-Enter toggles any DOS window between full and windowed view.)

Copying text from a MS-DOS box is now a simple procedure. Click on the Mark button, click and drag across the desired text, and click on the Copy button.

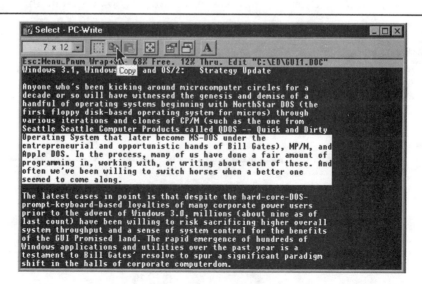

3. If the DOS box's toolbar isn't showing, turn it on by clicking in the upper-left corner of its window (on the MS-DOS icon) and choosing Toolbar.

4. Click on the Mark button.

5. Holding the mouse button down, drag the pointer over the desired copy area, dragging from upper left to lower right. As you do so, the color of the selection will change to indicate what you're marking.

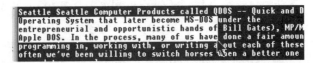

6. Release the mouse button. The selected area will stay highlighted.

7. Click on the Copy button. The information is now on the Clipboard.

NOTE

Notice that there isn't a Cut button because you can't cut from a DOS application in this way. Cutting has to be done using the DOS program's own editing keys, and it won't interact with the Windows Clipboard.

TIP

As soon as you click on the Mark button, the DOS box's title bar changes to read *Mark*. Once you start marking the selection, the word *Select* precedes the program's name in the title bar, indicating that you're in select mode. Typing any letter on the keyboard terminates the selection process.

That's all there is to copying information from an application that's running in the DOS box. Of course, the normal procedure will apply to pasting what was just copied. You just switch to the destination application (which, incidentally, can be a DOS *or* a Windows program), position the cursor, and choose Edit ➤ Paste to paste in the Clipboard's contents at the cursor position. (For a DOS application as the destination, you'd use the Paste button on the DOS box's toolbar. This is explained later in this chapter.)

Doing Screen Captures with Clipboard

You can capture the screen image while running an application. Screen captures are useful for creating program documentation, software education materials, or for putting out promotional material about software.

Clipboard is handy for capturing screen images in lieu of purchasing a special-purpose screen-capture program. The price is right, and it works, albeit with some limitations.

 TECH TIP

Professional programs designed for screen capture help you organize, crop, and edit your screen captures, among other things. If you regularly do screen captures, you might want to check these programs out. I used Collage Complete for the screens in this book. Other programs you might want to explore are Tiffany, PixelPop, Hotshot, and Hijaak. These programs give you a lot of latitude with capture techniques, file formats, color settings, grayscaling, and so forth, none of which the old Clipboard workhorse affords you.

Whether you're capturing a DOS or Windows-based application, the capture is converted to bit-mapped format for pasting into page layout or graphics programs such as PageMaker, Paint, and so forth.

 TIP

Though you can't edit your files or add borders and nice stuff like that using this economy approach to captures, you can save a file to disk for later use. The Clipboard and the Clipbook both let you save files on disk for later use. Please refer to "Saving the Clipboard's Contents in a File" and "Working with the Clipbook" later in this chapter.

To copy the screen image onto the Clipboard, do the following:

1. Get the desired application open and running in a window and adjust and size the window as needed.

2. Press the PrintScreen key. The image is copied to the Clipboard.

NOTE

All the computers I used this technique on responded as expected when these keys were pressed. However, some older PC keyboards use slightly different codes, requiring the user to press Shift-PrintScreenor Alt-PrintScreen instead.

Using the Paste Command

Once you have some information on the Clipboard, Windows 98 offers you several options for working with it. Here are the three routes you'll be able to take:

- Paste the information into a document you're working with (or that you open subsequently).
- Save it to a Clipboard (.clp) file for using later.

The last two choices are described later in this chapter. For standard pasting there are two options:

- You can paste information into Windows applications.
- You can paste into DOS applications (when they are in a window rather than running full-screen).

Let's look at these two individually because they require distinctly different techniques.

Pasting Information into Windows Applications As you are probably aware, the great majority of Windows applications' Edit menus include a Paste command. As the name implies, this is the command you'll use to paste material from the Clipboard into your documents. Of course, this command won't be usable unless there is something already on the Clipboard that can be accepted by the document you're working with at the time.

TECH TIP

Some heavier-duty programs have their own internal Clipboard that's not connected at all to the system's Clipboard. This isn't usually the case, so you don't have to worry about it with most applications. However, to accommodate proprietary data types and large amounts of data, some programs do use their own. Word for Windows, for example, does have a so-called large clipboard that it uses when you cut or copy a sizable bulk of material. In such an application, data you thought you were making available to the entire Windows system might not be. But this caveat will probably apply less to 32-bit applications than to 16-bit ones.

To successfully paste information from the Clipboard, here's what to do. Of course there may be some variation from application to application, but you'll figure that out as you use them. This basic approach works almost all the time.

1. First, you must set up the right conditions. That means cut or copy material onto the Clipboard.

2. Next, switch to the destination program or document—the one that will receive the information.

3. Now position the cursor or insertion point. In a text-based program this means position the I-beam cursor where you want it and click the left or primary mouse button.

4. Finally, choose Edit ➢ Paste or (in most programs) press Ctrl-V. The Clipboard's contents then appear in the destination window. Figure 6.4 shows an example.

FIGURE 6.4

Typical pasting operation, showing the Paste selection on the Edit menu

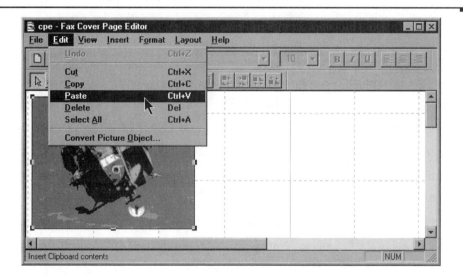

The Clipboard's contents remain static only until you copy or cut something new, so repeated pasting of the same material is possible. Just keep selecting insertion points and choosing Edit ➢ Paste.

Pasting into a DOS Box As weird as this seems, you can also paste into DOS applications. I say weird because most DOS applications were invented way before the Windows Clipboard was even a twinkle in Bill Gates' eye. There are certain limitations to this technique, such as only being allowed to paste text (no graphics). This is for obvious reasons—pasting graphics into a DOS application would be a nightmare. It simply wouldn't work because there is no standard agreement among DOS applications about treatment of on-screen graphics. Even with text, the results of pasting may be less than expected because DOS applications don't all accept data the same way.

NOTE

You should be aware that all text formatting will be lost when you paste text into a DOS document. This is because formatting (bold, italics, fonts, bullets, and so forth) is application-specific information (specially coded for each program), and most applications just don't speak the same language at this point.

TIP

Though you can't paste graphics directly into DOS applications, here's a workaround. Simply paste the graphic into a windows-based graphics program like Paintbrush or CorelDRAW. Then save the graphic in a file that's readable by the DOS graphics program. Most DOS programs can read `.bmp` or `.pcx` files, and most Windows graphics programs can save files in these formats.

When it comes time to actually do the pasting into a DOS application, here are the steps:

1. Put the desired text on the Clipboard by cutting or copying it from somewhere.

2. Toggle the destination DOS application so it's a window (this can't be done full-screen).

3. Position the DOS application's cursor at the location where you want to insert the Clipboard's material. This *must* be the location where you would next type text into the DOS document.

4. Click on the DOS box's Paste button.

Figure 6.5 shows an example in which I've inserted Clipboard text copied from a Help screen into a PC-Write file running in a window.

FIGURE 6.5

To paste text into a DOS application running in a window, position the cursor and click on the Paste button.

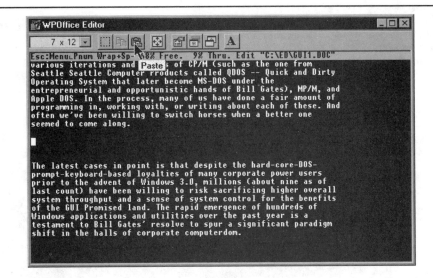

TECH TIP

The internals of the process of pasting into a DOS box are interesting. The text on the Clipboard is sent to the portion of the operating system that's responsible for buffering keyboard data entry. When you paste, the application thinks you have typed in the new text from the keyboard. For the procedure to work correctly, however, the recipient program has to be written in such a way that it doesn't balk at receiving information at the speed a supernormal typist could enter it.

Right-Click Shortcuts for Cut, Copy, and Paste

As mentioned earlier, the cut, copy, and paste scheme is implemented throughout Windows 98, even on the Desktop, in the Explorer, in folder windows, and so forth. This is done using right–mouse-button shortcuts. Many applications offer this feature too.

As explained in the last chapter, right-clicking on a file in a folder window and choosing Copy puts a pointer to the file on the Clipboard. Right-clicking on another location, such as the Desktop, and choosing Paste drops the file there (e.g., on the Desktop). Try clicking the secondary (normally the right) mouse button on icons or on selected text or graphics in applications to see if there is a shortcut menu. Figure 6.6 shows an example of copying some text from a Word for Windows document using this shortcut.

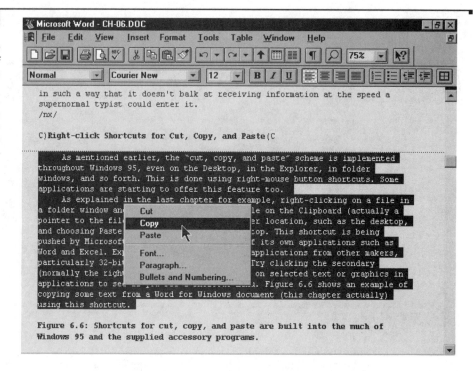

FIGURE 6.6

Shortcuts for cut, copy, and paste are built into much of Windows 98 via the right-click menu. Windows applications are beginning to implement this feature, too, as you see here in Word for Windows.

Figure 6.6: Shortcuts for cut, copy, and paste are built into the much of Windows 95 and the supplied accessory programs.

Working with the Clipboard's Viewer

Once data is on the Clipboard, you may not want to paste it immediately, or you might want to see what's there. There's a program supplied with Windows that makes this really easy. Clipboard Viewer can be found in the Accessories folder (choose Start ➤ Programs ➤ Accessories ➤ Clipboard Viewer). This program lets you do some useful Clipboard-related things, such as:

- view the Clipboard's contents
- save and retrieve the Clipboard's contents to/from a file
- clear the Clipboard's contents
- set up pages of the Clipboard, each storing things you plan to use later or want to make available to networked colleagues

Let's look at each of these simple tasks in order.

Viewing the Clipboard's Contents

Sometimes you'll simply forget what information is on the Clipboard because you won't remember what you cut or copied last. And before you go ahead and paste it into an application (especially if that application doesn't have an Undo command), you might want to check out what's going to get pasted. Another time when viewing is useful is when you're trying to get a particular item into the Clipboard and don't know how successful you've been. Bringing up the Viewer and positioning it off in the corner of the screen can give you instant feedback as you cut and copy.

Actually, there are two different utilities that let you examine the Clipboard's contents: Clipboard Viewer and Clipbook Viewer. You won't have Clipbook Viewer, however, unless you installed Windows 98 as an upgrade over an earlier version of Windows (3.11 or 95).

If you don't see Clipboard Viewer in your Accessories folder, you can install it from the Control Panel's Add/Remove Programs icon. Choose Windows Setup, then click on System Tools. Click on Details, turn on Clipboard Viewer, and then OK twice.

Here's how to view the Clipboard's contents.

1. Click on the Start button and choose Programs ➣ Accessories ➣ Clipboard Viewer.

2. The Clipbooard Viewer window comes up, displaying the Clipboard's current contents. Figure 6.7 shows typical Clipboard contents; in this case, a portion of an image I had just copied from the Paint program.

Changing the View Format

It's possible that the contents of the Clipboard will look different from how they look in the application you copied or cut from. For example, graphics may appear mottled or distorted, text may appear with incorrect line breaks, fonts, and so forth. You see, graphics and text can contain substantial amounts of formatting, such as font type and size, indents, colors, resolution settings, grayscaling, and so on. But there are some limitations to the amount of information that will actually be transferred through the Clipboard. It's the job of the source application to inform Windows 98, and thus the

Clipboard, of the nature of the material. The Clipboard tries its best to keep all the relevant information, but it doesn't necessarily display it all in the Viewer window.

FIGURE 6.7

The Clipboard's contents being displayed in a window within the Clipbook Viewer

Let's take an example. A Paint picture can be passed on to another application as what Windows calls a bitmap, a picture, or a Windows Enhanced Metafile. (In addition to this, there can be information that pertains to Object Linking and Embedding, but these aspects don't appear in the Viewer window.)

When you first view the Clipboard's contents, the Viewer does its best to display the contents so they look as much as possible like the original. However, this isn't a fail-safe method, so there may be times when you'll want to try changing the view. To do this:

1. Open the View menu (or the Display menu in Clipboard Viewer).

2. Check out the available options. They'll vary depending on what you've got stored on the Clipboard. Choose one and see how it affects the display. The Default setting (called *Auto*) returns the view to the original display format the material was first shown with. However, none of them will affect the Clipboard contents—only its display.

NOTE

When you actually go to paste into another Windows application, the destination program tries to determine the best format for accepting whatever is currently on the Clipboard. If the Edit menu on the destination application is grayed out, you can safely assume that the contents are not acceptable. (Changing the Clipboard's view format as described above won't rectify the situation, either. In fact, it doesn't have any effect on how things actually get pasted.)

Storing the Clipboard's Contents in a File

When you place new material onto the Clipboard, reboot, or shut down the computer, the Clipboard contents are lost. Also, because the Clipboard itself is not *network aware* (meaning it can't interact with other workstations on the network), you can't share the Clipboard's contents with other networked users. You'll want to take advantage of Clipbook pages for that (see below). However, there is one trick left. You *can* save the Clipboard's contents to a disk file. Clipboard files have the extension .clp. Once the Clipboard's contents are stored in a disk file, it's like any other disk file—you can later reload the file from disk. If you do a lot of work with clip art and bits and pieces of sound, video, text, and the like, this technique can come in handy. Also, if you give network users access to your .clp file directory, they can, in effect, use your Clipboard.

TIP

The Clipboard CLP files use a proprietary file format that is readable by virtually no other popular programs. So, to use a CLP file, you have to open it in Clipboard and *then* paste it where you want it to appear. This might all seem like a hassle, and it is. Actually, the Clipbook Viewer, explained later in this section, offers a hassle-free way to archive little things you regularly want to paste.

In any case, here's how to save a Clipboard file:

1. First make sure you have run the Clipboard Viewer, as explained above.

2. If you're using Clipbook, activate the Clipboard window within the Clipbook Viewer. The easiest way to do this is to choose Clipboard from the Window menu. You could also double-click on the Clipboard icon if you see it at the bottom of the Clipbook Viewer window.

3. Choose File ➢ Save As. A standard Save As dialog box will appear.

4. Enter a name. As usual, you can change the folder, name, and extension. Leave the extension as .clp because Clipboard uses this as a default when you later want to reload the file.

5. Click on OK, as you see in Figure 6.8. The file is saved and can be loaded again as described below.

Saving a Clipboard file

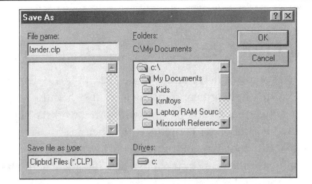

Retrieving the Contents of a Stored Clipboard File

As I mentioned, once the CLP file is on disk, you can reload it. Use these steps.

WARNING

When you reload a CLP file, anything currently on the Clipboard will be lost.

1. Run Clipboard Viewer.

2. If using Clipbook, choose Clipboard from the Window menu.

3. Choose File ➢ Open. The Open dialog box will appear.

4. Select the file you want to pull onto the Clipboard. (Only legitimate CLP files can be opened.)

5. If there's something already on the Clipboard, you'll be asked if you want to erase it. Click on OK.

6. Change the display format via the View menu if you want to (assuming there are options available on the menu).

7. Paste the contents into the desired destination.

Clearing the Clipboard

You might want to keep in mind, while using the Clipboard, that the information you store there, even temporarily, can impact the amount of memory available for use by the system and other applications. If you're cutting and pasting small bits of text and graphics as most people do during the course of a workday, this shouldn't be a concern, especially because Windows new memory management is more efficient than its predecessor's.

However, be aware that some items you might place on the Clipboard can be large. For example, graphics, video, sound samples, or large amounts of formatted text take up considerable space on the Clipboard. Some items are stored in a number of formats for pasting into different kinds of destinations and thus may hog more memory than you might expect.

The moral of the story is that if you're running into memory shortages, you may occasionally want to clear the contents of the Clipboard using the technique explained below.

NOTE

You can run the System Monitor program from the Accessories ➤ System Tools folder if you need to keep track of memory (and many other system resource) usages. The System tools are discussed in Chapter 23.

To clear the Clipboard:

1. If using Clipbook Viewer, select the Clipboard view by double-clicking on the Clipboard icon or clicking on its window. If using Clipboard Viewer, skip to step 2.

2. Choose Edit ➤ Delete, as you see in Figure 6.9.

3. Click on OK in the resulting dialog box to actually clear the board. The Clipboard's contents will be deleted.

Object Linking and Embedding under Windows 98

The ability to run numerous programs, simultaneously switching between them at will and copying data between documents, marked a major advance in desktop computing, especially on the PC. Merely for its task-switching capabilities, Windows has been embraced by thousands of DOS diehards who don't even like Windows per se. They use Windows just to switch between multiple DOS programs!

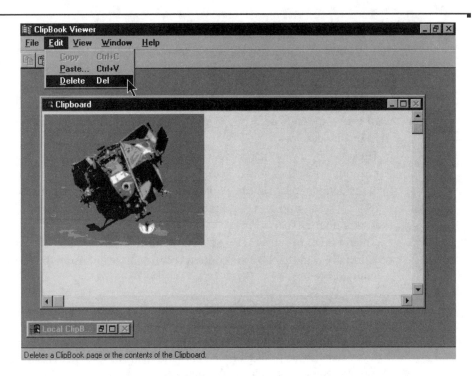

FIGURE 6.9

Clearing the contents of the Clipboard

However, the Clipboard and Clipbook impose severe limitations on truly "transparent" data sharing between applications. If you've been following Windows developments over the past several years, you'll know that post-Windows 3.0 products (Windows 3.1, Windows for Workgroups, Windows NT, Windows 95, and now Windows 98) have taken data sharing several steps further with a scheme called *Object Linking and Embedding* (OLE).

By the same token, though, many veteran Windows users have only the barest awareness of OLE, considering it some kind of black art (along with, unfortunately, such simple tasks as using a modem or getting their printer to work). So why should they care about OLE? The vast majority of folks don't understand OLE's nuances and stick instead with the tried-and-true Clipboard when it comes to passing data between applications. (Want a chart in that report? Paste it in!)

And for good reason. *Live* data sharing such as that offered by Windows OLE is the stuff computer-science conventions are made of. There are some highly technical distinctions to grasp, not to mention that not all Windows applications are *OLE aware* or implement OLE in the same way when they are. Add to this some confusion concerning OLE's use over a PC network, and you've got a topic in need of clarification!

In hopes of dispelling some of the confusion, this section offers a brief OLE primer. I'll fill you in on why you'd want to use OLE, and actually how easy OLE makes creating flashy documents that really take advantage of all that power your computer has under its hood.

Advantages of OLE

Just to give you an idea of what I'm even talking about here with all this technical talk, consider an example when the regular old Clipboard doesn't cut the mustard, and where you might want to use OLE instead.

Let's assume you're applying for a grant from an arts council and they want to see a professional-looking, attractive business plan as part of your application. You'll be using a Windows word processor such as WordPerfect, Word, or AmiPro to write the text, and you'll also need to incorporate financial projections for your project using data taken from a spreadsheet. Got the picture?

Okay. So you *could* just copy numbers from the spreadsheet into your text document. But there's a problem—your projections are changing daily as you update and refine your spreadsheet. What to do? Well you can just paste in the cells at the last minute before printing the grant application. But there's a more elegant solution. You can *link* the relevant cells from the live spreadsheet directly to the document. Then, whenever you alter any numbers in the spreadsheet, they'll be automatically updated in your grant application. Figure 6.10 shows an Excel spreadsheet linked to a Word for Windows document.

This is basically what OLE is all about—splicing pieces of documents (called *objects*) from different applications into a single *compound* document. And this splicing (called *linking*) keeps the documents connected so editing one will affect any other documents that are linked to it.

There's one other major nicety of OLE: You can edit a linked addition to a document just by double-clicking on it. In the example above, this means if you wanted to enter new figures in the spreadsheet, there's no need to run Excel and open the source spreadsheet file. You just double-click on the portion of the spreadsheet that's in your word-processing document. Windows knows that Excel created this portion of the document and dishes up the correct tools for you to edit with. Once you've entered your changes, you save them, and you're dumped back into your word-processing document. Windows takes care of updating any related documents.

FIGURE 6.10

Data linked between an Excel spreadsheet and a Word for Windows document

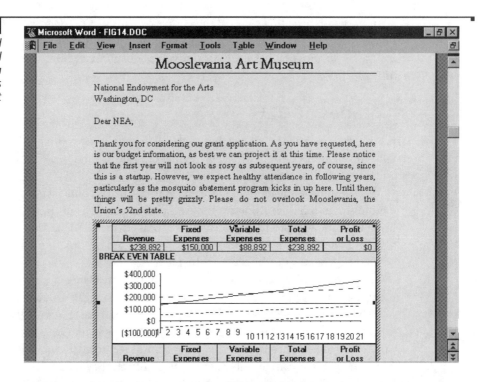

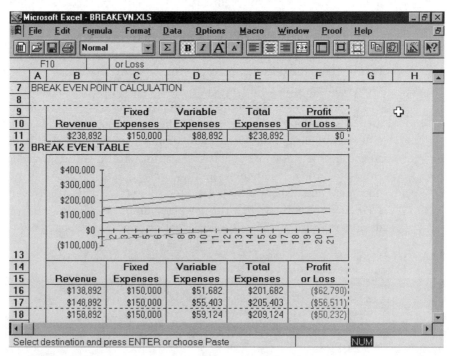

TECH TIP

Technically, in the above example, Excel becomes the active application, not Word. Excel actually runs, takes over the active window, changes the menus, and accepts the edits. When you exit, the window returns to Word. To the user, it looks as though only the menus and toolbars have changed.

The catch is that programs must be intentionally designed with OLE. But more and more of them are these days, so you shouldn't have trouble finding chart, graphics, sound, and even video programs that'll all work together. For example, you might want to add a chart from that same spreadsheet program to your business plan to communicate the numeric information graphically or a sound clip that when clicked on explains a concept in the author's own voice. And because Windows now supports networks so well, linked documents can be spread out all over the network. The art department's latest version of the corporate logo could be loaded into the annual report you're about to print without your having to even make a phone call.

Basic OLE Concepts

It's important that you have a working understanding of OLE terms and concepts before you try creating documents with OLE. Also, it's important that you understand that there are differences between OLE 1.0 and OLE 2.0. As of this writing, most sophisticated applications are 2.0 enabled. Although OLE 2.0 is backward-compatible with 1.0, meaning you can mix and match the two, the techniques you'll use to create compound documents differ somewhat. In this section I'll explain all you need to know to use OLE to put together some fancy compound documents.

So let's start with objects. What *is* an object, really? An *object* is any single block of information stored as a separate bundle but incorporated into a document. An object can consist of as little as a single spreadsheet cell, database field, or graphic element; or as much as an entire spreadsheet, database, or a complete picture or video clip.

Next, there's the issue of the differences between *linking* and *embedding*. With OLE, you have the option of using either one. You either link *or* embed an object—not both. Linking and embedding are different in functionality. Also you work with linked objects differently than you do with embedded ones. Study Figure 6.11 for a moment.

In the case of linking, two separate files exist—the spreadsheet and the word-processing files. The spreadsheet data can be edited either from within the word-processor document or separately from its source file in the spreadsheet application.

FIGURE 6.11

*A linked and
embedded
document*

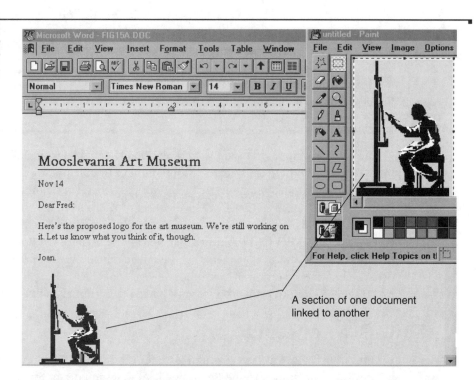

A section of one document
linked to another

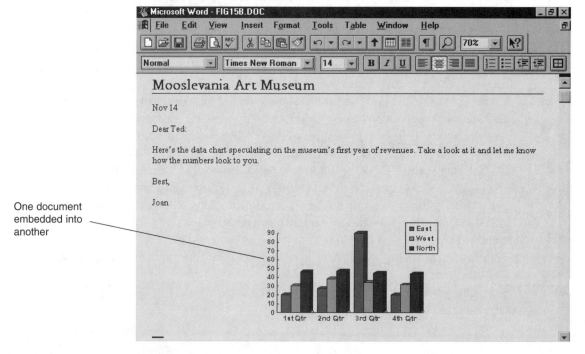

One document
embedded into
another

By contrast, the second figure displays an *embedded* object. The embedded graphic is more intimately connected to the word-processing document. In fact, it is contained *within* the word-processing file itself. Although the embedded picture can still be edited, it doesn't have a life outside of the word-processing document that contains it.

Regardless of whether the objects in the word-processing document are linked or embedded, the resulting larger document is called a *compound* document. A compound document is any document composed of two or more dissimilar document types joined via OLE.

Servers, Clients, Containers, and Other Terms

Let's look a little more closely at how applications work together to create compound documents. First consider that there are two separate and distinct roles played by programs in the process of sharing information through OLE. One program originates the object that is to be embedded or linked. This is called the OLE *server*. The other program accepts the object. This is called the OLE *client*. For example, in Figure 6.10, Lotus 1-2-3 is the originating (server) program and the word processor is the accepting (client) program.

Sophisticated Windows applications usually will work both as OLE servers and as clients. As an example, consider a spreadsheet program such as Excel. This program can supply charts and worksheet objects to a word processor or desktop-publishing program—acting as an OLE server. Excel can also accept embedded database objects from, say, Access.

This bidirectionality isn't always the case, however. For example, Windows Write and WordPad can function only as clients, while programs such as Paint, Media Player, and Sound Recorder can only behave as servers.

Two final terms you'll need to know are: the *source document* is the one in which an object is originally created, while a *destination document* is the one into which you place the object. I'll be using these terms in this chapter as we get into the procedures for creating compound documents.

Object Packages

In addition to the two basic OLE options I've described above—linking and embedding—there is a third variation of OLE called *packaging*. Packaging is a technique you can use to wrap up an object into a cute little bundle represented by an icon. Then you drop the icon into the destination document. For example, you might want to drop a sound clip or video clip into a document in this way. When the reader of the container document comes across the icon, he or she just double-clicks on it and it unwraps, so to speak. The video clip runs in a window, a sound clip plays, and so forth. Of course, this is only useful if the document is being viewed on a computer because nothing happens when you double-click on a piece of paper! It's particularly useful when sending e-mail messages because it keeps the messages smaller. Figure 6.12 shows an example of a WordPad document with a sound-file package embedded in it.

You add a package to a document using the Explorer, the File Manager, or the Object Packager program.

FIGURE 6.12

*Packaging a docu-
ment iconizes it for
later replay when
double-clicked on.*

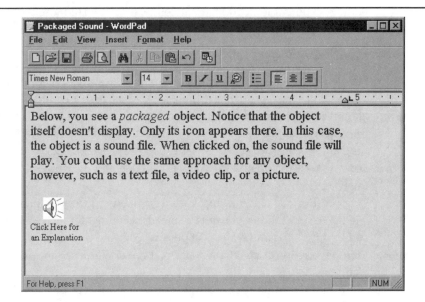

Embedding Objects

The difference between linking and embedding throws people sometimes, so let's talk about that for a minute. It might help to think of embedding an object as almost identical to pasting a static copy of it from the Clipboard in a regular old non-OLE document. This is because neither embedding nor pasting involves a link to external files. Once a chart is embedded into your word-processing file, it becomes part of that file. The only difference between standard Clipboard cut and paste and OLE embedding is that once embedded, an object can easily be edited by double-clicking on it or via some other command. Even though the object (let's say a graph) isn't something the container application (let's say Word) knows how to edit, the object contains a pointer to a program that can edit it.

Here are the basic steps:

1. Open the source application and document. (The application must be able to perform as an OLE server.)

TIP

You might want to try this using some OLE applications, such as Word, Excel, 1-2-3, Wordpad, or Sound Recorder, just to name a few.

2. Select the portion of the document you want to embed in another.

3. Switch to the destination application and document. Position the insertion point and choose Paste Special. When you do so, you may see a dialog box giving you some choices about what you want to do. For example, here are two Paste Special boxes, one from Word and one from Excel.

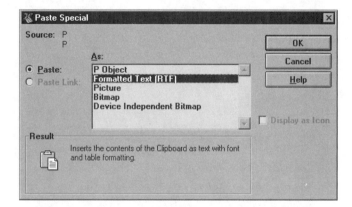

As I said before, you might have to do a little head scratching to figure out which option to choose, but here are some tips. As a rule, if the option says just plain Paste, that won't get you anything more than a normal paste job—which isn't what you want. What you want is some choice that does *not* say Link, but *does* say something about an *object*. So, for example, in Word's dialog box you'd choose the first option and click on OK. In the Excel box you'd choose Object and click on Paste (not on Paste Link, because that will link the object rather than embedding it). Some dialog boxes will let you choose to display the pasted information as an icon rather than as the item itself. For example, normally an embedded video clip will appear in a box that displays the first video frame of the clip.

After doing the Paste operation, and assuming both applications are OLE aware, you might get what looks like a static copy of the material (such as a bitmap), but the destination application will know from whence it was received and thus it can be easily edited. Figure 6.13 shows an example of an MS-Graph file embedded in a Word document.

After pasting an object into Word, the graph appears in the container document.

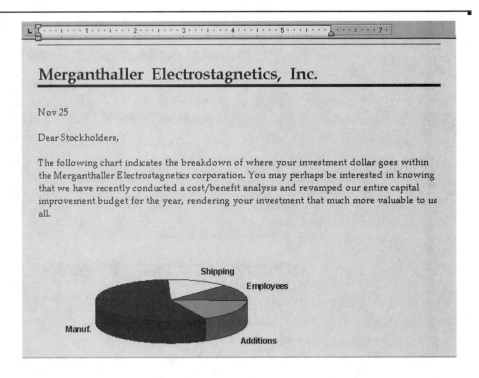

TIP

With some OLE applications you can embed an object using a command choice, such as Insert ➢ Object. This leads to a dialog box from where you choose the type of object (all the OLE-aware programs on your system are listed). When you choose, the source application runs and you can then create the object and exit. When you exit, the object is placed in the container document you were previously working in.

Editing an Embedded Object

Now assume you've got an object embedded in a document; anyone viewing the document can see it, or you can print it out, and so forth. If it's a video clip or sound clip, double-clicking on it brings up a suitable program—such as Sound Recorder or Media Player—running the clip and allowing the reader of the document to pause, stop, rewind, and replay the clip as needed. For other types of objects, double-clicking makes the object really easy to edit. For example, say you have a graph in your Word document.

1. Double-click on the embedded item. Depending on whether the applications involved are OLE 1.0 or OLE 2.0, several different scenarios may occur. If both applications are 2.0 aware, what ideally happens is that the toolbar, menus, and commands in the application you're working with (the container application) change to those of the object. Use them just as if you were working in whatever program created the object. If one or both of the applications are only OLE 1.0 aware, the object's source application will run in its own window, and the object will be loaded into it. Edit as you normally would.

NOTE

Note that in some cases, such as a sound or video clip, double-clicking on an object will "play" the object rather than edit it. You'll have to edit it via another means, such as right-clicking on it and choosing Edit or selecting it, opening the File menu, and choosing Edit Object or some similar command.

2. Choose File ➢ Update and then File ➢ Exit, or just File ➢ Exit and then answer Yes to any resulting dialog boxes about updating.

As an alternative to the above technique, an application may have an Edit menu option for editing the object. Select the object first, then check the Edit menu.

Linking Objects

Recall that linking an object is similar to embedding it, but there's one important difference. When linking, the object and the container both "live" in separate files on your hard disk somewhere. However, there is a connection between the linked document and the container it's linked to. This connection is called, not surprisingly, the *link*. So, instead of copying the object's data to the destination document, the link tells the destination application where to find the original source file.

As long as the link isn't broken, it is kept live by Windows, even between sessions. You can edit the linked object by double-clicking on it in the container document, just as you can an embedded object. However, the object will open in a separate window for editing—even if both the server and client applications are OLE aware.

You can also edit the object separately using the program that created it, even if the container document isn't open. For example, if the linked item is a spreadsheet file, editing it at its source (say by running 1-2-3, opening the file, editing the spreadsheet, and saving it) will still work. What's more, any changes you make to the file independently will show up in any and all linked files. Because of this, linking is the technique to use when you want to use data that must always be identical in two or more documents.

To link two files:

1. Create or find the server document you want to link (the source document). For example, you could open Paint and draw something.

NOTE

Before a file can be linked, it has to be given a name and saved on disk. Windows won't let you link a file that's still called Untitled (the default name of many documents before they are saved).

2. Select the portion of the document you want to pull into the container document.

3. Choose Edit ➤ Copy to put it onto the Clipboard.

4. Switch to the destination document.

5. Move the insertion point to the place where you want to insert the linked item.

6. Open the container's Edit menu and choose Edit ➤ Paste Link (not Paste). If there isn't a Paste Link command, look for Paste Special and the relevant linking option. You'll likely see a dialog box something like one of the two on the next page.

Up and Running

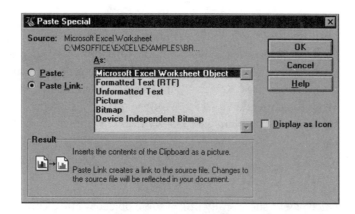

Choose options from the box as you see fit. Whatever the case, because you want to link rather than embed, choose a Paste Link option, as illustrated above.

 **NOTE**

Some friendlier Paste Special dialog boxes explain what effect the various format options will have when you paste the link. The default choice (the one that comes up highlighted when the box first appears) is usually your best bet. However, you might prefer one of the other choices, particularly if you want the linked material to have the exact same look as the source. When linking to a spreadsheet, for example, if you want the headings, grid, and exact font in which the spreadsheet is displayed, you'd choose Bitmapped Picture. Note however, that linking data as a picture rather than text will take up much more room on the disk, making your file much larger. Importing data as formatted text is much more space efficient.

7. If you want to establish a second link, repeat steps 4 through 6, selecting a different destination document in step 4.

The linked item should now be added to the container document in the correct position. If everything went as planned, the object will appear in its original form. That is, a graphic looks like a graphic, cells look like cells, and so forth. In some cases, when OLE applications aren't communicating properly, you'll see the source application's icon instead. This can happen with older applications such as Windows 3.x's Write program and Word for Windows 2.0. If this happens, you're better off just pasting in the text as plain text. Otherwise what you get is essentially a packaged object (see the sections below on packaging).

Editing a Linked Object

Once you've successfully linked some object(s) into a container document, you can check out how well it works. Adjust both windows so you can see both sets of the same data (source and destination). Try altering the source and notice how, in a few seconds, the linked version of the data (stored in the container document) is updated as well.

But what about editing the linked stuff right from the container document? No problem. Just as with editing embedded objects, you simply double-click. The result, however, is different because changes you make to a linked object appear in all the documents you've linked it to.

Here's the basic game plan for editing a typical linked object.

1. In any of the documents the object has been linked to, simply double-click on the object. The source application will open in a window, with the object loaded. For example, Figure 6.14 shows some linked spreadsheet cells that opened in Excel when I double-clicked on them from a WordPad document.

As an alternative, check the Edit menu. If you click on the object once and open the Edit menu, it may have an option such as Edit Object on it. Many Windows 9x applications are also supporting the right–mouse-click approach to editing. Click on the item, then click the right mouse button. You're likely to see an option such as Edit Lotus 1-2-3 Worksheet Link.

2. In the source application's window, make your edits.

3. Choose File ➢ Save, then File ➢ Exit. Changes you made should appear in all destination documents containing links to this source material.

FIGURE 6.14

Editing a linked object is usually as easy as double-clicking on it. You can also try right-clicking or check the Edit menu for a special editing command.

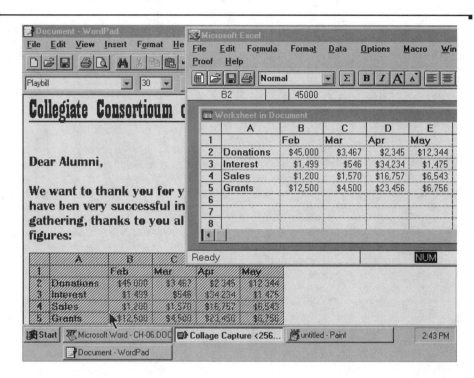

PART II

Exploring Windows 98

CHAPTERS:

7. Basic Customizing with the Control Panel

8. Printers and Printing

9. Using Fonts Effectively

10. Windows Multimedia

11. Object Properties and the Right-Click

12. Working with the File System and Windows Explorer

Chapter

7

Basic Customizing with the Control Panel

FEATURING

Accessibility options

Adding new hardware

Adding and removing programs

Audio control

Setting the date and time

Customizing your screen display

Adjusting the mouse

Basic Customizing
with the Control Panel

There are numerous alterations you can make to customize Windows to your liking—adjustments to screen colors, modems, mouse speed, passwords, key repeat rate, fonts, and networking options, to name just a few. Most of these adjustments are not necessities as much as they are niceties that make using Windows just a little easier. Others are more imperative, such as setting up Windows to work with your brand and model of printer, setting up Windows Messaging preferences for your e-mail, or getting your mouse pointer to slow down a bit so you can reasonably control it.

Preferences of this sort are made through Windows 98's Control Panel. Once you change a setting with the Control Panel, alterations are stored in the Windows configuration Registry. The settings are reloaded each time you run Windows and stay in effect until you change them again with the Control Panel.

A few Control Panel settings can be altered from other locations throughout Windows. For example, you can set up printers from the Start ➤ Settings ➤ Printers command, you can make Windows Messaging settings from within Exchange, and you can change your screen's settings by right-clicking on the Desktop. However, such approaches essentially run the Control Panel option responsible for the relevant settings, so the Control Panel is still doing the work. Running the Control Panel to make system changes is often easier because it displays in one place all the options for controlling your system. This chapter discusses how you run and work with the Control Panel and delves into what the multifarious settings are good for.

Opening the Control Panel

You open the Control Panel by clicking on the Start button, choosing Settings, and choosing Control Panel. The Control Panel window then opens, as shown in Figure 7.1.

TECH TIP

The Control Panel can also be reached from My Computer or from the Explorer. From the Explorer, scroll the left pane to the top and click on the My Computer icon. Then double-click on the Control Panel in the right pane.

FIGURE 7.1

The Control Panel window. Each item opens a window from which you can make adjustments.

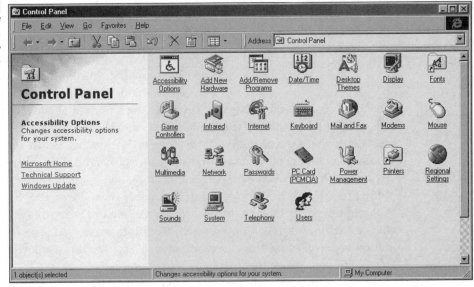

In your Control Panel there will be as many as twenty or so items to choose from, depending on the hardware in your computer and which items you opted for during installation of Windows 98. As you add new software or hardware to your system, you'll occasionally see new options in your Control Panel, too. Or your mouse icon might look different from the one you see in the figure. One of my computers has a Microsoft Ballpoint mouse, so the icon looks like a trackball rather than a tabletop mouse.

Each icon in the Control Panel runs a little program (called an *applet*) when you double-click on it, typically bringing up one or more dialog boxes for you to make settings in. Below is a list of all the standard Control Panel applets and what they do.

Accessibility Options Lets you set keyboard, mouse, sound, display, and other options that make a Windows 95 computer easier to use by those who are visually, aurally, or motor impaired.

Add New Hardware Installs or removes sound, CD-ROM, video, MIDI, hard- and floppy-disk controllers, PCMCIA sockets, display adaptors, SCSI controllers, keyboard, mouse, printers, ports, and other device drivers.

Add/Remove Programs You can add or remove modules of Windows 95 itself and sometimes add or remove other kinds of programs. Also lets you create a start-up disk to start your computer with in case the operating system on the hard disk gets trashed accidentally.

Date/Time Sets the current date and time and which time zone you're in.

Desktop Themes These combine custom sounds, color schemes, screen savers, and cursors into easily chosen settings groups.

Display Sets the colors (or gray levels) and fonts of various parts of Windows' screens, title bars, scroll bars, and so forth. Sets the background pattern or picture for the Desktop. Also allows you to choose the screen saver, display driver, screen resolution, and energy-saving mode (if your display supports it).

Fonts Adds and deletes typefaces for your screen display and printer output. Allows you to look at samples of each of your fonts. Fonts are discussed at length in Chapter 9.

Game Controllers Adds, removes, and adjusts settings for "joysticks" and other types of game controllers.

Infrared Configures and monitors infrared (wireless) communications.

Internet Settings for all Internet-related activities such as Web, mail, newsgroups, your home page location, etc. See Chapters 15 and 17 for details.

Keyboard Sets the rate at which keys repeat when you hold them down, sets the cursor blink rate, determines the language your keyboard will be able to enter into documents, and lets you declare the type of keyboard you have. Covered in Chapter 29.

Mail As explained in Part III and Chapter 25, profiles are groups of settings that control how your faxing and e-mail are handled. This applet lets you manage these profiles.

Microsoft Mail Postoffice If you are connected to a network that has a Microsoft Mail Postoffice, this applet lets you administer the postoffice or create a new postoffice. Postoffices are used as a central repository for mail on a network. This is covered in Chapter 17.

Modems Lets you add, remove, and set the properties of the modem(s) connected to your system. Covered in Chapter 15.

Mouse Sets the speed of the mouse pointer's motion relative to your hand motion and how fast a double-click has to be to have an effect. You can also reverse the functions of the right and left buttons, set the shape of the various Windows 95 pointers, and tell Windows 95 that you've changed the type of mouse you have.

Multimedia Changes the Audio, MIDI, CD music, and other multimedia device drivers, properties, and settings. See Chapter 10 for details.

Network Function varies with the network type. Typically allows you to set the network configuration (network card/connector, protocols, and services), add and configure optional support for Novell, Banyan, Sun network support, and network backup hardware, change your identification (workgroup name, computer name), and determine the manner in which you control who gains access to resources you share over the network, such as printers, fax modems, and folders. See Part V for details.

Passwords Sets up or changes log-on passwords, allows remote administration of the computer, and sets up individual profiles that go into effect when each new user logs onto the local computer. Passwords and security are covered in Chapter 26.

PCMCIA Lets you stop PCMCIA cards before removing them, set the memory area for the card service shared memory (very unlikely to be needed), and disable/enable the beeps that indicate PCMCIA cards are activated when the computer boots up. This icon only appears on laptops or on desktop machines configured with PCMCIA slots.

Power Management If you have a battery-powered portable computer or an energy-efficient desktop machine, this applet provides options for setting the Advanced Power Management details and viewing a scale indicating the current condition of the battery charge.

Printers Displays the printers you have installed on your system, lets you modify the property settings for those printers, and lets you display and manage the print *queue* for each of those printers. Use this applet to install *printer drivers*. (Installing new printer drivers and managing the print queue are covered in Chapter 8.)

Regional Settings Sets how Windows displays times, dates, numbers, and currency.

Sounds Turns off and on the computer's beep or adds sounds to various system events if your computer has built-in sound capability. Lets you set up sound *schemes*— preset collections of sounds that your system uses to alert you to specific events.

System Displays information about your system's internals—devices, amount of RAM, type of processor, and so forth. Also lets you add to, disable, and remove specific devices from your system, set up hardware profiles (for instance, to allow automatic optimization when using a docking station with a laptop), and optimize some parameters of system performance such as CD cache size and type. This applet also provides a number of system-troubleshooting tools. The use of the System applet is rather complex and thus is covered in Chapters 22, 23, and 29.

NOTE

All the Control Panel setting dialog boxes have a ? button in their upper-right corner. Remember from Chapter 3 that you can click on this button, then on an item in the dialog box that you have a question about. You'll be shown some relevant explanation about the item.

I'll now discuss the Control Panel applets in detail. Aside from the Accessibility settings, the applets here are the ones you're most likely to want to adjust.

Telephony Lets you delete your location, your dialing prefixes for an outside line, and other attributes relating to telephone-dependent activities that rely on the TAPI interface. Refer to Chapter 13 for more details.

Users Enables your computer to set up for use by other people, allowing each of them to have their own Desktop icons, background, color choices, and other settings. See Part V.

PART

II

Exploring Windows 98

Accessibility Options

Accessibility means increasing the ease of use or access to a computer for people who are physically challenged in one way or another. Many people have difficulty seeing characters on the screen when they are too small, for example. Others have a disability that prevents them from easily typing on the keyboard. Even those of us who hunt and peck at the keyboard have it easy compared to those who can barely move their hands, are limited to the use of a single hand, or who may be paralyzed from the neck down. These people have gotten the short end of the stick for some time when it came to using computers unless they had special data-entry and retrieval devices (such as speech boards) installed in their computers.

Microsoft has taken a big step in increasing computer accessibility to disabled people by including in Windows 95 proper, features that allow many challenged people to use Windows 95 and Windows programs without major modification to their machines or software. (Accessibility add-ons for Windows 3.*x* and NT have been available for some time, but as add-ons.)

The Accessibility applet lets you make special use of the keyboard, display, mouse, sound board, and a few other aspects of your computer. To run the Accessibility option, double-click on its icon in the Control Panel. The resulting dialog box looks like Figure 7.2.

FIGURE 7.2

Accessibility dialog box

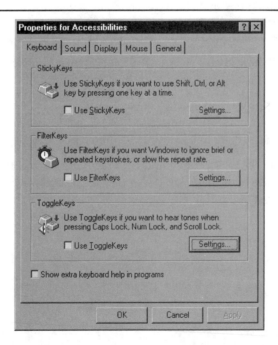

NOTE

As of Windows 98, several new accessibility features have been added, including support for screen readers, larger high-contrast font displays, screen magnification, and more. Most of these features are available via the Accessibility Wizard, which is an entry point and interface for the settings described in this section. To reach this wizard, click Start ➤ Programs ➤ Accessories ➤ Accessibility. For more information about Microsoft's ongoing advancements in accessibility support, and for API information, please see http://microsoft.com/enable.

Keyboard Accessibility Settings

Probably all of us have some difficulty keeping multiple keys depressed at once. Settings here help with this problem and others.

1. Click on the Keyboard tab (if it's not already selected). There are three basic setting areas:

StickyKeys	Keys that in effect stay pressed down when you press them once. Good for controlling the Alt, Ctrl, and Shift keys.
FilterKeys	Lets you filter out quickly repeated keystrokes in case you have trouble pressing a key cleanly once and letting it up. This prevents multiple keystrokes from being typed.
ToggleKeys	Gives you the option of hearing tones that alert you to the Caps Lock, Scroll Lock, and Num Lock keys being activated.

2. Click on the box of the feature you want your Windows 98 machine to use.

3. Note that each feature has a Settings button from which you can make additional adjustments. To see the additional settings, click on the Settings button next to the feature, fine-tune the settings, and then click on OK. The most likely setting changes you'll make from these boxes are to turn on or off the shortcut keys.

4. After you have made all the keyboard changes you want, either move on to another tab in the Accessibility box or click on OK and return to the Control Panel.

PART

II

Exploring Windows 98

You can turn on any of these keyboard features—StickyKeys, FilterKeys, or ToggleKeys—with shortcuts at any time while in Windows 98. To turn on StickyKeys, press either Shift key five times in a row. To turn on FilterKeys, press and hold the right Shift key for eight seconds (it might take longer). To turn on the ToggleKeys option, press the Num Lock key for five seconds.

When StickyKeys or FilterKeys are turned on, a symbol will appear on the right side of the Taskbar indicating what's currently activated. For example, here I have the StickyKeys and FilterKeys both set on. StickyKeys is indicated by the three small boxes, representative of the Ctrl, Alt, and Shift keys. FilterKeys is represented by the stopwatch representative of the different key timing that goes into effect when the option is working.

Turning on FilterKeys will make it seem that your keyboard has ceased working. You have to press a key and keep it down for several seconds for the key to register. If you activate this setting and want to turn it off, the easiest solution is to use the mouse or switch to Control Panel (via the Taskbar), run the Accessibility applet, turn off FilterKeys, and click on OK.

Unless you disable this feature from the Settings dialog box, you can turn off StickyKeys by pressing two of the three keys that are affected by this setting. For example, pressing Ctrl and Alt at the same time will turn StickyKeys off.

Sound Accessibility Settings

There are two Sound Accessibility settings—Sound Sentry and Show Sounds (see Figure 7.3). These two features are for the hearing impaired. What they do is simply cause some type of visual display to occur in lieu of the normal beep, ding, or other auditory alert that the program would typically produce. The visual display might be something such as a blinking window (in the case of Sound Sentry) or it might be some kind of text caption (in the case of ShowSounds).

FIGURE 7.3

*The two Sound
Accessibility settings*

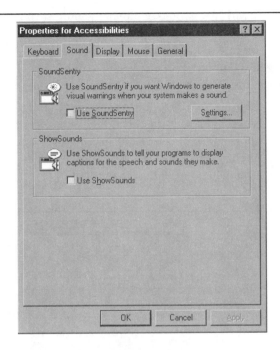

The Settings button for Sound Sentry lets you decide what will graphically happen on screen when a program is trying to warn you of something. For example, should it flash the window, flash the border of the program, or flash the whole screen? If you really don't want to miss a beep-type warning, you might want to have it flash the window. (Flashing the whole screen doesn't indicate which program is producing the warning.)

NOTE

Not all programs will work cooperatively with these sound options. As more programs are written to take advantage of these settings, you'll see more *closed captioning*, for example, wherein sound messages are translated into useful captions on the screen.

Display Accessibility Settings

The Display Accessibility settings pertain to contrast. These settings let you set the display color scheme and font selection for easier reading. This can also be done from the normal Display setting, described below, but the advantage to setting it here is

PART

II

Exploring Windows 98

that you can preset your favorite high-contrast color scheme, then invoke it with the shortcut key combination when you most need it. Just press Left-Alt, Left-Shift, Prnt-Scrn. This might be when your eyes are tired, when someone who is sight impaired is using the computer, or when you're sitting in an adverse lighting situation. Figure 7.4 displays the dialog box:

1. Turn on the High Contrast option box if you want to improve the contrast between the background and the characters on your screen. When you click on Apply or OK, this will kick in a high-contrast color scheme (typically the Blue and Black) scheme, which will put black letters on a white work area. (You can't get much more contrast than that!)

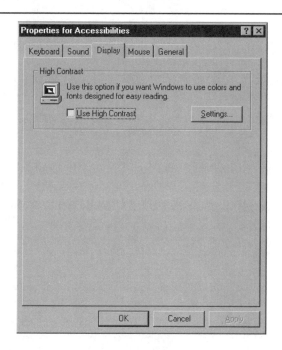

FIGURE 7.4

The dialog box for setting Display Accessibility

2. Click on the Settings button if you want to change the color scheme that'll be used for high contrast or if you want to enable or disable shortcut-key activation of this feature. This option may come in handy because some of the schemes have larger fonts than others and some might show up better on your screen than will others.

TIP

You can experiment more easily with the schemes in the Display applet than here. You can even create your own custom color scheme with large menus, title bar lettering, and dialog box lettering if you want. I explain how to do all this in the Display section.

3. Click on Apply if you want to keep making more settings from the other tab pages or on OK to return to the Control Panel.

Mouse Accessibility Settings

If you can't easily control mouse or trackball motion, or simply don't like using a mouse, this dialog box is for you. Of course, you can invoke most commands that apply to dialog boxes and menus throughout Windows and Windows programs using the Alt key in conjunction with the command's underlined letter. Still, some programs, such as those that work with graphics, require you to use a mouse. This Accessibility option turns your arrow keys into mouse-pointer control keys. You still have to use the mouse's clicker buttons to left- or right-click on things, though. Here's what to do:

1. Click on the Mouse tab in the Accessibility dialog box. You'll see the box displayed in Figure 7.5.

PART

II

Exploring Windows 98

FIGURE 7.5

The Mouse Accessibility dialog box

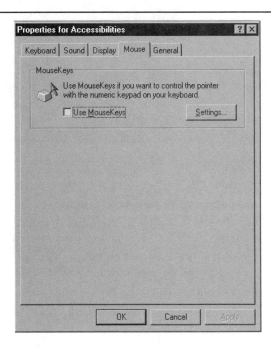

This is a great feature for laptop users who are on the road and forgot the mouse. If you have to use a graphics program or other program requiring more than simple command choices and text entry, use the Mouse Accessibility tab to turn your arrow keys into mouse-pointer keys.

2. Turn on the option if you want to use the arrow keys in place of the mouse. You'll probably want to adjust the speed settings for the arrow keys, though, so the pointer moves at a rate that works for you. The Settings button brings up the box you see in Figure 7.6. Note that you can also set a shortcut key sequence to activate MouseKeys.

FIGURE 7.6

Additional Mouse Accessibility settings

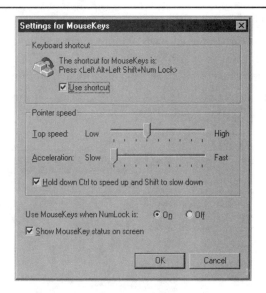

3. Play with the settings until you like them. The Top Speed and Acceleration settings are going to be the most important. And note that you have to set them, click on OK, then click on Apply in the Mouse dialog box before you can experience the effect of your changes. Then go back and adjust your settings if necessary. Notice that one setting lets you change the tracking speed on the fly while using a program, by holding down the Shift key to slow down the pointer's motion or the Ctrl key to speed it up.

4. Click on Apply if you want to keep making more settings from the other tab pages or on OK to return to the Control Panel.

 TIP

> The pointer keys that are used for mouse control are the ones on a standard desktop computer keyboard's number pad. These are the keys that have two modes—Num Lock on and Num Lock off. These keys usually have both an arrow and a number on them; for example, the 4 key also has a ← symbol on it. Most laptops don't have such keys because of size constraints. However, many laptops have a special arrangement that emulates these keys, providing a ten-key numeric keypad (and arrows when NumLock is off).

Wheel Mouse Support

One particularly crucial accessibility improvement in Windows 98 is the inclusion of support for the Microsoft "wheel mouse" (a.k.a. the Intellimouse™). That's a mouse with a little wheel sticking up between the mouse buttons. As mentioned in Chapter 3, when you spin the wheel with some newer programs it scrolls the contents of the active window; it relieves you of having to position the pointer on the scroll bar. Spinning the wheel one increment causes text to scroll several lines (default: three) per wheel detent.

Just because a window has a scroll bar doesn't mean it will work with the wheel. The program has to be "wheel aware." Some wheel-aware programs, including the programs in Office 97, will zoom in or out (cause the document to be displayed larger or smaller) if you rotate the wheel and hold down the Ctrl key at the same time.

Some wheel-aware applications (such as Internet Explorer or an Office 97 program) also offer "panning mode": you press down on the wheel to enter this special mode. When in panning mode, the mouse cursor changes to a special panning cursor, and just moving the mouse forward or backward will start the document scrolling in its window. The scroll speed is determined by how far you pull the mouse away from the position where you activated panning mode. When you want to exit the panning mode, simply press any mouse button.

Other Accessibility Settings

The last tab in the Accessibility box is called General (Figure 7.7).

FIGURE 7.7

The last of the Accessibility settings boxes

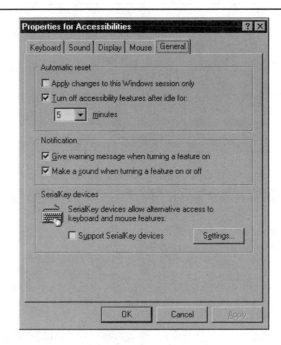

The box is divided into three sections pertaining to:

- When Accessibility functions are turned on and off. Notice that you can choose to have all the settings you've made during this Windows session apply only to this session (that means until you restart Windows).

- How you are alerted to a feature being turned on or off. You have the choice of a visual cue (a little dialog box will appear) and/or a sound.

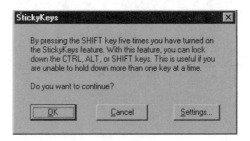

- Acceptance of alternative input devices through the serial (COM1 through COM4) ports on your computer.

Adding New Hardware

If you have a computer that is Plug-and-Play compatible, this section won't be of a lot of use to you, and you should celebrate. That's because, as I discussed in Chapter 1, Plug and Play ensures that by simply plugging a new card or other device into your computer, it will work. The Plug-and-Play software in Windows 98—in concert with software coding in the computer and add-on cards and devices—takes care of installing the appropriate hardware device driver file and making the appropriate settings so your new device doesn't conflict with some other device in the system. That's the good news.

TECH TIP

Of course, there are a limited number of IRQs, ports, and DMAs. Plug in enough Plug-and-Play cards, and one or more is guaranteed not to be installed by the system because Plug and Play will not enable a device unless resources are available for it.

The bad news is that there are a zillion non–Plug-and-Play PC cards and devices floating around in the world and just as many pre–Plug-and-Play PCs. This older hardware isn't designed to take advantage of Windows 98's Plug-and-Play capabilities. The upshot of this is that when you install such hardware into your system, many computers won't detect the change. This will result in disappointment when you've carefully installed some piece of new and exciting gear (such as a sound card) and it just doesn't work—or worse, it disables things that used to function just fine.

NOTE

If you're installing a new printer, please read Chapter 8 as well.

Microsoft has added a nifty feature that tries its best to install a new piece of hardware for you. All you have to do is declare your new addition and let Windows 95 run around and try to detect what you've done. Luckily, the Add Hardware applet is pretty savvy about interrogating the hardware you've installed—via its Install Hardware Wizard—and making things work right. You can also tell it exactly what you have in order to save a little time and ensure that Windows gets it right.

NOTE

Notice the applet is only for adding new hardware, not for removing hardware and associated driver files. Removing drivers is done through the System applet. Note that there are other locations throughout Windows for installing some devices, such as printers, which can be installed from the Printers folder via My Computer. However, the effect is the same as installing these devices from this applet.

TIP

Microsoft maintains a Windows 98 driver library that contains new, tested drivers as they are developed for printers, networks, screens, audio cards, and so forth. You can access these drivers through the Microsoft website, CompuServe, GEnie, or the Microsoft Download Service (MSDL). You can fax MSDL at (425) 936-6735. You can also order the entire library on disk by calling Microsoft at (800) 426-9400.

Running the Install Hardware Wizard

If you've purchased a board or other hardware add-in, first read the supplied manual for details about installation procedures. There may be installation tips and an install program supplied with the hardware. If there are no instructions, then install the hardware and follow the steps below (but *only* if there are no instructions).

NOTE

I suggest you install the hardware before you run the Wizard, or Windows 98 won't be able to validate that the hardware is present. Also, unless you follow these procedures, simply putting new hardware into your computer usually won't change anything. This is because Windows has to update the Registry containing the list of hardware in your system, it has to install the appropriate device-driver software for the added hardware, and it often has to reboot before the new hardware will work.

1. Close any programs you have running. You're probably going to be rebooting the machine, and it's possible that the detection process will hang up the computer, possibly trashing work files that are open.

2. Look up or otherwise discover the precise brand name and model number/name of the item you're installing. You'll need to know it somewhere during this process.

3. Run the Control Panel and double-click on the Add New Hardware applet. You'll see its dialog box, looking like the one in Figure 7.8.

FIGURE 7.8

The Add Hardware Wizard makes installing new hardware pretty easy, usually.

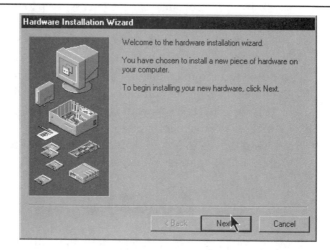

4. There's nothing to do but click on Next. The wizard looks for any new Plug-and-Play hardware, and will list anything new that it finds. The next box, as shown in Figure 7.9, requires some action on your part, though.

FIGURE 7.9

Choose the type of hardware you want to install.

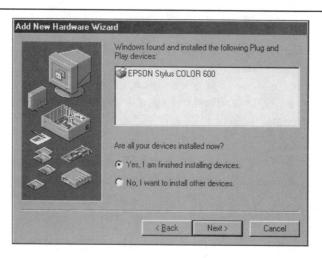

5. If the item(s) list looks complete, click Yes, I am finished and click Next. Follow instructions on screen. If you are not satisfied with the list and want some other stuff installed, click No, then next, and move to step 6.

6. Now, if you want the Wizard to run around, look at what you have, and notice the new item you installed, just leave the top option button selected and click on Next. You'll be warned that this could take several minutes and be advised to close any open programs and documents. Keep in mind that the Wizard is doing quite a bit of sleuthing as it looks over your computer. Many add-in cards and devices don't have standardized ID markings, so identifying some hardware items isn't so easy. The Microsoft programmers had to devise some clever interrogation techniques to identify myriad hardware items. In fact, the results may even be erroneous in some cases. Regardless, while the hardware survey is underway, you'll see a gauge apprising you of the progress, and you'll hear a lot of hard-disk activity. In rare cases, the computer will hang during this process, and you'll have to reboot. If this happens repeatedly, you'll have to tell the Wizard what hardware you've added, as explained in the next section.

7. When completed, you'll either be told that nothing new was found or you'll see a box listing the discovered items, asking for confirmation and/or some details. Respond as necessary. You may be prompted to insert one of your Windows 98 diskettes or the master CD-ROM so the appropriate driver file(s) can be loaded. If nothing new was found, click on Next, and the Wizard sends you on to step 2 in the section below.

Telling the Wizard What You've Got

If you're the more confident type (in your own abilities rather than the computer's), you might want to take the surer path to installing new hardware. Option two in the previous Wizard box lets *you* declare what the new hardware is. This option not only saves you time, but even lets you install the hardware later, should you want to. This is because the Wizard doesn't bother to authenticate the existence of the hardware: It simply installs the new driver.

1. Follow steps 1 through 5 above.

2. Now choose the second option button, *Install specific hardware*.

3. Scroll through the list to get an idea of all the classes of hardware you can install via this applet. Then click on the category you want to install. For this example,

I'm going to install Creative Lab's Sound Blaster sound card because that's a popular add-in item.

TIP

If you don't know the class of the item you're installing, you're not sunk. Just choose Other Devices. Find and click on the manufacturer's brand name in the left-hand list; most popular items made by that manufacturer will be displayed in the right-hand list. Then choose your new hardware from this list.

4. Click on Next. This brings up a list of all the relevant drivers in the class you've chosen. For example, Figure 7.10 lists the sound cards from Creative Labs, the people who make the Sound Blaster cards.

PART

II

Exploring Windows 98

FIGURE 7.10

After choosing a class of hardware, you'll see a list of manufacturers and models.

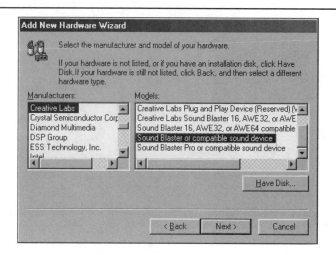

5. First scroll the left list and click on the manufacturer. Then find the correct item in the Model list and click on that.

6. Click on Next. What happens at this point depends on the type of hardware you're installing:

- If the hardware is Plug-and-Play compatible, you'll be informed of it, and the Wizard will take care of the details.

- For some non–Plug-and-Play hardware, you'll be told to simply click on Finish, and the Wizard will take care of installing the necessary driver.

- In some cases, you'll be shown the settings that you should adjust your hardware to match. (Add-in cards often have switches or software adjustments that control the I/O port, DMA address, and other such geeky stuff.) For example, Figure 7.11 shows the message I got about the Sound Blaster card. Your job is to read the manual that came with the hardware and figure out how to adjust the switches, jumpers, or other doodads to match the settings the Wizard gives you.

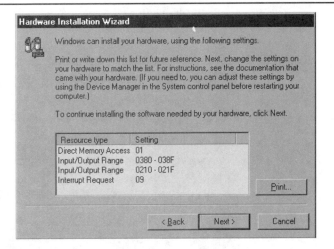

If for some reason you don't want to use the settings suggested by the Wizard, you can set the board or device otherwise. Then you'll have to use the System applet's Device Manager to change the settings in the Windows Registry to match those on the card. See Chapter 29 for coverage of the Device Manager.

- In some cases, you'll be told there's a conflict between your new hardware and what's already in your computer (Figure 7.12). Despite the dialog box's message, you have *three* choices, not two. In addition to proceeding or canceling, you could also back up and choose a different piece of hardware, such as a different model number or a compatible make or model that might support a different port, DMA address, or whatnot. If you decide to continue, you'll have to resolve the conflict somehow, such as by removing or readdressing the conflicting board or device. In that case you'll be shown a dialog box that lets you run the *conflict troubleshooter*. This is a combination of a Help file and the System applet's Device Manager. The Help file walks you through a series of questions and answers.

FIGURE 7.12

You have three options when the Wizard detects a conflict: the two choices offered and the Back button to try another piece of hardware.

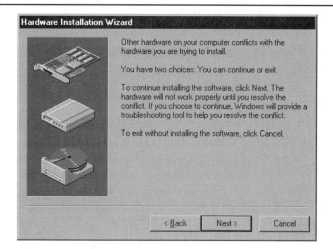

PART

II

Exploring Windows 98

7. Next, you may be prompted to insert a disk containing the appropriate software driver. Windows remembers the disk drive and directory you installed Windows 98 from, so it assumes the driver is in that location. This might be a network directory, your CD-ROM drive, or a floppy drive. In any case, just supply the requested disk. If the driver is already in your system, you will be asked if you want to use the existing driver. This is okay assuming the driver is up to date and you aren't trying to install a new one.

8. Finally, a box will announce that the necessary changes have been made and you can click on Finish. If you haven't physically installed the hardware already, you'll see this message:

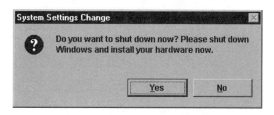

If the hardware is already installed, you'll probably see a message asking you to shut down and restart.

When Your Hardware Isn't on the List

Sometimes your new hardware won't be included in the list of items the Wizard displays. This means that Microsoft hasn't included a driver for that device on the disks that Windows 98 came on. This is probably because your hardware is newer than Windows 98, so it wasn't around when Windows 98 went out the door from Microsoft. Or it could be that the manufacturer didn't bother to get its product certified by Microsoft and earn the Windows "seal of approval." It's worth the few extra bucks to buy a product with the Windows 95 or 98 logo on the box rather than the cheapie clone product. As mentioned above, Microsoft makes new drivers available to users through several channels. However, manufacturers often supply drivers with their hardware, or you can get hold of a driver from a BBS, an information service such as CompuServe, or Microsoft Network.

If you're in this boat, you can just tell the Add New Hardware Wizard to use the driver on your disk. Here's how:

1. Run the Add New Hardware applet and choose the correct class of hardware, as explained above.

2. Click on the Have Disk button.

3. Enter the location of the driver (you can enter any path, such as a directory on the hard disk or network path) in this box.

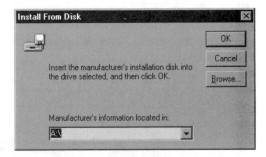

Typically, you'll be putting a disk in drive A, in which case you'd use the setting shown here. However, don't type the file name for the driver, just its path.

Usually this will be just A:\ or B:\. If the driver is on a hard disk or CD-ROM and you don't know which letter drive or which directory it is, use the Browse button and subsequent dialog box to select the source drive and directory. When the path is correct, click on OK.

4. Assuming the Wizard finds a suitable driver file (it must find a file called OEMSETUP.INF), choose the correct hardware item from the resulting dialog box and follow on-screen directions (they'll be the same as those I described above, beginning with step 6).

TECH TIP

If you're not sure which ports and interrupts your other boards are using, rather than use the old trial-and-error method, Windows 98 comes with a great tool for sleuthing this out—see Chapter 29 for a discussion of the Control Panel's System applet. Double-clicking on the Computer icon at the top of the Device Manager page in that applet will reveal a list of IRQs and ports that are currently in use.

Adding and Removing Programs

The topic of adding and removing programs is discussed in Chapter 5, in the context of the Program Manager and ways to organize your programs and documents. The applet has three functions:

- Installing and uninstalling programs that comply with Windows 98's API for these tasks. The API ensures that a program's file names and locations are recorded in a database, allowing them to be reliably erased without adversely impacting the operation of Windows 98.

- Installing and removing specific portions of Windows 98 itself, such as Windows Messaging.

- Creating a start-up disk that will start your computer in case the operating system gets trashed beyond functionality for some reason. With a start-up disk, you should still be able to gain access to your files and stand a chance of repairing the problem that prevents the machine from starting up.

Installing New Programs

The applet's first tab page is for installing new programs.

1. Run Control Panel, then the Add/Remove Software applet. You'll see the box shown in Figure 7.13.

FIGURE 7.13

The Wizard for adding and removing software can be reached from the Add/Remove Programs applet (only programs that comply with Windows 98 installation standards).

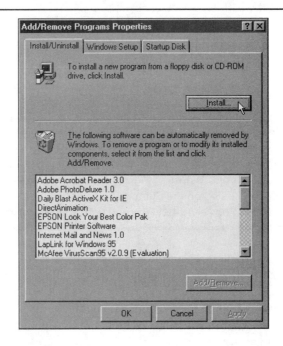

2. Click on Install. Now a new box appears, telling you to insert a floppy disk or CD-ROM in the appropriate drive and click on Next. Assuming an appropriate program is found (it must be called *install* or *setup* and have a `.bat`, `.pif`, `.com`, or `.exe` extension), it'll be displayed as you see in Figure 7.14.

3. Click on Finish to complete the task. The new software's installation or setup procedure will now run. Instructions will vary depending on the program. If your program's setup routine isn't compatible with the applet, you'll be advised of this. After installation, the new program will appear in the list of removable programs only if it's compatible with Windows 98's install/remove scheme.

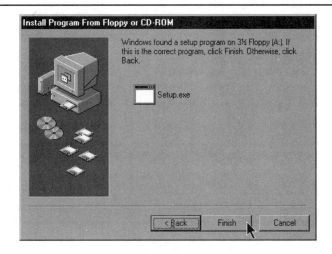

FIGURE 7.14

The Wizard looks for a likely installation program on your CD-ROM or floppy, and displays the first one it finds.

Removing Existing Programs

With time, more programs will be removable via the Control Panel. This is because the PC software industry at large has heard much kvetching from users and critics about tenacious programs that once installed are hard to remove. Some ambitious programs spread themselves out all over your hard disk like olive oil in a hoagie, and there's no easy way of reversing the process to return your system to a pristine state. The result is often overall system slowdown, unexplained crashes, or other untoward effects.

To this end, aftermarket utilities such as Uninstaller have become quite popular. Uninstall utility programs monitor and record just exactly what files a new software package adds to your hard disk and which internal Windows settings it modifies. It can then undo the damage later, freeing up disk space and tidying your Windows system.

In typical fashion, Microsoft has incorporated such a scheme into Windows 98 itself. Time will tell if its mousetrap is as good as the competition's. Probably not, but it will be "close enough for jazz," as the saying goes. Programmers are befinning to write installation routines that work with Windows 9*x*'s Add/Remove Software applet, so it looks like we're in luck.

Use of the uninstall feature of the applet is simple:

1. In the bottom pane, select the program(s) you want to uninstall.

2. Click on Remove.

3. Answer any warnings about removing an application as appropriate.

PART

II

Exploring Windows 98

NOTE

Once removed, you'll have to reinstall a program from its source disks to make it work again. You can't just copy things out of the Recycle Bin to their old directories because settings from the Start button—and possibly the Registry—will have been deleted.

TIP

Always check a program's disk or program group (from the Start button) for the possible existence of its own uninstall program. Such programs are frequently more thorough than the Windows Add/Remove Software approach.

Setting the Date and Time

NOTE

You can also adjust the time and date using the TIME and DATE commands from the DOS prompt, or by double-clicking the time in the System Tray on the end of the Taskbar.

The Date/Time icon lets you adjust the system's date and time. The system date and time are used for a number of purposes, including date- and time-stamping the files you create and modify, scheduling fax transmissions, and so on. All programs use these settings, regardless of whether they are Windows or non-Windows programs. (This applet doesn't change the format of the date and time—just the actual date and time. To change the *format*, you use the Regional applet as discussed in Chapter 29.)

1. Double-click on the Date/Time applet. The dialog box in Figure 7.15 appears.

2. Adjust the time and date by typing in the corrections or clicking on the arrows. Note that you have to click directly on the hours, minutes, seconds, or am/pm area before the little arrows to the right of them will modify the correct value.

3. Next, you can change the time zone you are in. Who cares about the time zone, you ask? Good question. For many users it doesn't matter. But because people fax to other time zones, and some programs help you manage your transcontinental and transoceanic phone calling, it's built into Windows 98. These programs need

to know where in the world you and Carmen Sandiego are. So, click on the Time Zone tab and you'll see a world map (Figure 7.16).

FIGURE 7.15

Adjust the date, time, and local time zone from this dialog box. A shortcut to this box is the double-click on the time in the Taskbar.

Set month from drop-down list

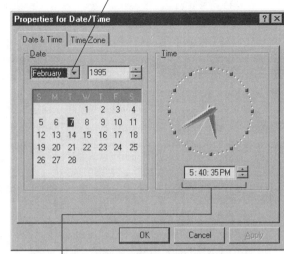

Click in desired area and use the little arrows to adjust

FIGURE 7.16

Check and set your time if necessary. Some programs will use this information to help you schedule mail or fax transmissions to other time zones. For laptop users who travel, this can be a great boon. Just point to your new location and click. The computer's time is automatically adjusted.

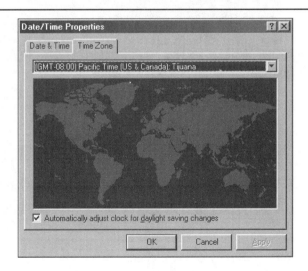

PART

II

Exploring Windows 98

Desktop Themes

The Desktop Themes applet combines sound schemes, color schemes, screen savers, and cursors for your Windows 98 system. It isn't much different from what you can achieve using the Sounds, Display, and Mouse applets from the Control Panel. The advantage of Desktop Themes is that settings from these three areas are pulled into one applet called Desktop Themes, making it easy to recall many settings at once. If you've installed Desktop Themes (use Control Panel's Add/Remove Software applet, then choose Windows Setup), you'll have several preset themes to choose from, some of which are fairly artistic.

Desktop Themes isn't just a tool for organizing your own settings into groups. You also get some great sounds and Desktop backgrounds; you also get cute new icons for My Computer, the Recycle Bin, and Network Neighborhood.

Running the applet brings up the dialog box shown in Figure 7.17.

FIGURE 7.17

Desktop Themes provides a means for coordinating various elements of the Windows 98 environment and saving them under a single name. An interesting variety of Desktop Themes is supplied with the Microsoft Plus! package.

You can create your own schemes by setting up the screen saver, sounds, cursor, and Desktop the way you like and then saving them using the Save As button at the top of the box. However, you might find that the supplied themes give you all the variation you need. Choose a theme from the drop-down list box to see what it looks like. You can preview the screen saver, pointers, and sounds using the two Preview buttons in the upper right corner.

Because some of the visuals are actually photo-realistic, some of the schemes may look pretty bad on your monitor, even in 256 colors, if you don't switch to a high-color or true-color setting. High-color themes are marked as such. If you *don't* have a high-color video driver, you might as well remove these schemes; it will save a significant amount of disk space (about 9MB).

In the Settings portion of the box, you'll see eight checkboxes for things like Screen Saver, Sound Events, and so on. Each scheme includes settings for all these options. However, you might not want to load all these features when you change schemes; for example, you might like the sounds you already have but want everything else from one of the Desktop Themes. To do this, turn off the Sound Events option before clicking on Apply or OK.

To switch back to the ordinary Windows 98 settings, choose the Windows Default master theme at the bottom of the list of themes.

Customizing Your Screen Display

The Display icon is accessible either from the Control Panel **or** from the Desktop. Right-click on an empty area of the Desktop and choose Properties.

The Display applet packs a wallop under its hood. For starters, it incorporates what in Windows 3.*x* were the separate Color and Desktop Control Panel applets for prettying up the general look of the Windows screen. Then, in addition, it includes the means for changing your screen driver and resolution—functions heretofore (in Windows 3.*x*) available only from the Setup program. If you were annoyed by getting at all these areas of display tweaking from disjunct venues, suffer no more. Microsoft has incorporated all display-related adjustments into the unified Display applet. If you are among the blessed, you will even have the option of changing screen resolution on the fly. If you've been using Windows 95, well, there's new stuff her for you, too.

Here are the functional and cosmetic adjustments you can make to your Windows 98 display from this applet:

- Set the background and wallpaper for the Desktop.
- Set the screen saver and energy conservation.
- Set the color scheme and fonts for Windows elements.
- Set the display device driver and adjust resolution, color depth, and font size.
- Change the icons you want to use for basic stuff on your Desktop such as My Computer and the Recycle Bin.
- Set color management compatibility so that your monitor and your printer output colors match.
- Decide which Web goodies you want alive on your Desktop, such as stock quotes, news, the Channel Bar, and so forth.

Let's take a look at this dialog box page by page. This is a fun one to experiment with and will come in handy if you know how to use it.

First run the applet by double-clicking on it.

Setting the Background and Wallpaper

The pattern and wallpaper settings simply let you decorate the Desktop with something a little more festive than the default screen. Patterns are repetitious designs, such as the woven look of fabric. Wallpaper uses larger pictures that were created by artists with a drawing program. You can create your own patterns and wallpaper or use the ones supplied. Wallpapering can be done with a single copy of the picture placed in the center of the screen or by tiling, which gives you multiple identical pictures covering the whole screen. Some of the supplied wallpaper images cannot be used if you are low on memory. This is because the larger bit-mapped images take up too much RAM.

Loading a Pattern

To load a new pattern,

1. Click on the Background tab of the applet's dialog box.
2. Scroll the Wallpaper list to a pattern you're interested in and highlight it. A minuscule version of your choice will show up in the little screen in the dialog box (Figure 7.18).

FIGURE 7.18

Simply highlighting a pattern will display a facsimile of it in the dialog box's tiny monitor screen.

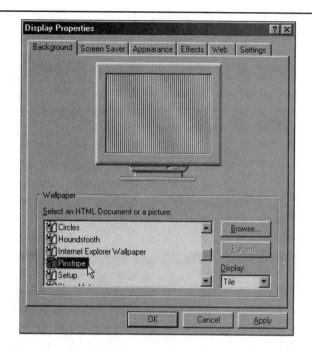

3. To see the effect on the whole screen, click on the Apply button. This keeps the applet open and lets you easily try other patterns and settings. (If you want to leave it at that, click on OK. Then the applet will close, and you'll be returned to the Control Panel.)

Open the Display drop-down list and choose Center, Tile, or Stretch to position the chosen item. If the picture is rather large, you'll want to use Center. Tile repeats the graphic across the screen in a mosaic, so that every inch is covered. Stretch will ensure that a single copy of the graphic fills the entire screen. This can look pretty ghastly, since usually the dimensions of the graphic become disproportional.

You can have a *pattern* on your Desktop rather than wallpaper, if you want. Patterns give the Desktop a nice texture rather than placing a whole picture there. And they easily fill up the whole Desktop if you use the Tile setting.

To choose a pattern, follow these steps:

1. Select None in the list on the left.

2. Click on Pattern.

3. From the resulting list, choose a pattern you like.

4. Click on OK.

NOTE

For a pattern to show up, wallpaper has to be set to None or be smaller than the full-screen size. This is because wallpaper always sits on top of the Desktop's pattern.

Editing a Pattern

If the supplied patterns don't thrill you, make up your own with the built-in bitmap editor. You can either change an existing one or design your own. If you want to design your own, choose None from the Name drop-down list before you begin. Otherwise, choose a pattern you want to play with:

1. Click on the Edit Pattern button. A new dialog box appears.

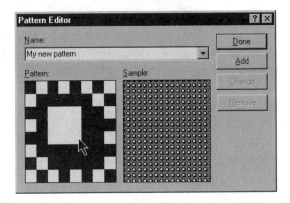

2. In the Name text box, type in a name for the new pattern.

3. Create the pattern by clicking in the box on the left. What you are doing is defining the smallest element of the repeated pattern (a cell). It is blown up in scale to make editing easier. Each click reverses the color of one pixel. The effect when the pattern is applied across a larger area and in normal size is shown in the Sample section to the right.

4. When you like the pattern, click on Add and the pattern will be added to your list of patterns.

5. Click on Done when you're through creating new patterns.

If you later want to remove a pattern, select the pattern while in the editor and click on Remove. If you want to edit an existing pattern, get into the editor, select an existing pattern, make changes to it, and click on Change.

TIP

If you want to abandon changes you've made to a pattern, click on the Close button (X) and answer No to the question about saving the changes.

Loading a New Slice of Wallpaper

If you don't like the wallpaper you see, you can go hunting. Click on Browse, and look around for something else to use. A nice improvement over Windows 95 is that you can now use pictures other than BMP (Microsoft Paint) files. So in addition to BMP files, GIF and JPG files will work. HTML files (a.k.a. Web pages) will also display as wallpaper on your Desktop. Well, most of them will. They may not link properly or scroll correctly, but they'll show up. With all these file types accepted as Desktop wallpaper, the sky's the limit. For example, you could use a scanned color photograph of your favorite movie star, a pastoral setting, some computer art, a scanned Matisse painting, or a photo of your pet lemur. Figure 7.19 shows an example of a custom piece of wallpaper.

PART

II

Exploring Windows 98

FIGURE 7.19

A custom piece of wallpaper Arthur Knowles, the technical editor of this book sent to me over the Microsoft Network. This is a .bmp file of the Apollo 11 base cam on the moon.

In Microsoft Paint's File menu there's a choice for setting the currently open bit-mapped file to Wallpaper. Chapter 21 covers the Paint program.

If you have some other form of picture file, such as a `.tif` or `.pcx` file that you want to use, you can, but you'll have to convert the file to `.bmp`, `.jpg`, or `.gif` format first using another graphics program such as Collage Image Manager, Publisher's Paintbrush, Paintshop Pro, or other.

Setting the Screen Saver

A Screen Saver will blank your screen or display a moving image or pattern if you don't use the mouse or keyboard for a predetermined amount of time. Screen savers can prevent a static image from burning the delicate phosphors on the inside surface of the monitor, which can leave a ghost of the image on the screen for all time no matter what is being displayed. They can also just be fun.

Many modern computer monitors have an EPA Energy Star, VESA, or other kind of energy-saving strategy built into them. Because far too many people leave their computers on all the time (although it's not really true that they will last longer that way), efforts have been made by power regulators and electronics manufacturers to devise computer–energy-conservation schemes. If your monitor has an Energy Star rating and your video board supports this feature, the screen saver in Windows 98 can power the monitor down after it senses you went out to lunch or got caught up at the water cooler for a longer-than-expected break.

The screen-saver options allow you to choose or create an entertaining video ditty that will greet you when you return to work. You also set how much time you have after your last keystroke or mouse skitter before the show begins. And a password can be set to keep prying eyes from toying with your work withl you're away.

TECH TIP

For an energy-saving screen saver to work properly, you'll have to set the Energy Star options from the Control Panel ➤ Display ➤ Settings ➤ Advanced Properties ➤ Monitor tab. Also, the monitor must adhere to the VESA Display Power Management Signaling (DPMS) specification or to another method of lowering power consumption. Some LCD screens on portable computers can do this. You can assume that if your monitor has an Energy Star emblem, it probably supports DPMS. Energy Star is a program administered by the U.S. Environmental Protection Agency (EPA) to reduce the amount of power used by personal computers and peripherals. If you notice that your screen freaks out or the display is garbled after your power-management screen saver turns on, you should turn off this check box.

Loading a Screen Saver

Here's how it's done:

1. Click on the Screen Saver tab. The page appears as you see in Figure 7.20.

PART

II

Exploring Windows 98

FIGURE 7.20

Setting up a screen saver

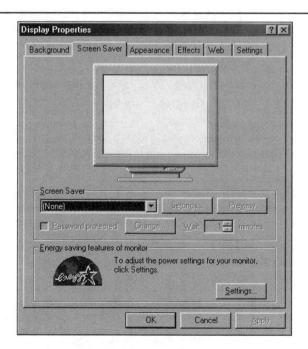

2. Choose a name from the drop-down list. The saver will be shown in the little screen in the dialog box. (The 3-D Pipes are particularly dazzling.)

3. Want to see how it will look on your whole screen? Click on Preview. Your screen will go black and then begin its antics. The show continues until you hit any key or move your mouse.

4. If you want to change anything about the selected screen saver, click on Settings. You'll see a box of settings that apply to that particular screen saver. For example, for the Mystify Your Mind saver, this is the Settings box:

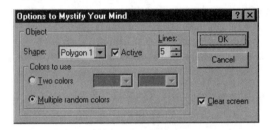

Most of the option boxes have fun sliders and stuff you can play with to get an effect you like. Depending on which screen saver you chose, you'll have a few possible adjustments, such as speed, placement, and details pertinent to the graphic. Play with the settings until you're happy with the results and OK the Setting box.

5. Back at the Screen Saver page, the next choice you might want to consider is Password Options. If you set password protection on, every time your screen saver is activated you will have to type your password into a box to return to work. This is good if you don't want anyone else tampering with your files or seeing what you're doing. It can be a pain, though, if there's no particular need for privacy at your computer. Don't forget your password, either, or you'll have to reboot to get back to work. Of course, anyone could reboot your computer to get to your files, so this means of establishing security is somewhat bogus. Click on the Password Protected check box if you want protection and go on to the next two steps. Otherwise skip them.

6. Click on the Change button to define or change your password. In the dialog box that appears, type in your new password.

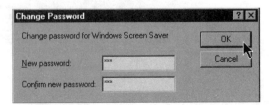

You won't see the letters, just an asterisk for each letter (to preserve confidentiality). For confirmation that you typed it correctly, type it again (don't copy the first one and paste it; a mistake in the first one can result in your being locked out of your computer) in the Confirm New Password text box. If there is a discrepancy between the two, you'll get an error message. Reenter the password. (If you're changing a password, the steps will be approximately the same. Enter your old password first, then the new one and its confirmation.) When it is correct, click on OK.

7. Back at the Desktop dialog box, set the number of minutes you want your computer to be idle before the screen saver springs into action. Next to Wait, either type in a number or use the up and down arrows to change the time incrementally.

8. Next you have the Energy Star options. Energy Star monitors need an Energy Star-compatible video card in the computer. If your screen setup supports this, the options will not be grayed out. Otherwise they will be. Assuming you can gain access to the settings, click on Configure. That will bring you to the Power Management dialog box. Here you have two choices: when the low-power mode kicks in and when total power off kicks in. You don't want total power down to happen too quickly because the screen will take a few seconds (like about ten) to come back on when you move the mouse or press a key, which can be annoying. So make the two settings something reasonable, such as 15 minutes and 30 minutes.

9. When all the settings are correct, click on Apply or OK.

Some Energy Star displays require the "Blank Screen" screen saver in order to shut down.

Adjusting the Appearance

The Appearance page lets you change the way Windows assigns colors and fonts to various parts of the screen. If you're using a monochrome monitor (no color), altering the colors may still have some effect (the amount will depend on how you installed Windows).

Windows sets itself up using a default color scheme that's fine for most screens—and if you're happy with your colors as they are, you might not even want to futz around with them.

However, the color settings for Windows are very flexible and easy to modify. You can modify the color setting of just about any part of a Windows screen. For those of you who are very particular about color choices, this can be done manually, choosing colors from a palette or even mixing your own with the Custom Colors feature. Once created, custom colors and color setups can be saved on disk for later use or automatically loaded with each Windows session. For more expedient color reassignments, there's a number of supplied color schemes to choose from.

On clicking on the Appearance tab, your dialog box will look like that shown in Figure 7.21. The various parts of the Windows graphical environment that you can alter are shown in the top portion and named in the lower portion. As you select color schemes, these samples change so you can see what the effect will be without having to go back into Windows proper.

FIGURE 7.21

The dialog box for setting the colors, font, and metrics of the Windows environment

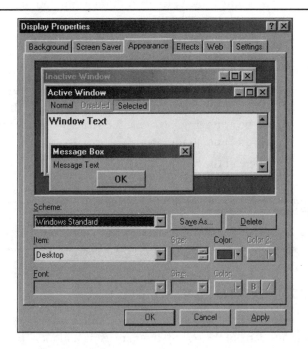

Loading an Existing Color Scheme

Before playing with the custom color palette, first try loading the supplied ones; you may find one you like:

1. Click open the drop-down Color Schemes list box.

TIP

You can always toggle a drop-down list box open and closed from the keyboard by pressing Alt-↓ or Alt-↑.

2. Choose a selection whose name suits your fancy. The colors in the dialog box will change, showing the scheme. Try them out. Some are garish, others more subtle. Adjusting your monitor may make a difference, too. (You can cycle through the different supplied color schemes without selecting them from the drop-down list: with the Color Schemes space highlighted, just press the ↑ and ↓ keys. The sample screen elements will change to reflect each color scheme as its name appears in the Color Schemes box. There is an amazing variety!)

3. Click on Apply or OK to apply the settings to all Windows activities.

Microsoft has incorporated a few color schemes that may enhance the operation of your computer:

- On LCD screens that you'll be using in bright light, you might try the setting called High-Contrast White.

- If your eyes are weary, you may want to try one of the settings with the words Large or Extra Large in the name. These cause menus, dialog boxes, and title bars to appear in large letters.

Choosing Your Own Colors and Other Stuff

If you don't like the color schemes supplied, you can make up your own. It's most efficient to start with a scheme that's close to what you want and then modify it. Once you like the scheme, you may save it under a new name for later use. Here are the steps:

1. Select the color scheme you want to modify.

2. Click on the Windows element whose color you want to change. Its name should appear in the Item area. You can click on menu name, title bars, scroll bars, buttons—anything you see. You can also select a screen element from the Item drop-down list box rather than by clicking directly on the item.

3. Now click on the Color button to open up a series of colors you can choose from.

4. Click on the color you want. This assigns it to the item. Repeat the process for each color you want to change.

5. Want more colors? Click on the Other button. This pops up another 48 colors to choose from. Click on one of the 48 colors (or patterns and intensity levels, if you have a monochrome monitor) to assign it to the chosen element.

6. Once the color scheme suits your fancy, you can save it. (It will stay in force for future Windows sessions even if you don't save it, but you'll lose the settings next time you change colors or select another scheme.) Click on Save Scheme.

7. Type in a name for the color scheme and click on OK.

TIP

If you want to remove a scheme (such as one you never use), select it from the drop-down list and click on the Delete button.

Before I get into explaining custom colors, there are two other major adjustments you can make to your display—the fonts used for various screen elements, and Windows metrics, which affect how big or small some screen elements are.

In Windows 3.*x* this wasn't possible, but since Windows 95 you can choose the font for elements such as title bars, menus, and dialog boxes. You can get pretty wacky with this and make your Windows 98 setup look very strange if you want. Or, on the more practical side, you can compensate for high-resolution monitors by making your menus more easily readable by using large point sizes in screen elements. In any case, you're no longer stuck with boring sans serif fonts such as Arial or MS Sans Serif. For an example, see Figure 7.22

1. On the Appearance page, simply click on the element whose font you want to change, such as the words "Message Box."

2. In the lowest line of the dialog box, the current font for that element appears. Just open the drop-down list box and choose another font if you want. You may also change the size, the color, and the style (bold or italic) of the font for that element.

3. Be sure to save the scheme if you want to keep it.

FIGURE 7.22

You can use any installed fonts when defining your screen elements.

Finally, consider that many screen elements—such as the borders of windows—have a constant predetermined size. However, you might want to change these settings. If you have trouble grabbing the borders of windows, for example, you might want to make them larger. If you want icons on your desktop and in folders to line up closer or farther apart, you can do that, too.

1. Simply open the list and choose the item whose size you want to adjust. Some of the items are not represented in the upper section of the dialog box. They're things that appear in other parts of Windows 95, such as vertical icon spacing or selected items. You'll have to experiment a bit to see the effects of these items.

2. Click on the up or down size buttons to adjust.

3. Click on Apply to check out the effects of the changes. You might want to switch to another application via the Taskbar to see how things look.

4. If you don't like the effects of the changes you've made, just return to the Control Panel and click on Cancel. Or you can just select another color scheme, because the screen metrics are recorded on each color scheme.

Making Up Your Own Colors

If you don't like the colors that are available, you can create your own. There are 16 slots at the bottom of the larger color palette for storing colors you set using another fancy dialog box called the color refiner. Here's how:

1. Click on the Color button and then choose Other. This opens the enlarged color-selection box.

2. In that box, click on Define Custom Colors. Now the Color Refiner dialog box appears (see Figure 7.23).

FIGURE 7.23

The custom color selector lets you create new colors.

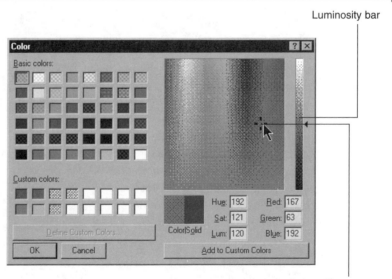

Luminosity bar

Color-refiner cursor

There are two cursors that you work with here. One is the luminosity bar and the other is the color refiner cursor. To make a long story short, you simply drag these around one at a time until the color in the box at the lower left is the shade you want. As you do, the numbers in the boxes below the color refiner will change. Luminosity is the amount of brightness in the color. Hue is the actual shade or color. All colors are composed of red, green, and blue. Saturation is the degree of purity of the color; it is decreased by adding gray to the color and increased by subtracting it. You can also type in the numbers or click on the arrows next to the numbers if you want, but it's easier to use the cursors. When you like the color, click on Add Color to add the new color to the palette.

You can switch between a solid color and a color made up of various dots of several colors. Solid colors look less grainy on your screen but give you fewer choices. The Color|Solid box shows the difference between the two. If you click on this box before adding the color to the palette, the solid color closest to the actual color you chose will be added instead of the grainier composite color.

Once a color is added to the palette, you can modify it. Just click on it, move the cursors around, and then click on Add Color again. Click on Close to close the dialog box. Then continue to assign colors with the palette. When you are content with the color assignments, click on OK. If you decide after toying around that you don't want to implement the color changes, just click on Cancel.

Effects

The settings on this tab page were inherited from the Plus! program that used to be sold as an add-on for Windows 95. Among other creature comforts like font smoothing and full-window drag, Plus! lets you install what Microsoft calls Desktop "themes."

> Full-window drag and font smoothing are included in Windows 98; they just aren't settable from the Display applet. Open any folder window, choose View ➤ Options ➤ Advanced, and look for the options *Smooth edges of screen fonts* and *Show windows contents while dragging.*

Themes were combinations of color settings, wallpaper, and icons designed for your Desktop. The fancy icons are what this option is about. Instead of being stuck with the same boring icons as everyone else, you can change them to something more your style.

1. Click on Effects from the Display Properties dialog box (see Figure 7.24).

Change the look of your Desktop icons from here.

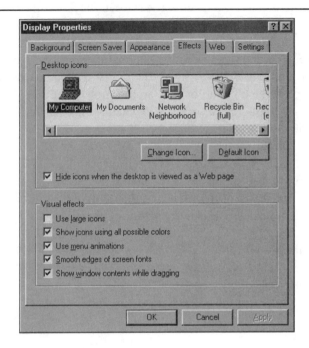

2. Click on the icon you want to alter, then click Change Icon or Default Icon (to return to the factory setting). You'll get a resulting list of icons you can choose from, and you can also browse for icon replacements. (Where to look? Use the Browse box's "Files of type" selector to set the type of file as you're cruising. You can pick up an icon from an existing program (.exe), library (.dll), or icon (.ico) file.

The Internet is a good source of icons. One way to find them is to do a search for the phrase *Icons* or *.ICO.*

The file Windows Explorer.exe (in the Windows directory) contains a bunch of icons. In fact, these are the old Windows 95 default icons, the ones you get if you click the Default Icon button when reassigning icons. To get back to the newer Windows 98 icons, use the file \windows\system\cool.dll.

The Visual Effects portion of the Effects tab page offers an assortment of other options. If you want your icons to be larger and more easily seen, set the *Large icons* checkbox on. You can click Apply to see the results. If you don't like them looking large on your Desktop horizon, just turn off the checkbox and click Apply again.

You can force Windows 98 to display icons in their full glory with the last checkbox, *Show icons using all possible colors*. This is normally on, so there typically isn't a problem.

In addition to the icon settings, this portion of the Effects tab also offers the following settings:

- **Use menu animations:** When this setting is on, menus will open up in a little more artistic manner. Instead of just popping up, they'll slide open.

- **Smooth edges of screen fonts:** Makes larger fonts look smoother on the screen. (See the sidebar on this topic in Chapter 3.)

- **Show window contents while dragging:** Keeps each window's contents visible while you are dragging or resizing it on screen.

Web

This tab page lets you set up your Active Desktop. Active Desktop is the feature in Windows 98 that lets you pull in stuff from the Web and have it display on the Desktop. This is discussed in Chapter 18.

Driver Settings

The last tab page of the Display applet tweaks the video driver responsible for your video card's ability to display Windows. These settings are a little more substantial than those that adjust whether dialog boxes are mauve or chartreuse because they load a different driver or bump your video card up or down into a completely different resolution and color depth, changing the amount of information you can see on the screen at once (see Figure 7.25).

PART

II

Exploring Windows 98

NOTE

This option is also the one to use for installing a Windows 3.*x* video driver for your video card just in case there isn't a Windows 98 driver for it.

NOTE

Changing the color depth or palette on some systems requires rebooting before the changes will take effect.

FIGURE 7.25

The Settings page of the Display applet controls the video card's device driver. With most video systems, the slider lets you adjust the screen resolution on the fly. Changing color depth requires a restart, however.

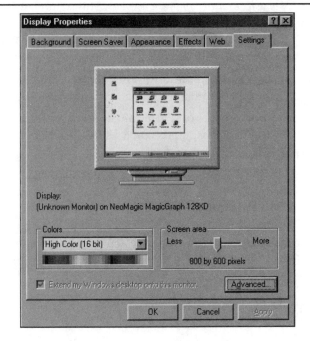

Color Palette

Let's start with the color palette. Assuming your video card was properly identified when you installed Windows 98, this drop-down list box will include all the legitimate options your card is capable of. As you may know, different video cards are capable of displaying differing numbers of colors simultaneously. Your monitor is not the limiting factor here (with the exception of color LCD screens like those on laptops, which do have limitations); the limitations have to do with how much RAM is on your video card. All modern analog color monitors for PCs are capable of displaying 16 million colors, which is dubbed True Color.

It's possible that the drop-down list box will include color amounts (called depths) that exceed your video card's capabilities, in which case such a choice just won't have any effect. On the other hand, if your setting is currently 16 colors and your screen can support 256 or higher, Windows will look a lot prettier if you choose 256 and then choose one of the 256-color schemes from the Appearance tab page.

When you move the Desktop Area slider to the right, the resolution setting increases, right? True, but usually this will also lower the color palette setting to 256 or 16 colors (unless you have a really fancy display card). If after this you choose a lower resolution, such as 640 by 480, and you want to return to the richer color depth, you'll have to reset the color palette to a higher setting manually, by opening the color palette drop-down list.

Desktop Area

The Desktop Area setting is something avid Windows users have been wanting for years. With Windows 3.x, changing this parameter (essentially the screen resolution) meant running Windows Setup, choosing a different video driver, and rebooting the machine and Windows. Windows 95 made this much easier. Now, with the right video card, you can change the resolution as you work. Some jobs—such as working with large spreadsheets, databases, CAD, or typesetting—are much more efficient with more data displayed on the screen. Because higher resolutions require a tradeoff in clarity and make on-screen objects smaller, eyestrain can be minimized by going to a lower resolution, such as 640-by-480 pixels (a pixel equals one dot on the screen). Note that there is a relationship between the color depth and the resolution that's available. This is because your video card can only have so much RAM on it. That RAM can be used to display extra colors or extra resolution, but not both. So, if you bump up the colors, you won't have as many resolution options. If you find the dialog box won't let you choose the resolution you want, try dropping the color palette setting to 16 colors.

To change the Desktop area:

1. Run Control Panel and run the Display applet.

2. Choose the Settings tab page.

3. Grab the slider and move it right or left. Notice how the little screen in the box indicates the additional room you're going to have on your real screen to do your work (and also how everything will get relatively smaller to make this happen, because your monitor doesn't get any larger!). Figure 7.26 illustrates.

Change your screen resolution by dragging the slider. Here I've chosen 800 by 600.

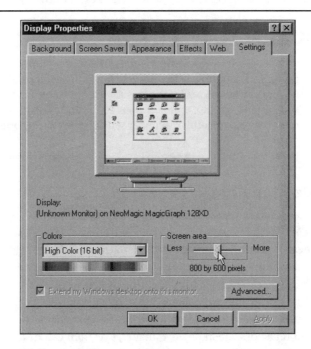

4. Click on Apply. You'll now see this message:

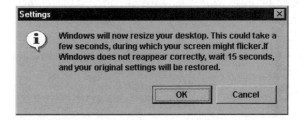

Go ahead and click on OK to try the setting. If your screen looks screwy and you can't read anything, don't worry. It will return to normal in about 15 seconds. If, on the other hand, you like what you see, there will be another dialog box asking you to confirm that you want to keep the current setting. Confirming that box makes the new setting permanent until you change it again.

Font Size

As you may know, some screen drivers use different size fonts for screen elements such as dialog boxes and menus. When you switch to a high Desktop-area resolution, such as 1,280 by 1,024, these screen elements can get quite small, blurry, and difficult to read. For this reason, you can adjust the font size. Of course, you can do this via the Fonts settings on the Appearance page as discussed earlier. But doing it here is a little simpler. If you select a Desktop area above 640 by 480, you'll have the choice of Small Fonts or Large Fonts. Especially for resolutions of 1,024 by 768 or above, you might want to check out the Large Fonts selection from this drop-down list box. If you want, you can also choose a custom-size font by clicking on the Custom button, which lets you declare the amount that you want the fonts scaled up. The range is from 100 to 200 percent.

Advanced Properties

Finally, the Advanced... button in the Settings box leads you to the Advanced Settings page, which allows you to actually change a bunch of nitty-gritty stuff like the type of video card and monitor that Windows thinks you have, the refresh rate, and some performance factors. If you install a new video card or monitor, you should update this information.

You may have noticed on the Advanced Settings page the option "Show settings icon on Taskbar." This is a very spiffy addition to Windows 98. Turn this checkbox on, and you'll get a little monitor icon next to the clock in the Taskbar. Click on the icon and you're able to immediately choose the color depth and Desktop area from a popup menu.

If your screen is flickering, you'll want to check the refresh rate fore sure!

WARNING

If you specify a refresh rating that is too high for your monitor, trying to expand the Desktop area to a larger size may not work. You'll just get a mess on the screen. If this happens, try using a setting with a lower refresh rate, such as 60 Hz or *interlaced.* The image may flicker a bit more, but at least it will be clearly visible.

TIP

If you have just received a new driver for your video adaptor card or monitor and want to use that instead of the one supplied with Windows 95 (or Windows 95 doesn't include a driver), click on the Have Disk button and follow the directions.

Click on the Advanced Properties button, and you'll see something like Figure 7.27.

FIGURE 7.27

You can make some hairy alterations to your monitor setup from here. You should investigate all the tab pages. If you're into monitors, you'll really like what's available from this box.

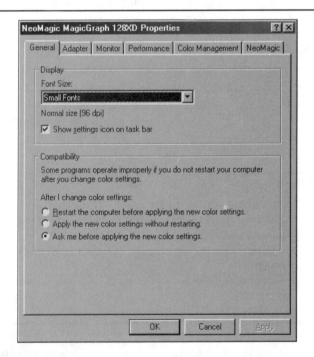

This stuff isn't for the novice, but if you're like me, you've waited a long time for settings like these to be easily available. Windows NT started the trend, and now it's migrated to Windows 98. The first tab page tells you more stuff about your display card than you may have wanted to know, such as the chipset and DAC (Digital to Analog Converter) type, which exact driver files are being used, and amount of RAM on your card. Useful, maybe. Boring, definitely. But the refresh rate, now that's a biggie in my book. In case you don't know, the refresh rate is how many times per second the screen is redrawn by the electron gun in the back of the monitor. Translation: It determines whether the screen appears to be flickering like an old-fashioned movie or not, and whether your eyes get tired looking at the screen for hours on end. Anything under 70Hz is too slow, say the experts, and I agree. In fact, I prefer 72Hz or above. But beware! Not all monitors can work that fast (that electron gun has to move really fast to paint all those dots on the screen), especially at resolutions above 800 by 600. Even if your display card can put out the right refresh signal, the monitor might not be able to handle it. And this can fry a monitor after some time. So if after setting the correct monitor on the Monitor tab page, you don't have the desired refresh available from the Refresh Rate drop-down list, take heed—your monitor probably can't cut the mustard, and Windows is trying to save you from damaging the monitor. Try living with a slower refresh like 70, or get a new monitor (or possibly just a new card). Or choose Optimum. The Adapter Default setting will accept whatever speed the display card is currently set to, or boots up in. This is more than likely not an optimal setting.

Thinking of Buying a New Monitor or Display Card?

If you're thinking about purchasing a new monitor or card, check the specs on both the monitor *and* the card. For both the monitor and the card, you'll want to be ensured that you can:

- display at 72Hz or above, while
- displaying your favorite resolution (a.k.a. Desktop size, such as 1024 × 768), while
- displaying your favorite color depth (such as 64,000 colors or 16 million colors). At least 64,000 colors are necessary for photo-like display.

Make sure the monitor has a dot pitch value smaller than .28, preferably .26. If you have a big wallet, check out the new flat-panel displays just coming out from the likes of NEC and Viewsonic. These are *super* sharp and clear, and refresh isn't even an issue with them.

If you notice that the adapter setting for your computer is wrong, click on the Change button on the Adapter tab page. This will run a wizard. Depending on your choices here you may see a list of compatible boards. For example, on my computer the adapter is listed as S3. The S3 is a popular video chip, installed on my display adapter. But hey, my adapter is a Diamond Stealth 64 PCI. My guess is that the driver that Windows 98 assigned is some generic S3 chipset driver. When I clicked on Change, I saw this:

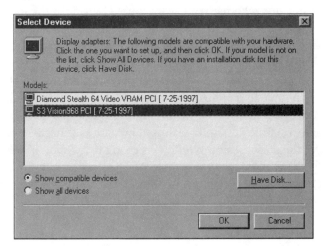

Looks like the Diamond Stealth is compatible, and there is a later date on the driver, so I think I'll try that. This driver was provided by the Diamond company and sent to Microsoft for inclusion in Windows 98.

If you want to see all the possible drivers to choose from (including ones that *won't* work with your card), click on Show All Devices. But typically this won't be useful unless you're planning to install another driver, power down, change display cards, and then boot up again.

Monitor Tab

Bought a new monitor? Here's the place to tell Windows 98 about it. Or at least to see what monitor it *thinks* you have. Click on the Monitor tab on the Advanced Display Properties dialog, and you'll see something like Figure 7.28.

FIGURE 7.28

The Monitor tab of the Advanced Display Properties box

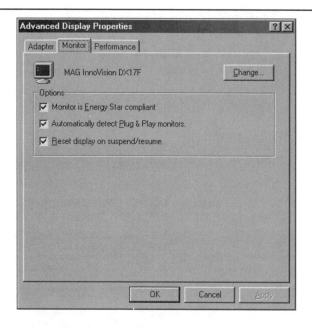

Click on Change if the monitor is reported wrong. Then choose the correct monitor. You might have to use Show All Devices to see your brand. What's that? You say your monitor isn't listed, or you have a no-name monitor? If that's the case, choose Show All Devices, then select the topmost manufacturer type in the list ("Standard monitor types"), and choose the generic brand that most closely matches your monitor's maximum screen resolution and refresh rate at that resolution. You may have to look in your monitor's manual to figure this out.

NOTE

Notice there is a *Television* choice in the Standard monitor types. This may seem a little strange at first. But more and more computers are now equipped with a video output that can drive a TV set as your monitor.

The other options on this tab are also interesting:

- **Monitor is Energy Star compliant:** If yours fits this description, set this. It affects other Power Management settings in your computer.

- **Automatically detect Plug & Play monitors:** Windows runs around and detects Plug & Play hardware once in awhile (when booting up, for example). In some cases this can cause PnP monitors to flash wildly. If yours does this, try turning off this checkbox.

- **Reset display on suspend/resume:** Does your computer have the ability to go into a suspended state (low power state)? I mean the whole computer, not just the screen. If it does, and your screen flickers or freaks out when your computer "wakes up," turn this checkbox off. It may help.

Performance

When you click the Performance tab, you'll see a dialog box that looks like Figure 7.29.

FIGURE 7.29

Tweaking the performance of your monitor/card duo can be achieved from this box.

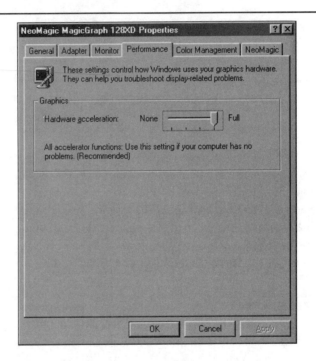

If speed is your concern (and who isn't concerned with their computer's speed?), make sure the slider is set to Full. This is recommended for most computers. Occasionally a computer/card combo (the monitor has nothing to do with this) won't be able to take advantage of all the graphics speed-up routines that Windows is capable of for things like moving lots of graphics around the screen quickly ("bit blitting") and such. If you're seeing display anomalies, you might try slowing this setting down a bit, clicking OK, and closing the Display Properties box. Then see if anything improves.

Adjusting the Mouse

You can adjust six aspects of your mouse's operation:

- left-right button reversal
- double-click speed
- look of the pointers
- tracking speed
- mouse trails
- mouse type and driver

Switching the Buttons and Setting Double-Click Speed

If you're left-handed, you may want to switch the mouse around to use it on the left side of the computer and reverse the buttons. The main button then becomes the right button instead of the left one. If you use other programs outside of Windows that don't allow this, however, it might just add to the confusion. If you only use the mouse in Windows programs and you're left-handed, then it's worth a try.

1. Run the Control Panel and double-click on Mouse. Then click on the first tab page of the dialog box (Figure 7.30).

PART

II

Exploring Windows 98

FIGURE 7.30

First page of the Mouse setting. Here you can reverse the buttons for use by left-handed people. You can also adjust the double-click speed.

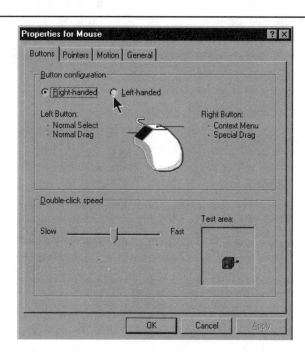

2. Click on the Left-handed button as shown in the figure. Then click on Apply to check it out. Don't like it? Revert to the original setting and click on Apply again.

On the same page, you have the double-click speed setting. Double-click speed determines how fast you have to double-click to make a double-click operation work (that is, to run a program from its icon, to open a document from its icon, or to select a word. If the double-click speed is too fast, it's difficult for your fingers to click fast enough. If it's too slow, you end up running programs or opening and closing windows unexpectedly. Double-click on the Jack-in-the-box to try out the new double-click speed. Jack will jump out or back into the box if the double-click registered. If you're not faring well, adjust the slider and try again.

NOTE

You don't have to click on Apply to test the slider settings. Just moving the slider instantly affects the mouse's double-click speed.

Setting Your Pointers

Your mouse pointer's shape changes depending on what you are pointing at and what Windows 98 is doing. If you are pointing to a window border, the pointer becomes a two-headed arrow. If Windows 98 is busy, it becomes a sandglass. When you are editing text, it becomes an I-beam, and so on.

You can customize your cursors for the fun of it or to increase visibility. You can even install animated cursors that look really cute and keep you amused while you wait for some process to complete.

To change the cursor settings:

1. Click on the Pointers tab page of the Mouse dialog box (see Figure 7.31).

2. The list shows which pointers are currently assigned to which activities. To change an assignment, click on an item in the list.

3. Next, if you've changed the shape and want to revert, click on Use Default to go back to the normal pointer shape that Windows 95 came shipped with. Otherwise, choose Browse and use the Browse box to load the cursor you want. When you click on a cursor in the Browse box, it will be displayed at the bottom of the box for you to examine in advance—a thoughtful feature. Even animated cursors will do their thing right in the Browse box. (Cursors with the .ani extension are animated ones.)

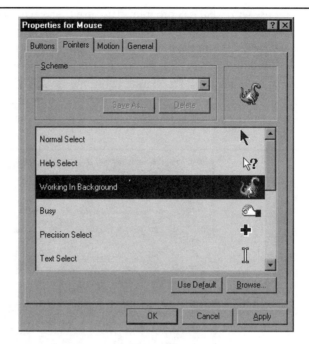

PART

II

Exploring Windows 98

FIGURE 7.31

Choose pointer shapes for various activities here. As you can see, I have a couple of weird ones installed, such as the walking dinosaur instead of the sandglass.

4. Click on Open. The cursor will now be applied to the activity in question.

You can save pointer schemes just as you can colors. If you want to set up a number of different schemes (one for each person in the house, for example), just get the settings assigned the way you like, enter a name in the scheme area, and click on Save As. To later select a scheme, open the drop-down list box, select the scheme's name, and click on Apply or OK.

Setting the Pointer Motion

Two very useful adjustments can be made to the way to the mouse responds to the motion of your hand—speed and trails (Figure 7.32).

Pointer speed is the speed at which the mouse pointer moves relative to the movement of the mouse. Believe it or not, mouse motion is actually measured in *Mickeys*! (Somebody out there has a sense of humor.) A Mickey equals 1/100 of an inch of mouse movement. The tracking-speed setting lets you adjust the relationship of Mickeys to pixels. If you want to be very exact in your cursor movement, you'll want to slow the tracking speed, requiring more Mickeys per pixel. However, this requires more hand motion for the same corresponding cursor motion. If your desk is crammed and your coordination is very good, then you can increase the speed (fewer Mickeys per pixel). If you use the mouse with MS-DOS programs that use their own mouse driver, you might want to adjust the Windows mouse speed to match that of your other programs so you won't need to mentally adjust when you use such non-Windows programs.

Incidentally, if you think the mouse runs too slowly in your non- Windows applications, there may be a fix. Contact your mouse's maker. For example, if you're using a Logitech mouse, a program called Click that is supplied with the Logitech mouse lets you easily control its tracking. See the Logitech manual for details.

FIGURE 7.32

You can adjust the speed at which the mouse pointer moves and whether you'll see trails.

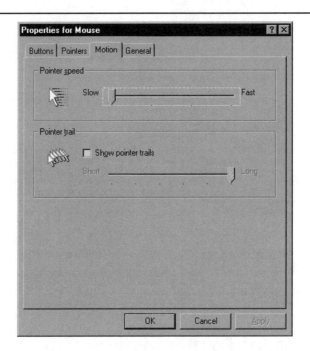

The other setting—Mouse trails—creates a shadow of the mouse's path whenever you move it. Some people find it annoying, but for those who have trouble finding the pointer on the screen, it's a blessing. Mouse trails are particularly helpful when using Windows on passive-matrix or dual-scan laptop computers, where the pointer often disappears when you move it.

Here are the steps for changing these items:

1. Drag the speed slider one way or another to increase or decrease the motion of the pointer relative to your hand (or thumb in the case of a trackball) motion. Nothing may happen until you click on Apply. Adjust as necessary. Try aiming for some item on the screen and see how well you succeed. Having the motion too fast can result in straining your muscles and holding the mouse too tight. It's ergonomically more sound to use a little slower setting that requires more hand motion.

2. If you want trails, click the option box on and adjust the slider. You don't have to click on Apply to see the effects.

3. Click on OK or Apply to make it all official.

General Mouse Settings

The last tab page lets you change the mouse's software driver and possibly make changes that the driver has built in. The type of mouse is listed in the box. If this looks wrong or you're changing the mouse to another type, click on Change and choose the desired mouse type from the resulting Select Device box. See the discussion about changing the Display Adaptor, above, if in doubt about how to use the Select Device dialog box.

In some cases, you'll have an Options button on this tab page. The options will vary from mouse to mouse. They may include such things as choosing to have the mouse pointers be black rather than white or be transparent rather than opaque. For example, the Options for my Ballpoint mouse are shown in Figure 7.33.

PART

II

Exploring Windows 98

FIGURE 7.33

Some mouse drivers have additional options built in. The last tab page of the Mouse applet gives you access to them.

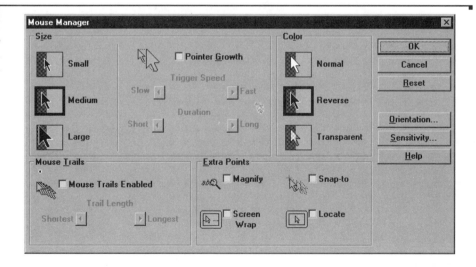

Chapter

8

Printers and Printing

FEATURING

Print Manager basics

Installing and configuring a printer

Sharing a printer

Removing a printer

Printing from your programs

Viewing the print queue

Pausing and resuming print jobs

Printing to a disk file

Chapter

8

Printers and Printing

I f your printer is of the Plug-and-Play variety, your Windows system will probably have a so-called default printer driver already installed. This means you'll be able to print from any Windows program without worrying about anything more than turning on the printer, checking that it has paper, and choosing the File ➤ Print command from whatever programs you use. If your printer isn't Plug-and-Play compatible, wasn't plugged in at the time of installation, or you weren't upgrading over a previous version of Windows for which you had printers set up already, you'll have to manually set up your printer before you can print. This chapter tells you how to do that and how to manage the use of your printer to get your work done.

As with Windows 3.1, Windows 95, and Windows NT, unless you specify otherwise, Windows programs hand off data to Windows 98, which in turn *spools* the data to a specified printer. Spooling means temporarily putting on the hard disk the information that's really headed for the printer. Your document then gets sent out to the printer at the slowest speed that the printer can receive it. This lets you get back to work with your program sooner. You can even print additional documents, stacking up a load of jobs for the printer to print. This stack is called a *queue*.

In Windows 3.x, a program called Print Manager was responsible for doing the spooling and managing the print jobs. Windows 98 nomenclature dispenses with the term "Print Manager," even though the same functionality is provided. Now you simply look at what's "inside" a printer by clicking on the printer's icon. This opens a window and displays the print queue for that printer. In reality, however, there *is* a spooler program and Print Manager-like thing in Windows 98, and that is how I'll refer to the window that displays and works with the print queue.

TECH TIP

Unlike Windows NT, Windows 95 doesn't always prevent a program from writing directly to the printer port. (In Windows NT, any such attempt by programs to directly write to hardware, such as an LPT port, is trapped by the security manager.) Windows 98 offers less security in this regard. Applications can directly access a port. Also, if you shell out of Windows 98 and run MS-DOS mode, direct port access is allowed.

NOTE

MS-DOS programs can also be spooled so you can get back to work with your DOS or Windows programs while printing happens in the background.

When you print from a Windows program, Print Manager receives the data, queues up the jobs, routes them to the correct printer, and, when necessary, issues error or other appropriate messages to print-job originators. You can use the Print Manager user interface to manage your print jobs, making it easy to check out what's printing and see where your job(s) are in the print queue relative to other people's print jobs. You may also be permitted to rearrange the print queue, delete print jobs, or pause and resume a print job so you can reload or otherwise service the printer.

Each printer you've installed appears in the Printers folder, along with an additional icon called Add Printer that lets you set up new printers. Printer icons in the folder appear and behave like any other object: You can delete them at will, create new ones, and set their properties. Double-clicking on a printer in the folder displays its print queue and lets you manipulate the queue. Commands on the menus let you to install, configure, connect, disconnect, and remove printers and drivers.

This chapter explains these features, as well as procedures for local and network print-queue management. Some basics of print management also are discussed, providing a primer for the uninitiated or for those whose skills are a little rusty.

A Print-Manager Primer

Windows 98's Print Manager feature mix is quite rich. Here are the highlights:

- You can add, modify, and remove printers right from the Printers folder (available from My Computer, Explorer, the Start button, or Control Panel).

- An object-oriented interface using printer icons eliminates the abstraction of thinking about the relationship of printer drivers, connections, and physical printers. You simply add a printer and set its properties. Once added, it appears as a named printer in the Printers folder.

- Once set up, you can easily choose to share a printer on the network so others can print to it. You can give it a useful name such as *LaserJet in Fred's Office* so people on the network know what it is.

- If you're on a network, you can manage network-printer connections by displaying available printers, sharing your local printer, and connecting to and disconnecting from network printers.

- Because of Windows 95's multithreading and preemptive multitasking, you can start printing and immediately go back to work; you don't have to wait until spooling for Print Manager to finish. (This won't be true for older 16-bit programs.)

- While one document is printing out, other programs can start print jobs. Additional documents are simply added to the queue and will print in turn.

- Default settings for such options as number of copies, paper tray, page orientation, and so forth are automatically used during print jobs so you don't have to manually set them each time.

- For the curious, a window can be opened displaying jobs currently being printed or in the queue waiting to be printed, along with an indication of the current print job's progress.

- You can easily rearrange the order of the print queue and delete print jobs.

- You can choose whether printing begins as soon as the first page is spooled to the hard disk or after the last page of a document is spooled.

- You can temporarily pause or resume printing without causing printer time-out problems.

PART

II

Exploring Windows 98

Adding a New Printer

If your printer is already installed and seems to be working fine, you probably can skip this section. In fact, if you're interested in nothing more than printing from one of your programs without viewing the queue, printing to a network printer, or making adjustments to your current printer's settings, just skip down to *Printing from a Program*, below. However, if you need to install a new printer, modify or customize your current installation, or add additional printers to your setup, read on to learn about how to:

- add a new printer
- select the printer port and make other connection settings
- set preferences for a printer
- install a printer driver that's not listed
- set the default printer
- select a printer when more than one is installed
- delete a printer from your system

About Printer Installation

As I mention in the appendix, before installing hardware, including printers, you should read any last-minute printed or on-screen material that comes with Windows 98. Often such material is full of useful information about specific types of hardware, including printers. Open the files `Setup.txt` and `Printers.txt` on your Windows 98 CD-ROM, then look through the files for information about your printer.

With that said, here is the overall game plan for adding a new printer. It's actually a really easy process thanks to the Add a Printer Wizard that walks you through it.

1. Run Add a Printer from the Printers folder.
2. Declare whether the printer is local (directly connected to your computer) or on the network.
3. Declare what kind of printer it is.
4. Select the printer's port and relevant port settings.
5. Give the printer a name.
6. Print a test page.
7. Check and possibly alter the default printer settings, such as the DPI (dots per inch) setting and memory settings.

After these steps are complete, your printer should work as expected. Once it's installed, you can customize each printer's setup by modifying its properties, such as:

- specifying the amount of time you want Windows to keep trying to print a document before alerting you to a printer problem

- specifying the share name for the printer so other network users can find it when they search the network for printers

- setting job defaults pertaining to paper tray, two-sided printing, and paper orientation

- stipulating a *separator file* (a file, usually one page long, that prints between each print job)

- selecting the default printer if you have more than one printer installed

- choosing whether your printer should substitute its own fonts for certain Windows TrueType fonts

- selecting printer settings relevant to page orientation, color matching, greyscaling, size scaling, type of paper feed, halftone imaging, and when file-header information (such as a PostScript "preamble") is sent to the printer

- set whether you want to share the printer for use by others on the network

- set whether documents will go directly to the printer or will go through the spooler

The good news is that normally you won't have to futz with any of these settings. The other good news is, unlike in Windows 3.x, getting to any one of these settings is now a piece of cake. You don't have to wind your way through a bevy of dialog boxes to target a given setting. The Properties dialog box has tab pages, so it's a cinch to find the one you want.

TIP

The Properties box has context-sensitive Help built in. Click on an element in a dialog box and press F1, or click on the ? button, then on the item. A relevant Help topic will appear.

PART

II

Exploring Windows 98

NOTE

Advanced printer-security issues—such as conducting printer-access auditing and set-ting ownership—are not features of Windows 98. Windows 98 *does* support use of a password when sharing a printer, however, which is explained later in this chapter.

About Adding Printers

Before running the Wizard, let's consider when you'd need to add a new printer to your Windows 98 configuration:

- You didn't tell Windows 98 what kind of printer you have when you first set up Windows.
- You're connecting a new printer directly to your computer.
- Someone has connected a new printer to the network and wants to use it from your computer.
- You want to print to disk files that can later be sent to a particular type of printer.
- You want to set up multiple printer configurations (preferences) for a single physical printer so you can switch between them without having to change your printer setup before each print job.

Notice that a great deal of flexibility exists here, especially in the case of the last item. Because of the modularity of Windows 98's internal design, even though you might have only one physical printer, you can create any number of printer defini-tions for it, each with different characteristics.

TECH TIP

These definitions are actually *called* printers, but you can think of them as printer names, aliases, or named virtual devices.

For example, you might want one definition set up to print on legal-sized paper in landscape orientation while another prints with normal paper in portrait orientation. Each of these two "printers" would actually use the same physical printer to print out on. While you're working with Windows 98's manual, online help, and this book, keep this terminology in mind. The word "printer" often doesn't really mean a physi-cal printer. It usually means a printer setup that you've created with the Wizard. It's a collection of settings that typically points to a physical printer, but it could just as well create a print file instead.

About Printer Drivers

And finally, consider that a printer can't just connect to your computer and mysteriously print a fancy page of graphics or even a boring old page of text. You need a printer *driver*. The printer driver (actually a file on your hard disk) translates your text file to commands that tell your printer how to print your file. Because different brands and models of printer use different commands for such things as *move up a line, print a circle in the middle of the page, print the letter A*, and so on, a specialized printer driver is needed for each type of printer.

NOTE

> Because some printers are actually functionally equivalent, a driver for a popular brand and model of printer (for example, an Epson or a Hewlett-Packard) often masquerades under different names for other printers.

TECH TIP

> DOS programs require a print driver for the application, too. For instance, WordPerfect 5.1 running in a DOS session under Windows 98 will use a DOS printer driver *and* a Windows 98 printer driver to work under Windows 98.

When you add a printer, unless you're installing a Plug-and-Play–compatible printer, you're asked to choose the brand and model of printer. With Plug-and-Play printers, if the printer is attached and turned on, Windows queries the printer and the printer responds with its make and model number. Virtually all new printers are Plug-and-Play compatible, but if yours isn't, you'll have to tell Windows what printer you have so it will install the correct driver.

A good printer driver takes advantage of all your printer's capabilities, such as its built-in fonts and graphics features. A poor printer driver might succeed in printing only draft-quality text, even from a sophisticated printer.

If you're the proud owner of some offbeat brand of printer, you may be alarmed when you can't find your printer listed in the box when you run the wizard. But don't worry, the printer manufacturer might be able to supply one. The procedure for installing manufacturer-supplied drivers is covered later in this chapter.

NOTE

If your printer isn't included in the list, consult *"When You Don't Find Your Printer in the List,"* later in this chapter.

Running the Wizard to Add a New Printer

Microsoft has made the previously arduous chore of adding a printer something that's much more easily mastered by a majority of computer users. Here's what you have to do:

1. Open the Printers folder by clicking on the Start button and choosing Settings ➤ Printers. Two other paths are from My Computer and from Control Panel.

TECH TIP

Depending on the type of access control you stipulate from the Access Control tab of the Network applet in the Control Panel, you may want to password-protect your printer when you share it on the network. This helps guard against a printer being continually tied up with print jobs from an unauthorized user somewhere on the network. Just share your printer with password protection as discussed later in this chapter, or if part of an NT domain, restrict access to your resources via the Control Panel applet mentioned above (see Part V of this book).

2. Double-click on Add Printer, as shown in Figure 8.1.

3. A dialog box like that in Figure 8.2 appears. Click on Next.

4. You're asked whether the printer is *local* or *network*. Because here I'm describing how to install a network printer, choose Network, then click on Next. (If you are setting up a local printer that is connected directly to your computer, at this point you should skip down to the next section, *Adding a Local Printer*.)

5. You'll now be asked two questions, as shown in Figure 8.3.

NOTE

For a printer to appear in the network listing, it has to have been added to the host computer's setup (the computer the printer is directly attached to) using the steps in *"Adding a Local Printer,"* below. It must also be shared for use on the network.

FIGURE 8.1

Run the Wizard to add a printer.

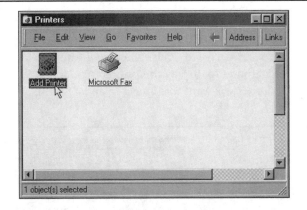

FIGURE 8.2

Beginning the process of adding the printer

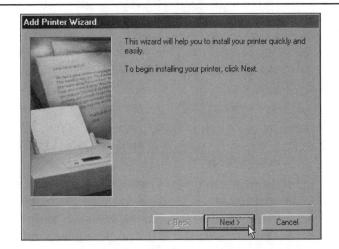

FIGURE 8.3

When choosing a network printer, you have to specify the printer's path and declare whether you can print from DOS programs.

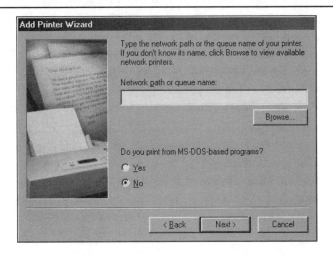

6. You don't have to type in the complicated path name for the location of the printer on the network. Just click on Browse, and up comes a list of the printers on the network. For example, in Figure 8.4 you see the network printer *Apple*. You may have to double-click on Entire Network or click on the + sign next to a computer to display the printer(s) attached to it. Either way, just highlight the printer you want to connect to and click on OK.

FIGURE 8.4

The Browse box graphically displays computers that have shared net-worked printers available for others to use. Click on the printer you want, then click OK.

If the network printer is currently *offline*, you'll be told that you have to wait until it comes back online before you can use it but that you can go ahead and install it if you want. However, as long as it's offline, you'll be asked to specify the brand and model of the printer because the Wizard can't figure out what kind of printer it is when it is unavailable for your computer to question. If you can alert the owner of the printer to put it online (they have to right-click on the printer's icon at their computer and turn off the Work Offline setting), then you won't have to specify these settings. If this isn't possible, just select the brand name and model from the resulting list.

7. Back at the Wizard dialog box, decide whether you want to print from DOS applications or not.

- If you choose Yes, click on Next, and you'll be asked to choose a printer port to associate the output with (such as LPT1, LPT2, and so on). Usually this will be LPT1. However, if you have a local printer attached to your computer using LPT1, you should choose a different port, such as LPT2. This doesn't mean the printer has to be connected to your LPT (parallel) port, it only tells Windows 98 how to fake the DOS program into thinking that it's printing to a normal parallel port. Click on Capture Printer Port, choose accordingly, and click on OK. Then click on Next.

- If you won't be printing from DOS applications to this new printer, choose No, and you won't be asked about the port. Just click on Next.

8. Now you're asked to name the printer (Figure 8.5). This is the name that will show up when you're setting up to print from a program such as a word processor, spreadsheet, or whatever. Type in a name for the printer; the maximum length is 32 characters. Typically, the type of printer, such as HP Desk Jet 320, goes here. There's also a description line in which you can be even more descriptive about the printer, accepting up to 255 characters. Specifying the location of the printer in this box is a good idea so network users can find a printer when browsing and will know where to pick up their hard copy when a print job is completed.

Name the printer and choose whether it's going to be your default printer.

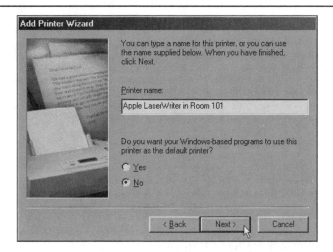

9. In this same dialog box you'll have to decide whether you want the printer to be the *default* printer. The default printer is the one that programs will assume you want to print to. Some programs don't let you choose which printer a document will print out on, so setting the default printer can be important. If you want this network printer to be the default printer, remember that the computer the printer is directly connected to (in the example here, that would be the computer called Samson) has to be up and running for the printer to work. So, if you

Exploring Windows 98

have a local printer on your machine as well, it's better to make that the default printer.

10. Finally, you're asked if you want to print a test page. It's a good idea to do this. Turn on the printer, make sure it has paper in it, and click on Finish. You may be prompted to supply a printer driver for the printer, depending on the type of network you're connecting to and whether a driver is already on your machine. If you're told that a driver file for the printer is already on your machine, you'll be asked if you want to use it or load a new one from the Windows 98 CD-ROM or floppy disks. It's usually easier to use the existing driver. If the driver isn't on your hard disk, you'll be instructed to insert the disk containing the driver.

11. The test page will be sent to the printer; it should print out in a few minutes. Then you'll be asked if it printed OK. If it didn't print correctly, click on No, and you'll be shown some troubleshooting information containing some questions and answers. The most likely fixes for the malady will be described. If the page printed OK, click on Yes, and you're done.

If all went well, you now have a network printer set up and ready to go. The new printer appears in your Printers folder. If there is a checkmark over the printer, this means you've set it as the default printer.

Adding a Local Printer

If you want to add a local printer rather than a networked printer, the steps are a little different from what I explained above.

1. Follow the first three steps in the section above.

2. In the box that asks whether the printer is local or networked, click on Local. Then click on Next.

3. You're presented with a list of brands and models. In the left column scroll the list, find the maker of your printer, and click on it. Then in the right column choose the model number or name that matches your printer. Be sure to select the exact printer model, not just the correct brand name. Consult your printer's manual if you're in doubt about the model. What you enter here determines which printer driver file is used for this printer's definition. Figure 8.6 shows an example for an HP LaserJet 4.

FIGURE 8.6

Choosing the printer make and model: here I'm choosing a Hewlett-Packard LaserJet 4.

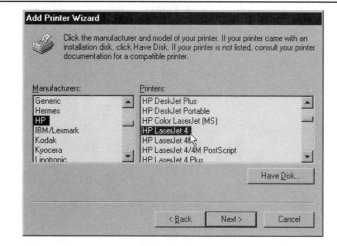

4. Click on Next. Now you'll see a list of ports. You have to tell Windows which port the printer is connected to. (A port usually refers to the connector on the computer—but see Table 8.1 for the "file" exception.)

Most often the port will be the parallel printer port called LPT1 (Line Printer #1). Unless you know your printer is connected to another port, such as LPT2 or a serial port (such as COM1 or COM2), select LPT1 as in Figure 8.7.

5. Click on Next. Now you can give the printer a name (see Figure 8.8).

NOTE

If the printer will be shared with DOS and 16-bit Windows users (such as people running Windows for Workgroups 3.11), you might want to limit this name to twelve characters because that's the maximum length those users will see when they are browsing for printers.

PART

II

Exploring Windows 98

FIGURE 8.7

Choosing the port the printer's connected to is the second step in setting up a local printer.

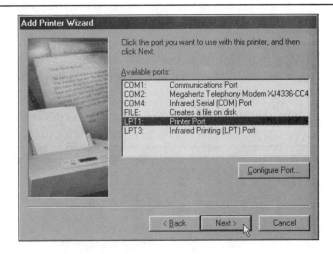

FIGURE 8.8

Give your new printer a name that tells you and other people something about it.

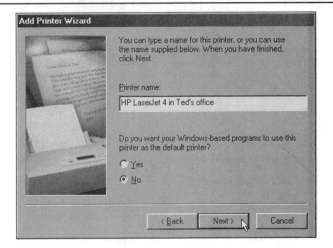

6. Also set whether the printer will be the default printer for Windows programs.

7. Finally, you're asked if you want to print a test page. It's a good idea to do this. Turn on the printer, make sure it has paper in it, and click on Finish. If the driver file for your printer is in the computer, you'll be asked if you want to use it or load a new one from the Windows 98 CD-ROM or floppy disks. It's usually easier to use the existing driver. If the driver isn't on your hard disk, you'll be instructed to insert the disk containing the driver.

TABLE 8.1: PRINTER PORTS

Port	Notes
LPT1, LPT2, LPT3	The most common setting is LPT1 because most PC-type printers hook up to the LPT1 parallel port. Click on Configure Port if you want to turn off the ability to print to this printer from DOS programs.
LPT3 Infrared printing port	If your computer is equipped with an infrared port you may have this option.
COM1, COM2, COM3, COM4	If you know your printer is of the serial variety, it's probably connected to the COM1 port. If COM1 is tied up for use with some other device, such as a modem, use COM2. If you choose a COM port, click on Configure Port to check the communications settings in the resulting dialog box. Set the baud rate, data bit, parity, start and stop bits, and flow control to match those of the printer being attached. Refer to the printer's manual to determine what the settings should be.
File	This is for printing to a disk file instead of to the printer. Later, the file can be sent directly to the printer or sent to someone on floppy disk or over a modem. When you print to this printer name, you are prompted to enter a file name. (See the section in the chapter titled *Printing to a Disk File Instead of a Printer.*)

8. The test page will be sent to the printer. It should print out in a few minutes, then you'll be asked if it printed OK. If it didn't print correctly, click on No, and you'll be shown some troubleshooting information containing some questions and answers. The most likely fixes for the malady will be described. If the page printed OK, click on Yes, and you're done.

The new icon for your printer will show up in the Printers folder now.

TECH TIP

Windows 98 remembers the location you installed Windows 98 from originally. If you installed from a CD-ROM, it's likely that the default location for files is always going to be the CD-ROM drive's logical name (typically some higher letter, such as E or F). If you have done some subsequent installs or updates from other drives or directories, those are also remembered by Windows 98 and will be listed in the drop-down list box.

PART

II

Exploring Windows 98

When You Don't Find Your Printer in the List

When you're adding a local printer, you have to supply the brand name and model of the printer because Windows 98 needs to know which driver to load into your Windows 98 setup to use the printer correctly. (When you are adding a network printer, you aren't asked this question because the printer's host computer already knows what type of printer it is, and the driver is on that computer.)

What if your printer isn't on the list of Windows 98-recognized printers? Many off-brand printers are designed to be compatible with one of the popular printer types, such as the Apple LaserWriters, Hewlett-Packard LaserJets, or the Epson line of printers. Refer to the manual that came with your printer to see whether it's compatible with one of the printers that *is* listed. Some printers require that you set the printer in compatibility mode using switches or software. Again, check the printer's manual for instructions.

Finally, if it looks like there's no mention of compatibility anywhere, contact the manufacturer for their Windows 98-compatible driver. If you're lucky, they'll have one. It's also possible that Microsoft has a new driver for your printer that wasn't available when your copy of Windows was shipped. Contact Microsoft at (206) 882-8080 and ask for the Windows 98 Driver Library Disk, which contains all the latest drivers, or, better yet, check the Microsoft Web site www.microsoft.com/support/printing.

NOTE

All existing printer setups should actually have been migrated from Windows 95 to Windows 98 when you upgraded, so if it was working under Windows 95, it will probably work fine under Windows 98. This is true for other types of drivers, too, such as video display cards, sound boards, and so on.

Also remember that Windows 98 can use the 16-bit drivers that worked with Windows 3.x. So, if you had a fully functioning driver for your printer in Windows 3.x (that is, your printer worked fine before you upgraded from Windows 3.x to Windows 98), you should be able to use that driver in Windows 98.

Locate the Windows 3.x driver disk supplied with your printer or locate the driver file. (Sometimes font or other support files are also needed, incidentally, so it's not always as simple as finding a single file.)

Assuming you do obtain a printer driver, do the following to install it:

1. Follow the instructions above for running the Add a Printer Wizard.

2. Instead of selecting one of the printers in the Driver list (it isn't in the list, of course), click on the Have Disk button. You'll see this box:

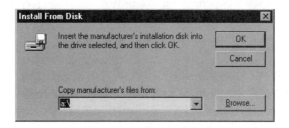

3. The Wizard is asking you to enter the path where the driver is located (typically a floppy disk). Insert the disk (or make sure the files are available somewhere), enter the path, and click on OK. Enter the correct source of the driver. Typically, it'll be in the A or B disk drive.

The Wizard is looking for an file with an `.inf` extension, incidentally. This is the standard file extension for manufacturer-supplied driver information files.

4. Click on OK.

5. You might have to choose a driver from a list if multiple options exist.

6. Continue with the Wizard dialog boxes as explained above.

If none of the drivers you can lay your hands on will work with your printer, try choosing the Generic *text-only* driver. This driver prints only text—no fancy formatting and no graphics. But it will work in a pinch with many printers. Make sure the printer is capable of or is set to an ASCII or ANSI text-only mode, otherwise your printout may be a mess. PostScript printers typically don't have such a text-only mode.

Altering the Details of a Printer's Setup—The Properties Box

Each printer driver can be fine-tuned by changing settings in its Properties dialog box. This area is difficult to document because so many variations exist due to the number

PART

II

Exploring Windows 98

of printers supported. The following sections describe the gist of these options without going into too much detail about each printer type.

The settings pertaining to a printer are called *properties*. As I discussed earlier, properties abound in Windows 98. Almost every object in Windows 98 has properties that you can examine and change at will. When you add a printer, the Wizard makes life easy for you by giving it some default properties that usually work fine and needn't be tampered with. You can change them later, but only if you need to. It may be worth looking at the properties for your printer, especially if the printer's acting up in some way when you try to print from Windows 98.

1. Open the Printers folder.

2. Right-click on the printer's icon and choose Properties. A box such as the one in Figure 8.9 appears.

 **TIP**

You can also type Alt-Enter to open the Properties box. This is true with many Windows 98 objects.

3. Notice that there is a place for a comment. This is normally blank after you add a printer. If you share the printer on the network, any text that you add to this box will be seen by other users who are browsing the network for a printer.

4. Click on the various tab pages of your printer's Properties box to view or alter the great variety of settings. These buttons are confusing in name, and there's no easy way to remember what's what. But remember that you can get help by clicking on the ? in the upper-right corner and then on the setting or button whose function you don't understand.

Sharing a Printer for Network Use

You have to *share* a printer before it becomes available to other network users. Sharing is pretty simple: First off, the printer must be a local printer. Then you share it by right-clicking on it and choosing Share, or via its Properties box. Here are the details:

1. Add the printer as described earlier in this chapter.

FIGURE 8.9

Each printer has a Properties box such as this, with several tab pages. Options differ from printer to printer.

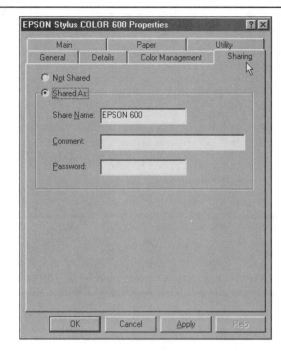

2. Right-click on the printer's icon and choose Properties or Sharing.

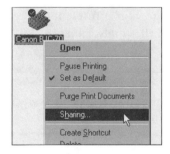

3. Now you'll see the box in Figure 8.9. Click on the Sharing tab if it's not selected.

4. On the Sharing page, click on Shared As.

5. A *share name* based on the Printer Name is automatically generated. You can leave the share name as is or give it another name. DOS-based network users see this name, which must conform to DOS file-naming rules. Other users will see this name, too, though some may see the other comments about the printer. The name can't be more than twelve characters long and mustn't contain spaces or characters not acceptable in DOS file names, such as ?, *, #, +, |, \, /, =, > , < , or %.

6. Fill in a comment about the printer, such as the location of the printer so users know where to pick up their printouts.

7. Fill in a password only if you want to restrict the use of the printer. If a password is entered here, other network users will be prompted to enter it at their machine before they can print to your printer. Make a list of people whom you want to give printer access to and tell them what the password is. This is one way to prevent overuse of a given printer. If you don't enter a password, protection is not in effect.

Another approach to preventing overuse of a given printer (at least temporarily) is to right-click on its icon and choose Pause Printing. Not a very elegant way to deter people from printing to your printer, but it *will* stop print jobs.

8. Click on OK. If you entered a password, you'll be prompted to verify it by reentering. Then click on OK, and your printer is shared! Its icon now has a hand under it. Pretty soon you'll start to see someone else's print jobs rolling out of your printer.

QMS-PS 810

To unshare your printer, open the Properties box again, choose the Sharing page, and click on Not Shared.

If you forget the password, don't worry. You can change it by simply entering a new password from the Share tab page.

Connecting to a Network Printer

Assuming your Windows 98 network system is successfully cabled and running, network printing should be possible. Before a network user can access a network printer, the following must be true:

- The printer must be cabled to the sharing computer.
- The printer must be created and working properly for local use.

- The printer must be shared.
- The printer's security settings and network users wishing access must match.

By default, new printer shares are given a security setting that gives all users access for printing. Only the creator and administrators can *manage* the printer, however. Managing the printer means rearranging the print-job queue: starting, stopping, and deleting print jobs.

How to Delete a Printer from Your Printers Folder

You might want to decommission a printer after you've added it, for several reasons:

- You've connected a new type of printer to your computer and you want to delete the old setup and create a new one with the correct driver for the new printer.
- You want to disconnect from a network printer you're through using.
- You've created several slightly different setups for the same physical printer and you want to delete the ones you don't use.

In any of these cases, the trick is the same:

1. Open the Printers folder (the easiest way is using Start ➤ Settings ➤ Printers).
2. Right-click on the icon for the printer setup you want to delete and choose Delete (or just press Del).

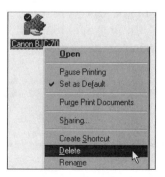

You will see at least one confirmation box before the printer is deleted. You may see another warning if there are print jobs in the queue for the printer.

PART

II

Exploring Windows 98

NOTE

If you have stipulated that the computer can keep separate settings for each user (via Control Panel ➤ Passwords ➤ User Profiles), the removal process removes only the printer setup from Windows 98's Registry for the currently logged-in user. Also note that the related driver file and font files are not deleted from the disk. Therefore, if you want to re-create the printer, you don't have to insert disks, and you won't be prompted for the location of driver files. This is convenient, but if you're tight on disk space, you might want to remove the printer fonts and drivers. To remove fonts, use the Fonts applet in the Control Panel, as described in Chapter 9.

How to Print Out Documents from Your Programs

By now your printer(s) are added and ready to go. The procedure for printing in Windows 98 is simple. Typically, you just open a document, choose File ➤ Print, and make a few settings, such as which pages to print, and click OK. (You might have to set the print area first or make some other settings, depending on the program.) If you're already happy with the ways in which you print, you might want to skim over this section. However, there *are* a couple of conveniences you might not know about, such using drag and drop to print or right-clicking on a document to print it without opening the program that created it.

About the Default Printer

Unless you choose otherwise, the output from both Windows and DOS programs are routed to the Print Manager for printing. If no particular printer has been chosen (perhaps because the program—for example, a DOS app or Notepad—doesn't give you a choice), the default printer is used.

NOTE

The default printer can be set by right-clicking on a printer icon and choosing Set as Default.

Exactly how your printed documents look varies somewhat from program to program because not all programs can take full advantage of the capabilities of your printer and the printer driver. For example, simple word-processing programs like

Notepad don't let you change the font, while a full-blown word-processing program such as Ami Pro or Word can print out all kinds of fancy graphics, fonts, columns of text, and so forth.

NOTE

> Here's something to consider. If you choose as a default a printer that your DOS programs can't work with, your print jobs could bomb. Suppose you're running WordPerfect 5.1 for DOS and have it installed to print to an HP LaserJet, but the default printer is a Postscript laser printer. This would cause your printouts to be nothing but a listing of PostScript commands, such as ERROR: undefined, OFFENDING COMMAND: |ume STACK {-pop-, and so on. On another type of printer, you might see garbage printouts such as @#$@$%G$V%B^YB&M(OM instead of readable text. Just make sure your DOS programs can work with your default printer (or change the default printer).

When you print from any program, the file is actually printed to a disk file instead of directly to the printer. Print Manager then spools the file to the assigned printer(s), coordinating the flow of data and keeping you informed of the progress. Jobs are queued up and listed in the Print Manager window, from which their status can be observed; they can be rearranged, deleted, and so forth.

Printing from a Program

To print from any program, including Windows 3.x and Windows 95 programs, follow these steps (which are exact for Windows programs but only approximate for other environments):

1. Check to see that the printer and page settings are correct. Some program's File menus provide a Printer Setup, Page Setup, or other option for this. Note that settings you make from such a box temporarily (sometimes permanently, depending on the program) override settings made from the Printer's Properties dialog box.

2. Select the Print command on the program's File menu and fill in whatever information is asked of you. For example, in WordPad, the Print dialog box looks like that in Figure 8.10.

PART

II

Exploring Windows 98

When you choose Print from a Windows program, you often see a dialog box such as this that allows you to choose some options before printing. This one is from WordPad, a program supplied with Windows 98.

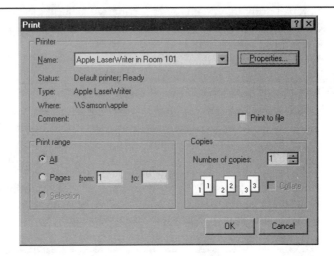

Some programs have rather elaborate dialog boxes for choosing which printer you want to print to, scaling or graphically altering the printout, and even adjusting the properties of the printer. Still, you can normally just make the most obvious settings and get away with it:

- correct printer
- correct number of copies
- correct print range (pages, spreadsheet cells, portion of graphic, etc.)
- for color printers, which ink cartridge you have in (black & white or color)

3. Click on OK (or otherwise confirm printing). Windows 98 intercepts the print data and writes it in a file, then begins printing it. If an error occurs—a port conflict, the printer is out of paper, or what have you—you'll see a message such as this:

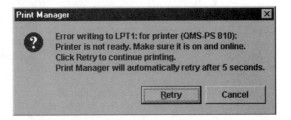

Check the paper supply, check to see that the printer is turned on, that it's online (there may be a switch on the printer for this). If it's a network printer, make sure it's shared and that the computer it's connected to is booted up and has shared the printer for use.

When printing commences, a little printer icon will appear in the Taskbar next to the clock. You can double-click on this icon to see details of your pending print jobs.

Printing by Dragging Files onto a Printer Icon or into Its Window

You can quickly print Windows program document files by dragging them onto a printer's icon or window. You can drag from the Desktop, a folder, the Find box, the Windows Explorer, or a File Manager window. This will only work with documents that have an association with a particular program. (See Chapter 3 for a discussion of associations.) To check if a document has an association, right-click on it. If the resulting menu has an Open command on it (not Open With), it has an association.

1. Arrange things on your screen so you can see the file(s) you want to print as well as either the printer's icon or its window (you open a printer's window by double-clicking on its icon).

You can drag a file into a shortcut of the Printer's icon. If you like this way of printing, keep a shortcut of your printer on the Desktop so you can drag documents to it without having to open up the Printers folder. Double-clicking on a shortcut provides an easy means of checking its print queue, too.

2. Drag the document file(s) onto the Print Manager icon or window (Figure 8.11 illustrates). The file is loaded into the source program, the Print command is automatically executed, and the file is spooled to Print Manager. The document isn't actually moved out of its home folder, it just gets printed.

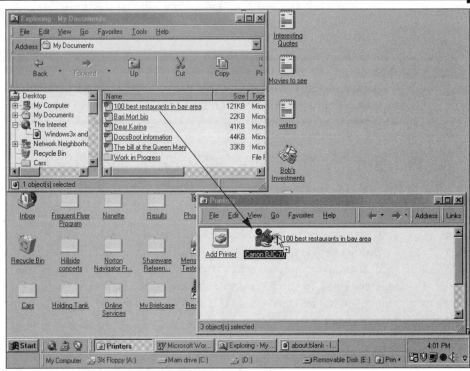

If the document doesn't have an association, you'll see an error message:

Also, a nice feature of this approach is that you can drag multiple files onto a printer's icon or open window at once. They will all be queued up for printing, one after another, via their source programs. You'll see this message asking for confirmation before printing commences:

One caveat about this technique: as you know, some programs don't have a built-in facility for printing to a printer other than the default one. Notepad is a case in point: Try to drag a Notepad document to a printer that isn't currently your default printer, and you'll see this message:

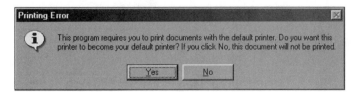

The drag-and-drop method can be used with shortcuts, too. You can drag shortcuts of documents to a printer or even to a shortcut of a printer, and the document will print.

Printing by Right-Clicking on a Document

Finally, you can print some documents using another shortcut that doesn't even require you to have a printer icon in view; instead, you use the right-click menu. Here's how:

1. Right-click on the icon of any document you want to print and notice whether the right-click menu has a Print command on it.

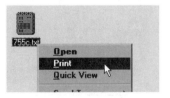

2. If there's no Print command, press Esc to cancel the menu. You can't print the document using this technique. If there is a Print command, choose it. The file will open in its source program and start printing right away. Once spooled to the Print Manager, the document will close automatically.

PART

II

Exploring Windows 98

Working with the Print Queue

If you print more than a few files at a time, or if you have your printer shared for network use, you'll sometimes want to check on the status of a printer's print jobs. You also might want to see how many jobs need to print before you turn off your local computer and printer if others are using it. Or you might want to know how many other jobs are ahead of yours.

You can check on these items by opening a printer's window. You'll then see:

Document Name: Name of the file being printed and possibly the source program

Status: Whether the job is printing, being deleted, or paused

Owner: Who sent each print job to the printer

Progress: How large each job is and how much of the current job has been printed

Start at: When each print job was sent to the print queue

Figure 8.12 shows a sample printer with a print queue and related information.

FIGURE 10.12

A printer's window with several print jobs pending.

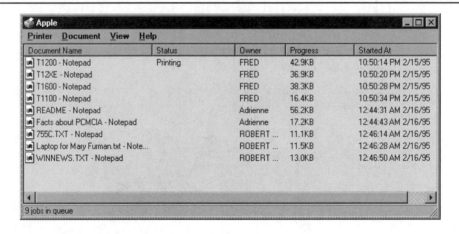

Document Name	Status	Owner	Progress	Started At
T1200 - Notepad	Printing	FRED	42.9KB	10:50:14 PM 2/15/95
T12XE - Notepad		FRED	36.9KB	10:50:20 PM 2/15/95
T1600 - Notepad		FRED	38.3KB	10:50:28 PM 2/15/95
T1100 - Notepad		FRED	16.4KB	10:50:34 PM 2/15/95
README - Notepad		Adrienne	56.2KB	12:44:31 AM 2/16/95
Facts about PCMCIA - Notepad		Adrienne	17.2KB	12:44:43 AM 2/16/95
755C.TXT - Notepad		ROBERT ...	11.1KB	12:46:14 AM 2/16/95
Laptop for Mary Furman.txt - Note...		ROBERT ...	11.5KB	12:46:28 AM 2/16/95
WINNEWS.TXT - Notepad		ROBERT ...	13.0KB	12:46:50 AM 2/16/95

9 jobs in queue

To see the queue on a printer:

1. Open the Printers folder.

2. Double-click on the printer in question.

3. Adjust the window size if necessary so you can see all the columns.

If the print job originated from a DOS program, the Document Name will not be known. It's listed as Remote Downlevel Document, meaning that it came from a workstation that doesn't support Microsoft's RPC (Remote Procedure Call) print support. Additional cases in point are Windows for Workgroups, LAN Manager, Unix, and Netware.

You can resize the columns in the display to see more data in a small window. Move the pointer to the dividing line in the header display and drag the line left or right.

If the printer in question is a network printer, and the printer is offline for some reason, such as its computer isn't turned on, you'll be forced to work *offline*. An error message will alert you to this, and the top line of the printer's window will say *User intervention required—Work Offline*. Until the issue is resolved, you won't be able to view the queue for that printer. You can still print to it, however.

Refreshing the Network Queue Information

The network cabling connecting workstations and servers often is quite busy, so Windows usually doesn't bother to add even more traffic to the net by polling each workstation for printer-queue information. This is done when necessary, such as when a document is deleted from a queue. So, if you want to refresh the window for a printer to get the absolute latest information, just press F5. This immediately updates the queue information.

Deleting a File from the Queue

After sending a file to the queue, you might reconsider printing it, or you might want to re-edit the file and print it later. If so, you can simply remove the file from the queue.

1. Open the printer's window.

2. Select the file by clicking on it in the queue.

NOTE

I have found, especially with PostScript laser-type printers, that after deleting a file while printing, I'll have to reset the printer to clear its buffer or at least eject the current page (if you have a page-eject button). To reset, you'll typically have to push a button on the printer's front panel or turn the printer off for a few seconds, then on again.

3. Choose Document ➤ Cancel Printing, press Delete, or right-click and choose Cancel Printing. The document item is removed from the printer's window. If you're trying to delete the job that's printing, you might have some trouble. At the very least, the system might take some time to respond.

NOTE

Of course, normally you can't delete someone else's print jobs on a remote printer. If you try to, you'll be told that this is beyond your privilege and that you should contact your system administrator. You *can* kill other people's print jobs if the printer in question is connected to *your* computer. But if you want to be able to delete jobs on a remote computer, someone has to alter the password settings in the remote computer's Control Panel to allow remote administration of the printer. Remote administration is covered in Part V.

NOTE

Pending print jobs will not be lost when computers are powered down. Any documents in the queue when the system goes down will reappear in the queue when you power up. When you turn on a computer that is the host for a shared printer that has an unfinished print queue, you will be alerted to the number of jobs in the queue and asked whether to delete or print them.

TIP

When an error occurs during a print job, Windows tries to determine the cause. For example, the printer might be out of paper, or the printer might be offline or unplugged from the AC outlet. You may be forced to work offline until the problem is resolved. Opening the printers queue should display an error message approximating the nature of the problem to the best of Print Manager's capabilities. Check the printer's File menu to see if the Work Offline setting has been activated. When you think the problem has been solved, turn this setting off to begin printing again.

Canceling All Pending Print Jobs on a Given Printer

Sometimes, because of a megalithic meltdown or some other catastrophe, you'll decide to bail out of all the print jobs that are stacked up for a printer. Normally you don't need to do this, even if the printer has gone wacky. You can just pause the queue and continue printing after the problem is solved. But sometimes you'll want to resend everything to another printer and kill the queue on the current one. It's easy:

1. Select the printer's icon or window.

2. Right-click and choose Purge Print Jobs, or from the printer's window choose Printer ➤ Purge Print Jobs. All queued jobs for the printer are canceled.

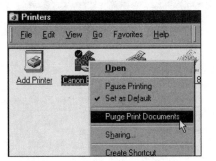

WARNING

Make sure you really want to cancel the jobs before you do this. This is a good way to make enemies if people on the network were counting on their print jobs being finished anytime soon.

Pausing (and Resuming) the Printing Process

If you're the administrator of a printer with a stack of jobs in the print queue, you can temporarily pause a single job or all jobs on a particular printer at any time. This can be useful for taking a minute to add paper, take a phone call, or have a conversation in your office without the noise of the printer in the background. The next several sections explain the techniques for pausing and resuming.

Pausing or Resuming a Specific Print Job

You can pause documents anywhere in the queue. Paused documents are skipped and subsequent documents in the list print ahead of them. You can achieve the same effect by rearranging the queue, as explained in the section titled *Rearranging the Queue Order*. When you feel the need to pause or resume a specific print job:

1. Click on the document's information line.

2. Choose Document ➤ Pause Printing (or right-click on the document and choose Pause Printing as you see in Figure 8.13). The current print job is temporarily suspended, and the word "Paused" appears in the status area. (The printing might not stop immediately because your printer might have a buffer that holds data in preparation for printing. The printing stops when the buffer is empty.)

FIGURE 8.13

Pause the printing of a single document with the right-click menu. Other documents will continue to print.

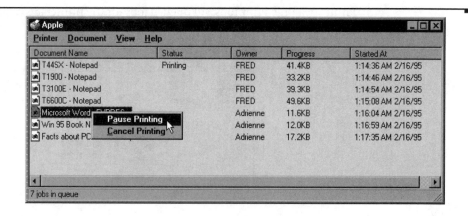

3. To resume printing the document, repeat steps 1 and 2 to turn off the check mark next to Pause Printing.

Pausing or Resuming All Jobs on a Printer

In similar fashion, you can temporarily pause all jobs on a given printer. You might want to do this for a number of reasons including:

- to load paper or otherwise adjust the physical printer
- to alter printer settings from the printer's Properties dialog box

Follow these steps to pause or resume all jobs for a printer:

1. Deselect any documents in the printer's window; press the Spacebar if a document is selected.

2. Choose Printer ➤ Pause Printing. The printer window's title bar changes to say "Paused."

3. To resume all jobs on the printer, choose Printer ➤ Pause Printing again to turn off the check mark next to the command. The *Paused* indicator in the title bar disappears, and printing should resume where the queue left off.

Rearranging the Queue Order

When you have several items on the queue, you might want to re-arrange the order in which they're slated for printing.

1. Click on the file you want to move and keep the mouse button depressed.

2. Drag the file to its new location. The name of the document moves to indicate where the document will be inserted when you release the mouse button.

3. When you release the mouse button, your file is inserted in the queue, pushing the other files down a notch (see Figure 8.14).

PART

II

Exploring Windows 98

FIGURE 8.14

You can shift the order of a document in the queue by dragging it to the desired position and dropping it.

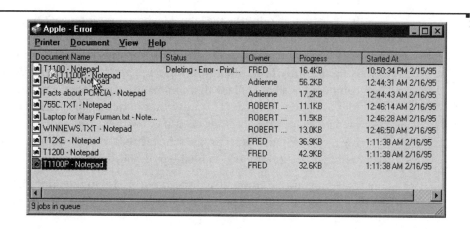

Printing to a Disk File instead of a Printer

There are times when you may want to print to a disk file rather than to the printer. What does this mean? When you print to a disk file, the codes and data that would normally be sent to the printer are shunted off to a disk file—either locally or on the network. The resulting file typically isn't just a copy of the file you were printing; it contains all the special formatting codes that control your printer. Codes that change fonts, print graphics, set margins, break pages, and add attributes such as underline, bold, and so on are all included in this type of file. Print files destined for PostScript printers typically include their PostScript preamble, too—a special file that prepares the printer to receive the instructions that are about to come and the fonts that are included in the document.

Why would you want to create a disk file instead of printing directly to the printer? Printing to a file gives you several options not available when you print directly to the printer:

- Print files are sometimes used by programs for specific purposes. For example, printing a database to a disk file might allow you to more easily work with it in another application. Or you might want to print an encapsulated PostScript graphics file to be imported into a desktop- publishing document.

- You can send the file to another person, either on floppy disk or over the phone lines, with a modem and a communications program such as Terminal. That person can then print the file directly to a printer (if it's compatible) with Windows or a utility such as the DOS **copy** command. The person doesn't need the program that created the file and doesn't have to worry about any of the printing details—formatting, setting up margins, and so forth. All that's in the file.

- It allows you to print the file later. Maybe your printer isn't hooked up, or there's so much stuff on the queue that you don't want to wait, or you don't want to slow down your computer or the network by printing now. Print to a file, which is significantly faster than printing on paper. Later, you can use the DOS **copy** command or a batch file with a command such as **copy *.prn lpt1 /b** to copy all files to the desired port. This way you can queue up as many files as you want, prepare the printer, and then print them without having to be around. Be sure to use the **/b** switch. If you don't, the first Ctrl+Z code the computer encounters will terminate the print job because the print files are binary files.

In some programs, printing to a disk file is a choice in the Print dialog box. If it isn't, you should modify the printer's configuration to print to a file rather than to a port. Then, whenever you use that printer, it uses all the usual settings for the driver but sends the data to a file of your choice instead of to the printer port.

1. In the Printers folder, right-click on the printer's icon and choose Properties.

2. Select the Details tab page.

3. Under *Print to the following port*, choose FILE:

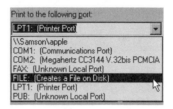

4. OK the box. The printer's icon in the Printers folder will change to indicate that printing is routed to a disk file.

 Now when you print a file from any program and choose this printer as the destination for the printout, you'll be prompted for a file name.

Epson LX-80

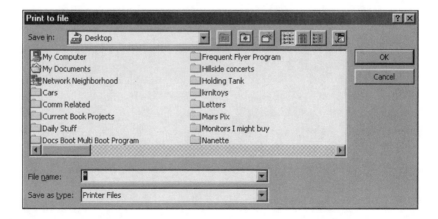

If you want to print the file as ASCII text only, with no special control codes, you should install the Generic/Text Only printer driver. Then select that as the destination printer.

If you want to print to an encapsulated PostScript file (`.eps`), print to a printer that uses a PostScript driver (the Apple LaserWriter or the QMS PS-810, for instance) or set up a phony printer that uses such a driver. (No physical printer is needed.) When prompted for a file name, specify an EPS extension.

Chapter

9

Using Fonts Effectively

FEATURING

What are fonts and what is True Type?

Building a font collection

Adding and removing fonts

Some basic guidelines for using fonts

Deleting font files from your hard disk

Using Fonts Effectively

One of the most compelling characteristics of Windows—possibly even the single ability that most ensured the acceptance of Windows as *the* PC standard GUI—is the convenience of having a single system for displaying and printing text that works with all Windows programs. Though at the time Windows 3.0 appeared some ordinary MS-DOS programs could display and print high-quality fonts, they have had to rely on a bewildering hodge-podge of different printer drivers and font formats to achieve any success in this arena. Worse yet, each program solved font dilemmas in its own way, not sharing their wealth of fonts or font-management utilities with other MS-DOS programs.

By contrast, Windows programs (especially as of Windows 3.1, when True Type fonts were introduced) need only a single printer driver and one pool of fonts. Thus, Lotus 1-2-3 for Windows, Ami Pro, Microsoft Access, Excel, Word, and PowerPoint on a Windows system can all share the same fonts and print with them to a number of printers without difficulty. Because fonts are so readily available at this point—in shareware packages, on BBSs, or on those economy CD-ROM packages down at the local computer discount store—getting your paws on some interesting fonts is a cinch.

Like other Windows versions, Windows 98 comes with a set of stock fonts such as Courier New, Times New Roman, and Arial. You may be happy with these relatively banal, though useful, choices and possibly never feel the need to add to them. More likely, though, you'll want to augment these rudimentary fonts with a collection of your favorites to spruce up your documents. In this chapter I'll explain how to add and remove fonts from your system, how to choose and use fonts wisely, ways to procure new fonts, and even how to create fonts of your own.

Font Management in Windows 98

Fonts are highly desirable to most users. Suddenly having the Gutenbergian power to lay out and print aesthetically sophisticated correspondence, books, brochures, and newsletters is one of the great joys of computerdom. But installing, removing, and managing fonts threw a kink in the works for many Windows 3.x users, especially once they installed a zillion fonts and realized how much that slowed down their system. Windows 3.x initially loaded much more slowly once you'd hyped up your system with a lot of fonts because all the fonts, font names, and font directories have to be checked out and loaded.

Microsoft has included much-improved font management since Windows 3.x. It's not perfect, but it's better. Choosing Fonts from the Setting menu or My Computer, or selecting the Fonts directory in Windows Explorer will present options such as:

- installing and removing fonts
- viewing on screen or printing an example of each font in various point sizes
- listing only font families rather than each variation of a font, eliminating redundant listings (for instance, Times New Roman, Times New Roman Bold, and Times New Roman Italic)
- listing all fonts similar in appearance to a given font, such as all fonts similar to Arial
- toggling between a listing of actual font file names and the font's common name

What Are Fonts and What Is TrueType?

Fonts are the various type styles that you can use when composing a document, viewing it on the screen, or printing it on paper. Fonts add visual impact to your documents to help you express your words or numbers in a style that suits your audience. They can also increase readability.

As an example of some fonts, Figure 9.1 shows several popular type styles. Fonts are specified by size as well as by name. The size of a font is measured in *points*. A point is 1/72 of an inch. In addition, fonts styles include **bold**, *italic*, and underlining.

FIGURE 9.1

Various fonts and point sizes

Times New Roman
12 point

Brush Script
33 point

Times New Roman Italic
12 point

Gill Sans
28 point

Shelley Allegro
30 point

Casper Open Face
20 point

Windows comes supplied with a reasonable stock of fonts, some of which are installed on your hard disk and integrated into Windows during the setup procedure. The number and types of fonts installed depend on the type of screen and printer you have. When you install a printer into your Windows setup (see Chapter 8), a printer driver is installed. The printer driver includes a set of basic fonts for your printer.

Some programs, such as word processors, may have additional fonts supplied with them—fonts not included with Windows—that you may want to use. Fonts can also be purchased separately from companies that specialize in typeface design, such as Bitstream, Inc., Adobe Systems, Inc., and Microsoft.

Font packages usually come with their own setup programs, which will automatically install the fonts into your Windows system for you. When installing fonts with these programs, just follow the instruction manual supplied with the font package. If there is no such installation program, use the Control Panel's Fonts applet as explained later in this chapter.

General Classes of Fonts

There are several basic classes of fonts that are used in Windows, and an understanding of them will help you manage your font collection. Windows fonts break down into the following groups:

Screen fonts control how text looks on your screen. They come in predefined sizes, such as 10 points, 12 points, and so forth.

Printer fonts are fonts stored in your printer (in its ROM), stored on plug-in cartridges, or downloaded to your printer by Windows when you print. Downloaded fonts are called *soft fonts*.

Vector fonts use straight line segments and formulas to draw letters. They can be easily scaled to different sizes. These are primarily used on printing devices that only draw lines, such as plotters.

TrueType fonts are generated either as *bitmaps* or as soft fonts, depending on your printer. The advantage of TrueType fonts is that they will print exactly as seen on the screen. (TrueType fonts were first introduced with Windows 3.1 to solve problems associated with differences between how fonts appear on screen and how they print.)

Before Windows 3.1, both printer and screen fonts often had to be added for each type style you wanted to add to your setup. TrueType fonts simplify matters because adding a TrueType font installs both printer and screen fonts simultaneously. In addition, TrueType fonts will look identical (though perhaps with differences in smoothness or resolution) regardless of the printer with which you print them.

When you print a document, Windows checks your printer driver file to see if it includes the fonts you put in the document. If the printer or printer driver does not supply the font, Windows attempts to find a happy solution. In most cases, Windows will handle day-to-day printing jobs just fine. If your printer has a soft font already in it (from plug-in font cartridges or in its ROM) and Windows doesn't have a screen font of that type, Windows will usually substitute another, similar screen font with the correct size for displaying your work on screen. Even though it might not look exactly like the final printout, the line length and page breaks on your screen should be accurate.

About TrueType Fonts

With the addition of TrueType fonts in Windows several years ago, typefaces could be scaled to any size and displayed or printed accurately on virtually all displays and printers—without the addition of any third-party software. And because of the careful design of the screen and printer display of each font, TrueType provides much better WYSIWYG (What You See Is What You Get) capabilities than previous fonts. Furthermore, you no longer have to ensure that you have fonts in your printer that match the fonts on screen.

In the past, if you used a printer like the LaserJet II, you might have been limited to the two fonts that come standard with that printer (Courier and Line Printer). If you wanted to print any other fonts, you had to buy a cartridge containing a few additional fonts, or you had to buy soft fonts. These fonts had to be individually rendered by the vendor in each size that might be required. This was often costly and required a tremendous amount of hard-disk space. If you wanted to display the fonts on screen, you had to create yet another set of screen fonts that matched the printer fonts.

With TrueType, any printer that can print graphics can print the full range of TrueType fonts—all orchestrated by Windows. And the results will look more or less the same, even on different printers. Although different printers provide different resolutions, the essential characteristics of a TrueType font will remain consistent whether it is printed on a 9-pin dot-matrix printer or a high-resolution image setter.

TrueType also allows users of different computer systems to maintain compatability across platforms. For example, because TrueType is also integrated into Mac System 7 and System 8 (Macintosh operating systems), a document formatted on a Macintosh using TrueType fonts will look exactly the same on a Windows-equipped PC.

Finally, because TrueType is an integrated component of Windows, any Windows program can make use of TrueType fonts. These fonts can be easily scaled (increased or decreased in size), rotated, or otherwise altered.

Comparing TrueType Fonts to Bit-Mapped and Vector Fonts

So much for TrueType fonts. Now let's consider other types of fonts, namely bit-mapped and vector fonts. First let's see how these two kinds of fonts work as screen fonts. Then I'll discuss printer fonts.

PART

II

Exploring Windows 98

NOTE

Recall from the list above that printer fonts are those built into the printer or those sent to the printer by the computer to print a document. Screen fonts are the fonts Windows uses to display text on the screen.

There are two types of screen fonts: bit-mapped and vector. Each is quite different from the other and serves a distinct purpose.

Bit-Mapped Fonts

Bit-mapped fonts are essentially a collection of bitmaps (pictures), one for each character you might want to type. These bitmaps cover the entire character set and range of styles for a particular typeface in a limited number of sizes. Examples of bit-mapped fonts in Windows are Courier, MS Serif, MS Sans Serif, and MS Symbol. When you install Windows, these fonts are automatically copied to the appropriate Windows FOLDER by Setup. Windows comes with a number of versions of these fonts. Based on the resolution of your video adapter, Windows chooses the font files that take best advantage of your particular display. Figure 9.2 shows a character map of a bit-mapped font (MS Serif).

NOTE

Some of your programs may not display the list of bit-mapped fonts in their Font boxes. They may only show a list of TrueType fonts. This doesn't mean they aren't there, only that your program isn't displaying them. If you try other programs, such as MS Paint (when using the Text tool), you'll see a larger list, including such bit-mapped fonts as MS Serif.

FIGURE 9.2

A bit-mapped font

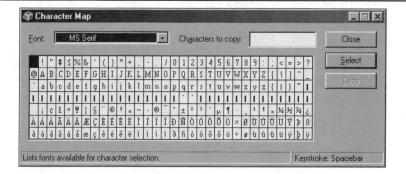

Because bit-mapped fonts are dependent on the bitmaps included in their font files, you are limited to displaying these fonts in the sizes provided or in exact multiples of their original sizes if you want the font to look good. For example, MS Serif for VGA resolution includes bitmaps for display at 8, 10, 12, 14, 18, and 24 points. Opening the Size box for a bit-mapped font will display a limited list of sizes such as this list for Courier:

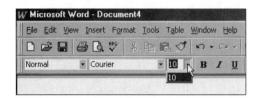

Even though the list of sizes for a bit-mapped font is usually limited, you can type in any number you want. Windows will do its best to scale the font to the approximate size you ask for, but it will likely look pretty icky. There's one exception to this: bit-mapped fonts can scale acceptably to exact multiples. So if 10 is on the list (as in the example above), you could get decent-looking 20-, 30-, or 40-point renditions, although the results will not look as good as a TrueType font at the same size.

Vector Fonts

Vector fonts are more suitable for devices like plotters that can't use bit-mapped characters because they draw with lines rather than dots. Vector fonts are a series of mathematical formulas that describe a series of lines and curves (arcs). They can be scaled to any size, but because of the process involved in computing the shape and direction of the curves, these fonts can be quite time consuming to generate. PostScript fonts are actually vector fonts, but because the PostScript printer itself is optimized to do the computing of the font sizes and shapes, performance is fairly good. Examples of vector fonts are Modern, Roman, and Script.

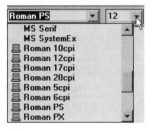

Variations of Printer Fonts

Just as there are different types of screen fonts, there are also several different types of printer fonts:

- device fonts
- printable screen fonts
- downloadable soft fonts

Device fonts are those fonts installed in your printer, either factory defaults or members of a font-cartridge collection. Printable screen fonts are bit-mapped and vector fonts that can be used not only on screen but also sent to the printer. Downloadable soft fonts are fonts that, like TrueType, are stored on your PC's hard disk and can be sent to the printer as needed. Unlike TrueType fonts, though, they are specific to your printer and are generally provided in limited styles and sizes.

Adobe Sytems was the first popular seller of scalable fonts, called Type 1 fonts. These were a part of the PostScript page-description language. Partly to avoid the costs of having to license Type 1 fonts from Adobe, and partly to challenge Adobe's position in the fonts market, Microsoft pioneered TrueType fonts. Both systems provide approximately the same advantages—namely, with a single font file you can make the type appear in whatever size you want, both on screen and printed. This tug of war between the two manufacturers is finally about to end, so rumor has it. An agreement between Microsoft and Adobe is supposed to lead in the near future to a new type format called Open-Type. Intended to be a superset of Type 1 and TrueType, the system will convert your older Type 1 or TrueType fonts to the new format. It also provides some additional features that resolve some of the limitations of the other formats; for example, OpenType will provide ligatures (special character pairs to improve readability), alternative versions of the same characters within the same font, and embedding of compressed font information into documents. The latter feature will enable Web pages to rapidly display whatever fonts the designer wishes.

How Does TrueType Work?

TrueType fonts are similar to both bit-mapped and vector fonts. They contain a description of the series of lines and curves for the typeface—like a vector font. When you press a key in a Windows word processor, for example, that application asks Windows to generate the bitmap of the appropriate character in the right font and size at a particular spot on screen. Windows' Graphical Device Interface (GDI) creates a bitmap in memory that best represents that character. But the job of creating the character is only half done.

Like bit-mapped fonts, TrueType fonts include a number of bit-mapped "hints" that help Windows when rendering the font in smaller point sizes. Hints are an extremely important element of TrueType. Because the resolution of even an SVGA monitor is somewhat less than that of a 300-dpi laser printer, many fonts simply don't look right on screen. There just aren't enough pixels to accurately reproduce the font at smaller point sizes.

When Windows displays a character at a small point size, it uses the hinting instructions located in a TrueType font to cheat a bit by reshaping the character so lines or curves aren't missing or misshapen. But hints are not just important for screen display. Look closely at a page of small text generated by your printer. If it prints 300 dots per inch, chances are you'll notice slight imperfections in characters. An *O* may not be perfectly round; the slant of a *W* may not be truly straight. Hinting ensures the highest possible quality of fonts despite the resolution limits of most common output devices.

You may notice that when you select a different font or a new point size that Windows pauses for a moment. During this delay, it creates bitmaps for the entire character set in the new size or style. This happens only once during a Windows session. After first generating the bitmaps, Windows places them into a memory cache where they can be quickly accessed the next time they are required.

TIP

If you have a number of documents you created using fonts that you no longer have, you don't need to go through the documents and change your formatting. You can force Windows to substitute appropriate replacements. Load `win.ini` into an editor like Notepad. If you look at the [FontSubstitutes] section of the file, you'll notice lines like `TmsRmn=MS Serif`. Add any associations you like, keeping the old name on the left of the equation and the new name on the right. Windows will automatically fill requests for the old font with the new font.

Elements of TrueType Typography

As discussed earlier, *font* is now used freely to describe a number of different typographical elements. Font is often used to mean the same thing as *typeface*, a group of fonts that are closely related in design. Technically, a font is a specific set of characters, each of which shares the same basic characteristics. For example, Arial is a typeface. In turn, Arial comprises the fonts Arial, Arial Bold, Arial Bold Italic, and Arial Italic. When you pick Arial from your word processor's font dialog box and then choose to italicize text, you are selecting the font Arial Italic.

Basic TrueType Font Families

As with other types of fonts, all TrueType fonts can be generalized into font families. These are a group of typefaces with similar characteristics but that are much more loosely related than the members of a typeface. Windows recognizes five font families: Decorative, Modern, Roman, Script, and Swiss.

The most common of these families are Roman and Swiss. The Roman font family contains the majority of serif fonts. Sans-serif fonts like Arial are generally members of the Swiss family. Figure 9.3 shows fonts from the Roman and Swiss families. (Serifs are discussed below, in *Classes of Font Styles*.)

FIGURE 9.3

A Roman font (Times New Roman) and a Swiss font (Arial)

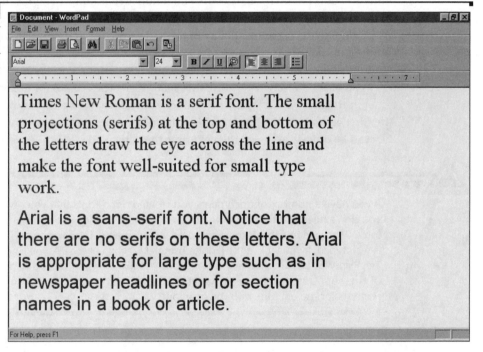

Special Characters

Each TrueType font contains a number of special characters like trademark (™) and yen (¥), punctuation such as the em dash (—) and curly quotes (""), and foreign (æ) and accented (ñ) characters. But Windows 98 also includes two special fonts you should become familiar with: Symbol and WingDings.

Symbol contains a number of mathematical symbols such as not-equal-to (≠) and plus-or-minus (±). It also contains a complete Greek alphabet for scientific notation.

WingDings is quite a bit more versatile. It contains a wide range of symbols and characters that can be used to add special impact to documents. Instead of printing *Tel.* next to your phone number, why not place a telephone symbol? WingDings includes several religious symbols: a cross, a Star of David, and a crescent and star, as well as several zodiac signs. Figure 9.4 displays all of the characters of these two fonts.

FIGURE 9.4

Symbol and WingDings are two TrueType fonts worth checking out. They contain characters you might find useful in your documents. You may even want to use one of these for your personal or corporate logo.

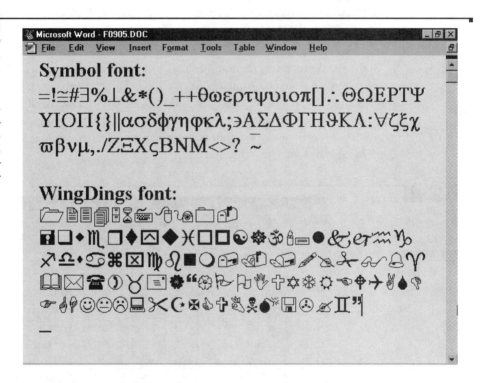

PART

II

Exploring Windows 98

You can access these special characters in several different ways. The easiest is to select WingDings or Symbol in any TrueType-compatible application, then type characters from the keyboard. For example, the universal symbol for *airport* corresponds to a *Q* in WingDings. This method requires a bit of memorization or a handy reference chart to keep the associations straight.

Alternately, you can enter keys by using the Alt key with your numeric keypad. Each character in a font is associated with a numeric value between 0 and 255. By holding down the Alt key while entering that number, you can insert the appropriate character. For example, to insert an em dash (—), hold down the Alt key and press the numbers 0151 on the keypad. This will not work with the number keys at the top of your keyboard, and you must remember to preface the number with a 0. Again, you will need a reference chart for the particular font you're using to take advantage of this method.

TIP

The Fonts option from the Control Panel lets you examine all the characters in a font, too. You can read about that later in this chapter, under "Adding and Removing Fonts Using Control Panel."

Many word processors include a function called Insert Symbol. This feature allows you to choose a character from a table of all the characters in a particular font. You just highlight the character you want and click on OK (or double-click on the character), and it appears instantly in your document. This is not the quickest way to enter a symbol, but it is the easiest if your word processor offers it. Figure 9.5 shows the Insert Symbol table in Word for Windows 6.0.

FIGURE 9.5

A typical Insert Symbol table in a word-processing application

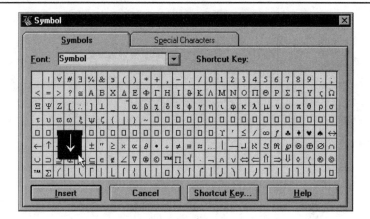

If your application lacks an Insert Symbol feature, you can open the Character Map accessory discussed in Chapter 22 and copy the symbols you want to the Clipboard. Then switch back to your application and paste the symbols where you want them. While not the easiest way to insert symbols, this method is adequate for most uses. However, sometimes the font "loses" its font family name when it's copied in this way; once pasted, you may have to select the character and reset its font.

TrueType Font Embedding

What if you get a document from a friend or a business associate that was formatted with TrueType fonts you don't have on your system? One of the most important features of TrueType is the ability to *embed* fonts in documents. So when you send a document to someone else, the fonts you use go with it.

NOTE

Beware: Although Windows itself supports embedded TrueType fonts, not all Windows applications do. Most programs will be able to display embedded TrueType fonts, though an occasional program won't be able to embed them.

When you load a document that contains embedded TrueType fonts, Windows copies those fonts into memory temporarily. They can then be used in conjunction with that document specifically. Depending on the attributes set by the font vendor, a font can have one of three embedding options—read-only embedding, read-write embedding, or no embedding at all.

The most common type of font will most likely be read-only. If you load a document containing read-only fonts—and you don't have those fonts yourself—you will only be able to print or view the document. You won't be able to alter it. This prevents nonowners of a font from using it without paying for it.

However, the fonts supplied by Microsoft in Windows 98 and Microsoft's TrueType Font Pack are read-write fonts. Documents containing these fonts can be printed, viewed, and edited regardless of whether the fonts themselves are installed on the system. Also, Windows provides the ability to save the fonts themselves for use with future documents. Obviously, this approach is not popular with commercial developers who make their livings selling their fonts, but a quick scan of public-domain TrueType fonts that have popped up on online services like CompuServe and AOL shows that most free fonts are read-write enabled.

On the other end of the spectrum, vendors may choose to disallow embedding of their fonts. If you try to save a document that contains one of these typefaces, your word processor will simply not include the fonts. Essentially, this would create documents similar to those containing no font information other than the name of the original font.

TrueType's greatest advantage is that it ensures that the fonts you see on screen are the fonts you get on paper. Embedded TrueType takes this one step further by ensuring that the fonts used to create a document are the ones used to view, edit, and print it.

PART

II

Exploring Windows 98

TECH TIP

If when you send another person a document, you want to ensure that he or she will be able to actually edit the document using the fonts you have used to create it, either use popular fonts that all Windows users have on their systems, such as Times New Roman, Arial, or Courier New; or check that your application is set to embed fonts. For example, in Microsoft Word this is done with the Tools ➤ Options menu.

Which Fonts Should I Use?

You can install bit-mapped, vector, and scalable fonts into Windows. But as long as your printer can print graphics and is not a plotter, you should stick to scalable fonts like TrueType and ignore bit-mapped and vector fonts entirely—in fact, you can remove them from your system, as discussed later.

Bit-mapped fonts look good on your screen, but only at the particular size they're designed for; when you display them at another size, they appear distorted and jagged. In addition, because you need one file for every size of a given typeface you want to display, one set of bit-mapped fonts can consume a great deal of valuable territory on your hard disk. It's also inconvenient to keep track of all the files involved.

Vector fonts are worth using only if your output device is a plotter. While the files aren't overly large, and while you can print vector fonts at any size, they have an unattractive, noticeably angular appearance. One plus: vector font files are quite small.

TrueType and other scalable fonts, by contrast, look great when displayed or printed at any size. If you decide that a particular document requires, say, a 13.5-point rendition of Times, all you have to do is request it, and Windows will generate it automatically. Although TrueType font files are fairly large, typically around 60K, you only need one file for each typeface. Font files of other scalable font formats such as Type 1 PostScript and FaceLift tend to be somewhat smaller.

How Your Fonts Get Used by Windows

Most Windows programs that print text let you specify the font you want. In some cases, as in most word-processing programs, you can change fonts with every text character, while other programs restrict you to one font for each block of text or field or impose some other limitation. For example, in the accessory program Paint, once text is laid into a picture, its font can't be altered.

Ideally, Windows should let you select only from the fonts your printer can actually print. Unfortunately, this isn't always the case if you install more than one printer driver. In this situation, many Windows programs offer you all the fonts available with every installed printer driver, leaving it to you to figure out which ones are appropriate for your printer. Or they might switch the list of fonts available when you change the default printer to a new printer, but a list of MRU (most recently used) fonts may still display fonts from the previous default printer. Word 6 has such a list at the top of its font list.

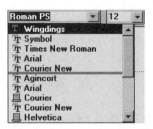

All the fonts above the double line are recently used fonts.

In any case, once you've chosen a font, what you see on the screen depends on the class in which the font falls. If you've selected a TrueType or other scalable font, Windows will generate the appropriate screen font for you so you'll always get a close match between the screen and the final printout. On the other hand, if you're using a nonscalable font, Windows must look for a screen font that corresponds to the one you'll be printing with. If it can't find a match, Windows will substitute the most similar screen font it can find. Depending on the font you've chosen and your screen font collection, this substitute screen font may not look anything like the printed version. Nevertheless, at least the line lengths and page breaks you see on your screen will be accurate.

When you print the document, Windows checks your printer driver file and the win.ini file, looking for the fonts you specified. If the fonts exist, Windows will know whether they're already resident in the printer or must be scaled or downloaded from the hard disk. If a font is missing, Windows will again make an effort to substitute a similar one.

Building a Font Collection

Windows comes with a set of very attractive TrueType fonts that will serve you well in most situations, whether you're writing letters, preparing reports or grant proposals, or adding text to charts or graphics. So why buy more fonts?

PART

II

Exploring Windows 98

Broadly stated, the reason to enlarge your font collection is simple: to improve your ability to communicate. Typographers claim the fonts you use can influence the impact of your message on your readers, even if they're not consciously aware of their reactions. With more fonts to work with, you'll be better able to select ones that suit the mood of whatever document you're preparing. Some fonts, such as Bodoni or Times New Roman, have a decidedly formal appearance, ideal for serious business correspondence. But these same fonts are just too stuffy for a letter to a friend; for this you'd be better off using a font with a casual look, such as Dom Casual or Tekton.

In addition, looking beyond the stock Windows fonts helps you create an identifiable style for your printed documents. Like a logo, the typefaces you choose become associated with you or your business in the minds of those who read your documents regularly. Using the same typeface that everyone else does will make it harder to establish your own typographic identity.

Expert Font Sets

Most fonts you'll pick up for free don't have some of the bells and whistles that professionals often need to set up their fancy documents for printing. If you're going to pay actual real money for a typeface you should know about these three gotta haves:

- **Ligatures:** In some letter combinations beginning with the letter *f*, the *f* touches the subsequent letters in a clumsy way (for example, with the *fi* combination in *"fine"*). Ligatures are multicharacter replacements for these unsightly combinations. For instance, compare the use with and without an fi ligature in the following two words: finger, finger.

- **Small caps:** An actual alternate series of uppercase letters that look better than simply using a smaller point size for corporate names and the like—for example, SYBEX versus SYBEX.

- **Old-fashioned numerals:** Number characters in most fonts look kind of funky. They are designed to perform nicely in tables, spreadsheets, and so forth. But they don't have a polished look that conveys professionalism. Nifty number typefaces actually have descenders, just like lowercase letters such as *y* and *g* do. They are also proportionally spaced rather than monospaced. For example, 2567 West Goshen Lane versus 2567 West Goshen Lane.

What about Other Scalable Type Alternatives?

TrueType fonts are the most convenient kind of scalable fonts for anyone who uses Windows because TrueType technology is built right into the Windows environment. However, you have several other choices in scalable-font formats.

TrueType's biggest competitor is the Type 1 or PostScript format. Type 1 fonts produce very high quality screen fonts and printed output. Vast numbers of fonts are available in the Type 1 format from many different manufacturers, including some of the most respected typographic houses, and they cover an extremely wide range of beautiful designs.

NOTE

PostScript fonts used with Adobe Type Manager are referred to as Type 1 fonts to distinguish them from another PostScript font format, Type 3. Don't get Type 3 fonts unless you have a PostScript printer or a way to convert them to Type 1.

Since the release of Windows 3.1, TrueType has become very popular, even to the point of being implemented widely on the Macintosh. Although the selection of True-Type fonts was limited only a few years ago, this is no longer the case. Still, there is at least one other reason to consider using Type 1 fonts instead of TrueType fonts: PostScript is still the established standard for very high resolution typesetting devices used in professional publishing. If you stick with Type 1 fonts, you can use the exact same fonts for printing drafts on a desktop laser printer and outputting final typeset copy on a Linotronic or other digital typesetter. This means you can be confident that, aside from lower resolution, your draft will look exactly like your final document.

To use Type 1 fonts to your best advantage, you need a utility program called Adobe Type Manager (ATM). ATM scales Type 1 fonts to the requested size faster than Windows does. It also provides a number of useful options for handling the fonts that you don't get with Windows' built-in font manager.

Other scalable font choices for Windows are less attractive, though you might want to consider them in special circumstances. If you have access to a library of fonts in another scalable font format, it may make sense to purchase a font-scaling utility that allows you to use your font collection with Windows. Like ATM, other font-scaling utilities take over from Windows the job of creating the correctly sized final fonts for the screen and printer.

The runner-up font-scaling utility with the broadest appeal for Windows users is probably Intellifont-for-Windows (by Hewlett-Packard). It works with the Intellifont scalable-font format designed for their LaserJet III through LaserJet 6 printers. If you have a

PART

II

Exploring Windows 98

LaserJet III, IIID, or IIISi and use Intellifont fonts with your non-Windows programs, it may make sense to use Intellifont-for-Windows and stick with a single set of fonts.

SuperPrint (by Zenographics) is the Rosetta stone of font-scaling utilities. It works interchangeably with most of the major font formats—including Type 1, FaceLift, Intellifont, Fontware, and Nimbus Q—although reviews have judged output quality to be lower than that from ATM or FaceLift. As a bonus, SuperPrint speeds up Windows graphics printing significantly and allows you to print sophisticated graphics on non-PostScript printers.

Finally, if you have a limited font budget, consider Publisher's Powerpak for Windows (by Atech Software) and MoreFonts (by MicroLogic Software, Inc.). The fonts that work with them are much, much less expensive than most TrueType, Type 1, and FaceLift fonts.

Choosing Specific Fonts

Once you've settled on the font format you're going to use, your next task is to decide which specific fonts to buy. The number of typeface designs available for Windows totals in the thousands and is still growing. With that much variety, selecting a set of fonts that's right for you can be a daunting proposition.

For this reason, it makes sense to stick to the tried-and-true favorites of typographic professionals when you're starting to build a font library. Figure 9.6 offers a few suggestions; you can't go wrong with any of the fonts shown here. Another simple solution is to buy one of the font sets available from vendors such as Adobe Systems and Monotype. Each of these packages comes with several fonts chosen for a specific type of document, along with design tips for using the fonts appropriately.

Classes of Font Styles

As Figure 9.6 suggests, fonts can be classified into various styles, or looks, too. Even if you choose your fonts from a style chart, such as Figure 11.6, a basic understanding of the classifications is a good idea before you start buying fonts and designing your own documents.

The simplest division in the font kingdom is between serif and sans-serif designs. As a look at the table will show you, serifs are the little bars or lines that extend out from the main parts of the characters. A sans-serif font lacks these lines. It's important to choose a few fonts from each category because almost any combination of a serif and a sans-serif font will look good together, but two sans-serif or two serif fonts will clash.

PART

II

Exploring Windows 98

FIGURE 9.6

The typefaces in the top two groups are proven designs that work well in many types of documents. To be safe, start with these faces. It's more difficult to recommend display faces because you must choose them carefully for the particular mood you want to convey. Still, they are high-quality designs, popular among professional designers, and they cover a considerable range of moods.

Serif typefaces for body text

Baskerville Caslon

Garamond Palatino

San-serif typefaces for general use

Futura Gill Sans

Optima Univers

Display and decorative faces

Benguiat Industria

LITHOS Peignot

Another simple classification for fonts depends on the space allotted to each character. In a *monospaced* font, every character occupies the same amount of space in the horizontal dimension. That is, an *i* takes up just as much room on a line of text as a *w*. In a *proportionally spaced* font, characters occupy differing amounts of space. Proportional fonts are easier to read and allow you to fit more text in a given space. (The typefaces in this book are proportional.) The only reason to use monospaced fonts is when you're printing reports or tables in which the alignment of columns is determined by spaces (by pressing the spacebar on the keyboard).

NOTE

The numerals in most proportionally spaced fonts are monospaced, allowing you to line up columns of numbers easily.

Still another way to classify fonts has to do with their intended purpose, such as for:

- body text
- headlines
- ornamental special effects
- nonalphabetic symbols

Body fonts have highly legible characters and work well for long blocks of text. Although any body-text font can be used for titles and headlines, display or headline fonts are specifically meant for that purpose (such as those used in this book). They boast stronger, more attention-getting designs, but for that reason don't work well for body text.

Two remaining font types—*ornamental* and *display* fonts—aren't shown in Figure 9.6 because they don't have universal application. The distinction between ornamental (or novelty) fonts and display fonts is arbitrary. Still, the idea is that an ornamental font is so highly stylized that it might distract the reader's attention from your message. Use ornamental fonts with care when you want to set a special mood. Symbol or pi fonts contain special symbols such as musical notes, map symbols, or decorations instead of letters, numbers, and punctuation marks, as explained earlier.

Procuring Fonts

The explosion of interest in typography generated by desktop-publishing technology has, in turn, resulted in a proliferation of font vendors. Even Microsoft is offering free TrueType fonts on the Internet. You can search for "free truetype fonts" using your favorite search engine, or go to the site: www.microsoft.com/truetype/fontpack/win.htm.

Many other leading font vendors, including Bitstream and SWFTE, have brought out TrueType versions of their font collections. You can find these in most software stores. Shareware sources of TrueType fonts abound. Be aware though, that not all TrueType fonts have sophisticated hinting built in and may not look as good as fonts from the more respectable font foundries. Also, some users report that badly formed TrueType fonts can sometimes wreak havoc on your system.

If you're looking for fonts on the cheap side, check out one of your local BBSs or an online service like CompuServe or GEnie. The Windows sections of these networks hold a number of free fonts that are yours for the taking. Many of the fonts are PostScript Type 1 fonts that have been converted to TrueType. The quality of these fonts is generally not as good as the commercial fonts, but in most cases, you'll be hard-pressed to notice the difference. I've seen numerous cheapie CD-ROMs that pack hundreds of TrueType fonts on them in several computer stores.

TIP

Here's a great source for typefaces: www.microsoft.com/truetype/links. This website links to a couple hundred sources of fonts, font-related shareware, "type-o-zines" (Web-based magazines about fonts), tips about using fonts; it also links to numerous type designers.

Adding and Removing Fonts Using Control Panel

Now that you have the basics of fonts under your belt, let's get down to the business of managing and maintaining your font collection. As mentioned earlier, the Control Panel's Fonts applet (also available from Explorer if you display the \Windows\Fonts directory) is the tool for the job. The Fonts applet lets you:

- add fonts to your system so your programs can use them
- remove any fonts you don't use, freeing disk space
- view fonts on screen or print out samples of each font you have
- display groups of fonts that are similar in style

Adding Fonts

If no installation program came with your fonts or if you want to add some TrueType fonts to your system that you downloaded from some BBS or otherwise acquired, here's how to do it.

1. Run Control Panel by clicking on Start ➤ Settings ➤ Control Panel.

2. Double-click on the Fonts icon. A window now appears as shown in Figure 9.7. All your installed fonts appear in a folder window that looks like any other folder. (This is a departure from Windows 3.*x*, which had a nonstandard Font dialog box.) You can choose the form of the display from the View menu as with any other folder, too. There are a couple of extra menu options, though, as you'll see.

NOTE

If you have installed special printer fonts for your particular printer, these fonts may not appear in the Fonts folder. They will still appear on font menus in your programs. They just won't show up in the Fonts folder because they probably aren't stored in that folder.

NOTE

Bit-mapped and vector fonts are stored on disk in files with the extension .fon; True-Type font files have the extension .ttf.

FIGURE 9.7

All of your installed fonts are displayed when you choose Fonts from the Control Panel. Because fonts are actually files, they appear the same way other files on your disks do. The TrueType fonts have the TT icon. The fonts with the A icon are bit-mapped or vector fonts.

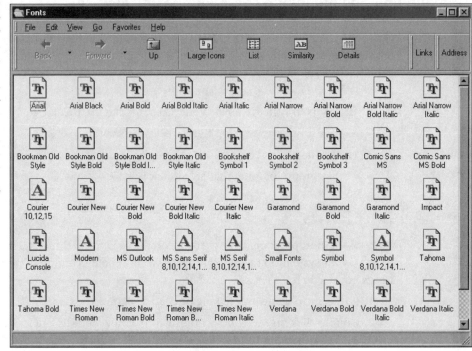

3. Open the File menu and choose the Install New Font option.

A file dialog box appears, as shown in Figure 9.8. Choose the correct drive and directory where the fonts are stored. Typically the fonts you'll be installing are on a CD-ROM or on a floppy disk drive, so you'll have to select the correct drive by clicking on the drive selector.

4. Choose the fonts you want to add. If you want to select more than one, extend the selection by Shift-clicking (to select a range) or Ctrl-clicking (to select individual noncontiguous fonts). Noticed that I have selected several fonts to install at once. If you want to select them all, click on Select All.

FIGURE 9.8

Choose the drive, directory, and fonts you want to install. consider whether you want the fonts copied into the Windows font directory, typically \Window\Fonts. *You can select multiple fonts to install at once, using the Shift and Ctrl keys.*

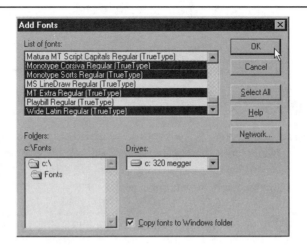

NOTE

If the fonts you want to install are on a network drive somewhere, you have to choose the correct network drive from the Drive list. If the drive isn't in the list, this means you have to *map* the network drive to a local hard-disk name (D, E, F, and so forth) by clicking on Network and filling in the resulting box (mapping drives is covered in Part V).

5. When fonts are installed, they're normally copied to the \Windows\Fonts directory. However, font files are pretty large. If the fonts you're installing are already on your hard disk in another folder, you might want to leave them in their current home, especially if your hard disk is low on space. If this is the case, turn off the Copy Fonts to Windows Folder check box. The fonts will still be installed, but they'll be listed in the Fonts folder with shortcut icons rather than normal font file icons.

You should *not* turn off this box if the files are being installed from a CD-ROM, a floppy, or from another computer on the network (unless the network drive is always going to be available). You'll want the fonts on your own hard disk so they'll always be available.

6. Click on OK. The font(s) will be added to your font list, available for your Windows applications.

If you try to install a font that's already in your system, the installer won't let you, so don't worry about accidentally loading one you already have.

TrueType Options

As mentioned above, TrueType fonts take up a fair amount of disk space. They can also be slower to print than fonts that are built into your printer. For example, PostScript printers often have 35 or so built-in fonts that are very similar to popular TrueType fonts like Courier, Times New Roman, and Arial. If you use the basic cast of TrueType fonts a lot, you may be able to speed your print jobs by telling Windows 95 to use a font-substitution table that uses the printer's built-in fonts rather than downloading TrueType fonts to the printer each time you print something. The substitution table will, for example, use the internal Helvetica font in place of the TrueType font Arial. Line breaks and page appearance should print as you see them on the screen, though minute details of the font may differ a bit. Some other kinds of printers, such as HP LaserJet's for example, have TrueType options too.

For examples of typical dialog boxes with options that affect TrueType printing, study Figure 9.9. It shows the TrueType options for a PostScript printer (such as an Apple Laserwriter) and for an HP LaserJet IV.

FIGURE 9.9

Options for TrueType printing are available for some printers. Setting these correctly can speed up printing. As a rule, these settings have already been optimized when you install Windows 98.

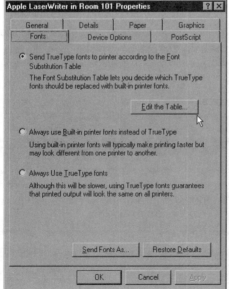
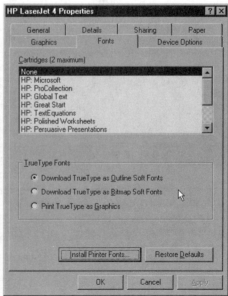

These dialog boxes are reached via the Printers folder. Open the folder, right-click on a printer, choose Properties, and then choose the Fonts tab.

NOTE

Font options will vary from printer to printer, depending on the printer driver. Some printers won't even have a font tab page.

TIP

Normally you will do just fine by not even adjusting the settings in these boxes. If you are curious, you can click on the buttons such as the Edit Substitution Table button or Send Fonts As button. You'll see a lot of options, many of which may be confusing at first. You can always click on the ? button on the title bar of the dialog box, then on the item in question to learn about the options. Some interesting bits of information about the options will pop up, including advice about how best to set them.

One last point about TrueType font options: in Windows 3.*x*, the Fonts applet in the Control Panel gave you two systemwide options controlling TrueType fonts. You could disable TrueType fonts to economize on RAM usage, and you could elect to show only TrueType fonts in your applications, eliminating confusion on the font menus by hiding vector and bit-mapped fonts. Both of these options were dropped in Windows 95, mostly because of improvements in Windows 95's memory management and the standardization of TrueType fonts industrywide. Windows 95 and 98 just don't bog down as much when TrueType fonts are enabled, and because the majority of Windows machines these days are using TrueType fonts, disabling other fonts isn't as advantageous as it once was.

Displaying and Printing Examples of Fonts with the Font Viewer

Once you have a large selection of fonts, it can be difficult to remember what each looks like. Windows 98's built-in font viewer provides an easy way to refresh your memory.

1. Open the Fonts folder.

2. Double-click on any icon in the folder. The font will open in the font viewer. In Figure 9.10 I've displayed a font called Desdemona and maximized the window.

FIGURE 9.10

The font viewer kicks ion when you double-click on any font in the fonts folder. The small numbers in the left margin indicate what point size is displayed to the right. Information about the font's maker appears in the upper portion of the window.

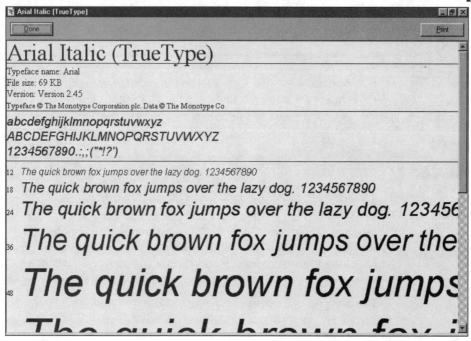

Arial Italic (TrueType)

Arial Italic (TrueType)

Typeface name: Arial
File size: 69 KB
Version: Version 2.45
Typeface © The Monotype Corporation plc. Data © The Monotype Co

abcdefghijklmnopqrstuvwxyz
ABCDEFGHIJKLMNOPQRSTUVWXYZ
1234567890.:,;("*!?')

12 The quick brown fox jumps over the lazy dog. 1234567890
18 The quick brown fox jumps over the lazy dog. 1234567890
24 The quick brown fox jumps over the lazy dog. 123456
36 The quick brown fox jumps over the
48 The quick brown fox jumps

3. You can open additional fonts in the same manner and arrange the windows to compare fonts to one another.

4. Sometimes it's useful to have a printout of a font. You can compile a hard-copy catalog of all your fonts for easy reference if you work with a healthy stable of fonts regularly. To print a single font, double-click on it and click on Print (or right-click on it and choose Print).

To print all your fonts (or multiple fonts) in one fell swoop, select them in the Fonts window with Edit ➤ Select All. Then choose File ➤ Print (or right-click on one of the selected icons and choose Print). You'll get a one-page printout for each font.

Actually, the font viewer will work from any directory. So, if you have a floppy with some fonts you're thinking of installing but you want to see each font first, just open the floppy disk folder and double-click on the fonts one at a time.

TIP

Like other objects in Windows 98, fonts have properties. Right-click on a font's icon and choose Properties to view details about the font's size, creation date, location, type, DOS attribute settings, and so forth. Chapter 11 discusses object properties in detail.

Viewing Font Families

Each variation on a typeface is stored in a separate file. That means a separate font file is required for normal, bold, italic, and bold italic versions of each font.

When you're viewing the contents of the Fonts folder, it can be helpful to see only one icon per font family instead of four. This way, you can see more clearly and quickly just which fonts you have. To do this, open the View menu and choose Hide Variations:

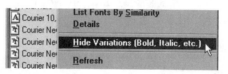

Try it with your fonts and notice how it clears up the display. Unless all four files required for a complete font family are installed, a name won't appear in the listing now. So, if you've installed only Garamond Bold but not Garamond, Garamond Italic, and Garamond Bold Italic, you won't see Garamond listed at all. You will still see an icon for the one type you installed, but such icons won't be named. Double-clicking on an unnamed icon will still display the font in the font viewer so you can identify it.

To return the view to showing all font files listed separately, choose the command again to toggle the check mark off in the menu.

Viewing Fonts by Similarities

Many TrueType fonts contain within them something called *Panose* information. Panose information helps Windows 98 classify a font by indicating a font's general characteristics, such as whether it is a serif or sans-serif font. Based on this information, Windows can group together fonts that will appear somewhat similar on screen and when printed. It can be a boon to have Windows list the fonts that are similar in look to, say, Arial, in case you're looking for an interesting sans-serif font that everyone hasn't seen already.

PART

II

Exploring Windows 98

NOTE

Some older TrueType fonts, as well as all bit-mapped and vector fonts, won't have Panose information stored in them. This is also true of symbol fonts, such as WingDings and Symbol. The font folder will simply display *No Panose information available* next to the font in this case.

To list fonts according to similarity:

1. Open the Fonts folder, one way or another. You can do this most easily from the Control Panel, as described earlier, or from Explorer.

2. Choose View ➢ List Fonts by Similarity. If the folder's toolbar is turned on, you'll have a button that will render the same effect.

3. The folder window will change to include column headings and a drop-down list. The list box is for choosing which font will be the model to which you want all the others compared. Open this list box and choose the desired font. The font must be one endowed with Panose information, otherwise Windows 95 will have nothing with which to compare other fonts. The results will look like Figure 9.11.

FIGURE 9.11

Font listing by similarity. Notice three categories of similarity: Very similar, Fairly similar, and Not similar.

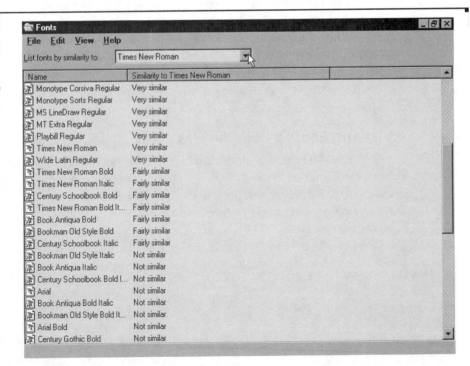

4. You may want to turn off the Hide Variations setting on the View menu to eliminate unnamed icons in the window.

Removing Fonts

Fonts consume space on your hard disk. A typical TrueType font consumes between 50 and 100K (one thousand bytes) of disk space. Deleting individual fonts or font sets increases the available memory in your computer, letting you run more programs and open more documents simultaneously. If you are having memory-limitation problems, you could gain some room by eliminating fonts you never use. If you never use the Italics versions of some fonts, for example, you might want to remove the Italic and Bold Italic versions specifically, leaving the normal version installed. A little-known fact is that even if an italic or bold font has been removed, Windows 98 can still emulate it on the fly. It won't look as good as the real thing, but it will work.

To remove a font, follow these steps:

1. Open the Fonts folder. All the installed fonts are displayed.

2. To remove an entire font family (normal, Bold, Italic, and Bold Italic), turn on the View ➤ Hide Variations setting. If you want to remove individual styles, turn this setting off so you can see them.

3. Select the font or fonts you want to remove.

4. Choose File ➤ Delete or right-click on one of the selected fonts and choose Delete.

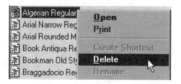

Don't remove the MS Sans Serif font set; it's used in all the Windows dialog boxes.

5. A dialog box asks you to confirm the removal. Choose the Yes button. The font is moved to the Recycle Bin.

PART

II

Exploring Windows 98

CAUTION

You shouldn't remove or install fonts just by dragging them from and to the Fonts folder. Using the Install command from the File menu ensures that the fonts will be registered properly in the Windows Registry and the internal list of fonts that applications draw on for displays in their menus and dialog boxes. Always use the Install New Font command to add fonts and the Delete command to remove them.

Some Basic Guidelines for Using Fonts

Whether you rely on the fonts supplied with Windows or put together a sizable font collection, you should follow a few simple guidelines when formatting your documents. Attractive fonts by themselves aren't enough—the chief goal is readability:

- Allow plenty of space between lines. The space between two lines of text should be about 20 percent greater than the size of the font. Thus, if you're using a 12-point font, you should set the line spacing or *leading* to 14 points. This guideline doesn't hold true for headlines, in which the line spacing should usually be about the same as the font size.

- Don't mix too many fonts in one document. It's often best to stick with one font for the main body of your text and a larger, bold version of the same font for headlines. If you want to mix fonts, use a serif font for the body of your text and a sans serif for the headlines, or vice versa. You can get away with using a third font for sidebar text, but you'll run the risk of clashing font designs.

- If you use two or more font sizes, be sure they contrast adequately. If your main text is in 12-point Times New Roman, use at least 14-point type for the subheadings.

- Use italics or boldface type to indicate emphasis. Avoid underlining and capitalizing letters, both of which make it harder to read your text.

- Make your margins generous. One of the most common mistakes that causes an amateurish-looking document is text that crowds too closely to the edge of the paper. Allow plenty of space between columns as well.

- Following these few guidelines will help you avoid the most glaring errors of document layout. For more detailed advice, consult your bookstore or library for treatises on the topic of desktop publishing or graphic and printing design.

Deleting Font Files from Your Hard Disk

While a variety of high-quality fonts can definitely lend a professionally typeset look to your printed documents and make it easier to understand the information on your screen, a big font collection isn't necessary to run Windows. In fact, you don't even need all the fonts that come with Windows.

In Windows 3.*x* there were three critical system fonts you had to have on your hard disk; Windows simply wouldn't work if you deleted certain important fonts used in dialog boxes, menus, and DOS boxes. In Windows 95 and 98, because you can use TrueType fonts for just about every aspect of a window, including DOS boxes, you can bag any fonts you're not using. Remember, however, that I don't just mean fonts you're not using in your documents; your Windows screen display (set or checked via the Control Panel's Display applet) uses fonts as well. But if disk space is at a premium and the appearance of your text isn't critical for the work you do with Windows, you can remove unused fonts from your Windows setup, saving valuable disk space in the process.

Using Control Panel's Fonts applet, you can remove all the fonts you find unnecessary from your Windows installation and delete their files on disk at the same time. However, I recommend you keep at least the fonts that have the *A* icon (bit-mapped fonts)—such as all the ones that start with *MS*, as in MS-Sans Serif—in the dialog box because various error dialog boxes and some programs will use these from time to time. If they are missing, Windows will substitute a system font that you may find harder to read.

After removing all the fonts from the Control Panel list, you can then check your disk for any remaining `.fon` or `.ttf` files. They may be scattered around in different directories. You can use Start ➤ Find to assist you in the search.

Font Utility Programs

If you are a font nut, you might like to know about a few classes of font programs that can assist you in managing and expanding your type library. This section describes some of them.

Managing Large Numbers of Fonts

Font aficionados and typography professionals typically have no trouble acquiring a bevy of typestyles that range from the sublime to the absurd. The upside of this method is that you'll always have just the right typestyle available when you need it.

But managing hundreds of fonts can be tedious, and Windows' performance can be negatively impacted if you have a large number of fonts installed in the system and active at one time. Windows start-up time can become sluggish, and some applications may also be bogged down by too many installed fonts. Aside from performance issues, scrolling through a gargantuan font list in your word-processing program just to find a common font such as Times New Roman is a nuisance. If you have a healthy font collection (more than 50 fonts), you'll want to lay your hands on a good font-organizer program. There are a number of programs on the market.

TECH TIP

Some Windows 3.*x* font-utility programs expect to find fonts in the \Windows\System directory. Windows 95 and 98 now places fonts in the\Windows\Fonts directory, which could throw a wrench into some font-manager programs. You should contact the manufacturer of a font-utility program about its compatibility with Windows 95 or 98 before purchasing or using it.

At the time of this writing one of the best font managers is Ares Software's Font-Minder. Unfortunately, Adobe has recently purchased it and is putting it out to pasture. (Too bad, since it was quite useful, letting you group fonts together into "packs" for separate projects.) You may want to check into Adobe's Type Manager Deluxe, which, though similar, is not quite as useful in my opinion.

NOTE

Many fonts are copyrighted and not in the public domain. It is illegal to copy and use these fonts without buying them or buying site licenses for them.

The other primary font-management program of note is called FontHandler, from Qualitype. This program also lets you set up packs (groups) of predefined fonts and subgroups of fonts, much like the Explorer has folders and subfolders. It provides an elegant means for viewing, printing, searching for, installing and uninstalling, and viewing details about each of your fonts. Four different sample page styles can be printed. Figure 9.12 shows one of the installed fonts being displayed.

Up to nine fonts can be displayed at once, which is a nice feature, allowing quick comparison. ATM, Printer, and TrueType fonts are supported.

Beyond this, FontHandler offers something not found elsewhere. Unless a document has embedded TrueType fonts, a problem arises when you try to open a document that includes a font not currently installed in your system. Windows will do its best to locate

FIGURE 9.12

FontHandler lets you quickly scroll through and display fonts.

a font that will suffice as a replacement, but it rarely looks very good. If the font called for in the document is actually on your computer, but not installed, a utility in Font-Handler called *Font Sentry* can save the day. It sits in the background, quietly watching and waiting for any program or document to request a font that is not currently available. When a request for a missing font is detected, Font Sentry goes out and *AutoInstalls* the needed font on the fly, with the application or document never missing a beat or being aware of anything having been wrong.

Once a font is installed in this way, it will appear as available in all Windows programs. Such AutoInstalled fonts can be declared *temporary* or *permanent*, defined by the user, so that AutoInstalled fonts are either automatically forgotten when Windows is restarted or fully installed as if you'd done it from the Control Panel's Fonts applet or Explorer.

QualiType also offers two other font utilities. One is a keyboard remapping program, for rearranging which letters and characters are triggered when you press the keys on your keyboard. The other is for moving fonts between drives and folders. QualiType Software can be found on the Web at www.qualitype.com. Their phone number is (313) 822-2921.

Chapter

10

Windows
Multimedia

FEATURING

What is multimedia?

New multimedia developments in Windows 98

Upgrading to multimedia

Using DVD Player

Assigning system sounds

Using Media Player

Using Sound Recorder

Using CD Player

Using TV Viewer

Windows Multimedia

Windows 98 is more *multimedia-ready* than any previous version of Windows. Gone are the days when upgrading your PC for multimedia meant days of intense hardware analysis. And because Windows 98 has built-in, high-performance, 32-bit support for digital video, digital audio, MIDI, game controllers, and even TV, developers and users no longer need to worry about installing special drivers and programs to squeeze maximum multimedia out of their Windows machines.

PC-based multimedia has grown dramatically in the last several years. Not only do practically all mainstream software packages (including Windows 98 itself) now come to us on CD-ROMs, many of them also have on-line multimedia tutorials to teach basic skills. These often include music, video or animation, as well as voice coaching. We've come a long way from the old days when a program consisted of a single floppy disk and a big, boring manual, thanks to the cooperative efforts of many hardware and software engineers. And this is just the tip of the multimedia iceberg. Internet-based multimedia games, music education programs, video telephone conferencing, 360-degree panoramic-view Web sites, streaming audio and video Web sites are some of the nifty features that are becoming common.

Improvements in Plug-and-Play (PnP) technology have decreased the hassle of upgrading your system to add stuff like CD-ROMs, audio cards, microphones, and speakers. You're almost guaranteed nowadays that any new PnP multimedia device you add will install itself with little or no hassle. You're also more likely to meet with success when plugging in some older piece of gear, due to improved detection of "legacy" (a.k.a. old) hardware by Windows 98.

With few exceptions, today's PCs are multimedia PCs, complying with standards that were primarily developed by Microsoft and a few other industry giants. The "multimedia PC standard" proposed a few years back has been widely adopted by PC makers partly by design and partly as the result of mass popularity of specific pieces of hardware. (For example, most PC sound systems are "SoundBlaster" compatible. Manufactured by Creative Labs, Inc., SoundBlaster was one of the first add-in sound cards. Even without being endorsed by other hardware and software companies, it has become a de facto industry standard thanks to the sheer number of installed units in the field.) Windows 98 has helped solidify the standards for multimedia by adding multimedia APIs to Windows. By writing their code around the APIs, software developers only have to write one version of a program regardless of the hundreds of possible combinations of video, audio, MIDI, or other multimedia hardware that may be included in users' computer systems. Windows and the installed device drivers take care of the rest.

A multimedia PC equipped with Windows 98 can:

- Display cable and broadcast television in a resizable window or full-screen with better-than-TV quality, and even capture the closed-captioning text of a show to a text file for later perusal.
- Play DVD movies, complete with display of embedded textual or other material that the producer may add.
- Record, edit, and play sounds in a variety of formats from highly compressed monaural voice grade to CD-quality stereo.
- Play MIDI sequences on your synthesizer or other MIDI device.
- Play fancy CD-ROM titles such as interactive encyclopedias that talk or adventure games such as Myst.
- Display streaming video and audio from Web broadcasts such as live concerts or news shows.
- Display live video and audio teleconferencing over the Internet using NetMeeting or other compatible programs.
- Respond to voice commands (with the right third-party hardware).

All such capabilities and the hardware and software that make them work fall into the category of *Windows multimedia*. This chapter will answer your questions about Windows 98's multimedia abilities and how you can best take advantage of them. Please keep in mind while reading this chapter that talking about Windows multimedia is like shooting at a moving target. Changes are taking place so rapidly in the field that book publishers would need unrealistically brisk turnaround times (akin to that of magazines) to accurately reflect the state of the industry. Therefore, to spare you the annoyance of reading out-of-date material, I'll focus this chapter on the multimedia features of Windows 98 itself and deal only fleetingly with issues of secondary, after-market products.

Exactly What Is Multimedia?

Multimedia—alias *interactive media* or *hypermedia*—is difficult to define, which accounts for much general confusion on the topic. The practical definition changes each time I write a book about Windows, and that's about every year or so. Actually, multimedia simply means two or more simultaneous types of display. Regular old TV is a good example—it's a multimedia device since it integrates audio and video. But computers are capable of more advanced levels of multimedia amalgamating animation, graphics, video, MIDI, digitally recorded sounds, and text—and can also interact with people while they view the presentation.

It's interesting to chronicle the breakneck rate of multimedia advancements. Just two years ago, updating a system to multimedia meant adding a CD-ROM drive. This year, any decent PC (even most laptops) have them built in, along with speakers, and even accelerated video display cards capable of 30 frame-per-second high-speed animation, and texture mapping.

Some multimedia programs are *interactive* and some are not. Interactivity means that through some input device such as keyboard, mouse, voice, or external controller—for example a Musical Instrument Digital Interface (MIDI) keyboard—you interact with the system to control aspects of the presentation. Most of today's software is still primarily based on text display, though it's increasingly permeated with graphics, charts, and clip art. With the added capabilities of stereo sound, animation, and video, multimedia computing offers a much richer and more efficient means of conveying information.

As an example of a simple interactive program, consider the Windows tour, which demonstrates Windows fundamentals for the newcomer. (You launch it by choosing Start ➤ Programs ➤ Accessories ➤ System Tools ➤ Welcome to Windows. Then click on Discover Windows 98.) The tutorial demonstrates rudimentary multimedia, integrating animation, text, and voice. It does not incorporate live-action video clips. Now imagine expanding such a tutorial to include music, realistic 3-D animation, and moving video images just as if you were watching TV. As you probably know by now, animators, musicians, designers, writers, programmers, audio engineers, industry experts, and video producers have joined forces to create multimedia applications such as:

- A WordPerfect document that lets you paste in video clips (with audio) from a VCR tape you've made; instead of displaying just a still graphic, the document will be "alive" with sight and sound.

- A music-education program on a CD-ROM from Microsoft that plays Beethoven's Ninth Symphony while displaying informative and educational text about each passage and about the composer.

- A dictionary, thesaurus, book of quotations, and encyclopedia on a CD-ROM from Microsoft that not only contains a huge amount of textual information but actually pronounces the dictionary entries; reads quotations aloud in the voices of Robert Frost, Carl Sandburg, T.S. Eliot, e.e. cummings, Dylan Thomas, and John F. Kennedy; and illustrates scientific phenomena with animation.

- Programs that teach you how to play the piano using a MIDI keyboard connected to your PC. The computer senses whether you play the lesson correctly and responds accordingly with a recorded high-quality voice. Similar programs teach music theory.

- Interactive company annual reports, product demonstrations, presentations, or corporate training manuals for new employees.

- *Moving catalogs* from mail-order houses, displaying everything from cars to coats via high-quality video and audio.

- An interactive geography test used at the National Geographic Society Explorer's Hall in Washington, D.C.

- Interactive high-speed, random-access books, newspapers, or catalogs for the blind, using high-quality voice synthesis or recorded voices.

- Interactive training for hard-to-teach professions such as medical diagnosis, surgery, auto mechanics, and machine operation of various types.

- Complex interactive games and children's learning programs that incorporate stereo sound effects, flashy visuals, and the ability to move through synthetic virtual worlds.

In fact, most of these multimedia products already exist. The explosion of multimedia CD titles has been enormous in the last two years.

What's New in Windows 98 Multimedia

Windows 98 adds a number of new features as well as enhancing some of the better features of Windows 95 multimedia:

- Built-in support for compressed video allows playback of video files (such as AVI and QuickTime) without installation of additional licensed drivers.

- AutoPlay support lets users simply insert a CD and it will begin to run, eliminating the need to enter the correct command or find and click on the correct program icon in the CD's file directory.

- 2-D and 3-D graphics support is now provided through improved DirectX 5, a set of tools that help developers take advantage of new capabilities of Windows 98 such as multiple monitors, Intel Pentium MMX extensions, use of the USB (Universal Serial Bus) interface for gaming device input, faster texture mapping, and anti-aliasing.

- DirectShow, a streaming media player technology, allows Windows 98 to efficiently play back a variety of multimedia file types: AVI video, MPEG compressed video, Apple QuickTime video, and WAV audio. MPEG-compressed video can be played back on PCs that have no decompression hardware; Windows 98 can achieve decompression quickly enough.

- NetShow, a streaming media player, plays unicast and multicast streaming audio and video that comes over the Web. It's compatible with existing RealAudio and RealVideo formats as well as with Microsoft's own NetShow format.

- A DVD (Digital Video Disk) player program is included. If you have a (hardware) DVD player attached to your system, you can play DVD, CD-sized disks that contain huge amounts of data, such as audio, several hours of video, and optional text.

- Surround Video allows software developers an easy way to create programs that let users interact with objects, images, patterns, and live action video in a 360-degree view in a synthetic environment.

- CD-ROM support: Windows 98 includes 32-bit drivers for support of faster CD-ROM drives, while still supporting older drives and 16-bit Windows 3.x drivers (MSCDEX). Also supported is the new CD-PLUS specification developed by Sony and Phillips, which puts text (including biographies and music program notes), video, and other enhancements on the same CD with the usual audio material. These new CD titles can be played on a Windows 98 machine.

- Windows 98 "broadcast-enables" your computer. You can receive Web pages that contain video and audio content as well as view television programming from cable, over-the-air, and satellite networks.

- Smoother 32-bit multitasking and better codec (compression/decompression) software make it possible to display even full-screen video simultaneous with MIDI or audio playback—something not possible only a few years ago. Even modest-priced laptops have fast enough electronics to support this.

For more information about streaming video and audio broadcasts over the net , visit `http://www.microsoft.com/hwdev/ver4/desinit/bcast1.htm`. For more information on broadcasts of Internet-standard information over regular television signals, visit `http://info.internet.isi.edu/in-drafts/files/draft-panabaker-ip-vbi-02.txt`.

Upgrading to Multimedia

With Windows 3.*x*, working with multimedia required purchasing Microsoft's Multimedia upgrade kit or buying an expensive and hard-to-find MPC (multimedia PC). MPCs were manufactured by only a few vendors and were not generally available on the clone market. Whether upgrading an existing computer or buying an MPC, the results were about the same: you got the Microsoft multimedia extensions (drivers), a CD-ROM drive, audio card, and a good VGA video card. Either solution was pricey, often amounting to thousands of dollars, and in the end you didn't have much to write home about.

Beginning in Windows 95, Microsoft started to bundle multimedia drivers with their operating systems and include related utility programs (such as Sound Recorder) in the hope that this would accelerate the development of multimedia Windows applications. Setting up the MPC specification helped set some standards for what a multimedia PC should look and act like, and the PC add-on market did the rest. A vast profusion of multimedia hardware, applications, and utilities have subsequently become prevalent, many of which are now incorporated into Windows 98.

The magazines now inundate us with ads for newer and faster CD-ROM drives, 128-bit coprocessed video cards, high-resolution energy-efficient monitors, and fancy sound cards—some even have samples of real orchestral instruments built in. The MPC moniker has fallen by the wayside, and now what's really more important is whether a system is fully Windows 9*x*-compatible or not. After that, the rest is icing on the cake: How big is the screen, how good do the speakers sound, how clear is the image, and overall, how fast does the *whole system* (not just the CPU chip) perform?

You'll have to rely on the magazines for these kinds of test comparisons. Don't rely on the guys in the store. One brand of 166-MHz Pentium machine might actually be faster than another one that's got a 233-MHz Pentium under the hood, because of the vagaries of hard-disk controllers, type of internal bus, memory caching, or speed of the video card.

If you already own a multimedia-ready machine with a couple of speakers and a CD-ROM drive, you might as well skip this section and move down to the next major section in this chapter, "Supplied Multimedia Applications and Utilities." But if you don't have such a machine, and you're thinking about endowing your machine with the gift of gab, some fancy video graphics capabilities, and the ability to watch TV or play DVDs, stay on track here.

There are three basic ways to upgrade your computer: buy a whole new computer, buy an "upgrade-in-a-box," or mix and match new components that exactly fit your needs. As of this writing, there were about twenty upgrade-in-a-box products to choose from. You'll typically get a CD-ROM drive, speakers, a sound card, a microphone, and maybe some CDs in the package. The sound card has the SCSI (Small Computer Systems Interface, pronounced "scuzzy") connector that hooks the CD-ROM drive to the computer. Mixing and matching is for us total control-freak geeks who must have the best or who don't like the idea of other people controlling our purchase decisions. The obvious downside is that sorting through the sea of components in the marketplace is a big waste of time. I've spent too many hours testing video boards, trying to get a SCSI upgrade to my sound card to work with my CD-ROM drive, or running around listening to speakers. In any case, here are a few points about the pros and cons of the three upgrade routes.

NOTE

You might want to check out Chapter 2 for more about choosing and adding hardware to your system, because some of those topics apply to multimedia.

In your shopping, you may wonder what the minimal requirements of a multimedia system should be. With the technology changing so quickly, it's hard to predict what the pickings will look like a year from now and what the latest and greatest version of Riven (or some other multimedia game you'll want as your major distraction from work) will crave in the way of MM nuts and bolts. Still, here's Bob's rule of thumb about buying new computer stuff:

> The best balance between price and performance lies just in the wake of the technology wave.

That is, if price is an issue, eschew the cutting edge! State-of-the-art gear is too expensive and usually still has some bugs to be worked out or ends up becoming an "industry standard" with a half–life of about 9 months before being dropped like a hot potato. When a product hits the mainstream, that's the time to buy; prices usually take a nosedive at that point, often about 50 percent.

TABLE 10.1: APPROACHES TO MULTIMEDIA UPGRADING			
Question	New Computer	Kit in a Box	Mix and Match Components
What is it?	A whole computer system that is designed for multimedia Windows 98 from the ground up and includes a fairly zippy computer, color screen, speakers, microphone, sound card, fast video display card capable of TV tuning and video capture, built-in Zip drive, and a CD-ROM drive. Options will be CD writers and DVD players.	A box of stuff you get at a computer store or by mail order. Everything works together and costs less than $200. Includes a sound card, CD-ROM drive, microphone, and speakers. (For more money you can get a DVD drive instead of a CD-ROM drive. Most DVD drives can play normal CDs as well as DVD disks.)	CD-ROM drive, optional DVD drive, sound board, speakers, microphone, cabling, and possibly necessary software drivers. Purchase parts separately. $300-$500. Add an additional $300 minimum for a CD writer.
Who should buy?	Owner of an older computer who has already decided to purchase a new computer either because existing computer isn't worth upgrading to a faster CPU and larger hard disk, or because an additional computer is needed.	Average owner of non-multimedia computer that's acceptably endowed in terms of the CPU and hard-disk (e.g., a Pentium and 1GB hard disk or larger) but needs multimedia capability to run multimedia games and standard productivity applications.	Power user who wants the best selection of components—or who already has one or two essential components, such as a CD-ROM drive, and now wants the rest. May be a professional (such as a musician, application developer, or graphic artist) who needs one element of the multimedia upgrade to be of very high quality.

Continued ▶

TABLE 10.1: APPROACHES TO MULTIMEDIA UPGRADING (CONTINUED)			
Question	**New Computer**	**Kit in a Box**	**Mix and Match Components**
How much hassle?	No hassle. Everything is installed and working. Get the system with Windows 98 installed and working if you can, and you're really set.	You'll have to remove the cover to the computer, remove some screws, insert a couple of cards, hook up some cables and the CD-ROM drive (if the drive is the internal type), and then hook up the speakers. If the cards and computer are not Plug-and-Play compatible, you'll have to make IRQ and DMA settings. This may take some homework. You might have conflicts with existing hardware; if so you should have Windows 98 detect and install drivers for the new hardware, or use supplied drivers.	About the same amount of hassle as a box upgrade, but you'll have to deal with separate documentation for each component and figure out how to get everything working together, unless they are Plug-and-Play components. IRQ and DMA conflicts are likely otherwise.
Advantages?	Low hassle factor. You can start getting work done instead of poring over magazines and manuals. Your church (or kid) gets your old computer (which means you get an easy tax write-off), and you get more sleep, and have only one vendor to deal with at service time.	You don't have to sell your existing computer. You might even get some free CD-ROM software in the box.	You can have exactly what you want. 24-bit TrueColor graphics, direct video capturing, video conferencing, great sound, superfast display at 1,600 by 1,280—you name it.

Continued

PART

II

Exploring Windows 98

TABLE 10.1: APPROACHES TO MULTIMEDIA UPGRADING (CONTINUED)			
Question	New Computer	Kit in a Box	Mix and Match Components
Disadvantages?	You have to buy a whole new system. You'll probably be compromising somewhat on the components for the low hassle factor.	It will take some work to install it, unless it comes from the same people who made your computer (e.g., a Dell upgrade to a Dell computer). Again, some compromise on the components is likely. You may not have the best-sounding speakers, fastest video, greatest color depth, or CD-ROM drive.	Price and installation hassle can be high, but PnP is making things much easier. Multiple dealers to reckon with at service time.
Price?	Less than $2000 for most systems, which is not much more for a multimedia system than for those without multimedia. A few hundred additional dollars is typical. Tricked-out systems with all options and lots of memory and large hard disk will be between $3000 and $4000.	Typically between $150 and $300 for fast CD-ROM drive, 16-bit sound card, speakers, and a few extras.	Difficult to predict. Bottom-of-the-line but functional clone parts could run you as little as a few hundred dollars. Or you could pay well into the thousands for the best brands.

What does that mean in the current market? Well the now old and crusty MPC specification requires at least a machine with 4 MB of RAM, a 130-MB hard disk, and a fast processor such as a 486 or Pentium. But that's now a joke. You'll be hard pressed to find a PC with that little RAM these days. On the next few pages are my suggestions to keep in mind when you're shopping for multimedia components and systems.

Computer   I'd suggest at *least* a 486DX2/50 CPU, a local bus video card, and a 500-MB hard disk (EIDE or SCSI), with 16 MB (preferably 32 MB) of RAM. A SCSI hardware interface is even better because you can also hook up as many as seven devices to most SCSI controllers, not just hard disks, and they run faster. But the bulk of machines these days have EIDE hard disks, and they are fast enough for most purposes short of doing real-time video capture. Remember, this is a minimum configuration.

Of course, if you're buying a new computer, you're probably going to get at least a Pentium 133 with a 1.6GB hard disk. For any serious work (or play) I'd recommend that kind of speed or faster.

CD-ROM Drive   Get at least an 8x speed drive. (The x means how many times faster the data can be read from the disk relative to the first CD drives, which are considered 1x.) As of this writing, affordable 24x drives are common. Windows 98 caches your CD-ROM drive data, so that it will help slower drives keep up with the data-hungry demands of applications that display video, for example.

If you want to be able to connect to a laptop or move the drive between computers, get a lightweight portable external job, maybe even a Zip or Jaz drive. You'll pay a little more for it, but prices are plummeting anyway, so the difference won't be that much. Make sure the drive supports multisession Kodak photo format. This lets you not only view photographs in CD-ROM format on your computer but also take an existing photo CD-ROM to your photo developer and have them add new pictures to it. You might want up-front manual controls on the player so you can listen to audio CDs without running the CD Player program that comes with Windows.

PART

II

Exploring Windows 98

Photos and Windows 98

If you're among the gadget happy, you'll probably be procuring yourself a digital camera soon, or at least want your photos on disk or in your computer somehow. That way, you can futz with your pictures using nifty software such as Adobe PhotoShop, Goo Power Tools, or other programs that let you make art out of common photographs. Or, so you can email pictures of Horny, your pet iguana, to your friends back home.

If you already have a CD-ROM drive in your computer, the easiest way to get your pix into the computer is to take your next roll of film down to the photo finisher's and request your snaps back on disk as well as on paper. Though some will give them to you on floppies, most services will provide the shots on CD. The standard format is the Kodak CD format.

Continued

CONTINUED

Once you get the CD, check it for the info that tells you how to view the pictures. If all else fails, you may be able to simply click on the picture files using Windows Explorer, but better to use some software front-end to do it. The pictures usually show up as JPG or GIF files, and there may be numerous resolutions for each picture (thus, a set of files for each picture).

Digital cameras always come with Windows software that you can load up, and instructions for getting your pictures from the camera into your computer. I like using the cameras that have a pop-out memory card that I can plug into the PC card slot on my laptop. Then I don't have to hassle with wires (and thus the relatively slow download speed of the pictures over a wire). Two of the cameras I've tested (Panasonic Cool Shot and Kodak DC 210) used these cards, and they were interchangeable. I just took some pictures and then popped the card out of the camera and then into the computer. Windows 98 recognizes the card automatically and treats it like a disk drive, which makes it easy to display the contents in Windows Explorer or in a Browse box from a photo display program or other imaging program.

NOTE

There are two flavors of Photo CD you should know about: *single-session* and *multi-session*. With a multi-session Photo CD, you can just bring in your existing CD to your photo finisher's shop and ask them to add your new pictures to the same disk. Single-session doesn't let you do that; it's a write-once format.

CD Writer   Among the latest goodies in the CD-ROM drive market are the now-affordable writers that will "burn" (record) a custom CD for you. These used to cost thousands of bucks, and were affordable by only recording and software magnates could afford them. Now, creating your own music CDs (I create CD compilations of my fave dance tunes for parties), or backing up tons of data on CDs is something anyone can do, if they have a CD-R (CD Recording) drive. The blank disks cost only a few dollars, and you can put 650 MB on one. But the drives that record them are about three times the price of standard CD-ROM reader. I bought a CD-R kit recently (called the "Smart and Friendly" kit) for just a few hundred dollars at Costco/Price Club. Such a deal. It installed with only a little hassle, and the bundled Adaptec Easy CD Pro software was simple to use. Check the magazines and get a kit that has everything you might need, right in the box. You might be buying more than you need, but you'll be avoiding headaches in the long run. For example, I paid for the extra SCSI card they bundle with the drive (I already have a faster one), just so I knew I had a complete one-stop solution. Also note that CD-R drives tend to be slower at reading CD-ROMs than the fancy 24x drives are. Mine reads at only 6x and writes at a measly 2x. So I have two CD-drives: a regular 24x and the CD-R at 2x/6x. Many CD-Rs require a SCSI interface, but not all do. Many EIDE units are also available. Most of the SCSI units come with a simple SCSI adapter card. It doesn't have to be a fancy fast SCSI card (fast/wide/ultra or any of that), since speed isn't an issue. If you already have a SCSI card, it will likely work with the a CD-R drive.

NOTE

> The CD-R format allows you to record once, and that's all. Once a CD is written, it can't be erased and rewritten. With some formats you can add more data later, until the disk is full, but you can't erase. Another format, CR-RW (rewritable) uses *much* more expensive media to allow you to write and rewrite disks again and again.

PART

II

Exploring Windows 98

DVD   DVD drives are the new hot item on the market. However, DVD is a technology in such an emerging state that manufacturers can't even agree what DVD stands for. (Some say Digital Video Disk while others say Digital Versatile Disk.) Regardless, we're going to see a lot more of them in next few years to come. Many households in the US will have DVD players in their computers and on their TV set tops even before this book goes to print. As of this writing, set-top DVD players run about $500 and support lots of nifty features such as:

- 500 lines of horizontal resolution (more than twice as sharp as standard TV)
- 8 sound tracks (for different languages, instruction, etc)
- 32 sets of subtitles
- Multiple movie viewing formats (standard, letterbox) and angles
- Theater sound
- 2 hours of video per side (up to 4 hours max)
- Dolby digital sound

Adding a DVD drive to your PC lets you view movies and educational titles on the PC, with the superior resolution of your computer's monitor (instead of the pretty funky resolution of a standard TV). In addition, you'll be able to interact with DVD titles designed for computers. Windows 98 supports DVD drives and has a DVD player program (similar to its CD player program) for playing DVD titles.

A few DVD add-in kits are available today for your PC. We'll see more and more PCs with DVD as an option or standard fare very soon. And writable DVDs will appear after that. Currently they are very expensive. But once those appear, editing your own homebrew movies will be a snap.

Speakers   The larger the better, usually. Little speakers will sound tinny, by definition. Listen before you buy if possible. Listen to a normal, speaking human voice—the most difficult instrument to reproduce. Does it sound natural? Then hear something with some bass. If you're going to listen to audio CDs, bring one with you to the store and play it. Speakers that are separate (not built into the monitor) will allow a nicer stereo effect. Separate tweeter and woofer will probably sound better, but not always. It depends on the electronics in the speaker. Magnetic shielding is important if the speakers are going to be within a foot or so of your screen; otherwise, the colors and alignment of the image on the screen will be adversely affected. (Not permanently damaged, though. The effect stops when you move the speakers away.) Of course, instead of buying speakers you can use your stereo or even a boom box if it has high-level (sometimes called *auxiliary*) input. Some boom boxes and virtually all stereos do have such an input. Then it's just a matter of using the correct wire to attach your sound card's *line* output to the stereo's or boom box's Aux input and setting the volume appropriately. The easiest solution is to purchase a pair of amplified speakers designed for small recording studios, apartments, or computers. For about $150 you can find a good pair of smaller-sized shielded speakers (4- or 5-inch woofer, separate tweeter) with volume, bass, and treble controls. For $300 you can get some that sound very good. If you like real bass, shell out a little more for a set that comes with a separate larger subwoofer you put under your desk.

Sound Board   This should have 16-bit, 44.1-KHz sound capability for CD-quality sound. Some newer boards (also called "cards") boast "20-bit sampling." (Above 16-bit, the audible advantages are debatable, in my opinion.) You'll want line-in, line-out, and microphone-in jacks at least. Typical cards also have a joystick port for your game controller. The card should be compatible with Windows 9x, with the General MIDI specification, and with SoundBlaster so it will work with popular games. This means it should have protected-mode 32-bit drivers for Windows 9x, either supplied with Windows 98 or with the card. If it doesn't, you'll be stuck using 16-bit drivers that take up too much conventional memory space, preventing many DOS-based games and educational programs from running. I've seen this problem with cards, such as the Sound-Blaster Pro, that prevent a number of games such as the Eagle-Eye Mystery series from running. Fancy cards such as those from Turtle Beach don't sound like cheesy synthesizers when they play MIDI music because they use samples of real instruments stored in *wave tables* instead of using synthesizer chips, but you'll pay more for them. Wave-table cards are easy to find now. Even Turtle Beach makes one for $49.

Video Card and Monitor   The video card goes inside the computer and produces the signals needed to create a display on the monitor. A cable runs between the video card and the monitor. For high-performance multimedia, you'll want a *local bus* video card (typically VLB or PCI) capable of at least 256 colors at the resolution you desire. VLB has fallen from grace, so if you're looking for a new computer, don't get one with a VLB bus. Go for the current industry standard local bus format called PCI, a standard developed by Intel.

TIP

Local bus cards only work in computers that have a local bus connector slot, so check out which kind of slots your computer has before purchasing a video card upgrade.

Standard resolution (number of dots on the screen at one time, comprising the picture) for a PC is 640 (horizontal) by 480 (vertical). Most new video cards these days will support that resolution at 256 colors. If you have a very sharp 15-inch screen or a 17-inch screen, you may opt for a higher resolution, such as 800 by 600 or 1,024 by 768. When shopping for a video card, make sure it displays at least 256 colors (and preferably in the thousands of colors) at the resolution you want *and has at least a 70-Hz noninterlaced refresh rate at that resolution and color depth.* The correct refresh rate prevents screens from flickering, which can cause headaches and/or eye fatigue. Video cards with graphics coprocessor chips on them will run faster than those that don't. High speed is necessary when you move objects around on the screen or display video clips. Make sure the board will work well with Windows 98, preferably with the 32-bit video driver that comes with Windows 95 or 98, not an old driver designed for Windows 3.*x*. You don't have to worry about any monitor's ability to display colors because any color monitor will display all the colors your card can produce. What you *do* have to check on are a monitor's dot pitch, controls, and refresh rate. The monitor should ideally have a dot pitch of .25 or .26, be at least 17 inches (though 15 inches will do), and run all your desired resolutions at 70-Hz refresh or higher to avoid flicker. Beware of the refresh-rate issue: False or misleading advertising is rampant. Many monitors and video cards advertise 72-Hz or higher refresh rates, but the fine print reveals that this is only at a low resolution such as 640 by 480. Bump up the resolution, and the refresh on cheaper cards or monitors drops to a noticeably slow 60 Hz. Get a monitor that has low radiation emissions, powers down automatically when it isn't being used (a so-called green monitor), and has a wide variety of controls for size, picture position, brightness, contrast, color, and so forth.

PART

II

Exploring Windows 98

TIP

If you expect to view lots of TV or play the latest games, get a video card with 2D and 3D acceleration, video capture, a TV tuner, and video in and out. The ATI All-In Wonder card is currently my card of choice. It works well with Windows 98's TV tuner programs, and has a slew of video resolutions, and works right out of the box with Windows 98. It's about $150, street price.

That's the basic rundown on multimedia upgrading. Now let's look at what's supplied with Windows 98 in the way of multimedia programs and utilities.

The Supplied Multimedia Applications and Utilities

Here's what you get in the way of multimedia programs and utilities with Windows 98:

Sound Settings   This Control Panel applet lets you assign specific sound files (stored in the .wav format) to Windows system events such as error messages, information dialog boxes, and when starting and exiting Windows.

Media Player   This application, which you'll find in the Start ➢ Programs ➢ Accessories ➢ Multimedia folder, lets you play a variety of multimedia files on the target hardware. In the case of a device that contains data, such as a CD-ROM or video disk, Media Player sends commands to the hardware, playing back the sound or video therein. If the data is stored on your hard disk (as are MIDI sequences, animation, and sound files), Media Player will send them to the appropriate piece of hardware, such as a sound board, MIDI keyboard, or other device.

TECH TIP

The Media Player only works with MCI (Media Control Interface) devices and thus requires MCI device drivers.

Sound Recorder   This is a simple program for recording sounds from a microphone or auxiliary input and then editing them. Once recorded, sound files can be used with other programs through OLE or used to replace or augment the generic beeps your computer makes to alert you to dialog boxes, errors, and so forth. Sound Recorder is also the default program used to play back WAV files.

TIP

> You can find more elaborate WAV file editors. For my CD recording projects I use a shareware program called Cool Edit, which you can find and download from the Web. Another capable shareware WAV file program is called WaveWorks.

CD Player   Assuming your computer's CD-ROM drive and controller card support it (most do), this accessory program lets you play back standard audio CDs. This can be a great boon on long winter nights when you're chained to your PC doing taxes or writing that boring report. You'll find coverage of this program in Chapter 22 along with the other Accessory odds and ends.

DVD Player   If the DVD drive you purchase, whether by upgrade or built-in, says it is Windows 98 compatible, then it will have a DVD player program supplied. Whether you choose to use that player or the one supplied with Windows 98 is up to you; they all work similarly. You just have to compare their respective features, as some have more bells and whistles than others. In this chapter I'll cover the player that comes with Windows 98.

Adding Drivers   The System and Add New hardware applets in the Control Panel let you install drivers for many add-in cards and devices such as CD-ROMs, MIDI interface cards, and video-disk controllers if they are not detected automatically once you plug them in. Drivers for most popular sound boards such as the SoundBlaster (from Creative Labs, Inc.) and Ad Lib (Ad Lib, Inc.) and popular MIDI boards such as the Roland MPU-401 (Roland Digital Group) are supplied. Other drivers can be installed from manufacturer-supplied disks using this option. Even if your hardware is physically installed, it won't work unless the proper driver is loaded.

A few programs have either been covered elsewhere in this book or were seen in Windows 3.*x* but have been dropped from Windows 95. They are:

Volume Control   The volume control accessory, available from the Taskbar, simply lets you control the balance and volume levels of the various sound sources that end up playing through your computer's speakers. This is covered in Chapter 22.

MIDI Mapper   This was included as a separate Control Panel applet in Windows 3.1 and NT, but has been hidden in Windows 98 because it is rarely used. Its purpose was to declare settings for your MIDI device, such as channel assignment, key remapping, and patch-number reassignment for nonstandard MIDI instruments. The assumption now is that most MIDI instruments comply with the General MIDI standard for these parameters and thus the Mapper is rarely needed. If you have a nonstandard MIDI instrument that you're running from Windows programs (this won't affect DOS programs), check out Control Panel ➢ Multimedia ➢ MIDI ➢ Custom Configuration ➢ Configure. It will lead you to the rather complex remapping facilities.

Doing It All with DVD Player

As mentioned earlier in the chapter, Windows 98 includes support for DVD (Digital Versatile Disk / Digital Video Disk) drives. DVD and CD-ROM use very much the same technology (micro laser to read the disk), so besides being able to play DVD disks on your computer, you should be able to use a DVD drive to read your current CD-ROM and audio CD disks (this depends, however, on how early you buy; first-generation DVD drives could not read as many CD formats as the current generation). Pricewise, this will be an almost unnoticed transition, at least for new system buyers. A computer equipped with a DVD drive will probably cost only $100 to $200 more than one equipped with a CD-ROM drive instead. (If it weren't for the need for a decoder card to play DVD movies on your computer, the difference would be more like $100.) DVD drives will probably start to be offered as standard equipment in PCs by the end of 1998, as they begin to replace the now common CD-ROM drive.

Some DVD Specifics

I already sang the praises of DVD earlier in the chapter. However, as there is some confusion about different generations of DVDs, I want to make sure we have the basics understood before I discuss the DVD Player program supplied with Windows 98.

DVD is going to be the content-providing medium of choice over the next few years. The research group called IDC, from Framingham, Massachusetts, predicts that 13 percent of all PC software will be available on DVD by the end of this year (1998). Sure, CDs will still be around, but even with the giganto capacity of 650MB on a CD, some programs actually require multiple CDs! (Hard to believe, but true.) In addition, megadatabases such as national phone directories, the catalog of the Library of Congress, the complete Oxford English Dictionary, photo stock house collections, museum and gallery holdings photographed in high resolution, and fonts packages span multiple CD-ROMs. These are all prime candidates for appearing on DVD.

And then, of course, we've got movies—the hands-down winners of the disk-consumption sweepstakes. With a maximum capacity of 17GB (yes, gigabytes), an innocent DVD (which looks almost identical to a CD) can store two hours of video that displays more clearly (and has groovier options) than VHS, LaserDisk, or video CD-ROMs. DVD movies will boast multichannel surround sound, subtitles, multiple alternative audio tracks (for different languages), multiple video playback formats, and even, in some cases, user-selectable camera angles.

How does a DVD pack all that information onto a five-inch disk? Well, first, the optical pits on a DVD disk are stuffed in twice as close to one another as on a CD, and so are the tracks. Also, more of the surface is recorded on. *And* error correction is more rigorous! All this increases the data storage capacity from a CD's 650MB to a DVD's 4.3GB. But wait! That's only for one layer! DVDs can have *two* layers per side. By focusing the read laser carefully, a second layer can be used, adding another 4.3GB, for a one-side total of approximately 8.4GB. But wait! DVDs can have data written on *both sides*, so by flipping the disk over, the 8.4GB is doubled.

Another compelling point about DVD is its versatility. CD-ROM suffers from a plethora of competing and often incompatible formats: multisession, Photo CD, Mode 1, Mode 2, Joliet, CD-I, and CD+, to name but a few. The DVD spec is, well, versatile (as the name implies: Digital Versatile Disk). A new disk file format that was devised for DVD, called Universal Disk Format (UDF), ensures compatibility between disk and player, regardless of content. (Well, almost. As the saying goes, some limitations apply.) A single DVD drive should be able to read most existing CDs, as well as text, data, and video DVD formats. Even CD-R and CD-RW disks should be readable by most second-generation DVD drives.

Shop Carefully!

If you're thinking about buying a DVD, check the specs thoroughly, and ask around before you drop your cash. We're just beginning to see the third round of drives (Spring 1998), so you'll probably want to skip buying a first- or second-generation drive. The differences lie mostly in the formats they can read. Second-generation drives can read CD-R (recordable CDs) and CD-RW (recordable/eraseable CDs), whereas first-generation drives can't. Third-generation drives will probably read a greater variety of recordable and re-recordable formats, including (hopefully) the yet-to-be-standardized "writeable DVD" (DVD-RAM and DVD+RW) formats.

As for speed, don't worry. As long as they can play back a movie, you'll have speed to burn. The latest crop of DVD drives (2× DVD) played CDs at the equivalent speed of a 24× CD-ROM drive.

Installation of DVD can be tricky. I suggest you purchase a complete upgrade kit or purchase a computer with the DVD built in. I upgraded piece by piece. It cost me more, and was a hassle to get working. Read the requirements for an upgrade carefully. Typically you'll need at least a 166MHz Pentium with 16MB of RAM; you'll also need a bus-mastering PCI slot, an empty drive bay for the drive, and an open EIDE connector. (Although some DVDs are SCSI drives, most are EIDE. Besides, most motherboards support four EIDE drives, and you probably don't have four hard disks connected; so why buy a SCSI disk controller if you don't need it?) Most DVD drives don't care whether they are "slave" or "master" drives.

TIP

As a rule, just look for a kit or computer that is Windows 98-compatible, and follow the instructions supplied with the unit.

In addition, until you can buy a video card that is tailored to support DVD video playback, you'll need a *decoder card* to be able to watch DVD movies on your computer. (If you aren't planning to play video DVD disks, neither of these is necessary.) The decoder card plugs into the PCI bus (typically) and connects to your existing video card (via a ribbon cable) to translate the video data into the analog signals needed for display on your monitor. Among other things, such as decoding Dolby Surround-Sound audio, and handling copy-protection schemes, the decoder decompresses the MPEG-1 or MPEG-2 compressed video in real time. This takes some serious computing speed. Some DVD drives come with "software" decoders which they say can be used instead of a decoder card, but don't expect smooth performance from them, even on a fast Pentium 266 machine. The computer's CPU just can't keep up with the data stream very well, and ends up dropping frames to keep up.

Running the DVD Player

Typically the DVD player that comes with the drive will have all the basic controls found on a VCR, plus some number of additional bells and whistles, such as searching tools, audio controls for bass, treble, and volume, a viewing angle selector, child-proofing locks, video format selector, "chapter" and "title" features, and so on. Most of them are used in similar ways; you'll just have to compare the features of each. In this section, I'll provide the basic instructions for running the player that comes with Windows 98.

First, I'll assume that you've got your hardware installed (or someone at the factory did it for you), as discussed earlier. If your drive is in working order, then here are the basics of running the Microsoft DVD player:

1. Insert a DVD disk as you would insert a disk into any other drive, and shut the door. Windows will detect the disk; if the disk is a video disk, the DVD player will start; if it's an audio disk, the CD player will start (as discussed earlier in this chapter).

2. If a disk has been inserted and nothing happens, run the DVD player explicitly by choosing Start ➢ Programs ➢ Accessories ➢ Entertainment ➢ DVD Player. Then click the Options button and choose Select Disk. You'll see this dialog box:

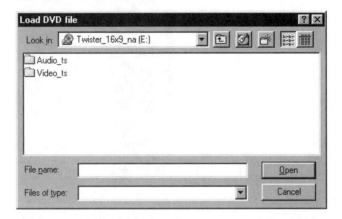

3. If you've set the option that prevents someone from running a movie without authorization (see the Tip following this step), you'll see a logon dialog box:

TIP

You can create a new logon password by choosing the Options button on the player. Typically, you might create a password to prevent children from playing your disks.

4. To start playing a disk, click on ➢ button on the player toolbar. You should experiment with the other various controls by clicking on them as well, just as you might in the CD player application or on a VCR. You can play, stop, pause, fast forward, fast rewind, eject, etc. (There are also buttons here for "very fast forward" and "very fast rewind.") If you're better with words than icons, you

PART

II

Exploring Windows 98

can display a textual list of all of the commands available from the player tool-bar by right-clicking on any one of the controls:

To see a full-screen view of the movie you are watching, click on the little icon of the television set in the toolbar. The toolbar disappears. You can access the tools again by right-clicking anywhere on the screen. That action pops up the following menu:

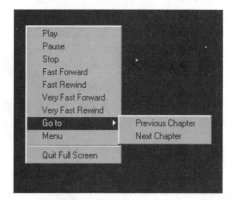

Choose the Quit Full Screen command to see the toolbar again, or choose any of the other commands as you wish. Alternatively, to cancel this menu and return to full-screen view, click anywhere outside of the menu.

Chapters and Titles   Typically you'll watch video DVDs just as you would a VHS tape; that is, you'll start it, pause it once in a while to get up for more popcorn, then sit down and click on Play to start it up again. But as more interesting DVDs start to hit the market, you may want to jump to specific *titles* and *chapters*. Think of a title as, say, one of several shows on the disk. A chapter, then, is a subset of a title: perhaps a lesson, a scene in the movie, a section of a tutorial, etc. Once a disk is inserted, you can quickly choose to search for sections by title or chapter by right-clicking on the display, as shown on the next page.

- If you choose Title, this handy little box lets you jump to a specific title and to any portion of the title track by entering its time value:

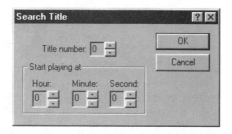

- If you choose Chapter, you'll see the following box, which also expects you to enter a time value:

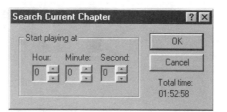

Just enter the hour, minute, and second of the spot you want to jump to (and if you're in the Title box, enter the title number), and click OK.

Selecting Language and Subtitles   Some disks will have subtitles (nice for when you're talking on the phone; that way nobody can hear what's distracting you), and some disks will have multiple languages (i.e., multiple alternative audio tracks), as I mentioned earlier. You can make choices for these features from the Options button:

The procedure is a no-brainer:

1. Click Options.

2. Choose SubTitles or Language.

3. Set the subtitle or language option as desired, and click Close.

For example, suppose I wanted to see English subtitles (assuming my disk offered them). The Options ➢ SubTitles command might show the following choices:

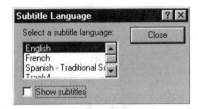

I'd just click on English, then on the Show Subtitles checkbox. For language choice, I might see the following little box. I'd just choose the audio language I'm interested in listening to:

Ending a DVD Session   When you're finished listening to, using, or viewing the disk, you can either press the Eject button on the front of the drive or click the Eject button on the DVD Player toolbar. Then close the DVD Player program.

Assigning Sounds with the Control Panel's Sound Utility

You can use the Control Panel's Sound utility for assigning sounds to system events, such as warning dialog boxes, error messages when you click in the wrong place, and so on. Once you've installed a sound board, you can personalize your computer's beep to something more exciting. If your computer had a sound card when you installed Windows 98, it's likely Windows established a default set of rather boring sounds for your system, most of which you're probably tired of already. Besides making life more interesting, having different sounds for different types of events is also more informative, because you can assign sounds to many more events than Windows does by default. You know when you've made an error as opposed to when an application is acknowledging your actions, for example.

Of course, to add basic sounds to your Windows setup, you need a Windows 98-compatible sound card. The sounds you can use must be stored on disk in the .wav format. Most sounds you can download from BBSs or get on disk at the computer store are in this format. Also, the Sound Recorder program explained later in the chapter records sounds as WAV files. Windows 98 comes with more than a few sound files. In fact, just as with the color schemes you can create and save with the Control Panel's Display applet (covered in Chapter 7), you can set up and save personalized sound schemes to suit your mood. Microsoft has supplied us with several such schemes, running the gamut from happy nature sounds to futuristic, mechanistic robot utterances to the sonorities of classical musical instruments.

NOTE

You have to do a Custom installation to get all the sound schemes loaded into your computer. You can do this after the fact by running Control Panel ➤ Add/Remove Programs ➤ Windows Setup. Then click on Multimedia to select it and click on the Details button. The Multimedia Sound Schemes are located near the bottom of the list.

Despite this diverse selection, you may still want to make or acquire more interesting sounds yourself or collect them from other sources.

TIP

See Chapter 7 for a discussion of the Desktop Themes option which in addition to neat visual features, adds some spiffy sounds to your system.

To record your own, you'll need a sound board that handles digital sampling. I have messages in my own voice, such as, "You made a stupid mistake, you fool," which—for a short time—seemed preferable to the mindless chime. If your system lets you play audio CDs, you should be able to directly sample bits and pieces from your favorite artists by popping the audio CD into the computer and tapping directly into it rather than by sticking a microphone up to your boom box and accidentally recording the telephone when it rings. Check out the Volume Control applet and adjust the slider on the mixer panel that controls the input volume of the CD. Then use the Sound Recorder applet to make the recording.

TIP

Any time your sound isn't working correctly (if there's no sound, for example), check the following: Are your speakers connected and turned on? Is the volume control on them (if they have it) turned down? Has the sound worked before? If so, it's probably the mixer settings that are wrong. Right-click on the speaker icon near the clock in the TaskBar and choose Open Volume Controls. Check the settings. Don't forget to choose Options ➢ Properties and poke around. Don't change the mixer device, but notice that you can choose to see the Recording mixer controls, and choose which sliders are on either the recording or playback controls. Make sure the source that isn't working properly isn't muted.

Like any good sound-o-phile, I'm always on the lookout for good WAV files. You'll find them everywhere if you just keep your eyes open: cheap CDs at the local Compu-Geek store, on the Internet, on CompuServe, even on other people's computers. Usually these sound files aren't copyrighted, so copying them isn't likely to be a legal issue. Most WAV files intended for system sounds aren't that big, either. But do check out the size, using the Explorer or by showing the Details view in a folder, before copying them. Sound files *can* be super large, especially if they are recorded in 16-bit stereo (about 172K bytes per second of CD-quality audio). As a rule you'll want to keep the size to a minimum for system sounds because it can take more than a few seconds for a larger sound file to load and begin to play.

Once you're set up for sound and have some WAV files, you assign them to specific Windows events. Here's how:

1. Open the Control Panel and run the Sounds applet. The dialog box shown in Figure 10.1 appears.

2. The top box lists the events that can have sounds associated with them. There will be at least two classes of events—one for Windows events and one for Explorer events. (Scroll the list to the bottom to see the Explorer events.) As you purchase and install new programs in the future, those programs may add their own events to your list. An event with a speaker icon next to it already has a sound associated with it. You can click on it and then click on the Preview button to hear the sound. The sound file that's associated with the event is listed in the Name box.

3. Click on any event for which you want to assign a sound or change the assigned sound.

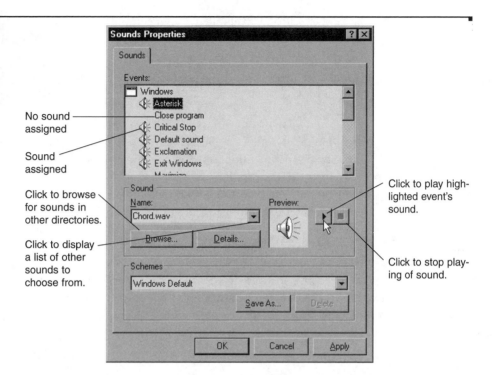

FIGURE 10.1

Use this dialog box to choose which sounds your computer makes when Windows events occur.

No sound assigned

Sound assigned

Click to browse for sounds in other directories.

Click to display a list of other sounds to choose from.

Click to play highlighted event's sound.

Click to stop playing of sound.

4. Open the drop-down Name list and choose the WAV file you want to use for that event. Some of the event names may not make sense to you, such as Asterisk, Critical Stop, or Exclamation. These are names for the various classes of dialog boxes that Windows displays from time to time. The sounds you're most likely to hear often will be Default sound, Menu Command, Menu Popup, Question, Open Program, Close Program, Minimize, Maximize, Start Windows, and Exit Windows.

The default directory for sounds is the \Windows\Media directory. That's where the WAV files that come with Windows 98 are stored. If you have WAV files stored somewhere else, you'll have to use the Browse button to find and assign them to an event. I find it's easier to copy all my WAV files into the \Windows\Media directory than to go browsing for them when I want to do a lot of reassigning of sounds.

5. At the top of the list of available sounds there is an option called <none> that has the obvious effect—no sound will occur for that event. Assigning all events to <none> will effectively silence your computer for use in a library, church, and so forth. You can also quickly do this for all sounds by choosing the No Sounds scheme as explained below.

6. Repeat the process for other events to which you want to assign or reassign sounds.

7. Click on OK.

Keep in mind that different applications will use event sounds differently. You'll have to do some experimenting to see when your applications use the default beep, as opposed to the Asterisk, Question, or the Exclamation.

Clicking on the Details button displays information about the WAV file, such as its time length, data format, and copyright information (if any).

Loading and Saving Sound Schemes

Just as the Control Panel's Display applet lets you save color schemes, the Sounds applet lets you save sound schemes so you can set up goofy sounds for your humorous moods and somber ones for those gloomy days—or vice versa. The schemes supplied with Windows 98 are pretty nice even without modification.

To choose an existing sound scheme:

1. Click on the drop-down list button for schemes, down at the bottom of the box:

2. A list of existing schemes will appear. Choose a sound scheme. Now all the events in the upper part of the box will have the new sound scheme's sounds. Check out the sounds to see if you like them.

3. If you like the sound scheme, click on OK.

You can set up your own sound schemes by assigning or reassigning individual sounds, as I've already explained. But unless you *save* the scheme, it will be lost the next time you change to a new one. So, the moral is: once you get your favorite sounds assigned to system events, save the scheme. Then you can call it up any time you like. Here's how:

1. Set up the sounds the way you want. You can start with an existing scheme and modify it or start from scratch by choosing the No Sounds scheme and assigning sounds one by one.

2. Click on the Save As button.

3. In the resulting dialog box, enter a name for the scheme. For example, here's one I made up and saved:

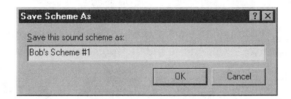

4. Click OK in the little dialog box, and your scheme is saved. Now you can create additional schemes and save them or just OK the large dialog box to activate the new scheme.

You can delete any existing sound schemes by choosing the doomed scheme from the list and then clicking on the Delete button. You'll be asked to confirm the deletion.

Playing Multimedia Files with Media Player

Media Player is a little application that plays multimedia files, such as digitized sounds, MIDI music files, and animated graphics. It can also send control information to multimedia devices such as audio CD players or video disk players, determining which tracks to play, when to pause, when to activate slow motion, and so on.

Obviously, you can only use Media Player on devices installed in your system and for which you've installed the correct device drivers (see "Installing New Drivers," below), so first see to that task. Then follow these instructions for playing a multimedia file:

1. Run Media Player from the Start ➢ Programs ➢ Accessories ➢ Entertainment ➢ Media Player. The Media Player's control panel appears, as shown here:

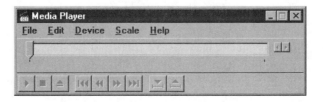

2. Open the Device menu and choose the type of device that's going to receive the information.

3. If the type of device you've chosen has an ellipsis (...) after it, a File Open dialog box will appear, asking for the name of the file you want played and displaying the files with the correct extension for the selected device. This only happens with devices that play a file stored on hard disk (this type of device is called a *compound* device). Choose the file you want played. If the device you selected has no ellipsis after it, it's a *simple* device. This means the data to be played are already in the drive—as in the case of a CD-ROM or video disk—and don't have to be chosen (no File Open box will appear). When you load a file for a compound device, the Media Player's appearance will change slightly to display a scale and tick marks indicating the length of the item:

You can jump to a particular location in the piece by dragging the scroll bar, clicking at the desired point in the scroll bar, or using ↑, ↓, ←, →, PgUp, and PgDn. Also, check the Device menu for options pertaining to the device you are using.

4. Now you can use the buttons in the dialog box to begin playing the piece. The buttons work just as on a VCR or cassette deck; if in doubt, the buttons have pop-up descriptions. The Eject button works for most devices with an Eject feature, like an audio CD player. However, not all devices will respond to the Eject button. It depends on the device and the driver.

5. If you want to open another file for the same device (in the case of compound devices), use the File ➤ Open command to do so. If you want to play a file intended for another device, you'll have to change the device type first from the Device menu, which will then bring up the File ➤ Open command for you to open a new file.

6. You can change the scale (tick marks) above the scroll bar to show *tracks* instead of time. Track display may be useful when you're playing audio CDs or video disks arranged by track. Do this from the Scale menu. Track tick marks will then replace the time tick marks. To change tracks, drag the scroll bar, click on the scroll buttons, or use →, ←, PgUp, and PgDn.

7. When you're done playing, close the application from the Exit menu.

NOTE

Compound devices will stop as soon as you quit Media Player; simple devices will continue to play.

Media Player has a few options worth noting. Check out the Edit ➤ Options and Device ➤ Configure options. Choose Device ➤ Volume control to bring up the volume control and mixer for your particular sound board.

NOTE

Use of the Volume Control accessory is covered in Chapter 22.

Recording and Editing Sounds with Sound Recorder

Sound Recorder is a nifty little program that lets you record your own sounds and create WAV files. To make it work, you need a digital sampling card such as the SoundBlaster and some kind of input, such as a microphone. The program also lets you do some editing and manipulation of any WAV files you might have on disk. You can do this even if you don't have a microphone.

The resulting WAV files can be put to a variety of uses, including assigning them to system events or using them with other multimedia applications, such as Media Player. Once a file is recorded, you can edit it by removing portions of it. Unfortunately, you cannot edit from one arbitrary spot to another, only from one spot to either the beginning or the end of the file. You can also add an echo effect to a sample, play it backwards, change the playback speed (and resulting pitch), and alter the playback volume.

Playing a Sound File

Follow the steps below to play a sound file:

1. Make sure your sound board is working properly. If it's been playing sounds, such as the one that plays when Windows starts up, it probably is. If not, check that you've installed the correct driver and that your sound board works (Chapter 7 discusses how to add new hardware and drivers).

2. Run Sound Recorder by choosing Start ➢ Programs ➢ Accessories ➢ Entertainment ➢ Sound Recorder. The Sound Recorder window will appear, as shown here.

3. Choose File ➢ Open and choose the file you want to play. Notice that the length of the sound appears at the right of the window and the current position of the play head appears on the left.

4. Click on the Play button or press Enter to play the sound. As it plays, the wave box displays the sound, oscilloscope style. The Status Bar also says Playing. When the sound is over, Sound Recorder stops and the Status Bar says Stopped. Press Enter again to replay the sound. You can click on Stop during a playback to pause the sound, and then click on Play to continue.

5. Drag the scroll button around (see below) and notice how the wave box displays a facsimile of the frequency and amplitude of the sample over time.

You can also click on the rewind and fast-forward buttons to move to the start and end of the sample or press the PgUp and PgDn keys to jump the play head forward or backward in longer increments.

Recording a New Sound

This is the fun part, so get your microphone (or line input) ready. Suppose you want to make up your own sounds, perhaps to put into an OLE-capable application document such as Wordpad or Word so that it talks when clicked on. Here's how:

1. Choose File ➢ New.

2. You may want to check the recording format before you begin. Choose File ➢ Properties. Select Recording Formats, then click on Convert Now. A dialog box appears, showing some details about the recording format. Click on the Convert Now button to see the dialog box shown in Figure 10.2. A combination of data-recording format (e.g., PCM, Microsoft's ADPCM, and so forth) and sampling rate (e.g., 8 KHz 4-bit mono) are shown. Together these comprise a format scheme.

FIGURE 10.2

Choosing a data scheme for a new sound recording

Choose a pre-existing format scheme here.

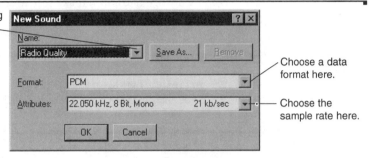

Choose a data format here.

Choose the sample rate here.

NOTE

The Attributes list shows the amount of disk space consumed per second of recording. You'll want to consider this when making new files, as recording in high-fidelity stereo can suck up precious disk room, rendering sound files quite unwieldy. Also, for most purposes, you are best served by choosing one of the preexisting sound schemes— CD-Quality, Radio Quality, or Telephone Quality—for your recordings. All three use the PCM recording technique but employ different sample rates. If you are recording only voice, use either the Radio or Telephone setting. The CD-quality setting will only use up more disk space than you need to. If you are planning to record from an audio CD player, you'll probably want to choose the CD-quality setting unless you want to conserve disk space. If you accidentally record at a higher quality level than you wanted to, don't worry. You can convert to a lower quality and regain some hard disk space via the File ➢ Properties ➢ Convert Now button. You can save recording and playback settings with the Save As button in the dialog box.

3. Click on the Record button. The clock starts ticking, counting the passing time. Begin talking into the microphone that's plugged into your sound card, playing whatever is connected to your AUX input (a.k.a. *line in*) on the sound card, or playing the audio CD that's in the CD-ROM drive. You'll have to use the volume control applet to set the relative balance of the various devices. Typically you'll be able to mix these disparate audio sources into a single recording if you use the mixer deftly. The maximum recording time will vary, depending on your recording format. In the default setting (PCM, 22.050-KHz 8-bit mono) you can record for up to one minute. Be cautious about the length of your sounds, as they tend to take up a large amount of disk space. For example, a one-second sample at CD Quality in stereo consumes about 172K.

4. Click on Stop when you are finished recording.

5. Play back the file to see if you like it.

6. Save the file with File ➢ Save As. You'll see the familiar File dialog box. Enter a name (you don't have to enter the WAV extension; the program does that for you).

When recording a voice narration, make sure to speak loudly and clearly, particularly if you notice that playback is muffled or buried in noise.

A simple way to create a new sound file is to right-click on the Desktop and choose New ➢ Sound File. Name the file, then double-click on it. Then click on the Record button.

Editing Sounds

You can edit sound files in several ways. For instance, you can:

- Add echo to a sample.
- Reverse a sample.
- Mix two samples together.
- Remove unwanted parts of a sample.
- Increase or decrease the volume.
- Increase or decrease the speed and pitch.
- Convert it to another format for use by a particular program.

You may run out of memory if your file becomes very long because of inserting files into one another. The amount of free physical memory (not virtual memory) determines the maximum size of any sound file.

To edit a sound file:

1. Open the sound file from the File menu.

2. Open the Effects menu to add echo, reverse the sound, increase or decrease volume, or increase or decrease speed. All the settings except echo can be undone, so you can experiment without worry. You undo a setting by choosing its complementary setting from the menu (e.g., Increase Volume instead of Decrease

Volume) or by choosing Reverse. Some sound quality can be lost by doing this repeatedly, however.

3. To cut out the beginning or ending of a sound—i.e., to eliminate the lag time it took you to get to the microphone or hit the Stop button—determine the beginning and ending points of the sound, get to the actual starting position of the sound, and choose Edit ➢ Delete Before Current Position. Then move the scroll button to the end of the desired portion of the sample and choose Edit ➢ Delete After Current Position.

4. To mix two existing sounds, position the cursor where you'd like to begin the mix, choose Edit ➢ Mix with File, and choose the file name. This can create some very interesting effects that are much richer than single sounds.

5. To insert a file into a predetermined spot, move to the spot with the scroll bar, choose Edit ➢ Insert File, and choose the file name.

6. To put a sound on the Clipboard for pasting elsewhere, use Edit ➢ Copy.

7. To return your sound to its original, last-saved state, choose File ➢ Revert.

Note that not all sound boards have the same features. Some won't let you save a recording into certain types of sound files. Also, the quality of the sound differs from board to board. Some boards sound "grainy," others less so. This is determined by the sampling rate you've chosen, the quality of the digital-to-analog converters (DAC), and the analog amplifiers on the board.

Some programs require a particular sound file format to use sounds. For example, the Voxware plug-in for Web browsers (which lets you put sound clips on your Web pages) expects sound files in its proprietary Voxware format. You can convert an existing sound file by opening it in Sound Recorder. Then choose File ➢ Properties. Click on Convert Now and choose the correct setting from the Format list. Then click OK. Then save the file. It should be in the new format.

NOTE

Typically programs that require proprietary sound formats supply their own conversion tools, and it's often better to use those tools when they are available than a little accessory such as Sound Recorder.

Playing Tunes with CD Player

The CD Player accessory turns your computer's CD-ROM drive into a music machine: With it, you can play standard audio CDs with all the controls you'd expect on a "real"

PART

II

Exploring Windows 98

CD player, and then some. Of course, you'll need speakers (or at least a pair of head-phones) to hear the music. Here's what CD Player looks like:

With CD Player, you can:

- Play any CD once through or continuously while you work with other programs.
- Play the tracks in sequential or random order, or play only the tracks you like.
- Move forward or in reverse to any desired track.
- Fast forward or rewind while a track is playing.
- Stop, pause, and resume playback, and (if your CD-ROM drive has the capability) eject the current CD.
- Control play volume if you're playing the CD through a sound card (this only works with some CD-ROM drives).
- Control the contents of the time display (you can display elapsed time, time remaining for the current track, or time remaining for the entire CD).
- Catalog your CDs (after you've typed in the title and track list for a CD, CD Player will recognize it when you load it again, displaying the titles of the disk and the current track).

Getting Started with CD Player

To run CD Player, begin from the Start menu and choose Programs ➢ Accessories ➢ Entertainment ➢ CD Player. Load your CD-ROM drive with an audio CD, turn on your sound system or plug in the headphones, and you're ready to go.

CD Player can tell when your CD-ROM drive is empty or doesn't contain a playable audio CD. In this case, it will display the message:

```
Data or no disc loaded
Please insert an audio compact disc
```

in the Artist and Title areas in the middle of the window.

Basic Playing Controls

The CD Player window looks much like the front panel of a typical CD player in a sound system. The large black area at the top left displays track and time information. On the left, the faux LED readout tells you which track is currently playing, while on the right it keeps a running tally of how many minutes and seconds have played in the track (you can change the contents of the time display as detailed below).

If you've ever worked a standard CD player, the control buttons (to the right of the track and time display) should be immediately familiar.

On the top row are the essential stop/start controls:

Play: The largest button with the big arrow starts or resumes play.

Pause: The button with the two vertical bars pauses play at the current point in the track.

Stop: The button with the square stops play and returns you to the beginning of the current track.

On the second row, the first four buttons have double arrows pointing to the left or right. These let you move to other parts of the disc.

You can move directly to a specific track by choosing it from the list in the Track area near the bottom of the CD Player window. See "Playing Discs with the Play List" later in the chapter.

Previous and *Next Track:* At either end of this set of four buttons, the buttons with the vertical bars move to the beginning of the previous or next track. The one at the left end—with the left-pointing arrows—moves to the beginning of the previous track (or if a track is playing, to the beginning of the current track). The one at the right—with the right-pointing arrows—moves to the beginning of the next track.

Skip Backward and *Skip Forward:* The two center buttons in the set of four have double arrows only; these are for moving quickly through the music while the disc plays in the reverse or forward direction.

The *Eject* button is the last button at the far right of the second row, with the upward-pointing arrow on top of a thin rectangle. Click here to pop the current disc out of your CD-ROM drive. Of course, this will only work if your drive is capable of ejecting automatically.

Display Options

Like other Windows programs, CD Player has a Toolbar with buttons for other common commands (we'll cover these in a moment). The Toolbar may not be visible when you first run the program; choose View ➢ Toolbar to turn it on and off. Here's how the CD Player window looks with the Toolbar visible:

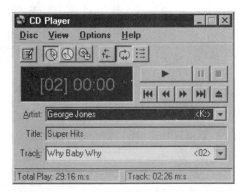

When the Toolbar is on, you can get a brief description of each button's function by placing the mouse pointer over the button.

Two other elements of the CD Player window can also be turned off and on via the View menu. These are the Status Bar and the area displaying the artist and disc and track titles.

When visible, the Status Bar runs along the bottom of the window. It offers Help messages when the mouse pointer passes over a menu choice or rests over a button on the Toolbar for a few moments. Otherwise, it displays the total play time for the disc and current track. To turn the Status Bar off or on, choose View ➢ Status Bar.

Once you've cataloged a disc, CD Player displays the artist, disc title, and title of the current track in the middle of its window. If you want to hide this information, perhaps to make the window small enough to stay on your screen while you work with another program, choose View ➢ Disc/Track Info.

TIP

You can choose between two font sizes for the numerals in the track and time read-out. See "Setting CD Player Preferences" later in this discussion.

You can also control the display of time information in the main readout of the CD Player window. The standard setting shows elapsed time for the track currently playing. If you prefer, you can instead see the time remaining for the current track or for the entire disc. To select among these options, open the View menu and choose one of the three relevant options: Track Time Elapsed, Track Time Remaining, or Disc Time Remaining. The currently active choice is checked on the View menu. Or, if the Toolbar is visible, you can click on the button corresponding to your time-display choice.

Other Play Options

You have several commands for determining the play order for a disc's tracks. Three of these are available as items on the Options menu or as buttons on the Toolbar:

Random order: Plays the tracks randomly. This is often called *shuffle* mode on audio-only CD players.

Continuous play: Plays the disc continuously rather than stopping after the last track.

Intro play: Plays only the first section of each track. You can set the length of this intro with the Preferences command, covered below.

NOTE

If you have a multiple-disc CD-ROM drive, you'll find an additional Multidisc Play choice on the Options menu. Select this if you want to hear all the discs loaded in the drive rather than just the currently active disc.

You can select these playback options in any combination. To turn them on or off, open the Options menu and choose the desired item; they are active when checked. Alternatively, click on the button for that command (the button appears pressed when the command is active). Here are the buttons you use:

If none of these commands are active, CD Player plays the tracks in full and in sequence, stopping after the last track.

Other play options include whether or not the current disc keeps playing when you close CD Player (covered in "Setting CD Player Preferences," below) and playing a custom list of tracks, covered in the next section.

Cataloging Your CDs and Creating Play Lists

If you're willing to do a little typing, CD Player will keep a "smart" catalog of your disc collection. Once you've entered the catalog information, such as the disc title, the artist, and the track titles, CD Player automatically displays these details whenever you reload the disc:

Note that if you have a multidisc CD-ROM drive (or more than one unit), you can choose from the available drives by letter using the list in the Artist area.

Cataloging a Disc   When you load a disc that hasn't been cataloged, CD Player displays generic disc information. The Artist area reads *New Artist*, and the Title area says *New Title*. Tracks are titled by number (*Track 1, Track 2,* and so on).

 To enter the actual information for the current disc, choose Disc ➢ Edit Play List, or, if the Toolbar is visible, click on the corresponding button (the one at the far left, shown here on the left). The dialog box shown in Figure 10.3 will appear.

FIGURE 10.3

The Disc Settings dialog box

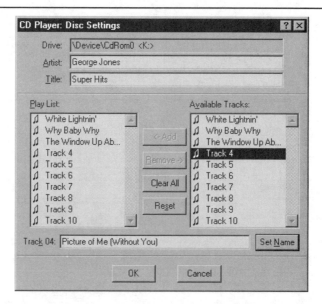

The top area in this dialog box, labeled Drive, identifies the location of the disc being cataloged. If you have a multidisc player, you can double-check whether you're working with the correct disc here.

Type in the artist and title of the CD in the appropriate areas at the top of the dialog box. To type in track titles:

1. Select a track in the Available Tracks box (the one at the *right* of the dialog box).

2. Type in the track title in the Track area at the bottom of the dialog box.

3. Click on the Set Name button to change the current name.

You can change any of this information at any time. When you're satisfied with your entries, go on to create a play list as described below or click on OK to return to CD Player. The disc information will appear in the appropriate areas of the window.

Creating a Play List   The typical CD has some great songs, a few that are good to listen to but aren't favorites, and one or two that are just terrible. CD Player lets you set up a custom play list for each disc so you never have to hear those dog songs again. If you like, you can even play your favorites more often than the others (be careful, you might get sick of them).

Here's how to create a play list:

1. In the Disc Settings dialog box (Figure 10.3), the Play List box on the left side of the window displays the tracks in the play list. Initially, the box displays all the tracks on the disc in order.

2. If you just want to remove one or two tracks, drag each track off the list as follows: Point to the track's icon (the musical notes) in the Play List box, hold down the mouse button, and drag to the Available Tracks box. Alternatively, you can highlight each track in the Play List box and click on the Remove button. To remove all the tracks and start with an empty list, click on Clear All.

3. You can add tracks to the play list in two ways:

   • Drag the track (or tracks) to the Play List box using the same technique for deleting tracks but in the reverse direction: Starting from the Available Tracks box, drag the track to the desired position in the play list. You can add a group of tracks by dragging across them to highlight them, releasing the mouse button, and then dragging from the icon area to the play list.

   • Use the Add button: Highlight one or more tracks in the Available Tracks box and click on Add. In this case, the added track always appears at the end of the list.

4. If you want to start again, click on Reset. The Play List box will again show all the tracks in order.

5. Click on OK when you've finished your play list to return to the main CD Player window.

Playing Discs with the Play List   CD Player always selects the tracks it plays from the play list. Before you make any modifications, the play list contains all the tracks on the disc, and you'll hear every track when you play the disc. Once you've created your own play list, though, CD Player plays only the tracks on the list. If you select Random Order play, the program randomly selects tracks from the play list, not from all the tracks on the disc.

The play list tracks are accessible individually in the Track area near the bottom of the CD Player window. To move to a particular track, just select it in the list. If the disc is already playing, the selected track will start. Otherwise, click on the Play button to start it.

Setting CD Player Preferences

Use the Preferences dialog box to change miscellaneous CD Player settings. To display it, choose Options ➤ Preferences. Here's what the Preferences dialog box looks like:

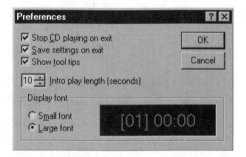

Here are the available preference settings and their effects:

Save settings on exit: When this box is checked, the settings you make on the View and Options menu and in the Preferences dialog box are saved when you close the program. If you clear this box, changes in settings affect only the current session—the previous settings are restored the next time you start CD Player.

Show tool tips: Check this box if you want pop-up descriptions (also known as tooltips) and Help messages in the Status Bar when the mouse pointer rests on a button for a few moments. Clear it if you find these messages annoying.

Intro play length: Use the arrow controls to set the number of seconds at the beginning of each track that CD Player will play when you activate the Intro Play command.

Display font: Choose a large or small font for the LED-like track and time readout by choosing the appropriate radio button.

TV Viewer

One of my favorite multimedia applications in Windows 98 is the TV Viewer. It's probably not installed in your system, because it's an option. To install it from the CD, run Control Panel ➢ Add/Remove Programs ➢ Windows Setup ➢ TV Viewer. You may be prompted to reboot the computer several times before the installation is complete, so close up any work in advance.

TV Viewer works in conjunction with special TV cards and video capture cards/drivers that are compatible with DirectShow 2.0 and WDM (drivers that are built into Windows 98). Even if you don't have a video capture card or TV display card, you can still take advantage of the program listing guide, which downloads TV listings from the Web and displays them in various fomats that put *TV Guide* (even the online version) to shame. You can search for shows, times, show types (sci-fi, drama, specials, etc.), and set reminders so your computer reminds you not to miss a show.

With the appropriate hardware, you can select and tune among hundreds of analog (broadcast and cable) or digital satellite television programs, and navigate to Web channels and other information broadcast through these networks. For satellite reception, drivers specifically written for the Broadcast Architecture are required. Check with your satellite TV provider to see whether their service is compatible with TV Viewer.

You will need a PC system capable of running Microsoft Windows 98 or Windows NT Workstation 5.0, including:

- A Pentium-class PC with at least 16MB RAM
- Microsoft Windows 98 or Windows NT Workstation 5.0
- Television or standard VGA monitor (large screen monitor optional)
- Supported TV tuner and video card(s)
- Wireless remote control device (optional)
- Modem and Internet connection (optional)

For more information on supported hardware, search the Microsoft Web site for Broadcast Architecture. (When I wrote this chapter, the information was in a password-protected area of the site, for registered beta-testers, but it should be publicly accessible by the time you read this.) For the latest information about Microsoft's plans to integrate digital TV, the Web, and your PC, visit http://www.microsoft.com/windows/tv/home.htm.

What's So Cool about TV Viewer?

For starters, you watch TV either on the whole screen or in a window while you work, and the quality is very high. The picture is much sharper than on a standard TV; and some of the TV cards perform "line doubling," drawing twice as many lines on the screen as on a normal TV. This results in a better-looking picture, especially since you are typically watching from just a couple of feet from your screen. Most TV tuner cards decode stereo sound, so the sound will be good as well. Further, you also get the benefit of *enhanced TV* viewing. Here are some of the potential benefits of enhanced TV viewing (once this technology is more firmly developed):

- News and weather reports can be accompanied by local or other specialized information that satisfies the needs of limited audiences.

- Educational programs could spice things up with references and links to other programs, and locations on the Web.

- When watching dramas and comedies, you could read cast information, recaps of past episodes, links to related Internet and bulletin board sites, and other such background information.

- When watching sporting events, you could read statistics, or even create your own data sheets for personalized tracking of favorite players or teams. You could hear or read additional syndicated commentary.

- Music-only channels can add background graphics containing song title, album, and artist information, so you know what you are listening to and how to find it again.

- Shows can be enhanced by letting the viewer respond and interact. Viewers can then play along with game shows, enter contests, take quizzes, vote on issues presented in the show, express opinions, and take part in polls. Consumers using a back channel can actually investigate and purchase things from the comfort of their living rooms.

NOTE

Of course, your Internet connection must be correctly configured and working to download Program Guide information from the Web and to interact with shows. To verify your connection, confirm that you can successfully view content from some popular Web pages such as http://www.microsoft.com with Internet Explorer.

How It Works

At its simplest, TV Viewer simply picks up TV signals from an antenna or cable TV input plugged into your TV tuner card and displays the result in a resizable window.

Windows 98 provides the TV tuner program to make this happen. If your TV tuner card is supported, Windows 98 also supplies all the drivers. If not, you'll get them in the box with the card.

Going a step beyond that, if you're on a digital satellite system, you'll probably have to get a special accompanying card (either external or mounted inside the PC) that decodes the digital signals and then pumps them into the TV card.

You can download your program listings either from a broadcast channel or over the Web. It's much faster over the Web. The TV Viewer program is set up to decode the broadcast listings from StarSight and load them into the Program Guide.

Using TV Viewer

To run the program, first install it as I explained above. Then run it either by clicking on the TV set icon in the Quick Launch bar or choose Start ➣ Programs ➣ Accessories ➣ Entertainment ➣ TV Viewer. The first thing you'll notice upon running the program is that it takes a bit of time to load. You'll see the TV Viewer "splash screen" first and after a little wait you'll be walked through setting up the program the first time (see Figure 10.4). There a man's voice telling you what to do. Just listen and follow the instructions.

PART

II

Exploring Windows 98

FIGURE 10.4

TV Viewer

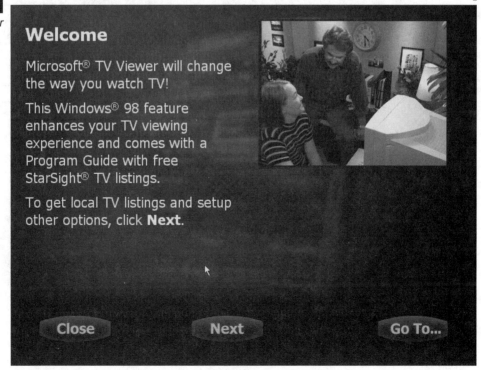

Welcome

Microsoft® TV Viewer will change the way you watch TV!

This Windows® 98 feature enhances your TV viewing experience and comes with a Program Guide with free StarSight® TV listings.

To get local TV listings and setup other options, click **Next**.

Close   Next   Go To...

If you're already hooked up to a good TV source (antenna, cable, satellite), have the wizard scan for channels. I have found that when I'm using a cheesy antenna, I have to input the channels manually or they don't get registered because the signals aren't strong enough. (I'll show you how to do that shortly.) And if you have a Web connection, choose that as the source for your Program Guide data, not the broadcast option, which can take hours to download, though you may be able to do this in the background. If you download from the Web, you'll have to answer a few questions about your zip code and perhaps specify what your source of TV signal is (which cable company, which local broadcast area), as in Figure 10.5.

After a few minutes of downloading, the Web page should tell you that the process is now complete. You can start using the program, and you'll see something like what I have in Figure 10.6. It looks totally unlike anything else in Windows 98, so get ready, since the interface is completely new and a little annoying at first. But it's pretty easy to learn, so don't worry.

FIGURE 10.5

Specifying your broadcast medium when using the StarSight Program Guide Web download

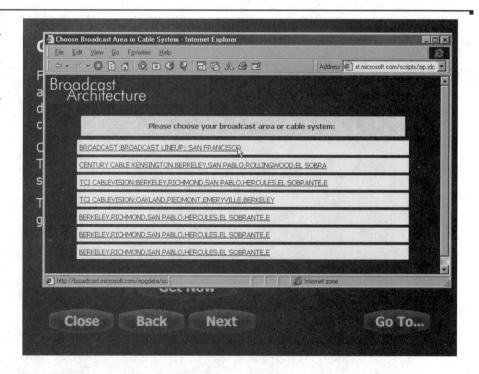

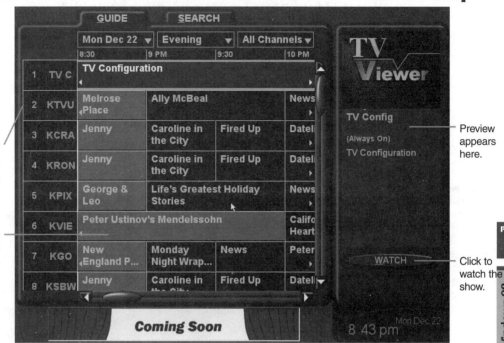

FIGURE 10.6

Typical Program Guide appearance. Click on a green area to preview a show on the right. Click on Watch to remove the guide from view.

Click here to see what is currently on this channel (useful if you can't download schedule info).

Click in a light-green area to preview the show.

Preview appears here.

Click to watch the show.

NOTE

Only the shows displayed in green are being broadcast currently. Other times are displayed with a blue background. Clicking on them does nothing.

TIP

You may not have program listings, either because you aren't connected to the Web and therefore can't download them from the Net, or you don't live in an area that broadcasts the listings over the air. Not to worry. If you don't have program listings you can still watch TV. You just click on the TV channel number over to the left, or press the PageUp and PageDown keys to change channels. If you have no channels except 1 and 99 showing, you have to add your channels manually. See that section below.

Adding (and Removing) Channels Manually

Just like when you set up a new TV or VCR, the automatic scan option can add channels you don't want, or can skip over weak channels and not add them. To manually add or remove channels, do this:

1. With the TV Viewer window active (or full screen) Press Alt or F10. This brings up a big toolbar with a few icons on it.

2. Click on Settings in the toolbar. In the resulting dialog box, click on Add Channels. Add and enter the number, as you see in Figure 10.7. To remove a channel, select it and click Remove.

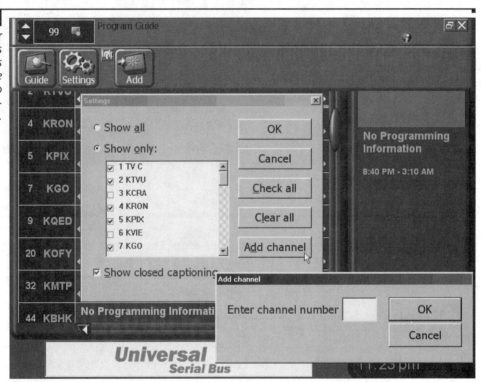

FIGURE 10.7

You can add or remove channels using the Settings box. You also choose which channels to display in the Program Guide.

Tips for Using TV Viewer

Here are some tips to make using TV Viewer easier.

Online Documentation

Use the online help. It's pretty good. Just press F1 while you're in TV Viewer.

Avoid Channel 1

Channel 1 is the Setup channel. Choosing it by clicking on it, or (more likely) by landing on it while pressing PgUp and PgDn to channel-surf, runs the wizard again and starts talking you through the setup routine. Unless you want to hear all that and download the Program Guide again, or choose your video options (like for assigning a VCR or camera to a channel), just skip to another channel quickly.

FIGURE 10.7

You can add or remove channels using the Settings box. You also choose which channels to display in the Program Guide.

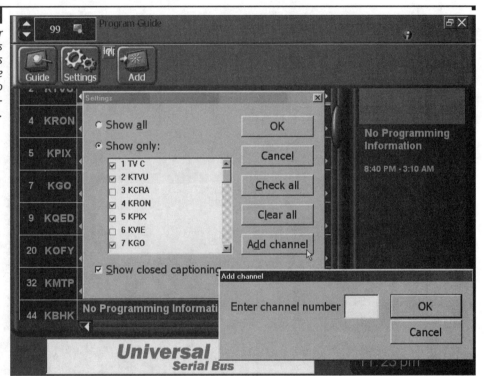

PART

II

Exploring Windows 98

Channel 99 is always the Program Guide.

Scrolling the Display

Note the scroll buttons on the display. You can grab them and slide just as you do with other windows. When you do so, you'll see an indication of where you're headed. They work in both the horizontal (time) and vertical (channel) directions. See Figure 10.8.

TIP

You can size the display to any size you want, including full screen. The correct height/width proportion of the image is maintained as you resize. See the keystroke table below for how to toggle between full screen and a window. While in a window, size it just as you would any other.

FIGURE 10.8

Use the scroll bars to get around your Program Guide.

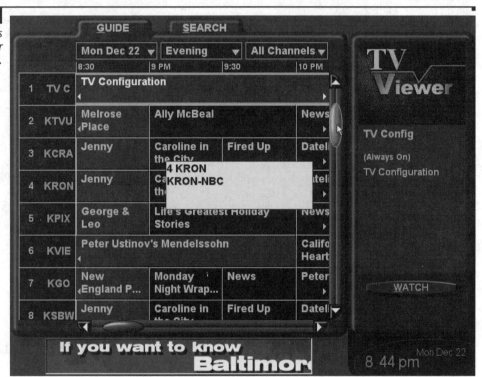

Searching for a Show

How many times have you wondered, "Hey when is *X-Files* (or the *Price is Right*, or something else) on? Now you don't have to scan the whole *TV Guide*. Just use the Search option.

1. Click on the Search tab near the top of the TV Viewer window.
2. Click in the Search area at the bottom left.

3. Enter the show you're looking for. Then click Search.

You'll see shows that match the name, on all stations in your area. You can then choose to set reminders (see below), or tune to it immediately. You can also click on Other Times to see a list of other times and channels when the same program is going to be on.

Looking for a Category of Shows

Looking for a drama, something educational, maybe a musical? Instead of just channel surfing and taking pot luck with a regular TV remote control, why not search by category and get what you're really looking for, like when you go to the video store?

1. Click the Search tab.

2. Click on the desired category in the left pane.

3. Pull down the left time menu at the top:

4. Choose the time slot you're thinking of.

After choosing a time slot, you'll only see listings for that time. The time slot you choose stays active until you change it or go back to the Guide Page by clicking on the Guide tab. So, clicking on other categories will also display only shows in the chosen time slot.

Reading about a Program

Wondering if you've seen the program before? A spiffy feature of the Program Guide is that is also contains lots of information about shows it lists. You can click on a show in the Program Guide, and over to the right, under the preview screen you'll see some stuff about the show, such as the rating, whether it's a rerun, a synopsis of content, etc. Figure 10.9 shows an example. Note the location of the pointer.

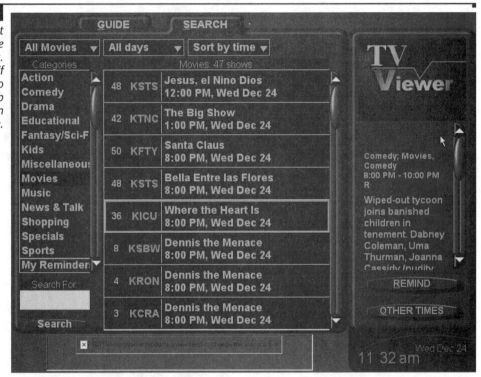

If you're online with the Internet, you can click on the name of the program just under the preview window to quickly conduct a search of pages that contain the name of the show. Sometimes you get useful information about the show, fan pages, and so on.

Setting Reminders

Want to be alerted before a show comes on, so you can tape it or watch it? Easy. You just set a reminder:

1. Click on a program in Program Guide.

2. Click on the REMIND button in the lower right. You'll see a dialog box:

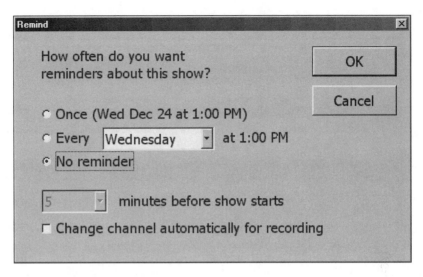

3. Fill in the relevant info and click on OK.

A dialog box will appear on the screen to remind you of the upcoming show, at the time(s) you choose.

NOTE

The TV Viewer program has to be running in order to give you reminders.

Adding Favorite Channels to Your Toolbar

You can have up to five favorite channels in your toolbar, making it easy to switch between favorite channels. If you have five and add another, the oldest one disappears and is replaced by the new one.

1. Display the toolbar.

2. Select a channel you want, using one of the various techniques.

3. Click on Add:

The new channel appears on the toolbar. Click it now to switch to that channel.

TIP

When you're viewing full-screen, just move the pointer to the top of the screen and wait a second. The toolbar will appear. If you then move it away from the top of the screen, the toolbar will disappear after a few seconds. Pressing Esc always makes the toolbar go away, too.

Remote Controls and Special Keys While Watching

The TV Viewer is designed to work with remote controls available (or to-be-available) from your computer manufacturer (not your standard TV remote!) If you don't have a computer remote control, you're not alone. As an alternative, you can use the keystrokes listed in Table 10.2 with the TV Viewer application: The most frequently used keys are listed first.

TIP

If you have a Gateway Destination entertainment sytem, your remote control will work with the TV Viewer. The only exception is that the Recall button on the Gateway remote control has no function.

TABLE 10.2: KEYSTROKE CONTROLS FOR TV VIEWER

Keystroke	Action
F10	Brings up toolbar menu (favorites, guide, logins, preferences, etc. are accessible from the toolbar)
F6	Toggles windowed/full screen mode. Windowed mode is useful for displaying video while using desktop applications.
0-9	Used for changing channels. Channels are three digits.
Enter	Confirms selection
↑, ↓, ←, →	Scrolls up/down when viewing programming grid.
Win	Brings up Start menu
Win-Ctrl-Shift-z	Shows the Program Guide (grid view)
Win-Ctrl-z	Brings up TV Viewer if not yet started, otherwise toggle between desktop and full screen

Continued ▶

TABLE 10.2: KEYSTROKE CONTROLS FOR TV VIEWER (CONTINUED)

Keystroke	Action
Win-Ctrl-v	Volume Up (on Master Mixer)
Win-Shift-v	Volume Down (on Master Mixer)
Win-v	Toggle Mute (on Master Mixer)
Win-Ctrl-Alt-z	Channel Up
Win-Ctrl-Alt-Shift-z	Channel Down
Win-Ctrl-Alt-Shift-f	Arrow Left (some apps may interpret as REWIND)
Win-Ctrl-Alt-Shift-p	Arrow Up (some apps may interpret as PLAY)
Win-Ctrl-Alt-f	Arrow Right (some apps may interpret as FORWARD)
Win-Ctrl-Alt-Shift-g	Recall (some apps may interpret as EJECT)
Win-Ctrl-Alt-p	Arrow Down (some apps may interpret as STOP)
Win-Ctrl-Alt-g	PAUSE

* "Win" means the Windows key on your keyboard if it has it. Older keyboards do not have this key.

Future Plans for TV Viewer, IE, and Webcast Receivers

A technology called Broadcast Architecture is built into Windows 98. It's both flexible and powerful, and it allows data to be broadcast to computers in a number of ways. The chapters on Internet Explorer and the Active Desktop talk about this as it pertains to the use of IE. However, Microsoft and others are working on ways to integrate TV broadcasts into the list of media through which Web-style information can be downloaded to your computer. One application that takes advantage of this "filter and store" architecture is the Webcast receiver.

Webcast receiver exists on channel 720 in the Program Guide. Through it you can subscribe to content which may be broadcast over your LAN, local TV stations, or Direct Broadcast satellites. Then again, you may not have this option in your area, in which case 720 won't appear as a station in your Program Guide listing.

Continued

PART

II

Exploring Windows 98

CONTINUED

The Webcast receiver application is also available through the Webcast Channel in the Internet Explorer Channel Bar, incidentally.

Here's how it works. Just as when you subscribe to a site or channel in Internet Explorer, the upshot is that Web pages are downloaded to your computer in the background. When you're ready to view pages, they are there for your viewing pleasure, even if you're not online. After you subscribe to a site, the Webcast filter constantly listens for content, and when received, will automatically store this content in your Internet Explorer cache. Unlike an Internet Explorer subscription, which "hits" the requested Web pages and downloads them semi-automatically, Channel 720 waits for this information to arrive through a broadcast interface.

As of this writing, the feature wasn't fully implemented, but was being tested through participating broadcast television networks in selected cities, as well as through direct broadcast satellite networks.

Managing Multimedia Drivers and Settings

When you add a new piece of hardware to your system, such as a sound board, CD-ROM controller, MIDI board, or other piece of paraphernalia, you'll have to alert Windows to this fact by installing the correct software device driver for the job. Some drivers simply control an external player as though you were pushing the buttons on the device's control panel by hand. These types of devices are called Media Control Interface (MCI) devices and include audio CD players, video disc players, MIDI instruments, and others. Other drivers actually send the sound or video data to the playback card or hardware, as well as control the playback speed and other parameters.

You use the Add New Hardware option in the Control Panel to install the device driver. Drivers for popular multimedia items are included with Windows and will often be detected when you've added the hardware, especially if the hardware is Plug-and-Play compatible.

**TIP**

As a rule, when you're purchasing new stuff, avoid non–Plug-and-Play hardware like the plague.

Chapter 7 covers the use of the Add New Hardware applet; refer to that chapter if you have added new multimedia hardware to your system and it isn't being recognized.

If you are having trouble running your multimedia hardware or need to make adjustments to it, you'll have to examine the Properties of the item and its driver. Device property dialog boxes can be reached from several locations. For example, the Edit menu in the Sound Recorder applet will take you to your sound card's Properties settings, though you could also use the System applet in the Control Panel to get there. Properties are discussed in Chapter 11.

When in doubt, always contact the manufacturer of your multimedia hardware to obtain drivers and driver updates for use with Windows 98. You can often download new drivers over the Web, but not always. Sometimes a phone call is required.

Chapter

11

Object Properties
and the Right-Click

Right-clicking to reveal quick menu choices

Object properties boxes

Object Properties
and the Right-Click

In this chapter, I'll discuss Properties boxes and the use of the right-click as a means for getting your work done faster and for adjusting object properties. Let's start with a brief recap of right-clicking.

Right-Clicking around Windows

As you are well aware by now, right-clicking on objects throughout the Windows 98 interface brings up a shortcut menu with options pertaining to the objects at hand. The same options are typically available from the normal menus but are more conveniently reached with the right-click.

NOTE

These button names will, of course, be reversed if you are left-handed or have reversed the mouse buttons for some other reason. If you have a trackball, a GlidePoint, or other nonstandard pointing device, your right-click button may be somewhere unexpected. You may have to experiment a little to find which one activates the right-click menus.

Right-clicking isn't only part of the Windows 98 interface; it's been incorporated into recently written Windows programs, too. For example, Microsoft Office programs such as Word and Excel have had right-click menus for some time. Some of the accessory programs supplied with Windows 98 have context-sensitive right-click menus, too. In general, the contents of the right-click menus change depending on the type of object. Options for a table will differ from those for a spreadsheet cell, frames, text, graphics, and so on.

As a rule, I suggest you start using the right-click button whenever you can. You'll learn through experimentation which of your programs do something with the right-click and which don't. Many older 16-bit Windows programs won't even respond to the click; others may do the unexpected. But in almost every case, right-clicking results in a pop-up menu that you can close by clicking elsewhere or by pressing Esc, so don't worry about doing anything dangerous or irreversible.

A good example of a right-clickable item is the Taskbar. Right-click on an empty place on the Taskbar, and you'll see this menu:

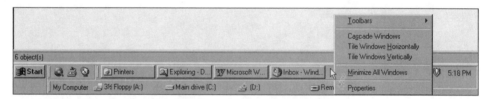

Now right-click on the Start button, and you'll see this menu:

Here are a few other right-clicking experiments to try:

- Right-click on My Computer and notice the menu options.

- Right-click on a document icon. If you right-click on a DOS batch file (any file with a BAT extension), you'll have an edit option on the menu. What an easy way to edit a batch file!

- Right-click on a program file, such as Pbrush.exe in the Windows directory or on a DLL (Dynamic Link Library) file. The Quick View option (available only if you have the Quick Viewers installed) lets you read information about the program, such as how much memory it requires to run and when it was created. A Properties option may tell you even more.

- When you right-click on a printer in the Printer's folder, you can quickly declare the printer to be the default printer or to work offline (not actually print yet, even though you print to it from your applications) or go online with accumulated print jobs. Right-click on the Desktop to set the screen colors, screen saver, and so forth.

- Right-click on any program's title bar and notice the menu for resizing the window or closing the application.

- Right-click on a minimized program's button down in the Taskbar. You can close the program quickly by choosing Close.

- Right-click on the time in the Taskbar and choose Adjust Date/Time to alter the date and time settings for your computer.

Right-click menus will often have Cut, Copy, Paste, Open, Print, and Rename choices on them. These are discussed in Chapters 4, 5, and 6.

Many objects such as folders, printers, Network Neighborhood, and Inbox have a right-click menu called Explore that brings up the item in the Windows Explorer's format (two vertical panes). This is a super-handy way to check out the object in more detail. You'll have the object in the left pane and its contents listed in the right pane. In some cases the contents are print jobs; in other cases they are fonts, files, folders, disk drives, or computers on the network. (The Windows Explorer is covered in Chapter 12.)

Sharable items, such as printers, hard disks, and fax modems will have a Sharing option on their right-click menus. The resulting box lets you declare how an object is shared for use by other users on the network. (Sharing a printer is covered in Chapter 8. Additional discussion of sharing can be found in Part 6.)

Property Sheets

Just as most objects have right-click menus, many also have property sheets. Properties pervade all aspects of the Windows 98 user interface, providing you with a simple and direct means for making settings to everything from how the screen looks to whether a file is hidden or what a shared printer is named.

Virtually every object in Windows 98—whether a printer, modem, shortcut, hard disk, folder, networked computer, or hardware driver—has a *property sheet* containing such settings. These settings affect how the object works and, sometimes, how it looks. And property sheets not only *display* the settings for the object, but usually allow you to easily *alter* the settings.

You've probably noticed that many right-click menus have a Properties choice down at the bottom. This choice is often the quickest path to an object's property sheet—not that there aren't other ways. Many dialog boxes, for example, have a

PART

II

Exploring Windows 98

Properties button that will bring up the object's settings when clicked on. And the Control Panel is used for setting numerous properties throughout Windows 98. Still, as you become more and more comfortable with Windows 98, you'll find the right-click approach most expedient.

Who Will Use Property Sheets?

The majority of Windows 98 users will rarely bother viewing or making changes to property-sheet settings because Windows 98 is well-enough behaved to govern itself (for example, repairing shortcuts when the target file or folder has been moved) and to prompt you when necessary for details about objects. As a case in point, when you install Windows 98 for the first time, or when you add new hardware or create a new printer, Wizards conscientiously assume the responsibility of setting up properties appropriately. The upshot is that tweaking Windows 98's internals and objects isn't nearly as necessary as it was in Windows 3.x. And in those rare instances when it is, unearthing the required dialog box for the job isn't an exercise reminiscent of dismantling a Chinese box puzzle.

Certainly any self-respecting power user will want to know all about properties for easily performing tasks such as sharing a folder on the network, changing the name of a hard-disk volume, checking the status of the computer's ports, displaying a font or other file's technical details, or checking the amount of free disk space on a hard disk.

TIP

To even more quickly see an object's properties, highlight the object and press Alt-Enter.

Trying Out a Few Properties Boxes

The Properties option is always the last command on a right-click menu. For example, if you right-click on My Computer, you'll see this menu:

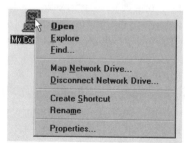

Or right-click on the clock in the Taskbar, and you'll see this:

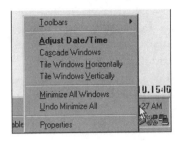

Just choose the Adjust Date/Time command to easily set the time, date, and time zone for your computer, ensuring that all your files are properly date and time stamped and your Taskbar displays the time correctly.

Here's another everyday example. Suppose you're browsing through some folders (or the Windows Explorer) and come across a Word document. Wondering what it is, when it was created, and who created it, you just right-click and choose Properties. The file's property sheet pops up, as shown in Figure 11.1. There are several tab pages on the sheet because Word specifically stores additional property information in its files.

FIGURE 11.1

A typical property sheet for a document file. This one is for a Word 97 file, so it has several pages listing its editing history, who created it, keywords, title, and so forth.

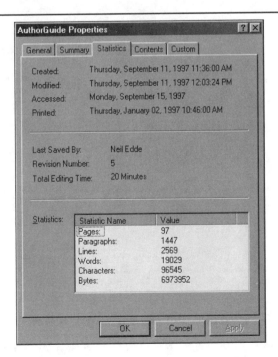

Property sheets for other kinds of files may only have a single tab page with less than a copious amount of information. In fact, most document property sheets are truly useful only if you want to examine the history of the file, determine its shorter MS-DOS file name, or set its DOS attributes such as whether it should be read-only (to prevent others from using it), hidden from view in folders, or if its *archive bit* should be set. (A check mark in the Archive box means the file hasn't been backed up since it was last altered or since it was created.) My point is that you can usually only *view* the status of the document, not *alter* it.

Property sheets for objects other than documents often let you make more substantive changes to them. A shortcut's property sheet, for example, lets you adjust some goodies about how the shortcut works, the file it points to, and so on, as shown in Figure 11.2.

FIGURE 11.2

Shortcuts have property sheets with a second tab page listing the particulars of the shortcut and allowing modification. Here you can change settings that control how the document or program will run when the shortcut is double-clicked on.

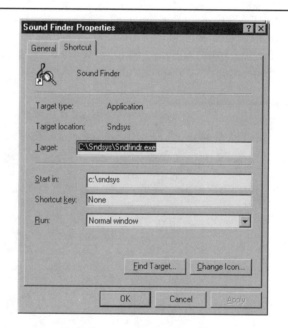

There is now a way to ensure that a program (whether DOS *or* Windows) defaults to a certain directory. In the dialog box shown in Figure 11.2, you can use the Start In field to set the default directory for a program. When you start the application from the shortcut, the File ➤ Open and File ➤ Save As commands will then default to this directory. In Windows 3.x, setting this variable was only possible for DOS programs. Now it's possible for Windows programs too.

This property sheet is somewhat similar to the old PIF files in Windows 3.x, though those only affected the running of DOS programs. Shortcut property sheets can affect any program or document. You can use the ? button for help on any of the options, but I'll just say that the two handiest items here are Shortcut Key and Run. Shortcut Key lets you assign a key combination that will run the shortcut from anywhere. For example, to jump to My Computer without having to minimize all your other windows first:

1. Get to the Desktop. Then right-click on My Computer and choose Create Shortcut. This creates a new shortcut on the Desktop called Shortcut to My Computer.

2. Right-click on the new shortcut and choose Properties.

3. In the Properties dialog box, click on the Shortcut tab, then click in the Shortcut Key field.

4. Press Ctrl-Alt-C to assign the shortcut key to Ctrl-Alt-C.

5. OK the box.

Now whenever you want to open My Computer, just press Ctrl-Alt-C. It takes a little manual dexterity, but it's quick. Use the same trick for any object you use regularly and find you're fishing around to open.

The Run field in a Shortcut's property box just determines whether the object will open in a maximized, minimized, or normal (floating) window.

Another interesting property sheet belongs to the Recycle Bin. See Chapter 22 for details.

Making Property Settings from My Computer

Probably the most powerful property sheet is reachable directly from My Computer. Clicking on My Computer and choosing Properties brings up the box shown in Figure 11.3.

Examine the four tab pages here. The first page tells you some useful information about the version of Windows you are running, how much memory your computer has, and what type of CPU chip is in your machine. This will come in handy the next time someone asks you what's in the computer you're running: Instead of drumming your fingers on the desk, feeling like a dufus, you can open this box and read what it says.

The second tab page lists all the devices in the whole computer, many of which you probably didn't even know you had. Clicking on a + sign opens up a device to display more attributes about it. Clicking on a device and then on the Properties button tells you more about the highlighted device.

PART

II

Exploring Windows 98

A grand overview of your computer's attributes is available by right-clicking on My Computer and choosing Properties. Use some caution with these settings. This box is also available from the System applet in the Control Panel.

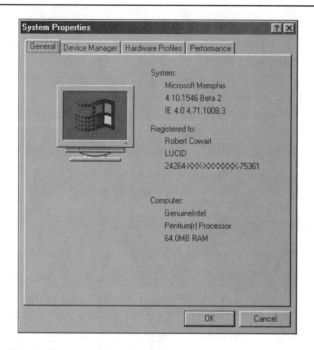

The third and fourth tab pages are about setting up specialized system profiles (collections of settings to match different hardware arrangements, such as when a laptop is docked into a base unit or running around in the field) and for fine-tuning your system's virtual memory management, file system, and video graphics display speed.

WARNING

As a rule, don't toy with the System Properties settings unless you know what you're doing. Examining all the dialog boxes is fine if you just cancel them. But adjusting the file system and virtual memory settings will more likely negatively impact your system's performance than accelerate it.

Chapter

12

Working with the File System and Windows Explorer

FEATURING

A review of DOS directories

Exploring the Explorer

Working with folders, files, and disks

Using network drives, files, and disks

Working with other objects in Explorer

Working with the File System and Windows Explorer

Most application programs nowadays consist of numerous files. Add to this the plethora of documents and programs you're likely to collect, and suddenly your hard-disk directory looks like that ugly snake-filled chamber in *Raiders of the Lost Ark*. With the advent of affordable high-capacity hard disks (2, 4, or even 10 gigabytes), one of the more challenging maintenance issues with any computer operating system is the job of managing your files.

If you find that the folder system is a nuisance because of the circuitous routes it takes you through at times, read on, because in the following pages, I'm going to reveal the pleasures of the Windows Explorer. If you're just upgrading from Windows 3.*x*, you can think of Windows Explorer as a sort of supercharged File Manager. It's a very powerful tool that does almost any Windows 98 system task, from making Control Panel settings to adding printers, viewing and mapping network drives, creating and managing folders and documents, opening Web pages, or running programs. If you want to truly master Windows 98, the Explorer is *the* vantage point from which to do it. You'll benefit greatly in your day-to-day tasks by understanding how to use it.

A Review of DOS Directories

But first a little review. For the most part this chapter assumes you understand the basic filing system used by a "Wintel" computer (i.e., a computer running Windows on an Intel or Intel-compatible CPU, formerly known more loosely as "IBM-compatible computers"). The file system for storing data on your disks comes from MS-DOS, which predates Windows. It's based on the idea of directories, which since Windows 95 have been called *folders*. If you're a little rusty on the topic DOS directory layout, here's a thumbnail primer for directory (folder) workings.

NOTE

Although Microsoft would like us all to forget we ever heard the terms "directory" and "subdirectory," any discussion of the Windows Explorer has to at least acknowledge that most of what the program does is display and manipulate your DOS directories in various ways. Because of the historical linkage between DOS "directories" and Windows "folders," I'll use the terms *folders*, *directories*, and *subdirectories* interchangeably, though I'll favor the newer term.

Despite the fancy graphical user interface, Windows 98 is still tacked on top of an updated version of the old MS-DOS, which even has some crusty old 16-bit code in it. It's DOS (which stands for Disk Operating System) that is responsible for managing all those files and folders on your disk. As you know, a folder is simply a collection of files—programs, documents, fonts, system files, or what have you. Even Windows with all its bells and whistles is nothing but a bunch of files spread out across many, many folders. As you also know, folders let you keep related files nested together. With occasional limitations imposed by specific programs, you can organize your files however the spirit moves you.

Folders are organized in a system that is supposed to be analogous to a tree, as illustrated in Figure 12.1. In fact, the organization of folders, which is called the *directory tree*, is a little misguided, insofar as most systems represent the tree upside down, with the "root" at the top of the display and the branches growing downward rather than upward. The folders are organized in a hierarchical manner, from the the most basic level (the *root*) to various branches off the root (the *folders*) and branches off those branches (the *subfolders*). (Actually, when you think about it, the concept of "root" is also misbegotten in this analogy, as there are many roots on a real tree; a better term would have been "trunk." (Where were the simile police when we needed them most?)

The Faces of Explorer

Windows 98's Explorer has even more personalities than it possessed in Windows 95. Technically, the Windows Explorer is sort of a jack of all trades and the heart of the display system in Windows. It's responsible for running the taskbar, displaying all folders, including desktop which is really just another specialized folder, and it's now even integrated with the Internet Explorer (IE) Web browser. This is why typing **C:**\ into an IE window will display the contents of drive C, for example, and why typing a URL into the address bar of a folder window displays the URL's contents in that folder. Even your Start button menus and Favorites list (bookmarks in IE) are displayed and manipulated by the Windows Explorer. And finally, the Windows Explorer program is simply the same Explorer with yet another face, one that's more like the old File Manager from Windows 3.*x* days. Now that we have two Explorers (Internet Explorer and Windows Explorer) we run the risk of additional confusion. When I use the term Explorer, I'm referring to the Windows Explorer program run from Start ➤ Programs ➤ Windows Explorer.

FIGURE 12.1

The DOS directory-tree structure. Folders are organized from the root outward.

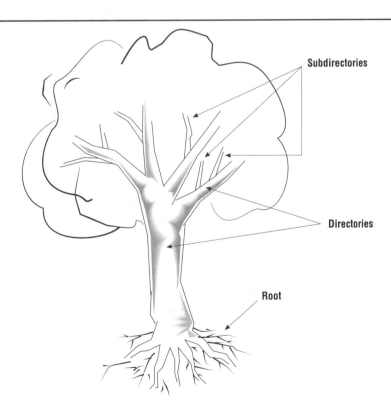

Subdirectories

Directories

Root

It is possible that you've never taken much advantage of folders before. This is because, theoretically, you can cram all your work files into one folder.

As discussed in Chapter 5, it's much wiser to divide things up according to projects. For one thing, it makes finding your projects that much easier. It's also a little safer; you don't lose all of your work if you accidentally erase a single folder.

The root folder in DOS and File Manager was indicated by a single backslash (\). In Explorer it's indicated by the drive's icon:

All other folders have names that you or some program (such as an application's installation program) create. For example, the Windows Setup program created a folder branch called Windows. Subordinate to Windows, it created another branch called System. The official name of the system folder is C:\Windows\System. This is called the folder's *path name*. The name describes the path you'd take to get to the folder, just as if you were climbing the tree—from the root up to the particular branch. Notice that the backslash (\) character (indicating the root) precedes the folder name and that branches in the path name are also separated by a backslash.

In working with folders, the main thing to keep in mind is the "you can't get there from here" rule. To switch between distant branches, there are times when you have to remember their relationship to the root; I explain this in Chapter 3 in "File Dialog Boxes." For example, if you were working in the \Windows\System folder and wanted to save a file in the \Letters\Personal folder, you'd typically have to back up to the root level first, select the Letters folder, and finally select the Personal folder. Just like when climbing a tree, if you want to get from one branch to the next, you have to go back to the trunk, then out the other branch.

Exploring the Explorer

To run the Explorer, click on the Start button and choose Programs ➢ Windows Explorer. The Explorer will load.

> **TIP**
>
> If you use the Windows Explorer often, add a shortcut icon on the Quick Launch bar, or on the Start menu. See Chapters 3 and 4 if you don't remember how to do this.

Maximize the window and it will look something like Figure 12.2. Of course, the folders in your window will be different from those shown in this figure.

FIGURE 12.2

The basic Explorer screen, showing the major items on the left and the contents on the right.

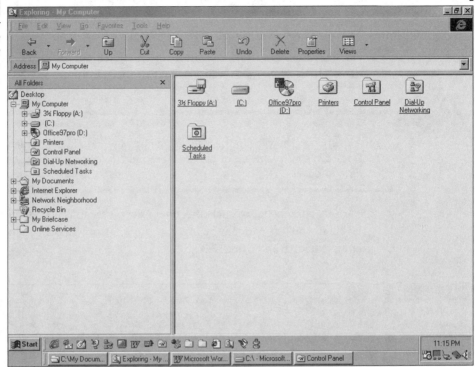

Unlike the old Windows 3.*x* File Manager, Explorer doesn't let you open multiple windows. However, that's not necessary because Explorer is more flexible in design. You can copy files, folders, or other objects from anywhere to anywhere without needing multiple windows.

Actually, if you prefer to work with multiple windows for a drive or folder, you can simply run multiple "instances" of Windows Explorer. That is, just run it as many times as you need to. Then just adjust the windows as necessary to see them.

Displaying the Contents of Your Computer

When you run the Explorer, all the objects constituting your computer appear in the list on the left. Some of those objects may have a plus sign (+) next to them, which means the object is collapsed; it contains sub-items that aren't currently showing. For example, my hard disk drive in Figure 12.2 is collapsed. So are Network Neighborhood (which you won't see unless you have network options installed) and the floppy drive (drive A). Here's how to check out the contents of such an item:

1. Click on the item itself, not on the + character. For example, click on your C drive's icon. Now its contents appear in the right pane as a bunch of folders.

TIP

You can change the view in the right pane just as you do in any folder. Click on the Toolbar icons over to the left or use the View menu to display large icons, small icons, list view, or details.

2. Another approach is to click directly on the plus sign (+). This opens up the sublevels in the left pane, showing you the relationship of the folders in a tree arrangement as in Figure 12.3.

FIGURE 12.3

Click on a plus sign (+) to display folders and other sub-objects.

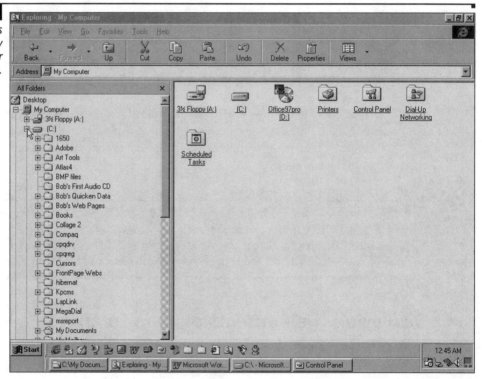

3. Notice that the plus sign is replaced with a minus (–), indicating that the object's display has been expanded. Click on it again, and it collapses.

4. To collapse everything, click on the minus sign next to My Computer.

5. Click on the Desktop icon up at the top of the tree. Notice that all the objects on your Desktop appear in the right pane.

The tree is a graphical representation of your disk layout. Each file folder icon symbolizes one folder, and the straight lines connecting them indicate how they're related. The name of each folder appears after the icon. If you have more folders than can be seen at one time, the window will have a scroll bar that you can use to scroll the tree up and down. Notice that there are two scroll bars—one for the left pane and one for the right. These scroll independently of one another, a feature that can be very useful when you are copying items from one folder or drive to another.

Also notice the Toolbar. It's just like the ones for individual folders. Refer to Chapter 4 for a discussion of the buttons' functions. The View ➤ Explorer option is a new feature in Windows 98. Leave this alone for the time being. I'll talk about it a bit later in this chapter, and more in Chapter 16, on the Internet Explorer.

You may or may not see a status line at the bottom of the window, displaying information about the item(s) you have selected in the right or left panes. You can turn this on or off with the View ➤ Status Bar command. Turning it off frees up a little more screen space for displaying folders and files, though having it on gives you some useful information such as how much free disk space you have. Choose View ➤ Toolbars to choose which toolbars will display. Turning off button text and/or the Address bar are options I sometimes use to see more files at one time.

Working with Folders

To work with folders and files, the first task is to select the correct drive, whether a local hard disk, a floppy drive, or a networked drive. Once you have the correct drive selected, you can drag and drop files, run programs, open documents that have an association, and use right-click menu options for various objects. For example, you can right-click on files or folders and choose Send To ➤ 3½" Floppy to copy items to a floppy disk.

Selecting the Correct Drive and Choosing a Folder

To select the drive whose contents you want to work with:

1. Scroll the left pane up or down until you see the drive you want. Use the scroll bar in the middle of the window to do this. If the drive you want isn't showing, you may have to expand the My Computer icon by clicking on its plus sign. At least one hard drive (and probably a floppy) should be visible.

2. Click on the name or icon of the drive whose contents you want to work with. The right pane then displays its contents. On a hard disk, you'll typically see a bunch of folders there, not files. (Floppies often don't have folders on them.) Folders are always listed first, followed by files. If you scroll the list a bit, you'll reach the files. Remember, at this point you are in the root directory of the selected drive. You have to find a specific folder before you get to see what's in it.

3. If the drive has folders on it, you now have a choice. You can double-click on one of the folders in the right pane, or you can expand the drive's listing in the left pane by clicking on its plus sign.

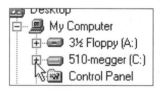

Which option you choose doesn't really matter. You can get to the same place either way. The advantage of expanding the drive in the left pane is simply that it gives you a more graphical view of how your disk is organized and also lets you drag items from the right pane into destination folders. Go ahead and click on the drive's plus sign if it's showing (Figure 12.4). Note that I've changed the right pane's view to show small icons so I can see more items at once. I've also turned off the View as Web Page option (View ➤ View as Web Page).

4. Now suppose you want to see which fonts you have in your Fonts folder. I suspect the Fonts folder is a subfolder of the Windows folder. Finding it from My Computer would take a little hunting around, but with Explorer it's easy. If necessary, scroll the left list down, using the scroll box in the left pane's scroll bar, until you see the Windows folder.

FIGURE 12.4

Clicking on a drive's plus sign opens it. Here you see my C drive.

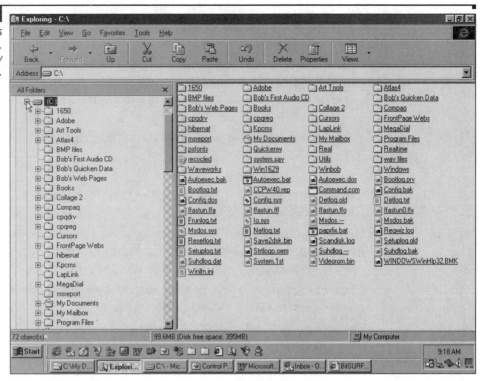

5. Because the Windows directory has subfolders, click on the plus sign. Its subfolders now show.

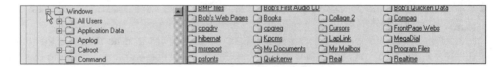

6. Psfonts is one of the subfolders under Windows. Click on it to see which font files are in the directory and consequently which fonts are installed on your system. The Psfonts directory works a little differently than other directories, letting you install and display fonts by similarity. You'll notice some menu commands that are different from other directories. You can double-click on a font name in the right pane and a window will open displaying all the characters in that font style.

7. Click on the Cursors folder to see which cursors are in your system. These are the shapes Windows has available for your mouse pointer.

PART

II

Exploring Windows 98

Try clicking on Desktop to see the list of items on your desktop, or Help to see all the Windows Help files. (There are quite a few!)

Here are a few tips when selecting folders:

- Only one folder can be selected at a time in the left pane. If you want to select multiple folders, click on the parent folder (such as the drive icon), and select the folders in the right pane. Use the same techniques described in Chapter 4 for making multiple selections.

- When a folder is selected in the left pane, its icon changes from a closed folder to an open one.

- You can move to a folder by clicking on it, typing a letter on the keyboard, or moving the highlight to it with the arrow keys. When selected, the folder icon and name become highlighted.

- You can jump quickly to a folder name by typing its first letter on the keyboard. If there is more than one folder with the same first letter, you can press the key again to advance to the next choice that starts with that letter.

- Click on the plus sign to expand a folder tree one level down. Click on the minus (–) sign to collapse a folder's tree up a level.

- The fastest way to collapse all the branches of a given drive is to click on that drive's minus sign.

Notice that every time you select a folder, its contents are displayed in the folder-contents side of the window. The contents will include subordinate folders (listed first and looking like little folders just as they do in the left window), followed by the list of files.

WARNING

When selecting folders and files, be careful not to drag them accidentally! The icons are small and this is easy to do, especially in the left pane. Dragging one folder on top of another folder will dump the first one into the second one (complete with all of its subfolders, if it has any), rearranging the directory tree. This could make programs and files hard to find; worse, some programs might not work. In short, it will generally be an annoyance. If you think you have accidentally dragged a folder into the wrong place, open the Edit menu immediately. The first choice will probably read *Undo move*. Choose it and the folders or files you dragged will be returned to their previous locations.

If you want to change the order in which files are sorted (by name, extension, etc.), you can only do it in Details view. Change to Details view via the View menu, the

right-click menu, or the Toolbar; then click on the appropriate column heading. For
example, to sort files by size, click here:

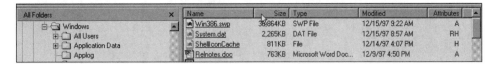

The first time you click, the files list in ascending size. A second click reverses the
order. And just as with most column headings of this style, you can resize any column
by dragging the dividing line between two column headings.

You can easily move between folders you have visited by clicking on the toolbar's Back
and Forward buttons, and by the File menu, which lists the last seven folders you
viewed.

Creating a New Folder

As explained in Chapter 5, organizing your projects often involves making up new
folders. You already know how to do this using My Computer. In keeping with Windows 98's consistency, Explorer uses the same techniques.

Creating a folder is easy, and because of the graphical nature of the folder tree, for
many people it's easier to visualize what you're doing in Explorer than when creating
folders from My Computer when you have windows scattered all over the screen.

1. From the left (tree) pane, select the folder in which you want to create a subfolder. If you select a drive icon at the top of a tree (the root), the folder will be
   created directly off of it. Make sure you click on the folder or drive, not just on
   its + or - sign. Its contents should display in the right pane.

2. Now here's the trick. Click in any empty space in the right pane, then create a
   new folder just as you do from My Computer. That is, choose File ➤ New, or
   right-click and choose New ➤ Folder.

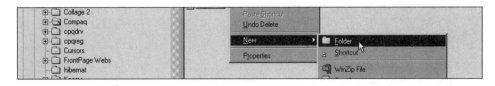

A new blank folder is created, waiting to be named:

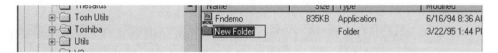

3. Type in the name for your folder, replacing the default name New Folder, which is really only a placeholder. When you finalize the name by pressing Enter, it will show up in the left pane when you expand its parent folder branch.

Deleting a Folder

In Explorer, just as from My Computer, deleting a folder is quite simple; you can do it in one step. But because it's so easy, you should be careful—you can easily trash an entire directory. The good news is that you can reverse the action with the File ➤ Undo command—at least until you delete something else. And of course, you can examine the Recycle Bin and return individual items to their former locations until you empty the trash.

You should know that only programs designed to take advantage of the Recycle Bin will safely move files there, rather than irrevocably deleting them. Deleting a file in the old File Manager or from the MS-DOS prompt, for example, will definitely erase the file. As a rule, most programs designed for Windows 9*x* support the functionality of the Recycle Bin.

You'll be asked if you want to delete an item or group of items before it gets trashed; you have the option of turning the confirmation request off, but it's a reasonable safe-guard. Techies who don't want to be bothered with the Recycle Bin or confirmation messages may turn them off from the Recycle Bin's property sheet. (Right-click on the Recycle Bin and notice the Global Settings, last option box.)

To quickly erase an entire floppy, right-click on the drive's icon and choose Format ➤ Quick erase ➤ Start.

1. In either the left or the right pane, right-click on the folder you want to delete and choose Delete. As an alternative, highlight it (point or click depending on

Web view or Classic view) and then choose File ➤ Delete or press Del. A confirmation box such as this will appear, asking for your permission:

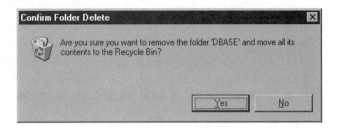

2. If you really want to delete the folder and all its files, click on Yes. The contents of the folder (including any and all subfolders!) will be moved to the Recycle Bin.

If you click on Yes in the above dialog box with the confirmation messages set on, you will need to keep clicking on Yes for each file before it is deleted. If you click on Yes to All, all files will be deleted with no further ado, with one exception. When Windows 98 detects that you are trying to erase an application program (any file with an EXE, COM, or BAT extension), it will ask for additional confirmation:

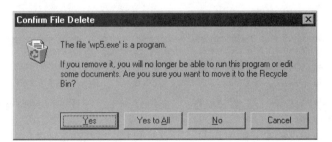

Click on Yes to delete the named program. Click on Yes to All to skip these messages while the folder is being deleted.

Moving Folders

In addition to enabling you to move files easily, Windows Explorer lets you move complete folders or folder branches. When you move a folder, all items in the folder (including other folders) are moved automatically.

You can select the folder to be moved either from the tree pane or from the folder (file) pane. Just drag the folder from either pane and drop it into the new destination:

- When you move a folder to another folder, Windows adds it as a new branch, *below* the destination folder.

PART

II

Exploring Windows 98

- When you move a folder from one drive to another, Windows adds it below the current folder in the destination drive. And the folder is *copied,* not moved, unless you press the Shift key before you drop the item.

Frequently, people want to move folders around on the same drive, a bit like rearranging their living-room furniture. This is extremely easy with the Windows Explorer.

1. Select the folder you want to move (in either pane) and drag it to its new location. As you slide the mouse over possible targets, the target becomes highlighted, indicating where the folder will land if you release the mouse button.

2. When you release the mouse button, the folder will be added as a subfolder one level below the destination folder (and any subfolders will be arrayed below it as before).

Moving Multiple Folders Simultaneously

You can move the contents of more than one folder at a time, but unless they are connected by a descending branch, you have to do this from a folder (file) pane, not from the tree pane. For example, suppose you wanted folders named 1997 Reports, 1998 Reports, and 1999 Reports to be subfolders under a folder called Eagle Inc Reports. Let's say the current arrangement looked like this:

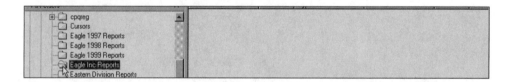

You could consolidate the folders by dragging one folder at a time as explained above. But especially if you have lots of folders, it's faster to do it in one fell swoop. This requires a trick, though, since you can't select multiple folders in the left pane. You have to display the root drive's contents in the right pane, so that the Eagle folders will display there and can be selected. First, scroll up to the C drive icon and click on it, then select the three folders in the folder pane. Drag them as a group to Eagle Inc Reports in the tree pane. Figure 12.5 shows the process of dragging, and Figure 12.6 shows the change to the folder tree.

FIGURE 12.5

Dragging multiple folders into a destination folder. The source folders will become subfolders of the destination folder.

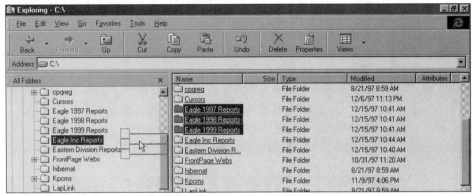

FIGURE 12.6

The result of moving Eagle 1997 Reports, Eagle 1998 Reports, and Eagle 1999 Reports into Eagle Inc Reports. Notice the altered folder tree.

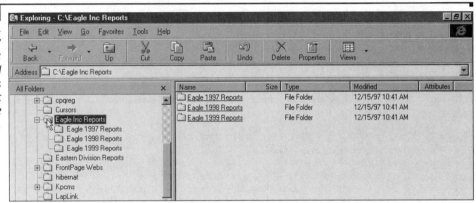

Working with Files

So what about working with files? It's simple. All the rules of working with files in standard folders (as discussed in Chapter 5) apply to Explorer. Once you've selected the correct drive and folder, you do all your work with files by selecting them in the right pane. Just select the file(s) and then cut, copy, paste, run, open, print, quick-view them, or change their properties using the right-click menu or commands from the

File and Edit menus. You can also drag files around to relocate them or right-click and drag them to move, create shortcuts, or copy them.

All these techniques were covered in Chapter 5. But to give you a feel for dragging a file from one folder to another, here's a little exercise. Try moving a file, using the drag-and-drop approach.

1. In the left pane, click on the Windows folder. Then make sure it's expanded to show its subfolders.

2. Then click on the Media folder, which is a subfolder of Windows. In the right pane, you should see a lot of sound (WAV) files.

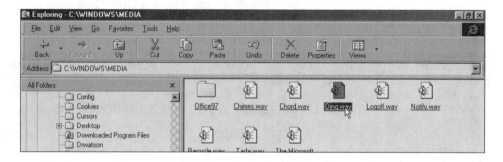

3. Now look for the file ding.wav. We can experiment with this file because it's not terribly important.

4. Let's say you wanted to move this file to the Cursors folder. Scroll the left pane up or down until you see Cursors (another subfolder of Windows).

5. Now drag ding.wav on top of the Cursors folder. The Cursors folder is the target folder and must be highlighted before you release the mouse button, so keep the mouse button depressed until the word Cursors is highlighted, then release.

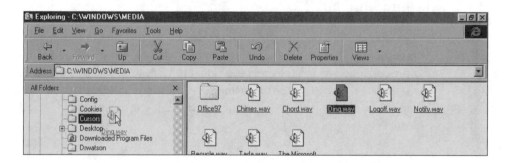

6. Just to check that it worked, now view the contents of the Cursors folder by clicking on it. Among all your icon files you'll now see the Ding.wav file.

7. Now, for purposes of good housekeeping, you should return the file to its origin. Sometimes Windows want to find this file where it belongs. (Windows uses the "ding" wav file sound to alert you of events.) Choose Edit ➣ Undo Move (or drag the file back to the into the Media folder).

Refreshing the Directory

Sometimes other programs will affect the contents of an open drive window. For example, you might switch away from Explorer into an application window such as Word, Excel, or whatever, and create a new document in a folder that's displaying back in the Explorer. Or you might edit a file that's also displayed in the folder's window, changing its size (in bytes). Normally Windows takes care of updating the information in the display; however, there are times when this doesn't happen reliably. Particularly when you are connected to a network, Windows may have trouble detecting that a folder's contents have changed. This will also be an issue if you change floppy disks and want to see the folder on the new disk. If you suspect that a folder may have been changed in some way that isn't reflected in the folder pane, just choose View ➣ Refresh or press F5.

Selecting Files

Before you can work with the files in a folder, you have to select one or more of them. As with other objects in Windows, you select files by highlighting them. Here are various methods of selecting (and deselecting) files:

In the Classic view:

To select one file: Click once on the file. Notice that the status line (the last line in the File Manager window) indicates that one file is selected.

To select multiple nonconsecutive files: Click on the first file to select it and Ctrl-click on additional files.

To select a group of consecutive files: (This is easiest in the List or Details view because objects are in a list.) Click on the first file in the series, then Shift-click on the last item you want to select. As an alternative, you can draw a box around the files you want to select.

To select several groups of consecutive files: Select the first group as described above. To select the second group, hold down the Ctrl key and click on the first file in the second group. Hold down Shift and Ctrl keys simultaneously and click on the last file in the second group. Repeat for each additional group.

To select all the files in a folder: Choose File ➢ Select All. You can then deselect specific files by Ctrl-clicking.

To invert the selection of files: Select the files you want to omit from the selection. Then choose Edit ➢ Invert Selection.

In the Web view:

To select one file: Point to the file. Notice that the status line (bottom of the window) indicates that one file is selected.

To select multiple nonconsecutive files: Point to first file to select it. Then hold down Ctrl and point to additional files.

To select a group of consecutive files: (This is easiest in the List or Details view because objects are in a list.) Point to the first file in the series, then hold down Shift and point to the last item you want to select. (As an alternative, you can draw a box around the files you want to select.)

To select several groups of consecutive files: Select the first group as described above. To select the second group, hold down the Ctrl key and point to the first file in the second group. Hold down the Shift and Ctrl keys simultaneously and click on the last file in the second group. Repeat for each additional group.

To select all the files in a folder: Choose File ➢ Select All. You can then deselect specific files by Ctrl-pointing.

To invert the selection of files: Select the files you want to omit from the selection. Then choose Edit ➢ Invert Selection.

Once highlighted, a file or group of files can be operated on by using the mouse or by using the commands on the File and Edit menus. For example, you can drag a group of files into another folder, delete them, copy and paste them somewhere else, or print them (assuming they are documents). All these commands are covered in Chapter 4, but here's a quick recap of the commands and clicks:

- *Run* a program or *open* a document by double-clicking (in Classic view) or single-clicking (in Web view) on it. Alternatively, highlight a file and press Enter.

- *Print* a document by choosing File ➢ Print. Alternatively, right-click on it and choose Print.

- *View* a file (document, program, font, etc.) with File ➢ Quick View or by right-clicking and choosing Quick View. In some cases you'll have other choices, such as Play, if the file is a sound or video file, or View in Same Window if it's an

HTML (Web page) file. If the QuickViewers are not installed in your computer, you won't see this option. You'll have to install them. See Chapters 5 and 7 for details.

- *Edit* a BAT file with File ➤ Edit or by right-clicking and choosing Edit.

- *Send* selected file(s) to a floppy drive or your Briefcase (or to other programs that you can add to the Send To menu) with File ➤ Send To or by right-clicking and choosing Send To.

- Create a *new* document or shortcut or certain types of registered documents with File ➤ New or by right-clicking and choosing New. You can also create a new shortcut for the selected item(s) with File ➤ Create Shortcut. Then you can copy or move the resulting shortcut to wherever you like, e.g. the desktop, Start button, or Quick Launch bar.

- *Paste a shortcut* for the selected item(s) by first copying the item(s). Then move to the destination and choose Edit ➤ Paste Shortcut. Alternatively, right-click-drag and choose Shortcut from the pop-up menu when you release the mouse button.

- *Delete* the selected item(s) with File ➤ Delete, the Del key, or by right-clicking and choosing Delete. This sends items to the Recycle Bin. Clicking on the X button in the Toolbar has the same effect.

- *Rename* items with File ➤ Rename, by right-clicking and choosing Rename (or by a slow double-click on their name, if in Classic View). Edit the name, and then press Enter to finalize the new name.

- Check a file's *Properties* by clicking the Properties button on the Toolbar. Or, as a quicker way, highlight it and press Alt-Enter. You could also choose File ➤ Properties or right-click on the file and choose Properties from the menu that appears. (Properties are covered in Chapter 11.)

- *Copy* a file by clicking the Toolbar's Copy button. (You could instead choose Edit ➤ Copy, or right-click and choose Copy.) To paste the file where you want it, select the destination (folder or drive), and click Paste on the Toolbar. (You could instead choose Edit ➤ Paste or right-click and choose Paste.)

- *Move* selected item(s) from one location to another by dragging and dropping or choose Edit ➤ Cut followed by Paste (using the Toolbar is easiest).

- *Undo* your last action with the Edit ➤ Undo command.

For viewing options, setting up associations, or refreshing the directory listing, please refer to Chapter 5.

PART

II

Exploring Windows 98

In Explorer and in My Computer folders, pressing Backspace always moves you up a level in the folder hierarchy. This is an easy way to move back to the parent directory of the current folder. After several presses, you'll eventually end up at the My Computer level, the top level on any computer. At that point, Backspace won't have any effect.

When moving files around, keep these points in mind: The new destination can be a folder window that you opened from My Computer, a folder in the left pane of Explorer, or a folder in the right pane. Many programs that support drag-and-drop will let you drag from Explorer into them, too. To open a Word file in an existing Word window, for example, drag the file onto the Title Bar of the Word window. You can even drag a document onto a printer's window, icon, or shortcut. The general rule is this: If you want to move it, try selecting it and dragging it to the new location. If the action isn't allowed, Windows will inform you and no damage will have been done. If you're trying to move the item and get a shortcut instead, right-click-drag the item and choose Move from the resulting menu.

Moving Files to Another Disk Drive

Moving or copying files to another disk drive uses much the same technique as when moving or copying to another folder on the same drive. The basic game plan is that you select the source files and drag them into the destination drive icon as described below.

1. Open the source drive and folder and select the files in the right pane.

2. If it's not showing, scroll the tree pane so you can see the destination drive's icon.

3. Click open the drive if you need to target a particular folder on it.

4. Drop the files on the target. If you're moving the folders or files to a floppy drive, make sure you have a formatted disk in the drive, or you will get an error message.

When you drag files (or folders) between *different* drives, Windows assumes you want to copy them, not move them. That is, the originals are left intact. You can tell that a copy is about to be made because the dragged icon has a + character next to it. When you drag files between folders on the *same* drive, Windows assumes you want to move them, not copy them (you won't see a plus sign).

Working with Disks

Explorer has a few features that apply specifically to managing your disks, particularly floppy disks. These commands make the process of formatting disks and copying disks a bit simpler. There's also a way to easily change the volume label of a disk, the optional name that each floppy or hard disk can be assigned (typically for archival purposes).

Formatting Disks and Making System Disks

As I mentioned in Chapter 5, floppy disks must be formatted before they can be used in your computer. Many disks you buy in the store are preformatted, so this isn't an issue. Some are not, however. Also, you more than likely have many disks with old defunct programs and files on them that you'd like to reuse. To gain maximum room on such a disk, you'll want to erase all the old files, something you can most efficiently achieve with a "quick format" procedure. Finally, you may want to create a disk that is capable of booting the computer. In this section I explain how to do all these things.

WARNING

Formatting erases all data from the disk! Reversing the process is difficult if not impossible.

Here's how to format a disk:

1. Put the disk to be formatted in the floppy drive.

2. Open the My Computer window or Windows Explorer. Right-click on the floppy disk and choose Format.

3. The dialog box shown in Figure 12.7 appears. Use the drop-down lists to set the drive and disk capacity of the floppy.

4. For *Format type* and *Other options*, choose accordingly:

   • *Quick:* Simply deletes the file-allocation table and root folder of the disk, but the disk is not scanned for bad sectors. It doesn't actually erase the whole disk and reinitialize it or check for errors in the disk medium itself. Quick formatting can only be done on a disk that has been formatted in the past, and for a PC. You can't quick-format a Mac disk, for example, though you could do a full format on it.

- *Full:* Checks the entire disk's surface to make sure it's reliable. Any bad spots are omitted from the directory table and won't be used to store your data. This kind of format isn't fast, but it better ensures that valuable data is stored properly on the disk.

NOTE

Disks can actually lose some of their formatting information with time. If you are going to use an old disk, it's best to full-format it it to prevent data loss down the road. And if you do not know where it has been, it's a good idea to full format it to prevent any possible viruses from spreading. If the disk has been around some strong magnets, such as electric motors or unshielded loudspeakers, it is best to full format then, too.

- *Copy system files only:* Doesn't format the disk. It just makes the disk bootable. That means it can start up your computer from the A drive in case your hard disk is having trouble. The necessary hidden system files will be copied to the floppy disk. (Don't use this option to create an emergency backup disk. That's done using the Add/Remove Programs applet in the Control Panel.)

- *Label:* Lets you enter a name for the diskette if you're really into cataloging your disks. All floppy and hard disks can have a volume label. This is not the paper label on the outside, but a name encoded into the folder on the disk. It shows up when you type **DIR** at the DOS prompt and in some other programs. The label really serves no functional purpose other than to identify the disk for archiving purposes. You can change the label from the disk's Properties box at any time.

- *No Label:* Clears any existing label from the disk.

- *Display summary when finished:* Causes a dialog box listing particulars of the diskette, such as how much room is available on it, bad sectors found, and so on, after formatting.

- *Copy system files:* Works similarly to *Copy system files only*, except that you use this option when you want to copy the system files in addition to formatting the disk.

5. Click on Start. You may see a confirmation message. A gas gauge at the bottom of the dialog box will keep you apprised of the progress of the format. A typical full format will take a minute or so.

FIGURE 12.7

Right-click on a floppy drive and choose Format to reach this dialog box. A disk must be formatted before you can store files on it.

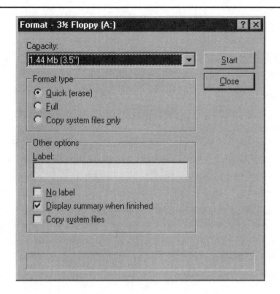

Copying Disks

You can make copies of disks in any of four basic ways—from My Computer, from Windows Explorer, from the DOS prompt, or from the old Windows 3.x-style File Manager.

Using Explorer or My Computer will work most easily:

1. Just right-click on a floppy drive's icon, and you'll see a Copy Disk command. Choose it, and a little dialog box pops up asking for the destination drive. If you only have one drive, that's okay. Just click on Start.

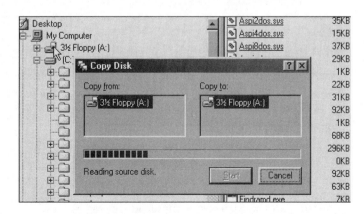

2. You may have to swap the source and destination disks, but you'll be prompted if this is necessary.

If you're an old DOS hand, you might prefer this approach:

1. Choose Start ➢ Programs ➢ MS-DOS prompt.

2. Type the following command:

```
diskcopy x: y:
```

where *x* is the drive that contains the disk you want to copy and *y* is the drive that contains the disk you want to copy to. For example:

```
diskcopy a: b:
```

**TIP**

You can use the same drive letter for both drives if you have only one floppy drive. For more information, type **diskcopy /?** at the command prompt.

Finally, you can also use the Windows 3.*x* File Manager to copy disks if the disk formats and sizes are the same:

1. Run File Manager by choosing Start ➢ Run and entering **winfile** in the Run box.

2. Click on the floppy drive up in the menu bar and choose Disk ➢ Copy Disk. If you have two drives, you'll have to choose the destination drive from the dialog box. If you only have one drive, you'll have to swap the disks a few times.

**WARNING**

Be aware that all of these methods erase everything on the destination disk before creating an exact copy of the source disk.

Making Sure There's Enough Room on a Floppy Disk

When you are moving files about, particularly to a floppy disk, there may not be enough room on the floppy for all the source files. Explorer shows you how many bytes you've got selected in the Status Bar of its window. So, select the files you're going to copy, then look at the Status Bar.

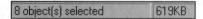

Remember this number for a moment. Then in the left pane, click on the destination drive and check its properties before doing the copy.

Using Network Drives, Files, and Disks

NOTE

As explained further in Part V, Windows 98 can be used on either *peer-to-peer* or *client/server* networks. The first type, usually found in smaller businesses, is much simpler and can be maintained by its users. Client/server networks are usually the responsibility of administrators; if you are on such a network, you probably don't have to worry too much about connecting to or disconnecting from network drives, or sharing resources, as described in this section, though you may still have such options. (Some network administrators can be very controlling about such operations.) In either case, networked drives will be visible in Windows Explorer just as if they were part of your own computer.

If you are on a network, Windows Explorer lets you browse around and explore it, too. This is a brilliant feature of Explorer. Networks are covered in great detail in Part V, but here I'll just introduce you to simple use of Explorer for examining and working with networked objects.

Here's the general game plan. You can *share* your drives and folders (printers and fax machines, too, as discussed in Part V) for use by coworkers on the net. Likewise, you can hook up to the resources other people have shared. With Explorer, scanning the network to see what's available is straightforward. It's just like looking at your own computer's contents.

Many everyday tasks, such as using a document or program on a network file server or another workstation's hard disk can be done right from the folder system or the Windows Explorer without any fancy footwork. You just open Network Neighborhood from the Desktop or from the Explorer (open the drop-down list in Explorer or any folder and choose Network Neighborhood) and see what's on the net:

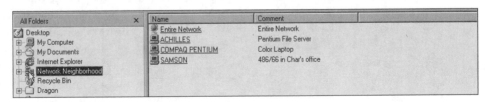

If the network is operational and people are sharing stuff on their workstations, there will be computers listed in the right pane. Click on one of them and start browsing. Examining someone else's drives and folders is *exactly* like looking at your own. For example, I clicked on Samson and saw the contents of Figure 12.8.

Note that you'll only see *shared* items on any networked computer, not *everything* on that computer. This scheme allows users to protect confidential items. Password protection is another option, limiting access of shared objects to specific users. All of the folders in Figure 12.8 (as well as the printer) were intentionally shared by the person who maintains Samson.

FIGURE 12.8

Here you see the shared folders and drives on the networked computer named Samson.

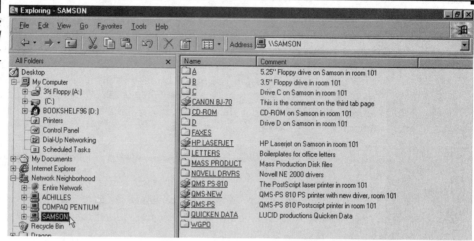

Another point about using Explorer on the network concerns *connecting* to or "mapping" networked drives. If you're an upgrader from Windows for Workgroups 3.11, note that with Explorer you don't have to map a networked drive to a logical drive letter (such as D, E, etc.) before you can work with it. You simply browse any networked computer to see what's been shared on it. Some programs may need you to map a shared folder to a drive letter so you can open a document or perform some other action, but there's an easy way to do this from Explorer, from folders, and from some older-style File dialog boxes that have a Network button on them.

Virtually all Windows 9*x* programs will let you use networked drives and folders with no hassle. For example, say I wanted to open a Notepad file that's stored on

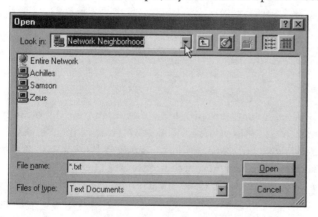

someone else's computer. I simply find the file and double-click, just as if it were on my computer. If I'm already in, say, Word-Pad and I want to use its File ➢ Open command to open a file, no problem. Consider the dialog box on the left.

Notice that I've selected Network Neighborhood in the drop-down list, and the stations on the net show up. Just choose a workstation and look for the document you want. Of course, the same approach applies to saving a document with File ➤ Save.

Mapping a Drive from a Windows 3.*x* File Dialog Box

With some older programs, such as Windows 3.*x*-style ones, you won't have the same luxuries because the File dialog boxes aren't as savvy about networking. You'll more often see something like this dialog box:

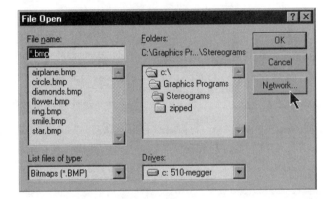

To gain access to a workstation's shared folder, you first have to map the network folder to a drive letter (such as D, E, F). Basically, mapping is just a way to fake your computer and your applications into thinking it has another hard disk on it so you can use older File dialog boxes with networked folders. Mapping is also necessary for some other procedures, such as when an application expects to find support files on a logically lettered drive. In any case, the necessity is a throwback to DOS days.

Click on Network, then fill in the dialog box below. In the lower text area, type in the network path name of the shared directories. You can also use the drop-down list of previous mappings, assuming you've made this connection before. Then select or choose the disk letter you want to assign to this folder or remote drive.

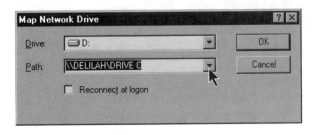

When you OK this box, you'll have a new disk-drive letter to choose from when you open or save a document from any application. Here's what happened when I mapped Delilah's drive C to my local drive D:

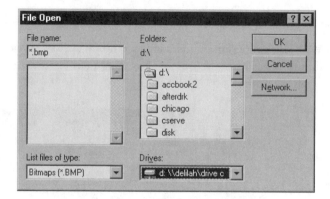

NOTE

Now even Explorer and My Computer will show the newly mapped drive as a "network" drive D until it is disconnected as explained below.

Mapping a Drive from Explorer—The Easy Way

The approach explained above is necessary at times, and it's handy because many File dialog boxes in 3.x applications have a Network button right there. But it's sometimes a hassle to remember the network path name of a particular folder and to enter it. Notice above that the path name syntax is \\computer name\path. In a complex path name there are a lot of slashes to enter and potential for typos. Also, there's no Browse button to let you cruise the network and find a folder to map.

Opening Network Neighborhood from the Desktop or Explorer makes mapping a network drive much simpler.

1. Open Network Neighborhood.

2. Browse to the folder you want to map.

3. Right-click on it and choose Map Network Drive (or click on the Map Network Drive button in the Toolbar).

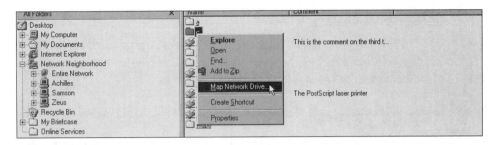

4. Choose the drive letter.

5. Click on Reconnect at Logon if you want to always have this mapping made when you boot up your computer. Of course, the remote workstation will have to be running when you boot up for this to work properly, but it won't harm anything if it isn't. You just won't have access to the drive.

NOTE

If the folder you're trying to connect to is password protected, you'll be prompted to enter a password.

Now you'll have an additional icon in Explorer and in your My Computer folder, representing the new drive letter. For example:

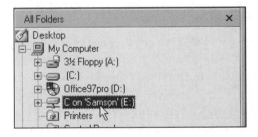

Network drives have their own style of icon, similar to the hard-disk icon but with a network cable attached. Not that it will behave as a local drive would. For example, open its Properties box to see how much free space is left on it.

TIP

For easy Mapping and Unmapping of network drives, you can add two buttons to the toolbar. From Explorer (or any folder window) choose View ➢ Folder options. Click the View tab. Turn on the network drive mapping button option.

Disconnecting from a Network Drive or Folder

When you're through with a mapped network drive, you'll probably want to disconnect from it. There's no sense in staying connected unless you regularly use the drive and expect to always have the setup available.

WARNING

On a client-server network, connections are usually permanent; so you should not attempt to disconnect without checking with your administrator.

Use the following steps to disconnect a network drive:

1. Click on the mapped networked drive either from My Computer or Explorer.

2. If the network drive buttons are displayed on your toolbar, click on Disconnect.

If buttons aren't there, choose Tools ➤ Disconnect Network Drive, or right-click and choose the same.

If you currently have any files open on the mapped drive, attempting to disconnect will result in a warning. Make sure you're not running a program, editing a file, or otherwise accessing the mapped drive that you're about to disconnect. If you get such a warning, cancel the box, close any suspicious programs or documents, and try again. In my experience, this warning can actually be erroneously triggered (i.e., when no files are open). As long as you know you're not going to lose data, go ahead and disconnect.

Sharing Folders and Drives

You can share drives and folders on the network for others to use. Before other workgroup members can use your files, though, you have to share the drive or directory containing them. Shared items can have passwords, and they also can have specific privileges (read-only or read-write). If you have a bunch of files that you want people to be able to see but not alter, just put them into a new folder and share it as read-only.

If you want only specific people to be able to alter the files, share them protected by a password. Take the following steps to share your drives and folders.

NOTE

Again, if your network has an administrator, that person is probably responsible for setting and maintaining access rights to network resources.

1. In My Computer or Explorer, right-click on the folder or drive you want to share.

WARNING

Because sharing a hard disk itself (from the root level) allows network users into all directories on the disk, doing so can be dangerous. Clicking on a disk icon in the Explorer or My Computer and sharing it is certainly the easiest way to share all files and folders on your computer. However, it allows any connected user to alter or erase everything you have on your hard disk. Your only defenses are to share files and folders with password protection or marked "read only" via their Properties box.

2. Choose Sharing. A dialog box appears, as shown in Figure 12.9. Click on Shared As.

FIGURE 12.9

To share a folder or drive, just click on Shared As and OK the box.

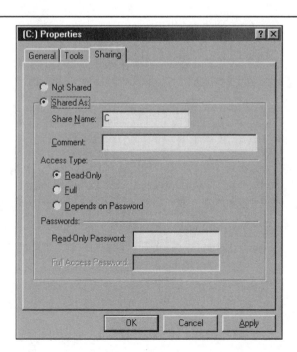

3. You don't have to do anything other than click on OK. The icon of the folder or drive will change to include a little hand under it, a suggestion of sharing.

The other options in the dialog box provide better detailed control of how the object is shared:

- The Share Name is, by default, the same name as the directory itself. This should be limited to a DOS 8.3-character name if others on the network will be using an operating system that doesn't display long file names, such as Windows 3.11 or DOS.

Even if you choose to limit the Share Name to the DOS 8.3 file-naming convention, you might want to elaborate on the directory name a bit. For example, while still conforming to DOS file-naming conventions (spaces and some characters are illegal), you could lengthen Reports to Reports.98.

- You can add a comment line that network users will see, perhaps explaining who the file is for or what is in the shared folder. This will show up when someone checks out your computer in Network Neighborhood or Explorer in the Details view. This line can be approximately 50 characters long and include spaces and punctuation.

- Next, you have the option of setting specific permissions to restrict the use of the directory by others.

If you don't manually set the permissions, although anyone can access the directory, nobody will be able to edit the files in it or make other changes that an application might require, such as recording changes to a style sheet or creating a temp file in the directory. If you are sharing a folder that has applications in it for use by workers on the net, this could cause a problem. Consider carefully whether you should share the directory with Full permission to prevent potential application or document problems.

Set the Access Type by clicking on the appropriate button. You have three choices:

Read: Enables viewing file names, copying information, running applications in the directory, and opening document files.

Full: All permissions listed above, plus the ability to delete files, move files, edit files, and create new subdirectories.

Depends on Password: The type of access will be determined by which password option is chosen and which password is entered by the person attempting to use the disk or folder.

WARNING

Be careful not to share directories that have subdirectories unless you want those to become accessible with the same level of restriction. A user has the same rights to all the subdirectories as they have to the shared parent directory.

- Finally, there are the password settings:

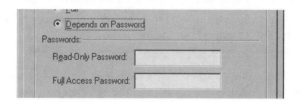

With Read-Only or Full selected, you can enter a password in the appropriate spot. Anyone trying to use the folder will be prompted to enter a password. If you choose the Depends on Password option, the level of access the remote user is granted (Read-only or Full) is determined by the password he or she enters.

NOTE

Access to shared objects can be further controlled from the Network applet in the Control Panel. Using this applet, you can control whether access is granted on a user-by-user basis or on a group basis. Group access control is discussed in Part V of this book.

Changing a Share's Properties

You can change permissions or other settings pertaining to the share after the fact, if necessary. For example, you might decide to limit the number of people who use the shared folder by requiring passwords to be entered. You might want to change the passwords on a regular basis to ensure security. Or you might decide to stop sharing a folder altogether.

1. Right-click on the directory or disk in Explorer or My Computer's File Manager and choose Sharing.

2. The Share dialog box that appears, letting you make changes, is the same one that appeared when you originally shared the directory.

3. Click on Not Shared to stop sharing the object. If workgroup users are currently connected to the directory, you see a message indicating this and warning you against terminating the share. If you really want to terminate, click on Yes, but be aware that other users might lose their data—particularly if the dialog box indicates that files are open. Closing a shared directory like this is a great way to lose friends, so normally you would click on No, get the other user to sign off from your directory, and then try again later.

You might want to contact users of the directory to alert them of your intention to remove the drive from the network.

If you want to know what's really going on with a directory (that is, who's using it and whether files are open), run the NetWatcher program found in the Programs ➢ Accessories ➢ System Tools folder. This program isn't installed by default, so you might have to load it from your master Windows 98 disk(s). This is covered in Chapter 23.

Working with Other Objects in Explorer

As I mentioned at the top of this chapter, Explorer has many talents. You can explore and set properties not only for files, folders, and disks, but also for printers, the Control Panel, the Recycle Bin, Dial-Up Networking, and Briefcase. Try experimenting with each of these objects by clicking on them. You'll find most of them at the bottom of the Explorer's tree in the left pane. As you'd expect, the Explorer simply provides another view of these items, even though functionally the effect is no different from working with them in ways discussed elsewhere in this book. For example, Figure 12.10 shows the result of clicking on the Control Panel. You can run the Control Panel applets from the right pane by double-clicking as usual.

Another notable addition to Windows 98's Explorer is its ability to view Web pages. There are numerous ways you can do this. If Internet Explorer is installed, it is listed in the left pane along with your drives and Network Neighborhood. Just click on it and, if you're connected to the Internet (see Part III), you may be surprised by what you get. The Microsoft home page (or whatever home page you have chosen in Internet Explorer) will appear, as shown in Figure 12.11.

FIGURE 12.10

Other computer-
related objects such
as the Control Panel
can be accessed via
Explorer, too.

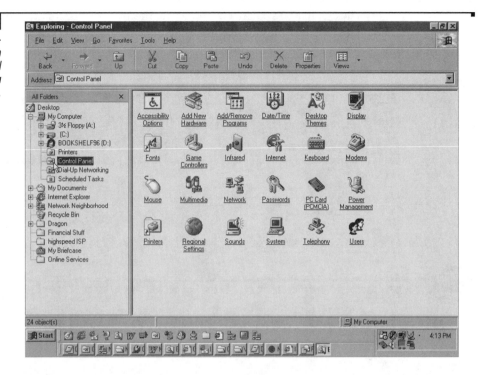

FIGURE 12.11

Internet Explorer is
integrated into
Windows Explorer.

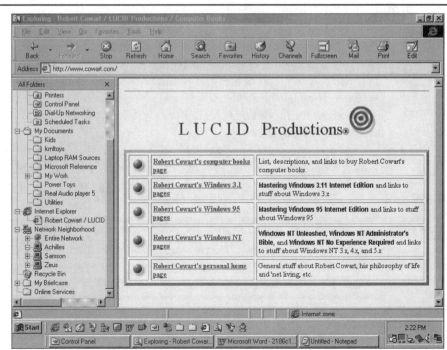

Just click on it, and you are now browsing the Web. Notice that the toolbar and menus change a bit. You can now use the Address bar to enter Web addresses, and change the left pane's contents (also called the *Explorer bar*) via the toolbar buttons (Search, Favorites, History, Channels) or by the View ➢ Explorer Bar menu choices.

 **TIP**

To stop Web browsing and get back to the normal folders and files view in Explorer, choose View ➢ Explorer Bar ➢ All Folders. Then click on a folder in the left pane.

Preview and Thumbnails View

A nifty new feature of Windows Explorer is that it can give you a little preview of certain types of files without having to actually open the file in a program. This is especially useful with graphics files and HTML (Web) pages. Sound and video files can be previewed as well. When a file's format can't be displayed, you'll at least see some information about the file or folder. All this is activated only if you've set the right pane to display as a Web page.

There are two levels of previewing in this manner: previewing a single file, or previewing a whole mess of them at once in a screenful of "thumbnails." Other programs offer this feature, but now it's integrated into the Explorer.

 NOTE

Incidentally, this preview option is also available when using the My Computer folders view rather than in Windows Explorer. Just make sure the View as Web Page option is on for the folder.

Let's start with the preview of a single file:

1. Choose View ➢ As Web Page. A middle pane now appears, displaying some additional info.

2. Choose different directories and notice how they display. If you choose Control Panel, you'll see some useful information about it. I've chosen a directory where I store Web pages, since it may have a .gif file I am looking for.

3. Highlight the file you hope to see previewed. Figure 12.12 shows an example, with the preview to the left of it:

FIGURE 12.12

Using the As Web Page view in Explorer.

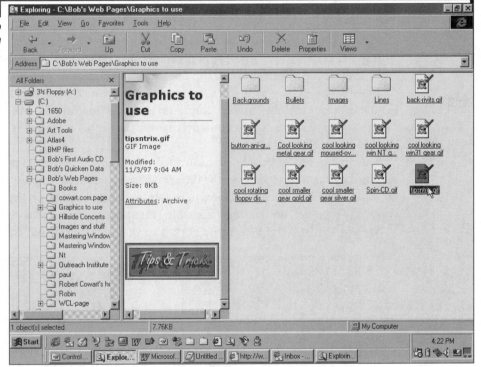

If the file were a sound, then you'd see a preview display like this:

PART
II

Exploring Windows 98

You can click on the Play button here to hear the sound. The "Release this file" link lets the file be used by another program, since as long as the preview is showing, the sound file is actually loaded into the multimedia player program and will be locked, preventing use by other programs. You can click on the Attributes link to see or set the properties for the file (hidden, read-only, archive, or system).

Other files will display in other forms. Sometimes you'll only see text describing the file, the author of the file (in the case of Microsoft Word), the date of creation, or the size of the file.

That's the first step of previewing. Now for the best part: Thumbnails.

Enabling Thumbnail View

Typically, people store files of like kind in the same folder. For example, I have a folder with lots of graphics in it. Another of my folders has HTML files I'm designing for the Web. Another has screen shots for this book. It is sometimes very useful to see a listing of these files in such a way that it's immediately clear which file is which, not requiring me to open each one and say "Nope, not that one" repeatedly, until I find the one I want. A graphical view of the contents of every file (rather than one at a time) *is* possible, using the Thumbnails view.

You can turn on the thumbnails feature for individual folders, but it's normally turned off, since it takes time to generate the thumbnail views, and it uses up disk space. To turn on thumbnails for a folder, you have to enable it by right-clicking on the folder's icon, choosing Properties, and setting the Enable Thumbnails option on, as in Figure 12.13.

Now the toolbar's and View menu's options will have a new friend: Thumbnails:

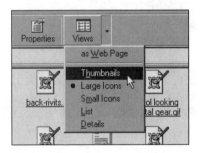 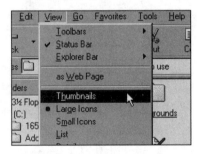

Now if you explore the folder with this view chosen, you'll see something like Figure 12.14.

FIGURE 12.13

*Enabling Thumb-
nails via a folder's
property sheet.*

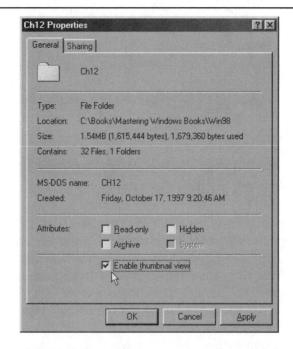

FIGURE 12.14

*A typical Thumb-
nails view of a
folder that contains
lots of graphics.*

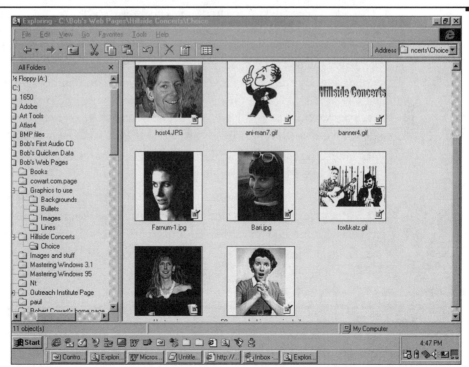

If your folder contains lots of graphics, it may take some time for Explorer to generate the little thumbnail pictures. It actually looks at each file, determines whether it can present a thumbnail image, and does its best to do so. The results are stored in a file called `thumbs.db` in the same folder. The file can be fairly large if you have lots of images in the folder. You may have to refresh the view (press F5) to enable the view the first time.

For nongraphic files or folders, you'll just see a little folder or icon in the thumbnail. An HTML page will display as a thumbnail version of the Web page it represents, assuming the graphics and other linked files it needs are available in the directories the links point to.

Customizing a Folder

As mentioned in Chapter 1, to take advantage of the Web and thumbnail views, you can customize individual folders in Windows 98 using HTML programming code. You essentially create a Web page that is used by Explorer to display your files and stuff. What, you're not a programmer? No problem. Later in this book we'll show you how to use FrontPad, a lightweight HTML editor, to create Web pages for the Internet as well as for displaying stuff on your Active Desktop and in Explorer folders.

Explorer actually uses a basic HTML template to display your files in thumbnails and Web view previews. When you choose "Display as Web page" for a folder, the default HTML code is generated for the folder, and goes into effect. That's how the little cloud image on the left of the display comes up, and the size and other aspects of the selected file(s) and folder(s) manage to appear.

Even without any HTML programming know-how, you can do some customizing of any folder on your disks. It's easy, since there is a wizard that does it for you. You just make a few selections about the color of the background, and perhaps a background image you want to use. It's like setting the color and wallpaper on the desktop, only it applies to a folder. Each file can have its own settings, too. Here's how you do it:

1. Get to the folder you want to customize, either using Explorer or a standard folder (e.g. from My Computer).

2. Choose View ➤ Customize this folder. You'll see the dialog box in Figure 12.15.

3. Click on the second option and then click on Next. In the next box, choose a background image. Browse around to other folders and drives if you need to.

4. You'll also have the option of choosing the color for text under the icons as well as an optional color for the background little square of background *behind* each icon.

NOTE

Setting a background color is a good idea if you choose a dark picture for the folder's background and want dark colored text; otherwise the icons' descriptions sort of disappear.

FIGURE 12.15

*Creating a custom
look for a folder's
display*

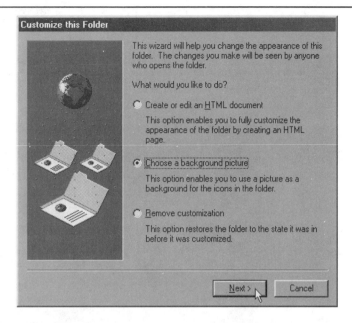

Figure 12.16 shows the choices I made and the effects after I finished. Notice I used a light background for the icons and a dark colored text. I could have used no background color and white text.

FIGURE 12.16

*The results of a cus-
tom background.*

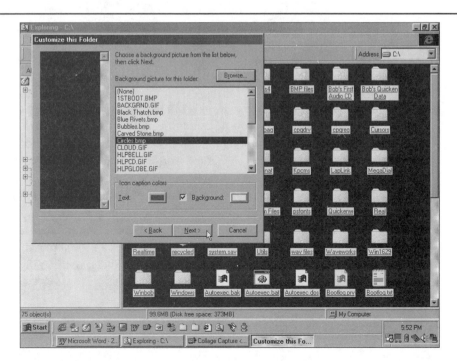

5. Click on Finish and the custom look is made for you. It will be applied to both folder and Explorer views as long as the Display as Web page setting is active from the View menu or button.

When/if you want to eliminate the special look for a folder, run the wizard again and choose Remove Customization:

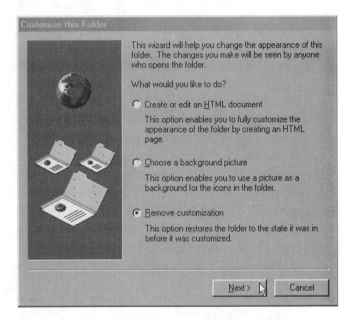

Keep Experimenting with Windows Explorer

In summary, there is much to learn about using Explorer. It's quite powerful, and offers you a sort of bird's-eye view of your entire computer. Don't be afraid to experiment with its many features, and try poking around to look at things, from the Recycle Bin to Web pages on the other side of the world. If you use the Web, be sure to check out the Search, Favorites, History, and Channel options. We'll talk more about these in the Internet part of the book, but in the meantime, take a few minutes to see what happens when you choose the options.

And remember to be careful about dragging things around, particularly folders. I have a touchpad on my laptop, and as I said earlier, a little slip of the finger and I've dragged a folder accidentally onto a neighboring folder. Get friendly with the Undo command!

Remember also that you can run programs by clicking on them from Explorer, and you can open any registered file types, such as Word files or graphics files. Typically, TIF, JPG, and GIF files will open in the Internet Explorer window; HTML files that you might save from the Web will open in an IE window as well. Any .TXT files will open in Notepad. You'll get the idea if you just experiment.

If, on the other hand, you just want to get your work done without learning all the ins and outs of your computer, that's cool too. I would suggest that you continue to use the folder system from My Computer, if that's how you like to work. It's a little less powerful, but it's also a little less distracting.

PART III

Communications and Using the Internet with Windows 98

CHAPTERS:

13. Introduction to Windows Communications

14. Communicating Using HyperTerminal

15. Getting Connected to the Internet

16. Browsing the World Wide Web with Internet Explorer 4

17. Communicating with Outlook Express News and Mail

18. Using the Active Desktop and Tuning In to Channels

19. Using NetMeeting

Chapter

13

Introduction to Windows Communications

FEATURING

What's new in Windows 98 communications

The Windows Telephony Interface

Installing a modem

Introduction to Windows Communications

A few years ago when people bought a new computer, they only planned to do things like word processing, financial record keeping, maybe financial analysis, and of course play some games on it. They'd tap information into the keyboard, the computer would do its thing, and after a while, it would print the result on a piece of paper or display it on the screen. PCs were typically stand-alone devices, not connected to any other computers. If you needed to exchange data with somebody else, you could use a floppy disk to move files from one machine to the other (a technique sometimes called "sneakernet").

But when you start connecting them together, stand-alone computers become extremely flexible communications tools. Relatively early in the development of computer technology, people figured out that it wasn't particularly difficult to transfer information through a wire from one computer to another. As long as the computers on both ends use the same technical standards, you can move messages, programs, text, video, audio and other data files back and forth. And when you connect a *lot* of computers together through a network, you can communicate with any other computer on the same network, just as you can reach any other telephone connected to the global telecommunications system from the phone on your desk.

Under the broad category of "communications," your PC can send and receive text, program files, sounds, and images. It can also exchange images of fax pages with a distant fax machine. This data can enter and leave your PC through a modem, a network interface card, or a direct cable connection to another computer.

Communications capability has been part of DOS and Windows since the earliest IBM PCs. Windows 98 pushes the limits of today's technology and now includes an extensive set of communications tools that allow you to exchange electronic mail with other computers, look at potentially millions of Web sites, even use your computer to make international video and audio phone calls for free. This chapter introduces the communications features of Windows 98 and tells you how to configure Windows to work with your modem, making it all possible. Once your modem is installed and configured, then you can find more specific information about communications applications such as Hyperterminal, Outlook Exchange (for e-mail and newsgroups), Internet Explorer (for browsing the Web), and NetMeeting (for video and audio conferencing) in the subsequent chapters.

NOTE

Another avenue of communications, TV viewing, has now been integrated into Windows 98 with the TV Viewer application, if you have the correct hardware. Chapter 10 covers TV Viewer as one of Windows 98's multimedia features.

What's New in Windows 98 Communications?

Windows 98 includes some major improvements over the way Windows 3.*x* handled communications and a few over what was bundled in Windows 95. Let's look at Windows 3.*x* first. Windows 98 is a lot happier about sending and receiving data at high speeds, transferring data in the background doesn't interfere with other applications, and you don't have to shut down a program that waits for incoming messages or faxes before you try to use the same modem to place an outgoing call. In addition, Microsoft has replaced the old Terminal program in Windows 3.*x* with a completely new set of applications for connecting to distant computers and for sending, receiving, and managing messages and various data forms. As the basis for many communications tasks, it incorporates a Telephony Applications Program Interface (TAPI) that integrates your PC with a telephone system. Microsoft has also included easy access to its own online information service, called the Microsoft Network, as well as to other information services such as AOL, Prodigy, AT&T WorldNet, and CompuServe. Windows 98 goes a long way toward turning your stand-alone computer into a tool that can be linked to other computers, and other communications devices anywhere in the world.

The Windows 9*x* communications suite has undergone a handful of updates, and, quite frankly, some serious revisions on the part of Microsoft. Some of these revisions have been confusing to computer professionals in the field and certainly to many average users. In Microsoft's defense, PC communications is an emerging field, a moving target. Microsoft has been almost single-handedly responsible for catalyzing the emergence of communications standards from which we will all benefit. However, often it seems Microsoft is trying to conquer the communications racket by the shotgun method, pushing too many products at us that perform the same task, or at least have overlapping functionality. The result is confusion, wasted expense and effort, and additional training overhead for private and corporate users. As this book went to press, it wasn't clear what a few of the communication details would look like when Windows 98 was released.

Let's look at a little history. The first version of Windows 95 included an e-mail and faxing system called Microsoft Exchange. In its nascent stages, it sported so many options and functions that testers couldn't even figure out how to install the program, much less use it constructively. The program took forever to load, and consumed enormous amounts of disk space. As testing progressed, features dropped out and the interface became somewhat simpler. Still, Exchange introduced new data formats for storage of e-mail (not compatible with other existing and popular e-mail programs such as Pegasus, Netscape, Eudora, and even Microsoft Mail). With the second major version of Windows 95 (OSR2), Exchange was renamed Windows Messaging. Internal fixes were made, and a few features and updates were added. In the meantime, Microsoft had released several other e-mail client programs such as Microsoft Internet Mail (bundled with Internet Explorer 3), and the upscale interface for Windows Messaging called Outlook (bundled with Microsoft Office). The neat thing about Outlook was that it could share data files with Exchange/Messaging. Thus, whether you chose to use Outlook or Messaging/Exchange, your mail, fax, and address books were up-to-date in either program. On the other hand, neither Exchange/Messaging nor Outlook have support for reading Internet "newsgroups" (special-interest bulletin boards). Microsoft has yet to provide a communications client program that does e-mail, newsgroups, *and* fax. (*Client* and *server* are terms you'll encounter frequently in discussions of the Internet and computer communications. *Client* means the software on the receiving end, such as your browser. *Server* software is used at the Internet Service Provider's end.)

Enter Windows 98. We were all expecting Windows 98 to include a newer version of Messaging, with some performance improvements and perhaps some bug fixes. But instead, the bundled e-mail client is called Outlook Express. The good news is that Outlook Express (or OE for short) is clean and simple, and works nicely. It supports

PART

III

Communications and
Using the Internet

multiple e-mail accounts *and* (this is the biggie) it's also a news reader, meaning you can use it to interact with special interest groups (called *newsgroups*) on the Internet. It also has an "Inbox assistant" that can automatically organize your incoming mail.

The bad news is that it doesn't use the same file format for e-mail that Outlook and Exchange/Messaging do. It can import mail from those programs, but really you should decide to use one program or the other. I suggest you convert over to using Outlook Express. If Microsoft is hoping you'll buy Microsoft Office and upgrade to the full Outlook product, they haven't done their homework, since Outlook (at least Outlook 97) doesn't do newsgroups.

Then there is the issue of fax. Windows 95 had built-in faxing capabilities. If you had a fax-capable modem attached to your computer, you could send and receive faxes without needing a fax machine or paper. A neat feature. As of this writing Windows 98 did not include a means for faxing. The Kodak Imaging program in the Accessories group lets you *view* faxes, but at least at this point, you'd have to purchase another fax program such as Delrina's WinFax to send and receive them.

NOTE

If you upgraded from Windows 95, and you had Exchange or Messaging installed in Windows 95, it will be pulled into Windows 98. You'll still have everything, including faxing if that was set up before.

Well, that's it in a nutshell. Don't let this cast a bleak tinge over Windows communications abilities. You can still, of course, use any popular programs you like, and in fact this discussion will be moot to you if you're a Netscape enthusiast, since you're probably already using Netscape Communicator for your mail, Web browsing, and news reading. Ditto for folks who dig Eudora, Pegasus, or the AOL tools. All these tools will work fine, and probably faster in Windows 98 since some settings that slowed down Internet data transmission to and from your computer were tweaked for Windows 98.

And in case most of this tech talk is over your head, don't worry! Once you've read the next several chapters, all these buzzwords will make perfect sense, and you'll soon be browsing the Web, communicating with your friends over e-mail, and reading newsgroups—all using the supplied tools, which are certainly adequate. Internet Explorer 4, in fact, is quite likely the best Web browser available today, and so well integrated into Windows that the Department of Justice charged Microsoft on anti-trust grounds. That's Microsoft's problem. But for you and me, at least in the meantime, it means we have some powerful communications tools to work with. Now let's get down to learning about them.

Regarding Fax and Microsoft Mail on the LAN

Because the mail client has been changed in Windows 98 to Outlook Express, several issues are raised, as discussed previously. Notably, there's the disappearance of built-in fax software. Another wrinkle regards compatibility with office e-mail on LANs (local area networks), since many LANs have mail systems based on the Microsoft Mail product.

Accessing a LAN e-mail account may still be fairly easy, depending on what you are using for your LAN e-mail. If your LAN e-mail server supports the popular Internet POP3 and SMTP standards (for example, Microsoft Exchange Server), Outlook Express can access those e-mail accounts without incident. If not, it is a little more complicated. If you are using an MS Mail Postoffice, unfortunately, accessing it from Outlook Express will not be possible. But here's an alternative. As of this writing, Microsoft promised that there will be a directory on the Windows 98 CD-ROM with MS Mail Postoffice support, the old Windows Messaging program, and MS Fax.

Since Messaging is included on the disk, you may choose to install it. Messaging is more complex than Outlook Express, doesn't read or write mail in HTML (formatted text), and doesn't give you access to Internet newsgroups. But it can be set up to use Microsoft Word as your e-mail editor (a nice feature if you have macros or other editing niceties set up), and you won't have to learn to use new e-mail client software if you're already used to it. Since coverage of Messaging is a large topic, I won't discuss it here. Look for instructions in the related directory (I don't know what it's going to be called, but it should be obvious) on the CD. For use of Messaging, if you can lay your hands on the previous edition of this book (*Mastering Windows 95*), you'll find a full discussion there.

The other advantage of Messaging, obviously, is that it has fax send and receive capabilities. It even supports fax sharing: a user on the LAN can share his or her fax modem so all workstations on the LAN can send and receive faxes from one telephone line.

The Windows Telephony Interface

Windows 98 includes a set of software "hooks" to applications that control the way your computer interacts with the telephone network. TAPI is an internal part of the Windows 9*x* operating system rather than a specific application program—it provides a standard way for software developers to access communications ports and devices such as modems and telephone sets to control data, fax, and voice calls. Using TAPI, an application can place a call, answer an incoming call, and hang up when the call is

PART

III

Communications and
Using the Internet

complete. It also supports things like hold, call transfer, voice mail, and conference calls. TAPI-compliant applications will work with conventional telephone lines, PBX and Centrex systems, and with specialized services like cellular and ISDN.

By moving these functions to a common program interface, Windows prevents two or more application programs from making conflicting demands for access to your modem and telephone line. Therefore, you no longer need to shut down a program that's waiting for incoming calls before you use a different program to send a fax.

Unless you're planning to write your own communications applications, you won't ever have to deal directly with TAPI, but you will see its benefits when you use the communications programs included in the Windows 98 package—such as HyperTerminal, Outlook Express, Phone Dialer, and Remote Access—and when you use Windows 9*x*-compatible versions of third-party communications programs such as ProComm and WinFax.

Windows 98 includes a relatively simple telephony application called Phone Dialer, but that just scratches the surface of what TAPI will support, in the same way that, say, WordPad has fewer bells and whistles than Word for Windows. Phone Dialer is much simpler than some of the other programs that will appear in the near future. Programs from some third parties based on Windows Telephony can now handle control of all your telephone activities through the Windows Desktop. For example, some let you use the telephone company's caller ID service to match incoming calls to a database that displays detailed information about the caller before you answer, or use an on-screen menu to set up advanced call features like conference calling and forwarding that now require obscure strings of digits from the telephone keypad.

Installing and Configuring a Modem

For most individuals and small businesses, the most practical way to connect is through a dial-up telephone line and a modem. *Modem* is a made-up word constructed out of *mod*ulator-*dem*odulator. A modem converts digital data from a computer into sounds that can travel through telephone lines designed for voice communication (that's the modulator part), and it also converts sounds that it receives from a telephone line to digital data (that's the demodulator part).

Choosing a Modem

For reasons of economy, convenience, or simplicity, you've decided to go with an inexpensive connection to the Internet through a modem and a telephone line. What now? If you bought your computer in the last year or two, it probably has an internal modem already. (If you're planning to buy a new computer, the following guidelines will help you find one with a modem that meets your needs.) If you don't already have a modem, go find one. There are three things to consider when you choose a modem: speed, form, and compatibility.

Modem Speed

The speed of a modem is the maximum number of data bits that can pass through the modem in one second. You might find some extremely inexpensive 9600 bps (bits per second) modems, but that's really too slow for programs like Internet Explorer. Don't waste your time or money. Anything slower than 9600 bps is most useful as a paperweight.

Today, almost all new consumer-grade modems have maximum speeds of either 33,600 bps or 56,000 bps. As a general rule, buy the fastest modem you can afford. Modem connections, even at 56,000 bps, are a lot slower than dedicated data circuits such as frame relay. But a fast modem is good enough for many users, especially because most households and offices already have at least one telephone line, so there's no added expense for running new cabling to your house or business from the phone company switching office.

Modem Form

Modems come in three forms: internal, external, and on a credit-card size PCMCIA card (also known as a PC Card). Each type has specific advantages and disadvantages.

- Internal modems are expansion cards that fit inside your PC. They're the least expensive type of modem, and they don't require special data cables or power supplies. However, they're a nuisance to install, and they don't include the status lights that show the progress of your calls.

- External modems are separate, self-contained units that are easy to install and move between computers. They cost more than internal modems, and they need a separate AC power outlet. In order to use an external modem, your computer must have an unused serial (COM) connector. Make sure you have an unused COM port before you purchase an external modem, or find a device that lets you share a COM port with two or more external devices. (Typically this device will be in the form of a switch box with a dial on the front of it.)

- PC Cards are small, lightweight devices that fit into the PCMCIA slots on many laptop computers. They're the most convenient modems for people who travel with their PCs, but they're also the most expensive. Some have cell-phone connectors on them. If you have a cell phone and want to send and receive data through it, make sure you get a card that is guaranteed to work with your brand and model of phone! Some cards even come with the cable for your phone already in the box.

PART

III

Communications and
Using the Internet

Cell phones connected to PCMCIA modems must be set to run in "analog" mode, and in the best of circumstances you will only get 9600 bps throughput because of limitations in the cellular technology.

Modem Compatibility

The third thing to consider when you choose a modem is compatibility with standards. In order to connect your computer to a distant system, the modems at both ends of the link must use the same methods for encoding and compressing data. Therefore, you should use a modem that follows the international standards for data communication. The important standard for 28,800 bps modems is called V.34; the standard for slower modems is V.32bis. Don't even consider a modem that doesn't follow one of these standards. Some newer modems are boasting that they are twice as fast as the competition, but if the Internet Service Provider (ISP) you are considering doesn't support that kind of modem, there will be no advantage to using such a modem. If you do purchase a 56K modem, make sure your ISP uses the same format (X2 and 56K Flex are competing standards and are currently incompatible), find out if they charge extra for you to connect at that speed, and check whether there is a local or toll-free number for the 56K access.

After you physically connect the modem to your computer, you must also notify the operating system that there's a new modem in place. It also can be advantageous to alert Windows 98 to the type of modem you have, since some modems have special properties, such as the ability to compress data before sending it, to effectively increase the speed of transmission. Telling Windows what kind of modem you have can help ensure that these options are optimally used.

Installing a Modem into Windows 98

Every time you installed a new communications application in Windows 3.*x*, you had to go through another configuration routine—you had to specify the port connected to your modem, the highest speed the modem could handle, and so forth. Because there was no central modem control, each program required its own setup.

This changed in Windows 95 and carries into 98, because they use a *universal modem* driver called *Unimodem*. Unimodem is the software interface between all of your computer's 32-bit Windows 9*x*-compatible communications applications (including the ones that use TAPI) and your modem or other communications hardware. It includes integrated control for port selection, modem initialization, speed, file-transfer protocols, and terminal emulation. The modem configuration is handled by Unimodem, so you only have to specify setup parameters once.

If you're using third-party communications applications left over from earlier versions of Windows, they'll work with Windows 98, but you'll still have to configure them separately. When you replace them with newer, Windows 98-compatible updates, they'll use the settings already defined in Windows.

If your modem follows the Plug and Play (PnP) specification, Windows 98 should automatically detect it when you turn on your computer, assuming the modem is connected and turned on at the time. If you have a PCMCIA (credit-card style) modem, simply inserting the card, even while the computer is on, should result in Windows detecting it and loading the appropriate software driver (consult the manual that comes with the modem).

However, if you're using an older modem ("older" means anything that was made before late 1995 and isn't PnP-aware), you may need to add it to the configuration manually, by following these steps:

1. Click Start ➢ Settings ➢ Control Panel.

2. When the Control Panel window opens, open the Modems applet. The Modems Properties dialog box, shown in Figure 13.1, will appear.

FIGURE 13.1

The Modems Properties dialog box identifies the modem currently installed in your system.

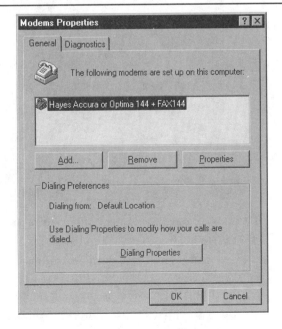

Communications and
Using the Internet

3. If Windows 98 has already detected your modem, its name will appear in the Modems Properties dialog box.

- If the correct modem is already listed, you can close the dialog box now—skip to step 6.

- If there is no modem listed, or if the name on the list does not match the modem you want to use, click on the Add button to run the Install New Modem wizard.

4. The wizard now runs, and asks you if you have a PCMCIA modem or "Other," which means an internal (card you had to install) or external modem connected by a cable. Choose an option and click Next.

- If you chose PCMCIA you are instructed to insert the modem.

- If you chose Other, you can let the wizard look for a modem or you can specify it yourself. Let it look around first. The wizard will look for a modem on each of your COM ports. If it fails to find a modem, it will ask you to specify the make and model and the port to which the modem is connected.

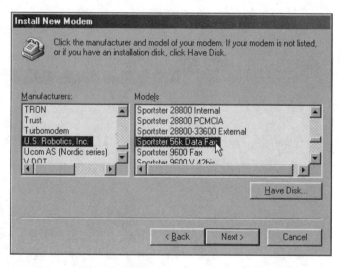

If it finds a modem, but does not recognize the make and model, it will use one of the Standard Modem Types options.

- If your modem came with a Windows 9*x* installation diskette, put the diskette in your computer's drive and click on the Have Disk button to load the configuration software for your modem.

- If you don't have a disk, don't worry about it; the Standard Modem Types settings will almost certainly work just fine.

5. When the wizard completes the installation, it will return you to the Modems Properties dialog box, which should now include the modem you just installed in the list of modems.

6. Click on the Close button and close the Control Panel to complete the installation.

NOTE

If the list shows more than one modem, you can select the ones you're not using and click on the Remove button, but it's not really necessary; Windows 98 will identify the active modem every time you turn on your computer. I have two or three modems installed in my system, and use different ones with different programs, phone lines, and COM ports. When you create your dial-up-networking (DUN) settings for accessing services such as an ISP, at that time you'll get to stipulate which modem you want to use for that connection.

TIP

Windows 98 supports the use of multiple modems simultaneously (for higher throughput), which is a feature called *modem aggregation*—ganging up modems to increase the speed of your connection. This is a little tricky and requires multiple phone lines and multiple ISP accounts to work, as well as an ISP that supports synchronization of multiple modems.

Changing Modem Properties

Once you've installed your modem, all of your Windows 98 communications programs will use the same configuration settings. When you change them in one application, those changes will carry across to all the others. In general, you won't want to change the default modem properties, which specify things like the loudness of the modem's speaker and the maximum data-transfer speed. If you replace your modem, or if you use different modem types in different locations, you can install an additional modem from the Control Panel.

To change the modem properties after installation is complete, open the Control Panel and double-click on the Modems icon. When the Modems Properties dialog box appears, select the modem and click on the Properties button to display the dialog box in Figure 13.2.

PART

III

Communications and
Using the Internet

FIGURE 13.2

Use this Properties dialog box to change your modem configuration.

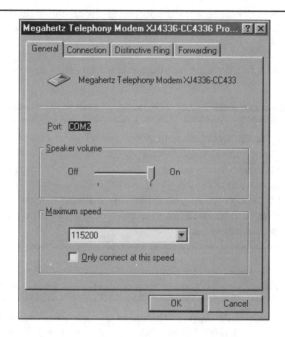

General Properties

The General tab has three settings:

Port   Use the drop-down Port menu to specify the COM port to which your modem is connected. If you don't have a drop-down list box, there is no choice of port. This will be the case for PCMCIA modems.

Speaker Volume   The Speaker Volume control is a slide setting that sets the loudness of the speaker inside your modem. In some cases, you will only have Off and On as options, rather than a variable speaker volume.

Maximum Speed   When your modem makes a connection, it will try to use the maximum speed to exchange data with the modem at the other end of the link. As a rule, if you have a 9,600 bits-per-second (bps) or faster modem, the maximum speed should be three or four times the rated modem speed (e.g., set your modem speed to 38400) to take advantage of the modem's built-in data compression.

If you don't want to accept a slower connection, check *Only connect at this speed*.

Connection Properties

Choose the Connection tab to display the dialog box in Figure 13.3.

FIGURE 13.3

Use the Connection dialog box to change communication parameters.

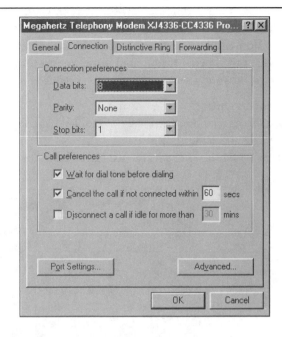

The Connection dialog box has several options:

Connection Preferences   The Data bits, Parity, and Stop bits settings must be the same at both ends of a data link. The most common settings are 8 data bits, no parity, and one stop bit.

Call Preferences   The three *Call preferences* options control the way your modem handles individual calls. Place a checkmark in each box if you want to use that option.

Port Settings   Clicking on this button brings up the Advanced Port Settings dialog box.

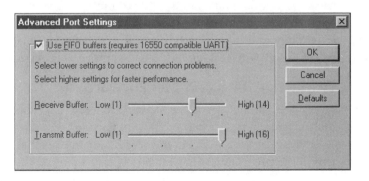

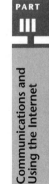

PART

III

Communications and
Using the Internet

These settings determine how the incoming and outgoing data are buffered (lined up in the queue during transmission), and should probably be left alone unless you have information from your ISP or modem manufacturer to the contrary. If you do experiment, and your throughput drops, return to this screen and click on Defaults to set the sliders and checkbox back to the original suggested settings.

Advanced Options The Advanced Connection Settings are options that you will probably set once and then leave alone. They manage error control, flow control, and additional special settings.

Figure 13.4 shows the Advanced Connection Settings dialog box.

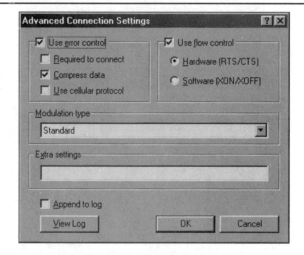

The *Extra settings* section is a place to send additional AT commands to your modem. In most cases, you won't need to add any special commands. Because different modem manufacturers use slightly different command sets, you'll have to consult your modem manual for specific commands. If you are using a cellular phone with the modem, set the *Use cellular protocol* option on. Cell phones use special data error compression and correction protocols to increase connection speed. The modem will still work with this off, but it may improve the connection if turned on.

Distinctive Ring and Call Forwarding

The two remaining tabs on the Modem Properties box let you set up features that your modem and phone line may or may not have.

Distinctive ring is a service from your phone company that provides different ring patterns for different kinds of incoming calls. Depending on the kind of modem you have, you can have between three and six numbers, or addresses, for one telephone line. Each number can have a distinctive ring pattern. You can also assign each ring pattern to a specific type of program. For example, if you have two rings assigned for fax calls, any call received with that ring pattern could be automatically sent to your fax program. Some phone companies have distinctive ring patterns based on the duration of the ring rather than the number of rings. Some modems support this scenario. In general, choose the desired number of rings for each kind of incoming call based on settings you get from your phone company. Then check your modem's manual for details on using this feature. You'll have to enable the distinctive ring feature first by clicking on the checkbox before you can alter the ring settings.

Use the second tab to tell the computer that your modem line has call forwarding installed. For instructions on how to forward calls from your telephone, contact your phone company. Call forwarding is useful if you are away from your computer and want to receive calls at a different number. The computer can actually activate the call forwarding feature and pass on an incoming data or fax call to another phone number that you specify. Activate the feature with the checkbox, and enter the necessary codes, supplied by your phone company.

Diagnostic Properties

Click on the Diagnostics tab back in the original Properties for Modems dialog box to display the dialog box in Figure 13.5. The Diagnostics dialog box identifies the devices connected to each of your COM ports.

FIGURE 13.5

Click on the Diagnostics tab to see the devices connected to your COM ports.

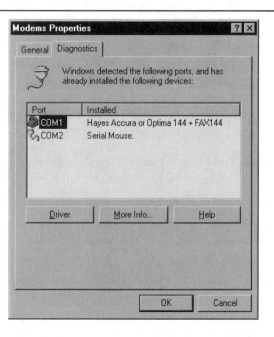

PART

III

Communications and
Using the Internet

Click on the Driver button to see information about the Windows communications driver program. Highlight a COM port and click on the More Info button to display the information in Figure 13.6. This information can be extremely useful when you are trying to configure additional communications devices.

The More Info window shows detailed information about COM port and modem configuration.

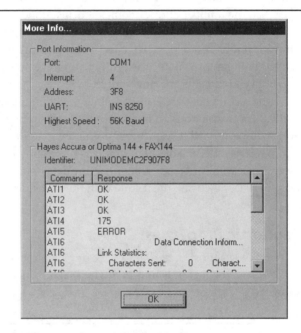

Dialing Properties

If you're using a portable computer, you may need to change the information about your location. You can open the Dialing Properties dialog box in Figure 13.7 from the General tab of the modem's property sheet or from most Windows 98 communications programs.

The Dialing Properties dialog box includes these fields:

I Am Dialing From   This field specifies the name of each configuration set. To create a new configuration, use the New button and type a name in the Create New Location dialog box.

The Area Code Is   Type your own area code in this field.

FIGURE 13.7

*The Dialing Prop-
erties dialog box
controls the way
communications
programs place
telephone calls.*

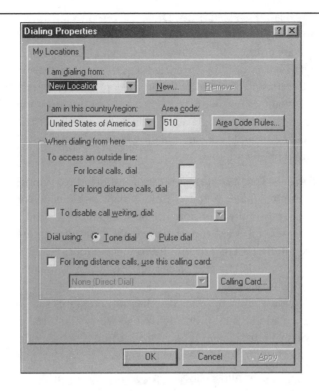

I Am in This Country/Region   This field contains a drop-down menu that lists the international dialing codes for most countries of the world. Choose the name of the country from which you will be originating calls. The United States, Canada, and many Caribbean countries all use the same Country Code.

The Area Code Rules button lets you set details about use of an area code, specifically the use of the "1" prefix for certain exchanges. If you have to dial 1 (but no area code) for certain areas, you can add those prefixes.

When Dialing from Here   If your modem line is in an office where you must dial **9** for an outside line or some other code for long distance, type those numbers in these fields. If you have a direct outside line, leave these fields blank.

NOTE

The only time you will need to use the *For long distance calls, dial* field is when your modem is connected to a PBX or other telephone system that uses a special code for toll calls. Do not use this field for the "1" prefix that you dial before long-distance calls. The dialer will add that code automatically.

PART

III

Communications and
Using the Internet

To Disable Call Waiting, Dial   If your phone service has call waiting, this can be a nuisance and cause your data connection to fail when a phone call comes in while you are online. Most call waiting services let you turn off the service for the duration of the current call by entering *70, 70#, or 1170 before making the call. If you have call waiting, you should turn on this option and enter the code your phone company tells you, or choose the correct code from the drop-down list. Often your local telephone directory will have the necessary code listed. The comma after the code causes a 1- or 2-second pause after dialing the special code, often necessary before dialing the actual phone number.

Tone vs. Pulse Dialing   Most push-button telephones use tone dialing (known in the United States as Touch-Tone™ dialing). However, older dial telephones and some cheap push-button phones use pulse signaling instead. Tone dialing is more efficient because it takes less time. Chances are, your telephone line will accept tone dialing even if there's a dial telephone connected to it. Therefore, you should go ahead and select Tone dialing and place a test call to see it if works. If it doesn't, choose Pulse dialing instead.

Because all Windows 95 application programs use the same modem-configuration information, you'll probably have to worry about the stuff in this section only once, when you install your modem for the first time. After that, TAPI uses the existing information when you load a new program.

Dial Using Calling Card   This section of the dialog box deals with automatic billing to a calling card (a telephone company credit card) when traveling. Of course, in many urban areas, calls to an ISP are local. If your ISP has many points of presence (has local dial-up numbers all over the country), these settings can be skipped. But if your ISP doesn't have a local number, and you're traveling with a laptop and accessing your ISP out of the area, you might want to bill to your calling card.

To pay for a call with a calling card you must dial a special string of numbers that includes a carrier access code, your account number, and the number you're calling. In some cases, you have to call a service provider, enter your account number, and wait for a second dial tone before you can actually enter the number you want to call.

NOTE

Calling card options have changed significantly since Windows 95. Many more options are available now.

To use your calling card, select the For Long Distance Calls Use This Calling Card option and choose the card type from the drop-down list. There are a zillion card types listed, even multiple ones for the same company, so be sure to choose the right one. You can further fine-tune the settings (such as for specifying your calling card PIN) by clicking on the Calling Card button. This brings up the Calling Card dialog box in Figure 13.8. Check the entries here. Enter your Personal ID Number (PIN) if necessary. Not all Calling Card options require it, so this option may be grayed out.

FIGURE 13.8

Use the Calling Card dialog box to specify your telephone credit card type and number.

When you choose a calling card from the menu, the program automatically uses the correct calling sequence for that long-distance carrier. But if you need a special calling sequence, click the *Long Distance Calls* or *International Calls* button and choose the sequences for long distance or international calls in the Dialing Rules dialog box. (Figure 13.9.)

To enter a specific sequence of digits, choose "Specified Digits" from the drop-down list for a given field. Then enter the digits in the resulting text box.

PART

III

Communications and
Using the Internet

Use this box for stipulating very specific dialing instructions for the use of calling cards for international and national calls. Only use this box if the presets do not work.

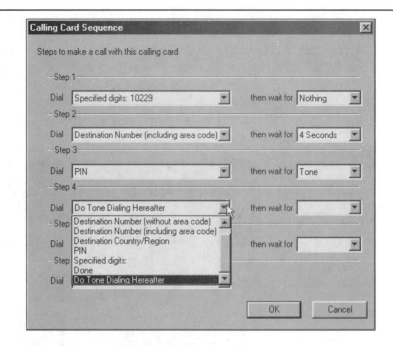

You can not only change the sequence of events, but also enter any specific numbers or other codes (see below). When you make the call, the events will progress from the top (step 1) to the bottom (step 6).

The Tone option available in the "then wait for" part of the dialog box means to wait for the "bong" tone that you hear after calling the long distance carrier. Most services require waiting for this tone before you proceed with the dialing sequence and PIN input. If the tone your carrier plays isn't detected by your modem, you may have to use a pause of a second or two instead. Try experimenting with different pause lengths. You typically are allowed a few seconds to enter the remainder of the sequence so the pause amount may not be critical as long as you have waited for the bong to sound.

If a connection isn't working, and you're fine-tuning these events, it sometimes helps to lift the receiver of a phone on the same line and listen (or turn on the modem's speaker), monitoring the sounds. You'll be better able to figure out where a sequence is bombing out.

Advanced users can, if necessary, use the following codes for variables within a calling sequence. Add these to the "specified digits" sequence. However, most of these scenarios can now be handled by the drop-down lists in the dialog box shown in Figure 13.9.

E	Country Code
F	Area Code
G	Destination Local Number
H	Calling-card number
W	Wait for second dial tone
@	Wait for a ringing tone followed by five seconds of silence
$	Wait for a calling-card prompt tone (the "bong" tone)
?	Display an on-screen prompt

For example, the default calling sequence for long-distance calls using an AT&T calling card is 102880FG$H:

10288	specifies AT&T as the long distance carrier
0	specifies a credit-card call
F	specifies the area code
G	specifies the local telephone number
$	specifies a wait for the calling-card prompt
H	specifies the calling-card number

Now that you have your modem fully configured, in the following chapters we'll explore the Windows 98 communications features of Outlook Express, Internet Explorer, Phone Dialer, FTP, Netmeeting, and more!

PART

III

Communications and
Using the Internet

Chapter

14

Communicating Using HyperTerminal

FEATURING

Setting up a HyperTerminal connection

Choosing communications settings

Sending and receiving data

Ending a communications session

Chapter

14

Communicating Using HyperTerminal

Γ

he HyperTerminal program supplied with Windows 98 lets you and your PC make contact with other computers to exchange or retrieve information. With the advent of the Internet, specialized e-mail programs, and proprietary information service programs like AOL and CompuServe, communications programs such as HyperTerminal are not as popular as they once were. But if you have a need to dial into a BBS (bulletin board system), or make a direct connection with a dial-up service of some sort, you'll definitely be glad it's included in Windows 98. With HyperTerminal and the right hookups, you can communicate with other computers whether they are in your own house, around the block, or on the other side of the world. The kinds of information you might share in this way run the gamut from electronic mail through instant stock quotes to complex document files (such as word-processing or spreadsheet documents). Or you might join an online chat group or get technical support from a computer company's bulletin board.

NOTE

You can't use HyperTerminal to cruise the Web or send e-mail. You need special Internet programs for that. Check the next few chapters for coverage of the Internet, Web browsing, and email. HyperTerminal is also probably not the program you'd use to connect to your company LAN when calling in from a remote site; for that you'll probably use Dial-Up Networking (see Chapter 28).

Working with HyperTerminal

Unlike some communications programs, HyperTerminal is document-centric. Once you create a setup for a given remote computer system, the settings are stored in a file that you can easily run again. You don't have to re-enter all the technical settings into the program to get hooked up to the remote computer. Connecting again is as simple as double-clicking on its icon in the HyperTerminal Connections folder. I'm just a click away from CompuServe, MCI Mail, or AT&T Mail, or from setting up a new account for use with another dial-up system, such as the mainframe at work.

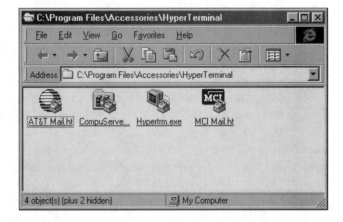

Figure 14.1 shows how the main window looks when HyperTerminal starts. Like many other Windows programs, it has a Toolbar at the top full of buttons for one-click access to common commands. At the bottom is the Status Bar, which keeps you informed of the progress of your communications session. (You can shut the Toolbar and Status Bar off if you prefer—we'll talk about that later.)

FIGURE 14.1

*The main
HyperTerminal
window*

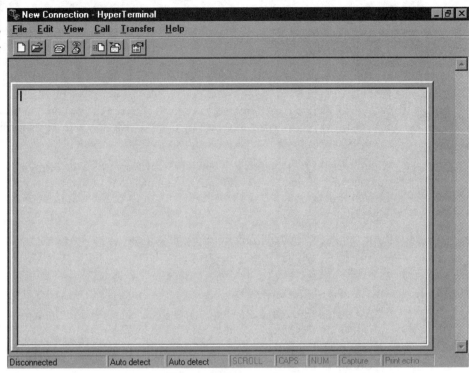

Within dialog boxes, you can click on the Help button at the upper right and then
on a button or setting of interest to get a quick help message.

NOTE

The information in this chapter is necessarily somewhat general. Because a communications program such as HyperTerminal can be used to connect to an almost endless
variety of information services and computers, it's impossible to cover all the specific
situations. What's more, each service typically has its own way of logging on, transmitting and receiving files, and so on. So, instead of demonstrating exact procedures,
I'll discuss all the aspects of the HyperTerminal program and explain the general steps
you'll need to understand to use it effectively.

PART

III

**Communications and
Using the Internet**

For Windows 3 Users

If you've upgraded to Windows 98 from Windows 3.11 and you've been relying on the Terminal program, making the transition to HyperTerminal will be easy. But before you decide to switch to HyperTerminal, you should compare the two programs to see which one really fits your needs best. You may find that sticking with Terminal makes more sense, especially if you're already very familiar with how it works.

While HyperTerminal offers a few meaty improvements over Terminal, most of the changes have to do with making your communications sessions easier and better looking. On the other hand, some of Terminal's most useful features aren't available in HyperTerminal.

If you do plan to switch to HyperTerminal, you can make the transition as efficient as possible by importing the settings from your Terminal setup (.TRM) files. To open a Terminal setup file:

1. Choose File ➢ Open.

2. At the bottom of the Select Session File dialog box, choose Terminal files from the list in the *Files of type* box.

3. Locate the Terminal file you want, select it, and click on Open. HyperTerminal reads its settings.

4. Make any necessary adjustments to the settings via the Properties dialog boxes.

5. Choose File ➢ Save As to save the settings as a HyperTerminal connection (session file).

Once you've completed these steps, you can use the new settings just as you would any other HyperTerminal connection.

Setting Up Your Communications System

In most cases, you'll be using HyperTerminal to communicate across a telephone line. You might connect to the Internet, to a commercial dial-up service such as CompuServe, Dow Jones News/Retrieval, the Source, or MCI Mail, or you might call up a friend's or colleague's computer to exchange files. The other computer can even be of a different type, such as a Macintosh.

To communicate in this way from a distance via the telephone line (as opposed to communications between computers connected directly together with a cable), you'll need a modem. A *modem* is a device that provides the electronic connection between a computer and the phone line. The modem attached to your computer converts digital information from the computer into an *analog* signal that travels over the phone line. On the other end of the line, the receiving modem does just the reverse. The word *modem* stands for *modulator/demodulator*, as the process of converting digital information to an analog signal is called modulation.

Though you can always run the HyperTerminal program to experiment with it, you can't use it over the phone line without a modem.

To connect a modem, you'll need either:

- an external modem, a cable, an unused serial port (where you plug in the cable), and an unused COM port (the electronics that permit communications at a specific computer *address*)

- *or* an internal modem installed inside your computer plus an unused COM port

In either case, the general installation procedures are similar. You install the modem, plug your telephone line into it, and run a communications program (in this case, HyperTerminal). Chapter 13 covers the installation of modems.

The main distinguishing factor among modems is the speed at which they can transfer data over the phone lines. As of this writing, modems that transmit data at speeds from 28,800 to 56,000 bits per second are the most popular, though many slower modems are still in use, and faster ones (such as DSL and cable modems) are available. (When it comes to bits-per-second ratings, the larger the number, the faster the transmission.)

NOTE

You'll sometimes see the word *baud* used as a synonym for bits per second as a rating of modem speed. Technically, the two terms aren't strictly synonymous, and you can avoid confusion by sticking with bits per second (*bps*) and kilobits per second (*Kbps*). (To make matters worse, people often leave off the abbreviation, and just mention the number; when people speak of a "28.8" modem, they're actually referring to a modem that transmits at 28.8Kbps.)

Setting Up a HyperTerminal Connection

Make sure you have your modem connected to, or installed in, your computer properly, following instructions in the modem's manual, before continuing. Incorrect modem installation (most often caused by improper switch settings) is a frequent cause of communications problems. Then, before doing anything else, find the telephone number your modem must dial to connect to the information service, BBS, or computer you're trying to reach. Be sure you have the number for modem communications—in printed material it may be labeled the *modem* or *data* number. *Voice* or *fax* numbers won't work.

While you're looking for the number, see if you can locate any details on the communications setting in force at the computer you want to connect to. Your system must be set up to match, as detailed later in this chapter.

Starting HyperTerminal

To access HyperTerminal, begin from the Start menu and choose Programs ➢ Accessories ➢ Communications ➢ HyperTerminal. This will display the contents of the HyperTerminal folder. This window will look like the one shown earlier in this chapter.

Open the HyperTerminal icon (`Hypertrm.exe`) to run the program and prepare to set up a new connection, as covered below. Once a specific connection has been set up, you'll be able to double-click on its icon to start a communications session with that connection.

Defining a New Connection

When you start from the program icon (rather than from an existing connection icon), HyperTerminal asks you to define a new connection in the dialog box shown here:

TIP

You can also set up a new connection once you're working with the main HyperTerminal window by choosing File ➢ New Connection or clicking on the New button on the Toolbar to display the above dialog box.

Your first step is to give the new connection a name. Keep it simple—something like *MCI* or *The Chem Lab* will do. Then pick out an appropriate icon for the connection from the scrolling list and click OK to go on.

Entering a Phone Number

Next you must supply the phone number your modem should dial to make the connection. HyperTerminal displays the Phone Number dialog box, shown here:

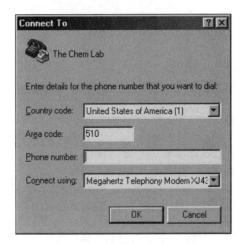

Type in the phone number for the new connection. You have your choice of styles. If the phone number for the new connection is local, that's all you have to do—Windows has already entered your settings for the country code and area code based on your current Telephony settings. If you're dialing out of the area or out of country, use the first two boxes to set the correct country and area code. And if you have more than one modem connected to your computer, choose the one you want to use for this connection from the list at the bottom of the dialog box.

Click on OK when all the settings are correct.

PART

III

Communications and
Using the Internet

Setting Dialing Properties

Once you've set the phone number, HyperTerminal assumes you want to dial it and presents you with the following dialog box:

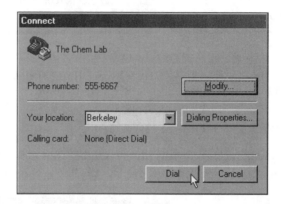

At this point, it's safe to go ahead and click on Dial to see if the setup works. But don't be too surprised if nothing happens. In many cases, you'll need to change other settings before you can connect successfully.

Take a look at the area labeled *Your location*. Here, you should select the choice that describes where you are at this moment. The first time you use HyperTerminal, the only choice available is the nondescript selection *Default location*. This corresponds to the area code and country you entered when you set up Windows itself, so if you haven't moved, it may well be correct for those items.

If you use a portable computer, however, you may be thousands of miles from your default location. And besides, there are other considerations: Do you have to dial 9 to get an outside line? Are you dialing from a customer's office, so it will be necessary to use your telephone credit card? Or are you at a friend's place who doesn't believe in high technology and never installed a push-button phone? If so, tone dialing won't work.

To change any of these properties for the default location or to set up new locations from scratch, click on Dialing Properties. For information about the dialog box and dialog properties, see Chapter 13, in the section "Installing a Modem."

Insert commas into the phone number to tell your modem to pause before moving ahead to the next digit. On Hayes-compatible modems, each comma results in a two-second pause. At least one comma is necessary when you have to dial a special number to reach an outside line. So, **9,** would be a typical entry in the boxes for accessing an outside line.

Choosing Communications Settings

Unfortunately, there are no set standards covering all aspects of the technology required for modem communications. But look on the bright side: Once you've figured out the correct settings for a given connection, HyperTerminal will remember them. From then on, all you have to do is start up the connection, and you're guaranteed success.

If you are in doubt about how to set these options, there's a simple solution. Just find out what the settings are on the computer at the other end of the line and set yours accordingly. If you can't find out what those settings are, go ahead and try the standard settings by dialing the connection and seeing if you can communicate. If that doesn't work, then start systematically altering the settings one at a time, testing for a good connection each time.

To change the communications settings, choose File ➤ Properties or click on the Properties button on the Toolbar.

You'll see the Properties dialog box showing settings for the current connection, as shown in Figure 14.2.

FIGURE 14.2

Use the Properties dialog box to change communications settings.

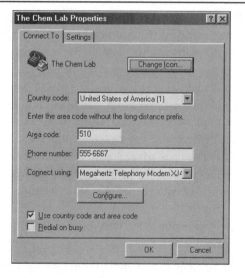

PART

III

Communications and Using the Internet

NOTE

To alter settings for another connection, you must open the Properties dialog box for that connection first. You can set the Properties for any connection from the Hyper-Terminal folder (the fast way: right-click on the connection's icon and choose Properties from the pop-up menu). Alternatively, when HyperTerminal is already running, switch to another connection by choosing File ➤ Open, selecting a pre-existing connection, and then choosing File ➤ Properties or click on the Properties button on the Toolbar.

Changes you make here apply only to the specific connection you're working with at the time. As you can see, the Properties dialog box has two tabs, one called Connect to, the other called Settings.

The settings you may need to change to connect successfully fall into the following categories:

Basic Communications   For setting the speed and format for commands and data sent between the two connected computers.

Terminal Emulation   For choosing between the types of terminals that HyperTerminal can simulate (terminals are defined below). Both the remote computer and your software must be set to the same terminal type to communicate correctly.

In addition, you can control a variety of settings that are a matter of preference, as detailed at the end of this section.

Choosing Basic Communications Settings

What I'm calling basic communications settings control the fundamental "language" of modem-to-modem communications. They determine such critical characteristics as how fast information flows between the modems, how they signal each other, and how each modem can tell one nugget of information from another.

One fundamental principle bears repeating: Most of these settings must be identical on both ends of the communications link (I'll note the exceptions as they come along). Because you probably have no control over the settings at the other end of the line, you're stuck with making sure your settings match. Actually, most connections will work without any changes—HyperTerminal's default settings are the most popular ones, in use by most of the major commercial information ser vices. But if you experience problems or if you know the other computer's settings are different, you'll need to alter the standard settings.

All the basic communications settings are controlled via the modem Properties dialog box. Access it as follows:

1. Display the Properties dialog box for the connection you're working with (Figure 14.2).

2. In the list labeled *Connect using*, choose the modem you want to use for the connection.

3. Click on the Configure button. You'll see the Properties dialog box for this particular modem, as shown in Figure 14.3.

FIGURE 14.3

The Properties dialog box for modem settings

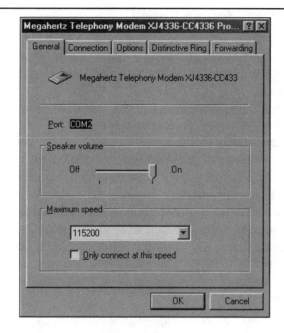

The modem Properties dialog box has five tabbed pages: General, Connection, Options, Distinctive Ring, and Forwarding.

The Port Setting

The first setting on the General page of the modem Properties dialog box is Port. Here, you tell HyperTerminal which *port* your modem is connected to. Most PCs have at least two communications ports, called COM1 and COM2. Some systems have COM3 and COM4 ports as well. Each modem is assigned to one of these ports when you first install the modem. If the port has changed, you can change the setting to match by choosing from the list here.

NOTE

There's a subtle but important distinction between the communications or COM ports, which are circuits that permit communications at a particular computer address, and the *serial* ports on the back of your computer, which are the physical receptacles into which you plug devices like external modems. Each serial port is assigned to a specific COM port. On the other hand, you may not have a serial port for every COM port—devices such as internal modems can access a COM port directly.

PART

III

Communications and Using the Internet

Setting Modem Speed

The speed at which your modem transfers information makes a big difference in how much work you can get done during a communications session. Just how fast information can travel between two modems depends on two things: the top speed of the *slower* modem and the quality of the telephone line.

In any HyperTerminal connection, the theoretical speed limit is set by the slower modem—obviously, it won't do you any good to have a super-fast modem when you're communicating with an old, slow unit. Usually, though, you don't need to know the speed of the other modem. Because most modems can sense the speed of the other modem, automatically adjusting themselves to match, you may be able to leave yours set to its maximum speed.

Note that some information services charge more for your connection time when you use a fast modem. You'll save money if you take advantage of the faster communications speed to get your work done quicker. On the other hand, if you just like to dial up and browse through the available options, you may save money at a slower speed.

To change the speed setting, display the modem Properties dialog box (shown earlier in Figure 14.3). Then:

1. In the Maximum speed area, choose the speed you want. The setting is labeled *Maximum speed* on the assumption your modem can auto-adjust to lower speeds to match its counterpart on the other end of the line. If you choose the Highest Possible option, Windows will try to connect at the fastest speed your modem and computer can handle.

2. If you're sure you don't want to connect at a slower speed than the one you've set, check the box labeled *Only connect at this speed*. This can be useful if you'd rather call back later to take advantage of a higher speed if the receiving modem is too slow at the moment. This choice is available only if your modem's auto-adjust feature can be turned off.

Specifying the Data Format Settings

Three key settings pertain to the way the two modems in a connection define and detect individual chunks of data. The two modems must agree on the same format for data, or they will speak completely different languages.

The individual data-format settings—data bits, parity, and stop bits—are described in separate paragraphs below. To change any of these settings:

1. Display the Properties dialog box for the connection you're working with (Figure 14.2).

2. In the list labeled *Connect using*, choose the modem you want to use for the connection, then click on the Configure button. In the Properties dialog box for this modem click on the Connection tab. The dialog box should now display the page shown in Figure 14.4.

FIGURE 14.4

The Connection page of the modem Properties box

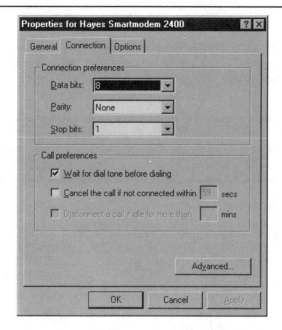

3. For each of the three settings in the *Connection preferences* area, select the choice you want from the list.

Setting Data Bits   The *Data bits* setting refers to the number of *bits* (the smallest division of computer information) you want to send out in each separate chunk of data. This setting is almost always going to be 8 and must be 8 if you are intending to transfer binary files between computers. Binary files include all programs and any documents that consist of more than plain ASCII characters. Thus, formatted word-processing documents, spreadsheets, and graphics documents are binary files. The other popular standard is 7 bits, which allows you to send plain text files slightly faster. The 4-, 5-, and 6-bit options are rarely used. Change this setting only if you are specifically told that the other system uses a setting other than 8 bits.

Setting Parity   *Parity* is a means by which the communications software can perform a rudimentary check to see if an error has occurred in the transmission of each byte of data. Parity checking isn't commonly used, and the standard setting is None. If you are specifically told that the system with which you're communicating uses parity checking, change this setting to match.

Setting Stop Bits   *Stop bits* are used by the computers on both ends to indicate the end of one character and the beginning of the next. You can probably leave this set to 1. Change this setting if you are specifically told that the other system uses 2 or 1.5 stop bits.

Special Dialing Settings Two settings control the way your modem interacts with the telephone line. You'll need to change these settings if your modem is unable to dial for you even when other settings are correct. This can happen with certain types of phone systems that have nonstandard dial tones—or no dial tone at all—or that require you to dial outside calls via the operator.

NOTE

Because they only affect your own modem, these dialing settings are an exception to the rule about matching your settings to those at the other end of the line.

The two settings are:

Wait for dial tone before dialing: This check box is located on the Connection page of the modem Properties dialog box. It's available only if Windows knows how to control your modem's ability to recognize the dial tone. The box should be checked if there's a delay before the dial tone comes on—otherwise HyperTerminal will start dialing too soon. Clear the box if the system uses a nonstandard dial tone, if there is no dial tone at all, or if you will be dialing yourself or with the operator's help.

Operator assisted or manual dial: This check box is located on the Options page of the modem Properties dialog box. Check it only if you need to dial the phone yourself or via the operator. When this box is checked, HyperTerminal displays a message telling you to dial the number after you click on Dial in the Dial dialog box:

As the message indicates, you should then dial the number (directly, or with the operator's help). When you hear the modem at the other end of the line answer, click on the Connect button and hang up the receiver.

Specifying Advanced Settings

A number of the basic communications settings are accessible in a separate window for advanced settings. These settings are perhaps more technically complex than the ones described above, but they can be just as critical to successful communications. They include:

- error-control settings
- flow-control settings
- low-speed settings
- custom-initialization commands

To access these settings, begin from the Connection page on the modem Properties dialog box (see Figure 14.4). Click on the Advanced button to display the Advanced Connection Settings dialog box, shown here.

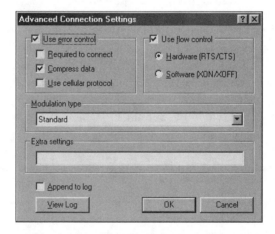

When you're through making changes to the advanced settings, click on OK to return to the modem Properties dialog box. From there, you can change other settings or click on OK again to return to HyperTerminal.

Selecting Error-Control Settings   Some modems come with built-in circuits that detect and correct errors in transmission and that *compress* data, reducing the amount of information that must be sent and, in turn, speeding up the transfer process. If your modem has these features, you can turn them on or off in the Advanced Connection Settings dialog box. Use the four check boxes in the area labeled *Use error control*.

To access any of these error-control features, you must first check the *Use error control* box. The remaining choices are:

Required to connect: Even if your modem has error-control features, you may not be able to use them for a given connection—the modem at the other end of the line may not have them or some other problem may interfere. Check this box if you don't want to proceed with a connection unless the error-control features are working. If the box is clear, HyperTerminal will go ahead and connect even if error control isn't available.

Compress data: Check this box if you want to use the data-compression feature. At each end of the connection, information is compressed by the sending modem and then *decompressed* by the receiving modem. Data compression speeds up transmission significantly and appears to work reliably, so this box should be checked unless you have some specific reason to do otherwise.

Use cellular protocol: Some modems include a special error-control method for cellular communications, which are prone to more glitches than communications over standard phone lines. If you're communicating "cellularly," checking this box may be necessary for a successful connection. On the other hand, the extra error-control procedures will slow you down, so clear the box when you return to a regular phone line.

Setting the Flow-Control Method   In the process of receiving and sending data, your computer often has to attend to other tasks as well, such as storing information on disk. Sometimes these tasks can distract the computer from handling incoming data. The *Use flow control* setting in the Advanced Connection Settings dialog box determines how *your* computer interacts with *your* modem to manage such situations. It provides a way for the computer and the modem to agree when to stop and start the sending process so other contingencies can be dealt with.

NOTE

This setting has no effect on the interaction between your modem and the remote computer, so you don't need to match the other computer's setting.

Unless you know the system will work otherwise, leave the *Use flow control* box checked. Beneath the check box, choose one of the available flow-control protocols. The hardware method is more reliable, so choose its radio button unless your modem isn't able to respond via hardware.

Setting the Low-Speed Modulation Protocol   At speeds above 2,400 bps, modems use a standard international signaling (modulation) protocol. At 1,200 bps and 2,400 bps, however, there are two sets of signaling protocols in wide use: Bell and CCITT. The Bell protocols are the ones to use in the United States, while the CCITT are for Europe and many other parts of the world (outside the United States and Europe, you'll need to check locally). Choose the appropriate option in the drop-down list in the Advanced Connection Settings dialog box.

Specifying Initialization Settings   If you need to send special commands to your modem before you begin a communications session—*initialization* commands—type them into the area labeled *Extra settings* in the Advanced Connection Settings dialog box. For example, you may want to tell your modem how many rings to try before giving up trying to connect with the remote computer. Or, if you don't have Touch Tone™ service, you can tell the modem to use pulse dialing instead. Check your modem's manual for the commands it uses.

NOTE

The initialization command may or may not pertain to settings in effect at the other end of the line.

By the way, you can send commands to your modem at any time from the main HyperTerminal window. Just type the command and press Enter. As an example, you can set up the modem to answer an incoming call after four rings with the command ATS0=4.

Choosing Terminal Settings

Before PCs were invented, people used *terminals* to communicate with large mainframe computers. Terminals are essentially nothing but a screen and keyboard with which data can be entered and displayed. They have no internal computing power or disk storage as does your PC. Because more than one manufacturer made terminals, conflicting standards developed regarding how data were displayed on the terminal screens and how keyboards worked.

These standards remain valid today. They apply to communications setups using PCs as well as to terminals. As its name implies, *HyperTerminal* can make your PC act like an old-style terminal. But because your computer has more brains and storage capabilities than a terminal, your PC is something of a chameleon—it can *emulate* more than one type of terminal with a change of options in a dialog box.

For successful telecommunications, two computer systems must use the same terminal standard. This almost always means that you'll be setting up your connection to match the terminal standard used by the remote system.

To set or check the settings pertaining to *terminal emulation* and related attributes in HyperTerminal, begin by choosing File ➢ Properties or clicking on the Properties button on the Toolbar. In the Properties dialog box for this connection, click on the Settings tab to display the page shown in Figure 14.5.

NOTE

Some of the settings on the Settings page have more to do with personal taste than ensuring successful communications. Still, because HyperTerminal lumps them together, I'll cover them in this section.

PART

III

Communications and
Using the Internet

FIGURE 14.5

*The Settings page
for a HyperTerminal
connection in the
Properties dialog box*

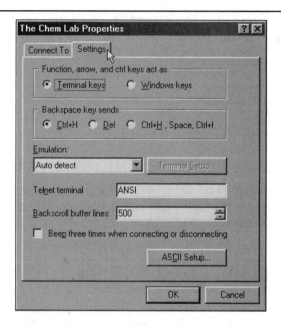

Controlling the Function, Arrow, and Ctrl Keys

HyperTerminal gives you a choice around how some of the keys work when you're communicating with another computer. In the area labeled *Function, arrow, and ctrl keys act as*, choose the Terminal keys radio button if you want HyperTerminal to send the codes for these keys to the other modem. Choose the Windows keys radio button to have HyperTerminal *trap* these keys so they're still available to control Windows. For example, pressing Ctrl-Esc would still work to open the Start menu.

Selecting a Terminal-Emulation Setting

The Emulation setting lets you choose which type of terminal Hyper Terminal should emulate (work like) for this connection. The standard setting, Auto detect, usually works—HyperTerminal can tell what type of terminal the remote computer expects and sets everything up for you automatically. If the Auto detect setting doesn't work or if you simply want manual control over your system, choose the correct terminal type from the drop-down list.

Here are descriptions of some of the more popular terminal standards:

TTY (for teletype): This is the least sophisticated choice and therefore has the highest level of compatibility. It makes your PC emulate what's known as a *dumb* terminal, meaning that the only formatting codes it uses in communicating to the remote computer are carriage return, Backspace, and Tab characters.

If you do not know which terminal emulation to use or if you see strange characters on your screen during a session, try this.

VT52: This emulates the DEC VT-52 terminal. Use this for information services such as CompuServe, BBSes, electronic mail services, and so on.

VT100: This emulates the DEC VT-100 terminal. Select this for communicating with mainframes as though you were using a DEC VT-100, VT-220, or VT-240 terminal or compatible.

ANSI: This recognizes a set of standard commands, or *escape sequences*, governing screen displays. Most BBSes optionally allow you to use these ANSI escape sequences to display their menus and other screen elements in color. ANSI stands for American National Standards Institute, an industry body that establishes voluntary standards for many products.

Choosing Options for a Specific Terminal Emulation   If you choose a specific type of terminal in the Emulation area, you can then set various options concerning its operation. To do this, click on the Terminal Setup button. The available options are different for each terminal-emulation setting. Here's an example:

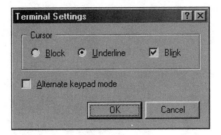

Often, as in the above example, you can choose whether the Hyper Terminal cursor appears as a block or underline and whether or not it blinks. When you change the cursor setting, it changes for all the other terminal emulations. Settings unique to a given terminal emulation remain even after you select a different emulation; when you change back to the first emulation, the previous settings are restored.

Setting the Backscroll Buffer Size

HyperTerminal records all the text that it displays in its main window, storing it so you can scroll back to see earlier material at any time. The recorded text is preserved in a backscroll buffer even when you exit Hyper Terminal so you can see text from a previous day's communication sessions.

You can control how many lines of text the program records on the Settings page of the Properties dialog box for the current connection. The standard setting is the maximum, 500 lines. To change it, type in a new number or click on the small arrow controls to increase or decrease the value.

Turning Sound On or Off

The *Beep three times when connecting or disconnecting* check box at the bottom of the Settings page toggles Hyper Terminal's beep off and on. You may or may not want to be alerted of successful connection, or disconnection (intended or accidental). I like to know if the connection was successful, or if the line goes down for some reason.

Controlling How Text Is Sent and Received

Seven settings control the way HyperTerminal handles text transferred between your modem and its counterpart at the other end of the line. To access these settings, click on the ASCII Setup button, found on the Settings page of the Properties dialog box. The ASCII Setup dialog box appears, as shown here:

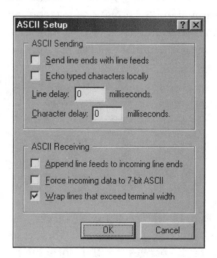

Five of the seven choices are check boxes, meaning you can turn them on or off individually by checking or clearing the box. Two let you enter values. Here's how they work:

Send line ends with line feeds: Computer systems differ in how they register the end of a line of text. Sometimes the system you're sending text to won't be able to detect the end of a line unless HyperTerminal sends a special character called a *line feed* after each line. If that turns out to be the case, check this box.

Echo typed characters locally: When this box is checked, the characters you type on your keyboard appear on your screen so you can see what you're typing. It may sound strange, but in some communications sessions you may find you can't see what you're typing unless this setting is turned on. That's because the remote computer isn't sending the characters it receives from you back to your screen. On the other hand, if you see double characters on the screen (such as *HHEELLLLOO!!*), clear this box.

Line Delay: Some slower systems need a short delay to the end of each line sent to the remote computer, or else the first character or two of the next line gets omitted.

Character Delay: This is the same idea as line delay, but a little delay is added between each character instead. If your transmission has random lost characters, try adding a few (starting with 1 or 2 and working up to, say, 5) milliseconds delay here.

Append line feeds to incoming line ends: If all the incoming text appears on a single line that gets continually rewritten, or if the cursor moves to the right margin and seems to get stuck, try checking this box. What's happening is that the other computer isn't sending the special line-feed character to move the cursor down after each line is complete. When you turn this setting on, Hyper-Terminal moves the cursor down every time it receives a finished line. If this box is checked and the text you receive is double-spaced, clear the box.

Force incoming data to 7-bit ASCII: On a PC, each character is represented by 8 bits of data, providing a total of 256 different characters. Although the first 128 characters have been standardized internationally, characters numbered 128 and above (*high-ASCII characters*) vary from country to country and from computer system to computer system (in fact, they are different in DOS and Windows). So if you see strange characters on your screen, it may help to check this box. HyperTerminal will then translate high-ASCII characters according to the International Stan dards Organization (ISO) 7-bit codes. Normal letters, numbers, and punctuation marks are left as is.

Wrap lines that exceed terminal width: Checking this box causes incoming text that is longer than the width of your screen to wrap to the next line.

Setting Other HyperTerminal Preferences

A smattering of other settings control various aspects of HyperTerminal's operation according to your preferences—these settings don't affect your ability to transfer information successfully. You can:

- Control your modem's speaker volume
- Control how long HyperTerminal waits to make a connection

PART

III

Communications and
Using the Internet

- Have HyperTerminal hang up automatically if no information is being transferred
- Control the display
- Change the font for the main window

Setting Speaker Volume

Many modems are equipped with speakers, allowing you to monitor the progress of a call audibly. If your modem has a speaker and Windows knows how to control the speaker (this varies by type of modem), you can change the volume as follows:

1. Choose File ➢ Properties or click on the Properties button to display the Properties dialog box for this connection (Figure 14.2).
2. Click on Configure to display the Properties dialog box for the selected modem (Figure 14.3).
3. Change the volume with the sliding *Speaker volume* control.

Setting Call Preferences

Two settings let you set waiting periods governing HyperTerminal's behavior in certain calling and communications situations. When dialing, you can specify the number of seconds HyperTerminal waits for a connection before giving up. After a connection is made, you can tell HyperTerminal to disconnect if no information has been transferred after a specified number of minutes.

Change these settings as follows:

1. Choose File ➢ Properties or click on the Properties button to display the Properties dialog box for this connection (Figure 14.2).
2. Click on Configure to display the Properties dialog box for the selected modem (Figure 14.3).
3. Click on the Connection tab (Figure 14.4).
4. To have HyperTerminal stop trying to connect after a given waiting period, check the box labeled *Cancel the call if not connected within* and type in the number of seconds. To have HyperTerminal disconnect after a period of inactivity, check the box labeled *Disconnect a call if idle for more than* and type in the number of minutes. (If Windows can't control the settings in question, they will be unavailable.)

Controlling the HyperTerminal Display

Several settings are available for controlling what you see in HyperTerminal and when.

For one thing, you can choose whether or not to display the Toolbar or the Status Bar. Just choose the appropriate item on the View menu to turn either bar on or off.

You can also decide whether the Dial dialog box appears when you first start HyperTerminal and whether to view a window showing modem status when HyperTerminal dials a number. To access these settings:

1. Choose File ➤ Properties or click on the Properties button to display the Properties dialog box for this connection (Figure 14.2).

2. Click on Configure to display the Properties dialog box for the selected modem (Figure 14.3).

3. Click on the Options tab. You'll see the settings shown in Figure 14.6.

FIGURE 14.6

The Options page of the Properties dialog box

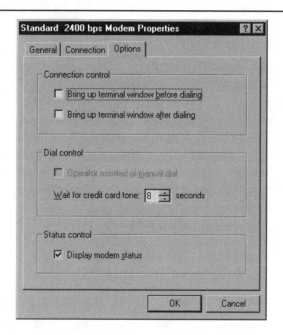

4. The check boxes in the area labeled *Connection Control* determine whether or not HyperTerminal displays the terminal window (the main portion of the HyperTerminal display) before dialing the connection or after the call is concluded. In the *Status control* section, the check box labeled *Display modem status* turns the message window on and off (shown below) that tells you how a connection is

PART

III

Communications and Using the Internet

progressing when HyperTerminal dials. (The *Dial control* settings on the Options page are covered earlier in this chapter.)

Choosing a Font

Another cosmetic option, this one determines which font and type size HyperTerminal will use to display both incoming and outgoing characters. This is actually a thoughtful feature, giving tired eyes a break when you're doing a lot of telecommunications. If you increase the font size beyond a size that will allow a complete line of text to fit in the window, scroll bars will allow you to scroll horizontally to see it. However, it's rather a nuisance to do this, and it's better to stick with a smaller size, such as 12 or 14 points.

To make a font change, choose View ➤ Fonts. Select the font, style, and size in the standard Fonts dialog box that appears, then click on OK.

Saving Your Settings

HyperTerminal automatically saves the changes in settings you make as soon as you click on OK in the Properties dialog box for the current connection as well as in the modem Properties dialog box. However, you can save the settings yourself just to be sure they're recorded. More practically, you can save the current settings as a new connection. That makes it easy to use existing settings to connect with a different service or computer—all you have to do is change the phone number and then use the Save As command.

To save the current settings for the connection that's already active, just choose File ➤ Save. To save them as a new connection, choose File ➤ Save As. The familiar Save As dialog box will appear. Give your connection a name, preferably one that will help you remember which information service or computer the settings are for, and click on OK.

Making Connections

Assuming you've completed all the setup steps properly, the process of actually making a connection couldn't be simpler. All you do is click on the Dial button on the Dial dialog box:

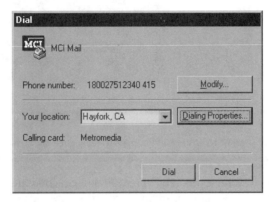

NOTE

By the way, if HyperTerminal has displayed the Dial dialog box but you don't want to make the connection at this time, just click on Cancel to go to the main HyperTerminal window.

HyperTerminal displays the Dial dialog box first each time you start the program from an existing connection. There are other ways to bring up the Dial dialog box to start a new communications session:

- When you're creating a new connection, the Dial dialog box will appear after you've named the connection, chosen its icon, and typed in a phone number.
- Once you're working with the main HyperTerminal window—perhaps after completing a previous communications session—you can display the Dial dialog box again by choosing Call ➢ Connect or clicking on the Dial (Connect) button.

When you click on the Dial button, HyperTerminal immediately starts the dialing process. You'll see the Connect message window, informing you of the progress of the call, as shown on the next page.

PART

III

Communications and
Using the Internet

If you want to stop the dialing process, click on Cancel in the Connect window.

Behind the scenes, HyperTerminal begins by sending a series of commands to the modem to prepare it for dialing. These are determined by the settings you've chosen, as detailed in the previous section.

Then HyperTerminal sends the command to dial the number. At this point, if your modem's speaker is on, you'll hear the telephone being dialed. When the phone on the other end is answered, you may hear some high-pitched tones indicating that the modems are "talking" to each other.

If the connection is successful, the message *Connected* will appear briefly in the Connect window and you'll hear three quick beeps. The Connect window will then disappear. If you have the Status Bar visible, you'll see the message *Connected* at its far left followed by a time indicator showing how long your computer has been connected to the remote machine in hours, minutes, and seconds.

At this point, if both modems are set up properly, and depending on how the other computer is programmed, you're likely to see messages from the connection on your screen. From now on, everything you type on the keyboard will be sent to the other computer. You can respond to these messages—or initiate messages of your own—by simply typing whatever you like. And you're now ready to transfer files from disk in either direction, as discussed later in the chapter.

What Might Go Wrong

A variety of problems can prevent you from successfully communicating. Here are the broad categories and some brief tips on how you can track down the specific problem:

- If you receive a message that no lines are available, or if the Connect window never displays the *Dialing* message, something is wrong with your modem or its connection to your computer. The modem may not be connected properly, it may not be turned on, or the COM port settings may be incorrect. Your modem could even be broken, though this is by far the least likely problem.

- If HyperTerminal is able to dial your modem, but can't establish a connection, it will eventually give up. You'll see the message *Busy* in the Connect window. Typical reasons for failure at this point are the following:

  - There was a busy signal.
  - The call didn't go through. Check to be sure the phone number is correct and that you've set up the Dialing Properties dialog box to dial the proper numbers to connect you to an outside line and to dial using your calling card, if you're using one.
  - The other phone never answered.
  - The other phone was answered, but not by a modem (you dialed a voice line or a standard fax machine, or the other modem was turned off). You may have entered the wrong number or area code.
  - The modems are set at different speeds so they didn't recognize each other.

When any of these problems occur, the Connect window remains on your screen. The Dial Now button becomes active, so if you want to try again, just click on it.

- If a connection is made but you see gibberish on your screen, your modem settings don't match those of the other party. See "Choosing Communications Settings" above for details on changing modem settings.

Disconnecting

After you've completed a communications session, it's time to break the connection between your system and the other modem. When possible, the graceful way to do this is by telling the other computer you want to end the session. Most information services and BBSes let you type a command such as **EXIT** or **BYE** for this purpose. When you do, the other computer sends the *disconnect* command to your modem, and you are disconnected automatically.

Sometimes, though, it's necessary to break off a connection manually. All you have to do is click on the Disconnect button on the Toolbar or choose Call ➤ Disconnect.

Making a Different Connection

Of course, after opening HyperTerminal from one connection icon and completing your communications session with that computer, you don't have to shut down the program to call a different destination. All you need do is choose File ➤ Open or click

PART

III

Communications and
Using the Internet

on the Open button on the Toolbar. Pick the connection (session) file you want to open, click on Open, and click on the Dial button to place the call.

Connecting via Cable

While you'll usually use HyperTerminal to communicate over the telephone lines, the program will also work to transfer information when you connect your computer to another computer directly, via a *serial cable*. All you need is the right type of cable: a *null-modem* cable, with jacks that fit the serial ports on the backs of the two computers (a modem is not required, and should not be used).

If you are connecting two Windows 9*x* computers directly to each other (without using modems), the most reliable approach is to use the Direct Cable Connection program discussed in Chapter 28. The following section is more widely applicable to anyone using a Windows 3.*x* or Windows 9*x* machine.

When you plug in the cable to your computer, be sure you know which COM port you've connected it to. Then, in HyperTerminal, proceed as follows:

1. Open the Properties dialog box for this connection to set up the program for that port. On the Phone Number page, select the correct COM port from the list at *Connect using*.

2. Click on the Configure button. You'll see the dialog box full of settings for this COM port in Figure 14.7. Select the maximum speed that the two computers can reliably handle—direct connections are usually much faster than modem-based connections. The other settings work the same as they do for modems and are described earlier in the chapter. All of them should be set the same on both computers.

3. Click on OK twice to return to the main HyperTerminal window.

4. Click on the Connect button or choose Call ➢ Connect to establish the connection. HyperTerminal immediately proceeds with the connection—you won't see a Dial dialog box or anything similar. If all the settings are correct, you should be able to send messages back and forth between the two computers by typing on their keyboards. You can now send and receive text and files just as in a modem-based connection.

FIGURE 14.7

Configure the
COM port with
the settings in
this dialog box.

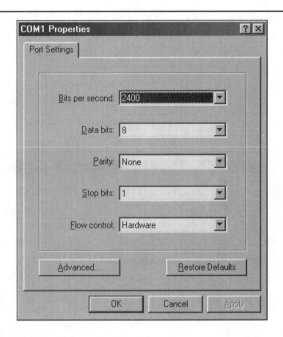

Sending and Receiving Data

Once you've made a successful connection, you can begin to transfer data between the two computers. What you do now depends entirely on what the other computer expects from you. If you are calling an information service, BBS, or a mainframe computer, you will typically have to sign on to the remote system by typing your name and possibly a password. If you are calling a friend's or associate's computer, you can just begin typing whatever you want to say. In any case, once the initial connection is made, there are several ways that you can begin to transfer data between the two computers. The next several sections describe these techniques and how to use them.

Communicating in Interactive Mode

The simplest way to communicate information is directly from your keyboard. As mentioned earlier, once you're connected to the other computer, everything you type is automatically sent to the other end of the connection. Conversely, characters typed at the other computer will be sent to your computer, showing up on your screen. Sending and

PART

III

Communications and
Using the Internet

receiving data this way is called working in *interactive* or *terminal* mode. Communication sessions often begin in terminal mode, with each person typing to the other's screen.

Terminal mode is often used, too, when connecting to many of the information services and electronic-mail services that are interactive in nature. With these, you type certain commands to the host computer, and it responds by sending you some data. As information comes over the line to your computer, it will appear on the screen, as shown in Figure 14.8. As you type, your text will appear on the screen as well.

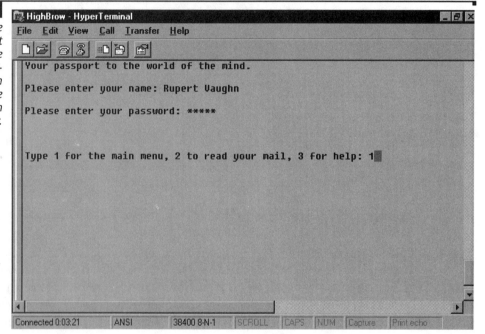

FIGURE 14.8

A typical interactive session. Notice that the user entered the number 1 at the bottom of the screen in response to the prompt from the sender.

How HyperTerminal Displays and Stores Text

As each new line of text is received or typed in by you, the cursor moves down a line in the HyperTerminal window. Once it reaches the bottom of the window, each new line shifts the previous text up so the oldest line disappears from view. This is just as text behaves in a word-processing program such as WordPad (Chapter 20).

But the older text isn't gone forever. HyperTerminal remembers the last 500 lines in its *backscroll buffer*. To see text that has scrolled off the screen, use the vertical scroll bar or the standard cursor-movement keys. Then scroll back down to continue interacting with the other computer. (You can scroll through previous text when you're not connected, too.)

Capturing Text

There will be times when you'll want a way to save data you see on your screen while you're working in terminal mode so you can work with it later. You can *capture* incoming text at any time during a communications session with the Receive Text File command on the Transfer menu and save it in a disk file for later reading, printing, or editing. Here is the basic procedure for capturing text:

1. Choose Transfer ➤ Capture Text.

2. A small dialog box appears, asking you to name the file in which you want the captured text stored. Type in the name (you can use the Browse button to select a new directory) but don't press Enter yet.

3. Click on OK. The file will be opened. If the Status Bar is visible, the Capture message becomes highlighted, indicating the capture is in progress.

4. Continue with your session. All incoming text, along with whatever you type as well, will be captured in the file you chose. When you want to stop capturing text, choose Transfer ➤ Capture Text again to display a new submenu (only available when a capture is currently in progress). Here, choose either:

   - *Stop* to close the file, or

   - *Pause* to temporarily discontinue capturing text while leaving the file open for more. To resume the capture, choose Transfer ➤ Capture Text ➤ Resume.

By the way, after you stop a capture, you can add or append more text to the same file by simply restarting the capture process and specifying the file again. If you don't want the new text to go into the previous capture file, you must enter a different file name when you restart the capture process.

Capturing Selected Portions of Text

During text capturing there may be sections of text you don't want to save interspersed with portions you do. There are two ways to selectively capture portions of the text that appears in the HyperTerminal window:

- You can use the Pause feature of the Capture command to stop the capture process whenever you're receiving information you don't want to keep. When you expect more "good" information, use Resume.

- Alternatively, you can dispense with the Capture command and just allow HyperTerminal to store the text in its backscroll buffer. You can then scroll through the buffer to copy the information you want to keep to a document in a text-editing program such as Windows Notepad. See "Manipulating Text in the HyperTerminal Window" below for details.

PART

III

Communications and
Using the Internet

Sending and Receiving Text Files

Receiving text files sent from the other computer is easy: You just use the Capture command described in the previous section. When you're connected to a BBS or information service, you'll first have to type whatever commands are needed to get the other computer to send you the file you want.

It's convenient to *send* short messages by typing them on your keyboard, but obviously, this would be an inefficient way to send larger quantities of text. HyperTerminal gives you an alternative: You can send documents already prepared by a word processor or other program and stored on disk. By composing your messages first with a word processor or text editor, you can drastically reduce the connection time (and resultant cost). And it's much easier than typing them using the primitive editing features of HyperTerminal.

There are two ways to do it. One method uses error correction to ensure that the other computer receives your file without any loss of data, and it also allows you to transfer complete documents. This is discussed in the next section. The other technique does not use error correction and can send *only* text, but it is compatible with a wider variety of computers.

The Send Text File command on the Transfer menu is the method for sending text only, *without* error correction. Use this command to send memos, letters, and so forth when the content alone of your text, without any fonts or formatting, will suffice.

WARNING

You cannot use the Send Text File command to send formatted documents or to send programs. Send such files as binary files, as described in the next section.

Files you can send with this command are called, of all things, *text-only* files, also known as ASCII files. (Sometimes they're just called *text files*, but this can be a little confusing because a word-processing document might also be considered a text file.) Text-only files are the standard means of communicating on most electronic-mail services such as MCI Mail. There are several ways to create text-only files:

- You can use a text editor such as Windows Notepad (see Chapter 22).

- Most word-processing programs, including WordPad, let you save a document as a text-only file. Remember that when you save a word-processing document as a text-only file, all formatting—including fonts, type styles, and spacing settings such as margins and indents—are lost.

- Files stored with HyperTerminal's Capture Text File command (described in the previous section) are also text-only files, and they'll work too.

Checking Settings for Text-File Transfers

Before sending or receiving a text file, you might want to check the pertinent settings for this connection. To do so:

1. Choose File ➤ Properties or click on the Properties button on the Toolbar. When the Properties dialog box for this connection appears, switch to the Settings page.

2. Click on the ASCII Setup button. A small dialog box appears.

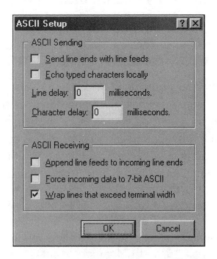

Only the first choice, *Send line feeds with line ends*, pertains to sending text-only (ASCII) files. If you need to add a line feed to the end of each line of text you send, check this box. You might have to talk with the person running the other computer to determine whether line feeds should be added or not. The three choices in the section labeled *ASCII Receiving* pertain to receiving text-only files. You can figure out which settings are correct based on the appearance of the text you receive.

3. Click on OK twice to close the dialog boxes.

Sending a Text File

Once you've selected the correct settings, you're ready to actually send the text file. Connect to the other computer if you haven't already done so. Then follow these steps:

1. Prepare the other computer to receive the text. If you're sending an e-mail letter via a BBS or commercial service, for example, type whatever command the service requires to prepare itself for the message. You might need to enter a command such as *Create* or *Send mail*, and then enter the name and electronic address of your recipient. Consult the service for details.

2. When the other computer is ready to receive your text, choose Transfer ➢ Send Text File.

3. A standard Windows file dialog box will appear. Select the file you want to transfer, then click on OK. The text from the file will appear on your screen as it is sent to the other computer.

4. When the entire file has been sent, type whatever command the other computer requires to indicate the end of the message or go on to send another file.

Sending and Receiving Documents and Other Files

Most of the files stored on your computer's disks do *not* consist of only text. Instead of simple sequences of characters arranged in lines, the typical file—whether it's a document created by your word-processing or spreadsheet program or the program itself—contains all sorts of information in encoded form. This information is perfectly understandable by your computer (with the right software), but it usually looks like complete gibberish to you and me. Such files are called "binary" files.

Most e-mail programs these days allow you to "attach" binary files to your email. See Chapters 13, 15, and 17 for more about e-mail.

That's why you can't transfer most files with HyperTerminal's Capture Text and Send Text File commands. You need the Send File and Receive File commands instead. These commands transfer the entire document just as it is, without trying to interpret it as text. In the bargain, they detect and correct errors that have crept in during the transfer.

By the way, it's perfectly okay to send and receive text-only files via the Send File and Receive File commands to get the benefits of error correction. The only drawbacks: you won't see the text on your screen, and the process takes a tad longer.

It's not uncommon for data transmission errors to occur during the transmission process over telephone lines, particularly from noise or static. In response to this, computer scientists have devised numerous error-detection and error-correction schemes to determine whether errors have occurred in transmission and to correct them if possible. These schemes are referred to as *file-transfer protocols* because they also manage other aspects of the file-transfer process. HyperTerminal lets you choose from several of the most popular of these file-transfer protocols with its Receive File and Send File commands.

Understanding File-Transfer Protocols

To detect and correct errors, file-transfer protocols divide a file into a series of small sections, called *blocks*. The blocks are then sent sequentially, and each one is accompanied by a mathematically calculated code based on the contents of the block. After getting the block, the receiving computer sees whether its contents match this calculated code. If they do, the sending computer is advised to send the next block. If there is a discrepancy, the receiving computer asks the sending computer to retransmit the block until it's received properly. This process continues until the entire file is transmitted error free.

Some file-transfer protocols, such as Zmodem, keep track of how far along the file transfer is from moment to moment. If the connection is broken, they can pick up the file transfer where it left off so that you don't have to start all over again from scratch.

Choosing a File-Transfer Protocol

When you transfer a file with the Send File or Receive File commands, HyperTerminal lets you choose which of several file-transfer protocols to use for the transfer. Although each of the file-transfer protocols has its own characteristics, the critical point should sound familiar by now: To send or receive a file successfully, you need to use the same protocol as the other computer.

Often, when you're transferring files to or from a commercial service or BBS, you'll be able to tell the other computer which protocol to use. Whether or not you select the other computer's protocol, just be sure to set HyperTerminal to match.

Here's a list of the file-transfer protocols available in HyperTerminal:

Xmodem was the first widely used error-detection and correction scheme. It was devised by Ward Christensen, who placed it in the public domain in 1977 for use on microcomputers, which were just then becoming available. Xmodem is available on most information services, such as CompuServe. The 1K version is a bit faster than the standard version.

Ymodem is similar to Xmodem but a little faster and more reliable.

Kermit may be the only protocol available when you communicate with some larger computers such as the minicomputers at a university. It's usually slower than the others, so this protocol would be a second or third choice.

Zmodem is the fastest and most capable of HyperTerminal's protocols. Use this choice if the other computer permits it.

PART

III

Communications and
Using the Internet

Sending Files

To send a file, follow these steps:

1. Make sure you're online (connected).

2. Make sure the receiving computer is ready to receive the file. How you do this depends on the computer system, BBS, or information service to which you are connected. If you are sending a file to another PC, you may want to type a message in HyperTerminal mode telling the operator of the other computer to do what is necessary to prepare for receiving the file.

3. Choose Transfer ➤ Send File or click on the Send button on the Toolbar.

A small dialog box appears:

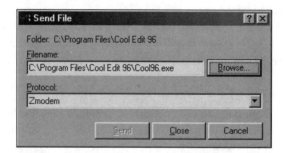

4. Enter the name of the file you want to send (or click on Browse, locate and select the file, and click on OK to go back to the Send dialog box). Then choose the error-detection protocol you want (the one in use by the receiving system).

5. Click on OK to begin the file transfer.

You'll now see a large window reporting the progress of the transfer, as shown in Figure 14.9. At the top, the name of the file being sent is displayed. Next come several readouts on the error-checking process—these are pretty technical, and you can usually ignore them. If something goes seriously wrong, HyperTerminal will halt the transfer. At that point, you may be able to diagnose the problem by reading the message displayed at *Last error*.

The (slightly) more interesting part of the display is the lower half. Here, HyperTerminal shows you graphically and in numbers how quickly the transfer is going. The bar graph at File expands to the right giving you a quick sense of how much of the file has been sent so far, relative to its total size. Next to the graph, you're shown how much of the file has been sent in numbers. Below are counters showing how much time has elapsed since the transfer began, how much time is remaining (assuming all goes well, and if HyperTerminal is able to calculate this), and, in the Throughput area, your current "speed." By clicking on the cps/bps button, you can set the display units for throughput speed: characters per second (cps) or bits per second (bps). Characters per second is actually a measure of the number of bytes (8-bit information units) being transferred each second.

FIGURE 14.9

You'll see a window like this during file transfers.

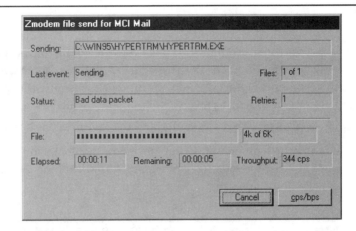

To cancel a file transfer before it has finished, click on the Cancel button at the bottom of the window. If the transfer completes normally, you'll hear a single beep as the window disappears.

NOTE

You can't pause a binary transfer, but you can end it in midstream by clicking on Stop or choosing Stop from the Transfers menu.

As a recap of sending binary files, consider the following: a binary file will arrive just as you sent it, with no modifications (for example, no adding or stripping of line feeds). All types of files, including program files, can be sent and received as binary files. Formatted text as well as program files must be transmitted as binary files, or information will be lost.

Receiving Files

You'll want to use the Receive File command to transfer document and program (non-text) files to your computer from the computer at the other end of the line. The process of receiving such a file is very similar to sending one:

1. After connecting to the other computer, tell the sending computer to send the file and which file-transfer protocol to use in the process. How you do this

depends on the computer and program(s) involved. If you're connected to a BBS or information service, you can usually control the process from your computer. If you're connected to another individual's computer, you ask the person at the other end of the line to type in the command to send you the file.

2. Choose Transfer ➤ Receive File or click on the Receive button on the Toolbar.

3. The Receive File dialog box appears. Choose the *directory* where you want Hyper-Terminal to store the received file (not the actual file name, which will be set by the other computer). Type in the directory name or use the Browse button to find it. Then select the file-transfer protocol that matches the one used by the other computer. And do all this quickly because the other computer is already trying to send the file. It will wait, but usually not too long.

4. Click on OK or press Enter, and the transmission should begin.

Once the transfer is underway, a window that looks and works very similar to the one you see when sending files (Figure 14.9) will appear. See the previous section for details on its use.

WARNING

Depending on the file-transfer protocol you're using, HyperTerminal may not know the size of the file being sent to it. In this case, you won't be able to check to see whether you have enough disk space for the file, and you may run out of disk space while receiving it. This is a real hassle, particularly if you've spent half an hour receiving most of a large file only to get an error message saying there isn't enough room on your disk for the rest of it. When this happens, HyperTerminal will abort the receiving process. So make sure the disk you choose to store the file on has enough free space on it before you begin the transfer.

Ending a Communications Session

Once you've finished your work (or play) during a session, you should end it by following some simple rules:

1. If you want to save the settings you've made, choose File ➤ Save and name the file.

2. If you are logged on to an information service, electronic mail provider, or BBS, follow the system's instructions for signing off. This may be important to free up a connection for other users or to ensure that the service will cease billing you for connect time.

3. Choose Call ➢ Disconnect.

4. Close HyperTerminal by double-clicking on its Control box.

Despite great strides in the field of communications, mostly due to conveniences spurred by the personal computer market, communications is still a bit of a black art. Chances are good that you'll run into some problem or other while transferring files, sending mail, or whatever it is you end up doing with HyperTerminal. The fault will not necessarily lie with HyperTerminal (or yourself), but much more likely will be the result of improper wiring, faulty modems, noisy telephone lines, incorrect log-on procedures, or incompatible software on the other end of the line. If you're trying to connect to a BBS or information service, don't hesitate to call them (the old-fashioned way) for help with making things work right. You can also get help from your company's computer expert, your computer store, or an experienced friend.

Chapter

15

Connecting to the Internet

FEATURING

Types of connections to the Internet

Setting up your modem

Choosing an Internet Service Provider

Configuring a Dial-up Networking connection profile

Making connections with more than one online service

Adding Internet access to an MSN account

Chapter

15

Connecting to the Internet

Before you can use Internet Explorer (or
any other Internet application program),
you must connect your own computer
to the Internet. In this chapter, you will find information about choosing an Internet
Service Provider; making the connection through a modem, a LAN, or other link; and
installing and configuring your system for a TCP/IP connection.

If you already have an Internet connection that supports other TCP/IP Internet client
programs, you may be able to use it with Internet Explorer, Outlook Express NetMeeting,
and the other Internet tools discussed in this book. If that's the case, you can skip this
chapter.

NOTE

> TCP/IP is the networking software (protocol) established during the 70s that allows
> many different kinds of computers to interact with one another regardless of type and
> operating system. First debuted in 1978 for use on the ARPANET (the predecessor of
> the Internet), TCP/IP remains the most widely used network protocol software today,
> and it forms the basis of the Internet. It is not owned by any one agency or company.

What Kind of Connection?

Choosing a way to connect your computer to the Internet is a trade-off between performance and cost; more money gets you a faster link between your own system and the backbone. (Just like in the human body, the Internet's backbone forms the core high-speed communications channel on which the Internet is built.) While the difference between file transfers through a modem and a high-speed link can be dramatic, the cost of improved performance may not always be justified. For most home users and many small businesses, a dial-up telephone line and a 33.6Kbps (kilobits per second) or 56Kbps modem is still the most cost-effective choice.

If it's available in your area, you might want to consider ISDN (Integrated Services Digital Network) as an alternative to conventional POTS (Plain Old Telephone Service) lines. ISDN is more expensive and complicated to install and configure, but once it's in place, it offers substantially faster network connections. Your Internet Service Provider (ISP) can tell you if ISDN service is available and explain how to order the lines and obtain the necessary interface equipment.

Microsoft offers an easy means for establishing an ISDN hookup. Go to `http://www`
`.microsoft.com/` and look around or search the site for "Get ISDN." You should find
a page with an online Wizard that will find the nearest ISDN provider and let you
order service. I used this approach to get my ISDN service, and it was pretty painless.

In a larger business, where many users can share the same link to the Internet, a connection with more bandwidth is probably a better approach. Many users can share a single high-speed connection through a LAN, so the cost per user may not be significantly greater than that of a second telephone line.

If your PC is already connected to a LAN, you should ask your network administrator or help desk about setting up an Internet account; it's likely that there's already some kind of connection in place.

As with most decisions related to data communications, the simple answer to "What kind of connection should I use?" is "The fastest that you can afford." With the drastic increase in the number of Internet users, and growing awareness of how aggravating a slow connection can be, alternatives are beginning to crop up. A wide variety of higher-speed access vendors have appeared in recent months. Cable modems that use existing cable-TV service wires, digital satellite dish systems, and new telephone-system technologies such as ADSL (Asymetrical Digital Subscriber Line) are among the most promising. Table 15.1 lists several types of connections and speed(s) you can expect from each. The prices are in flux, obviously. Also, don't forget that hardware equipment is needed for all of these solutions. You can buy an analog modem for about $100, but some of the other solutions will cost you thousands for your hardware. Some of these solutions, such as satellite hookup, do not include the ISP costs, either. They only supply the hookup to their system, one stop short of the Internet.

TABLE 15.1: POPULAR MEANS FOR CONNECTION TO THE INTERNET

Technology	Speed / Notes	Speed relative to 28.8modem (approx)	Typical cost
Standard 14.4Kbps–56Kbps dial-up service over standard POTS lines	14.4Kbps–33.6Kbps or so. Rarely is 56Kbps achieved due to noise on phone lines. Legally, 53Kbps is the top limit as of this writing.	1x	$20/month + telephone connect charges
ISDN	56Kbps–128Kpbs	2x–4x	$20–$50/month + connect time (typically 1 cent/ minute)
Satellite	Varies, typically 400Kbps, some as high as 27Mbps	8x–900x	$20/month + ISP charges
T-3	45Mbps	1,500x	$32,000/month
T-1	1.54Mbps	50x	$3,300/month
Frame relay	Available in 64Kbps increments, up to 1.5Mbps	As high as 50x	$200–$500/ month depend- ing on speed
xDSL— includes ADSL, IDSL, SDHL, HDSL, VDSL, RADSL	Asymetrical Digital Subscriber Line (ADSL) can deliver up to 8Mbps over the 750 million ordinary existing "twisted pair" phone connections on earth. Actual speed offerings of these technologies range from 1.5Mbps to as high as 60Mbps on VDSL.	50x–2000x	$75/month (128Kbps), $250/month (768Kbps) + ISP service
Cable modem, using existing TV cable systems	10Mbps maximum. In reality probably about 1.5Mbps with typical number of users. Some systems offer only 500Kbps. Most systems require separate phone line for uplink since they only *receive* data over the cable. Others are bi-directional.	50x	$40/month

TIP

For a good source of information on high-speed Internet connections, and the inside scoop, check this site: http://www.teleport.com/~samc/cable1.html. It's *extremely* complete. Another good site is http://www.specialty.com/hiband/.

Now come back down to Earth for a moment and stop daydreaming about how fast your connection to the Internet *could* be. For the time being, it will probably be either 56Kbps using one of the three 56Kbps standard modem types (but you'll probably only get about 33Kbps maximum connect speed) or 128Kbps using ISDN. But I expect that a combination of ISDN, ADSL, and cable modems will dominate the market for high-speed seekers within two years. Even then, good old POTS line dial-ups will continue to be very popular since they work on virtually any phone line and accounts are cheap.

However, the telcos (that's short for telephone companies) have a vested interest in stopping people from tying up phone lines with modems all day, since the telephone system was designed for relatively short-term connections and works most economically that way. ADSL is a terrific solution for delivery of data and even video, since it uses the existing phone wires (no cable wiring necessary), *and it doesn't tie them up for other uses*. What, you say? That's right, you can pick up the regular old phone and make calls while your computer stays online downloading Web pages at T-1 speeds. This is because the Internet data is carried inside a high-frequency carrier signal that rides on top of the phone lines regardless of whether low-frequency voice calls are going on.

With that background, let's get down to the job of getting your modem hooked up and maybe even getting you online.

Choosing a Service Provider

As you know, the Internet is the result of connecting many networks to one another. You can connect your own computer to the Internet by obtaining an account on one of those interconnected networks.

Several different kinds of businesses offer Internet connections, including large companies with access points in many cities, smaller local or regional ISPs, and online information services that provide TCP/IP connections to the Internet along with their own proprietary information sources. You can use popular programs such as Internet Explorer with a connection through any of these services.

When you order your account, you should request a PPP connection to the Internet. PPP is a standard type of TCP/IP connection, which any ISP should be able to supply.

The Information Superhighway version of a New Age gas station, ISPs are popping up all over the country (and all over the world, for that matter). And like long-distance telephone companies, they offer myriad service options. If you're not among the savvy, you may get snowed into using an ISP that doesn't really meet your needs. As with long-distance telephone providers, you'll find that calculating the bottom line isn't that easy. It really depends on what you are looking for. Here are some questions to ask yourself (and any potential ISP):

- Does the ISP provide you with an e-mail account? It should.

- Can you have multiple e-mail accounts (for family members or employees)? If so, how many?

- Do they offer 56Kbps support? If so, which format? It should match your modem.

- Will they let you create your own *domain name*? For example, I wanted the e-mail address `bob@cowart.com` rather than something cryptic like `bobcow@ic .netcim.net`. Sometimes creating your own domain name costs extra, but it gives your correspondents an easier address to remember. You can decide if it's worth it.

- Does the ISP provide you with a news account so you can interact with Internet *newsgroups*? It should, and it shouldn't restrict which newsgroups you'll have access to unless you are trying to prevent your kids from seeing "dirty" messages or pictures.

- Do you want your own Web page available to other people surfing the Net? If so, does the ISP provide online storage room for it? How many "hits" per day can they handle, in case your page becomes popular? How much storage do you get in the deal? Do you want them to create the Web page for you?

- What is the charge for connect time? Some ISPs offer unlimited usage per day. Others charge by the hour and/or have a limit on continuous connect time.

- Do they have a local (i.e., free) phone number? If not, calculate the charges. It may be cheaper to use an ISP that charges more per month if there are no phone company toll charges to connect.

- Do they have many points of presence or an 800 number you can use to call into when you are on the road?

- Do they have too much user traffic to really provide reasonable service? Ask others who use the service before signing up. This has been a major problem with some ISPs, even biggies like AOL. Smaller providers often supply faster connections. Remember that even if you can connect without a busy signal, the weakest link in the system will determine the speed at which you'll get data from the Net. Often that link is the ISP's internal LAN that connects their in-house computers together. It's hard to know how efficient the ISP really is. Best to ask someone who's using them.

- Are they compatible with the programs you want to use? Can you use Internet Explorer or Netscape Web browsers? Which newsgroup and mail programs are supported?

If you have access to the Web, try checking the page http://www.thelist.com/. You'll learn a lot about comparative pricing and features of today's ISPs, along with links to their pages for opening an account. Another good site is http://www.boardwatch.com/.

Using a National ISP

The greatest advantage of using a national or international ISP is that you can probably find a local dial-in telephone number in most major cities. If you want to send and receive e-mail or use other Internet services while you travel, this can be extremely important.

The disadvantage of working with a large company is that it may not be able to provide the same kind of personal service that you can get from a smaller, local business. If you must call halfway across the continent and wait 20 minutes on hold for technical support (especially if it's not a toll-free number), you should look for a different ISP.

Many large ISPs can give you free software that automatically configures your computer and sets up a new account. Even if they don't include Internet Explorer in their packages, you should be able to use some version of the program along with the application programs they do supply.

You can obtain information about Internet access accounts from the national service providers listed in Table 15.2.

Many local telephone companies and more than a few cable TV companies are also planning to offer Internet access to their subscribers. If it's available in your area, you should be able to obtain information about these services from the business office that handles your telephone or television service. In San Jose, California, a local UHF TV station is using TV broadcasting technology to deliver high-speed Internet service, for example.

TABLE 15.2: NATIONAL INTERNET SERVICE PROVIDERS		
ISP	**Phone Number**	**Web Address**
AT&T WorldNet	1-800-WORLDNET (1-800-967-5363)	`http://www.att.com/worldnet/`
MCI Internet	1-800-955-6505 (for Business Use) 1-800-550-0927 (for Home Use)	`http://www.mci.com/`
SPRYnet	1-800-SPRYNET (1-800-777-9638)	`http://www.sprynet.com/`
PSInet	1-800-774-0852	`http://www.psi.net/`
Netcom	1-800-353-6600	`http://www.netcom.com/`
Earthlink Network	1-800-395-8425	`http://www.earthlink.com/`
Concentric Networks	1-800-745-2747	`http://www.concentric.net/`
IBM Internet	1-800-821-4612	`http://www.ibm.net/`

Using a Local ISP

The big national and regional services aren't your only choice. In most metropolitan areas and in a growing number of other places, smaller local service providers also offer access to the Internet.

If you can find a good local ISP, it might be your best choice. A local company may be more responsive to your particular needs and more willing to help you get through the inevitable configuration problems than a larger national operation. Equally important, reaching the technical support center is more likely to be a local telephone call.

But, unfortunately, the Internet access business has attracted a tremendous number of entrepreneurs who are in it for the quick dollar—some local ISPs are really terrible. If they don't have enough modems to handle the demand, or if they don't have a high-capacity connection to an Internet backbone, or if they don't know how to keep their equipment and servers working properly, you'll get frequent busy signals, slow downloads, dropped lines, and unexpected downtime rather than consistently reliable service. And there's no excuse for unhelpful technical support people or endless time on hold. If a deal seems too good to be true, there's probably a good reason.

To learn about the reputations of local ISPs, ask friends and colleagues who have been using the Internet for a while. If there's a local computer user magazine, look for schedules of user group meetings where you can find people with experience using the local ISPs. If you can't get a recommendation from any of those sources, look back at the previous Tip regarding lists of ISPs on the Web (assuming you already have Web access, which I realize is sort of a Catch-22).

PART

III

Communications and Using the Internet

Connecting through an Online Service

One of the welcome additions to later versions of Windows 95 has continued into Windows 98. It's the inclusion of easy signup software for the major information services in the United States. Evidently this was done in reaction to complaints that Microsoft Corp. was gaining unfair advantage by bundling software for their own service, The Microsoft Network. The services included are America Online, CompuServe, AT&T Worldnet, and Prodigy. Any one of these services will get you connected to the Internet, using a "name brand" so to speak.

With the exception of Worldnet, which offers little more than a standard ISP connection, these services not only get you connected to the Internet—they sell you *content* too. Content providers such as CompuServe have been around for years now (I think I signed up with them about 10 years ago, before the Internet was used by anyone except universities and government agencies). In essence, these outfits are their own isolated mini Internet, with e-mail, bulletin boards, chat groups, and so forth. They typically provide you with special software that makes the whole process of working online simpler than using the more generic software tools designed for e-mail, newsgroups, and the Web. The proprietary information content supplied on services such as AOL and Prodigy is also a bit more supervised than what is available on the Internet at large. On the other hand, you're often somewhat crippled, since you may not be able to use the latest Web browsers.

In addition to supplying their own content, all the major services such as AOL now will connect you through to the Internet, so you can use the Web, newsgroups, and Internet mail. I'd want to use a generic ISP such as Netcom, myself, since I want to be allowed the choice of Web browser I use (Netscape, Internet Explorer, Mosaic, etc.) and which mail reader (Eudora, Netscape, Outlook, Pegasus Mail, and so on). Services such as AOL and CompuServe don't give you a big choice there. But if a service lets you use the latest versions of Internet Explorer or Netscape for Web browsing, and the mail program they give you is decent (has folders to organize your mail, has a decent editor, and displays or deals reasonably with attachments such as gif and jpg pictures), then go for it, especially if they make it easy to get hooked up.

Be careful, though. Generally speaking the most expensive way to connect to the Internet has been through one of these national providers. I used to pay $6/hour to be connected to CompuServe, for example. And that amounted to a monthly bill far and away more expensive than the $19 I pay to Netcom now to get unlimited hours on the Internet. AOL and CompuServe are now keeping up with the Joneses (or down, rather) and offering $20 rates too. Read the fine print though to see just what you *do* get for that 20 bucks. Also check the access numbers to see that you won't be paying additional hourly phone connect charges. Then choose.

NOTE

Note that by selecting an online service provider listed in this folder (not the MSN icon), you will be establishing an account with that online service provider and not with Microsoft Corporation. Therefore, your payment will be due to the online service provider. The online service provider you select will provide you with specific payment instructions.

If you decide to select one of the online service providers listed in this folder, just click the icon for that online service provider; this will begin setting up your computer for access with that provider. Here's how:

1. Clear the desktop by clicking on the Desktop icon in the Quick Launch bar at the bottom of the screen, or by any other method.

2. Look for a folder called Online Services and open it.

3. Run the icon of the service you want to check out. A "splash" screen about the product will appear, or you'll be prompted to insert your Windows CD-ROM, or take some other action, depending on the service. You should ensure your modem is on and connected to the telephone line, since a phone call will be made to sign you up. You'll need a credit card number, too, so get that ready.

4. Once signed up, you'll see instructions about what your services will include, how to proceed, and how to connect with the Internet.

WARNING

There may be specific instructions for how to run their software with Windows 98. Be sure to carefully answer any questions or read relevant instructions about the operating system you are using. For example, AOL has different versions of its software for Windows 3.11 than for Windows 95 or 98. Read carefully.

PART

III

Communications and
Using the Internet

Getting Directly on the Internet—Finding a Local ISP

Suppose you don't want to use one of the big content providers such as AOL, CompuServe, or AT&T, and you just want onto the Internet. Then what? As you probably know, there are thousands of smaller ISPs out there in the world, especially in the United States. These are the folks that don't supply "content" like AOL and CompuServe do, but that's OK. Maybe all you want is to get onto the Internet, not join clubs on AOL. So why pay for AOL or CompuServe features you don't need, or be limited by their regulations or in some cases, censorship of the material they'll provide you? Or be limited by the types of Web browser or mail or news readers they support?

These are some reasons why many folks get directly onto the Internet via a local or even national ISP. I, for one, use Netcom, probably the nation's largest ISP. They have dial-up numbers almost everywhere in the country, which is great. I can travel and still plug in my laptop, make a local call, and get my mail. For my ISDN line, I use a different provider, called Verio, in Berkeley, California. They are only local, but it's affordable ISDN service.

So, if you've decided that you can get cheaper or better service through a generic ISP, Microsoft has made it easy to get connected to the Internet via a little Wizard called Get on the Internet. Normally you'd have to find out on your own who your local ISPs are, and call them or otherwise contact them to get signed up for service. This can be a hassle. Depending on where you live, some local newspapers or computer rags sometimes list all the ISPs in the area. (This is true here in the San Francisco Bay Area where I can find a huge chart of all the local ISPs in the *Computer Currents* magazine.) Microsoft decided to make this process easier by providing a Web page that lists ISPs around the country.

So, how do you get connected to an ISP? It's easy. In fact, if you don't have some dial-up connections to the Internet already, and you've tried running Outlook Express or Internet Explorer, you've probably already seen the Get Connected dialog box that has been insistently trying to sign you up with an ISP.

Have your Windows 98 Setup CD handy. The Wizard may need to install some Windows 98 files in order to set up your Internet connection.

1. Click Start ➤ Programs ➤ Internet Explorer ➤ Connection Wizard. You'll see the Wizard.

2. Click on Next. You'll see the dialog box shown in Figure 15.1. Choose which kind of setup you want. Referring to the figure, the choices in order are:

- Shows you a list of ISPs and helps get you signed up with them.

- Sets up the computer for use with your current ISP account, assuming you have one.

- Quits the Wizard without doing anything.

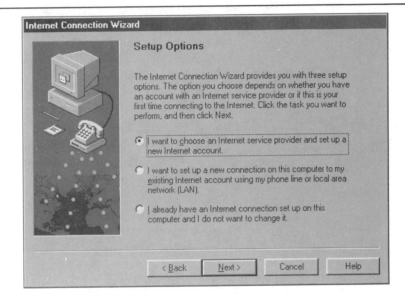

3. You'll be asked a few things, such as which modem to use, where you are located, the first three digits of your phone number, and so on. Then it will try to dial your modem and call an 800 number that lists ISPs in your area. If you are having trouble connecting, click on Help in the dialog box and this will run the Internet Connection Wizard Help with troubleshooting tips.

4. When you finally connect to the 800 number, the Wizard runs Internet Explorer and displays a list of ISPs with some facts about each, as shown in Figure 15.2. Since they will undoubtedly be modified from time to time, I won't try to second guess what the remote instructions will say when you read them. Just follow the instructions you find there. If you click on a service's More Info or Sign Me Up button and want to get back to the previous list, look for an icon on the screen that says "Back" or "Return" and click on it. If you want to quit the whole shebang and sign up later, scroll down to the bottom of the listing page (the one in Figure 15.2) and click on Cancel.

PART

III

Communications and
Using the Internet

FIGURE 15.2

Typical ISP display resulting from using the Internet Connection Wizard

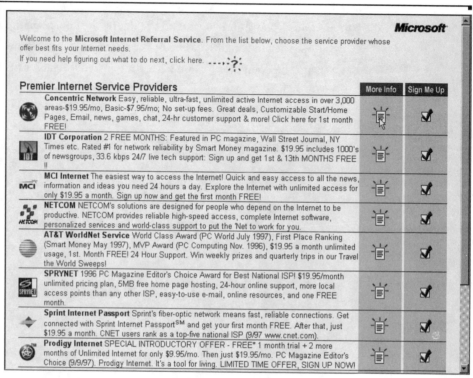

It's likely that you'll see the more national ISPs and information services listed here. No big surprise, I guess. It probably takes some doing to get on the Microsoft list. As I said earlier, you might have to sleuth around to find the smaller fry ISPs in your local area. Once you do, they will tell you what to do to get connected with Windows 98.

Setting Up Windows 98 Dial-Up Networking

The premium ISPs that show up when you run the Connection Wizard create ready-to-roll Dial-up Networking profiles for you. By the time you're through entering all your identification and billing information, and clicking on some buttons, all the dirty work previous versions of Windows required is done automatically.

But what if you're using a little backwoods ISP? Then you have a little more work to do. As a rule, simply ask the ISP for some printed material about how to set up your Dial-up Networking connection to work with their service. They undoubtedly have printed matter about this or can walk you through the necessary steps over the phone. There are several hairy dialog boxes you get to via the Dial-up Networking (DUN) folder (My Computer ➤ Dialup Networking) and via Control Panel ➤ Network icon.

Creating a new profile is not difficult, but it's a little more complicated than simply clicking on an option in the Setup Wizard. Here are the basics, just so you know what you're talking about when you do contact the ISP, or if you have the info already and want to get set up to configure a Dial-up Networking connection profile, you must complete two separate procedures: load the software and create a connection profile.

Loading the Software

If you didn't load Dial-up Networking when you installed Windows 98, you must add it before you can connect to the Internet. Follow these steps to add the software:

1. Open the Control Panel.

2. Open the Add/Remove Programs icon.

3. Click on the Windows Setup tab to display the Windows Setup dialog box.

4. Select the Communications item from the Components list and click on the Details button.

5. Make sure there's a checkmark next to the Dial-up Networking component and click on the OK button.

6. When you see a message instructing you to insert software disks, follow the instructions as they appear.

7. When the software has been loaded, restart the computer.

8. The Control Panel should still be open. Open the Network icon.

9. Click on the Add button to display the Select Network Component Type dialog box, shown in Figure 15.3.

FIGURE 15.3

Use the Select Network Component Type dialog box to set up Dial-up Networking.

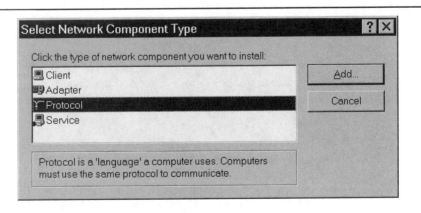

10. Select Protocol in the list of component types and click on the Add button.

11. Select Microsoft from the list of manufacturers and TCP/IP in the list of network protocols. Click on the OK button.

12. You should see TCP/IP in the list of network components. Click on the OK button to close the dialog box.

Creating a Connection Profile

Once you've added support for TCP/IP networking, you're ready to set up one or more connection profiles. Follow these steps to create a profile:

1. Start Dial-up Networking from either the My Computer window on the desktop or the Programs ➢ Accessories menu.

2. Double-click on the Make New Connection icon.

3. The Make New Connection Wizard will start. The name of the computer you will dial is also the name that will identify the icon for this connection profile in the Dial-up Networking folder. Therefore, you should use the name of your ISP as the name for this profile. If you have separate profiles for telephone numbers in different cities, include the city name as well. For example, if you use SPRYnet as your access provider, you might want to create profiles called SPRYnet Chicago and SPRYnet Boston.

4. Click on the Next button to move to the next screen, and type the telephone number for your ISP's PPP access.

5. Click on the Finish button to complete your work with the Wizard.

6. You will see a new icon in the Dial-up Networking window. Right-click on this icon and select the Properties command.

7. When the Connections Properties dialog box, shown in Figure 15.4, appears, click on the Server Type button.

8. When the Server Types dialog box, shown in Figure 15.5, appears, choose the PPP option in the drop-down list of dial-up server types.

9. Make sure there are checkmarks next to these options:
   • Log on to network.
   • Enable software compression.
   • TCP/IP (you can turn off NetBEUI and EPX/SPX if you are only connecting to the Internet. Those are used for networking with IBM PCs running Novell and Microsoft networking protocols on a LAN).

FIGURE 15.4

Use the Connections Properties dialog box to configure Dial-up Networking.

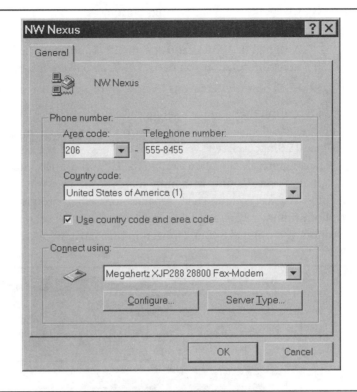

FIGURE 15.5

Use the Server Types dialog box to set up a PPP connection.

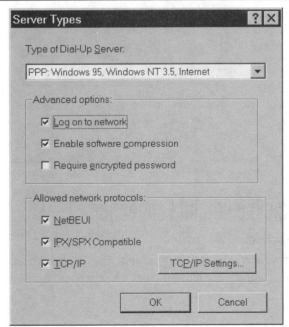

PART

III

Communications and
Using the Internet

10. Click on the TCP/IP Settings button.

11. Ask your ISP how to fill in this dialog box. You will probably use a Server Assigned IP Address and specific DNS addresses, but your ISP can give you the exact information you need. *This is an important step!*

12. Click on the OK buttons to close all the open dialog boxes.

To confirm that you have set up the connection profile properly, turn on your modem and double-click on the new icon. When the Connect To dialog box, shown in Figure 15.6, appears, type your user ID and password and click on the Connect button. Your computer should place a call to the ISP and connect your system to the Internet.

If you have accounts with more than one ISP, or if you carry the same computer to different cities, you can create separate connection profiles for each ISP or each telephone number. By choosing a connection profile before you start any Winsock application, you can make your connection through a profile other than the default.

FIGURE 15.6

The Connect To dialog box shows the name and telephone number of your ISP.

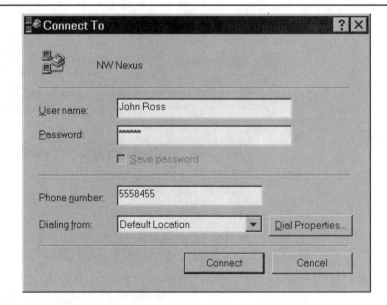

Changing the Default Connection

When setup is complete, you will have a Dial-up Networking connection profile for each of your ISPs. Internet Explorer and other Winsock-compliant or Internet-dependent programs will use the current default to connect your computer to the Internet whenever you start the programs. But what if you have several connections, and want to declare which one will be the default that Windows should use?

To change the default, follow these steps:

1. Open Control Panel and then run the Internet applet.

2. When the Internet Properties dialog box appears, click on the Connection tab to display the left dialog box shown in Figure 15.7.

3. Click on Connect to the Internet using a modem. You'll see the right-hand dialog box in Figure 15.7.

4. Open the drop-down list and choose the connection that you want as the default.

5. OK the dialog boxes and close the Control Panel.

FIGURE 15.7

Use the Connection tab to change the default connection profile.

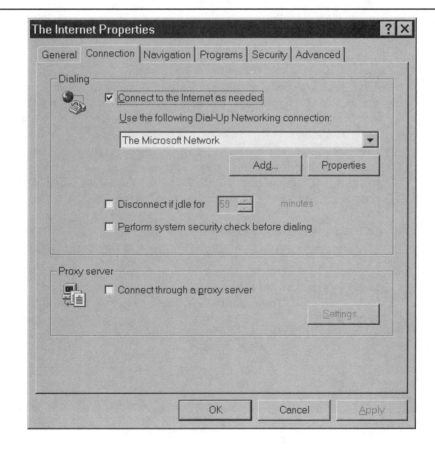

PART **III** Communications and Using the Internet

Telling Internet Programs NOT to Dial the Phone!

Notice in Figure 15.7 that you can choose to connect via the local area network rather than by a modem. This is intended for workstations connected to a local area network running the TCP/IP protocol and which has a connection to the Internet via a router, or some other approach such as Microsoft Small Business Server, or Windows NT Server. But you can use this setting to your advantage, even if you've just got a lowly stand-alone computer.

Here's why: It can be annoying when you open your mail program or IE or Netscape and suddenly the phone is being dialed by Windows in hopes of making life easy for you by connecting automatically to the Internet to carry out your wishes. Maybe you're on the phone already, talking to someone, and don't want your modem blasting into your ear. Or you want to ensure that if you're not home, but you've left your computer on, that your e-mail program doesn't cause Windows to dial the phone and stay online accidentally racking up connect-time charges.

If you choose "connect to the Internet using a local area network" in the dialog box on the left side of Figure 15.7, running IE, or OE, or Netscape will not run the phone dialer to try to log you on. Actually, nothing will happen except that you'll most likely eventually get an error message from your program saying a connection couldn't be made. Make your connection to the Net manually, by running the DUN profile from My Computer ➢ Dial-up Networking. Once connected, then you can run your Internet programs without having them try to dial the phone. In fact, what I do is tell any Internet programs (i.e., Winsock-compatible programs) that they are not to bother connecting to the Internet except through the LAN. (How you do this depends on the program. Some have no settings, and rely on the default setting explained above.)

Anyway, this arrangement can give you much more flexibility. For example, when I want to connect to the Internet, I run the DUN profile for the connection I want at the time. Sometimes I want a fast connection, so I dial up with my ISDN connection. Other times I want to be on all day with minimal cost, so I use my analog Netcom connection ($19.95/month unlimited connect time). The programs I'm using don't know how the connection was made. All they know is that the TCP/IP connection to the Internet is active. As long as the little connection icon appears down on the task bar's right edge,

Continued

CONTINUED

all popular Winsock Internet programs such as Netscape, Eudora, Pegasus Mail, Internet Explorer, WS_FTP, etc. should work fine. When it's time to get off the connection, I have to do that manually, too (or face the consequences). I double-click on the little connection icon,

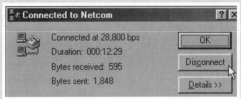

and click Disconnect.

Chapter

16

Browsing the World Wide Web with Internet Explorer 4

Finding your way around Internet Explorer

Browsing the Web off-line

Adding items to your Favorites menu and organizing them

Setting up subscriptions to websites

Defining the subscription schedule, content, and notification method

Browsing Active Channels in Internet Explorer

Subscribing to an Active Channel

Searching the Web using keywords or by topic

Searching the Web in the Explorer bar

Browsing the World Wide Web with Internet Explorer 4

Internet Explorer is your window not only to your own computer and network, but also to the World Wide Web and all you'll find there. Although it's really "just a browser," you'll see in this chapter that Internet Explorer does a lot more than simply display pages from the Web. In fact, you'll find that Internet Explorer is now an integral part of Windows, just as the worldwide network called the Internet is now an integral part of our lives.

Inside Internet Explorer

You'll find that Internet Explorer has many similarities to other Windows programs you have used, especially those in Microsoft Office (Word, Excel, Access, and so on). The primary difference between Internet Explorer and other programs you use is that you use it for viewing files, not editing and saving them. Let's begin by seeing how you can start Internet Explorer.

Starting Internet Explorer

Like just about all Windows programs, Internet Explorer can be started in many ways. You can also run more than one copy of the program at a time, which allows you to view the pages from multiple websites or different sections of the same page.

To start Internet Explorer at any time, simply choose it from the Windows Start menu. In a standard installation, choose Start ➤ Programs ➤ Internet Explorer ➤ Internet Explorer. The program will start and open its *start page*, which is the page Internet Explorer displays first whenever you start it in this way.

NOTE

To specify a different start page for Internet Explorer, choose View ➤ Internet Options, choose the General tab. Enter the URL to the start page in the Address field. You can instead click Use Current to use the URL currently displayed in Internet Explorer, or click Use Blank to display a blank page each time Internet Explorer starts.

If the start page is available on a local or networked drive on your computer or if you are already connected to the Internet, Internet Explorer opens that page immediately and displays it.

If you use a modem to connect to the Internet, however, and the start page resides there but you're not currently connected, Internet Explorer opens your Dial-Up Networking connector to make the connection to the Internet.

Here are some ways you can start Internet Explorer:

- Open an HTML file (one with an htm or html file name extension) in Windows Explorer, and that file will be opened in Internet Explorer (assuming that Internet Explorer is the default browser on your computer).

- Open a GIF or JPEG image file, which are associated with Internet Explorer, unless you have installed another program that takes those associations.

- While in another program, click (activate) a hyperlink that targets an HTML file to open that file in Internet Explorer. For example, while reading an e-mail message you have received in Outlook Express (as shown below), click a hyperlink in the message that targets a website, and that site will be opened in Internet Explorer.

Making Internet Explorer Your Default Browser

If you have installed another browser since installing Internet Explorer, Internet Explorer may not be set as your default browser, and that other browser will be called upon to open any Web pages you request. If you want to make Internet Explorer your default browser and keep it that way, here's how to do it.

In Internet Explorer, choose View ➢ Internet Options. On the Programs tab, you'll find an option called "Internet Explorer should check to see whether it is the default browser." Select this option, and close the Internet Options dialog box.

Now whenever you start Internet Explorer, it will check to see if it is still the default browser. If it finds that it isn't, it will ask if you want it to become the new default browser. If you choose Yes, it will change the Windows settings to make it the default. Now when you open an HTML file—for example, by clicking a hyperlink in a Word document that targets a Web page—Internet Explorer will be the program that opens it. You'll also get the "e" icon on your Desktop for starting Internet Explorer with a single click.

If you later install another browser that makes itself the default, the next time you start Internet Explorer, it will check to see if it is the default and prompt you accordingly.

To close Internet Explorer, choose File ➢ Close as you would in many other programs. Unlike a word processor or spreadsheet program, when you have been viewing sites on the Web in Internet Explorer, there are normally no files to save before exiting the program.

NOTE

When you started Internet Explorer, it may have caused Dial-Up Networking to make the Internet connection. In that case, when you later exit Internet Explorer, you will be asked if you want to disconnect from the Internet. You can choose to stay connected if you want to work in other Internet-related programs. In that case, don't forget to disconnect later by double-clicking the Dial-Up Networking icon in the system tray of the Windows taskbar. Then click the Disconnect button in the dialog box.

The Components of Internet Explorer

Now we'll look at the features and tools that make up Internet Explorer. Figure 16.1 shows Internet Explorer while displaying a Web page. As you can see, the Internet Explorer window contains many of the usual Windows components.

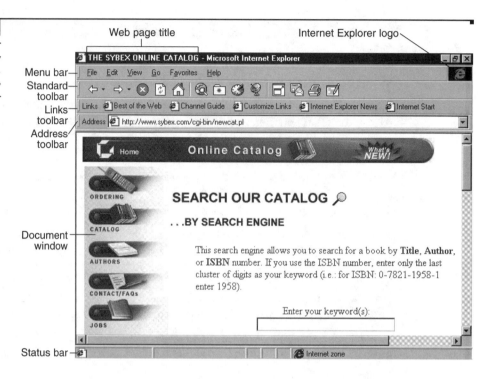

FIGURE 16.1

The Internet Explorer program window contains many components that are common to other Windows programs.

Web page title

Internet Explorer logo

Menu bar

Standard toolbar

Links toolbar

Address toolbar

Document window

Status bar

NOTE

A company or an Internet service provider (ISP) can customize Internet Explorer to make it look and act as though it were their own browser and then distribute it to employees or customers. So if your ISP or your employer gives you a copy of Internet Explorer, it may not look exactly like the one shown in Figure 16.1.

When you want to show as much of the Web page as possible, try the View ➤ Full Screen command, or click the Full Screen button on the toolbar. Internet Explorer will be maximized to occupy the entire screen, it will lose its title bar, status bar, two of its toolbars, and even its menu bar. (You can right-click a toolbar and choose Menu Bar to display it again.)

NOTE

To view or adjust the various options and settings for Internet Explorer, choose View ➤ Internet Options. For example, if you want to have Internet Explorer always start in its full-screen mode, select the Advanced tab in this Internet Options dialog box, and then select the option called "Launch browser in full screen window."

You can switch back to the normal view by choosing the Full Screen command again. The full-screen mode is the default when you open a channel from the desktop (channels are discussed later in this chapter), when it's formally called the Channel Viewer. Here are the parts of Internet Explorer that are labeled in Figure 16.1:

Title Bar: At the top of the window is the usual title bar. It displays either the title of the Web page you are viewing or the document's file name, if it is not a Web page. On the right side of the title bar are the Minimize, Maximize/Restore, and Close buttons; on the left side is the System menu.

Menu Bar: Beneath the title bar is the menu bar, which contains almost all the commands you'll need in Internet Explorer. Keyboard shortcuts are shown next to those commands that have them. For example, you can use the shortcut Ctrl-O instead of choosing the File ➢ Open command.

Toolbars: By default, the toolbars appear beneath the menu bar and contain buttons and other tools that help you navigate the Web or the files and other resources on your computer. The three toolbars are Standard, Links, and Address (top, middle, and bottom in Figure 16.1). The Internet Explorer logo to the right of the toolbar is animated when the program is accessing data.

Document Window: Beneath the menu and toolbars is the main document window, which displays a document such as a Web page, an image, or the files on your computer's disk. If Internet Explorer's program window, which encompasses everything you see in Figure 16.1, is smaller than full-screen, you can resize it by dragging any of its corners or sides. The paragraphs in a Web page generally adjust their width to the size of the window.

TIP

You cannot display multiple document windows in Internet Explorer. Instead, you can view multiple documents by opening multiple instances of Internet Explorer (choose File ➢ New ➢ Window). Each instance of the program is independent of the others.

Explorer Bar: When you click the Search, Favorites, History, or Channels button on the toolbar (or choose one of those commands from the View ➢ Explorer Bar menu), the Explorer bar will appear as a separate pane on the left side of the window. This highly useful feature displays the contents for the button you clicked, such as the search options shown in Figure 16.2. This allows you to make choices in the Explorer bar on the left, such as clicking a link, and have the results appear in the pane on the right. To close the Explorer bar, repeat the command you used to open it, or choose another Explorer bar.

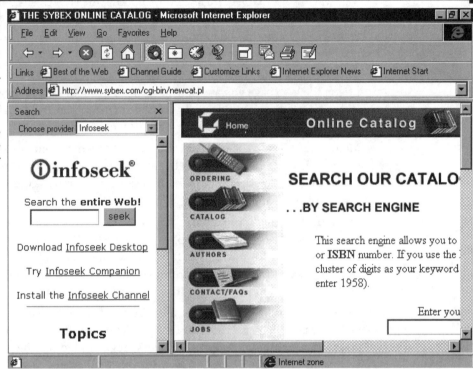

Scroll Bars: The horizontal and vertical scroll bars allow you to scroll the document window over other parts of a document that is otherwise too large to be displayed within the window.

Status Bar: At the bottom of the Internet Explorer window is the status bar. It displays helpful information about the current state of Internet Explorer, so keep an eye on it. For example, when you are selecting a command from the menu bar, a description appears on the status bar. When you point to a hyperlink on the page (either text or an image), the mouse pointer changes to a hand, and the target URL of the hyperlink is displayed on the status bar. When you click a hyperlink to open another page, the status bar indicates what is happening with a progression of messages. Icons that appear on the right side of the status bar give you a status report at a glance. For example, you'll see an icon of a padlock when you have made a secure connection to a website.

You can use the Toolbars and Status Bar commands on the View menu to toggle on or off the display of the toolbars and status bar.

Some Commands You'll Use Frequently

Here's a short list of the Internet Explorer commands that you'll use on a regular basis, or would use if you knew they existed:

- File ➤ Open opens an existing file (an HTML file on your hard disk) in the current Internet Explorer window.

- File ➤ New ➤ Window opens an existing file in a new Internet Explorer window, while leaving the first window open. You can switch between open windows in the usual ways, such as by pressing Alt-Tab.

- File ➤ Save As lets you save the current document to disk as an HTML file.

- File ➤ Properties displays the Properties dialog box for the current document.

- File ➤ Work Offline lets you browse without being on-line, as data is opened from your Internet Explorer cache on your local disk.

- Edit ➤ Cut/Copy/Paste lets you copy or move selected text or images from Internet Explorer to another program.

- Edit ➤ Page opens the current page for editing in your default HTML editor, such as FrontPage Express if it is installed.

Don't forget that you can access some of these commands from the buttons on the Standard toolbar. Also, try right-clicking on an object in Internet Explorer, such as selected text, an image, or the page itself, and see what choices are offered on the shortcut menu.

- Edit ➤ Find (on this page) lets you search for text in the current page, just as you can do in a word processor.

- View ➤ Stop cancels the downloading of the current page, or press Esc.

- View ➤ Refresh updates the contents of the current page by downloading it again, or press F5.

- View ➤ Source displays the HTML source code for the current page in your default text editor, such as Notepad, which is a great way to see the "inner workings" of a page and learn more about HTML, the HyperText Markup Language.

- View ➤ Internet Options lets you view or change the options for Internet Explorer (the command is called View ➤ Folder Options when you are displaying the contents of your local disk).

- Go ➤ Back/Forward lets you move between the pages you've already displayed, or use the buttons on the toolbar.

- Favorites lets you open a site that you have previously saved as a shortcut on the Favorites menu.

- Favorites ➤ Add to Favorites lets you add the current URL to the this menu, and establish a subscription to the site, if you wish.

- Favorites ➤ Organize Favorites opens the Favorites folder so you can rename, revise, delete, or otherwise organize its contents.

Using the Toolbars

The three toolbars in Internet Explorer (Standard, Links, and Address) are quite flexible. You can change the size or position of each one in the trio, or you can choose not to display them at all. In fact, the menu bar is also quite flexible and can be moved below one or more toolbars, or share the same row with them.

- To hide a toolbar, choose View ➤ Toolbars and select one from the menu; to display that toolbar, choose that command again. Or right-click any of the toolbars or the menu bar, and select a toolbar from the shortcut menu.

- To hide the descriptive text below the Standard toolbar buttons, choose View ➤ Toolbars ➤ Text Labels, or right-click a toolbar and choose Text Labels. Choose the command again to display the text.

- To change the number of rows that the toolbars use, point to the bottom edge of the bottom toolbar; the mouse pointer will change to a double-headed arrow. You can then drag the edge up to reduce the number of rows or drag it down to expand them.

- To move a toolbar, drag it by its left edge. For example, drag the Address toolbar onto the same row as the Links toolbar, as shown below.

- To resize a toolbar when two or more share the same row, drag its left edge to the right or left.

NOTE

> Remember, you'll also find these three toolbars when you are browsing the files and folders on your local computer; the Address and Links toolbars are also available on the Windows taskbar.

Standard Toolbar

The buttons on the Standard toolbar in Internet Explorer (the toolbar just beneath the menu bar in Figures 16.1 and 16.2) are shortcuts for the more commonly used commands on its menus. For example, you can click the Stop button to cancel the downloading of the current page, instead of using the View ➤ Stop command, or click the Home button as a shortcut for the Go ➤ Home Page command.

Point at a button to see its name appear in a ToolTip. You can also have each button's name displayed beneath it in the toolbar by choosing View ➤ Toolbars ➤ Text Labels.

Links Toolbar

Each of the buttons on the Links toolbar is a hyperlink to a URL (you can also access these links from the Links command on the Favorites menu). By default, they all target Microsoft websites on the WWW that serve as gateways to a wealth of information on the Web (if you received a customized version of Internet Explorer, these hyperlinks may point to other locations).

For example, the Best of the Web button displays a useful collection of links to reference-related websites, where you might look up a company's phone number, find an e-mail address of a long-lost relative, or find sites that will help you with travel arrangements or personal finance. All the Links buttons are customizable:

- To modify a button's target, right-click it and choose Properties from the shortcut menu, and then choose the Internet Shortcut tab.

- To change any aspect of a button, including its display text, choose Favorites ➤ Organize Favorites and then open the Links folder, where you'll see the names of all the buttons on the Links toolbar. Rename a button just as you rename any file in Windows, such as by selecting it and press F2. Delete a button by selecting its name and pressing Del.

- To add a new Links button, simply drag a hyperlink from a Web page in Internet Explorer onto the Links toolbar. When you release the mouse button, a new button will be created that targets the same file as the hyperlink.

- To rearrange the buttons, drag a button to a new location on the Links bar.

PART

III

Communications and
Using the Internet

Once you've tried these buttons and have a feeling for the content on each of the sites, you can revise the buttons or create new ones that point to sites that you want to access with a click. An example is shown below.

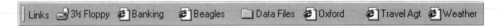

Address Toolbar

The Address toolbar shows the address of the file currently displayed in Internet Explorer, which might be a URL on the Internet or a location on your local disk. You enter a URL or the path to a file or folder *and then press Enter* to open that website or file.

NOTE

When you are entering a URL that you have entered once before, Internet Explorer's AutoComplete feature recognizes the URL and finishes the typing for you. You can either accept the URL or continue to type a new one. Or right-click in the Address toolbar, choose Completions from the shortcut menu, and then select one of the possibilities from the menu.

To revise the URL, click within the Address toolbar and use the normal Windows editing keys. Then press Enter to have Internet Explorer open the specified file. The arrow on the right side of the Address toolbar opens a drop-down list of addresses that you've previously visited via the Address toolbar. They're listed in the order you visited them. Select one from the list and Internet Explorer will open that site.

Getting Help

Internet Explorer offers the usual variety of program help, with a few touches of its own. Choose Help ➢ Contents and Index to display its help window, where you can browse through the topics in the Contents tab, look up a specific word or phrase in the Index tab, or find all references to a word or phrase in the Search tab.

To see if there is a newer version of any of the Internet Explorer software components, or to add new components, choose Help ➢ Product Updates, which is an easy way to keep your software current—immediately and on-line.

To work through a basic online tutorial about browsing the Web, choose Help ➢ Web Tutorial. Internet Explorer goes on-line to a Microsoft website and opens the tutorial page, where you can click your way through the lessons.

To find answers to your questions or problems, choose Help ➢ Online Support. This will open Microsoft's online support page for Internet Explorer. It's packed with tips, troubleshooting guides, answers to common questions, and much more. It's a great place to go for up-to-the-minute solutions and fixes.

The items under Help ➢ Microsoft on the Web each takes you on-line to the Internet, and should prove to be quite valuable. For example, the Best of the Web command displays Microsoft's Exploring page, which offers a wide variety of links to interesting and useful sites. The Send Feedback command lets you post a comment about Internet Explorer for Microsoft. You can report a bug or send in a request for a special feature you'd like to see in the program. The Microsoft Home Page command takes you to Microsoft's ever-so-humble home page for Internet Explorer, where you can catch up on the latest Microsoft news, read about their products, and link to other Microsoft sites.

NOTE

The Microsoft Home Page command is *not* the same as the Go ➢ Home Page command (or the Home button on the Toolbar), which opens your chosen start page.

Moving between Pages

The feature that perhaps best defines the whole concept of browsing in Internet Explorer is your ability to move from page to page, winding your way through the Web. The most common way to do so is by clicking a hyperlink, but this section will also show you some other ways to jump to another page.

Making the Jump with Hyperlinks

You can click an embedded hyperlink (either a text link or a graphic image link) in a page on the Web or your intranet to open the target file of that link. The target can be anywhere on the Web or your local computer. Clicking a link in a page that's on a server in Seattle might open a page on the same server or on a server in London, Tokyo, Brasilia—or maybe next door.

When you point to a text or to an image link with your mouse in Internet Explorer, the pointer changes to a small hand. Click here to jump to the link destination. Clicking a hyperlink with your mouse is the usual way to activate a link, but you can activate a link in Internet Explorer in several other ways.

- For example, you can press Tab to move to the next hyperlink in the page; you'll see a dotted outline around the currently selected link. Press Enter to activate the selected link.

- Right-click a hyperlink and choose Open from the shortcut menu.
- Choose Open in New Window to open the target in a new Internet Explorer window.
- Choose Save Target As to save the target of the link to disk (you will be prompted for a location). In this case, Internet Explorer will not display the target.
- Choose Print Target to print the target of the link without opening it.

You can use any of these methods to open the target of a hyperlink, whether the link is text, an image, or an image map.

In many cases, the target of a hyperlink will be another Web page, which will probably have hyperlinks of its own. Sometimes, however, the target will be another kind of resource, such as an image file or a text file that contains no links of its own. You'll have to use the Back button to return to the previous page.

Another type of target uses the *mailto* protocol. For example, many Web pages have a link via e-mail to the Webmaster—the person who created or maintains the site. The link target might look like the one shown here on the status bar, where the target uses the mailto protocol.

When you click such a link, your e-mail program, such as Outlook Express, opens a new message with the address of the target already entered in the recipient field. You can then fill out the subject and body of the message and send it in the usual way.

Other Ways to Move between Pages

Although clicking a hyperlink in Internet Explorer is the usual way to open another resource (a file, such as a Web page or an image), you'll undoubtedly use other means on a regular basis.

Using the Back and Forward Commands

Once you jump to another page during a session with Internet Explorer, you can use the Back and Forward commands to navigate between the pages you've already visited. You can either use those commands on the Go menu, or the Back and Forward buttons on the toolbar.

You can right-click either button or click the down-arrow to its right to see a menu of the places that button will take you. The first item on the menu is the site you would visit if you simply click the larger button. Select any site from the menu to go directly to that site.

NOTE

The Back and Forward buttons work exactly the same when you are browsing your local or network drive in an Explorer window. As you display various folders, you can use these buttons to open folders that you have already visited.

Using the Address Toolbar

As mentioned before, you can also jump to another page by entering its URL into the Address toolbar and pressing Enter. Keep the following in mind when you do:

- Spelling counts! The bad news is that if you do not type in the address exactly right, Internet Explorer will not be able to open the site and will display an error message to that effect. The good news is that the URL you typed might take you to some new and exciting place on the Web. Good luck!

- If you're entering a complete URL including a file name with a trailing file name extension, watch that extension. Some websites use the traditional four-letter extension for a Web page, HTML. Other sites may have adopted the three-letter extension, HTM.

TIP

One way to take advantage of the Address toolbar is by also taking advantage of the Windows Clipboard. For example, you can copy a URL from a word-processing document and paste it into the Address toolbar—after that, all you need to do is press Enter to go to that site.

Choosing from Your Favorites Menu

In Internet Explorer, you can create a list of your favorite websites or other destinations, such as folders on your local disk, by adding each one to the appropriately named Favorites menu. You don't need to remember a site's URL in order to return to that site—simply select it from the Favorites menu.

You'll learn more about adding to and organizing the Favorites menu later in this chapter in "Returning To Your Favorite Pages." In the section named "Subscribing to Your Favorite Web Sites," you'll learn how to subscribe to sites when you add them to

PART

III

Communications and Using the Internet

your Favorites menu, so that you'll be notified when the site's content has been updated. After that section, you can read about subscribing to channels, which are subscriptions that are defined by each site's publisher, and can bring you unique and timely information.

Digging into the History and Cache Folders

Internet Explorer keeps track of both the URLs you visit and the actual files that are downloaded:

History: It keeps a list of the URLs you visit in its History folder; the default location is C:\Windows\History. You can access these URLs in Internet Explorer with the View ➢ Explorer Bar ➢ History command or by clicking the History button on the toolbar. Your past history will be displayed in chronological order in the Explorer bar in the left-hand pane of the Internet Explorer window, where you can select one of the URLs to open that site in the right-hand pane.

Temporary Internet Files: It saves the files it downloads in a folder on your local drive, which serves as a cache. By default, this folder is C:\Windows\Temporary Internet Files. When you return to a site, any content that has not changed since the last time you visited that site will be opened directly from the cache on your drive. This saves a lot of time, compared with downloading those files again (especially images). You can also open this folder and then open or otherwise use any of the files it contains. Choose View ➢ Internet Options, select the General tab, click the Settings button, and then click the View Files button.

NOTE

When multiple users share one computer, each may have their own History and Temporary Internet Files folders, which will reside within each of their folders within the C:\Windows\Profiles folder.

Browsing Off-line

When you have saved a Web page from the Internet to your local hard disk, you can open that page at any time in Internet Explorer; there's no need to be connected to the Internet to do so. However, think about what happens when you click a link in that page. You opened the page itself from your local hard disk, but more than likely the target file of that link is still back on the Web and not on your disk. To open that file, Internet Explorer needs access to the Internet.

If you have a full-time Internet connection, you might not even notice that Internet Explorer had to go out on the Internet to open that file. If you have a dial-up connection, however, Internet Explorer will first have to make the call and connect to the Internet before opening the file, as shown in Figure 16.3.

The Dial-Up Networking connector offers two choices:

Connect: Go ahead and connect to the Internet so Internet Explorer can find the targeted file.

Stay Offline: Remain off-line, even though you may not be able to access the file.

 If you choose the second option, you'll still see the Working Off-line icon on the status bar, as shown here, and Internet Explorer will attempt to open and display the specified file from your Temporary Internet Files folder (the cache). Remember that most of the files that are opened while you're browsing the Web are saved in this cache folder, as explained in the previous section, so the requested file might be available off-line.

If the file isn't found there, however, Internet Explorer displays the dialog box shown below.

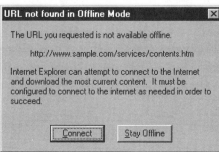

PART

III

Communications and
Using the Internet

As before, you can choose to connect to the Internet to find the file. In that case, the Working Off-line icon disappears once you're connected. If you choose to stay off-line, the requested file will not be opened because it does not reside locally.

You can also choose File ➤ Work Offline at any time, which will again display the Working Off-line icon on the status bar. Internet Explorer will not attempt to connect to the Internet when you request a file, but will look only in its cache.

NOTE

Sites you've never visited or haven't visited recently can't be accessed while off-line, but chances are, files for those sites you visit frequently are still in your cache.

When you're browsing Web pages from your cache in the offline mode, you'll notice that when you point to a link in a page whose target file is *not* available locally in the Internet Explorer cache, the mouse pointer changes to the little hand, as usual, but also displays the international "No" symbol (as shown here). This reminds you that you won't be able to open the target of this link while you are off-line.

When you want to return to browsing on-line when needed, choose File ➤ Work Offline again. The next time you request a file that is on the Internet, a connection will be made in the usual way. You can also click the Connect button in the Dial-Up Connection dialog box (see Figure 16.3) when you have requested a file that is not available locally. The connection will be made and you will no longer be working in the offline mode.

Being able to browse off-line without worrying about Internet Explorer trying to make a connection is especially valuable when you have subscribed to various web-sites and have chosen to have their content downloaded automatically. Automatic downloading will be explained in Chapter 18.

With subscriptions and offline browsing, you don't need to go out of your way to return to sites to see if they've been updated, or wait at the keyboard while large files are downloaded, perhaps from a site that is busy during the times you normally access it. Instead, you can set up Internet Explorer to check the sites you want at any time of the day or night, notify you that those sites have been updated, and optionally down-load any new pages.

So you can browse those sites off-line and let Internet Explorer load the pages and assorted files directly from your Temporary Internet Files folder (the cache). Not only will these sites load almost instantly, but you can also view them while sitting in your beach chair near the breaking waves.

Returning to Your Favorite Pages

If you've browsed in Internet Explorer for more than a few hours, you've undoubtedly run into what is perhaps the easiest thing to do on the Web—lose your place and be unable to find your way back to a page that you really, really want to visit. Whatever your reasons for wanting to return to a specific page, the Favorites menu offers the best solution for finding your way back.

The Structure of the Favorites Menu

On the Favorites menu you can store the names of any sites, folders, or other resources that you might want to return to. To visit a one again, simply select it from the Favorites menu. Remember that you'll also find the Favorites menu on the Windows Start menu, and you can access your Favorites folder from just about any Files dialog box in a Windows program.

This menu is put together in much the same way as your Windows Start menu. For example, the Favorites menu is built from the Favorites folder within your Windows folder, just as the Start menu is built from the Start Menu folder. The items on the Favorites menu are actually shortcuts that reside in the Favorites folder. You can create submenus on the Favorites menu to help you organize items into relevant categories. The submenus are actually folders within the Favorites folder.

Don't forget that you can also display your Favorites menu in the Explorer bar. Choose View ➢ Explorer Bar ➢ Favorites, or click the Favorites button on the toolbar. You'll be able to click a link in your Favorites menu in the Explorer bar and see the target open in the pane on the right.

Adding Items to the Favorites Menu

When you browse to a page or other resource that you just might want to return to, the smart thing to do is add it to your Favorites menu. To do so, choose Favorites ➢ Add to Favorites, or right-click anywhere within the page and choose Add to Favorites. You are then presented with the Add Favorite dialog box, shown in Figure 16.4, in which you can:

- Specify the name of the page as it should appear on the menu.
- Choose to place the new item in a submenu on the Favorites menu.
- Choose to subscribe to this page so that Internet Explorer will automatically check the site and either notify you of new content or notify you and optionally download any new pages that you can then view off-line (subscriptions are discussed a little later in this chapter).

When you add an item to the Favorites menu, you can specify the name that will appear on the menu as well as the submenu (folder) in which it should appear.

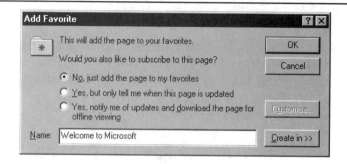

Naming an Item for the Favorites Menu

When you are adding a Web page to the Favorites menu, Internet Explorer by default uses the page's title as its name on the Favorites menu. In Figure 16.4, the page's title was *Welcome to Microsoft*. If you are viewing a file or folder from your local or network drive, the file or folder name will be used as the default name for the Favorites menu.

In either case, you are free to revise the name to make it more recognizable when you later want to find it on the menu. For example, in Figure 16.4, you could probably shorten the name to *Microsoft*. Not only is this name quite recognizable, but it will also be alphabetized appropriately on the menu.

Try to keep names short and descriptive. Any menu works best when you can quickly scan it to find the item you want. Additionally, the Favorites menu displays only the first 40 characters or so of any long names.

Choosing a Submenu for the New Item

When you add an item to the Favorites menu, it appears on the top-level menu by default, so you'll see that item when you first open the menu. However, this is usually *not* the best place to add new items. In the real world, you'll end up with dozens or, more likely, hundreds of items on your Favorites menu. Opening that menu and finding one long list could soon be less than helpful.

You can avoid this by adding a new item within a submenu, so that the item appears "farther down" in the nest of menus. Again, this is the same concept and mechanism as your Windows Start menu.

Keep at least one submenu that serves as a catchall for items that you can't readily categorize. You can call that submenu something like *Temp* or *Misc*. Then, when you can't decide in which submenu to place a new item, don't put it on the top-level menu. Put it in the catchall menu instead, where it will be out of the way so that you can deal with it later when you organize your Favorites menu.

In most cases, when you're creating a new item in the Add Favorite dialog box (as shown earlier in Figure 16.4), you'll want to click the Create In button, which opens a view of your Favorites folder and the folders it contains. Click your way to the folder you want for the new item, so that the folder icon appears opened. Then click OK.

If a suitable folder does not yet exist in your Favorites folder, click the New Folder button in the Add Favorite dialog box. Enter a name for the new folder and click OK. The new folder is created within the currently selected folder. You can then select the new folder and add the new item to it.

TIP

If you create a new item in the Favorites Links folder, that item appears as a new button on the Links toolbar.

Organizing Your Favorites Menu

When you add a new item to the Favorites menu, you can change its name, place it in a submenu off the Favorites menu (a subfolder of the Favorites folder), or create a new submenu (folder) for it.

The Favorites menu isn't static, however. You can change it whenever the need arises. You can make most changes right from the menu simply by right-clicking a menu item to access its shortcut menu. So if you want to delete an item from the Favorites menu, rename it, or change its target, just right-click it.

If you want to make several changes to the menu, you'll probably find it easier to choose Favorites ➤ Organize Favorites. You'll see the Organize Favorites dialog box, as shown in Figure 16.5. Before we look at the changes you can make to the Favorites menu, you should consider the ways you might organize your menu.

You'll want to organize your Favorites menu every bit as well as you do your day-to-day files on your hard disk. Keeping the things you need well organized, whether they are items on the Favorites menu or files on your hard disk, will make your daily routines much more efficient. So what's the best way to organize your Favorites menu? The answer is "Any way you want."

The trick is to create categories (folders) that are relevant to the types of sites you are collecting and the way you would naturally group them. No doubt you'll be creating new subfolders and rearranging the existing ones on a regular basis. In fact, the more you browse the Net, the more you'll realize how powerful a well-organized Favorites menu can be.

PART

III

Communications and
Using the Internet

FIGURE 16.5

You can make changes to the files or folders in the Favorites folder with the Organize Favorites dialog box.

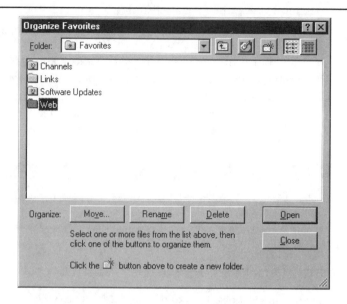

The menu item named Web in the Organize Favorites dialog box in Figure 16.5 was created so that all the other Web-related categories could fall beneath it as submenus. This adds a layer of menu each time you select an item, but it also keeps the top-level Favorites menu uncluttered. As time goes by, you might instead choose to have several main categories on the Favorites menu that lead to multiple submenus.

In the Organize Favorites dialog box, you select items as you always do; so you can select multiple items with Shift-Click or Ctrl-Click. You can perform just about any file operation on the selected items, using either the buttons in the dialog box or the commands on the shortcut menu when you right-click a selected item.

For example, you can move an item from one menu (folder) to another, or delete an item to remove it from the menu. Once you've become familiar with a website, you might want to rename its shortcut on your Favorites menu to make it shorter or more recognizable.

Subscribing to Your Favorite Websites

The one constant to the World Wide Web is that it seems to grow faster every day. This is a great boon for all of us, but it also introduces some rather hefty problems: How do we stay in touch with a website so we know when it has new information, without having to go back and visit it on a regular basis?

Internet Explorer in Windows 98 offers two answers: subscriptions and channels. Subscriptions are a way for you to let Internet Explorer check websites for new content without your involvement.

Channels are Internet Explorer's way of implementing *Webcasting*, a technology by which content from a website seems to be *pushed* to you, instead of your having to go and get it. In fact, channels are really just a more sophisticated form of subscriptions, in which the parameters for a subscription are set by the website and are, therefore, tuned specifically for that site. Channels are discussed later in this chapter; we'll start with subscriptions.

Using Subscriptions to Stay in Touch

Traditionally, when you *subscribe* to something, such as a magazine or a newspaper, it regularly arrives on your doorstep or in your mailbox—daily, weekly, or monthly.

In the new world of the Internet, the concept of needing a traditional subscription no longer exists—if you want to see what's happening on the Times of London website, just go look at it! There's no need to wait by your mailbox for the next edition.

NOTE

Because of the ease with which a website can be updated, many online newspapers add content to their site several times throughout the day. If this sounds totally modern and high-tech, don't forget that back in the old days, big-city newspapers printed several updated editions throughout the day. Extra! Extra!

But the ease with which you can access data on the Internet creates substantial hurdles. We tend to access not just a few sites, but we regularly access dozens or hundreds. It's not just *The Times* of London but *The New York Times*, *The Los Angeles Times*, and who knows how many other *Times* throughout the world? The list goes on and on.

How do you find out if a site has new content without actually going there, and how do you then find the time to download it all at the less-than-thrilling speeds of our normal Internet connections?

Signing Up for a Subscription

The answer is the *subscription*, which is the way Internet Explorer 4 and Windows 98 can keep you up-to-date with your chosen websites—automatically. When you subscribe to one of the sites on your Favorites menu, you're telling Internet Explorer that you want to keep in touch with that site, be notified when it has new material, and, optionally, have that material delivered to you.

PART

III

Communications and
Using the Internet

The term *subscription* is a little misleading, because traditionally we subscribe to something by contacting the owners or publishers. But a site subscription is internal to Internet Explorer; it does not involve the publishers of a website. It's just a convenient term that describes an important part of the traditional subscription terminology: getting information regularly.

Subscribing to a site in Internet Explorer saves you time and effort in several ways:

- Internet Explorer will automatically check each subscribed site to see if it has any content that is new since the last time you visited that site. And you can have it do its checking at any time of the day or night. Imagine how much time it would otherwise take you to trudge manually from site to site, wondering if new material might be there.

- When a subscribed site changes or has new material, Internet Explorer notifies you and can automatically download all the new content.

- When Internet Explorer updates the content from a subscribed site, it stores the new content on your local drive. You can then access that new content *without* being connected to the Internet and downloading that content over your Internet connection. This means that you can do without that wire that binds you to the Net, and that you can access the data from your hard disk many times faster than you could access it from the Internet.

The bottom line is that you can come into work Monday morning and find that Internet Explorer has updated all your subscribed sites with their new content.

Subscribing to a Site

As discussed in the previous chapter, when you're adding a site to your Favorites menu, you choose whether to subscribe to that site in the Add Favorite dialog box, which was shown earlier in Figure 16.4. There are three subscription choices (the site is added to your Favorites menu no matter which one you choose):

No is the default choice, so that no subscription is set up.

Yes, but only tell me will have you notified when the site has new content.

Yes and download will have you notified when there is new content, and that new content will also be downloaded to your local disk.

If you want to subscribe to the site you're adding to your Favorites menu, pick either of the Yes options and then click the OK button to accept the default subscription settings. Alternatively, you can click the Customize button, which starts the Subscription

Wizard. It will take you through the steps of defining the subscription in the following categories (you'll read about all of these later in the chapter):

Notification: The manner in which you will be notified when Internet Explorer finds new data on the site. By default, the item's icon in the Favorites menu displays a starlike gleam.

Download: How much of any new data will be downloaded.

Schedule: The schedule Internet Explorer will follow to check the site for new content. By default, if you have a LAN connection to the Internet, the site is checked automatically without your intervention. If you have a dial-up (modem) connection, by default you'll have to update the subscription manually, although you can choose to have the site checked automatically. You can also specify a custom schedule or choose to manually update this subscription no matter how you connect to the Internet.

You can also subscribe to a site that's already on your Favorites menu. The easiest way to do so is to find the site on your Favorites menu in the usual way, but don't open it. Instead, right-click on that item in the menu and then choose Subscribe from the shortcut menu that pops up.

Choosing Subscribe displays the Subscribe Favorite dialog box, which is similar to the Add Favorite dialog box. Choose to be notified when the site has new content or to have that content downloaded, as well. Then click OK to accept the default settings, or click Customize to adjust them.

Whether you subscribe to a new or existing site on the Favorites menu, the result is the same. In the next section, you'll see how to browse a subscribed site without actually going there.

Browsing Your Updated Subscriptions

Let's take a short tour of how subscriptions work to give you a feel for why subscriptions can be so important. You'll learn about all these steps later in the discussion of subscriptions.

When you subscribe to a website, Internet Explorer automatically checks that site for new content, either when you specifically ask it to (a manual update) or according to the schedule you've chosen. If the site has new content, Internet Explorer downloads as much of the new material as you specified in the subscription settings (none, by default) and then notifies you by the method you chose, such as by displaying a star on the item's icon on the Favorites menu.

PART

III

Communications and
Using the Internet

When you highlight a subscription on the Favorites menu that has new content available, you'll see a ToolTip that displays the date and time when Internet Explorer last updated it (checked it for new content).

To view all your subscriptions, choose Favorites ➢ Manage Subscriptions. An Explorer window then displays a list of your subscriptions. You can see which ones have been updated recently, open one as you would any Internet shortcut, or right-click a subscription to view or revise its properties.

Here's where the second half of the subscription trick kicks in. If you chose to have Internet Explorer download a subscription's new content, you can browse that updated website while off-line—you don't need to be connected to the Internet. Internet Explorer has already downloaded all the new material from that site, and it is waiting for you on your local hard disk.

Browsing Your Subscriptions while Off-Line

When trying to browse files off-line, you may sometimes see an error message indicating that the file you requested is not available off-line. The amount of offline browsing you can do for any subscribed website depends on how much of that website is already on your computer in the Temporary Internet Files folder (the cache folder for Internet Explorer).

If you browse to that site regularly or have that site's new content downloaded frequently via a subscription, a great deal of that site's content should now be available. Nonetheless, a large website can have huge amounts of data hiding many links down in the site, farther than a subscription can reach (as you'll read later). Some links might target files external to the site, that were not included in the subscription download.

So if you click a link that targets a file that you don't have on your local computer, Internet Explorer must connect to the Internet to get that file, as described earlier in this chapter in "Browsing Off-Line."

Being able to browse without being connected to the Internet means that you might let Internet Explorer update your subscriptions on your portable computer the night before you plan to travel. The next morning, you can unplug your portable from the network or telephone line and head for the airport. Once you've settled into your seat on the plane, you can browse those updated websites as though you were connected to them over the Internet. Not only are you free of a network connection, but Internet Explorer opens websites at hard-drive speeds. You will have to wait barely a second for a site to open.

Canceling a Subscription

A subscription remains in effect until you revise or cancel it completely. You'll learn how to revise one in the sections that follow; here's how to cancel one. Find the item on the Favorites menu, right-click it, and then choose Unsubscribe from the shortcut menu. You'll be prompted about the impending removal of the subscription. Choose Yes to remove the subscription, or choose No to leave it as it is.

You can also cancel a subscription in the Organize Favorites dialog box in the same way. If you're going to be canceling or otherwise revising several subscriptions, it might be more convenient to do this within the Subscriptions dialog box (choose Favorites ➢ Manage Subscriptions). Right-click the site you want, and choose Properties from the shortcut menu (there is no Unsubscribe command). Choose the Subscription tab, and then click its Unsubscribe button.

When you unsubscribe to a site, you're only canceling the subscription. The site remains on the Favorites menu as before, but Internet Explorer does not check it for new content.

Viewing Your Current Subscriptions

To open a list of all your subscriptions at any time, choose Favorites ➢ Manage Subscriptions. This opens an Explorer window that lists all your subscriptions, as shown in Figure 16.6. Notice the icons to the left of each item in the list. Some are Web pages, others are channels, and still others are channels that have their own unique icon. The channels you subscribe to are essentially special websites that define their own subscription download schedule, but they are nonetheless subscriptions, as you'll read later in this chapter.

The columns of information in the list of Subscriptions are mostly from the various settings in each subscription's properties dialog box, and they allow you to see these settings at a glance. You can easily see which subscriptions have new content, how many of them are updated daily, weekly, or manually, or which ones were updated most recently. To change the settings for a subscription, right-click it and choose Properties from its shortcut menu.

FIGURE 16.6

To view or modify your current subscriptions, choose Favorites ➢ Manage Subscriptions.

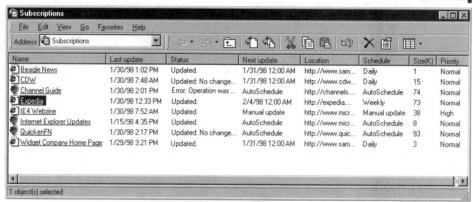

Click a column title to sort the list of Subscriptions by that column. For example, click the Last Updated column title to sort the list by the dates in that column. Click the column title again to sort in the opposite order (ascending or descending).

The Subscriptions list (or folder) is the place to go when you want to update a few but not all of your subscriptions. Simply select the subscriptions you want to update, and choose File ➢ Update Now, or right-click a selected subscription and choose Update Now.

When you want to go offline to browse the downloaded content of your subscriptions, you could look for each subscribed site on your Favorites menu that has the "gleam" on its icon, which indicates new content. But browsing through all the menus could be quite tedious, and the gleam doesn't tell you if a subscription includes downloading the content to your disk.

It's much easier to open your Subscriptions folder, where you'll have access to all your subscriptions with no other sites in the way.

Defining Your Subscriptions

As mentioned earlier, when you subscribe to a new site, you can choose to have Internet Explorer notify you when that site has new content, or download that content, as well. You'll be notified that there's new material at a site by the "gleam" on the item's icon in the Favorites menu. You can either choose the default schedule for that site or set your own custom schedule.

In the sections that follow, you'll learn how to modify all these settings for any existing subscriptions on your Favorites menu or when you create a new subscription.

When creating a subscription for a new site on your Favorites menu, click the Customize button in the Add Favorite dialog box (look back at Figure 16.4), which starts the Subscription Wizard.

Here's how to change the settings for an existing site subscription on the Favorites menu:

1. Find the site on your Favorites menu (or in the Organize Favorites dialog box or in the Subscription folder).

2. Right-click the site and choose Properties.

3. In the Properties dialog box, you'll find three subscription-related tabs with which you can view or revise the subscription settings.

   Subscription displays the current settings for the subscription.

   Receiving lets you choose how to be notified when Internet Explorer finds new content on the subscribed site and whether that new content should be downloaded. You can also limit how much content is downloaded so that you don't end up being surprised by who knows how many megabytes of new material!

   Schedule lets you choose the schedule that Internet Explorer will follow when checking the site for new content.

4. Make any changes you want to the subscription and click OK when finished.

The following sections will show you how to adjust all the subscription options so that you'll be able to tune any subscription to fit your need for updated content from that site.

Viewing Current Subscription Settings

To look at the current subscription settings for an Internet shortcut, open its Properties dialog box and select the Subscription tab, as shown in Figure 16.7. Here you'll see the name of the item as it appears on the Favorites menu, its URL, the type of notification you'll receive when the site has been updated, whether any data will be downloaded, the update schedule, and the date and time when the site was last updated and when it will be updated next.

On this tab you'll find the Unsubscribe button, which you can click to remove the subscription from this site.

PART

III

Communications and
Using the Internet

FIGURE 16.7

The Subscription tab in the Properties dialog box shows you the current settings and status of a subscription.

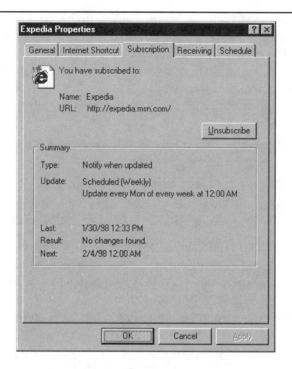

Choosing How You Want to Be Notified

When you are subscribing to a new website and choose only to be notified, clicking the Customize button in the Add Favorite dialog box (refer to Figure 16.4) opens the first dialog box of the Subscription Wizard, which is shown in Figure 16.8. (When you have chosen to download pages, this step of the Wizard comes a little later in the process.)

Here you choose whether you want an e-mail message sent to you when Internet Explorer finds new content at this site. By default, the No option is selected.

If you choose Yes, Internet Explorer notifies you by e-mail when it finds new content at this site. If you normally use an HTML-enabled mail program, such as Outlook Express, the e-mail message will actually contain the Web page. Otherwise, you will receive a plain text message that includes the URL of the subscribed site.

If you then click Change Address, you can enter a different e-mail address and mail server that Internet Explorer should use. If you're traveling, you could have Internet Explorer check your subscriptions from your desktop computer and then notify you by e-mail when a subscription has new content.

With either choice, when this site has new content you'll be notified by a starlike gleam on this item's icon on the Favorites menu. This simply lets you know that there's something new at this site.

FIGURE 16.8

The first dialog box of the Web Site Subscription Wizard lets you choose whether new content should be downloaded when Internet Explorer checks this site.

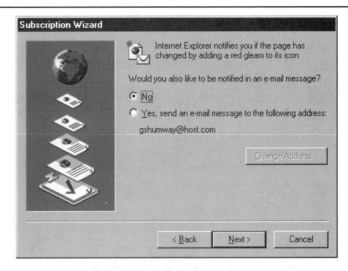

When you're revising the settings for an existing subscription, look on the Receiving tab in the Properties dialog box for the Notification options; it's shown in Figure 16.9. If you want to be e-mailed when this site has new content, select that checkbox. If you need to change the e-mail address, click the Change Address button. In the next section, we'll discuss how you can have Internet Explorer download any new content it finds at a subscribed site.

FIGURE 16.9

In the Receiving tab in the Properties dialog box, you can change a subscription's method of notification and specify whether new content will be downloaded.

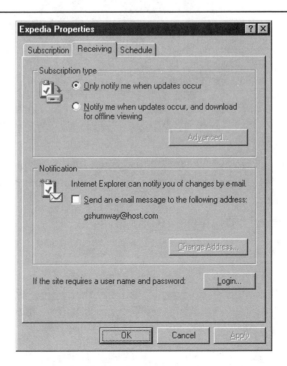

PART

III

Communications and Using the Internet

Choosing How Much Content Should Be Delivered

When you're defining a new subscription or revising the settings for an existing one, you can limit how much new content Internet Explorer will download. As mentioned earlier, if you have chosen only to be notified, Internet Explorer simply checks the site for new content but does not download any. You can browse to the site in the usual fashion and see the new content that way. Let's look at the ways you can have Internet Explorer download that content for you—automatically and even while you're not at your computer.

When you're creating a new subscription, you have two options for downloading new content, as shown in Figure 16.10:

- Download this page.

- Download this page and pages linked to it.

The Subscription Wizard lets you choose how much new content to download.

If you choose "Download this page," Internet Explorer downloads only the one page that is the target for this item on the Favorites menu. For example, if the URL for this item is:

www.widget.com/default.htm

only the page named DEFAULT.HTM is checked and, if there is new content, downloaded to your computer.

If you choose "Download this page and pages linked to it," the targets of any links on this page are also downloaded. In other words, if there are ten links on this page, you'll receive 11 downloaded pages, or whatever files are the targets for those links.

Obviously, unless you know a site well, you really have no idea how many pages might be downloaded.

When you choose this second option and click the Next button, you'll see the dialog box shown in Figure 16.11, which asks you how many links "deep" you'd like to have downloaded. The default is 0 (the maximum is 3), so that only the target of each link is downloaded. If you set this option to 1, not only is the target of each link downloaded, but so are all the targets of all the links found on any of those pages.

FIGURE 16.11

Internet Explorer will follow links to the number of levels you specify, and download their targets.

Subscription Wizard

In addition to this page, Internet Explorer can download linked pages.

For example, if this page links to three pages, Internet Explorer will download all three to your computer.

How many linked pages deep do you want to download?

1   pages

Warning: If you download one or two links deep from this page, it can increase your Internet connection time and decrease the amount of disk space on your computer.

< Back   Next >   Cancel

WARNING

When you specify a certain number of pages deep, you're creating a potential situation that is not unlike the family tree of fruit flies multiplying in a biology classroom. If the site has lots of good links, you might be committing to a lifetime's supply of pages! Use caution even when specifying a depth of two pages. Once you're very familiar with a site and how many links it tends to have, you can increase the depth as needed.

You have even more download options when you revise the settings for an existing subscription. As you saw in Figure 16.9, the Receiving tab in the Properties dialog box has a group of options labeled Downloading. If you choose the "Notify and download" option, you can then click the Advanced button to access the Advanced Download Options dialog box, shown in Figure 16.12.

Communications and
Using the Internet

FIGURE 16.12

In the Advanced Download Options dialog box, you can specify exactly how much content you want Internet Explorer to download from a subscribed site.

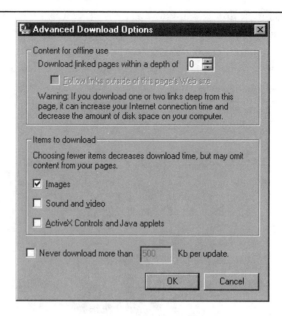

This dialog box gives you a wide range of options for limiting the amount of data that Internet Explorer downloads from this site.

As you can when you're specifying a new subscription, you can choose to download the pages targeted by the links on this page. Again, use caution with this option until you are familiar with this site. If you choose to download links, use even more caution when you choose the option to download linked pages even when they reside outside the subscribed page's website. This is definitely an option to leave disabled until you are familiar with a site and the links it contains. You wouldn't want Internet Explorer to attempt to download the entire World Wide Web!

In the next group of options, Items to Download, you can choose the type of content to include or exclude from the download. To avoid lengthy downloads, deselect some or all of these options. If a page contains a deselected item, such as a video or an audio clip, you'll have to do without that content. When you select any of the other data types, download times could increase drastically.

The last option lets you limit the amount of data that is downloaded when Internet Explorer updates this site. By default, there is no limit, so if you want to specify one, select this option and enter the maximum number of kilobytes that should be downloaded (remember that 1000 kilobytes (KB) is 1 megabyte (MB)).

Setting a Subscription Schedule

When you are subscribing to a new website and have chosen to download new content, one of the last dialog boxes in the Web Site Subscriptions Wizard (shown in Figure 16.13) lets you specify the schedule by which this site will be updated. You have three choices:

Scheduled You can set the precise schedule, such as at a specific time each day, every hour during the nighttime hours, once each Monday, once a month, and so on.

Manually You must specifically choose to update one or more sites, which you can do at any time.

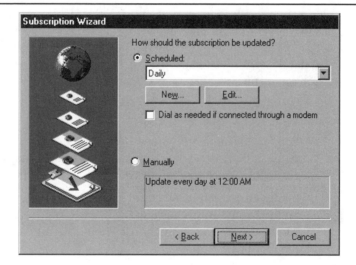

FIGURE 16.13

You can specify a schedule for a new subscription or choose to update it manually.

Let's look at two disparate scenarios for scheduling the updating of your subscriptions. Suppose you have a network connection to the Internet that is always "live" and available and that you tend to leave your computer on 24 hours a day. In this case, you can set just about any schedule you want.

NOTE

You can create your own, customized schedules by clicking the New button in the Subscription Wizard's scheduling dialog box. The name of each custom schedule will appear on the drop-down menu of schedule types so you can apply them to other subscriptions.

PART

III

Communications and
Using the Internet

Whenever the scheduled time rolls around, Internet Explorer automatically connects with the Internet, goes to each subscribed site, and downloads whatever content you specified. You can schedule these updates for the evenings or weekends when they won't get in the way of your daily work routine and when the Internet and your network may be less busy, as well.

At the opposite end of the spectrum, suppose that you connect to the Internet with a modem, that you pay for your connection by the hour, and that you tend to turn your computer off at the end of the day. In this case, you'll probably want to update your subscriptions manually while you're working at the computer, as described in the next section.

Updating Your Subscriptions Manually

You can update any or all of your subscriptions at any time by doing so manually. If a subscription is set to be manually updated, this is the only way you can have this site checked for new content. But even if a site has a custom schedule, you can still choose to update it manually at any time.

You can manually update sites in several ways:

- To update all your subscriptions, in any Explorer window choose Favorites ➢ Update All Subscriptions.

- To update a single subscribed site, right-click that site's item on the Favorites menu and choose Update Now. Or if you have already opened that site's Properties dialog box, choose the Schedule tab, and click the Update Now button.

- To update multiple subscriptions, open your Subscriptions folder in an Explorer window by choosing Favorites ➢ Manage Subscriptions. Select one or more subscriptions and choose File ➢ Update Now; or right-click one and choose Update Now.

When the update begins, you'll see the Downloading Subscriptions dialog box similar to the one shown in Figure 16.14. If you click the Details button, which was done in this figure, you'll see a list of all the sites being checked and the status of each one. To cancel the updating, click the Stop button. To cancel it for just one site, select that site in the details list and click the Skip button.

NOTE

The Downloading Subscriptions dialog box is a separate process (program) that you can minimize or otherwise ignore while it does its job.

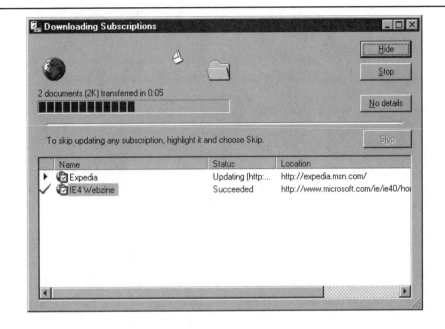

FIGURE 16.14

The Downloading Subscriptions dialog box shows you the status of the subscriptions update.

Viewing and Subscribing to Active Channels

So far we've looked at two ways to retrieve information from the Web:

- By explicitly visiting a website, such as by entering a URL into the Address toolbar or by following a hyperlink
- By subscribing to a website

Now we'll look at a third technique, which builds on the concept of subscriptions. This was a major new feature of Internet Explorer 4 called Active Channels. It can deliver just the information you want and on a timely basis, where *timely* is defined by the publisher of that information.

The term *channel* suggests TV quality or TV attributes, but the technology is not quite there at this point (for which we may yet give thanks). A channel is not a site that broadcasts information (thus, the term *channel* is confusing, to say the least). It is actually a regular website that provides information through regular Web pages. In fact, you can generally view a site that is a channel just as you would view any website; the trick becomes evident when you choose to subscribe to a channel.

When you subscribe to a Web page, Internet Explorer visits that site from time to time and checks that site's content to see whether it has changed. You can subscribe to any site, even if it was created prior to the release of Internet Explorer 4. A channel is similar, but you can only subscribe to a channel when that site has been configured as a channel.

You subscribe to a channel simply by linking to a file that contains the site's Channel Definition Format (a CDF file). This file is provided by the publisher of the site and automatically defines the subscription to this channel in Internet Explorer. You'll see how all this works in the sections that follow.

You can also customize channels. Besides viewing a channel in Internet Explorer, either on-line or off-line (if you have chosen to download its contents), you can make a channel an item on your Active Desktop or part of the Channel screen saver.

Before we get into the details, let's see how channels are used. By looking at a few examples, you will be able to better understand the differences between channels and subscriptions, as well as the advantages of channels over plain browsing.

Viewing a Channel in Internet Explorer

As mentioned earlier, you can view a channel in several ways. First, you can simply go to a website that happens to be a channel, in any of the usual ways. In fact, you may often encounter websites quite by accident that are set up to be used as channels; whether you subscribe to a channel is your decision.

When you installed Windows 98 and Internet Explorer, links to a variety of channels were also installed, which you can access in a number of ways. In Internet Explorer, choose View ➢ Explorer Bar ➢ Channels, or click the Channels button on the toolbar, and your list of channels will be displayed in the Explorer bar. To close the Explorer bar, click that button again.

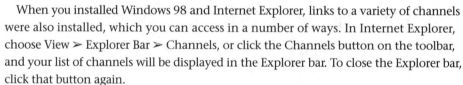

NOTE

The Channel Guide channel is a Microsoft site at which you will find additional channels. You'll see shortly how to visit a channel so you can subscribe to it.

You can also use the Favorites ➢ Channels command in Internet Explorer. That menu of channels is also available with the Favorites ➢ Channels command on the Windows Start menu. Selecting a channel in this way opens the channel in Internet Explorer.

Viewing a Channel in the Channel Viewer

When the Quick Launch toolbar is displayed on the taskbar, you can click the View Channels button to open Internet Explorer in a full-screen mode known as the Channel Viewer, which is shown in Figure 16.15. The Explorer bar is displayed on the left side of the screen, as shown in the figure. You can also launch a channel in the Channel Viewer by selecting the channel from the Channel bar on the desktop, as discussed in the next section.

NOTE

> The channels you'll see in your own Explorer bar will probably vary from those shown in Figure 16.15, in the same way that we can each have our own list of favorite websites. As Internet Explorer 4 is used by more and more people, you'll undoubtedly find that many websites will now offer you the option to subscribe to their channels from within their home page.

You can close the Explorer bar by clicking the Channels button on the toolbar, but in the Channel Viewer, the Explorer bar will automatically slide out of the way when your mouse is not over it. Simply point to the left side of the screen to have the Explorer bar slide open again. To prevent the Explorer Bar from hiding, click the pushpin button that you'll find on the right side of the Explorer bar's title bar.

FIGURE 16.15

The Channel Viewer is Internet Explorer's special full-screen mode that offers the maximum amount of viewing area.

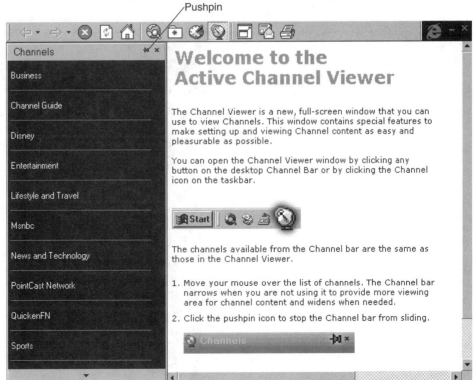

PART

III

Communications and
Using the Internet

When you're using Internet Explorer in Channel Viewer mode, almost all the tools in Internet Explorer are hidden, by default, leaving as much room as possible for the Web page. Only the standard toolbar is displayed, and you can even hide that by choosing the Auto Hide command from the shortcut menu when you right-click the toolbar. The other toolbars, the status bar, and even the menu bar are hidden! This really is a full-screen mode, because even the Windows taskbar is hidden.

You can turn on these features in the usual ways. For example, right-click the toolbar and choose Menu Bar to display the menus, or use the View menu to turn on the status bar or the other toolbars. To return to the normal view in Internet Explorer, choose View ➤ Full Screen, or click that button on the toolbar.

Viewing a Channel from the Channel Bar

Yet another way to access a channel is from the Channel bar, which can be displayed on the Active Desktop. It offers the same choices that you'll find on the Channels menu or in the list of channels in the Explorer bar, only they're conveniently placed as icons in the Channel bar (shown in Figure 16.16) which you can access from the desktop. When you open a channel in this way, it is displayed in Internet Explorer's Channel Viewer, as discussed in the previous section.

FIGURE 16.16

You can access a channel by clicking its icon in the Channel bar; some channels offer sub-categories, as well.

We'll discuss the Active Desktop in detail in Chapter 18, but if you don't see the Channel bar on your Active Desktop, here's how to display it. First, you may have disabled the Active Desktop entirely, so right-click the desktop and choose Active Desktop from the shortcut menu. On the submenu that is displayed, the View as Web Page item should have a checkmark next to it. If not, select it to turn on the Active Desktop.

If you still don't see the Channel bar, you need to add it to the Active Desktop, using the following method (you can also turn on or off other items on the Active Desktop in this way):

1. From the Windows Start menu, choose Settings ➢ Active Desktop ➢ Customize My Desktop, or right-click the desktop and choose Properties to open the Display Properties dialog box, and then select the Web tab, which is shown in Figure 16.17.

2. In the list of items, select the Internet Explorer Channel Bar by clicking its checkbox.

3. The option named "View my Active Desktop as a Web page" should also be selected if you already used the View as Web Page command discussed earlier. Otherwise, select this option.

4. Click OK to close the Display Properties dialog box.

The Channel Bar should now appear on your desktop.

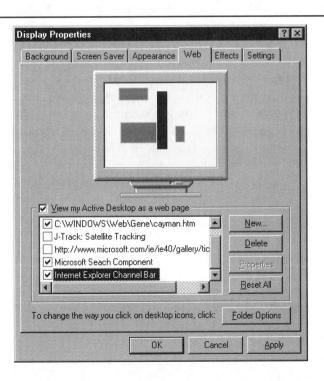

FIGURE 16.17

The Web tab in the Display Properties dialog box, where you can add items to the Active Desktop.

PART

III

Communications and Using the Internet

Subscribing to an Active Channel

In most cases, the first time you access a channel, such as by clicking its button in the Channel bar, an introductory screen at that site invites you to subscribe to the channel. Unless you're informed otherwise, no cost is involved, and most channels don't even require a registration. You simply answer a few questions for Internet Explorer, just as you do when subscribing to a website.

Internet Explorer organizes many channels into categories. For example, when you are viewing the Channel bar on the desktop or in the Explorer bar in Internet Explorer and click the News & Technology button, you will see the names of the channels in that category, such as:

- CMPNet
- CNN Interactive
- The CNET Channel
- The New York Times
- Wired
- ZDNet

These channels are all related to the news and technology category. In the right pane of the Internet Explorer window, you will see the icons that correspond to these channels. To subscribe to the CNET channel, for example, first click its button (in either pane) to access that site. If you are in the Channel Viewer (full-screen mode), the Explorer bar with its list of channels slides to the left and is hidden (unless you leave the mouse pointer resting on it), and CNET's opening screen appears and invites you to subscribe, looking something like the one shown in Figure 16.18.

To subscribe to the CNET channel, click the Click Here to Subscribe button. Most channels will have a similar way to subscribe, although it might be called something like "Add Active Channel". This button links to a Channel Definition Format file (CDF), which will trigger Internet Explorer to create what is essentially a channel subscription.

The process of adding active channels may vary, depending on the settings and content of each site, but Figure 16.19 shows a typical case, where the Add Active Channel dialog box is displayed. The process is very much like adding a website to your Favorites menu and creating a subscription to the site, but in this case it's for a channel.

FIGURE 16.18

CNET invites you to subscribe to its channel.

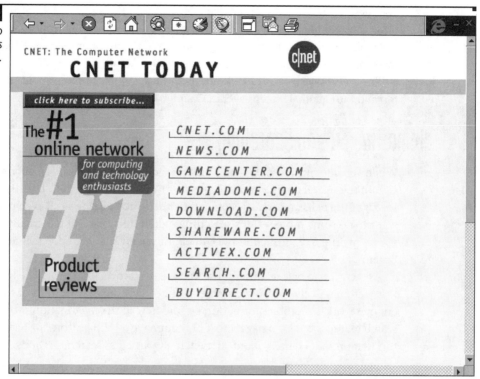

FIGURE 16.19

Subscribing to a channel is similar to subscribing to a website.

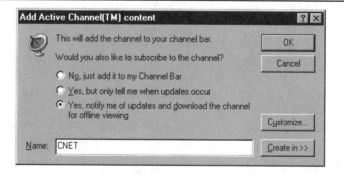

In most cases, as in this example, the subscription to the channel will include the downloading of new content, with the schedule being established by the publisher of the channel. You can click the OK button to accept the new subscription.

After completing the subscription process to the CNET channel, you will see the CNET home page, and a new icon for the channel will appear in the Channel bar on

PART

III

Communications and
Using the Internet

your desktop and in the Explorer bar. You'll also find this channel listed along with your other subscriptions when you choose Favorites ➤ Manage Subscriptions.

Finally, you'll find that some channels have a component for the Channel screen saver, or that can be added to the Active Desktop. Some channels offer these as options, while others make them available automatically. You'll read more about the Active Desktop and the Channel screen saver in Chapter 18.

Some Tips on Web Searching

When you conduct a search from the Explorer bar, you'll see only an abbreviated version of the search engine you choose, over in the bar on the left. Usually you won't see all of the bells and whistles offered by the search engine's full Web page. If you want to do some more serious searching, you'll find it useful to actually go to the search engine's site. (Just enter the URL of the engine into the address line and press Enter.)

As mentioned before, different search engines work differently. The information in this section will give you a very general understanding of how most of today's search engines work; for more information be sure to read the information provided at each search engine's full Web page. Most of them have a Help button or a Search Tips button that provides details about that engine's particular search methods.

Keywords

Most search engines work by providing a blank area where you can type in keywords that represent the information you want to find. For example, typing in **Hale-Bopp Comet** *should* find websites with information about that comet. Typing in **Comet**, by itself, would match every website with any information about comets.

A keyword is simply one word that represents information you want to find. A keyword is generally a noun, but may also be a verb or some other part of speech. When you use a search engine, you are searching a database for documents that have words that match the keyword(s) you've entered.

NOTE

The most common words, such as conjunctions ("and," "but," etc.), pronouns ("I," "he," etc.), and prepositions ("of," "for," "into," etc.) are ignored by search engines.

Typically, you may enter as many keywords as you want. The engine will search for all the words and find any document that contains one or more of those words. Multiple keywords are treated as having an implicit Boolean "OR" operator. For example, if you entered these keywords:

Chevy Impala

then the server would return documents that contain the word "Chevy" *or* the word "Impala," and would therefore include pages containing mention of *Chevy Impala*, some pages containing mention of *impala* (probably natural wildlife pages, actually, since an impala is an animal), and pages that merely include mention of *Chevy* (without necessarily including *Chevy Impala*). Note that pages containing both words would be ranked higher, and appear first in the resulting list.

NOTE

Most search engines ignore the capitalization of your request.

Notice that for the OR search of the preceding paragraph you did not have to enter the word "OR." To search only for pages that contain both Chevy *and* Impala, however, you would have to insert the word "AND" between the two words:

Chevy and Impala

Even with the AND approach, however, you might still turn up pages that don't mention Chevy Impalas; it's possible you'll turn up pages describing somebody's trip across the country to photograph wild animals (lions, wildebeest, impala) from the back of their Chevy station wagon. If you only wanted to find pages that contain the words *Chevy* and *Impala* together as a phrase (okay, I admit I should have told you this up front—but, hey, I'm using this example as a teaching tool), then you should put the words together between quotes:

"Chevy Impala"

But see the discussion later in this section concerning "Exact Matches"; there are some variations on this approach from one search engine to another.

Combining Criteria

Many engines let you combine criteria in complex ways. Here's a typical example. Suppose you wanted to find pages about *child safety* that do *not* discuss *adolescents*. Proper use of the words AND and OR will help you:

child *and* safety *not* adolescents

Wildcards

Most engines will let you enter partial keywords by means of "wildcards." Here's an example. Suppose you were doing research about a car company, and wanted to see any and all pages about it. You might want listings of any occurrences of *Chevy* or *Chevrolet*.

You could do two separate searches, one for each. Or to be more expedient, you could use a wildcard in your search:

Chev*

The * character applied at the end of a partial keyword will match all documents that contain words that start with the partial word.

Exact Matches

Often you'll want to search for an exact match of the words you enter. For example, you might want to find pages that contain the entire phrase *Hubble telescope repair*. Typically, you would specify that you want an exact match of this phrase by enclosing it with quotes (') or double quotes ("). Some engines, however, want you to use the + sign between the words instead. Thus, depending on the search engine you're using, you may have to try

'Hubble telescope repair'

or

"Hubble telescope repair"

or

Hubble+telescope+repair

One of these should find pages that contain that exact phrase.

As a general game plan, when you're doing complex searches, start out with a *simple* search (it's faster and easier), and then check the first ten pages or so that result to see what they contain. In many cases, this will provide you with whatever you need, and you won't have spent your time concocting a complex set of search criteria. Of course, if too many pages are found and only a few of them are meeting your actual needs, you'll have to start to narrow the search. On the other hand, if no pages are resulting, ("no matches found"), you'll have to try again by widening the search.

Searching vs. Browsing

Some search engines, such as InfoSeek and Yahoo! offer a Browse option as well as a Search option. That means that in addition to being able to search for keywords, you can look through topics by category, such as *business*, *entertainment*, or *magazines*, just to see what is available. This is great if you are interested in seeing what's out there in a general category instead of searching for a specific topic.

Endlessly Indexing the Web

The ability to search the Web for specific sites or files relies on one tiny factor: the existence of searching and indexing sites that you can access to perform the search. These sites are often known as Web spiders, crawlers, or robots, because they endlessly and automatically search the Web and index the content they find.

Search sites literally create huge databases of all the words in all the pages they index, and you can search those databases simply by entering the keywords you want to find. Despite the size of this vast store of information, they can usually return the results to you in a second or two.

This is definitely a Herculean task, because the Web is huge and continues to grow with no end in sight. Plus, a search engine must regularly return to pages it's already indexed because those pages may have changed and will need to be indexed again. Don't forget that many pages are removed from the Web each day, and a search engine must at some point remove those now invalid URLs from its database.

To give you an idea of just how big a job it is to search and index the Web, the popular AltaVista search site at

```
www.altavista.digital.com
```

recently reported that its Web index as of that day covered 31 million pages from 1,158,000 host names on 627,000 servers. AltaVista also had indexed 4 million articles from 14,000 newsgroups. On top of that, this search site is accessed more than 30 million times each day.

Keeping track of what's on the Web is definitely a job for that infinite number of monkeys we've always heard about.

Searching in the Explorer Bar

Let's perform a keyword search in Internet Explorer. Although you could open one of the search sites, the easiest place to begin is with the Explorer bar. Select View ➢ Explorer Bar ➢ Search, or click the Search button on the toolbar. Internet Explorer opens its Explorer bar, the separate pane on the left side of its window, while the page you had been viewing is displayed in the right pane. Figure 16.20 shows Internet Explorer with its window split into two panes.

PART

III

Communications and
Using the Internet

FIGURE 16.20

The Explorer bar allows you to perform a search in one pane and then sample its results while keeping those results on the screen.

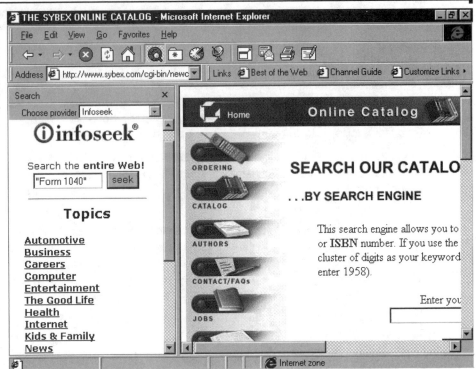

You can close the search bar by choosing View ➣ Explorer Bar ➣ None, clicking the Search button on the toolbar, or clicking the Close button at the top of the Explorer bar. In this way, you can toggle the search bar open or closed while still retaining the results of the last search you performed.

Once the Explorer bar is open, performing the search is as easy as selecting a search site from the list and entering the keywords you want to search for. For example, in Figure 16.20, we selected the site named Infoseek and entered the search criteria **Form 1040** in the text-entry field. To perform the search, simply click the Seek button.

In a second or two (or more if the Internet or the search site you chose is having a busy day), the results of the search will appear in the Explorer bar, as shown in Figure 16.21.

In this example, some 2,224 results were found, although only the first 10 are displayed in the search bar. You can click a link at the bottom of the results to view the next 10.

NOTE

If none of the results looks right, you can create an entirely new search by entering new keywords into the text-entry field and clicking the Seek button, or by selecting a different search site and starting from that one.

FIGURE 16.21

After you click the Seek button, the results of the search will appear as links in the search bar.

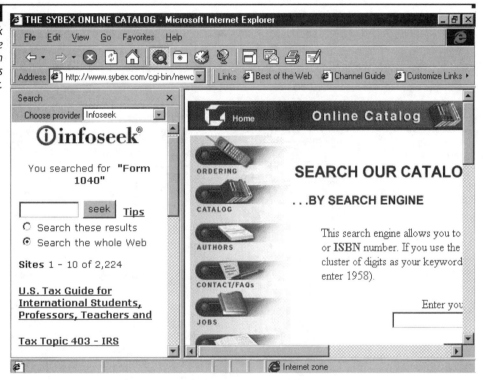

Each result is a link to the page that was found to contain the keywords you entered. The Infoseek search site, like most others, arranges the resulting links in order of their likelihood of matching your query. If you point to one of the links with your mouse, a ToolTip displays information about it, as shown below:

Tax Topic 403 - IRS

Interest Received Topic 403. [Click for Text Only Version].
Generally, any interest that you receive or that is credited to
your account and can be withdrawn is taxable income. ...
73% (Size 8.4K)
http://www.irs.ustreas.gov/basic/tax_edu/teletax/tc403.html

- A short description of the target page, or the first few lines of text found on that page
- A percentage that describes the likelihood that this page meets your search criteria
- The size of the result's target file, which gives you fair warning before you decide to open it
- The URL of the target page, so you'll have an idea of where this file resides

You can click a link in the Explorer bar to open its target in the right pane. Figure 16.22 shows Internet Explorer after one of the links in the Explorer bar was clicked. The target page appears on the right, where you're free to work in it as you would with any other page. In fact, if this looks like a page you'll want to spend some time with, click the Search button to close the Explorer bar so you'll have the entire screen for the target page.

FIGURE 16.22

When you click a link in the Explorer bar, its target is opened in the pane on the right.

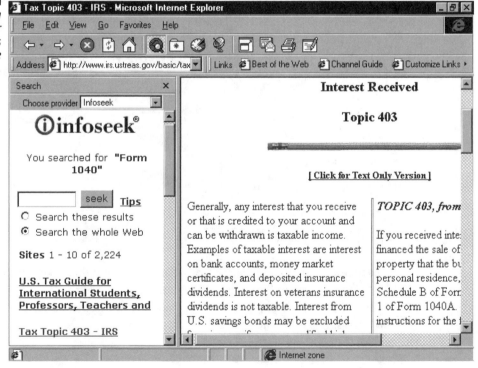

Common Search Engines

This section describes some of the most common search engines on the Web.

AltaVista
www.altavista.com

Digital Equipment Corporation's AltaVista claims to be the largest search engine, searching 31 million pages on 476,000 servers, and four million articles from 14,000 Usenet newsgroups. It is accessed over 29 million times per weekday.

Infoseek
www.guide.infoseek.com/

Combines two powerful search systems, as well as a great news search engine that enables you to search wire services, publications, and more.

- **Ultrasmart** offers comprehensive query results. So you can narrow your results quickly, each new Ultrasmart query you perform searches within your previous results (unless you specify otherwise).

- **Ultraseek** offers the speed, accuracy and comprehensiveness of Ultrasmart, only in a streamlined form. It's aimed at power users who know what they want and want it fast.

- **News Center** offers the latest headlines listed by category. You can also "personalize" your news so you see only what interests you every time you return to Infoseek, including local weather, TV listings and more. You may also search its "News Wires" (from Reuters, Business Wire, and PR News Wire) or "Premier News" (today's news from seven major national news organizations).

Lycos
www.lycos.com/

Searches not only text, but also graphics, sounds, and video!

Yahoo!
www.yahoo.com

Started by two graduate students at Stanford, Yahoo! is considered the first search engine and still one of the most comprehensive. If you are looking for the address for a website, such as the New York Times website, this is a good way to find it.

PART

III

Communications and
Using the Internet

EXCITE
www.excite.com/

If you can't describe exactly what you're looking for, Excite's unique concept-based navigation technology may help you find it anyway. Excite's Web index is deep, broad, and current: it covers the full text of more than 11.5 million pages and is updated weekly.

Magellen
www.mckinley.com/

A different concept in search engines. This one ranks the results using its own independent system in an effort to help you make more refined searches.

Search.com
www.search.com/

This search engine lets you search up to eight search engines at one time. This is a pretty unique and powerful approach to searching. If nothing else, you'll probably get lots of results from almost any search! It's also a good site for linking to other engines.

NetSearch
home.netscape.com/home/internet-search.html

Perhaps the most easily accessible because it is available through a button in Netscape (if you happen to use Netscape!).

Point
www.pointcom.com

Another engine that rates website matches according to its own system.

Starting Point
www.stpt.com/

Lets you select a subject area for your search.

Webcrawler
www.webcrawler.com/

Offers a speedy Web search engine and a "randomlinks" feature to find new and unusual sites. It also features a list of the 25 most visited sites on the Web.

Dejavu News
www.dejanews.com/

Enables you to search through millions of postings to Usenet newsgroups.

BigBook
www.bigbook.com

National Yellow Pages listing nearly every business in the U.S., with detailed maps of their locations.

WHO/WHERE?
www.whowhere.com/

This is a comprehensive White Pages service for locating people, e-mail addresses, and organizations on the Net. WhoWhere? intuitively handles misspelled or incomplete names, and it lets you search by initials.

WWWomen
www.wwwomen.com/

The premier search directory for women.

Environmental Organization Web Directory
www.webdirectory.com/

The categories in this Web directory cover topics such as animal rights, solar energy, and sustainable development.

C|NET'S Shareware Directory
www.shareware.com/

This one makes it simple to find trial and demo versions of software. More than 170,000 files are available for easy searching, browsing, and downloading from shareware and corporate archives on the Internet.

The Electric Library
www.elibrary.com/

This address searches across an extensive database of more than 1,000 full-text newspapers, magazines, and academic journals, images, reference books, literature, and art. (This is a pay-subscription site, but a free trial is offered.)

**Homework help
tristate.pgh.net/~pinch13/

This website was put together by a nine-year-old boy (with the help of his dad) and provides a comprehensive collection of online information designed to help students with their homework. This excellent reference has won many awards.

An invaluable spot for comparing computer prices is www.computers.com.

Chapter

17

Communicating with Outlook Express News and Mail

FEATURING

Getting connected

Using Outlook Express Mail

Attaching files to messages

Using Address Book

Using Outlook Express News

Reading news off-line

Customizing Outlook Express

Communicating with Outlook Express News and Mail

Outlook Express is an Internet standards-based e-mail and news reader you can use to access Internet e-mail and news accounts. In this chapter, we'll look first at how to use Outlook Express Mail. We'll then look at Outlook Express News and conclude by showing you how to customize Outlook Express so that it works the way you want to work with your computer.

You can access Outlook Express from your Desktop, from Internet Explorer, and from any program that includes a Go menu. From the desktop, choose Start ➢ Programs ➢ Internet Explorer ➢ Outlook Express, click the Launch Outlook Express icon on the Quick Launch toolbar, or click the Outlook Express shortcut on your Desktop. (Windows created this shortcut during installation.) To go to Outlook Express from within Internet Explorer, click Mail and then choose one of the options from the drop-down menu. From a Go menu, choose Mail or News.

A Quick Tour of Outlook Express

When you first open Outlook Express, you see the window shown in Figure 17.1.

If you click Read Mail, Outlook Express opens your Inbox in Preview Pane view, and you may well have a message or two from Microsoft, as Figure 17.2 shows.

FIGURE 17.1

The Outlook Express window

Toolbar

Outlook Bar

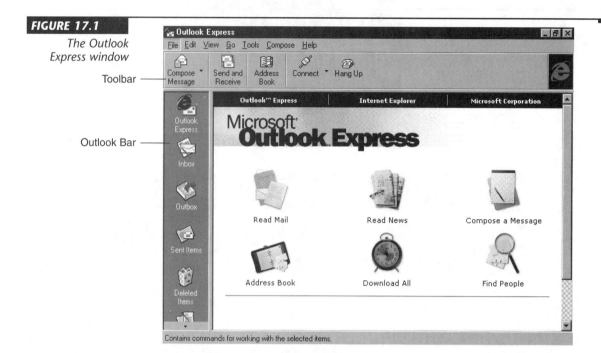

FIGURE 17.2

The Outlook Express window in Preview Pane view

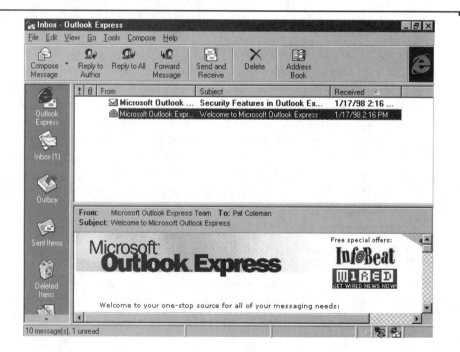

The Preview Pane

By default, the Preview Pane is split horizontally; header information is in the upper pane, and the message is displayed in the lower pane. To change this arrangement, as well as other parts of the Outlook Express user interface, choose View ➢ Layout to open the Window Layout Properties dialog box:

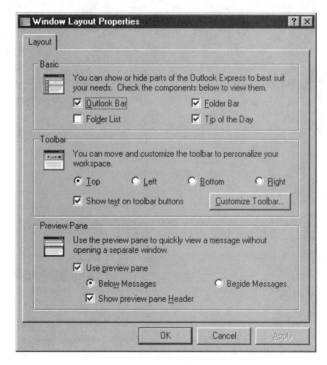

As you can see, in the Basic section of this dialog box, you can choose to display the Folder Bar, the Tip of the Day, and the Folder List in addition to the Outlook Bar. If you check Folder List and then click Apply and OK, the window in Figure 17.2 changes to show the Folder List.

NOTE

We'll look at the Toolbar section of the Window Layout Properties dialog box later, in the section "Customizing Your Toolbar."

You use the options in the Preview Pane section to select how you want to display header information and messages. Check and uncheck these options until the user interface is to your liking and fits the way you like to work when reading messages. You can also adjust the area for the Preview Pane and the Message List by dragging the divider between them.

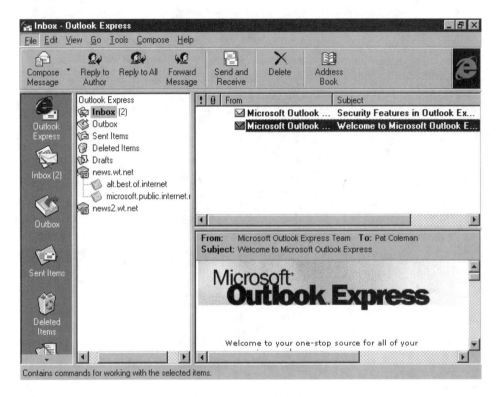

The Outlook Bar

As you can see from Figure 17.1, the Outlook Bar at the left side of the Outlook Express window contains several icons that correspond to folders in the Folder List:

Inbox contains newly received messages and messages you have not yet disposed of in some way.

Outbox contains messages that are ready to be sent.

Sent Items contains messages that you have sent (a handy feature if you send a lot of e-mail).

Deleted Items contains messages that you chose to delete after reading. (The messages are not yet permanently deleted—you'll find more on this in the "Deleting a Message" section later in this chapter.)

Drafts contains messages you are working on but which are not yet ready to be sent.

News contains articles that you have retrieved from newsgroups.

Getting Connected

Before you can actually use Outlook Express to send and receive messages or to read and post news articles, you must set up an Internet e-mail account and an Internet news account. Doing so tells Outlook Express how to contact your e-mail and news servers. You can initially set up one account or multiple accounts, and you can always add more as the need arises.

NOTE

This chapter assumes that you are setting up a dial-up account. If you are using Outlook Express on a local area network, see your Network Administrator for details.

Establishing an Account with an ISP

To set up an Internet e-mail or news account, you must have an account with an Internet service provider. If you don't have an account with an ISP, getting one may be as simple as checking out the Technology section of your local newspaper. Unless you live in a remote area, you may have access to any number of local Internet providers. Chapter 15 covers all the aspects of acquiring an ISP.

We recently established a new account with a local provider and completed the whole operation in a matter of minutes. We called the phone number listed in the newspaper, told the operator that we wanted an account for mail, news, and Internet access, asked about the charges, gave her our credit card number and told her the e-mail name and password we wanted to use, and within 15 minutes we were on-line. For unlimited access, we pay about 16 dollars a month.

You can also find ISPs listed in local trade publications, in national publications such as the *Wall Street Journal* and computer magazines, and on-line. Check out these URLs for a list of ISPs (you can even search by region of the country):

```
thelist.com
www.cybertoday.com/cybertoday/isps/
wings.buffalo.edu/world/
```

In general, we've found that local publications are the best source for pointers to local ISPs. The large, online lists don't seem to be as up-to-date.

PART

III

Communications and
Using the Internet

WARNING

Be sure you clearly understand what you are getting and what you are paying for. Some ISPs provide an e-mail account for as little as $5.00 a month. Others charge by the hour for connect time. If you don't have unlimited access, you can rack up some serious charges by surfing the Net a lot. Additionally, be sure that your provider allows you to connect through a local phone number or an 800 number.

You can also use the Windows Internet Connection Wizard to establish an Internet account. To do so, choose Start ➤ Programs ➤ Internet Explorer ➤ Connection Wizard. The Wizard may ask for your Windows 98 CD during this process, so have it handy.

Setting Up an E-Mail Account

Once you have an account with an ISP, you need to have the following information ready to set up an e-mail account in Outlook Express:

- Your e-mail address and password
- Your local access phone number
- The type of server that will be used for incoming mail
- The names of the servers for incoming mail and outgoing mail

When you have this information, you can start setting up your e-mail account with the Internet Connection Wizard:

1. In Outlook Express, choose Tools ➤ Accounts ➤ Add ➤ Mail to open the Internet Connection Wizard:

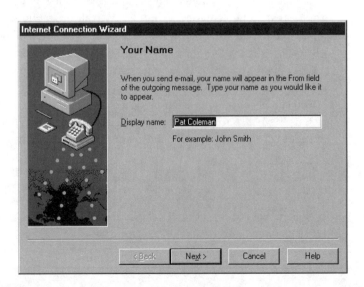

2. In the Display Name text box, enter the name that you want to appear in the From field of outgoing messages, and click Next.

3. In the E-mail Address text box, enter the e-mail address that your ISP assigned you, and click Next.

4. The Internet Connection Wizard asks you to specify the type of server that will be used for incoming mail and the names of the servers for incoming mail and outgoing mail. Enter this information and click Next.

5. In the Internet Mail Logon dialog box, enter the e-mail address and password that your ISP assigned you. If your ISP requires Secure Password Authentication, click the Log On Using Secure Password Authentication (SPA) button. When you are done, click Next.

6. In the Friendly Name dialog box, enter a name for your e-mail account in the text box, and click Next.

7. In the Choose Connection Type dialog box, click the option button that corresponds to your type of Internet connection—phone line, local area network, or manual—and then click Next.

8. The Wizard selects the type of modem you are using on your system. If the Wizard's selection is incorrect, click the down arrow and select another modem from the list. Once the correct modem is selected, click Next.

9. In the Dial-Up Connection dialog box, click the option button that applies in your situation. Are you creating a new dial-up connection or connecting to an existing one? Then click Next.

POP3, IMAP, and SMTP Explained

POP3 is an abbreviation for Post Office Protocol 3, a popular method used for storing Internet mail. Many Internet mail applications require a POP3 mailbox in order to receive mail.

SMTP is an abbreviation for Simple Mail Transfer Protocol, the TCP/IP protocol used for sending Internet e-mail.

IMAP is an abbreviation for Internet Message Access Protocol, the protocol that allows a client to access and manipulate electronic mail messages on a server. It does not specify a means of posting mail; that function is handled by SMTP.

PART

III

Communications and
Using the Internet

10. If you are creating a new dial-up connection, the Wizard displays the Phone Number dialog box. Enter the phone number of your ISP, and then click Next.

11. The Wizard again asks for your user name and password; enter them and then click Next.

12. In the Advanced Settings dialog box, leave the No option button selected unless your ISP has indicated that it does not use the default settings, and then click Next. If you choose the Yes option button, the Internet Connection Wizard steps you through a series of dialog boxes in which you can change the settings.

13. In the Dial-Up Connection Name field, enter a name for your dial-up connection, and click Next.

14. Finally, in the Congratulations dialog box, click Finish.

You have now set up an Internet e-mail account and can send and receive messages.

Setting Up a News Account

Before you can read newsgroups, you have to connect to a news server. You set up a news server account in much the same way that you set up a mail server account.

Before you set up a news account, you must have already established an account with an ISP and obtained the name of the news server(s) you plan to use. Also, ask your ISP if you need a user name and password to log on to the news server. After you do this, you can follow these steps:

1. Start Outlook Express, choose Tools ➢ Accounts.

2. In the Internet Accounts dialog box, select the News tab and then choose Add ➢ News to open the Internet Connection Wizard.

3. In the Display Name field, enter the name that you want to appear when you post an article or send an e-mail message to a newsgroup, and then click Next.

4. In the E-mail Address field, enter your e-mail address and click Next.

5. Now, in the Internet News Server Name dialog box, enter the name of the news server that you received from your ISP (typically something like News.Myisp.com). If you have to log on to this server with an account name and password, check the *My news server requires me to log on* checkbox. Click Next.

6. In the Friendly Name dialog box, the Internet Connection Wizard fills in the Internet News Account Name field with the name of the server you entered in the previous screen. Accept this name or enter any name you want, and then click Next.

7. In the Choose Connection Type dialog box, check the option button that corresponds to the type of connection you are using, and click Next.

8. In the Choose Modem dialog box, the Wizard selects the type of modem you are using on your system. (If the Wizard's selection is incorrect, click the down arrow and select another modem from the list.) Click Next.

9. In the Dial-Up Connection screen, click the option button that applies in your situation. If you are creating a new dial-up connection, you will be asked to enter the phone number. Click Next, and then click Finish.

NOTE

If your ISP has more than one news server that you reach via the same connection, click Use an Existing Dial-Up Connection if you have already established the connection.

You have now set up an Internet news account, and you can read, subscribe to, and participate in newsgroups.

Do You Want to Use Your Real Name, or an Alias?

If you want to remain anonymous while cruising newsgroups, you can enter a fake name in the Display Name field in the first Internet Connection Wizard dialog box. You can use anything you want, but we suggest that you let the limits of good taste guide you. Remember: If you can use a fake name, so can anybody else.

If you want to be even more anonymous, enter a fake e-mail address as well. Some ISPs have policies about this; so check to be sure that entering a fake name does not violate these policies.

Using Outlook Express Mail

Once the domain of business and industry, e-mail is now used by all kinds of people all over the world. (We have friends who keep in touch with their seven children and four grandchildren primarily via e-mail!) Now, Outlook Express brings a new dimension to what you can do with e-mail. Not only can you type and send messages lickety-split, you can also send the following:

- Embedded URLs
- Web documents

PART

III

Communications and
Using the Internet

- Messages in HTML format
- Images
- Colorful, fanciful formatting
- Multiple attachments, including sound files

You can even use Outlook Express Mail to manage multiple e-mail accounts, both business and personal. You can check them one at a time or all at once.

To start the mail program, click Read Mail in the Outlook Express window.

Reading and Processing Messages

If you still have the welcome message from Microsoft in your Inbox and if you still have the default configuration of your Preview Pane, you will see the header information in the upper pane, and the message in the lower pane.

NOTE

If you have a different configuration, double-click a message header to read the message.

After reading a message, you can do any of the following:

- Print it
- Mark it as read
- Mark it as unread
- Move it to another folder in the Outlook Express bar
- Save it in a folder
- Forward it to someone else
- Reply to it
- Delete it

For some of these tasks, you use the File menu, and for some of them you use the Edit menu. In addition, you can take care of some tasks by simply clicking a toolbar icon.

Printing, Marking, and Moving Messages

Printing, marking, and moving messages are simple, straightforward tasks, so we'll start with them.

Printing Messages

On occasion, you may want a paper file of e-mail messages that you have sent or received. For example, you might work on a large project that involves people who aren't using e-mail, or you may want to maintain paper files as a backup. To print a message, open it, place your cursor in the message, and then click the Print tool, choose File ➤ Print, or press Ctrl-P.

Marking Messages

When you first receive a message, a closed envelope icon precedes its header, which is in boldface.

After you read the message, Outlook Express marks it as read by changing the icon to an open envelope and changing the header from bold to lightface type. If, for whatever reason, you want to change a message from Read to Unread, select the message header and choose Edit ➤ Mark As Unread. You can change it back to Read if you want by selecting it and choosing Edit ➤ Mark As Read. (You might want to do either of these to call attention to a message that you want to review.) To mark all messages as read, choose Edit ➤ Mark All As Read.

Moving Messages

You can easily move messages from one folder to another by dragging and dropping. For example, if you receive a message that you want to modify and send to someone else, first select the message header; then drag it to the Draft folder. You can now revise it to your heart's content, move it to your Outbox, and send it on its way. (We'll look at how to send messages in the "Sending Your Message" section, a bit later in this chapter.)

Saving Messages

With Outlook Express, you can save messages in folders you created in Windows Explorer, and you can save messages in Outlook Express folders. You can also save attachments as files.

Saving Messages in Windows Explorer Folders

To save messages in Windows Explorer, follow these steps:

1. Select the header of the message you want to save.

2. Choose File ➤ Save As.

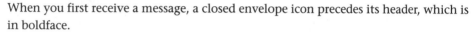

PART

III

Communications and
Using the Internet

3. In the Save Message As dialog box, select a folder in which to save the message. Outlook Express places the subject line in the File Name box. You can use this name or type another one.

4. You can save the message as e-mail (with the .eml extension) or as text (with the .txt extension). Select the file type, then click Save.

Saving Messages in Outlook Express Folders

Although Outlook Express saves messages in the Deleted Items, Inbox, Outbox, and Sent Items folders, you can create your own folders in which to save messages. To do so, follow these steps:

1. Choose File ➢ Folder ➢ New Folder.

2. In the Create Folder dialog box, type a name for the new folder and click OK.

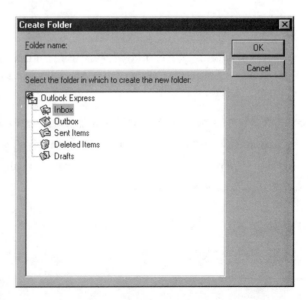

You now have a new folder in your Folder List, and you can drag any message from any other folder to it—or from it to any of them.

You have at your disposal, however, an even easier and more efficient way to save messages. If you rely heavily on e-mail to get your job done, you'll want to take advantage of this feature. You can use Inbox Assistant to tell Outlook Express Mail exactly what to do with messages you receive. For details, see the section "Taking Control of Your Mail with Inbox Assistant," later in this chapter.

Reading and Saving Attachments

An attachment is a file that is appended to an e-mail message. You'll know that a message has an attachment if the header is preceded by the paper clip icon. When you open the message, you'll see an attachment icon at the bottom followed by the name of the file and its size.

To read an attachment, simply double-click its icon (if the attachment is a text file). To save an attachment, follow these steps:

1. With the message open, choose File ➢ Save Attachments.

2. Click the file name to open the Save Attachment As dialog box.

3. Select a folder and a file name, and click Save.

Backing Up Your Message Files

In the likely event that the only messages you will lose are those most important to you, back up your message folders regularly. Here are the steps:

1. Select a folder, and then choose File ➢ Folder ➢ Compact. Doing so decreases the amount of disk space that each folder requires.

2. Find the files on your computer that have the extensions .idx and .mbx.

3. Copy the files to a backup disk.

To compact all folders, choose File ➢ Folder ➢ Compact All Folders.

Replying to a Message

When a message is selected, you can reply to it in the following ways:

- Click the Reply to Author icon in the toolbar.
- Click the Reply to All icon in the toolbar (if the message has carbon copy or blind copy recipients or multiple senders).
- Choose Compose ➢ Reply to Author (Ctrl-R) or Compose ➢ Reply to All (Ctrl-Shift-R).

PART

III

Communications and
Using the Internet

By default, Outlook Express Mail does not include in your reply all the text of the message to which you are replying. If you want that message included, follow these steps:

1. In the Outlook Express window, choose Tools ➤ Options to open the Options dialog box. (The Options dialog box will be discussed in more depth later.)

2. Select the Send tab, and click Include Message in Reply.

3. Click Apply, and then click OK.

To include only selected portions of the message in your reply, leave the Include Message in Reply option checked and follow these steps:

1. Click the message header to open the message.

2. Click the Reply to Author icon. You will see the message header and the text of the message to which you are replying. The message is now addressed to its original sender.

3. In the body of the message, edit the message so that the portions you want are retained and then enter your response.

4. Click the Send icon on the toolbar to send your reply. (Sending messages will be discussed in more depth later.)

Forwarding a Message

Forwarding an e-mail message is much easier than forwarding a letter through the U.S. mail, and it actually works. You can forward a message in three ways:

- Click the Forward icon on the toolbar.
- Choose Compose ➤ Forward.
- Press Ctrl-F.

To forward a message, follow these steps:

1. Open the message.

2. Click the Forward icon.

3. Enter an e-mail address in the To field. (You can also add your own comments to the message, if you choose.)

4. Click Send.

Deleting a Message

You can delete a message in three ways:

- Select its header and click the Delete icon on the toolbar.
- Select its header and choose Edit ➢ Delete.
- Open the message and click the Delete icon.

The message is not yet permanently deleted, however; Outlook Express has simply moved it to the Deleted Items folder. To delete it permanently, follow these steps:

1. Select the Deleted Items folder.
2. Select the message you want to delete.
3. Choose Edit ➢ Delete or click the Delete icon.
4. Outlook Express asks if you are sure you want to delete the message. If you are sure, click Yes.

NOTE

As you will see in the "Customizing Outlook Express" section later in this chapter, you can also specify that all messages in the Deleted Items folder be deleted when you exit Outlook Express Mail.

WARNING

Outlook Express has no Undelete command, so be sure you *really* want to delete a message when you delete it from the Deleted Items folder.

Creating and Sending Messages

By now, you must be champing at the bit to create and send your own messages, so let's do that next. In a later section, you will explore the many options you have when composing messages. In this section, you'll compose a simple message and send it.

Composing Your Message

You can begin a new message in a couple of ways:

- Choose Compose ➢ New Message (Ctrl-N).
- Click the Compose Message icon in the toolbar.

When you begin a new message, Outlook Express displays the New Message window, as shown in Figure 17.3.

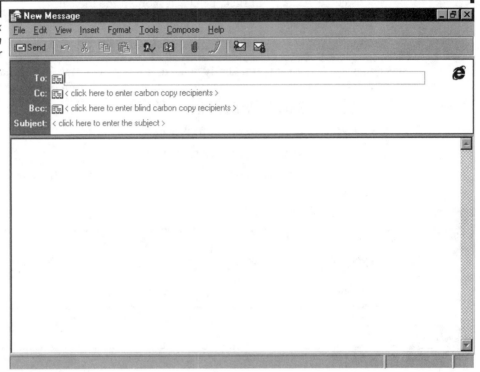

Header Information

The header section of the New Message window has four fields:

- To
- Cc
- Bcc
- Subject

The only field that you must fill in is the To field. All recipients can see the addresses you enter in the Cc, or carbon copy, field. The blind carbon copy recipient can see who was Cc'd, but the carbon copy recipients and the primary recipient cannot see the address of the person who was Bcc'd.

If you do not fill in the Subject field, Outlook Express displays a message box asking if you really want to send the message with no subject line. When Outlook Express saves your message in a folder, it uses the subject line as the filename.

Creating Your Message

To enter header information and compose your message, follow these steps:

1. Enter the e-mail address of the primary recipient in the To field. If you are sending a message to more than one primary recipient, separate their addresses with semicolons.

NOTE

If you have addresses in your Address Book, you can click the Address Book icon and select an address rather than typing it. We'll look at how to use the Address Book in detail in a later section.

2. Optionally, enter e-mail addresses in the Cc (carbon copy) and Bcc (blind carbon copy) fields.

3. Enter a subject line for your message.

4. Enter the text of your message. You can create e-mail messages in Plain Text or Rich Text (HTML) format. (We'll look at this in detail later.)

You can also set a Priority for your message. By default, the Priority is set to Normal. To set it to High or Low, choose Tools ➤ Set Priority, and select from the drop-down list.

If you set the priority to High, an exclamation mark precedes the message header in your recipient's mailbox. If you set the priority to Low, the message header is preceded by a down arrow.

Your message is now complete, and you are ready to send it.

Sending Your Message

You can send your message in several ways:

- Click the Send icon on the toolbar in the New Message window.
- Choose File ➤ Send Message or File ➤ Send Later.
- Click the Send and Receive icon on the toolbar in the main Outlook Express window (more about this option in a later section).

When you choose File ➤ Send Later, Outlook Express places the message in your Outbox. You can then send it later by clicking the Send and Receive icon on the toolbar in the main Outlook Express window. You might want to do this if you are composing several message off-line, for example.

PART

III

Communications and
Using the Internet

Retrieving Your Mail

Before we get into all the neat ways you can format messages and how you can send elements other than straight text in them, let's look at the ways in which you can retrieve your e-mail. You can do so in several ways:

- Choose Tools ➢ Download All.

- Choose Tools ➢ Send and Receive, which sends any messages in your Outbox and retrieves any messages waiting on your e-mail server.

- Click the Send and Receive icon on the toolbar, which works the same as choosing Tools ➢ Send and Receive.

Received messages are placed in your Inbox or in other folders that you have specified using the Inbox Assistant. You can also choose to display only newly received messages. To do so, choose View ➢ Current View ➢ Unread Messages.

You can now process your mail using all the techniques we looked at earlier in the "Reading and Processing Messages" section.

See the "Using Inbox Assistant" section for details on how to place incoming mail in specific folders.

Creating Designer E-Mail Messages

Now that we have covered the basics of reading, responding to, creating, and sending messages, let's look at some bells and whistles you can employ.

To see some of the possibilities available to you, compose a new message. Click the Compose Message icon to open the New Message window, and then choose Format ➢ Rich Text (HTML). You'll see the screen shown in Figure 17.4. Notice the Formatting toolbar, which contains many of the same tools you see and use in your Windows word processor. You'll also see the Font and Font Size drop-down list boxes that are present in your Windows word processor.

One tool that you may not see in your word processor is the Insert Horizontal Line tool. Click this tool to insert a horizontal line that spans the width of your message.

FIGURE 17.4

The New Message screen ready for Rich Text formatting

Formatting toolbar

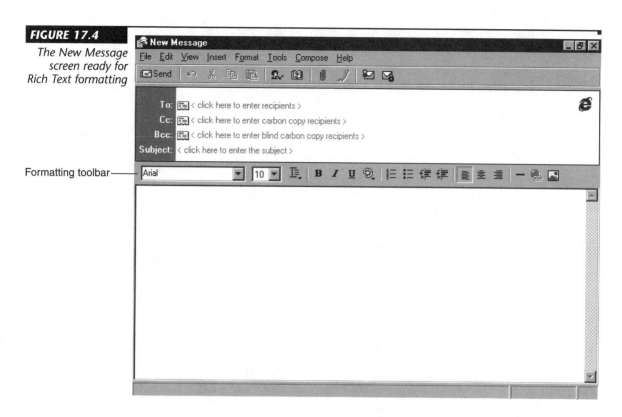

As you create your message, just pretend that you're using a word processor, and use the Formatting tools to apply emphasis to your message.

You can format an e-mail message in the same ways that you format any other document. All the usual design rules apply, including the following:

- Don't use too many fonts.
- Remember, typing in all capital letters in e-mail is tantamount to shouting.
- Don't place a lot of text in italics. It's hard to read on the screen.
- Save boldface for what's really important.

NOTE

If you send an HTML message to someone whose mail program does not read HTML, Outlook Express prompts you to send the message as plain text.

Using Stationery

In addition to the formatting you've just seen, you have another way to add some class or some comedy to your e-mail messages: stationery. Choose Compose ➢ New Message Using. You'll see a list of predesigned formats, including the following:

- A party invitation
- A holiday letter
- A formal announcement
- A festive border
- Colorful, textured backgrounds

Play around with these a bit, and you'll probably think of an occasion for which this would be really useful.

Adding a Signature to Your Message

Unless you're new to e-mail, you are probably in the habit of signing your messages in a particular way. If you want, however, you can create a signature that will be automatically added to all messages that you send. To do so, follow these steps:

1. In the main window, choose Tools ➢ Stationery to open the Stationery dialog box:

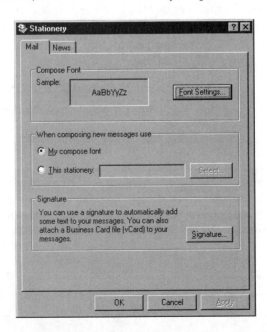

2. In the Signature section, click Signature to open the Signature dialog box:

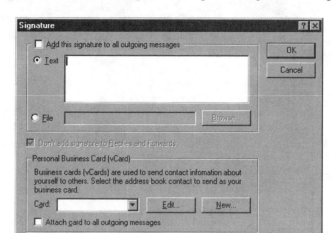

3. To create a text-only signature, click the Text radio button, and type your signature in the text box. To use a file as your signature, click the File radio button, and select a file.

You can also add an electronic business card to your messages. To do so, follow these steps:

1. In the Personal Business Card section of the Signature dialog box, click New to open the Properties dialog box. Next, enter information about yourself in the name and e-mail fields. Click OK when you are done.

2. Click the down arrow in the Card drop-down list to select your name from the list.

3. Check the *Attach card to all outgoing messages* option to automatically attach your business card to every message that you send.

NOTE

Leave the *Attach card to all outgoing messages* option unchecked if you want to attach a signature or business card to only selected messages. When you have composed your message, in the New Message window choose Insert ➢ Signature or Insert ➢ Business Card.

Adding a Picture to Your Message

Many of the picture-editing features of Microsoft Office 97 are included with Outlook Express. You can insert pictures, size them, and move them around. Figure 17.5 shows a message that has a flower file from Microsoft Office 97 Clip Art inserted into it.

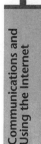

PART

III

Communications and
Using the Internet

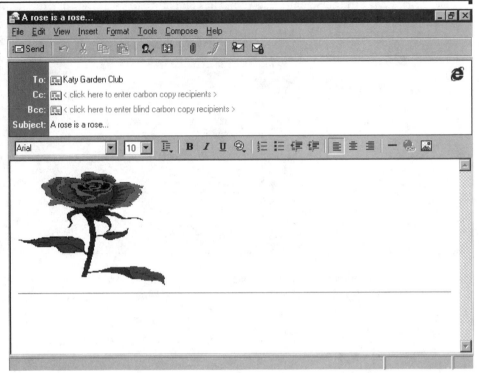

You can insert a picture in a message in two ways:

- As a background over which you can type text.
- As a piece of art.

To insert a picture as a background, choose Format ➤ Background ➤ Picture. Outlook Express Mail displays the Background Picture dialog box shown in Figure 17.6. Enter the file name of an image that you want to use as background, and click OK.

To insert some decorative art in your message, follow these steps:

1. Place the cursor in the body of your message, and click the Insert Picture icon on the Formatting toolbar to open the Picture dialog box:

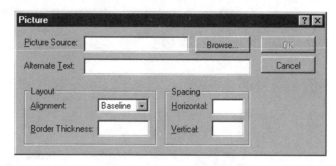

2. If you know the name of the file you want, enter it in the Picture Source box. If you don't know the file name, click Browse and select an image.

3. If you are sending this message to several recipients, some of whom may not be able to view the image, type text to substitute for the image in the Alternate Text box.

4. Specify layout and spacing and click OK.

Adding a Background Color to Your Message

To apply a color to the background of your message, choose Format ➢ Background ➢ Color, and select a color from the drop-down list. The screen in the message body is filled with the color you selected.

Now type something. Can you see it on the screen? If not, you have probably chosen a dark background and your font is also a dark color—most likely black if you haven't changed it from the default.

To make your text visible, you need to choose a light font color. To do so, click the Font Color icon and choose a light color. (We chose white.) Now type something else. You should see light-colored letters against a dark background. Impressive for an e-mail message, huh?

Attaching Files to Your Messages

In Outlook Express Mail, sending files along with your messages is painless and simple.

To attach a file to a message that you are sending to a recipient who has an Internet e-mail address, follow these steps:

1. In the New Message window, choose Insert ➢ File Attachment.

PART

III

Communications and
Using the Internet

2. In the Insert Attachment dialog box, select the file you want to attach, and click Attach. (You can select multiple files to attach, but be aware that some recipients' e-mail programs might not be able to handle multiple attachments.)

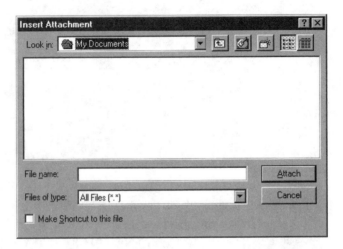

Your message now contains an icon indicating that a file is attached, the name of the file, and its size.

NOTE

As an alternative to the File ➢ Attachment approach, you can drag and drop files from any folder window into the message pane.

TIP

If you accidentally attach the wrong file, select the attachment icon, and press Delete.

In addition to attaching a file, you can insert part of a file's text in a message, which is a handy way to avoid retyping something that you already have stored on your computer. To insert only a portion of a text file in your message, follow these steps:

1. In the New Message window, choose Insert ➢ Text from File.

2. In the Insert Text File dialog box, select the file you want, and click Open. A copy of the text file opens in the body of your message.

3. Edit the file so that your message contains only the text you want.

Setting Up and Using Your Address Book

Before you get too far out in e-mail cyberspace, you'll want to set up your Address Book. It's the repository for all sorts of information that you can use on-line and off-line:

- E-mail addresses
- Voice, fax, modem, and cell phone numbers
- Home and business addresses
- Home page addresses

 TIP

You can print out your Address Book and take it with you.

Once an e-mail address is in your Address Book, you no longer need to type it in the To, Cc, or Bcc fields. You simply click the Select Recipients from a List icon and select the address you want.

In addition, you can use your Address Book to look for e-mail addresses in Internet service providers' address books, and you can use it to create distribution mailing lists.

If you already have a Windows Address Book, Outlook Express Mail uses it. If you have an Address Book (or messages) in any of the following, you can import them:

- Eudora Pro or Light Address Book (through version 3)
- LDIF-LDAP Data Interchange Format
- Microsoft Exchange Personal Address Book
- Microsoft Internet Mail for Windows 3.1 Address Book
- Netscape Address Book (version 2 or 3)
- Netscape Communicator Address Book
- A text file that has comma-separated values

To import one of these address books, follow these steps:

1. Choose File ➢ Import ➢ Address Book.
2. In the Address Book Import Tool dialog box, select the file you want to import, and click Import.

Accessing Address Book

You can open Address Book in the following ways:

- Choose Tools ➤ Address Book (press Ctrl-Shift-B).
- Click the Address Book icon on the toolbar.
- From a New Message window, click the Select Recipients from a List icon.

Creating a New Address Book from Scratch

If you don't currently have a Windows Address Book or an Address Book that you can import, you can create one from scratch. If you're thinking that typing in all that information from your organizer would be a monumental task, you're right. But you don't have to do it all at once, and, in fact, you'll soon see an easy way to add to your Address Book as you receive messages.

Open the Address Book now, and let's get started. You'll see the Windows Address Book window, as shown in Figure 17.7. We've already entered addresses in our Address Book, but obviously if you haven't, the bottom portion of this window will be empty.

FIGURE 17.7

The Windows Address Book window

You can add a name to your Address Book in two ways:

- Choose File ➢ New Contact (Ctrl-N).
- Click the New Contact icon on the toolbar.

Regardless of the method you use, Windows displays the Properties dialog box:

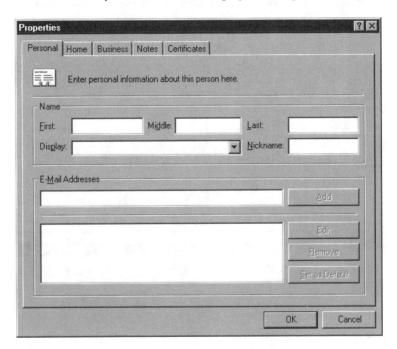

Entering Personal Information

As you can see, the Properties dialog box has six tabs, and when you enter new contact information, the Personal tab is selected by default. To enter information, follow these steps:

1. Enter the person's first, middle, and last names.

Press tab to move from one field to another. As you enter names, they appear in the Display field.

2. Now enter the person's e-mail address and press Enter. If the person has more than one e-mail address, click Add and continue entering addresses.

TIP

> To make one of multiple e-mail addresses the default, select it and click Set As Default. If the person has only one e-mail address, it is automatically the default.

If you make a typing mistake, click Edit and fix the address. Or, if you change your mind altogether, get rid of the address by clicking Remove.

If this is all the information you want to store for now, click OK. You'll now see the information for this person listed in the Windows Address Book window, and you can simply click the Send Mail icon if you want to compose a message to him or her.

If you want to continue entering more information about this person, however, you can select one of the other tabs. For our purposes here, let's select the Home tab.

Entering Home-Related Information

When you select the Home tab, you will see the window shown in Figure 17.8. Enter as much or as little information as you need.

FIGURE 17.8

The Home tab of the Properties window in Address Book

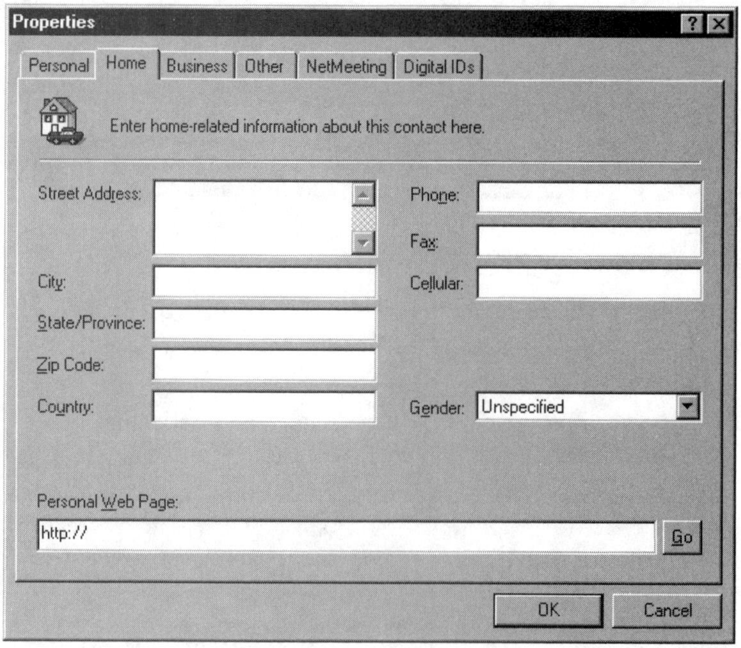

If this person has a personal home page, you can enter the URL in the Personal Web Page text box. If you are connected to the Internet, you can then click Go to open this contact's home page in a browser window.

Now let's also assume that you want to enter some business-related information for this person.

Entering Business-Related Information

Select the Business tab (shown in Figure 17.9), and enter as much or as little information as you think you need. Remember, you can always come back to this tab and change, delete, or add information.

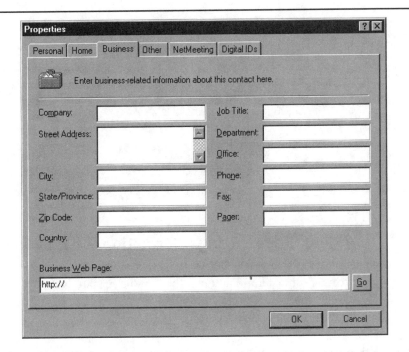

If this person has a business Web page, you can enter the URL in the Business Web Page text box. When you are connected to the Internet, you can then click Go to open this home page in a browser window, just as you can with a personal Web page address.

Making a Note about This Person

Do you also need to store some information for which you haven't yet seen a convenient spot? Perhaps, for example, you want to enter the names of a client's spouse and children or make some other comment that's important to remember about the client. You can put all this on the Other tab, as shown in Figure 17.10. Select the Other tab and then simply enter any additional information.

FIGURE 17.10

The Other tab of the Properties dialog box of Address Book

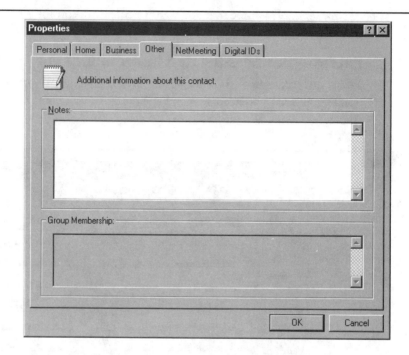

Adding Conferencing Information for Your New Contact

If you know that you will be getting together with this person via NetMeeting, you can enter contact information in the NetMeeting tab, as shown in Figure 17.11. Enter the person's conferencing e-mail address in the Select or Add New text box, and enter the name of the server in the Add New text box.

See Chapter 19 for details about NetMeeting.

Adding, Removing, and Viewing Digital IDs for This Person

You use a digital ID (certificate) when you want to show that you wrote a message, to show that the message has not been tampered with, and to prevent others from signing your name to messages that you did not write.

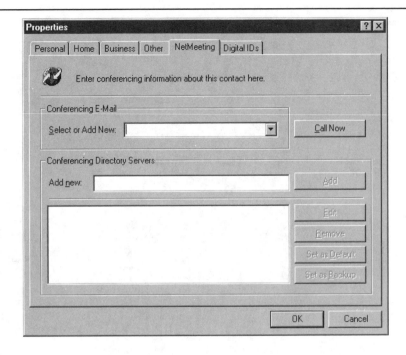

FIGURE 17.11

The NetMeeting tab of the Properties dialog box of the Address Book

When you use a digital ID, you encrypt your message. Only a person who also has your certificate can read your message. If you want another person to have your certificate, you usually send it as an e-mail message attachment. When you send e-mail to a contact that has the certificate, that person uses the certificate to decrypt the message.

You use the Digital IDs tab to add, view, and remove certificates (see Figure 17.12).

If you are entering information about someone in your Address Book and you receive a certificate from that person, the certificate will be in a file on your computer and will probably have the extension .pub. To enter it on this tab, click Import.

Now that you've seen how to add information about an individual to your Address Book, let's look at how to set up a group.

You obtain a digital ID from a qualified certifying organization such as the Internet security company VeriSign. For more information about digital certificates and for information about applying for one, see VeriSign's website at www.verisign.com.

PART

III

Communications and Using the Internet

FIGURE 17.12

The Digital IDs tab of the Properties dialog box of Address Book

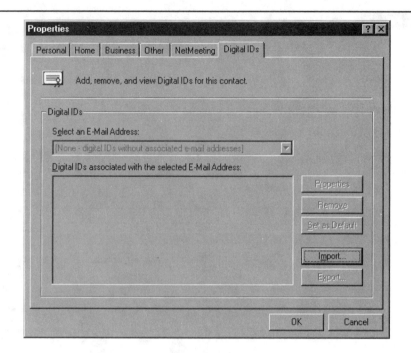

Setting Up a Group in Address Book

When you use a group, you can send the same message to several people at once; in other words, it's a distribution list.

You might set up a group for any number of purposes. For example, you might want to remind the Thursday night duplicate bridge club in your office that this week you'll be playing at Joe's house and that it's BYOB. Or you might set up a group that consists of the staff in your department.

To set up a group, open Address Book and click the New Group icon on the toolbar. You'll see the Group tab of the Properties dialog box, as shown in Figure 17.13.

To create a group, follow these steps:

1. In the Group name box, type a name for the group.

Be sure to make the name descriptive so that you know exactly which people are getting what. You probably don't want to invite the entire sales department to a baby shower for someone in your aerobics class.

FIGURE 17.13

*The Group tab of
the Properties dialog
box of Address Book*

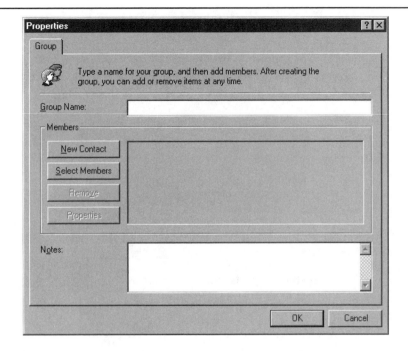

2. If you want to add to the group a person who is not yet in your Address Book, click New Contact to open the Properties dialog box.

3. Click Select Members to open the Select Group Members dialog box, and select members whose information is already in your Address Book.

4. In the Notes section, you can enter comments. For example, if you're setting up a group named New Products Task Force, you might make a note that this group meets every Wednesday at noon over lunch.

5. To place members in the group, select the person's name and then click Select. The names of the members begin to accumulate in the Members section.

6. When you have selected all the names you want, click OK. Outlook Express again displays the Properties dialog box for the group you are creating. If the list is to your liking, click OK.

You will now see the name of the group you just created in the Windows Address Book window. To send mail to the group, select the group name and click the Send Mail icon.

Customizing Your Address Book Window

If you have entered several contacts, you might have noticed that in the Address Book window they appear in the order in which they were entered. This is probably not the most useful way to maintain this list, especially if you have many contacts and many groups. You can change this order using the View menu:

To change the order, choose View ➢ Sort By. You'll see the options shown below:

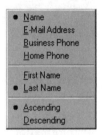

Click an option, and Outlook Express sorts your list accordingly.

But you have still other ways to customize this window. You can choose Large Icon, Small Icon, or List view. If you choose View ➢ List, you will see only the names, not the e-mail addresses and phone numbers.

Searching for Names in All the Right Places

Although your Address Book may be where you look for addresses most often when sending e-mail, you have some other powerful places to search called directory services. A directory service is something akin to a giant telephone book on the Internet, except that it also contains e-mail addresses.

When you install Windows, you can search the following directory services:

- Four11
- Bigfoot

- InfoSpace
- InfoSpace Business
- SwitchBoard
- Verisign
- WhoWhere

TIP

To add a directory service to this list, choose Tools ➢ Accounts. In the Internet Accounts dialog box, select the Directory Service tab and then choose Add ➢ Directory Service to open the Internet Connection Wizard, which walks you through the process.

To check this out, open Address Book, and click the Find icon on the toolbar. You will see the Find People dialog box:

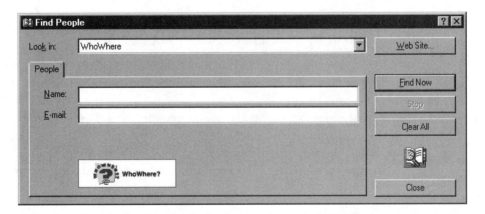

Let's take a break and have some fun. In the Find People dialog box, type your name in the Name box; click the Look In down arrow, and from the drop-down list, select WhoWhere and click Find Now. Can you find your name in the list that appears at the bottom of your screen?

When you're searching for real, you can add any address you find to your Address Book by clicking Add to Address Book.

Printing from Your Address Book

On occasion, you may need a printed copy of your Address Book. For example, you might want to take a printed copy on a trip. To print the entire contents of every contact in your Address Book, follow these steps:

1. Open Address Book.
2. Choose Edit ➤ Select All.
3. Click the Print icon.
4. In the Print dialog box, click the Memo option button (if it isn't already selected), and then click OK.

You'll get a printed copy showing the name of each contact (in alphabetical order by last name), followed by that person's information (both home and business).

To print only business-related information about a single contact or your entire list, click the Business Card option. If you want to print only names and phone numbers, click the Phone List option.

Taking Control of Your Mail with Inbox Assistant

Have you ever wished for a way to prevent unwanted telephone calls from even ringing? If you have caller ID, you can choose not to answer an identifiable sales call, but the phone still rings.

With Outlook Express Mail, however, you can set up a list of rules to govern which messages you receive and where messages go when they are received. You can even set up automatic replies. You do all this, and more, with the Inbox Assistant.

To open Inbox Assistant, choose Tools ➤ Inbox Assistant. Outlook Express displays the Inbox Assistant dialog box:

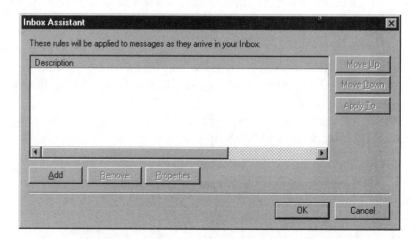

To start setting up the rules for your mail, click Add. Outlook Express Mail displays the Properties dialog box:

You can use Inbox Assistant to perform myriad housekeeping tasks; we can't possibly cover (or even think of) all of them here. We will give you some suggestions, though, for using Inbox Assistant to make at least your e-mail life a little easier and certainly more efficient.

For starters, let's take care of mail that you know you don't want to read. Perhaps you've repeatedly received some advertising that annoys you. If you know the sender's e-mail address or have an old message that includes the subject line, you can enter one or both in the To and Subject fields. Now, check the Delete Off Server checkbox. Mail from those particular folks will never find its way into your mailbox again.

If you get lots of mail from certain people, you might want to set up folders for each of them so that incoming messages are placed directly in these folders. Follow these steps:

1. Choose Tools ➤ Inbox Assistant ➤ Add to display the Properties dialog box.

2. In the From field, enter the person's e-mail address.

3. Check the Move To checkbox, and click Folder.

4. In the Move dialog box, click New Folder to create a folder, select the folder, click OK, and then click OK again.

Using Outlook Express News

If you've subscribed to any of the commercial Internet service providers, you've no doubt browsed online newspapers and magazines and seen a news flash when you sign on to the service. That's not what we're talking about in this section.

This section concerns *newsgroups,* collections of articles about particular subjects. Newsgroups are similar to e-mail in that you can reply to what someone else has written (the newsgroup term for this is *posted),* and you can send a question or a response either to the whole group or to individuals.

To read newsgroups, you need a *newsreader,* and that is what Outlook Express News is. But before we get into the nuts and bolts of how to use Outlook Express News to read newsgroups, we want to look at the kinds of newsgroups that are available and give you a bit of background about how they work, what they are, and what they are not.

WARNING

If you are new to newsgroups, be aware that they are uncensored. You can find just about anything at any time anywhere. No person has authority over newsgroups as a whole. If you find certain groups, certain articles, or certain people offensive, don't go there. You'll see later in this chapter how you filter out such articles. But remember that anarchy reigns. Forewarned is forearmed.

Newsgroups and the Internet

The primary (but not sole) source of newsgroups is Usenet, which is accessed by millions of people every day, in more than 100 countries. Usenet is a worldwide distributed discussion system consisting of newsgroups that have names which are classified hierarchically by subject. Newsgroup names fit into a formal structure in which each component of the name is separated from the next by a period. For example, `rec.crafts.metalworking` is a recreational group devoted to the craft of metalworking. The leftmost portion represents the largest hierarchical category, and the name gets more specific from left to right.

Table 17.1 lists the major top-level newsgroup categories and explains what topics each discusses.

TABLE 17.1: THE MAJOR NEWSGROUPS	
Newsgroup	**What It Discusses**
alt	Newsgroups outside the main structure outlined below
comp	Computer science and related topics, including operating systems, hardware, artificial intelligence, and graphics
misc	Anything that does not fit into one of the other categories
news	Information on Usenet and newsgroups
rec	Recreational activities such as hobbies, the arts, movies, and books
sci	Scientific topics such as math, physics, and biology
soc	Social issues and cultures
talk	Controversial subjects such as gun control, abortion, religion, and politics

Currently, there are thousands and thousands of newsgroups on every conceivable topic. For an extensive listing of them, go to:

sunsite.unc.edu/usenet-i/hier-s/master.html

Figure 17.14 shows the opening page at this site. As you can see if you start to scroll this list, newsgroup topics are wide ranging and far reaching. To go to one of these newsgroups, simply click its link.

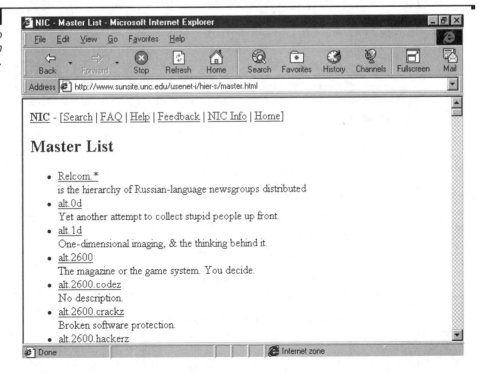

FIGURE 17.14

Click a link to go to any newsgroup in this massive list.

A Little Background

Usenet is a contraction from User Network, and it preceded the emergence of the Internet. (Usenet has been around some 17 years.) Although Usenet and the Internet are closely related, they are not the same thing. Not every Internet computer is part of Usenet, and not every Usenet system can be reached from the Internet. The Internet is used to transfer groups back and forth among computers, but that's because it is a convenient method for doing so.

For detailed information about what Usenet is and is not, go to `ftp://rtfm.mit .edu/pub/usenet/news.answers/usenet/what-is/part1`.

You access newsgroups by accessing the server on which they are stored. Not all servers store the same newsgroups. The network administrator or the owner of the site determines what to store.

Almost all news servers "expire" articles after a few days or, at most, a few weeks because of the tremendous volume. Although they might be archived at the site, these articles are no longer available to be viewed by users.

Using Outlook Express as Your News Reader

Unlike most of the other areas we're exploring in this book, newsgroups are text-only. You won't see any fancy formatting or flashy graphics, hear any background sounds, or pick up any video. What you see is what you get, and that's just plain text.

That seems simple enough, but if you spend any time in newsgroups, you'll soon see the value of having some tools to automate some processes and make others more manageable.

When you use Outlook Express News as your newsreader, you have tools to do the following:

- Find newsgroups that interest you
- Browse newsgroups quickly and easily
- View, expand, and collapse threads (details about threads are in the "Reading Newsgroups" section)
- Sort the message list
- Track what you have and haven't read
- Send messages
- Add a personal signature to messages

- Filter out newsgroup messages that don't interest you
- Subscribe to your favorite newsgroups
- Connect to multiple news servers
- Download newsgroups to view later off-line
- View articles in HTML

Starting Outlook Express News

You can start Outlook Express News in any of the following ways:

- From the Outlook Express windows, click Read News.
- Click News in the Outlook Bar.
- Choose Go ➢ News.

Connecting to Newsgroups

Connect to your ISP and open Outlook Express. In the Outlook Bar, click the icon for your news server to open this dialog box:

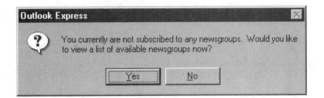

Click Yes to download a list of the newsgroups available on your news server. While this takes place, you will see a message similar to the following:

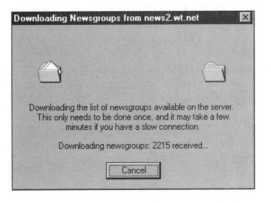

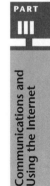

Depending on the speed of your connection, this downloading process should only take a few minutes. Watch as the counter increases—you'll be amazed at the number of newsgroups.

Once this list is downloaded, your Newsgroups dialog box will look similar to this:

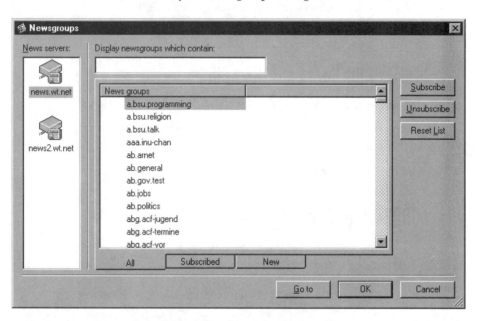

Only the names of the newsgroups are downloaded to your computer; their contents remain on the news server. Periodically, you can update this list by clicking Reset List.

Finding a Newsgroup of Interest

Well, now that you have all this at your disposal, how do you find something that you're interested in? It reminds us of having to go to a department store to select what you're going to wear to work every morning. With so many choices, how can you decide (if money's no object, of course)?

You can select a newsgroup to read in two ways:

- You can scroll through the list (this could take some time).
- You can enter a term to search on.

Just for the sake of doing it, scroll the list a bit. As you can see, it's in alphabetic order by hierarchical categories. Now let's assume you don't see anything right away that strikes your fancy. Not to worry—you can search for something. To search for a topic, enter the word or words in the Display Newsgroups Which Contain box.

WARNING

Type your entry and then *don't do anything!* Wait a second, and groups containing what you entered will appear in the Newsgroups area. You don't need to press Enter, choose OK, or do anything else. Just wait a nanosecond.

We entered the word *internet,* and Figure 17.15 shows the results.

FIGURE 17.15

A list of newsgroups that appeared when we searched on internet.

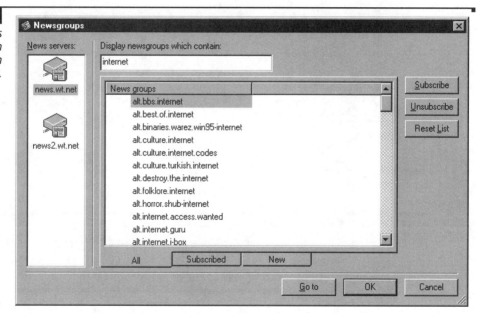

Reading a Newsgroup

Now you can select a newsgroup to read. To do so, follow these steps:

1. Click the name of the newsgroup.

2. Click Go To.

We chose to read `microsoft.public.internet.news`, and this is what we got:

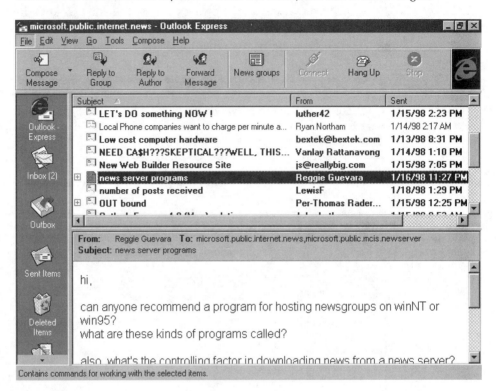

NOTE

Unfortunately, Outlook Express News doesn't maintain the list that your search found in the Newsgroups dialog box. If you want to select another newsgroup that was in the found group, you have to repeat your search.

To read an article, simply click its header.

Replying and Posting

While you're reading a newsgroup, you can respond to an individual author of a message or you can reply to the entire group. Choose the method most appropriate to the topic and the subject of the newsgroup.

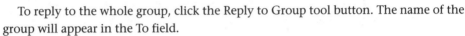

You will occasionally see requests that responses be directed toward the individual and not the group; you should honor these requests.

To respond to an individual author, follow these steps:

1. Click the Reply to Author tool button.

2. In the message window, type your message.

3. Click Send.

To reply to the whole group, click the Reply to Group tool button. The name of the group will appear in the To field.

To post a new message to a group, click the Compose Message tool button. To reply both to the author and to the newsgroup, choose Compose ➢ Reply to Newsgroup and Author. You can also use the Compose menu to forward articles and to forward articles as attachments.

Subscribing and Unsubscribing to Newsgroups

When you read a newsgroup, it appears as a subfolder in your News folder. When you exit Outlook Express, these folders are deleted from the Folder List.

When you *subscribe* to a newsgroup, it also appears as a subfolder in your News folder. When you exit Outlook Express News, however, this folder is retained in the Folder List. The next time you access your news server, you can simply click this folder to open the newsgroup.

You can subscribe to newsgroups in the following ways:

- In the Newsgroups dialog box, select a group and click Subscribe.

- With the newsgroup open, choose Tools ➢ Subscribe to This Newsgroup.

When you no longer want to subscribe to a newsgroup, follow these steps:

1. Click the News Groups tool button.

2. In the Newsgroups dialog box, select the Subscribed tab.

3. Select the name of the newsgroup, and click Unsubscribe.

While viewing a newsgroup, you can unsubscribe by choosing Tools ➢ Unsubscribe from This Newsgroup.

Communications and
Using the Internet

Rules for Posting to Newsgroups

Although newsgroups are not controlled by any single entity, there are some established rules for using them:

- Lurk before you post; get a sense of the group's culture and style.
- Never forget that the person on the other side is human.
- Don't blame system administrators for their users' behavior.
- Never assume that a person is speaking for his or her organization.
- Be careful what you say about others (as many as 3 million people may read what you say).
- Be brief.
- Your postings reflect upon you; be proud of them.
- Use descriptive titles.
- Think about your audience.
- Be careful with humor and sarcasm.
- Post a message only once.
- Summarize what you are following up.
- Use Mail; don't post a follow-up.
- Be careful about copyrights and licenses.
- Cite appropriate references.
- Don't overdo signatures.
- Avoid posting to multiple newsgroups.

Filtering Out What You Don't Want to Read

As we've mentioned, most newsgroups are not censored in any way. Outlook Express News, however, provides a way that you can be your own censor. You can choose which newsgroups appear on the message list and are downloaded to your computer.

NOTE

Some groups are *moderated;* that is, someone is in charge of the newsgroup and reads posts and replies. That person applies certain specified criteria, and only those messages that meet these guidelines appear in the newsgroup. When a newsgroup is moderated, you'll see a message to that effect when you open the newsgroup.

Selecting newsgroups and messages that you don't want to appear on your computer is called *filtering*. You might choose to filter groups and messages for any number of reasons, including the following:

- To avoid scrolling through messages on topics about which you have no interest.
- To screen out messages that have been around a long time.

To filter newsgroups and messages, follow these steps:

1. Choose Tools ➢ Newsgroup Filters to open the Newsgroup Filters dialog box:

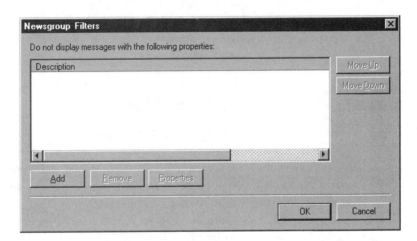

2. Click Add to open the Properties dialog box:

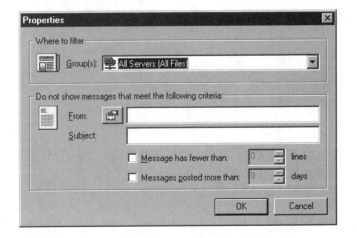

3. Click the down-arrow in the Groups drop-down list box to choose the groups you want to filter.

4. To filter messages from specific e-mail addresses, enter the address in the From field.

5. To filter messages by subject, enter the subject in the Subject field.

6. Check the Message Has More Than *x* Lines checkbox and select a number to filter out messages that have more than the specified number of lines.

7. Check the Messages Posted More Than *x* Days checkbox to filter out messages older than the specified number of days.

8. When you are satisfied with your selections, click OK, and then click OK again in the Newsgroup Filters dialog box.

Viewing, Marking, and Sorting Messages

As is the case with Outlook Express Mail, by default your Preview Pane is split horizontally, with header information in the top pane and messages displayed in the bottom pane. To change this format, choose View ➢ Layout to open the Window Layout Properties dialog box. In the Preview Pane section of this dialog box, select the options that correspond to the way you want to display messages.

You can also choose to display only certain messages. Choose View ➢ Current View, and then select an option from the drop-down menu:

You can choose to display the Subject, From, Sent, Size, and Lines fields in headers. Follow these steps:

1. With a newsgroup displayed, choose View ➢ Columns to open the Columns dialog box.

2. To remove information from the display, select what you want to remove, and then click Remove.

3. When the display is to your liking, click OK.

To return to the default display, click Reset.

Browsing for Messages

You can look for messages using the scroll bar, and you can go to certain messages by choosing View ➤ Next and selecting from the drop-down menu:

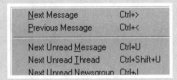

<u>N</u>ext Message	Ctrl+>
<u>P</u>revious Message	Ctrl+<
Next Unread <u>M</u>essage	Ctrl+U
Next Unread <u>T</u>hread	Ctrl+Shift+U
Next Unread Newsgroup	Ctrl+J

As you can see, you can choose the next or previous message or choose the next unread message, thread, or newsgroup.

When reading a message, you can click the up and down arrows at the top of the message to go to the previous or next message in the newsgroup.

Interpreting the News Icons

When you view a newsgroup, you'll notice that some messages are preceded by a plus sign (+). This means that this message is part of a thread. To view the thread, simply click the plus sign. The message that is part of the thread is displayed. It may also be preceded by a plus sign if it is part of a further, ongoing thread.

When you click a thread to display the further messages, it becomes a minus sign (–). Click the minus sign to once again collapse the thread.

For an explanation of the many, many other news icons, choose Help ➤ Contents and Index, select the Contents tab, select Tips and Tricks, and then click Message List Icons for Outlook Express.

PART

III

Communications and
Using the Internet

Terminology

Header: The information displayed in the message window. The header may contain information such as the name of the sender, the subject, the newsgroups to which it is posted, and the time and date the message was sent or received.

Thread: An original message and any posted replies. If you reply to a message and change the title, however, you start a new thread.

Marking Messages

Although Outlook Express marks messages as you read them and indicates which messages you have not read, you can manually mark messages. As you will see in the section "Customizing Outlook Express," you can use the Read tab of the Options dialog box to have Outlook Express automatically mark all messages as read when you exit a newsgroup. You can also mark messages using the Edit menu:

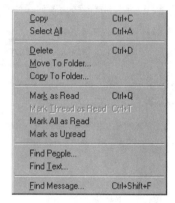

Select a message header, click Edit, and select one of these options.

Sorting Messages

By default, Outlook Express displays messages in ascending alphabetic order by subject. For example, in a software engineering newsgroup, a message header about Hungarian notation appears before a header containing "IBM Kasparov vs. Deep Blue."

You can change the order in which messages are displayed. Choose View ➤ Sort By and then choose an option from the drop-down menu:

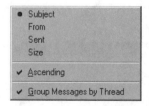

To display the most recently sent messages first, choose View ➤ Sort By ➤ Sent. To display the list so that all messages by any one sender are grouped together, choose View ➤ Sort By ➤ From. (Sorting and grouping headers can make for some interesting reading.)

Reading the News Off-Line

If you're hearing the clinking of coins as you're cruising the newsgroups, you have a couple of options. You can try to find an ISP that gives you unlimited access for a flat fee, or you can read news off-line. To read off-line, follow these steps:

1. Choose Tools ➢ Download This Newsgroup to open the Download Newsgroup dialog box:

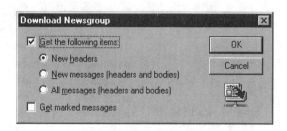

2. Click Get the Following Items, and then choose to download headers, messages, or both. You can also retrieve marked messages.

Outlook Express then connects to your news server and retrieves what you've requested. You can then read all your messages off-line, at your leisure.

Customizing Outlook Express

You can customize many aspects of Outlook Express so that it works the way you like to work. For example, you can place buttons for the tasks you most commonly perform on the toolbar, and you can choose not to display those you rarely need. And you can establish all sorts of rules for Outlook Express to follow while you are composing, sending, and receiving messages.

Let's look first at the ways you can customize the toolbar.

Customizing the Toolbar

When you first install Outlook Express, the toolbar in the main window looks like this:

To add or delete buttons or to rearrange them, choose View ➤ Layout to open the Window Layout Properties dialog box.

From the Toolbar section of the Layout dialog box, you can select to display the toolbar at the top of the window, at the left, at the bottom, or at the right. You can also choose to show or hide the toolbar labels.

To add or delete buttons, click Customize Toolbar, and Outlook Express displays the Customize Toolbar dialog box:

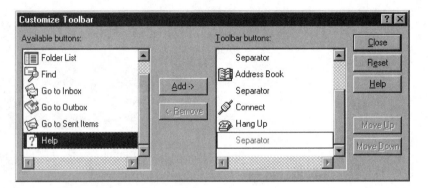

To add a button, follow these steps:

1. Select the button in the Available Buttons list.

2. Click the Add button.

3. Click Close.

4. In the Window Layout Properties dialog box, click Apply, and then click OK.

The button now appears on your toolbar.

You can return your toolbar to its original format at any time. In the Customize Toolbar dialog box, choose Reset and then Close. Then, in the Window Layout Properties dialog box, click Apply and then click OK.

Customizing Mail and News Options

You can use the Options dialog box to establish your preferences for both Outlook Express Mail and Outlook Express News. Let's start by looking at the General options.

NOTE

Depending on your installation of Internet Explorer 4, the default settings may differ. Before you start using Outlook Express extensively, take a moment to see which options are checked by default on your system.

The General Tab

When you choose Tools ➢ Options, Outlook Express displays the Options dialog box with the General tab selected:

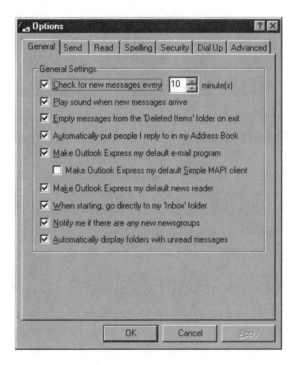

Table 17.2 shows the options that you can set up in the General tab.

TABLE 17.2: THE OPTIONS IN THE GENERAL TAB OF THE OPTIONS DIALOG BOX

Option	What It Does
Check for New Messages Every *x* Minutes	Check this item and then click the drop-down arrow list to select a time interval. This works only when you are connected to your server (or when the last option in the Dial Up tab is enabled).
Play Sound When New Messages Arrive	Of course, this works only when you are connected to your e-mail server. If you don't want to be notified when new mail arrives, uncheck this option. You can customize the sound via Control Panel ➤ Sounds.
Empty Messages from the "Deleted Items" Folder on Exit	Messages are placed in this folder when you select a message and choose Delete. Check this item if you want the Deleted Items folder emptied when you exit Outlook Express.
Automatically Put People I Reply to in My Address Book	Check this option if you want the names and e-mail addresses of everybody you reply to in your Address Book.
Make Outlook Express My Default E-Mail Program	Uncheck this item to make another e-mail program, for example, Outlook, your default e-mail program.
Make Outlook Express My Default Simple MAPI Client	Specifies whether Outlook Express is used when you choose File ➤ Send in other applications. Selecting this checkbox disables Microsoft Exchange and Outlook.
Make Outlook Express My Default News Reader	Uncheck this item to make another new program your default newsreader.
When Starting, Go Directly to My "Inbox" Folder	Check this item to go immediately to your Inbox when you start Outlook Express.
Notify Me If There Are Any New Newsgroups	Check this option if you want Outlook Express to check for new newsgroups and download their names when you access a news server.
Automatically Display Folders with Unread Messages	Check this option if you want to display only unread messages.

Sending Mail and News

To set your preferences for sending mail and news, select the Send tab:

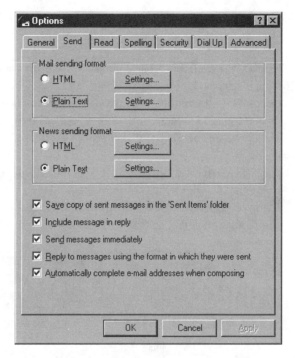

In the Mail Sending Format section of the Send tab, you specify whether you want to send mail in HTML or Plain Text format. If you want all messages composed and sent in HTML, check this option and click the Settings button to open the HTML Settings dialog box:

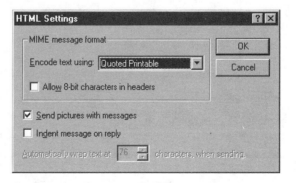

PART

III

Communications and
Using the Internet

In the Encode Text Using drop-down list box in the MIME Message Format section, you have three choices:

- None
- Quoted Printable
- Base 64

These are the available bit and binary formats for encoding your message. Quoted Printable is selected by default.

The Allow 8-Bit Characters in Headers checkbox is unchecked by default. This means that foreign character sets, high ASCII, or double-byte character sets (DBCS) in the header will be encoded. If this checkbox is checked, these characters will not be encoded.

In the lower half of this dialog box, you can choose to send pictures with messages and to indent the original text of messages to which you reply.

When you select Plain Text as your mail sending format and click Settings, Outlook Express displays the Plain Text Settings dialog box:

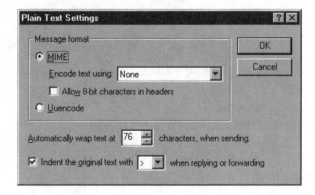

In the Encode Text Using drop-down list in the Message Format section of this dialog box, you have three choices:

- None
- Quoted Printable
- Base 64

None is selected by default.

NOTE

Unless your system administrator or ISP instructs you to do so, don't change these settings.

The Allow 8-bit Characters in Headers checkbox is unchecked by default. This means that foreign character sets, high ASCII, or double-byte character sets (DBCS) in the header will be encoded. If this checkbox is checked, these characters will not be encoded.

By default, when you send messages in plain text format, lines wrap at 76 characters. To change this format, click the drop-down list arrow and select a greater or lesser number of characters. Also by default, the original text of a message to which you reply is preceded by an angle bracket. To select another character, click the drop-down list arrow.

In the News Sending Format section of the Send tab, you can choose whether to post articles in HTML or Plain Text. Selecting Plain Text is a wise choice if you are posting to a widely read newsgroup. Most newsreaders cannot display articles in HTML. Selecting either HTML or Plain Text and clicking the Settings button opens the Settings dialog box for that selection. In either case, you'll see the same dialog boxes that open when you select that option for sending mail.

Table 17.3 lists and explains the other options in the Send tab.

TABLE 17.3: ADDITIONAL OPTIONS IN THE SEND TAB

Option	What It Does
Save Copy of Sent Messages in the "Sent Items" Folder	This is handy for verifying that you really sent a message that you intended to send. If it is unchecked, you can still keep a copy by including yourself on the Cc or Bcc line.
Include Message in Reply	If you check this option, you can edit the message to which you are replying so that it retains only the pertinent sentences or paragraphs. This device comes in handy when you are responding to a sender's questions.
Send Messages Immediately	If you check this item, messages are sent when you click the Send button rather than being saved in your Outbox until you send them.
Reply to Messages Using the Format in Which They Were Sent	To send a message in a different format, uncheck this item.
Automatically Complete E-Mail Addresses When Composing	If you check this option, Outlook Express completes the e-mail address you are typing as soon as it recognizes a series of characters, if this address is in your Address Book.

PART

III

Communications and
Using the Internet

Reading Mail and News

Select the Read tab, and Outlook Express displays this dialog box:

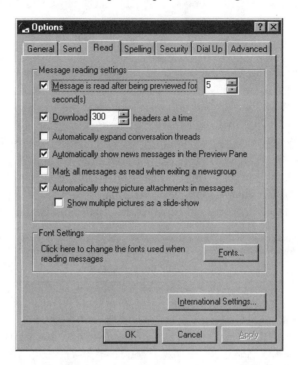

Table 17.4 shows the options in the Read Tab.

TABLE 17.4: THE OPTIONS IN THE READ TAB	
Option	**What It Does**
Message Is Read after Being Previewed for 5 Second(s)	You can change the number of seconds, and you can uncheck this option to manually mark messages as read.
Download x Headers at a Time	Set at 300 by default. You can set this option to a minimum of 50 and a maximum of 1000. (Would you really want to download 1000 headers?) If you uncheck this option, all headers in the newsgroup are down-loaded, regardless of the number.
Automatically Expand Conversation Threads	If you select this option, threads and all replies are dis-played when you open a newsgroup.
Automatically Show News Messages in the Preview Pane	If you uncheck this option, select the header and then press the spacebar to display the message body.

Continued ▶

TABLE 17.4: THE OPTIONS IN THE READ TAB (CONTINUED)	
Option	**What It Does**
Mark All Messages as Read When Exiting a Newsgroup	When you select this option, you choose to read only messages marked as unread when you return to this newsgroup.
Automatically Show Picture Attachments in Messages	If you have a low-bandwidth computer, you might want to disable this option.
Show Multiple Pictures as a Slide-Show	When this option is checked, multiple attached pictures are displayed one at a time, with forward and back buttons.

You use the Font Settings section of the Read tab to change the fonts used when reading messages. When you install Outlook Express, messages you read are formatted in the Western Alphabet using Arial as the proportional font (when you are using the HTML format), using Courier New as the fixed-width font (when you are using the Plain Text format), and a medium font size. To change any of this, click the Font Settings button. Outlook Express displays the Fonts dialog box, as shown in Figure 17.16. Click the down arrows to survey your choices.

FIGURE 17.16

The Fonts dialog box

Normally, Outlook Express can display messages or articles in the language in which they were composed and sent. If it cannot, you can change the character set for the displayed message. Choose View ➢ Language, and in the dialog box, choose Yes. To remove the mapping to this character set, click the International Settings button in the Read tab of the Options dialog box to open the International Settings dialog box.

Checking Spelling

If you send and receive lots of e-mail, you're probably used to seeing and, for the most part, ignoring typos. In the early days of e-mail, the only way to check what you were sending was to stop, read it over, and, with minimal editing features available, fix your errors.

This was a time-consuming task associated with a powerful time-saving application, and most people just didn't (don't?) bother. If you're simply communicating with colleagues down the hall or buddies in your bowling league, maybe it doesn't matter. But if you're sending a trip report to your boss or posting a major announcement to a newsgroup, it matters. You want to appear professional, and you certainly don't want to embarrass yourself with a couple of transposed letters.

NOTE

Outlook Express uses the spelling checker that comes with Microsoft Office 95 or Office 97 programs. If you don't have one of these programs installed, the Spelling command is unavailable.

Using the spelling checker, you can quickly give your messages the once-over before they wend their way to the outside world. Click the Spelling tab to display your options:

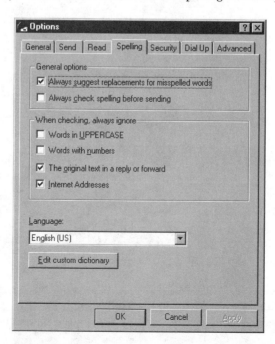

Table 17.5 shows the options available in the Spelling tab.

TABLE 17.5: THE OPTIONS IN THE SPELLING TAB	
Option	**What It Does**
Always Suggest Replacements for Misspelled Words	With this option checked, Outlook Express checks your spelling as you go along and suggests replacements.
Always Check Spelling before Sending	Check this option if you want Outlook Express to quickly look for typos before a message is sent.
Words in UPPERCASE	When this option is checked, words entirely upper-cased are ignored in the spelling check.
Words with Numbers	When this option is checked, words that include numeric characters are ignored in the spelling check.
The Original Text in a Reply or Forward	When this option is checked, only your message is spell checked, not the message you are forwarding or to which you are replying.
Internet Addresses	If you've ever had your spell checker come to a halt every time it reaches a URL, you'll want to keep this option turned on.

By default, your messages are checked against a U.S. English dictionary. If you want to choose British English, click the Language down arrow. To create or change a custom dictionary, click Edit Custom Dictionary.

Enhancing Security

You use the Security tab to establish security zones and to specify how Outlook Express handles digital certificates (also know as digital IDs).

PART

III

Communications and
Using the Internet

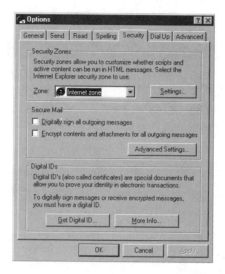

With Internet Explorer 4, you can assign websites to zones that have varying levels of security. If you have a digital certificate (as discussed earlier in the "Adding, Reviewing, and Viewing Digital IDs for This Person" section), you can add it to all outgoing messages by using the options in the Secure Mail section of this tab.

To obtain a digital ID, click the Get Digital ID button in the Digital IDs section.

Your Dial-Up Options

As we mentioned early in this chapter, we are assuming a dial-up connection to the Internet. You use the options in the Dial Up tab to specify how you connect to your ISP when you start Outlook Express:

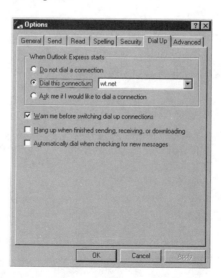

Table 17.6 lists and explains these options.

TABLE 17.6: THE OPTIONS IN THE DIAL UP TAB	
Option	**What It Does**
Do Not Dial a Connection	If you select this option, connect to the Internet by clicking the Dial button on the toolbar.
Dial This Connection	This option specifies which connection Outlook Express uses when connecting to the Internet (useful if you have more than one dial-up connection).
Ask Me If I Would Like to Dial a Connection	If you check this option, Outlook Express displays a message asking if you want to connect.
Warn Me before Switching Dial Up Connections	If you check this option, Outlook Express displays a message that allows you to cancel a connection that isn't working.
Hang Up When Finished Sending, Receiving, or Downloading	When this option is selected, Outlook Express automatically disconnects from your ISP after sending, receiving, or downloading.
Automatically Dial When Checking	Check this item if you want Outlook Express to connect when automatically checking for new messages at a specified time.

The Advanced Tab

You use the options in the Advanced tab to determine how your local message files are stored:

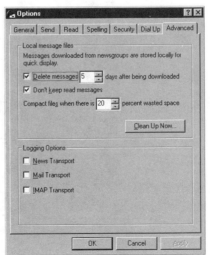

Table 17.7 lists and explains these options.

TABLE 17.7: THE OPTIONS IN THE ADVANCED TAB

Option	What It Does
Delete Messages *x* Days after Being Downloaded	Set at five days by default. You can choose a minimum of one day and a maximum of 999 days. (You could easily have a new computer by then!) When you select this option, Outlook Express deletes from your computer all newsgroup articles that meet your specification when you exit Outlook Express.
Don't Keep Read Messages	With this option selected, Outlook Express deletes all read messages from your computer when you exit Outlook Express.
Compact Files When There Is *x* Percent Wasted Space	Set at 20 percent by default. You can choose a minimum of 5 percent and a maximum of 100 percent.
News Transport	If you select this option, all commands sent to and from your news server are saved in a log file.
Mail Transport	If you select this option, all commands sent to and from your mail server are saved in a log file.
IMAP Transport	If you select this option, all commands sent to and from your IMAP server are saved in a log file.

Now let's look at the Clean Up Now button on this tab. When you click this button, Outlook Express News displays the Local File Clean Up dialog box:

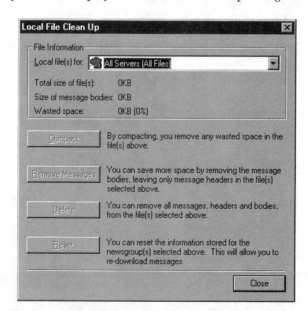

In this dialog box, first specify the files you want, and then click the appropriate buttons to do the following:

- Compact the files.
- Remove the message bodies but leave the headers in the file.
- Remove all messages, headers and bodies, from the file.
- Reset the information stored for the selected newsgroups so that you can download messages again.

Chapter

18

Using the Active Desktop and Tuning In to Channels

FEATURING

Understanding the Windows Desktop

Understanding the features of the Active Desktop

Working with the Active Desktop toolbars

Turning on or off the components on the Active Desktop

Adding items to the Active Desktop

Adding items from the Active Desktop Gallery

Using the Channel screen saver

Browsing your computer and the Internet with Explorer

Displaying your folders in Web view

Customizing a folder's Web view

Using the Active Desktop and Tuning In to Channels

As the Internet has worked its way into virtually every aspect of our lives, Microsoft has obliged by incorporating the World Wide Web into Windows 98, via a new dimension to the Windows interface called the *Active Desktop*. It's what all the fuss was about when Microsoft first introduced Internet Explorer 4 and its Windows-wide influence.

This chapter introduces you to the Web-related Desktop features in Windows 98, and the techniques you can employ to take advantage of them. When you see how you can add Web pages to your Desktop or browse the Web within Windows Explorer, you'll most likely be surprised at the extent to which Windows has absorbed the Internet (or is it the other way around?).

Understanding the Active Desktop

The *Active Desktop* is the term Microsoft uses to describe its new approach to the Windows Desktop. You can choose to enable or disable several key features of the Active Desktop, and at any time you can return to the previous, Windows 95 version of the Desktop.

NOTE

As you've learned, the Windows Desktop is much like a real desk. It's the area that lies beneath (or behind, if you prefer) all the programs you open, so that everything you do in Windows happens on the Desktop. Because everything occurs there, the term *Desktop* is often used to describe the broader concept of the interface that Windows presents to us. You should think of the Active Desktop in the same light—it refers to the actual Windows Desktop on which you work, as well as the tools and techniques that make up the Windows interface.

The Active Desktop is based on Microsoft's Active Platform strategy, which attempts to combine three World Wide Web–based concepts: HTML, scripting, and objects or components (ActiveX or Java). It's these three parts that make your Windows Desktop. For example, later in this chapter, you'll see how to place one or more HTML pages on your Windows Desktop. You can view these Active Desktop items as though each were being displayed in Internet Explorer. You can also place programmable objects on the Desktop, built from Java applets or ActiveX controls. Figure 18.1 shows a stock ticker on the Desktop above the Taskbar. There's even a new screen saver that displays your active channels, one after another. You'll read more about this exciting new dimension to Windows later in the sections "Adding Content to Your Active Desktop" and "Using the Channel Screen Saver."

FIGURE 18.1

You can place HTML and active content objects on the Active Desktop, such as this stock ticker.

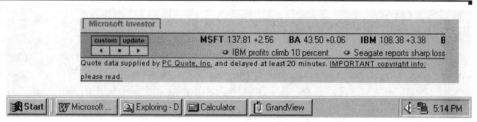

NOTE

If several users share one computer, each can have his or her own customized Active Desktop, because the Desktop is part of each user's personal profile. You can add user names and passwords by opening the Password tool in the Control Panel. To allow each user to have a custom Desktop, go to the User Profiles tab and select the "Users can customize their preferences…" option.

You'll find that the Active Desktop complements the Windows Desktop interface. Perhaps the most significant enhancement is the way that Windows Explorer and Internet

Explorer have merged into what feels like a single exploring window. Previously, you used Windows Explorer to "browse" the resources on your computer, and Internet Explorer to browse the resources on the Internet. Now the distinction between these two has all but disappeared, and the Internet is now another resource available to you, along with your disk drives, the Control Panel, your Printers folder, and so on. You can even create HTML pages within folders so that opening a folder is akin to opening a page on the Web.

To Single-Click or Not to Single-Click

If you read Chapters 3, 4, and 5, you've probably already tried the new single-click, Web-like interface that comes with Windows 98 and the Active Desktop. If not, it will most likely take you awhile to get used to pointing at an object to select it and single-clicking to open it. Here's how this works when you're viewing the files in a folder on your disk drive. As you move the mouse pointer over a file name or a folder name, the pointer changes to the little hand that you see when you point to a link in a Web page (as shown here), and the file name is underlined, just like a link. This tells you that something will happen if you click that link (the file name).

If you pause the mouse pointer over a file name (also called *hovering*) for more than a fraction of a second, that name is selected (as shown here), as though you had clicked on it in pre–Active Desktop days. If you click a file name, the result is the same as clicking a link in a Web page—the file is opened, just as though you had double-clicked it in pre-AD days.

Selecting a Block of Items in Single-Click Mode

To select a block of contiguous items, such as several files in Explorer, hover the mouse over the first or last item in the group that you want to select, which will select that single item. Then hold down the Shift key and hover the mouse over the item at the other end of the group of items you want to select, which will select the entire group.

To select noncontiguous items in a list, hold down the Ctrl key and hover the mouse over each item you want in the selection. Release the Ctrl key between selections to avoid selecting items you happen to pause over. It's easy to deselect an item, though; simply hover over it a second time while holding down the Ctrl key.

Switching Between Single-Click and Double-Click Modes

If you find that planet single-click is not a hospitable world (especially when you've got an hour until deadline), remember, you can easily return to the double-click world that we all grew up with. To recap the discussions from Chapters 3, 4, and 5, let's review the choices you have available.

You can access the Active Desktop interface options from the Start menu by choosing Settings ➤ Folder Options. You can also access them while in Windows Explorer (in other words, while viewing files, folders, or other resources on your computer) by choosing View ➤ Folder Options. In the Folder Options dialog box, choose the General tab, as shown in Figure 18.2. Here you can switch between the single-click and double-click mode in two ways:

Web Style lets you continue to use the "Web view" in Windows, so that you can single-click to open a file, customize folders to appear as Web pages, and so on.

Classic Style returns Windows to its earlier Windows 95 behavior, including returning to the double-click mode.

Custom lets you select between the interface-related options. Most important, you can choose between single- and double-clicking while keeping the Web-view interface. With single-click enabled, you can also choose to have all files and folders, or only those you select, underlined as links.

NOTE

The Web view in Windows Explorer that we're discussing here is unrelated to the HTML objects you can place on the Desktop. You can take advantage of one feature without the other if you so choose.

The Active Desktop Work Area

The Desktop work area in the environment of the Active Desktop includes everything in the Windows 95 Desktop: the Windows Taskbar, the Start button, any open program windows, and icons for files and shortcuts to files. You can treat all these items much as you did in the earlier, classic Windows Desktop.

The big change is the addition of a new HTML layer on the Desktop, which lies beneath (or behind) the traditional icon layer. It is on this new layer that you can place a new type of Desktop object: an HTML component. In a nutshell, you can place one or more Web pages directly on your Desktop, and also assign a Web page to be the Desktop's background, just as you can assign colors to the traditional background.

FIGURE 18.2

You can choose between the single-click world or the double-click world via the View ➤ Folder Options command.

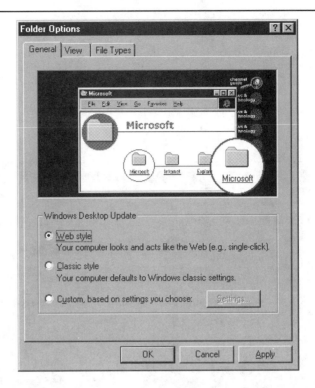

When you're connected to the Internet in the usual way, you can work in any HTML Desktop object as though you were working within Internet Explorer. For example, you can click links, download files, fill out forms, copy data from the page and paste it into another document, and so on.

NOTE

If you don't want to see any of the icons on the Active Desktop, select the "Hide icons when Desktop is viewed as Web page" option. You'll find this on the View tab when you choose View ➤ Folder Options in Windows Explorer, and also on the effects tab in the Display Properties dialog box (right-click the Desktop).

Figure 18.3 shows a personalized example of an Active Desktop.

- The Desktop background is no longer a Web page (although there are other Web pages on the Desktop), which cuts down on the clutter, and it has been assigned a color.

Communications and Using the Internet

- A stock ticker has been placed just above the Taskbar and regularly updates the prices and headlines it displays from the Internet.

- The Channel bar, which was discussed in Chapter 16, has been placed on the right side of the screen, where you can click a button to view a channel or set up a subscription to one.

- Various Web pages have been placed on the Active Desktop and await your online interaction.

FIGURE 18.3

The Active Desktop can display Web pages and other HTML objects along with the usual icons, program windows, and so on.

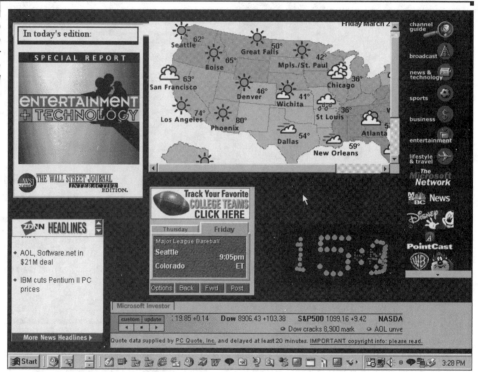

Again, any of the Desktop Web objects can be on-line and connected to the Internet, as though each had been opened in Internet Explorer. Later in this chapter in "Adding Content to Your Active Desktop," you'll learn how to add items such as these to the Desktop.

The Active Desktop May Be More Active Than You Want

Placing Web objects on the Active Desktop is a powerful new dimension of Windows 95. But, as always, there is a caveat or two. First, having more than a few Web objects on the Desktop can use up lots of your computer's RAM and processor capacity. You may have to do some experimenting to see how many Web objects and of what type your computer (and you) can handle.

Also, each time you start your computer, your Active Desktop may want to connect to the Internet to update one or more of the Desktop Web items. You might find this inconvenient or annoying if you use Dial-Up Networking to connect to the Internet via a modem.

If your Active Desktop proves to be too much when you need to dedicate more of your computer's power to other tasks, you can choose to turn off the display of all Desktop Web objects.

Simply right-click anywhere on the Desktop and choose Active Desktop ➢ View as Web Page from the shortcut menu (or use the Settings command on the Start menu). All Web objects will be removed from the Desktop, and their connections to the Internet will be broken, as though you had closed Internet Explorer and the Web page it displayed.

To put the Active Desktop back in place, simply choose that command again.

The Windows Taskbar

The Taskbar in the Active Desktop environment includes several new toolbars and features, some of which are shown below.

You can now have multiple toolbars displayed along with the Taskbar, on one, two, or multiple rows. As before, the Taskbar displays a button for each open program. You can still drag the Taskbar to other locations on the Desktop, and right-clicking it produces a shortcut menu. Here are some of the new features:

- One of the new toolbars, the Quick Launch toolbar, is just to the right of the Start button in the upper row of the Taskbar. You can add buttons to it (there are four in the example shown above) for starting programs that you tend to use regularly.

- The new Show Desktop button is displayed in the Quick Launch toolbar—click it to minimize all windows and reveal the entire Desktop; click it again to restore the windows.
- The Address toolbar behaves as it does in Internet Explorer. Enter a URL and press Enter to open that file.

You can display several other toolbars on the Taskbar, and you can also move them to any other location on the Desktop. You can create your own custom toolbars of buttons that can open just about anything: programs, documents, folders, Web pages, and more. You'll read more about the new toolbars later in this chapter in "Using the Active Desktop Toolbars."

The Windows Start Menu

The Start menu has been enhanced in several ways in the Active Desktop. First, you'll find your Favorites menu there, the same one that you see in Internet Explorer. This allows you to open one of your favorite websites or other resources in the appropriate program in one step.

When you choose Start ➢ Find, you'll see two new commands: On the Internet and People. The first command opens Internet Explorer and displays the search page you see when you choose Go ➢ Search the Web (as discussed in Chapter 16).

The People command opens the Find People dialog box. You first choose whether to search for a person in your Windows Address Book or in one of several online search sites on the Internet. You then enter the name of the person you want to find (the more information you can supply in the fields in the dialog box, the more accurate the search will be) and click the Find Now button. If you choose one of the Internet search sites, a connection to the Internet is made, the query is sent to the search service, and in a matter of seconds the results of the search appear in the Find People dialog box.

NOTE

The Find People dialog box is discussed in Chapter 22.

Another new aspect of both the Start and Favorites menus allows you to move an item on the menu to another location, simply by dragging it there. For example, you could drag the command that opens your word processor so that it appears on the very first menu that opens when you click the Start button.

Finally, there's another task you can perform without opening your Start or Favorites menu in an Explorer window. You can now right-click an item on the menu to access its shortcut menu. This means you can rename the item, delete it, or open its Properties dialog box.

Program Windows

Program windows behave the same under the Active Desktop, only now they might be hiding even more valuable Desktop information! But that's why the Show Desktop button was added to the Quick Launch toolbar—so that you can reveal the Desktop with a single click of the mouse or put it back the way it was with another click. And don't forget that you can click a program's button on the Taskbar to make it the active window and click the button again to minimize that window.

Icons

Icons still play an important role on your Active Desktop. By default icons are displayed on top of any Web objects so that the icons are not hidden. If you find that the icons get in the way of other objects on your Desktop, remember that you can hide the icons by choosing the "Hide icons when Desktop is viewed as Web page" option in the Folder Options dialog box, as discussed earlier.

Perhaps the most important feature to keep in mind when you're working on the Desktop is the single-click action, if you have enabled it. You simply point at an icon to select it and then single-click to open it. For those of us who have spent the past decade clicking items to select them and double-clicking to open them, it's just a little too easy to mess up in the Active Desktop.

With that said, when you're just starting out with the single-click rule enabled, don't be surprised if you find yourself opening a variety of items when you least expect it. Just be thankful you don't have any icons called "Format Hard Disk Now, Immediately!"

HTML Web Objects

You can place just about any Web object that you can view in Internet Explorer onto the Active Desktop, as you saw earlier in Figure 18.3. An item on the Desktop behaves just as it would in Internet Explorer, although you have almost none of Internet

Explorer's commands available. For example, you can't access the toolbars in a Desktop page, nor is there a way to add a page to your Favorites menu.

However, a few commands are available on the shortcut menu for a page on the Desktop. For example, you can select all the text and images on the page, print the page, edit the page's underlying HTML code, and reload the page from its server with the Refresh command.

TIP

You can also reload the Active Desktop by right-clicking it (but outside any Desktop components) and choosing Refresh from the shortcut menu.

Even though a Web object is not contained within a normal window, you can still adjust its size and position on the Desktop. When you pass the mouse pointer over the object, a box appears around it with a title bar (shown here) that serves as a temporary window. You can drag any side or corner of the box to change the size of the object, and drag the title bar to move the object.

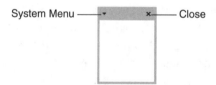

You'll also find a system menu button on the left side of the title bar, and a Close button on the right side that you can click to hide this object. Doing so will also deselect this object in the Web tab of the Display Properties dialog box, where you can add or remove any Web content in your Active Desktop. You'll see how to do this in the section "Adding Content to Your Active Desktop," a little later in this chapter.

When a Web item on the Desktop is not large enough to display the entire page it contains, horizontal or vertical scroll bars appear as needed. For example, in Figure 18.3, you can see that the Bank of Grand Cayman page has a vertical scroll bar.

Using the Active Desktop Toolbars

As mentioned earlier in this chapter in "The Windows Taskbar" section, the toolbars you can display in Internet Explorer are also available on the Active Desktop, along with several other toolbars. You can choose to display the new toolbars either as part of the Taskbar or separately, elsewhere on the Desktop.

Displaying Other Toolbars on the Desktop

To display a toolbar, right-click the Taskbar or another toolbar (but not on a button) and choose Toolbars from the shortcut menu. Then select the toolbar you want to display. The toolbar choices include Address and Links, which are the same toolbars you can display in Internet Explorer, as well as the following:

Desktop displays a button for each icon on your Desktop, giving you access to those icons without minimizing all program windows.

Quick Launch gives you a toolbar for displaying program or document icon buttons for which you want quick and easy access.

New Toolbar lets you create a new toolbar for any resource or folder you can access from your computer.

The Quick Launch toolbar is particularly helpful. When you first display it, several buttons are already on it. To add more buttons, simply drag a file or folder onto the toolbar. You can also drag a shortcut from a Web page onto the Quick Launch toolbar, giving you quick access to the target of that link.

The icon buttons on the Quick Launch toolbar are really shortcut files in the folder:

`C:\Windows\Application Data\Microsoft\Internet Explorer\QuickLaunch`

If you copy other shortcuts there, they will appear on the Quick Launch toolbar. If you share a computer with other users and sign in with a password, you'll find this folder at:

`C:\Windows\Profiles\[user name]\Application Data\Microsoft\Internet Explorer\Quick Launch`

When you choose Toolbars ➢ New Toolbar, you are presented with a folders window. You can either enter a URL of the file you want, or browse all the folders available to your computer. Click the one you want and a new toolbar is created containing a button for each item in that folder.

Manipulating Desktop Toolbars

The toolbars you place on the Desktop are quite flexible, and you can adjust them to suit the way you work with the Windows Desktop. By default, when you display a toolbar, it appears within the Taskbar, sharing that portion of the Desktop. The Quick Launch and Address toolbars are shown here, as displayed in the Taskbar.

Grippers

PART

III

Communications and Using the Internet

When toolbars are sharing the same space, you can manipulate them in a number of ways:

- To expand or shrink a toolbar, drag its *gripper* to the left or right (the gripper is the set of vertical bars at the left edge of a toolbar). Watch for the mouse pointer to change to a double-headed horizontal arrow when you point to the gripper.

- To display or hide the toolbar's name, right-click the toolbar (but not a button) and choose Show Title.

- To display or hide text descriptions of each button on a toolbar, right-click the toolbar and choose Show Text. (The added text can take up a lot of room.)

- When you point to a button, a ToolTip displays its name.

- To change the size of the buttons on a toolbar, right-click the toolbar, choose View from the shortcut menu, and then choose either Large or Small.

- To rearrange the toolbars, point just to the right of a gripper and click. The pointer changes to a four-headed arrow. Now drag the toolbar where you want it, relative to the others.

- To expand a toolbar to the entire width of the Taskbar, double-click the toolbar's gripper. The Taskbar and any other open toolbars shrink so that only their grippers and names are displayed. Double-click the toolbar's gripper again to shrink that toolbar so it is just wide enough to display its buttons. If the toolbar's title is displayed, this will shrink the toolbar completely, so that only its gripper and title are displayed.

- To display the Taskbar and toolbars in multiple rows, drag the top edge of the Taskbar upward.

- To close a toolbar, right-click it and choose Close from the shortcut menu.

 NOTE

Once you close a custom toolbar that you created with the New Toolbar command, that toolbar is gone. You'll have to create it again if you want to use it.

You can also detach a toolbar from the Taskbar and display it on its own, anywhere on the Desktop. Point to the toolbar's gripper or title and then drag the toolbar off the Taskbar to any other area in the Desktop (not into a program window). Once a toolbar is free of the Taskbar, you can move or change its size in the usual ways. To reattach a toolbar to the Taskbar, just drag it there by its title bar.

Adding Content to Your Active Desktop

When you first install Windows 98, only the Channel bar is displayed on the Desktop by default. But the Desktop is ready for you to add more objects at any time.

You add, remove, or revise components to your Active Desktop via the Web tab of the Display Properties dialog box, which is shown in Figure 18.4. You can access this tab in several ways. Right-click the Desktop and choose Active Desktop from the shortcut menu, and then choose Customize my Desktop. You'll also find this command by choosing Settings from the Start menu. You can open the Display Properties dialog box by opening the Display icon in the Control Panel, or by right-clicking the Desktop and choosing Properties.

The Web tab has a list of all the items that have been placed on the Active Desktop, but only those with their checkbox selected are currently displayed on the Desktop. Notice the preview image of your Desktop above the list. When you select an item in the list, its location on the Desktop will be shown in that preview.

FIGURE 18.4

You can add to or remove components from the Active Desktop in the Web tab of the Display Properties dialog box.

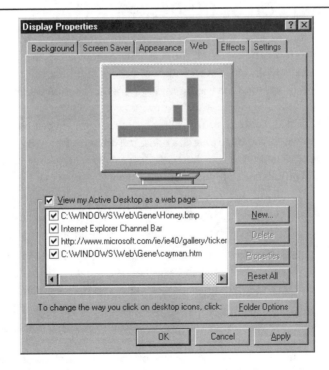

Your Active Desktop Is Contained in the File *DESKTOP.HTT*

The entire Active Desktop is defined within the single file DESKTOP.HTT, which resides as a hidden file in the same Internet Explorer folder where the Quick Launch folder is located (as described earlier in "Displaying Other Toolbars on the Desktop").

When you add or remove a Web-related item to your Active Desktop, the change appears within this file. For example, if you add a picture to the Desktop, an <IMG> tag is inserted into this file that defines the new image's position and size on the Desktop.

It's best to leave this file alone, but if you were to open it in Internet Explorer, you'd see that it looks much like your Active Desktop.

Turning On or Off Desktop Components

Before we look at how you can take advantage of the Active Desktop, let's see how to turn it off and return to the standard Windows Desktop. We mentioned earlier that a Desktop full of live Web components can significantly drain your computer's memory and processor. One way to mitigate this is to remove some components and see if that improves your computer's performance.

If your computer runs well most of the time, instead of trying to fine-tune the Desktop when you need an extra boost in performance, you can simply turn off *all* Desktop components. You'll be left with the pre–Active Desktop Windows Desktop.

You can turn off your Active Desktop in two ways:

- In the Web tab of the Display Properties dialog box, deselect the option named "View my Active Desktop as a Web page." You can later select this option to display the Web items on the Active Desktop once again.

- Right-click the Desktop, choose Active Desktop from the shortcut menu, and select View As Web Page. This is a toggle command, so selecting it again displays your Active Desktop. You'll also find this command by choosing Start ➤ Settings.

NOTE

When you turn on the display of active components on the Desktop, one or more of them may need to connect to the Internet to load its page or fetch some data. If you have a Dial-Up Networking connection to the Internet, remember that your modem's telephone line will be taken over to make the connection.

Adding an Item to the Desktop

The Web items that appear on the Active Desktop are the ones that are selected in the list of components in the Web tab of the Display Properties dialog box (shown earlier in Figure 18.4). Remember, if the "View my Active Desktop as a Web page" option is not selected, none of the components appears on the Desktop.

You can deselect a component in the list at any time to remove that object from the Desktop. Simply select it when you want to display it again.

NOTE

Clicking a Web item's Close button on the Desktop removes that item from the Active Desktop, while also deselecting the item in this list.

Here's how you can add a new Web item to the Active Desktop. The item can reside on your local disk, your network, or somewhere on the Internet.

1. Open the Display Properties dialog box and access its Web tab, such as by right-clicking the Desktop and choosing Active Desktop ➢ Customize my Desktop.

2. Click the New button, and you'll see a dialog box asking if you want to visit Microsoft's Active Desktop Gallery on the Web, where you can install one of its Web items. You'll read about adding new items from this gallery a little later in this chapter.

3. If you choose No, you'll see the New Active Desktop Item dialog box, in which you specify the URL of the object you want to place on the Active Desktop.

You can add four types of files to the Active Desktop (the accepted file name extensions are shown in parentheses):

- Internet Shortcut (URL) opens a URL.
- Channel Description File (CDF) displays a channel.
- HTML Document (HTML or HTM) displays a Web page.
- Picture (GIF, JPEG, or BMP) displays a graphic image.

4. In the dialog box, enter the URL of the item you want to place on the Active Desktop. You can instead browse your local disk by clicking the Browse button and selecting the file in the Browse dialog box. By default, only acceptable files are shown in the list (the file types mentioned above). Select the file you want and then click the Open button. Once you've entered the URL, click the OK button.

5. If the item you're adding is a file on the Web, you'll be presented with the dialog box shown in Figure 18.5, which tells you that you are setting up a subscription

to this new item. You can either accept the default subscription settings for this item or customize them, just as you can do when you're creating a subscription for a new item on the Favorites menu, as described in Chapter 16. You can modify the subscription settings later by selecting the item in the list in the Web tab and clicking the Properties button.

6. When you're finished with the subscription settings dialog box, click OK. The Web page will be downloaded and then you'll see the new item appear in the list of Desktop items in the Display Properties dialog box.

7. Click OK to close the dialog box, or click Apply to apply the changes but leave the dialog box open.

You'll see the new item on your Desktop. Remember that you can move an item by dragging its title bar. Drag any of its sides or corners to change its size.

FIGURE 18.5

When you add an item from the Web to your Active Desktop, you are also setting up a subscription to it.

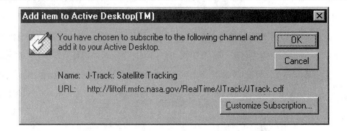

NOTE

One of the limitations of placing items on the Active Desktop is the Desktop itself— there just isn't enough of it. You can control the size of your Desktop by changing your screen's resolution—the higher the resolution, the more room you'll have for Desktop components. For example, if you're working with a standard VGA screen resolution of 640×480, there won't be much room on the Desktop. You can change your screen resolution (within the limitations of your video hardware) in the Settings tab of the Display Properties dialog box. See Chapter 7 for details.

Using a Web Page as the Desktop Background

Prior to Internet Explorer 4 and Windows 98, you could decorate your Desktop by displaying a picture in the Desktop background (called the wallpaper) or by changing the background's color or pattern. Now you can actually incorporate a Web page into the background of the Active Desktop.

Don't confuse this background Web page with the Web pages that you can place on the Active Desktop, as illustrated earlier in Figure 18.3. The background page literally serves as a background to anything else you place on the Desktop.

Open the Display Properties dialog box (right-click the Desktop and choose Properties) and choose the Background tab. You'll see a list of available bitmap images and Web pages that you can use as the Desktop's wallpaper. To use a new page as the wallpaper, either select the page from the list or click the Browse button to find the file.

The item you selected will appear in the Wallpaper list and will be selected; a preview of it will appear above the list. Click OK to accept this page as your new background. Any icons or Web items on your Desktop will appear over this page.

TIP

> If this Web page came from a file on your network, others could share the same Desktop background. This could be a convenient way to send these users reminders, news, or other timely notices—you would only need to update that Web page, and whenever someone started Windows, he or she would see the new page.

Removing Desktop Components

You can remove Web items or pictures from the Active Desktop in two ways: hide them or actually delete them. As discussed earlier in "Turning On or Off Desktop Components," you can deselect one or more items in the list in the Web tab of the Display Properties dialog box. When you close the dialog box, those items will be gone from the Desktop. To display them again at any time, select them in the list. You can also remove an item from the Active Desktop by clicking the Close button on its title bar.

You can actually remove an item from the list in the Web tab by selecting it and clicking the Delete button. This will remove it both from the list and from the Desktop. The file on which the component was based, however, is *not* actually removed from wherever it happens to reside. Therefore, if you remove an item that is stored on your local disk and you don't need that file any more, delete it in the usual way.

Adding Content from the Active Desktop Gallery

Microsoft has a website called the Active Desktop Gallery that is dedicated to Desktop components for the Active Desktop, where you can go to download components for your own Desktop. It's a site to behold and will give you a good introduction to what the Active Desktop can do for you.

Find this site in Internet Explorer at:

`www.microsoft.com/ie/ie40/gallery/`

You can also access this site when you're adding a new item to the Active Desktop, as mentioned in step 2 earlier in this chapter in "Adding an Item to the Desktop."

Installing the Investor Ticker

Let's download the Microsoft Investor Ticker from Microsoft's Active Desktop Gallery and install it on the Active Desktop (look back at Figure 18.3). Once installed, it will display the current price (delayed about 20 minutes) of the stocks you specify, as well as some headline news. When you're connected to the Internet, you can click a stock to see more information about that company, or you can click a headline to open that article in Internet Explorer.

This stock and headline ticker is cute and handy and will illustrate how easy it is to download and install a new item for the Desktop:

1. Either go to the Web Gallery site in Internet Explorer (the URL was shown earlier), or open the Web tab in the Display Properties dialog box, click the New button, and then click Yes to open the Active Desktop Gallery in Internet Explorer.

2. Click the News button hyperlink to display a page of news-related Desktop components. Several components will be listed, one of which should be the Microsoft Stock Ticker there.

3. Click a component to learn more about it, such as the stock ticker. If you then decide you want to install it, click the Add to Active Desktop button.

4. This will open the same dialog box shown earlier in Figure 18.5 when you're manually adding a new item from the Web to your Active Desktop. You can click OK to accept the default subscription settings, or click Customize to adjust them. Click OK when you're finished.

5. The ticker file will be downloaded to your computer; the download progress dialog box will show you the status of the download. When it's finished, the new ticker will be installed on your Desktop, as though you had added it yourself.

Feel free to take a look at any of the components on the Active Desktop Gallery website, and check back regularly to see what's new. The preview you see when you click a component will give you an idea of how that component looks. If you decide to download a component but later decide you don't want it, you can remove it from your Desktop, as described earlier in this chapter.

Let's look at one more Desktop component that you might find even more useful than the ticker.

Installing the Web Search Component

The Web Search Desktop component (shown here) lets you search the Internet right from your Desktop, without first opening Internet Explorer. You can choose from a diverse selection of search sites.

Go to the Active Desktop Gallery in Internet Explorer, and click the Cool Utilities button to display the components in that category. Then click the Microsoft Search Component link. You follow the same procedure described in the previous section for the ticker component. When you're finished, the Search component will be installed on your Desktop.

When you conduct a search in this Desktop component, you can choose from many search engines and "high-content" websites. To see how it works, try searching for upcoming tour dates for your favorite musician or group.

1. In the text-entry field in the Search component on your Desktop, enter the text you want to search for.

2. To select the search site, click the Click Here button to display a menu of choices (shown here).

3. Choose Entertainment ➢ Band Tours, and you'll see that Band Tours now appears to the right of the Click Here button, indicating the type of search you'll be making.

4. Finally, click the Go button to begin the search.

This will open Internet Explorer and the appropriate Web page where the search will be made. For this type of search, the Pollstar site is currently being used. Follow any instructions at this site for completing the query, and the site will display the upcoming concert dates for the artist or group you specified. You can follow links from here as you normally would to see more about an individual concert date.

Using the Channel Screen Saver

One outgrowth of the Active Desktop is an active screen saver, a new feature of your normal Windows 95 screen saver. Instead of displaying a fish tank, your favorite cartoon characters, or flying waffle irons, the Channel screen saver displays any of the eligible channels you have in your Channel bar, one after another.

You access the screen saver on the tab of that name in the Display Properties dialog box—right-click the Desktop and choose Properties. In the drop-down menu of screen savers, choose Channel Screen Saver (as shown here). As with any Windows screen saver, you specify the number of minutes of keyboard and mouse inactivity that should pass before the screen saver starts (10 minutes in this example).

Running the Channel Screen Saver

When the Channel Screen Saver starts, it displays the first Web page on the entire screen, covering all other windows and even the Taskbar. The screen saver displays each page for the number of seconds you specified in its options (as explained in the next section) before displaying the next page.

If you have a dial-up connection to the Internet, keep in mind that the Channel Screen Saver may need to connect to the Internet in order to update its content. If your computer is offline, the screen saver will simply use whatever content is already in your Temporary Internet Files folder.

NOTE

If you have a dial-up connection to the Internet, keep in mind that the Channel Screen Saver may need to connect to the Internet if you want the content to be up-to-date. If your computer is off-line, the screen saver will simply use whatever content is already in your Temporary Internet Files folder.

When the Channel Screen Saver is active, moving the mouse or pressing a key won't cancel it, as they would with most other screen savers, but will instead display a Cancel button in the upper-right corner of the screen. Click this button to cancel the screen saver and return to your normal display. Being able to use your mouse during this period of so-called "inactivity" allows you to click any interesting links, just as you would do in Internet Explorer.

Setting Up the Channel Screen Saver

You can adjust the options for the Channel Screen Saver by opening the Screen Savers tab in the Display Properties dialog box, and then clicking the Settings button to open the Screen Savers Properties dialog box, as shown in Figure 18.6.

WARNING

The first time you click the Settings button for the Channel Screen Savers, the screen saver will need to go on-line to download all relevant content from the channels you have in your Channel bar. The download could take many minutes at modem speeds, so be prepared for a delay.

The Channels list displays all the channels in your Channel bar that offer content for the Channel Screen Saver. You can select just those you want displayed while the screen saver is active.

Beneath that list, you specify the display interval for each screen. If you connect to the Internet with a modem, don't make this time too short, or you'll never see an entire screen displayed in full. A minute or two should give each page enough time to download the current content it needs. Once each screen has updated its content from the Internet, each should be displayed in a matter of seconds.

PART

III

Communications and
Using the Internet

FIGURE 18.6

In the Screen Saver Properties dialog box, you select the channels to include, the number of seconds that each should be displayed, and whether the screen saver will be canceled when you move the mouse.

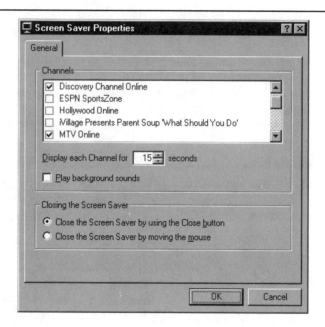

You can also choose whether any background sounds attached to a page should be played when the page is opened (keep in mind that silence is often golden, especially when your computer is trying to sleep).

Finally, you can choose whether moving the mouse should close the screen saver. By default it won't, so you can follow any links. You must use its Close button to cancel the screen saver. Even if you choose to have the screen saver closed when you move the mouse, you can hold down the Alt key and move the mouse without closing it.

WARNING

A word to the wise: Exercise caution when using the Channel Screen Saver in an office environment. None of us can remember exactly which of our channels are included in the screen saver. Do you really want this screen saver showing the entire office exactly what sort of sites you like to visit regularly?

Browsing Resources with Windows Explorer

One of the more subtle but quite important advances that came to Windows with Internet Explorer 4, and is now in Windows 98, was the joining of the personal computer with the Internet. The so-called Active Desktop that we're discussing in this chapter is the attempt to merge our own, personal Desktop (everything we do in Windows) with the worldwide network of the Internet.

In this section, we'll look at the way the Web browser, Internet Explorer, has been merged with your computer browser, Windows Explorer, so that the resources on your own computer—files, folders, printers, the Control Panel, and so on—have become almost indistinguishable from resources on the Internet—files, websites, FTP sites, and other content you can download.

 NOTE

Internet Explorer and Windows Explorer have almost merged into one Explorer. There's still a distinction, however, depending on whether you're viewing Web-related items or the files, folders, and other resources on your computer. You'll find differences in the commands on their menus, the options in their dialog boxes, and the buttons on their toolbars. That's why I generally use the two names instead of simply Explorer.

The Personal Computer Merges with the Networked Terminal

In the early days of the Computer Age, a person's "computer" was really nothing more than a terminal connected to the actual computer, which may have been down the hall, in another building, or in some other city. The terminal let the user input data to the computer via a keyboard and receive output via a monitor or printer.

When the personal computer came along in the late 1970s, the terminal and the computer merged into one unit, and the processing took place right on your desk. Gone were the connecting cables that joined many users on terminals to a main computer. Something was gained in that transition, but something was lost, too. When many people all had their own computers, the ability to share information or programs was greatly impeded.

Over time, however, more and more individual personal computers were networked together so that they could share information. When the Internet exploded onto the commercial and end-user market from its roots in universities and research centers, a whole new concept in personal computers and networking took hold. It suddenly became quite evident that an amazingly powerful combination had been reached—allowing personal computers all over the world to share the same network, the Internet.

Today in Windows 98, your personal computer and the Internet have been shuffled together into one concept. The idea is to allow you to browse resources on your own computer as easily as you browse resources on the World Wide Web.

Browsing Your Computer

The Windows Explorer, shown in Figure 18.7, has been your primary tool for working with the resources on your Windows 95 or 98 computer. At the top of the Explorer window you have a menu and toolbar, with two panes below them.

NOTE

The first indication you might notice that both Explorers are merging into one is the Explorer toolbars. Even when you're browsing files and folders, you'll find many familiar buttons from the Internet Explorer toolbars. For example, you can use the Back and Forward buttons to open other folders you've visited, just as you do with Web pages.

The pane on the left side of Explorer lists resources on your computer, such as its disk drives, file folders within a drive, Control Panel, Recycle Bin, Printers, and so on. The pane on the right lists the contents of the selected resource on the left. In Figure 18.7, the Windows folder has been selected in the left pane, and you can see its contents in the right pane.

TIP

If that left pane looks familiar, that's because it is now considered an Explorer bar. While you're browsing folders and files, you can choose View ➢ Explorer Bar ➢ All Folders to hide or display that left pane. You can also choose to display one of the other types of content in the Explorer bar, such as Favorites or Channels.

FIGURE 18.7

The Windows Explorer has been the tool by which you view, open, or manipulate the resources on your computer.

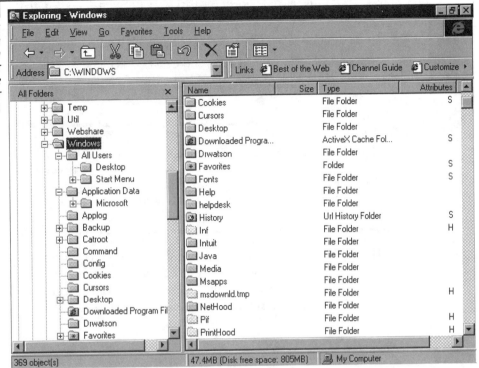

The left pane shows the resources in a *hierarchical* view; that is, subfolders are indented beneath the folder that contains them, and are hidden from view in the list until you click the plus sign to the left of the folder's name.

Let's have a quick review of a few ways you can move, copy, delete, and rename files or folders in Windows Explorer:

- To move one or more selected items (files that aren't programs or folders) to another folder, simply drag them to their destination. Or choose Edit ➤ Cut, switch to the destination, and then choose Edit ➤ Paste (remember that these commands are also available on the shortcut menu when you right-click a selected file).

- To move or copy items or to create shortcuts to them, hold down the right mouse button as you drag the items to the destination. When you release the button, choose the appropriate command from the shortcut menu. Use this method when you want to move a program file, or move any files to another disk, as simply dragging will create a shortcut to it.

PART

III

Communications and
Using the Internet

- To copy items, hold down the Ctrl key while you drag them to their destination, or use the Edit ➤ Copy and Paste method.

- To delete selected items, press Del or choose Edit ➤ Cut.

- To rename the selected item, choose File ➤ Rename or press F2.

- To view or modify the properties of a selected resource, choose File ➤ Properties.

NOTE

When you choose View ➤ Folder Options, you'll find the Advanced Settings options on the View tab. These affect the display of folders in an Explorer window, such as hiding all file name extensions for known file types (those with associations) and whether or not the current display settings for a folder should be remembered when you return to it.

The single-click method for opening files or folders is another indication that browsing the Web and browsing your computer are now much the same thing. But the two concepts in browsing really merge when you can actually browse the Internet as one of the resources displayed in Windows Explorer, which is discussed next.

Browsing the Internet

With Windows 98, you'll find that a new resource appears in the left pane of Windows Explorer—Internet Explorer (its icon is shown here).

When you select Internet Explorer in Windows Explorer left-hand pane, it quite logically displays your normal start page in the right pane. If that page is on the Internet, it will connect to the Internet in the normal way, such as by using your Dial-Up Networking connector.

All of a sudden, your Windows Explorer has become suspiciously similar to Internet Explorer, as shown in Figure 18.8. The menus and toolbar change to show that you're now viewing a Web page (Sybex's home page in this example), and they are the same as you would see in Internet Explorer. You can click your way through the links in the page that is displayed in the right pane, open the shortcut menu for any item on that page, and open a new resource from your Favorites menu.

The only difference between this view of the Internet and the one you get in Internet Explorer is that you can still see the other resources available to you in the left pane of the Explorer window.

TIP

Here's a quick-and-easy way to take advantage of this view of the Internet and your other computer resources: Simply drag a link from the Web page to a folder on your local disk (or to the Quick Launch bar, Start button, or Desktop) to create a shortcut to the target of that link.

As you open more pages in the right-pane of the Explorer window, you'll see the route you've taken appear indented beneath the Internet resource in the left pane.

FIGURE 18.8

When you view the Internet in Windows Explorer, the Web page appears in the right pane, while the rest of your computer's resources are still displayed in the hierarchical view in the left pane.

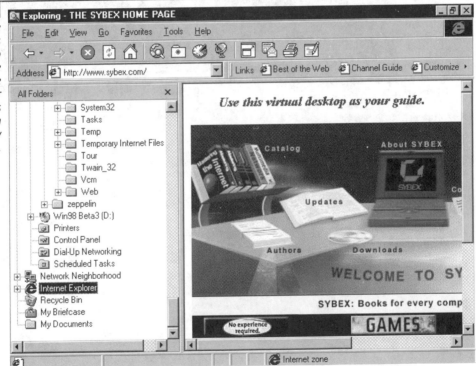

Browsing in Web View

When you open a folder, including My Computer (or whatever name you have given to My Computer) and Control Panel, you can choose to view that folder either in the standard view or in the Web view. From the menu bar or the shortcut menu, choose View ➤ As Web Page to switch between the two views, or choose that command from the menu for the Views button on the toolbar.

When in Web view, you'll see more information about each resource. For example, Figure 18.9 shows Control Panel in Web view. Each icon is displayed in the right pane of the window, while the left pane displays a brief description of the currently selected item. Note that the view is the same no matter how you open Control Panel, such as in an Explorer window or from the Start ➤ Settings menu.

Another connection to the Internet appears within the Web view of Control Panel. You can click the Technical Support button in the left pane to connect to Microsoft's technical support website, where you can find helpful information about the Control Panel or other issues.

FIGURE 18.9

In the Web view of Control Panel, icons are displayed in the pane on the right, and a short description of the selected icon is displayed on the left. You can click the Connect button to access Microsoft's technical support website.

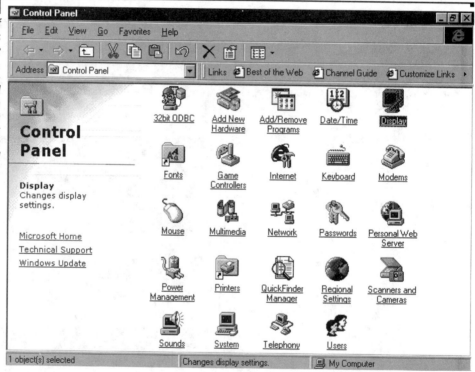

When you're viewing a folder in the Web-view mode and select a file, a "thumbnail" preview (a small image) of the contents of that file will be displayed in the folder pane of Explorer, which gives you a quick look at the contents of the file. If it is an image file, such as a bit-mapped, GIF, or JPEG file, you'll see a small version of the image. If the file is a page-oriented document, such as a word processing or HTML file, you'll see an image of its first page.

NOTE

This feature will display many, but not all, file types, just as Windows' Quick View feature will. Keep in mind that on a modern computer, the preview will appear almost instantaneously for moderately sized files (say, less than a megabyte). For larger files or on a slower computer, you may find that the time it takes to display the preview of the selected file may diminish the value of that preview.

You can also choose to see a preview of *all* files when you open a folder, although you will probably want to use this option only for a few special folders, in consideration of speed and convenience. Open the Properties dialog box for a folder and select the option called "Enable thumbnail view," and then click OK to close the dialog box. The next time you open this folder, you'll find a new command on the View menu called Thumbnails. Choose it to see a thumbnail preview of each viewable file in the folder.

An example is shown in Figure 18.10 (the Explorer bar containing the folders is turned off). The first item is a folder within this folder, the second is an HTML Web page, and the other files are image files. You can work with the files in this thumbnail view just as you always can, the only difference is that instead of seeing an icon or name for each file, you see a glimpse of its contents.

FIGURE 18.10

The Thumbnail view shows a preview of each file in the folder.

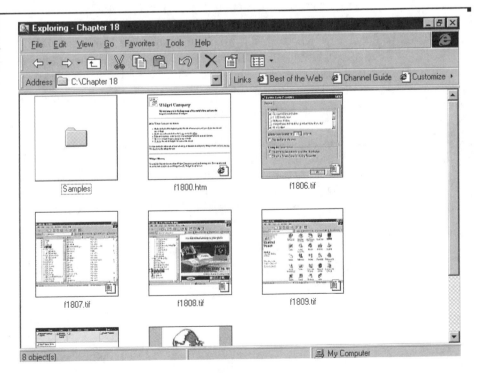

PART

III

Communications and Using the Internet

The first time you choose the Thumbnails command for a folder, a new, hidden file called THUMBS.DB is created in that folder, which contains the thumbnail preview of each file. This will take a few seconds, but on subsequent visits to this folder, the previews will already reside in this file and will be displayed quickly. If you ever turn off the thumbnails view for a folder by deselecting that option in the Properties dialog box, you can then delete the THUMBS.DB file.

Customizing a Folder

Another aspect of Windows 98 and its Active Desktop shows how browsing the Web has merged with browsing your own computer's resources. You saw in the previous section how you can view any folder in the Web-view mode, when a default Web page displays the contents of the folder, so all folders share the same default Web view. But you can also create a customized Web view in any folder you can view in Explorer. Thus, if you customize a folder, you have a unique view for just that folder, while other folders will continue to use the default Web view.

This not only allows you to create a distinctive look for a folder, but it also allows you to personalize a folder so that its resources (files and subfolders, for example) reside in a more friendly and informative place. On the other hand, it does help if you're an experienced HTML or Java programmer, as the customization process is not otherwise straightforward. This can be especially useful when multiple users share the same folder. New software you install could customize its own folder, so that when you open that folder, you might be presented with the company logo, instructions about using the files, or other helpful information.

Keep in mind that you'll still be viewing the same old files and folders, but on a custom background and surrounded by custom information.

Figure 18.11 shows Windows Explorer displaying a customized folder that comes with Windows 98—the Windows folder. The left pane shows the usual list of folders and other resources, but the contents of the folder in the right pane is now displayed in a customized Web page.

In this case, instead of seeing the files in this folder, you see only a message warning that you should not make changes to the contents of this folder. This is quite appropriate, because this is the folder in which the Windows operating system "lives," and making changes to it could have repercussions on your computer. Note, however, that there is a hyperlink beneath the message that you can click to display the files in this folder in the usual way.

FIGURE 18.11

The customized Windows folder illustrates how you can customize a folder as though it were a Web page.

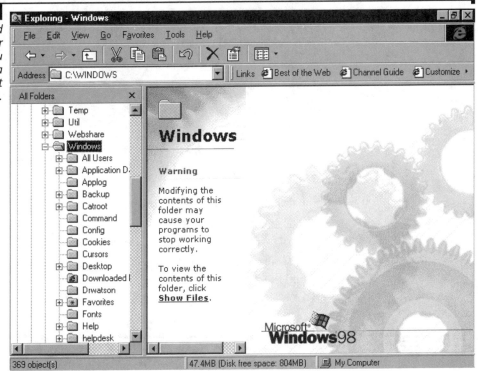

To customize the selected folder, choose View ➢ Customize this Folder, or choose that command from the shortcut menu when you right-click within the right pane. This opens the Customize This Folder Wizard, whose first dialog box is shown in Figure 18.12.

PART

III

Communications and Using the Internet

FIGURE 18.12

A Wizard helps you customize a folder either by specifying a background picture or by creating an HTML document.

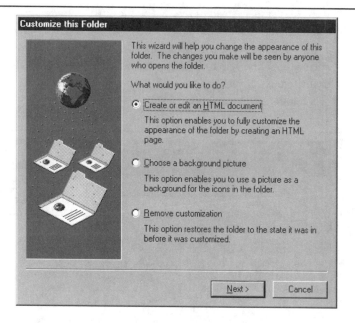

You can choose from two types of customization here:

- Select "Create or edit an HTML document" to create a Web page in which the folder's contents will be displayed, or to revise the existing Web page.

- Select "Choose a background picture" to specify a background image that will appear behind the files and folders within this folder. If the folder is already displayed as a Web page, the picture will appear as the background of that page.

NOTE

You can choose the Remove Customization option to eliminate the HTML page or background picture that was used to customize this folder.

When you choose to create a Web page for the folder and click Next, the Wizard's next dialog box explains the process. When you click the Next button this time, the Wizard opens a new page in your default editor for HyperText Template (HTT) files. This will be FrontPage Express if you have installed it, or whatever HTML editor you have installed that is associated with this type of file. Otherwise, Notepad will be used. The page will already contain HTML code, ActiveX controls, and ActiveX and Java scripts, which you should not attempt to edit unless you are quite adept at that type of programming.

Unless you want to make changes to this page (experience required), choose File ➢ Exit in FrontPage Express (or whatever editor you are using). The Wizard will already have stored this file as FOLDER.HTT in the folder that it customizes, so don't change its name or location.

The last step of the Wizard tells you what you just accomplished; you can click the Finish button to return to Explorer, where you'll see your custom folder displayed in the right pane.

NOTE

While viewing a customized folder, you can return to the standard folder view by choosing View ➢ As Web Page. When that command is not enabled, a folder you have customized will look like any other uncustomized folders.

You can revise a folder's custom Web page at any time. Right-click anywhere in the list of files and choose Customize this Folder; then follow the steps described above for creating a new Web page for the folder.

Rearranging Details View

Another way to customize the look of any folder, regardless of whether you have created a Web page for it, is by rearranging the columns in the Details view of that folder (choose View ➢ Details). It's as easy as dragging a column title to a new location.

This is especially useful when the window is not wide enough to display all the columns of the Details view, because you can place the most important columns on the left side of the list of files, as in the examples shown below.

Name		Size	Type		Modified	Attributes
Type		Size	Modified	Name		Attributes
Modified	Name	Size	Type			Attributes

Of course, you can also expand or contract a column by dragging the right edge of its title. If you want to return all columns to their default widths, press Ctrl-+, using the plus key on the numeric keypad.

Chapter

19

Using NetMeeting

New stuff in NetMeeting 2.x

System requirements and platform compatibility

Installing NetMeeting

Using NetMeeting

Using NetMeeting

Microsoft NetMeeting is a real-time Internet-based telephone and application-sharing program that lets multiple people connect with one another over the Internet to get work done in an ingenious manner. It's sort of like bringing several people into the same room, where they can work on documents together (through interactive applications), write on a blackboard they all can see (only in this case the term is whiteboard), and talk to each other—all at once. They can even see each other if they happen to have a compatible video camera. NetMeeting includes support for international conferencing as well as domestic hookups, and incorporates international standards. It provides true multi-user application-sharing and data-conferencing capabilities. The newest version of NetMeeting, version 2.*x*, adds H.323-based video-conferencing capabilities to the pre-existing audio telephone conferencing features.

 NOTE

Unfortunately, as far as the telephone aspect of NetMeeting goes, I should mention that, as with most Internet phone applications, the voice quality isn't quite up to what you're probably used to on a real telephone. Utility and software companies have been working seriously to provide higher quality Internet telephony as of this writing, however.

One way of describing NetMeeting is to say it takes the power of your PC running some powerful applications, and adds the power of the telephone and the global reach of the Internet. Although I'm risking sounding too much like a Microsoft advertisement, I will say it could actually transform the way telecommuters do their everyday work, the way clubs hold meetings, and the way schools present instructional material.

Some of the companies in the video conferencing field who have been working on add-ins or competing products include Creative Labs, Inc.; Intel; PictureTel; VDOnet Corp.; and White Pine Software, Inc.

Besides using NetMeeting straight out of the box to share apps and to conference with other NetMeeting users, there are various ways that NetMeeting can be tailored to specific uses. If you procure the *NetMeeting SDK* (the NetMeeting Software Developers Kit), you can use it to add conferencing support to your own Web pages (using JScript or Visual Basic Scripting Edition) or to Visual Basic applications (as well as to other ActiveX-enabled documents and applications). If you're a hotshot software developer, you can also use the SDK to add conferencing functionality to your own applications.

New Stuff in NetMeeting Version 2.x

NetMeeting 2 offers the following benefits/upgrades over NetMeeting 1:

- Changes to the user interface. For instance, there is no longer a separate window for the directory listing. Instead, the interface is consistent with Outlook 97 and Outlook Express, using a bar down the left-hand margin for the directory listing.
- Adds support for standards-based video conferencing. With NetMeeting 2.x, a user can send and receive real-time video with other users of NetMeeting 2.x, or compatible videophone products.
- Enables people to call you by clicking a link in your Web page.
- Allows you to place calls via the Windows Explorer.
- Integrates standards-based audio, data, and video conferencing to make communicating over the Internet almost as good, perhaps even better, than being there in person.
- Provides standards-based Directory Service.
- Supports Windows NT.

Now with Video!

Since video's been added, it's now pretty easy to have "face to face" meetings with friends, family, or business acquaintances around the world, as you can see in Figure 19.1. Finally, after all the competing video products out there, Microsoft has done it again. I don't always like the control Microsoft has on the industry, but they are making it easy to get into audio and video conferencing, so can you complain? Because NetMeeting 2.*x* works with any video capture card or camera that supports Video for Windows, there is a wide range to choose from. (For example, some black-and-white video cameras for the PC start at just $99, with color starting at around $199. Personally, I'm using a $99 Philips Easy Video card that was a snap to install, and lets me use my own color camcorder as the camera. I can also capture moving video and still pictures to files on the disk using this inexpensive card.)

FIGURE 19.1

Example of video and chat session in NetMeeting 2.x. I could see the guy I was talking to.

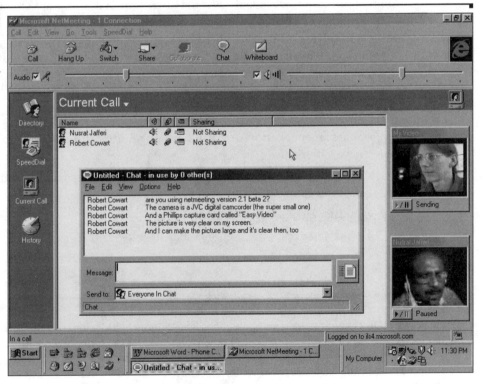

Following are some features of NetMeeting 2.*x* video support:

- Compliant with the ITU H.323 standard, which enables interoperability with other video conferencing products, such as the Intel Internet Video Phone.

- Support for H.323 makes NetMeeting multipoint-enabled to support audio *and* video with multiple people, through the use of a multipoint conferencing bridge service.

- Works with any video capture card or camera that supports Video for Windows.

- Allows you to receive video even if you do not have a video capture card or camera for sending video.

- Integrates with System Policy support in Windows 95, Windows 98, and Windows NT 4.0 to enable IS organizations to centrally control and manage video settings.

How You'll Use It

Supporting one or more people over the Internet or over a corporation's intranet, NetMeeting provides an effective way to communicate and collaborate in real time. ("Real time" means there is little or no delay, as there is with e-mail.) NetMeeting uses existing standards of *multipoint data conferencing* to let you accomplish the following:

- Talk to others on a speaker phone or headset (half or full duplex, depending on your sound card).

- See each other while talking (limited to a pair of users), or just see one party.

- Share an application that you have on your machine with people who don't have it on theirs.

- Collaborate with others using the shared application, to create and revise a document together.

- Transfer files back and forth as you talk.

- Write and display pictures on a shared whiteboard.

- Type to each other from the keyboard in chat mode.

TIP

Don't confuse the term *application sharing* under NetMeeting with the way the term is used in the context of LANs. In the world of LANs the term only means letting people use the same program without having to have it on their local machine, by making it available on a server computer that they can all access. In the context of NetMeeting, application sharing takes on the additional meaning of people actually editing the same documents on those applications—while being able to see each other's changes in real time! Even if the application isn't a true "multi-user" program, NetMeeting lets multiple people run the program and work on the same documents simultaneously.

Consider how most of us normally work with our computers now. You're probably limited to using your PC pretty much for getting your work done on your local drive, maybe printing over a network, and sending copies of your files to lots of people. When you really have to collaborate with one person or a group of people, it comes down to picking up the phone, "doing lunch," or "taking a meeting." Rarely are people patient enough to crowd behind your desk in order to crane their necks over your shoulder while you try to show them something complicated on your computer screen. With NetMeeting you have a fistful of new options. Imagine these scenarios:

- **Technical support**, allowing support organizations not only to *see* the scenario or situation on a remote user's computer, but also to be able to *correct* a problem during a support call without having to physically go to the remote PC.

- **Virtual meetings**, allowing users to be in different locations and conduct meetings as if everyone were in the same room.

- **Presentations**, allowing one expert to use her graphing or spreadsheet program to demonstrate different what-if scenarios to a group of remote users, while driving home her points by drawing diagrams on the whiteboard.

- **Document collaboration**, allowing users to collaborate on documents or information in real time.

- **Telecommuting**, allowing users to extend their presence beyond file sharing or e-mail while on the road or in remote branch offices.

- **Customer service**, allowing users to communicate directly with customer service from a website or to be able to see graphic information as part of a telephone call.

- **Distance learning**, allowing presentations to me made or information to be disseminated to numerous people at the same time over the Internet or intranets.

- **Deaf or hard of hearing** individuals can use NetMeeting 2.*x* to communicate more effectively in real-time with others in the workplace, the classroom, and the home—gaining substantial benefits over using traditional TTY devices.

As mentioned, NetMeeting has *multipoint capability*. This means that, unlike most of the phone and video toys running around on the Net, which are point-to-point, a group of folks can interact all at once, and not just with their voices. I don't mean to downplay the usefulness of the Internet phone products that have been introduced in the last couple of years. They are actually great for letting you converse for virtually no charge (other than your connect time over the Internet) with anyone around the world who is similarly equipped, and they can be an incredible boon for families with members in foreign countries, or even for businesses with remote offices. Not so good for the long-distance carriers, but that's another story. NetMeeting can earn its keep pretty quickly even if used only for this purpose.

It should be obvious how NetMeeting can improve the productivity of users in a corporate environment by extending the telephone call to include data-conferencing capabilities. Now imagine the effect that integrating NetMeeting into Web pages could have. Until you have NetMeeting you're limited in how you can interact with companies or individuals via their Web pages. Sure, you can read stuff, fill in some fields asking for data (essentially interacting with databases), order products, and leave e-mail. But, as mentioned earlier, the SDK for NetMeeting lets developers and Web site producers put rich data-conferencing capabilities into their pages. Web site creators could program conferencing capabilities directly into a Web page using the NetMeeting ActiveX control for conferencing. Web sites and Internet service providers can also create communities through conferencing services, by providing a directory of users with common interests via an *Internet Locator Server*, or *ILS* (more on this later in the chapter).

NetMeeting and Standards

Another attraction of NetMeeting is that it is based on *preexisting standards*—for once, it appears that Microsoft did not create any significant "new standards" that nobody else adheres to. Theoretically, NetMeeting can interact with other existing programs. The list of companies that are building products and services compatible with NetMeeting continues to grow, and Microsoft will be updating its information about them as it becomes available. For the latest information about compatible products and services, along with additional information about NetMeeting itself, point your browser to the Microsoft NetMeeting website on the Internet at the following URL:

```
http://www.microsoft.com/netmeeting/
```

NetMeeting 2 now supports the following industry standards that have been ratified or proposed through the International Telecommunications Union (ITU) or the Internet Engineering Task Force (IETF):

- **T.120**—Set of ITU protocols for transport-independent, multipoint data conferencing.
- **RTP/RTCP**—Real-time protocol (RTP) and real-time control protocol (RTCP), both from IETF. Packet format for sending real-time information across the Internet.
- **H.320**—Set of ITU protocols for audio, video and data conferencing over ISDN. Integrates with T.120.
- **H.324**—Set of ITU protocols for audio, video and data conferencing over analog phone lines (POTS). Integrates with T.120.
- **H.323**—Set of ITU protocols for audio, video and data conferencing over TCP/IP networks. Includes RTP/RTCP. Integrates with T.120.

System Requirements and Platform Compatibility

These are the minimum and recommended system requirements for NetMeeting version 2.*x*:

- 486/66 personal computer (Pentium or Pentium II recommended).
- 8 MB of RAM (12 MB recommended).
- Windows 95, 98, or NT. (To run any of the foreign-language versions of Microsoft NetMeeting, users must be using the same language version of Windows 95.)
- 14,400 bps modem (minimum) or LAN. If you're using a modem you're best off with at least a 28,800, 33K, 56K, or ISDN modems. If you're among the rich or lucky, you'll want one of these high-speed connections: T1, TV-broadcast, or cable-modem. You'll notice that screen redraws, video picture updates, and sound will be smoother with ISDN or faster connection.
- Sound card, speakers and microphone. (Required for real-time voice.)
- Videocam is required for transmitting video, but not for receiving video.

TECH TIP

Since NetMeeting 2 supports any video capture card or camera that supports Video for Windows, that gives you a wide range of products to choose from. Prices start from as low as around $99 for some tiny black-and-white video units that mount on top of your monitor or clip on your laptop screen. Some newer ones aimed specifically at Windows 98 connect quite easily to the USB port and don't tie up your parallel printer port or require you to open the computer and plug in a card or anything nasty like that.

Although it isn't necessary to have Microsoft Internet Explorer to use NetMeeting, the integration of conferencing functionality with websites works best with Microsoft Internet Explorer. Not surprisingly, therefore, NetMeeting is included with Microsoft Internet Explorer through many different distribution mechanisms. Windows 98 comes bundled with NetMeeting, so you don't have to worry about downloading it, unless you desire a newer version which may become available after this writing. During installation of Windows, NetMeeting will likely be installed by default. If you don't have it, see the directions below for installing it from the distribution CD.

One requirement you may have to consider relates to whether you plan to use NetMeeting for data only or for data plus voice and/or video. Data-conferencing features of Microsoft NetMeeting work with a 14,400bps or better modem connection, TCP/IP networks, and IPX networks. Real-time voice and video are designed for TCP/IP networks only (such as the Internet and corporate LANs).

NetMeeting supports more than 20 language versions, including Brazilian Portuguese, Chinese (simplified), Chinese (traditional), Czech, Danish, Dutch, Finnish, French, German, Greek, Hungarian, Italian, Japanese, Korean, Norwegian, Polish, Portuguese, Russian, Slovenian, Spanish, Swedish, and Turkish.

Although NetMeeting 1.0 worked only on the Windows 95 platform, NetMeeting 2.*x* is targeting Windows 95, Windows 98, and Windows NT 4.0. According to Microsoft, plans are in the works for a Mac version, too.

Installing NetMeeting

Before you can begin using NetMeeting, you have to install it. This section explains how to do that, and then how to use the various aspects of the program.

When you installed Windows 98 (or when it was installed by someone else), there was a dialog box for fine tuning what Windows software and accessories you wanted installed (see the installation appendix). NetMeeting is one of the options in the Communications category of software. You'll know if you have it by clicking Start ➢ Programs and looking for Microsoft NetMeeting (Figure 19.2).

FIGURE 19.2

Determining if you have NetMeeting installed

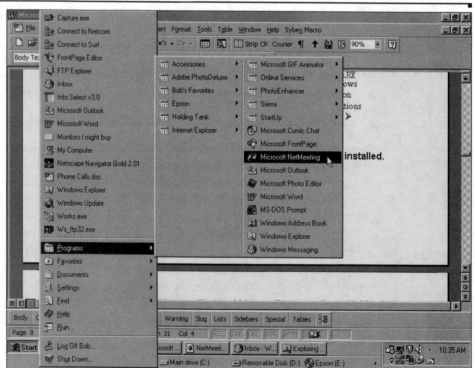

If you don't see NetMeeting there, you'll have to install it from the Windows 98 CD-ROM or download it over the Internet if you do not have the CD.

To download from the Internet, point your browser to location:

`http://www.microsoft.com/netmeeting/`

To install from the CD, follow these instructions:

1. Insert the CD into your drive.

2. Choose Start ➢ Settings ➢ Control Panel ➢ Add / Remove Software. After a few long moments (you may have to wait a little bit) you'll see a list of the Windows modules that are in your system already.

3. Click on Communications, then click on Details.

4. In the resulting list, ensure that the NetMeeting checkbox is turned on.

5. Click on OK to close both boxes. The NetMeeting installation will begin.

If you're installing from a file you download from the Internet, follow the instructions supplied with that file.

Running NetMeeting for the First Time

Once you've obtained the program, follow these steps to install it:

1. Choose Start ➢ Programs ➢ NetMeeting. A box appears touting the cool features of NetMeeting. Read it if you want.

2. Click on Next.

3. Now you're asked which "directory server" you want to use, and if NetMeeting should log into that directory automatically when you run it. Typically you'll want to have it log you in automatically, and you can choose any of the servers. You'll find out through experience which one you like most, probably the one that the people you're going to connect to use. In the meantime, just choose one of the microsoft.com servers, such as `ils3.microsoft.com`.

4. Click on Next. Now you'll see the dialog box shown in Figure 19.3. Fill in your name and other information asked for in the box. Then click Next.

5. Now you're asked to declare what category of activity you're going to be engaging in with NetMeeting: business, personal, or adult. (Adult means sexual, in case you didn't know!) The choice you make here determines how you are listed in the directory listings that other people will scan. Make a choice and click Next.

FIGURE 19.3

*Filling in your identi-
fication information*

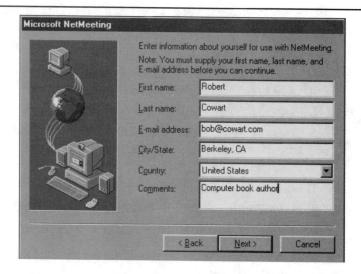

6. Next, you're asked what your Net connection speed will be: 14.4, 28.8, ISDN, or LAN. If you're connected to the Net though your local area network (typical scenario in an office setting where you don't have a modem on your computer dialing out), choose LAN. Otherwise choose the type of modem you have. NetMeeting will do some internal fine tuning to best work with the data transfer rate you'll be using. This setting will affect the quality of the video and audio delivered to your computer. Then click Next.

7. Click Next again, to move on to sound settings. Now you'll be asked to set the Play volume and to try recording some sound. See Figure 19.4. Make sure your microphone is set up, then click the Test button and adjust the volume.

8. Click Next, read the test sentence out loud into your microphone, and then click Next again. Presumably you successfully recorded some sound and the sound level was set automatically. If it didn't take, you'll be told about it and advised what to do. You can return to the previous dialog box by clicking Back, and try again, once you plug in your mic, fix your sound card, or whatever

TECH TIP

Some sound cards are capable of *full duplex sound*, letting you talk and listen at the same time like on a normal telephone (as opposed to half duplex, which switches back and forth from transmitting and receiving like a CB radio). Full duplex gives a more natural feeling to the conversations that you may have over NetMeeting. If you use NetMeeting a lot for voice communication, you should look into upgrading to a full duplex sound system. Depending on the kind of card you now have, you may be able to just purchase an additional half-duplex sound card. In other cases, you'll have to remove or disable your current card and replace it with a full-duplex card.

PART

III

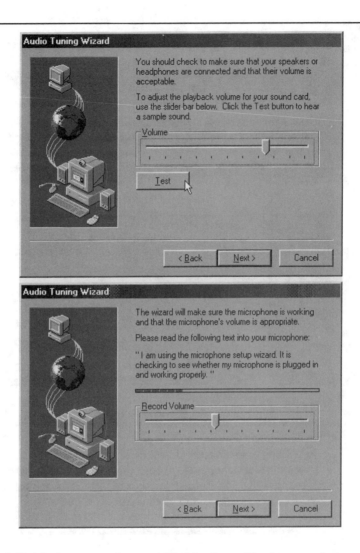

FIGURE 19.4

Record a few seconds of sound in order for the computer to adjust the record level.

9. Click Finish. In a second or two, NetMeeting will appear, ready to roll, as you see in Figure 19.5. Two new icons appear down next to the clock on your Taskbar. The blue one is the Intel Connection Advisor (it reports the status of and has controls for your audio and video connections). The green icon simply indicates that NetMeeting is running. Double-clicking on it brings up the Net-Meeting window if it's not in view.

If you're not connected to the Net, then you'll see an error message about that. Connect one way or another. Then move to the next section.

Communications and
Using the Internet

FIGURE 19.5

NetMeeting ready to roll

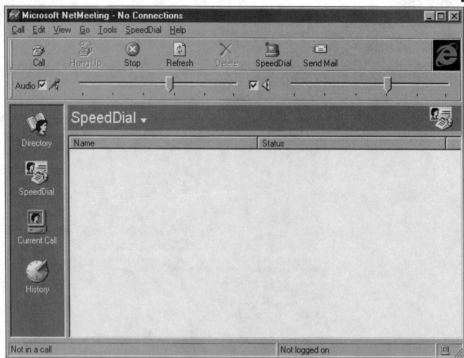

For a listing of sound and video cards, as well as other NetMeeting-compatible products, check the NetMeeting site http://www.microsoft.com/netmeeting/prodguide. There's a WHOLE LOT of stuff listed there that's compatible with NetMeeting, including a dozen or so cameras, lots of audio gear such as headsets, group conferencing add-ons, conferencing servers and bridges, call center integration, and more.

Using NetMeeting

The niftiest features of NetMeeting are best demonstrated on-line when you're connected to another party. That is, when you're having a "meeting," be it social or business. So, as soon as you can, you should connect to someone and try it out. This means you have to get a friend (preferably one whose computer has a sound card, and possibly a video camera) to install and start NetMeeting, or look for someone else who on the Net has already installed it, by checking the Directory. Let's assume the latter. It's probably going to be a stranger, but that's the fun of it.

About Internet Locator Service

The Directory (formerly called the User Location Service or ULS and now also called the ILS for Internet Locator Service) enables you to find people to talk to on the Internet. Just as with sending e-mail to someone, other users do not have to be on the same directory server as you. The ILS computers talk to one another. So, which ILS you are logged in to is of little consequence. However, before you can communicate with one or more people, you *do* have to log on to some server. Which one NetMeeting logs you on to is determined by the settings you make via the Call tab of the Tools ➣ Options dialog box. The Internet Locator Server (ILS) makes it relatively easy for NetMeeting users to find other users of NetMeeting with whom to connect and communicate. The trick that it has to perform is to provide a means of connecting a user's name with a unique network address (the IP address in the case of TCP/IP on the Internet), which is like dialing a person's phone number to connect to their house. The problem is that IP addresses for most folks are usually *dynamic*—the address is different each time they connect to the Internet. The ULS provides up-to-date information that ensures an accurate way to contact other users and for them to contact you. Internet service providers and Microsoft are working on ways to implement this service more fully.

Microsoft operates a number of ILS servers for NetMeeting users. Microsoft NetMeeting is the first product to use the ILS, in fact. Now other companies such as Four11 are setting them up, too, so we'll begin seeing more and more of them. In fact, you can set up your own, if you're the technical type. For example, if you're a Webmaster using Microsoft's Internet Information Service (IIS), you can set up your own User Location Service as a means of providing a way for visitors who are visiting your site to find each other.

1. Start NetMeeting if it isn't already running. You'll probably see the window shown in the previous figure (19.5), which is what you see before you're connected to an ILS and have displayed the directory of who's available for a meeting.

2. Check the Status line at the bottom of the screen. Over on the right side, it should say you're logged in to some server. If not, open the Tools menu, select Options, and click on the Calling tab and choose the server you want to log to. When you OK the box, you'll be logged in. It might take a few seconds to log you in.

Communications and
Using the Internet

3. Now choose the server whose directory you want to see, so you can choose someone to call. First click on the large Directory icon in the left column. Then open the Server list either by clicking as shown here:

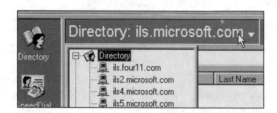

or by using the drop-down list in the upper right area of the window:

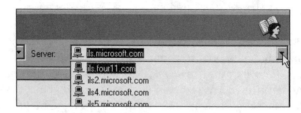

If you're on-line, in a few seconds you'll see a list of people on-line and conferencing, as shown in Figure 19.6. (If you're not on-line, the NetMeeting status line will say so. You'll have to choose Call ➤ Log onto [server name] to get on-line.) It may take a minute or two for the list to be completely download. If there are no names displaying in the window, click on Refresh in the toolbar. That should get the names rolling in. There might be lots of weird characters (letters, not people!) in the listing, due to foreign language usage by some of the international users, or by tricks people play to be listed first (sort of like naming your company AAAA Rent-A-Car in the yellow pages).

If you see an error message that you couldn't be logged on, try another server. Sometimes servers are off-line or dead in the water for mysterious reasons. Another possibility is that you are connected to the net through a company LAN that has a *firewall* that is intended to prevent unauthorized Internet access. Check with your system administrator about workarounds.

FIGURE 19.6

Clicking the Directory icon displays a listing of folks currently on line and registered with your currently set ILS. You can filter the listing using the Category drop-down list.

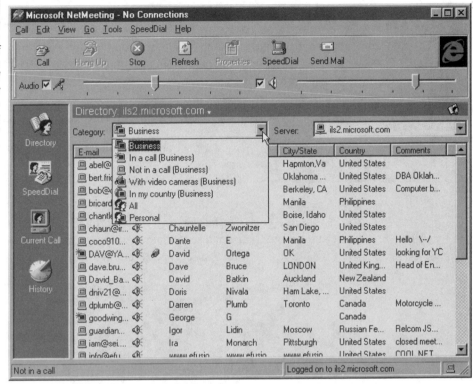

Notice that from the drop-down Category list you can choose the *category* of people to display. This can eliminate the folks whom you're not interested in communicating with. Remember a few steps back when you were setting up NetMeeting and you had to choose a category for yourself such as personal, business, or adult? Choosing Business from this list will display only the folks who chose Business when setting up *their* system. Notice too that you can select *not in a call* to list people who are currently available to receive a call. This saves you the hassle of ruling out people who are busy and won't bother answering your ring until they are finished with their current call. Those people's little computer icon is blue and has a little flashy thingy beside it, incidentally, like this:

A little speaker icon in a person's listing means they have sound. A little camera means they have a video camera hooked up and working.

You can click on any of the column headings to sort the list according to that column head. Clicking on the camera icon, for example, lists all the video folks first.

You can see better if you maximize the NetMeeting window, and resize the columns a bit, showing more of the comments.

4. Find a person you want to call, click his or her e-mail name, and then click Call (or just double-click on the person's name). You can also right-click on the name and choose Call. You'll see a dialog box similar to this one, listing the person's ILS address (which is a server and e-mail address combined), like this:

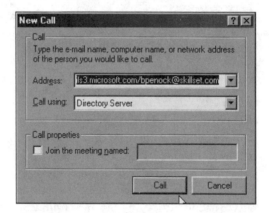

This box has several options you might want to check out if you're not using a typical Internet hookup. (If you're using an in-house ILS server, for example, over your intranet.) Click on the ? button, then on the option you're wondering about. Typically, though, all you'll have to do is click on OK, since NetMeeting has filled in the blanks for you. Once a person is called, your status line at the bottom of your NetMeeting window will indicate that the callee is being paged. Their computer will ring or beep or display a message alerting them that you are trying to reach them for a conference. If they don't want to answer your call, or for some reason simply don't respond (they're eating lunch or something and forgot to log out) you'll see the box on the next page.

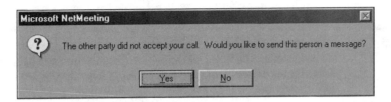

You have the option of bailing or sending them an e-mail message via your e-mail package. You might also be warned that the person has an earlier version of Net-Meeting. This just means some features might not work.

If they do answer, your names will appear in the list as in Figure 19.7. It might take a few seconds for things to link up. If you both have the hardware necessary to use the audio features of NetMeeting, you can talk with your friend by using your computer's microphone and speakers.

FIGURE 19.7

Your names are added to the active participants once a call connects.

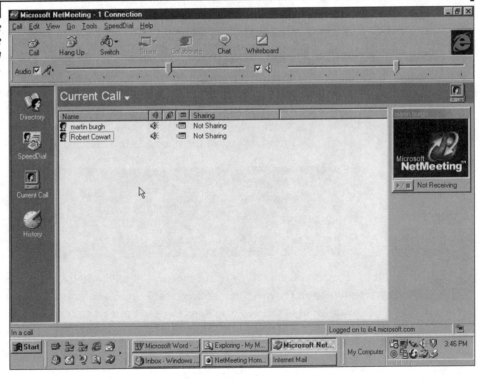

If you don't connect the first time, try making the call again with Call ➢ New and selecting Automatic in the Call Using drop-down list. This will ensure that NetMeeting uses the correct protocol.

You can right-click in the directory and choose Refresh to refresh the directory listing to reflect users who have logged off or to stop loading a new directory listing.

You can place a NetMeeting call from Windows Messaging Inbox. Just choose Tools ➢ Place a NetMeeting Call.

Not everyone on the listings can receive NetMeeting calls. Some folks are using other software that is not compatible with NetMeeting, or your version of NetMeeting. If this is the case when you try to call someone, you'll see a dialog box explaining that the person can't communicate with you over NetMeeting, or there might be some limitations. Try someone else, or send an e-mail message to your contact. Some people can't use either audio *or* video, and if you call them, you'll see a message warning you about that:

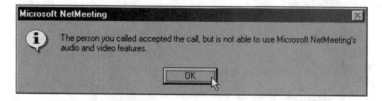

If the person you are calling is in a meeting, you'll be alerted to this fact, and asked if you want to join the meeting. Clicking on Yes puts you into the meeting.

If someone tries to call you, you'll hear a beep through your speakers and see a dialog box identifying the person at the other end, along with a button that lets you choose whether or not to pick up.

If you have trouble hearing your friend or being heard, adjust the speaker and microphone volume sliders in the NetMeeting window. If the problems persist, click the Tools menu, and then click Audio Tuning Wizard.

NOTE

Everyone in your conference should be using the same screen resolution if possible. Otherwise, things can get confusing, especially if one person maximizes or adjusts the size of a window beyond the capabilities of the other participants' monitors. People with smaller monitors or lower resolution can end up having windows that they can't see all of.

Hanging Up

When you've finished with your call, don't forget to hang up. Of course you should say bye first, either on the Chat board or with your voice. When you're ready to finally terminate the call click on the Hangup button on the toolbar.

Adjusting Your Audio and Video

Invariably you're going to have to make some modifications to your sound and video setups. As unexciting as it is, many conversations start with some replay of the old Alexander Graham Bell conversation over the first telephone. I always seem to end up doing 10 minutes of "Can you hear me?" before we really start having a real conversation or getting useful work done. Likewise, video often takes some adjusting as well. Here are some points to remember.

Sound Adjustments   To start with, adjust your speakers or use a headset, and make volume adjustments that are reasonable. The system works best if you keep your local volume turned fairly low. Well, not booming, anyway. If you're using a half-duplex system, earphones are best, since then the incoming sound doesn't trigger your microphone to turn on. The program is fairly good about this, and doesn't trigger super easily, but this is something to be a little careful about. You can control the speaker volume from a couple of places. My speakers have a volume control right on them, so I usually just crank the knob down a little bit. I'll also turn down the bass a little and bring up the treble a bit. This makes the voice more intelligible on my system. Yours may be different. The other place is just below the toolbar on the NetMeeting window. It's the slider on the right, next to the little speaker icon.

PART

III

Communications and
Using the Internet

Next, you should check the Microphone muting option. This is adjusted from the volume control applet, available from Control Panel, or easier yet, from the Taskbar. Double-click on the little speaker in the System Tray, down by the system clock. This brings up the volume control. Check for the following:

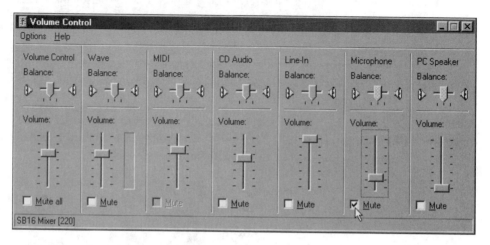

The microphone Muting should be turned on, as you see here. Muting prevents the mic from playing through your speakers and producing feedback.

WARNING

Don't turn this button off if your mic and speakers are on! You'll get a blast of high-pitched squealing in your ears. Not very enjoyable, and possibly damaging to your ears.

Next, even though the Wizard adjusted my sound settings when I first ran Net-Meeting, I've ended up having to tweak two sliders to get sound working right, especially since I have a fair amount of background noise in my office. The first setting is this one, right on the toolbar:

You might need to try adjusting this up or down a bit if people say either that you're coming in distorted or you are too quiet. Test your settings with a number of people before you make the definitive decision about your volume setting, though. It might just be that the other person's speakers are set too low or high!

Finally, the biggie is the microphone sensitivity control, which you get to from the Tools ➤ Options ➤ Audio tab.

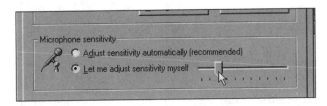

This control determines how loud your voice has to be in order to switch your microphone on. If set too high, any sound in the room will trigger your transmission, in effect drowning out the other people in the conversation, unless you all have full-duplex cards. You'll have to futz a bit with this setting. First click on the Let Me Adjust Sensitivity Myself button. Then start in on dragging the slider a bit. You want it as low as possible, but still up enough to switch on when you start talking. Try different settings, but no drastic changes from the way it was set. The wizard probably did a fairly good job at setting this originally. As a rule, talk fairly close to the mic and try to keep the sensitivity down. Then adjust the mic volume as needed so people can hear you loudly enough.

NOTE

Watch the little sound indicators to the right of the little microphone on the main NetMeeting page when you're talking. It should show several animated lines when you are talking, and drop to no lines when you stop talking. If a line or two are showing when you are not talking, the sensitivity or the mic volume is up too high. Try readjusting, or running the audio tuning wizard from the Tools menu again.

There are a couple other interesting settings on the audio tab. Here are some notes about them:

- The Enable Auto Gain Control should normally be left on. This helps compress your voice level to that even when you are talking quietly, the other parties can hear you.

- Only turn on Full-Duplex if you know you have a card that supports it.

- *Advanced* settings are for the brave only. Make sure you know what you're doing before messing with these. The list controls the order in which NetMeeting will attempt to use popular compression/decompression algorithms when sending and receiving sounds.

- Calling a telephone using NetMeeting. This option provides a place for you to type the address of the H.323 gateway server that NetMeeting will use to place your telephone call. These systems, wedding traditional, standard telephones and the Internet are beginning to appear as of this writing. Check with your network administrator or other telephony professional who is conversant in your setup for more info.

Video Adjustments You'll probably make some of your video adjustments through software that comes with your camera. For example, my system (the Phillips Easy Video card) has a couple of control programs to fine-tune my video capture. If you have a Connectix camera, you'll have a different set of controls, and so forth. Refer to the docs that come with your system for possible suggestions about appropriate NetMeeting settings.

If all is well, when you make a call to someone with a camera you'll see your image up top, and his or hers down below. (See Figure 19.8.)

FIGURE 19.8

A typical video phone call using NetMeeting

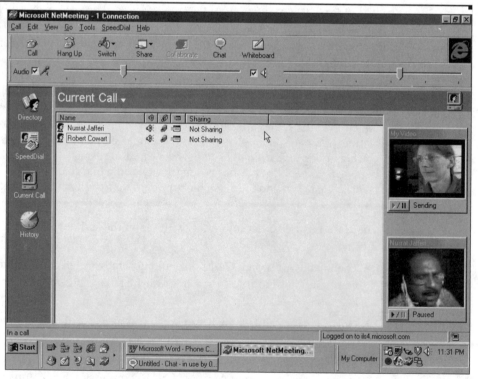

You can drag the pictures out onto the main section of the screen if you want, and resize them. However, then they are in separate windows. It's easy to manage everything with the pictures attached to the NetMeeting window, over in the right side of the screen, as they are in the screen shown in Figure 19.8.

Here are some video settings you can adjust:

- You can click on the pause and play buttons at the bottom of each video window to pause or restart the video you are sending and receiving. Pausing video input and output can improve on sound if the voices are starting to break up. This is because the video consumes large amounts of data bandwidth, often causing the audio to be delayed or lost.

- Right-click on either video window and you'll see a number of settings, including Properties, which brings up a bunch of settings to play with, as shown in Figure 19.9. The Detach From NetMeeting option just means display this window as a separate window rather than in the NetMeeting window.

- As a rule, the smaller the display size, and the fuzzier the image you send (faster video), the less data has to be transmitted per frame of video. So, if things are getting bogged down, try the small image size.

- If you don't mind having strangers see your image before you see theirs, turn on the Automatically Send Video checkbox as well as the Automatically Receive Video (which is on by default). Then you'll both see each other when you make or receive a video call.

FIGURE 19.9

Lots of video settings to play with. The defaults are probably the best bet.

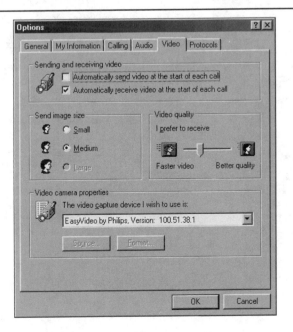

Chat

Chat provides a text-based mechanism to communicate with participants in a conference. Chat always seems to work. Thus it's a good way to get started talking to someone in case your sound (and possibly video, in version 2) isn't working. You can use Chat by itself if you want, to communicate about common ideas or topics with fellow conference participants, or you can use it to augment your conference proceedings, as you would record meeting notes and action items to distribute later as the minutes of your meeting.

To use Chat, just do this:

1. Click on the Chat button in the tool bar, or choose Tools ➤ Chat. You'll see a window with two sections.

2. Type a message into the bottom section, then press Enter (or click on the large button to the right of the text entry area). Actually, until you press Enter you can edit your message in the usual ways. It's only after pressing Enter that your message is sent, at which point you'll see your message appear next to your name in the upper window.

You can see in Figure 19.10 a chat I had on-line while I was testing NetMeeting 2.*x*.

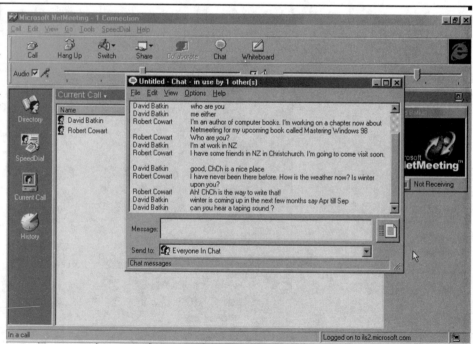

Whiteboard

Need a visual aid to make your point? Use the Whiteboard feature to draw a picture that the other people in the conference can see. You can paste onto the whiteboard from another application, or copy an active window, or copy any portion of the screen and drop it into the whiteboard. Several people can even draw on the picture at the same time. It also sports a few drawing tools, so you can sketch diagrams, organization charts, flow charts, or display other graphic information and share it with other people in a conference. Since the program is object-oriented (versus pixel-oriented) you can move and manipulate the contents by clicking and dragging with the mouse. A cute little remote pointer (in the shape of a pointing finger) and a highlighting tool can be used to point out specific contents or sections of shared pages. This is a great tool for ad hoc collaborations!

To use this feature, click on the Whiteboard icon in the toolbar or choose Tools ➢ Whiteboard. The whiteboard appears on both your and your friends' screens. Any time any one of you makes a change to the whiteboard, it is transmitted to the others.

If you want to copy something to your whiteboard (such as a picture or the contents of a window) do this:

1. Open that item in another window. If it's a picture, for example, open it in a drawing or graphics-viewing program.

2. Switch to the Whiteboard program and choose Tools ➢ Select Area (or click the Select Area button in the toolbar, on the left side of the Whiteboard window).

3. Switch to the program displaying the stuff you want to display on the whiteboard. Notice that you now have a crosshair cursor. Select the desired area by clicking and dragging with the crosshair, releasing the mouse button when finished. Now everything in the boxed area you just selected appears on the whiteboard, which means the other folks can see it too.

Anyone in the conference can point to stuff on the whiteboard by clicking on the pointing finger in the toolbar on the left side and then clicking in the screen. You can also move the hand around—but you have to intentionally drag the pointer hand and drop it before the other folks see the effect.

You can highlight stuff with the highlighter pen tool in the toolbar, too—second column, second row. Very useful. See Figure 19.11. Don't forget to try the Zoom control too, from the View menu, when you want a close-up.

FIGURE 19.11

You can use the highlighter tool to emphasize a portion of the whiteboard.

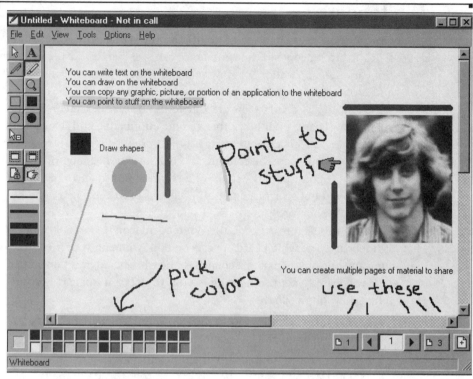

You can create multiple pages of stuff to share. If the whiteboard gets full with material that you don't want to erase just yet, simply create a new page by clicking on the Add page button. Then work from there. If you don't care about what's on a page and are running out of room, just clear the page by choosing Edit ➢ Clear Page.

TIP

Let's say you're working with a colleague and you have to sign off. It's the end of the work day, or you have lunch waiting. You can save a page or pages for later use in your next session. Just choose File ➢ Save As, and name the file. It gets a WHT extension on disk. You open it later by opening the Whiteboard, choosing File ➢ Open, and browsing for the document. By default it goes in My Documents \ Work In Progress.

Sharing Documents and Applications

You can actually share the programs running on your computer with other people in a conference. NetMeeting works with existing Windows-based programs that you already have, and you don't need any special knowledge of conferencing capabilities to share them. You just run any old program normally, and then share it. Other people you're connected to (are in "conference" with) then see your actions as you use that program, such as editing a document and so forth. They see your cursors as you edit content, scroll through information, and so forth. In addition, if you're running the program you can choose to allow others to *collaborate*, so others in the conference can take turns editing or controlling the application.

The amazing thing is, everyone can collaborate on a document even if only one person has the program being shared! So, for example, if I want an architect and my wife to help out on an AutoCAD drawing of a house we're working on, as long as each of us has NetMeeting on our machines and one of us has AutoCAD on their system, we're set.

Some examples of how the application sharing capability in NetMeeting can be used to improve productivity:

- You could share a Word or other word-processing program so that multiple people could collaborate on editing a document.

- Two or more programmers could share a programming language, working together to create a new program.

- Several people could share a spreadsheet program to work together on verifying and updating information.

Here's how to get NetMeeting to share your running applications, so that others in the conference can see what you're doing.

1. Start the application you want to share. The program does *not* have to know how to be NetMeeting "aware." Any program will do; it could be Word, it could be Photoshop, it could be the Calculator, etc. Also, it's not necessary for each person to have the application on their computer—it only has to be on the computer that is sharing it.

2. Switch back to NetMeeting and click on the Current Call icon in the left margin.

3. Click on the Share button in the toolbar or choose Tools ➢ Share Application, and then click the name of the application. (This command will be grayed out if you are not currently connected to another party.)

PART

III

Communications and
Using the Internet

4. Start working in the application you have shared; for example, typing numbers into Calculator. (In Figure 19.12, we're using Notepad.) Your friend will be able to see your work.

FIGURE 19.12

Sharing an application. In this case, it's Notepad. Two of us are editing the document together.

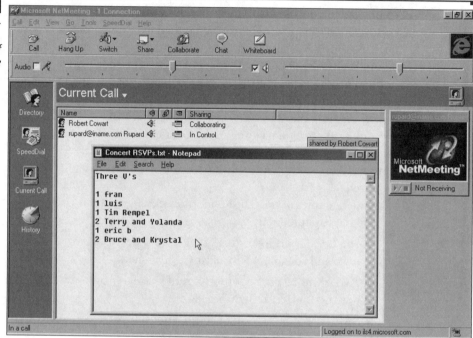

When you share an application, it is by default shared in Work-Alone mode, which means that only *you* can work in it. If you want, you can let others work with you to get things done more quickly. You do this by *collaborating*, as follows:

1. The person sharing the app (in this case, you) has to click on the Collaborate button in the toolbar (or choose Tools ➤ Collaborate). This enables Collaboration mode.

2. Next, anyone who wants to collaborate must *also* choose this command from their side. The other people in the conference are now able to take control of the shared application and work in it. All they have to do is double-click within the shared application window to grab control of the pointer. At this point the mouse pointer's shape will change, now showing the initials of the person in control of it. That person can use the pointer to move the window around, use the menus, move the insertion point and start typing, and take control of the shared program in any way.

3. To regain control of your shared program, just double click *your* mouse in the window. The initials below it will disappear and it will become functional to you again.

4. To end collaboration—that is, to regain and *keep* control of the program—click the Collaborate button again, or press Esc.

It's always good to issue a voice or chat warning that you want to take control of the mouse. Otherwise it becomes a free for all, with people trying to get the mouse control away from each other.

To share the document that results from this collaboration, you must send the final file to the participants in the meeting. See Doing File Transfers, below.

Click the NetMeeting icon in the System Tray (by the clock), and a little toolbar appears. It has icons for sharing, collaborating, chat, and whiteboard. This is called the quick-access toolbar. It's especially useful when you want to minimize NetMeeting to allow more room for displaying a shared application, the Whiteboard, or the Chat window on your screen, while still having the necessary NetMeeting commands available.

Sharing Your Clipboard

Here's another nifty feature. Two or more people can quickly share the contents of their Clipboards (remember, you put stuff on the Clipboard by using the Cut or Copy command from an application) regardless of whether they're set up to share applications. You just have to be connected to someone else using NetMeeting. This "sharing" via the Clipboard protects you from being vulnerable to the other person(s) with whom you're connected. If you haven't shared an application per se, but only your Clipboard, you can share only as much of a document as you want to, by copying it to your Clipboard—there is no danger of someone seeing all of your document unless you want them to.

Here's how this feature is used:

1. Get into the program containing the information you want to "share" with another.

2. Using your Edit menu, the right-click menu, or other appropriate function in the program, cut or copy the information you want to share. This will put it on your Clipboard. Interestingly enough, it also puts it on the Clipboard of people you are sharing applications with. It's as though you've taken over their Windows Clipboard without even knowing about it. (They can do the same thing to your Clipboard, so a little communication about what you're doing might be the polite way to go about this.)

3. Now the other people you're connected with can use an Edit ➢ Paste command in any application they have on their local machine to paste the material into their own documents. (And of course, you can do the same with applications on your machine.)

4. Until someone else copies or cuts something to their Clipboard, the material remains on each participant's Clipboard, and each person can paste the material elsewhere in as many places as they want.

NOTE

Clipboard sharing also happens automatically if you *have* set up an application to share or collaborate on.

Doing File Transfers to Other Participants

While you're in a meeting with folks, it's often useful to be able to send files to one another, or to disseminate files to everyone in the meeting, quickly. You can do this in NetMeeting. It's effortless. In fact, since NetMeeting is being used as a social meeting house on the Net, I've seen lots of people sending pictures of themselves to each other, or utility programs, or resumes, using this approach. Since the file transfers happen in the background, you can keep right on talking or chatting, while the files are being transmitted. The intended recipients have the option of accepting or declining receipt of a file being sent to them—an important consideration since files could be carrying viruses. As usual, plan to do a virus check on every file you accept via NetMeeting.

TECH TIP

The file-transfer capability in NetMeeting is fully compliant with the T.127 standard.

There are two basic approaches to sending a file in NetMeeting:

- You can right-click on a person in the conference and choose to send them a file,

- or you can drag a file from any Explorer folder window into the Microsoft Net-Meeting window to have that file automatically sent to each participant in a conference.

Here's the step-by-step rundown:

1. Get into a conference and click on the Current Call icon in the left margin if it isn't already active.

2. Click Tools ➢ File Transfer ➢ Send File, choose the file or files. The file(s) will be sent to everyone in the meeting. Or, if there is more than one person in the conference you can send to an individual. In the Current Call window, just right-click on the person you want to send to and choose Send File.

3. As each file is sent, a dialog box on the recipient's computer asks for confirmation to receive the file, and reports the progress, as shown in Figure 19.13.

FIGURE 19.13

After accepting a file (note the virus warning), transmission progress is reported in this box. By default, the file is placed in the Netmeeting\ Received files folder.

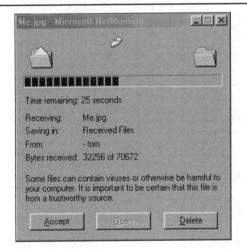

PART

III

Communications and
Using the Internet

NetMeeting is an OLE-compliant program, so you can drag files from an Explorer window (any folder window or from Windows Explorer proper) and drop them onto the conference window. All participants of the conference (excluding yourself) will then receive the files.

Speed Dial, Viewing Dial History, and Sending E-Mail

You may have noticed that whenever you connect with someone successfully, their name is added to the Speed Dial list. Click on Speed Dial in the left margin, and the list appears. You can easily reconnect with a past contact by double-clicking on their name now. The Speed Dial list has to be updated to reflect the status of the party, indicating whether they are currently on line or not. If the status indicates they are not on-line, no sense trying to call them.

Another feature lists all the calls you've made, even if they haven't been successful. Click on the History icon in the left margin and you'll see the list of everyone you tried to contact (as shown in Figure 19.14). You can easily hit someone up again this way, without seeking them out.

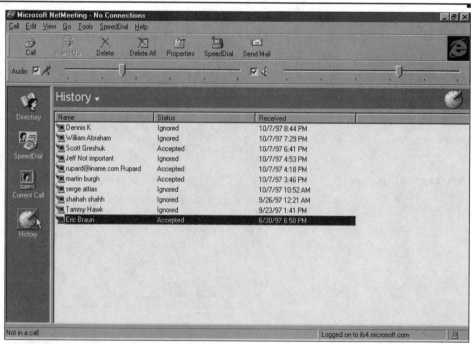

One final note: When you can't reach someone, you can send e-mail to anyone using NetMeeting, assuming they've filled in their real e-mail name in the personal properties box. Some people disguise their identities when using NetMeeting, so this doesn't always work. But many times it does. Just right click on a person's listing (in any listing—Directory, Speed Dial, Current Call or History) and choose Send Mail. Your mail program will come up, waiting for you to fill in the e-mail and send it. If a person is using a bogus address in NetMeeting to remain anonymous, the e-mail address entered in the missive won't look right, typically missing some final letters. I've seen some such as bob@bye. This obviously isn't a complete e-mail address. Nothing you can do about it, short of asking the person over NetMeeting what his/her real e-mail address is.

For More Information about NetMeeting

For general information, try this website:

`http://www.microsoft.com/netmeeting/`

For information about the NetMeeting SDK, try the Internet Developers website:

`http://microsoft.com/netmeeting/sdk/`

Additional information for developers can be found at this site:

`http://microsoft.com/netmeeting/authors/`

For information about the international standards used in NetMeeting, there are several organizations in the industry responsible for defining, approving, and communicating standards. Following are some of the key organizations:

- **International Telecommunications Union.** The ITU, headquartered in Geneva, Switzerland, is an international organization through which governments and the private sector coordinate global telecom networks and services. ITU activities include the coordination, development, regulation, and standardization of telecommunications, and organization of regional and world telecom events. Check out their website:

  `http://www.itu.ch/`

- **Internet Engineering Task Force.** The IETF is the protocol engineering and development arm of the Internet. The IETF is a large, open, international community of network designers, operators, vendors, and researchers concerned with the evolution of the Internet's architecture and the smooth operation of the Internet. For information, go to:

  `http://www.ietf.org/`

- **International Multimedia Telecommunications Consortium Inc.** The IMTC is a nonprofit corporation founded to promote the creation and adoption of international standards for multipoint document and video teleconferencing. The IMTC and its members promote a Standards First initiative to guarantee compatibility between aspects of multimedia teleconferencing. For more info, check out:

  `http://www.imtc.org/imtc/`

PART

III

Communications and
Using the Internet

PART IV

Using the Supplied
Programs

CHAPTERS:

20. Using WordPad for Simple Word Processing

21. Using Paint and Kodak Imaging

22. The Other Windows Accessories

23. Maintaining Your System with the System Tools

Chapter

20

Using WordPad for Simple Word Processing

FEATURING

Creating a document

Entering text

Inserting the date or time in a document

Formatting paragraphs

Working with tabs

Reformatting the whole document

Using Undo to reverse mistakes

Using WordPad for
Simple Word Processing

I f you're like most people, you'll end up using your computer for writing more than for any other task. Writing letters, memos, and reports with your computer is much more efficient—and much more fun—than banging them out on a typewriter. To get you started, Windows 98 comes with a simple yet capable *word processor*, called WordPad, for editing and printing text documents.

WordPad lacks the frills of the hefty word processing programs like Microsoft Word for Windows, WordPerfect, or Word Pro, but it works fine for most everyday writing chores. WordPad gives you all the essential tools you'll need for editing word processing documents of virtually any length; it is limited only by the capacity of your disk drive. Like the high-end programs, it even lets you move text around with the mouse, a feature called drag-and-drop editing. WordPad accepts, displays, and prints graphics pasted to it from the Clipboard; it also lets you edit those graphics right in your document using OLE (see Chapter 6 for more about OLE). WordPad may not offer all the bells and whistles of the market leaders, but it's no toy—and besides, the price is right.

This chapter begins with a tutorial that gives you the opportunity to learn how to create and edit a word processing document. Along the way, you can experiment with the major procedures involved in a simple Windows-based word processor. Many of the techniques discussed in this chapter are applicable to other Windows programs as well.

After entering and editing your document, we'll extend your skills by discussing the various formatting features you can easily apply to your documents. Included in the discussion is information on how to perform the following:

- Insert the date and time in documents.
- Format paragraphs by changing line spacing, indents, and margins.
- Format individual characters with font, style, and size alterations.
- Set the tab stops to aid you in making tables.
- Quickly search for and replace specific text.
- Incorporate and edit graphics.
- Copy text between two WordPad documents.
- Save and print files.

Tips for Windows 3.1 and NT 3.xUsers

If you have ever used Windows Write, the word processor included with earlier versions of Windows, you'll notice how crude it seems compared with WordPad. But while WordPad would clobber Write in a beauty contest, and WordPad's fancier button bars make it easier to use, Write actually has several important features that WordPad lacks. If your word-processing needs don't justify buying a high-end program such as WordPerfect or Microsoft Word, you should consider keeping Write handy in case you need these capabilities.

Present in Write but missing from WordPad are:

- Repeating headers and footers for information you want to display on every page. Write lets you insert a page-number marker that automatically numbers each page for you.
- Full paragraph justification (so that text is flush on both the left and right sides of a paragraph).
- Double-spacing and $1\frac{1}{2}$-spacing for paragraphs (WordPad permits only single-spaced paragraphs).
- Decimal tabs, allowing you to line up columns of decimal numbers.
- Superscript and subscript character formats.
- A *Regular* character format command, allowing you to remove all styles (bold, italic, underlining, superscripts, and subscripts) from selected text with a single command.

Continued ▐▶

CONTINUED

- A *page break* command, allowing you to force text that follows to the top of a new page, regardless of how you edit previous text (useful for creating documents with sections).

- The ability to find text that matches the capitalization (case) of your entry in the Find dialog box and the ability to find text that is found only if it occurs as a separate word (not as part of a longer word).

- The ability to search for paragraph markers, page breaks, and tabs with the Find command. Among other uses, this lets you reformat DOS-style plain text documents much more easily.

By the way, you should know that although WordPad can open Write documents, items that WordPad doesn't recognize are converted or discarded. For example, WordPad converts decimal tabs to ordinary tabs, and it simply discards headers or footers.

Creating a Document

To start a new WordPad document, begin from the Taskbar. Choose Programs ➢ Accessories ➢ WordPad. The WordPad window will appear with a new, empty document window open for you. If the WordPad window isn't already maximized, maximize it so it fills the whole screen. Your screen should now look like that shown in Figure 20.1.

FIGURE 20.1

The initial WordPad screen with no text in the document

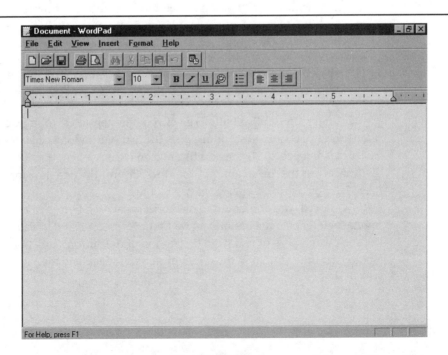

Getting Help in WordPad

Before going any further, it bears repeating that on-screen help is always a mouse click or key press away while you're working in WordPad. To activate WordPad help, press F1 or choose Help ➤ Help Topics. When the standard Windows Help application appears, choose the Contents, Index, or Find tabs, then locate the topic you need help with and double-click on it.

You can also get help for any item in a dialog box by using the right mouse button. Click over the item with the right button to pop up the What's This? button. Click on the button to display a short help message.

Finally, WordPad displays brief help messages when you pass the mouse pointer over certain items on the screen. These include menu choices and the buttons on the toolbar and Status bar (those rows of buttons at the top of the screen).

Working with the WordPad Window

There are several things to notice on your screen. As usual, up at the top of the Word-Pad window you see the menu and title bars. The menu bar offers options for writing, editing, and formatting text.

Referring to your screen or to Figure 20.1, notice that the title bar shows *Document* as the filename because you haven't named the document yet.

The Toolbar

Just below the menu bar you should see a row of buttons, each with a small graphical icon. This is the *toolbar,* shown below. If you don't see the toolbar, someone has turned it off. Display it by choosing View ➤ Toolbar.

Clicking on the toolbar buttons gives you one-step access to some of the most common WordPad commands. For instance, the first button (on the far left) shows a single sheet of blank paper. Clicking on this button creates a new, blank document. About halfway across the row of buttons, the Find button—the one showing a pair of binoculars—lets you search for specific passages of text.

In WordPad, you don't need to memorize what each button does. Just position the mouse pointer over the button and wait for a few seconds. WordPad will display a small text box with a one- or two-word description of the button's function. In addition, the Status bar at the bottom of the screen displays a longer help message.

Displaying and Hiding Control Bars with the View Menu

WordPad offers several other bar-like sets of controls and readouts to speed your work and give you quick information on your document. The View menu lets you display or remove each of these control bars individually. If the item isn't currently visible, choose its name from the View menu to display it. Do exactly the same to remove the item if it's already displayed (if, for example, you want more space for editing text).

Notice that when you display the View menu, you'll see a checkmark to the left of each control bar that is currently visible. If there's no checkmark, the corresponding bar is currently hidden.

The Format Bar

Like the toolbar, the *Format bar* offers a set of graphical buttons, but it also contains (at the far left) two drop-down list boxes for selecting font and type size:

All of the Format bar's controls affect aspects of your document's appearance. Besides the font and type-size controls, various buttons let you set such characteristics as type style (such as boldface and italics) and paragraph alignment (such as left-aligned or centered).

The Ruler and the Status Bar

The *ruler*, another control bar available from the View menu, lets you see and modify paragraph indents and tab stops. See the "Formatting Paragraphs" section for instructions on working with the ruler.

The *Status bar* is a thin strip at the very bottom of the WordPad window. It displays messages from WordPad on the left. On the right are indicators showing when the CapsLock and NumLock keys are depressed.

Repositioning the Toolbar and Format Bar

You can reposition the toolbar and Format bar if you like. Just position the mouse pointer over any part of the bar that's not a button and drag the bar where you want it. If you drag the bar to the bottom of the WordPad window, the bar will merge with the lower portion of the window. You can also drag the toolbar to the right side of the window so it becomes a vertical strip fused with the right window edge. (This won't work with the Format bar because the list boxes for typeface and size are too wide to fit in the narrow strip.) If you drag either bar into the document area or outside the WordPad window altogether, it becomes a separate movable window with its own title bar, as shown in Figure 20.2.

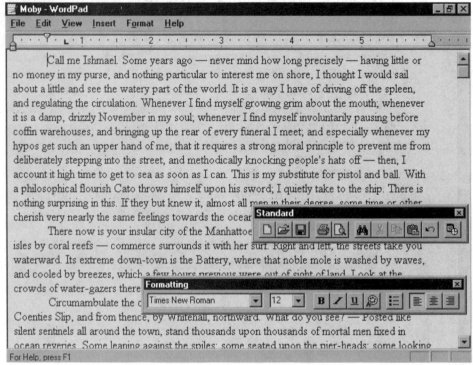

FIGURE 20.2

Here's how the toolbar and Format bar look when you "tear" them from their standard locations, thereby turning them into separate, movable windows.

Entering Text

Notice the main document area of the WordPad window. Because you haven't typed in anything yet, the only item to look at here is the blinking cursor in the upper left corner. This *insertion point* indicates the place where new text will appear when you type.

Now begin creating a document. Of course, you're free to type in anything you want. However, to establish a consistent text to refer to later on in this chapter, try entering the following text, a hypothetical news story. (For later steps in the tutorial, keep the two misspelled words, *Pizza* and *sight*, as they are.) If you are at all unfamiliar with word processors, first read the steps that follow this text:

NEWS FLASH

Society for Anachronistic Sciences
1000 Edsel Lane
Piltdown, PA 19042

The Society for Anachronistic Sciences announced its controversial findings today at a press conference held in the city of Pisa, Italy. Pizza was not chosen as the sight for the conference because of its celebrated position in the annals of Western scientific history. The Society has made public its annual press conferences for well over 300 years and, as usual, nothing new was revealed. According to its members, this is a comforting fact and a social service in an age when everything else seems to change.

Begin entering the text into your new file, following the steps outlined here. If you make mistakes while you are typing, use the Backspace key to back up and fix them. If you don't see an error until you have typed past it, leave it for now. You'll learn how to fix any mistakes later:

1. Type **NEWS FLASH** on the first line.

2. Next, press Enter twice to move down a couple of lines to prepare for typing the address. Notice that pressing Enter is necessary to add new blank lines in a word-processing document. Pressing the ↓ key will not move the cursor down a line at this point or create new lines; you will only hear an error beep from your computer if you try this.

3. Type the first line of the address, then press Enter to move down to the next line. Repeat this process for the last two lines of the address.

4. Press Enter twice to put in another blank line.

WARNING

Don't insert two spaces (that is, don't press the spacebar twice) between sentences as you would with a typewriter. WordPad will automatically add enough space to clearly separate each sentence. If you add two spaces, your text will print with unsightly gaps between sentences.

5. Begin entering the body of the story. Don't forget to leave in the spelling mistakes so we can fix them later on. When you get to the end of a line, just keep typing. You shouldn't press Enter, because WordPad will automatically move text that overflows to the next line for you. This is called *word wrapping*. All you need to do is keep typing—and leave only one space between sentences, not two.

When you've finished entering the sample text, the WordPad window should look something like Figure 20.3.

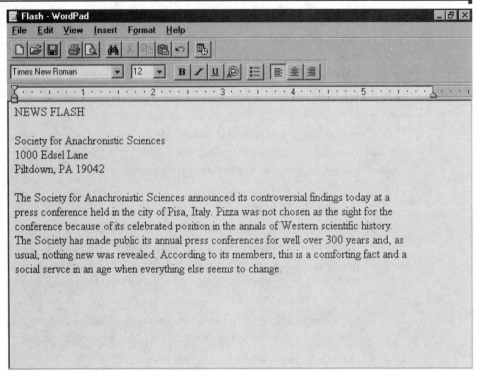

Editing Your Text

The first step in editing is learning how to move around in the text. If you followed the instructions above, you moved the cursor only by pressing Enter and, perhaps, by pressing Backspace to delete a character or two after you made a mistake. For the most part, you left the cursor alone, and it moved along by itself as you typed. But now you'll want to move up and down to fix misspelled words and make other changes. After all, it's the ability to move around freely in your document and make changes at will that makes a word processor so much more capable than a typewriter.

Moving the Cursor

The *cursor* marks the position where letters appear when you type. As noted before, this is the insertion point. Editing your text involves moving the insertion point to the correct location and then inserting text, removing words, fixing misspellings, or marking blocks of text for moving, copying, or deletion.

The easiest way to move the cursor is just to point and click. When the mouse pointer is over the document window, it looks like a large letter *I* or a steel beam (this shape is often called the *I-beam pointer*). Move the I-beam pointer so that the vertical line is over the place in the text where you want to begin editing or typing. When you click, the blinking insertion point will jump from wherever it was to this new position.

NOTE

After positioning the cursor with the mouse, don't forget to click; otherwise, you'll end up making changes in the wrong place.

You can also use the arrow keys to move the cursor. This is often quicker than using the mouse when you need to move the cursor by only a few characters or lines.

Here are some exercises in cursor movement using both the mouse and the keyboard:

1. Move the mouse pointer to the second line of the story and click immediately to the left of the *t* in the word *sight*.

2. Press the right arrow key and hold it down for a few seconds. Notice that the cursor moves one character to the right, pauses briefly, and then moves rapidly to the right. When it gets to the end of the first line, it wraps around to the start of the second line, continuing to the right from that point.

3. Press the left arrow key and hold it down. The cursor moves steadily to the left until it reaches the beginning of the line, then jumps to the end of the previous line. When the cursor gets to the beginning of the document, your computer starts to beep because the cursor can't go any farther.

4. Press the down arrow key to move the cursor down a line. If you hold down the key, the cursor will keep moving down until it reaches the last line in the text. (If a document has more text than will fit in the window, the text will scroll up a line at a time until the end of the document is reached.)

5. To move up one line at a time, press the up arrow key. Again, the text will scroll when you get to the top of the window until the cursor reaches the very first line.

6. Press Ctrl-right arrow. Each press of the arrow key moves the cursor ahead one word. Ctrl-left arrow moves it a word at a time in the other direction.

7. Press Ctrl-Home. The cursor jumps to the very beginning of the document. To jump to the end of the text, press Ctrl-End.

Because writing relies heavily on the keyboard, WordPad provides several keyboard combinations that can be used to move the insertion point. These are listed in Table 20.1, along with the single keystrokes for moving the cursor.

TABLE 20.1: KEYS FOR MOVING THE INSERTION POINT IN WORDPAD	
Key combination	**Moves the insertion point...**
↑	Up one line
↓	Down one line
←	Left one character
→	Right one character
Ctrl-←	Left one word
Ctrl-→	Right one word
Ctrl-Home	Beginning of document
Ctrl-End	End of document
Ctrl-PgUp	Top left of current window
Ctrl-PgDn	Bottom right of current window

Scrolling in the Document

Like other Windows programs, WordPad gives you a variety of ways to scroll through your document when the entire text doesn't fit in the window. Depending on the size of your WordPad window, the sample press release you've typed in probably does fit.

With the mouse, you scroll using the scroll bars. You can also use the arrow (cursor) keys to move right and left a character at a time or up and down a line at a time. Use the PgUp and PgDn keys to scroll your text a screen at a time.

Scrolling with the Mouse

When your entire document won't fit in the WordPad window, scroll bars appear in the work area along the right edge or at the bottom. A vertical scroll bar indicates the text is *longer* than the window; a horizontal bar means the text is *wider*. Because the sample document you've entered in this chapter fits in the maximized WordPad window, scroll bars will only be visible if you make the window smaller, as shown in Figure 20.4.

Consider the vertical scroll bar to be a sort of measuring stick for your document, with the top of the bar representing the beginning of your document and the bottom of the bar the end. The elevator, that rectangular object that you slide along the scroll bar, shows you the relative position of the current window's text within the document.

By dragging the elevator to the approximate relative position you want to scroll to, you can get close to your desired spot quickly. You can also scroll by clicking in the scroll bar above or below the elevator.

The horizontal scroll bar works the same way as the vertical bar but is only visible when you document is wider than the WordPad window.

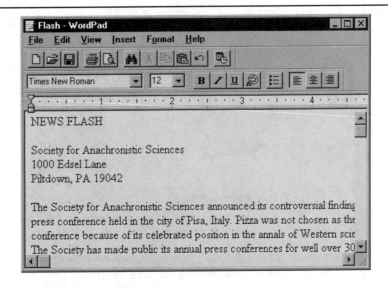

FIGURE 20.4

*This resized window
has both horizon-
tal and vertical
scroll bars.*

Scrolling with the Keyboard

Scrolling with the keyboard can be more efficient than using the mouse because you
don't need to take your hands off the keyboard.

Hold down the ↑ or ↓ key to move one line at a time. When you reach the top or bottom of the window, the text scrolls a line at a time as long as you hold down the key.

Pressing PgUp moves you up one window toward the beginning of your document.
Pressing PgDn has the opposite effect.

Making Selections in WordPad

Much of editing with a word processor centers around manipulating blocks of text. A
block is a section of consecutive text characters (letters, numbers, punctuation, and so
on). Blocks can be of any length. Many of the commands in Windows programs use
this idea of manipulating blocks of information.

You must *select* a block before you can work with it. When you select a block, it
becomes the center of attention for WordPad. As shown in Figure 20.5, WordPad highlights the block. Until you deselect it, WordPad treats the block differently than the
rest of the document. For example, some menu commands will affect the selection
and nothing else.

FIGURE 20.5

The highlighted passage is a selected block of text.

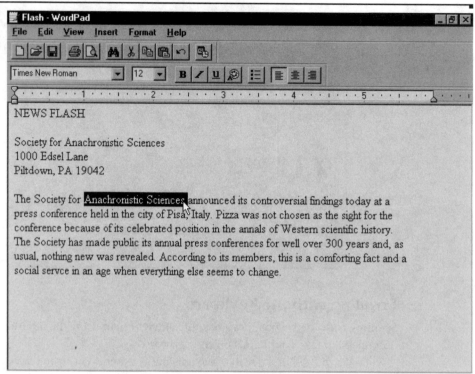

There are two main ways to select a text block: with the mouse, by dragging over the area you want to select, and with the keyboard, by holding down the Shift key while you move the cursor. We'll cover both methods in detail in a moment. You *deselect* when you click elsewhere, select elsewhere with the mouse, or move the cursor after releasing the Shift key.

Once you've selected a block, be careful about the keys you press. If you type *A*, for example, the text of the whole block (the *selection*) will be replaced by the letter *A*. If this happens accidentally, choose Edit ➤ Undo or click on the Undo button on the toolbar *before doing anything else*, and your text will be returned to its previous state.

After selecting a block of text, you can manipulate it in any number of ways: you can cut or copy it, change its font size, alter the paragraph formatting, and so forth. Try the following exercises to get the hang of selecting blocks.

Selecting an Arbitrary Text Area with the Mouse

Selection is particularly intuitive and simple with the mouse. Try this:

1. Deselect any selections you may have made already by clicking anywhere in the text.

2. Move the pointer to the beginning of a word somewhere.

3. Hold the left mouse button down and move the pointer down several lines. As you move the mouse, the selection extends. You'll notice that as soon as the pointer touches any part of each word in turn, the entire word becomes selected (unless someone has changed the relevant setting—see the section "Selecting Measurement Units and Controlling Word Selection" later in the chapter for more information). When you release the mouse button, the selection is completed.

4. Click anywhere again to deselect the selection.

The *anchor point* is the point you first clicked. Dragging downward extends the selection downward from the anchor point. If you were to keep the mouse button down and drag *above* the anchor point, the selection would extend from the anchor point upward.

Selecting an Arbitrary Text Area with the Shift Key

You can also use the Shift key in combination with the arrow keys or the mouse to select an arbitrary amount of text:

1. Deselect anything you have already selected.

2. Move the cursor to the beginning of any word in the first paragraph and press Shift-→. The selection advances one letter with each press (unless you hold the key down too long, in which case it moves by itself and selects several letters).

3. Press Shift-↑ five times. Notice that as you move up past the anchor point, the selection reverses, moving upward in the text.

4. Press Shift-Ctrl-→. As the cursor jumps a word to the right, WordPad removes the selection highlighting from the characters it passes over.

5. Release the keys and click somewhere to deselect.

6. Click on the first word in the second paragraph (with the method you're testing now, this sets a new anchor point there).

7. Hold down the Shift key.

8. Click on a word in the middle of the paragraph. This changes the selection. It now extends from the new anchor point to the point where you clicked.

Selecting a Word or a Paragraph at a Time

Often, you'll want to select a word or paragraph quickly, either to delete it or to change some aspect of it, such as its font size. You can do this easily by double-clicking (to select a word) or triple-clicking (for a paragraph). If you keep clicking rapidly, the selection alternates between the whole paragraph and the word under the pointer.

Selecting a Line or Series of Lines

There's a shortcut for selecting an entire line or quickly selecting a series of entire lines:

1. Move the mouse pointer into the left margin. It changes into an arrow pointing to the top right. This margin is called the *selection area*.

2. Position the pointer to the left of the first line of the first paragraph and click the mouse to select the entire line.

3. Starting from the same place, hold down the mouse button and drag the pointer down along the left margin. This selects each line the pointer passes.

Selecting an Entire Paragraph: An Alternative Method

Here's another shortcut for selecting an entire paragraph:

1. Move the cursor into the selection area (left margin) next to the first paragraph.

2. Double-click, and the entire paragraph will be highlighted.

Holding down the Shift key while you drag the pointer in the margin selects additional paragraphs.

Selecting an Entire Sentence

If you need to change a particular sentence in its entirety, you can do so easily:

1. Hold down the Ctrl key.

2. Click anywhere in the document. The whole sentence containing the location you clicked will be selected.

Selecting an Entire Document

Sometimes you'll want to select the whole document. This can be useful for changing the font size or type of all the text or changing other attributes, as discussed in the following sections. You have several choices for selecting an entire document. From the menu, you can choose Edit ➤ Select All. But try these simpler methods as well:

• Move the pointer into the selection area (the left margin of the document window). Hold down Ctrl and click the mouse. The entire document will be selected. Click anywhere in the text to deselect it.

• Move the pointer back to the selection area. This time, triple-click to select the whole document. Again, deselect it by clicking elsewhere.

• Use the keyboard shortcut for selecting the whole document: Ctrl-A.

Making Some Changes to the Text

Now that you know how to get around and select portions of text, you can begin to correct some of the typos in your letter.

Deleting Letters

Let's start with the second sentence of the first paragraph, where the word *site* is misspelled as *sight*:

1. Position the cursor between the *i* and *g* in *sight*.

2. Press Delete. This removes the misplaced *g*. Notice also that the space closed up where the *g* was when you deleted the letter, pulling the letters to the right to close the gap.

3. Press Delete again to remove the *h*.

4. Move the cursor one character to the right and add the *e*.

Notice that the line opened up to let the *e* in. Unlike on a typewritten page, lines on a computer screen are flexible. You may have noticed that WordPad rewraps all the lines of the paragraph almost instantly as you insert text.

Many simple errors can be fixed using the Delete or Backspace key. But suppose you wanted to delete an entire word, sentence, or paragraph. You could do this by moving to the beginning or end of the section you wanted to erase and then holding down Delete or Backspace, respectively, until the key repeated and erased all the words, letter by letter. But this is a slow and potentially risky method. If you're not careful, you may erase more than you intended to. This is where selecting a text block comes in, as you'll learn shortly.

Deleting Words

For our second change, find the word *not* in the second sentence, the one that now begins "Pizza was not chosen...". So the paragraph makes more sense, delete the *not* as follows:

1. Select the word *not* with one of the techniques you learned earlier.

2. You have several choices for removing the word. You can press Delete or Backspace to remove the offending word permanently. Choosing Edit ➢ Clear has the same effect, it just takes a little longer.

**TIP**

If you delete a word accidentally with any of these techniques, you can retrieve it by choosing Edit ➢ Undo or clicking on the Undo button before you make any other changes. And if you want to remove a word but save it on the Clipboard for later use, you cut it instead of deleting or clearing it. You'll learn how to cut selected blocks a bit later.

Replacing Words

But what if you wanted to *replace* a word, not just delete it? WordPad gives you a short-cut method for doing just that.

1. Select the misspelled *Pizza* in the first sentence.

2. With *Pizza* highlighted, type in *Pisa*. Notice that as soon as you type the first letter, *P*, it replaces the entire selection. This saves the extra step of pressing Delete or choosing Clear from the Edit menu. (You may need to add a space after the word, depending on how you selected *Pizza*.)

All of this may seem like a lot of work just to change a few letters, but for larger selections you will find it's worth the effort.

Inserting Letters

You can insert any number of letters, words, or paragraphs wherever you want within a document. This is called *inserting* because as you type new characters, they appear within the existing text, which is pushed to the right as you type.

Some word processors allow you to deactivate insertion in favor of *overwriting*, where newly typed letters replace the old ones instead of pushing them to the right. WordPad does not let you do this. The advantage is that you will never accidentally type over some text you want to keep. The disadvantage is that you will need to take some action to delete unwanted text.

TIP

If you need to insert characters that aren't available on your keyboard—such as a ™, ©, or ¥ symbol—use the Character Map accessory, covered in Chapter 9.

Moving Selected Blocks

The editing process often involves moving large portions of text, such as sentences and paragraphs, within a document. Rather than inserting a block of text by retyping it, you can pick it up and move it from one place to another with the Cut, Copy, and Paste commands covered here. And WordPad also gives you a snazzy drag-and-drop method for moving text around with the mouse.

Moving Blocks with Cut and Paste Commands

Here's an example of the Paste command that will reverse the order of the first two paragraphs in our letter:

1. Move to the top of the document.

2. Select the "News Flash" line (this is a one-line paragraph) with whatever technique you prefer, and carefully select the blank line immediately below the

paragraph, too, because you want a blank line between the paragraphs after the move. This second line is also a *paragraph* as far as WordPad is concerned. If you're selecting by dragging, just drag the mouse a little further down. If you double-clicked in the margin to select the first paragraph, press Shift to retain the paragraph selection and then double-click to the left of the blank line. You'll know the blank line is selected when a thin strip at the left margin becomes highlighted (this is the normally invisible *paragraph mark* associated with the blank line):

Every paragraph has a paragraph mark. Paragraph attributes such as alignment, tab settings, and margins are contained in it. Copying this mark is an easy way of copying attributes from one place to another.

3. Now it's time to cut the block. You have three choices: choose Cut from the Edit menu, click on the Cut button on the toolbar (shown here), or press Ctrl-X on the keyboard.

4. Move the insertion point to the place where you want to insert the paragraph, which happens to be just before the *T* of the word *The* in the first main paragraph.

5. Paste the paragraph back into your document. You can click on the Paste button on the toolbar (the one that shows a small piece of paper and a clipboard, shown here), choose Edit ➤ Paste, or press Ctrl-V.

Sometimes, after moving paragraphs around, you may need to do a little adjusting, such as inserting or deleting a line or some spaces. You can always insert a line by pressing the Enter key. If you have extra blank lines after a move, you can delete them by putting the insertion point on the first space of a blank line (the far left margin) and pressing the Backspace key.

NOTE

Just a reminder: once you've placed text (or any other information) on the Clipboard, you can reuse it as many times as you like because it stays on the Clipboard until you replace it with new information by using the Cut or Copy commands.

Moving Blocks Using the Right Mouse Button

In WordPad, clicking the right mouse button over the document pops up a small menu offering immediate access to the most common editing commands, as shown in Figure 20.6.

FIGURE 20.6

WordPad's pop-up menu is displayed when you click the right mouse button.

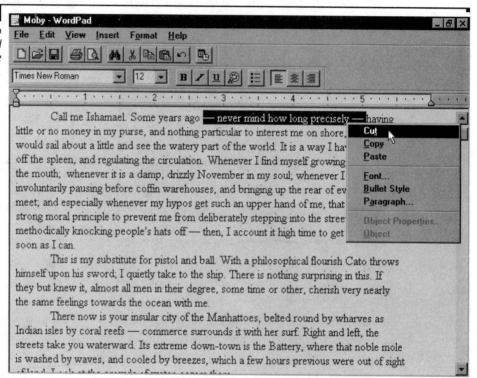

Here's how to move the paragraph back with this method:

1. Select the paragraph again.

2. Click the right mouse button anywhere over the selected block. The pop-up menu shown in Figure 20.6 appears.

3. Choose Cut from the pop-up menu.

4. Position the pointer where you want the text to go and click, again with the right button. From the pop-up menu, choose Paste.

Copying Blocks of Text

When you want to move existing text to a new location without deleting the original, you need the Copy command. After selecting a block of text, use Copy instead of Cut to place a copy of the text on the Clipboard. Then move the cursor to the spot where you want the copy and paste it in. As usual, you have several alternatives for copying a selected block to the Clipboard:

- Click on the Copy button, the one that shows two overlapping pieces of paper.
- Click the right mouse button, then choose Copy from the pop-up menu.
- Choose Edit ➢ Copy.
- Press Ctrl-C.

After you've copied the text to the Clipboard, you paste it in just as you would when moving a text block.

Moving Blocks with Drag and Drop

WordPad gives you yet another method for moving a block of text within a document. With drag-and-drop editing, you pick up the block with the mouse and drop it into place without ever fussing with menus, buttons, or keyboard commands.

This time, move the third full paragraph in the story to the very end of the document. Here's how:

1. Select the paragraph.
2. Click anywhere within the selection and hold the mouse button down.
3. Very slowly (just for this exercise), begin to move the pointer while holding the button down. Notice that the pointer becomes a white arrow with a dotted line at its tip and a small, dotted rectangle at its base as soon as you begin to move it.
4. Move the pointer so that the dotted line is over the very end of the document (once you get to the bottom of the window, the text will scroll automatically if the end isn't visible) and release the button. The paragraph reappears at its new location.

A couple of points about drag-and-drop editing bear mentioning. First, no matter where you click on a selected block as you start to drag it, the entire block will appear—beginning at the pointer location—when you release the mouse button.

Second, don't panic if you realize you've made a mistake after you've started dragging a block. One way out is to press the Esc key before releasing the mouse button. You can also move the pointer back to the original block, releasing it anywhere in the block.

The insertion point moves to the spot where the pointer is, but the block itself remains in place. Finally, you can let up on the mouse button wherever you happen to be when you discover your mistake and immediately use Undo to restore the block to its original location.

Inserting the Date or Time in a Document

One of WordPad's few frills is a special command that automatically inserts today's date or the current time into your document. For dates, you have many choices for the style WordPad uses. Depending on the document's intended audience, you can pick an abbreviated format, such as 12/12/98, or let WordPad write out the full date, as in December 12, 1998. For the time, you can choose between two versions of the 12-hour AM/PM format that most people use and the 24-hour military format.

NOTE

WordPad always records the complete current time—down to the second—in your text. You probably won't want the seconds to appear in most documents, so you'll need to delete them after closing the Insert Date and Time dialog box.

To insert the date or time, follow these steps:

1. Choose Insert ➢ Date and Time, or if the toolbar is visible, click on the Date and Time button (shown here). The Insert Date and Time dialog box appears.

2. In the dialog box, choose your preferred style for the date or time from the list. The list offers more choices than will fit in the box, so scroll through it if you don't see the style you want.

3. Click on OK to insert the chosen information in your document.

Formatting Paragraphs

Paragraphs are the most essential division of your text when it comes to *formatting*, which simply means controlling the appearance of your document. A paragraph is defined by WordPad as any text terminated by pressing the Enter key. So even a single letter, line, or word will be treated as a paragraph if you press Enter after typing it. For that matter, pressing Enter on a completely blank line creates a paragraph, albeit an empty one.

WordPad handles each paragraph as a separate entity, with its own formatting information. The press release you created early in the chapter uses a standard block-paragraph format typical of many business letters. In that format, a paragraph's first line is not indented, so you separate paragraphs with an empty paragraph. Also notice that the right margin is *ragged*, rather than aligned evenly—or *justified*—as it is on the left margin.

These and other qualities affecting the appearance of your paragraphs can be altered while you are entering text or at any time thereafter. As you change the format settings, you immediately see the effects. Bold letters will look bold, centered lines centered, italic letters look slanted, and so forth.

For most documents, you may find that you are satisfied with WordPad's default format. WordPad applies the standard default format for you, carrying it from one paragraph to the next as you type. If you decide you would rather use a different format for a new document, just alter some settings before typing anything. Then everything you type into the new document will be formatted accordingly until you change the settings again.

Using the Ruler as Your Guide

The *ruler* (shown below) helps you keep track of where you are typing on the page, much like the guide on a typewriter. It also lets you alter the format of paragraphs by clicking on various symbols displayed within its boundaries. These alterations can also be made from the Paragraph menu and from the pop-up menu displayed when you click the right mouse button, but making changes on the ruler is probably easiest.

The ruler may be off (*hidden*), but you can turn it on or off at will by choosing View ➤ Ruler. This command is a *toggle*, which means that if the ruler is off, choosing the command displays it; if it is already on, choosing this command hides it.

Hiding the ruler lets you see extra lines of your text in the document window, but the ruler is useful to have around. The ruler has markings on it to help you gauge where your text will fall across the printed page and to help you set up tab stops. Each inch is marked with a number, and each tenth of an inch is marked by a small line. (You can change the ruler to show centimeters or other units via the Options dialog box.)

Notice the small markers at either end of the ruler. On the left are two triangular shapes: one along the top of the ruler, the other along the bottom. The lower one rests atop a small block. At the right side of the ruler, there's a single upward-pointing marker.

The lower markers at either end indicate the current paragraph's left and right indents (these are sometimes called *margin settings*, but remember that they affect the current paragraph, not the whole page). The upper marker on the left indicates the setting of the first-line indent for each paragraph. Actually, these markers do more than mark the current settings—you can use them to change the settings as well.

The ruler also shows tab settings. WordPad's built-in tab stops are marked by tiny gray dots along the lower border of the ruler. When you set your own tab, it appears on the ruler as a heavy black L-shaped mark within the ruler.

Paragraph formatting falls into three categories with WordPad: alignment, spacing, and indents. The following sections explain and illustrate these categories. Unless otherwise noted, the examples here use inches as the basic unit of measure. If you wish to indicate another unit, such as centimeters, you can use the View ➢ Options command to do so.

Adjusting Alignment

Alignment refers to where the text in a paragraph sits within the margins. *Left* is the default, causing text to be flush with the left margin (and ragged along the right margin). *Center* centers every line of the paragraph. *Right* causes text to be flush with the right margin (and ragged along the left margin).

To display or modify the settings for a given paragraph, click anywhere on it and then view or change the setting, either from the Format bar or from the Format Paragraph dialog box. Anytime you position the insertion point in a paragraph, the rulers and menu will reflect that paragraph's current settings.

NOTE

WordPad does not permit you to create fully justified paragraphs; that is, paragraphs with text that is flush along both the right and left margins. If you want justified paragraphs, you'll need to use another word processor.

Viewing Paragraph Alignment

To see the current paragraph alignment setting, move the insertion point to the paragraph in question and click. If the Format bar is visible, you can simply look at the bar to see the alignment. The alignment buttons will indicate the current setting—the button for that setting looks like it has been pressed, as shown below.

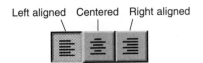

You can also discover the current settings for a paragraph by displaying the Format Paragraph dialog box, shown in Figure 20.8. To open the Format Paragraph dialog box, choose Format ➤ Paragraph, or click the right mouse button with the pointer over the paragraph and then pick Paragraph from the pop-up menu. At the bottom of the Format Paragraph dialog box, you'll see the current paragraph's alignment setting.

FIGURE 20.8

The Format Paragraph dialog box, like the buttons in the Format bar, indicates the settings for the current paragraph.

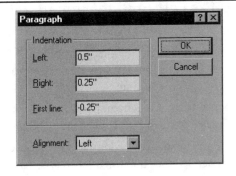

Changing Paragraph Alignment

You can change the settings for a paragraph almost as easily as you can display them:

1. Move the insertion point to the paragraph or select several paragraphs (even a portion of each paragraph will suffice).

2. Open the Format Paragraph dialog box (choose Format ➤ Paragraph or right-click and choose Paragraph). In the Alignment drop-down list box, choose the alignment setting you want.

3. As an alternative, if the Format bar is visible, click on one of its three alignment buttons (this is faster).

Setting Indents

Indents fall into three categories: right, left, and first-line indent. Every paragraph has settings for each, and each paragraph's settings can be different. As with the other paragraph settings, these are carried from one paragraph to the next as you type, or you can change them after the fact. You set indents via the Paragraph menu's Indents command or by dragging the indent symbols on the ruler, shown below.

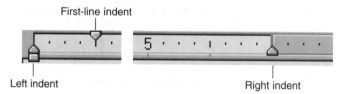

The settings determine how far in from the left and right margins your text will appear. They do not determine how far from the edge of the page the text will appear, however. That's established by the *margins*, discussed later in this chapter. The first-line indent determines the starting position of the first line of each paragraph.

Setting the Left or Right Indent with the Dialog Box

You can change the left or right indent by either typing new settings into the Format Paragraph dialog box or using the ruler. Here's the first method:

1. Place the insertion point in a paragraph or select several paragraphs whose settings you want to change.

2. Choose Format ➢ Paragraph or right-click and choose Paragraph from the pop-up menu. The Format Paragraph dialog box (shown in Figure 20.8) will appear.

3. Type in the desired indent and click on OK. If you just type in a number, it's assumed to be in inches. You can type **cm** after the number to indicate centimeters, **pt** to indicate typesetter's points, or **pi** for typesetter's picas.

If the number you enter isn't acceptable, WordPad will tell you. This usually happens when you accidentally enter a value that is too large for the paper your printer driver is set up for.

Setting the Left or Right Indent with the Ruler

You can also use the ruler to change the left or right indent:

1. Place the insertion point in the paragraph or select several paragraphs whose settings you want to change.

2. Turn on the ruler, if it's off, by choosing View ➢ Ruler.

3. Drag the left-indent marker in the ruler—the lower triangular symbol—to its new position. First, try grabbing the block *underneath* the triangular portion of the marker. This moves the block, the triangle that rests on it, *and* the other triangular marker, the one at the top of the ruler. When you let go of the mouse button, the paragraph's left indent moves to the new location. Notice that the first line has moved, too, even if it had been indented or outdented. It retains its indent relative to the left indent of the other lines.

4. Now try dragging the left indent marker by grabbing the lower triangle. This time, the top triangle remains where it is; when you release the button, all the other lines move to align with the new left indent.

Setting the First-Line Indent

On a typewriter, you press the Tab key if you want to indent the first line of each paragraph. This works in WordPad, too, but it's easier to let WordPad do it for you with its first-line indent setting. This also lets you modify the look of a document after you've written it, because you can adjust the size of the first-line indents.

The first-line indent setting establishes the relative indent for the first line of each new paragraph. Note that the setting is *in addition to* the left indent. So if the left indent is 1 inch and the first-line indent is 0.5 inch, the first line will start 1.5 inches from the left margin. Incidentally, setting the first-line indent to a negative number, such as -0.5, will cause it to hang out that amount from the left indent. This is sometimes called a *hanging indent* or an *outdent*.

To change the first-line indent, follow these steps:

1. Place the insertion point in the paragraph, or select several paragraphs whose settings you want to change.

2. Choose Format ➤ Paragraph or right-click and choose Paragraph. The Format Paragraph dialog box will appear.

3. Type in the first-line indent amount and click on OK.

As an alternative, you can drag the first-line indent marker (the upper triangle on the left side of the ruler) to the new indent position instead of going through the Format Paragraph dialog box.

WordPad will immediately reformat the paragraph in accordance with the new settings. Figure 20.9 shows examples of three different indent setups.

Creating Bulleted Paragraphs

One of the most common conventions in business and technical writing is the use of *bullets* to set off the items in a list. The standard bullet—and the one WordPad uses—is a heavy circular spot. But a bullet can be any symbol offset to the left of a paragraph. Bulleted text is useful for, and illustrated by, the following items:

- Calling attention to the individual benefits or features of a product or service

- Listing a set of options

- Itemizing the parts or supplies needed for a given job

FIGURE 20.9

Paragraphs with three different indent setups

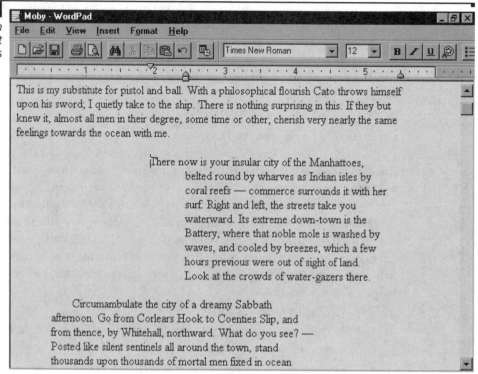

WordPad can automatically add a bullet to any paragraph or to each paragraph in a selected block of text. WordPad places the bullet at the original left indent of the paragraph, shifting the rest of the paragraph to the right (the position changes are accomplished by adjusting the left indent and first-line indent settings, as you can see on the ruler).

To apply bullets to an unbulleted paragraph or group of paragraphs, place the cursor in the paragraph to be bulleted or select a group of paragraphs and choose Format ➤ Bullet Style, or if the Format bar is visible, click on the Bullet button shown here.

The Bullet Style command works as a toggle—if the paragraph already has a bullet, the Bullet command removes the bullet.

Formatting Characters

WordPad includes commands for altering the look of the individual letters on the printed page. This is called *character formatting*. You can use character formatting to emphasize a section of text by making it bold, underlined, or italicized, or you may want to change the size or the font.

NOTE

As with all Windows programs, WordPad measures character sizes in *points*. Typical point sizes are 9 to 14 for ordinary text. Newspaper headlines may appear in anything up to 60 points or so.

Just as with paragraph formatting, WordPad starts you off with a standard character format: a conventional, unobtrusive font (Times New Roman) at a standard size (10 points). But you can change character formatting to your heart's content. Word-Pad gives you three ways to modify character formatting:

- From the Format bar
- From the Fonts dialog box
- With shortcut Ctrl-key combinations to change type styles

You can change the formatting of individual characters, selected blocks of text, or the whole document. Character formatting applies to paragraphs as a whole only if the paragraphs are actually selected.

Formatting Existing Characters

To change the formatting of characters you've already typed, begin by selecting the text character(s) to be altered. You can select a single letter, a sentence, a paragraph, the whole document, or any arbitrary sequence of characters. Now you have three choices:

- Use the controls on the Format bar to alter individual format characteristics (font, size, and so forth). This is a quick way to control any aspect of character format.

- Use keyboard shortcuts to modify the text style (boldface, italics, or underlining). This is the quickest way to change these particular styles.

- Use the Fonts dialog box to set all the format characteristics from a single window. This lets you see a sample of how your text will look as you experiment with different formatting choices.

WARNING

Expect lower print quality if you add boldface or italics when you don't have separate fonts installed for those styles. Windows 98 lets you add boldface or italics to any installed font, even if you haven't installed the bold or italics versions of the font. When the actual bold font is missing, Windows just makes the characters thicker. When the italics font is missing, it simply slants the regular font.

Changing Character Formats with the Format Bar

Here's how to use the Format bar to change character formatting:

1. If the Format bar isn't already visible, choose View ➢ Format Bar to display it.

2. To change the font of the selected text, choose the new font name from the drop-down list box at the left side of the Format bar.

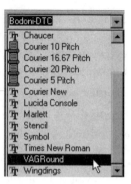

> **NOTE**
>
> The icon next to the font name tells you whether it is a TrueType or Printer font. Note that the type of font you choose affects the range of available sizes. Scalable fonts such as TrueType and PostScript (Type 1) fonts can be used in virtually any size; other fonts have a set number of specific font sizes available.

3. To change the text size, pick a new size from the next list box or type in the size you want (WordPad only allows integer font sizes; fractional values won't work).

4. To turn styles (boldface, italics, or underlining) on or off, click on the appropriate button. When the style is active, the appropriate button looks like it has been pressed.

5. To change the color of the selected text, click on the button that displays an artist's palette and pick your color from the list that appears.

Note that you can change these settings in any combination. For example, a single selection can be italicized, underlined, and displayed in fuschia—if you're willing to take some serious liberties with typesetting etiquette.

After you've returned to your document and deselected the block, the Format bar shows you the current formatting of the character or selection. If the character or selection has been italicized, for example, the button for italics appears pushed.

You can see at a glance if a selected block contains more than one style, font, or font size. For example, if only part of the block is set to bold, the Format bar button for bold appears translucent. If the block contains two or more different fonts, the entry in the box for fonts will be blank.

Changing Character Formats with the Fonts Dialog Box

The Fonts dialog box lets you see a sample of your character-formatting choices before you apply them. Otherwise, if your formatting experiments prove unsuccessful, you'll need to reset each setting for the selected block individually.

To modify character formatting with the Fonts dialog box, follow these steps:

1. With the text selected, choose Format ➤ Fonts or right-click and choose Fonts. You'll see the Fonts dialog box.

2. In the dialog box, you can make changes to any of the character-formatting settings you wish.

3. When you're finished setting character formats, click on OK.

Changing Character Formats with Keyboard Shortcuts

You can also use keyboard shortcuts (these also are toggles) to modify the character styles (bold, italics, and underlining) of a selected block, as follows:

- Ctrl-B for bold
- Ctrl-I for italics
- Ctrl-U for underlining

Formatting Characters As You Type

You can also change the appearance of text as you type. Subsequent characters will be entered with the new settings, and the settings will remain in effect until you change them.

For instance, you would press Ctrl-B once to start typing bold characters and then press it again when you're ready to type more unbolded text. The same procedure applies to the other character formats.

Working with Tabs

As with a typewriter, you can vary WordPad's tab settings to suit your needs. For complex multicolumn tables, you'll probably want to set up your own custom tab stops.

Default tab stops are already set up across the page in half-inch increments. If you haven't set tabs yourself, the half-inch markers—small gray dots on the ruler's lower border—indicate the locations of the default tabs.

For each paragraph, or any selected group of paragraphs, you can also place as many as 32 of your own tabs. These show up as heavy L-shaped markers in the ruler, as you can see in the ruler portion shown here.

 **NOTE**

When you set a tab manually, WordPad automatically eliminates all default tab stops to its left.

You can set and alter tabs from the Tabs dialog box or from the ruler. If you're good with the mouse, setting tabs is much easier and faster with the ruler. With the ruler on screen (choose View ➤ Ruler if it's not already visible), click inside the ruler at the place where you want the tab. You can drag the tab marker left and right to adjust its placement any time. The text affected will be adjusted immediately.

To set tabs from a dialog box, choose Format ➤ Tabs or right-click over the paragraph or selection and choose Tabs from the pop-up menu. A dialog box appears, as shown in Figure 20.10.

FIGURE 20.10

You can set the 32 possible tabs from the Tabs dialog box.

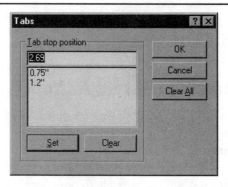

Type in the exact location for each new tab stop and choose Set. You can set tabs in any order (for example, you could set a tab at 4.5 inches, then set a second at 2.5 inches). When you choose Set, WordPad inserts the tabs in order as shown in Figure 20.10. Type the position in inches (or whatever measurement unit you're using in the Options dialog box). Three custom tabs are shown in Figure 20.10: .75 inch, 1.2 inches, and 2.69 inches.

After you click on OK, the tabs will be set. The ruler will have new tab markers in it to indicate the new tab positions, and the text will be adjusted immediately.

Repositioning Existing Tab Stops

It's easy to adjust existing tabs to improve the layout of a table or list without retyping columns, or adding or deleting spaces between them.

The quickest way to change a tab's location is with the ruler. Just drag the tab to its new location. If you want more precision, you can use the Tabs dialog box, but you must first clear the existing tab stop, then set a new one at the desired location.

Clearing Custom Tab Stops

You can clear any of your custom tab stops at any time, either from the ruler or from the Tabs dialog box. To clear a tab from the ruler, simply drag the tab marker from the ruler down into the document, as though you were pulling it off the ruler. It will disappear. Any text formerly aligned at that tab will move right to the next custom tab stop. If there are no remaining custom tab stops, the text moves to the appropriate default tab.

To clear tabs from the dialog box, follow these steps:

1. Choose Format ➤ Tabs. The Tabs dialog box appears.

2. Find the tab stop you want to clear in the list box and click on it. It will appear in the entry box above the list.

3. Choose Clear to zap the tab stop, removing it from the screen.

4. Click on OK. Any text aligned at deleted tabs will move right to the next one.

To remove all your custom tab stops in one step, choose the Clear All button in the Tabs dialog box.

Reformatting the Whole Document

You may want to reformat an entire document. For example, you might print the document, look at it, and realize you should have used larger (or smaller) type or perhaps that it should have smaller (or larger) first-line indents.

To make a format change that affects the entire document, first select the whole document. You can do this by choosing Edit ➢ Select All, pressing Ctrl-A, or triple-clicking in the selection area. After the document is selected, change the format settings, as described in the previous sections.

Using Undo to Reverse Mistakes

WordPad makes allowances for our imperfections via the Undo command. In a split second, a slip of the mouse—choosing Clear instead of Cut—can send a large block of text to oblivion instead of to the Clipboard.

Undo is, quite understandably, the first selection on the Edit menu. But you can access Undo even faster if the toolbar is visible. Just click on the button showing an arrow with a curved stem.

Undo can reverse the following:

- Block deletions made with the Delete command from the Edit menu or the Delete key on the keyboard.

- Individual or multiple letters that you erased using the Delete or Backspace keys. Unfortunately, it will return only the last letter or series of letters erased. Once you move the cursor to another location using any of the cursor-movement keys and delete again, the text in the previous deletion is lost.

- Selected blocks directly deleted and replaced by typing new text on the keyboard.

- New text that you typed in. This can be undone back to the last time you issued a command.

- Character- and paragraph-formatting changes (if you select the Undo command immediately after making the change).

When you realize you've done something that you regret, select Edit ➢ Undo or click on the Undo button on the toolbar. But remember, the Undo command can recall only the last action. If you decide you have made a mistake, either while entering or deleting, you must undo the damage before using any other editing or formatting commands.

Searching for and Replacing Text

WordPad offers Find and Replace commands to look for specific letters, words, or series of words in your text. After the word processor finds the text, you can have it automatically replace that text with other text if you wish. Although WordPad calls these commands Find and Replace, this type of operation is also referred to as *search and replace*.

You can also use searching to get to a particular place in your document quickly. If you put unique markers (for example, *##1* or *aaa*) in your text, you can search for them to move from one part of a document to another specific point.

TIP

Using Find and Replace together, you can replace abbreviations with words. For example, you could selectively replace *W* with *Windows* and *wp* with *word processor*. This eliminates a lot of repetitive typing.

Finding a Specific Word or Text String

Here's how to use Find to locate a specific word or group of words:

1. Choose Edit ➢ Find, press Ctrl-F, or, if the toolbar is visible, click on the Find button (the one showing binoculars).

2. The dialog box shown in Figure 20.11 will appear. Type the text you're searching for and press Enter or click on Find Next. The cursor moves to the next instance of that text.

FIGURE 20.11

The Find dialog box. Type the word you want to find. Here, it is Anachronistic.

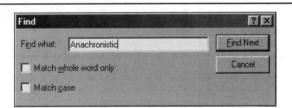

3. To find out if there are any other occurrences of the text, click Find Next again or just press Enter. WordPad will try to find the text again. WordPad always remembers the last word you searched for, so you can repeat the action more easily. It also scrolls the document for you so you can see the text if and when it's found.

TIP

Here's a shortcut for finding other occurrences of text in your document: Select the text, then bring up the Find dialog box. WordPad will have entered the text for you in the Find What area, so you can immediately click on Find Next.

4. When there are no further occurrences of the text you're searching for and the entire document has been searched, a dialog box will appear saying, "WordPad has finished searching the document." Just press Enter or click on OK.

The Find command always starts at the current cursor location and searches to the end of the document. Then it wraps around to the beginning and continues until it reaches the cursor again.

You can move the Find dialog box around the screen. Although WordPad automatically moves the Find dialog box so that you can see text that has been found, you may want to move the Find dialog box so you can see other parts of the document. The Find dialog box stays on the screen, ready for searching, until you close it.

Another handy command lets you repeat the previous search without the Find dialog box. After using Find to search for your text the first time, close the dialog box. Now whenever you want to repeat the search, either choose Edit ➢ Repeat Last Find or simply press F3.

Replacing Specific Words

To replace a text string with another text string, you use the Replace dialog box:

1. Choose Edit ➢ Replace or press Ctrl-H. A Replace dialog box appears, which is similar to the one for Find. There is an additional text area in the dialog box called Replace With. This is where you type in the text that you want the found text to be changed to.

2. Now click on Find Next, Replace, or Replace All. Here's what each does:

- Find Next finds the next occurrence of the word, but doesn't change anything.

- Replace changes the next or currently highlighted occurrence of the word and then moves on to find and highlight the next occurrence.

- Replace All automatically finds and changes all occurrences of the word. You don't see what's happening.

3. Depending on which option you chose, you may want to continue the process by clicking again on the Find Next, Replace, or Replace All button.

4. Close the dialog when you're finished by clicking on Close.

Copying between Two Documents

You may often need to copy portions of text between two documents. Many professionals use word processors because they can use *boilerplate text* to piece together new documents from existing ones. This is particularly useful for constructing legal documents or contracts that regularly include standard clauses or paragraphs. A more domestic example is creating a series of somewhat similar letters to a number of friends.

Because Windows lets you have multiple programs running at once, you have a fair amount of flexibility here. Although WordPad doesn't let you open more than one *document* at a time, Windows *will* let you run more than one *session* of WordPad. So you can run WordPad for each document you want to open.

Once your documents are open, you can select text from one, copy or cut it, and then open another window, position the cursor, and paste it in. Adjust the windows so that you can see enough of each document to easily select and insert text. Figure 20.12 shows an example of two WordPad documents open simultaneously.

FIGURE 20.12

You can run multiple copies of WordPad and load a different document into each window. This lets you transfer material easily between them or switch between writing tasks.

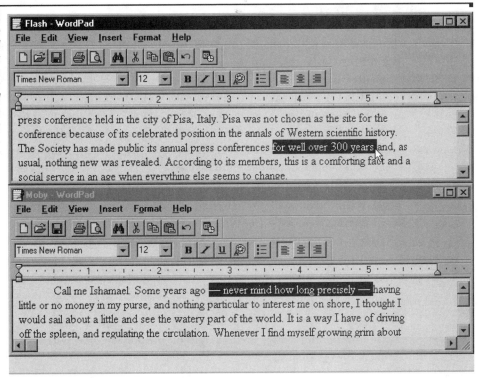

Of course you can use the multiple WordPad windows for simply writing or viewing more than one document at a time, too. For example, you may be working on several news stories, letters, or chapters of a book. Just minimize the documents you're not actively working on but want to have close at hand.

Here are the general steps for opening two WordPad documents and transferring material between them:

1. Minimize any other running applications. The quick way to do this is to click with the right button over any empty part of the Taskbar and choose Minimize All Windows from the pop-up menu that appears.

2. Run WordPad and open the first document (or just leave the window as is if you're creating a new document).

3. Run another copy of WordPad from the Start menu and open the file from which you're going to be cutting or copying.

4. Adjust the windows so you can see both. The quick way is to right-click on the Taskbar, then choose Tile Horizontally from the pop-up menu.

5. You can now move information between the windows to your heart's content.

Hyphenating Text

WordPad does not hyphenate your text automatically. As a result, some lines will be too short because WordPad has to push an entire large word to the next line. In WordPad, the only cure for such layout problems is to insert the missing hyphens manually. You should do this as the very last step you take before printing a document. Otherwise, if you make any further changes in your text—whether it's adding or deleting text or changing paragraph or character formatting—the line layout will likely change, and the entire word you hyphenated will now appear on a single line with the hyphen still visible (if this happens, just delete the hyphen).

Here's what you should do:

1. Find the optimal hyphenation point in the long word at the beginning of the next line, move the cursor to that point, and type a hyphen.

2. Then move the cursor to the beginning of the line and press Backspace. The newly hyphenated word will split, with the first section being pulled up to join the last word on the previous line. Press the spacebar to separate the two words again.

You may find that when you press Backspace, the last word from the previous line jumps down to join the hyphenated word. If this happens, it means that even the first part of the hyphenated word will not fit on the previous line. Go back to the word and remove the optional hyphen.

If you edit your text or change the formatting after hyphenating it, be sure the changes don't cause hyphenated words to move to locations where the hyphens are inappropriate. The easiest way to check for this is to use the Find command to search your document for all occurrences of a hyphen.

Adding Graphics to Your WordPad Document

Although it's sort of a bare-bones word processor, WordPad does allow you to insert pictures or graphics and all kinds of other *objects,* such as charts, video sequences, and sounds, into your documents. We'll focus on graphics for the moment, but the steps you'll learn here apply to other types of objects as well.

With this insertion feature you can add your company logo to every letter you print, put your picture on your letterhead, or put a map on a party announcement. Figure 20.13 shows examples of graphics inserted into a WordPad document.

FIGURE 20.13

Examples of graphics in a WordPad document. Graphics are imported from the Clipboard and then can be moved and sized.

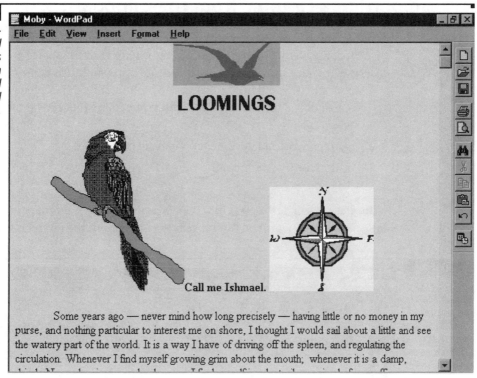

You can't create graphics with WordPad itself. You must get your pictures from other applications such as Paint. But you can use just about any kind of image in your WordPad documents. To add a photo, for example, you would have the photograph digitized with a scanner, then copy the picture onto the Clipboard and paste it into WordPad.

Once you've inserted graphics in the document, you can then cut, copy, or paste them. You can also change a graphic's size or move it around.

The simplest way to handle graphics in WordPad is to treat them as isolated items copied as independent chunks directly into the document via the Clipboard. But with a little more effort, you can maintain a connection between the graphic and the other application that created it. That way, you can edit the graphic from within WordPad— you won't need to return to the application that created the picture to make changes and then recopy the graphic to WordPad. Windows calls this feature *object linking* and *embedding*, or OLE. Chapter 6 covers OLE in detail.

Importing a Graphic from the Clipboard

To import a graphic into your document, follow these steps:

1. Place the picture on the Clipboard by switching to the source application, such as Paint, and choosing the Copy or Cut commands. (In Paint and many other applications, you'll need to select the portion of the image you want before you copy or cut). You can then paste almost any image that can be cut or copied into WordPad.

2. Open the WordPad document or activate its window.

3. Position the insertion point on the line where you want the picture to start and select Edit ➤ Paste.

The graphic will be dropped into the document at the insertion point. Figure 20.14 shows an example. Now you can move it or resize it with the methods explained next.

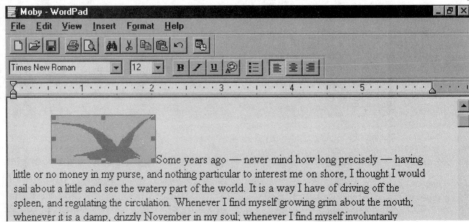

Positioning the Graphic

After you've pasted a graphic into WordPad, you have only crude control over positioning it where you want it in the document. You can't move a graphic around with the mouse, and there's no menu command for this purpose. Instead, you must "push" the picture around in your document with ordinary typing.

NOTE

WordPad automatically adjusts the spacing between lines so that the graphic fits without overlapping the line above it, just as it does if you change the text size.

It helps to know that WordPad treats an inserted graphic or other object as if it were a single text character. The bottom edge of the graphic sits on the line of text marked by the insertion point.

If you insert a graphic into a separate paragraph—so that it's the only "character" in the paragraph—you can use WordPad's paragraph alignment commands to position the image. With the insertion point on the same line as the graphic, click on any of the alignment buttons on the Format bar or use the Format ➤ Paragraph command to choose the correct alignment.

An alternative is to move the graphic by typing characters to the left or right on that same line. If the right edge of the graphic passes the right indent setting for the current paragraph, WordPad wraps the graphic down a line, repositioning it on the left side, just as when wrapping text.

To move a graphic, begin by positioning the insertion point to its left, and then:

- Press Backspace to move it to the left (or up a line, if it's already at the left side of the paragraph).

- Press the spacebar or Tab key to move it to the right.

- Press Enter to move it down in the file.

Another way to change the *vertical* location of a graphic is to select it (by clicking on it), cut it to the Clipboard, click where you want to move the graphic, and paste it into place.

Sizing the Graphic

You can resize a graphic in WordPad, too. Here's how:

1. Select the graphic by clicking on it. The rectangular frame indicating the boundaries of the graphic appears, with small black squares called *handles* at the corners and at the center of each side.

2. Drag the handles to resize the graphic. You can resize in both the horizontal and vertical dimensions by dragging a corner handle. Drag a side handle if you want to resize in one dimension only.

3. When you're finished stretching or shrinking the image, release the mouse button. If you don't like the results, Undo will return the graphic to its previous size.

Notice that you can distort the picture if you want to by making it long and skinny or short and fat. In general, you'll get best results by trying to maintain its original proportions, or *aspect ratio*, by changing both the width and height by the same percentage.

To avoid distortion when the picture is printed, keep the x and y values (in the status line) the same, and keep them in whole numbers rather than fractions.

Also, be aware that bitmapped images, such as Paint pictures and scanned photos, never look as good when resized. If you shrink them, you lose detail; if you stretch them, curved edges look blocky.

Inserting Graphics as Objects

When you place a graphic into a WordPad document using the Clipboard, the connection between the image and Paint (or whatever application created it) is broken. If you need to edit the graphic, you'll need to delete it from WordPad, then start all over in Paint.

Unless you're sure the graphic is final, it makes more sense to insert it using Windows 98's OLE capability. That way, the graphic remains *live* in your document—you can edit it in place without leaving WordPad. See Chapter 6 for step-by-step instructions on how to link and embed objects into your documents.

Saving Your Work

WordPad stores your document in memory while you work on it. However, memory is not a permanent storage area; you will lose your work when you turn off your computer unless you first save it to disk.

You save your documents with two commands: File ➢ Save and File ➢ Save As. The first time you save a document, WordPad will ask you for a name to give your document—in this situation, the Save and Save As commands work the same. After the initial save, WordPad assumes you want to use the current name unless you indicate otherwise by using the Save As command.

Remember to save your work frequently. Nothing hurts like losing forever an afternoon's inspired writing. Taking a few moments to save your document every five or ten minutes is much easier on the psyche.

There are three ways to save a file: File ➢ Save, the Save button (the one with the picture of a floppy disk, shown below) and the Ctrl-S key combination.

No matter which of these methods you use to start the process, the Save As dialog box, shown in Figure 20.15, appears because this is the first time you've saved this file.

FIGURE 20.15

The Save As dialog box appears when you choose to save a file. After making sure the drive and directory are correct, type in the filename.

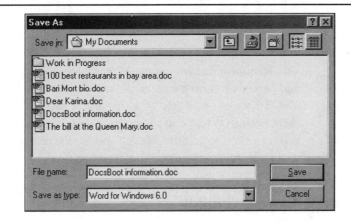

WordPad has assigned a generic name, Document, but you can change it. Finish saving your file as follows:

1. Type in a more descriptive name in the File Name box.

2. Ensure that the correct drive and directory are selected.

3. If you wish to change the type of file you'll be saving, do so by picking a new choice from the Save as Type drop-down list box.

4. Click on OK.

The Save as Type drop-down list box is normally set to store your document in the Word for Windows 6 format. Different programs use different coding systems, or *formats,* to store the document's text, its character and paragraph formatting, any graphics or other objects, and other miscellaneous information. You shouldn't alter this setting unless you want to create a document that other word processors or other types of programs can read.

NOTE

There are two distinct uses for the term *format*: It can refer to the way a document is stored in a disk file or to the appearance of text in a document.

The following are the various formats in which you can save a WordPad document:

- Word for Windows 6.0 format stores the document in the same format used by Microsoft Word for Windows, version 6.0. If you open the document with Word, all the text, character and paragraph formatting, graphics, and other objects will be preserved.

- Rich Text Format is used as a common format for exchanging documents between word processors, but none of them use it as their primary format (it's sort of like Esperanto for word processors). The Rich Text Format preserves the appearance as well as the content of your document. Graphics and other objects are saved in the file along with the text, but they may be lost when you open the file with another application.

- Text Files format saves the file with only text and without any of the character and paragraph formatting you've added. Such files are also known as *plain* text files. They can be opened by a text editor such as Notepad. You can also open them with DOS text editors such as PC-Write, WordStar, or Sidekick (although you may need to add line breaks, and special characters such as bullets will not display or print properly).

Opening Other Documents

Once a WordPad document has been saved on disk, you can come back to it at any future time. To *open* a document—moving the information stored on disk into RAM so you can work with it again—use the Open command.

Keep in mind that in WordPad, unlike fancier word processors, you can only work with one document at a time. When you open a document, it replaces the one you were working with, if any. If you want to keep the changes you made in a document, you must save that document before opening a new one. But don't worry—WordPad will remind you to save before it lets you open another document.

As usual, you have several options for opening existing documents: choose File ➤ Open, press Ctrl-O, or click on the Open button (the one with a picture of a file folder opening, shown below) on the toolbar.

Regardless of which technique you use, you'll see the Open dialog box. After listing any subdirectories, this dialog box shows you all the files in the current directory matching the setting in the Files of Type drop-down list box. Unless someone has changed the entry, you'll see a list of all files stored in the Word for Windows format, WordPad's preferred format.

To open a document, double-click on it in the list or click once on the document and then click on Open. At this point, if you haven't already saved the previous document, WordPad asks if you want to do so. Choose Yes or No, as you prefer.

A Shortcut for Opening Recent Documents

WordPad lists the last four documents you've opened on the File menu. If you want to reopen any of these documents, do it the quick way: open the File menu, then choose the document by name from the menu.

WordPad will open the document immediately without displaying the Open dialog box (you'll still receive a message asking if you want to save the current document if you haven't done so yet).

Opening Documents Stored in Other Formats

Although WordPad's standard format for storing documents on disk is the Word for Windows 6.0 format, WordPad can also open documents stored in several other formats. Formats WordPad can open include:

- Windows Write format (Write was a simple word processor included with earlier versions of Windows)
- Rich Text Format
- Text-only files

If you know the format of the document you want to open, select that format in the Files of Type drop-down list box. If you're unsure of the format, choose All Files instead, and WordPad will display all the files in the current directory. Once you locate the correct document in the list, double-click on it to open it.

WordPad automatically opens Word for Windows, Windows Write, and Rich Text Format files, even those incorrectly named. If someone has improperly renamed say, a Word for Windows-format document, the Open dialog box may not show it even when the Files of Type setting is correct. However, WordPad can still open the document if you locate it with All Files selected in the Files of Type box or if you type in the document's name in the File Name box.

All other documents are opened as text-only files. If the document contains formatting information from some other application, WordPad will display the entire document, including the formatting information, as ordinary text. You'll likely see gibberish mixed in with intelligible text.

Converting ASCII Files

When opening most text-only files created by DOS programs, WordPad interprets each line of text as a separate paragraph (in these *ASCII* files, paragraphs are typically set apart by a blank line).

The only way to fix the problem is to delete the unwanted paragraph dividers once you open the document into WordPad. It's best to do this systematically, immediately after you open the document.

Follow these steps to fix each paragraph. Skip paragraphs that are only one line long:

1. Move the cursor to the end of the first line of the paragraph. Press Delete to remove the paragraph division. This will pull up the previous line to the cursor.

2. Press the spacebar to add a space between the two words on either side of the cursor, if necessary.

3. Repeat the above steps on all lines of the paragraph *except* the last one.

Opening a New Document

Whenever you start WordPad, the program opens a new, empty document for you. To create a new document after working with an existing one, however, you need the New command. Here's how to do it:

1. Choose Edit ➢ New or click on the New button on the toolbar—it's the one that looks like a blank sheet of paper.

2. If you haven't already saved the current document, WordPad gives you a chance to do so.

3. WordPad now asks you what format you want to use for the new document: Word for Windows, Rich Text, or Text Only. Select the desired format in the list and choose OK. The new document will appear in the window.

Display Options

You have some choices about the way the WordPad window looks and works. As you learned earlier, the View menu lets you turn on or off any of the individual control bars: the toolbar, the Format bar, the ruler, and the Status bar. Other display options are available via the Options dialog box.

To open the Options dialog box, choose View ➢ Options. You'll see the dialog box shown in Figure 20.16.

The Options dialog box is tabbed. One tab covers general options; the remaining tabs apply to the various document types (file formats) that WordPad can handle.

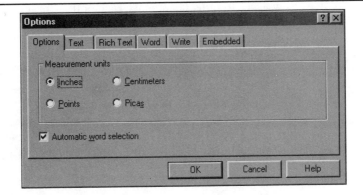

FIGURE 20.16

The Options dialog box lets you set measurement units for the ruler and for spacing settings, among other choices.

Selecting Measurement Units and Controlling Word Selection

Click on the tab labeled Options in the Options dialog box to set measurement units for your document. You can choose from inches, centimeters, points, and picas (the last two units are used by typesetters). If the ruler is visible, it will be displayed with the selected measurement units. In addition, spacing settings in the Paragraph Spacing and Page Setup dialog boxes will be listed in the chosen unit.

Regardless of the Measurement Units setting in the Options dialog box, you can enter new settings in the Paragraph Spacing and Page Setup dialog boxes in any unit by typing the unit abbreviation after the value. For example, type **1.5 in** to enter a left margin of 1.5 inches, **2.3 cm** to enter a right margin of 2.3 centimeters.

The only other choice on the Options tab is a checkbox labeled Automatic Word Selection. With this setting checked, the mouse selects entire words when you drag the pointer across two or more words. You can still select a group of characters within a single word by holding down Shift while pressing the arrow keys. Remove the check in the Automatic Word Selection box if you want the selection to cover only the characters you actually drag the pointer across.

Choosing Display Options for Each Type of Document

Aside from the page labeled Options, the other pages in the Options dialog box pertain to the various types of documents that WordPad can open—Word for Windows 6.0, Windows Write, Rich Text Format, and text-only files, as well as WordPad documents embedded via OLE in other documents. Each of these pages offer identical choices, as shown in Figure 20.17.

The Options dialog box offers these choices for each type of file WordPad can handle.

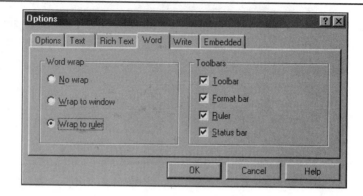

The checkboxes on the right let you select which of the control bars (the toolbar, Format bar, ruler, and Status bar) WordPad will display automatically when you open a document of the type indicated by the tab.

On the left side of each tabbed panel are radio buttons for selecting the way Word-Pad wraps your text from line to line on the screen. Note that none of these choices affects the way your document prints:

No Wrap: If this button is selected, WordPad doesn't wrap your text at all. As you add text anywhere within a line, the line keeps expanding toward the right, regardless of the right indent and right margin settings. On printed copies, the text still wraps according to the indent and margin settings.

Wrap to Window: With this button selected, WordPad wraps the text to fit within the document window, ignoring the right indent and margin settings. Choose this setting to see all your text, even when the WordPad window is nar-rower than the paragraph width set by the ruler. Again, this doesn't affect printed documents.

Wrap to Ruler: When this button is selected, the displayed text wraps according to the right indent and right margin settings as shown on the ruler (whether or not the ruler is visible).

Printing Your Documents

Generally speaking, the ultimate goal of all your typing and formatting is a printed copy of your document. Printing a WordPad document is a straightforward process. Like the major-league word processors, WordPad lets you see a preview of your document as it will appear in print, and you can fix your mistakes before they appear on paper.

Seeing a Preview of Your Printed Document

Instead of wasting paper on a document with an obvious layout mistake, use Word-Pad's Print Preview command to inspect your work before you print. This command displays your document on screen just as it will look when printed. You can look at entire pages to check the overall layout or zoom in on a particular portion to check details.

To see a preview, choose File ➢ Print Preview, or click on the Print Preview button in the toolbar—it's the button with the picture of a magnifying glass over a sheet of paper, shown below.

The WordPad window fills with a mock-up of your document, fitting two full pages into the available space, as shown in Figure 20.18. A special toolbar offers quick access to a number of special commands, and the mouse pointer becomes a magnifying glass.

FIGURE 20.18

WordPad's Print Preview window

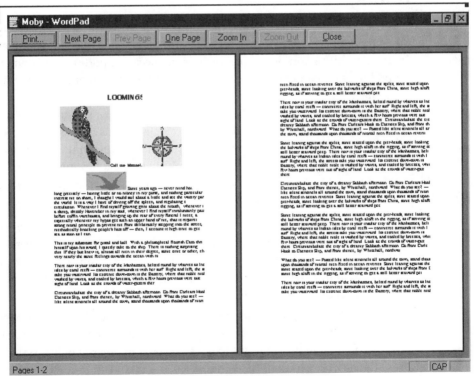

At this level of magnification, you can't read ordinary-size text, but you can check for problems with page margins, paragraph alignment, and spacing. Clicking anywhere on the document window changes the magnification, cycling through the three available levels. Starting from the full-page view, the first click zooms you in on the portion of the page you clicked on, the second gives you a life-size close-up of a still smaller area, and the third click returns you to the full-page view. You can also change the magnification by clicking on the Zoom In or Zoom Out buttons in the toolbar.

To page through the mock-up of your document, click on the Next Page button. You can move back toward the beginning with the Prev Page button. To display only a single page of the document instead of two, click on the One Page button. You can switch back to the two-page view by clicking on the same button, which will now read Two Page. You can also page through the mock-up with the PgUp and PgDn keys.

When you're satisfied that the document looks as you expected, click on the Print button to begin the actual printing process, covered in the next section. On the other hand, if you find mistakes, click on the Close button to return to editing the document.

Printing

When you are about ready to print, don't forget to save your file first just in case the computer or the printer goes berserk in the process and you lose your file. If you want to print only a portion of your document, select that portion. And don't forget to turn on the printer and make sure it has paper and is ready to print (in other words, that it is *online*).

First, choose File ➤ Page Setup, and check that paper size and paper source are correctly set. (Notice that you can print envelopes via this setting.) Then choose File ➤ Print, press Ctrl-P, or click on the Print button from the Print Preview window. You'll be presented with a dialog box asking you about the following options:

Name (of Printer): If the printer you plan to use isn't already chosen in this box, choose it from the drop-down list of your installed printers.

Properties: This button takes you to the Printer Properties dialog box for the selected printer. From this dialog box, you can choose the paper orientation (portrait or landscape), paper size and feed, print quality (for text) and resolution (for graphics), and other options available for your printer. See the discussion of printer properties in Chapter 8 for details.

Print Range: If you want to print all the pages, click on All. If you want to print specific pages only, click on Pages and type in the range of page numbers you want to print in the From and To boxes. If you want to print only text that you selected, click on Selection.

Copies: Specify the number of copies of each page to be printed.

Collate: Choose whether each complete copy should be printed one at a time, in page order (more convenient but slower), or all copies of each page should be printed before moving onto the next page (quicker but requires you to hand collate). This option applies only if you're printing more than one copy of the document.

When you've made your choices, press Enter or click on OK. If the printer is connected and working properly, you should have a paper copy of your document in a few moments.

Quick Printing with the Print Button

If you're sure the settings in the Print dialog box are already correct and you want a copy of the entire document, you can streamline the printing process via the toolbar's Print button—it's the one showing the picture of a printer ejecting a page.

When you click on the Print button, WordPad immediately begins sending your document to the printer via the Windows Print Manager. You don't need to deal with the Print dialog box.

Chapter

21

Using Paint and Kodak Imaging

FEATURING

Kinds of Images

Basic painting techniques

Manipulating areas of a picture

Zooming in for detail work

Editing the color scheme

Printing

Working with GIFs, JPGs, Photos, and Fax

Using Paint
and Kodak Imaging

T his chapter will cover two programs you
get for free with Windows 98: *Microsoft
Paint* and *Kodak Imaging*. Microsoft Paint
(Paint, for short) is the fourth generation of a program that's been supplied with Windows since version 3.0. It's a bitmap image editing program you can use to draw or
edit simple graphics (.BMP files) of various types such as doodles or sketches, or even
complex works, if you have the patience. Paint's emphasis is on freehand drawing.

Kodak Imaging is a recent addition and was written by Kodak (the camera and film
people) and licensed to Microsoft for inclusion with Windows 98. It's the default "quick
viewer" for looking at image files in Windows. It's also capable of creating, scanning, faxing, or emailing single- or multiple-page graphical documents. Imaging lets you annotate (mark up with text) and do freehand drawing on images. For the most part, you
could think of Imaging as a viewer program or organizational tool for existing documents, though you can create new works with it.

There are better programs for doing all that these two do, but then again, you'll pay
big time for programs like Adobe Illustrator, Adobe Photoshop, or CorelDRAW. Paint
and Imaging come free with Windows 98.

Let's look at both of these freebies, and what you can do with them.

Using Paint

Paint is a program for the artist in you. It's a simple but quite capable program for painting and drawing images on your computer screen, and optionally printing them out. You can brush on colors free-form, draw lines and geometric shapes, and even add text to your pictures. A variety of nifty special effects are at your command, too.

Here are some ideas for things you can do with Paint:

- Create printed signs.
- Create illustrations for printed matter.
- Create images for use in other Windows programs.
- Design invitations.
- Enhance digitized images or photographs.
- Draw maps.
- Make wallpaper images for your Windows Desktop.
- Edit clip art (pre-drawn images you can buy in collections).
- Clean up "digital dust" from scanned images.
- Edit graphics embedded or linked into documents created by other programs (see Chapter 6).

Starting a New Document

To bring up Paint:

1. Beginning from the Taskbar, choose Start ➢ Programs ➢ Accessories ➢ Paint.
2. The Paint window appears. Maximize the window. Figure 21.1 shows the Paint window and its component parts.

The *work area* is the main part of the window where you do your painting. Along the left side, the *Tool Box* provides a set of buttons for activating the tools you use to paint. You choose colors from the *Color Box* at the bottom of the window. The Status Bar offers help messages on menu choices and displays the coordinates of the mouse pointer.

FIGURE 21.1

The Paint window

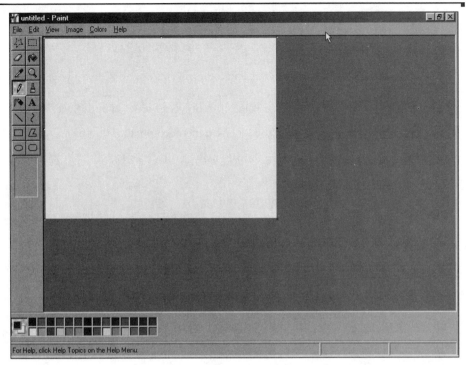

Update Notes from 3.x and Windows 95

Compared to its Windows 3.x predecessor, Paintbrush, Paint has more features, it looks a little snazzier, and some of the commands and buttons have changed. Still, Paint will seem very familiar if you've worked with Paintbrush. The one big difference that you might not notice is this: You can paint with the *right* mouse button, not just the left (using the right button paints with the background color). Aside from that, most of the tools work about the same as they did in Paintbrush.

Though they aren't earth shattering, new features are plentiful in Paint. You get two new tools: the eyedropper and the pencil. Manipulating selections is much easier now that they have resize handles, and you can rotate them or even use them as a brush shape. Print Preview lets you check your work before you print, saving paper and time. It's easier to work with text by virtue of the Text Toolbar (for setting font, size, and style). And you can Undo three previous commands, not just one.

Continued

CONTINUED

You give up some features, too. The color eraser tool is gone. You can't save files in the PCX (PC Paintbrush) format, and you can't use shadow or outline styles with text. Paintbrush let you print headers and footers, Paint does not. But if you are enamored of any of these features, you don't have to give them up. Because both programs can open the same files, you can keep Paintbrush on your hard disk and use it when the need arises.

Here's a list of some of the tools and menu commands that have changed:

In Paintbrush	In Paint
Paint roller	Paint Can
Shrink and Grow	Stretch
Tilt	Skew
Inverse	Invert Colors

Additions new to Windows 98 are the ability to save files in JPG and GIF formats in addition to the usual bitmapped (BMP) formats, but only if the appropriate Office97 Graphics Import Filters are installed. If you have installed Office 97 with those options, the Open and Save As dialog boxes will include GIF and JPG extensions. Otherwise only BMP files are supported. Also, a few menu rearrangements such as the Options menu being replaced by a Colors menu.

Understanding Computer Art

Before going any further, let's pause a minute for a little background on how Paint works—it will help you to get the results you want from your artistic creations. In the personal-computer world there are two basic classes of pictures, or graphics: *bitmapped* and *object-oriented*. Paint can create and edit only bitmapped graphics, so let's focus there (more on object-oriented graphics in a moment).

In programs like Paint, you create a picture on the computer screen as if you were painting on a canvas with paint. Imagine yourself painting the Mona Lisa. With each stroke of the brush, the paint you apply to the canvas sticks irreversibly, covering up whatever was there before.

In Paint, you use colored dots on the screen as your paint, but the process is otherwise quite similar. Once you've placed anything on the screen (and unless you use Undo immediately), it becomes an integral part of the image. It remains there until you cover it up with something else.

Here's why Paint works this way. Your computer's screen is divided into very small dots (*pixels* or *pels*) that are controlled by the smallest division of computer information—bits. A bit map is a collection of bits of information that creates an image when assigned (*mapped*) to dots on the screen. This is similar to a sports scoreboard that can display the score, a message, or even a picture by turning on and off specific lightbulbs in a grid.

The point is, the only thing Paint knows about the image on your screen is which dot should be displayed in which color. When you change the picture, Paint doesn't keep track of whether you paint a line, draw a circle, or type some text. Instead, it simply changes its map of colored dots—the new dots blend into all the other ones.

What all this means is that bitmapped graphics can be incredibly detailed because you can control the color of each and every dot in your picture if you want to (with the Zoom command). That's why bitmapped graphics are used to create artwork with the rich detail of a real painting and to store photographic images that have been recorded by a scanner.

On the other hand, there are some limitations to keep in mind. Once you paint a shape, you can't move it independently. True, you can use the computer to remove an area of the painting and place it somewhere else—as if you were cutting out a piece of the canvas and pasting it elsewhere. But *all* the dots in the area get moved, not just the ones in the shape you're interested in. Also, because a bitmapped graphic has a fixed number of dots, its resolution is fixed—you can't make it look sharper by printing it on a higher-resolution printer, for example.

By contrast, in object-oriented graphics, the computer stores each shape as a separate entity—it's something like those felt boards you used in grade school. Each line, circle, and text character retains its identity as a separate object. These objects can later be moved, sized, cut, copied, and otherwise altered without affecting anything else in the picture. In addition, object-oriented graphics always display and print at the maximum possible resolution of the device you're using.

With object-oriented graphics it's harder to do detailed work, especially involving random shapes and color blends, than with bitmapped graphics. On the other hand, this type of computer art is great for line drawings, logos, and poster-like illustrations.

Windows 98 doesn't come with an object-oriented graphics program. Popular programs of this type include CorelDRAW, Adobe Illustrator, and Micrografx Designer. Also, simple object-oriented graphics modules are included in many word processors and spreadsheets.

Enough theory.

Opening an Existing Picture

To open an existing picture for editing, do the following:

1. Choose File ➢ Open.

2. Select the picture by name in the Open dialog box. Windows 98 comes with many BMP files scattered around through various folders. I used the Start ➢ Find ➢ Files or Folders command to find one. I entered *.BMP as the "named" section of the Find box and found 953 BMP files. The file open in Figure 21.2 I found in my Program Files\Chat directory.

FIGURE 21.2
A picture file opened and displayed in the work area

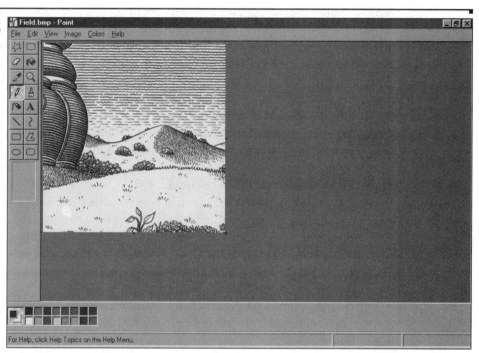

Now you can edit the picture and save it again or copy any part of it to the Clipboard for use with other programs.

Paint remembers the last four pictures you've opened or saved, listing them by name at the bottom of the File menu. To open one of these pictures without slowing down for the Open dialog box, just choose the picture from the File menu.

Paint can only open pictures stored in its own format (also known as the BMP format). If you want to open pictures stored in other formats, such as PCX or TIF, you'll have to translate them to the BMP format with conversion software first. If you've installed Microsoft Office with the GIF and JPG converters options installed, your Open and Save dialog boxes will have the ability to open GIF and JPG files:

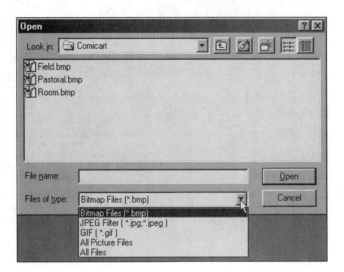

Seeing More of the Picture

If the picture is too big to fit in the work area, you can, of course, scroll to see any part of the image. But scrolling is a nuisance. You can also take steps to see more of the picture all at once, as detailed in the following sections.

Removing and Tearing Off the Tool and Color Boxes

The simplest method to increase your viewing area is to remove the tools along the left side and bottom of the Paint window. Actually, you don't have to give them up entirely—you can "tear them off" as floating windows that are easy to reposition on the screen.

To tear off the Tool Box or the Color Box, click on any part of the box's background. Hold down the mouse button and drag the window outline that appears into the work area. As shown in Figure 21.3, the box becomes a separate floating window that you can move around as needed to work with your picture.

If you don't need the Tool Box or Color Box—not very likely, but once in a while this may be the case—you can turn them off altogether. Open the View menu and choose the corresponding menu command. You can also remove the Status Bar at the very bottom of the screen this way. To turn on an item back on, just choose its command again from the View menu.

NOTE

When a screen item (Tool Box, Color Box, or Status Bar) is visible, the View menu displays a checkmark beside the item's command; there's no checkmark if the item has been turned off.

Alternatively, if you've torn off a box, making it a separate window, you can remove it from the screen by clicking on its close box. To turn it on again, choose the corresponding item on the View menu. It will appear on the screen in its last location.

Displaying Only the Picture

If you just want to look at as much of your picture as possible, choose View ➢ View Bitmap. The picture fills the entire Paint window—all the other screen elements, including the title bar, menu bar, and scroll bars disappear. You still may not be able to see the whole picture, of course, but this is as good as it gets. And all you can do is look at the picture—you can't make any changes. Clicking anywhere on the screen or pressing any key returns you to the working screen.

Creating a New Picture

To start a new picture, choose File ➢ New to erase the previous image, then choose Image ➢ Attributes to set the picture size and select *color* or *black-and-white.*

If another picture is open, choose File ➢ New to begin work on a new, blank "canvas." If you haven't already saved the previous picture, Paint will ask if you want to do so. The existing image will then disappear, leaving the work area empty.

Setting a Picture's Basic Characteristics

Before you actually start painting, decide whether you want to change any of Paint's standard settings governing the picture's basic characteristics: its size and whether it's a color or black-and-white image. To change the settings for either of these characteristics, choose Image ➢ Attributes to display the Attributes dialog box shown below.

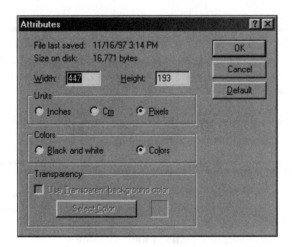

Setting Picture Size

The first thing you should decide when starting a new picture is how big it should be. If you're creating a picture to fit snugly into another document, or if you have an idea of how much room you'll need to express your ideas, defining the picture's size now may save you some work down the road. It's easy to change the size of a picture, so don't spend much time on this decision.

Keep in mind that the size of the image you see is tied to the resolution of your screen. Actually, the size settings control only the number of dots in the picture (even though you can set the size in inches or centimeters in the Attributes dialog box). If you increase the resolution of your screen (see Chapter 7), the picture will look smaller because each component dot is smaller.

Likewise, the image will almost certainly print smaller than it appears on your screen because most printers have much higher resolution than even an SVGA or XGA monitor.

 **TIP**

If you're planning to print the image, choose size settings according to the printed size you plan, not the screen size. For example, if you want the image to be 3×5 inches on the printed page and your printer's resolution is 300 dots per inch, you would enter a width of 900 pixels and a height of 1,500 pixels. Remember too that if your picture is wider than it is tall, and if its printed width is more than about 8 inches, you'll need to change the page orientation for printing from Portrait to Landscape. Choose File ➤ Page Setup and select the appropriate button.

 NOTE

The maximum size of a picture is limited by the amount of memory available in your computer. Maximum size also depends on the color scheme: black-and-white pictures use far less memory than color pictures do, so they can be much larger. Paint will let you know if you set a picture size that's too large to fit in memory.

 NOTE

When you change the size of a picture, Paint remembers the new dimensions. From then on—until you make further size changes—Paint uses these dimensions whenever you choose File ➤ New to create a new picture. This is true even if you open other larger or smaller pictures in the meantime.

You can resize a picture with the mouse or by typing entries in the Attributes dialog box. Using the mouse is easier if the entire picture fits in the work area, but many pictures are bigger than that. Besides, whereas the mouse isn't very accurate, you can type exact dimensions. At any rate, you use the same resizing techniques whether you're working with a brand new picture or an existing one.

To set the size of your picture with the Attributes dialog box:

1. Choose Image ➢ Attributes. The Attributes dialog box appears.

2. Decide on the measurement units you want to use and click on the corresponding radio button. Pixels (screen dots) is the standard unit, but you can choose inches or centimeters instead.

3. Type in new width and height values. At any time, you can return to the standard size values—equal to the size of your screen—by clicking on Default.

4. Click on OK to return to Paint. The size of your canvas will change according to your entries, though you can only see this if the entire canvas fits within the work area.

To resize a picture with the mouse:

1. Find the picture's sizing handles, the small squares at the bottom-right corner of the picture and along the bottom and right edges. If the picture is larger than the work area, you'll have to scroll down or to the right to see the sizing handles. (The handles at the other three corners and along the other edges do nothing.)

2. To change the picture's width, drag the handle on the right edge to the left (to make the picture narrower) or to the right (to make the picture wider). To change the height, drag the bottom-edge handle up or down. To change both dimensions simultaneously, drag the handle at the bottom-right corner.

Setting the Image to Color or Black-and-White

Paint can handle both color and black-and-white images. Of course, if you want to create a cartoon or line drawing, you can do it with a color picture by painting with a black brush only. The only real reason to set the picture itself to a black-and-white "color" scheme is to save memory or disk space. Black-and-white pictures consume one-fourth as much memory and disk space as the simplest color pictures. If you need a very large image, and memory or disk space is limited, black-and-white may be your only choice.

NOTE

Paint's black-and-white setting restricts you to two "colors" only, black and white (the speckled-looking choices on the color palette are patterns of black and white dots). A black-and-white image is *not* the same thing as a gray-scale image, in which you can paint with 16 or more separate shades of gray. To create a grayscale image, you must place the desired shades of gray on the palette—see *Editing the Color Scheme* later in this chapter.

You're not likely to get great results when converting an existing color image to black-and-white. Paint converts light colors to white and darker colors to black, and you have no control over the process. In most cases, you'll lose much of the image detail.

WARNING

You can't undo a change from color to black-and-white. Be sure you want to make the change. If you're working with an existing color picture, make a backup copy before you convert it to black-and-white.

To set up a new black-and-white picture, or to convert an existing color picture to black-and-white:

1. Choose Image ➤ Attributes to open the Attributes dialog box.

2. Choose the *Black-and-white* radio button and click on OK. Any existing colors in the picture will be converted to either black or white.

Remember, this change is permanent.

NOTE

New pictures always open in color, even if you changed a previous picture to black-and-white.

Basic Painting Techniques

Once you've created a new, empty painting, you're ready to try your hand at computer art. Feel free to play with the tools as much as you want—you can't hurt anything, and the learn-by-doodling approach is fun.

In this section I'll explain each of the on-screen controls in the Color Box and Tool Box and suggest some tips and tricks to make your work easier. You might want to sit at your computer and work with each of the tools as you read, changing colors to suit your fancy along the way. Pretty soon you'll have a good high-tech mess on your screen, at which point you can just choose File ➤ New again to clear it and be ready for more experimentation. (When asked about saving your work, click on No unless you really like it.)

Setting the Foreground and Background Colors

NOTE

The term *color* describes either a color or a colored pattern selected from the Color Box. If you are using a black-and-white screen, colors in the Color Box may appear as shades of gray or varying densities of dot patterns.

One of the most fundamental techniques to learn is selecting a color to paint with. In Paint, you control both foreground and background colors independently.

Understanding Foreground and Background Colors

The foreground or drawing color is the main color you paint with. For example, when you add strokes with Paint's paintbrush, draw lines or shapes, or even when you type text, these items appear in the currently selected foreground color.

The term *background color* is somewhat different. Once you have a picture on your screen, many of the tools (such as the Brush, Pencil, and the shape tools) let you paint with the so-called background color just as you would with the foreground color. All you have to do is hold down the right mouse button instead of the left one as you paint. The background color also determines the fill color for circles, squares, and other enclosed shapes, the fill color inside text frames, and the color with which you erase existing parts of the picture. If you select a section of the picture and drag it to another location, the resulting "hole" will be filled with the background color. You can change the background color as many times as you like.

Choosing a Color Scheme: Basic Tips

You'll get the best results if you stick with solid colors. Here's the scoop: the number of separate solid colors you can use depends on the capabilities of your display hardware and the specific software driver setting you've chosen. Most screens allow at least 256 colors these days, and many will displays roughly 64,000 ("high color") or even 16.7 million colors ("true color").

On some older systems that can only display 16 colors, Paint uses patterns made up of dots of different colors to represent hues that it can't display as solid colors. These patterns tend to look murky or fuzzy in your pictures. Avoid them when possible.

Also, keep in mind the color capabilities of your printer when you choose colors for your picture. An image that looks great on your screen can become a blurry gray soup when you print it out on a black-and-white printer. When Windows prints to a black-and-white printer, it attempts to translate colors into contrasting shades of gray (actually, gray shades are simulated with different densities of black dots). Sometimes the translation gives you good results, but if not, experiment with the color scheme until you find one that produces a clear image in print—even if the colors clash horribly on the screen. If that doesn't work, just stick with painting in black on a white background.

Viewing and Changing Color Settings

The current settings of the foreground and background colors are shown in the area at the left side of the Color Box. In this area, the box on top toward the upper left shows the foreground color. The box in back, toward the lower right, shows the background color. The default colors are a black foreground on a white background, and they always come up that way when you open a new or existing picture.

You choose new foreground and background colors by selecting them in the Color Box, as described below. Alternatively, you can use the Eyedropper tool, described later, to use a color from the picture as the new foreground or background color.

Setting the Foreground and Background Colors

Set the foreground color as follows:

1. Point to the color or pattern you want.

2. Click the *left* mouse button. Now whatever you paint with the tools using the left mouse button will appear in this color. Notice that the foreground color box at the left side of the Color Box reflects your color choice.

To set the background color:

1. Point to the color or pattern in the Color Box.

2. Click the *right* mouse button. The background color box at the left side of the Color Box changes accordingly.

WARNING

You can't change the color of an existing picture's actual background by changing the background color with the Color Box.

TIP

If you want to start a new picture with a certain color as the "canvas," here's how. Before painting anything on the picture, choose the correct background color and click anywhere over the work area with the Paint Can tool, described below. The entire picture area will change to that color. Now start painting. Alternatively, after choosing the desired background color, draw anything in the work area, then choose Image ➤ Clear Image.

Selecting Colors with the Eyedropper Tool

An alternative technique for selecting colors: the Eyedropper tool.

The Eyedropper lets you "suck up" a color that already appears in the picture. That color becomes the new foreground or background color for use with any of the painting tools.

Be aware, though, that the Eyedropper can only detect solid colors. If the shade you're interested in is a composite of two or more solid colors, the Eyedropper will select only one of those colors, not the shade.

Here's how to use the Eyedropper:

1. Click on the Eyedropper tool in the Tool Box.

2. In the picture, click over the desired color with the left button to select it as the foreground color, with the right button to make it the background color. The Color Box display changes accordingly.

You can now paint with the chosen color using any of the painting tools as detailed in the next section.

Using the Painting Tools

Here's a brief description of how each of the tools in the Tool Box works:

1. Click on the tool you want to use. This selects the tool.

2. Position the pointer in the work area where you want to start painting, selecting, or erasing, and then click and hold the mouse button.

3. Drag to paint, select, or erase. Release the mouse button when you are through.

Paint's Tool Box offers a slew of useful controls to help you realize your artistic vision. Here's the Tool Box:

To choose a tool, you simply click on its button in the Tool Box. The tool is then activated (and highlighted), and the pointer changes shape when you move back into the work area. In most cases, the tool stays selected until you choose another one.

When some of the tools are selected, the area below the grid of buttons provides options for the selected tool. The options are different for each tool. For example, if you're drawing with the line tool, you can choose how thick the line should be by clicking on an icon in this area. If there are no options associated with a tool, this area is empty.

The following sections will describe each of the painting tools.

The Brush

The Brush is the basic painting tool. It works like a paint brush, pen, or marker. Use this tool to create freehand art.

With the Brush, you can paint in either the foreground or the background color, switching between the two by simply changing which mouse button you press. All of the painting tools that add lines, strokes, or enclosed shapes work this way.

Here's how to use the Brush:

1. In the Color Box, select the foreground and background colors you want to paint with by clicking on them with the left button and right buttons, respectively.

2. Choose the Brush button in the Tool Box.

3. Pick a size and shape for your brush from the tool options area in the bottom of the Tool Box. The diagonal brush shapes produce lines that vary in width depending on which direction you move the brush—it's a calligraphic pen effect.

4. Move the pointer over the work area so it becomes a crosshair. Press and hold the left button to paint with the foreground color, the right button to paint with the background color. Paint by dragging the mouse around in the work area. Release the button when you want to stop painting. Repeat the process as often as you like.

In Figure 21.4 you can see a simple design created with the brush.

FIGURE 21.4

A freehand design made with the brush

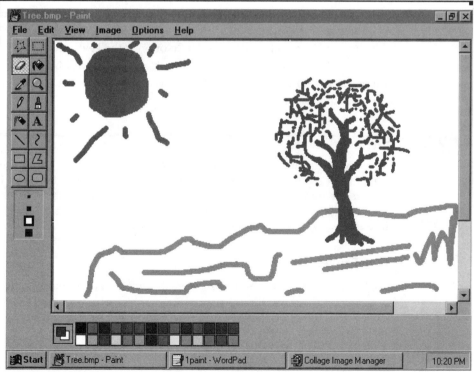

NOTE

You can also paint with a custom brush that you create by copying it from the picture. This brush can be any shape and can contain multiple colors. You don't use the Brush tool for this—see "Sweeping" later in this chapter for the technique.

TIP

The status bar reports the location of the cursor while you draw. This can be useful for doing precision work. A second readout farther to the left is only active when you're drawing shapes such as boxes, ellipses, and polygons or when you're selecting an area of the picture. This set of coordinates tells you where the mouse pointer is relative to the location where you started drawing the shape or where you began selecting.

Undoing Mistakes   Each addition you make to a picture ultimately loses its individual identity, becoming part of the image. Paint does keep track of the most recent additions, though, as separate items, giving you a chance to undo your mistakes.

You can use the Undo command to eliminate the last *three* additions to the picture. Each time you make a new change, Paint "forgets" the fourth most recent change, and it becomes permanent.

To activate Undo, choose Edit ➢ Undo or press the keyboard shortcut, Ctrl-Z.

Paint will even let you redo changes you've removed with Undo. To restore what you previously undid, choose Edit ➢ Repeat or press F4. Again, you can restore as many as three changes.

TIP

Here's another way to undo your mistakes: If you realize something is wrong in the middle of any painting operation, such as using the Brush, drawing a line, or even using the Eraser, click the *right* mouse button *before* you release the left button. Whatever changes you were in the process of making disappear—it's as if you never started.

The Eraser

The Eraser works like the eraser on a pencil—only you don't have to rub.

Just pass it across an area, and it erases whatever it touches, leaving nothing but the background color behind. Use the Eraser whether you want to obliterate a major section of your picture or just touch up some stray dots or lines.

> Even the smallest Eraser size covers more than a single dot in your picture. To erase (change) individual dots, use the Pencil tool (see the next section), setting the *foreground* color to the desired erasure color.

The Pencil

The Pencil works much like the Brush for freehand art, except that it only paints lines that are one dot (pixel) wide.

You can produce essentially the same effect with the Brush by choosing the smallest circular shape for the Brush (at the top right of the Brush-shape display), but the Pencil is often a convenient way to draw fine lines freehand while leaving the brush for wider swaths.

You can force the Pencil to draw straight vertical, horizontal, or diagonal lines, something you can't do with the Brush. After selecting the Pencil tool, hold down the Shift key while you drag the mouse. The direction you initially move establishes the line's direction—as long as you hold down Shift, you can only lengthen the line, not change directions (this is different from the way the Line tool works, as described below).

> For precise, dot-by-individual-dot editing, make it easy on yourself—zoom in on your picture to see the detail. See "Zooming In for Detail Work" below.

The Airbrush

Here's a tool that's a legal outlet for repressed graffiti artists.

The Airbrush works like the real thing, or like a spray can, spraying a mist of paint that gets thicker the longer you hold it one place. Think of the mouse button as the button on the top of the spray can. Just set the foreground and background colors, click on the Airbrush tool, move into the picture area and start spraying.

> Moving the mouse quickly results in a finer mist, while letting it sit still or moving very slowly plasters the paint on.

The Line Tool

Use the Line tool to draw straight lines (and only straight lines). You have five line widths to select from.

Hold the Shift key down to force the line to be vertical, horizontal, or at a 45-degree angle.

Below is an example of a drawing made up only of lines.

The Curve Tool

Use the Curve tool for drawing curves, of course. But don't expect to master this tool quickly—it will seem downright strange at first. Start by laying down a straight line, just like you would with the Line tool. Then you get two chances to "stretch" that line into a curve—once from one location and once from another. The result might be an arc, an S curve, or even a pretzel-y shape. You do this by clicking on any part of the line and dragging the crosshair cursor around. The line will stretch like a rubber band. Release the button when the bend is correct.

The Box Tool

The Box tool draws boxes—or rectangles, if you prefer.

You can draw three types of boxes: hollow boxes with borders only; filled, bordered boxes, and solid boxes without borders. Choose the option from the toolbar after you click the tool.

1. Click where you want one corner of the box to start. This sets the anchor.

2. Drag the crosshair down and to one side. As you do, a rectangular outline will appear.

3. Release the mouse button when the size is correct.

TIP

If you draw with the right button instead, the border and interior colors are reversed.
This applies to the other tools for drawing enclosed shapes as well.

TIP

To constrain boxes to be perfect squares, hold down the Shift key as you draw. This
applies to filled boxes as well as to hollow ones.

The Rounded Box Tool

The rounded Box tool works exactly like the regular Box tool described in the previous
section, but it creates boxes with rounded corners, rather than crisp right angles.

The Ellipse Tool

This tool also works just like the Box tool, except that it creates ellipses (ovals).

Use the same basic drawing technique. The rules regarding the fill and border colors
of boxes apply to ellipses, too. Here are some bubble-like objects created with the Ellipse
tool. The perfect circles were created by holding down the Shift key while drawing with
the Ellipse tool.

The Polygon Tool

With the Polygon tool you can create an endless variety of polygonal shapes.

As with the Line tool, you manually draw straight lines—the difference being that
you keep adding endpoints until you complete the polygon's edges.

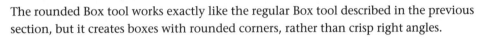

TIP

To constrain any line of the polygon to be vertical, at 45 degrees, or horizontal only,
hold down the Shift key as you draw.

1. If you're drawing a bordered polygon, select the Line tool and choose a line
width for the border.

2. Then choose the polygon tool and choose the type of polygon you want to draw (border only, filled and bordered, or solid with no border).

3. Click and hold the button down. Drag the mouse pointer to the endpoint for the side and release the button. The line you've drawn defines the first side of the polygon.

4. Press and hold the mouse button again as you drag to the endpoint of the next side (or just click over this next endpoint). Paint draws the second side. Continue adding sides in this way, but *double-click* to mark the endpoint of the next-to-the-last side (for example, the fourth side of a pentangle). Paint connects this endpoint with the original anchor point, filling in the polygon if appropriate.

Note that a polygon's sides can cross. You can haphazardly click all over the screen, and, until you double-click, Paint will keep connecting the dots regardless.

You can create a cubist artistic effect with this tool because of the way Paint calculates an enclosed area. It starts at the top of the screen and begins filling areas. If your polygon has a lot of enclosed areas from multiple lines overlapping, Paint alternates the fills. Thus adjacent enclosed areas will not all be filled. Using the tool with the cutout tools and the Invert command can lead to some rather interesting geometrical designs (inverting is covered later in the chapter). Figure 21.5 shows an example of the possibilities.

FIGURE 21.5

A geometric design created with the Polygon tool using filled polygons

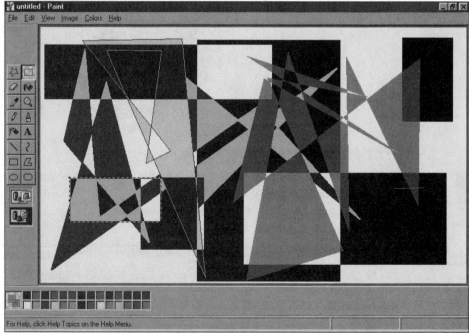

Filling Areas with the Paint Can

The Paint Can will fill in any enclosed area with the foreground color. An *enclosed area* can be defined by any lines or curves in the work area. So three separate lines set up to form a triangle constitute an enclosed space just as much as a box's border does. Because the entire work area is also considered an enclosed space, you can use the Paint Can to change the background of the picture. Letters you create with the Text tool (discussed next) can be filled, too. Just point the tip of the spilling paint into the area to be filled and click. The enclosed area will be filled with the foreground color if you click with the left button, with the background color if you click with the right.

Note that the color flows to fill the entire enclosed area. If there is a "leak" in what you thought was an enclosed area, the paint will seep through the crack, so to speak, and fill everything until it is stopped by a complete boundary. You may accidentally fill the entire work area. If this happens, just choose Undo.

The Text Tool

The Text tool lets you add words to your pictures, which is great when you're designing flyers, invitations, maps, instructions, and the like. This is a good tool for annotating pictures created in other programs. (Kodak Imaging is good for this, too.)

You can add text in two ways: as text only, so that only the characters you type are added to your picture; and as text on a solid rectangular background that covers up whatever was there in the picture. These two styles are also called *transparent* and *opaque*.

1. Choose the color for the text by clicking in the Color Box with the left button (text always appears in the selected foreground color). If you plan to add opaque text (on a solid-color background), choose the color for the background by clicking on it with the right button.

2. Choose the Text tool in the Tool Box.

3. In the tool-options area at the bottom of the Tool Box, choose the icon for opaque or transparent text. The top one turns on the opaque style.

4. Draw your text frame using either mouse button. When you let go, *handles* appear on the dashed rectangular frame at the corners and along the edges, and, if you chose the opaque text style, the frame fills with the background color. The Fonts Toolbar (also known as the Text Toolbar) appears. Figure 21.6 shows a text frame and the Fonts/Text Toolbar.

You can resize or reposition this frame, change color, or change the font type and size at any time until you finalize your text entry by clicking outside the text box.

PART

IV

Using the Supplied Programs

FIGURE 21.6

The Paint "Fonts" toolbar, which serves as the Text tool's toolbar

5. Choose the font, size, and styles for your text from the Text Toolbar. You can use bold, italic, and underline in any combination.

> **TIP**
>
> If the Text Toolbar isn't visible, choose View ➢ Text Toolbar to restore it to the screen.

6. Click again over the new text frame to make the insertion-point cursor reappear. Now type whatever you like. When your text reaches the right edge of the text frame, Paint wraps down to the next line. You can use standard Windows text-editing techniques to move the insertion point, select characters or words, and cut, copy, and paste (see the section on Notepad in Chapter 22 for a summary).

7. As long as the rectangular outline of the text frame remains on the screen, you can change its size and location and the colors of the text and the frame background, and edit the text:

To resize the frame: Drag any of the handles, the little squares at the corners and along the sides of the frame. The mouse pointer becomes a double-headed arrow when it's directly over a handle, indicating that you can move the handle.

To move the frame: Drag any part of the frame outline that isn't a handle. The mouse pointer becomes an arrow when it's over the outline. As you drag, a solid gray rectangle represents the moving frame, which appears at the new location when you release the button.

To change colors: On the Color Box, click the left button to change the color of the text, the right button to change the frame background's color. You can also switch between a transparent and opaque text frame by clicking on the appropriate icon in the tool-options area or by choosing Image ➢ Draw Opaque.

8. Click outside the text frame to finalize your text entry. You can no longer edit the text.

Manipulating Areas of a Picture

So far, you've learned how to add and change colors and shapes with the various painting tools. But your creative options don't stop there. Paint gives you a variety of tools and commands for working with a specific portion of the picture as a unit. First you must first define, or *select*, the area you want to work, as detailed in the next section. If you don't select an area to manipulate, many of the commands covered in this section will affect the entire picture.

Selecting an Area

The Tool Box offers two tools for selecting specific portions of a picture for further manipulation. Appropriately enough, they're collectively called the *selection tools*. They are the top two buttons on the Tool Box. The one on the left with the star-shaped outline is for selecting irregular shapes; it's called the Free-Form Selection tool. The one on the right with the rectangular outline, the Select tool, is for selecting rectangular areas.

Once you've selected an area with either tool, you can cut, copy and paste, it, or drag it around in the picture. You can also perform many other manipulations on a selection, such as inverting its colors or rotating it.

Selecting Rectangular Areas

The easiest way to select an area—or define a cutout, if you prefer—is with the Select tool, the one with the dotted rectangular outline at the top right of the Tool Box.

All you have to do is:

1. Select the Select tool (how's that for computerized English?).

2. Move to the upper-left corner of the boxed area you want to select. Click and hold down the left mouse button.

3. Drag the mouse down and to the right. As you draw, a dotted rectangular outline indicates the selection area.

4. Release the button. After a moment, the dotted outline appears, indicating the selection.

TIP

Don't use the handles to redefine the selection area—they're for resizing the image within the area.

Once you've selected an area, it remains selected until you click outside the dotted outline around it (the *selection rectangle*) or until you choose another tool.

Selecting Irregular Areas

The Free-Form Select tool lets you select any area of the picture by drawing a line free-hand around the area.

It allows you to select exactly the part of the picture you're after, hugging the edges of the element that interests you, and avoiding others you want to leave unaffected. As you hold the mouse button down, draw a line completely around the area. If you make a mistake in defining the selection, press the right mouse button and make the selection again. When you're through, Paint displays a dotted rectangular outline large enough to contain the entire selection, even though the irregular shape is all that is selected.

Moving a Selected Area

Once you've selected an area, the simplest thing you can do with it is to move it elsewhere in the picture. All you have to do is drag it where you want it to go: Press the left mouse button down anywhere within the selection, or cutout, move to the new location, and release the button. I've adjusted the letters in the word Plain:

Even after dragging, an item remains selected until you click outside the selection rectangle, so you can move it again or perform other manipulations.

If you previously changed the background color for an interim operation, be sure to change it back to the "real" background color, or you'll get shape of an unwanted color in your picture left behind when you drag the selection.

To move a *copy* of the selection, leaving the original in place, just hold down the Ctrl key while you drag the cutout to its new home. This is a good trick for duplicating any shape quickly.

Opaque vs. Transparent Placement

When you move a selection by dragging it, you can choose between *opaque* and *transparent* placement at the new location. In opaque placement, the selection will completely replace whatever you place it on top of in the picture—nothing of what was previously there will show through.

In transparent placement, the selection's background disappears, so only the foreground elements in the selection appear at the new location. But this only works if you select the background color of the selection as the background color in the Color Box (by clicking in the Color Box with the right button). Select the correct background color before you move the selection.

Sweeping

Sweeping a selection is a neat trick that deposits multiple copies of the cutout (selection) across the picture as you move the mouse. You can use this technique to suggest motion of an object or to create interesting artistic effects:

Just as when you move a single copy of a selection, you can do opaque or transparent sweeping. Again, the background color of the cutout and the current background color have to be the same for transparent sweeping to work as you'd expect. Just drag the selection while holding the Shift key down. Copies of the cutout are made as you drag the cursor around.

Using the Clipboard with Selections

Paint uses the Windows Clipboard just like any other program does. You can copy and paste stuff too and from a Paint picture. You can also move parts of your picture around using the Windows Clipboard as an alternative to dragging it around. It's usually easier to drag, but if you want to paste the item a number of times, or cut a design from one picture, then open another picture and paste it in, use the clipboard.

To cut or copy a selection to the Clipboard, define the area with one of the Selection tools, then choose Edit ➢ Cut or Edit ➢ Copy, or just press the standard Windows keyboard shortcuts for these commands (Ctrl-X and Ctrl-C, respectively). Paste the contents with Edit ➢ Paste, or Ctrl-V. It appears in the upper right corner of the screen as a selection. Then drag it where you want it.

NOTE

When you cut a selection to the Clipboard, Paint fills in the space left behind with the currently selected background color.

Saving and Retrieving a Selection

You can save a selection as a disk file for later use. Using this technique, you can create a stockpile of little graphics (like clip art) that you can call up from disk to drop into new pictures. Here are the steps to save and retrieve a selection:

1. Define the selection with either of the selection tools.

2. Choose Edit ➢ Copy To. A file box pops up. Name the file as you wish.

3. When you want to reload the cutout, choose Edit ➢ Load From and click on the picture file containing the selection from the file box. It will appear in the upper-left corner of the current picture on screen.

4. Reposition the selection by dragging it.

Flipping and Rotating Selections

Paint lets you *flip* the selection (or the entire picture) on its vertical or horizontal axis. Flipping produces a mirror image. If you flip horizontally, the pattern is still right-side up, while if you flip vertically, it's upside down. Another option, rotate, simply rotates the image around a central axis, sort of like how the hands on a clock rotate around the clock's center.

You'll understand better how these commands work if you just play with them. You can select an area of the drawing, or not. Then choose Image ➢ Flip/Rotate. The Image Flip and Rotate dialog box appears.

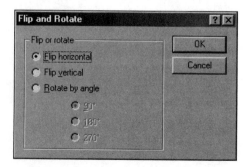

Try each of the buttons to see the effect. You can always undo it if you don't like it. You can use these commands to create reverse images by defining a selection, copying it to the Clipboard, pasting it back in, then flip or rotate it. Figure 21.7 shows an example.

FIGURE 21.7

After selecting and copying the car to the clipboard, it was pasted in, flipped or rotated, and then positioned.

Inverting Colors

The Image ➢ Invert Colors command *reverses* the colors in the selected area (or, if nothing is selected, in the entire picture). Black turns to white and white will turn to black. If you're working in color, the colors will turn to their complements. *Complementary colors* are defined here as being the color on the opposite side of the RGB (Red, Green, Blue) color wheel. This is a really fun tool. Try selecting several slightly overlapping squares of a picture and inverting them in sequence. Or try inverting sections of photograph, as shown in Figure 21.8.

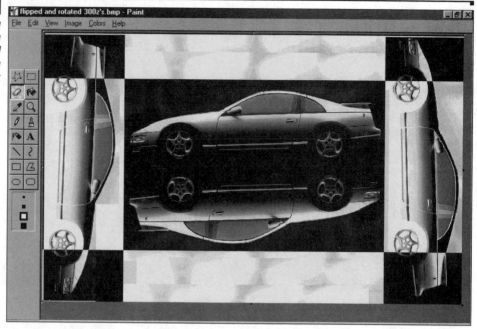

Stretching, Shrinking, and Slanting

Paint lets you change the size of a selection with the mouse, or by typing values into a dialog box. You can also slant or *skew* the image. Figure 21.9 shows a selection that has been shrunken, stretched, and skewed. Just select an area (or none, for the entire picture) and choose Image ➤ Stretch/Skew. Then fill in the numbers. A shortcut for sizing is to grab the handles on the selection carefully (a *two*-headed arrow must appear first), then drag the handle. You can't skew using the mouse; use the dialog box for that.

You can repeatedly resize a selection until you click elsewhere to deselect the area. Just remember that the more you stretch or shrink the area, the more distorted it will look.

WARNING

When you change the size of a bitmapped image (or any part of it), you create unavoidable distortions in the image look. Even if you maintain the area's proportions perfectly, shrinking it will result in loss of detail and a coarse appearance, while enlarging it will make curved lines appear more jagged.

FIGURE 21.9

In this picture, the car has been pasted in several times. The copies were (top to bottom) shrunken, stretched, and skewed.

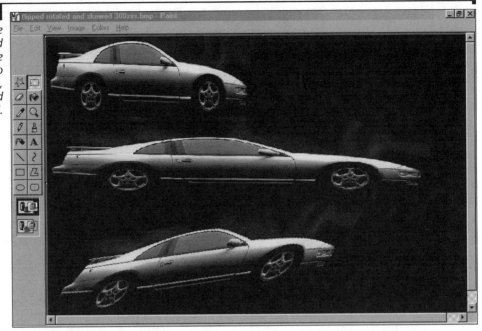

Zooming In for Detail Work

Sometimes you need a magnified view of your picture, either to see fine detail or to make precise changes more easily. Open the View ➢ Zoom dialog box to check it out. You can choose from five magnification levels: normal, 2×, 4×, 6×, and 8×. Figure 21.10 shows a picture at highest magnification, 8× (800%), with the grid marks and thumbnail options turned on.

 TIP

You can also click on the magnifier tool and then on one of the options below the toolbox to choose the magnification.

FIGURE 21.10

Here's a screen image showing what a magnified picture looks like. The network of horizontal and vertical lines the grid, designed to make precision editing easier. The little thumbnail window shows some of the magnified area at its normal, unmagnified size.

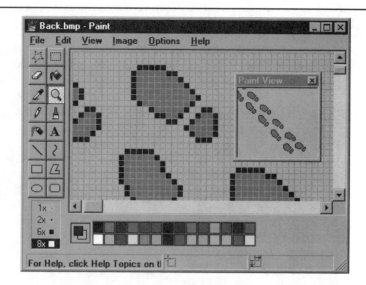

You can use any of the standard painting tools at any magnification level. Use the Pencil tool to best change the color of one dot at a time. The highest magnification is best for editing individual dots. This kind of microsurgery is useful for smoothing out lines, creating minute patterns, and eliminating single stray dots that often appear in scanned images.

NOTE

The Grid setting (choose View ➤ Zoom ➤ Show Grid) is only available at higher magnification levels 4× and above. It displays a grid of lines that indicates the location of each individual dot in your picture, making it easier to do very detailed work with your painting tools.

Creating Custom Colors

Don't like the colors in the color box? No problem. Often I'll just use the dropper tool to work with new colors, but if you are starting from scratch, that won't work, since you have no colors to pick up. To create new colors, or black-and-white patterns (if you are working in black and white), double-click on a color in the color bar. This brings up a color selector box. Then click on Define Custom Colors. The box expands to a color refiner box. Please see Chapter 7 for details on using the refiner. It works the same way as in the Control Panel, Display applet.

A custom color set remains active only with the current picture. Once you close the program, the custom settings in the color bar are lost. Paint restores the standard, or default, color set when you run it again.

Saving Your Work

If you're painting for posterity—or at least have some use in mind for your work other than doodling—remember to save your work to disk regularly. Of course, you can open pictures you've worked on before for further editing—or just to admire them.

You can save pictures as disk files in several formats, all of them variations of the basic Paint (BMP) format (unless you have MS Office's GIF and JPG file filters installed in which case you can save as GIF and JPG also). Normally, you can just let Paint choose the correct format for you. But there may be times when knowing which format to use comes in handy.

Here are the available formats and their descriptions:

Monochrome Bitmap: Use when you have only two colors (black and white) in your picture.

16-Color Bitmap: Use when you have 16 colors or fewer in your picture.

256-Color Bitmap: Use when you have more than 16 and fewer than 257 colors in your picture.

24-Bit Bitmap: Use when you have more than 256 colors in the picture.

Why change a picture's format? The most common reason: you have a picture and you like its design, but it looks cartoonish because it has too few colors. By saving it in a format with more colors, you'll be able to modify it with a much richer, more realistic color palette. But this only works if your screen can display the additional colors and is set up in Control Panel to do so (see Chapter 7 for instructions). Note that the more colors you save, the larger the files become and the more disk and RAM space they'll need.

WARNING

Saving a picture with a format that has fewer colors may ruin it. When you save (for example, if you save a picture with 16 colors as a monochrome bitmapped file), Paint translates each color in the original picture into the closest match in the new format. Clearly, you're likely to lose a significant amount of detail, especially when going to the monochrome format—the picture may well come out looking like a sea of black with a few white dots, or vice versa.

After you've saved a new picture, or if you're working with a picture you opened from disk, Paint can tell Windows to use the picture as wallpaper. From then on, the picture will appear as the backdrop for your Windows Desktop. Just choose File ➢ Set as Wallpaper (Tiled). If want the whole screen filled with multiple copies of the image. Choose File ➢ Set as Wallpaper (Centered) if you want a single copy of the image centered on the Desktop.

Printing

Finally, you might want to print out your artwork! Here's how you do it:

1. Open the picture document, if it's not already open.

2. Turn on the printer and get it ready to print.

3. If you want to change the page margins or paper orientation, choose File ➢ Page Setup and make the necessary entries in the dialog box.

4. To see how the picture will look on the printed page, choose File ➢ Print Preview. You'll see a mock-up of the printed page on your screen. This works exactly like the Print Preview function in WordPad (see Chapter 20).

5. When you're ready to print, choose File ➢ Print, or, from Print Preview, click on the Print button. The standard Windows Print dialog box will appear, allowing you to choose the correct printer, specify which pages should print and how many copies, and change the printer's settings (by clicking on the Properties button).

Using Kodak Imaging

While Paint is good for drawing and pixel editing (detail work), Kodak Imaging isn't much of a drawing program at all. Though you can do some rudimentary drawing with Imaging, its drawing tools are mostly for marking up pictures with annotations and notes. Imaging's main jobs are viewing graphics files, scanning pages of text or pictures, highlighting and annotating images, and optionally faxing them off to other people. Think of Imaging as a combination of Visioneer's PaperPort (for scanning documents), a graphics image viewer such as LView Pro, and Delrina's WinFax Pro (for some faxing abilities).

The primary areas I'll cover here are:

- Viewing images
- Annotating images
- Scanning images
- Faxing

Setting Kodak Imaging As Your Default Program for Graphics Files

Depending on your system settings Kodak Imaging may or may not be the default on-screen viewer for today's popular image formats, including GIF, TIF and JPG, XIF, PCX, DCX, BMP, WIF, and AWB files. Opening one of these files from Windows Explorer or a folder window can be set to run Imaging and display the picture. Also, if your Windows settings are appropriately configured, right-clicking on such a file and choosing Preview can open the file in Imaging's Preview mode.

As explained elsewhere in this book, it is the system file "associations" that determines which program will be used to open or edit a file. So, since I don't know what image programs you may have installed, I can't predict how your system will behave. For example, if you have Internet Explorer installed, then GIF and JPG files will be displayed in an IE window by default. (TIF files will still be displayed in Kodak Imaging.)

If you want to set your default image viewer to Kodak Imaging, do this:

1. Run Imaging.
2. Choose Tools ➢ General Options.
3. To set your default viewer, click either Imaging or Preview. When you set your default viewer to Imaging for Windows, all the editing features are available when you view the image. If you choose Preview, images open in Preview mode. It's faster this way, but you'll have to switch to Imaging mode to create a new document, to add pages to an existing document, or to annotate a document.
4. Click OK to close the dialog box.

Viewing Images

The most common use of Imaging will be to view or preview existing documents. In Windows Explorer, when you see a TIF, GIF, JPG, BMP, PCX, DCX, WIF, XIF, or AWB file, right-click the document name, then click **Preview**.

This should bring up the file in the Imaging Preview window as you see in Figure 21.11.

FIGURE 21.11

Imaging has two modes: Preview and Edit. This is the Preview screen.

NOTE

AWB is the extension Windows 98 uses for its fax file format. Images are compressed and converted to 200×200 dpi gray scale images for efficient disk storage and faxing when you store them in this format.

Rotating and Zooming

Often you'll want to adjust the display to see more, or possibly to rotate the picture if it's in the wrong axis. The Preview toolbar has four buttons that affect the view:

Trying clicking on the buttons to see the effects. Each click on the + or – minus buttons increases or decreases the zoom. The Zoom menu has additional zoom options.

If you want to rotate all the pages in a multi-page document, choose Page ➢ Rotate all Pages.

Imaging can redisplay a black-and-white image in grayscale format. A grayscale display makes black-and-white text documents easier to read, and is most effective at a zoom percentage of less than 100%. Choose View ➢ Scale to Gray. When the command has a checkmark next to it, all pages of the document are displayed in grayscale. The setting won't affect color images or documents.

Opening the Image for Editing

Once an image is open, you can make some modifications, such as annotations, add rubber stamp marks (e.g. "Draft"), etc. Just click on the edit button to switch to the editing window:

(You can alternatively choose File ➢ Open Image.)

Imaging only lets you edit TIF, AWB, or BMP files. You can view GIF and JPG files, but you have to save them as TIF before you can annotate or otherwise edit them.

You'll be asked if you always want the option of editing files you preview in the future:

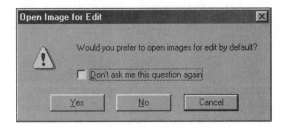

It's up to you. If you edit lots of images using Kodak Imaging, then click Yes. In Figure 21.12 you can see a TIF file in the Imaging edit window.

FIGURE 21.12

The editing window. New toolbars appear, one at the top and one at the bottom.

Different Views while Editing

Once in the Editing screen, you can alter the view in additional ways. Click on each of the three buttons just above where my pointer is in Figure 21.12.

- Page view: just show the image
- Thumbnail view: just show a small thumbnail of the image
- Page and Thumbnail view: show images and thumbnails

When a document has a number of pages, using thumbnail view is very useful, since simply clicking on one of the thumbnails displays its page.

When the document is too large to fit in the window, you can use the scroll bars to see the rest of it, or use the Drag feature. Click on the Drag button:

The pointer changes to a hand. Place the hand on the image, click and hold the mouse button, and drag the image up, down, left, or right.

To the right of the Drag button is the selection tool. To select an area of a document:

1. Click on the selection button.

2. Drag the crosshair across the desired section, and release. A box appears, marking the selection.

3. Choose a command:

   - Cut, Copy, Paste do as you would expect (actually the same as in Paint)

   - Click the Zoom to selection button in the toolbar. The view zooms in to show just the selected area.

Scanning Images

TWAIN devices are supported by this program. So, if your scanner has a TWAIN driver, you're in luck. You can scan documents into imaging without having to use another program like Photoshop. This can save you some hassle, since Imaging is a relatively small program. Then again, some other super useful programs such as PaperPort Deluxe are great for organizing your documents and will scan quite efficiently using TWAIN devices.

NOTE

TWAIN Acronym for *Technology (or Toolkit) Without An Interesting Name,* is a standard driver interface between scanners/cameras and Windows. It provides a means for graphics editing programs to import data from a scanner, without having to know what scanner or camera you're using. Nearly all scanners come with a TWAIN driver, which makes them compatible with any TWAIN-supporting software.

Imaging let you create multiple-page documents by scanning. Once a document is scanned, you can edit it, fax it, etc. You can also scroll through the pages using the page buttons on the toolbar, or the thumbnails, if they are displayed.

To scan:

1. Turn on your scanner and insert the page, photo, etc.

2. Click on the appropriate scan button: there are four.

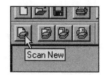

Annotating Images

Once you have an editable document on the screen, you can annotate it. You can think of annotations as an overlay on your document that can be moved, edited, or removed. Once you make the annotations permanent, though, they are set.

If the status title bar of the Imaging window says *(Read Only)* after the document name, you won't be able to annotate. You are viewing a file format that Imaging can only display—not edit or save. Save the file first as a TIF, BMP, or AWS document, then open it. Then you can annotate.

Notice down at the bottom of the window, there is an annotation toolbar:

If it's not there, click View ➤ Toolbars and turn on Annotation. While you're there, notice the other settings on the dialog box for future reference.

The Annotation toolbar does the following things (buttons, left to right):

- Select an existing annotation to delete, copy, move, etc. Use this once you have created some annotation. Good for dragging things around, resizing boxes, sticky notes, etc.

- Draw a freehand line of any shape. Use this to draw a line, just like using the pencil or brush in Paint (see earlier in this chapter). Set the color and line width with the properties options (see below).

- Draw a highlighted rectangular area.

- Draw a straight line. Use this for drawing labels on pictures.

- Draw a hollow box. Good for drawing a box around an object or doing flow diagrams. You can specify the line color and whether the color is transparent or not.

- Draw a filled box.

- Draw a box with text in it. Draw the box, then type in the text. You can change the font and text color.

- Draw a sticky yellow note. Like the text box, but it's yellow, with a shadow behind it. You can change the color of the note's background, the text font.

- Draw a box containing text that's stored in a file. Click on the image and a dialog box comes up asking you for file containing the text. Must be a .TXT file. You can change the font.

- Rubber stamp the document with one of several terms. Click the tool and choose of the five four stamp options: Approved, Draft, Received, Rejected, or you can click Properties to create your own text stamp or an image stamp.

Making Annotations Permanent

Until you nail down annotations, they can be moved, edited, and have their properties reset. To make them permanent, choose Annotations ➤ Make Annotations Permanent.

TIP

If the Make Annotations Permanent menu command is unavailable, make sure that annotations are displayed. When annotations are hidden, you can't make them permanent. Choose Annotations ➤ Show Annotations.

You should make annotations permanent before you export a document to an application that does not recognize annotations, or save the document in another file format that doesn't recognize annotations. Otherwise they'll be lost.

WARNING

If you convert a color image to black-and-white, colored annotations will also be converted. Remember that light or pale colors will be converted to white (most likely) and darker colors will be converted to black. So if the background of a text box, for example, is dark red, after the conversion text may be obscured by the resulting black.

Setting Annotation Properties

Each kind of annotation has its own properties. Once you make an annotation, you can right-click on it and choose Properties. You'll then see a dialog box. For example clicking on a text box or sticky note brings up this box:

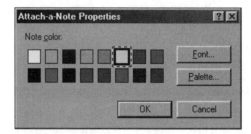

Or, for a text box you'll see this:

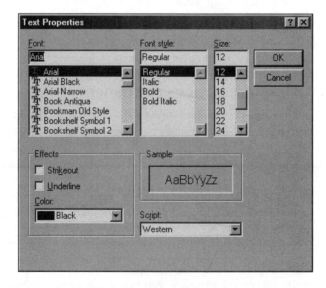

To set the properties for a line's width and color, you have to click directly on the line. This applies to lines around boxes as well as straight and freehand lines.

You can set the properties for the whole picture as well. Right-click on the picture or page, then fill in the boxes. Use this technique to change a color picture to a gray scale or black-and-white, change the compression, the size, or the resolution of an image. See "Starting a New Document" later in this chapter for details.

TIP

You can specify the default annotation for any one of the tools, including setting color, line width, and font settings. Right-click the button on the annotation toolbar, then choose Properties.

You can make new rubber stamps by right-clicking on Stamp tool, choosing Properties and using the buttons in this box:

Notice that a stamp can be a graphic as well as custom text. Make a small graphic using Paint, or another drawing program, save it as a TIF, GIF, BMP, JPG, WIF, PCX, DCX, XIF, WIF format, and click the Browse button to assign it to a new rubber stamp.

PART

IV

Using the Supplied Programs

TIP

The characters %x in a stamp's text will print the current date as part of a stamp. Examine the Received stamp's settings, and you'll see that it's "Received %x," which will print in the form "Received 10/10/98" on the image.

Starting a New Document

You can start a new document from scratch. When you do, you're asked to set the document properties with this box.

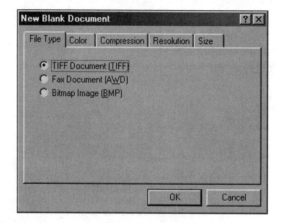

As you can see there are several tabs here, each with a number of settings. In general, simply choosing the file type and color should be enough to get you going. Details about compression and resolution are handled automatically. Note also that files can be very large if you are not careful. I pasted a couple of JPG files in to a document and before I knew it I had a 10MB file.

If you want to create a multi-page file, follow these steps:

1. Start a new file, either TIF or Fax (not BMP).

2. Choose Page ➤ Insert ➤ Existing Page, or Page ➤ Append ➤ Existing Page.

3. Browse to the existing page you want to insert. "Page" means a graphics file, or a specific page in a multi-page graphic document such as multi-page TIF or pre-existing Fax file stored in AWD format. The Browse box lets you choose among many types of graphics files, if you open the Files of Type drop-down list.

TIP

If you have questions about the other settings, use the ? button as explained in Chapter 3.

Saving Documents

Don't forget to save your documents if you want to use them again later. Once you modify a document, unless you just faxed it and are happy with the outcome (like it reached its destination) and want to trash the file, then you'll want to choose File ≻ Save, and give it a name. You can then open it later in Imaging, or if it's a TIF file, in any program that reads TIFs.

You may want to change the format of the document you have open. For example you may simply want to open a TIF file and save it as a GIF file, or a JPG with a certain amount of compression, or new resolution. To do that:

1. Open the file

2. Right click on the image and choose Properties.

3. Adjust the settings as necessary and click on OK.

TIP

If you want to convert between formats (for example, a JPG to a TIF) open the JPG file. Then choose Save As. Then choose TIF from the Save as Type list.

Chapter

22

The Other Windows
Accessories

FEATURING

Using Notepad for simple text files

Using the calculator

Entering special symbols with Character Map

Adjusting volume control

Phone Dialer

Finding people on the Internet

The Other Windows Accessories

In this chapter, you'll learn the miscellaneous accessories included with Windows 98. These accessories are fairly modest programs, but each is genuinely useful in its special niche. If you take the time to acquaint yourself with their basic functions, you'll know where to turn when you need help with a problem they can solve.

 **NOTE**

As you may have noticed by now, quite a few programs and utilities came along with Windows 98. Clicking on Start ➢ Programs ➢ Accessories and then choosing Communications, Entertainment, or System Tools will reveal a great many selections. The number of selections you have depends on what's been installed on your machine from the Windows 98 CD. (See Chapter 7 for how to add software modules of Windows.) This chapter deals with those programs and utilities that do not fall into other category chapters, such as system tools (Chapter 23), entertainment programs (Chapter 10), or communications tools (Chapters 13 through 19).

Jotting Down Notes with Notepad

Like WordPad, Notepad lets you type and edit text. But the two programs have different missions. Notepad is a tool for text editing *only*, while you use WordPad to make the text you type look good (that is, to *format* your text). To use the appropriate jargon, Notepad is a *text editor,* while WordPad is a *word processor.* (WordPad is covered in Chapter 20.)

In Notepad, you can type text, but you can't change the fonts, add bold, italics, or color, modify the tab settings, center a paragraph—well, you get the point. So why bother with Notepad? After all, you could type your text in WordPad and simply not use that program's formatting features.

Notepad's main advantage over WordPad is that it's *lean*—it takes up much less memory than WordPad, and it starts up faster, too. It's small enough to keep open all the time so you can jot down quick notes whenever you need to. And it's a perfect tool to call up whenever you need to view a text file.

So, What's a Text File?

Notepad can only open and save *text-only* files—files that contain only text characters. That is, text-only files *don't* contain any of the formatting codes used by word processors to store information about the looks and layout of a document. Text-only files are also known as plain text files, ASCII or plain ASCII files, or simply as *text files*, which is what Windows calls them.

Before I explain more about text files, here is some practical information: Windows recognizes a text file as such only if it is stored on disk with the file-name extension .txt. Files having the .txt extension appear in your folders with the text-file icon, shown to the left. Text files often have other extensions, however. Note that Windows will recognize files having the .doc extension as WinPad documents even if they actually contain plain text only. You may wish to rename such files to avoid this conflict.

Though text files look fairly boring, they do have some important advantages over fancier, formatted text documents. The most important one is their universality: Text files provide the lowest common denominator for exchanging text between different programs and even between different types of computers. Every system has a way to create and display text files. That's why they remain the medium for most of the electronic-mail messages passed back and forth on the Internet and other information services, as well as those posted to electronic bulletin boards.

In addition, most programs have text files on the installation disk named something like READ.ME, README.TXT, or README.DOC. Such files usually contain important information about the software that was added after the manual was printed, including tips on installation, details on new features or bugs in the software, and corrections of errors in the manual. Again, these messages are stored as text-only files because that way, everyone can read them.

Text files are also good for storing the "source code" used to generate computer programs. When a programmer writes the source code, he or she types it in using a text editor such as Notepad, saving the work in a text file. That way, the instructions needed to create the final program aren't mixed up with extraneous formatting information that would confuse the *compiler* or *interpreter* (software that converts the source code into a working program).

You may not be a programmer, but you do sometimes deal with program files of a sort—your system-configuration files, including win.ini, sys.ini, protocol.ini, config.sys, and autoexec.bat. These text files qualify as programs because they tell your system how to operate. You can edit them with Notepad.

Notepad's Limitations

Just so you won't use it for the wrong tasks, here's a summary of Notepad's limitations:

- It has no paragraph- or character-formatting capability. It can wrap lines of text to fit the size of the window, however, which is a nice feature. (Although, for some reason, the default is no-wrap.)

- Files are limited to text only. Notepad can't open formatted documents created with WordPad, Microsoft Word for Windows, WordPerfect, or any other word processor (actually, it can open the files, but they won't look right).

- Files are limited in size to about 50K. This is fairly large, accommodating approximately 15 pages of solid single-spaced text—20 or so pages of regularly spaced material.

- It doesn't have any fancy pagination options, though it will print with headers and footers via the Page Setup dialog box.

Running Notepad

To run Notepad, double-click on the Notepad icon; it's in the Accessories group. Notepad will appear on your screen, and you can immediately begin typing in the empty work area (Figure 22.1).

FIGURE 22.1

The Notepad window

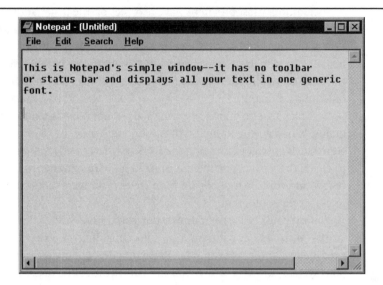

> **TIP**
>
> If you have Notepad files that you use regularly—for example, a file for your random notes—you might want to put them into a folder for easy access. If you use them very regularly, put them into the start-up folder so they are loaded when you start up Windows. You can assign each one a shortcut key for rapid access.

Alternatively, you can double-click on any document that Windows recognizes as a text file. As it starts up, Notepad will open that file automatically, and you'll see the text in the work area.

Opening Files

Once Notepad is up and running, opening another text file is as simple as choosing File ➢ Open and selecting the file you want from the Open dialog box.

> **NOTE**
>
> Of course, you can choose File ➢ New to start a new file at any time. If you've made changes in the previous file, Notepad gives you the expected opportunity to save it before creating the new file.

Keep in mind, though, that Windows may not recognize the file you want to open as a text file. When you initially bring up the Open dialog box, it's set to display only files stored with the .txt extension (note the setting in the *Files of type* area). To locate a text file with another extension, choose All files in the Files of type area.

If you try to open a file that is too large, Notepad will warn you with the message:

```
This file is too large for Notepad.
Would you like to use WordPad to read this file?
```

Clicking on Yes will automatically run WordPad, which will open the chosen file.

WARNING

Be careful about opening non-text files with Notepad. While it's fine to browse through a non-text file to see if you can make sense of it, don't make any changes and, above all, *don't save the file*. If you do, the file may be unusable even by the program that originally created it.

Notepad will go ahead and open any file you specify, even if it doesn't contain only text. If you open a non-text file, it will probably look like unintelligible garbage.

Entering and Editing Text

You can enter and edit text in Notepad as you would expect, with a few exceptions. To enter text, just start typing. The insertion point will move, just as it does in WordPad. However, as you reach the end of the window, the text will not wrap. Instead, Notepad just keeps adding new text to the same line, scrolling the window to the right so that the insertion point is always visible. When you press Enter, the window will pan back to the far left again, ready for the next line of text. Figure 22.2 shows an example of text in this state.

This is a rather inconvenient way to enter your text because you can't see much of what you just typed. To fix the problem, choose Edit ➢ Word Wrap. When you do, the text will wrap within the constraints of the window. If you resize the window, the text will rewrap to fit the available space. Figure 22.3 shows the same long line of text reformatted with Word Wrap turned on.

NOTE

Certain types of program files, such as .bat, .ini, and config.sys files, are line-oriented and are better edited with Word Wrap off. This allows you to distinguish more clearly one line from the next in the case of long lines.

FIGURE 22.2

Each paragraph of text will normally stay on one long line unless Word Wrap is turned on.

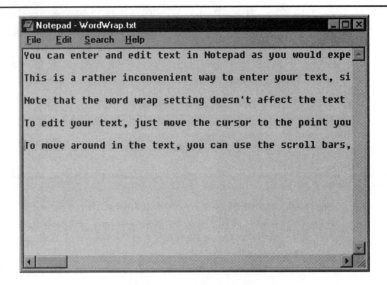

FIGURE 22.3

Text will wrap within a window if Word Wrap is turned on.

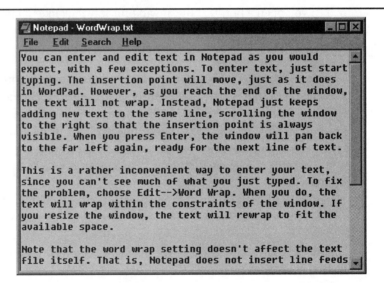

Note that the word-wrap setting doesn't affect the text file itself. That is, Notepad does not insert line feeds or carriage returns at the points where the lines wrap.

To edit your text, just move the cursor to the point you want to change. You can select, cut, copy, and paste text with the mouse, using the same techniques described in Chapter 20. To select all of the text in the file, choose Edit ➤ Select All.

To move around in the text, you can use the scroll bars, of course. You can also use
the following keys:

Key	Moves Insertion Point to
Home	Start of the line
End	End of the line
PgUp	Up one window
PgDn	Down one window
Ctrl-Left Arrow	Start of previous word
Ctrl-Right Arrow	Start of next word
Ctrl-Home	Start of the file
Ctrl-End	End of the file

Entering the Time and Date in Your Text

A common use of a Notepad-type program is to take notes pertaining to important
phone conversations or meetings with clients or colleagues, or to type up memos.
Typically, you'll want to incorporate the current time and date into your notes to document developments as they happen. The Time/Date command on the Edit menu does
this quickly.

To enter the time and date at the cursor:

1. Position the insertion point where you want the time and date inserted.

2. Choose Edit ➢ Time/Date or press F5.

Searching for Text

You can search for specific text in a Notepad file, but you can't replace it automatically. Follow these steps to search:

1. Choose Search ➢ Find. The dialog box shown below will appear.

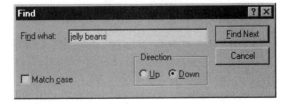

2. Type in the text you want to search for.

3. Check the Match Case box if you want to find text only having the same capitalization as your text. If you want the search to ignore capitalization, leave the box clear.

4. Click on Up if you want to search the portion of text above the current insertion point. Down is the default setting—Notepad searches from the insertion point to the end of the file and stops. Unlike WordPad, Notepad does not wrap around to the top of the file and continue the search down to the insertion point.

5. If you want to search again for the same word, choose Search ➤ Find Next or, better yet, press F3.

Setting Margins and Adding Headers and Footers

While its formatting capabilities are crude, Notepad does let you change the page margins and set up headers and footers. Here's how:

1. Choose File ➤ Page Setup command. You'll see the small dialog box shown here:

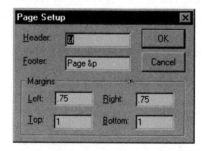

2. To change the margins, type in the new settings in inches.

Margin changes and header and footer settings aren't visible on the screen but will show up in your printed document.

3. To add a header or footer, type in any text you want to appear on every page. You can also use special codes to have Notepad place various information in the header or footer for you. Note the standard header and footer settings in the Page Setup dialog box shown above. These standard settings print the file name at the top of the page and the page number at the bottom. Here's a list of the codes you can enter:

Code	Effect
&d	Includes the current date
&p	Includes the page number
&f	Includes the file name
&l	Makes the subsequent text left align at the margin
&r	Makes the subsequent text right align at the margin
&c	Centers the subsequent text
&t	Includes the time of the printing

You can enter as many of these codes as you like.

Printing a Notepad File

To print a Notepad file, do the following:

1. Make sure the printer is ready.

2. If you're not sure that the correct printer is selected or if you want to make changes to its settings, choose File ➤ Page Setup, then click on the Printer button. You can now choose a different printer (if more than one is installed) or change settings by clicking on the Properties button.

3. Choose File ➤ Print to print the file. Notepad immediately starts the printing process and always prints the entire document—you don't have an opportunity to select which pages will print or how many copies.

Performing Calculations with the Calculator

The Calculator is a pop-up tool that you can use to perform simple or complex calculations. There are really two calculators in one—a Standard Calculator and a more complex Scientific Calculator for use by statisticians, engineers, computer programmers, and business professionals.

To run the Calculator, find it in the Accessories group on the Start menu and select it from the menu. A reasonable facsimile of a handheld calculator will appear on your screen, as shown in Figure 22.4. If your Calculator looks larger, it's the Scientific one. Choose View ➤ Standard to switch back to the basic calculator. The program always remembers which type was used last and comes up in that mode.

FIGURE 22.4

*The Standard
Calculator*

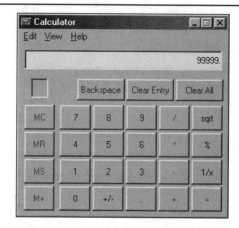

NOTE

Changes to the Calculator in Windows 98: It now uses an infinite-precision math package to eliminate binary integer math precision errors. Also, Factorial works for non-integers and odd roots of negative numbers.

Getting Help with the Calculator

For quick tips on how to use any calculator button, just click the right mouse button over the calculator button of interest. A little *What's this* button appears. Click on this, and you'll see a pop-up Help window. Of course, you can also choose Help ➢ Help Topics to display the main Help text.

Calculating a Result

To perform a typical calculation, follow these steps:

1. Clear the calculator's display by pressing Esc or clicking on the Clear All button.

2. Enter the first value in the calculation by clicking on the numbers or using the keyboard. (If you set the keypad's Num Lock setting on, you can use it to enter the numbers and the four mathematical operators. This is easier than using the number keys across the top of the keyboard.) You can use the Backspace key to fix mistakes, click on Clear All to clear the calculator and start again, or click on Clear Entry to clear only the current entry but preserve the previous result.

3. After entering the first number, click on the mathematical operator you want to use. (The asterisk represents multiplication, SQRT calculates the square root, and 1/*x* calculates the reciprocal. The others are self-evident.)

4. Enter any additional numbers followed by the desired operators. In this way, you can perform a sequence of operations using the result of each computation as the beginning of the next one.

5. Press Enter or click on the calculator's equals (=) button. The answer appears in the display.

TIP

To add up a series of numbers or to find their mean, you may prefer to use the statistical functions on the Scientific Calculator. This way, you can see all the numbers in a list before you perform the calculation instead of having to enter them one at a time. And don't let the idea of statistics make you nervous—the technique is very simple.

Most of the operations on the standard calculator are self-explanatory, but a couple of them—square roots and percentages—are just a bit tricky. They are explained below, as are the functions of the scientific calculator.

Using the Memory Keys

The memory keys work just like those on a standard calculator. MS stores the displayed number in memory, MR recalls the memory value to the display for use in calculations, M+ adds the current display value to the existing memory value, and MC clears out the memory, resetting it to zero.

When the Calculators' memory contains a value, an *M* appears in the small area just above the MC button. If no value is in memory, this area is empty.

Copying Your Results to Other Documents

To enter the number displayed in the Calculator readout into another document, just use the standard Windows copy and paste commands. Use the Calculator for your computations, and then, when the result you want is in the display, choose Edit ➢ Copy (or press Ctrl-C). The value will be copied to the Clipboard. Then switch back to your document, position the cursor where you want the result, and paste it in.

Copying Calculations from Other Documents to the Calculator

Although the Calculator doesn't keep records of your computations for reference or reuse, you can get around that limitation via the Clipboard and a text editor such as Notepad or your word processor. Here's what to do:

1. In the text editor, type in the entire equation using the special symbols listed in Table 22.1.

2. Copy the equation to the Clipboard.

3. Switch to Calculator.

4. Click on the Clear All button to clear the Calculator, then press Ctrl-V or choose Edit ➢ Paste.

If you've written out the equation correctly, the Calculator will compute the answer for you.

TABLE 22.1: KEYBOARD SHORTCUTS FOR THE CALCULATOR

Calculator button	Equivalent keyboard key	Calculator button	Equivalent keyboard key	Calculator button	Equivalent keyboard key
%	%	cos	o	MS	Ctrl-M
(	(	Dat	Ins	n!	!
)	)	Dec	F6	Not	~
*	*	Deg	F2	Oct	F7
+	+	dms	m	Or	|
+/-	F9	Dword	F2	PI	p
-	-	Exp	x	Rad	F3
.	. or ,	F-E	v	s	Ctrl-D
/	/	Grad	F4	sin	s
0-9	0-9	Hex	F5	SQRT	@
1/x	r	Hypo	h	Sta	Ctrl-S
=	= or Enter	Int	;	Sum	Ctrl-T
A-F	A-F	Inv	i	tan	t
And	&	ln	n	Word	F3
Ave	Ctrl-A	log	l	Xor	^
Bin	F8	LSH	<	x^2	@
Byte	F4	M+	Ctrl-P	x^3	#
Back	Backspace	MC	Ctrl-L	x^y	y
Clear All	Esc	Mod	%		
CD	Del	MR	Ctrl-R		

Here's how a simple calculation might look, ready for copying from the text editor to Calculator:

((2+4)+16)/11=

or

(2+(4+16))/11=

Note that you must surround each pair of terms in parentheses to indicate the calculation sequence. This is true even if you would have gotten the right answer had you typed in the numbers into the Calculator without the parentheses.

If you don't like the parentheses, you can try this format instead:

2+4=+16=/11=

Note that this time you have to insert an = after each arithmetic operation; the Calculator gets confused if you don't.

You can use the following special characters in an equation to activate various Calculator functions:

:c	Clears the Calculator's memory
:e	If the Calculator is set to the decimal system, this sequence indicates that the following digits are the exponent of a number expressed in scientific notation; for example, 1.01:e100 appears in the Calculator as 1.01e+100
:m	Stores the number currently displayed in the Calculator's memory
:p	Adds the number currently displayed to the number in memory
:q	Clears the calculator
:r	Displays the number stored in the Calculator's memory
\	Places the number currently displayed into the Statistics box, which must already be open

Computing Square Roots and Percentages

To find a *square root*, just enter the number whose square root you want and click on the SQRT button. That's all there is to it—the only thing to remember is that this is a one-step calculation. You don't need to click on the = button or do anything else.

Percentages are a little trickier. Let's say you want to know what 14 percent of 2,875 is. Here's how to find out:

1. Clear the Calculator of previous results. This is a key step—you won't get the right answer if you leave a previous result in memory when you start.

2. Enter the number you're starting with, 2875 in this case.

3. Click on or type * (for multiplication) or *any* of the arithmetic operators. It actually doesn't matter which one you use—this step simply separates the two values you're entering.

4. Enter the percentage; in this case, 14. Don't enter a decimal point unless you're calculating a fractional percentage, such as 0.2 percent.

5. Now click on or type %. The Calculator reports the result.

Using the Scientific Calculator

In the Standard view, the Calculator may seem a fairly simple affair, but wait 'til you see the Scientific view—this is an industrial-strength calculating tool that can handle truly sophisticated computations. Figure 22.5 shows how the Scientific calculator appears on your screen. To display it, choose View ➤ Scientific.

FIGURE 22.5

The Scientific Calculator

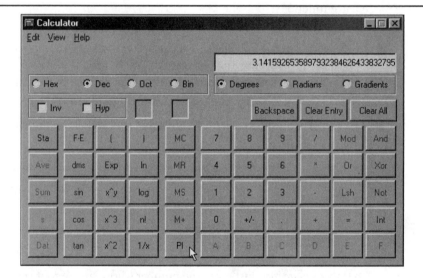

The term "scientific" is somewhat misleading because the functions available here cover programming and statistics as well as the operations traditionally used by scientists. With the Scientific Calculator, you can do the following:

• Perform complex computations, grouping terms in up to 25 levels of parentheses.

• Display and perform calculations on values expressed in scientific (exponential) notation.

• Raise numbers to any power and find any (nth) root.

- Calculate logarithms and factorials.
- Perform trigonometric functions such as sine and cosine, displaying values as degrees, radians, or gradients.
- Insert the value of pi into your calculations.
- Perform calculations in four bases (hexadecimal, octal, and binary, in addition to decimal) and translate values between the bases.
- Perform bitwise operations (logical and shift operations on individual bits in a value) such as And, Or, Not, and Shift.
- Calculate standard deviations and other statistical computations.

Details on the individual functions of the Scientific Calculator are beyond the scope of this book—if you're rocket scientist enough to use them, you probably don't need me to explain them to you. An introduction to operating the program is in order, however.

Accessing Additional Functions with the Inv and Hyp Check Boxes

The Inv check box at the left side of the Scientific Calculator functions something like the Shift key on your keyboard: checking it alters the function of some of the Calculator's buttons. This means you have access to additional functions that aren't obvious from the button labels.

For example, to find the arcsine of the value currently displayed in the readout, you would check the Inv box, then click on the sin button. Similarly, to find a cube root, enter the number, check the Inv box, and then click on the x^3 button. Instead of raising the value to the third power, you've calculated the cube root.

As you can guess, Inv stands for *inverse*, and it causes most buttons to calculate their inverses. With some buttons, though, checking the Inv box simply accesses a related function.

The Inv box is automatically cleared for you after each use.

Immediately to the right of the Inv box is the Hyp (for hyperbolic) check box, which works similarly. Its function is to access the corresponding hyperbolic trigonometric function when used with the sin, cos, and tan buttons.

Working with Scientific Notation

To enter a number using scientific (exponential) notation:

1. Begin by entering the significant digits (the base number).
2. When you're ready to enter the exponent, click on the Exp button. The display changes to show the value in exponential notation with an exponent of 0.

3. If you want to enter a negative exponent, click on the +/– button.

4. You can now enter the exponent. The Calculator accepts exponents up to +/- 307. If you enter a larger number, you'll get an error message in the display and you'll have to start over.

You can switch back and forth between exponential and standard decimal notations for numbers with absolute values less than 10^{15}. To do so, just click on the F–E button.

Working with Different Number Bases

The Scientific Calculator lets you enter and perform calculations with numbers in any of four commonly used number base systems: decimal (base 10), hexadecimal (base 16), octal (base 8), and binary (base 2). To switch to a different base, click on the appropriate radio button from the group at the upper left. The value currently in the display will be translated to the new base.

Many of the Scientific Calculator's operators and buttons work only while the decimal numbering system is active. For example, you can only use scientific notation with decimal numbers. The letter keys (A–F) at the bottom of the Scientific Calculator's numeric button pad are for entering the hexadecimal digits above 9 and only work in hexadecimal mode.

You have three display options when each number base system is active. The choices appear as radio buttons at the right side of the Calculator.

When the decimal system is active, you can display values as degrees, radians, or gradients. These are units used in trigonometric computations, and for other work you can ignore the setting.

NOTE

If the display is set for Degrees, you can use the dms button to display the current value in the degree-minute-second format. Once you've switched to degrees-minutes-seconds, you can translate back to degrees by checking the Inv box, then clicking on the dms button.

The choices for the other three bases are:

Dword: Displays the number as a 32-bit value (up to 8 hexadecimal places).

Word: Displays the number as a 16-bit value (up to 4 hex places).

Byte: Displays the number as an 8-bit value (up to 2 hex places).

When you switch to an option that displays fewer places, the Scientific Calculator hides the upper (more significant) places but retains them in memory and during calculations. When you switch back, the readout reflects the entire original number, as modified by any calculations.

Grouping Terms with Parentheses

You can use parentheses to group terms in a complex calculation, thereby establishing the order in which the various operations are performed. You can *nest* parentheses inside other parentheses to a maximum of 25 levels.

Aside from the math involved, there's nothing tricky about using parentheses—except keeping track of them as your work scrolls out of the display area. In this regard, the Scientific Calculator does provide one bit of help: It displays how many levels "deep" you are at the moment in the small area just above the right parenthesis button.

Performing Statistical Calculations

The Scientific Calculator can also perform several simple statistical calculations, including standard deviations, means, and sums. Even if you're not savvy with statistics, the statistical functions provide a good way to add or average a series of values. You get to enter the numbers in a list, where you can see them all, and then click on a button to get the result.

You access the statistical functions via three buttons at the left of the Scientific Calculator: Ave, Sum, and s. These buttons only work when you display the Statistics box, as detailed in the general instructions below. The functions of each button are listed after the instructions.

Now you're ready for the general method for performing any statistical calculation:

1. Click on the Sta button to display the Statistics box, shown here:

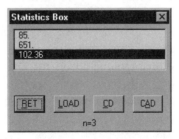

2. Position the Statistics box and the Calculator on your screen so you can see the box and have access to the Calculator buttons and readout.

3. Place each value in the Statistics box by entering the value and clicking on Dat. Repeat this for all the values you want to perform the calculation on.

4. To delete an entry in the Statistics box, highlight it, then click on CD (clear datum). You can delete all the entries by clicking on CAD (clear all data).

5. When you've entered all the correct values, click any of the three statistics buttons to perform the selected calculation. The answer appears in the Calculator's main readout.

Each of the statistical function buttons performs two functions: one "regular" function and a second function if you check the Inv box above before clicking on the button. Here are the buttons' functions:

Button	Normal function	Function with Inv
Ave	Calculates the mean	Calculates the mean of the squares
Sum	Calculates the sum	Calculates the sum of the squares
s	Calculates the standard deviation using $n-1$ as the population parameter	Calculates the standard deviation using n as the population parameter

Never heard of the population parameter? You're not alone....

Entering Special Symbols with Character Map

The Character Map program lets you choose and insert into your documents those oddball characters such as foreign alphabetic and currency symbols and characters from specialized fonts such as Symbol and Wingdings. With Character Map, you can easily view and insert these symbols even though there aren't keys for them on your keyboard.

Here are some everyday examples. Suppose that instead of the standard straight quotes (like "this") you'd prefer to use real open and close quotes (like "this") for a more professional-looking document. Or perhaps you regularly use the symbols for Trademark (™), Registered Trademark (®), Copyright (©); Greek letters, or the arrow symbols ↑, ↓, ←, and ➢ that we use in this book. These, as well as fractions and foreign-language accents and the like, are included in your Windows fonts and can most likely be printed on your printer.

Character Map is a small dialog box that displays all the symbols available for each font. You select the symbol(s) you want, and Character Map puts them on the Clipboard for pasting into your document. Figure 22.6 displays some examples of special characters.

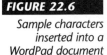

FIGURE 22.6

*Sample characters
inserted into a
WordPad document
using Character Map*

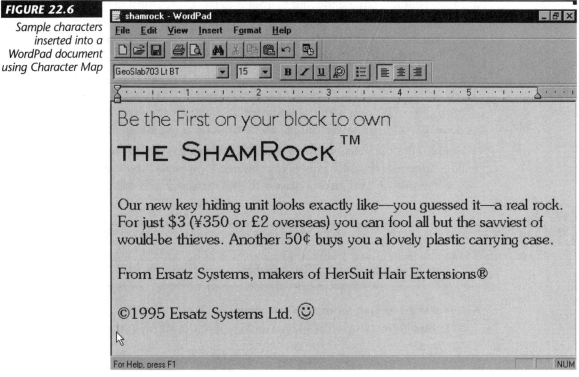

Using Character Map

Here's how to use Character Map:

    1. Run Character Map (it's in the Accessories group). The Character Map table comes up, showing all the characters included in the font currently selected in the Font list (a font can contain up to 224 characters).

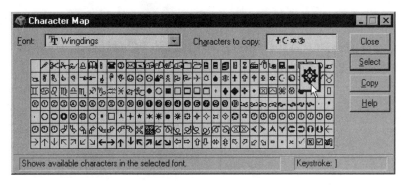

2. In the Font list, choose the font you want to work with. Most of the fonts have the same characters, but some special fonts have completely different *character sets*. For example, the Symbol font includes all sorts of special math and Greek symbols, while the Wingdings font consists of a wacky set of little pictures.

3. To make it easier to see the individual characters, you can click on a character box and hold the mouse button down to magnify the symbol. You can accomplish the same thing with the keyboard by moving to the character using the arrow keys. With this technique, each character is magnified as you select it.

4. Double-click on a character to select it, transferring it to the *Characters to copy* box. Alternatively, once you've highlighted a character, you can click on the Select button or press Alt-S to place it in the Characters to copy box.

NOTE

You can change fonts at any time. Just be aware that this will affect the characters you previously placed in the Characters to copy box, not just new characters.

5. If you want to grab more than one character, keep adding them in the same way. Each new character is added to the end of the string in the *Characters to copy* box.

6. Click on the Copy button. This places everything in the Characters to copy box onto the Clipboard.

7. Switch back to your destination application and use the Paste command (typically on the application's Edit menu) to insert the characters into your document. You may then have to select the inserted characters and choose the correct font to format the characters correctly.

Of course, once you've entered a character in this way, you're free to change its font and size as you would any character you typed in.

Entering Alternate Characters from the Keyboard

Notice that the bottom of the Character Map dialog box includes a line that reads

`Keystroke:`

When you click on a character in Character Map, this line displays the keys you would have to press to enter the character directly from the keyboard rather than from Character Map. For the characters in the first three lines—except the very last character on the third line—the keystroke shown will be a key on your keyboard. If you're working with a nonstandard font such as Symbol, pressing the key shown will enter the selected symbol into your document. With Symbol, for example, pressing the *j* key enters the cheery symbol shown here.

For all the other characters, Character Map instructs you to enter a sequence of keys in combination with the Alt key. For example, say you wanted to enter the copyright symbol (©) into a Windows application document. Note that with a standard text font like Arial or Times New Roman selected in Character Map, the program lists the keystrokes for the copyright symbol as Alt-0169. Here's how to enter the character from the keyboard:

1. Press Num Lock to activate the numeric keypad on your keyboard if the keypad is not already active.

2. Press Alt and as you hold it down type **0 1 6 9** (that is, type the 0, 1, 6, and 9 keys individually, in succession). When you release the Alt key, the copyright symbol should appear in the document.

Not all Windows application programs accept characters in this way, but it's worth a try as a shortcut to using the Character Map.

Character Sets: ANSI vs. IBM

Normally you'll be using Character Map with Windows applications. However, you may have some success dropping special characters into non-Windows applications. The basic technique is simple:

1. Copy the desired characters to the Clipboard.

2. Display the non-Windows application in a window if it isn't windowed already.

3. Paste the Clipboard contents into your application using the application window's Control menu (choose Edit ➤ Paste or click on the Paste button).

That's easy enough, but whether or not you see the desired characters depends on several factors. Here's the situation: Windows uses the American National Standards Institute (ANSI) character set to display characters on the screen and assign them to the keyboard. This includes 256 characters, numbered 0 to 255. By contrast, when your PC runs DOS *text mode* or *character-based* programs, the computer uses a different character set called the IBM extended character set.

In the United States, at least, the ANSI and IBM sets are identical for the characters numbered between 32 and 127, which correspond to the letters, numbers, and symbols on a standard U.S. keyboard. However, the two sets differ dramatically when it comes to the other characters. For example, in the ANSI set the British pound symbol (£) is character 163, whereas in the IBM extended character set it is 156.

With me so far? Okay, here's how Character Map and your non-Windows programs interact. When you copy a character from a standard Windows text font to a non-Windows application, Windows tries to translate the character into one that the non-Windows program can display. Sometimes this works, sometimes it doesn't. Here are the possible scenarios:

- If the symbol is present in the IBM character set, you may be in luck—it should appear in the non-Windows document as is. For example, if you select and copy the British pound symbol, Windows translates it to the correct code for that same symbol in the IBM character set. So far so good. But what happens when that code gets pasted into your non-Windows program is up to the program. Some programs can accept any character code you throw at them. Others display some codes as expected but react strangely to others, perhaps by executing some menu command. Still others ignore all characters except the standard ones.

- If Windows has no exact equivalent in the IBM character set, Windows converts it to the character it thinks is the closest. Thus, a copyright symbol becomes *c*, the registered trademark becomes *r*, and so on. Again, depending on the character code after the conversion, your non-Windows application may or may not accept it when you paste it in.

By the way, Windows performs these translations on all Clipboard text you paste to a non-Windows program, not just characters copied from Character Map.

It's usually easier to enter the non-keyboard characters into a non-Windows application directly, rather than copying them from Windows—that way, you'll avoid all the pitfalls I've just described. Check your non-Windows application's manual to see whether it includes information about entering non-keyboard characters from the keyboard. If you don't find any specific advice, you can try entering them as follows:

1. Look up the code for the character you want to insert. There are several places to look:

   - In Character Map's Font box, select the font called Terminal, which is used to display text in your windowed non-Windows programs. This font includes all the characters of the IBM set, although Character Map doesn't display the first 31 of them. Again, the necessary code appears at the bottom of the Character Map window.

   - Character codes are usually listed in your computer's manual or your DOS manual.

   - You can get pop-up utilities (I'm talking non-Windows utilities) that display the characters and their codes on the screen. Usually referred to as *ASCII tables*, these utilities are available as shareware or freeware from many bulletin boards and shareware distributors.

2. Once you've found the code, press Num Lock to activate the numeric keypad on your keyboard if the keypad is not already active.

3. To enter the character, press the Alt key, hold it down, and type the three-digit code on the numeric keypad. Note that these are *three*-digit codes, not four-digit codes as in Windows. All Windows keycodes require entry of an initial 0, the fourth digit. For example, to enter the British pound symbol in a non-Windows program, you would enter Alt-156, *not* Alt-0156. If the three-digit code does start with a 0, go ahead and enter that.

Note that you can use a Windows program such as WordPad or Notepad to open text files saved by a non-Windows application, even if they contain extended characters. In general, however, the extended characters will be represented by small solid or hollow boxes—in other words, you'll lose them. The rest of your text should remain intact, however.

Audio Control

This accessory is a pretty simple one. When you run it, it pops up volume controls, balance controls, and the like for controlling your sound card, if you have one. If you don't have a sound card, this accessory won't be available, or won't do anything. There are two sets of controls—one for recording and one for playback.

1. Run the accessory from Start ➢ Programs ➢ Accessories ➢ Multimedia ➢ Volume Control. You can more easily run it by double-clicking on the little speaker

icon in the Taskbar. Your sound system's capabilities will determine the format of the volume control(s) you'll see. On first running the accessory on my machine, I see the screen shown below.

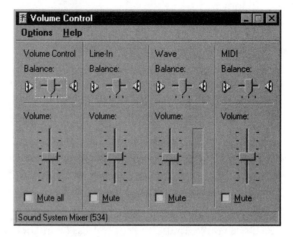

2. Change any volume control's setting by dragging the volume up or down. Change the balance between right and left channels by dragging the Balance sliders left or right.

3. Check out the Properties menu. It may have options that will provide an expanded view of the volume controls. The graphic below shows a typical Properties box allowing alteration of which volume controls display.

NOTE

Some of the sliders in one module are linked to sliders in other modules. Adjusting the Volume setting on one will affect Volume settings on the other mixers, for example.

Because audio controls operate differently for different sound cards, check out any Help files that might be available from your audio controls. Typically there will be a Help button to press.

Here's a tip. To quickly kill the sound output from your system (useful when the phone rings), click on the little speaker icon in the Taskbar:

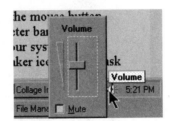

You'll be able to adjust the master volume from here and even mute the sound by clicking on the Mute box.

Using the Phone Dialer

Phone Dialer is a simple application that places outgoing voice telephone calls through your modem. You can tell Phone Dialer what number you want to dial by typing the number, choosing it from a Speed Dial list, or clicking numbers on an on-screen keypad. After you've called a number, you can select it from a list of recent calls. After it dials the call, Phone Dialer connects the line through to the telephone set plugged into the phone jack on your modem so you can pick up the handset and start talking.

You'll have to decide for yourself whether pressing keys on your computer keyboard is any improvement over pressing buttons on a telephone, but the speed-dial feature can be quite convenient for frequently called numbers. Of course, you're out of luck if you normally use separate telephone lines for voice and data.

Starting Phone Dialer

Phone Dialer is in the Windows Accessories menu, so you can start it by clicking on the Start button and then choosing Programs ➢ Accessories ➢ Phone Dialer. If you use Phone Dialer frequently, you can create a shortcut for this application.

When you start the program, the main Phone Dialer screen in Figure 22.7 appears. To make a call, either type the number or click on the numbers on the on-screen keypad. If you want to call a number you've called before, you can display recently dialed numbers in a drop-down menu by clicking on the arrow at the right side of the *Number to dial* field. When the complete number you want to dial is in this field, click on the Dial button.

The Phone Dialer screen offers several ways to enter a telephone number.

Dialing a number with Phone Dialer is exactly like dialing the same number from your telephone. Therefore, you must include all the prefixes required by the phone company for this kind of call, such as a **1** for prepaid long-distance calls or a **0** for operator-assisted calls. On the other hand, if you're using an office telephone that requires **9** or some other access code for an outside line, you can use the Dialing Properties dialog box to add the code for all calls. You can open the Dialing Properties dialog box from Phone Dialer's Tools menu.

Programming the Speed Dial List

The eight entries in the Speed Dial list are push buttons. Click on one of the names in the list to dial that person's number. When you click on an unassigned button, the Program Speed Dial dialog box in Figure 22.8 appears. Type the name you want on the button in the *Name* field and the complete telephone number in the *Number to dial* field. Click on the Save button to save the new number and return to the main Phone Dialer screen or the Save and Dial button to call the number from this dialog box.

FIGURE 22.8

*Use the Program
Speed Dial dialog
box to assign names
and numbers to the
Speed Dial list.*

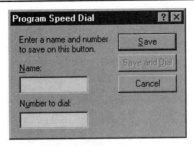

You can program several Speed Dial buttons at one time or change the name or number of a previously assigned button by choosing Speed Dial from the Edit menu. When the Edit Speed Dial dialog box in Figure 22.9 appears, click on the button you want to change and then type the name and number you want to assign to that button. After you have configured as many of the eight buttons as you want to use, click on the Save button.

FIGURE 22.9

*Use the Edit Speed
Dial dialog box to
add or change
Speed Dial items.*

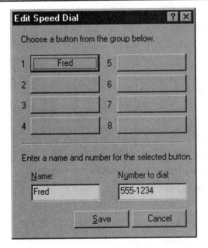

Placing a Call

When you place a call through Phone Dialer, the Dialing dialog box in Figure 22.10 appears. If you entered the number from the Speed Dial list, the dialog box will display the name of the person you're calling. Otherwise, it will report the call destination as *unknown*. If you wish, you can type the recipient's name and a few words about the call to keep a record of this call in the Phone Dialer log.

FIGURE 22.10

This dialog box appears when you place a call with a Phone Dialer.

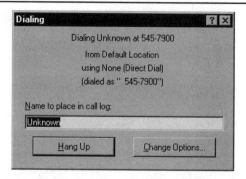

As Phone Dialer places the call, you will hear the dialing tones (or pulses) and the ringing signal or busy signal through the modem's speaker. A *Call Status* window will let you know when the call has gone through. To transfer the call to your telephone set, click on the Talk button and pick up the handset or click on Hang Up to break the connection. If the modem detects a busy signal, you will see a *Call Failed* window instead.

After you pick up the receiver and click on the Talk button, your call passes through the modem to your telephone set. At this point, there's no real difference between a Phone Dialer call and one placed directly from the telephone itself. To end the call, hang up the telephone.

Finding People on the Internet

In Chapter 4 I talked a bit about using the Start ➤ Find command as a way to locate programs you want to run or files you want to open. Find is a super useful utility that you'll use at least several times a day once you realize how much time it can save you. We misplace files in our computers so often that it's really a godsend, especially with today's multi-gigabyte drives that can store many thousands of files.

Find has been expanded in Windows 98 to include finding people and stuff on the Web as well as files and computers. We'll cover finding computers in the networking section and finding stuff on the Web in the Internet Explorer section. Right here, I want to tell you about finding people.

How often have you lost friends because they moved, they changed phone numbers, you forgot to stay in touch, or you lost your address book? Lots, right? The answers to all these questions, believe it or not, lies a few clicks away, assuming you have a connection to the Internet.

Short for **Lightweight Directory Access Protocol**, LDAP is a set of protocols for accessing information directories. Although not yet widely implemented, LDAP should eventually make it possible for almost any application running on virtually any computer platform to obtain directory information, such as e-mail addresses. Because LDAP is an open protocol, applications don't have to know about the type of server that's hosting the directory. Though only now emerging, LDAP will enable anyone to locate organizations, individuals, and other resources such as files and devices in a network, whether on the Internet or on a corporate intranet.

LDAP is called "lightweight" because it's a smaller version of DAP (which stands for Directory Access Protocol). DAP is part of a more extensive directory system called "X.500," a directory services standard used in large networks. LDAP doesn't include the same levels of security that DAP does. LDAP was brainstormed by folks at the University of Michigan and has been endorsed by at least 40 companies, including Netscape, Microsoft, and Novell.

Some popular search engines on the Web have conspired to provide this standard lookup methodology to provide 'net users with data about the people in their databases. Databases are compiled using all kinds of publicly-available information such as local telephone books and using e-mail addresses gathered from who knows where. Think of LDAP as a combination of white pages and a few indirect services such as e-mail addresses, greeting cards, and flowers thrown in.

Here's how find an individual or business:

NOTE

If you don't have an Internet connection, please read Chapter 15, "Getting Connected to the Internet."

1. Assuming you're connected to the Internet already, click on Start ➢ Find ➢ People.

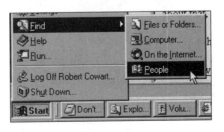

2. You'll see the box shown below. Choose the LDAP server you want to use. Notice that some are for business listings, though most are for individuals.

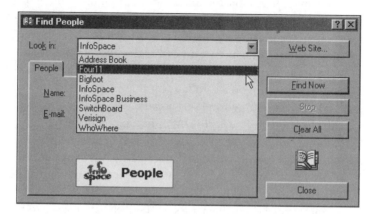

Even though one LDAP service may not find the person or business you're looking for, another might succeed. Try several.

3. Enter the name or, alternatively, the e-mail address of the person you're looking for. You can search either way. Then click Find Now. I searched for John Smith. Using Four 11, there were no finds, and I got an error message and a beep. But in Bigfoot, I found 40, as you can see in Figure 22.11

You can enlarge the Find box by dragging its corners or sides, to see more. There isn't a maximize button on the window, though; you have to size it manually.

4. Double-click on an entry in the list, and you'll see a Properties sheet with all kinds of information about that entry. For example, I'll search for Computer Literacy Bookshop. I got two listings and displayed one (Figure 22.12).

As of this writing, most of listings I could get were limited to people's e-mail addresses. As LDAP becomes the accepted format for directory listings on the Internet, you'll see more option boxes on the other tabs of the Properties box filled in. Notice the NetMeeting tab. If a person uses NetMeeting, this is a way to figure out how to get them into a NetMeeting conference with you.

FIGURE 22.11

*A list of John Smiths
dished up by Bigfoot
LDAP service*

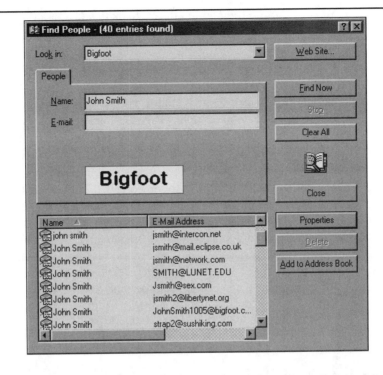

FIGURE 22.12

*If the information
you want isn't
showing already,
you can click on
the Properties but-
ton or double-click
the entry to display
the Properties for
the individual or
business.*

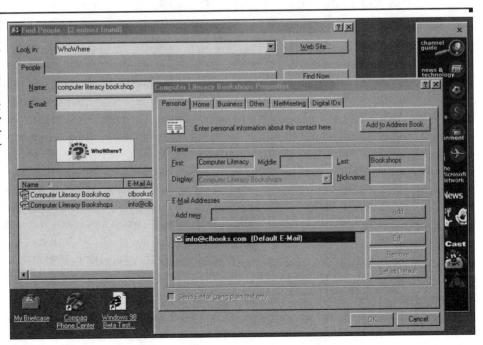

You can click on the Add to Address Book to add a found person or business to your personal address book (used by Outlook Express, Microsoft Outlook, or Windows Messaging/Exchange).

If you want to conduct more extensive searching for people, select a service from the Look In box and click on the Web Site button. That will take you to the LDAP server's more exhaustive search engine. For example, many sites such as Switchboard will have access to national Yellow Pages. Other sites have reverse phone number listings to look up a person's address from their phone number. And suppose you're headed to see a friend or client and just don't know how to navigate to their location (physical location) and want to see a map showing their exact location, or suppose you wanted to send a card or flowers to someone without the hassle of going to the store or calling a florist. Some of the websites will let you do all these with the click of your mouse, once a person is found.

 **TIP**

You can search for someone in your personal address book (the one in your Outlook Express or Microsoft Exchange, if you're using one of those e-mail programs), by choosing Address Book as the Look In: option.

How to Get Registered in LDAP

We all search for ourselves the first time around. So don't be shy about it. Just try looking for yourself in the listings. Try each service, then try each Web page. You'll find your clones there, too. Didn't know so many people had your name, did you?!

Is your information wrong? Or did you not appear at all? Maybe it's time to get listed, unless of course, you want the anonymity. There is no central repository of LDAP listings, as far as I know, at this time. The easiest way to get into the listings is to visit the various people search engine Web pages and sign up. Each has a link on them for registering yourself as a living, breathing, e-mail-using, Internet entity. It's up to you how much information you enter about yourself. Some of the pages will ask you for info about where you went to school and God knows what else, such as what you mother's maiden name was. Offer only what you feel comfortable putting out to everyone on the Internet, as you can be sure that these lists get passed around between search engine companies or just gleaned by individuals and dumped into databases for various purposes, such as spamming (bulk e-mailing). On the other hand, if you want to be findable by loved ones or business clients and prospective clients, go for it.

Microsoft Chat [formerly Comic Chat]

Microsoft Chat, previously dubbed Comic Chat, is a cute little program that you (or your kids, or the kid in you) will find hilarious and entertaining. As discussed in the chapter on NetMeeting and mentioned elsewhere, "chatting" is the activity that lets you carry on real-time typed conversations over the Internet. It's sort of like a slow-motion telephone call, but with the added attraction that it doesn't cost any extra to have it be a party line (i.e., to have numerous participants). With Chat, nobody hears your voice, and you have time to edit your thoughts before broadcasting them (a luxury we don't have on the phone). If you've ever been in an AOL chat room, you know what the chat experience is all about.

Most chat programs (including the generic version of Chat on the Internet called IRC, for *Internet Relay Chat*) are text-only programs, displaying your and others' comments simply as text in a window. Pretty boring. Some inventive (frustrated?) animators and illustrators at Microsoft came up with a better mouse trap: a program they dubbed Comic Chat. At least that was the old name. As of IE4, its new moniker is simply—what else?—Microsoft Chat. In any case, the two are the same: You get to participate in a comic strip where you are one of the characters. You can choose a face (a character) to participate with others who are already in the strip. And, even more fun, you have a range of emotions to choose from, to add a little umph to your conversations. The program takes care of putting you in the frames of the cartoon strip as you interact with your new friends. It's pretty lively.

WARNING

No one is monitoring most of these conversations for adherence to FCC guidelines, or to any other standards of decency, for that matter. If they were to be rated, these comic-strip conversations would run the range from Kiddy to XX. User beware.

Running Chat

To run Chat and get into a conversation, follow these steps:

1. Get online to the Internet in whatever way you normally do. (See Chapter 15 if you're in need of Internet access help.)

2. Click Start ➤ Programs ➤ Internet Explorer ➤ Microsoft Chat. You'll see the window and dialog box displayed in Figure 22.13.

3. Choose which chat room you want to go to. The simplest choice is to accept the default and just click on OK. Click on *Show all available rooms* if you want to see a list of the rooms from which you can choose.

FIGURE 22.13

*The opening
Chat screen*

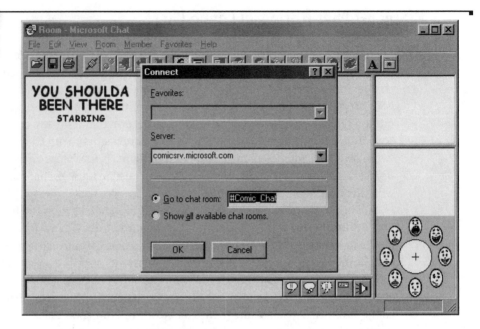

4. You'll next be prompted to enter a nickname for yourself. This name will be displayed on each participant's computer so they can see who else is in the cartoon chat session. If the name you enter is in use already, you'll be advised that you have to choose a different name.

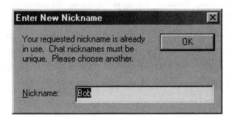

If in step 3 you chose to see all available rooms, you should now see an extensive listing of discussion groups currently on line, as shown here in Figure 22.14.

NOTE

When you choose to show all chat rooms, you may frequently notice lots of weird letters in the listing. This is normal. People use weird letters in the room descriptions sometimes to get attention; also, foreign alphabets sometimes display as strange symbols in English.

FIGURE 22.14

*A scrollable list of
all the chat rooms
currently active*

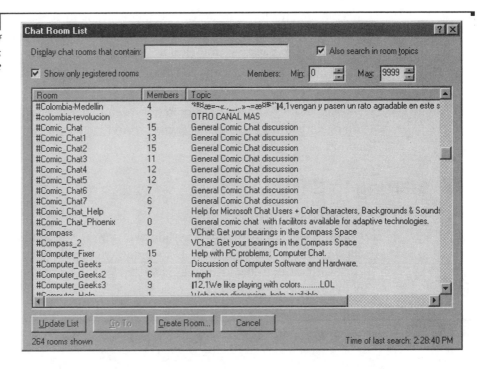

Notice that the chats that are listed are actually Internet IRC chat rooms. Other participants in some of these rooms will probably be using an IRC program other than Microsoft Chat to interact with you, so they won't see the comic characters. That's okay. They'll still see the text you write. You may notice, though, as in the listing I've shown, that there are quite a few Comic Chat rooms, since the popularity of Microsoft Chat is on the rise.

There are a few useful settings on this window to check out:

- You can search for rooms of a certain description. In the *Display chat rooms that contain:* box at the top of the window, type in a search word to filter the list. For example, type in the word *nice* and you stand a better chance of engaging in some civilized conversation:

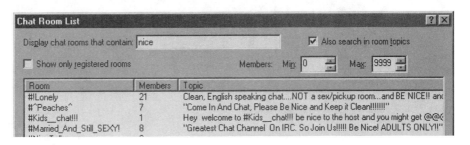

- You can limit the listing to "registered" rooms. These are rooms monitored by the Internet server that hosts the room. By checking this option, you stand a better chance of eliminating scatological or pornographic chat rooms from the list.

- You can exclude rooms with too few or too many users, via the Members Min and Max settings.

- You can create your own chat room (for meeting new friends, or having a pre-arranged time for your friends to meet you) by clicking on the Create Room button.

Starting to Chat

Ready to chat? Follow these steps:

1. Choose a room (skip this if you already went with the default room), by double-clicking on it in the Chat Room List window. You should see a currently active chat, with cartoon characters (see Figure 22.15). The list on the upper right side of the window shows who's in the room.

FIGURE 22.15

What you'll see once you get into a chat room

2. Just as before interacting with newsgroups, watch (lurk) for a while to see what's going on. Then decide whether you want to jump in. You're likely to be either "hit on" or at least acknowledged once you sign in, and someone might even try to "whisper" to you. (More about whispering in a bit.) Just ignore them until you are comfortable with the topic and know you want to participate.

3. When you're ready to interact, you can go with the character you were assigned, or you can choose one you like better (by choosing View ➤ Options ➤ Character). Unfortunately, the possibility exists that you could choose one that is already in use, which could create confusion. Lurking for a while should give you an idea of which characters are already represented in the chat.

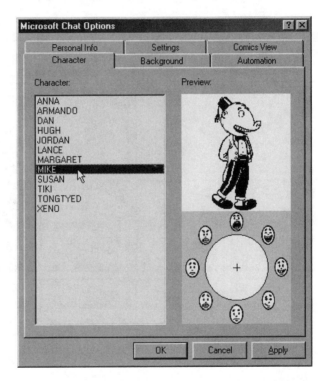

4. Each time you send a message, your character's emotion will change. If you want to *choose* an emotion to match or emphasize your comment, you must click on the emotion first (lower right corner of the window) before sending the text of your comment.

5. Type your message in the bottom line of the window (you can edit it before you send it), then send it by pressing Enter for a normal spoken balloon, or by clicking on the thought bubble or the Action button.

6. When you're ready to leave the room, choose Room ➤ Leave Room. To enter a new room, choose Room ➤ Room List and choose a new room from the list.

Additional Chat Features

Here are a few Chat tricks you might want to check out:

- You can enlarge the display so you see more panels at once. Choose View ➤ Options ➤ Comics View, and change the number of panels, then maximize the Chat window. On an 800 × 600 screen, you'll be able to see four columns of panels (see Figure 22.16).

FIGURE 22.16

You can display more panels at one time via the View ➤ Options settings.

- If you don't want to see the comic characters, click on the text-only icon in the toolbar, or choose View ➤ Plain Text.
- If you want to have a private conversation with someone, click on his or her name in the member list in the upper right corner of the window. Then click on

the Whisper icon or press Ctrl-W. (You can also right-click on the person's character in the comic pane and choose Whisper Box from the right-click's pop-up menu.) The other party will automatically be invited to converse with you in private. They will have the option of ignoring the request, though, so don't be surprised if your overtures are not reciprocated. If they accept your invitation, a private Whisper window will appear. This is a text-only window in which you can type your private conversation.

- You can play a sound on everyone else's Windows computer as the mood strikes you. The sound has to be on their computers, so the only choices are sounds that everyone has:

- You can point to a person in the graphic display to identify who they are; their name will pop up under the cursor. This is especially useful when several people have taken the same display character.

- Choose Room ➢ Create Room to set up a new room. You are the room host then, and can invite people into the new room, if you want.

- Choose View ➢ Member List ➢ Icon to change the member list display to an icon list. It's easier to see who is who this way.

- The toolbar is a shortcut to many of the right-click and other features.

- You can right-click on a person's character and find out a number of things about the person or engage them in another type of forum:

NOTE

When you right click on a character in a chat panel, you can send the person a file, send them e-mail, visit their personal home page, invite them to whisper with you (private chat), or run NetMeeting to place a NetMeeting call to the other party. Except for whispering, all these options require the other person to have filled in a *profile* of themselves when they logged on, indicating their e-mail address and other coordinates.

Chapter

23

Maintaining Your System with the System Tools

FEATURING

Correcting disk errors with ScanDisk

Backing up files with Backup

Increasing disk capacity with DriveSpace

Compression Agent

Disk Defragmenter and Disk Cleanup

Drive Converter (FAT 32)

Tracking system resources with System Monitor

NetWatcher

Task Scheduler

Maintenance Wizard

Windows Update

System Information Tool

Maintaining Your System with the System Tools

Windows 98 includes a very full set of software tools designed to improve the performance of your system and protect your vital information against breakdowns, damage, theft, or loss. The tools are listed in the following table. Some of the utilities are rather high-end tools for techie power users, and would be difficult to present adequately in a book of this scope; they must be left to another edition. The rest of the programs, however, are covered in depth in this chapter.

To see the plethora of tools, open the System Tools folder as you see in Figure 23.1. The programs are described in Table 23.1.

Correcting Disk Errors with ScanDisk

While your PC's disks give you a reliable place to store vast amounts of information, they are vulnerable to glitches of various types that can make the information unusable or reduce the space available for storing new data. The ScanDisk accessory can find these problems and take remedial action either by correcting the problem directly or locking out problem areas on the disk. It can't fix all possible errors, but it will notify you of every problem it discovers.

FIGURE 23.1

The plethora of system tools

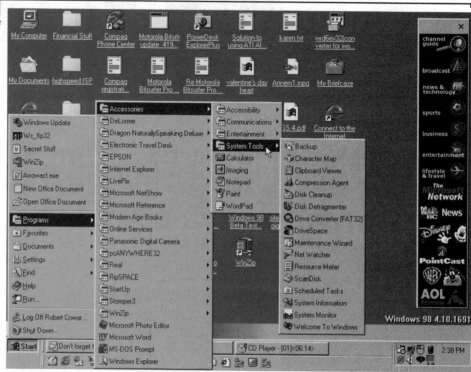

TABLE 23.1: SYSTEM TOOLS IN WINDOWS 98

System Utility Program	Purpose
ScanDisk	For detecting and correcting errors on your disks that might otherwise cause you to lose information or waste disk space.
Backup	For making backup copies of the files on your hard disks onto floppy disks or tape. If your computer or hard disks ever break down or get stolen, you'll be able to retrieve the files using Backup and the backup copies.
DriveSpace	For increasing the amount of storage space available on your disks by compressing the information in your files.
Disk Defragmenter	For speeding access to the files on your hard disks. It works by reorganizing the disks so each file is stored as a single contiguous block on one area of the disk instead of in sections scattered over different parts of the disk.
System Monitor	For displaying technical information about the activity of your system, showing you how your system resources are being used on a moment-to-moment basis (this is only available if you install Network Administrator Tools).

Continued ▶

TABLE 23.1: SYSTEM TOOLS IN WINDOWS 98 (CONTINUED)

System Utility Program	Purpose
Drive Converter (FAT 32)	Installs an enhancement of the File Allocation Table (FAT or FAT 16) file system format on your hard disk, improving disk space efficiency on large drives (512 megabytes to 2 terabytes). Typically increases your drive's capacity by about 25%.
Compression Agent	On drives compressed with DriveSpace 3, use Compression Agent to compress selected files using the settings you specify. With Compression Agent, you can save disk space by compressing files, or improve performance by changing the level of compression on your files.
Disk Cleanup	A simple utility to quickly free up space on your hard disk by erasing specific temporary files.
NetWatcher	Lets you see which workgroup users are currently using resources on your computer; also lets you share folders and/or disconnect users from your workstation.
System Information	A substantial set of tools for reporting information about your computer and for running a number of useful system tools. The tools include *Registry Checker* (which automatically scans your Registry and repairs problems as directed) and the *System File Checker* (for verifying the integrity of your operating system files, restoring them if they are corrupted, and extracting compressed files, such as drivers, from your installation disks). Also includes *Dr. Watson* (familiar to power users of earlier versions of Windows), *Windows Report Tool*, *System Configuration Utility*, *ScanDisk*, and *Version Conflict Manager*.
Maintenance Wizard	Lets you schedule times for Windows to optimize your programs to run faster, run ScanDisk to check your hard disk for problems, and run Disk Cleanup to free up hard disk and Compression Agent (if a DriveSpace 3 volume is present on the system).
Windows Update	Helps keep your Windows 98 system tuned and up-to-date by automating driver and system updates from one place on the Web.
Windows Reporting Tool	Winrep is a means for quickly producing and submitting a bug report to Microsoft about a problem with Windows.
System Troubleshooting Wizards	Fifteen built-in troubleshooters for solving problems with Dial-Up Networking, Direct Cable Connection, DirectX, Display, DriveSpace, Hardware Conflicts, Memory, Modem, MS-DOS Programs, Networking, PC Card, Print, Sound, Startup and Shutdown, The Microsoft Network.

You can run ScanDisk manually, when you suspect there might be trouble with your disk, or you can have the Maintenance Wizard (covered in this chapter) do it automatically on a regular schedule. It's likely that ScanDisk will also be run pretty regularly without your intervention. Why? If you challenge Windows 98 by running lots of programs or more specifically, buggy programs, you're likely to have a system "crash" once in a while, causing an ungracious shutdown. Whenever Windows 98 isn't shut down properly (you should choose Start ➤ Shutdown the command), or if the power goes out suddenly, ScanDisk runs the next time you boot up. Disk errors, if any, are found and fixed (without notifying you or requiring keystrokes). The system will restart without user intervention.

TECH TIP

After an automatic execution of ScanDisk after a bad shutdown, any fixed data, such as cross-linked files, are still on the hard disk, and will be stored as files (see below). Thus, if you need to run advanced data-recovery utilities you can once the system boots.

NOTE

This version of ScanDisk performs functions similar to those of the DOS-based programs SCANDISK and CHKDSK (SCANDISK was included with MS-DOS 6, and CHKDSK is available in every version of DOS and came with Windows 95 as well). The big difference is, you can use the current version of ScanDisk from within Windows and it can repair more problems. Also the DOS-based CHKDSK won't work with FAT 32-formatted disks.

To run ScanDisk, first close any programs you're using. Then, click Start ➤ Programs ➤ Accessories ➤ System Tools ➤ ScanDisk. You'll see the main ScanDisk window, shown in Figure 23.2.

TIP

If something has gone seriously wrong with your hard disk, it may help to run ScanDisk more than once. In some cases, the program is able to find and repair additional errors on each of several passes.

FIGURE 23.2

*The main ScanDisk
window*

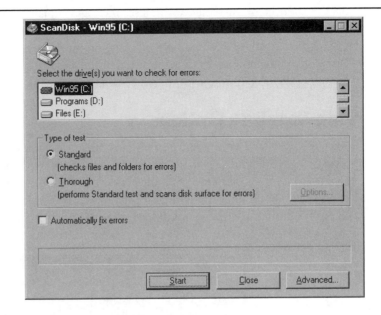

You have only a few choices to make in this window. Choose the disk you want to analyze from the list at the top of the window. Check the Automatically Fix Errors box if you want ScanDisk to correct the errors it finds for you without any further input from you. Clear this box if you want a chance to determine how ScanDisk handles each error.

The two radio buttons in the center let you select either a standard test, which simply checks for errors and inconsistencies in the records Windows keeps on folders (directories) and the files they contain; or a "thorough" test which in addition checks the actual disk surface itself for problems with the magnetic media on which information is stored.

I'll explain more about the various types of checks that ScanDisk performs and why they're necessary in a bit. For now, a quick word of advice on how to choose between these two options is in order. The standard test is *much* faster than the thorough test, and the problems it detects occur far more frequently than flaws in the disk surface. You should run the standard test regularly—every day when you start your PC, if you're a heavy user, or once a week if you only use your computer occasionally. Running the thorough test once a week (for heavy users) to once a month (for occasional users) should be enough to catch most disk-surface errors before you lose data.

Testing a Disk

To begin a disk test, click on the Start button at the bottom of the ScanDisk window. As the program analyzes your disk, it reports its progress in the area above the buttons near the bottom of the window. You'll see messages explaining what ScanDisk is doing at the moment plus a graphical meter of how much of the analysis is complete.

You can stop a test at any time by clicking on the Cancel button. Otherwise, Scan-Disk displays the message "Complete" when it finishes the analysis. Depending on how you've set the display options, you may see a summary of its findings.

Setting ScanDisk Options

ScanDisk's standard settings are best for most users, and you probably won't need to change them. But choice is the name of the game. ScanDisk lets you select settings for a variety of options pertaining to both standard and thorough tests.

To review and change the settings for standard disk tests, click on the Advanced button in the ScanDisk window. You'll see the ScanDisk Advanced Options dialog box, shown here:

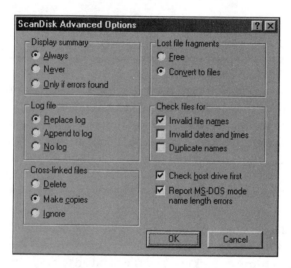

The dialog box is divided into four main areas: one for specifying display options, one for controlling how files are analyzed, and two for specifying how ScanDisk handles specific types of errors. In addition, there's a checkbox near the bottom of the dialog box that pertains only to compressed drives.

Setting Display Options

The Display Summary area offers radio buttons for three settings that determine when you will see a summary of ScanDisk's findings. Choose:

> **Always:** If you want to see the summary when ScanDisk finishes testing a disk, whether or not it finds any errors.

Never: If you never want to see the summary.

Only if errors found: If you want to see the summary only if ScanDisk found any errors.

Handling Cross-Linked Files

One long-familiar PC problem that can still bedevil your Windows disks is *cross-linked files*. Because of quirks in the way DOS and Windows store information about files, errors can creep into the master record that shows where each file is located on the disk. When files are cross-linked, the record shows that two or more files share a common part (cluster) of the disk. Files are always supposed to be independent entities, so this is clearly a mistake. When the system tries to access a cross-linked file, it will likely read the wrong information. Your documents may open looking like garbage, or your whole system may come to a halt.

ScanDisk lets you decide how to handle the cross-linked files it discovers as it combs through the disk's master record. However, these settings only apply if you have checked Automatically Fix Errors in the main ScanDisk window (if not, ScanDisk will let you decide how to handle each cross-linking problem on a case-by-case basis as described just below).

Choose one of the radio buttons in the Cross Linked Files area as follows:

Delete: If you want ScanDisk to erase the cross-linked files. You won't have to worry about them again, although you'll lose the data they contain.

Make copies: If you want ScanDisk to copy each cross-linked file to a new location on the disk in hopes of preserving the original information. When two or more files are cross-linked, the disk cluster they have in common contains valid information from only one of the files, at most. (In some cases, all of the information in the shared cluster is garbage.) If you're lucky, copying the files will restore one of them to its original condition. In any case, you may be able to retrieve some of the contents if they are copied word-processor or database files. To try this, open them in a text editor or word processor and copy any valid information you find to a new file.

Ignore: If you want ScanDisk to leave the cross-linked files as is. This is a choice for advanced users who may wish to use other disk tools to examine the contents of the problem files in hopes of retrieving more of their data. Normally, you shouldn't select this option—if you leave the cross-linked files in place, you're very likely to lose even more of the information they contain, and the problem may spread to other files.

If the option Automatically Fix Errors is not checked, ScanDisk displays a dialog box similar to this one when it detects cross-linked files:

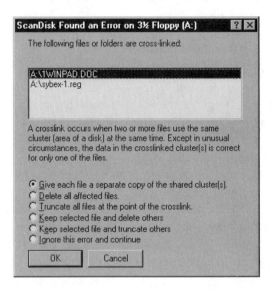

Handling Lost File Fragments

Lost file fragments are portions of the disk containing information that doesn't belong to any specific file. Somehow, the master record for the disk has gotten muddled. While the record indicates that these areas hold data, it doesn't show which files they belong to. As ScanDisk checks the master record, it finds these free-floating chunks of information by checking the entry for each cluster against the list of files and their locations.

If you have checked the Automatically Fix Errors box in the main ScanDisk window, ScanDisk will deal with the lost file fragments it finds according to the setting in the Lost File Fragments area. Choose:

Free: If you want ScanDisk to delete the lost file fragments, freeing up the space on disk for other files.

Convert to files: If you want ScanDisk to convert the fragments to valid files. ScanDisk names the files according to the pattern file0000.chk, file0001.chk, and so on, placing them in the top-level folder (the root directory) of the current disk drive. After you finish with ScanDisk, you can use a file-viewing program to examine their contents.

If the Automatically Fix Errors box isn't checked, you'll receive a message when ScanDisk encounters lost file fragments, allowing you to decide then how to deal with the situation.

File-Checking Options

The Check Files For area has two checkboxes having to do with the types of errors Scan-Disk checks for when analyzing individual files. You can check them in any combination.

Invalid filenames: If you want ScanDisk to find files with invalid characters in their names.

Invalid dates and times: If you want ScanDisk to find files whose date and time information is invalid (e.g. 14/13/98).

Duplicate names: If you want ScanDisk to find duplicate broken files on your disk. (It doesn't report all files of the same name, just ones that are broken that share the same name.) Setting this option on immediately results in a warning that it can take a long time to check for duplicate names on a drive containing many files.

Other options: Click on the ? button, then on the checkbox for helpful information about other less common options.

If you have checked the Automatically fix errors box on the main ScanDisk window, ScanDisk will fix the types of errors you've chosen automatically. If not, you'll be shown a message describing the problem and giving you options for dealing with it, as in this example:

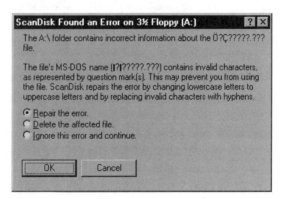

Options for Compressed Drives

The checkbox labeled *Check host drive first* in the ScanDisk Advanced Options dialog box applies only to compressed drives. If you're testing a drive that has been compressed for more storage space by DriveSpace (included with Windows 95), DoubleSpace (included with DOS 6), or DriveSpace 3, you might want to change this setting.

When the box is checked, ScanDisk tests the actual disk—the *host* drive—where the compressed drive is located before checking the files and folders of the compressed drive. You should leave this box checked for most work because the host drive may be hidden and because errors on a compressed drive are commonly caused by problems with the host drive. Clearing the box will make the test run faster.

Options for Thorough Disk Tests

If you select a thorough test on the main ScanDisk window, the Options button becomes available. Click on it to display the Surface Scan Options dialog box, shown here:

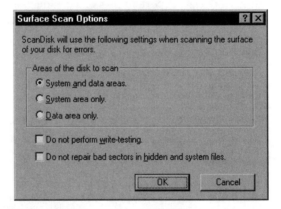

In the bordered area labeled *Areas of the disk to scan*, choose the radio button for the type of test you want to perform:

System and data areas: If you want to scan the entire disk.

System area only: If you want to scan only the sections of the disk that store system information, such as the boot (start-up) programs and the master records of the file and folders. Much of the information stored here cannot be moved, so ScanDisk will be unable to fix problems here. If errors in the system area are found, the disk probably should be junked.

Data area only: If you want to check the bulk of the disk area, where your files can be stored, but not the system area. This choice scans the entire data area, including areas not currently storing files. When it finds a faulty location, Scan-Disk can often preserve the information stored there by moving the data elsewhere. The faulty location is then marked as "bad" so it won't be used in the future. If the problem isn't caught early enough, however, data at the faulty location may be unreadable, in which case it's gone for good (ScanDisk will still mark the bad spot).

Because the system area occupies only a small part of the entire disk, testing the system area takes much less time than testing the data area or the full disk.

The Surface Scan Options dialog box also has two checkboxes:

Do not perform write-testing: When this box is cleared, ScanDisk tests each location on the disk exhaustively. It reads the data stored at that location, writes the data back to the same spot, then rereads the information to check it against the original copy. If you check the box, ScanDisk simply checks to be sure it can read the data. This may not be enough to catch and correct some errors before the information becomes unusable.

Do not repair bad sectors in hidden and system files: When this box is cleared, ScanDisk attempts to relocate the data stored in all damaged locations on the disk, even if the information belongs to a hidden or system file. The problem is, some programs expect to find certain hidden system files in a specific disk location. If these files (or any part of them) are moved, the program stops working. In the early days of the PC, this was a fairly common *copy-protection scheme,* a technique to keep people from making unauthorized copies of software. If you have such programs, you may wish to check this box. ScanDisk will then leave hidden and system files where they are even when they are found on damaged areas of the disk. The programs will find their special files in their expected locations—but because of the disk problems, they may not work anyway.

Options for File Names That Are Longer Than They Should Be

Notice the option in the Advanced box called: *Report MS-DOS mode name length errors.* When this option is set on, ScanDisk alerts you if some file names or folders are longer than the maximum length for use by non-Windows programs, such as DOS files. Since Windows automatically truncates long file name for use by DOS or older Windows programs, the most common offender will be long pathnames for folders. Here's an example:

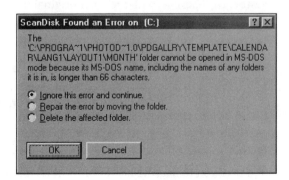

By default, this option is off. If long folder paths are a problem with some of the programs you use, you can turn this option on, do a ScanDisk, and have them checked. Normally you won't want to delete the folders that are found. You'll move them to another location, closer to the root directory.

Backing Up Your Files with Backup

You're probably sick of people telling you how important it is to back up the work you do with your computer. Well, it's true. If you're not backing up your work regularly, you're putting it all at risk. Learn how to do it now, and you could potentially save your business from turning into a total loss.

NOTE

In case you're new to computers, you should know that backing up is a critical every-day task. Any information you store on a disk is vulnerable to damage or loss from a host of dangers, ranging from theft, fire, and water to magnetic or mechanical failure of the disk itself. The greatest threat to your data is you—choosing the wrong command can wipe out hours of work in an instant. Your most effective weapon in the battle to protect your data is to make backup copies of everything you keep on your disks, especially the documents and other files you create yourself. Should disaster strike and wipe out your front-line data, you can fall back on the backups—but only if you've made them.

Backup simplifies the process of backing up your disks and of *restoring* the backed-up files should the originals ever be lost. With Backup you can do any of the following:

- Back up to floppy disk or on tape.
- Specify which files are backed up.
- Create sets of files for repeated backup as groups.
- Compress the backed-up files so fewer floppy disks or tapes are required.
- Restore the backed-up files to their original folders or to new locations.
- Compare the backed-up files with the current versions on disk.

One caveat is important to mention here: Don't rely on your backups until you've tested the entire process of backing up and restoring data. Back up a set of files including programs and some data. After restoring them, check that the programs still run properly and that the other files will still open and still contain valid information. This is the only way you can be sure that Backup and your backup hardware are working properly.

Also, be aware that backup tapes and floppies can go bad as they age. Although it should be fine if your daily backup sessions only back up files that are new or have changed, I urge you to back up *all* your files at regular intervals.

NOTE

NEW FOR WINDOWS 98   Windows 98's backup program is essentially the same program supplied with Windows 95, with the addition of support for more devices. It now supports SCSI tape devices and many other new backup devices, such as QIC-80, QIC-80 Wide, QIC 3010 (and wide), QIC 3020 (and wide), TR1, TR2, TR3, TR4, DAT (DDS1, 2, and 3), DC 6000, 8mm, DLT, and drives by Conner, Exabyte, HP/Colorado, Iomega, Micro Solutions, Seagate, Tandberg, WangDAT, and Wangtek. In addition, Windows 98 Backup supports backups to local, removable, and network drives. At this time there is no support for CD writers.

Running Backup

NOTE

Backup is not installed on your drive by default, so you may need to install it yourself. Go to Start ➢ Settings ➢ Control Panel ➢ Add/Remove Programs ➢ Windows Setup ➢ System Tools ➢ Details. Turn on the Backup option and OK the boxes. You will most likely be prompted to insert the Windows 98 CD or specify the path of the setup files.

To run Backup, begin from the Start menu and choose Programs ➢ Accessories ➢ System Tools ➢ Backup.

TIP

If you install a new tape drive after running Backup for the first time, you must choose Tools ➢ Redetect Tape. Backup will re-initialize itself, repeating the search for a working tape drive.

The first time you run Backup, it examines your system, looking for a working tape drive. You may hear some gruesome noises from your floppy drives as Backup probes to see just what kind of devices they really are. If Backup can't find a working tape drive, you won't be able to access the tape-related commands, but you'll have access to other commands. You can actually back up to another hard disk or floppy, or network drive if you want, so don't worry. In fact, hard drives are so much faster than tape that I'd suggest using something like a Jaz drive, or even a Zip drive rather than tape.

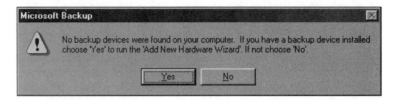

If you have installed new hardware and it's not been detected, you can run the hardware Wizard and set up the drivers for it and then come back and run Backup again. Click Yes. (Refer to Chapter 7 for use of the Add New Hardware Wizard.) Clicking on No still gets you into the program and you choose the destination for your backup.

Running Backup via the Wizard

When the Backup screen appears, a Wizard helps walk you through the process of backing up (or restoring data from a backup you did earlier). See Figure 23.3. You can bail on the Wizard and run Backup manually, if you want. Just click on Close. Skip to the section below called "Running Backup without the Wizard." (You can start the Wizard again, if you want, by choosing Tools ➤ Backup Wizard from the Backup window.)

*The first step in
making a backup*

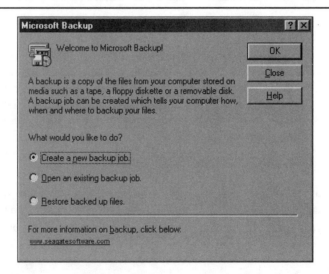

Choose the option you want. The first and third options are self-explanatory. The second option lets you choose from different backup scenarios that you might have created and saved in the past. (People who do lots of backups have different needs for different situations.) For the purposes of illustration here I'll assume you're starting a new backup.

TIP

If you're connected to the Web, the hyperlink on the dialog box will take you to additional information about the Backup program on a site run by Seagate. (Seagate is the company that made the Backup program.)

Next you're asked what it is you want to back up:

- **My computer:** If you have room on the destination drive to do a complete backup, choose the first option. Everything in your computer, including the zillions of Windows files will be backed up—which is not a bad idea in cases where you really want to be protected against major disaster. You can use Backup's emergency recovery feature to restore the whole system if your hard disk does a major swan song.

- **Selected files:** If you only want to back up certain critical directories, choose this option.

If you chose My Computer, you're given the opportunity to choose all files or just ones that are new or have changed since the last backup (an *incremental* backup).

If you chose Selected Files you'll first see a directory-tree listing of files and folders to choose from. *Then* you get to choose whether you want to do an incremental backup, or back up all the files in the folders you indicated. The file and folder box is shown in Figure 23.4. The object is to put a checkmark in the box next to the items you want to back up.

FIGURE 23.4

If you choose to back up selected files you'll see this box. Click on the items you want to back up.

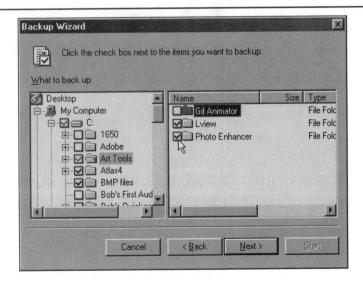

Here are some tips for using this box effectively:

- Click on a + sign to open a drive to see its folders, just like in Windows Explorer.

- If you put a checkmark in a disk drive's box, *everything* in the drive will be backed up.

- If you put a checkmark in a folder's box, *everything* in the folder will be backed up.

- If you click on a folder's icon, it will open the right pane and you can choose individual files.

- If you select specific folders rather than an entire disk, Backup places a check-mark in the disk's box, too, but it is gray, not blue. Similarly, if you pick out sep-arate files within a folder, the folder's box will be checked with a gray checkmark.

- Incremental backups save time in subsequent passes. If you are going to back up a large amount (such as an entire disk) on a regular basis, use the "new or changed" option. Then, only new or changed files get backed up. This can save considerable time.

After that choice is made, the Wizard now asks for the backup destination. Where is the backed up stuff going to be stored?

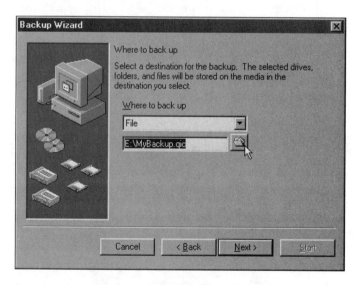

Here I've chosen to store the backed up stuff in a file, and it's going to be on drive E. That drive is a ZIP disk in my case. (Click where you see my pointer to choose the location of the file and name it. You'll get a normal File dialog box to work with.) As you can see above, a file named MyBackup.QIC is going to be created, containing all the files I'm having backed up. A QIC file is a specially compressed file that can con-tain a whole mess of backed-up files.

Clicking on Next brings up these choices:

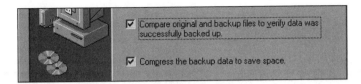

Normally these are both on.

- You can turn off compression if the files you are backing up are already compressed. This will save space on the backup media. However, for uncompressed data, this option should be left on.

- You can speed up the backup process by not verifying the data. It takes a little time, but it's worth knowing whether your backup was successful, so I'd leave comparison turned on.

Next you get to name the job. Giving it a name makes it easier to repeat this backup procedure.

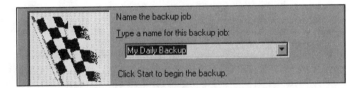

Check all the settings reported in the box and make sure they are correct. If not, click Back to reach the relevant box and fix the settings. Then click Next as many times as necessary to get back to this box.

Click Start and the backup will begin. You'll see a progress report as it moves along. After the backup is complete, the verification process begins.

Assuming all went OK, you'll see a message stating "Backup successful, no errors." If there is some other problem, you'll be alerted. You can click on OK, then close the program if you're all done. The next time you run Backup, the Wizard will start, and you'll have the option of running the saved backup job again without filling in all the boxes. Choose this option:

Choose the job from the resulting list, then insert your backup media and run the job by clicking on Start (see instructions below for more about what the screens will look like since the Wizard goes away and you're in manual mode at this point).

Running Backup without the Wizard

If you prefer to run without the Backup and Restore Wizard, you'll have substantial control over Backup. You'll see the window in Figure 23.5.

FIGURE 23.5

The basic Backup window

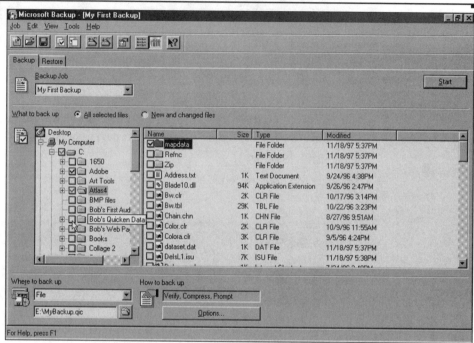

Note that there are two pages to this window: Backup and Restore. Click on the Backup tab to choose the information you want to back up and where you want to store it as well as to initiate the actual backup process.

> The Options button lets you set a wide variety of optional settings controlling details of the backup process. See "Setting Backup Options" later in this section.

1. Click on the Backup Job button, or choose Job ➤ New.

2. Select the items you want to back up: entire disks, their folders, or individual files, in any combination. The display works just like the one in Explorer, showing disks and folders in a tree view on the left and listing subfolders and individual files in the currently selected disk or folder on the right. Unlike Explorer, however, Backup displays a small checkbox next to each item. To select an item for backup, click on the square for that item (in either side of the window) so a checkmark appears there. As you can guess, checking a disk selects all the folders and files on that disk for backup. If you select specific folders rather than an entire disk, Backup places a checkmark in the disk's box, too, but it's gray, not blue. Similarly, if you pick out separate files within a folder, the folder's box will have a gray checkmark.

3. Choose either All Selected Files or New and Changed Files (see discussion above in the Wizard section).

4. Move to the Where to Back Up section. Open the drop-down list and choose the device, or the word *File* to back up to a file (you'll use this when backing up on a hard disk, network disk, floppy disk, or removable disk media such as Zip or Jaz). Set the file name if you want to give it a name other than the default name. Either type in the full name and pathname or click on the little folder graphic and you'll use a File box to browse to the destination.

5. Select any options you might want (options are covered below).

Finishing the Backup

Before you go any further, prepare the disks or tapes you'll be using for the backup:

1. Get out enough of them to hold all the data. (Backup displays the total size of all the selected files at the bottom right. If you turn the compression option on, you may need half this much capacity or less on your backup tapes and disks.)

If you need to format your tapes or erase existing data from tapes or disks, use the commands on the Tools menu described in "Formatting, Erasing, and Other Operations for Backup Media" below.

2. Label the first tape or disk with the date, a set name, and the number 1.

3. To proceed to the actual backup step, click on Start. (You may be prompted to save your settings first, and give the backup job a name for later use. Just do it.) The backup will begin and you'll see a progress report as it happens. If all the files won't fit on the first target disk or tape, Backup notifies you and asks you to insert another disk or tape (before you do, label it with the date and set name and number it in proper sequence). The process continues in this way until all the files in your file set have been backed up.

NOTE

If Backup encounters any problems during the backup process, you'll see error messages describing the glitch.

TIP

Sometimes you'll get an error message when you start a backup, saying there are other backup file sets on the same drive or media and asking if you want to overwrite. You're allowed to have multiple backup sets on a media, just not ones with the same name. Use the Job ➤ Save As command to save your new job under a new name, and enter a new file name in the *Where to Back Up* field. Then try again. You can prevent this in the future by always starting new backup jobs with step 1, above.

NOTE

In the Windows 95 version of Backup, you had the option of saving backup sets or not. In Windows 98's version, you *have* to save the set before you can actually perform the backup.

Formatting, Erasing, and Other Operations for Backup Media

The Tools ➤ Media ➤ menu has several useful subcommands, depending on your backup medium. If you are using File as the backup medium, you don't have any of these commands, which apply mostly to tape backup units.

- **Identify**: Shows you the name of the device, and of the medium. You can view the medium's existing backup sets by clicking View media in the Identify Progress window. If the see the indicator "N/A" in the Capacity section, this means that the device can't estimate the amount of free and used space on the medium.

- **Format**: Formats a standard QIC medium. Just as with a floppy disk, all data will be permanently erased. Use caution. You'll be given a chance to bail out, since you have to confirm the format.

- **Initialize**: Like Format, but for non-QIC devices. Erases and prepares the medium for recording on. Again, take caution, since any existing data will be trashed. If there is existing data, you're asked to confirm the process.

- **Erase**: For SCSI devices, this trashes existing data. You're asked to confirm.
- **Retension**: For tape systems, this tightens up the tape and removes any slack in the tape by performing a fast-forward and rewind procedure.
- **Rename**: Lets you see and rename the tape currently inserted. To rename your QIC tape, enter a new name in the text box, then click OK.

Formatting can take 30 minutes to several hours, so do it when you aren't in a hurry. You can work on other things on the computer while this is happening, though it may slow down the computer's response time.

By the way, you can set up Backup so that it *always* automatically erases existing data from tapes and/or disks before each new backup operation. See "Changing Backup Options" later in this section.

The Windows 95 version of Backup accommodated drag-and-drop techniques for initiating backups. This feature has been dropped in Windows 98.

Restoring Files from Your Backups

You may never need the backups you've so diligently made, day after day, week after week. If your hard disk never breaks down, if you never delete a file by mistake, if your computer never gets stolen, consider yourself lucky and the time you spent backing up as inexpensive insurance.

But if you ever do lose data, your backups suddenly will seem to you precious jewels of infinite value. After your computer is running again—or you've gone out and bought another—slip the backup disk or tape into the machine, do a restore, and with luck your vanished files will be miraculously recovered.

With Backup, restoring files is a piece of cake. As with making the backups, there are two ways to restore from them: Using Wizard, and manually, without the Wizard.

Restoring with the Wizard

1. Find the set of tapes or disks containing the lost files and insert disk or tape #1.

2. Run the Backup program and choose Restore, or if the program is already up, choose Tools ➤ Restore Wizard. You'll see the this dialog box.

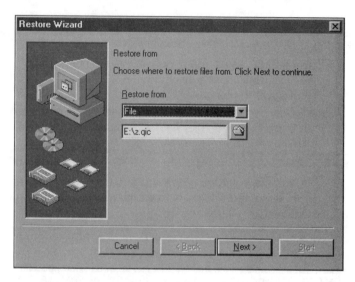

3. Choose the device in the upper box. Change the file name, if needed, by clicking on the little folder to the right of the lower box and browsing for it, or by typing it in.

4. Click Next. In a few seconds you'll be asked to click on the backup set you want to restore.

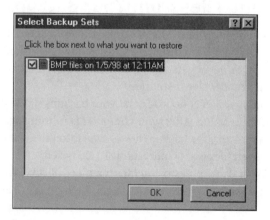

Select it and click OK.

5. Now you'll see a two-paned box like the one you used to do the backup. You can now select which drives, folders, or files you want to restore. As usual, you open drives by clicking on the + sign. You open subfolders the same way. To see the contents of a folder, right-click on it—its contents appears in the right pane. From there you can select a single file to restore if you want to. Clicking on the highest level (for example the C drive) without opening any folders, will restore *everything* you backed up. In this example, I'm only selecting three files, since those were the ones I lost.

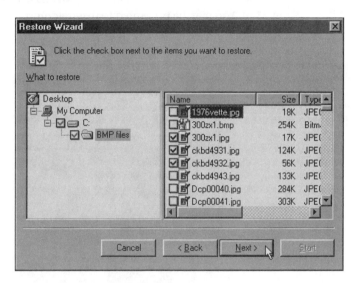

6. Click on Next. Now you're asked where you want to restore the data to. Typically this will be to the original location. But if you choose Alternate Location, you can specify the location.

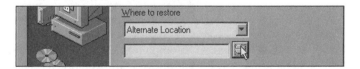

7. Click on Next and you'll be asked one more set of questions before beginning the restore:

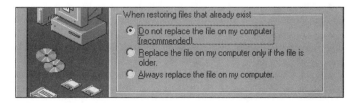

This will take some thinking. I can't tell you the answer. Obviously if you are trying to restore a file or folder that was trashed somehow, and is still on the computer, the first option is not what you want. You *want* to replace existing files. So you'll at least choose the second option. But even then, if the trashed or corrupted one on your disk has a newer date, then the file won't be restored. You'll have to use option 3.

8. Click Start. You're now prompted to insert the backup media in the source drive. Do so, and the restore process begins. Progress is reported in a window (see Figure 23.6). You may be prompted to insert additional backup media if the backup set spans multiple tapes or disks.

FIGURE 23.6

Progress is reported as the restore takes place.

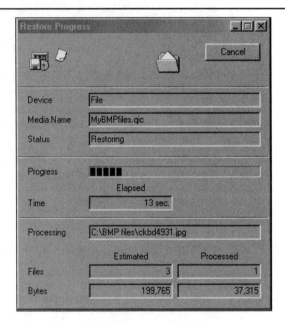

9. When the process is complete you'll be alerted. Remove the media and count your blessings. The backup/restore process worked. Maybe it even saved you your job!

10. Use Windows Explorer or My Computer to check the restored files on your hard disk to make sure they are there.

Restoring without the Wizard

Restoring without the Wizard is simple. You'll have to use many of the same steps the Wizard takes you through, so try it once with the Wizard. Then if you like flying solo, use the manual approach.

1. Run Backup and maximize the window.

2. Click on the Restore tab, shown in Figure 23.7.

FIGURE 23.7

Use this page to restore damaged or lost files.

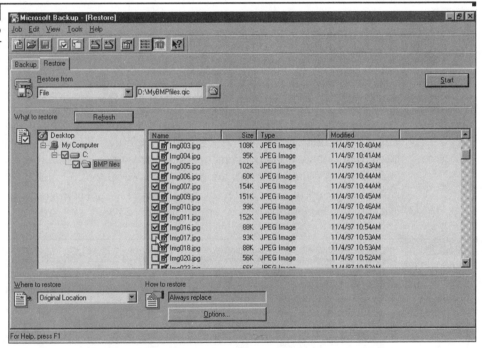

3. Choose the device and backup set file in the Restore From area. (Click on Refresh subsequent to changing these settings. This is necessary so that Backup rechecks the contents of the chosen set.)

4. After Backup checks the set, the window shows the set's disks and folders. Just as when backing up, select the information you want to restore, and click in the little boxes next to each displayed item. If you check the box of the top item in the left-hand list, all the disks, folders, and files contained in the set will be restored. Otherwise, you can check individual disks, folders, and files in any combination. To display an item's contents in the right side of the window, click directly on the item (not its checkbox).

5. Check the setting in the Where to Restore area. Click on it and change it if necessary. (See notes above in the Wizard restore section for discussion on this.)

6. Set any options you want, by clicking the Options button. If you assigned a password when you created the backup, you'll be asked to type it in now.

7. The restoration begins. You'll be informed of its progress and notified when it completes. Depending on how you've set the options, you may be asked for permission to overwrite existing files with the same names as the ones you're restoring.

NOTE

The Windows 95 version of Backup had an option to let you speed up file selection for a backup or restore called *filtering.* This feature has been dropped from the Windows 98 version.

Backup and Restore Option Settings

Each of the two pages on the Backup window (Backup and Restore) has its own set of advanced options. Most folks won't need to alter these. But you might want to, or need to. If you use Backup much, you should at least know what they are since they may save you some time or hassle. You can see the options by clicking the Options button at the bottom of each of the two pages. There are many more options for Backup than for Restore, as you can see in Figure 23.8.

FIGURE 23.8

Option boxes for Backup and Restore

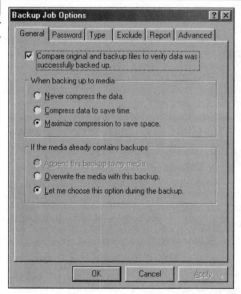
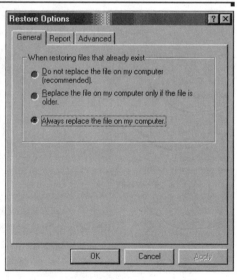

Use the What's This? Button in each option box to learn more about the various options.

Increasing Disk Capacity with DriveSpace 3

The DriveSpace system tool helps you stay ahead of the ever-increasing demand for information storage capacity. DriveSpace *compresses* the files on your disk, storing them in an encoded form so they take only about half as much space as they normally would.

No matter how big a hard disk you buy, it always fills up faster than you expected. It's easy to see why. Windows 98 itself takes up close to 100 MB of hard disk space or more, depending on which components you install—that's roughly ten times as much as a sparse Windows 3.1 installation. Programs are constantly growing larger, too. And if your system software and programs haven't eaten up all the available room, wait 'til you save some multimedia files such as video clips or high-resolution still images, which can easily consume tens of megabytes of disk space.

With DriveSpace, there *is* a free lunch: It roughly doubles the available space on any disk, leaving you with a compressed disk that operates exactly as normal and *maybe even faster*. Of course, you'll still run out of disk space faster than you planned.

NOTE

FAT 32 conversion can also gain you 25% or so of space, but won't work with Drive-Space. That's covered later in this chapter.

DriveSpace has been around in some form in MS-DOS and Windows for about 5 years now. DriveSpace 3 is the latest version and is an enhancement to the DriveSpace program that was supplied with earlier versions of Windows.

How DriveSpace Works

Disk compression is essentially a coding system for the information in your files. As it stores a file on disk, DriveSpace examines the data for repeated sequences that it can represent with shorter codes. Files containing long repeating sequences wind up more compressed than files in which the information has no consistent pattern. When it reads a compressed file, DriveSpace translates the codes back into the original sequences. DriveSpace works with all your files, programs and documents alike.

NOTE

Compression utilities such as PKZIP and LHA work by encoding and decoding files the way DriveSpace does, but only when you specifically tell them to. Such utilities can create significantly smaller compressed files than DriveSpace does, which is great for storing large files you rarely use. Because you have to operate them manually, though, these utilities are far too time consuming and inconvenient for ordinary use.

Techniques for Freeing Up Disk Space

System slowing down to a crawl and you don't know why? Seeing messages about your hard disk not having enough space? Here's the laundry list of methods for clearing up space.

- Use Disk Cleanup to remove unneeded files.
- Use ScanDisk to check for errors that may be using up disk space.
- Remove Windows components that you no longer use.
- Remove programs that you no longer use.
- Create more disk space by converting to FAT 32 or using DriveSpace disk compression.
- If you compress a drive with DriveSpace, use Compression Agent to specify some files to be extra compressed.
- Back up unneeded files and remove them from your hard disk.

DriveSpace works behind the scenes without any intervention on your part. When you run a program, copy a file, or save or open a document, Drive Space steps in automatically to handle the compression or decompression. In the jargon of the day, Drive-Space provides *on-the-fly* compression.

As the discussion implies, DriveSpace actually compresses files, not disks. When it "compresses" a disk, it creates one large special file on the disk to hold the compressed files it then stores there. This special file is set up to act just like a real disk in Windows. It is assigned a letter, just like any other disk drive. The original disk that contains the special file is called the *host* drive.

The file containing the compressed disk must exist on a single unbroken area of the hard disk (that is, it must not be *fragmented*—see "Disk Defragmenter" later in this chapter for more on fragmentation). For this reason, DriveSpace must defragment the hard disk to consolidate its free space before the actual compression process. It also checks the disk for errors before proceeding.

When to Use DriveSpace

My advice is to go ahead and use DriveSpace on any hard disks that are not FAT 32 formatted, but to preserve some uncompressed space—say about 10 to 20 megabytes—on the C drive that's used to boot your computer. Disk compression really does work, it's very reliable, it doesn't slow your system down, and it's free—so why not take full advantage of it?

Although DriveSpace can compress floppy disks, ZIP disks, Jaz disks, or other external, removable media, keep in mind that you can only use these floppies on computers that also have DriveSpace. Other computers won't be able to read them.

On the Incompatibility of DriveSpace and FAT 32

Why are DriveSpace and FAT 32 mutually exclusive? This was a decision on the part of Microsoft. Basically, among users, there are two camps: those who want fastest performance, and those who want maximum storage space. With FAT 32 you get best performance, and pretty good space savings (about 25% better than FAT 16), without having to compress anything at all. With DriveSpace you'll practically double your disk space, but it will cost you some in performance. Also, the kind of space loss that FAT 16 causes is minimized on a DriveSpace compressed drive because there is essentially only one file (the host compressed file). The space lost on FAT 16 drives is the result of partially empty clusters in small files, not a problem with the one large compression file that DriveSpace creates as a storage container for any number of files.

New Features of DriveSpace 3

If you had installed Plus! for Windows 95, or were running Windows 95 OSR2 (also known as version 950b), you already had DriveSpace 3 in your system before installing Windows 98. The major advantage DriveSpace 3 has over its predecessor is that it uses more-advanced compression algorithms for providing even more space on your hard disk.

When creating a new compressed drive, DriveSpace 3 works essentially the same way as DriveSpace. The major differences are that some options such as HiPack and a Settings button have been added, allowing Exceptions and some other advanced options. Together with the Compression Agent (later in this chapter), the new enhancements let you:

- Customize the type of compression used to save files to a compressed drive. You can save files uncompressed, in the Standard compression format, in the new HiPack format, or double-compressed in the new UltraPack format.

- Create compressed drives that are up to 2 gigabytes in size. (To create a 2-gigabyte compressed drive, you need an uncompressed drive that is at least 900 MB in size.)

- Recompress a currently compressed drive using a single compression method or compress each individual file and folder using a separate method for each.

- Uncompress an entire disk or only specific files and folders.
- Specify highest compression for files you seldom use, medium compression for files you use more frequently (access will be quicker).

Likely candidates for highest compression are all Help files (HLP) and setup-information (INF) files. These files are not often used; the Help files are particularly large, sometimes as much as 2 MB.

WARNING

According to Microsoft, "If you compressed your hard disk with Microsoft Plus! and then upgraded to Windows 98 and you need to reinstall Plus!, do *not* use the Re-Install All option in Plus! Setup. If you need to reinstall Plus! and your disk is compressed, you must delete your Setup.STF file (which should be in your \Program Files\Plus!\Setup folder) and then rerun Plus! setup."

For Windows 3.*x* Users

DriveSpace 3 recognizes and works fine with existing compressed disks created by the DOS version of DiskSpace that came with MS-DOS 6.22 or the DoubleSpace utility included with MS-DOS 6.0 or 6.2. You'll no longer need your DOS-based tools to manage these disks because DriveSpace can handle compression-related chores, while ScanDisk (covered earlier in this chapter) can check for and repair errors on the compressed disks.

Windows 98 will recognize disks compressed with other compression software such as Stacker. However, keep two limitations in mind: ScanDisk can't check these "foreign" compressed disks for compression errors, and you can't use DriveSpace and another compression utility at the same time.

Compressing a Drive

Before you compress a disk for the first time, it makes a lot of sense to back up the entire disk just in case something goes wrong during the compression process. After all, you should be backing up regularly anyway, so just think of this as a good time to do your regular backup. You can use the Backup utility, covered earlier, to do the job.

WARNING

Be prepared to wait a long time—possibly many hours—if you compress a disk that already contains a lot of files. And don't think you can walk away from your computer while it works because you may need to respond to messages from the program many times during the process. Why does it take so long? DriveSpace starts by creating a small, uncompressed disk from the available free space. It then goes through a cycle of copying some uncompressed files to the compressed disk, erasing them from the uncompressed disk, and enlarging the compressed disk, repeating this sequence over and over. The best time to compress a disk drive is *before* you install programs other than Windows.

When you use the standard method for compressing a drive, DriveSpace converts nearly all of the original (host) drive to the new compressed drive. All existing files are copied to the compressed drive, leaving only about 2 megabytes of free space uncompressed on the host. If you like, however, you can control how much free space is left uncompressed. You can also use an alternative method, covered later, to create a compressed drive using only the remaining free space on the host.

Now, another point: You can't compress a disk formatted with the FAT 32 file system. So, you better check on that first. When you try to compress a drive, DriveSpace 3 will alert you to such a conflict. Or, for a quick check on your own, open My Computer, right click on the drive in question, and choose Properties. If you see "FAT 32" in the Properties box, you're out of luck. If you see "FAT" you're OK.

Once that's out of the way, you can get down to compressing.

1. To run DriveSpace, begin from the Start menu and choose Programs ➢ Accessories ➢ System Tools ➢ DriveSpace. You'll see the main Drive Space window, consisting simply of a menu bar and a list of the disk drives on your system:

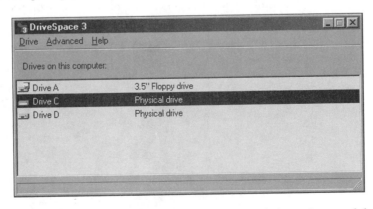

The DriveSpace menu choices let you compress new disks, activate and deactivate them, remove existing compressed disks, and adjust various settings. These options are covered in detail below.

2. To see information about any disk in the list, double-click on the entry for the disk or choose Drive ➤ Properties. You'll see the window shown in Figure 23.9.

FIGURE 23.9

*The Compression
Information window*

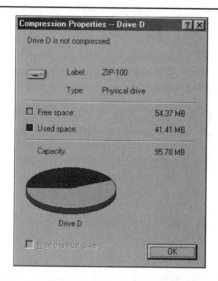

3. The window tells you whether or not the disk is compressed and displays a pie graph showing how much space is in use and how much is free for new programs and documents. You also get a numeric readout of the used and free space and of the total disk capacity. OK the window to close it.

4. To compress a drive using the standard method, select the drive from the list in the DriveSpace window, then choose Drive ➤ Compress. You'll see the window shown in Figure 23.10. This before-and-after window shows you graphically and in numbers how much more room you'll have on the disk after you compress it.

FIGURE 23.10

*The Compress a
Drive window*

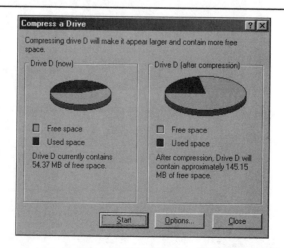

5. Check the Options by clicking on Options. You'll see this dialog box:

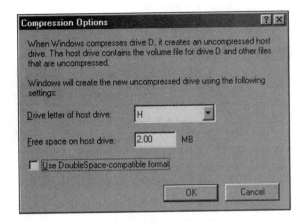

6. Before compressing, you can review the compression settings and change them if you like; click on Options in the Compress a Drive window.

Your choices include:

- **Drive letter of host drive:** DriveSpace will automatically assign the next available drive letter to the host drive. If you want to assign a different drive letter, select it from this list. For example, if you know the letter DriveSpace has chosen will be used by a network drive or a new, real hard disk you plan to install, you would select another letter.

- **Free space on host drive:** If you want to change the amount of uncompressed free space DriveSpace automatically preserves on the host drive, type in the new amount here. I recommend that you keep at least 5 MB uncompressed on the drive used to start your system (originally drive C). After the compression process is complete, you should copy some essential utility programs such as a non-Windows text editor and a disk manager such as Xtree to the noncompressed drive, just in case something ever goes wrong with Drive Space and you need a way to get at your machine without Windows. (As a safeguard against even more serious problems, make sure you have made two or more start-up diskettes.) If you're using a program that requires uncompressed disk space for its work files, as some do, you'll need to increase this amount. The other host drives require little or no free space.

- **Use DoubleSpace-compatible format:** Check this box to have DriveSpace create a compressed drive that is compatible with the compression formats in Windows 95 and MS-DOS version 6.0 or 6.2. If you will use this disk on a computer that will also be booting up in Windows 95 or MS-DOS 6.0 or 6.2, make sure this box is checked.

7. Click on OK to confirm any new settings you've made and return to the Compress a Drive dialog box.

8. Click on Start to compress the drive. You'll be prompted to make a current emergency startup disk:

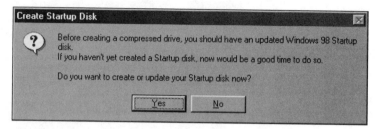

Get a floppy (it doesn't have to be blank, but you have to be willing to lose anything on it), and insert into your floppy drive and click on Yes, or if you already have a startup floppy (or want to take your chances), click on No.

9. Now you're given the option of backing up any existing files on the disk you're about to compress, or just go ahead and compress. If you click on Backup, that runs the Backup program. (See the previous section to learn how to use it and make your backup. When you finish the backup, you're returned to this point.) If you click on Compress Now, the job begins. First the drive is checked for errors. If there are serious errors, you'll be alerted to fix them running ScanDisk (see this chapter, ScanDisk section), then start the compression again. After checking for errors, the drive is setup for compression, then existing files are compressed. When the whole thing is finished, you'll see a box like this:

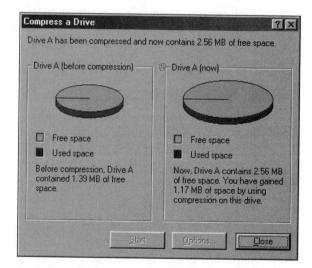

WARNING

Compression takes a long time on a large drive, especially if it contains lots of files. Get ready to wait for hours. Start big compression jobs before you leave work or go to bed. And yes, you can compress a parallel-port Zip drive, but it takes forever since the parallel port is so slow. Use a SCSI ZIP drive if you must compress one. Compressing a blank floppy, however, only takes a few minutes, and nets you about 2.56 MB as opposed to the normal 1.44 MB of storage space.

TIP

When DriveSpace compresses a drive the new compressed drive is assigned the drive letter that had been used by the original uncompressed drive, the host. The host receives a new letter but is then *hidden* so it won't appear in Windows Explorer, My Computer, and File dialog boxes such as Open and Save As (after all, the host hardly has any usable space).

Adjusting the Amount of Free Space

After you've compressed a drive, it may turn out that you need more uncompressed free space on the host. Or perhaps you realize that you don't need as much uncompressed space as you thought you would and you really should compress the surplus to get more capacity. Fortunately, DriveSpace lets you shift unused capacity back and forth between a compressed drive and its uncompressed host.

To change the distribution of free space, highlight either the compressed drive or its host in the main DriveSpace window. Then choose Drive ➢ Adjust Free Space. You'll see a window like the one shown in Figure 23.11.

The window shows you graphically and in numbers how much free space is currently available on the two drives. Use the slider control at the bottom of the window to shift free space between them. You can set the slider with the mouse or by pressing the → and ← keys. As you do, the graph changes to show you how free space would be distributed with the new settings.

When you're satisfied, change the setting in the *Hide this host drive* box if you like and then click on OK. DriveSpace makes the necessary adjustments and returns you to its main window.

FIGURE 23.11

The Adjust Free Space window

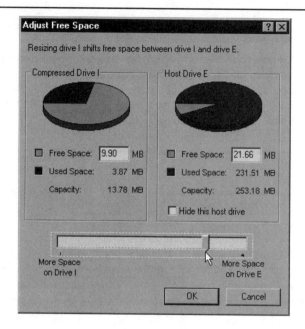

Uncompressing a Compressed Drive

Just in case you ever need to, you can restore a compressed drive to its original, uncompressed state. DriveSpace will transfer the files contained on the compressed drive to the host, reset the host to its original drive letter, and show the host if it was hidden.

There's only one potential fly in the ointment, but unfortunately it's rather large: If you've been using the compressed drive for its intended function—storing files—there's a good chance those files won't fit on the uncompressed drive. In this case, if you want to go through with uncompressing the drive, you'll need to move the excess files to another disk somewhere before uncompression can proceed. If your computer is connected to a network, a drive somewhere else on the network may be a good place to try.

To uncompress a compressed drive, highlight it in the main DriveSpace window, then choose Drive ➢ Uncompress. DriveSpace displays a window showing a before-and-after graph of the used and free space on the compressed drive and the host. If the projected results meet your expectations, click on Start to proceed.

Creating an Empty Compressed Drive from Free Space

If you prefer, you can have DriveSpace compress only the free space on an existing drive rather than compressing the entire drive. This is often a *much* quicker way to get more space, because DriveSpace doesn't have to copy all the existing files to the new compressed drive. On the other hand, if the existing disk contains a lot of files, you won't have much free space to work with and the compressed drive will be relatively small.

NOTE

> The only drives on which you can create an empty compressed drive from free space are non-removable, non–FAT 32 drives.

Because it is created from free space, the new compressed drive is empty. The host drive retains its original letter while the compressed drive is assigned a new letter. This is the opposite of the way things work when you compress a drive with the standard method as described above.

To create an empty compressed drive from free space, select the uncompressed drive where the free space is located in the main DriveSpace window. Choose Advanced ➢ Create Empty. You'll see the dialog box shown in Figure 23.12.

FIGURE 23.12

The Create New Compressed Drive dialog box

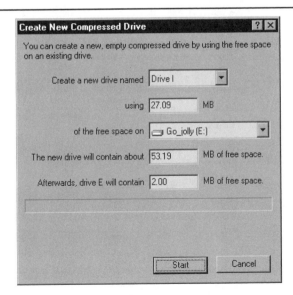

DriveSpace assumes you want the new drive to occupy all but 2 MB of the free space now available on the uncompressed drive. You can change the new drive's size in any of the three areas listing megabyte amounts. The first of these three areas, labeled *using*, indicates the amount of uncompressed free space to be compressed; the second area, *The new drive will contain about*, gives an estimate of how much space will be available on the compressed drive; while the third area, *Afterwards, drive "X" will contain*, shows you how much free space will be left on the host. Typing a new number into any of these areas changes all three areas. If you enter a value that's too large, DriveSpace adjusts it to the maximum valid value.

You can choose a different drive letter for the new drive if you need to in the first area. When you're through making changes, click on Start to create the new compressed drive. It will take some time. After the disk is checked for errors (which can take some time), the system will reboot and the final results will be reported.

Deleting a Compressed Drive

If you know you won't ever need the information on a compressed drive, or if you've backed up all the files you want to preserve, you can summarily delete the drive. This is a quicker way of restoring the host drive to its original state than using the Uncompress command because DriveSpace doesn't have to copy all the compressed files back to the host.

To delete a compressed drive, select it in the main DriveSpace window, then choose Advanced ➤ Delete. DriveSpace will warn you that this command will delete all the information on the drive. To proceed, click on Yes.

Mounting and Unmounting Compressed Drives

Mounting a compressed drive means to activate it so that the drive and the files it contains are accessible. Normally, DriveSpace automatically mounts all compressed drives, including those on floppy disks and removable hard-disk cartridges. If you turn off this automatic mounting feature, however, you'll have to mount the drives yourself. This doesn't make much sense for most people.

To mount a compressed drive, select its uncompressed host drive in the list in the main DriveSpace window. Then choose Advanced ➤ Mount. DriveSpace will search the disk for the special files that contain compressed disks. If it finds any unmounted compressed drives, it displays them in a list box (if there are two or more of these files, you can pick the one you want to mount from the list). DriveSpace shows you which drive letter it plans to assign to the selected disk. You can select a different letter by clicking on Options and choosing the desired letter from the list box that appears at the bottom of the same window.

Of course, you can *unmount* any compressed drive any time you like. Each mounted compressed drive uses a small amount of system memory, so if you're not using the drive, you may want to unmount it. You might also unmount a drive to keep other people who use the computer from accessing it, though anyone familiar with DriveSpace could find and mount the drive. The best reason to unmount a drive is when you need to change its letter designation, because you can't select a new letter for a drive that is currently mounted.

Changing the Estimated Compression Ratio

Because the amount of compression varies from file to file, DriveSpace can only estimate how much free space is available on a compressed drive. When you store an average mix of files, DriveSpace's standard estimate is about as good as you can expect. If you store many files of a particular type, however, you can improve on the estimate's accuracy. This will help you figure out how much more information the compressed drive will hold.

Select the compressed drive and choose Advanced ➢ Change Ratio. DriveSpace displays this window:

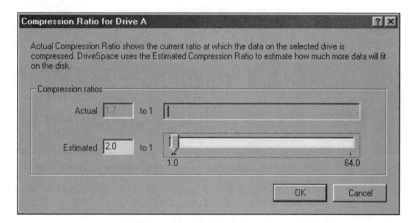

Here you can see the actual compression ratio for the files currently stored on the drive, along with DriveSpace's current setting for the estimated ratio it uses to calculate the remaining free space. If the actual ratio varies from the estimate and you're pretty sure you'll be using the disk in about the same way, you should change the estimated ratio. Use the slider control, dragging it to the new value with the mouse or pressing the ← and → keys.

Advanced Settings: Compression Amounts and Auto Mounting

Choose the Advanced ➤ Settings command to display the following dialog box in Figure 23.13.

You set the advanced compression options and turn off automatic mounting of drives from here.

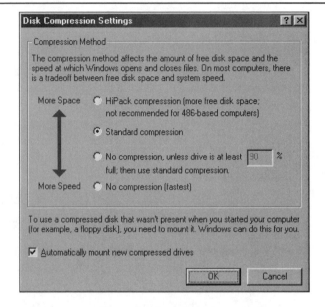

Setting Advanced Compression Options

There are four buttons that let you select various amounts of compression for the highlighted compressed drive. Here are what they mean:

HiPack Compression: This option searches your disk for repetitive data and provides better compression than Standard while still giving you minimal slowdowns when opening files. However, because a larger portion of your disk is searched for repetitive data, compressing your drive may take longer. HiPack files are, on average, compressed to one-half their original size—a little smaller than Standard.

Standard Compression: The normal method of compression used by Windows 98. Files are typically compressed to a little more than 50 percent of original size.

No Compression Unless drive is at least xx% full: When available disk space drops below the entered amount, compression will begin. Standard compression is used.

No Compression: Files will not be compressed.

NOTE

As mentioned above, a utility called Compression Agent provides an additional compression type: *UltraPack Compression.* See the next section for coverage of this type.

Auto-Mount Settings

Normally, DriveSpace automatically activates, or mounts, new compressed drives immediately after you create them. If you want to mount new compressed drives manually, clear the *Automatically mount new compressed drives* box at the bottom of the dialog box.

Compression Agent

Compression Agent is a utility program that you use in conjunction with DiskSpace-compressed drives. It lets you really fine tune the compression settings for the drive. For example, suppose you want to super compress files you rarely use, while not compressing others you use more frequently, so they open more quickly. Compression agent also has an option that uses optimal compression technology to provide maximum space savings on your hard disk.

To use Compression Agent, first check to see if it might not already be set to run automatically—look in your Windows Maintenance Wizard and Task Scheduler settings. If it's not running, create a DriveSpace 3 compressed drive, or upgrade an older compressed drive to the DriveSpace 3 format by running DriveSpace 3 and choosing the Drive ➢ Upgrade command.

NOTE

Accessing UltraPacked files may be slow if you are using a 486-based computer because the file crunching takes advantage of certain Pentium-processor abilities.

To further compress a drive:

1. Choose Start ➢ Programs ➢ Accessories ➢ System Tools ➢ Compression Agent. If you have multiple compressed drives you'll see a box like this, asking which drive you want to recompress:

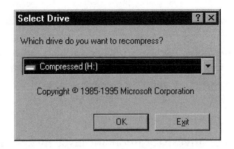

Only drives that have already been compressed will be selectable from the drop-down list. If you want to compress an uncompressed drive, use DriveSpace 3, not ExtraPack.

2. Choose the desired drive and click on OK. Now you'll see the Compression Agent main screen, with lots of zeros on it, since no recompressing has been done yet.

3. You can change a number of defaults that affect Compression Agent's choices about recompression before you begin. Click on the Settings button to check them out:

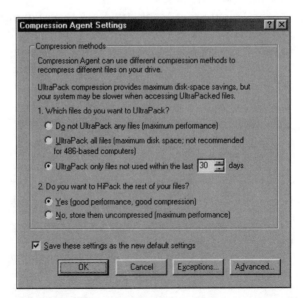

Study these options carefully before changing them; the default settings work for most users. You can click on the Advanced and Exceptions button for a few more. The Exceptions button lets you specify files (or complete folders) you don't want compressed or want compressed using a specific compression technique. Use this option when you want to accelerate access to files you use frequently, particularly if you have noticed a performance penalty after compression. (You can revisit this dialog box later if you find there are files whose compression properties you need to alter. Just run Compression Agent again and select the same drive.) If you are befuddled by the range of options, just go with the defaults. The default setting of UltraPacking files not used for 30 days is a sensible one.

4. Click on Start in the main ExtraPack dialog box. While files on your drive are being recompressed, Compression Agent updates information in a table to reflect how your disk space changes as files are moved from one compression method to another. (See Figure 23.14.)

FIGURE 23.14

Compression Agent's screen reports additional space savings as it recompresses a previously compressed drive.

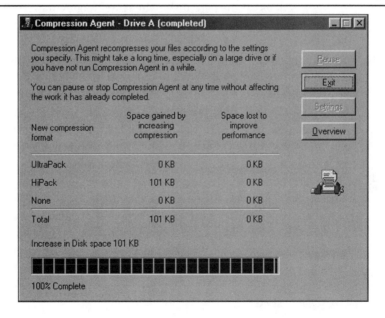

TIP

Unlike normal DriveSpace compression which ensures that all files placed on the compressed drive get compressed, Compression Agent's extra recompression only happens when you run the Compression Agent program. So, to keep new files or changes recompressed, you'll have to with run Compression Agent manually, or have it run automatically somehow, such as by adding it to the Task Scheduler. The Task Scheduler (explained below) can be automatically set to run Compression Agent on any preexisting compressed drives, giving you additional space without your intervention. You could set the process to kick in after the computer has been on and left idle for, say, twenty minutes.

Disk Defragmenter

Disk Defragmenter keeps your system performing at its best by detecting and correcting *fragmentation* on the hard disks. The term "fragmentation" sounds a little scary—after all, who wants their hard disk to break into little pieces? Actually, though, it refers to the files stored on the disk, not the disk itself.

When Windows stores information on your disk in a file, it begins *writing* the information onto the first place it can find that isn't already occupied by another file. If the disk already contains a lot of other files, however, that location may not be large enough for the whole file Windows now wants to store. If this is the case, Windows must search for another open spot on the disk for the next section of the file. The process goes on in this way until the entire file has been written to the disk into as many pieces, or fragments, as necessary. Of course, Windows keeps track of the location of all the fragments, and when you need the file again, it can find all the pieces for you without your ever knowing where they are stored.

Actually, this system for breaking files up into fragments when necessary has important performance benefits. If Windows had to stop and find a single section of the disk big enough for each entire file, your system would steadily slow down as the hard disk filled up. Also, you would wind up with less usable disk space. Eventually there would come a time when the disk still had many free areas, but none of them big enough to fit a reasonably sized file.

So what's the problem? Well, fragmentation also slows your hard disk down. To access information stored on a disk, the disk drive must move mechanical parts over the location where the information is stored. It takes only a fraction of a second to move these parts, but those fractions add up when a file is broken into many fragments. As more and more files become fragmented, you may begin to notice the slowdown, especially when Windows opens and saves files.

Disk Defragmenter remedies the problem by reorganizing the disk so that each and every file is stored as a complete unit on a single area of the disk. To do this, it identifies any remaining free areas, moves small files there to open up more space, and uses this newly opened space to consolidate larger files. It continues to shuffle files around in this manner until the entire disk is defragmented. All of this takes place behind the scenes. Though the files have been moved physically on the disk, they remain in exactly the same place "logically"—you'll find all your files in the same folders they were in before running Defragmenter.

When Should You Use Disk Defragmenter?

After wading through this long technical explanation, you may feel let down when I tell you that you may not ever really need to defragment your hard disk. Yes, it's true that fragmentation puts a measurable drag on file access if you time the system electronically. But in real life, you'll probably detect a slowdown only if you have very large, very fragmented data files. The reason is simply that today's hard disks are so fast.

WARNING

Keep in mind also that the defragmenting process itself can take quite a bit of time (on the other hand, you can run Disk Defragmenter overnight or while you're out to lunch).

Anyway, the point is simply that you shouldn't worry about a drastic performance loss if you don't defragment your disk regularly.

All that said, here are some tips for deciding when to use Disk Defragmenter:

- Disk Defragmenter itself can help you decide when to defragment. When you run the program, it analyzes the disk to detect fragmentation and offers a recommendation about whether or not to proceed (more on that in a moment).

- The slower your hard disk, the more you'll notice the performance hit caused by fragmentation and the more often you should defragment it. If you're still using a disk with an access time of 25 milliseconds or greater, you'll probably detect an improvement after defragmenting a heavily fragmented disk.

- The greater the percentage of data files (documents, pictures, database files, and so on) on your hard disk—as compared to program files—the more likely you'll need to defragment. After you install them, your program files stay put. Data files, on the other hand, are constantly being revised and saved anew, and are much more vulnerable to increasing fragmentation. (If you frequently install and then remove programs, the risk for significant fragmentation also rises.)

Running Disk Defragmenter

To run Disk Defragmenter:

1. Click Start ➢ Programs ➢ Accessories ➢ System Tools ➢ Disk Defragmenter. A small Window appears:

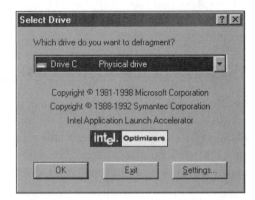

2. Choose the hard disk you want to defragment from the drop-down list.

3. Click Settings to check the settings.

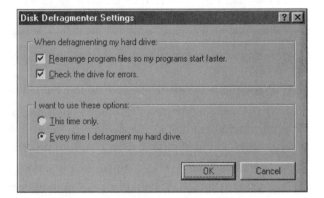

The default settings shown here are good for most situations. Checking the drive for errors is a good idea before the program starts moving data around, or you could lose some important information in the process of the shuffling. If you want to change the settings for a single instance of running the program, click on This Time Only. The first option in the box groups your most often used programs together on the disk so they start easily without the drive heads running around too much.

4. OK the Settings box.

5. Click on OK to start defragmenting the drive. If the drive doesn't need defragmenting, you'll be told as much and you can cancel. If it does, the program starts analyzing the drive. If it detects a serious error in the drive, you'll see a report such as this:

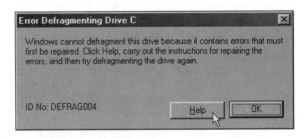

Mostly likely you'll have to run ScanDisk to repair the error. If there are no errors detected, Defrag starts to rearrange the data on the drive. You'll see a progress bar creep across the screen.

The Defragmentation Process

Click on Defragment (or Defragment Anyway) in the Defragmentation dialog box to begin the process. You'll see yet another little dialog box informing you of the program's progress:

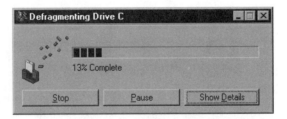

As Disk Defragmenter does its work, the indicator shows you graphically how far along you are in the process, and the percentage complete is displayed as well. Three buttons are available:

Stop: Stops the defragmenting process and returns you to a dialog box titled Are You Sure. The choices are similar to those of the Defragmentation dialog box: you can click on Resume to return to defragmenting, Select Drive to pick another drive to defragment, Advanced to set defragmentation options, or Exit to close Disk Defragmenter.

Pause: Temporarily stops the defragmenting process. The Pause button appears pushed in while Disk Defragmenter remains paused. To continue where you left off, click on it again.

Show Details: Displays a large window showing you exactly what's going on during the defragmentation process (Figure 23.15). This window represents the disk contents as a grid of little colored boxes, each of which stands for a single *cluster* (usually 2,048 bytes). The various colors signify the status of each cluster: those containing information that needs to be moved, those that are already defragmented, those that are free (containing no file information), and so on. To see a legend showing the meanings of the block colors, click on the Legend button:

FIGURE 23.15

This is the window you'll see if you choose Display Details during defragmentation. It graphically represents every cluster on your hard disk.

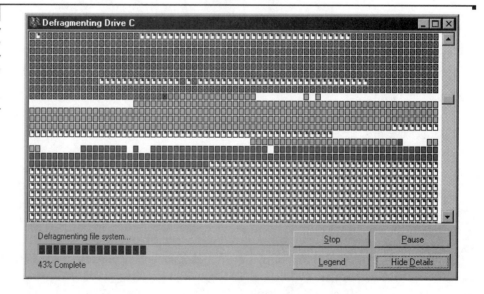

As Disk Defragmenter moves information around, the map gives you a moment-by-moment readout of which clusters are being read and written to, and the resulting disk organization. The bottom of the window displays a progress indicator and readout and includes Stop and Pause buttons. You can close the large map window at any time by clicking on Hide Details.

Because Disk Defragmenter continues its work whether or not the program window is visible, you can switch to another program to continue your work. You'll hear the hard disk chattering more or less continuously during the defragmentation process, and your system will probably seem a little sluggish at times when it waits for Disk Defragmenter to give it access to the disk. Otherwise, however, you can use Windows just as you normally would.

Disk Cleanup

How many times have you wanted to install a new program, download some files off the 'Net, or saved a document and gotten an error message about not having enough disk space? You just want a little more room, fast, with no lengthy defragging or compression sessions, and no sleuthing around with Windows Explorer. Disk Cleanup is the right tool for this job. It's a simple system utility that can recover some disk space for you in a jiffy by killing off relatively unimportant temporary files and a few other goblins that tend to grow, munching up precious hard disk space. Some of these files you probably didn't even know were on your disk; others, like the ones in the Recycle Bin, you did, but forgot about.

Here's how to use it.

1. Open Windows Explorer or My Computer.

2. Right-click the disk you want to free space on, and then click Properties.

3. On the General tab, click Disk Cleanup. In a few seconds, you'll see a report of how much disk space you can free up.

4. Click the unnecessary files you want to remove. When you work with the Web on the Internet, lots of files are downloaded and cached (stored temporarily) on your hard disk to speed up viewing those pages the next time you look at the same website. How many Web pages are cached on your hard disk is determined by settings in your browser program. In any case, you can usually free up a bunch of space by cleaning out the cache of "temporary Internet files."

5. You can read a description of each file type in the area under the list, by clicking on the file item. Clicking on the View button brings up a folder window with the files listed. Then you can view them, or delete them individually if you want to.

6. Once you've selected the file types you want to remove, Click OK. You'll recover the amount of space that the program reported. In my case, I got back 10 megabytes of space. Not bad for so little work.

Finding Even More Space

What? Not enough space, still? You need more. OK, click on the More Options tab in the Disk Cleanup dialog box. You'll see this box:

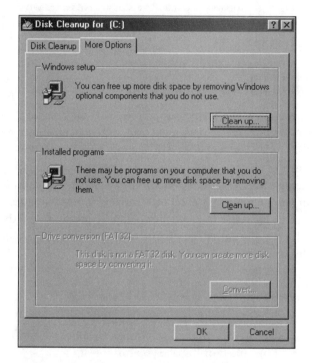

You have three major options here:

- **Remove Windows optional components:** Click on Cleanup, and the Control Panel ➤ Add/Remove Programs ➤ Windows Setup box appears. The system has to do an analysis of what modules of Windows you have installed, then lists them. Now scroll through the listing and consider what you might chuck. Look for the big ticket items that are using lots of space. Caution is advisable here, you don't want to eliminate something you really use. Take a look at Figure 23.16. I've clicked on Internet Tools since it looks like they are using up about 15 MB of space. Then I clicked on Details to see the list of Internet Tools I have installed. Hmmm. Looks like Front Page Express is using up 4.6 MB. Since

I have MS Front Page 98 on my machine already, why keep Front Page Express? I think I'll zap it. If you don't do any Web page designing, you could, too. Then again, you may not have installed it, so it wouldn't be in your listing. Another likely candidate for the kill list is the Internet Tool called Web Based Enterprise Management. Or, in the first box, Desktop Themes (just above Internet Tools), TV Viewer (if you're not using it), which will get you 33 MB back. You get the idea. If there is a checkmark in the box next to an item, it's installed. If you turn off the check, it will be removed, freeing up disk space. If in doubt about removing something, leave it in. If you *do* remove something you needed, it's not terrible. You can go back to this box (do it from Control Panel ➢ Add/Remove Programs ➢ Windows Setup) and add the item.

PART

IV

Using the Supplied Programs

FIGURE 23.16

You can free up hard disk space by removing Windows components. Use some caution when choosing what to eliminate, since you may still have a need for a component.

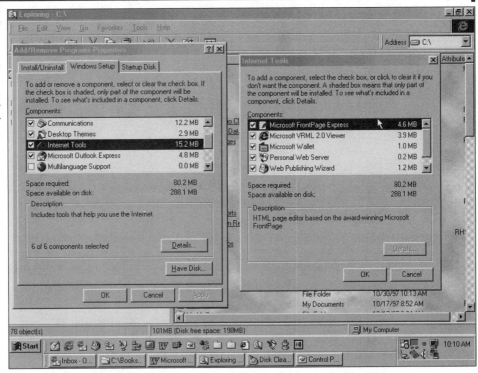

- **Remove Installed Programs:** Click Cleanup and you're taken to the *first* tab of the Control Panel ➢ Add/Remove Software applet (the option above opened the second tab). Now you can look around for stand-alone programs (as opposed to stuff that comes with Windows proper) you don't use anymore. Programs that comply with Windows' uninstall features will be listed here. Other programs that don't, won't, so this isn't a way to jettison them. They may have their own uninstall feature or instructions. But for complying programs, flushing them is pretty simple. Look around and see if there isn't an entry here for a program you no longer use or want. The amount of space you'll save isn't listed – a little shortcoming, but you're guaranteed *some* space reclamation at least. Click on anything you want to remove and then click Add/Remove. If the program has an uninstall program, you may be prompted to insert its CD, or make some choices. Typically, you'll just be asked to confirm that you want to trash the program. Microsoft Office is a good example of a program that will ask for the CD. It's also a good example of a program that can release *lots* of disk space if you choose the right options, such as removing examples, clip art, extra templates, Wizards, online help, and so forth.

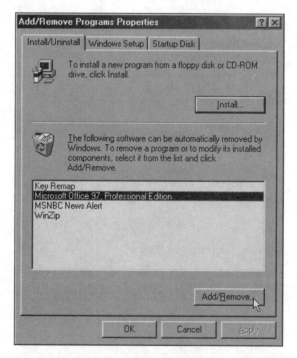

- **Convert to FAT 32:** This option reformats your hard disk non-destructively (no data is lost) in the FAT 32 format, for more efficient data storage, resulting in approximately 25% additional space on most drives. See the coverage of FAT 32 conversion on the following page. In the picture above, this option is grayed out since my drive is already converted to FAT 32. Yours may be also.

Notice that using DriveSpace 3 isn't offered as an option from the Disk Cleanup window, but it's a good choice nonetheless, since, it will almost *double* your disk space! Microsoft is just trying to get you to move to FAT 32, and since FAT 32 doesn't work with DiskSpace, it's not suggested in the box.

Drive Converter (FAT 32)

FAT 32 is the new file system for Windows 9*x* operating system. It debuted with what's called OSR2, an update to Windows 95 that came out in 1997. FAT 32 has nothing to do with being fat. The FAT stands for *file allocation table* (the means of organizing the data on your hard disk). FAT 32 is designed to break through the 2.1 gigabyte DOS barrier imposed by the older FAT 16 system and it is more efficient at using space on hard drives.

In imposing a certain structure on the disk, the FAT system has always caused some loss of usable data space. For a one to four gigabyte hard drive—the sizes that most new computers are being equipped with these days—FAT 16 typically renders 10 to 20 percent of the drive's capacity useless. In the past users could reduce this percentage by partitioning their hard drives into three or more logical drives, so as to maintain a reasonable ratio of lost space to used space.

FAT 32 uses space on large hard drives more efficiently than other file allocation systems. With FAT 32, it is possible to increase your usable hard drive space by about 25 percent, because the cluster size (the minimum amount of space that the tiniest file can occupy) is much smaller than it is under the FAT arrangement. As a result there's less file "overhang": the situation that occurs when you have with tiny files each taking up a full cluster, as when a file of say 1 kilobyte still takes up a full 32 kilobytes on a large hard disk. The cluster size used on FAT 32 drives depends on the size of the drive or logical partition. The defaults and comparisons are shown in Table 23.2.

TABLE 23.2: COMPARISONS OF FAT 32 AND FAT 16		
Partition size	**FAT 16 Cluster size**	**FAT 32 Cluster size**
512 MB to 1024 MB	16 KB	4 KB
1024 MB to 2 GB	32 KB	4 KB
513 MB to 8 GB	Not possible	4 KB
8 GB to 16 GB	Not possible	8 KB
16 GB to 32 GB	Not possible	16 KB
Greater than 32 GB	Not possible	32 KB

Space savings are dependent upon the FAT 16 cluster size and the number of small files you have on disk. The small files are the ones producing the most wasted space in FAT 16 partitions.

NOTE

To track files and usable/unusable space on a drive, the FAT uses *pointers*. Since current FAT pointers are only 16-bit and there are some that have special uses, the number of pointers or clusters per partition is limited to 65,520. With its maximum of 64 sectors per cluster and each sector limited to 512 bytes, drive capacity under FAT is 2.1 gigabytes. FAT 32 increases the maximum capacity of a drive by providing 32-bit pointers, which raises the maximum number of clusters per partition to 4,294,967,296. At 8 sectors per cluster instead of 64, and 512 bytes per sector, you could have drives as large as 2 terabytes.

In addition to saving space, FAT 32 is usually faster than FAT 16. According to Microsoft, "...converting to FAT 32 will result in applications starting up to 50% faster than on a FAT 16 disk."

The Downside of FAT 32

Along with all the great stuff, there are some drawbacks to FAT 32:

- Once you convert your hard drive to the FAT 32 format, you can't return to using the FAT 16 format unless you repartition and format the FAT 32 drive or use another program such as Partition Magic.

- If you have a compressed drive, or want to compress your drive in the future, you should not convert to FAT 32. If you have a removable disk that you use with another operating system, don't convert it to FAT 32, since the other operating system probably won't be able to read it.

- Laptop computers often have a Hibernate feature. Converting to FAT 32 will prevent portables from being able to hibernate anymore, since the BIOS chip in the portable (responsible for doing the hibernate) probably doesn't know about FAT 32 (check with the manufacturer). Windows 98 supports Hibernate, but not if you've converted the laptop's hard disk to FAT 32. One workaround: If your laptop has interchangeable hard disks, you could convert one for experimentation and have another one still able to support Hibernate.

- FAT 32 formatted drives are not compatible with the current versions of NT and NT's special NTFS (NT File System).

- If you convert your hard drive to FAT 32, then you cannot uninstall Windows 98 and revert to the previously installed operating system, even if you enabled the Uninstall option during setup (see Appendix A).

PART
IV

Using the Supplied
Programs

- Although most programs are not affected by the conversion from FAT 16 to FAT 32, some disk utilities that depend on FAT 16 do not work with FAT 32 drives. Contact your disk utility manufacturer to see if there is an updated version that is compatible with FAT 32.

- In real-mode MS-DOS or when you're running Windows 98 in Safe Mode, FAT 32 is considerably slower than FAT 16. If you run lots of applications in MS-DOS mode, don't convert. Or at least load Smartdrv.exe in your Autoexec.bat to increase speed when using those programs.

- If you convert your hard drive to FAT 32, you can no longer use dual boot to run earlier versions of Windows (Windows 95 [Version 4.00.950], Windows NT 3.*x*, Windows NT 4.0, and Windows 3.*x*). However, if you are on a network, earlier versions of Windows can still gain access to your FAT 32 hard drive through the network.

- The FAT 32 Drive Converter will not work on drives under 512 MB.

TIP

As mentioned, NT 4.0 can't boot from or access FAT 32 drives. However, NT 5 will probably support FAT 32 in some form, if only via an upgrade path. So if you don't mind upgrading any NT 4 installations you have to NT 5, the NT issue should not be a consideration in whether to convert or not.

Why Not NTFS?

If you're an NT user, you might be wondering why the designers of Windows 98 didn't choose Windows NT's fancy NTFS file system for replacing FAT 16, rather than introduce yet another file system? Good question. NTFS is a fine file system, with lots of protection, security, file-by-file compression, journaling, and other goodies. But according to Microsoft, to support NTFS under MS-DOS would take a significant amount of very limited MS-DOS memory. Thus, it would impair the ability of Windows to continue to support MS-DOS–based games and applications. Implementing NTFS without MS-DOS support would require two disk partitions: a FAT partition to start from and the main NTFS partition. Because NTFS has such a different on-disk format than FAT, FAT 32 is much less likely to introduce application compatibility problems.

Check Your Non-Microsoft Disk Utilities!

Changes to the boot record's cluster size and FAT pointers make some current applications, especially disk utilities, incompatible and therefore dangerous with FAT 32. Most existing applications that need to read file structures, such as Symantec's Norton Disk Doctor, will have to be updated. Expect that many companies have or will be creating new versions that address FAT 32. For example, Norton Utilities Version 2.0 and later for Windows 9*x*, is compatible. And of course Microsoft's own utilities that it bundles with Windows 98 (ScanDisk, for example) have been revised to support the new file system—with the notable exception of the DriveSpace disk compression utility, which I discussed earlier in this chapter.

Some programs won't display free space on a disk properly. Since there used to be a limitation of 2 GB on drives under FAT 16, some older programs will top out at 2 GB and not report free disk accurately, even on larger FAT 32 drives. These applications show the correct free space up to 2 GB, but after that point they continue to show 2 GB.

Other programs that may need watching are any utility tools that access the hard drive directly in order to increase performance. Many games fall into this category. If you have any doubts about which programs to install, you should consult the software maker before installing these programs.

WARNING

Unless your disk utility packages (like Norton Utilities and PC Tools) specifically mention that they have been upgraded to work with Windows 98, Windows 95 OSR2, FAT 32, or the 32-bit filing system, it is not safe to install those utilities.

Can't Use DriveSpace 3

As mentioned several times (repetition is a great teaching device), DriveSpace is *not* compatible with FAT 32. If you try to compress a FAT 32 drive with DriveSpace or DriveSpace 3, you will receive an error message such as:

```
Drive C cannot be compressed because it is a FAT 32 drive.
ID Number: DRVSPACE378
```

Microsoft says the cause of this is that DriveSpace was designed to work with the FAT12 and FAT 16 file systems and cannot be used with drives using the FAT 32 file system. Duh. OK, just accept it. DriveSpace is provided only in case you plan to use Windows 98 with FAT 16 drives in order to have compatibility with earlier versions of Windows, DOS, and Windows NT.

Microsoft is supposedly considering updating DriveSpace to work with FAT 32 for possible inclusion in a future release of Windows, but they won't commit to it.

Dual Booting Considerations

Because virtually no other operating systems know what FAT 32 is, you can't expect to dual boot two or more systems with it. Well, actually you could dual boot Windows 95 OSR2 (on FAT 32) if it's stored in another directory than Windows 98. But it takes some doing, and since I don't recommend it, I won't even go into it here.

If you're using a FAT 16 drive, on the other hand, you can dual boot between Windows 98 and earlier versions of MS-DOS by using the same F4 dual boot that Windows 95 supports. Just press F4 while Windows 98 is booting and choose what you want to do from the resulting menu. However, if you have other FAT 32 partitions, they will not be visible to operating systems other than Windows 98.

But, you could maybe think of a way to turn this hidden partition to your advantage. See the following tip.

TIP

Actually, using FAT 32 isn't a bad way to hide some data on a drive. If you have dual-boot capability using something like Boot Commander or Partition Magic 3, you could have a machine default-boot into DOS, Windows 3.*x*, or Windows 95 build 950 (i.e., the pre-OSR2 version) instead of Windows 98—in which case your system couldn't see the FAT 32 volume, and thus you could keep prying eyes from seeing what's on that volume. To see the volume, reboot, taking whatever measures are necessary to boot into Windows 98. There is an exception to this tip. A non-Windows 98/non-FAT 32 machine *on a network* can access a FAT 32 partition if that partition is on a Windows 98 machine on the network. This is similar to a WIN9x machine accessing an NTFS partition on a NT server.

As I mentioned, Windows NT version 4.0 and earlier can't access or start from a FAT 32 drive. Although you can't dual boot with Windows NT, you can have non-boot disks formatted with FAT 32, assuming you don't need to access it from Windows NT.

Check for Equipment Compatibility

Is FAT 32 compatible with your equipment? The main issue here is your motherboard. The motherboard BIOS must support LBA mode to be compatible with FAT 32—that is, LBA mode must be enabled. Many 486 motherboards do not support LBA mode.

For more information on the FAT 32 file system, advantages, drawbacks, and compatibility issues, check out the Microsoft Knowledge Base article Q154997 on the Internet. You can find it at the site www.microsoft.com/kb.

If you convert an Iomega Jaz disk with FAT 32 your Jaz Tools software may not work properly. According to Microsoft the following symptoms were seen with Iomega's Jaz Tools software with dates prior to 6/25/96 when used on a FAT 32–formatted Jaz cartridge: The software-eject JAZ drive, write-protect disk, and password-protect media commands did not function correctly. If you have these problems, contact Iomega for an updated version of the Jaz Tools software.

There is no method for converting from FAT 32 to FAT 16 built into either Windows 98 or Windows 95. The best tool for doing this is Partition Magic from PowerQuest. The next best approach is to back up, FDISK, reformat, and restore. Here's another solution to converting backwards to FAT 16 if you have another spare drive that is large enough: Create a FAT 16 partition on a second drive and copy the contents of the C drive, which is FAT 32 to it, using xcopy32 or another program. Then change the slave to master and reboot. You'll ended up with the exact configuration you had before, but with a 16-bit FAT drive.

Running the FAT 32 Converter (FAT 32)

Unlike the Windows 95 technique for conversion from FAT 16 to FAT 32 which was pretty messy, Windows 98 comes with a Wizard to do it for you. When you run the FAT 32 converter, it then boots into DOS to perform the conversion work, then boots back to Windows 98 and defragments your hard disk. It may take several hours to defragment your drive. You can stop the defragmenter and run it at another time, but your system performance may be degraded until you allow the defragmenter to complete to defragment the converted partition. Beware, the whole process can take quite a long time! It's not something to do over a coffee break.

Here's how to convert your drive to FAT 32.

1. Click Start ➢ Programs ➢ Accessories ➢ System Tools ➢ FAT 32 Converter. You'll see this dialog:

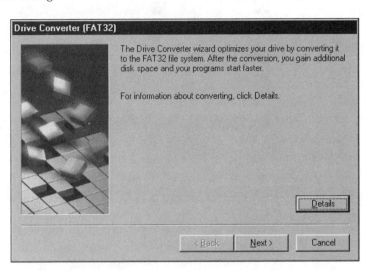

2. Click Next. You'll see this box, listing your drives:

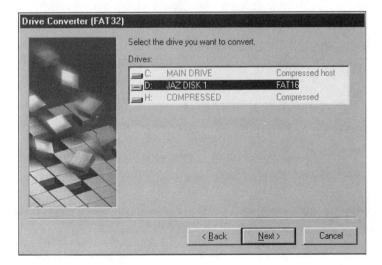

3. Click the drive you want to convert and click on Next. You'll see a couple of warnings:

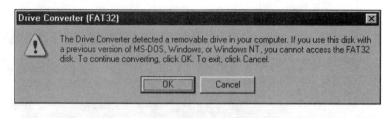

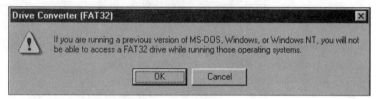

4. Click Next and the Wizard will look for programs such as virus checkers that are not compatible with FAT 32. If it finds any, it will list them and alert you can click on Details to read about what to do.

5. Click Next. You are now given an option to run a backup before doing the conversion (just as when doing a DiskSpace 3 compression). Do it if your data is of any particular value to you. See the Backup section in this chapter if you don't know how to run a backup.

6. Click on Next. Close all open programs and save any open documents.

7. Click Next again. A DOS box opens and ScanDisk runs, and a bunch of other conversions take place.

8. In a few minutes you'll be prompted to restart your computer. Let it restart, and sign in if prompted to. Defragmenting will now start. This can take quite a while, depending on how many files are on the disk, and how fragmented they are.

9. When the conversion is over, you'll be told it was successful.

Microsoft says that if you run into a bad sector while converting, you'll be told that you cannot convert to Fat 32. They say this is "by design" and prevents unnecessary data loss. Some people have had success using Partition Magic to solve the problem and even recover some "bad" sectors that ScanDisk had marked as unusable on the drive. They then used Partition Magic to convert to FAT 32 instead of using Microsoft's FAT 32 Converter.

Memory Shortage Error Messages During Conversion

When attempting conversion, you may get a message about shortage of memory space. Since the conversion is done in MS-DOS mode, you're actually running a DOS program, and the program needs about 440 KB of conventional DOS memory. You must have enough conventional memory space to run the converter. If you get a message during one of the conversion phases saying you're short on memory and need to REM (remark) out items in your Autoexec and Config files, reboot and try again, do this. Find someone who knows about PCs and can figure out for you which device drivers and programs can be removed from these two startup files. Then reboot, and rerun the program. If that still doesn't do the trick, then examine Dosstart.bat (if it exists), which could be loading additional memory-consuming drivers or programs. Cull that as necessary, or temporarily remove it or rename it. Then reboot and run the program again.

In real-mode MS-DOS or when you're running Windows 98 in Safe Mode, FAT 32 is considerably slower than FAT 16. If you run applications in MS-DOS mode, load Smartdrv.exe in Autoexec.bat to increase speed.

If you use OnTrack Disk Manager on a system that starts from a FAT 32 drive, you may experience a long pause at startup. This pause can occur because the drive is also set to run in compatibility mode. In version 7.0*x*, you can use the **/L=0** option with Disk Manager to avoid this pause. If you are running an earlier version of Disk Manager, you should update to at least version 7.04 and use the **/L=0** option if you use FAT 32.

System Monitor

System Monitor is a *real-time* analysis tool that lets you monitor Windows' activities from one moment to the next. If you are trying to track down a performance problem, say with unexpected memory shortages, or if you just want to keep tabs on what Windows is up to, try System Monitor. You can use it on your own system or across a network to monitor other computers.

There's a good chance System Monitor is not yet installed on your hard disk. If you need to install it, begin by placing the install disk in your floppy or CD-ROM drive, choosing Add/Remove Programs in the Control Panel, and switching to the Windows

Setup page. Highlight Accessories, then click on Details. In the list that appears, check the box for System Monitor. When you click on OK, the program will be installed.

Once System Monitor has been installed, run it by choosing Programs ➤ Accessories ➤ System Tools ➤ System Monitor from the Start menu. You'll see the System Monitor window, as shown in Figure 23.17.

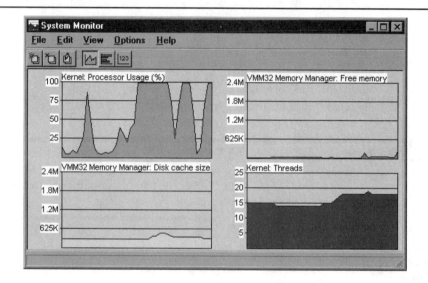

The main part of the window is divided into areas for each type of information you choose to monitor. When you first run the program, it displays its reports as shaded line graphs, but you can select bar graphs or numeric displays instead. You can click on any displayed item to get a report of its last and peak values in the Status Bar at the bottom of the window.

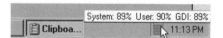

Note that System Monitor has its own little button bar for quick access to commonly used commands. The buttons are displayed in two groups of three buttons each. The first group (on the left) includes buttons for adding, removing, and editing individual items on the display; the second group lets you pick between the two graph types and a numeric readout.

System Monitor continuously updates the information it displays at a rate you can control. To change the frequency of updates, choose Options ➤ Chart and use the slider to set the Update Interval.

Choosing Items to Display

You have your choice of twenty-odd types of system information you can track with System Monitor. To add a new item, click on the Add button or choose Edit ➤ Add Item. You'll see the dialog box shown here:

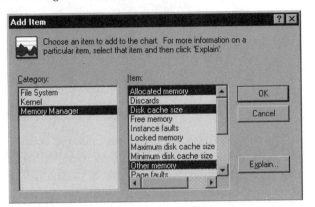

Select a category of system information from the list on the left. When you do, a list of the individual items available for display appears on the right. Be forewarned: Unless you're technically oriented, the terms you see here may look completely foreign to you. You can learn something about what an item means by selecting the item and clicking on Explain. System Monitor will then display a slightly longer—but also highly technical—description of the term.

When you're ready to choose one or more items, select them in the list. You can select more than one item at a time by dragging across consecutive items with the mouse or by holding down the Ctrl key while you click on individual items anywhere on the list. However, you can only select items from one category at a time.

Click on OK to return to System Monitor. The items you chose will now appear, each in its own area on the screen. As you add more items, System Monitor reduces the size of each item's graph.

Editing an Item's Display Properties

System Monitor lets you control some aspects of the graphical display of each item.

To see or change the current settings:

1. Click on the Edit button or choose Edit ➤ Edit Item. You'll see a list of all the items currently displayed.

If you double-click on the item you want to edit, then the Chart Options dialog box automatically opens for that item.

2. Select the item you want to work with and click on OK. A Chart Options dialog box appears:

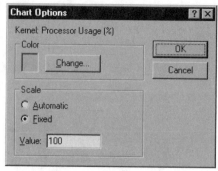

3. Here you can choose the graph color and control its scale. The pair of radio buttons on the left let you switch between letting System Monitor adjust the scale automatically based on the current values for the item and fixing the scale to cover a range you specify by typing in the scale maximum at Value. The right pair of radio buttons switches between linear and logarithmic display.

4. Click on OK to confirm your choices. System Monitor adjusts the item's graph to match.

Choosing the Display Type

To select a different type of display for all the items in the window, click on the button for the type of display you want (line graph, bar graph, or numeric). Alternatively, you can choose the desired type from the View menu.

Removing Items from the Window

To remove an item from the System Monitor display, click on the Remove button or choose Edit ➢ Remove Item. You'll be presented with a list of all the items currently displayed. Choose the item or items you want to remove and click on OK.

Other Display Options

To reset all items to zero, removing all the current graphs and starting the analysis again from scratch, choose Edit ➢ Clear.

You can control whether the Toolbar and Status Bar are visible. Choose the corresponding command on the View menu to turn either item off or on.

To remove System Monitor's title bar, menu bar, Toolbar, and Status Bar so only the graphs remain visible, press Esc or choose View ➢ Hide Title Bar. To restore the window to its normal state, double-click anywhere in the window or press Esc again.

To keep the System Monitor visible no matter what other programs you use, choose View ➢ Always on Top. If you choose this option, you may wish to resize the window so it won't block your view of your other programs.

Task Scheduler

Task Scheduler lets you set up any program to be run automatically at predetermined times. This utility is most useful for running some of the system maintenance programs discussed in this chapter. For example, you could set Task Scheduler to defragment your hard disk with the Disk Defragmenter, recompress a drive with Compression Agent, or run the Windows Maintenance Wizard (see below). Of course, if you have other programs you want to run, such as batch files or scripts (Windows 98 lets you create scripts that run programs), you can do that, too. I'll leave that part up to you. Of course, tasks can't run unless the computer is on. So don't expect to be able to recompress a hard disk in the middle of the night if the computer is shut down, or even if it's in a suspended state.

What I'll explain here is how to assign tasks to the Scheduler, and what some of its options are.

NOTE

If you upgraded from Windows 95 and had installed the Plus! pack, you already had a similar program called System Agent on your computer. When you upgraded to Windows 98, all of System Agent should have converted over to Task Scheduler.

1. Run the Task Scheduler by clicking Start ➢ Programs ➢ Accessories ➢ System ➢ Scheduled Tasks. You'll see this window:

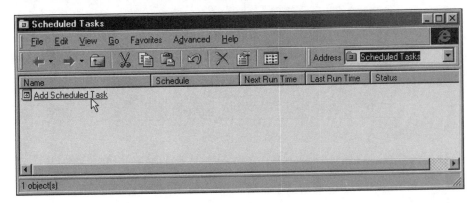

If you have any scheduled tasks, they'll be in the list already. Mine was empty.

2. Click on Add Scheduled Task. This invokes a Wizard that walks you though adding a new task. For this exercise, I'll set up Compression Agent.

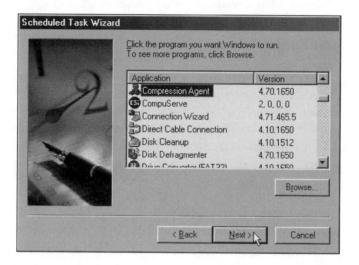

You can choose the program from the list that Task Scheduler finds, or you can browse for it using the Browse button.

3. Click Next and choose how often you want the program run. Click Next again, and then specify applicable time options, such as time of day, as required.

4. Click Finish. It's done, and the task is added to the list. Switch to the Task Scheduler window, or double-click on the Task Scheduler icon in the Taskbar by the clock and you'll see the new item in the window:

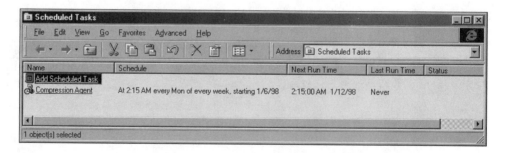

PART

IV

Using the Supplied
Programs

You may have noticed the button for setting advanced options. You can always adjust the settings for a task after they are set. Just open the window and open the task (or right-click and choose properties). You'll see a dialog box such as this:

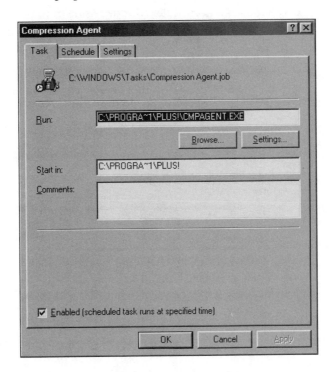

Check out the three tab pages. You can change the scheduled time as you like, from the second page. Note that on the first page you can disable the task temporarily, without having to delete it. Actually, you can suspend all tasks by right clicking on the Task Scheduler icon in the system tray and choosing Pause.

You can remove a task by right-clicking on it in the Task Scheduler window and choosing Delete. This doesn't remove it from your hard disk, incidentally, so don't worry. It just removes it from the list of tasks to be executed.

Running a Task Immediately

You may want to run one of your tasks immediately. Do this:

1. Open the Task Scheduler window. Aside from the Start menu way, you can also do it by double-clicking My Computer and then opening the Scheduled Tasks folder.

2. Right-click the task in question and choose Run.

3. You can end the task by clicking the File menu, and then clicking End Scheduled Task.

Task Scheduler tasks are actually stored in the Windows\Tasks directory. Each file has the extension of .JOB.

You can view scheduled tasks on a remote computer by opening the Network Neighborhood, opening the computer in question and opening the Scheduled Tasks folder. See the Windows Help file for information if you want to be able to modify the task settings on a remote computer.

NetWatcher

Net Watcher is a program that allows you to monitor resources you have shared on your LAN. You'll want to run this program if there is heavy traffic on your shared items such as files or printer. For one thing, it lets you know what the consequences might be if you need to shut down your computer. You'll see who is attached to your resources, and what they are using. Secondly, it can help you analyze your LAN traffic flow, and possibly determine why your computer is acting a little sluggish (lots of folks are using the contact database!).

You cannot only see who is currently using resources on your computer, but also disconnect them from specific files if need be, or easily share new folders.

1. Start NetWatcher by clicking Start ➤ Programs ➤ Accessories ➤ System Tools ➤ NetWatcher. The program appears:

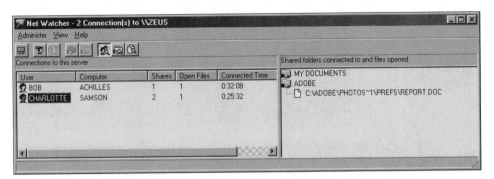

Notice that there are two users using stuff on my machine now, Bob and Charlotte. Clicking on a person in the left pane displays (in the right pane) what they are using.

2. Clicking on the Shared button will show what you currently have shared (they aren't necessarily being used):

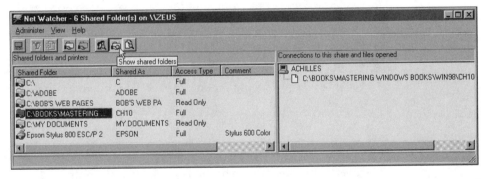

3. Click on the Open Files button or choose View ➤ Open files to see a listing of open files, who is using them, and what the share status is.

TIP

If you don't have NetWatcher on the System Tools menu, it's not installed. You'll have to go to Control Panel ➤ Add/Remove Programs ➤ Windows Setup and add it from there. You can find NetWatcher under System Tools.

To stop sharing a file or resource, click on the resource and click on the Stop Sharing button in the toolbar (or choose Administer ➤ Stop Sharing). You'll be asked to confirm. To disconnect a specific user, choose the user display mode, click on the user, and click on the disconnect user button (or choose Administer ➤ Disconnect User). You'll be advised that this could spell trouble for the user.

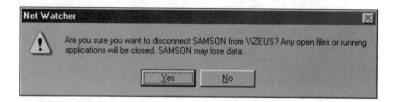

Checking Resources on Another Computer

In case you're administering other computers on a LAN, you can also check out the activity on another's computer workstation. First, make sure the remote computer is set up for remote administration. Secondly, ensure you're set up as an administrator (given access permission). You do these things from the Control Panel ➤ Passwords applet. Next,

1. Double-click Network Neighborhood.

2. Click the name of the computer on which you'd like to view shared resources.

3. On the File menu, click Properties.

4. Choose Tools ➤ NetWatcher.

5. On the NetWatcher View menu, click the type of information you want to see. You'll be asked to supply a password, since remote administration always requires a password.

If NetWatcher is already running, you can choose Administer ➤ Server and enter or browse to the server you want to remotely administer.

Maintenance Wizard

Probably because people's Windows 95 PCs got so loaded up with programs, and due to the vagaries and anomalies of hard disks and other hardware, Microsoft decided to put together a program that can try to help tune up your computer. Called the Maintenance

Wizard, it runs a number of goodies, all of which I've discussed already. In fact, you can add this program to the Task Scheduler, and probably catch some demonic little monsters before trouble comes a knockin' at your computer's door. So this program can automate lots of the stuff you've learned about in this chapter.

The Wizard ensures that:

- Your programs run as fast as possible (runs ScanDisk and Disk Defragmenter)
- You have maximum hard disk space (removes old files via Disk Cleanup)
- System performance is optimal (runs Compression Agent (if you have a Drive-Space 3 volume on your system)

To start the Windows Maintenance Wizard:

1. Click Start ➢ Programs ➢ Accessories ➢ System Tools and choose Maintenance Wizard. Depending on how it's been configured, a message may pop up asking if you want to run Maintenance now or to change your settings. If you do get this message, choose to change your settings.

2. You're given a choice of using Express or Custom settings in the Maintenance Wizard. Choose the Custom option.

3. The Wizard lists any programs you have in your Startup group and suggests that you can make Windows start up faster by removing them from the Startup group. It's mainly a question of what's convenient for you. Click Next after you make your decision.

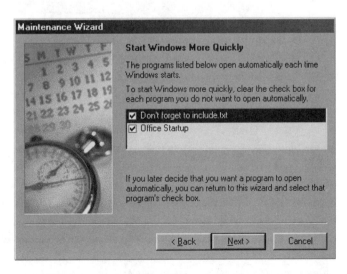

4. Follow the instructions for setting the time when tune-ups should happen. Though the suggestion is to leave your computer on all the time, you may not

want to do that. After all, it wastes energy, unless you have a computer that is miserly on power consumption. Then again, having the computer tune itself up when you're trying to use it is going to be a disappointment. System performance will degrade past the point of livability. So whatever time you choose for tune-ups, make sure the computer is on and you're not trying to get any work done on it.

5. When you're finished setting the time, you'll see a summary of what you've selected.

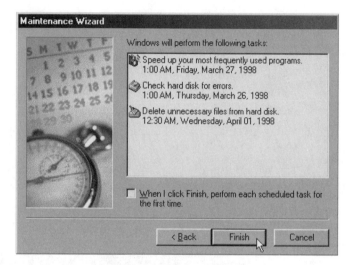

Note that you can opt to have a tune-up begin upon clicking Finish, if you set the checkbox on. Don't do this unless you're ready to take off for a few hours and leave the computer on.

6. When you click on Finish, three or four new tasks are added to the Task Scheduler, as you see here:

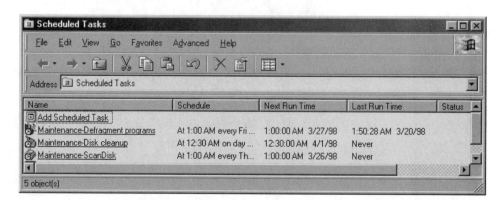

Windows Update Wizard

If you've been a slave to computers for any length of time, you've undoubtedly heard about system files that go out of date or get lost, or about drivers that need replacing to reflect the latest upgrades. In the olden days (a couple of years ago) you had to call some manufacturer such as Microsoft to have them send you a disk, or dial up a electronic BBS to download files. Now with the almost universal availability of the Web, not only can manufacturers supply files online, they can even sell complete software titles, or check your computer automatically to see whether you're running the right stuff. Although this could be seen as an invasion of technical privacy, the advantages are obvious.

Microsoft has embraced this kind of online technology to help reduce the number of glitched-out Windows 98 systems in the world. The Windows Update Wizard helps you keep your Windows 98 system tuned and up-to-date by automating driver and system updates from one place on the Web. In addition, if you're a registered Windows user, you'll be able to locate the latest information on using Windows 98, and answers to frequently asked Windows 98 questions.

 NOTE

You have to be connected to the Web to use this service.

To open the Windows Update website:

1. Connect to the Internet.

2. Click Start ➢ Settings ➢ Windows Update. Or open your browser and enter this URL:

   `http://www.microsoft.com/windowsupdate/default.asp`

3. You can register to become a Windows Update user the first time you select an item on the Windows Update home page.

4. Click on Update Wizard on the Web page, as shown in Figure 23.18.

5. You will probably see a security alert about downloading and/or running the Active X program. Just say Yes.

6. If you're not registered, the Wizard knows this, and you'll see a dialog box asking you if you want to register. (Resist paranoia. Whether you've registered is stored in your computer program and the Active X applet checks this.) The Windows registration screen will come up and walk you through registering. You can register, or put it off until later by clicking Register Later.

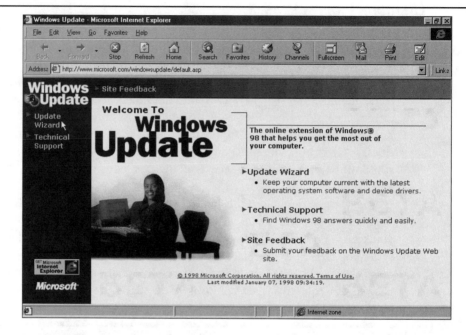

7. The Update Wizard screen will now appear, asking what you want to do. Click on Update. This will check on possible updates for your system. This may take a few minutes. You may eventually see some windows asking if you want to download something such as the Windows 98 Update Wizard Control, or the like. Again, just say Yes. Eventually the program will start searching your system files. It's building a database of what you have, the dates and sizes of the files, and comparing them to the database on the Microsoft company site. You'll see a list of anything that's newer than what you have in your computer, such as you see in Figure 23.19.

8. Click on an item (if there are any) in the left pane to see its description in the right pane. Follow instruction on screen to install the item(s) you want to update.

9. Close the Browser window after you're finished updating your system.

The Restore button on the page returns your system to the state it was in prior to the update. If you discover that the computer doesn't work correctly after the update, then find the Restore button and click it. This should work even after you close the browser, get off the net etc. To restore your older system files, just get to the update page again and click Restore. On the screen, you'll see instructions for updating and restoring your files.

FIGURE 23.19

Typical results of the Update Wizard's scan of a system

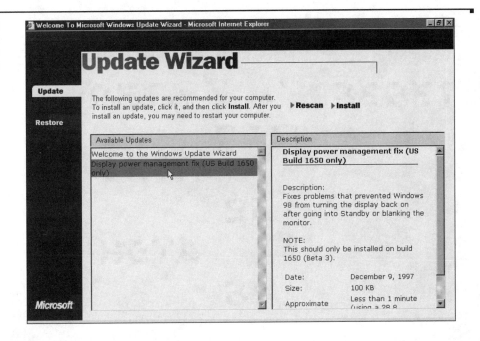

The System Information Utility

The System Information utility is a powerful control center for system analysis, configuration, and troubleshooting. Several tools that were previously available as stand-alone utility programs have been rolled into it, such as the Registry Checker and System File Checker. A few programs that are also available from other locations within Windows 98, such as the System Update and ScanDisk utilities described earlier in this chapter, are available from the Tools menu in this utility. All in all, the System Information utility is a one-stop shop for the system technician or troubleshooter.

If you're a typical user, you should not need to use this package of programs. However, it is quite possible that if you place a call to Microsoft's hotline for technical support, they will send you rooting around with this utility's Windows Report ("Winrep") tool, which can not only generate a bug report and create a list detailing your hardware and operating system configuration, but also send them to Microsoft for further assistance. Actually, even typical users can benefit from occasionally running the utility's System File Checker (which helps detect damaged system files that could bring Windows to a halt or otherwise be ruinous) and the Registry Checker (which replaces the Registry with a backup version if it detects Registry problems at bootup). Other programs in the System Information suite were not fully implemented at the time of this writing, but it was expected to include the Dr. Watson problem reporting utility (from previous versions of Windows), Signature Verification, and the Version Conflict Manager, among others; check the Microsoft online help for more information.

PART V

Networking
with Windows 98

CHAPTERS:

24. An Overview of Windows 98 Networking

25. Planning Your Windows 98 Network

26. Setting Up a Peer-to-Peer Windows 98 Network

27. Internetworking Windows 98 Workstations with NT

28. Extending Your Reach with Dial-Up Networking

29. Troubleshooting Your Windows 98 Network

Chapter

24

An Overview of
Windows 98
Networking

FEATURING

New features of Windows 98

The OSI reference model

The Windows 98 networking model

An Overview of Windows 98 Networking

As microcomputers become increasingly ubiquitous in the workplace, demands on their efficiency continue to grow. These demands extend into the area of local-area networks (LANs) and LAN administration. Growing on the base of past products such as Windows for Workgroups (Windows 3.11) and Windows 95, yet also borrowing from the more advanced technology of Windows NT, Windows 98 has become a fairly mature networking product. It has inherited some high-performance aspects, such as more 32-bit code. It boasts a unified user front-end, regardless of protocol being used (Novell, Microsoft, TCP/IP), and also has decent remote access capabilities. Remote administration of Windows 98 clients across a LAN has received attention from Microsoft as well, in their attempt to create the "thin client" and the "zero administration client."

Windows 98 has all the features necessary to make it the perfect network citizen. Right out of the box—with no additional software required—your PC and Windows 98 are capable of connecting to 32 Windows 98 workstations. They are also capable of interoperating with all major network operating systems (NOSs) and can function either as a client, as a server, or as both simultaneously. Because of its modular approach to networking software and its true multitasking ability, Windows 98 is capable of simultaneously speaking multiple network languages (called *protocols*) and even using multiple network interface cards. You could, for example, simultaneously access a database on your company's mainframe, print a report on your office's Novell print server, and cruise the Web on the Internet, all while one or more other users are accessing files located on your PC's hard drive. Moreover, these various network connections can take place via any combination of the following: standard network adapters and cable, high-speed digital phone lines, "normal" phone lines and a modem, or even directly attached to your PC via either a serial or a parallel port. And because the networking features are truly integrated parts of Windows 98, you can access drives and printers located on a variety of different networks from any Windows application—always in the same way, regardless of the type of computer or network to which you are connected. Being able to network—or rather, *internetwork*—with other computer systems in exactly the same manner, whether you're at the office, at home, or even on the road using your laptop, opens almost endless possibilities for extending the usefulness of your computers.

Networking Features of Windows 98

The networking possibilities supplied by Windows 98 truly are exciting. Never before have so many ways to so easily network with other computers been brought together like this in one product, let alone within a popular, graphical operating system.

Here are a few of the networking capabilities and features that Windows 98 has to offer:

- Using 32-bit underpinnings (drivers, protocols, client software) offers a means for users to easily share data, hard disk, and printing resources.

- The ability to use multiple protocols and redirectors, and drivers at the same time, allows administrators to integrate different types of network cards, software, and computers on a single Windows 98–based network.

- Simple integration with Windows 95, Windows 3.11, Windows NT, Microsoft LAN Manager, and Novell clients and servers (both 3.*x* and 4.*x* servers as well as peer sharing) using 32-bit drivers. Real-mode (16-bit) supplied drivers can integrate Banyan Vines, DEC Pathworks, and SunSoft PC-NFS clients. All of these clients can be connected to a single Windows 98 workstation client simultaneously. Regardless of the protocol or network type a given workstation is networking with, the users' interface remains the same. For example, a user on a Windows 98 PC connecting to a Novell PC and a Mac will see the same dialog boxes for printer and file sharing, regardless of the machine to which they are connecting. This consistent interface approach minimizes learning time for new users and cuts confusion for experienced users working with multiple platforms.

- Integration of the Internet into Windows 98 is simple and seamless. TCP/IP protocol (the networking protocol for data exchange popularized by Unix and the Internet) is built in and installed by default. Windows 98 includes a fast, 32-bit TCP/IP "stack" for connecting to the Internet via either a modem or your LAN connection. Also included is a 32-bit "winsock" (Windows Sockets) interface so you can use all the popular winsock-compatible programs such as Eudora, Pegasus, Netscape, Internet Explorer, and so on with no additional hassle.

- Integration of Apple Macintosh workstations is possible but only through an NT Server box running the Mac-compatible file services, which serves as the intermediary.

- Remote access dial-up ability, using the Windows Dial-Up networking, letting you connect remotely to Microsoft, UNIX, or NetWare machines and networks when you are out of the office.

- Support for SLIP (Serial Line Internet Protocol), and PPP (Point-to-Point Protocol). These are the two most popular software protocols necessary for connecting to the Internet.

- Support for PPTP (Point-to-Point Tunneling Protocol), also called Virtual Private Networking (or VPN), letting you use the Internet as the intermediary for wide-area networking between remote offices.

- Remote administration that allows system managers to remotely configure, query, and monitor workstations from a remote location. Working at a single Windows 98 PC, a network administrator can determine the hardware and software complement in the network, diagnose workstation and network problems, and monitor and tweak network performance.

- Simple network installation of Windows 98 from a server. Administrators can opt to remotely install Windows 98 from their server onto remote network workstations ("push"). Or they can "pull" the Windows setup files from a networked PC from the server.

- Networking now allows a manager to set up "NC" (network computer) workstations that run Windows 98 from a server machine where all the system files are stored and maintained by the Net administrator. This is the "thin client" apprach. Running from a server lets users take their personal settings, data, and applications with them from PC to PC as they move around, since all their settings are stored in the central Registry on the server.

In this and following chapters, we will look closely at the networking capabilities of Windows 98 and discuss step by step how to install, configure, and use them. If you are

PART

V

Networking with
Windows 98

interested less in the details and more in how to quickly set up your networking components, you may want to skip ahead to the "how-to" sections in the following chapters.

Windows 98, as I have said, can share your local hard drive(s) and printer with other users, acting as a server on a peer-to-peer network. In this role, a Windows 98 workstation allows other computers to use its resources such as files, printers, and (in certain respects) modems. Additionally, Windows 98 can act as either a Dial-Up Networking client or as a host so you can use regular phone lines to extend the reach of your network. This allows you to be on the road (or at home—or anywhere) and dial into your office network and have the same resources available as if you were sitting right at your desk.

If your computer supports Plug and Play, when you install a Plug-and-Play–compatible network adapter card, Windows 98 will automatically load and configure all the necessary software to place your computer on a network—all without any user intervention apart from selecting the desired protocols. This includes PCMCIA cards for mobile computers. Getting a PC connected to a network has never been so easy, assuming you're using Plug-and-Play cards. Simply plug in the card and start the computer (unless it's a PCMCIA card since those can be inserted with the computer on), and Windows 98 will prompt you for any necessary driver disks (typically the install CD-ROM).

Roughly, protocols can be thought of as the various languages that different networks use to communicate. The protocol implementation manages such tasks as requesting data from file and application servers, providing resources to other workstations, and placing data onto the network. Each of these tasks uses a specific protocol or layer of a protocol, and Windows 98's networking software ensures that it uses the correct protocol at the correct time. While this may sound complex (behind the scenes, it *is* complex), Windows 98 makes it very easy to choose, install, and make use of the protocol(s) you need. In the next section, we discuss protocols in more detail. You *can* configure and use Windows 98 without a thorough knowledge of networking protocols, but having at least a passing familiarity with networking protocols and related concepts will be helpful in getting the best performance out of your network.

A protocol, in general, is really nothing more than a set of rules and conventions for accomplishing a specific task. In the case of computer networking, a protocol defines the manner in which two computers communicate with each other. As an analogy, consider the protocol you use to place a phone call. Before you dial, you first make sure no one else is using the phone line. Next you pick up the phone and listen for a dial tone. If you are at your office, you might have to dial 9 and again wait for a dial tone. Then you can dial either a seven-digit number for a local call or a 1 followed by a 10-digit number for a long-distance call. You then wait for the other person to answer. But if you do not follow this protocol correctly—for example, you do not dial a 9 for an outside line when at the office—you will be unable to place your phone call.

In the world of computers, a protocol works exactly the same way. If a client does not structure and send a request in the exact manner in which the server expects it—and we all know how particular computers can be—it will never establish the connection.

When you first activate the networking component on your computer, Windows 98 installs the NetBEUI and IPX/SPX protocols by default. Besides these two, Windows 98 allows you to install several other protocols that—depending on the design of your network and type of applications you run—might provide better performance or other advantages. To help you make the best choices possible for your Windows 98 network, I next present an overview of how LANs work—both in theoretical and practical terms. I do this by first talking about networking models and then looking at how Windows 98 implements these concepts. Finally, I delve into the most common protocols themselves and help you choose the best for your particular environment.

The OSI Reference Model

In the early years of networking, each vendor defined its own standard for communication between its computers. The primary goal was to maximize the performance on a particular vendor's hardware (and lock you into their products) rather than to provide compatibility with other vendors' products. This caused problems because these systems did not share a common protocol and so could not interact with each other. In the late 1970s, the networking community came together in an effort to replace these closed systems with open systems. This would allow IS (Information Systems) shops to mix and match their hardware so users could access the desired resources on other vendors' products. The result was the Open System Interconnect (OSI) model developed by the International Standards Organization (ISO). While no network fully implements this model in the exact manner described by the ISO committee, it is the common framework for discussing networking in theoretical terms. Its strongest asset is that it provides an excellent way of comparing two different networking technologies because it provides a common measuring stick.

The OSI reference model (often referred to simply as the OSI model) takes a modular approach to networking by identifying and defining seven separate processes that any network—whether local- or wide-area—must accomplish. In OSI lingo, each process is a *layer*. Figure 24.1 shows the seven layers of the OSI model.

Each of these seven layers is responsible for a specific and discrete aspect of networking. The OSI model describes the flow of network data from the top layer—the user's application—to the bottom layer—physical connections of the network. Because no network follows the OSI model exactly, some networks may use only four separate pieces to cover the same functionality as the seven layers of the OSI model. Others may segment it into nine parts.

FIGURE 24.1

The seven layers of
the OSI reference
model

As data flow across a network, the OSI model stipulates that each layer communicate only with the layers immediately above and below it. This serves two purposes. First and foremost, it creates modularized layers. Each layer needs to know none of the details of how the other layers work; it only needs to know what its input will look like and how it must format its output so the next layer can understand it. Second, modularizing prevents *feature creep*—layers growing excessively complex and taking on functions that other layers should accomplish.

When creating a message, each layer assumes it is in direct communication with its peer layer on the other side. For example, when the transport layer needs to send an error across the network, it sends the message directly to the transport layer on the other side. This virtual communication further streamlines the process.

Before delving into the individual layers of the OSI model, let's look at the process of network communication in everyday terms. A good way to look at network communication is simply as a message: requesting a database row, opening a file for access, or sending someone an e-mail message. Now, imagine that this message is nothing more than a letter to Gramma Gertrude that needs to pass through several layers to get from you to her.

After deciding to write the letter, you need to get out some paper and a pen and write the message: "Thanks for the lovely dress. I wear it to church every Sunday." Now you must place it in a container—an envelope. Next, you place a stamp on the envelope. After that, you address it so it can get to the correct place. Finally, you drop it into the mailbox and from there the post office bundles it with all the other messages and delivers it. If you want to ensure that the letter is delivered, you might send it via certified or registered mail with a return receipt; otherwise, you have no guarantee that the letter will reach its destination.

A Matter of Terminology: Packets and Frames

Depending on the amount of traffic on the systems involved in transmitting and receiving the data between the sender and intended recipient (there may be various intermediate computers and processes between the origin and ultimate destination), the amount of data that is received from moment to moment differs. The amount of information that comes in as a single discrete chunk is referred to as a *packet*. In our Gramma Gertrude example, the packet may be the entire letter you've written to your grandmother, or it might be a whole page, or it might be a single paragraph. The packet will consist of numerous *frames* of data, each of which is a highly organized arrangement of a tiny amount of data. You might think of data frames as the individual sentences in the letter you're writing to your grandmother (albeit sentences loaded with extraneous numbers and codes). Each frame contains, in a specific sequence, the start bit, the data bits, the stop bits, and perhaps other specialized bits denoting such useful things as the frame address and error-checking values.

The Application Layer

The application layer is at the top—closest to the end user—of the OSI model. This layer directly supports any application that wants to access a network resource for any reason—be it a file, a printer, or another application. In other words, any time any user's application—regardless of type—needs to communicate with any resource across the network, it must begin here.

In the example of the letter to Gramma Gertrude, this layer systematically encompasses your decision to write the letter thanking her for the dress. Explorer, Exchange, and Dial-up Networking provide application-layer services in Windows 98.

The Presentation Layer

The presentation layer acts primarily as a translation agent. In doing so, it determines the best way for two computers to communicate with one another. When data are going down to the physical layer, the application layer relies on the presentation layer to translate the data sent from the application layer into an intermediary format. Here the presentation layer resolves character set (ASCII, EBCDIC, Unicode) differences, adds any security, and compresses the data. Conversely, when data come up from the physical layer, the presentation layer reverses the process and removes the encryption, re-expands the data, and gives it to the application layer using a data set that the application layer can directly use.

Back in the Gramma Gertrude example, translating the message content from your mind to written words represents the activities of the presentation layer. When you first start up your computer and log into an NT network, Windows 98 encrypts your password so no one can steal it as it goes across the network wire—this is the presentation layer at work.

The Session Layer

The session layer manages the dialogue between two logical addresses. It allows applications on a network to initiate, use, and terminate a connection—called a *session*—with another computer or another process. The layer also is responsible for name recognition between computers.

Once two computers have established a session, the session layer synchronizes the communication between them. Essentially, it sets the ground rules defining whose turn it is to send data and sets a limit on how long one side may monopolize the communication before it must yield to the other computer.

When you place the letter to Gramma Gertrude in the envelope, you are, in OSI terminology, *initiating a session*—passing control over to the session layer.

The Transport Layer

The transport layer ensures end point–to–end point data integrity by managing error recognition and, if necessary, correction and recovery throughout the data transfer. This layer ensures accuracy by adding Error Correcting Code (ECC), typically a Cyclic Redundancy Checksum (CRC). This CRC is a calculated value based on an accumulation on a byte-per-byte basis of the data being sent.

Once the transport layer receives a packet of data, it first calculates the Cyclic Redundancy Checksum (CRC) for that packet. If the CRC calculated in real time does not match the CRC the other side originally placed in the data packet, it knows there has been an error in the transmission. If an error occurred, the data will be sent again until an acknowledgment is received. If several attempts to transmit the data fail, an error message will be displayed.

In our letter example, placing a stamp on the envelope and requesting the return receipt is the proxy for the transport layer. Here you are providing a means of ensuring the message gets through snow, sleet, and rain. If it encounters an error along the way, you will get the message back; otherwise, you will get a signed receipt indicating your grandmother received (and hopefully read) your letter.

The Network Layer

The network layer manages addressing the message. Once it has resolved the address, it routes the message using a cost-based algorithm. On the addressing side, the network layer translates the logical address it originally received from the session layer into a physical address the data layer can understand. When data come back up the chain, the network layer reverses the process, replacing the physical address with a logical one. By doing so, it provides connections between two open systems regardless of the type of physical link between the two. Packages coming from the upper layers need only contain the logical address, thus freeing these layers from concerning themselves with the peculiar addressing schema of various network technologies.

In your letter to Gramma, you performed the task of the network layer when you put the address on the letter. If you wanted to send it via the U.S. Postal Service, you would include a zip code and possibly the carrier route.

The Data Link Layer

The data link layer is responsible for providing error-free transmission of this frame between any two destinations over the physical layer. (This differs from the data integrity provided by the transport layer. The transport layer, remember, is concerned with the data throughout the transmission.) As a data frame flows down to the physical layer, the data link layer takes the frames sent to it from the network layer and places them bit by bit onto the physical layer.

The address in the data link layer differs from that in the network layer in that it is a simpler address, one that the data link layer on the other side will recognize. To understand the difference between the addresses, you can think of the network layer address as the street name and the data layer address as the street number.

The Physical Layer

The physical layer's job is to send individual bits—usually impulses of light or electricity—from one end of the physical medium (the wire) to the other. The physical layer defines the data-flow rate, the type of cable over which the data flow, the topology, the number of pins, and the voltage flowing through those pins. Common specifications for the physical layer include 10Base-T Ethernet, Token Ring, and FDDI (optical fiber). In the letter example, the mail carrier would be considered our network physical layer as he or she drives down to your grandmother's house to deliver your letter.

The Windows 98 Networking Model

Now that I have covered networking on the theoretical level, I can discuss the networking architecture built into Windows 98 and the protocols it supports. Just like the OSI model, Windows 98 takes a layered approach to networking as shown in Figure 24.2.

FIGURE 24.2

Layers of the Windows 98 networking model

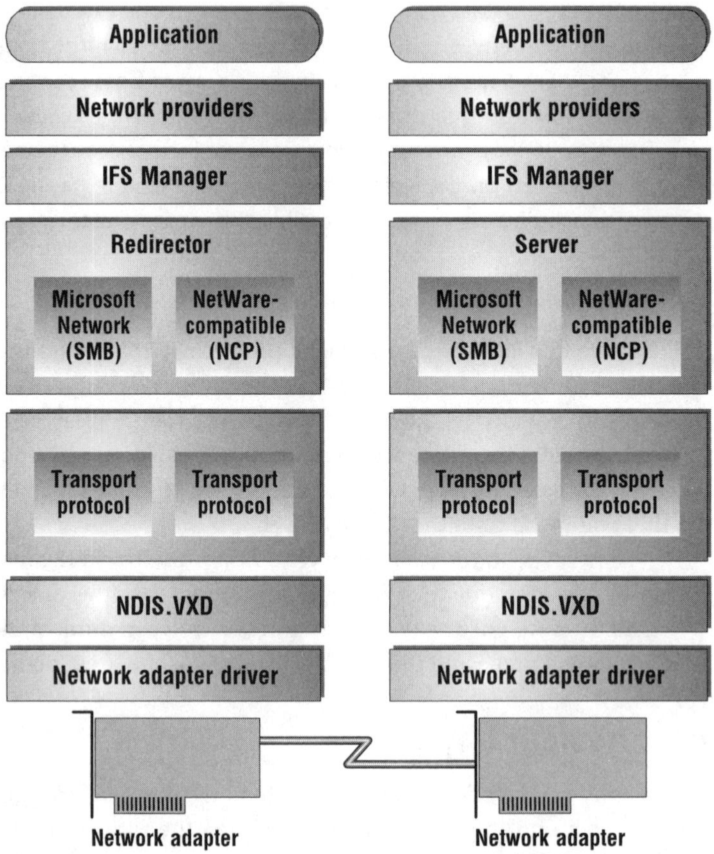

The Network Drivers Interface Specification (NDIS) is key to Microsoft's layered network. It provides the vital link between the protocol and the network interface card driver. While the protocol and the network interface card drivers provide separate functions, they remain fundamentally linked. The protocol (discussed in more detail in a later section) determines how your computer structures data sent across the network. The network adapter card drivers define how your computer interacts with the card, which, in turn, actually places the data on the network.

Network Drivers Interface Specification (NDIS)

A network interface card fulfills the most basic requirement of networking—a physical connection to other computers. Before your computer can use this card, you must load a device driver for it just as you would load a driver for your video card or CD-ROM drive. The driver is a piece of software that instructs the computer how to interact with the network card—how to drive it, if you will. Because each vendor's cards differ from those of another vendor, each type of card requires a driver tailored to its peculiarities. This driver takes the data packets sent from the upper layers of the network architecture and packages them for the physical layer.

Microsoft provides two types of NDIS drivers, NDIS 2.0 and NDIS 3.1. The primary difference between these drivers is that an NDIS 2.0 driver is a real-mode driver and is loaded in your `autoexec.bat` or `config.sys` files, while an NDIS 3.1 driver is loaded in Windows 98 as a 32-bit, protected-mode driver. This protected-mode driver is designed as a dynamically loadable virtual device driver (VxD) and will perform better than the real-mode NDIS 2.0 drivers.

Open Datalink Interface (ODI)

As a universal client, Windows 98 also supports the Open Datalink Interface (ODI) standard put forth by Novell and Apple in addition to NDIS. Essentially, ODI and NDIS provide the same functionality in different ways. The only practical difference from a user perspective is that Windows 98 implements ODI as a real-mode device driver, where NDIS is a 32-bit, protected-mode driver. If you plan to connect to a NetWare server, you might need to stick with the ODI drivers for compatibility reasons as some network applications are very particular about the network drivers. I recommend trying NDIS drivers first, though, keeping in mind you may need to change to ODI if any of your networking applications begin misbehaving. The performance gain of using the 32-bit, protected-mode NDIS drivers makes having to use ODI (which executes in real-mode) rather undesirable. But, if you absolutely need the most compatibility, the ODI drivers are there and can be installed just as easily as the NDIS drivers.

With an understanding of Windows 98's networking model, we can now look at the various transport protocols available as you set up your Windows 98 network.

Which Protocol to Use?

Right out of the box, Windows 98 gives you a choice of 12 transport protocols. These protocols fall into two broad groups. First, open-systems protocols such as NetBEUI and IPX/SPX allow you to connect to several vendors' networks. With them you can communicate over a Windows 98 peer-to-peer network or over another vendor's network. The second type of transport protocols are the proprietary protocols used to support specific vendors' networks such as Banyan Vines and DEC Pathworks. Because the choice of protocols becomes important only in open systems (if you have DEC Pathworks, for example, you already know what protocol you are going to use), I discuss the open protocols in this chapter. In later chapters I cover the other proprietary protocols.

NOTE

Although it is somewhat confusing, when network managers refer to a *transport protocol*, they usually mean the functions provided by both the transport and network layers. The reason these two layers are combined into one term (besides sloppiness) is that they are interrelated; between the two of them they are responsible for transporting your data through the network. The upper layers are more closely tied to the application requesting the network services. The lower physical layer, because it is the only layer with a tangible presence (unless you are using a wireless net where there is no tangible presence except for the network interface card), is not lumped into *transport protocol*.

Whenever you are installing Windows 98 networking support (either initially or at any later point), Windows 98 allows you to select protocols as shown in Figure 24.3. Here Windows 98 gives you the choice of nine built-in protocols. Five of them are of the most interest: IPX/SPX, DLC, NetBEUI, TCP/IP, and IPX/SPX with NetBIOS.

FIGURE 24.3

List of Microsoft-supplied protocols when installing a network

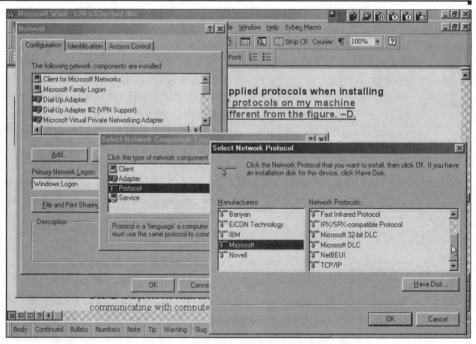

Before going into more detail on the particulars of each protocol, I'll quickly look at the typical uses of each protocol:

- IPX/SPX is the protocol Novell uses to connect to their NetWare file servers.

- IPX/SPX with NetBIOS adds support for the NetBIOS application programming interface (API) to the standard IPX/SPX protocol stack.

- Microsoft 32-bit DLC and Microsoft DLC (16-bit) are for communicating with IBMs or other mainframes. DLC (data link control) provides an interface between Windows 98 machines and mainframes as well as network printers. Network managers handle this type of protocol.

- NetBEUI is a protocol originally developed by IBM and used by Windows for Workgroups and LAN Manager.

- TCP/IP is a protocol often used over wide-area networks and for communicating with computers running some flavor of the Unix operating system.

- ATM Call Manager, ATM Emulated LAN, and ATM Lan Emulation Client are all new entries for Windows 98. ATM stands for Asynchorous Transfer Mode. Some large companies use ATM for their data transmission backbones. It doesn't typically make an appearance at the desktop machine, but it's becoming more popular as a desktop option. ATM Lan Emulation Client is a software layer that lets workstations emulate a LAN over the ATM backbone. This is similar to VPN using the Internet. You need an ATM card in your PC to take advantage of this high-speed networking option. If you are using ATM, you'll no doubt have a network administrator who will have explicit instructions about how to install it.

- Fast Infrared Protocol allows you to network with other devices and computers using IrDA (infrared) ports. Some "wireless" networking devices use infrared transmission for this purpose. In the past you had to install proprietary device drivers to use such products.

IPX/SPX and IPX/SPX with NetBIOS Protocols

Xerox originally developed the Internetwork Packet Exchange/Sequenced Packet Exchange (IPX/SPX or just IPX) protocol as part of its XNS protocol suite. Novell decided to use it as the base protocol for connecting to its NetWare file servers and currently maintains the specifications and ongoing enhancements to the protocol. In Windows 98 you can use the IPX protocol to connect to NetWare 2.x, 3.x, and 4.x (with bindery emulation) servers. You can also use it to connect to Windows for Workgroups 3.x, Windows NT 3.x, and of course Windows 98 computers running the IPX protocol.

NOTE

Windows 98 allows you to install either Microsoft's own version of IPX/SPX or one supplied by Novell.

Where NetBEUI was the default protocol in Windows 3.*x*, Windows 95 and Windows 98 install IPX as the default. IPX works for small to medium networks because it is small and fast, besides being *routable*. A routable protocol is one you can use to send data to computers on different LAN segments. (I discuss what constitutes a LAN segment in the following chapter.) The IPX stack that Microsoft includes is compatible with Novell's implementation, works with NT and Novell servers, and with almost any other network hardware that expects it, including routers and bridges. Its fully 32-bit code also includes "packet-burst" capability that speeds up transmission across the network cabling.

The IPX protocol can support larger networks than other nonroutable protocols. It allows network managers to break down larger networks into smaller segments to achieve significant performance gain, with packets being automatically forwarded (routed) to the correct segment. However, IPX is not suitable for networks consisting of more than 500 workstations or networks connected over a WAN, because IPX workstations regularly send out "hey, I'm still here" messages, called *broadcasts*, that tell other servers and stations on the network that their connections are still active. On large networks, these broadcasts alone generate quite a bit of network traffic and thus reduce the performance of the network as a whole.

Network Basic Input/Output System (NetBIOS) is a programming interface that implements many of the functions provided by the session layer. Sytek originally developed it for IBM's broadband computer networks and included it in the ROM of its network adapter cards. Since then, many other companies have developed their own version of NetBIOS, making it a de facto standard.

NetBIOS allows applications to communicate over any protocol compliant with NetBIOS. Many server-based applications, such as Lotus Notes, use NetBIOS to communicate with clients over a network. Because IPX does not directly support NetBIOS, you must load it separately. Previously, to use NetBIOS over the IPX protocol, you had to use a Novell-provided terminate-and-stay-resident (TSR) driver called `netbios.exe`. Like all other TSRs, you had to load it before starting Windows if you wanted any of your Windows applications to take advantage of it. As such, it not only took up valuable conventional memory (below the 640K limit), but it also forced Windows to switch into real mode to communicate with NetBIOS applications.

Fortunately, Windows 98 provides a full 32-bit protected-mode implementation of NetBIOS for use with the IPX protocol called NWNBLink (NetWare NetBIOS Link). It is fully compatible with the Novell version and provides significantly improved performance simply because it is 32-bit and executes in protected mode. In addition, Windows 98 can support Windows Sockets over IPX. (Like NetBIOS, Windows Sockets is another network programming interface—in this case, based on the sockets standard used on several other operating systems, Unix in particular.) When communicating with other computers using NWNBLink, Windows 98 can support sliding windows and PiggyBackAck (acknowledging previous frames in later response frames).

In Windows NT 3.5 (both flavors), the service that allows it to act as a peer-to-peer server (not to be confused with the product NT Server) supports IPX without NetBIOS. The service that provides peer-to-peer *workstation* support (not to be confused with the product NT Workstation), however, does *not* support IPX without NetBIOS. Therefore, a Windows 98 client running IPX without NetBIOS can connect to a Windows NT *server*; however, a Windows NT *workstation* will not be able to connect to a Windows 98 machine running IPX without NetBIOS. If you install IPX with NetBIOS support on both sides, you will always be able to communicate over the IPX/SPX protocol. Here are the pros and cons of IPX/SPX:

Advantages of IPX/SPX	Disadvantages of IPX/SPX
Compatible with Novell products	Not as fast as NetBEUI
Routable	Not as routable as TCP/IP
Single protocol support for mixed NetWare and Microsoft networks	More overhead than NetBEUI
	Regular broadcasts take up limited bandwidth

DLC (Data Link Control)

Networks based on IBM Token Ring claim most of the users of the Data Link Control protocol. Actually, DLC really is not properly a transport protocol; rather it is a data link layer protocol that behaves much like a transport protocol. You cannot, for example, use DLC to share files and printers on Windows 98 networks. However, Windows 98 machines can use DLC to send print jobs to printers located directly on the network (rather than attached to a printer server), such as HP LaserJet IVs with a JetDirect card installed. And Microsoft has also included DLC to enable your Windows 98 machines to connect directly to IBM mainframe computers. Here are the pros and cons of DLC:

Advantages of DLC	Disadvantages of DLC
Compatible with IBM mainframes	Not compatible with standard Microsoft file and print services

PART

V

Networking with Windows 98

NetBEUI

The NetBIOS Extended User Interface (or NetBEUI), first introduced by IBM in 1985, is a protocol written to the NetBIOS interface. Microsoft first supported NetBEUI in MS-Net, its first networking product, when it introduced the product in the mid-1980s. It was the default protocol for all Microsoft networks from Windows for Workgroups to LAN Manager up through Windows NT 3.1. NetBEUI is a small and very fast protocol—in fact, the fastest protocol shipped with Windows 98—because it requires very little overhead. Overhead in this context refers to the additional network-control information such as routing and error checking that the protocol adds to the data that the application layer wants to send across the network.

NOTE

NetBEUI is not NetBIOS. It is easy to confuse NetBIOS and NetBEUI. The confusion stems not only from the similar naming but from the fact that earlier implementations of NetBEUI provided NetBIOS as an integral part of the protocol driver. When I refer to NetBEUI here, I am referring to the transport-layer protocol, not the NetBIOS programming interface. NetBEUI is a sufficient but not a necessary requirement for using NetBIOS because other protocols also support NetBIOS. In other words, if you use NetBEUI, you can run NetBIOS applications. On the other hand, if you have another protocol such as IPX *with* NetBIOS (which obviously includes support for NetBIOS), you can completely remove the NetBEUI protocol and still run your NetBIOS applications.

One reason for NetBEUI's lower overhead is that NetBEUI only provides what is called *unreliable communication*. Don't worry, unreliable is something of a misnomer; the connection is still reliable. Unreliable communication means that the protocol does not require an explicit acknowledgment (ACK) of each frame before it sends the next. Rather, the receiving computer bundles up several acknowledgments and sends them all at once. In our example of the letter to Gramma Gertrude, you would have had unreliable communication had you decided not to send the letter registered but waited to hear that she had received your card as part of some future message like a holiday card.

Were a protocol to require an ACK for each packet, it would waste the majority of the networks' resources because an ACK is so small it would use very little of the network's bandwidth. Rather than require an acknowledgment for each frame, NetBEUI dynamically determines (through a process called Sliding Windows) the number of frames the sender can transmit before receiving an ACK, based on the current network conditions.

NOTE

Actually, the NetBEUI shipped with Windows 98 and Windows NT is not really Net-BEUI. Rather, it is a NetBIOS Frame protocol (NBF), sometimes referred to as NetBEUI 3.0. NBF is completely compatible with the "real" NetBEUI used in Windows for Workgroups and LAN Manager. In addition to supporting the NetBEUI specification, NBF is completely self-tuning, provides better performance across slow links such as telephone lines, and eliminates the 254-session limit of the original NetBEUI. Because the Windows 95 documentation refers to NBF as NetBEUI, we will too; for all practical purposes, they are identical.

Because of its speed and ability to self-tune through Sliding Windows, NetBEUI provides an excellent protocol for small networks such as regional sales offices. While Net-BEUI is fast on small networks, you cannot use it effectively on large networks. The main reason for the poor performance over large networks is its addressing scheme. For Net-BEUI, your computer's address is the very name you entered as your computer's name in the Network Identification dialog box. Obviously, this prevents a network from having two computers with the same name—something quite difficult to achieve on a large network while still giving computers meaningful names. Another, not quite as obvious, implication is that you cannot route it although you can bridge it. A bridge provides the same basic functionality as a router by providing the ability to combine multiple network segments into one logical segment. Here are the pros and cons of NetBEUI:

Advantages of NetBEUI	Disadvantages of NetBEUI
Compatible with Windows for Workgroups and LAN Manager	Not routable
Small memory footprint	Poor performance on large networks
Good error checking	Difficult to give meaningful names to computers on large networks
Fastest protocol in Windows 98	Tuned for small networks

TCP/IP

Quite simply, Transmission Control Protocol/Internet Protocol (TCP/IP) is the most complete, most widely accepted protocol in the world. And strictly speaking, TCP/IP is not a single protocol but a suite of protocols, usually referred to singularly as TCP/IP, that defines various interactions between computers sharing the protocol. TCP/IP originated as the protocol the U.S. Department of Defense developed in the late 1970s to connect computers to the Advanced Research Projects Agency Network (ARPANet), the precursor to the Internet. In 1983, in an effort to ensure all its computers could talk to each other,

PART

V

Networking with Windows 98

the Department of Defense mandated that all its new networking products support TCP/IP. Overnight, it created an instant market for TCP/IP. Soon after, one of the three major Unix vendors, Berkeley Software Design, Inc. (BSDI), released Unix version 4.2BSD, which incorporated TCP/IP into its core operating system, thus making it the lingua franca of midrange computers.

Until recently, that's where TCP/IP stayed—on midrange computers. In the last few years, however, the PC began to replace the dumb terminal as the standard in desktop computing. This forced network managers to find ways of integrating PCs into the rest of their corporate network, which included TCP/IP-based midrange computers. Because PCs use an open architecture rather than the proprietary ones in legacy systems, the obvious choice was to bring the PCs to the legacy systems via TCP/IP. Thus, just like the Department of Defense, many network administrators began demanding TCP/IP support for all their new PCs.

Windows 98 includes an easy-to-configure version of all the standard TCP/IP connectivity and diagnostic tools and applications such as FTP, telnet, ping, route, netstat, nbstat, ipconfig, rexec, rcp, rsh, tracert, and so on.

NOTE

For an in-depth discussion of TCP/IP configuration in Windows 98, see Chapter 15.

While TCP/IP has a reputation as a difficult protocol to configure and manage, new implementations are making it easier. In the TCP/IP arena, support for servers running Dynamic Host Configuration Protocol (DHCP) represented probably the most important advance in Windows 95 over Windows 3.x, and this carries over to Windows 98. Without DHCP, network managers have to assign the four-byte IP addresses to each machine manually. With DHCP enabled, a DHCP server manages a range of IP addresses and assigns one to each workstation as it logs onto the network.

NOTE

Currently only Windows NT Server provides the DHPC server required by the DHCP client in Windows 98. However, Windows 98 can provide the Windows Internet Name Service (WINS) server to resolve NetBIOS computer names to IP addresses. WINS provides the same functionality as the Unix Domain Name System (DNS) service. A Windows 98 computer can support a single DNS server and up to two WINS servers.

The TCP/IP protocol included with Windows 98 supports Windows Sockets 2. Windows Sockets is a programming interface (not a protocol) similar to NetBIOS but specifically designed for client/server applications because of its scalability. Windows Sockets 2 follows the Windows Open System Architecture (WOSA) and among other advances, isn't limited to supporting TCP/IP as was Windows Sockets 1.1. The upshot for most users is that Windows 98 can better receive video and audio transmissions (such as real-time multimedia communications) over the Internet as well as via other network protocols, using the same Winsock interface.

Microsoft TCP/IP supports NetBIOS by encapsulating—providing a wrapper—around the NetBIOS request within the TCP/IP protocol. Here are the pros and cons of TCP/IP:

Advantages to TCP/IP	Disadvantages to TCP/IP
Most widely used	More overhead than NetBEUI
Routable	Can be difficult to administer
Interoperates across hardware and software platforms	Not as fast as NetBEUI on small networks
Provides Internet connectivity	Supports Windows Sockets 1.1

Subsequent chapters examine many of the networking features in much more detail to help you either design a new network around Windows 98 workstations or integrate Windows 98 clients into your existing network.

PPTP: Point-to-Point Tunneling

Point-to-Point Tunneling is a protocol that allows disparate networks to communicate with each other securely (privately) using public networks like the Internet as the transmission medium. This is a relatively new technology, one which can save corporations big bucks by eliminating the need for proprietary leased lines between cities or even countries. It also allows remote users (such as telecommuters) to connect to corporate mainframes to check e-mail or transmit data files without requiring special wiring and without making long-distance calls over conventional telephone lines. And since public transmission media such as the Internet can support higher speeds of transmission than typical voice-grade telephone lines, using PPTP with a high-speed connection to, say, the Internet can provide quite respectable throughput over long distances.

Windows 98 networking includes PPTP support. Multiple protocols are supported, so you could have, for example, two Novell PC networks in distant locations, connected across the Internet using two PCs running Windows 98. Even Windows NT security via domain names and logins are operational across the link.

Chapter

25

Planning Your Windows 98 Network

FEATURING

Ethernet networks and cabling technologies

Which LAN topology to implement

Choosing your cards

Planning Your Windows 98 Network

This chapter is a fast track to designing your Windows 98 network. Although there are several network-technology choices you can make, I am only going to look at Ethernet networks. This is because Ethernet networks are easier to manage and less expensive to implement than token ring. Token-ring networks require more hardware than Ethernet, are more expensive to implement, and are only advantageous if you have to interface your network clients with IBM mainframes.

In this chapter, I first take a look at the two most likely network-cable topologies that home consumers and small-business owners use, and then I help you pick the best network interface card (NIC) for your computer.

If you are setting up a new Windows 98–based network, one of the first decisions you will have to make is what technology you will use to physically connect your computers. If you are integrating Windows 98 computers into an existing network (or if someone else has specified the network technology), you can skip ahead to the section on selecting your network adapter card.

If your network will have more than 30–40 workstations, you will probably need to split it into multiple sections, called *segments*. You then connect each segment to the other segments of the network through a series of routers or bridges. I mention the implications your decisions will have on both segmented and nonsegmented networks, but segmented networks are outside the scope of this book. Although there are indeed several excellent books on the subject, I have found that enterprise-wide network specialists design more successful networks than network managers who try to do everything themselves. Because these sorts of networks are exceedingly complex with no clear guidelines, many consultants resort to a trial-and-error design methodology. When looking for a network consultant, try to find one who has executed a trial-and-error period with a previous client.

Ethernet Networks and Cabling Technologies

Ethernet is what network professionals call a Carrier-Sense Multiple Access with Collision Detection (CSMA/CD) network. The University of Hawaii developed this model in the late 1960s when it was trying to place multiple computers on a campuswide wide-area network (hence *Multiple Access*). Their network controlled access by requiring each computer to listen to the wire and wait until no one else was transmitting (the *Carrier Sensing* part). Once the network was free, a station could go ahead and send its data. If another station tried to send at the same time and the transmissions collided, the computers realized this (*Collision Detection*), and each waited a random period of milliseconds before trying to resend. Whichever computer had the shorter random period of time got to transmit first.

When designing the physical side of your local-area network (LAN), you have two main decisions to make. You need to select which type of cable you will use to connect your computers together, and you need to choose which LAN technology you will employ to send data over this cable. In the next section I deal with the first question—the wiring. After that I discuss each of the technologies I highlighted above in more detail.

Which Type of Cable to Use?

In the past decade or so, network managers have installed LANs that run on every type of wiring imaginable. We limit our discussion to looking at coaxial cable, often referred to as Thin Ethernet, and unshielded twisted-pair cable. These two cabling mediums are most widely used today, and each offers unique strengths and weaknesses.

Coaxial Cable

Up through the late 1980s, almost every LAN (at least every one that I saw) used coaxial cable, usually referred to as "coax." Coax has only a single center conductor—usually solid copper wire—with a thick insulation surrounding the center and a layer of wire-mesh braid over this insulation. A final, outer layer of plastic insulation covers the wire braid and is what you normally see when you look at a piece of coax. The wire-braid layer further insulates the inner conductor from possible interference. As you can see in Figure 25.1, this coax looks very much like the round cable that connects your TV set to your antenna. In fact, network coax (especially thin coax) is quite similar to the coax used by ham and CB radio and TV antennas.

FIGURE 25.1

Coaxial cable

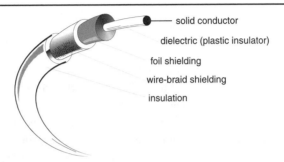

- solid conductor
- dielectric (plastic insulator)
- foil shielding
- wire-braid shielding
- insulation

Coax is fairly inexpensive and very easy to install. One complicating factor, however, is that each LAN technology uses a slightly different specification (called an RG number—such as RG-58). As a result, your existing cabling may not work with a new technology. However, for a home consumer or small-business owner this technology will provide usable network services for many years to come. Here are the pros and cons of using coax:

Advantages of Coax	Disadvantages of Coax
Simple to install	Low security, easy to tap
Good signal-to-noise ratio, particularly over medium distances	Difficult to change topologies
	Limited distance and topology
Low maintenance costs	Easily damaged

Unshielded Twisted Pair

Unshielded twisted pair (UTP) is similar to the cable that connects your phone to the wall jack. Each pair of wires is twisted around each other, as shown in Figure 25.2, to create a magnetic field that provides better transmission capabilities. Because the wire is unshielded, it is open to electrical interference, so you should be careful about how you route the cable. For instance, never run your cables next to a power transformer or an overhead lighting system.

FIGURE 25.2

Unshielded twisted-
pair cabling

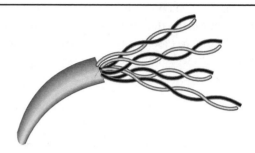

You should never use a low-quality cable type for your network. For instance, never use a telephone patch cord in your network segment. Although a telephone cable looks just like a network cable (RJ-45), they have different properties. Telephones will run on almost anything that carries a current; high-speed data networks, however, are very finicky. If the cable is not perfect, the data will garble up and bring your network to its knees. A single six-foot patch cable constructed from the standard untwisted telephone cabling that runs between your wall jack and phone (called *silver satin*) will usually prevent the entire LAN from sending any data across the entire segment.

To clean up the confusion over what constitutes acceptable network cable and to prevent installation mistakes, the Electronics Industries Association/Telecommunications Industry Association (EIA/TIA) released a system differentiating the varieties of unshielded twisted pair. The EIA/TIA system ranks cable from Grade 1 at the low end to Grade 5 at the high end:

- **Levels 1 and 2:** These grades are not appropriate for high-speed digital transmissions and should only be used for voice.

- **Level 3:** You can safely use Level 3 for low- to moderate-speed data such as 4Mbps (megabits per second) token ring and 10Mbps 10Base-T. If your network is in a location where it will be subjected to a great deal of electrical interference, you probably will want to use at least Level 4 even for speeds of 10Mbps.

- **Level 4:** When you start getting up above 10Mbps speeds such as 16Mbps token ring, you must use at least Level 4.

- **Level 5:** This top-of-the-line cable can be used for all transmission speeds, even up to the 100Mbps rate of Fast Ethernet. One word of caution: When you start using the new, high-speed technologies, be sure to use a top-rated cable-installation firm; a high-quality installation becomes essential at these speeds.

So what level should you choose? For the past several years, I have been recommending nothing other than Level 5. Because installing cable is labor-intensive (at least three-quarters of the total installation cost is directly related to labor; even more in complex, multifloor jobs), it only makes sense to make sure that whatever you use will last as long as possible. By saving a few hundred dollars in cable costs, you run the risk of having to rip it all out and pull all new cable if your cable is not up to supporting the newest LAN technologies. Remember, like any physical plant, you would like your cable to last at least 10 years, so it behooves you to plan for your network's future traffic.

NOTE

Every now and then one of my clients tells me one of their (usually previous) vendors told them they could not use Level 5 for token ring and 10Base-T because the specification called for Level 3. This misunderstanding is due to a misreading of the spec that sets the minimum acceptable EIA/TIA grade rather than the required grade. You can—and usually should—use a higher grade any time a lower grade is specified.

The following lists the maximum data-transfer rates for each of the EIA/TIA grades for unshielded twisted pair:

EIA/TIA Level	Maximum Data-Transfer Rate
1	0Mbps
2	1Mbps
3	10Mbps
4	10Mbps
5	100Mbps

All told, unshielded twisted pair is probably your best choice if you are using a cabling contractor to install your network cable in a business office or if you are building a new home and can have the cable installed before you put the wallboard up. If you are just trying to connect several computers in the same room or have short cable runs between rooms, coax cable is the better choice. Here are the pros and cons of UTP:

Advantages of UTP	Disadvantages of UTP
Easy to add additional nodes to the network	Limited bandwidth
	Requires a new cable to be run from hub to each new node
Break in a wire disables just one node on network	Limited distance
Well-understood technology	Low security, easy to tap
Inexpensive	Requires hubs
Can be used to support phones	Supports many topologies

Wireless LANs

You may have seen advertisements for products that claim to set up "wireless" LANs. Some of these use radio waves to connect the workstations, while others utilize infrared light sources and receivers, bouncing invisible light around your office space. Such alternatives to physical wiring have been reviewed in the trade press and are reported to work acceptably.

Be aware, however, that the data throughput (speed of data transfer across the link) is likely to take a substantial hit, so your network performance will suffer. This is partly due to limitations in the technology itself. Also, there may be a performance penalty due to interference of one sort or another during transmissions over the unconventional medium.

For example, infrared technology requires a "line of sight" between the sending station and receiving station. If you happen to be standing between the transmitter and receiver, the computers will keep retrying the transmission and will not be successful until you move out of the way. This is similar to using a TV remote control when someone is standing in between you and the television. Radio-based units can suffer from metal walls and fire doors, metal reinforced concrete, or by various external sources of radio interference.

In some cases where the cost or practicality of wiring is truly prohibitive, one of these alternatives may just be the only solution, however. As a rule, whatever method of "wiring" you use, compare the actual throughput to that of the day's leading NICs (typically 10Mbps–100Mbps as of this writing).

Which LAN Topology to Implement?

Now that you understand the physical media, you need to decide which LAN topology you will use to create your network. There are basically two types to be considered in our discussion:

- A bus topology for thin Ethernet or coax cabling
- A star topology for unshielded twisted pair

Thin Ethernet (10Base-2)

Thin Ethernet uses the main network cable, or *bus*, to connect each person's PC to the network. Each PC connects to this main cable by splicing the cable and terminating it with a bayonet nut connector (BNC), which is then connected to a T connector on the back of the network card. This essentially creates a single network cable that runs from the first PC to the last PC on the network.

You can create a Thin Ethernet segment for up to 185 meters (about 600 feet) and connect up to 30 stations to it. The cable itself must have an impedance of 50 ohms and be terminated with a 1/2watt 50-ohm (±1 ohm) resistor at each end. To prevent ground loops, you should also ground one (and only one) end of the cable as shown in Figure 25.3.

PART

V

Networking with
Windows 98

FIGURE 25.3

*A typical Thin
Ethernet segment*

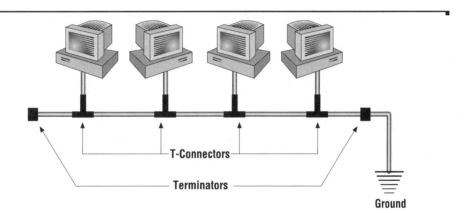

Thin Ethernet quickly became one of the most popular LAN technologies primarily because of its high performance-to-cost ratio and its relative ease of installation. In the early 1990s it began to lose favor to a newer variant of Ethernet, which runs on twisted pair rather than coax.

The real problem with 10Base-2 comes not from the coax cable but from the bus topology, where every computer is connected to a single cable. Whenever a computer wants to send data, it places a signal on the wire. This signal or *bus* then travels the length of the cable. As the bus passes each computer, the computer checks the destination address to see if it matches its own. If it matches, it reads the message; otherwise, it ignores it. If the cable breaks or otherwise becomes inoperable, suddenly every computer between the break and the terminator can no longer communicate with any of the stations on the other side of the break.

This is the primary reason I no longer recommend Thin Ethernet for business use outside of training rooms. If you only have three or four computers to connect, or the network cable can be easily routed from computer to computer and is very accessible, thin Ethernet is a good choice. Otherwise, by all means go with 10Base-T or 100Base-T.

Twisted-Pair Ethernet (10Base-T)

In the late 1980s, LANs moved out of the domain of the tightly controlled corporate MIS departments and into the departmental workgroup where everyone was connected to a network. Not only did the likelihood of the cable breaking increase as more computers were put on the network but so did the costs of downtime as more and more users began to depend on consistent network access.

In an effort to address these problems, vendors began offering Ethernet running on twisted pair using a star bus topology (see Figure 25.4). In a star bus network, each workstation is connected directly to a multiport repeater, sometimes called a *hub* or a *concentrator*. The concentrator basically acts as a traffic cop, directing incoming messages out to the correct computer. Each hub usually supports either eight or 16 computers, but some hubs can handle up to 128. If you need to add more computers than your concentrator can handle, or if you want to segment network traffic, you can connect several hubs together.

FIGURE 25.4

A network based on the star bus topology

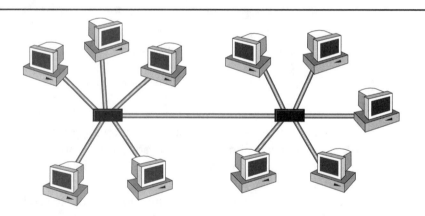

The benefit of a star topology is that if the cable fails at any point, only the computer directly served by that cable loses its connection. The downside, however, is that if the multiport repeater (*hub*) fails, then all the workstations attached to it lose their connection to the network also. In my opinion, you should not view this as a deterrent to installing a star rather than a bus network.

A failed hub in a star bus topology has the same effect as a cable break in a regular bus-style network: A lot of people lose their connection to the network. However, a failed hub is almost always easier to troubleshoot than a broken cable. With bus-style networks, you have no idea where your cable might have broken; it may be right at someone's computer or it may be up in the ceiling between the third and fourth floors. Once you have located the point of failure, hub problems are easy to fix—just swap in a new one. It is not that easy with cable because you cannot replace it; you need to fix it by splicing in a good piece of cable.

While twisted-pair Ethernet only requires two pairs, typical networks use 8-pin (four pairs) cable with an RJ-45 connector. Some networking professionals suggest using the extra wires for voice so you do not have to pull separate cables for your phones. Although this is technically possible, I don't think it's a good idea. Rather than use the extra wires for voice, use them for future expansion or as a backup in case a wire breaks. Better yet, you may be able to use them as part of your new 100Mbps Ethernet cabling.

With twisted-pair starting to catch on, computer managers quickly jumped at the opportunity to upgrade their cables to twisted-pair Ethernet, and the IEEE 802.3 committee created a new specification for Ethernet called 10Base-T. Among other things, this specification stipulates a workstation running 10Base-T must be within 100 meters (330 feet) of a concentrator and connected to it by cable meeting or exceeding the EIA/TIA UTP Level 3 grade.

Although twisted-pair networking hardware was initially quite a bit more expensive than coax-based equipment, mass production and the move to 100Base-T networks have pushed the price of 10Base-T network cards and hubs down to astonishingly low prices, even including the cost of the required additional hub. The price differential between 10Base-T and 10Base-2 has disappeared. I've seen network cards advertised for as little as $15 each.

As for the hubs themselves, you are better off sticking with the eight- or 16-port variety rather than going with the larger ones. By using more hubs, you can reduce the workload on each one. At press time, you can get these hubs for around $10 per port. In addition to the RJ-45 jacks for the twisted pair, some have a BNC or AUI (attachment unit interface) connector on the back so you can attach it to ThickNet or fiber backbones. If you are adding on to an existing ThinNet network, this is an essential feature; the additional cost is less than $20.

As your network grows, you will want to look at hubs with built-in management features. Although costing more, they are a great benefit to harried network managers because they allow them to remotely check the status of and administer each port on the hub. However, remote management adds $50–100 *per port* to the cost of each hub, so this feature will only make sense in a network with dozens or hundreds of hubs, or to networks that really need to be managed from a remote location.

I would recommend 10Base-T for your Ethernet network; unless you have a huge investment in thin Ethernet, or you need the greater speed of a 100Base-T network. The other options just are not worth it.

Table 25.1 summarizes the specifications of each of the LAN technologies discussed.

TABLE 25.1: THINNET (10BASE-2) AND TWISTED PAIR (10BASE-T) SPECIFICATIONS		
	ThinNet (10Base-2)	**Twisted Pair (10Base-T)**
Topology	Bus	Star Bus
Cable	RG-58	UTP
Impedance	50 ohm	N/A
Termination	50 ohm ± 2 ohm	UTP 85–115 ohm
Maximum length/segment	185 m	100 m
Maximum segments	5	N/A
Maximum stations/segment	30	N/A
Minimum distance between stations	.5 m	2.5 m (between hub and station)

Fast Ethernet (100Base-T)

Fast Ethernet, or 100Mbps Ethernet, is really "10Base-T The Next Generation." The engineers who brought us 10 Mbps figured out how to bring us 100 Mbps for really not much more in cost. Although it's hard enough for a single PC to keep up with data delivered at 10 Mbps, what this extra speed buys is the ability for many PCs to talk to several servers at once without the limitations of the network getting in the way. That is, although one user might not notice the difference, a few dozen will.

Hubs vs. Switches

10Base-T hubs are "dumb," and simply repeat every bit of data they hear from one port out to all of the others. This preserves the illusion that all of the computers on the network are connected together on a common wire, like coax-based networks. However it's not the most efficient use of your expensive network wiring.

Imagine how phone service would be if only one person could speak at a time, and everyone else in town had to listen! Since our phones no longer share a "party line," but we each have our own private wire right to the phone company's office, the telephone company can *switch* our conversations just between the phones involved in given conversation.

Many 100Base-T hubs have a similar ability to "switch" data as well, allowing several servers to send data to several network segments at the same time, since each has an independent connection to the switch. This, in addition to the higher speed used by the wiring, and *full duplex,* or simultaneous send/receive, give 100Base-T networks a tremendously improved data-carrying capacity.

Most of the discussion about 10Base-T applies to 100Base-T as well, with a few differences:

100Base-T	10Base-T
Enough speed for *big* networks or video feeds	Suitable for smaller, less data-intensive networks
Requires Cat-5 cabling	Can operate with less expensive Cat-3 cabling
Hardware about 3 to 5 times the cost of 10Base-T	Hardware is dirt cheap
Supports *full-duplex* or simultaneous send and receive, for even greater throughput	Normally half-duplex
Tricky or expensive to mix in with 10Base-T or 10Base-2 legacy network segments	Mixes easily with 10Base-2 network segments

In a small office network, you would be hard pressed to ever tell the difference between these two technologies. With Internet access, you will be limited to the speed of your Internet connection, which will be *much* slower than your LAN connection, so there is even less of a chance of noticing the speed difference. However, there are three reasons you might want to install a 100Base-T network:

- You have 50 or more computers on your network
- You will be using videoconferencing over your LAN (not just over the Internet)
- You have several servers and several high-intensity users

If any of these conditions apply and you're installing a new network, consider using 100Base-T. Even if you decide not to do so now, install Cat-5 cabling so that you can upgrade all or part of your network later. You will save lots of time and money if you start with adequate wiring and need only change network cards and hubs.

If any of these conditions apply, and you're upgrading an existing network, consider using a 100Mbps card in your server or servers, connecting these to a 100Mbps "switching" hub, and dividing your existing network into several small segments, each of which connects to the switching hub. You can connect individual workstations or existing hubs to the new switching hub. Then your server can send data to each of the segments virtually simultaneously.

If you do mix 10Base-T and 100Base-T in the same network, be sure that the hub you use to connect these disparate network types is a true "mixed-speed" hub, not one that forces the whole network to run at the lowest common denominator. Both types of hubs are being sold as "Dual Speed" hubs. If you have any doubt, ask the vendor if the hub can support both speeds simultaneously on a port-by-port basis.

Choosing Your Cards

Now, with the LAN, protocol, technology, and topology decisions behind you, you only have one more decision to make before you can start installing your network: How will you connect your PCs to this physical network you have just designed?

A few years ago, network designers often agonized over this decision. They would pore over manufacturers' spec sheets, then dutifully design a whole set of tests so they could compare the performance of various cards from various manufacturers. Finally, they would spend days laboriously putting the cards into each model computer on site and running the tests.

Why put forth such an effort? Well, although the costs of cards only varied by about 25 percent, the performance difference between a good card and a bad card could vary as much as 300 percent. Nowadays, most manufacturers use standard chip sets so the performance differences are quite small.

When choosing a card, by far the most important factor should be whether there is an NDIS 3.1 or (preferably) 4.1 driver available for the card. If not, you will either not be able to use the card with Windows 98, or you will have to use 16-bit real-mode drivers rather than the faster 32-bit protected-mode drivers.

NDIS 4.1

NDIS (Network Driver Interface Specification) version 4.1 supersedes NDIS 3.1 that was used in Windows NT 4 and Windows 95. NDIS 4.1 adds:

- Additional Plug-and-Play enhancements allowing network drivers to be installed and removed without rebooting
- Support for ATM network cards
- Compatibility with the "mini-driver" model used in NT, reducing the amount of program code a network card vendor has to write for their card to work in Windows 98

Really, if the card does not have at least an NDIS 3.1 driver available, don't even consider buying the card. Using 16-bit real-mode drivers will deprive you of one of

Windows 98's major benefits—the speed of 32-bit protected-mode drivers—every time you need to access the network. If possible make sure it's Plug and Play, and has an NDIS 4.1 driver.

Microsoft ships Windows 98 with drivers for many of the most popular token ring and Ethernet cards on the market. But if you find Windows 98 does not have a driver for an existing card, you do have a few options. First, check to see if Microsoft has recently released a driver. You can get all the latest Microsoft drivers from the following sources:

- **CompuServe:** Windows 98 Driver Library
- **CD-ROM:** \Drivers subdirectory (some but not all drivers)
- **Internet:** FTP to ftp.microsoft.com (131.107.1.11)
- **Internet:** Go to www.microsoft.com and search for "drivers"
- **Microsoft Download Servers:** Data (206) 936-6735 (No parity, 8 data bits, 1 stop bit)
- **Microsoft Product Support Services:** Voice (206) 637-7098 if you do not have a modem
- (In addition, you will probably be able to download the drivers from the Microsoft Network.)

If Microsoft does not have a driver available, you can contact your card's manufacturer directly. Be warned, however, this is a real hit-or-miss prospect. In some cases, the hardware manufacturers produce excellent drivers for their hardware—they, after all, know its ins and outs better than anyone else. In other cases, the manufacturer will have put very little effort into producing a quality driver. Rather, it simply wants to say Windows 98 supports its hardware with little regard for how buggy the hardware is and how often it crashes your system.

You will also want to consider the flexibility of your cards. You want a card that supports multiple network media and one you can configure with software. Until recently, manufacturers made separate cards for Thin coax and twisted pair. Now many manufacturers offer cards that support both of the popular media (these are called *combo* cards). If your network runs on multiple technologies, you definitely want cards that will support all of them.

I refuse to purchase a manufacturer's cards if I cannot configure them on the fly with software. As recently as two years ago, you could only change a card's configuration—interrupt, I/O address, DMA channel—by getting the forceps out and changing the jumpers. Most leading manufacturers now allow you to either hard configure your NIC with jumpers or soft configure with software. Until all your cards are Plug-and-Play compliant, soft configuration is the best available option.

PART

V

Networking with
Windows 98

You also need to match your network adapter card to your computer's system bus. Bus types are fairly easy to identify as there are only five from which to choose:

- 16-bit Industry Standard Architecture (ISA)
- 32-bit Extended Industry Standard Architecture (EISA)
- 16- and 32-bit Micro Channel Architecture (MCA)
- VESA (VL-Bus) Local Bus
- Intel Peripheral Component Interconnect (PCI) Local Bus

If you are not sure what type of bus you have, chances are it is an Industry Standard Architecture (ISA) machine, and it probably has PCI slots as well. Currently ISA (sometimes called AT-bus or AT-compatible because it originated when IBM first released the IBM Personal Computer AT) is by far the mostly widely used architecture. ISA machines have both 8- and 16-bit slots. If you have any PCI slots still available, get a PCI network adapter card. Although it will not double your throughput, switching from an 16-bit ISA card to a PCI card will produce a noticeable improvement. (8-bit ISA network cards still exist, but then, so do 300 baud modems).

The Extended Industry Standard Architecture (EISA) standard was *supposed* to be the successor to the ISA standard. In addition to the standard 8- and 16-bits slots used in ISA machines, EISA adds support for 32-bit cards. Unfortunately, it never gained market acceptance because the additional performance failed to justify the (substantial) extra cost. These days you only see EISA machines in file and database servers. Although you can use both 8- and 16-bit ISA cards in an EISA machine, you should take advantage of the EISA bus and use 32-bit EISA cards. (But see the comments below about EISA network cards.)

IBM also tried to create the successor to ISA with MCA. Like EISA, the costs outweighed the benefits. To make matters worse, if you have an MCA machine, you *must* use MCA cards (unlike EISA, which supports ISA cards). If you have an IBM P/S or any other computer that requires a reference disk, you probably have an MCA bus and therefore must use MCA cards.

If you purchased your computer in the last year or two, you might have local bus slots in addition to ISA or EISA slots. A local bus interface card can send and receive data at the full speed of your system bus (usually 25 or 33 MHz); it doesn't have the 8-MHz limit of standard ISA and EISA slots. Because of their faster throughput, local bus slots are a perfect candidate for I/O-intensive interface cards such as video and disk controllers.

There are two types of local bus machines on the market; those adhering to the VESA local bus standard (VL-Bus) and the PCI bus produced by Intel for its Pentium machines. If you have a VL-Bus machine, the benefits of a local bus network card are unclear, and it's even less likely that you'll find a supported VL bus network card. Use an ISA card instead.

Pentium machines built around the PCI local bus show much more promise when it comes to increasing network performance. First off, they support a full 64-bit data path, as opposed to the VL Bus' 32-bit path. Second, you can have any number of PCI local bus cards in your computer. Lastly, there is no uncertainly about the performance of PCI: It is definitely faster. If you have a PCI machine and find network cards that Windows 98 supports, buy them.

When choosing a manufacturer, I recommend that all my clients purchase a card from a leading vendor. For Ethernet you cannot go wrong with 3Com, Eagle, Intel, National Semiconductor, or SMC. These are the market leaders: Almost all software supports them, and they have the widest variety of drivers available. Although you might save a bit purchasing the GarageTech clone, it is not worth the possible incompatibilities to save 10–20 dollars.

Now that you have your physical network planned, in the following chapter we take a look at setting up a simple, yet complete, Windows 98 peer-to-peer network.

Chapter

26

Setting Up a
Peer-to-Peer
Windows 98 Network

FEATURING

Getting acquainted with peer-to-peer networking

Setting up the network

Network Neighborhood

Security overview and settings

Chapter 26

Setting Up a Peer-to-Peer Windows 98 Network

I n this chapter I will walk through setting up a simple peer-to-peer network of Windows 98 workstations. I will start with obtaining, configuring, and installing a network adapter card, then installing and configuring the correct network drivers, go on to discuss pros and cons of installing Windows 98 before or after installing your network card, and finally set up a small workgroup of at least two Windows 98 stations, which will be able to easily access each other's disk drives, printers, and modems.

Getting Acquainted with Peer-to-Peer Networking

Peer-to-peer refers to the fact that each station on the network treats each other station as an equal or a peer. There is no special station set aside to only provide file and print services to all the other stations. Instead, any printer, CD-ROM drive, hard drive, or even a floppy drive located on any one station can (if you wish) share access with all the other stations on the network. When you share a resource, such as a disk drive or printer, the computer that shares the resource becomes the server, and the computer that accesses the shared resource becomes the client. In a peer-to-peer network you can both share resources and access shared resources equally. In effect, your computer can be both a server and a client at the same time. Figure 26.1 illustrates a peer-to-peer network arrangement.

FIGURE 26.1

A typical peer-to-peer network topology: Notice that no particular station is designated as a standalone server.

Of course, there are security features as well, which will allow you to grant or remove access to shared resources on your computer. But first let's get the network up and running.

Networking without a Network Card

Amazingly, with Windows 98, it is *possible* to set up a peer-to-peer network of two computers with no additional hardware except a $5 cable! By installing the Direct Cable Connection (DCC) network driver supplied in Windows 98 and connecting a cable between available printer or serial ports on two PCs, you can quickly set up a simple yet full-featured, two-station network, actually sharing drives and printers just like the bigger networks.

The main drawback to this approach is that it is slow—copying a 1-MB file, for example, takes about one minute via a null-modem serial cable or about 25 seconds via a parallel cable. While this is much faster than networking via modem (an option that is also supported), it is significantly slower than most network interface cards (NICs). Generally, if you want to network two or more PCs on a regular basis, it will be worth the money to just buy network cards and cable and network the normal way. But whenever you need a convenient but temporary network connection, DCC provides you with a slick and easy built-in solution. I was *amazed* the first time I connected my laptop to desktop via parallel port and discovered I suddenly had several "neighbors" in my Network Neighborhood. Not only could I access resources such as my Desktop's CD-ROM drive and 5$\frac{1}{4}$-inch floppy drive, I also could print from my laptop directly to any network printer at the office, send faxes using another station's fax modem, and send and receive e-mail from the network mail server—all of this just using the parallel (printer) port. (The serial port could be used just as easily but is somewhat slower than using the parallel port, and it's usually easier to find an available printer port as serial ports tend to be already occupied by mice and/or modems.) In Chapter 28 I discuss DCC and its cousin—Remote Access Service (RAS)—in greater detail. For step-by-step instructions on setting up a direct-cable network connection, see that chapter.

Setting Up the Network

By way of example, let's assume in this chapter that we are setting up a new Windows 98 peer-to-peer network from scratch. For now, our goal will be to connect two or three stations together so we can share various drives and printers from each station to its peers. Let's assume that based on our reading of the previous chapter, we have decided to go with a 10Base-2 (coax) configuration. Accordingly, here is our shopping list of equipment and hardware we will need—other than Windows 98 and our soon-to-be-networked computers:

- One network interface card (NIC) for each station we want on the network
- One premade coax (RG-58) cable with BNC connectors on each end for each workstation to be connected. Cable-length requirements will be based on the distance between workstations, between 6 and 50 feet.
- One T-connector per network card

 **TIP**

Look in your local computer store for a Microsoft Windows 98 starter kit. Currently Microsoft sells just such a kit for Windows for Workgroups 3.11, and Windows 95, and I expect that when Windows 98 is made available to the public, Microsoft will continue these starter kits. The kit should include everything you need, aside from the computer, to get your network up and running: two software-configurable network cards, two T-connectors, a 25-foot roll of coax cable, two licenses for your operating system, and complete instructions. You can purchase additional add-on kits that include another network card, T-connector, coax cable, and software license to add additional single workstations as well.

Let's take a closer look at each of these items.

Buying Your Network Cards

First you'll need a network card for each station. If you're buying network cards for the first time, please note that these are also frequently referred to as network adapters or network interface cards (NICs). Your network cards will have a thin Ethernet connector (also called a BNC connector) on them, and you might want the flexibility of also having RJ-45 connectors and/or thick Ethernet connectors, if you foresee ever having to use these types of cable. You may find that the two- or three-connector cards cost almost as much individually as buying two separate single-connector network cards. But again, if you think you need the flexibility, nothing beats the convenience of being able to change cable type without (in many cases) even having to change software or card settings. Figure 26.2 shows what a typical NIC (network interface card) looks like.

FIGURE 26.2

This is a typical Network combo-card, sporting both RJ-45 and BNC thin coax connectors.

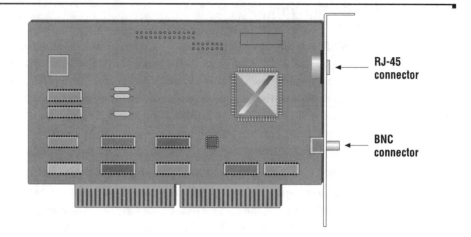

RJ-45 connector

BNC connector

At the time of this writing, typical 16-bit single-connector network cards range from $45 to $60 or more, with dual-connector (and triple-connector) cards ranging from $120 to $140, and high-speed PCI, VESA, and other 32-bit cards selling for around $130 or more. Be sure your cards either come with NDIS 3.1 (and preferably NDIS 4.1) drivers on diskette or (ideally) are supported with a Windows 98 built-in driver. Last, remember you want Plug-and-Play adapter cards (if available) or at least software-configurable cards, as these can save a lot of grief and aggravation when you start installing and configuring driver software.

Installing the Network Hardware

In this section I'll describe how to install and connect the basic hardware elements of your peer-to-peer network—the NIC and the cables.

 **TIP**

If you happen to be adding a non–Plug-and-Play network card (or any other hardware, for that matter) *after* Windows 98 is already running on your system, first use Windows 98 to print out a current System Summary Report, then shut down your system. This report can be printed by going into My Computer ➢ Control Panel ➢ System applet and clicking on the Device Manager tab. Click on the Print button, choose System Summary for report type, and click on OK. This will give you a handy listing of all current IRQs, DMA channels, port I/O addresses, and upper memory (the memory between 640K and 1024K) currently being used in your system.

Installing the Network Interface Card (NIC)

In the unlucky event you are working with a network card that still uses jumpers to configure it, we have a little work to do. First, open the card's manual to where it shows how to set the jumpers or switches to configure the card's settings. For now, don't make any changes, but do write down the current IRQ (interrupt) number, DMA channel, and memory address, as you will need these to configure the driver. Even if you have a card that doesn't have switches but lets you make changes to settings via software, you'll have to install the card. Follow these steps to do so:

1. Select your first PC "victim," make sure the power is turned off, unplug it to be really safe, and remove the PC's case. If you have questions about how to remove your computer case, refer to your owner's manual for a complete description.

WARNING

Don't forget to unplug your PC from the AC outlet before opening up the cover. This ensures you have the PC's power turned off, plus reduces the chance of electric shock. Having come this far, I don't want to lose you. Also, before you install the network card, be sure to ground yourself by touching the metal case of the computer to eliminate the possibility of static electricity zapping your network card.

2. You likely have all too much experience inserting and removing cards, but in any case, you'll have to remove the screw that holds the thin metal slot cover behind the connector you intend to use for your card. Don't drop the screw into the machine! If you do, you must get it out one way or another, such as by turning the machine over.

3. Insert the card gently but firmly until it is completely seated in the slot. You may have to wiggle the card a bit from front to back to ensure it seats firmly into the connector.

4. Next, store the metal slot cover somewhere for future use and screw the card in securely (this can be a hassle sometimes as the screw may not line up with the hole too easily).

WARNING

After installing your network card, it is imperative that you take the time to put the screw back in the bracket and tighten the card down securely. Otherwise, once you have the network cable attached to the card, a little tug on the cable could easily uproot the NIC, damaging it and your computer's motherboard (if the power is on). This is not fun. So take the extra time to put the screw back in.

5. If the PC in question is a laptop computer or a desktop that accepts PCMCIA cards, your chores are much easier. Simply plug the card into an available PCM-CIA slot. Your computer (and Windows 98) can even be running while you do this. (You might want to verify this first, however, by reading the manual or asking the salesperson, as there are a few early PCMCIA cards that should only be inserted when the unit is off.) And, of course, it won't hurt to insert the card before turning on the laptop. If the card is in next time Windows 98 starts up, the appropriate driver will be loaded immediately. But the ability to insert the card *while* Windows 98 is running is Plug and Play at its finest. If all goes well, network drivers appropriate to your card will get automatically loaded when you insert the card and unloaded when you remove it. The first time you plug the card in, however, you may be prompted to insert the master Windows 98 CD-ROM (or one of the diskettes) to load the correct network card driver.

NOTE

Some network cards may come with updated Windows 98 drivers included on a diskette. Read the documentation that came with your card (or call the manufacturer) to determine whether this is the case, and if so, insert this driver diskette into your drive when you are prompted to do so.

6. Repeat the above process with each PC you intend to network. When finished, place each PC's cover back on but do not put all the screws back into the case yet—anyone who's done this before will tell you that screwing the case back on before making sure everything works is the best way to ensure that things will *not* work. Unfortunately, even with Plug-and-Play network cards, you may still end up having to get back inside your PC to reconfigure that Sound Blaster or some other card that happens to be using a needed IRQ or DMA channel and is not itself Plug-and-Play compatible. (In my experience, sound cards are the most frequent problem.)

Installing the Cables

Connect the T-connectors to the back of each network card, then connect each workstation to the next with lengths of coax cable. The first and last stations must have a terminator attached to the free end of their T-connector. To guard against the possibility of voltage differences between workstations, some people suggest that you ground one of the terminators. That is, connect one end of a wire to a ground tap on an electrical outlet or a water pipe, and the other end to the out metal jacket of the T-connector. Ground only one terminator to prevent ground loops.

With a network card installed in each of your stations and each card connected via cable to the next, you are now ready to install and configure your Windows 98 software for networking. If all goes well, the hard part of your job is already complete.

Configuring Windows 98 for Networking

If you have not yet installed Windows 98 on your stations, you'll need to do so before continuing (see the Appendix for installation instructions). If all goes well, Setup will automatically detect your newly installed network card and, if you're lucky, will even determine the type of card and configure it for you. Windows 98's setup program is quite sophisticated in this regard, and it's likely that if you have a relatively new computer (only 2 years old or so), and a Plug and Play network card, Windows 98 will install most of what you need automatically. If it doesn't, you can just wait until Windows 98 is finished installing and then add the network drivers, as explained below.

Network operability is installed in Windows 98 by default, with Microsoft and Novell network support automatically included. If your network card was already installed when you ran Setup, it should have been detected and the necessary drivers installed. However, if you already have Windows 98 running but haven't installed your network card yet, shut down Windows (perhaps print out a system-configuration report first), then turn off the computer and install the network card. (See *Installing the Network Interface Card*, above, for details on installing your card.) You'll want to note the IRQ, I/O, and memory address of your card in case you need to manually enter these settings later. Most likely, however (especially if your card is new), after turning your computer back on, Windows 98 will come up and detect that you've added a network card, detect what kind it is, and configure it for you. If this is the case, you can skip down to *Network Neighborhood* now.

You can wing it and just skip to the Network Neighborhood section below, but it's a good idea to check the installed Network components first. You can access the network-configuration options in Windows 98 via the Control Panel by choosing My Computer ➢ Control Panel ➢ Network, as shown in Figure 26.3.

Installing Network Drivers after You've Installed Windows 98 Assuming you have opened the Network applet under the Control Panel, you should see the Network Properties dialog box (see Figure 26.4).

PART

V

Networking with
Windows 98

FIGURE 26.3

Accessing network options once Windows 98 is installed

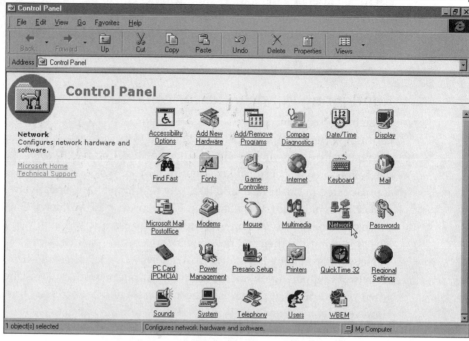

FIGURE 26.4

The Network Properties dialog box

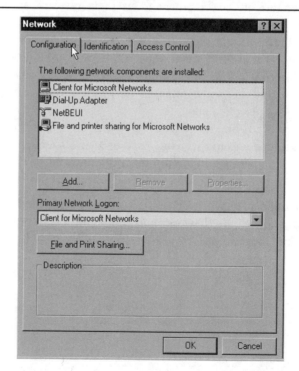

If Windows 98 Doesn't Detect Your Network Adapter Type

If Windows 98 did not detect your adapter correctly (or at all), do the following, making sure you have the diskette containing your network card's drivers:

1. Choose Control Panel ➤ Network and click on the Configuration tab.

2. Notice the adapters installed. If you see an incorrect network card installed, remove it by selecting it and then clicking on the Remove button.

3. Press the Add button to add your new adapter.

4. In the resulting Select Network Adapters dialog box, click on Have Disk.

5. When prompted, insert the driver disk and press Enter. Sometimes the diskette that shipped with your network card will contain drivers for a variety of different operating systems, each in a different subdirectory. When adding a new network card, if Windows 98 cannot find the correct drivers in the root directory of the diskette, you may have to help it along a little. Click on the Browse button and double-click on the correct subdirectory before letting Windows 98 continue.

6. For many non–Plug-and-Play cards, you will next be shown the desired settings for your network card. Make sure you write these down, because as soon as the drivers are installed, you will need to shut down Windows 98, remove your card, make sure all the jumpers are set to configure the card for the required settings, and then reinsert it. If your card is software configurable, just run the card's configuration program and verify that the settings are what Windows 98 wants them to be.

7. Windows 98 will probably let you know it needs to restart (reboot) to load your network drivers. Choose Yes to restart.

When Windows comes back up, the newly installed drivers will hopefully detect your network card and be able to communicate with it. If you do not see any error messages, you can proceed with the Network configuration procedure already in progress. (If you do have problems—an error message comes up, for example—first see if the message points to anything obvious you can fix; otherwise, flip to Chapter 29.)

PART

V

Networking with
Windows 98

1. Under the option *The following network components are installed* on the Configuration tab, make sure you have the following:

   • Client for Microsoft Networks

   • a driver specific to your network card

   • NetBEUI

   • File and Printer Sharing for Microsoft Networks

Because Windows 98 includes support for Novell networks right out of the box, the Client for Novell Networks and IPX/SPX (its default protocol) will show up in your list of installed *network components*. Remove the Client for Novell Networks and the IPX/SPX for now—unless you plan to connect to a Novell Network—and make sure NetBEUI is selected as the only protocol installed (unless you have a modem installed and intend to connect to the Internet, in which case having "TCP/IP → Dial-Up Adapter" is OK).

If you need to add anything to this list, just click on the Add button, select Client, Adapter, Protocol, or Service, then select the manufacturer and type. What you're aiming for is to have several things:

- Your specific network card to appear in the list, indicating its driver is installed. Example:
  - Nat Semi 4100 Infomover
- The NetBEUI protocol to appear in the list, linked to the network card. Example:
  - NetBEUI -> Nat Semi 4100 Infomover

Continuing with the network-configuration procedure, next do the following:

2. Again, on the main Network Configuration property sheet (shown in Figure 26.5), make sure for now that the Primary Network Logon says Client for Microsoft Networks.

3. Click on the File and Print Sharing button and make sure both options are checked; when finished, the dialog box should look like the one on the next page.

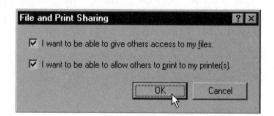

4. Now click on the Network Identification tab (see Figure 26.5). For the computer name, enter something descriptive of the computer—the important thing is that this name be different from others on the network. Select a descriptive name for your workgroup: This name needs to be the same for each station. Finally, add a computer description, if you like.

FIGURE 26.5

The Network Identification Properties sheet lets you specify how your computer will be known to other users and which workgroup you are a member of.

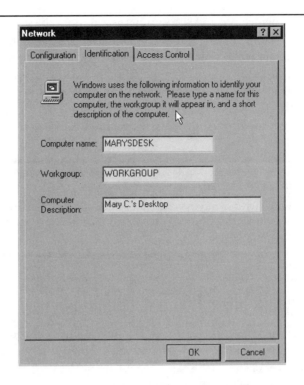

TIP

When configuring large numbers of Windows 98 machines, you may want to give more attention to the machine name you assign to each workstation. While the machine name itself is easy to change later, doing so can confuse all the other workstations that used to know the workstation under a different name. Also, all resource sharing is based on the computer name. Therefore, if your office has a high turnover rate, you do not want to be naming machine names after employees using each machine; rather, give each machine a name descriptive of its function within the workgroup it belongs to.

5. Now click on the Access Control tab. Again, at least for now, select the share-level access control. We'll look at user-level access control at the end of this chapter, under *Security Features*.

When you're finished setting these options, be sure to click on the OK button at the bottom of the Network Property dialog box. After the dialog box closes, you may be prompted to shut down and restart Windows 98. If so, go ahead and do it.

Repeat this network-configuration procedure on any other stations that need it.

If all goes well, either you or Windows 98 has successfully installed the appropriate network drivers on each of your peer-to-peer stations, and you are now ready to begin testing and configuring your network.

TIP

If all has *not* gone well, the most likely problem will be incorrect network-card settings. Try running the Network troubleshooter via Start ➢ Help ➢ Troubleshooting ➢ Networking. This will run a Wizard that will walk you though various questions and suggest possible fixes.

Moving into the Network Neighborhood

Start up Windows 98 on each of your stations, and you should now see the Network Neighborhood icon on each station's Desktop. Click on the icon, and you should see a number of computer-shaped icons with names matching those unique machine names you assigned to each station.

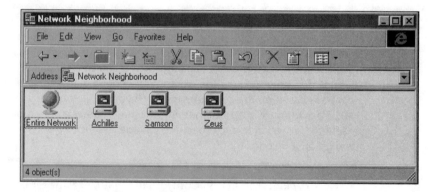

Each station on your network should appear in this Neighborhood folder. If any are missing, or worse, if you do not *have* a Network Neighborhood on your Desktop, you'll have to do some troubleshooting. The most common problem, aside from missing protocol(s) and incorrectly configured network cards, will be that one or more of your stations are not set to the same workgroup as all the others. As mentioned in the note above, Windows has a network troubleshooter built in. Check it out.

Sharing Resources on the Network

To make the resources from one station accessible to other stations on the network, you need to *share* the drive or printer. First we will look at sharing drives, then sharing printers, and, finally, we will look at how to use security features to restrict access to your shared resources.

NOTE

File and Print Sharing must be enabled before you can share files or printers to your network, as described earlier in this chapter.

Sharing Drives and Subdirectories

Using the Explorer and manipulating folders both provide an easy way to share information with other people on your network. In the following example, I'll share a station's hard drive. (If you are not currently on a station that has a hard drive, you may wish to switch to one on your network that does so you can try the example.)

Sharing from a Folder   The easiest way to share a folder object is to point to an object in the folder you wish to share and right-click on it. As shown below, this will bring up the right-click menu for that object, and you will see a menu option labeled Sharing.

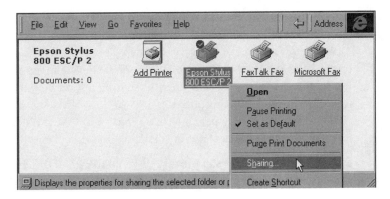

Select this, and you will go to the Properties dialog box (see Figure 26.6). Then just follow these steps.

The Sharing dialog box lets you specify how a shared drive (or folder) will be known to others on the network. It also allows you to specify a password and even which users and groups of users will be allowed to access the shared resource.

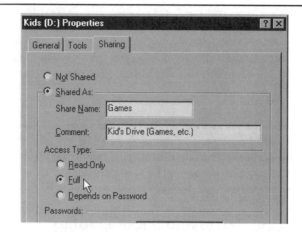

1. Click on the Sharing tab.

2. Type in a share name or just keep the default share name. If you like, you may add a comment describing the contents of this share.

3. Next you need to set the access type. Note the default is read-only, which only allows other users to open and view the contents but not to change them. The Full option lets anyone on the network both read and make changes to this folder. Keep in mind, by the way, that sharing a drive or folder shares all the subfolders below it as well.

4. If you want to restrict access to the share, assign a password. For now, let's leave access set to Full. We'll cover security shortly.

Another way you can bring up the share options is via the File menu. If you click on the drive or folder to be shared, then select the File menu option, you will see Sharing on this menu as well. Selecting this sharing option produces the same results as right-clicking and selecting Sharing.

Note the change in appearance of your drive or folder. When it is shared, the same icon appears, but as if held out in someone's hand.

Sharing from Windows Explorer   If you understand the above-mentioned ways to share from a folder, then you also know how to share using Windows Explorer. Both sides of the Explorer window support right-clicking to bring up property sheets (and from there you can select Sharing), and the File menu will also have the Sharing option, provided you've selected an object on the right side of the Explorer window (see Figure 26.7).

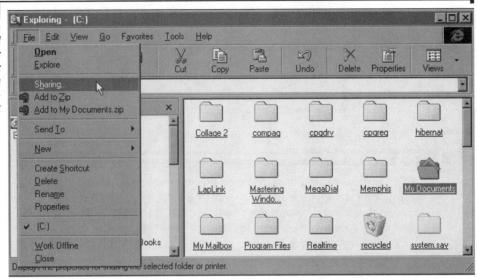

Before you go to another station to see if you can access the shared drive, bring up an MS-DOS prompt and type **NET VIEW *ComputerName*** where you replace *ComputerName* with the name of your computer. This will display a list of all the resources you have shared on your computer. If you can see the new shared resources, then go to another workstation and open Network Neighborhood, then open the computer that has the shared drive. If you now see the shared resource, congratulations. You can now go to each station and add shares to any local drive you want accessible from the network.

Don't forget you can also share floppy drives and CD-ROM drives in exactly the same way. Perhaps only one station has a 5¼-inch floppy or a CD-ROM drive. Share it via the network, and anyone now has access to both sizes of floppy drive and the CD-ROM drive. Of course, network etiquette will likely preclude frequent use of someone else's floppy or CD-ROM drive, but for occasional use—installing software, for example—having the ability to share even removable media drives can be wonderfully helpful. In the following illustration, I am about to share a CD-ROM drive.

PART

V

Networking with
Windows 98

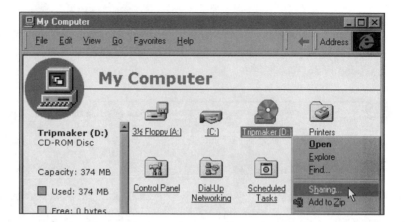

 NOTE

If you are going to share a read-only resource such as a CD-ROM drive, be sure to set the network access to read-only (the default). This will prevent a remote user from attempting to write to the CD-ROM drive. If you do not do this, your remote software may hang while attempting to write to read-only media, so it's best to make sure that read-only access is enabled.

Sharing Printers

Sharing printers is just about as easy—and is certainly as much fun—as sharing drives and subdirectories. Before a printer can be shared, of course, its driver must be installed on the station to which the printer is physically attached. Additionally, other stations needing to use this printer across the network must have the same printer driver installed on their stations. Therefore, let's next look at how to install the printer driver.

Installing the Printer Driver for a Shared Printer   Go to a station that has a local printer attached. If you haven't yet installed the driver for this printer, you will need to do this first. To install it, just open My Computer ➢ Printers ➢ Add Printer, and select the appropriate printer brand and model. If you are asked whether this is a network or local printer, select local. Depending on which printer you have, you might be asked for a Windows 98 driver diskette.

Once the printer driver is installed, the printer should show up in the Printers folder (located in My Computer). Using the right-click method, share the printer. Note that printers can also be shared from Explorer, just as drives and folders can.

Now, to share the printer, do exactly what you did to share a drive—namely, after right-clicking on the printer's icon, select the Sharing menu option. You have a set of sharing options quite similar to those for drive sharing. Type the name you want your printer known as on the network, provide a descriptive comment, if you like, and note the option to provide a password. If you do enter a password, your printer will only be available to users on the network who know the password. For now let's leave the password off, as this will make testing easier.

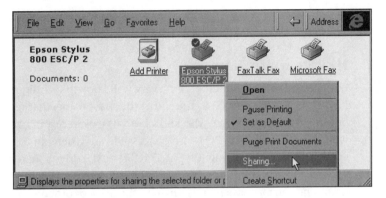

After you've shared the printer, go to another station—preferably one that has no local printer attached—and open Network Neighborhood. Double-click on the computer icon that has the shared printer, and you should now see the printer, plus any shared drive(s) for that station. If so, congratulations are once more in order. You can now go to any other stations that have a local printer and share those as well. Here's an example of what a shared printer will look like:

Having shared those printers you want accessible on the network, your users will now be able to print to any of them simply by choosing the Print option from any Windows application that supports printing. Of course, with more than one printer on the network, the desired printer can also be selected from any Windows application, usually by selecting File ➤ Print Setup from the application's menu. Additionally, note that any printer (local or network) can be set on each station as that station's default printer.

Now that your network printers are printing correctly (at least I hope they are!), I'll discuss using security features to control access to your shared drives and printers. For more about printers and printing with Windows 98, refer to Chapter 8.

Security Features

Although we've disabled all of them for clarity's sake, Windows 98 does have several means of restricting access to a station's shared resources.

Hiding Share Names

Let's start with the easiest (but not a very well known) technique. In any Share As name, if you add a dollar sign ($) to the end of the share name, that resource becomes invisible but still accessible to those who know both its existence and name. For example, if you want to make your CD-ROM drive accessible anywhere on the network but not have everyone using it, you might type CDROM$ as the drive's share name. Then, whenever you need to access this drive from another station, you would need to specify the share name and the machine name to map to the drive or otherwise access it. The access path would look similar to this: \\CD_STATION\CDROM$.

Obviously this technique is only as secure as the knowledge of the resource's share name (and location).

Share-Level and User-Level Access Control

A second means of restricting access is to use passwords with share-level control. This means you supply one password for each shared resource, and that password remains the same for all users who access the resource. (You set up the password in the Sharing dialog box for the resource simply by entering a password. When a remote user tries to access the resource, they'll be prompted for the password.) Again, there are limitations to this.

Although the simple effectiveness of the above two methods might be all that is needed on smaller networks, eventually you will need to consider *user-level* access control. This more-sophisticated security relies on Windows 98 verification of users by their log-on password. In other words, you specify exactly which users and groups of users are to have access to a given network resource, and then those users, once they have logged in, automatically gain access to that network resource. For Windows 98 to make use of user-level access, it must use a Windows NT Server user database.

Read-Level and Read-Write-Level Access Control

Both the user- and share-level control methods also allow read-only access as distinct from read-write access. Read-only access makes perfect sense for memoranda, static databases (perhaps a zip code database?), and backups.

Obviously, any such security is only as good as the confidentiality of the passwords. If security is of more than passing interest to you, you should encourage proper choice of user passwords. There are several good computer security books that discuss guidelines for selecting difficult-to-guess passwords. Additionally, keep in mind that you may want to combine share-name hiding with share-level or user-level passwords. In this way, even if someone logs on with a stolen ID and password, he or she may not know a particular resource exists. I wouldn't count on this, but on the other hand, I wouldn't discredit or overlook even small additional layers of security where they are called for.

Please bear in mind that Windows 98 was not designed to be a really secure operating system. If you do need something more secure, strongly consider using Windows NT—it is one of only a few operating systems that has security incorporated in it at every level, earning it a C2-level security rating. We will look at these and other features of Windows NT in Chapter 27.

PART

V

Networking with
Windows 98

Chapter

27

Internetworking
Windows 98
Workstations with NT

FEATURING

Workgroups

Domains

Adding Windows 98 workstations to the network

Printing

Mapping shared drives and folders

Internetworking Windows 98 Workstations with NT

As you connect more stations to your Windows 98 peer network, you will sooner or later want to interconnect with one or more Windows NT workstations or servers. My goal in this chapter is to show you how to network Windows 98 stations with one or more Windows NT stations functioning as a server for files, printers, and applications. Adding one or more Windows NT servers to your network provides you with an array of powerful options and tools that can help maximize the usefulness and productivity of your Windows 98 workstations—especially in the areas of security, performance, and network administration.

Some Networking Philosophy

In the preceding chapter you saw how each networked peer showed up in the Network Neighborhood as a computer icon. Each station's shared printers and folders were available to anyone who double-clicked on a particular computer or created a map to one of the shared drives or printers. This is great as far as it goes, but consider how it would be if you had two hundred, a thousand, even several thousand stations on the network all appearing in Network Neighborhood. Clearly, the neighborhood concept would become very confusing to use, and a *nightmare* for the network administrator. What is needed, then, is a way to organize these stations into groups, and perhaps groups of groups, so that visualizing and working with the stations becomes both more manageable and efficient: thus the concept of *workgroups*.

Workgroups

First introduced in Windows 3.11 (Windows for Workgroups), the subdividing of Windows workstations into workgroups helps free the members of each workgroup to maintain, support, and use only those resources needed by their workgroup. All other network resources may still be *physically* connected, but the workgroup sees and makes use of only those resources directly relevant to its area. From the user's vantage point, 95 percent of the clutter is removed from Network Neighborhood, and the neighborhood becomes a familiar metaphor once more. And where security is needed, passwords can be assigned within the workgroup on a per-resource or per-user basis (a single password can even be used by a group of users).

Small networks—say those with a total of fifty or fewer workstations—might find that the workgroup approach is a sufficient and easy enough means of subdividing and organizing the network resources and users, assuming they're subdivided into multiple workgroups. But with very large networks, workgroups are not adequate, because there's no way to oversee all the different workgroups. Managing the centralized networking resources on larger networks requires being able to access and configure user accounts and other network resources in a way that transcends the boundaries of individual workgroups.

Domains

For ease of organizing and managing large networks—say those with a total of fifty or more workstations—Microsoft came up with the idea of *domains*. Domains are similar to workgroups but provide the ability to group all users in a single user *database*. This database resides on the Windows NT Server *domain controller* (and, optionally, on *backup domain controllers*). When you log on to a domain from the Windows 98 log-on dialog box, you are authenticated as a specific user with specific access rights. These access rights are the basis for your ability to use shared resources on the network, such as a directory or printer.

NOTE

Throughout this chapter, I am speaking of NT version 3.5 or later. If you are still running NT or NT Advanced Server version 3.1, you will notice a marked performance increase and feature set by upgrading to version 4.0 or later. Although NT 5 was not yet available at the time of this writing, it will solve many of the ills of version 4.0, so I strongly recommend it for large enterprise settings. NT 5 will feature *Active Directory*, which replaces the SAM (Security Accounts Manager); Active Directory will make NT deployment within a large corporate setting a safe and reliable option for workstations and servers alike.

For more specific information on NT Server, take a look at my book on NT called *Windows NT Server 4.0: No Experience Required* (Sybex, 1997).

NT Workstation vs. NT Server

Although in this chapter I will be concentrating primarily on Windows NT in its capacity as a server, NT can also be used as a workstation and as a peer of Windows 95 and Windows 98 stations. In fact, Microsoft emphasizes these dual uses by currently selling two different "flavors" of NT, appropriately labeled NT Workstation and NT Server. While both can be used as servers and both can be used as workstations, each has certain optimizations that better suit it to one of the two uses.

Why, you may wonder, would you want to use NT on a workstation? To begin with, there are various reasons to choose Windows NT over Windows 98. For example, you will need Windows NT rather than Windows 98 if you require any of the following from your workstation:

- You plan to run NT services software or certain high-end graphics software.

- Or you need beefed-up security or support for non-FAT file systems.

- Or you have a non-Intel-compatible workstation.

Software developers, CAD users, and scientists doing math-intensive work might need or prefer Windows NT over Windows 98 for a combination of these features. Some programmers, for example, will have both Windows 98 and Windows NT installed on their stations, and can boot to one operating system or the other as needed to develop and test their software.

Let's look at the differences between NT Workstation and NT Server. First of all, while NT Workstation can function as a server, it has the following limitations when compared to NT Server:

- It cannot function as a domain controller.

- It has a maximum of ten simultaneous client connections.

- It does not provide gateway services to Novell Netware.
- It does not provide network services for Apple workstations.
- It has a limit of two CPUs (for "symmetric multiprocessing").

Let me clarify these briefly.

It cannot function as a domain controller. First, and perhaps most notably, although NT Workstation cannot be used as a domain controller, NT Workstation *can* log on to a domain and can function as an additional server within an existing domain. (As mentioned above, a domain controller is where the user database resides.)

NOTE

Despite its domain controller limitation, I do want to emphasize that NT Workstation can perform very ably as a server for a *workgroup* of Windows 98 stations. Thus, where cost is an issue and the ten-client limit is not a problem, NT Workstation might well be the best choice.

It has a maximum of ten simultaneous client connections. The ten-connection limit does not prevent NT Workstation from having more than ten user accounts or from recognizing more than ten other stations on a network. It simply means that no more than ten other workstations or servers can be *simultaneously* connected to its disk and printer resources.

It does not provide gateway services to Novell Netware. If you do have one or more Novell Netware servers, consider installing NT Server. NT Workstation (and of course Windows 95/98 stations themselves) can easily connect to and use Novell resources—and Windows 95/98 can even share files and printers back to Novell stations. But for the ultimate in all sorts of connectivity options between Windows and Novell network resources, you definitely want NT Server.

It does not provide network services for Apple workstations. If you have Apple workstations connecting to your network, you will need NT Server.

It has a limit of two CPUs (for "symmetric multiprocessing"). If you have a server computer with more than two CPUs, you will need NT Server.

NOTE

The above differences between NT Server and Workstation are by no means the only differences, but they are the main points to keep in mind if you're considering buying NT. For the rest of this chapter, I'll be discussing NT Server unless otherwise mentioned. Also, due to the similarities between Windows 95 and Windows 98, all references to Windows 98 in this chapter also apply to Windows 95 unless otherwise mentioned.

NT Server, as opposed to NT Workstation, provides for centralized administration, because all the user accounts and groups reside on the domain controller rather than on each individual NT workstation. However, one interesting point about Windows NT Server is that it can operate as a super workgroup server instead of as a domain controller. When NT Server is configured to run in server mode, instead of as a domain or backup controller, it does not perform any user authentication. In this mode it essentially works just like NT Workstation, but with unlimited user connections, and it still includes the rest of the NT Server functionality, like the Novell Gateway Service and Macintosh Services.

Adding Windows 98 Workstations to the Network

To allow your Windows 98 stations to communicate with an NT server, you must make sure they are using one of the protocols used by the NT server. In most cases, this will probably be either NetBEUI or IPX/SPX—or if you have a really big network, you may be using TCP/IP. Remember, on a small Windows-only network (where no connections to Novell or other systems are needed) NetBEUI will be your fastest protocol. Again, you just need to make sure the Windows 98 stations are talking the same language as your server.

Adding Workstations to an NT Server

Once the protocols have been configured, you need to take the following steps so your Windows 98 stations can share network resources with an NT server.

1. Use the right-click ➤ Share Properties dialog box on your Windows 98 stations to share any printers, drives, and/or folders that you want the NT station (and the other Windows 98 stations) to be able to access. Add any security restrictions (either share-level or user-level) desired.

NOTE

To employ user-level or group-level access rights, you must be part of a Windows NT domain or you must be using pass-through authentication with a Novell NetWare server.

2. Use NT's File Manager or Windows Explorer to share any drives or folders you want your Windows 98 stations to access.

3. Use NT's My Computer ➤ Printers folder to share any printer(s) you want your Windows 98 stations to access. Note that NT can share not only locally attached printers, but also any printers it has access to as long as they are located on another NT station (either Workstation or Server).

4. If the NT server is a domain server, you will also need to create a user account on the NT server for each Windows 98 user that will be needing access to resources on the NT server. Use NT's User Manager for Domains to create these accounts, and then set any desired file restrictions using NT's File Manager or Windows Explorer, and any desired printer or printing restrictions using NT's Print Manager.

5. Choose as appropriate:

- If you are using NT Server, set each Windows 98 station to log on to the NT domain and enter the correct domain in the domain field at each station. To do this, open Control Panel ➢ Networks and double-click on Client for Microsoft Windows Networks. Click on the Domain checkbox and type in the name of your NT domain (see Figure 27.1).

FIGURE 27.1

Configuring a Windows 98 station to log on to an NT Server domain

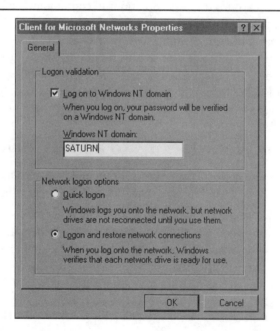

- If you are using NT Workstation, simply make sure you have the same workgroup name specified on the NT workstation as you do for each Windows 98 station that will be part of this workgroup.

After performing these steps, you should be able to open Network Neighborhood on any Windows 98 stations in the workgroup (or domain) and see an icon for the NT server. Also, when using the server browsers in either NT's Print Manager or File Manager, you should now see your Windows 98 stations appear as additional servers in the workgroup (or domain).

NOTE

If your office has one or more Novell Netware print servers and you are running NT Server, you can use the NT Printers folder to share Netware print servers. You must first install and configure the Netware Gateway Services software (supplied with NT Server) and then connect to the Netware print queue before trying to share it. In this way, Windows 98/95 stations (and even DOS, Windows 3.1, and Windows for Workgroups stations) will not need Novell-specific network drivers loaded to print on the Novell print queue. You will, however, need to use a printer driver for each printer you use.

Using Shared Printers

One of the major benefits of using Windows NT or Windows 98 is that they both provide the ability to connect to a network printer without installing a printer driver. You will of course need to install a printer driver on the computer that has the local printer attached to it, but your NT and Windows 98 clients do not need to have that printer driver installed locally. Instead, they will access the remote printer and use the printer driver installed on the remote computer. The only time you will need to install a printer driver is when you connect to a different type of print server, such as a Windows for Workgroups, Novell Netware Server, or Unix server. If you are unfamiliar with how to install a printer or connect to a networked printer, take a look at Chapter 8.

Mapping Windows 98 and Windows NT Shared Drives

At this point you might also wish to establish *persistent* drive mappings for the drives that are offered for share on either the NT server or your Windows 98 stations, or both. This will allow you to always have the same drive letters assigned to shared drives (or folders).

Windows 98

For Windows 98 stations, the fastest and easiest way, in my opinion, to map to any shared drive is to right-click on Network Neighborhood's icon and select the Map Network Drive option. In this dialog box, first you open the drop-down Drive list and select the drive letter you want the remote drive to map to (i.e., how does the drive appear in your Explorer window). Then, in the lower box, you have to enter the actual pathname of that drive as it appears on the network; thus, you must enter it in network drive syntax, which includes the computer name, in the format shown here:

    \\machine_name\drive_letter (or share_name)

For example, you might type **achilles****C** (no colon) if you are mapping a drive that is shared from a machine known as "achilles" on the network and its C: drive is shared by the name "C".

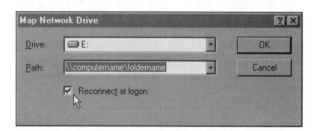

If you don't know the exact network pathname of the resource you are trying to map (for instance, you want to map a shared folder rather than an entire drive), don't fret. Network Neighborhood makes it easy to browse to and map a shared folder or drive. Try this approach:

1. Open Network Neighborhood, either in Windows Explorer or from the Desktop. The workstations available to you should now be listed.

2. Open the computer whose drive or folder you want to map for your use.

3. Now you'll see the list of folders and drives that the workstation has made public (i.e., has offered for sharing). Right-click on the one you want to map, and choose Map Network Drive.

4. You'll see a box like the one shown below (in this example, I've mapped the drive from Windows Explorer):

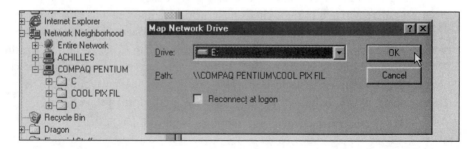

5. The drive letter that is already entered for you is by default the "next available" letter; you can change it to another letter using the drop-down list.

6. Enable the Reconnect at Logon checkbox if you want this mapping to be made automatically each time you boot up your machine. (This works only when the remote computer is already running.)

NOTE

If and when you ever need to disconnect from the remote drive, you can do it quite easily. Right-clicking on Network Neighborhood is, again, one way to do this, but for disconnecting mapped drives, I find the most straightforward way is to open Network Neighborhood and right-click on the shared drive's icon. Choose the Disconnect option, and you're done.

Windows NT 4.*x*

As of NT 4.0 (which has the Windows 95/98 interface), mapping drive letters to network (shared) drives is accomplished using the same techniques as presented above for Windows 98.

Windows NT 3.5

With NT 3.5, you map drives by using NT's File Manager, like this:

1. Open File Manager.

2. Select Drives ➤ Connect.

4. Select the drive letter you want to map to, then use the server browser (the list box in the lower half of the dialog box) to select which server and which shared drive to connect to. Or just type in the *machine_name**drive_name* path in the Path field (as described in the Windows 98 steps earlier in this section)—for example, type **achilles**\C (no colon) to map the drive shared as C on the machine known to the network as achilles.

5. Press the OK button.

6. At this point you may also need to enter a password if the directory being shared includes share-level password protection.

Using Your NT/98 Network

Assuming your NT station is going to function primarily as a server, you will probably place some or all of your workgroup's most frequently accessed data on the NT server, both to free up your workstations' loads somewhat and also to get the best performance because you now have a dedicated server. Just keep in mind that NT Workstation can only provide ten simultaneous connections, so its use as a dedicated server will only work well for modest networks.

Chapter

28

Extending Your Reach with Dial-Up Networking

Remote access

Windows 98 and Dial-Up Networking

Dial-Up Networking and system security

DCC (Direct Cable Connection) using a serial or parallel port

Chapter 28

Extending Your Reach with Dial-Up Networking

I n the past few years, the number of mobile computer users has increased dramatically, as advances in computer technology and changes in the business climate have made it easier to use a computer on the road. Improved manufacturing techniques have allowed miniaturization only dreamed of ten years ago—clearly, there would be far fewer mobile users if everyone still had to carry around a seventeen-pound Compaq luggable. And improved communication interfaces have allowed users to access other computers without having to memorize obscure Unix or AT modem commands.

On the business side, the near-universal reliance on computers, coupled with the downsizing and re-engineering trends that have forced users out of the office and into their home offices or onto the road to visit client sites, has created a demand for remote access at about the same time that advances in computer technology have provided the means.

Mobile users are everywhere. Because computer-toting travelers are ubiquitous these days, few self-respecting motels and hotels now fail to provide RJ-11 data jacks on their phones. I no longer ask if a hotel is modem-friendly; I simply assume that one of the reasons they are still in business is that they provide data jacks. While I still carry a telephone patch cable with alligator clips on one end, it has been more than a year since I stayed in a hotel so far in the Dark Ages that I actually had to splice their phone cord to be able to use it with my modem.

In this chapter, I will first cover the options Windows 98 provides for remote connections and help you choose the best one for your particular circumstance. Next, I'll examine the hardware requirements for effective remote commuting over phone lines and take an in-depth look at *Dial-Up Networking*, as Windows 98's remote-node client is called. Then, I'll cover specific issues you need to address when using remote access, such as security. Finally, I'll talk about the Direct-Cable-Connection utility program that lets you skip the modems altogether and connect two computers together as if networked, but without a LAN card and cabling.

Remote Access—What Is It?

Since remote use of computers has become so prevalent, Microsoft has seen to it that remote access is seamlessly integrated into the Windows 98 operating system, giving you simple access to essential system resources. Think of it this way: When you are in the office, using your computer that's attached to the local area network (LAN), Windows 98 takes care of the details when you want to print to a network printer or use some data stored on a hard disk somewhere across the network. The details of this process are handled smoothly by the Windows 98 networking architecture, system calls, and the user interface.

When you are using a Windows 98 computer away from the office, the operating system attempts to find other solutions when you ask for access to one of your office network's resources such as a printer. This is possible because Windows 98 supports multiple network protocols and adapters as discussed earlier in this part of the book. If you've set up your computer correctly, Windows 98 will attempt to reach the office LAN using Dial-Up Networking (DUN), essentially replacing the LAN cable and network interface card (NIC) with telephone wires and modems.

As in the case of normal Windows 98 LAN connections, Dial-Up Networking supports a broad base of network protocols. Using DUN, you can remotely connect to systems running TCP/IP (such as the Internet), NetWare-based servers, and NetBEUI-based servers.

One of the most popular uses for Windows 98's DUN is to connect to the Internet. As explained in Chapter 15, virtually anyone who uses a portable Windows 98 machine (or a desktop computer with a LAN connection to the Internet) to connect to the Internet for e-mail or Web access will use DUN to do it. See that chapter if all you want to do is get connected to the Internet.

Connections to Novell NetConnect servers via the NRN protocol or NT Servers using the RAS protocol are automatic. Industry-standard PPP (point-to-point protocol) and the newly added PPTP (point-to-point-tunneling protocol) are supported as well. Other protocols are easily added. All a software vendor has to do is write its code to support the Windows 98 Remote Accesses API. Microsoft, for example, supplies a SLIP protocol as part of the Windows 98 Resource Kit.

Remote Control vs. Remote Node

If you need to allow off-site users to connect to your network, you essentially have two choices: remote *control* or remote *node*.

- **Remote-control** programs use standard telephone lines and provide on-demand connections. Remote control works just as you would expect from the name. You sit down at the remote computer, it dials into a host computer, and then you can actually control the computer you dial into from the computer you have dialed in from. The leading remote-control products include Norton PCAnywhere, Carbon Copy, and Co-Session. When you type or move the mouse on the remote computer, the software sends the keystrokes and mouse movements to the host computer for processing. In turn, the software transmits any screen updates such as dialog boxes or drop-down menus from the host back to the remote computer for display. If the user wants to run an application, he or she launches the application on the host computer.

- **Remote node** works on an on-demand basis just like remote control, but rather than taking over the host computer, the remote computer uses the host computer as a *server*. This places the remote node directly on the network. In other words, the phone line becomes an extension of the network cable. This allows the user to request file and print services just as if he or she sat right next to the file server. When a user starts an application, it runs on his or her local computer, not on the host computer as it would when using remote-control systems.

Remote control and remote node both provide network connectivity, but they use two entirely different approaches to providing remote access. The primary difference between these two types of remote-access software is that remote-control software actually takes over complete control of the host system, while remote-node software just uses the modem to provide a network interface to the host system.

Windows 98's Style of Dial-Up Networking

As explained earlier, a mobile user can use Dial-Up Networking to seamlessly connect remote resources. While early versions of Windows included a version of Dial-Up Networking called *Remote Access Services* (*RAS*), it was clearly an add-on feature. To use it, you had to start it separately before accessing shared resources on a remote computer.

Installing Dial-Up Networking in Windows 98 places the remote-node software directly into the core operating system, so you can access remote resources just as you can local ones. Whenever you try to open a remote file (whether through the File ➤ Open dialog box or by double-clicking on the file), Windows 98 automatically starts Dial-Up Networking and establishes the remote connection with the host computer.

> If DUN is not installed, go to the Add/Remove Programs feature in the Control Panel, and choose Windows Setup ➤ Communications ➤ Dial Up Networking.

DUN and TAPI

Dial-Up Networking uses the Telephone Application Programming Interface (TAPI), Microsoft's proposed standard for integrating telephones and computers. Because TAPI allows multiple applications to share a single line, one application can wait for a call while another dials out.

What is the point?, you may ask. After all, when one application dials out, the line is busy, so waiting applications can't receive a call anyway. Well, suppose, for example, you have Microsoft Fax waiting to receive incoming faxes and you want to use Dial-Up Networking to download a file from a computer in a satellite office. In earlier versions of Windows, you would have had to shut down the fax software before you could use the modem for any other purpose. Because Dial-Up Networking uses TAPI, you can leave Fax running in the background as you connect to a remote computer. As soon as you finish with Dial-Up Networking, Fax will pick up any incoming faxes.

Dial Helper

Another benefit of TAPI is its support of *Dial Helper*, shown below, which allows you to define phone numbers in location-independent fashion.

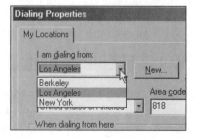

With Dial Helper, you can associate a single number with any resource. If you change locations, you simply change the Dial Helper location rather than having to reenter the number. When you want to call that number from the office, Windows 98 will, by default, prefix it with a 9 so your PBX can distinguish it from an internal call and thus give it an external line. When you're calling from home, Windows 98 will prepend (also by default) a *70 to turn off call waiting. Finally, when you're on the road, you can have it enter your calling-card information for you.

Along with its support of TAPI, Windows 98 further simplifies Dial-Up Networking by supporting the *Unimodem* infrastructure. You can think of Unimodem as the modem equivalent of the Windows printer subsystem. As you may recall, rather than require each application to manage its own printing, Windows 9*x* allows an application to send a print job to the printer subsystem, which then passes the job to a printer driver specifically designed for the printer in use. Unimodem does the same thing: it provides a single interface for any application requiring communication services. When an application wants to access a modem, it sends a packet, or "*communication job,*" to Unimodem, which then passes the packet off to the modem-specific driver.

Connecting

Any time you want to connect to a remote computer, you must keep three questions in mind. First, what type of server or host do you want to connect to? Second, how will you connect with it? And third, what communication protocol will you use? Luckily, Windows 98 supports the majority of the options available. Better yet, Dial-Up Networking will negotiate with the host and automatically configure itself using the best set of options that both it and the host support.

What Type of Server or Host?

Windows 98 supports the following remote-node servers:

- Windows 95/or 98 Dial-Up Server (one incoming connection only)
- Windows NT 3.*x* and 4.*x* RAS (up to 256 incoming connections possible)
- Novell NetWare Connect
- Microsoft LAN Manager Remote Access Servers
- Windows for Workgroups 3.*x* RAS (if you have the separate WFW RAS server installed)
- Shiva NetModem or LanRover (and compatibles) dial-up router
- Third-party PPP and SLIP servers, including Internet access providers

How Will You Connect?

If you are like the vast majority of Windows 98 users, you will use standard modems to establish asynchronous connections over Plain Old Telephone Service (POTS)—residential and business phone lines. To accommodate users with additional requirements, Dial-Up Networking also supports:

- PBX modems
- Integrated Systems Digital Network (ISDN), including aggregation of ISDN lines to gang two B channels for 128K throughput on internal ISDN adapters
- Parallel port or null modem over a serial connection

Which Protocol Will You Use?

Just as you may have a choice of protocols when plugging directly into your local-area network, you may have a choice of using one of the following protocols with Dial-Up Networking:

- NetBEUI
- TCP/IP
- IPX/SPX

If your network has either an NT Server or NetWare server, Windows 98 will fully support user-based security, allowing you to grant different users varying levels of access to your computer and the rest of the network. Additionally, if your server is running NT, Windows 98 supports domain-trust relationships and centralized network security administration.

Using Your Remote Connection

Once you have connected to a remote computer, you can use any of its shared resources, be they files, printers, or other modems (for faxing), just as if you were in the same office building connected with Ethernet or Token Ring.

Besides the resources on the single computer you're dialed into, you may also use the services of any other computer in the workgroup (or the NT domain)—assuming you've been given access. In other words, if you dialed into your office computer from home, you could copy the files from any computer that your office computer can see, or print a report on any printer your office desktop can access. Of course, an administrator can restrict access to specific machines and resources, so a RAS caller doesn't necessarily have access to all machines on the LAN.

Setting Up Your Modem for Dial-Up Networking

As with all other hardware, Windows 98 provides a Wizard for installing your modem(s). You can activate it either through the Hardware Installation Wizard or by double-clicking on the Modems icon in the Control Panel. The Modems approach is more direct.

NOTE

If you have a PCMCIA card modem, you can just plug it in. If you're really lucky, Windows 98 will detect it and all necessary drivers will be installed automatically. Then you can skip all the steps below.

1. If you have an external modem, make sure it is properly connected to your computer and turned on. If it's an internal modem, ensure that you've installed it properly, inserted any necessary screws, etc., as per the manufacturer's instructions.

2. Open up the Control Panel by selecting it from the Start ➤ Settings menu.

3. Double-click on Modems. If Windows does not recognize that there are any modems installed, you'll instantly see a box about adding a new modem. Otherwise, any modems that have been completely installed will be listed here. If yours is not listed, click on Add.

4. You're now asked if you are installing a PCMCIA (a credit-card-sized jobbie) or "other." Click on the appropriate button and click Next.

   - If you chose PCMCIA, you're prompted to insert the card. Insert it and click Finish. That's it, you're done.

   - If your modem is the "other" kind, you get to go through the Hardware Installation Wizard, as outlined in the next section.

Installing Your Modem via the Hardware Installation Wizard

You can choose to let Windows attempt to figure out what kind of modem you're adding, or just tell it yourself by clicking on the *Don't run the hardware installation wizard* checkbox. It's your call. I usually let Windows try to discern new hardware on its own. If it succeeds, there is a better chance the correct drivers, ports, and other settings will be installed. Things are a little iffier if you declare this on your own. Here's how to let Windows decide.

1. You can reach the Hardware Installation Wizard via the steps outlined for the Modems icon approach in the Control Panel (the steps directly preceding this one), or you can go directly to the Control Panel and choose Add New Hardware.

2. At the Add New Hardware Wizard welcome screen, select Next. You'll be prompted to let the Wizard check for any new PnP (Plug and Play) hardware. Let it do that by clicking on Next. If the device you're installing is in the list, click on it and then click Next and follow the resulting instructions. If it's not, simply click Next and go on to the next screen.

3. At this point, you can have Windows look around and try to guess what your modem is, or you can declare this, and how it's connected. Again, I usually let Windows try to detect the new modem, so I suggest pressing Next.

4. If the Hardware Installation Wizard finds your new modem, it will ask you to verify the modem type. If Windows correctly identified your modem, which is usually the case, skip to step 8.

   • If the Wizard has guessed wrong, or if it was not able to find the modem at all, then you pretty much have to step in and make your own declaration at this point. Click to see a list of hardware, select *Modems* and you'll see the window shown in Figure 28.1. (You may see another Modem dialog box or two before this one, but they are self explanatory to get to this box.)

FIGURE 28.1

Selecting a specific modem

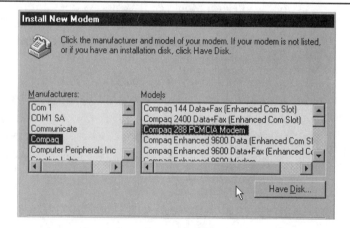

5. First, select the manufacturer of your modem. If it is not listed and you have an installation disk from the manufacturer, click the Have Disk button. If you do not have a disk, try using the Generic Modem driver appropriate for your modem speed. These drivers will work for most Hayes-compatible modems.

6. Next, choose the specific model or modem speed.

7. Click Next, and then choose the port the modem is connected to.

8. Press Finish. The modem driver is installed.

9. Now the Wizard will want to test the modem to make sure it works. You can skip this step if you want, though testing is advised. If the test fails, you'll be routed back to the earlier step of declaring the modem.

- If you've gotten this far but the modem has failed the Wizard's test (step 9), try testing the modem again before going all the way back to the beginning. Make sure you're declaring the correct port, that the modem is turned on, and that it's connected with a good cable! Power the modem off and then on again. If it's a PCMCIA card modem, eject it, wait a few seconds for any electrical charge to dissipate, and then reinsert it. The computer should beep to indicate you've inserted it.

NOTE

If you have a PCMCIA modem, you may find that Windows 98 installs a generic modem driver for it. This is because many modem manufacturers actually use the same internal chipsets. Also, PCMCIA modems should install automatically (avoiding all the above steps) in most machines, assuming your PCMCIA support drivers in Windows 98 are working properly.

Now that you have installed your modem, you can install and set up a Dial-Up Networking client and server. The client allows you to dial into other computers. The server portion allows other computers to dial into yours.

Setting Up Dial-Up Networking on Your Computer

To install the necessary Dial-Up Networking files from your Windows 98 CD, you use the Control Panel, as explained earlier in this chapter. (Note that DUN may already be installed on your computer. If it is, it will appear as a folder in My Computer. You should check this from your Desktop before proceeding.)

Once you have the Dial-Up Networking component installed, you need to set it up correctly for your particular use.

1. Open My Computer, then open the Dial-Up Networking folder. Now run Make New Connection. You'll see the screen below.

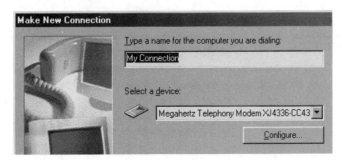

2. Give your connection a name, such as *Al's Desk in the East Wing*.

3. If you have more than one modem, select the modem you want to use.

4. Press Next. This leads you to the screen where you enter the particulars for this connection.

5. Enter the area code and phone number.

6. If necessary, change the country code.

7. Press Next.

8. You are now done. Verify the name and press Finish to save the connection.

Now that you have set up Dial-Up Networking, whenever you open up the Dial-Up Networking folder there will be two icons: the connection you just created—*Al's Desk in the East Wing* in my example—and *Make New Connection*. If you select this second icon, Windows 98 will use the same Wizard to lead you through setting up a connection to another remote-node server.

Now that you have Dial-Up Networking installed and configured, you can use the Dial-Up Networking client to dial into other computers. You are now ready for the next section where you will learn how to take full advantage of Dial-Up Networking.

Using Dial-Up Networking

As noted earlier, Dial-Up Networking allows you to leverage the near-universal reach of the phone system to extend your computer network; all your networked computers need is a phone line. But just because you *can* does not mean you *should*. You will need to exercise some caution when using remote resources over a dial-up connection, because your connection is much slower than a normal network connection. While you might not think twice about SUMing an XBase table (DBF) across a Token Ring connection, trying this over a Dial-Up Networking link will produce a very disappointing performance. The same goes for starting up applications that reside on the remote computer. In both cases, the cause of the poor performance is the same: Dial-Up Networking must transfer the entire application file over the phone link. For example, starting FoxPro from a remote computer requires the transfer of the entire 2.5MB executable file. Instead of taking a few seconds to load from a local hard disk, it takes about 10 minutes over a 28.8K modem connection!

Whenever you want to run an application during a Dial-Up Networking session, make sure you have the application on your local hard drive *and* in your DOS search path. This will ensure that you run the local version instead of passing the entire executable across the wire.

TIP

If you do need to run actual programs across a dial-in link, you should use a program designed for this purpose, such as PC Anywhere, from Symantec. It's surprisingly responsive and intelligent. You can dial directly into another computer's modem to make the connection, or even use the Internet as the intermediary link for long hauls. Such remote-control programs (there are others on the market too, such as Remote Control) actually let you see exactly what is on the remote computer's screen and interact with it to transfer files and run programs. You can even use it to remotely examine and adjust settings on the remote machine. This is a perfect tool for remote administration of systems by computer consultants and the like.

With Windows 98 you have three ways to establish a remote connection:

- Explicit
- Application-initiated
- Implicit

With an explicit connection, you must manually initiate the connection. An application-initiated connection, as you might expect, is started by an application calling the remote-node software. As for implicit connections, Windows 98 starts these when it can neither find a resource locally nor locate it on the physical network (i.e., via your network adapter card).

Explicit Connections

Connecting to a remote computer with an explicit connection is very similar to creating a RAS connection with Windows for Workgroups 3.11 or Windows NT.

When you create an explicit connection, you manually dial up the remote computer and log on. Once you have done this, the remote computer and all its share points show up in your Network Neighborhood. You can manipulate these resources just as you would any other computer's resources—except that it's much slower.

TIP

If, once you are connected, no remote resources show up or you get an error message about not being able to browse the network, and you know everything on the server side of the connection is set up correctly, then you most likely have a problem with the networking protocols set for your local computer. The most likely culprit would be that you're using different protocols on each end of the connection. For the connection to work, all machines must be using the same protocol, just as with a LAN connection. The setting of protocols is accomplished via the Control Panel's Network icon. Other chapters in this part explain the installation of protocols.

To use Windows 98 Dial-Up Networking to explicitly connect to a remote computer:

1. Open up the Dial-Up Networking folder (i.e., select My Computer and double-click on the folder).

2. Double-click on the icon you created in the previous section. This will bring up a dialog box like the one shown in Figure 28.2.

FIGURE 28.2

Connecting to a remote network

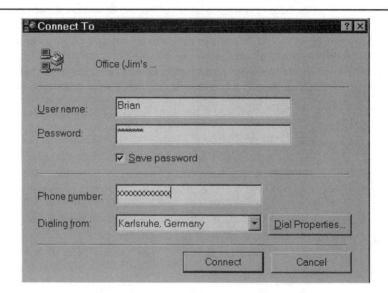

3. Enter the password, if any, for this resource. If you are connecting to a computer with user-based security, enter your log-in name and password.

4. Click on the Connect button.

Windows 98 will now initiate a process that will result—if all goes well—in a connection to the remote computer. As the negotiation between the two computers progresses, Windows gives you periodic updates to reassure you the process has not gone awry.

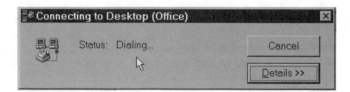

Now that you have manually initiated the connection, you will remain connected until you click on the Disconnect button (or until you "time out" your session connection—that is, until you let the connection run without input for a period of time that surpasses the timeout value that is set from the Connection tab on the DUN connection's property sheet). An icon will appear in the System Tray (near the clock in the Taskbar) to indicate when you are connected and online.

Double-click on this icon to displays the number of bytes transferred, or to manually disconnect, when you are through using the connection and don't want to incur additional telephone charges (important if you're in a hotel!).

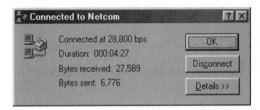

Application-Initiated Connections

Windows 98 also allows application developers to create programs that will establish Dial-Up Networking connections themselves rather than forcing the user to initiate the session manually.

A DUN-enabled application will take responsibility for automatically connecting to a DUN server as needed. The application uses Windows 98's Remote Access Session API to select a server, initiate a connection, and later disconnect the session. Besides allowing applications to initiate their own connections, the Remote Access Session API also reports the status back to the calling application. This way, if the server is unavailable for some reason (like the line being busy), the application can try again later.

The Outlook Express client provided with Windows 98 serves as an excellent example of an application that takes advantage of the Remote Access Session API. If you have configured Outlook Express for remote access, it will automatically use Dial-Up Networking to connect to your mail server anytime you try to access your mailbox. You can change Outlook's connection method by selecting Tools ➢ Options ➢ Dialup and choosing the desired DUN connection. As soon as it is connected to the mail server, Exchange will send all your outgoing mail, retrieve any new messages, and then disconnect.

 **TIP**

For more information on using Outlook Express, see Chapter 17.

Implicit Connections

Establishing a Dial-Up Networking implicit connection to a remote computer is just like connecting to that same computer in the office—simply double-click on the network object. Depending on the type of object you clicked on, Windows 98 may try to automatically create an implicit connection. That is, it's automatic, but initiated by Windows 98 itself, not a specific application. Whenever you have Dial-Up Networking installed, the following circumstances will cause Windows 98 to establish an implicit connection:

- You click on a link pointing to a remote resource.
- You try to use a network resource while disconnected from a network.
- Either you or an application you are using specifies a resource using a Universal Naming Convention (UNC) name (that is, *server_name**share_point*), and Windows 98 cannot find it on the local-area network. Windows 98 references printers via their UNC names (*server_name**printer_name*), so printing to a remote printer will also trigger an implicit connection.
- You try reconnecting to a remote OLE object (also known as a *DCOM* object) not located on the local network.
- An application tries to connect to a named pipe.

Whenever you try to access such a resource either by clicking it directly or through an application request, Windows 98 first tries to find it locally on your computer or out on your LAN. If it fails to locate the resource, Windows gives you the dial-in dialog box shown in Figure 28.3, asking if you want to connect to the resource through Dial-Up Networking.

FIGURE 28.3

*Windows 98 asks
the user if it should
connect to a remote
resource via Dial-Up
Networking.*

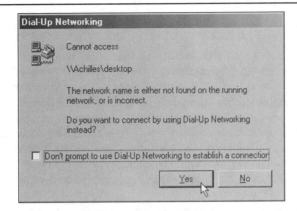

It then checks the Registry for the Dial-Up Networking entry for the server associated with the object. If it finds a server, it establishes the connection automatically. If it cannot find a server associated with the object, it prompts the user to either select the proper Dial-Up Networking connection for the object or to enter a new one, as shown below. With this information, Dial-Up Networking tries to establish a connection to the server.

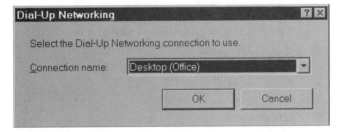

If it succeeds and successfully establishes a Dial-Up Networking connection, Windows 98 stores the name of the connector in the Registry so that the next time you click on the object or enter its name in a File ➢ Open dialog box, it does not have to prompt you to select the server.

NOTE

The decision concerning which of the three connection modes (explicit, application-initiated, or implicit) you should use most often depends on the type of work you do. If you are a network manager and your job requires you to manage several remote networks, you will probably find yourself using explicit connections most often, as they give you the greatest amount of control over your remote session. Less-technical users will probably rely on implicit connections because they are less hassle. Whether you use application-initiated connections depends on whether you are using any remote-access–enabled applications.

TIP

I often establish remote connections myself rather than relying on a remote-access–enabled application to do it for me. Why? Because once I have a connection to a remote server, I can do several tasks on-line rather than having each connection-enabled application simply hang up when it is done with the first task. How you tell an application to let you make the connection manually rather than doing it for you varies with the program. You'll have to read its documentation (ugh). In some cases, such as with Windows Messaging, you use the "connect using the LAN" setting rather than telling it to dial up by itself. Some recent programs from Microsoft have options such as "Let me make my own connection to the Internet," which makes a little more sense to the novice.

Advanced Configurations for Dial-Up Networking

When you're making or configuring Dial-Up Networking, there are several parameters you can edit:

- Dialing locations
- Server type
- Modem configurations (see Chapter 15)
- Scripting options
- Multilink options

I'll cover the first two of these here; the last two must be left to books directed at Windows developers.

Dialing Properties

When you initiate a dial-up connection, you can select a dialing location each time you establish a connection. Whenever you change locations, your location selection remains in effect for only that one connection. Then next time you connect, it will revert to your current location (as set in the Telephony applet in the Control Panel, which you can change as you travel about).

TIP

Modem installation and configuration is covered in Chapter 15, so I won't discuss those settings here. Suffice it to say you can alter the modem settings by clicking on the Configure button in the DUN connection's Properties box.

Server Type

The other parameter we'll discuss here is the server type. With the exception of ensuring you have the line speed set to the modem's maximum data rate, the Server Type options will have the greatest impact on the performance of Dial-Up Networking.

To bring up the Server Type properties:

1. Open the Dial-Up Networking folder from My Computer.

2. Right-click on the connection you want and select Properties.

3. Click on the Server Types tab. This displays the info shown in Figure 28.4.

FIGURE 28.4

*Editing the Server
Type Properties (new)*

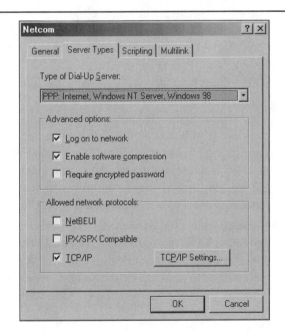

Obviously, you can configure a bunch of stuff here. Let's look at the most important ones.

Type of Dial-Up Server: Windows 98 will connect to four types of Dial-Up Networking servers:

- NRN (NetWare Connect)
- PPP (Point-to-Point Protocol servers, such as Windows 95, Windows NT, and Internet access providers)
- SLIP (Serial-Line Internet Protocol, used by UNIX systems)
- Windows for Workgroups and NT Server 3.1

Whenever Windows 98 establishes a Dial-Up Networking connection, it assumes the computer on the other end is a PPP server. If it isn't, Windows 98 cycles through the other three possibilities until it succeeds in making a connection or fails on all four. If you know the type of server to which you will connect (and you probably do), you will reduce your connection time by selecting the proper type in this field. A warning, however: If you change the default PPP setting and select the incorrect type of server, Windows 98 will not cycle through the other options. Rather, it will give up after trying your selection.

Enable software compression: As a rule, data compression will increase the effective data-transfer rate. These days, most modems support compression themselves, so you can have either the software (your computer) or the hardware (the modem) compress the data for you. For almost all types of data, software compression will provide superior performance to hardware compression. As you probably know, data compression works through a pattern-recognition algorithm that reduces redundancies in the data. Because Windows 98 provides more memory for storing patterns than your modem does, software compression has a better chance of recognizing complex patterns and thus of compressing the data as much as possible. The only time data compression does not increase performance—and in fact might reduce it—is when you transfer already highly compressed data such as ZIP files. If you plan to transfer ZIP files in a given Dial-Up Networking session, turn off software compression. Along the same lines, if you choose to use software compression, be sure to turn hardware compression off.

Require encrypted password: This is a security feature. By checking this box, Windows 98 will scramble your password as it transmits it across the phone lines so no one tapping your line can steal your password. (For additional information about Dial-Up Networking and security, see the following section.) If you check this box, make sure the server can understand and decrypt the password.

Protocols

The protocols section of the dialog box and the TCP/IP settings are both important, but they're covered in other chapters in this part (Part V). In brief, as I mentioned earlier in this chapter, computers on both ends of the connection must be running the same protocol. If you're connecting to the Internet, that will be TCP/IP. As a rule, I disable all non-applicable protocols whenever possible. This should increase security and possibly increase speed when using this connection. If you're using TCP/IP, typically you must set the TCP/IP settings (click on the TCP/IP Settings button) to match those of the host computer. That information is available from the system administrator or Internet service provider you dialing into.

> Windows 95 had a mistake in the Registry that slowed down data transmission when using DUN to connect to the Internet. The MTU setting (a variable which determines how many bits of data are sent at a time) didn't match most ISP's settings for the same variable most efficiently. As a result, a Windows PC wasted time negotiating repeatedly with the Internet when transmitting data such as Web pages and e-mail. Microsoft has now fixed this problem, so you needn't bother downloading utility programs or editing the MTU Registry setting if you're using Windows 98.

Dial-Up Networking and Security

Whenever you allow dial-in access to your network, you open it up to everyone who has a modem. Before you set up a Dial-Up Networking host, you need to take a good look at the risks involved and design your security model to minimize them. Some network managers go so far as to forbid dial-up access to any of their machines, regardless of the circumstances. While this is a draconian step, you do need to give security some thought.

Before setting up a Dial-Up Networking server, your first level of network security was not the user accounts and log-ins, but the more difficult hurdle of gaining *physical* access to your network. Dial-Up Networking effectively removes this major (and probably most effective) deterrent because the outside world is now physically connected to your network (or single-PC server). Anyone with the right skills may be able to break into your server.

For a system with remote access, your first line of defense becomes the relative obscurity of your modem's phone number. Before anyone can gain remote access to your network (at least through the telephone lines), the would-be hacker must know your data phone number. Accordingly, you should keep a tight grasp on who knows this number. You cannot, however, keep your modem number a secret. Hackers can (and will) set their modems to dial every number in a given prefix just to look for modems.

The next level in your security model is supplied by the user accounts and passwords. Regardless of how open your company is with its data, instituting a policy of secure log-ins and passwords on any network is a good precaution. This becomes essential when physical access is no longer a requirement for logging on to your network. How you implement this varies based on server type.

You can add security to your network by using Dial-Up Networking's callback feature. When using a Windows 98 Dial-Up Networking server with the callback facility turned on, as soon as the server authenticates a user, Windows 98 drops the line. It then calls the user back at a prearranged phone number. The obvious advantage to this feature is that simply figuring out the modem number and guessing the log-in and password combination is not enough to gain access to your network. An unauthorized user must also be at the prearranged phone number, which is not so likely.

This scenario also has an obvious drawback: It will not work for users who move around and thus do not have a consistent phone number, such as members of your sales force. There is also a less obvious security hole: The phone system is not all that secure, and talented phone hackers (phreakers) can reroute a phone call to any location.

NOTE

Many companies implement RAS callback features primarily as a means of controlling phone costs. Callback enables you to control who pays for the call and therefore provides a means of tracking costs. With callback, companies are able to centralize their telecommunications costs to one line (or a group of lines) so they can easily tell how much money they are spending to provide their free-spirited users with ready access to corporate resources. Additionally, callback allows them to route calls through the least-expensive channels available, whether it be WATS lines or lines purchased though a reseller.

On top of these security measures, you can use several third-party security devices such as random-number generators and encrypted-access modems with Dial-Up Networking to further bolster your security.

The best method for maintaining a secure environment is to regularly monitor your network's activity; not only the dial-in portion, but *all* activity. When you notice something unusual, such as repeated (yet unsuccessful) log-in attempts or abnormally high traffic at strange times, investigate it at once to find out the cause. While the answer may be simply an employee working late or someone who forgot his or her password, it may also be someone trying to break into your system.

Protecting Your Data While Connected to the Internet Using Dial-Up Networking

Finally, a little tip about settings for file sharing. Obviously, for a DUN connection to be used by, say, outside employees, you'll want to enable file sharing; otherwise a remote user won't be able to gain access to information on the server's hard disk. But when your DUN connection (*from* the server, not *to* it) is specifically for making a connection to an ISP (for the purposes of getting e-mail, surfing the Web, doing FTP transfers, etc.), you will *not* want to have file sharing turned on. Why not? Because it leaves a major gap in security for someone to break into your computer while you're sitting there connected to the world's largest network. Get used to thinking of the Internet as a huge LAN, with millions of users on it, any one of which could break into your system if you're not careful. Windows 98 may warn you of this danger if you have installed the TCP/IP protocol with file and printer sharing turned on. Or it might not. This is something you should manually check if you're only using your TCP/IP modem connection for Internet work. Here's how:

1. Open Control Panel and choose Network.

2. Find the entry "TCP/IP ≻ Dial-Up adapter" and click on it, and then click on the Properties button. (OK the resulting warning about your TCP/IP settings.)

3. Click the Bindings tab.

4. Make sure the *File and printer sharing* option is not enabled (i.e., make sure the x is cleared from the checkbox), as shown in Figure 28.5.

5. Close the dialog boxes and reboot.

PART

V

FIGURE 28.5

Ensuring that file sharing is turned off for TCP/IP over the dialup adapter can help protect your computer when you are connected to the Internet.

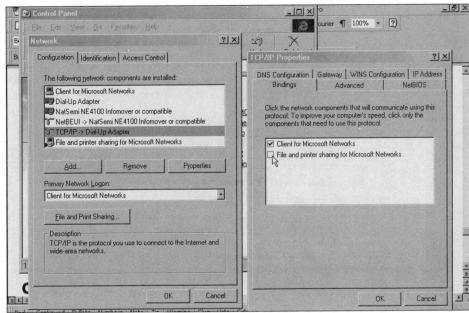

Networking with Windows 98

Can't I Share an Internet DUN Connection with Other User Stations on My LAN?

Ever wondered if you can share a modem connection among several workstations on your LAN? If you have, you're not alone. After all, you can share printers and even fax-modems in Windows 98 so that everyone on the LAN can use them. So why can't you share a modem's connection to the net? This could save you the extra expenses of additional modems, your ISDN or analog lines, and ISP charges, right? You'd only have to pay for one of each, and everyone on your small business LAN or home LAN could use it.

Not.

Here's the rub. You see, for normal LAN activities, each workstation has a discrete and *static* (non-changing) address. Say your workstation is called Alex's Computer. So, when your workstation needs to handle messages from, say, a printer about a print job you started, it knows how to find you—Alex's Computer. Or when you're copying a file from the server, the server knows where to copy it to—Alex's Computer.

Interacting with the Internet is different. For most mortal users (unless you pay big bucks for a static address), each time a modem logs on the Internet through an ISP, the ISP provides it with a *temporary* Internet address. It looks something like 123.456.789.012, and is called an *IP address* (for Internet Protocol address). Each modem dial-up connection to the ISP is given a single IP address, lasting only for the duration of the call. The address is not static, it's transitory.

Now, suppose two people on your office LAN were trying to get their respective e-mail through a shared modem connected to the Internet. Since there is only one IP address but two users, the messages would collide, and the data wouldn't know where to go once it comes across the modem. It would be like the mailman trying to deliver two people's mail but only finding one mailbox to put it in. Things could get very mixed up. Or imagine that you and I are at different workstations browsing different pages on the Web. Our displays would get all mixed up, with data from viewed pages intermingling.

As you might expect, there *is* a solution to this problem. You have to use a special kind of connection to the Internet called a *router*. A router is an intermediary computer and software (or a specialized router box) connected to your LAN. The router keeps track of which workstations on the LAN make data requests of the Internet, watches for the Internet's responses to those requests, and passes the packets of data to the respective workstations. In essence, the router acts as the local mailman. Routing can be done cheaply using inexpensive and wimpy computers; it's more elegant (and expensive) to use a dedicated router box.

Direct Cable Connect (DCC) Using a Serial or Parallel Port

Windows 98's DCC program (Direct Cable Connect) is a wonderful little feature that lets you have a fully operational network connection between any two PCs, connected only by their serial (modem/mouse) ports or parallel (printer) ports. Of course, if you have LAN cards in your computers already, you can forget about this feature. It's only a boon if you don't want to get into the hassle of setting up a network, or if you have a computer that *doesn't* have a LAN card in it. Since a LAN card can transfer data much faster than the DCC will (the slowness is due to the limitations of serial and parallel ports), you'll want to use the LAN option whenever possible. Even a relatively "slow" 10Megabit-per-second Ethernet card is super fast compared to a measly parallel port (and *super*-super fast compared to a serial port).

If you're one of the growing numbers of laptop users, you probably appreciate having the mobility of the laptop but still find times when you could really use a 5¼-inch floppy drive, or a CD-ROM drive, or just wish you could copy files up to the network or down to your laptop faster than with floppies. Using DCC, you can very easily connect that laptop to any other computer running Windows 98 (or Windows 95, since it works on that operating system too) as long as you have either a serial-to-serial or a parallel-to-parallel cable designed for data transfer between two computers (LapLink-style cables). There's a place where I live that sells nice long parallel cables for only $5, and if you find a similar deal, I'd recommend buying a few. It is really simple to connect the cable to the printer port on your laptop and to an office PC, start DCC on both PCs, and within seconds actually have a network connection, allowing you to access any shared resources on whichever PC is configured as the host.

1. The first thing you will need to do to set DCC up on your system, if you haven't done so already, is add the Dial-Up Adapter driver to your list of network components. Just open My Computer ➤ Control Panel ➤ Network, and then click on Add, click on Adapter, select Microsoft, and select Dial-Up Adapter. Click on OK, and DCC is ready to run.

2. To start up the DCC applet, click on Start ➤ Programs ➤ Accessories ➤ Communications ➤ Direct Cable Connection.

3. When you start up DCC for the first time, it will ask you to select whether this PC will be configured as a Guest PC or as the Host PC, as shown in Figure 28.6.

4. Finally, you have to select which port you want to use with DCC (see Figure 28.7). If at all possible, you should use a parallel port. Not only is it quite a bit faster than the alternative (a serial port), it will also usually be easier to find a parallel port available on the computers you'll be connecting to.

FIGURE 28.6

Configure one PC as Host, the other as Guest.

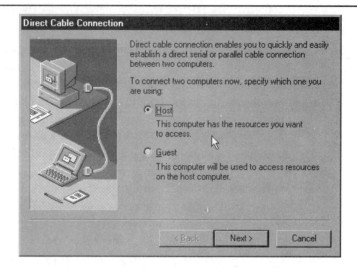

FIGURE 28.7

Configuring DCC to use a parallel port. Note that both PCs will need to be using the same type of port (either serial or parallel).

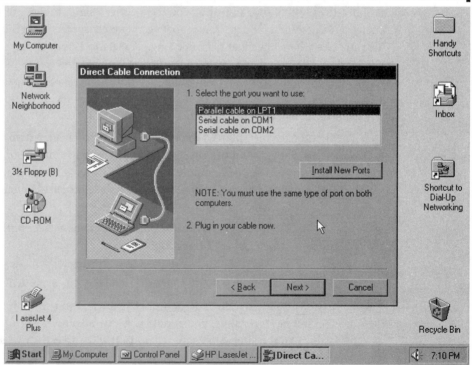

Once when I was installing DCC, no parallel ports showed up in the Ports list. After checking out my Device Manager list in Control Panel ➢ Devices, I discovered that the parallel port was disabled because it conflicted with a sound card. After reconfiguring the sound card to a different IRQ, the printer port showed up in DCC's list of available ports.

Now that you've configured one PC, you need to do the same on the other one, of course making sure you choose the same port type (either serial or parallel), and remembering which one you've decided to set up as Host and which one as Guest. Then, connect your cable between the two ports, click on Listen on the host PC, and click on Connect on the guest PC. After a few seconds, you should see a message similar to this:

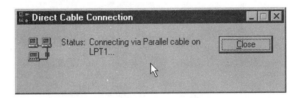

If you've entered a password (on both sides), you will next see the message "Verifying user ID and password," and then the connection will be established. Once the connection has been established, you can minimize the DCC Status dialog box on both PCs to get them out of the way.

At this point, you will be able to access the host PC from Network Neighborhood and thus can map drives, install a printer driver corresponding to any printers on the host side, and so on—just like we did back in the chapter about setting up the peer-to-peer network (Chapter 26).

If you will be using DCC frequently on a particular PC, you may want to drag the DCC icon from the Accessories ➢ Communications folder onto your Desktop for easy access. Or, if you prefer, drag and drop the DCC icon onto your Start button or Quick Launch bar.

By now you should have a good understanding of the many options Windows 98 gives you for interconnecting (networking) your computers. In the next chapter I'll discuss troubleshooting your networked Windows 98 computer.

Networking with Windows 98

PART V

Chapter

29

Troubleshooting Your Windows 98 Network

Diagnosing cable problems

Diagnosing NIC and driver problems

Restoring from a downed hard drive

What to do if your system can't boot

Troubleshooting Your Windows 98 Network

Aside from reducing your system bottlenecks, running backups, and dealing with daily user issues—such as creating new accounts, setting up new stations, adding servers, and so on—much of a network administrator's time is typically spent fixing various network problems. In this chapter, I will look first at the process of troubleshooting network problems, then step through several of the most frequent types of problems and show how to resolve them. At the end of this chapter, I'll discuss some procedures for getting a Windows 98 station back into operation after a hard-drive failure.

Not only are networking problems sometimes difficult to track down, they also typically require a quick resolution because frequently a network problem means downtime for one or more network users. When you first learn of a problem, it helps to assign it a priority by taking into account criteria such as the following:

- How many users are (or will be) affected?

- What type of work (emergency, critical, or lower priority) is affected?

- How difficult does the problem appear to be?

- Does the problem have a known solution (at your organization) or are you dealing with something new?

Dealing with networking problems—and with computer problems in general—is largely a matter of deduction, eliminating possibilities through questioning, trial and error, and adverting to past experience. This is why keeping a problem-and-resolution log can be so effective. If someone else is reporting the problem to you, write down what they say and ask questions while the situation is still fresh in their memory. Almost always, the first thing you should ask is, "When was the last time this equipment, software, or whatever, worked correctly?"

The second most helpful question to ask—assuming someone else is explaining the problem to you—is, "What were you doing when you noticed the problem?" (Avoid giving this question an accusatorial tone—you just want to know what led to the problem.) Besides helping to narrow your focus, these questions sometimes point you directly to the root cause of the problem. Sometimes, for example, users will try tightening the keyboard or mouse cables and end up loosening the network cable. Perhaps they turned off the computer without first shutting down. About half the time, the problem was caused by operator error, but if so, rather than chastising the user, show them how to avoid this problem in the future. As much as you may enjoy using computers, don't forget that to some users, they are probably a mystery and even an object of fear. Try to pass on your appreciation of computers whenever possible. A thorough and positive introduction to the computer and occasional user training can go a long way toward eliminating accidental damage to cables, keyboards, and other hardware and software.

Troubleshooting is also helped by having a good memory (or a good set of notes). When was the software on this station upgraded? Which network adapter (and drivers) is it using? When was this cable run? Again, knowing what to look for greatly reduces the number of possibilities you need to look at.

Certain applications may indirectly cause extra troubles for your organization. Maybe an older communications program insists on using an earlier version of Winsock, thus conflicting with Windows 98's built-in version of Winsock. Perhaps some application is opening files in exclusive mode, preventing other users from opening the same file.

Has a new piece of hardware or software recently been added to the station? If so, this is a good place to start looking. Until every system is fully Plug-and-Play aware and has only Plug-and-Play components installed, interrupt and I/O address conflicts will be an ongoing source of problems. The best weapons against such conflicts are these: using identical hardware for all workstations, using the same interrupts and I/O addresses for the same devices in each workstation as much as possible, documenting the card settings on a sheet of paper taped inside each computer, and lastly, making use of a POST (power-on self test) diagnostics card. Such a card fits into the bus of a problem PC and can perform a large array of tests on the computer, reporting the results via LEDs on the card. The Discovery Card from JDR Microdevices costs about $99 and can find IRQ- and DMA-related conflicts, while a more complex card may cost $1,200 to $1,500 and can identify all devices set to the same IRQ, bad SIMMs, errors on the motherboard, as well as problems with the power supply, serial and parallel ports, and so on. Such errors might otherwise take half a day or longer to diagnose, besides the productivity time wasted while the system is down. I have seen completely configured systems delivered with two serial ports configured to the same address, a network card conflicting with video memory, and even two parallel port adapters, both configured to LPT1, in the same PC. Obviously whoever configured these systems was not using a POST diagnostics card.

For the rest of this chapter, I'll look at some of the most common problems that can plague your Windows 98 network and how you can resolve them most efficiently.

Diagnosing Cable Problems

One of the nicest things about star-topology networks (such as 10BaseT) is the relative ease of diagnosing and fixing cable problems. If all stations on a particular hub suddenly lose their network connection, you should check out your hub. Check the connection from the hub to the server, in particular—assuming you have a dedicated server. If none of the cable connections have pulled loose, try swapping in a different hub. If the stations now connect to the network again, you've found the problem. You can see the practicality of keeping a spare hub around—ideally one identical to what's in use so you can immediately replace the hub if it ever becomes necessary. For diagnostic purposes though, even a hub with a small number of ports lets you try connecting a few stations. If it works, you know there's a problem with the other hub.

On a network using thin coax, however, things are a bit more hairy. First of all, it's much more likely for the whole segment to go down, because of the nature of the connection. Typically what you'll have to do then is perform *binary searching* for the location of the cable break by splitting the network segment in half, seeing which half still works when you connect it to the server, then splitting the bad subsegment in half and repeating this process until you locate the offending cable portion.

On a thin-net coax network, some additional things you'll want to check include making sure the terminators are still connected to each end and that one end is properly grounded, and verifying that the complete length of cable has the same RG number. I have seen strange connection problems surface only months later, and then only intermittently, when someone used a length of cable somewhere in the network that had slightly different impedance than the rest of the network cable.

When single stations lose their connection on a star-type configuration, again the problem-solving process is much easier. The first thing to do (obvious, but frequently effective) is to check that both ends of the cable are connected tightly. If this doesn't take care of the problem, try connecting the hub end of the cable to a different jack on the hub.

NOTE

One thing I really appreciate about Windows 95, 98, and NT is their ability to auto-reconnect when a connection is temporarily broken. This may seem like a small thing, but it's nice not to have to reboot the station each time; I can just double-click on Network Neighborhood or reopen a folder on a network drive.

If you still aren't able to establish a connection, try whichever of these is less trouble: either swap in a different cable or connect a different PC to the end of the existing cable (use a PC known to have no trouble getting on the network). Using these two tests, you can determine either that the cable is bad (if the new cable worked or the new PC did not) or that the original PC has a network-card problem (if the new PC worked, but the new cable did not work with the original PC). If you determine that the cable is the problem, you might try replacing the cable connector if you are adept at this and think it's a quicker solution than running a new length of cable.

Finally, if you are able to connect to the network, but transferring data across the network seems slow as molasses, you are likely dealing with an inferior quality (or damaged) network cable. Remember, nowadays you want level 5 cable, if possible (and at least level 3); otherwise, you can expect all sorts of problems with throughput on your network.

Diagnosing Network Interface Card (NIC) and Driver Problems

If you have reason to believe a network card may not be functioning properly, here are several things you can try in the order in which you'll most likely want to try them. First, if Windows 98 is already running, go into Control Panel ➤ Networks and check that all network components that should be installed actually are. If not, add them, shut down and restart Windows 98, and again try to get on the network. If this doesn't work, then just to get everything working, you could remove any network (software) components other than these three:

- the driver for the installed network card
- the protocol(s) you need to get on the network
- the appropriate client service (for example, Client for NetWare Networks or Client for Microsoft Networks)

The most important thing is to verify that the card settings match those configured on the driver. To do this, double-click on the card driver (while looking at the installed–network-components list). This should bring up the network card's Properties dialog box (see Figure 29.1). Click on the Resources tab and verify that the settings are correct. Also write down these settings in case you need to pull your network card later to verify that its settings correspond to these.

FIGURE 29.1

Verifying and configuring network-card settings

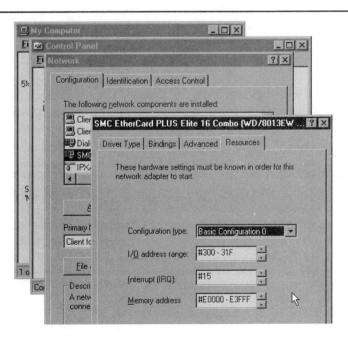

Another common problem is that the memory-address settings required by the adapter card are not excluded from use by the expanded memory manager. In our example above we would also want to make sure that the DEVICE=EMM386.EXE line in config.sys also included an X=E000-E3FF entry. Otherwise the expanded memory manager would map the NIC memory address to be used as upper memory and could cause connectivity problems. As a quick and easy test to determine an upper memory block (UMB) problem, comment out the expanded memory manager in config.sys. This can be accomplished by placing a REM in front of the DEVICE=EMM386.EXE if using Microsoft's expanded memory manager or DEVICE=QEMM386.SYS if using Quarterdeck's QEMM.

Next, click on the Driver Type tab. In almost all cases, you'll want the first radio button, *Enhanced mode (32 bit and 16 bit) NDIS driver*, selected—the only reason you ever need real-mode drivers is if you happen to be using a network card for which you cannot find Windows 98 protected-mode drivers or if you want to test network-connectivity problems. For instance, when attempting to solve a connectivity problem, you can install an NDIS 2.0 (real-mode) driver, boot Windows 98 to a command prompt, then try to log onto the network with a **NET LOGON** command. If that works, but the NDIS 3.1 (protected-mode) driver failed, you have at least identified the problem and can begin troubleshooting the protected-mode driver installation. In any case, make sure the setting matches what you need. Also, click on the Bindings tab and verify that a check mark is placed next to the protocol(s) you will need to get on your network.

If you notice any incorrect settings, after changing these you will next want to restart Windows 98 and see if you are now able to connect to the network. Otherwise, the next thing I'd recommend doing is printing out a handy list of equipment and resource settings, which can be done by going to Control Panel ➤ System ➤ Device Manager and clicking on Print.

If your network card is one that lets you software-configure the IRQ and I/O address, open a DOS window and run this software now. If the settings match what they should be, good. Otherwise, adjust them accordingly.

NOTE

Some cards that let you run a software-configuration utility also have one or more jumper settings that need to be set before your configuration software can work; otherwise it won't run at all, or when you try to make changes, they won't stick. In this case, refer to your card's documentation for information on enabling the software-configuration option.

If your network card is not software configurable, you'll need to remove the network card to visually inspect it and possibly make changes to it. Again, first print out the system summary report, as it will definitely be helpful in setting your card. Next, shut down Windows, turn off the PC and unplug it, remove the PC's cover, and take out the network card. If you're lucky, the network card will have the jumper settings silk-screened near the jumper pads. Otherwise, dredge up your card's documentation and flip to the jumper-settings diagram. Verify that the settings match what your driver is configured to. If not, make changes to the jumpers.

If your network card settings match your network driver settings and you are *still* not able to connect to the network, it's likely that either the IRQ or the I/O address conflicts with another card. If this is the case, refer to your system configuration report and select a different (unused) IRQ and I/O address for your network card. To see a list of IRQs and other potentially conflicted system resources, go to Control Panel ➢ System and click on the Device Manager tab. Double-click on Computer. You'll see a dialog box listing lots of goodies to help you, as shown in Figure 29.2.

PART
V

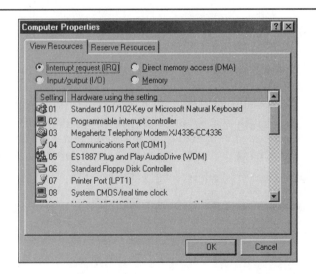

FIGURE 29.2

To help you determine resource conflicts, go to the Device Manager and click on Computer.

Networking with
Windows 98

When you've got your network card configured, gently reinstall it and tighten down the edge bracket with a screw. Replace the PC's cover (you don't want to replace all the screws holding the cover just yet—wait until your network card is verified operational). Then turn the computer back on and make any changes to the network-card driver to synch it with the changes you've made to the card. If you're prompted to shut down and restart Windows 98, do so.

NOTE

When attempting to get network support operational, you may want to start Windows 95 in *safe mode with networking support.* This disables other drivers that may conflict with your network card, reducing the number of factors that can interfere with initially connecting with the network. To boot Windows 98 in this mode, press the F6 key when the computer is first starting (when you see the Starting Windows 98 prompt), before you see the logo screen. (On a fast computer, you may have to act quickly, as the window of opportunity between "starting" and the logo is very small.) If the F6 approach doesn't work, try holding down the Shift key during bootup.

If you've got any patience left, and you're *still* not able to talk to the network at this point (you're probably a saint!), you might try swapping this network card into a PC that is talking to the network—and perhaps swap that PC's card into the problem PC. This, finally, will tell you one way or another what you need to know. Either the NIC from the bad PC will now work in the good PC, meaning there's still a conflict with another card in the bad PC, or the bad card will also refuse to work in the good PC. If it's a conflict, start removing other cards from the bad PC one by one, bringing up Windows 98 after each time, until you're able to get back on the network. If you're with a large-enough organization to have a POST diagnostic card, you will have put it to use before now, I am sure. Otherwise, you'll be wishing you had one at this point.

If you continue to have no success after futzing with IRQs and I/O addresses some more, try installing a different network card, preferably from a different vendor. If the first card was a jumpered card, do yourself a favor and try a newer card. By the time you're reading this, just about any new network card should at least be software configurable, if not fully Plug-and-Play. Just choose one of the top five or six brands, and you should be up and running again in no time. If not, your problems are way outside the scope of this book and you certainly deserve a prize of some sort for having come this far.

Restoring from a Downed Hard Drive

When you have a station that has undergone a disk crash or for other reasons has damaged system files, you will likely find the system refuses to get further than the initial logo screen before issuing an error message and then hanging at the system prompt. Of course the ideal thing at this point is to simply restore the system files from those backups you make every night. Here are the files you will need most if you need to restore from a damaged drive:

From the root directory of the boot drive:

- `config.sys` (if used)
- `autoexec.bat` (if used)
- `io.sys` (hidden, read only, system)
- `msdos.sys` (hidden, read only, system)
- `command.com`

From the \Windows directory (the directory where Windows 98 is installed):

- `win.ini`
- `system.ini`
- `protocol.ini`

NOTE

These next two are the most important (or the most likely to be damaged).

- `user.dat` (hidden, system)
- `system.dat` (hidden, system)

Try booting Windows 98 using the boot menu and selecting Safe Mode. To bring up the boot menu, press the F8 key (or Shift) while the system is first booting. The first thing I usually try running is the *logged to file* option, which tries starting Windows 98 again normally and also creates a file in the Windows 98 directory called BOOTLOG.TXT, which shows each step as it's trying to boot.

NOTE

If BOOTLOG.TXT isn't in your Windows 98 directory, look in the root directory of the boot drive. If you find it here, it will be marked as a hidden file.

If your system fails again while starting Windows 98, reboot, select *System Prompt only*, go into the Windows 98 directory, and check BOOTLOG.TXT for clues to why Windows wouldn't start. If this doesn't help, try booting using Safe Mode. As a last resort, try booting using *safe mode with command prompt only*. This will at least let you try the following technique.

When a Windows 98 station will not start Windows 98, the single most likely way to get the station up again fast is to go to the directory Windows 98 is installed in (usually \Windows or \Win98), run attrib -s -h on SYSTEM.* and USER.*, and then make a backup of SYSTEM.DAT and USER.DAT. Finally, copy SYSTEM.DA0 to SYSTEM.DAT, and USER.DA0 to USER.DAT. What this does is restore the backup copies of the system Registry files. If you're lucky, rebooting after doing this will allow you to get back into Windows 98. At that point, immediately run the System File Checker (Start ➢ Programs ➢ Accessories ➢ System Tools ➢ System File Checker).

If you still cannot get Windows 98 to start, and you've tried replacing the Registry files SYSTEM.DAT and USER.DAT from the backups automatically made by Windows 98, it's looking rather grim. You need to start thinking about reinstalling Windows 98. If you do have a recent full-system backup, try restoring all the files from the Windows 98 directory and all directories under it. If restoring from a backup won't work, your best bet is to dust off your Windows 98 CD-ROM or disks and run the install again. See the Appendix for installation.

If you are only able to boot to a system prompt, don't have an emergency startup disk with CD-ROM support, or do not have a CD-ROM drive locally attached, but have been (up 'til now) part of a network and using an NDIS 2.0 (real-mode) network driver, try going into the Windows 98 directory and typing NET START WORKSTATION. With luck, this will get you on the network and allow you to copy the Windows 98 install files from some other station on the network that *does* have a CD-ROM drive. Of course, you will need to have sufficient disk space available, plus space for installing Windows again.

For those systems on your network that can afford 70-some MB of disk space better than they can afford to be down for some time, copy the contents of the \Win98 install directory from your CD-ROM or diskettes into a unique directory on the hard drive and then reinstall from this directory if you ever need to reinstall Windows 98. You will find this to be noticeably faster than even the fastest CD-ROM drives.

When reinstalling Windows 98, first try installing to the same directory you originally installed to. This usually works fine and will let you keep most of your system settings (assuming they haven't been damaged).

What to Do If You Cannot Even Boot to a System Prompt

While rather rare, it is possible to have your system in such a state that it won't even boot but says *invalid system* or some such message. Before taking the extreme measure of reformatting your drive, try booting with the Windows 98 startup disk you made during setup. If you don't have one of these, go to another station on the network and make one. In case you're not familiar with the process, open Control Panel ➢ Add/Remove Programs, click on the Startup Disk tab, and click on the Create Disk button (after inserting a blank diskette).

NOTE

Unlike the Windows 95 startup disks, the Windows 98 startup disks include drivers for most CD-ROM devices. This solves a major problem that sometimes occurred with system crashes under previous versions of Windows—i.e., when your system crashes so badly that it doesn't recognize that it has a CD-ROM drive installed, it can be difficult to restore the files you need if they reside only on your installation CD. With CD-ROM support now available on the startup floppy, you'll be able to use your CD immediately after using the startup disk.

Once you've booted with the Windows 98 startup diskette and are at the command prompt, do the following:

1. Change to the System directory, which is under the Windows 98 directory.
2. Copy the file sys.com to your Windows 98 startup diskette.
3. Switch to drive A (or B if appropriate) and type **SYS** C:—this should allow your hard drive to at least boot to a Windows 98 command prompt.
4. Remove the diskette and attempt to reboot system.
5. If Windows 98 doesn't start normally, reboot and use the Safe Mode with command prompt only.

At this point, follow the above instructions for restoring the SYSTEM.DAT and USER.DAT Registry files. If this doesn't work, read the above section about reinstalling Windows 98.

PART

V

Networking with Windows 98

Ideally, you are reading this before any troubles arise and can see some ways to practice preventive medicine, such as keeping an extra hub, cables, and network cards handy for quick replacements in time of failure. You may realize that it makes more sense to use several smaller hubs rather than one or two large ones. And I'm sure you can now better see the utility of making Windows 98 startup diskettes and regular backups of the system Registry files, and running the System File Checker on a regular basis.

Check Chapter 23 for other system utilities that can help prevent system crashes. The Task Scheduler, System Update, and Maintenance Wizard can be of value in this regard.

Appendix

A

Installing Windows 98 on Your Computer

INSTALLING WINDOWS 98 ON YOUR COMPUTER

Chances are good that your computer came installed with Windows 98 already, in which case reading this appendix isn't necessary for you. On the other hand, if you are still using Windows 3.x or Windows 95, or have no version of Windows on your computer at all, you'll want to read this appendix. If at some point after you install Windows 98 you discover that you are missing some of the components discussed in this book, you can install them later from the Windows Control Panel's Add/Remove Programs applet, as explained in Chapter 7.

There are several basic scenarios when installing Windows 98:

- Installing on a new or newly formatted hard disk
- Installing over Windows 3.x
- Installing over Windows 95

Within each scenario, there are sub-scenarios, based on the source of the installation programs:

- Local CD-ROM or hard disk
- Local floppy disks
- Network CD-ROM or hard disk

In the vast majority of cases, you'll be installing from a local CD-ROM drive, over an existing Windows 3.x or Windows 95 installation.

NOTE

If you have a previous version of Windows on your computer, you can install from a DOS prompt, but Microsoft *recommends* installing from within Windows.

Although I don't recommend it, you can choose to install Windows into a directory other than the existing Windows directory. This lets you install a "clean" version of Windows 98, with no settings pulled in from the earlier installation. Although this assures you of having a fresh Registry, and might make you feel safer about trying out the new version, it will be a hassle in the long run. What I *do* recommend is upgrading *over* your existing Windows directory, by which I mean installing into the same directory; typically this would be C:\Windows. Besides, when you install over an existing version of Windows, you are offered the option of saving your old system files, so you can effortlessly revert to the old system if you want. (But be warned that if you're currently running Windows 95 it can take as much as 50 MB of additional space to perform this save, even though it is ultimately compressed to about 10 MB.)

When you opt to install over an existing Windows version (that is, 3.*x* or 95—see the note below about Windows NT), various important settings—such as program INI settings, file locations, program associations, program groups, and so forth—are transferred into your new version. The most important advantage of this approach is that you won't have to install all your applications (such as Microsoft Office) again for Windows 98. (If you install to a separate directory, things get pretty complicated, because with two separate versions of Windows on the same computer, the changes you make in one version don't carry over to the other.)

If you are installing on a computer that has Windows NT on it, read the NT section at the end of this appendix. You cannot install *over* NT, though 98 can coexist *with* NT on the same drive.

Microsoft has done a laudable job of making the Windows 98 installation process pretty painless, thanks to the Setup Wizard, which provides a pleasant question-and-answer interface. It's been made even simpler than in Windows 95 by asking only a few questions up front, and then doing the rest of the work on its own without your intervention. Therefore, I'll spare you the boredom of walking you through *every* step here on paper. Rather, I'll get you going and discuss some of the decisions you'll have to make along the way.

Setup requires approximately 120 MB of hard disk space to complete. Of this, about 45 MB is temporary space used only during setup, and will be freed up again after the installation process is complete.

WARNING

Microsoft strongly suggests that you back up any important existing data and programs before you install Windows 98, just to be safe. Also, be sure to take Setup's advice about making a new Startup disk. Startup disks that you may have created with Windows 95 are not compatible with some features of Windows 98.

Easiest Approach: A Full Upgrade from an Earlier Version of Windows

First off, you'll need to decide whether you are going to install from floppy disks, CD-ROM, or your local area network. I highly recommend using a CD (or networked CD or hard disk if one is available) rather than floppies. It will save you a lot of time and disk swapping. With floppies you have to stay by the computer for close to an hour, plugging in disks (though there's a way to reduce the wait somewhat; see the following Tip). With the other options you can get things going, then take a coffee break while the necessary files are copied in.

Before beginning, make sure you have at least 120 MB of free hard-disk space on the drive you're going to install Windows on. You can use Windows Explorer or File Manager or the DOS **dir** command to check this.

TIP

If you must take the floppy-disk approach, here's a way to make it a little less onerous. If you have *more* than 120 MB of free disk space (this approach requires an additional 1.8 MB per floppy), you can copy all the disks into a directory on your hard disk and then run Setup from there. This will speed up the install-by-floppy version of the process considerably. Just make sure you still have the requisite 120 MB of free space after copying the floppies to the hard disk.

To begin the setup process,

1. Boot your computer into Windows.

2. Insert the CD into the CD-ROM drive, or, if you're going with the floppy approach, insert the first diskette into the appropriate floppy drive.

TIP

As I mentioned earlier, if you're using the CD, the CD-ROM drive needn't be on your local computer. Furthermore, you can install over a local-area network or dial-up connection from a shared directory or drive that contains the CD (or a copy of all of its files). You simply switch to that directory (via File Manager in Windows 3.*x* or Windows Explorer in Windows 95) and run Setup.exe.

3. I recommend you read through two text files that contain last-minute information about Windows 98. These files might provide special tips about your brand of computer or cards, printers, and other accessories. The files are called readme.txt and setup.txt. They can be found on Disk 1 of the floppy set or in the \Win98 directory on the CD-ROM. To read these files, just get to them via the File Manager or Windows Explorer, then double-click on them.

4. If you're in Windows 3.*x*, switch to the File Manager or Program Manager, open the File menu, and choose Run. If you're running Windows 95, go to Start ➤ Run. Then enter whichever of the following commands is appropriate for your circumstance (i.e., depending on whether you're installing from a CD-ROM or floppy):

- If installing from a CD, enter **d:\win95\setup**

- If installing from a floppy, enter **a:setup**

(You may have to replace a: or d: in the above statements with the appropriate drive letter for your machine.) Alternatively, in File Manager or Windows Explorer you can look around for setup.exe and double-click on it. In a few seconds you'll be greeted with a fancy blue screen and some directions about installation (as in Figure A.1).

NOTE

If you install from the DOS prompt instead of from Windows, you will have more questions to answer than the ones you're asked from this series of screens, relating to your choice for the destination directory for Windows and concerning which components to install. If you're interested in this approach, see the section below, "Installing to a Fresh Disk or New Directory."

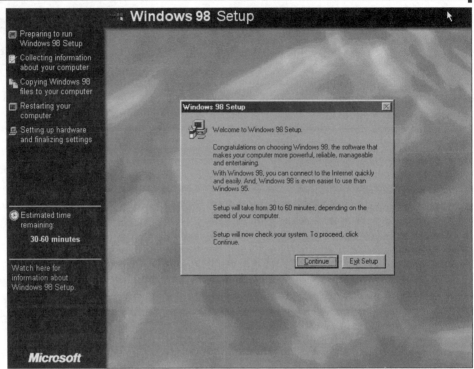

5. Click on Continue to let Setup check out your computer. If you have too little disk space, you'll be alerted.

   • You'll also be alerted to quit other programs if they are running. This is because Setup might bomb, in which case any work you have open in those programs could be lost. Switch to any program in which you have open work, save the work, close the program, and switch back to Setup.

6. Next, you'll see a license agreement. If you agree to the terms, click on Yes, then click on Next.

7. Setup now checks out what hardware is in your computer, and initializes the system's Registry file. It will check for installed components if you are upgrading from a previous version of Windows, and it will check to see that you have

enough hard disk space. Assuming there is enough disk space (you checked for that earlier, didn't you?), you won't see any error messages about that. If you do, see the "Removing Uninstall Files to Free up Disk Space" section later in this appendix.

You'll also be asked at this point if you want to save your "system files." This is so that you can uninstall Windows 98 if it doesn't work, or if you decide you don't like it, or if for some other reason you want to be able to go back to your old operating system. (See the "Reverting to the Previous Operating System" section later in this appendix.) Click on Yes or No. If in doubt, click on Yes, then Next.

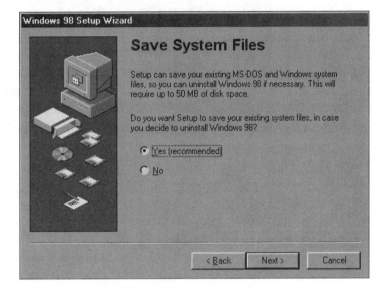

8. Your current system files will be backed up to a hidden, compressed file. If doing that would leave too little space for installation of Windows 98, you'll be alerted and given the option of skipping the backup in order to save disk space.

9. Next you're asked something about "channels," a question which pertains to using the Internet. For now, just click on the country you are in, and then click on Next. (Scroll the list if necessary.) Don't worry now about what this box is asking you; you'll learn about channels later. (It's covered in the chapter "Using the Active Desktop.")

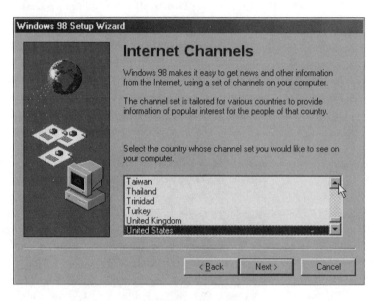

10. At this point Setup offers the opportunity to create an emergency startup disk. This is for starting your computer in case the hard disk is damaged or some system files get lost or corrupted. Since these are problems that could happen to even the best of machines, it's a good idea to make such a disk and keep it in a readily accessible drawer near your computer. This disk is also necessary for uninstalling Windows 98 in case the installation bombs. Just read the screen, then click on Next. Setup creates the list of files that will be put on the startup disk, but it doesn't make the disk yet.

11. You'll be prompted to insert a floppy disk in the disk drive and click on OK to make the disk. Anything on the floppy disk will be erased, so don't use one with something important on it. You can skip this procedure by clicking on Cancel, but I don't recommend it.

   • For reasons given earlier, it's a very good idea to proceed with the creation of the startup disk now. However, if you don't have a floppy with you, you cancel this process for now and continue with the rest of the installation. You can always return to Setup at some other time (even after you've been using Windows 98 for months) to make a startup disk later.

12. Now you'll move on to the main stage of the installation process: the copying of files from the source to your hard disk. This is the portion that takes the most time. Click on Next to start this process. A status bar keeps you abreast of the progress of the file copying operation.

At this point your computer will reboot. Remove the floppy disk, if you haven't already, and let the computer restart. If nothing happens for an extended period, you may have to turn the machine off and then on again. It will pick up where it left off.

Upon restarting, a Windows 98 screen appears with blue clouds on it, and the words "Getting ready to run Windows for the first time." This screen may stay there a *long time* (like 15 minutes or more) and your hard disk may sound like a garbage disposal (lots of activity), but that's okay. Really. Setup is doing some major housekeeping, and possibly defragmenting your hard disk. Just sit tight.

NOTE

I've actually had to sit for 20 minutes while waiting for Windows to do its initial house-cleaning. As long as the hard disk light is still lighting up, or you hear hard disk activity, all is well. Don't despair unless everything goes silent for multiple minutes.

Now you're in the phase in which hardware drivers are installed. Plug-and-Play devices are detected first, and then older, non Plug-and-Play hardware is detected.

Then the system may reboot again in order to load the hardware drivers it just set up. Devices such as PCMCIA cards should initialize. Again, if the system hangs (nothing happens for a long period of time), turn the computer off and on again using the power switch.

Next, a number of other things are adjusted:

- Control Panel options are set up.
- Programs on the Start menu are set up.
- Windows Help is installed.
- MS-DOS program settings are adjusted.
- Applications are set to start faster.
- Some system configuration is optimized.

The last activity, updating system settings, can take a bit of time, like five to ten minutes. But a progress bar lets you know how it's going. A few files may be copied from the CD at this time, so make sure the CD is still available.

Again the system restarts. The blue clouds will appear. It may take a couple of minutes for the Windows Desktop to appear. If you were updating from a previous version of

Windows, you should see the same Desktop background or wallpaper you had before. You'll be prompted to enter your user name and password.

> **TIP**
>
> You may choose a user name and password now and enter it if you like. Remember the password for the next time you log into Windows 98.

After that, the computer may even restart one more time. Once it does, you're up and running. Turn to Chapter 1 to begin learning what's new and exciting about Windows 98. I hope you enjoy the book!

Installing to a Fresh Disk or New Directory

You may prefer to install Windows 98 into a new directory for one of three reasons:

- You have no version of Windows on the machine.

- *Or* you have an existing version of Windows on the machine, but want to keep that version and set up Windows 98 too. Then, by changing directory names or using some third-party utility program such as Partition Magic or BootCom, you can choose which version boots up. (This option is for confident, advanced users.)

- *Or* you want to control what components of Windows get installed. When you install to a new directory you have many more options than when upgrading over an existing installation.

To control the destination directory, you must (1) run Setup from a DOS prompt, and (2) boot in such a way as to have access to the CD-ROM drive, or, if you're installing across a network, to the network drive. If you have Windows 95 on the machine, the best way to do this is to create a Windows 95 emergency startup disk and boot from that. (To create this disk, go to Control Panel ➢ Add/Remove Programs ➢ Startup Disk.) If you had a CD-ROM drive available to you when you created the startup disk, it should have CD driver support files on them. Once you've booted to DOS, switch to the Setup source disk and run setup.exe.

When running Setup from DOS, ScanDisk runs first, checking the hard disk media. Assuming that all is okay (see the following section if it's not), exit ScanDisk by typing X (for Exit) when prompted. Setup will proceed, temporarily in character mode, then in a GUI mode with graphics, blue background, and mouse functionality.

After accepting the terms of the license agreement, you'll be given the option of choosing a hard disk directory for your Windows 98 installation. The default will be the existing Windows directory if there is one, but you can create a different directory at this point by typing a name for it. Next, you'll see a series of screens asking for your input or verification concerning the following tasks:

- Choose which set of Windows 98 components to install: Typical, Portable, Compact, or Custom (your choice).
- Provide your name and company name.
- Select specific components.
- Provide or verify your network ID: computer name, workgroup, and workstation description.
- Verify your computer settings: Keyboard, Language, Regional Variants, and User Interface (Windows 98 or 3.1).
- Choose your Internet Channels. (You can simply choose the country at this point.)
- Create a Windows 98 Emergency Startup disk.

The rest of the installation will go as explained in the previous section.

If you have a situation that requires additional setup options—for example, you may be a LAN administrator and want remote setup capabilities—refer to the Microsoft Windows 98 Resource Kit.

Finding and Fixing Hard-Disk Problems during Installation

The Setup program automatically runs ScanDisk to check for problems on your hard disk before proceeding. If it finds problems on your hard disk, the setup process won't continue until they are fixed. It's also possible that you'll see a message during a later stage of the setup process that says you have to run ScanDisk to fix the problems. This section offers a couple of approaches to run ScanDisk most effectively.

The MS-DOS–based version of ScanDisk that Setup runs may detect long-filename errors, but it can't correct them. These errors will not prevent Setup from proceeding, but once it completes, you should run the new Windows version of ScanDisk from within Windows 98 to correct these errors.

1. Exit from the Setup program (and quit Windows if it's running).
2. Boot to a DOS prompt that offers access to the drive you're installing from.

3. Insert the CD (or floppy Setup Disk 1) into the drive, and from a DOS prompt, type the following:

`d:scandisk.exe /all`

(replacing the "d:" with the letter for the drive that contains the setup disk; for example, "a:" if you're working with a floppy).

4. Follow the instructions on your screen to fix any problems that ScanDisk finds.

5. Run Setup again (from Windows if it's available on your machine; otherwise, run it from a DOS prompt).

TIP

If you have problems or questions about Setup that are not covered in this appendix, check out the file called `setup.txt` on the CD or your floppy disks. On the CD you'll find it in the `readme` directory.

Reverting to the Previous Operating System

Assuming you opted during your Windows 98 setup to save your previous version's system files, you can revert to that version of Windows in case of a failed or unappreciated installation of Windows 98. (For exceptions to the "Saving System Files" scenario, see the sidebar nearby.)

To uninstall Windows 98 and completely restore your system to its previous versions of MS-DOS and Windows 3.x or Windows 95, follow these steps:

1. Choose Start ➢ Settings ➢ Control Panel.

2. Double-click Add/Remove Programs.

3. On the Install/Uninstall tab, click Windows 98, and then click Remove.

If you can't even get to the Start menu to begin the steps above (because of problems starting Windows 98), use your startup disk to start your computer and, from a DOS prompt, type **a: UNINSTAL** and press Enter. Here are a few notes to be mindful of when running `Uninstal`:

- The uninstall program needs to shut down Windows 98. If your computer starts to run Windows 98 again on reboot, try restarting it again and this time quickly pressing F8 when you see the message "Starting Windows 98." (Note, though, that you might only have a fraction of a second to do this, depending on how fast your machine is. Another approach that may work, depending on your computer, is to hold down the Shift key during the bootup process.) Then choose Command Prompt Only and run Uninstal from this command prompt.

If you've misplaced your startup disk but can get to the DOS prompt, you can run Uninstal from the hard disk instead. There should be a copy of the Uninstal program in your Windows directory on the hard disk.

- If you saved your files on a drive other than C, you can use the /w option to specify the drive where the files are located. For example, if your system files were saved to drive E during installation, type **Uninstal /w e:** to access them on that drive.

Why You Can't Always Save Your System Files

The option of saving your system files for a future uninstall is not always offered during setup. Here are some situations where Setup does not offer the option:

- You are upgrading over an earlier version of Windows 98 itself.
- *Or* you are installing to a new directory (in which case you don't need to *revert* to your previous version; instead, you can simply boot to the previous version's directory to run that version).
- *Or* you are running a version of MS-DOS earlier than 5.0 (in which case your system is automatically updated with the version of DOS that is used in Windows 98).

In most other situations, you are given the option to save your system files. When you choose this option, Setup saves your system files in a hidden, compressed file on your local hard drive. (They cannot be saved to a network drive or a floppy disk.) If you have multiple local drives, you will be able to select the one you want to use.

If you are not in one of the above exception situations but you see a message during setup about not being able to save your system files, refer to the "Setup Error Messages" section of the setup.txt file in the CD's readme directory or on the floppy installation disk.

Removing Uninstall Files to Free Up Disk Space

If you want to free up an additional 6 to 10 MB of disk space, you can remove the Uninstall files by following the steps below. Please note, however, that without the Uninstall files, you will no longer be able to uninstall Windows 98. In short, save this operation until you're sure you're going to keep Windows 98.

Here are the steps for removing the Uninstall files. Note that Windows 98 must be running to perform this operation.

1. Choose Start ➢ Settings ➢ Control Panel.

2. Double-click Add/Remove Programs.

3. On the Install/Uninstall tab, click Old Windows/MS-DOS System Files, and then click Remove.

Installing onto a Compressed Drive

If you have used compression software to compress your hard disk, or if a host drive or partition for your startup drive is compressed, you may get a message during setup that there is not enough space on the host partition of the compressed drive. If you get this message, you should free up some space on the specified drive, and then run Setup again. Note that if the drive was compressed with SuperStor or Stacker, you'll have to decompress the drive and remove the compression program before you can install Windows 98. If you used Microsoft DriveSpace, you were smart: you don't have to decompress in order to free up extra space—you just tell it to free up the space.

Here are some other steps to freeing up space for your installation:

- If you are setting up Windows on a compressed drive, try setting it up on an uncompressed drive if possible.

- Delete any unneeded files on your host partition.

- If you are running Windows 3.1 and have a permanent swap file, try making it smaller. In Control Panel, click the 386 Enhanced icon, and then click Virtual Memory. Then modify the size of your swap file.

- Use your disk compression software to free up some space on the host drive for the compressed drive.

And don't forget to check out the following subsections concerning particular compression programs.

WARNING

If you create a startup disk during setup, make sure you do not use a compressed disk for the startup disk.

SuperStor or Stacker Compressed Drive

If you have compressed your hard disk by using SuperStor, Setup may not be able to find your startup drive and install Windows 98. If you get a message about this during setup, uncompress your disk and then remove SuperStor, and then run Setup again.

Windows 98 will not run on a Stacker-compressed hard drive. If you currently have Stacker v. 4.1 installed on your computer, uninstall Stacker before you upgrade to Windows 98.

DriveSpace or DoubleSpace Compressed Drive

1. Quit Windows and get to a DOS prompt.

2. Run Drvspace.exe or Dblspace.exe (probably in your DOS or Windows directory).

3. Select the compressed drive on which you want to free up some space.

4. On the Drive menu, select Change Size.

NOTE

If you notice a discrepancy between the amount of free space reported by Setup and the amount of space you *think* is available on your host drive, it may be because Windows is reserving some space for a swap file.

XtraDrive Compression

If you have compressed your hard disk by using XtraDrive and you are upgrading over a previous version of Windows, you'll have to turn off XtraDrive's *write cache* before doing the install. Here's how to do that:

1. Exit Windows and get to DOS.

2. Run Vmu.exe (XtraDrive's Volume Maintenance Utility).

3. Click Advanced Options, and then press Enter.

4. Set the EMS cache size to 0.

5. Set the Conventional cache size to 1 (the minimum).

6. Set Allow Write Caching to **No**.

7. At the confirmation prompt, click Yes. You will see a message saying that you must restart your computer for the changes to take effect.

8. Quit the Volume Maintenance Utility, and then restart your computer.

9. Start Windows, and then run Windows 98 Setup again.

How to Install Windows 98 to a Machine Running Windows NT

Although you can install Windows 98 to a machine that is already running Windows NT, you must install it to a separate partition—you cannot install 98 *over* NT, or vice versa. (You may remember that you could install NT over Windows 3.*x* and share settings, associations, and so forth; Windows 98 does not work this way.) As a result, though you can have NT and Windows 98 on the same computer and boot either operating system as you like, they won't share INI settings, installed applications, and other settings. This may change in the future, but in the meantime, it's simply an annoyance, because it means you'll have to install most applications twice—once for NT and once for Windows 98.

If you're configured to multi-boot MS-DOS and Windows NT Boot to MS-DOS, and then run Windows 98 Setup from either MS-DOS or Windows 95. You will not be able to install Windows 98 to a partition with a shared Windows 95/Windows NT configuration; you will need to install Windows 98 to a different partition.

If you're not configured to multi-boot MS-DOS and Windows NT You must first configure your computer to multi-boot MS-DOS and Windows NT, and then follow the instructions above.

If you were planning to boot to MS-DOS from a floppy disk and then run Windows 98 Setup This approach permits you to install Windows 98 as you wish; however, you will no longer be able to boot to Windows NT. You can *restore* Windows NT, however, by booting from the Windows NT boot/repair disk and then selecting the Repair option.

NOTE

Windows 98 Setup will not run on OS/2. You need to boot to MS-DOS and then run Setup from the MS-DOS prompt. For more about installing over OS/2 see the setup.txt file on floppy disk 1 or in the readme directory on the CD.

INDEX

Note to the Reader: First-level entries are in **bold**. Page numbers in **bold** indicate the principal discussion of a topic or the definition of a term. Page numbers in *italic* indicate illustrations.

Numbers and Symbols

10Base-2 (thin Ethernet) networks, 1021–1022, *1021*, 1024
10Base-T (twisted-pair Ethernet) networks, 1022–1024, *1022*, **1025**
32-bit applications
  upgrading, 47–49
  writing for multiple platforms, 48
100Base-T (Fast Ethernet) networks, 1024–1026
➢ (arrows) in menus, 83
, (commas) in phone numbers for modem connections, 518
• (dots) in menus, 83
… (ellipses) in menus, 83
– (minus sign)
  in newsgroups, 677
  in Windows Explorer, 445
( ) (parentheses) in Scientific Calculator, 883, 887
+ (plus sign)
  in newsgroups, 677
  in Windows Explorer, 443–444
' or " (quotes or double quotes) in Web search engines, 618

A

access rights. *See* permissions
Accessibility Options applet, 16, 235, **238–247**. *See also* Control Panel
  defined, **16**, **235**, **238–239**, *238*
  Display tab, **241–243**, *242*
  FilterKeys options, 239–240
  General tab, 246–247, *246*
  High Contrast options, 241–243, *242*
  Intellimouse or wheel mouse support, 245
  Keyboard tab, *238*, **239–240**
  Mouse tab, **243–245**, *243*, *244*
  ShowSounds options, 240–241, *241*
  Sound tab, **240–241**, *241*
  SoundSentry options, 240–241, *241*
  StickyKeys options, 239–240
  ToggleKeys options, 239–240

accessories, 384–424, 871–898. *See also* applications; HyperTerminal; Kodak Imaging; Paint; System Tools; utilities; WordPad
  Calculator, **879–888**
    copying results from other documents into, 882–883
    copying results to other documents, 881
    defined, **879**, *880*
    entering numbers in scientific notation, 885–886
    grouping terms with parentheses, 883, 887
    Help, 880
    Inv and Hyp options in Scientific Calculator, 885
    keyboard shortcuts, 882
    memory keys, 881
    new features, 880
    performing calculations, 880–881
    Scientific Calculator, **884–888**, *884*
    square roots and percentages, 883–884
    Standard Calculator, 880, *881*
    starting, 879
    statistical calculations, 881, 887–888
    using different number bases, 886–887
  CD Player, **385**, **403–410**
    cataloging CDs, 408–409, *408*
    creating play lists, 409
    defined, **385**, **403–404**
    display options, 406–407
    play controls, 405–406, 407–408
    playing CDs from play lists, 410
    setting preferences, 410
    starting, 404
  Character Map, **344**, **888–893**
    ANSI versus IBM character sets and, 891–893
    defined, **888**, *889*
    entering special characters from the keyboard, 343–344, 890–891
    entering special characters in non-Windows applications, 891–893
    inserting symbols, 344
    Keystroke option, 890–891
    running, 889–890
  Clipboard Viewer, **208–211**
    changing the view format, 209–211, *210*
    defined, **208**
    viewing Clipboard contents, 209

Clipbook Viewer, **209**
DVD Player, **385**, **386–392**
   defined, **385**
   DVD defined, **386–387**
   ending DVD sessions, 392
   purchasing and installing DVD drives, 387–388
   running, 388–390
   selecting chapters and titles, 390–391
   selecting language and subtitles, 391–392
Media Player, **384**, **397–399**
MIDI Mapper, **385–386**
Notepad, **872–879**
   adding headers and footers, 878–879
   creating documents, 874
   defined, **872**
   entering date and time, 877
   entering and editing text, 875–877, *876*
   finding text, 877–878
   limitations of, 873
   margin settings, 878
   navigating from the keyboard, 877
   opening files, 874–875
   opening files in WordPad from, 875
   printing files, 879
   running, 873–874, *874*
   text files defined, **872–873**
   Word Wrap option, 875–876, *876*
overview of, 871
Phone Dialer, **492**, **895–898**
   defined, **492**, **895**
   placing calls, 897–898, *898*
   programming the Speed Dial list, 896–897, *897*
   starting, 895–896, *896*
Sound Recorder, **384–385**, **399–403**
   defined, **384–385**, **399**
   editing sounds, 402–403
   playing sound files, 399–400
   recording sounds, 400–402, *401*
TV Viewer, **17**, **411–424**
   adding favorite channels to the toolbar, 421–422
   adding and removing channels manually, 416, *416*
   avoiding Channel 1, 417, *417*
   Broadcast Architecture and, 411, 423
   defined, **17**, **411–412**
   finding shows, 418–419
   finding shows by category, 419
   future of, 423–424
   how TV Viewer works, 412–413
   keyboard shortcuts, 422–423
   online Help, 416
   reading Program Guide information, 414–415, *415*,
     420, *420*
   remote controls, 422
   scrolling the display, 417–418, *418*
   setting reminders, 420–421, *421*
   starting, 413–415, *413*, *414*, *415*
   system requirements, 411
Volume Control, **385**, **893–895**

Active Channels, 609–616
   Channel Definition Format (CDF) files, 610
   defined, **609–610**
   displaying Channel bar, 613, *613*
   subscribing to, 610, 614–616, *615*
   viewing, **610–613**
     from Channel bar, 612–613, *612*
     in Channel Viewer, 610–612, *611*
     in Internet Explorer, 610
Active Desktop, 183, 697–729. *See also* Desktop
   adding content, **700–701**, **709–716**
     Active Desktop Gallery website, 713–714
     adding items, 711–712, *712*
     deleting Desktop components, 713
     installing Microsoft Investor Tracker, 714–715
     installing Web Search component, 715–716
     listing items added to Active Desktop, 709, *709*
     overview of, 700–701
     screen resolution and, 712
     turning Desktop components on and off, 710
     using Web pages as backgrounds, 712–713
   advantages and disadvantages of, 703
   application windows, 705
   browsing resources with Windows Explorer, **719–729**
     browsing the Internet, 722–723, *723*
     browsing in Web view, 723–726, *724*, *725*
     browsing your computer, 720–722, *721*
     customizing folders, 726–729, *727*, *728*
     defined, **719**
     merging the personal computer with the networked
       terminal, 719–720
     rearranging columns in Details view, 729
     Thumbnails view, 724–726, *725*
   Channel Screen Saver, **716–718**
     defined, **716**
     running, 716–717
     setting up, 717–718, *718*
   defined, **697–699**, *698*
   DESKTOP.HTT file and, 710
   Display Properties dialog box, 709, *709*
   Favorites menu, 704
   Find People dialog box, 704
   hovering, **699**
   HTML Web objects, 705–706
   icons, 701, 705
   passwords, 698
   refreshing, 706
   single-clicking
     versus double clicking, 699
     selecting blocks of items with a single-click, 699–700
     switching between single-click and double-click
       modes, 700, *701*
   Start button menu, 704–705
   Taskbar, 703–704, 707
   toolbars, **703–704**, **706–708**
     Address toolbar, 704
     displaying other toolbars, 707
     manipulating, 707–708

Quick Launch toolbar, 703–704, 705, 707
Show Desktop button, 704, 705
user profiles for, 698
View menu options, 183
work area, **700–703**, *702*
ActiveMovie architecture, 17
Add New Hardware applet, **235**, **247–255**, **385**, **1073–1075**.
See also Control Panel
defined, **235**, **247–248**
installing modems, 1073–1075, *1074*
installing multimedia drivers, 385
running the Install Hardware Wizard, 248–250, *249*
telling the Wizard what hardware you have, 250–254, *251*
what to do if your hardware is not listed, 254–255
Add Printer Wizard, 298, 302–306
Add/Remove Programs applet, **235**, **255–258**. *See also*
Control Panel
defined, **235**, **255**
installing applications, 255–256, *256*, *257*
removing or uninstalling applications, 257–258
adding. *See also* entering; inserting; installing
background color to Outlook Express e-mail, 651
channels manually to TV Viewer, 416, *416*
conferencing information to Outlook Express address
books, 658, *659*
content to the Active Desktop, **700–701**, **709–716**
Active Desktop Gallery website, 713–714
adding items, 711–712, *712*
deleting Desktop components, 713
installing Microsoft Investor Tracker, 714–715
installing Web Search component, 715–716
listing items added to Active Desktop, 709, *709*
overview of, 700–701
screen resolution and, 712
turning Desktop components on and off, 710
using Web pages as backgrounds, 712–713
digital IDs or certificates to Outlook Express address books,
658–659, *660*
favorite channels to TV Viewer toolbar, 421–422
fonts, 353–356, *354*, *355*
headers and footers in Notepad, 878–879
to Internet Explorer Favorites menu, 591, *592*
local printers, 298, 306–309, *307*, *308*
network printers, 298, 302–306, *303*, *304*, *305*
notes to Oultook Express address books, 657, *658*
options to Start button, 143–145, *144*, *145*
options to Start button menus, 149–152, *149*, *150*, *152*
pictures to Outlook Express e-mail, 649–651, *650*
signatures to Outlook Express e-mail, 648–649
toolbars to Taskbar, 146–148, *147*
address books in Outlook Express, 653–664
adding notes to entries, 657, *658*
creating, 654–655, *654*
creating groups, 660–661, *661*
customizing the Address Book window, 662
defined, **653**
entering business-related information, 657, *657*
entering conferencing information, 658, *659*

entering, deleting, and viewing digital IDs or certificates,
658–659, *660*
entering home-related information, 656–657, *656*
entering personal information, 655–656
importing from other mail programs, 653
obtaining digital IDs, 659, 690
opening, 654
printing, 664
searching directory services, 662–663
Address toolbar
on the Active Desktop, 704
in Internet Explorer, 584, 587
on the Taskbar, 146–148, *147*
ADSL Internet connections, 555–556
advanced compression settings in DriveSpace, 952–953,
952
Advanced Configuration and Power Interface (ACPI),
17–18, **55**, **101**
Advanced Connection Settings dialog box, 500, *500*
Advanced Download Options dialog box, 605–606, *606*
Advanced Options dialog box in ScanDisk, 918–923
compressed drive options, 921–922
Cross-linked Files options, 919–920
Display Summary options, 918–919
file-checking options, 921
Lost File Fragments options, 920
Report MS-DOS Mode Name Length Errors option, 923
Surface Scan options, 922–923
Advanced Port Settings dialog box, 499–500
Advanced View menu settings, 179–182, *179*
Airbrush tool in Paint, 841
alert boxes, 84, *85*
aliases. *See also* shortcuts
defined, **168**
in e-mail and news accounts, 637
aligning paragraphs in WordPad, 792–793
Alt key
+ Enter (opening objects), 312
+ hyphen (-) or spacebar, 77
+ Tab (switching between applications), 140
entering special characters, 343–344, 890–891
AltaVista search engine, 619, 623
America Online Internet connections, 560–561
annotating images in Kodak Imaging, 862–866
Annotation toolbar overview, 862–863
making annotations permanent, 863–864
setting annotation properties, 864–866
ANSI character set, 891–893
ANSI terminal-emulation setting, 529
APIs
API calls and operating-system primitives, 35–37
TAPI (Telephony API), 491–492, 1070
Win32, Win32c, and Win32s APIs, 48–49
Apple Macintosh operating system, 7–8
application layer in OSI reference model, 999
application windows
in Active Desktop, 705
defined, **68**, *69*

application-initiated remote connections, 1079–1080
applications, 105–140. *See also* accessories; utilities
    Add/Remove Programs applet, **235, 255–258**
        defined, **235, 255**
        installing applications, 255–256, *256, 257*
        removing or uninstalling applications, 257–258
    compatibility of with Windows 98, 106
    DOS applications
        copying text and graphics to the Clipboard from,
          200–203, *201*
        default printer setting and, 317
        DOS session property settings, 131–136, *135*
        entering special characters in, 891–893
        FAT32 file system and, 973
        graphics mode, 201
        pasting from the Clipboard into, 206–207, *207*
        PIF settings, 133–136, *135*
        printing from, 296
        running, 35–40, 107–108, 127–130, *129, 130*
        and the virtual DOS machine (VDM), 38, 133
    installing, **255–256,** *256, 257*
    Intellimouse or wheel mouse-aware applications, 245
    internal Clipboards in, 204
    printing from, **317–319**
    running, **106–127**
        from batch files, 137
        by right-clicking the Desktop, 124–126, *125*
        from a document, 123–124, *123,* 126–127, *127*
        DOS applications, 35–40, 107–108, 127–130, *129,*
          130
        DOS session property settings, 131–136, *135*
        from File Manager, 114, 117–119, *118*
        from MS-DOS Prompt, 107–108, 129–136, *130, 135*
        from My Computer icon, 111–114, *112, 114*
        overview of, 106–107
        from Program Manager, 119–120, *120*
        remotely, 1076
        shell programs, 40–41
        from the Start button, 107–110, *109*
        from Start button Find option, 120–122, *122*
        from Windows Explorer, 114–117, *115, 116,* 456
    sharing in NetMeeting, 736, **759–761,** *760*
    shortcuts
        copying files and folders to floppy disk shortcuts, 176
        creating, **166–169, 457**
        defined, **136, 144**
        property sheets for, 434–435, *434*
    switching between, **137–140,** *139*
    and upgrading to Windows 98, **34–40**
        API calls and operating-system primitives, 35–37
        applications versus utilities, 34–35
        DOS applications and the virtual DOS machine (VDM),
          38, 133
        I/O permission bitmaps in Intel processors, 37
        running DOS applications and utilities, 35–40
        running shell programs, 40–41
        running Windows 3.x and 95 utilities, 41–46, *42*
        Win32, Win32c, and Win32s APIs, 48–49
        Windows 3.x applications and .ini files, 46
        Windows 32-bit applications, 47–49
    versus utilities, **34–35**
    Windows 3.x applications and .ini files, 46
    Windows 32-bit applications, 47–49
    writing 32-bit applications for multiple platforms, 48
arranging file and folder icons and listings in folders,
    177–179
arrow keys, HyperTerminal terminal-emulation settings for,
    528
arrows (➤) in menus, 83
art. *See* graphics
ASCII files. *See* text files
assigning sounds to Windows events, 394–396, *395*
associations, 124
AT&T Worldnet Internet connections, 560–561
attaching files to Outlook Express e-mail, 651–652
Attributes dialog box in Paint, 831–834
audio settings for NetMeeting, 751–754
Audio Tuning Wizard, 742, *743,* 750
autoexec.bat file, 11
AutoHide feature for Taskbar, 138–139
AutoInstalled fonts, 365
automatic ScanDisk execution after improper Shutdown,
    16, 916
auto-mount settings in DriveSpace, 953
avoiding Channel 1 in TV Viewer, 417, *417*
.AWB files, 858

B

Back command or button in Internet Explorer, 586–587
backgrounds
    background colors in Outlook Express e-mail, 651
    background colors in Paint, 835, 836–837
    Web pages as backgrounds in Active Desktop, 712–713
backing up
    before installing Windows 98, 1110
    Outlook Express e-mail messages, 641
backscroll buffers in HyperTerminal, 529–530, 540
Backspace key
    deleting text in WordPad, 785
    navigating folder windows with, 113, 458
Backup utility, 16, 914, 924–938
    backup and restore option settings, 938, *938*
    defined, **914**
    error messages, 932
    finishing backups, 931–932
    installing, 925
    new features, 16, 925
    overview of, 924–925
    restoring files from backups, **933–938**
        without the Wizard, 937–938, *937*
        with the Wizard, 934–936, *936*
    running, **925–931**
        overview of, 925–926

without the Wizard, 930–931, *930*
via the Wizard, 926–929, *926, 927*
Tools menu options, 932–933
batch files, running applications from, 137
baud rates, 515
BigBook search engine, 625
binary files
receiving with HyperTerminal, 544–545, 547–548
sending with HyperTerminal, 544–545, 546–547, *547*
bitmapped fonts, 336, 338–339, *338,* **346,** 353, 360
bitmapped graphics, 826–827
bits per second (bps), 515
black-and-white option in Paint accessory, 833–834
body fonts, 352
bold text in WordPad, 797, 798, *799*
boot failures, 1105–1106
Box tool in Paint, 842–843
bps (bits per second), 515
Broadcast Architecture, 17, 411, 423
Browse Folders as Follows options in View menu, 183
browsing. *See also* Internet Explorer
for newsgroups messages in Outlook Express, 677
off-line with Internet Explorer, 588–590, *589*
resources with Windows Explorer, **719–729**
browsing the Internet, 722–723, *723*
browsing in Web view, 723–726, *724, 725*
browsing your computer, 720–722, *721*
customizing folders, 726–729, *727, 728*
defined, **719**
merging the personal computer with the networked terminal, 719–720
rearranging columns in Details view, 729
Thumbnails view, 724–726, *725*
updated website subscriptions, 597–599
updated website subscriptions off-line, 598
with Web search engines, 618
Brush tool in Paint, 838–840, *839*
bulleting paragraphs in WordPad, 795–796
bus architectures for computers, 1028–1029
bus network topologies, 1021–1022, *1021*
business-related features, 21–22
business-related information in Outlook Express address books, 657, *657*
buying. *See* purchasing

C

C-2 security features in Windows NT, 28–29
cables, 1016–1020. *See also* networks
cable connections using HyperTerminal, 538, *539*
cable modem Internet connections, 555–556
coaxial cables, 1016–1017, *1017*
installing for peer-to-peer networks, 1038–1039
troubleshooting cable problems, 1097–1098
unshielded twisted pair cables (UTP), 1017–1019, *1018*
wireless networks, 1020

Calculator accessory, 879–888
copying results from other documents into, 882–883
copying results to other documents, 881
defined, **879,** *880*
Help, 880
keyboard shortcuts, 882
memory keys, 881
new features, 880
performing calculations, 880–881
Scientific Calculator, **884–888**
defined, **884–885,** *884*
entering numbers in scientific notation, 885–886
grouping terms with parentheses, 883, 887
Inv and Hyp options, 885
statistical calculations, 881, 887–888
using different number bases, 886–887
square roots and percentages, 883–884
Standard Calculator, **880,** *881*
starting, 879
call preferences in modem Properties dialog box, 499, 532
call waiting, disabling, 504
callback feature in Dial-Up Networking, 1085–1086
calling card options in modem Properties dialog box, 504–507, *505, 506*
calling with Phone Dialer, 897–898, *898*
canceling. *See also* deleting
all pending print jobs, 325
website subscriptions, 599
capturing
screen images, 203–204
text with HyperTerminal, 541
carrier-sense multiple access with collision detection (CSMA/CD) networks, 1016
CD Player, 385, 403–410. *See also* accessories; multimedia
cataloging CDs, 408–409, *408*
creating play lists, 409
defined, **385, 403–404**
display options, 406–407
play controls, 405–406, 407–408
playing CDs from play lists, 410
setting preferences, 410
starting, 404
CD writers (CD-R drives), 380–381
.CDF (Channel Definition Format) files, 610
CD-ROM drives, 379–380
cell phones, modems and, 494
certificates
adding, deleting, and viewing in Outlook Express address books, 658–659, *660*
obtaining, 659, 690
challenged user tools. *See* Accessibility Options applet
changing. *See also* editing; setting
Clipboard view format, 209–211, *210*
color settings in Paint, 836
default Internet connection profile, 568–569, *569*
display properties in System Monitor, 975–977
estimated compression ratio in DriveSpace, 951

Internet Explorer start page, 576
screen resolution, 279–281, *280*
shared object permissions and other properties, 471–472
website subscription settings in Favorites menu, 601
Channel 1 in TV Viewer, 417, *417*
Channel bar
defined, **67**
displaying, 613, *613*
viewing Active Channels, 612–613, *612*
Channel Definition Format (CDF) files, 610
Channel Screen Saver, 716–718
defined, **716**
running, 716–717
setting up, 717–718, *718*
Channel Viewer, viewing Active Channels in, 610–612, *611*
channels. *See* Active Channels
chapters in DVD Player, 390–391
character formatting in WordPad, 796–799
bold, italic, and underline text styles, 797, 798, 799
with Fonts dialog box, 797, 799
with Format bar, 775, 797–799
with keyboard shortcuts, 797, 799
overview of, 796–797
as you type, 799
Character Map accessory, 344, 888–893
ANSI versus IBM character sets and, 891–893
defined, **888,** *889*
entering special characters from the keyboard, 342–344, 890–891
entering special characters in non-Windows applications, 891–893
inserting symbols, 344
Keystroke option, 890–891
running, 889–890
chats
chat feature in NetMeeting, 756, *756*
Microsoft Chat, **903–910**
chat features, 908–910, *908*
chatting, 906–908, *906*
defined, **903**
starting, 903–906, *904, 905*
check boxes in dialog boxes, 88
check marks in menus, 83
checking spelling in Outlook Express, 688–689
child windows, 69, *70*
CHKDSK utility, 916
Classic view. *See also* Web view
double-clicking in, 111
selecting files in Windows Explorer, 455–456
switching with Web view, 96–97, *97,* 100
clearing. *See also* deleting
the Clipboard, 213, *214*
tab stops in WordPad, 801
Click Items as Follows options in View menu, 184
clicking the mouse, 63, 111
Client Services for NetWare, 22
client/server networks, 463, 468

clients
defined, **489**
OLE clients, **219**
Clipboard, 60, 197–213. *See also* copying and pasting; cutting and pasting; Object Linking and Embedding
capturing screen images, 203–204
clearing, 213, *214*
Clipboard Viewer accessory, **208–211**
changing the view format, 209–211, *210*
defined, **208**
viewing Clipboard contents, 209
Clipbook Viewer accessory, **209**
copying text and graphics from DOS applications, 200–203, *201*
defined, **60, 197**
how the Clipboard works, 197–198
importing graphics into WordPad from, 808, *808*
internal Clipboards in applications, 204
networks and, 211
versus Object Linking and Embedding, **213–214**
in Paint, 849–850
pasting into DOS applications, 206–207, *207*
pasting into Windows applications, 204–205, *205*
retrieving stored Clipboard file contents, 212
right-click shortcuts for Cut, Copy, and Paste commands, 207, *208*
saving Clipboard contents to files, 211–212
selecting, copying, and cutting in Windows applications, 198–200, *199, 200*
sharing Clipboard contents in NetMeeting, 761–762
using Clipboard contents multiple times, **787**
Close buttons, 71, *72*
.CLP files, 211
coaxial cables, 1016–1017, *1017*
colors
color depth of monitors, 383–384
in Outlook Express e-mail, 651
in Paint, **833–837, 851, 854–855**
creating custom colors, **854–855**
defined, **824**
foreground and background colors defined, **835**
inverting colors, 851, *852*
selecting color schemes, 835–836
selecting colors with Eyedropper tool, 837
setting color or black-and-white option, 833–834
setting foreground and background colors, 836–837
tearing off or turning off Color Box, 829–830, *830*
viewing and changing color settings, 836
COM ports, 521
combining keywords in Web search engines, 617
Comic Chat. *See* Microsoft Chat
command buttons in dialog boxes, 88–89
commands. *See* menus
commas (,) in phone numbers for modem connections, 518
communications features, 487–492. *See also* Active Desktop; HyperTerminal; Internet connections; Internet Explorer; Outlook Express

fax software, 490, 491
history of, 488–489
Microsoft Exchange/Windows Messaging, 489, 490, 491
Microsoft Outlook, 489, 490
modems, **236, 492–507**
    baud rate versus bits per second (bps), **515**
    cell phones and, 494
    defined, **492, 514–515**
    Dial-Up Networking support for, 1072
    installing, **494–497,** *495,* **514–515**
    internal and external modems, PCMCIA cards, 493–494
    modem speeds, 493
    multiple modem or modem aggregation support, 497
    null-modem cable connections, **538,** *539*
    purchasing, **492–494**
    setting up for Dial-Up Networking, **1073–1075,** *1074*
    sharing Internet modem connections, 1088
    speaker volume setting in HyperTerminal, 532
    Unimodem driver, 494–495, 1071
NetMeeting, **733–765**
    audio settings, 751–754
    Audio Tuning Wizard, 742, *743,* 750
    chat feature, **756,** *756*
    defined, **733–734**
    dialing history, 764
    downloading, 741
    file transfers, 762–763, *763*
    full duplex sound cards and, 742, 753
    hanging up, 751
    installing, **740–741,** *740*
    Internet Locator Service (ILS) and, 745
    microphone settings, 752–753
    mouse control, 761
    multipoint data conferencing and, 736, 737
    new features, 734–736, *735*
    Object Linking and Embedding and, 763
    saving Whiteboard work, 758
    screen resolutions and, 751
    sending e-mail, 764–765
    session example, 744–751, *747, 749*
    setting up, **741–744,** *742, 743, 744*
    sharing Clipboard contents, 761–762
    sharing documents and applications, 736, 759–761, *760*
    Speed Dial list, 764, *764*
    standards for, 738, 765
    system requirements, 739–740, 742
    telephone sound quality, 733
    uses for, 736–738
    video settings, 754–755, *755*
    video support, 735–736, *735,* 739
    websites about, 741, 744, 765
    Whiteboard feature, **757–758,** *758*
new features, 489–490
overview of, 487–488
Phone Dialer accessory, **492, 895–898**
    defined, **492, 895**

placing calls, 897–898, *898*
    programming the Speed Dial list, 896–897, *897*
    starting, 895–896, *896*
TAPI (Telephony API), 491–492, 1070
Telephony applet, **237**
compatibility
    of applications with Windows 98, 106
    of DriveSpace with other compression utilities, 942
    of FAT32 file system with DriveSpace, 941, 968–969
    of hardware with FAT32 file system, 969–970
    of modems, 494
compilers, **873**
composing Outlook Express e-mail messages, 643–645, *644*
compressed disk drives. *See also* DriveSpace
    installing Windows 98 on, 1120–1121
Compression Agent utility, 915, 953–956
CompuServe Internet connections, 560–561
computers
    bus architectures, 1028–1029
    rebooting, 61
    reset button, 61
    upgrading for multimedia, 379
    Windows 98 requirements, 49–50
concentrators, **1022**
conferencing. *See also* NetMeeting
    conferencing information in Outlook Express address books, 658, *659*
    multipoint data conferencing, **736, 737**
config.sys file, **11**
Configuration Registry. *See* Registry
configuring Windows 98 for peer-to-peer networks, 1039, *1040*
connecting. *See also* mapping network drives
    via HyperTerminal, **535–539**
        cable connections, 538, *539*
        disconnecting, 537
        making a different connection, 537–538
        overview of, 535–536
        troubleshooting, 536–537
    to Internet service providers (ISPs), 562–564, *563, 564*
    to network drives, 464–465
    to network printers, 314–315
    to newsgroups in Outlook Express, 669–670
connection profiles in Dial-Up Networking
    changing default connection profile, 568–569, *569*
    creating, 566–568, *567, 568*
Connection tab in modem Properties dialog box, 498–500
    Advanced Connection Settings dialog box, 500, *500*
    Advanced Port Settings dialog box, 499–500
    Call Preferences options, 499
    Connection Preferences options, 499
Control boxes, 77, *77*
Control Panel, 233–291. *See also* customizing; Display applet
    Accessibility Options applet, **16, 235, 238–247**
        defined, **16, 235, 238–239,** *238*
        Display tab, **241–243,** *242*
        FilterKeys options, 239–240
        General tab, 246–247, *246*

High Contrast options, 241–243, *242*
Intellimouse or wheel mouse support, 245
Keyboard tab, *238*, **239–240**
Mouse tab, **243–245**, *243, 244*
ShowSounds options, 240–241, *241*
Sound tab, **240–241**, *241*
SoundSentry options, 240–241, *241*
StickyKeys options, 239–240
ToggleKeys options, 239–240
Add New Hardware applet, **235**, **247–255**, **385**,
1073–1075
defined, **235**, **247–248**
installing modems, 1073–1075, *1074*
installing multimedia drivers, 385
running the Install Hardware Wizard, 248–250, *249*
telling the Wizard what hardware you have, 250–254,
251
what to do if your hardware is not listed, 254–255
Add/Remove Programs applet, **235**, **255–258**
defined, **235**, **255**
installing applications, 255–256, *256, 257*
removing or uninstalling applications, 257–258
Date/Time applet, **235**, **258–259**, *259*
Desktop Themes applet, **235**, **260–261**, *260*
Fonts applet, **235**, **353–363**
adding fonts, 353–356, *354, 355*
defined, **235**, **353**
deleting fonts, 361–362, 363
TrueType options, 356–357, *356*
viewing font families, 359
viewing fonts by similarities, 359–361, *360*
viewing and printing examples with font viewer,
357–359, *358*
Game Controllers applet, **235**
Infrared applet, **235**
Internet applet, **235**
Keyboard applet, **236**
Mail applet, **236**
Microsoft Mail Postoffice applet, **236**
Modems applet, **236**
Mouse applet, **236**, **287–291**
defined, **236**, **287**
General tab, 291, *291*
Motion tab, 289–291, *290*
Pointers tab, 288–289, *289*
right-hand and left-hand mouse settings, 287–288,
287
Multimedia applet, **236**
Network applet, **236**
opening, 234–235, *234*
overview of, 233–234
Passwords applet, **236**
PCMCIA applet, **236**
Power Management applet, **236**
Printers applet, **237**
Regional Settings applet, **237**
Sounds applet, **237**, **384**, **392–397**
assigning sounds to Windows events, 394–396, *395*

default directory for sounds, 395
defined, **237**, **384**, **392–393**
loading and saving sound schemes, 396–397
recording or downloading sounds, 393–394
troubleshooting sound problems, 394
System applet, **237**, 248, 385
Telephony applet, **237**
Users applet, **237**
converting
color images to black-and-white in Paint, 834
Drive Converter (FAT32) utility, **17**, **915**, **970–973**
defined, **17**, **915**, **970**
memory shortage error messages, 973
running, 971–972
FAT32 file system to FAT16 file system, 970
copying
calculations from other documents into Calculator,
882–883
Calculator results to other documents, 881
files and folders to and from floppy disks, **171–176**
copying to floppy disk shortcuts, 176
with My Computer, 172–175, *173, 174*
overview of, 171–172
with Send To command, 175, 457
floppy disks, 461–462
between folders, **158–162**, **454–455**, **457**
moving versus copying, 159–160, 458
moving and copying files, 160–162, *161, 162*,
454–455, 457
moving and copying folders, 158, *159*
versus moving, 159–160, 458
screen images into the Clipboard, 203–204
text between documents in WordPad, 804–806, *805*
text and graphics from DOS applications to the Clipboard,
200–203, *201*
text in WordPad, 789
copying and pasting. *See also* Clipboard
Clipboard and, **60**
files and folders, 184–187
into DOS applications, 206–207, *207*
into Windows applications, 204–205, *205*
keyboard shortcuts for, 198
in Paint, 849–850
URLs into Internet Explorer, 587
in Windows applications, 198–200, *199, 200*
cost
of laptop computers, 28
of upgrade and retraining, **25–27**
CPUs. *See* processors
creating
CD play lists in CD Player, 409
custom colors in Paint, 854–855
custom views, 182–184, *183*
documents
in Kodak Imaging, 866–867
in Notepad, 874
from Windows Explorer, 457
in WordPad, 773, *773*, 814

documents in Paint, **831–834**
    setting color or black-and-white option, 833–834
    setting picture size, 831–833
folders, 156–157, 449–450
groups in Outlook Express address books, 660–661, *661*
Internet connection profiles, 566–568, *567*, *568*
Outlook Express address books, 654–655, *654*
Outlook Express e-mail messages, 643–645, *644*
shortcuts, 166–169, 457
sound files with Sound Recorder, 400–402, *401*
special characters with Alt key, 343–344, 890–891
system disks, 459–460, *461*
Cross-linked Files options in ScanDisk, 919–920
CSMA/CD (carrier-sense multiple access with collision detection) networks, 1016
Ctrl key
    + Esc key (Start button), 119
    HyperTerminal terminal-emulation settings for, 528
    keyboard shortcuts for cutting, copying, and pasting, 198
    single-click selecting with, 699–700
Curve tool in Paint, 842
custom colors in Paint, 854–855
customizing. *See also* Control Panel
    the Desktop, 99
    folders
        on Active Desktop, 726–729, *727*, *728*
        with HTML code, 478–480, *479*
    Internet Explorer, 578
    Outlook Express, **631–632, 679–693**
        the Address Book window, 662
        advanced options, 691–693
        dial-up options, 690–691
        fonts for received messages, 687–688, *687*
        general options, 680–682
        Outlook Express window layout, 631–632, *631*, *632*
        reading mail and news, 686–688, *687*
        security options, 689–690
        sending mail and news, 683–685
        spell checker options, 688–689
        the toolbar, 679–680
    printer setup, 299
    Start button submenus, **149–156**
        adding options, 149–152, *149*, *150*, *152*
        Advanced options, 154–156, *155*
        deleting options, 153–154, *154*
    the Taskbar, 138–140, *139*, 146–148, *147*
    Web view, 98–99
cutting and pasting. *See also* Clipboard
    Clipboard and, **60**
    files and folders, 184–187
    into Windows applications, 204–205, *205*
    keyboard shortcuts for, 198
    in Paint, 849–850
    text in WordPad, 786–788
    in Windows applications, 198–200, *199*, *200*
c|net's Shareware Directory, 625

D

data bits setting, 523
data conferencing. *See* conferencing
data frames, 999
Data Link Control (DLC) protocol, 22, **1007**
data link layer in OSI reference model, 1001
dates. *See also* time
    DATE command in DOS, 258
    entering dates in Notepad documents, 877
    entering dates in WordPad documents, 790
    setting date and time, 235, 258–259, *259*
DCC (Direct Cable Connect) utility, 1034, 1089–1091, *1090*
DCOM (Distributed Component Object Model), 21–22
default browser, setting Internet Explorer as, 577
default directory for sounds, 395
default graphics viewer, setting Kodak Imaging as, 857
default Internet connection profile, 568–569, *569*
default printer, 305–306, *305*, 316–317
defining new HyperTerminal connections, 516–517
defragmenting disk drives
    defined, **36**
    Disk Defragmenter utility, **15, 914, 956–961**
        defined, **15, 914, 956–957**
        running, 958–961, *960*
        when to use, 957
    running DOS defragmenters, 36
Dejavu News search engine, 625
deleting. *See also* canceling; clearing; Recycle Bin
    Active Desktop components, 713
    all pending print jobs, 325
    applications, 257–258
    channels manually from TV Viewer, 416, *416*
    Clipboard contents, 213, *214*
    compressed drives, 950
    digital IDs or certificates from Outlook Express address books, 658–659, *660*
    drivers, 248
    e-mail in Outlook Express, 643
    files, 165–166
    files from print queues, 323–325
    floppy disk contents, 450
    folders, 166, 450–451
    fonts, 361–362, 363
    options from Start button menus, 153–154, *154*
    printers from Printers folder, 315–316
    text in WordPad, 785
    Windows 98 Uninstall files, 1119–1120
    from Windows Explorer, 457
Desktop. *See also* Active Desktop
    Channel bar
        defined, **67**
        displaying, 613, *613*
        viewing Active Channels, 612–613, *612*
    on computers with multiple users, 170
    customizing, 99
    defined, **63–64**, *64*, **65**, *698*

Desktop Themes applet, **235**, **260–261**, *260*
icons, **65–66**
placing items on, **166–169**
running applications
    by right-clicking the Desktop, 124–126, *125*
    from My Computer icon, 111–114, *112, 114*
saving files from programs to, **169–171**, *170*
shortcuts
    copying files and folders to floppy disk shortcuts, 176
    creating, **166–169**, **457**
    defined, **136**, **144**
    property sheets for, 434–435, *434*
storage of folders on, 156
DESKTOP.HTT file, 710
destination documents in OLE, 219
Details view in Windows Explorer, 448–449, 729
device drivers. *See* drivers
device fonts, 340
Diagnostics tab in modem Properties dialog box, 501–502, *501, 502*
Dial Helper, 1070–1071
dialing history in NetMeeting, 764
dialing options in Outlook Express, 690–691
Dialing Properties dialog box, 502–507. *See also* modem
Properties dialog box
  calling card options, 504–507, *505, 506*
  dialing properties for HyperTerminal, 518
  disabling call waiting, 504
  overview of, 502, *503*
  telephone number and dialing code options, 502–503
  tone versus pulse dialing, 504
dialing properties for Dial-Up Networking, 1082
dialog boxes, 84–94
  alert boxes, 84, *85*
  check boxes, 88
  command buttons, 88–89
  defined, **84**, *85, 86*
  drop-down list boxes, 89
  entering information in, **87–94**
  file dialog boxes, **89–94**
    defined, **89–91**, *90*
    newer-style file boxes, 92–94, *93*
    older-style file boxes, 91–92
  list boxes, 89
  MS Sans Serif font and, 361
  navigating, 85–87, *87*
  option buttons, 88
  text boxes, 88
Dial-Up Networking, 19–20, 564–571, 1067–1091
  defining new HyperTerminal connections, 516–517
  Dial Helper and, 1070–1071
  modem setup, **1073–1075**, *1074*
  modem support, 1072
  new features, **19–20**
  protocol support, 1072
  versus Remote Access Services (RAS), 1069–1070
  remote computing, **1067–1069**
    defined, **1068–1069**

overview of, 1067–1068
remote control versus remote node software, 1069
remote connections, **1076–1082**
  application-initiated connections, 1079–1080
  explicit connections, 1077–1079, *1078*
  implicit connections, 1080–1082, *1081*
  running applications remotely, 1076
security, **1085–1087**
  callback feature, 1085–1086
  Internet connections and, 1086–1087, *1087*
  overview of, 1085–1086
Select Network Component Type dialog box, 565–566, *565*
server or host support, 1071
setting up, **564–571, 1075–1076, 1082–1085**
  changing default connection profile, 568–569, *569*
  creating connection profiles, 566–568, *567, 568*
  dialing properties, 1082
  disabling automatic phone dialing by Internet programs, 570–571
  installing Dial-Up Networking software, 565–566, *565*
  overview of, 564–565, 1075–1076
  protocols, 1084–1085
  server types, 1083–1084, *1083*
sharing Internet modem connections, 1088
TAPI (Telephony API) and, 491–492, 1070
Unimodem driver and, 1071
digital cameras and photographs, 379–380
digital IDs
  adding, deleting, and viewing in Outlook Express address books, 658–659, *660*
  obtaining, 659, 690
dimmed menu commands, 83
Direct Cable Connect (DCC) utility, 1034, 1089–1091, *1090*
directories. *See* folders
directory services, searching, 662–663
disabled user tools. *See* Accessibility Options applet
disabling. *See* turning off
disconnecting
  from HyperTerminal, 537
  from network drives or folders, 468
Disk Cleanup utility, 915, 961–965, *963*
Disk Defragmenter utility, 15, 914, 956–961
  defined, **15, 914, 956–957**
  defragmenting disk drives defined, **36, 956–957**
  running, 958–961, *960*
  running DOS defragmenters, 36
  when to use, 957
disk drives. *See* floppy disks; hard disk drives
DiskSpace utility, 942. *See also* DriveSpace
Display applet, 235, 261–286. *See also* Control Panel; monitors
  Advanced Settings page, **281–286**
    Monitor tab, 284–286, *285*
    opening, 281
    overview of, 281–284, *282*
    Performance tab, 286, *286*

Appearance tab, **269–275**
    creating color schemes, 271–274, *273*
    creating custom colors, 274–275, *274*
    defined, **269–270**, *270*
    loading color schemes, 270–271
Background tab, **262–266**
    editing patterns, 264–265
    loading new wallpaper, 265–266, *265*
    loading patterns, 262–264, *263*
defined, **235**, **261–262**
Display Properties dialog box, 276–277, *276*
Effects tab, **275–277**, *276*
Energy Saving features, 267
Screen Saver tab, **266–269**
    loading screen savers, 267–269, *267*
    overview of, 266–267
Settings tab, **277–281**
    color palette options, 278–279
    defined, **277–278**, *278*
    Screen Area options, 279–281, *280*
    screen font size and, 281
Web tab, **277**
display fonts, *351*, **352**
display options
    in CD Player, 406–407
    Display Properties dialog box, 709, *709*
    display properties in System Monitor, 975–977
    Display Summary options in ScanDisk, 918–919
    Display tab in Accessibility Options applet, **241–243**, *242*
    in WordPad, **814–816**
        options for each type of document, 815–816, *816*
        overview of, 814, *815*
        selecting units of measurement and controlling word selection, 815
        word wrap options, 816
displaying. *See also* hiding; viewing
    Channel bar, 613, *613*
    free space on disks, 175, 462
    graphics full-screen in Paint, 830–831
    hidden and system files, 114
    items added to Active Desktop, 709, *709*
    Show Windows Contents While Dragging option, 76
    toolbars on the Active Desktop, 707
    toolbars in WordPad, 775
displays. *See* monitors
Distinctive Ring tab in modem Properties dialog box, 500–501
Distributed Component Object Model (DCOM), 21–22
DLC (Data Link Control) protocol, 22, 1007
.DOC files, 872
document windows
    in Internet Explorer, 579
    in Windows 98, 69, *70*
documents. *See also* files; folders
    creating from Windows Explorer, 457
    creating in WordPad, 773, *773*
    document-centric applications, 12
    property sheets for, 433–434, *433*

running applications from, 123–124, *123*, 126–127, *127*
sharing in NetMeeting, 736, **759–761**, *760*
source and destination documents in OLE, **219**
viewing with Quick Viewers, **163–165**, *163*
in WordPad
    copying text between documents, 804–806, *805*
    creating, **773**, *773*, **814**
    display options for each type of document, 815–816, *816*
    opening ASCII files, 813–814
    opening documents from File menu's Recently Opened Documents list, 813
    opening documents in other formats, 813
    opening new documents, 814
    previewing documents, 817–818, *817*
    printing documents, 818–819
    reformatting whole documents, 801–802
    saving, 810–812, *811*
    selecting entire documents, 784, 802
domains and domain controllers, **1056**, 1058
DOS
    CHKDSK utility, 916
    copying floppy disks, 462
    DOS32 operating system, 18
    DOS applications
        copying text and graphics to the Clipboard from, 200–203, *201*
        default printer setting and, 317
        DOS session property settings, 131–136, *135*
        entering special characters in, 891–893
        FAT32 file system and, 973
        graphics mode, 201
        pasting from the Clipboard into, 206–207, *207*
        PIF settings, 133–136, *135*
        printing from, 296
        running, 35–40, 107–108, 127–130, *129*, *130*
        and the virtual DOS machine (VDM), 38, 133
    DOS directory structure, **440–442**, *441*
    installing Windows 98 from, 1116–1117
    PIF settings, 133–136, *135*
    Report MS-DOS Mode Name Length Errors option in ScanDisk, 923
    running applications from MS-DOS Prompt, 107–108, 129–136, *130*, *135*
    TIME and DATE commands, 258
dots (•) in menus, 83
double quotes (") in Web search engines, 618
double-clicking the mouse, 63, 111
DoubleSpace utility, 942, 1121. *See also* DriveSpace
downloadable soft fonts, 336, **340**
downloading
    drivers, 248
    e-mail in Outlook Express, 646
    NetMeeting, 741
    sounds, 393–394
Downloading Subscriptions dialog box, 608, *609*
Dr. Watson utility, 16, **22**

dragging
  defined, **75**
  and dropping files, 160–162, *161*, *162*
  and dropping folders, 158–160, *159*
  and dropping text in WordPad, 789–790
  files onto the Printer icon or window, 319–321, *320*
  right-click dragging, 160
Drive Converter (FAT32) utility, 17, 915, 970–973
  defined, **17, 915, 970**
  memory shortage error messages, 973
  running, 971–972
drivers
  downloading, 248
  managing multimedia drivers and settings, 424–425
  in peer-to-peer networks
    installing network drivers, 1039–1044, *1040*
    installing printer drivers for shared printers, 1048–1050
  printer drivers, 301–302, 310–311, 1048–1050
  removing, 248
  selecting network interface card drivers, 1026–1029
  troubleshooting network interface card and driver problems, 1099–1102, *1099, 1101*
  TWAIN driver support, 861
  Unimodem driver, 494–495, 1071
  utilities for installing multimedia drivers, 385
  virtual device drivers (VxDs), **37**
  Win32 Driver Model (WDM), **21**
drives. *See* floppy disks; hard disk drives
DriveSpace 3 utility, 914, 939–953
  adjusting the amount of free space, 947, *948*
  advanced compression settings, 952–953, *952*
  auto-mount settings, 953
  changing estimated compression ratio, 951
  compatibility with other compression utilities, 942
  compressing drives, **942–947**, *944*
  compressing existing free space, 949–950, *949*
  compressing Zip drives, 947
  defined, **914, 939**
  deleting compressed drives, 950
  FAT32 file system incompatibility, 941, 968–969
  how DriveSpace works, 939–940
  Microsoft Plus! and, 942
  mounting and unmounting compressed drives, 950–951
  new features, 941–942
  ScanDisk utility and, 921–922
  selecting compression method, 952–953, *952*
  uncompressing compressed drives, 948
  when to use, 940–941
drop-down list boxes in dialog boxes, 89
dual boot systems, 969
DUN. *See* Dial-Up Networking
DVD drives, 381–382
DVD Player, 385, 386–392. *See also* accessories; multimedia
  defined, **385**
  DVD defined, **386–387**
  ending DVD sessions, 392
  purchasing and installing DVD drives, 387–388
  running, 388–390
  selecting chapters and titles, 390–391
  selecting language and subtitles, 391–392

E

ease of use features, 17–19
Edit menu. *See also* Clipboard
  Paste Special command, 224–226
  Undo command
    overview of, 187, 457, 785
    in Paint, 840
    in WordPad, 802
editing. *See also* changing
  embedded objects, 223
  in Kodak Imaging, 859–861, *860*
  linked objects, 226, *227*
  sounds in Sound Recorder, 402–403
  text in Notepad, 875–877, *876*
  from Windows Explorer, 457
  in WordPad, **778–790**
    copying blocks of text, 789
    deleting letters and words, 785
    dragging and dropping blocks of text, 789–790
    inserting letters and symbols, 786
    moving the cursor, 778–780
    moving text with cut and paste, 786–787
    moving text with right-click menus, 788, *788*
    replacing words, 786
    scrolling with the keyboard, 781
    scrolling with the mouse, 780, *781*
    selecting entire documents, 784, 802
    selecting lines of text, 784
    selecting paragraphs, 783, 784
    selecting sentences, 784
    selecting text with the mouse, 781–783, *782*
    selecting text with the Shift key, 783
    selecting words, 783, 815
EISA bus architecture, 1028
Electric Library search engine, 625
Ellipse tool in Paint, 843
ellipses (…) in menus, 83
e-mail in NetMeeting, 764–765
e-mail in Outlook Express, 637–652
  adding background color to, 651
  adding pictures to, 649–651, *650*
  adding signatures to, 648–649
  attaching files to, 651–652
  backing up, 641
  creating or composing, 643–645, *644*
  customizing mail reading options, 686–688, *687*
  customizing mail sending options, 683–685
  deleting, 643
  entering header information, 644–645
  formatting, 646–647, *647*
  forwarding, 642
  marking, 639
  moving, 639

overview of, 637–638
printing, 639
reading and saving attachments, 641
replying to, 641–642
retrieving or downloading, 646
saving in Outlook Express folders, 640–641
saving in Windows Explorer folders, 639–640
sending, 645
setting up e-mail accounts, **633–637**
    establishing an ISP account, 633–634
    POP3, IMAP, and SMTP defined, **635**
    setting up e-mail accounts, 634–636
    using real names versus aliases, 637
using stationery, 648
embedding. *See also* Object Linking and Embedding
editing embedded objects, 223
embedding objects, **220–223**, *222*
versus linking, **217–218**, *218*
TrueType fonts, 345–346
enabling. *See* turning on
encapsulated PostScript files (.EPS), 330
ending
backups, 931–932
DVD sessions, 392
HyperTerminal sessions, 548–549
NetMeeting sessions, 751
Enter key, Alt + Enter (opening objects), 312
entering. *See also* adding; inserting
date and time in Notepad documents, 877
header information in Outlook Express e-mail, 644–645
information in dialog boxes, 87–94
network passwords, 63
numbers into Calculator in scientific notation, 885–886
in Outlook Express address books
    business-related information, *657*, *657*
    conferencing information, 658, *659*
    digital IDs or certificates, 658–659, *660*
    home-related information, 656–657, *656*
    personal information, 655–656
phone numbers for HyperTerminal connections, 517
special characters
    from the keyboard, 343–344, 890–891
    in non-Windows applications, 891–893
text in Notepad, 875–877, *876*
text in WordPad, 776–777, *778*
entertainment and multimedia enhancements, 16–17
Environmental Organization Web Directory, 625
.EPS files, 330
Eraser tool in Paint, 840–841
error control settings for HyperTerminal, 525–526
error messages in Backup utility, 932
Esc key, Ctrl + Esc (Start button), 119
estimated compression ratio settings in DriveSpace, 951
Ethernet networks, 1016–1026
carrier-sense multiple access with collision detection
    (CSMA/CD) networks, **1016**
coaxial cables, 1016–1017, *1017*

Fast Ethernet networks (100Base-T), 1024–1026
hubs and switches, 1024
thin Ethernet networks (10Base-2), 1021–1022, *1021*, 1024
twisted-pair Ethernet networks (10Base-T), 1022–1024, *1022*, 1025
unshielded twisted pair cables (UTP), 1017–1019, *1018*
exact matches in Web search engines, 618
Exchange/Windows Messaging, 489, 490, 491
Excite search engine, 624
exiting
Internet Explorer, 577
Windows 98, 61, 100–102, *102*
explicit remote connections, 1077–1079, *1078*
Explorer. *See* Internet Explorer; Windows Explorer
Explorer bar in Internet Explorer, *579*, *580*, 619–622, *620*, *621*, *622*
extensions. *See* file extensions
external modems, 493–494
Eyedropper tool in Paint, 837

F

F5 key, updating window contents, 172, 455
FaceLift fonts, 350
Fast Ethernet networks (100Base-T), 1024–1026
FAT32 file system, 965–973
advantages of, 965–966
converting to FAT16 file system, 970
defined, **17, 965**
disadvantages of, 966–967
disk utilities and, 968
DOS applications and, 973
Drive Converter (FAT32) utility, **17, 915, 970–973**
    defined, **17, 915, 970**
    memory shortage error messages, 973
    running, 971–972
DriveSpace 3 incompatibility, 941, 968–969
dual boot systems and, 969
versus FAT16 file system, 965
hardware compatibility with, 969–970
Jaz drives and, 970
versus NTFS file system, 967
OnTrack Disk Manager utility and, 973
Partition Magic conversion utility, 970, 972
favorite channels, adding to TV Viewer toolbar, 421–422
Favorites menu
in Active Desktop, 704
in Internet Explorer, **591–594**
    adding to, 591, *592*
    changing website subscription settings in, 601
    moving between pages with, 587–588
    naming entries for, 592
    organizing, 593–594, *594*
    selecting submenus for new entries, 592–593
    structure of, 591
faxes, 490, 491, 858

file dialog boxes, 89–94. *See also* dialog boxes
defined, **89–91**, *90*
newer-style file boxes, 92–94, *93*
older-style file boxes, 91–92
file extensions
.AWB, 858
.CDF, 610
.CLP, 211
defined by file type, **164–165**
.DOC, 872
.EPS, 330
.FON, 353
for font files, 353
.LNK, 136, 167
.PIF, 133–136, *135*
registering, **123–124**
.TTF, 353
.TXT, 872
.WHT, 758
file formats
in Kodak Imaging, 858, 859, 867
in Paint, 829, 855
File Manager, 27, 114, 117–119, *118*
File menu Recently Opened Documents list, 813
file systems. *See also* FAT32 file system
NTFS file system, 967
files. *See also* documents; folders; ScanDisk; Windows Explorer
attaching to Outlook Express e-mail, 651–652
binary files
receiving with HyperTerminal, 544–545, 547–548
sending with HyperTerminal, 544–545, 546–547, *547*
Clipboard files
retrieving stored Clipboard file contents, 212
saving Clipboard contents to files, 211–212
copying to and from floppy disks, **171–176**
copying to floppy disk shortcuts, 176
with My Computer, 172–175, *173*, *174*
overview of, 171–172
with Send To command, 175, 457
cutting, copying, and pasting, **184–187**
deleting, 165–166
deleting from print queues, 323–325
DESKTOP.HTT file, 710
displaying hidden and system files, 114
file transfers with NetMeeting, 762–763, *763*
file-checking options in ScanDisk, 921
moving
versus copying, **159–160**, **458**
and copying between folders, 160–162, *161*, *162*, 454–455, 457
between drives, 458
opening in Notepad, 874–875
Photo CD formats, 380
previewing in Windows Explorer, **474–476**, *475*
printing to disk files, **328–330**
registering file extensions, **124**
renaming, **191–192**
running applications from batch files, 137

saving in root directory, 157
sorting and arranging file icons and listings in folders, 177–179
text files
ASCII Setup dialog box settings, 530–531
defined, **872–873**
how HyperTerminal displays and stores text, 540
HyperTerminal transfer settings, 543
opening into WordPad, 813–814
sending and receiving with HyperTerminal, 542–544
Thumbnails view in Windows Explorer, **476–478**, *477*, 724–726, *725*
Universal Disk Format (UDF), 387
Windows Explorer file operations, **453–458**
executing file operations, 456–457
moving files between drives, 458
moving files between folders, 454–455, 457
overview of, 453–454
refreshing folder contents, 172, 455
selecting files, 448, 455–456
viewing files, 456–457
filtering newsgroups in Outlook Express, 674–676
FilterKeys options in Accessibility Options applet, 239–240
Find option on Start button
overview of, 41–43, *42*
running applications from, 120–122, *122*
Find People dialog box, 704, 898–902
in Active Desktop, 704
defined, **898**
finding people or businesses, 899–902, *901*
getting registered in LDAP, 902
LDAP (Lightweight Directory Access Protocol) and, 899, 900, 902
finding
exact matches with Web search engines, 618
hard disk problems during Windows 98 installation, 1117–1118
names and addresses in directory services, 662–663
newsgroups, 670–671, *671*
options in Start button, 110
text in Notepad documents, 877–878
text in WordPad, 802–804, *803*
TV shows by category in TV Viewer, 419
TV shows in TV Viewer, 418–419
first-line indents in WordPad, *795*
fixing hard disk problems during Windows 98 installation, 1117–1118
flipping selections in Paint, 850–851, *851*
floppy disks. *See also* hard disk drives
copying files and folders to and from, **171–176**
copying to floppy disk shortcuts, 176
with My Computer, 172–175, *173*, *174*
overview of, 171–172
with Send To command, 175, 457
formatting, 174
installing Windows 98 from, 1110
quick erasing, 450
updating floppy disk window contents with F5 key, 172, 455

Windows Explorer floppy disk operations, **459–462**
copying disks, 461–462
formatting disks and creating system disks, 459–460, *461*
viewing free space on disks, 175, 462
write protecting floppy disks, 173–174, *174*
flow control settings for HyperTerminal, 526
folders, 156–166, 171–192. *See also* files; Windows Explorer
copying to and from floppy disks, **171–176**
copying to floppy disk shortcuts, 176
with My Computer, 172–175, *173, 174*
overview of, 171–172
with Send To command, 175, 457
creating, **156–157, 449–450**
customizing
on Active Desktop, 726–729, *727, 728*
with HTML code, 478–480, *479*
cutting, copying, and pasting, **184–187**
default directory for sounds, 395
deleting, **166, 450–451**
deleting printers from Printers folder, 315–316
disconnecting from networked folders, 468
DOS directory structure and, **440–442**, *441*
folder icons, 66
History and Temporary Internet Files folders in Internet
Explorer, 588
installing Windows 98 in a new directory, 1109,
1116–1117
moving and copying items between, **158–162, 454–455,
457**
moving versus copying, 159–160
moving and copying files, 160–162, *161, 162,*
454–455, 457
moving and copying folders, 158, *159*
My Computer folder. *See also* Dial-Up Networking
accessing the Control Panel via, 234
copying files and folders to and from floppy disks,
172–175, *173, 174*
navigating with Backspace key, 113, 458
previewing files, 474
property sheet for, 435–436, *436*
running applications from, 111–114, *112, 114*
viewing free space on disks, 175
navigating between folders in Windows Explorer, 449
navigating folder windows with Backspace key, 113, 458
Online Services Folder, **21**
renaming, **191–192**
saving files in the root directory, 157
selecting in Windows Explorer, 448–449
sharing subdirectories in peer-to-peer networks,
1045–1048
from folders, 1045–1046, *1046*
from Windows Explorer, 1046–1048, *1047*
storage of folders on the Desktop, 156
View menu options, **176–184**
Active Desktop options, 183
Advanced settings, 179–182, *179*
Browse Folders as Follows options, 183
changing Clipboard view format, 209–210, *210*

Click Items as Follows options, 184
creating custom views, 182–184, *183*
Customize This Folder command, 727
overview of, 176
Refresh command, 172, 455
sorting and arranging file and folder icons and listings,
177–179
turning text labels on and off, 182
View Web Content in Folders options, 183–184
Windows Explorer folder operations, **445–453, 478–480**
creating folders, 449–450
customizing folders with HTML code, 478–480, *479*
deleting folders, 450–451
moving between folders, 449
moving folders, 451–452
moving multiple folders simultaneously, 452, *453*
selecting drives, 446–447, *447*
selecting folders, 448–449
sharing folders, 468–471, *469*
viewing shared folders, 463–464, *464*
.FON files, 353
fonts, 333–365
AutoInstalled fonts, 365
bitmapped fonts, **336, 338–339,** *338,* **346,** 353, 360
body fonts, **352**
character formatting in WordPad, **796–799**
bold, italic, and underline text styles, 797, 798, 799
with Fonts dialog box, 797, 799
with Format bar, 775, 797–799
with keyboard shortcuts, 797, 799
overview of, 796–797
as you type, 799
defined, **334–336,** *335,* **341**
deleting, **361–362,** 363
device fonts, **340**
in dialog boxes, 361
downloadable soft fonts, **336, 340**
FaceLift fonts, 350
file extensions for font files, 353
font icons for TrueType versus printer fonts, 798
font management utilities, **363–365,** *365*
font smoothing, 275
font substitution, 336, 341, 356–357, *356*
Fonts applet, **235, 353–363**
adding fonts, 353–356, *354, 355*
defined, **235,** 353
deleting fonts, 361–362, 363
TrueType options, 356–357, *356*
viewing font families, 359
viewing fonts by similarities, 359–361, *360*
viewing and printing examples with font viewer,
357–359, *358*
font-scaling utilities, **349–350**
guidelines for using, 362
headline fonts, **352**
in HyperTerminal, 534
Intellifont-for-Windows utility, 349–350
ligatures, **348**

monospaced versus proportionally spaced fonts, **351**
MoreFonts utility, 350
numeral fonts, 348, 351
OpenType fonts, **340**
ornamental and display fonts, *351*, **352**
in Outlook Express, 687–688, *687*
overview of, 333–334
Panose information, **359–360**
PostScript fonts, **330**, **339**, **349**
printer fonts, **336**, **338**, **340**, **353**, 798
properties of, 359
Publisher's Powerpak for Windows utility, 350
purchasing, 347–348, 350, 352
scalable fonts, **346**, **349–350**
screen fonts
    defined, **336**, **338**
    printable screen fonts, **340**
    setting screen font size, 281
selecting, 346–347
serif versus sans-serif fonts, **350**, *351*
small caps, **348**
SuperPrint utility, 350
TrueType fonts, **336–337**, **340–346**
    versus bitmapped and vector fonts, 346
    defined, **336–337**, **340–341**
    embedding, 345–346
    file extension for, 353
    font icons for TrueType versus printer fonts, 798
    versus other scalable fonts, 349–350
    Panose information in, 360
    printers and, 337
    read-only versus read-write embedded fonts, 345
    special characters, Symbol and WingDing fonts,
      342–344, *343*, *344*
    TrueType font families, 342, *342*
    TrueType options in Fonts applet, 356–357, *356*
Type 1 PostScript fonts, **349**
versus typefaces, **341**
vector fonts, **336**, **339**, **346**, 353, 360
Windows 98 font management, 333–334, 346–347
footers in Notepad, 878–879
foreground colors in Paint, 835, 836–837
formatting
    characters in WordPad, **796–799**
      bold, italic, and underline text styles, 797, 798, 799
      with Fonts dialog box, 797, 799
      with Format bar, 775, 797–799
      with keyboard shortcuts, 797, 799
      overview of, 796–797
      as you type, 799
    e-mail in Outlook Express, 646–647, *647*
    floppy disks, 174, 459–460, *461*
    paragraphs in WordPad, **790–796**
      bulleting paragraphs, 795–796
      changing paragraph alignment, 793
      hanging indents or outdents, 795
      indenting with Format Paragraph dialog box, 794
      indenting with the ruler, 794–795
      overview of, 790–791
      setting first-line indents, 795
      types of indentation, 793–794, *796*
      using the ruler, 791–792
      viewing paragraph alignment, 792–793
    reformatting whole documents in WordPad, 801–802
Forward command or button in Internet Explorer, 586–587
forwarding e-mail in Outlook Express, 642
Forwarding tab in modem Properties dialog box, 501
frames of data, 999
Free-Form Select tool in Paint, 848
freeing up disk space, 940
full duplex sound cards, 742, 753
function keys, HyperTerminal terminal-emulation settings for,
    528

G

games
    Game Controllers applet, **235**
    support for, 18
General tab
    in Accessibility Options applet, 246–247, *246*
    in modem Properties dialog box, **498**
      Maximum Speed option, 498
      Port option, 498
      Speaker Volume option, 498
    in Mouse applet, 291, *291*
graphics. *See also* Kodak Imaging; Paint
    bitmapped versus object-oriented graphics, **826–827**
    copying from DOS applications to the Clipboard,
      200–203, *201*
    graphics mode in DOS applications, **201**
    Kodak Imaging as default graphics viewer, 857
    in Outlook Express e-mail, 649–651, *650*
    pasting into DOS applications, 206
    in WordPad, **807–810**
      importing from the Clipboard, 808, *808*
      inserting as objects, 810
      overview of, 807–808, *807*
      positioning, 809
      sizing, 809–810
grayed menu commands, 83
grayscale display in Kodak Imaging, 859
grayscale images in Paint, 833, 835–836
grouping terms with parentheses in Scientific Calculator,
    883, 887
groups in Outlook Express address books, 660–661, *661*

H

handicapped user tools. *See* Accessibility Options applet
hanging indents in WordPad, 795
hanging up NetMeeting, 751
hard disk drives. *See also* floppy disks
    changing shared object permissions and other properties,
      471–472

Disk Cleanup utility, **915**, **961–965**, *963*
Disk Defragmenter utility, **15**, **914**, **956–961**
    defined, **15**, **914**, **956–957**
    defragmenting disk drives defined, **36**, **956–957**
    running, 958–961, *960*
    running DOS defragmenters, 36
    when to use, *957*
disk space requirements for installing Windows 98, **51–52**,
    1109
DiskSpace utility, 942
DoubleSpace utility, 942, 1121
Drive Converter (FAT32) utility, **17**, **915**, **970–973**
    defined, **17**, **915**, **970**
    memory shortage error messages, 973
    running, 971–972
DriveSpace 3 utility, **914**, **939–953**
    adjusting the amount of free space, 947, *948*
    advanced compression settings, 952–953, *952*
    auto-mount settings, 953
    changing estimated compression ratio, 951
    compatibility with other compression utilities, 942
    compressing drives, **942–947**, *944*
    compressing existing free space, 949–950, *949*
    compressing Zip drives, 947
    defined, **914**, **939**
    deleting compressed drives, 950
    FAT32 file system incompatibility, 941, 968–969
    how DriveSpace works, 939–940
    Microsoft Plus! and, 942
    mounting and unmounting compressed drives,
        950–951
    new features, 941–942
    ScanDisk utility and, 921–922
    selecting compression method, 952–953, *952*
    uncompressing compressed drives, 948
    when to use, 940–941
finding and fixing disk problems during Windows 98
    installation, 1117–1118
installing Windows 98 on a new disk drive, 1109,
    1116–1117
mapping network drives
    mapping Windows 98 and Windows NT shared drives,
        1061–1063
    overview of, 464–465
    from Windows 3.x file boxes, 465–466
    from Windows Explorer, 466–467
moving files between drives in Windows Explorer, 458
selecting in Windows Explorer, 446–447, *447*
sharing, 468–471, *469*
sharing drives in peer-to-peer networks, **1045–1048**
    from folders, 1045–1046, *1046*
    from Windows Explorer, 1046–1048, *1047*
troubleshooting hard disk drive crashes, **1102–1105**
viewing shared drives, 463–464, *464*
Windows 98 requirements, **51–52**
hardware. *See also* printers
    Add New Hardware applet, **235**, **247–255**, **385**, **1073–1075**
        defined, **235**, **247–248**

installing modems, 1073–1075, *1074*
    installing multimedia drivers, 385
    running the Install Hardware Wizard, 248–250, *249*
    telling the Wizard what hardware you have, 250–254,
        251
    what to do if your hardware is not listed, 254–255
    FAT32 file system compatibility, 969–970
    hardware requirements, **49–55**
        computers and processors, 49–50
        hard disk drives, 51–52
        monitors and video cards, 52–53
        for NetMeeting, 739–740, 742
        other components, 55
        Plug-and-Play components, 53–55
        RAM, 50–51
        for TV Viewer, 411
    MMX processor support, 17
    multimedia hardware support, 16
headers
    in newsgroups, 677
    in Notepad, 878–879
headline fonts, 352
Help
    in Calculator, 880
    in Internet Explorer 4, 584–585
    in TV Viewer, 416
    Windows 98 HelpDesk, **14**
    in WordPad, 774
Hibernate option, 101
hidden files, displaying, 114
hiding. *See also* displaying; viewing
    share names in peer-to-peer networks, 1050
    Taskbar automatically, 138–139
    toolbars in Internet Explorer, 580, 582
    toolbars in WordPad, 775
High Contrast options in Accessibility Options applet,
    241–243, *242*
History folder, 588
home pages, changing in Internet Explorer, 576
home-related information in Outlook Express address
    books, 656–657, *656*
Homework Help search engine, 626
hosts, 1071
hovering, 699
hubs
    defined, **1022**
    star topology and, 1022–1023
    versus switches, 1024
Hyp option in Scientific Calculator, 885
hyperlinks in Internet Explorer, 585–586
hypermedia. *See* multimedia
HyperTerminal, 511–549
    defined, **511–513**, *513*
    importing Windows 3.x Terminal program settings, 514
    installing modems, 514–515
    making connections, **535–539**
        cable connections, 538, *539*
        disconnecting, 537

making a different connection, 537–538
overview of, 535–536
troubleshooting, 536–537
modem Properties dialog box settings, **519–534**
Advanced settings, 524–527
basic settings, **520–524**
call preferences settings, 524
Connection tab, **522–527**, *523*
data bits setting, 523
data format settings, **522–523**
error control settings, 525–526
flow control settings, 526
initialization settings, 526–527
low-speed modulation protocol settings, 526
modem speed setting, 522
opening, 520–521, *521*
overview of, 519–520
parity setting, 523
port setting, 521
stop bits setting, 523
preferences, **531–534**
call preferences, 532
display settings, 532–534, *533*
font settings, 532
modem speaker volume setting, 532
overview of, 531–532
saving settings, **534**
sending and receiving data, **539–549**
backscroll buffers and, 529–530, 540
capturing text, 541
ending communications sessions, 548–549
how HyperTerminal displays and stores text, 540
interactive or terminal mode sessions, 539–540, *540*
receiving binary files, 544–545, 547–548
selecting file-transfer protocols, 544–545
sending binary files, 544–545, 546–547, *547*
sending and receiving text files, 542–544
text-file transfer settings, 543
setting up HyperTerminal connections, **515–518**
commas (,) in phone numbers for modem connections, 518
defining a new connection, 516–517
entering phone numbers, 517
setting dialing properties, 518
starting, 516
terminal settings, **527–531**
ASCII Setup dialog box settings, 530–531
backscroll buffer size setting, 529–530
function, arrow, and Ctrl key settings, 528
overview of, 527, *528*
terminal-emulation setting, 528–529
terminals defined, **527**
turning sound on or off, 530
hyphen key, Alt key + hyphen (-), 77
hyphenation in WordPad, 806

I/O address conflicts, 1097
I/O permission bitmaps in Intel processors, 37
I-beam pointer, 779
IBM character set, 891–893
icons. *See also* Desktop
on Active Desktop, 701, 705
defined, **65–66**
font icons for TrueType versus printer fonts, 798
My Computer icon. *See also* Dial-Up Networking
accessing the Control Panel via, 234
copying files and folders to and from floppy disks,
172–175, *173*, *174*
navigating with Backspace key, 113, 458
previewing files, 474
property sheet for, 435–436, *436*
running applications from, 111–114, *112*, *114*
viewing free space on disks, 175
Network Neighborhood icon in peer-to-peer networks,
1044–1045
IETF (Internet Engineering Task Force), 765
ILS (Internet Locator Service), 745
IMAP (Internet Message Access Protocol), 635
implicit remote connections, 1080–1082, *1081*
importing
address books into Outlook Express, 653
graphics from the Clipboard into WordPad, 808, *808*
Windows 3.x Terminal program settings into
HyperTerminal, 514
**IMTC (International Multimedia Telecommunications
Consortium),** 765
Inbox Assistant in Outlook Express, 664–665
indenting paragraphs in WordPad, 793–795, *796*
index Web sites, 619
Infoseek search engine, 623
Infrared applet, 235
Infrared Data Association (IrDA) standard, 19
.ini files
font substitution in, 341
Windows 3.x applications and, 46
initialization settings for HyperTerminal, 526–527
Insert Symbol dialog box, 344, *344*
inserting. *See also* adding
date and time in WordPad documents, 790
graphics as objects in WordPad, 810
letters and symbols in WordPad, 786
insertion point in WordPad, 776
installing. *See also* Add New Hardware applet; adding;
setting up
applications, 255–256, *256*, *257*
Backup utility, 925
cables for peer-to-peer networks, 1038–1039
Clipboard Viewer accessory, 209
Dial-Up Networking, 565–566, *565*
DVD drives, 387–388

fonts, 353–356, *354, 355*
Microsoft Investor Tracker on Active Desktop, 714–715
modems, 495–497, *495,* 514–515
NetMeeting, 740–741, *740*
peer-to-peer networks
    installing cables, 1038–1039
    installing network drivers, 1039–1044, *1040*
    installing network interface cards, 1036–1038
printer drivers for shared printers in peer-to-peer networks, 1048–1050
printers, **298–311**
    Add Printer Wizard, **298, 302–306**
    adding local printers, 298, 306–309, *307, 308*
    adding network printers, 298, 302–306, *303, 304, 305*
    customizing printer setup, 299
    printer drivers and, 301–302, 310–311
    what to do if your printer is not listed, 310–311
    when you'll need to install printers, 300–301
System Monitor, 973–974
Web Search component on Active Desktop, 715–716
Windows 98, **16, 1108–1122**. *See also* upgrading to Windows 98
    backing up before, 1110
    on compressed drives, 1120–1121
    deleting Uninstall files, 1119–1120
    disk space requirements, 1109
    from DOS, 1116–1117
    finding and fixing hard disk drive problems during, 1117–1118
    from floppy disks, 1110
    full upgrades from earlier versions of Windows, **1109, 1110–1116**
    on a new disk drive or directory, 1109, 1116–1117
    new features, **16**
    on OS/2 systems, 1122
    overview of, 1108–1110
    running ScanDisk before, 1117–1118
    saving system files for future uninstalls, 1119
    uninstalling Windows 98, 1118–1119
    on Windows NT computers, 1122
Integrated Internet Shell. *See* Web view
Intellifont-for-Windows utility, 349–350
Intellimouse support, 245
interactive mode sessions in HyperTerminal, 539–540, *540*
interactive multimedia. *See* multimedia
interface. *See* Desktop; dialog boxes; menus; windows
internal Clipboards in applications, 204
internal modems, 493–494
International Multimedia Telecommunications Consortium (IMTC), 765
International Telecommunications Union (ITU), 765
Internet applet, 235
Internet connections, 553–571. *See also* Outlook Express
    ADSL connections, 555–556
    cable modem connections, 555–556
    connecting to ISPs, **562–564,** *563, 564*
    Dial-Up Networking security and, 1086–1087, *1087*

disabling automatic phone dialing by Internet programs, 570–571
    Internet Connection Wizard, 562–564, *563, 564,* 634–637
    ISDN connections, 554, 555–556
    PPP connections, 556
    selecting Internet service providers, **556–561**
        local ISPs, 559–560
        national ISPs, 558–559
        online services, 560–561
        overview of, 556–558
    setting up Dial-Up Networking, **564–571**
        changing default connection profile, 568–569, *569*
        creating connection profiles, 566–568, *567, 568*
        disabling automatic phone dialing by Internet programs, 570–571
        installing Dial-Up Networking software, 565–566, *565*
        overview of, 564–565
    setting up e-mail and news accounts, **633–637**
        establishing an ISP account, 633–634
        POP3, IMAP, and SMTP defined, **635**
        setting up e-mail accounts, 634–636
        setting up news accounts, 636–637
        using real names versus aliases, 637
    TCP/IP protocol and, 553
    types of connections, **554–556**
    websites about, 556, 558
Internet Engineering Task Force (IETF), 765
Internet Explorer 4, 575–626, 903–910
    Active Channels, **609–616**
        Channel Definition Format (CDF) files, 610
        defined, **609–610**
        displaying Channel bar, 613, *613*
        subscribing to, 610, 614–616, *615*
        viewing in Channel Viewer, 610–612, *611*
        viewing from Channel bar, 612–613, *612*
        viewing in Internet Explorer, 610
    browsing off-line, **588–590,** *589*
    changing the start page, 576
    copying and pasting URLs, 587
    customizing, 578
    and disconnecting from the Internet, 577
    document window, 579
    exiting, 577
    Explorer bar, 579, *580,* 619–622, *620, 621, 622*
    Favorites menu, **591–594**
        adding to, 591, *592*
        changing website subscription settings in, 601
        moving between pages with, 587–588
        naming entries for, 592
        organizing, 593–594, *594*
        selecting submenus for new entries, 592–593
        structure of, 591
    frequently used commands, 581–582
    Help, **584–585**
    menu bar, 579
    Microsoft Chat, **903–910**
        chat features, 908–910, *908*

chatting, 906–908, *906*
defined, **903**
starting, 903–906, *904*, *905*
moving between pages, **585–588**
with Address toolbar, 584, 587
with Back and Forward commands or buttons,
586–587
with Favorites menu, 587–588
with History and Temporary Internet Files folders, 588
with hyperlinks, 585–586
overview of program components, **577–580**, *578*, *580*
scroll bars, 580
search engines, **616–626**
AltaVista, 623
BigBook, 625
combining keywords, 617
common search engines listed, 623–626
c|net's Shareware Directory, 625
Dejavu News, 625
Environmental Organization Web Directory, 625
Excite, 624
finding exact matches, 618
Homework Help, 626
Infoseek, 623
installing Web Search component on Active Desktop,
715–716
keywords, 616–618
Lycos, 623
Magellan, 624
NetSearch, 624
Point, 624
Search.com, 624
search and index sites, 619
searching versus browsing, 618
searching with Explorer bar, 619–622, *620*, *621*, *622*
Starting Point, 624
The Electric Library, 625
using quotes (') and double quotes ("), 618
using wildcards, 617–618
Webcrawler, 624
Who/Where?, 625
WWWomen, 625
Yahoo!, 623
setting as the default browser, 577
starting, 575–577
status bar, 580
subscribing to websites, **594–609**
Advanced Download Options dialog box, 605–606,
606
browsing updated subscriptions, 597–599
browsing updated subscriptions off-line, 598
canceling subscriptions, **599**
changing subscription settings in Favorites menu, 601
defined, **594–596**
Downloading Subscriptions dialog box, 608, *609*
overview of, 600–601
selecting how much content should be delivered,
604–606, *604*, *605*, *606*

selecting how you want to be notified, 602–603, *603*
setting subscription schedules, 607–608, *607*
subscribing to sites, 591, *592*, **596–597**
Subscription Wizard, 602–608
updating subscriptions manually, 608, *609*
viewing current subscription settings, 601, *602*
viewing current subscriptions, 599–600, *600*
title bar, 579
toolbars, **579**, **580**, **582–584**
Address toolbar, 584, 587
Explorer bar, 579, *580*, 619–622, *620*, *621*, *622*
hiding, moving, and resizing, 580, 582
Links toolbar, 583–584
overview of, 579
Standard toolbar, 581, 583
versus Windows Explorer, **719**
Internet features in Windows 98, 19–21, 24
Dial-Up Networking improvements, 19–20
Integrated Internet Shell or Web view, 19, 24, *24*
Internet browser improvements, 20
Internet communication tools, 20
Online Services Folder, 21
personalized Internet information delivery, 20
PPTP (Point-to-Point Tunneling Protocol) support, 20,
1011
Internet Locator Service (ILS), 745
Internet Message Access Protocol (IMAP), 635
interpreters, 873
Inv option in Scientific Calculator, 885
inverting colors in Paint, 851, *852*
Investor Tracker, 714–715
IPX/SPX and IPX/SPX with NetBIOS protocols, 1005–1007
ISA bus architecture, 1028
ISDN Internet connections, 554, 555–556
ISPs. *See* Internet connections
italic text in WordPad, 797, 798, 799
ITU (International Telecommunications Union), 765

J

Jaz drives, 970

K

key combinations
in Calculator, 882
for character formatting in WordPad, 797, 799
for cutting, copying, and pasting, 198
in menus, 84
for moving the cursor in WordPad, 779–780
for StickyKeys, FilterKeys, and ToggleKeys, 240
in TV Viewer, 422–423
keyboard
entering special characters from, 343–344, 890–891
Keyboard applet, **236**

Keyboard tab in Accessibility Options applet, *238*, **239–240**
Keystroke option in Character Map, 890–891
navigating Notepad documents from, 877
scrolling in WordPad with, 781
keywords in Web search engines, 616–618
Kodak Imaging accessory, 490, 823, 856–867. *See also* accessories; graphics
    annotating images, **862–866**
        Annotation toolbar overview, 862–863
        making annotations permanent, 863–864
        setting annotation properties, 864–866
    creating documents, **866–867**
    defined, **823**, **856**
    editing images, 859–861, *860*
    faxes and, 490, 858
    file formats, 858, 859, 867
    grayscale display, 859
    overview of, 823, 856–857
    rotating images, 859
    saving documents, **867**
    scanning images, 861–862
    setting as default graphics viewer, 857
    TWAIN driver support, 861
    viewing images, 858, *858*
    zoom controls, 859

L

language option in DVD Player, 391–392
LANs. *See* networks
laptop computers
    Advanced Configuration and Power Interface (ACPI), **17–18, 55, 101**
    Control Panel Power Management applet, **236**
    cost of, 28
    Mouse Accessibility options, 243–245, *243*
    PCMCIA cards
        Control Panel PCMCIA applet, **236**
        purchasing, 493–494
        support for, 18–19
    power management improvements, 17–18
    Suspend, Standby, Hibernate, and OnNow options, **101**
LDAP (Lightweight Directory Access Protocol), 899, 900, 902
left-hand mouse settings, 287–288, *287*
ligatures, 348
Lightweight Directory Access Protocol (LDAP), 899, 900, 902
Line tool in Paint, 842
lines of text, selecting in WordPad, 784
linking. *See also* Object Linking and Embedding
    editing linked objects, 226, *227*
    versus embedding, **217–218**, *218*
    linking objects, **224–226**
Links toolbar in Internet Explorer, 583–584
list boxes in dialog boxes, 89

listing items added to Active Desktop, 709, *709*
.LNK files, 136, 167
loading sound schemes, 396–397
local area networks (LANs). *See* networks
local bus video cards, 383
local Internet service providers (ISPs), 559–560
local printer installation, 298, 306–309, *307*, *308*
Lost File Fragments options in ScanDisk, 920
low-speed modulation protocol settings for HyperTerminal, 526
Lycos search engine, 623

M

Macintosh operating system, 7–8
Magellan search engine, 624
mail. *See* e-mail
Mail applet, 236
Maintenance Wizard, 915, **982–984**
manually resizing windows, 75–76, *76*
manually updating website subscriptions, 608, *609*
mapping network drives. *See also* networks
    mapping Windows 98 and Windows NT shared drives, 1061–1063
    overview of, 464–465
    from Windows 3.x file boxes, 465–466
    from Windows Explorer, 466–467
margin settings in Notepad, 878
marking
    e-mail in Outlook Express, 639
    newsgroup messages in Outlook Express, 678
maximizing windows, 71–74, *72*, *75*
Maximum Speed option in modem Properties dialog box, 498
MCA bus architecture, 1028
measurement units in WordPad, 815
Media Player, 384, **397–399**
memory
    memory shortage error messages in Drive Converter (FAT32), 973
    Paint images and, 832
    Windows 98 requirements, 50–51
memory keys in Calculator, 881
menus, 80–84. *See also* right-click menus; Start button
    arrows (➤) in, 83
    check marks in, 83
    dots (•) in, 83
    ellipses (…) in, 83
    grayed or dimmed commands, 83
    in Internet Explorer, 579
    key combinations in, 84
    menu bars defined, **80**
    opening, 80–81, *81*
    selecting commands, 82, *82*
    underlined letters in, 81
    View menu, **176–184**
        Active Desktop options, 183

Advanced settings, 179–182, *179*
Browse Folders as Follows options, 183
changing Clipboard view format, 209–210, *210*
Click Items as Follows options, 184
creating custom views, 182–184, *183*
Customize This Folder command, 727
overview of, 176
Refresh command, 172, 455
sorting and arranging file and folder icons and listings,
177–179
turning text labels on and off, 182
View Web Content in Folders options, 183–184
messages. *See* e-mail; newsgroups
microphone settings in NetMeeting, 752–753
microprocessors. *See* processors
Microsoft Chat, 903–910. *See also* chats
chat features, 908–910, *908*
chatting, 906–908, *906*
defined, **903**
starting, 903–906, *904*, *905*
Microsoft Download Service (MSDL), 248
Microsoft Exchange/Windows Messaging, 489, 490, 491
Microsoft Investor Tracker, 714–715
Microsoft Mail Postoffice applet, 236
Microsoft NetMeeting. *See* NetMeeting
Microsoft Outlook, 489, 490
Microsoft Outlook Express. *See* Outlook Express
Microsoft Paint. *See* Paint
Microsoft Plus!, 942
Microsoft System Information utility, 15, **22,** 915, 987
Microsoft Windows 3.x
File Manager, 27, 114, 117–119, *118*
font options, 357
importing Terminal program settings into HyperTerminal,
514
mapping network drives from Windows 3.x file boxes,
465–466
Paintbrush accessory, 825–826
Program Manager, 27, 119–120, *120*
system files and the Registry, 45–46
Windows 3.x applications and .ini files, 46
Write program, 772–773
Microsoft Windows 95
features introduced in, 10–13
networking features, 12
Microsoft Windows 98. *See also* new features
advantages of, **13–14, 22–25,** *24*, **27–28**
configuring for peer-to-peer networks, 1039, *1040*
cost of upgrade and retraining, **25–27**
defined, **6,** *7*
history of, 8–10
installing, **16, 1108–1122**
backing up before, 1110
on compressed drives, 1120–1121
deleting Uninstall files, 1119–1120
disk space requirements, 1109
from DOS, 1116–1117

finding and fixing hard disk drive problems during,
1117–1118
from floppy disks, 1110
full upgrades from earlier versions of Windows, 1109,
1110–1116
on a new disk drive or directory, 1109, 1116–1117
new features, **16**
on OS/2 systems, 1122
overview of, 1108–1110
running ScanDisk before, 1117–1118
saving system files for future uninstalls, 1119
uninstalling Windows 98, 1118–1119
on Windows NT computers, 1122
versus Macintosh operating system, 7–8
versus NetWare, **29,** *29*
shutting down or exiting, **61, 100–102,** *102*
starting, **62–64,** *64*
tour of, 64
upgrading to
cost of, **25–27**
overview of, **8–9**
usability studies, **23**
versus Windows NT, **28–30**
Microsoft Windows 98 networking model, 1002–1011
defined, **1002,** *1002*
Network Drivers Interface Specification (NDIS),
1002–1003
Open Datalink Interface (ODI) standard, 1003
protocols, **1003–1011**
DLC (Data Link Control), 1007
IPX/SPX and IPX/SPX with NetBIOS, 1005–1007
NetBEUI, 1008–1009
PPTP (Point-to-Point Tunneling Protocol), 20, 1011
selecting which protocol to use, 1003–1005, *1004*
TCP/IP, 1009–1001
Microsoft Windows NT, 1055–1063, 1122
C-2 security features, 28–29
domains and domain controllers, **1056,** 1058
installing Windows 98 on Windows NT computers, **1122**
networking Windows 98 workstations, **1059–1063**
adding Windows 98 workstations to NT servers,
1059–1061, *1060*
mapping Windows 98 and Windows NT shared drives,
1061–1063
sharing printers, 1061
NTFS file system, 967
version 5, 1057
versus Windows 98, **28–30**
Windows NT Workstation versus Windows NT Server,
1057–1059
Write program in NT 3.x, 772–773
MIDI Mapper, 385–386
minimized window buttons in Taskbar, 66
minimizing windows, 71–74, *72,* **111**
minus sign (–)
in newsgroups, 677
in Windows Explorer, 445
MMX processor support, 17

modem **Properties dialog box, 236**, 495–507, 519–534
    Connection tab, **498–500**
        Advanced Connection Settings dialog box, 500, *500*
        Advanced Port Settings dialog box, 499–500
        Call Preferences options, 499
        Connection Preferences options, 499
    defined, **236, 497**
    Diagnostics tab, 501–502, *501, 502*
    Dialing Properties dialog box, **502–507**
        calling card options, 504–507, *505, 506*
        disabling call waiting, 504
        overview of, 502, *503*
        telephone number and dialing code options, 502–503
        tone versus pulse dialing, 504
    Distinctive Ring tab, 500–501
    Forwarding tab, 501
    General tab, **498**
        Maximum Speed option, 498
        Port option, 498
        Speaker Volume option, 498
    HyperTerminal settings, **519–534**
        Advanced settings, 524–527
        basic settings, **520–524**
        call preferences settings, 524
        Connection tab, **522–527**, *523*
        data bits setting, 523
        data format settings, **522–523**
        error control settings, 525–526
        flow control settings, 526
        initialization settings, 526–527
        low-speed modulation protocol settings, 526
        modem speed setting, 522
        opening, 520–521, *521*
        overview of, 519–520
        parity setting, 523
        port setting, 521
        stop bits setting, 523
    installing modems, **495–497**, *495*
modems, 236, 492–507. *See also* communications features;
    Dial-Up Networking; Internet connections; PCMCIA cards
    baud rate versus bits per second (bps), **515**
    cell phones and, 494
    defined, **492, 514–515**
    Dial-Up Networking support for, 1072
    installing, **494–497**, *495*, **514–515**
    multiple modem or modem aggregation support, 497
    null-modem cable connections, **538**, *539*
    purchasing, **492–494**
        internal and external modems, PCMCIA cards,
            493–494
        modem compatibility, 494
        modem speed, 493
    setting up for Dial-Up Networking, **1073–1075**, *1074*
    sharing Internet modem connections, 1088
    speaker volume setting in HyperTerminal, 532
    Unimodem driver, 494–495, 1071
moderated newsgroups, 674

monitors. *See also* Display applet
    capturing screen images, 203–204
    Channel Screen Saver, **716–718**
        defined, **716**
        running, 716–717
        setting up, 717–718, *718*
    display setting enhancements, 17
    Display tab in Accessibility Options applet, **241–243**, *242*
    Multiple Display Support, **18**
    purchasing, 283
    refresh rates and color depth, 383–384
    screen fonts
        defined, **336, 338**
        printable screen fonts, **340**
        setting screen font size, 281
    screen resolution
        Active Desktop and, 712
        defined, **383–384**
        NetMeeting and, 751
        setting, 279–281, *280*
    setting refresh rate, 281–282, *282*
    setting screen font size, 281
    upgrading for multimedia, 383–384
    Windows 98 requirements, 52–53
monospaced fonts, 351
MoreFonts utility, 350
Motion tab in Mouse applet, 289–291, *290*
mounting compressed drives, 950–951
mouse. *See also* right-click menus
    clicking and double-clicking, **63**, 111
    dragging
        defined, **75**
        and dropping files, 160–162, *161, 162*
        and dropping folders, 158–160, *159*
        and dropping text in WordPad, 789–790
        files onto the Printer icon or window, 319–321, *320*
        right-click dragging, 160
    hovering, **699**
    I-beam pointer, **779**
    Intellimouse or wheel mouse support, 245
    minimizing, maximizing, restoring, and closing windows,
        71–74, *75*
    Mouse applet, **236, 287–291**
        defined, **236, 287**
        General tab, 291, *291*
        Motion tab, 289–291, *290*
        Pointers tab, 288–289, *289*
        right-hand and left-hand mouse settings, 287–288,
            287
    mouse control in NetMeeting, 761
    Mouse tab in Accessibility Options applet, **243–245**, *243,*
        244
    pointing in Web view, 97–98, *98*
    right-click dragging, 160
    right-click menus
        Cut, Copy, and Paste commands, 207, *208*
        Display option, 261
        moving text in WordPad, 788, *788*

overview of, **429–431**
printing by right-clicking on a document, 321
Send To command, 175, 457
Taskbar options, 146–147
single-clicking on the Active Desktop
  versus double clicking, 699
  selecting blocks of items with a single-click, 699–700
  switching between single-click and double-click
    modes, 700, *701*
in WordPad
  scrolling with the mouse, 780, *781*
  selecting with the mouse, 781–783, *782*
moving
versus copying, 159–160, 458
the cursor in WordPad, 778–780
e-mail in Outlook Express, 639
files in Windows Explorer
  between drives, 458
  between folders, 454–455, 457
folders, 451–452
between folders
  moving and copying files, 160–162, *161, 162,*
    454–455, 457
  moving and copying folders, 158, *159*
multiple folders simultaneously, 452, *453*
selected areas in Paint, 848
Start menu options in Active Desktop, 704–705
text in WordPad
  with cut and paste, 786–787
  with drag and drop, 789–790
  with right-click menus, 788, *788*
toolbars in Internet Explorer, 582
between Web pages in Internet Explorer, **585–588**
  with Address toolbar, 584, 587
  with Back and Forward commands or buttons,
    586–587
  with Favorites menu, 587–588
  with History and Temporary Internet Files folders, 588
  with hyperlinks, 585–586
windows, 77
MSDL (Microsoft Download Service), 248
MS-DOS. *See* DOS
multimedia, 16–17, 236, 369–425. *See also* sound
ActiveMovie architecture, **17**
Control Panel Multimedia applet, **236**
defined, **371–372**
digital cameras and photographs, 379–380
International Multimedia Telecommunications Consortium
  (IMTC), 765
managing drivers and settings, **424–425**
MMX processor support, 17
new features, **16–17,** 369–371, 373–374
Photo CD formats, 380
upgrading to multimedia, **374–384**
  CD writers (CD-R drives), 380–381
  CD-ROM drives, 379–380
  computers and processors, 379
  DVD drives, 381–382

  monitors and video cards, 383–384
  purchasing components, 374–378
  sound cards, 382
  speakers, 382
multimedia applications and utilities, 384–424
CD Player, **385, 403–410**
  cataloging CDs, 408–409, *408*
  creating play lists, 409
  defined, **385, 403–404**
  display options, 406–407
  play controls, 405–406, 407–408
  playing CDs from play lists, 410
  setting preferences, 410
  starting, 404
DVD Player, **385, 386–392**
  defined, **385**
  DVD defined, **386–387**
  ending DVD sessions, 392
  purchasing and installing DVD drives, 387–388
  running, 388–390
  selecting chapters and titles, 390–391
  selecting language and subtitles, 391–392
  for installing drivers, 385
Media Player, **384,** 397–399
MIDI Mapper, **385–386**
Sound Recorder, **384–385, 399–403**
  defined, **384–385,** 399
  editing sounds, 402–403
  playing sound files, 399–400
  recording sounds, 400–402, *401*
Sounds applet, **237, 384,** 392–397
  assigning sounds to Windows events, 394–396, *395*
  default directory for sounds, 395
  defined, **237, 384, 392–393**
  loading and saving sound schemes, 396–397
  recording or downloading sounds, 393–394
  troubleshooting sound problems, 394
TV Viewer, **17, 411–424**
  adding favorite channels to the toolbar, 421–422
  adding and removing channels manually, 416, *416*
  avoiding Channel 1, 417, *417*
  Broadcast Architecture and, 17, 411, 423
  defined, **17, 411–412**
  finding shows, 418–419
  finding shows by category, 419
  future of, 423–424
  how TV Viewer works, 412–413
  keyboard shortcuts, 422–423
  online Help, 416
  reading Program Guide information, 414–415, *415,*
    420, *420*
  remote controls, 422
  scrolling the display, 417–418, *418*
  setting reminders, 420–421, *421*
  starting, 413–415, *413, 414, 415*
  system requirements, 411
Volume Control, **385,** 893–895
WAV file editors, **384–385**

Multiple Display Support, 18
multiple modem or modem aggregation support, 497
multipoint data conferencing, 736, 737
multi-session Photo CD format, 380
multitasking and multithreading, 10
My Computer icon. *See also* Dial-Up Networking; icons
    accessing the Control Panel via, 234
    copying files and folders to and from floppy disks,
        172–175, *173, 174*
    navigating with Backspace key, 113, 458
    previewing files, 474
    property sheet for, 435–436, *436*
    running applications from, 111–114, *112, 114*
    viewing free space on disks, 175

N—————————————————————————————

names in e-mail and news accounts, 637
naming
    files and folders, 191–192
    options for Internet Explorer Favorites menu, 592
    printers, 307
national Internet service providers (ISPs), 558–559
navigating
    dialog boxes, 85–87, *87*
    folder windows with Backspace key, 113, 458
    between folders in Windows Explorer, 449
    Notepad documents from the keyboard, 877
NDIS (Network Drivers Interface Specification), 1002–1003
NetBEUI protocol, 1008–1009
NetMeeting, 733–765
    audio settings, 751–754
    Audio Tuning Wizard, 742, *743*, 750
    chat feature, **756**, *756*
    defined, **733–734**
    dialing history, 764
    downloading, 741
    file transfers, 762–763, *763*
    full duplex sound cards and, 742, 753
    hanging up, 751
    installing, **740–741**, *740*
    Internet Locator Service (ILS) and, 745
    microphone settings, 752–753
    mouse control, 761
    multipoint data conferencing and, 736, 737
    new features, 734–736, *735*
    Object Linking and Embedding and, 763
    saving Whiteboard work, 758
    screen resolutions and, 751
    sending e-mail, 764–765
    session example, 744–751, *747, 749*
    setting up, **741–744**, *742, 743, 744*
    sharing Clipboard contents, 761–762
    sharing documents and applications, 736, 759–761, *760*
    Speed Dial list, 764, *764*
    standards for, 738, 765
    system requirements, 739–740, 742

    telephone sound quality, 733
    uses for, 736–738
    video settings, 754–755, *755*
    video support, 735–736, *735*, 739
    websites about, 741, 744, 765
    Whiteboard feature, **757–758**, *758*
NetSearch search engine, 624
NetWare
    Client Services for NetWare, 22
    versus Windows 98, **29**, *29*
    Windows NT Workstation and, 1058
NetWatcher utility, 915, 980–982
Network Drivers Interface Specification (NDIS), 1002–1003
network interface cards (NICs)
    bus architectures and, 1028–1029
    installing for peer-to-peer networks, 1036–1038
    purchasing for peer-to-peer networks, 1035–1036, *1036*
    troubleshooting network interface card and driver prob-
        lems, 1099–1102, *1099, 1101*
    what if Windows 98 does not detect your network inter-
        face card, 1041
network layer in OSI reference model, 1001
Network Neighborhood icon in peer-to-peer networks,
    1044–1045
network printers
    installing, 298, **302–306**, *303, 304, 305*
    installing printer drivers for shared printers, 1048–1050
    password-protecting, 302, 314
    sharing, 302, **312–314**, 1061
networks, 463–472, 993–1011, 1015–1029, 1096–1106. *See
    also* peer-to-peer networks
    adding Windows 98 workstations to Windows NT net-
        works, **1059–1063**
        adding Windows 98 workstations to NT servers,
            1059–1061, *1060*
        mapping Windows 98 and Windows NT shared drives,
            1061–1063
        sharing printers, 1061
    cables, **1016–1020**
        coaxial cables, 1016–1017, *1017*
        installing for peer-to-peer networks, 1038–1039
        troubleshooting cable problems, 1097–1098
        unshielded twisted pair cables (UTP), 1017–1019,
            1018
        wireless networks, 1020
    carrier-sense multiple access with collision detection
        (CSMA/CD) networks, **1016**
    client/server networks, **463**, 468
    the Clipboard and, 211
    concentrators, **1022**
    Control Panel Network applet, **236**
    domains and domain controllers, **1056**, 1058
    entering network passwords, 63
    Ethernet networks, **1016–1026**
        carrier-sense multiple access with collision detection
            (CSMA/CD) networks, **1016**
        coaxial cables, 1016–1017, *1017*
        Fast Ethernet networks (100Base-T), 1024–1026

hubs and switches, 1024
thin Ethernet networks (10Base-2), 1021–1022, *1021*, 1024
twisted-pair Ethernet networks (10Base-T), 1022–1024, *1022*, 1025
unshielded twisted pair cables (UTP), 1017–1019, *1018*
hubs
defined, **1022**
star topology and, 1022–1023
versus switches, 1024
installing fonts from network drives, 355
mapping network drives
mapping Windows 98 and Windows NT shared drives, 1061–1063
overview of, 464–465
from Windows 3.x file boxes, 465–466
from Windows Explorer, 466–467
network adapter cards, **1026–1029**
new features, **26, 993–997**
OSI reference model, **997–1001**
application layer, *999*
data link layer, 1001
defined, **997–998**, *998*
network layer, 1001
physical layer, 1001
presentation layer, 999–1000
session layer, 1000
transport layer, 1000
peer-to-peer networks, **12, 463**
refreshing network print queue information, 323
topologies, **1020–1026**
bus topologies, 1021–1022, *1021*
Fast Ethernet networks (100Base-T), 1024–1026
star topologies, 1022–1023, *1022*
thin Ethernet networks (10Base-2), 1021–1022, *1021*, 1024
twisted-pair Ethernet networks (10Base-T), 1022–1024, *1022*, 1025
troubleshooting, **1095–1106**
boot failures, 1105–1106
cable problems, 1097–1098
hard disk drive crashes, 1102–1105
I/O address conflicts, 1097
network interface card and driver problems, 1099–1102, *1099, 1101*
overview of, 1095–1097
Windows 95 features, 12
Windows 98 networking model, **1002–1011**
defined, **1002**, *1002*
DLC (Data Link Control) protocol, 1007
IPX/SPX and IPX/SPX with NetBIOS protocols, 1005–1007
NetBEUI protocol, 1008–1009
Network Drivers Interface Specification (NDIS), 1002–1003
Open Datalink Interface (ODI) standard, 1003
PPTP (Point-to-Point Tunneling Protocol), 20, 1011

protocols, **1003–1011**
selecting which protocol to use, 1003–1005, *1004*
TCP/IP =PP, 1009–1001
Windows Explorer network operations, **463–472**
changing shared object permissions and other properties, 471–472
connecting to or mapping network drives, 464–465
disconnecting from network drives or folders, 468
mapping drives from Explorer, 466–467
mapping drives from Windows 3.x file boxes, 465–466
password settings, 471
setting permissions, 470–471
sharing drives and folders, 468–471, *469*
viewing shared drives and folders, 463–464, *464*
wireless LANs, **1020**
workgroups, **1056**
new features, **10–22**. *See also entries for specific features*
business-related features, 21–22
Client Services for NetWare, 22
Distributed Component Object Model (DCOM), 21–22
DLC (Data Link Control) protocol support, 22
Dr. Watson utility, 16, 22
System Information utility, 15, 22, 915, 987
Upgrade Wizard, 22
Win32 Driver Model (WDM), 21
Windows Scripting Host, 21
Windows Update, 15, 21, 915, 985–986, *986, 987*
in Calculator, 880
communications features, 489–490
in DriveSpace 3 utility, 941–942
ease of use features, **17–19**
DOS32 operating system, 18
FAT32 conversion utility, 17, 915, 970–973
FAT32 file system, 17, 915, 970–973
game support, 18
Infrared Data Association (IrDA) standard support, 19
Multiple Display Support, 18
PCMCIA support, 18–19
power management improvements, 17–18
Remote Access Server, 13, 18
entertainment and multimedia enhancements, **16–17, 369–371, 373–374**
ActiveMovie architecture, 17
display setting enhancements, 17
hardware support, 16
MMX processor support, 17
television and broadcast network access, 17
Internet features, **19–21, 24**
Dial-Up Networking improvements, 19–20
Integrated Internet Shell or Web view, 19, 24, *24*
Internet browser improvements, 20
Internet communication tools, 20
Online Services Folder, 21
personalized Internet information delivery, 20
PPTP (Point-to-Point Tunneling Protocol) support, 20, 1011
in NetMeeting, 734–736, *735*
network features, **26, 993–997**

overview of, 13–14
in Paint accessory, 826
reliability and performance improvements, **14–16**. *See also*
Backup
  accessibility tools, 16
  automatic ScanDisk after improper Shutdown, 16
  Disk Defragmenter, 15, 914, 956–961
  Dr. Watson utility, 16, 22
  HelpDesk, 14
  installation improvements, 16
  Microsoft System Information, 15, 22, 915, 987
  Shutdown improvements, 16
  System File Checker utility, 15
  Windows Tune-Up Wizard, 14–15
  Windows Update utility, 15, 21, 915, 985–986, *986, 987*
in Windows 95, **10–13**
newsgroups in Outlook Express, 666–679
browsing for messages, 677
categories of, 667
connecting to, 669–670
customizing news reading options, 686–688, *687*
customizing news sending options, 683–685
defined, **666–668**, *667*
filtering, 674–676
finding, 670–671, *671*
headers, 677
marking messages, 678
moderated newsgroups, **674**
overview of Outlook Express News, 668–669
plus sign (+) and minus sign (–) in, 677
posting to, 672–673, 674
reading, 671–672, *672*
reading off-line, 679
replying to, 672–673, 674
setting up news accounts, **633–637**
  establishing an ISP account, 633–634
  POP3, IMAP, and SMTP defined, **635**
  setting up news accounts, 636–637
  using real names versus aliases, 637
sorting messages, 678
starting Outlook Express News, 669
subscribing and unsubscribing to, 673
threads, 677
Usenet and, 666–668
viewing messages, 676
NICs. *See* network interface cards
notebook computers. *See* laptop computers
Notepad accessory, 872–879. *See also* WordPad
adding headers and footers, 878–879
creating documents, 874
defined, **872**
entering date and time, 877
entering and editing text, 875–877, *876*
finding text, 877–878
limitations of, 873
margin settings, 878
navigating from the keyboard, 877
opening files, 874–875

opening files in WordPad from, 875
printing files, 879
running, 873–874, *874*
text files defined, **872–873**
Word Wrap option, 875–876, *876*
notes in Outlook Express address books, *657, 658*
NTFS file system, *967*
null-modem cable connections, 538, *539*
Num Lock key, ToggleKeys shortcut, 240
numbers. *See also* Calculator
numeral fonts, 348, 351

O

Object Linking and Embedding (OLE), 12, 195–196,
213–227. *See also* Clipboard
advantages of, 215–217, *216*
versus the Clipboard, **213–214**
editing embedded objects, 223
editing linked objects, 226, *227*
embedding objects, **220–223**, *222*
linking versus embedding, **217–218**, *218*
linking objects, **224–226**
NetMeeting and, 763
object packages, **219–220**, *220*
objects, **217**
OLE servers, clients, source and destination documents,
  219
overview of, 12, 195–196, 213–215
Paste Special command, 224–226
terms defined, **217–220**, *218*
object packages, 219–220, *220*
object-oriented graphics, 827
objects, 217
obtaining digital IDs, *659, 690*
ODI (Open Datalink Interface) standard, 1003
off-line browsing with Internet Explorer, 588–590, *589*
100Base-T (Fast Ethernet) networks, 1024–1026
online services
as Internet service providers, 560–561
Online Services Folder, 21
OnNow option, 101
OnTrack Disk Manager utility, *973*
opaque images in Paint, 845, 849
Open Datalink Interface (ODI) standard, 1003
Open System Interconnect model. *See* OSI reference model
opening. *See also* running; starting
Control Panel, 234–235, *234*
documents
  in Notepad, 874–875
  in Paint, 828–829, *828*
documents in WordPad, **812–814, 875**
  ASCII files, 813–814
  documents in other formats, 813
  from File menu's Recently Opened Documents list, 813
  new documents, 814
  from Notepad, 875
  overview of, 812

menus, 80–81, *81*
modem Properties dialog box, 520–521, *521*
Outlook Express address books, 654
Start button menu with Ctrl-Esc, 119
OpenType fonts, 340
operating-system primitives, 35–37
option buttons in dialog boxes, 88
organizing Internet Explorer Favorites menu, 593–594, *594*
ornamental fonts, *351*, **352**
OS/2 systems, installing Windows 98 on, 1122
OSI reference model, 997–1001
    application layer, 999
    data link layer, 1001
    defined, **997–998**, *998*
    network layer, 1001
    physical layer, 1001
    presentation layer, 999–1000
    session layer, 1000
    transport layer, 1000
outdents in WordPad, 795
Outlook, 489, 490
Outlook Express, **489–490**, **491**, **629–693**. *See also* Internet
  connections
    address books, **653–664**
        adding notes to entries, 657, *658*
        creating, 654–655, *654*
        creating groups, 660–661, *661*
        customizing the Address Book window, 662
        defined, **653**
        entering business-related information, 657, *657*
        entering conferencing information, 658, *659*
        entering, deleting, and viewing digital IDs or certifi-
          cates, 658–659, *660*
        entering home-related information, 656–657, *656*
        entering personal information, 655–656
        importing from other mail programs, 653
        obtaining digital IDs, 659, 690
        opening, 654
        printing, 664
        searching directory services, 662–663
    customizing, **631–632**, **679–693**
        the Address Book window, 662
        advanced options, 691–693
        dial-up options, 690–691
        fonts for received messages, 687–688, *687*
        general options, 680–682
        Outlook Express window layout, 631–632, *631, 632*
        reading mail and news, 686–688, *687*
        security options, 689–690
        sending mail and news, 683–685
        spell checker options, 688–689
        the toolbar, 679–680
    defined, **629**, *630*
    e-mail, **637–652**
        adding background color to, 651
        adding pictures to, 649–651, *650*
        adding signatures to, 648–649
        attaching files to, 651–652
        backing up, 641
        creating or composing, 643–645, *644*
        customizing mail reading options, 686–688, *687*
        customizing mail sending options, 683–685
        deleting, 643
        entering header information, 644–645
        formatting, 646–647, *647*
        forwarding, 642
        marking, 639
        moving, 639
        overview of, 637–638
        printing, 639
        reading and saving attachments, 641
        replying to, 641–642
        retrieving or downloading, 646
        saving in Outlook Express folders, 640–641
        saving in Windows Explorer folders, 639–640
        sending, 645
        setting up e-mail accounts, 634–636
        using stationery, 648
    Inbox Assistant, **664–665**
    versus Microsoft Exchange/Windows Messaging, **491**
    newsgroups, **666–679**
        browsing for messages, 677
        categories of, 667
        connecting to, 669–670
        customizing news reading options, 686–688, *687*
        customizing news sending options, 683–685
        defined, **666–668**, *667*
        filtering, 674–676
        finding, 670–671, *671*
        headers, 677
        marking messages, 678
        moderated newsgroups, **674**
        overview of Outlook Express News, 668–669
        plus sign (+) and minus sign (–) in, 677
        posting to, 672–673, 674
        reading, 671–672, *672*
        reading off-line, 679
        replying to, 672–673, 674
        sorting messages, 678
        starting Outlook Express News, 669
        subscribing and unsubscribing to, 673
        threads, 677
        Usenet and, 666–668
        viewing messages, 676
    Outlook Bar, 632–633
    overview of, **489–490**, **629–633**, *630*
    Preview Pane, *630*, 631–632, *631, 632*
    setting up e-mail and news accounts, **633–637**
        establishing an ISP account, 633–634
        POP3, IMAP, and SMTP defined, **635**
        setting up e-mail accounts, 634–636
        setting up news accounts, 636–637
        using real names versus aliases, 637
    starting, 629
    Window Layout Properties dialog box, 631–632, *631, 632*

P

packaging objects, 219–220, *220*
packets, 999
Paint accessory, 823–856. *See also* accessories; graphics
  Attributes dialog box, 831–834
  bitmapped versus object-oriented graphics and, 826–827
  Color Box, **834–837, 854–855**
      creating custom colors, **854–855**
      defined, **824**
      foreground and background colors defined, **835**
      selecting color schemes, 835–836
      selecting colors with Eyedropper tool, 837
      setting foreground and background colors, 836–837
      tearing off or turning off, 829–830, *830*
      viewing and changing color settings, 836
  creating documents, **831–834**
      setting color or black-and-white option, 833–834
      setting picture size, 831–833
  defined, **823–824**
  displaying only the picture, 830–831
  file formats, 829, 855
  grayscale images, 833, 835–836
  how Paint works, **826–827**
  inverting colors, **851**, *852*
  memory and, 832
  new features, 826
  opening documents, **828–829**, *828*
  printing documents, 832, **856**
  saving documents, **855–856**
  saving selected areas, 850
  selecting areas, **847–851**
      flipping and rotating selections, 850–851, *851*
      moving selected areas, 848
      opaque versus transparent placement, 845, 849
      saving and retrieving selections, 850
      selecting irregular areas with Free-Form Select tool, 848
      selecting rectangular areas with Select tool, 847–848
      sweeping selections, 849
      using Clipboard with selections, 849–850
  starting, **824**, *825*
  status bar, 824, 830, 840
  stretching and skewing images, **852**, *853*
  Tool Box, **824, 829–830, 837–846**
      Airbrush tool, 841
      Box tool, 842–843
      Brush tool, 838–840, *839*
      Curve tool, 842
      defined, **824**
      Ellipse tool, 843
      Eraser tool, 840–841
      Eyedropper tool, 837
      Free-Form Select tool, 848
      Line tool, 842
      Paint Can tool, 845
      Pencil tool, 841
      Polygon tool, 843–844, *844*

  Rounded Box tool, 843
  Select tool, 847–848
  tearing off or turning off, 829–830, *830*
  Text tool, 845–846, *846*
  undoing mistakes, 840
  using tools, 837–838
  versus Windows 3.x Paintbrush, 825–826
  work area, 824
  zoom controls, 853–854, *854*
Panose information in fonts, 359–360
paragraphs in WordPad
  formatting, **790–796**
      bulleting paragraphs, 795–796
      changing paragraph alignment, 793
      hanging indents or outdents, 795
      indenting with Format Paragraph dialog box, 794
      indenting with the ruler, 794–795
      overview of, 790–791
      setting first-line indents, 795
      types of indentation, 793–794, *796*
      using the ruler, 791–792
      viewing paragraph alignment, 792–793
  selecting, 783, 784
parallel ports, Direct Cable Connect (DCC) utility and, **1034, 1089–1091**, *1090*
parentheses ( ) in Scientific Calculator, 883, 887
parity settings, 523
Partition Magic FAT32 conversion utility, 970, 972
passwords. *See also* security
  for Active Desktop, 698
  Control Panel Passwords applet, **236**
  entering network passwords, 63
  password-protecting network printers, 302, 314
  for shared folders and drives, 471
Paste Special command in Edit menu, 224–226
pausing
  all print jobs, 327
  a print job, 326, *326*
PCI local bus architecture, 1028–1029
PCMCIA cards
  Control Panel PCMCIA applet, **236**
  purchasing, 493–494
  support for, 18–19
peer-to-peer networks, 12, 463, 1033–1051. *See also* networks
  defined, **463, 1033–1034**, *1034*
  with Direct Cable Connection (DCC) utility, 1034, 1089–1091, *1090*
  installing printer drivers for shared printers, **1048–1050**
  Network Neighborhood icon, **1044–1045**
  security, **1050–1051**
      hiding share names, 1050
      read-level and read-write-level access control, 1051
      share-level and user-level access control, 1050
  setting up, **1035–1044**
      configuring Windows 98, 1039, *1040*
      installing cables, 1038–1039
      installing network drivers, 1039–1044, *1040*

installing network interface cards, 1036–1038
overview of, 1035
purchasing network interface cards, 1035–1036, *1036*
what if Windows 98 does not detect your network
interface card, 1041
sharing drives and subdirectories, **1045–1048**
from folders, 1045–1046, *1046*
from Windows Explorer, 1046–1048, *1047*
in Windows 95, **12**
Pencil tool in Paint, 841
percentages in Calculator, 883–884
performance improvements, 14–16
permanent AutoInstalled fonts, 365
permissions
changing shared object permissions, 471–472
setting, 470–471
personal information in Outlook Express address books,
655–656
Phone Dialer accessory, 492, 895–898
defined, **492, 895**
placing calls, 897–898, *898*
programming the Speed Dial list, 896–897, *897*
starting, 895–896, *896*
phone numbers
entering for HyperTerminal connections, 517
modem Properties dialog box options, 502–503
phone sound quality in NetMeeting, 733
Photo CD formats, 380
physical layer in OSI reference model, 1001
physically challenged user tools. *See* Accessibility Options
applet
pictures. *See* graphics
PIF settings for DOS applications, 133–136, *135*
placing calls with Phone Dialer, 897–898, *898*
planning networks, 1015–1029
cables, **1016–1020**
coaxial cables, 1016–1017, *1017*
installing for peer-to-peer networks, 1038–1039
troubleshooting cable problems, 1097–1098
unshielded twisted pair cables (UTP), 1017–1019, *1018*
wireless networks, 1020
carrier-sense multiple access with collision detection
(CSMA/CD) networks, **1016**
hubs
defined, **1022**
star topology and, 1022–1023
versus switches, 1024
overview of, 1015–1016
selecting network interface cards and drivers, **1026–1029**
topologies, **1020–1026**
bus topologies, 1021–1022, *1021*
Fast Ethernet networks (100Base-T), 1024–1026
star topologies, 1022–1023, *1022*
thin Ethernet networks (10Base-2), 1021–1022, *1021*,
1024
twisted-pair Ethernet networks (10Base-T),
1022–1024, *1022*, 1025
play controls in CD Player, 405–406, 407–408

playing
CDs from CD Player play lists, 410
sound files with Sound Recorder, 399–400
Plug-and-Play. *See also* Add New Hardware applet
Plug-and-Play standard, 13
Windows 98 requirements, 53–55
plus sign (+)
in newsgroups, 677
in Windows Explorer, 443–444
Point search engine, 624
Pointers tab in Mouse applet, 288–289, *289*
pointing in Web view, 97–98, *98*
Point-to-Point Tunneling Protocol (PPTP), 20, 1011
Polygon tool in Paint, 843–844, *844*
POP3 (Post Office Protocol 3), 635
portable computers. *See* laptop computers
ports
Advanced Port Settings dialog box, 499–500
COM versus serial ports, **521**
Direct Cable Connect (DCC) utility and, 1034,
1089–1091, *1090*
Port option in modem Properties dialog box, 498
port setting for HyperTerminal, 521
printer ports, 296, 307, 309
positioning
graphics in WordPad, 809
tab stops in WordPad, 801
toolbars in WordPad, *775, 776*
Post Office Protocol 3 (POP3), 635
posting messages to newsgroups, 672–673, 674
PostScript files (.EPS), 330
PostScript fonts, 330, 339, 349
power management improvements, 17–18
Powerpak for Windows utility, 350
PPP Internet connections, 556
PPTP (Point-to-Point Tunneling Protocol), 20, 1011
preemptive multitasking, 10
presentation layer in OSI reference model, 999–1000
Preview Pane in Outlook Express, *630, 631–632, 631, 632*
previewing
documents in WordPad, 817–818, *817*
files in Windows Explorer, 474–476, *475*
primitives, 35–37
printable screen fonts, 340
printer fonts, 336, 338, 340, 353, 798
printers, 237, 295–316
connecting to network printers, **314–315**
Control Panel Printers applet, **237**
deleting from Printers folder, 315–316
and deleting print jobs, 324
installing, **298–311**
Add Printer Wizard, **298, 302–306**
adding local printers, 298, 306–309, *307, 308*
adding network printers, 298, 302–306, *303, 304, 305*
customizing printer setup, 299
printer drivers and, 301–302, 310–311
what to do if your printer is not listed, 310–311
when you'll need to install printers, 300–301

naming, 307
network printers
  installing, 298, **302–306**, *303, 304, 305*
  installing printer drivers for shared printers, 1048–1050
  password-protecting, 302, 314
  sharing, 302, **312–314**, 1061
overview of, **295–296**
password-protecting network printers, 302, 314
Print Manager features, *297*
printer ports, 296, 307, 309
Printer Properties dialog box, 311–312, *313*
setting the default printer, 305–306, *305*, 316–317
sharing network printers, 302, **312–314**
sharing printers in Windows NT networks, 1061
TrueType fonts and, 337
printing, 295–296, 316–330
from applications, **317–319**
by dragging files onto the Printer icon or window,
  319–321, *320*
by right-clicking on a document, 321
default printer and, 305–306, *305*, 316–317
to disk files, **328–330**
from DOS applications, 296
e-mail in Outlook Express, 639
to encapsulated PostScript files (.EPS), 330
in Notepad, **879**
Outlook Express address books, 664
overview of, 295–296
in Paint, 832, **856**
print queues, **322–327**
  canceling all pending print jobs, 325
  deleting files from print queues, 323–325
  pausing and resuming all print jobs, 327
  pausing and resuming a print job, 326, *326*
  rearranging the print order, 327, *327*
  refreshing network queue information, 323
  viewing, 322–323, *322*
from Windows Explorer, **456**
in WordPad, **818–819**
processors
I/O permission bitmaps in Intel processors, **37**
MMX processor support, 17
upgrading for multimedia, 379
Windows 98 requirements, 49–50
Prodigy Internet connections, 560–561
productivity-enhancement software, 34–35
profiles
for Dial-Up Networking
  changing default connection profile, 568–569, *569*
  creating connection profiles, 566–568, *567, 568*
user profiles for the Active Desktop, 698
Program Manager, 27, 119–120, *120*
property sheets, 431–436
changing shared object properties, 471–472
defined, **431–432**
Display Properties dialog box for Active Desktop, 709, *709*
display properties in System Monitor, 975–977
for documents, 433–434, *433*

for DOS sessions, 131–136, *135*
of fonts, 359
for My Computer, 435–436, *436*
Printer Properties dialog box, 311–312, *313*
setting annotation properties in Kodak Imaging, 864–866
for shortcuts, 434–435, *434*
viewing in Windows Explorer, 457
who uses, 432
proportionally spaced fonts, 351
protocols, 1003–1011
for Dial-Up Networking, 1072, 1084–1085
DLC (Data Link Control), 22, 1007
file-transfer protocols in HyperTerminal, 544–545
IMAP (Internet Message Access Protocol), 635
IPX/SPX and IPX/SPX with NetBIOS, 1005–1007
LDAP (Lightweight Directory Access Protocol), 899, 900,
  902
NetBEUI, 1008–1009
POP3 (Post Office Protocol 3), 635
PPTP (Point-to-Point Tunneling Protocol), 20, 1011
selecting which protocol to use, 1003–1005, *1004*
SMTP (Simple Internet Mail Protocol), 635
TCP/IP, 553, 1009–1001
Publisher's Powerpak for Windows utility, 350
pulse dialing, 504
purchasing
DVD drives, 387–388
fonts, 347–348, 350, 352
modems, **492–494**
  internal and external modems, PCMCIA cards,
    493–494
  modem compatibility, 494
  modem speed, 493
monitors and video cards, 283
multimedia components, 374–378
network interface cards for peer-to-peer networks,
  1035–1036, *1036*
PCMCIA cards, 493–494
push technology, 67

Q

quick erasing floppy disks, 450
Quick Launch toolbar
on the Active Desktop, 703–704, 705, 707
defined, **146–148**, *147*
quotes (') and double quotes (") in Web search engines,
  618

R

RAM. *See* memory
RAS (Remote Access Services), 13, **18**, **1069–1070**
reading. *See also* sending
customizing mail and news reading options in Outlook
  Express, 686–688, *687*

e-mail attachments in Outlook Express, 641
newsgroups, 671–672, *672*
newsgroups off-line, 679
TV Program Guide information, 414–415, *415*, 420, *420*
read-level and read-write-level access control in peer-to-peer networks, 1051
read-only versus read-write embedded fonts, 345
rearranging
columns in Details view, 729
print order of print jobs, 327, *327*
rebooting computers, 61
receiving data with HyperTerminal, 539–549
backscroll buffers and, 540
capturing text, 541
ending communications sessions, 548–549
how HyperTerminal displays and stores text, 540
interactive or terminal mode sessions, 539–540, *540*
receiving binary files, 544–545, 547–548
receiving text files, 542–544
selecting file-transfer protocols, 544–545
text-file transfer settings, 543
recording
sound files with Sound Recorder, 400–402, *401*
sounds for system events, 393–394
Recycle Bin, 187–191
deleting and, 187–188, 450
emptying, 190–191
logical drives and, 188
restoring files and folders from, 188–190, *189, 190*
refresh rate of monitors, 281–282, *282*, 383–384
refreshing
Active Desktop, 706
folder window contents, 172, 455
network print queue information, 323
Regional Settings applet, 237
Registry
defined, **11**
font installation and, 362
registering file extensions, **123–124**
Windows 3.x system files and, 45–46
reliability improvements, 14–16
Remote Access Services (RAS), 13, 18, 1069–1070
remote computing, 1067–1069. *See also* Dial-Up Networking
defined, **1068–1069**
overview of, 1067–1068
remote control versus remote node software, 1069
remote connections, 1076–1082. *See also* HyperTerminal
application-initiated connections, 1079–1080
explicit connections, 1077–1079, *1078*
implicit connections, 1080–1082, *1081*
running applications remotely, 1076
remote controls for TV Viewer, 422
removing. *See* deleting
renaming files and folders, 191–192, 457
replacing text in WordPad, 786, 804
replying
to e-mail in Outlook Express, 641–642
to newsgroup messages in Outlook Express, 672–673, 674

Report MS-DOS Mode Name Length Errors option in ScanDisk, 923
repositioning
tab stops in WordPad, 801
toolbars in WordPad, 775, *776*
reset button, 61
resizing
graphics in WordPad, 809–810
the Taskbar, 138
toolbars in Internet Explorer, 582
windows manually, 75–76, *76*
windows with Minimize, Maximize or Restore, and Close buttons, 71–74, *75*
resolution of monitors
Active Desktop and, 712
defined, **383–384**
NetMeeting and, 751
setting, 279–281, *280*
restoring files from backups, 933–938
without the Wizard, 937–938, *937*
with the Wizard, 934–936, *936*
restoring windows, 71–74, *72*
resuming
all print jobs, 327
a print job, 326, *326*
retrieving
e-mail in Outlook Express, 646
saved selections in Paint, 850
stored Clipboard file contents, 212
Rich Text Format (RTF) files, 812, 813, 815–816
right-click dragging, 160
right-click menus. *See also* menus; property sheets
Cut, Copy, and Paste commands, 207, *208*
Display option, 261
moving text in WordPad, 788, *788*
overview of, **429–431**
printing by right-clicking on a document, 321
Send To command, 175, 457
Taskbar options, 146–147
right-hand mouse settings, 287–288, *287*
rights. *See* permissions
rotating
images in Kodak Imaging, 859
selections in Paint, 850–851, *851*
Rounded Box tool in Paint, 843
RTF (Rich Text Format) files, 812, 813, 815–816
ruler in WordPad, 775, 791–792, 794–795
Run option in Start button menu, 117, 119–120, 121
running. *See also* opening; starting
applications, **106–127**
from batch files, 137
by right-clicking the Desktop, 124–126, *125*
from a document, 123–124, *123*, 126–127, *127*
DOS applications, 35–40, 107–108, 127–130, *129, 130*
DOS session property settings, 131–136, *135*
from File Manager, 114, 117–119, *118*
from MS-DOS Prompt, 107–108, 129–136, *130, 135*

from My Computer icon, 111–114, *112, 114*
overview of, 106–107
from Program Manager, 119–120, *120*
remotely, 1076
shell programs, 40–41
from the Start button, 107–110, *109*
from Start button Find option, 120–122, *122*
from Windows Explorer, 114–117, *115, 116*, 456
Backup utility, **925–931**
overview of, 925–926
without the Wizard, 930–931, *930*
via the Wizard, 926–929, *926, 927*
Channel Screen Saver, 716–717
Character Map, 889–890
Compression Agent, 954–956
Disk Defragmenter, 958–961, *960*
DOS applications and utilities, 35–40
Drive Converter (FAT32), 971–972
DVD Player, 388–390
Install Hardware Wizard, 248–250, *249*
multiple copies of WordPad, 805–806, *805*
Notepad, 873–874, *874*
ScanDisk, 916–917, *917*
ScanDisk before installing Windows 98, 1117–1118
scheduled tasks immediately, 980
Scheduled Tasks Wizard, 977–979
shell programs, 40–41
System Monitor, 974, *974*
Windows 3.x and 95 utilities, 41–46, *42*

S

sans-serif fonts, 350, *351*
saving
Clipboard contents to files, 211–212
documents
in Kodak Imaging, 867
in Paint, 855–866
in WordPad, 810–812, *811*
e-mail attachments in Outlook Express, 641
e-mail in Outlook Express folders, 640–641
e-mail in Windows Explorer folders, 639–640
files in the root directory, 157
HyperTerminal settings, 534
NetMeeting Whiteboard work, 758
in Paint
saving documents, 855–856
saving selected areas, 850
sound schemes, 396–397
Windows 98 system files for future uninstalls, 1119
scalable fonts, 346, 349–350
ScanDisk utility, 16, 913–923
automatic execution of after improper Shutdown, 16, 916
defined, **913, 914**
running, 916–917, *917*
running before installing Windows 98, 1117–1118

ScanDisk Advanced Options dialog box, **918–923**
compressed drive options, 921–922
Cross-linked Files options, 919–920
Display Summary options, 918–919
file-checking options, 921
Lost File Fragments options, 920
Report MS-DOS Mode Name Length Errors option, 923
Surface Scan options, 922–923
testing disks, 917–918
scanning images in Kodak Imaging, 861–862
Scheduled Tasks Wizard, 977–980
defined, **977**
running, 977–979
running tasks immediately, 980
scheduling website subscription updates, 607–608, *607*
Scientific Calculator, 884–888
defined, **884–885,** *884*
entering numbers in scientific notation, 885–886
grouping terms with parentheses, 883, 887
Inv and Hyp options, 885
statistical calculations, 881, 887–888
using different number bases, 886–887
screen captures, 203–204
screen fonts. *See also* fonts
defined, **336, 338**
printable screen fonts, **340**
setting screen font size, 281
screen resolution. *See also* monitors
Active Desktop and, 712
defined, **383–384**
NetMeeting and, 751
setting, 279–281, *280*
screen savers
Channel Screen Saver, **716–718**
defined, **716**
running, 716–717
setting up, 717–718, *718*
Screen Saver tab in Display applet, 266–267
scripts, Windows Scripting Host, **21**
scroll bars
in Internet Explorer, 580
in Windows 98, 78–80, *78*
scrolling
TV Viewer display, 417–418, *418*
in WordPad
with the keyboard, 781
with the mouse, 780, *781*
search engines, 616–626
AltaVista, 619, 623
BigBook, 625
combining keywords, 617
c|net's Shareware Directory, 625
Dejavu News, 625
Environmental Organization Web Directory, 625
Excite, 624
finding exact matches, 618
Homework Help, 626

Infoseek, 623
installing Web Search component on Active Desktop, 715–716
keywords in, 616–618
Lycos, 623
Magellan, 624
NetSearch, 624
Point, 624
Search.com, 624
search and index sites, 619
searching versus browsing with, 618
searching with Explorer bar, 619–622, *620, 621, 622*
Starting Point, 624
The Electric Library, 625
using quotes (') and double quotes ("), 618
using wildcards, 617–618
Webcrawler, 624
Who/Where?, 625
WWWomen, 625
Yahoo!, 623
searching. *See* finding
security. *See also* passwords
Dial-Up Networking security, **1085–1087**
callback feature, 1085–1086
Internet connections and, 1086–1087, *1087*
overview of, 1085–1086
in peer-to-peer networks, **1050–1051**
hiding share names, 1050
read-level and read-write-level access control, 1051
share-level and user-level access control, 1050
security options in Outlook Express, 689–690
Select Network Component Type dialog box, 565–566, *565*
Select tool in Paint, 847–848
selecting
blocks of items with a single-click on the Active Desktop, 699–700
chapters and titles in DVD Player, 390–391
color schemes in Paint, 835–836
colors with Eyedropper tool in Paint, 837
compression methods in DriveSpace, 952–953, *952*
drives in Windows Explorer, 446–447, *447*
files in Windows Explorer, 448, 455–456
file-transfer protocols in HyperTerminal, 544–545
folders in Windows Explorer, 448–449
fonts, 346–347
how much content should be delivered via website subscriptions, 604–606, *604, 605, 606*
how you want to be notified about website subscriptions, 602–603, *603*
Internet service providers, **556–561**
local ISPs, 559–560
national ISPs, 558–559
online services, 560–561
overview of, 556–558
language and subtitle options in DVD Player, 391–392
menu commands, 82, *82*
network interface cards and drivers, 1026–1029

in Paint, **847–851**
flipping and rotating selections, 850–851, *851*
moving selected areas, 848
opaque versus transparent placement, 845, 849
saving and retrieving selections, 850
selecting irregular areas with Free-Form Select tool, 848
selecting rectangular areas with Select tool, 847–848
sweeping selections, 849
using Clipboard with selections, 849–850
Start button options, 110
submenus for new entries in Internet Explorer Favorites menu, 592–593
which networking protocol to use, 1003–1005, *1004*
in Windows applications, 198–200, *199, 200*
in WordPad
entire documents, 784, 802
lines of text, 784
with the mouse, 781–783, *782*
paragraphs, 783, 784
sentences, 784
with the Shift key, 783
units of measurement, 815
words, 783, 815
Send To command, 175, 457
sending. *See also* reading
customizing mail and news sending options in Outlook Express, 683–685
data with HyperTerminal, **539–549**
backscroll buffers and, 540
ending communications sessions, 548–549
how HyperTerminal displays and stores text, 540
interactive or terminal mode sessions, 539–540, *540*
selecting file-transfer protocols, 544–545
sending binary files, 544–545, 546–547, *547*
sending text files, 542–544
text-file transfer settings, 543
e-mail in NetMeeting, 764–765
e-mail in Outlook Express, 645
posting messages to newsgroups, 672–673, 674
sentence selection in WordPad, 784
serial cable connections, 538, *539*
serial ports
defined, **521**
Direct Cable Connect (DCC) utility and, **1034,** **1089–1091,** *1090*
serif fonts, 350, *351*
servers
defined, **489**
Dial-Up Networking support for, 1071, 1083–1084, *1083*
OLE servers, **219**
session layer in OSI reference model, 1000
setting
annotation properties in Kodak Imaging, 864–866
CD Player preferences, 410
Clipboard view format, 209–211, *210*
color or black-and-white option in Paint accessory, 833–834
date and time, 235, 258–259, *259*

the default printer, 305–306, *305*, 316–317
dialing properties for HyperTerminal, 518
foreground and background colors in Paint, 836–837
indentation in WordPad, 793–795, *796*
Internet Explorer as the default browser, 577
Kodak Imaging as default graphics viewer, 857
passwords for shared folders and drives, 471
permissions for network drives, 470–471
picture size in Paint, 831–833
refresh rate of monitors, 281–282, *282*
reminders in TV Viewer, 420–421, *421*
screen font size, 281
screen resolution, 279–281, *280*
tab stops in WordPad, 800–801, *800*
website subscription schedules, 607–608, *607*
setting up. *See also* installing
  Channel Screen Saver, 717–718, *718*
  Dial-Up Networking, **564–571**, **1075–1076**, **1082–1085**
    changing default connection profile, 568–569, *569*
    creating connection profiles, 566–568, *567*, *568*
    dialing properties, 1082
    disabling automatic phone dialing by Internet pro-
      grams, 570–571
    installing Dial-Up Networking software, 565–566, *565*
    overview of, 564–565, 1075–1076
    protocols, 1084–1085
    server types, 1083–1084, *1083*
  e-mail and news accounts for Outlook Express, **633–637**
    establishing an ISP account, 633–634
    POP3, IMAP, and SMTP defined, **635**
    setting up e-mail accounts, 634–636
    setting up news accounts, 636–637
    using real names versus aliases, 637
  HyperTerminal connections, **515–518**
    commas (,) in phone numbers for modem connec-
      tions, 518
    defining a new connection, 516–517
    entering phone numbers, 517
    setting dialing properties, 518
  modems for Dial-Up Networking, 1073–1075, *1074*
  NetMeeting, 741–744, *742*, *743*, *744*
  peer-to-peer networks, **1035–1044**
    configuring Windows 98, 1039, *1040*
    installing cables, 1038–1039
    installing network drivers, 1039–1044, *1040*
    installing network interface cards, 1036–1038
    overview of, 1035
    purchasing network interface cards, 1035–1036, *1036*
    what to do if Windows 98 does not detect your net-
      work adapter card, 1041
Settings submenu on Start button
  Control Panel option, 234, *234*
  Folder Options, 700
  Taskbar option, 138–140, *139*, 143–145
shareware, 625
sharing. *See also* networks; peer-to-peer networks
  changing shared object permissions and other properties,
    471–472

  Clipboard contents in NetMeeting, 761–762
  documents and applications in NetMeeting, 736,
    759–761, *760*
  drives and folders, 468–471, *469*
  drives and subdirectories in peer-to-peer networks,
    1045–1048
    from folders, 1045–1046, *1046*
    from Windows Explorer, 1046–1048, *1047*
  Internet modem connections, 1088
  network printers, 302, **312–314**
  printers in Windows NT networks, 1061
  share-level access control in peer-to-peer networks, **1050**
  viewing shared drives and folders, 463–464, *464*
Shift key
  drawing with in Paint, 843
  selecting with in WordPad, 783
  single-click selecting with, 699
  StickyKeys and FilterKeys shortcuts, 240
shortcut keys
  in Calculator, 882
  for character formatting in WordPad, 797, 799
  for cutting, copying, and pasting, 198
  in menus, 84
  for StickyKeys, FilterKeys, and ToggleKeys, 240
  in TV Viewer, 422–423
shortcut menus. *See* right-click menus
shortcuts
  copying files and folders to floppy disk shortcuts, 176
  creating, **166–169**, 457
  defined, **136**, **144**
  property sheets for, 434–435, *434*
Show Desktop button on the Active Desktop, 704, 705
Show Windows Contents While Dragging option, 76
ShowSounds options in Accessibility Options applet,
  240–241, *241*
Shutdown. *See also* Start button
  automatic ScanDisk execution after improper Shutdown,
    16, 916
  new features, 16
  shutting down Windows 98, 61, **100–102**, *102*
  Suspend, Standby, Hibernate, and OnNow options, **101**
signatures in Outlook Express e-mail, 648–649
Simple Internet Mail Protocol (SMTP), 635
single-clicking on the Active Desktop
  versus double clicking, 699
  selecting blocks of items with a single-click, 699–700
  switching between single-click and double-click modes,
    700, *701*
single-session Photo CD format, 380
sizing
  graphics in WordPad, 809–810
  the Taskbar, 138
  toolbars in Internet Explorer, 582
  windows manually, 75–76, *76*
  windows with Minimize, Maximize or Restore, and Close
    buttons, 71–74, *75*
skewing images in Paint, **852**, *853*
small caps, 348

smoothing fonts, 275
SMTP (Simple Internet Mail Protocol), 635
soft fonts, 336, 340
software. *See* accessories; applications; utilities
sorting
    file and folder icons and listings in folders, 177–179
    newsgroup messages in Outlook Express, 678
sound. *See also* multimedia
    audio settings for NetMeeting, 751–754
    full duplex sound cards, 742, 753
    sound cards, 382
    sound quality in NetMeeting, 733
    Sound Recorder, **384–385, 399–403**
        defined, **384–385, 399**
        editing sounds, 402–403
        playing sound files, 399–400
        recording sounds, 400–402, *401*
    Sound tab in Accessibility Options applet, **240–241,** *241*
    Sounds applet, **237, 384, 392–397**
        assigning sounds to Windows events, 394–396, *395*
        default directory for sounds, 395
        defined, **237, 384, 392–393**
        loading and saving sound schemes, 396–397
        recording or downloading sounds, 393–394
        troubleshooting sound problems, 394
source documents in OLE, 219
spacebar, Alt key + spacebar, 77
spacing between sentences in WordPad, 777
speakers
    modem speaker volume setting in HyperTerminal, 532
    for multimedia, 382
    Speaker Volume option in modem Properties dialog box, 498
special characters. *See* Character Map accessory
Speed Dial list
    in NetMeeting, 764, *764*
    in Phone Dialer, 896–897, *897*
spell checker in Outlook Express, 688–689
square roots in Calculator, 883–884
Stacker compressed drives, 1121
Standard toolbar
    in Internet Explorer, 581, 583
    in WordPad, 774, 775
standards for NetMeeting, 738, 765
Standby option, 101
star network topologies, 1022–1023, *1022*
Start button. *See also* Taskbar
    on the Active Desktop, **704–705**
    adding options to Start button, **143–145,** *144, 145*
    customizing submenus, **149–156**
        adding options, 149–152, *149, 150, 152*
        Advanced options, 154–156, *155*
        deleting options, 153–154, *154*
    Find option
        overview of, 41–43, *42*
        running applications from, 120–122, *122*
    Find People dialog box, **704, 898–902**
        in Active Desktop, 704

    defined, **898**
    finding people or businesses, 899–902, *901*
    getting registered in LDAP, 902
    LDAP (Lightweight Directory Access Protocol) and, 899, 900, 902
    finding options in, 110
    opening with Ctrl-Esc, 119
    Run option, 117, 119–120, 121
    running applications from, **107–110,** *109*
    running applications from MS-DOS Prompt, 107–108, 129–136, *130, 135*
    selecting options, 110
    Settings submenu
        Control Panel option, 234, *234*
        Folder Options, 700
        Taskbar option, 138–140, *139,* 143–145
    Shutdown option
        automatic ScanDisk execution after improper Shutdown, 16, 916
        new features, 16
        shutting down Windows 98, **61, 100–102,** *102*
        Suspend, Standby, Hibernate, and OnNow options, **101**
start pages, changing in Internet Explorer, 576
starting. *See also* opening; running
    Calculator, 879
    CD Player, 404
    File Manager, 117–118, *118*
    HyperTerminal, 516
    Internet Explorer, 575–577
    Microsoft Chat, 903–906, *904, 905*
    Outlook Express, 629
    Outlook Express News, 669
    Paint, 824, *825*
    Phone Dialer, 895–896, *896*
    Program Manager, 119–120, *120*
    TV Viewer, 413–415, *413, 414, 415*
    Windows 98, **62–64,** *64*
    Windows Explorer, 115–116, 442–443, *443*
Starting Point search engine, 624
stationery for e-mail in Outlook Express, 648
statistical calculations in Scientific Calculator, 881, 887–888
status bar
    in Internet Explorer, 580
    in Paint, 824, 830, 840
    in Windows Explorer, 445
    in WordPad, 775
StickyKeys options in Accessibility Options applet, 239–240
stop bits setting, 523
stretching images in Paint, 852, *853*
subscribing
    to Active Channels, 610, 614–616, *615*
    to newsgroups, 673
    to websites, **594–609**
        Advanced Download Options dialog box, 605–606, *606*
        browsing updated subscriptions, 597–599
        browsing updated subscriptions off-line, 598

canceling subscriptions, **599**
changing subscription settings in Favorites menu, 601
defined, **594–596**
Downloading Subscriptions dialog box, 608, *609*
overview of, 600–601
selecting how much content should be delivered,
   604–606, *604*, *605*, *606*
selecting how you want to be notified, 602–603, *603*
setting subscription schedules, 607–608, *607*
subscribing to sites, 591, *592*, **596–597**
Subscription Wizard, 602–608
updating subscriptions manually, 608, *609*
viewing current subscription settings, 601, *602*
viewing current subscriptions, 599–600, *600*
substituting fonts, 336, 341, 356–357, *356*
subtitle option in DVD Player, 391–392
SuperPrint font utility, 350
SuperStor compressed drives, 1121
Surface Scan options in ScanDisk, 922–923
Suspend option, 101
sweeping selections in Paint, 849
switches, 1024
switching
   between applications, 137–140, *139*
   between Classic and Web views, 96–97, *97*, 100
   between single-click and double-click modes on the Active
     Desktop, 700, *701*
symbols. *See* Character Map accessory
System Agent. *See* Task Scheduler
System applet, 237, 248, 385
system bus architectures for computers, 1028–1029
system disks, creating, 459–460, *461*
System File Checker utility, 15
system files, displaying, 114
System Information utility, 15, 22, 915, 987
System Monitor utility, 914, 973–977
   changing display properties, 975–977
   defined, **914, 973**
   deleting monitors from the window, 976
   installing, 973–974
   running, 974, *974*
   selecting display type, 976
   selecting monitors to display, 975
system requirements. *See* hardware
System Tools, 913–987. *See also* System Monitor
   Backup utility, **16, 914, 924–938**
     backup and restore option settings, 938, *938*
     defined, **914**
     error messages, 932
     finishing backups, 931–932
     installing, 925
     new features, 16, 925
     overview of, 924–925
     restoring files without the Wizard, 937–938, *937*
     restoring files with the Wizard, 933–936, *936*
     running without the Wizard, 925–926, 930–931, *930*
     running via the Wizard, 925–929, *926*, *927*
     Tools menu options, 932–933

Compression Agent utility, **915, 953–956**
Disk Cleanup utility, **915, 961–965**, *963*
Disk Defragmenter utility, **15, 914, 956–961**
   defined, **15, 914, 956–957**
   defragmenting disk drives defined, **36, 956–957**
   running, 958–961, *960*
   running DOS defragmenters, 36
   when to use, 957
Drive Converter (FAT32) utility, **17, 915, 970–973**
   defined, **17, 915, 970**
   memory shortage error messages, 973
   running, 971–972
DriveSpace 3 utility, **914, 939–953**
   adjusting the amount of free space, 947, *948*
   advanced compression settings, 952–953, *952*
   auto-mount settings, 953
   changing estimated compression ratio, 951
   compatibility with other compression utilities, 942
   compressing drives, **942–947**, *944*
   compressing existing free space, 949–950, *949*
   compressing Zip drives, 947
   defined, **914, 939**
   deleting compressed drives, 950
   FAT32 file system incompatibility, 941, 968–969
   how DriveSpace works, 939–940
   Microsoft Plus! and, 942
   mounting and unmounting compressed drives,
     950–951
   new features, 941–942
   ScanDisk utility and, 921–922
   selecting compression method, 952–953, *952*
   uncompressing compressed drives, 948
   when to use, 940–941
Maintenance Wizard, **915, 982–984**
NetWatcher utility, **915, 980–982**
overview of, **914–915**, *914*
ScanDisk utility, **16, 913–923**
   automatic execution of after improper Shutdown, 16,
     916
   compressed drive options, 921–922
   Cross-linked Files options, 919–920
   defined, **913, 914**
   Display Summary options, 918–919
   file-checking options, 921
   Lost File Fragments options, 920
   Report MS-DOS Mode Name Length Errors option,
     923
   running, 916–917, *917*
   running before installing Windows 98, 1117–1118
   ScanDisk Advanced Options dialog box, **918–923**
   Surface Scan options, 922–923
   testing disks, 917–918
Scheduled Tasks Wizard, **977–980**
   defined, **977**
   running, 977–979
   running tasks immediately, 980
System Information utility, **15, 22, 915, 987**
Windows Update Wizard, **15, 21, 915, 985–986**, *986*, *987*

T

Tab key, Alt + Tab (switching between applications), 140
tab stops in WordPad, 800–801
    clearing, 801
    repositioning, 801
    setting, 800–801, *800*
TAPI (Telephony API), 491–492, 1070
Task Scheduler Wizard, 977–980
    defined, **977**
    running, 977–979
    running tasks immediately, 980
Taskbar. *See also* Start button
    on the Active Desktop, **703–704, 707**
    adding toolbars to, **146–148,** *147*
    Address toolbar, 146–148, *147*
    Auto Hide feature, 138–139
    customizing, **138–140,** *139,* **146–148,** *147*
    minimized window buttons on, 66
    Quick Launch toolbar, 146–148, *147,* 703–704, 705, 707
    resizing, 138
    right-click menu options, 146–147
    setting date and time, 258
    Settings submenu Taskbar option, 138–140, *139,* 143–145
TCP/IP protocol, 553, **1009–1001**
tearing off Tool and Color Boxes in Paint, 829–830, *830*
telephone numbers
    entering for HyperTerminal connections, 517
    modem Properties dialog box options, 502–503
    Phone Dialer accessory, **492, 895–898**
        defined, **492, 895**
        placing calls, 897–898, *898*
        programming the Speed Dial list, 896–897, *897*
        starting, 895–896, *896*
telephone sound quality in NetMeeting, 733
telephony. *See also* communications features
    TAPI (Telephony API), 491–492, 1070
    Telephony applet, **237**
television. *See* TV Viewer
temporary AutoInstalled fonts, 365
Temporary Internet Files folder, 588
10Base-2 (thin Ethernet) networks, 1021–1022, *1021,* 1024
10Base-T (twisted-pair Ethernet) networks, 1022–1024, *1022,* **1025**
terminal mode sessions in HyperTerminal, 539–540, *540*
Terminal program, importing settings into HyperTerminal from, 514
terminal settings for HyperTerminal, 527–531
    ASCII Setup dialog box settings, 530–531
    backscroll buffer size setting, 529–530
    function, arrow, and Ctrl key settings, 528
    overview of, 527, *528*
    terminal-emulation setting, 528–529
    terminals defined, **527**
    turning sound on or off, 530
testing disks with ScanDisk, 917–918

text. *See also* Notepad; WordPad
    copying from DOS applications to the Clipboard, 200–203, *201*
    Text tool in Paint, 845–846, *846*
text boxes in dialog boxes, 88
text files. *See also* files
    ASCII Setup dialog box settings, 530–531
    defined, **872–873**
    how HyperTerminal displays and stores text, 540
    HyperTerminal transfer settings, 543
    opening into WordPad, 813–814
    sending and receiving with HyperTerminal, 542–544
thin Ethernet networks (10Base-2), 1021–1022, *1021,* 1024
threads in newsgroups, 677
Thumbnails view in Windows Explorer, **476–478,** *477,* 724–726, *725*
time. *See also* dates
    entering time in Notepad documents, 877
    entering time in WordPad documents, 790
    setting date and time, 235, 258–259, *259*
title bars
    in Internet Explorer 4, 579
    in Windows 98 windows, 70–71, 77
titles in DVD Player, 390–391
ToggleKeys options in Accessibility Options applet, 239–240
tone dialing, 504
Tool Box in Paint, 824, 829–830, 837–846
    Airbrush tool, 841
    Box tool, 842–843
    Brush tool, 838–840, *839*
    Curve tool, 842
    defined, **824**
    Ellipse tool, 843
    Eraser tool, 840–841
    Eyedropper tool, 837
    Free-Form Select tool, 848
    Line tool, 842
    Paint Can tool, 845
    Pencil tool, 841
    Polygon tool, 843–844, *844*
    Rounded Box tool, 843
    Select tool, 847–848
    tearing off or turning off, 829–830, *830*
    Text tool, 845–846, *846*
    undoing mistakes, 840
    using tools, 837–838
toolbars
    on the Active Desktop, 703–704, 706–708
    adding favorite channels to TV Viewer toolbar, 421–422
    adding to Taskbar, 146–148, *147*
    Address toolbar
        on the Active Desktop, 704
        in Internet Explorer, 584, 587
        on the Taskbar, 146–148, *147*
    Annotation toolbar in Kodak Imaging, 862–863
    Channel bar
        defined, **67**

displaying, 613, *613*
viewing Active Channels, 612–613, *612*
in Internet Explorer, **579**, **580**, **582–584**
  Address toolbar, 584, 587
  displaying Channel bar, 613, *613*
  Explorer bar, 579, *580*, 619–622, *620, 621, 622*
  hiding, moving, and resizing, 580, 582
  Links toolbar, 583–584
  overview of, 579
  Standard toolbar, 581, 583
  viewing Active Channels from Channel bar, 612–613, *612*
in Outlook Express
  customizing, 679–680
  Outlook bar, 632–633
Quick Launch toolbar
  on the Active Desktop, 703–704, 705, 707
  defined, **146–148**, *147*
in WordPad, **774–775**
  displaying and hiding, 775
  Format bar, 775, 797–799
  Print button, 819
  repositioning, 775, *776*
  ruler, 775, 791–792, 794–795
  Standard toolbar, 774, 775
  status bar, 775
Tools menu options in Backup utility, 932–933
topologies, 1020–1026. *See also* networks
  bus topologies, 1021–1022, *1021*
  Fast Ethernet networks (100Base-T), 1024–1026
  star topologies, 1022–1023, *1022*
  thin Ethernet networks (10Base-2), 1021–1022, *1021*, 1024
  twisted-pair Ethernet networks (10Base-T), 1022–1024, *1022*, 1025
tour of Windows 98, 64
transparent images in Paint, 845, 849
transport layer in OSI reference model, 1000
Trash. *See* Recycle Bin
troubleshooting
  HyperTerminal connections, 536–537
  networks, **1095–1106**
    boot failures, 1105–1106
    cable problems, 1097–1098
    hard disk drive crashes, 1102–1105
    I/O address conflicts, 1097
    network interface card and driver problems, 1099–1102, *1099, 1101*
    overview of, 1095–1097
  system event sound problems, 394
TrueType fonts, 336–337, 340–346. *See also* fonts
  versus bitmapped and vector fonts, 346
  defined, **336–337, 340–341**
  embedding, 345–346
  file extension for, 353
  font icons for TrueType versus printer fonts, 798
  versus other scalable fonts, 349–350
  Panose information in, 360
  printers and, 337

read-only versus read-write embedded fonts, 345
special characters, Symbol and WingDing fonts, 342–344, *343, 344*
TrueType font families, 342, *342*
TrueType options in Fonts applet, 356–357, *356*
.TTF files, 353
TTY terminal-emulation setting, 528–529
Tune-Up Wizard, 14–15
turning off
  Active Desktop components, 710
  automatic phone dialing by Internet programs, 570–571
  call waiting, 504
  file and folder text labels, 182
  sound in HyperTerminal, 530
  Tool and Color Boxes in Paint, 829–830, *830*
  Web view, 100
turning on
  Active Desktop components, 710
  file and folder text labels, 182
  sound in HyperTerminal, 530
  Web view, 96–97, *97*
TV Viewer accessory, 17, 411–424. *See also* accessories; multimedia
  adding favorite channels to the toolbar, 421–422
  adding and removing channels manually, 416, *416*
  avoiding Channel 1, 417, *417*
  Broadcast Architecture and, 17, 411, 423
  defined, **17, 411–412**
  finding shows, 418–419
  finding shows by category, 419
  future of, 423–424
  how TV Viewer works, 412–413
  keyboard shortcuts, 422–423
  online Help, 416
  reading Program Guide information, 414–415, *415*, 420, *420*
  remote controls, 422
  scrolling the display, 417–418, *418*
  setting reminders, 420–421, *421*
  starting, 413–415, *413, 414, 415*
  system requirements, 411
TWAIN driver support, 861
twisted-pair Ethernet networks (10Base-T), 1022–1024, *1022*, **1025**
.TXT extension, 872. *See also* text files
Type 1 PostScript fonts, 349
typefaces, 341

U

uncompressing compressed drives, 948
underlined letters in menus, 81
underlined text in WordPad, 797, 798, 799
Undo command
  overview of, 187, 457, 785
  in Paint, 840
  in WordPad, 802

Unimodem driver, 494–495, 1071
uninstalling
    applications, 257–258
    Windows 98, 1118–1119
units of measurement in WordPad, 815
Universal Disk Format (UDF), 387
Unix applications, 30
unmounting compressed drives, 950–951
unshielded twisted pair cables (UTP), 1017–1019, *1018*
unsubscribing to newsgroups, 673
updating
    website subscriptions manually, 608, *609*
    window contents with F5 key, 172, 455
Upgrade Wizard, 22
upgrading computers for multimedia, 374–384
    CD writers (CD-R drives), 380–381
    CD-ROM drives, 379–380
    computers and processors, 379
    DVD drives, 381–382
    monitors and video cards, 383–384
    purchasing components, 374–378
    sound cards, 382
    speakers, 382
upgrading to Windows 98, 8–9, 25–27, 33–55. *See also*
  installing, Windows 98
    cost of, **25–27**
    hardware requirements, **49–55**
        computers and processors, 49–50
        hard disk drives, 51–52
        monitors and video cards, 52–53
        other components, 55
        Plug-and-Play components, 53–55
        RAM, 50–51
    overview of, **8–9, 1109, 1110–1116**
    software considerations, **34–40**
        API calls and operating-system primitives, 35–37
        applications versus utilities, 34–35
        DOS applications and the virtual DOS machine (VDM),
          38, 133
        I/O permission bitmaps in Intel processors, 37
        running DOS applications and utilities, 35–40
        running shell programs, 40–41
        running Windows 3.x and 95 utilities, 41–46, *42*
        Win32, Win32c, and Win32s APIs, 48–49
        Windows 3.x applications and .ini files, 46
        Windows 32-bit applications, 47–49
usability studies, 23
Usenet newsgroups. *See* newsgroups
user interface. *See* Desktop; dialog boxes; menus; windows
user profiles for the Active Desktop, 698
user-level access control in peer-to-peer networks, 1050
Users applet, 237
utilities. *See also* accessories; applications; System Tools;
  Wizards
    versus applications, **34–35**
    CHKDSK, 916
    Direct Cable Connect (DCC), 1034, 1089–1091, *1090*
    DiskSpace, 942

DoubleSpace, 942, 1121
Dr. Watson, 16, 22
font management utilities, 363–365, *365*
font-scaling utilities, 349–350
for installing multimedia drivers, 385
Intellifont-for-Windows, 349–350
MoreFonts, 350
OnTrack Disk Manager, 973
Partition Magic FAT32 conversion utility, 970, 972
Publisher's Powerpak for Windows, 350
running
    DOS utilities, 35–40
    shell programs, 40–41
    Windows 3.x and 95 utilities, 41–46, *42*
SuperPrint, 350
System File Checker, 15
Windows Update, 15, 21, 915, 985–986, *986, 987*
UTP (unshielded twisted pair cables), 1017–1019, *1018*

V

vector fonts, 336, 339, 346, 353, 360
VESA local bus architecture, 1028–1029
video
    NetMeeting video settings, 754–755, *755*
    NetMeeting video support, 735–736, *735,* 739
video cards. *See also* monitors
    local bus video cards, 383
    purchasing, 283, 383–384
    resolution of, 383
    upgrading for multimedia, 383–384
    Windows 98 requirements, 52–53
video conferencing. *See* NetMeeting
View menu, 176–184, 209–210. *See also* menus
    Active Desktop options, 183
    Advanced settings, 179–182, *179*
    Browse Folders as Follows options, 183
    changing Clipboard view format, 209–210, *210*
    Click Items as Follows options, 184
    creating custom views, 182–184, *183*
    Customize This Folder command, 727
    overview of, 176
    Refresh command, 172, 455
    sorting and arranging file and folder icons and listings,
      177–179
    turning text labels on and off, 182
    View Web Content in Folders options, 183–184
viewing. *See also* displaying; hiding
    Active Channels, **610–613**
        from Channel bar, 612–613, *612*
        in Channel Viewer, 610–612, *611*
        in Internet Explorer, 610
    Clipboard contents, 209
    color settings in Paint, 836
    computer contents in Windows Explorer, 443–445, *444*
    digital IDs or certificates in Outlook Express address books,
      658–659, *660*

files from Windows Explorer, 456–457
in Fonts applet
    font families, 359
    fonts by similarities, 359–361, *360*
    viewing and printing examples with font viewer,
       357–359, *358*
free space on disks, 175, 462
images in Kodak Imaging, 858, *858*
newsgroup messages in Outlook Express, 676
print queues, 322–323, *322*
property sheets in Windows Explorer, 457
shared drives and folders, 463–464, *464*
Web pages in Windows Explorer, 472–474, *473*
website subscription settings, 601, *602*
website subscriptions, 599–600, *600*
views. *See also* Web view
    changing Clipboard view format, 209–211, *210*
    Classic view
       double-clicking in, 111
       selecting files in Windows Explorer, 455–456
       switching with Web view, 96–97, *97*, 100
    creating custom views, 182–184, *183*
    Details view in Windows Explorer, 448–449, 729
    Thumbnails view in Windows Explorer, 476–478, *477*,
       724–726, *725*
virtual device drivers (VxDs), 37
virtual DOS machine (VDM), 38, 133
VL-Bus architecture, 1028–1029
volume controls
    modem speaker volume setting in HyperTerminal, 532
    Speaker Volume option in modem Properties dialog box,
       498
    Volume Control accessory, 385, 893–895
VT-52 and VT-100 terminal-emulation setting, 529

W

WAV file editors, 384–385
WDM (Win32 Driver Model), 21
Web pages as backgrounds in Active Desktop, 712–713
Web view, 19, 24, 94–100
    customizing, 98–99
    defined, **19, 24,** *24,* **94–95**
    pointing in, 97–98, *98*
    previewing files, **474–476,** *475*
    returning to Classic view, 100
    selecting files in Windows Explorer, 456
    turning on, 96–97, *97*
Webcrawler search engine, 624
websites. *See also* Internet Explorer
    Active Desktop Gallery website, 713–714
    International Multimedia Telecommunications Consortium
       (IMTC), 765
    International Telecommunications Union (ITU), 765
    Internet Engineering Task Force (IETF), 765
    about Internet service providers, 556, 558
    about NetMeeting, 741, 744, 765

subscribing to, **594–609**
    Advanced Download Options dialog box, 605–606, *606*
    browsing updated subscriptions, 597–599
    browsing updated subscriptions off-line, 598
    canceling subscriptions, **599**
    changing subscription settings in Favorites menu, 601
    defined, **594–596**
    Downloading Subscriptions dialog box, 608, *609*
    overview of, 600–601
    selecting how much content should be delivered,
       604–606, *604, 605, 606*
    selecting how you want to be notified, 602–603, *603*
    setting subscription schedules, 607–608, *607*
    subscribing to sites, 591, *592,* **596–597**
    Subscription Wizard, 602–608
    updating subscriptions manually, 608, *609*
    viewing current subscription settings, 601, *602*
    viewing current subscriptions, 599–600, *600*
    Windows Update Wizard website, **15, 21, 915, 985–986,**
       986, 987
wheel mouse support, 245
Whiteboard feature in NetMeeting, 757–758, *758*
Who/Where? search engine, 625
.WHT files, 758
wildcards in Web search engines, 617–618
Win32, Win32c, and Win32s APIs, 48–49
Win32 Driver Model (WDM), 21
Window Layout Properties dialog box in Outlook Express,
    631–632, *631, 632*
windows, 67–80
    application windows
       in Active Desktop, 705
       defined, **68,** *69*
    Close buttons, 71, *72*
    Control boxes, *77, 77*
    customizing Outlook Express window layout, 631–632,
       631, 632
    defined, **59,** *60,* **67,** *68*
    document or child windows
       in Internet Explorer, 579
       in Windows 98, 69, *70*
    manually resizing, 75–76, *76*
    minimized window buttons in Taskbar, 66
    minimizing all windows, 111
    minimizing, maximizing, restoring, and closing, **71–74,** *75*
    moving, 77
    navigating folder windows with Backspace key, 113, 458
    Restore buttons, 71, *72*
    scroll bars, scroll buttons, and scroll boxes, 78–80, *78*
    Show Windows Contents While Dragging option, 76
    title bars, 70–71, *77*
    updating window contents with F5 key, 172, 455
Windows Explorer, 441–481
    accessing the Control Panel from, 234
    in Active Desktop, **719–729**
       browsing the Internet, 722–723, *723*
       browsing in Web view, 723–726, *724, 725*
       browsing your computer, 720–722, *721*

customizing folders, 726–729, *727, 728*
defined, **719**
merging the personal computer with the networked
  terminal, 719–720
rearranging columns in Details view, 729
Thumbnails view, 724–726, *725*
defined, **441**
Details view, 448–449, 729
file operations, **453–458**
  executing file operations, 456–457
  moving files between drives, 458
  moving files between folders, 454–455, 457
  overview of, 453–454
  refreshing folder contents, 172, 455
  selecting files, 448, 455–456
floppy disk operations, **459–462**
  copying disks, 461–462
  formatting disks and creating system disks, 459–460, *461*
  viewing free space on disks, 462
folder operations, **445–453, 478–480**
  creating folders, 449–450
  customizing folders with HTML code, 478–480, *479*
  deleting folders, 450–451
  moving folders, 451–452
  moving multiple folders simultaneously, 452, *453*
  navigating between folders, 449
  selecting drives, 446–447, *447*
  selecting folders, 448–449
  sharing folders, 468–471, *469*
  viewing shared folders, 463–464, *464*
versus Internet Explorer, **719**
minus sign (–) in, 445
network operations, **463–472**
  changing shared object permissions and other proper-
    ties, 471–472
  disconnecting from network drives or folders, 468
  mapping or connecting to network drives, 464–465
  mapping drives from Explorer, 466–467
  mapping drives from Windows 3.x file boxes, 465–466
  password settings, 471
  setting permissions, 470–471
  sharing drives and folders, 468–471, *469*
  viewing shared drives and folders, 463–464, *464*
plus sign (+) in, 443–444
previewing files, **474–476**, *475*
printing from, 456
running applications from, **114–117**, *115, 116,* 456
sharing drives and subdirectories in peer-to-peer networks
  from, 1046–1048, *1047*
starting, 115–116, 442–443, *443*
status bar, 445
Thumbnails view, **476–478**, *477,* 724–726, *725*
viewing computer contents, **443–445**, *444*
viewing other objects, 472
viewing Web pages, 472–474, *473*
Windows Messaging, 489, 490, 491
Windows Scripting Host, 21
Windows Tune-Up Wizard, 14–15

Windows Update Wizard, 15, 21, 915, 985–986, *986, 987*
WingDing font, 342–344, *343, 344*
wireless networks, 1020
Wizards. *See also* accessories; Control Panel; System Tools;
  utilities
  Add Printer Wizard, 298, 302–306
  Audio Tuning Wizard, 742, *743,* 750
  Backup Wizard, 926–929, *926, 927*
  Customize This Folder Wizard, 727–729, *728*
  Internet Connection Wizard, 562–564, *563, 564,* 634–637
  Maintenance Wizard, 915, 982–984
  Restore Wizard, 934–936, *936*
  Scheduled Tasks Wizard, **977–980**
    defined, **977**
    running, 977–979
    running tasks immediately, 980
  Subscription Wizard, 602–608
  Upgrade Wizard, 22
  Windows Tune-Up Wizard, 14–15
  Windows Update Wizard, 15, 21, 915, 985–986, *986, 987*
word wrap
  in Notepad, 875–876, *876*
  in WordPad, 816
WordPad accessory, 771–819. *See also* accessories; Notepad
  copying text between documents, **804–806**, *805*
  creating documents, **773**, *773,* **814**
  display options, **814–816**
    options for each type of document, 815–816, *816*
    overview of, 814, *815*
    selecting units of measurement and controlling word
      selection, 815
    word wrap options, 816
  editing, **778–790**
    copying blocks of text, 789
    deleting letters and words, 785
    dragging and dropping blocks of text, 789–790
    inserting letters and symbols, 786
    moving the cursor, 778–780
    moving text with cut and paste, 786–787
    moving text with right-click menus, 788, *788*
    replacing words, 786
    scrolling with the keyboard, 781
    scrolling with the mouse, 780, *781*
    selecting entire documents, 784, 802
    selecting lines of text, 784
    selecting with the mouse, 781–783, *782*
    selecting paragraphs, 783, 784
    selecting sentences, 784
    selecting with the Shift key, 783
    selecting words, 783, 815
  entering text, 776–777, *778*
  finding and replacing text, **802–804**
    finding words or text strings, 803–804, *803*
    overview of, 802–803
    replacing text, 786, 804
  formatting characters, **796–799**
    bold, italic, and underline text styles, 797, 798, 799
    with Fonts dialog box, 797, 799

with Format bar, 775, 797–799
with keyboard shortcuts, 797, 799
overview of, 796–797
as you type, 799
formatting paragraphs, **790–796**
bulleting paragraphs, 795–796
changing paragraph alignment, 793
hanging indents or outdents, 795
indenting with Format Paragraph dialog box, 794
indenting with the ruler, 794–795
overview of, 790–791
setting first-line indents, 795
types of indentation, 793–794, 796
using the ruler, 791–792
viewing paragraph alignment, 792–793
graphics, 807–810
importing from the Clipboard, 808, *808*
inserting as objects, 810
overview of, 807–808, *807*
positioning, 809
sizing, 809–810
Help, 774
hyphenation, **806**
inserting date and time, 790
insertion point, **776**
opening documents, **812–814**
ASCII files, 813–814
documents in other formats, 813
from File menu's Recently Opened Documents list, 813
new documents, 814
overview of, 812
overview of, 771–772
previewing documents, 817–818, *817*
printing documents, **818–819**
reformatting whole documents, 801–802
RTF (Rich Text Format) files, 812, 813, 815–816
running multiple copies of WordPad, 805–806, *805*
saving documents, **810–812**, *811*
spacing between sentences, *777*
tab stops, **800–801**
clearing, 801
repositioning, 801
setting, 800–801, *800*

toolbars, **774–775**
displaying and hiding, 775
Format bar, 775, 797–799
Print button, 819
repositioning, 775, *776*
ruler, 775, 791–792, 794–795
Standard toolbar, 774, 775
status bar, 775
Undo command, 785, 802
versus Write program in Windows 3.x and NT 3.x, 772–773
work area
on the Active Desktop, 700–703, *702*
in Paint, 824
workgroups, 1056
workstations. *See* Microsoft Windows NT
World Wide Web. *See* Internet Explorer 4
Worldnet Internet connections, 560–561
wrapping text
in Notepad, 875–876, *876*
in WordPad, 816
Write program in Windows 3.x and NT 3.x, 772–773
write protecting floppy disks, 173–174, *174*
writing 32-bit applications for multiple platforms, 48
WWWomen search engine, 625

X

XtraDrive compressed drives, 1121

Y

Yahoo! search engine, 623

Z

Zip drive compression, 947
zoom controls
in Kodak Imaging, 859
in Paint, 853–854, *854*

How Do I . . .?

This book includes information at all levels, for beginners to experienced users. If you're a beginner to Windows, you'll find this handy chart to be particularly useful to getting yourself up and running.

Start up the computer?

Remove any floppy disks. Switch on the computer and the monitor. Wait for Windows to boot up. When prompted, type in your password (or press the Esc key to skip it).

Start a program?

Click on the **Start** button in the bottom left corner of thwscreen. Move the pointer up to **Programs**. A menu opens up. Move the pointer carefully to the right, staying on **Programs**. Now find the program you're looking for. It might be in a subgroup. Point to the program subgroup you want to open (don't click). When you see the program you want, click on it.

Adjust the position or size of a window?

The fastest way to maximize the window is to double-click on its title bar (the bar across the top of the window). Double-click again and the previous size is restored. Reposition the window by dragging its title bar.

Find windows that have disappeared or switch between windows?

Each running program or open folder has a button on the Windows Taskbar. Click on the button once to restore the window. Click again to minimize it.

Find the work I was doing last time?

Click the **Start** button. Point to **Documents**. Slide the pointer over to the list of recently used documents. Click on the one you want. If it's not there,

click **Start**, click **Find**, and fill in at least part of the file name. Click **Find Now**. Once Find has located it, double-click the document name.

Save my work without losing it?

In your application window, click **File ➢ Save**. (Name the file if prompted.) For future purposes, try to remember which folder you're storing it in.

Copy or move text from one place to another?

Select the text by dragging the cursor over it (or, using the keyboard, by pressing **Shift** and the arrow keys). Then click **Edit ➢ Copy** or **Edit ➢ Cut**. Click on the destination location, and click **Edit ➢ Paste**.

Format a floppy disk?

Insert the disk in the floppy drive. Show the Windows Desktop by clicking the **Desktop** icon in the Taskbar. Open **My Computer** (upper left corner of the screen). Right-click on the floppy drive, and from the pop-up menu, choose **Format**.

Adjust or turn off those annoying beeps?

Single-click on the speaker icon next to the clock in the Taskbar. Then either click **Mute** or drag the volume slider to an appropriate volume level.

Turn off the computer correctly?

Close and save all open work windows. (You can leave folders and the Explorer windows open.)